UNDERSTANDING FICTION

UNDERSTANDING FICTION

Judith Roof
Michigan State University

HOUGHTON MIFFLIN COMPANY Boston New York

Publisher: Patricia A. Coryell
Executive editor: Suzanne Phelps Weir
Sponsoring editor: Michael Gillespie
Associate editor: Bruce Cantley
Editorial assistant: Lisa Littlewood
Senior production editor: Rosemary Winfield
Editorial assistant: Jake Perry
Art and design coordinator: Jill Haber
Photo editor: Jennifer Meyer Dare
Composition buyer: Sarah Ambrose
Manufacturing coordinator: Carrie Wagner
Marketing manager: Cindy Graff Cohen
Marketing assistant: Wendy Thayer

Cover: Autumn Landscape with Boats by Wassily Kandinsky © Kristie's Images/Corbis.

Acknowledgments begin on page C-1, which constitutes an extension of the copyright page.

Printed in the U.S.A.

Library of Congress Catalog Card Number: 20033110121

ISBN: 0-618-38632-7

123456789-QWV-07 06 05 04

Brief Contents

Contents

Preface for Instructors

The past twenty years have witnessed exciting evolutions in the way instructors think, talk, and write about literature—the expanding canon, growing interest in literary and cultural theory, changing definitions of what a "text" is, the emergence of new technologies, and so on. Capturing the energy, relevance, and skills of literary study and transmitting them to undergraduate students is one of the most important things we do as English instructors. In creating *Understanding Fiction*, the aim has been twofold—to better address the ways instructors want to teach literature today and to better inspire in students the desire and skills to engage literature critically. In its reading selections, approach, apparatus, and integrated technology components, *Understanding Fiction* has been carefully crafted to uphold the best literary traditions while furthering innovations that engage a new generation of students and instructors.

The heart of any anthology is found in its reading selections. I have balanced favorite canonical works with an outstanding selection of thought-provoking contemporary writing. I think you will find some wonderful surprises in the table of contents that you will be eager to explore with your students. A wealth of relevant works of art and photographs—including color pages—enriches the study of fiction and culture. A media-rich CD-ROM and Web site—fully integrated with the text—further brings fiction to life and to better engage the learning styles of today's students.

I focus students on the necessary skills to perform close readings and to think critically about literary works. *Understanding Fiction* starts with discussions of the basic, formal elements students need to understand to analyze fiction. You will find discussions of reading fiction for plot construction, narrative point of view, characterization, setting, tone, style, symbolism, and irony. These formalist practices continue to be essential skills that introductory students must master as requisites to understanding and enjoying fiction. However, I feel it is important for today's students to move beyond basic readings toward more considered interpretations of literary texts. Therefore, through integrated, *accessible* discussions of critical approaches to fiction, *Understanding Fiction* encourages and supports students to explore ways in which fiction engages with critical understandings of nationalism, race, gender, sexuality, global multiculturalism, and other cultural and political frames. *Understanding Fiction* enables instructors to adopt a text more in step with the needs and interests of today's students and reflective of the ways many instructors organize their classes.

If you are an instructor who wants to engage your students with a lifelong enjoyment of fiction while encouraging them to reach beyond a reading of the words to more rewarding and interesting interpretations, then *Understanding Fiction* will meet your needs. I hope you find that *Understanding Fiction* empowers you to go where you want to go and do what you want to do.

Key Features of the Anthology

Understanding Fiction offers instructors a wealth of features that support the teaching of their classes.

Compelling Table of Contents

A rich array of the best fiction offers instructors a wonderful range of authors—from the cherished work of Faulkner, Hawthorne, O'Connor, and Walker to the fresh and contemporary voices of Paul Auster, Michelle Cliff, and Mark Leyner. *Understanding Fiction* gives you the flexibility you need to teach the selections that suit your class.

Important featured writers are treated in-depth to allow more focused study of a single writer and give students rich opportunities for writing and research assignments. Featured writers include James Baldwin, Virginia Woolf, William Faulkner, and Salman Rushdie.

Three unique chapters explore the broader connections between fiction and culture

- "Fiction Across Media: Film" (Chapter 17) explores the similarities and differences in how actions, characters, settings, and stories are treated in fiction and film. A case study compares the treatment of these elements in Julio Cortázar's short story "Blow-Up" with Michelangelo Antonioni's film *Blow Up*. A useful discussion of film concepts gives students guidance in analyzing film.
- "The Limits of Fiction: Autobiography" (Chapter 18) examines the connections between fiction and autobiography. Selections from Mark Twain, Carl Van Vechten, Jean Rhys, Chester Himes, W. S. Penn, and Nicole Brossard are given.
- "Writing Communities: The Beats" (Chapter 19) includes a range of dynamic writers, including William S. Burroughs, Diane Di Prima, and Jack Kerouac.

Wealth of Visual Texts

Numerous photos and works of art, including four pages of full-color work, are carefully placed throughout the text to help students explore the connections between written and visual texts.

Comprehensive Coverage of Approaches to Studying Fiction

Complete coverage of the formal elements of fiction gives students the knowledge they need to understand the basic features of fiction including plot, character, point of view, and theme. Multiple chapters are devoted to the study of these elements giving helpful explanations and accessible examples.

Unique, integrated coverage of contemporary critical approaches offers accessible, insightful discussions of how literary and cultural theories are used to explore meaning in fiction. Integrated throughout the anthology in "Critical Perspective" sections rather than placed in an appendix or special chapters, this coverage includes in-text discussions, casebooks, and excerpts from classic and contemporary critical essays that offer students accessible yet important critical perspectives into how literary theory can facilitate a deeper understanding of literary texts. Critical Perspectives can also be used as a springboard for class discussion and writing.

Emphasis on cultural, social, and historical contexts Reflecting the increased desire to view literature through the lens of culture, the text discussions offer students ample opportunities to analyze and interpret fiction using cultural, social, and historical events.

Thorough Coverage of Writing and Research

Three chapters are devoted to guiding students through the process of writing about literature and developing effective essays. Coverage includes general guidance, fiction-specific advice, and help with the research paper.

An annotated student paper provides an excellent model of strong student writing.

Topics for Critical Thinking and Critical Writing are integrated into the chapters followed by suggestions for class discussion and writing topics. Instructors may use these informally in class or assign them as writing projects.

Integrated CD-ROM and Web Site

New technologies are opening up new avenues of literary exploration. Technology cannot replace the pleasure of reading a print text, but it can certainly enhance certain aspects of its study—particularly for today's students who are more accustomed to integrating technology into their lives. By integrating print and technology components, *Understanding Fiction* taps into the strengths of various media to bring fiction to life for your students. Marginal icons throughout *Understanding Fiction* direct you and your students to the related resources on the CD-ROM and Web site that help support and expand the readings and pedagogy in the text.

A highly interactive CD-ROM with a wealth of audio and visual resources offers opportunities for in-depth study of fiction. The fiction unit walks students through the literary elements of Hawthorne's *The Birthmark*, teaching students how to interpret this story and to apply it to other works of fiction. The CD-ROM also includes resources for poetry and drama.

A resource-rich Web site helps students and instructors further explore the works, authors, artistic movements, and literary theories introduced in the anthology. The *Understanding Fiction* Web site provides helpful support for students including questions and writing assignments, insights into literary movements, supplemental biographical materials, and relevant photos and visual art.

Organized to be Flexible and Teachable

Understanding Fiction, rich with the finest classic and contemporary fiction, allows instructors the flexibility to tailor the text to suit their classroom needs. Some instructors may prefer to concentrate on the core chapters that cover the literary elements. These instructors will find ample classic content and selections that suit their students. Other instructors may choose to blend the classic chapters with chapters that explore the cultural, social, and historical topics along with topics such as metafiction, postmodernism, and intertextuality.

Understanding Fiction includes major works of fiction that invite students to engage in both reading for pleasure and reading for critical engagement. The stories cover a wide range from the beginnings of modern prose fiction through the best in contemporary short stories. You will find a multitude of authors, themes, and writing styles, including the best-loved classics from Nathaniel Hawthorne, Kate Chopin, Zora Neale Hurston, and William Faulkner to the contemporary voices of Julio Cortázar, Paul Auster, and Michelle Cliff. Part I covers the basic literary elements with chapters devoted to character, setting, plot, narrator and point of view, and theme. These chapters give students a sound footing in the formal workings of fiction. Part II, "Image, Style, Structure," discusses imagery, style, structure, and tone, which lead to more sophisticated explorations in interpretation. Part III, "Reading and Interpreting," raises questions about *how we read.* The stories included are from around the globe, and students are asked to read these stories by examining issues of language, representation, metanarrative, and intertextuality.

Writing Guidance

Understanding Fiction is not just a textbook on how to read and interpret great works of fiction; equally important, it also offers a practical guide to student writing. Part IV, on "Writing About Literature," introduces students to the art of critical writing from invention through final execution. Here you will find practical advice about every stage of the writing process, illustrated by sample student writing. In teaching the craft of critical writing, *Understanding*

Fiction addresses the key areas of critical thinking and composition including crafting effective thesis statements and employing evidence in argumentation. In addition to providing a general introduction to effective critical writing, *Understanding Fiction* offers an extensive discussion of college-level research writing.

Resources for Teaching *Understanding Fiction*

A wealth of instructor resources are available to help you in the classroom. A comprehensive instructor's guide discusses every author and nearly every reading selection in the text. The manual provides guidance for discussing the selections in class, answering in-text questions and writing assignments, making connections to other writing selections, incorporating more coverage of literary theory in the classroom, and using the technology components. You will also find additional instructor resources at the *Understanding Fiction* Web site.

For instructors who want to assign additional literary works in their course, special packaging options are available with the New Riverside Editions—a wonderful series that complements literary texts with relevant historical documents, cultural contexts, and critical essays. For a complete listing, please visit the Houghton Mifflin Web site at http://college.hmco.com.

Acknowledgments

I would also like to thank all the instructors and colleagues who helped throughout the development process of this book. Your feedback and ideas were invaluable, and every chapter of this book has benefited from your insight. I particularly appreciate the dedicated work of Brian W. Gastle, Western Carolina University; Michelle Glaros, Dakota State University; Ann C. Hall, Ohio Dominican College; John Marx, University of Richmond; Michele Peers, Northern Kentucky University; and Aimee Pozorski, Emory University.

I thank all of the reviewers, focus group participants, and class testers for their assistance in shaping this project: Linda B. Adams, Jefferson Community College; Frank Ancona, Sussex County Community College; Mike Anzelome, Nassau Community College; Todd Avery, University of Massachusetts–Lowell; Maryam Barrie, Washtenaw Community College; Robert Barton, Rutgers University; John Blair, Southwest Texas State University; Barbara Bonallo, Miami-Dade Community College–Wolfson Campus; Lisa Brandom, John Brown University; Richard Brodesky, Pima Community College; Terence Brunk, Columbia College; Robert Callahan, Temple University; Ruth Callahan, Glendale Community College; Ron Carter, Rappahannock Community College; Peggy Cole, Arapahoe Community College; Mark Garrett Cooper, Florida State University; Keith Coplin, Colby Community College; Gail S. Corso, Neumann College; Carol Ann Davis, College of Charleston; Kathy De Grave, Pittsburg State University; Gillian Devereux, Old Dominion University; Ken Donelson, Arizona State University; Tina D. Eliopulos, Community College of Southern Nevada; Sandra K. Ellston,

Eastern Oregon University; Nancy Esposito, Bentley College; Marilyn Falkenberg, Menlo College; Ray Foster, Scottsdale Community College; Phyllis Frus, Hawaii Pacific University; Mark Gellis, Kettering University; Karen Golightly, University of Memphis; John Granger, San Diego State University; Marlene Groner, State University of New York–Farmingdale; Jean Harper, Ball State University; Randall Howe, North Georgia College and State University; Bryon Lee Grigsby, Centenary College; Grant Jenkins, Old Dominion University; Suzanne Keen, Washington and Lee University; Linda Cooper Knight, College of the Albemarle; Jim Kosmicki, Central Community College; Wendy Kurant, University of Georgia; Eleanor Latham, Central Oregon Community College; Marilyn Levine, Suffolk County Community College; David Levy, Housatonic Community College; Sarah Littlefield, Salve Regina University; Jerry Bryan Lincecum, Austin College; Jack Lynch, Rutgers University; Diann V. Mason, Paris Junior College; Deborah Mael, Newberry College; Lisa Marcus, Pacific Lutheran University; Dennis D. McDaniel, Saint Vincent College; Thomas H. McNeely, Emerson College; Janice Okoomian, Brown University; Michael Overman, University of South Carolina–Columbia; Elizabeth Patterson, Yakima Valley Community College; Eva Mokry Pohler, University of Texas at San Antonio; Stephen D. Powell, Texas Christian University; William Provost, University of Georgia; Jean-Michel Rabaté, University of Pennsylvania; Ann Marie Radaskiewicz, Western Piedmont Community College; Jeff Rice, University of Florida; Donald Riggs, Drexel University; Susan Roberts, Boston College; Peter Burton Ross, University of the District of Columbia; Albert Rouzie, Ohio University; Deborah Schwartz, Lourdes College; Carl Seiple, Kutztown University of Pennsylvania; Larry Severeid, College of Eastern Utah; Margaret Songe, Louisiana State University—Baton Rouge; William Sullivan, Winthrop College; John K. Swensson, DeAnza College; Joanna Tardoni, Western Wyoming Community College; Donna Thomsen, Johnson and Wales University; Michael Thro, Tidewater Community College; John Wargacki, Seton Hall University; Robert A. Watts, Drexel University; Joy Wentz, College of the Desert; Sallie Wolf, Arapahoe Community College; Nancy J. Young, Curry College.

I would also like to thank the individuals who helped us on this project from the start. For their thoughtful work on the anthology and the instructor's resource manual, I thank Jaime Hovey, Amy Nolan, and Johanna Frank. At Houghton Mifflin, I thank June Smith, Kris Clerkin, and Pat Coryell for their unflagging support of *Understanding Fiction* from its earliest stages. I appreciate the editorial guidance of Suzanne Phelps Weir, Michael Gillespie, Katharine Glynn, and Bruce Cantley. Janet Edmonds and Beth McCracken ably developed the technology components, and Rosemary Winfield and Jake Perry worked tirelessly to keep the book on schedule through production. Nancy Lyman and Cindy Graff Cohen contributed their ideas and enthusiasm throughout the process, and Maria Maimone and Michael Farmer tackled the Herculean task of clearing all the permissions.

Why Study Literature?

Literature, as the Welsh poet Dylan Thomas famously remarked, is a "sullen art." Bound between the covers of a book, the writer's craft is made up of black marks that lie silent on the page. Yet according to Henry David Thoreau, literature also can empower you to "live deep and suck the marrow out of life." Robin Williams, in the guise of English teacher John Keating, declared in the film *Dead Poets Society* that he read literature because he was "a member of the human race and the human race is filled with passion! Medicine, Law, Banking—these are necessary to sustain life—but poetry, romance, love, beauty! These are what we stay alive for."

Higher education is a requisite, certainly, to becoming a doctor, lawyer, accountant, journalist, or business executive. Nevertheless, the kind of passion to be found from the fiction of Gabriel García Márquez, Zora Neale Hurston, Virginia Woolf, or Chinua Achebe just might point you toward becoming a more discerning professional, a more engaged citizen, a more thoughtful human being: someone—in short—who is more alive. A work of literature—whether a short story, a poem, or a play—is not just a form of entertainment or an amusement. Reading is not the same as consuming; reading is more radically transformative. Great literature, according to German poet Rainer Maria Rilke, makes you aware that "you must change your life."

In addition to experiencing literature, understanding it requires discipline and critical thinking skills. No one is born with the capacity to detect dramatic irony or to discern the difference between "theater in the round" and "theater of the absurd." Interpreting the complexities of an Elizabethan sonnet or a postmodern work of hyperfiction is not something that comes naturally to most people. It's an acquired art, much like mastering a sport or a musical instrument. The delight of critical thinking lies in both experiencing and understanding what literature can do on the page, at the microphone, and on the stage. This book will give you the tools you will need to enjoy great literature and, equally important, to write about it with greater precision and keener insight.

UNDERSTANDING FICTION

FICTION

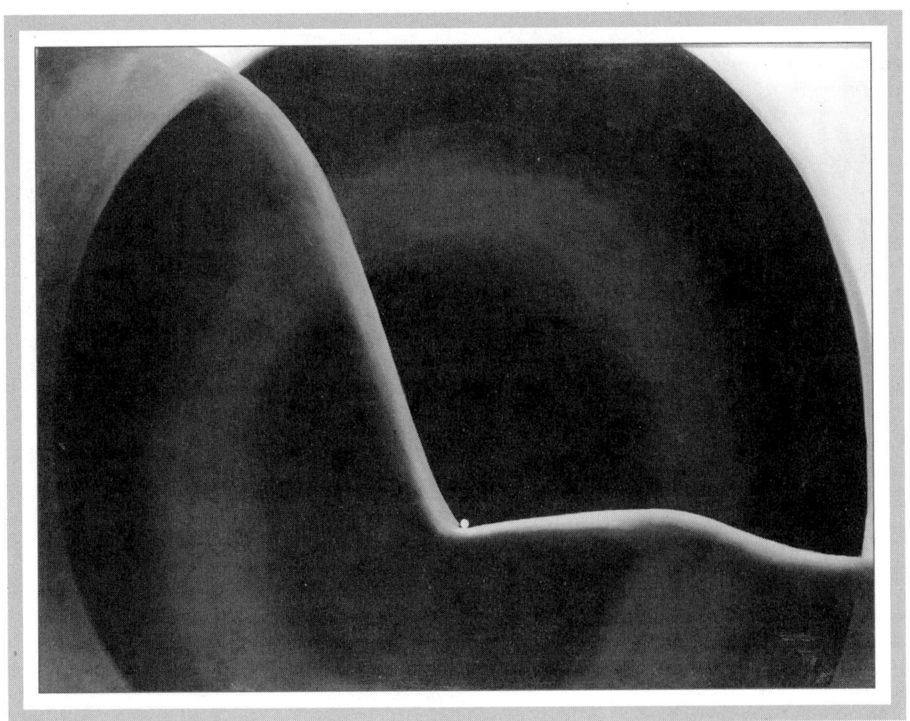

Part I
Form and Content

1 Introduction: Reading Fiction

Narrative Fiction

In the twenty-first century we are surrounded by fiction. Novels, short stories, comic books, movies, television shows, videos, folk tales, bedtime stories, and even jokes saturate our existence. Such genres (or kinds) of fiction as "mystery," "romance," "adventure," "science fiction," "comedy," "drama," and "literature" sort book and video store shelves. These forms of fiction are all narrative in that they organize events as a series of cause-and-effect relations in time: they tell stories. Most of us are avid consumers of stories and most of us know how they work: we are familiar with what the story is.

Fiction offers itself to be read, enjoyed, and interpreted. You might have noticed that most stories are not a simple recounting of events but embody an art in their telling. The study of fiction is the study of this art. It is a process of reading and analyzing both what a story says and how it says it. As we read,

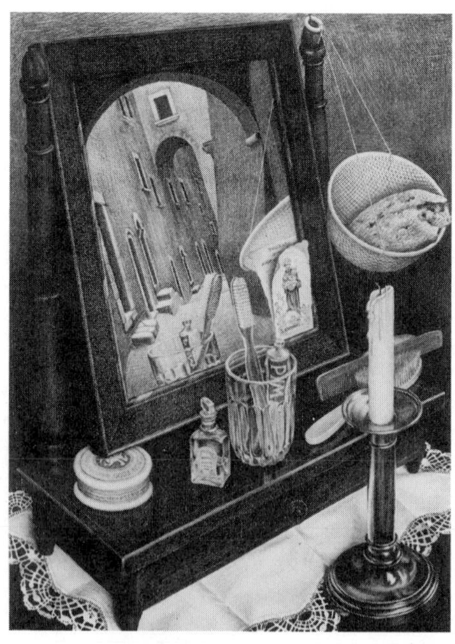

M.C. Escher, *Still Life with Mirror* (1934)

we notice these aspects of stories. Interpreting or analyzing stories is a way of explaining how they work as pieces of art—how they tell their story—and why we enjoy them. In other words, interpreting is a way of thinking about what we have already read and what we already know.

Fictional narratives are fictional in that they do not represent any specific historical event, though most stories transmit insights and truths about the nature of humanity and culture. While plays, poems, and stories in any medium (print, live performance, video, film) typically contain narratives, in discussions of literature the term *fiction* generally refers to fictional narratives in the form of written prose. Autobiography often embodies the blurry line between fiction and nonfiction.

In this section on fiction, we are concerned with prose fiction in the form of short stories or novellas (short novels). These genres of prose fiction accomplish most of the things the longer novel accomplishes except that they are shorter. Their relative brevity enables us to include them in their entirety. The skills readers use to interpret short stories are the same skills employed to interpret all prose fiction.

Characteristics of Fiction

All narratives share certain basic characteristics regardless of their medium. Let's use as an example a familiar—perhaps even an overly familiar and corny—story.

> A young white man, who has grown up in a big city, lives an aimless existence as a part-time prize fighter and collector for a loan shark. His striking boxing name catches the attention of the heavyweight champion who is looking for a man of the people to challenge. Wanting both the publicity and an easy victory, the champ, who is African American, invites the young man to fight him. The young man, unsure of his talent, decides to accept and begins a rigorous training regimen that includes drinking raw eggs, running through the streets, and pounding sides of beef. While in the midst of training, the young man falls in love with a shy young woman. Although he works hard and almost beats the champ, the young man is finally defeated. His courage, however, wins the heart of the crowd, and he realizes that in trying his hardest and winning the love of the woman, he has conquered after all.

Like all narratives, this story has characters, setting, and plot. Its characters consist of the young fighter, his trainer, the girl, and the champ. The story's setting is the big city, the boxing ring, and the young man's apartment. The story's plot involves the challenge, the young fighter's training and courtship of the young woman, the fight, and what the young man learns. Like all instances of narrative fiction, this story has a theme or unifying idea (or ideas) that hold it together. It focuses on the virtues of hard work and various understandings of what it might mean to win. It illustrates that although the young boxer doesn't win the bout, he gains love and self-respect. It also suggests that trying hard always pays off, even if in ways one doesn't expect.

Like most narrative fiction, this story also reflects in some fashion the ideas, biases, and social conditions of the period and culture in which it was written. The story of the boxer illustrates the possibilities or impossibilities of class mobility in American culture. It presents the saga of the classic underdog. It assumes our familiarity with the patterns of romance and the mechanisms of a society in which people can become stars or commodities. It works on (and in some ways counters) our assumptions about race and power.

All fictional narratives are involved in processes of reception (how readers react to a story), interpretation (the ways readers analyze and understand a story), and some contemplation of the story as a story and as part of a tradition of story telling (how the story relates to all other stories). The boxer's story, for example, depends on the reader sympathizing with the young boxer. His loss invites the reader to acknowledge the value of other kinds of triumph. It works in relation to our experience of all stories about underdogs, romance, sports, and the special reverence accorded the "common man" in American culture. And like all narratives, this one, minimal as it might seem, engages in the complex dynamics of telling a story. It employs a narrator (a presence in the story that tells the story), represents a point of view, and could recount events out of the order of their imagined occurrence, deploy images, symbols, motifs, repetition, and other devices to enhance and deepen the telling of the narrative.

The History of Prose Fiction

Prose fiction depends on written language as its medium of representation. Prose designed to be heard (such as orally transmitted folk tales and radio) tends to contain more repetition and simpler sentence structures than prose designed to be read. Prose for reading can take advantage of the fact that print media (including electronic forms) can be read as slowly as readers wish and that any part can be read over and over. The ease with which print enables the reader to peruse at will, to interrupt, read ahead, compare with other texts, and quote the text exactly means that prose fiction can be more linguistically complex. It can use more elaborate sentences, employ a wider and more varied vocabulary, and sustain a more complicated web of images. Prose fiction can also have a more complex mode of narration and might combine a greater number of different stories or plots. It can have, for example, one or more narrators and multiple narratives arranged together.

Of the various contemporary mediums devoted primarily to narrative, only orally transmitted folk tales are older than prose fiction. Written prose is an old medium compared to such relatively recent arrivals as radio, cinema, television, and the Internet. Both poetry and drama are ways of telling stories that have existed since ancient times. Until just after the Renaissance, the primary form for formal written storytelling was the long poem, a genre going back to antiquity. Shorter forms of prose fiction included folk tales, myths, and legends, which tended to be oral forms, and fables, which were written in either poetry or prose. From the seventeenth century on, prose fiction gained popularity, not only because of the continuing refinement of printing technologies that made books cheaper and more available but also because of the gradually widening audience of literate readers. **Web** Early forms of prose fiction, however, appeared mainly in the longer form of the novel and were often composed of a series of letters exchanged among characters (the epistolary novel). **Web**

Prose fiction in the form of the short story as we know it is a very recent genre. As twentieth-century writer Elizabeth Bowen suggests, "The short story is a young art. As we know it, it is a child of this century." That the novel was the favored form for prose writers and readers during the seventeenth, eighteenth, and nineteenth centuries was partly due to the vision and understanding of the role of fiction in culture during those eras. The rise of the novel—the genre employed by such writers as Jane Austen, Charles Dickens, George Eliot, and Mark Twain—accompanied the rise of the middle class and a coincident interest in history. This history consisted of tracking the causes and effects of various ideas, economic forces, and social conditions and describing relations within and among various social classes. The novel ultimately links the trends of history to society, and history's large movements to individual lives. Such a sense of the novel as the representation of "the shaping force of man's individual and collective history," as the eminent critic of the novel Ian Watt describes it, does not encourage serious writers to compose shorter, less panoramic works, nor are those shorter works perceived as worthy or serious art.

In contrast to the epic scale of the novel, shorter forms of fiction became prominent in the nineteenth century in America and in the 1880s in England. Cheaper to publish and circulate than the longer novel, short stories focused on the individual—often an outsider—and on more ephemeral expressions of social and cultural relations. In the nineteenth century, short fiction appeared primarily in periodicals. **Web** These short stories contrasted with the fairy tale, an ancient form that typically involves stereotyped characters with no specific consciousness or interior life, who take part in clear-cut events set in a remote or timeless world. In contrast to the fairy tale, the modern notion of the short story has, as Edgar Allan Poe suggests, "a unity of effect or impression." **Web** This unity was aided by the story's short length, which enabled readers to read it in two hours or less. There are many different definitions of the short story that add to Poe's insistence on unity. Critics suggest variously that the short story is defined by its "plot compression," its treatment of changes in character, its subject matter, or its tone. There are also many ways of looking at the short story.

Analyzing and Interpreting

Stories invite us to read and interpret, but we need the sets of concepts and vocabularies that permit us to think about and discuss the ways stories do what they do. There are many different ways of approaching a story. In this text, these various approaches are called Critical Perspectives. These perspectives, which come from an area of study called *critical* or *literary theory*, illustrate different ways of thinking about how literature works as an art. Understanding these perspectives will provide you with tools for interpreting prose fiction.

The range of skills and approaches needed to read, understand, analyze, and write about prose fiction are reflected in the organization and focus of the three sections on fiction. These three sections also roughly map the literary history of American, British, and Anglophone (stories written in English by writers who did not live in the British Isles or America) short fiction. Although the sections do not adhere strictly to either temporal or stylistic divisions, the tendency is to move from older, more realistic texts through modernism's emphasis on image and impression to more recent stories that are conscious of themselves as stories and reflect on what it means to write a story.

The first section, Form and Content, concentrates on the formal elements of short fiction and on some of the ideas, biases, and social conditions (the plight of women, poor people, or African Americans, for example) reflected in the stories—on what stories tell. Understanding the relation between how stories are shaped (their form) and what they tell is a basic and crucial starting point in interpreting prose fiction. This section centers primarily around nineteenth- and early twentieth-century American fiction, since the short story in English was mainly developed in America.

The second section, Image, Style, Structure, focuses on how stories are told. It examines the functions of images, symbols, motifs, style, and language as well as the structures and dynamics of narrating. It builds on the studies of form and content in the first section by inviting us to consider the ways language, image, and tone relate to both. The second section focuses on modernist and postcolonial fiction, including selections from English, American, and Anglophone writers.

The third section, Reading and Interpreting, raises questions about how we read. Centered around issues of language, representation, metanarrative, media, fictionality, and intertextuality itself, this section takes up issues of postmodernism in stories from Europe, America, and South America.

Each section encourages the reader to analyze stories and to understand and employ various critical perspectives as each builds on the basic skills and concepts of literary interpretation. (See, for example, the Study Project for *www* each chapter located on the Web **Web** or the intensive What to Do When Analyzing a Story included on the CD-ROM **CD-ROM**.) Part of this labor is to see writing itself as a mode of analysis and an engagement with various conversations and theories of literature. Whatever one writes or even says about literature inevitably assumes particular ideas about literature: how it works, what we should look at, the kinds of traits we are looking for. Part of the process of studying literature is to become conscious of what our assumptions about literature are, how these assumptions shape our perceptions and define the questions we ask, and how shifting our assumptions might enable us to gain new insights into what we read.

2 Overview: The Formal Elements of Fiction

When we analyze fiction, one of the first steps is to identify and characterize its formal elements. The **formal elements** include character, setting, plot, narrator, point of view, and theme. These are called formal elements for two reasons. First, defining the way a story employs each of these elements helps us characterize its **form:** what specific conventions a story uses. Second, studying a story's form is a way of describing how its elements come together as a whole work of art. We study each of these elements in more detail in the chapters that follow, but as a beginning it is useful to get a sense of how they all work together.

Stories present settings full of characters who do something. Characters may be people, animals, or even landscape or nature—the young boxer, the champ, or the young woman of the young boxer's story you read in the Introduction. Settings may be real places, imagined environments, or the imagination itself. In the young boxer's story, the settings are the city streets and the boxing ring. The deeds recounted make up the story's plot. These fundamental ingredients—characters, settings, and plot—provide readers with a basic sense of the story's subject—of *what the story tells.*

At first glance the three components of prose fiction are obvious. As apparent as these elements may be, understanding that they always work together with the story's other elements—narrator, point of view, themes, images, symbols, language, style, and tone—is critically important. Understanding how a story's formal elements work together is the beginning of the process of interpretation, which seeks both to understand the story's various meanings and to understand the story as a work of art.

Critical Perspectives: Formalism and New Criticism *www*

Web

Form (how a story's elements fit together) is one vantage from which a story might be interpreted. Analyses that employ form as their starting point are called **formalism.** Formalist critics begin with the assumption that literature's forms differentiate it from other modes of expression and that those forms and the ways various texts employ them tell us much about a story's art. Most literary interpretations consider some aspect of form in their analyses, and many approaches to fiction (feminist criticism, race criticism, Marxist criticism, queer theory) focus on the story's content or subject matter.

Criticism that studies how form and content relate to one another is called **New Criticism.** New Criticism assumes that a literary work can be read in itself, without additional contextual material such as author biography or history. It focuses on how all of the elements of a story work together to reflect, repeat, or sometimes contradict one another in ways that reflect what the story is about.

An example of the fledgling art of the short story is Nathaniel Hawthorne's "The Birthmark," which appeared in his second collection of short stories, *Mosses from an Old Manse* (1846), after originally appearing in *The Pioneer* in 1843. Hawthorne himself criticizes the collection in the book's Preface:

> These fitfull sketches with so little of external life about them, yet claiming no profundity of purpose—so reserved even when they sometimes seem so frank—often but half in earnest, and never, even when most so, expressing satisfactorily the thoughts which they profess to image—such trifles, I truly feel, afford no solid basis for a literary reputation.

But in a later edition of the book, author Henry James disagrees with Hawthorne's own assessment:

> [T]he valuable element in these things was not what Hawthorne put into them consciously, but what passed into them without his being able to measure it—the element of simple genius, the quality of imagination. This is the real charm of Hawthorne's writing—this purity and spontaneity and naturalness of fancy.

NATHANIEL HAWTHORNE

The Birthmark *(1854)*

In the latter part of the last century there lived a man of science, an eminent proficient in every branch of natural philosophy, who not long before our story opens had made experience of a spiritual affinity more attractive than any chemical one. He had left his laboratory to the care of an assistant, cleared his fine countenance from the furnace smoke, washed the stain of acids from his fingers, and persuaded a beautiful woman to become his wife. In those days, when the comparatively recent discovery of electricity and other kindred mysteries of Nature seemed to open paths into the region of miracle, it was not unusual for the love of science to rival the love of woman in its depth and absorbing energy. The higher intellect, the imagination, the spirit, and even the heart might all find their congenial aliment in pursuits which, as some of their ardent votaries believed, would ascend from one step of powerful intelligence to another, until the philosopher should lay his hand on the secret of creative force and perhaps make new worlds for himself. We know not whether Aylmer possessed this degree of faith in man's ultimate control over Nature. He had devoted himself, however, too unreservedly to scientific studies ever to be weaned from them by any second passion. His love for his young wife might prove the stronger of the two; but it could only be by intertwining itself with his love of science and uniting the strength of the latter to his own.

Such a union accordingly took place, and was attended with truly remarkable consequences and a deeply impressive moral. One day, very soon after their marriage, Aylmer sat gazing at his wife with a trouble in his countenance that grew stronger until he spoke.

"Georgiana," said he, "has it never occurred to you that the mark upon your cheek might be removed?"

"No, indeed," said she, smiling; but, perceiving the seriousness of his manner, she blushed deeply. "To tell you the truth, it has been so often called a charm that I was simple enough to imagine it might be so."

"Ah, upon another face perhaps it might," replied her husband; "but 5
never on yours. No, dearest Georgiana, you came so nearly perfect from the hand of Nature that this slightest possible defect, which we hesitate whether to term a defect or a beauty, shocks me, as being the visible mark of earthly imperfection."

"Shocks you, my husband!" cried Georgiana, deeply hurt; at first reddening with momentary anger, but then bursting into tears. "Then why did you take me from my mother's side? You cannot love what shocks you!"

To explain this conversation, it must be mentioned that in the centre of Georgiana's left cheek there was a singular mark, deeply interwoven, as it were, with the texture and substance of her face. In the usual state of her complexion—a healthy though delicate bloom—the mark wore a tint of deeper crimson, which imperfectly defined its shape amid the surrounding rosiness. When she blushed it gradually became more indistinct, and finally vanished amid the triumphant rush of blood that bathed the whole cheek with its brilliant glow. But if any shifting motion caused her to turn pale there was the mark again, a crimson stain upon the snow, in what Aylmer sometimes deemed an almost fearful distinctness. Its shape bore not a little similarity to the human hand, though of the smallest pygmy size. Georgiana's lovers were wont to say that some fairy at her birth hour had laid her tiny hand upon the infant's cheek, and left this impress there in token of the magic endowments that were to give her such sway over all hearts. Many a desperate swain would have risked life for the privilege of pressing his lips to the mysterious hand. It must not be concealed, however, that the impression wrought by this fairy sign-manual varied exceedingly according to the difference of temperament in the beholders. Some fastidious persons—but they were exclusively of her own sex—affirmed that the bloody hand, as they chose to call it, quite destroyed the effect of Georgiana's beauty and rendered her countenance even hideous. But it would be as reasonable to say that one of those small blue stains which sometimes occur in the purest statuary marble would convert the Eve of Powers to a monster. Masculine observers, if the birthmark did not heighten their admiration, contented themselves with wishing it away, that the world might possess one living specimen of ideal loveliness without the semblance of a flaw. After his marriage,—for he thought little or nothing of the matter before,—Aylmer discovered that this was the case with himself.

Had she been less beautiful,—if Envy's self could have found aught else to sneer at,—he might have felt his affection heightened by the prettiness of this mimic hand, now vaguely portrayed, now lost, now stealing forth again and glimmering to and fro with every pulse of emotion that throbbed within her heart; but, seeing her otherwise so perfect, he found this one defect grow more and more intolerable with every moment of their united lives. It was the fatal flaw of humanity which Nature, in one shape or another, stamps ineffaceably on all her productions, either to imply that they are temporary and finite, or that their perfection must be wrought by toil and pain. The crimson hand expressed the ineludible grip in which mortality clutches the highest and purest of earthly mould, degrading them into kindred with the lowest, and even with the very brutes, like whom their visible frames return to dust. In this manner, selecting it as the symbol of his wife's liability to sin, sorrow, decay, and death, Aylmer's sombre imagination was not long in rendering the birthmark a frightful object, causing him more trouble and horror than ever Georgiana's beauty, whether of soul or sense, had given him delight.

At all the seasons which should have been their happiest he invariably, and without intending it, nay, in spite of a purpose to the contrary, reverted to this one disastrous topic. Trifling as it at first appeared, it so connected itself with innumerable trains of thought and modes of feeling that it became the central point of all. With the morning twilight Aylmer opened his eyes upon his wife's face and recognized the symbol of imperfection; and when they sat together at the evening hearth his eyes wandered stealthily to her cheek, and beheld, flickering with the blaze of the wood fire, the spectral hand that wrote mortality where he would fain have worshipped. Georgiana soon learned to shudder at his gaze. It needed but a glance with the peculiar expression that his face often wore to change the roses of her cheek into a deathlike paleness, amid which the crimson hand was brought strongly out, like a bass relief of ruby on the whitest marble.

Late one night, when the lights were growing dim so as hardly to betray 10
the stain on the poor wife's cheek, she herself, for the first time, voluntarily took up the subject.

"Do you remember, my dear Aylmer," said she, with a feeble attempt at a smile, "have you any recollection, of a dream last night about this odious hand?"

"None! none whatever!" replied Aylmer, starting; but then he added, in a dry, cold tone, affected for the sake of concealing the real depth of his emotion, "I might well dream of it; for, before I fell asleep, it had taken a pretty firm hold of my fancy."

"And you did dream of it?" continued Georgiana, hastily; for she dreaded lest a gush of tears should interrupt what she had to say. "A terrible dream! I wonder that you can forget it. Is it possible to forget this one expression?—'It is in her heart now; we must have it out!' Reflect, my husband; for by all means I would have you recall that dream."

The mind is in a sad state when Sleep, the all-involving, cannot confine her spectres within the dim region of her sway, but suffers them to break forth, affrighting this actual life with secrets that perchance belong to a deeper one. Aylmer now remembered his dream. He had fancied himself with his servant Aminadab, attempting an operation for the removal of the birthmark; but the deeper went the knife, the deeper sank the hand, until at length its tiny grasp appeared to have caught hold of Georgiana's heart; whence, however, her husband was inexorably resolved to cut or wrench it away.

When the dream had shaped itself perfectly in his memory Aylmer sat in his wife's presence with a guilty feeling. Truth often finds its way to the mind close muffled in robes of sleep, and then speaks with uncompromising directness of matters in regard to which we practise an unconscious self-deception during our waking moments. Until now he had not been aware of the tyrannizing influence acquired by one idea over his mind, and of the lengths which he might find in his heart to go for the sake of giving himself peace.

"Aylmer," resumed Georgiana, solemnly, "I know not what may be the cost to both of us to rid me of this fatal birthmark. Perhaps its removal may cause cureless deformity; or it may be the stain goes as deep as life itself. Again: do we know that there is a possibility, on any terms, of unclasping the firm grip of this little hand which was laid upon me before I came into the world?"

"Dearest Georgiana, I have spent much thought upon the subject," hastily interrupted Aylmer. "I am convinced of the perfect practicability of its removal."

"If there be the remotest possibility of it," continued Georgiana, "let the attempt be made, at whatever risk. Danger is nothing to me; for life, while this hateful mark makes me the object of your horror and disgust,—life is a burden which I would fling down with joy. Either remove this dreadful hand, or take my wretched life! You have deep science. All the world bears witness of it. You have achieved great wonders. Cannot you remove this little, little mark, which I cover with the tips of two small fingers? Is this beyond your power, for the sake of your own peace, and to save your poor wife from madness?"

"Noblest, dearest, tenderest wife," cried Aylmer, rapturously, "doubt not my power. I have already given this matter the deepest thought—thought which might almost have enlightened me to create a being less perfect than yourself. Georgiana, you have led me deeper than ever into the heart of science. I feel myself fully competent to render this dear cheek as faultless as its fellow; and then, most beloved, what will be my triumph when I shall have corrected what Nature left imperfect in her fairest work! Even Pygmalion, when his sculptured woman assumed life, felt not greater ecstasy than mine will be."

"It is resolved, then," said Georgiana, faintly smiling. "And, Aylmer, spare me not, though you should find the birthmark take refuge in my heart at last."

Her husband tenderly kissed her cheek—her right cheek—not that which bore the impress of the crimson hand.

The next day Aylmer apprised his wife of a plan that he had formed whereby he might have opportunity for the intense thought and constant watchfulness which the proposed operation would require; while Georgiana, likewise, would enjoy the perfect repose essential to its success. They were to seclude themselves in the extensive apartments occupied by Aylmer as a laboratory, and where, during his toilsome youth, he had made discoveries in the elemental powers of Nature that had roused the admiration of all the learned societies in Europe. Seated calmly in this laboratory, the pale philosopher had investigated the secrets of the highest cloud region and of the profoundest mines; he had satisfied himself of the causes that kindled and kept alive the fires of the volcano; and had explained the mystery of the fountains, and how it is that they gush forth, some so bright and pure, and others with such rich medicinal virtues, from the dark bosom of the earth. Here, too, at an earlier period, he had studied the wonders of the human frame, and attempted to fathom the very process by which Nature assimilates all her precious influences from earth and air, and from the spiritual world, to create and foster man, her masterpiece. The latter pursuit, however, Aylmer had long laid aside in unwilling recognition of the truth—against which all seekers sooner or later stumble—that our great creative Mother, while she amuses us with apparently working in the broadest sunshine, is yet severely careful to keep her own secrets, and, in spite of her pretended openness, shows us nothing but results. She permits us, indeed, to mar, but seldom to mend, and, like a jealous patentee, on no account to make. Now, however, Aylmer resumed these half-forgotten investigations; not, of course, with such hopes or wishes as first suggested them; but because they involved much physiological truth and lay in the path of his proposed scheme for the treatment of Georgiana.

As he led her over the threshold of the laboratory, Georgiana was cold and tremulous. Aylmer looked cheerfully into her face, with intent to reassure her, but was so startled with the intense glow of the birthmark upon the whiteness of her cheek that he could not restrain a strong convulsive shudder. His wife fainted.

"Aminadab! Aminadab!" shouted Aylmer, stamping violently on the floor.

Forthwith there issued from an inner apartment a man of low stature, but bulky frame, with shaggy hair hanging about his visage, which was grimed with the vapors of the furnace. This personage had been Aylmer's underworker during his whole scientific career, and was admirably fitted for that office by his great mechanical readiness, and the skill with which, while incapable of comprehending a single principle, he executed all the details of his master's experiments. With his vast strength, his shaggy hair, his smoky aspect, and the indescribable earthiness that incrusted him, he seemed to represent man's physical nature; while Aylmer's slender figure, and pale, intellectual face, were no less apt a type of the spiritual element.

"Throw open the door of the boudoir, Aminadab," said Aylmer, "and burn a pastil."

"Yes, master," answered Aminadab, looking intently at the lifeless form of Georgiana; and then he muttered to himself, "If she were my wife, I'd never part with that birthmark."

When Georgiana recovered consciousness she found herself breathing an atmosphere of penetrating fragrance, the gentle potency of which had recalled her from her deathlike faintness. The scene around her looked like enchantment. Aylmer had converted those smoky, dingy, sombre rooms, where he had spent his brightest years in recondite pursuits, into a series of beautiful apartments not unfit to be the secluded abode of a lovely woman. The walls were hung with gorgeous curtains, which imparted the combination of grandeur and grace that no other species of adornment can achieve; and, as they fell from the ceiling to the floor, their rich and ponderous folds, concealing all angles and straight lines, appeared to shut in the scene from infinite space. For aught Georgiana knew, it might be a pavilion among the clouds. And Aylmer, excluding the sunshine, which would have interfered with his chemical processes, had supplied its place with perfumed lamps, emitting flames of various hue, but all uniting in a soft, impurpled radiance. He now knelt by his wife's side, watching her earnestly, but without alarm; for he was confident in his science, and felt that he could draw a magic circle round her within which no evil might intrude.

"Where am I? Ah, I remember," said Georgiana, faintly, and she placed her hand over her cheek to hide the terrible mark from her husband's eyes.

"Fear not, dearest!" exclaimed he. "Do not shrink from me! Believe me, 30
Georgiana, I even rejoice in this single imperfection, since it will be such a rapture to remove it."

"O, spare me!" sadly replied his wife. "Pray do not look at it again. I never can forget that convulsive shudder."

In order to soothe Georgiana, and, as it were, to release her mind from the burden of actual things, Aylmer now put in practice some of the light and playful secrets which science had taught him among its profounder lore. Airy figures, absolutely bodiless ideas, and forms of unsubstantial beauty came and danced before her, imprinting their momentary footsteps on beams of light. Though she had some indistinct idea of the method of these optical phenomena, still the illusion was almost perfect enough to warrant the belief that her husband possessed sway over the spiritual world. Then again, when she felt a wish to look forth from her seclusion, immediately, as if her thoughts were answered, the procession of external existence flitted across a screen. The scenery and the figures of actual life were perfectly represented, but with that bewitching yet indescribable difference which always makes a picture, an image, or a shadow so much more attractive than the original. When wearied of this, Aylmer bade her cast her eyes upon a vessel containing a quantity of earth. She did so, with little interest at first; but was soon startled to perceive the germ of a plant shooting upward from the soil. Then came the slender stalk; the leaves gradually unfolded themselves; and amid them was a perfect and lovely flower.

"It is magical!" cried Georgiana. "I dare not touch it."

"Nay, pluck it," answered Aylmer,—"pluck it, and inhale its brief perfume while you may. The flower will wither in a few moments and leave nothing save its brown seed vessels; but thence may be perpetuated a race as ephemeral as itself."

But Georgiana had no sooner touched the flower than the whole plant 35
suffered a blight, its leaves turning coal-black as if by the agency of fire.

"There was too powerful a stimulus," said Aylmer, thoughtfully.

To make up for this abortive experiment, he proposed to take her portrait by a scientific process of his own invention. It was to be effected by rays of light striking upon a polished plate of metal. Georgiana assented; but, on looking at the result, was affrighted to find the features of the portrait blurred and indefinable; while the minute figure of a hand appeared where the cheek should have been. Aylmer snatched the metallic plate and threw it into a jar of corrosive acid.

Soon, however, he forgot these mortifying failures. In the intervals of study and chemical experiment he came to her flushed and exhausted, but seemed invigorated by her presence, and spoke in glowing language of the resources of his art. He gave a history of the long dynasty of the alchemists, who spent so many ages in quest of the universal solvent by which the golden principle might be elicited from all things vile and base. Aylmer appeared to believe that, by the plainest scientific logic, it was altogether within the limits of possibility to discover this long-sought medium; "but," he added, "a philosopher who should go deep enough to acquire the power would attain too lofty a wisdom to stoop to the exercise of it." Not less singular were his opinions in regard to the elixir vitae. He more than intimated that it was at his option to concoct a liquid that should prolong life for years, perhaps interminably; but that it would produce a discord in Nature which all the world, and chiefly the quaffer of the immortal nostrum, would find cause to curse.

"Aylmer, are you in earnest?" asked Georgiana, looking at him with amazement and fear. "It is terrible to possess such power, or even to dream of possessing it."

"O, do not tremble, my love," said her husband. "I would not wrong either you or myself by working such inharmonious effects upon our lives; but I would have you consider how trifling, in comparison, is the skill requisite to remove this little hand."

At the mention of the birthmark, Georgiana, as usual, shrank as if a red-hot iron had touched her cheek.

Again Aylmer applied himself to his labors. She could hear his voice in the distant furnace room giving directions to Aminadab, whose harsh, uncouth, misshapen tones were audible in response, more like the grunt or growl of a brute than human speech. After hours of absence, Aylmer reappeared and proposed that she should now examine his cabinet of chemical products and natural treasures of the earth. Among the former he showed her a small vial, in which, he remarked, was contained a gentle yet most powerful fragrance, capable of impregnating all the breezes that blow across a kingdom. They were of inestimable value, the contents of that little vial; and, as he said so, he threw some of the perfume into the air and filled the room with piercing and invigorating delight.

"And what is this?" asked Georgiana, pointing to a small crystal globe containing a gold-colored liquid. "It is so beautiful to the eye that I could imagine it the elixir of life."

"In one sense it is," replied Aylmer; "or rather, the elixir of immortality. It is the most precious poison that ever was concocted in this world. By its aid I could apportion the lifetime of any mortal at whom you might point your finger. The strength of the dose would determine whether he were to linger out years, or drop dead in the midst of a breath. No king on his guarded throne could keep his life if I, in my private station, should deem that the welfare of millions justified me in depriving him of it."

"Why do you keep such a terrific drug?" inquired Georgiana in horror. 45

"Do not mistrust me, dearest," said her husband, smiling; "its virtuous potency is yet greater than its harmful one. But see! here is a powerful cosmetic. With a few drops of this in a vase of water, freckles may be washed away as easily as the hands are cleansed. A stronger infusion would take the blood out of the cheek, and leave the rosiest beauty a pale ghost."

"Is it with this lotion that you intend to bathe my cheek?" asked Georgiana, anxiously.

"O, no," hastily replied her husband; "this is merely superficial. Your case demands a remedy that shall go deeper."

In his interviews with Georgiana, Aylmer generally made minute inquiries as to her sensations, and whether the confinement of the rooms and the temperature of the atmosphere agreed with her. These questions had such a particular drift that Georgiana began to conjecture that she was already subjected to certain physical influences, either breathed in with the fragrant air or taken with her food. She fancied likewise, but it might be altogether fancy, that there was a stirring up of her system—a strange, indefinite sensation creeping through her veins, and tingling, half painfully, half pleasurably, at her heart. Still, whenever she dared to look into the mirror, there she beheld herself pale as a white rose and with the crimson birthmark stamped upon her cheek. Not even Aylmer now hated it so much as she.

To dispel the tedium of the hours which her husband found it necessary 50
to devote to the processes of combination and analysis, Georgiana turned over the volumes of his scientific library. In many dark old tomes she met with chapters full of romance and poetry. They were the works of the philosophers of the middle ages, such as Albertus Magnus, Cornelius Agrippa, Paracelsus, and the famous friar who created the prophetic Brazen Head. All these antique naturalists stood in advance of their centuries, yet were imbued with some of their credulity, and therefore were believed, and perhaps imagined themselves to have acquired from the investigation of Nature a power above Nature, and from physics a sway over the spiritual world. Hardly less curious and imaginative were the early volumes of the Transactions of the Royal Society, in which the members, knowing little of the limits of natural possibility, were continually recording wonders or proposing methods whereby wonders might be wrought.

But to Georgiana, the most engrossing volume was a large folio from her husband's own hand, in which he had recorded every experiment of his scientific career, its original aim, the methods adopted for its development, and its final success or failure, with the circumstances to which either event was attributable. The book, in truth, was both the history and emblem of his ardent, ambitious, imaginative, yet practical and laborious life. He handled physical details as if there were nothing beyond them; yet spiritualized them all and redeemed himself from materialism by his strong and eager aspiration towards the infinite. In his grasp the veriest clod of earth assumed a soul.

Georgiana, as she read, reverenced Aylmer and loved him more profoundly than ever, but with a less entire dependence on his judgment than heretofore. Much as he had accomplished, she could not but observe that his most splendid successes were almost invariably failures, if compared with the ideal at which he aimed. His brightest diamonds were the merest pebbles, and felt to be so by himself, in comparison with the inestimable gems which lay hidden beyond his reach. The volume, rich with achievements that had won renown for its author, was yet as melancholy a record as ever mortal hand had penned. It was the sad confession and continual exemplification of the shortcomings of the composite man, the spirit burdened with clay and working in matter, and of the despair that assails the higher nature at finding itself so miserably thwarted by the earthly part. Perhaps every man of genius, in whatever sphere, might recognize the image of his own experience in Aylmer's journal.

So deeply did these reflections affect Georgiana that she laid her face upon the open volume and burst into tears. In this situation she was found by her husband.

"It is dangerous to read in a sorcerer's books," said he with a smile, though his countenance was uneasy and displeased. "Georgiana, there are pages in that volume which I can scarcely glance over and keep my senses. Take heed lest it prove detrimental to you."

"It has made me worship you more than ever," said she.

"Ah, wait for this one success," rejoined he, "then worship me if you will. I shall deem myself hardly unworthy of it. But come, I have sought you for the luxury of your voice. Sing to me, dearest."

So she poured out the liquid music of her voice to quench the thirst of his spirit. He then took his leave with a boyish exuberance of gayety, assuring her that her seclusion would endure but a little longer, and that the result was already certain. Scarcely had he departed when Georgiana felt irresistibly impelled to follow him. She had forgotten to inform Aylmer of a symptom which for two or three hours past had begun to excite her attention. It was a sensation in the fatal birthmark, not painful, but which induced a restlessness throughout her system. Hastening after her husband, she intruded for the first time into the laboratory.

The first thing that struck her eye was the furnace, that hot and feverish worker, with the intense glow of its fire, which by the quantities of soot clustered above it seemed to have been burning for ages. There was a distilling apparatus in full operation. Around the room were retorts, tubes, cylinders, crucibles, and other apparatus of chemical research. An electrical machine stood ready for immediate use. The atmosphere felt oppressively close, and was tainted with gaseous odors which had been tormented forth by the processes of science. The severe and homely simplicity of the apartment, with its naked walls and brick pavement, looked strange, accustomed as Georgiana had become to the fantastic elegance of her boudoir. But what chiefly, indeed almost solely, drew her attention, was the aspect of Aylmer himself.

He was pale as death, anxious and absorbed, and hung over the furnace as if it depended upon his utmost watchfulness whether the liquid which it was distilling should be the draught of immortal happiness or misery. How different from the sanguine and joyous mien that he had assumed for Georgiana's encouragement!

"Carefully now, Aminadab; carefully, thou human machine; carefully, thou man of clay," muttered Aylmer, more to himself than his assistant. "Now, if there be a thought too much or too little, it is all over."

"Ho! ho!" mumbled Aminadab. "Look, master! look!"

Aylmer raised his eyes hastily, and at first reddened, then grew paler than ever, on beholding Georgiana. He rushed towards her and seized her arm with a grip that left the print of his fingers upon it.

"Why do you come hither? Have you no trust in your husband?" cried he, impetuously. "Would you throw the blight of that fatal birthmark over my labors? It is not well done. Go, prying woman! go!"

"Nay, Aylmer," said Georgiana with the firmness of which she possessed no stinted endowment, "it is not you that have a right to complain. You mistrust your wife; you have concealed the anxiety with which you watch the development of this experiment. Think not so unworthily of me, my husband. Tell me all the risk we run, and fear not that I shall shrink; for my share in it is far less than your own."

"No, no, Georgiana!" said Aylmer, impatiently; "it must not be."

"I submit," replied she, calmly. "And, Aylmer, I shall quaff whatever draught you bring me; but it will be on the same principle that would induce me to take a dose of poison if offered by your hand."

"My noble wife," said Aylmer, deeply moved, "I knew not the height and depth of your nature until now. Nothing shall be concealed. Know, then, that this crimson hand, superficial as it seems, has clutched its grasp into your being with a strength of which I had no previous conception. I have already administered agents powerful enough to do aught except to change your entire physical system. Only one thing remains to be tried. If that fails us we are ruined."

"Why did you hesitate to tell me this?" asked she.

"Because, Georgiana," said Aylmer, in a low voice, "there is danger."

"Danger? There is but one danger—that this horrible stigma shall be left upon my cheek!" cried Georgiana. "Remove it, remove it, whatever be the cost, or we shall both go mad!"

"Heaven knows your words are too true," said Aylmer, sadly. "And now, dearest, return to your boudoir. In a little while all will be tested."

He conducted her back and took leave of her with a solemn tenderness which spoke far more than his words how much was now at stake. After his departure Georgiana became rapt in musings. She considered the character of Aylmer and did it completer justice than at any previous moment. Her heart exulted, while it trembled, at his honorable love—so pure and lofty that it would accept nothing less than perfection nor miserably make itself contented with an earthlier nature than he had dreamed of. She felt how much more precious was such a sentiment than that meaner kind which would have borne with the imperfection for her sake, and have been guilty of treason to holy love by degrading its perfect idea to the level of the actual; and with her whole spirit she prayed that, for a single moment, she might satisfy his highest and deepest conception. Longer than one moment she well knew it could not be;

for his spirit was ever on the march, ever ascending, and each instant required something that was beyond the scope of the instant before.

The sound of her husband's footsteps aroused her. He bore a crystal goblet containing a liquor colorless as water, but bright enough to be the draught of immortality. Aylmer was pale; but it seemed rather the consequence of a highly-wrought state of mind and tension of spirit than of fear or doubt.

"The concoction of the draught has been perfect," said he, in answer to Georgiana's look. "Unless all my science have deceived me, it cannot fail."

"Save on your account, my dearest Aylmer," observed his wife, "I might wish to put off this birthmark of mortality by relinquishing mortality itself in preference to any other mode. Life is but a sad possession to those who have attained precisely the degree of moral advancement at which I stand. Were I weaker and blinder, it might be happiness. Were I stronger, it might be endured hopefully. But, being what I find myself, methinks I am of all mortals the most fit to die."

"You are fit for heaven without tasting death!" replied her husband. "But why do we speak of dying? The draught cannot fail. Behold its effect upon this plant."

On the window seat there stood a geranium diseased with yellow blotches which had overspread all its leaves. Aylmer poured a small quantity of the liquid upon the soil in which it grew. In a little time, when the roots of the plant had taken up the moisture, the unsightly blotches began to be extinguished in a living verdure.

"There needed no proof," said Georgiana, quietly. "Give me the goblet. I joyfully stake all upon your word."

"Drink, then, thou lofty creature!" exclaimed Aylmer, with fervid admiration. "There is no taint of imperfection on thy spirit. Thy sensible frame, too, shall soon be all perfect."

She quaffed the liquid and returned the goblet to his hand.

"It is grateful," said she, with a placid smile. "Methinks it is like water from a heavenly fountain; for it contains I know not what of unobtrusive fragrance and deliciousness. It allays a feverish thirst that had parched me for many days. Now, dearest, let me sleep. My earthly senses are closing over my spirit like the leaves around the heart of a rose at sunset."

She spoke the last words with a gentle reluctance, as if it required almost more energy than she could command to pronounce the faint and lingering syllables. Scarcely had they loitered through her lips ere she was lost in slumber. Aylmer sat by her side, watching her aspect with the emotions proper to a man the whole value of whose existence was involved in the process now to be tested. Mingled with this mood, however, was the philosophic investigation characteristic of the man of science. Not the minutest symptom escaped him. A heightened flush of the cheek, a slight irregularity of breath, a quiver of the eyelid, a hardly perceptible tremor through the frame,—such were the details which, as the moments passed, he wrote down in his folio volume. Intense thought had set its stamp upon every previous page of that volume; but the thoughts of years were all concentrated upon the last.

While thus employed, he failed not to gaze often at the fatal hand, and not without a shudder. Yet once, by a strange and unaccountable impulse, he pressed it with his lips. His spirit recoiled, however, in the very act; and Georgiana, out of the midst of her deep sleep, moved uneasily and murmured as if in remonstrance. Again Aylmer resumed his watch. Nor was it without avail. The crimson hand, which at first had been strongly visible upon the marble paleness of Georgiana's cheek, now grew more faintly outlined. She remained not less pale than ever; but the birthmark, with every breath that came and went lost somewhat of its former distinctness. Its presence had been awful; its departure was more awful still. Watch the stain of the rainbow fading out of the sky, and you will know how that mysterious symbol passed away.

"By Heaven! it is well nigh gone!" said Aylmer to himself, in almost irrepressible ecstasy. "I can scarcely trace it now. Success! success! And now it is like the faintest rose color. The slightest flush of blood across her cheek would overcome it. But she is so pale!"

He drew aside the window curtain and suffered the light of natural day to fall into the room and rest upon her cheek. At the same time he heard a gross, hoarse chuckle, which he had long known as his servant Aminadab's expression of delight.

"Ah, clod! ah, earthly mass!" cried Aylmer, laughing in a sort of frenzy, "you have served me well! Matter and spirit—earth and heaven—have both done their part in this! Laugh, thing of the senses! You have earned the right to laugh."

These exclamations broke Georgiana's sleep. She slowly unclosed her eyes and gazed into the mirror which her husband had arranged for that purpose. A faint smile flitted over her lips when she recognized how barely perceptible was now that crimson hand which had once blazed forth with such disastrous brilliancy as to scare away all their happiness. But then her eyes sought Aylmer's face with a trouble and anxiety that he could by no means account for.

"My poor Aylmer!" murmured she.

"Poor? Nay, richest, happiest, most favored!" exclaimed he. "My peerless bride, it is successful! You are perfect!"

"My poor Aylmer," she repeated, with a more than human tenderness, "you have aimed loftily; you have done nobly. Do not repent that, with so high and pure a feeling, you have rejected the best the earth could offer. Aylmer, dearest Aylmer, I am dying!"

Alas! it was too true! The fatal hand had grappled with the mystery of life, and was the bond by which an angelic spirit kept itself in union with a mortal frame. As the last crimson tint of the birthmark—that sole token of human imperfection—faded from her cheek, the parting breath of the now perfect woman passed into the atmosphere, and her soul, lingering a moment near her husband, took its heavenward flight. Then a hoarse, chuckling laugh was heard again! Thus ever does the gross fatality of earth exult in its invariable triumph over the immortal essence which, in this dim sphere of half development, demands the completeness of a higher state. Yet, had Aylmer reached a profounder wisdom, he need not thus have flung away the happiness which would have woven his mortal life of the selfsame texture with the celestial.

The momentary circumstance was too strong for him; he failed to look beyond the shadowy scope of time, and, living once for all in eternity, to find the perfect future in the present.

Nathaniel Hawthorne

(1804–1864)

Nathanel Hawthorne always wanted to be a writer. Born to an old New England family, Hawthorne graduated from Bowdoin College and returned to Salem, Massachusetts, to write. After producing children's fiction and encyclopedias, Hawthorne turned to serious writing, creating four novels, including *The Scarlett Letter*, and a series of short stories. A friend of President Franklin Pierce, Hawthorne served as United States Consul in England.

TOPICS FOR CRITICAL THINKING CD-ROM

1. What do the characters of "The Birthmark" stand for beyond themselves?
2. How does the story illustrate the clash of science and nature?
3. In what ways do the settings of "The Birthmark" reflect the story's conflicts?
4. Is Aminadab right? If so, why is this perspective voiced by him?
5. What is the role of Aylmer's dream in the story?
6. In what ways is the problem of perfection linked to issues of gender?

TOPICS FOR CRITICAL WRITING CD-ROM

1. Why is it that "The Birthmark" can have no other outcome?
2. Explain what it might mean that the birthmark is in the shape of a hand.

3 Character

Prose fiction solicits our interest in part through the intriguing characters it presents—figures that range from the resistant Bartleby to the chivalric grocery store clerk of "A & P." All stories have characters; and most stories have many characters who differ in the kinds of roles they play, their relative importance in the story, the detail with which they are drawn, and the degree to which readers are familiar with the stereotype they may represent. Characters who serve as the primary actors in a story and with whom readers are invited to sympathize are called **protagonists.** Rocky Balboa, Luke Skywalker, James Bond, Neo, and Bridget Jones are protagonists in film narratives, while Aylmer ("The Birthmark"), Betsey Lane ("The Flight of Betsey Lane"), Peyton Farquhar ("An Occurrence at Owl Creek Bridge"), and Marlow (*Heart of Darkness*) are protagonists in prose fiction whom you meet in this book.

Although it is usually clear which of several characters is a story's protagonist, sometimes the role shifts from one character to another (as it shifts from Luke to Han Solo in *Star Wars*) or is shared by more than one character. Both of the young travelers in Ernest Hemingway's "Hills Like White Elephants" could be considered protagonists, while in *Heart of Darkness*, the protagonist Marlow seeks the charismatic Kurtz who, in his own way, has served as hero (or demagogue) of the African bush. Determining which character is the protagonist of a story tells a lot about the story's plot and themes.

Another important role is that of the **antagonist,** the character who opposes the protagonist or whose actions conflict with the protagonist's aims or desires. Antagonists include such film characters as Austin Powers' enemy Dr. Evil, James Bond's nemesis Blofeld, and Luke Skywalker's opponent Darth Vader, or the literary villain The Misfit from Flannery O'Connor's "A Good Man Is Hard to Find." Although readers may often find an antagonist unsympathetic, occasionally antagonists are more interesting than protagonists—as perhaps The Misfit is or Iago from William Shakespeare's *Othello*. Although protagonists are usually human beings, antagonists sometimes appear as forces such as animals or nature. Jack London's stories often situate nature as an antagonist.

Protagonists and antagonists are usually main (that is, major or primary) characters in a story. They are fully drawn, often in some detail, and offer points of sympathy (or its opposite, in the case of the antagonist) and identification for the reader. In some stories, the narrator is the protagonist. These first-person narrator protagonists (those narrating using *I* or *we*) are also characters whose personalities are developed directly through comments they make about themselves and indirectly in the way they narrate events (see Chapter 6).

Other characters are presented in less detail, their more generalized qualities providing contrast to the main characters and enabling plot development. Minor characters frequently work with one another and with primary characters to produce a sense of time, place, and atmosphere or help with the development of plot details. As points of comparison to major characters, minor characters emphasize a main character's idiosyncrasies. As extensions of primary characters' influence and ability, they enhance major characters' importance, strengths, or even weaknesses. Other characters are functionaries, scarcely described, who fulfill such utilitarian roles as servant, authority figure, child, friend, or member of a crowd. These characters are almost part of *www* the story's setting. **Web**

Any type of character may be **stereotypical**—present a familiar type such as the bully; **allegorical**—stand for a concept, position, or one aspect of personality such as the greedy King Midas; or **structural**—serve as protagonist, antagonist, or narrator in the story. Characters sometimes fulfill more than one of these functions at a time. Many stories center on a single character, describing and developing the sense of a unique personality. In character-centered stories such as Herman Melville's "Bartleby the Scrivener" or *Heart of Darkness*, character dominates and defines other formal elements. The story's plot, for example, might track the actions and fate of a character or characters, and its setting might parallel or complement a character's traits and actions.

Critical Perspective: Psychological Criticism

Characters provide readers with a familiar fascination. As we do in other media such as television and movies, we are attentive to the characters' motivations—their reasons for doing things. Taking clues from the text, readers form theories about characters' behaviors based on what they know about how and why people behave in certain ways. Interpreting stories on the basis *www* of character motivation is called **psychological criticism.** **Web** Readers often treat characters as if they are real people; this is testimony to the power of the writer who creates such believable portraits. When stories are specifically about a character's motivations, character psychology is an important way of understanding how a story works. Not all stories, however, are about character psychology alone. Relying too much on character psychology sometimes prevents appreciation of a story's other elements or the ways all of its elements, including character, work together.

If we interpret a character's actions using the scientific categories of psychology (such as schizophrenia or depression), we are reading stories as clinical studies of people who are in trouble. Some stories invite such a reading, especially if they center on characters whose main difficulty seems to be psychological. We might interpret Bartleby's behavior as a symptom of depression, for example. In other stories focused on character, it is tempting to interpret characters psychologically because character psychology is a logic that can work anywhere. What, for example, motivates Betsey Lane to see the world? The many different schools of psychology (Freudian, Jungian, ego psychology, object relations psychology, to name a few) provide different models and vocabularies for understanding and talking about character motivation. Even if readers are not familiar with specific psychological terms, most still understand the basic motives of human behavior.

Critical Perspective: Myth Criticism

Another way of interpreting character is to understand characters as representative parts of a mythical pattern. This is called **myth criticism.** **CD-ROM**  Myths that concern creation, rites of passage (birth, puberty, marriage, death), or scapegoats are basic to Western culture and are shared in one form or another by many societies. Sometimes stories provide hints that characters might represent **archetypes** (the basic model for a particular character in a myth) through names, objects associated with characters, or actions that parallel the actions of mythical figures. For example, a character named Lucifer inevitably suggests evil, while a hooded figure carrying a scythe intimates death. Sometimes we discern mythical patterns through the prominence of a character who seems to be the embodiment of a mythical figure. An example of this would be Prometheus, who angers the gods by stealing fire and giving it to humanity. In other stories, we may discern a mythical pattern such as rebirth in spring, then fit the characters into their proper roles in the myth. Myth criticism thus involves our ability to match a specific instance of a pattern to a paradigm (or pattern) that is generally known. As with any kind of criticism, it's important to avoid trying to reduce a story to a simple pattern.

Stories About Character

While almost all stories involve some human characters, stories specifically focused on character may occasionally defy the conventional antagonist-protagonist patterns of plot (see Chapter 5). Such stories seem almost like character sketches or portraits whose main purpose is descriptive, but the often unusual whims of the featured character may permit a plot that runs counter to normal expectations. "Bartleby the Scrivener," first published in *Putnam's Magazine* in November–December 1853, is, on one level at least, a story about a character who refuses to participate in any conventional existence. "Bartleby" followed Melville's publication of seven novels, the first two of which focused on his experiences in the South Pacific.

Sarah Orne Jewett's "The Flight of Betsey Lane" was published forty years later in *Scribner's Magazine*. Jewett, who admired Harriet Beecher Stowe, often focused on female characters and their relationships. Tracking the decision of an elderly woman to take a trip to the Philadelphia Centennial, the story focuses on Betsey and her two retirement home friends, avoiding conventional narratives in which women's actions are traditionally more limited.

Herman Melville

Bartleby the Scrivener

(1853)

I am a rather elderly man. The nature of my avocations, for the last thirty years, has brought me into more than ordinary contact with what would seem an interesting and somewhat singular set of men, of whom, as yet, nothing, that I know of, has ever been written—I mean, the law-copyists, or scriveners. I have known very many of them, professionally and privately, and, if I pleased, could relate divers histories, at which good-natured gentlemen might smile, and sentimental souls might weep. But I waive the biographies of all other scriveners, for a few passages in the life of Bartleby, who was a scrivener, the strangest I ever saw, or heard of. While, of other law-copyists, I might write the complete life, of Bartleby nothing of that sort can be done. I believe that no materials exist, for a full and satisfactory biography of this man. It is an irreparable loss to literature. Bartleby was one of those beings of whom nothing is ascertainable, except from the original sources, and, in his case, those are very small. What my own astonished eyes saw of Bartleby, *that* is all I know of him, except, indeed, one vague report, which will appear in the sequel.

Ere introducing the scrivener, as he first appeared to me, it is fit I make some mention of myself, my *employés*, my business, my chambers, and general surroundings; because some such description is indispensable to an adequate understanding of the chief character about to be presented. Imprimis: I am a man who, from his youth upwards, has been filled with a profound conviction that the easiest way of life is the best. Hence, though I belong to a profession proverbially energetic and nervous, even to turbulence, at times, yet nothing of that sort have I ever suffered to invade my peace. I am one of those unambitious lawyers who never addresses a jury, or in any way draws down public applause; but, in the cool tranquillity of a snug retreat, do a snug business among rich men's bonds, and mortgages, and title-deeds. All who know me, consider me an eminently *safe* man. The late John Jacob Astor, a personage little given to poetic enthusiasm, had no hesitation in pronouncing my first grand point to be prudence; my next, method. I do not speak it in vanity, but simply record the fact, that I was not unemployed in my profession by the late John Jacob Astor, a name which, I admit, I love to repeat; for it hath a rounded and orbicular sound to it, and rings like unto bullion. I will freely add, that I was not insensible to the late John Jacob Astor's good opinion.

Some time prior to the period at which this little history begins, my avocations had been largely increased. The good old office, now extinct in the State of New York, of a Master in Chancery, had been conferred upon me. It was not a very arduous office, but very pleasantly remunerative. I seldom lose my temper; much more seldom indulge in dangerous indignation at wrongs and outrages; but, I must be permitted to be rash here, and declare, that I consider the sudden and violent abrogation of the office of Master in Chancery, by the new Constitution, as a——premature act; inasmuch as I had counted upon a life-lease of the profits, whereas I only received those of a few short years. But this is by the way.

My chambers were up stairs, at No.—Wall Street. At one end, they looked upon the white wall of the interior of a spacious sky-light shaft, penetrating the building from top to bottom.

5 This view might have been considered rather tame than otherwise, deficient in what landscape painters call "life." But, if so, the view from the other end of my chambers offered, at least, a contrast, if nothing more. In that direction, my windows commanded an unobstructed view of a lofty brick wall, black by age and everlasting shade; which wall required no spy-glass to bring out its lurking beauties, but, for the benefit of all near-sighted spectators, was pushed up to within ten feet of my window panes. Owing to the great height of the surrounding buildings, and my chambers being on the second floor, the interval between this wall and mine not a little resembled a huge square cistern.

At the period just preceding the advent of Bartleby, I had two persons as copyists in my employment, and a promising lad as an office-boy. First, Turkey; second, Nippers; third, Ginger Nut. These may seem names, the like of which are not usually found in the Directory. In truth, they were nicknames, mutually conferred upon each other by my three clerks, and were deemed expressive of their respective persons or characters. Turkey was a short, pursy Englishman, of about my own age—that is, somewhere not far from sixty. In the morning, one might say, his face was of a fine florid hue, but after twelve o'clock, meridian—his dinner hour—it blazed like a grate full of Christmas coals; and continued blazing—but, as it were, with a gradual wane—till six o'clock, P.M., or thereabouts; after which, I saw no more of the proprietor of the face, which, gaining its meridian with the sun, seemed to set with it, to rise, culminate, and decline the following day, with the like regularity and undiminished glory. There are many singular coincidences I have known in the course of my life, not the least among which was the fact, that, exactly when Turkey displayed his fullest beams from his red and radiant countenance, just then, too, at that critical moment, began the daily period when I considered his business capacities as seriously disturbed for the remainder of the twenty-four hours. Not that he was absolutely idle, or averse to business, then; far from it. The difficulty was, he was apt to be altogether too energetic. There was a strange, inflamed, flurried, flighty recklessness of activity about him. He would be incautious in dipping his pen into his inkstand. All his blots upon my documents were dropped there after twelve o'clock, meridian. Indeed, not only would he be reckless, and sadly given to making blots in the afternoon, but, some days, he went further, and was rather noisy. At such times, too, his face flamed with augmented blazonry, as if cannel coal had been heaped on anthracite. He made an unpleasant racket with his chair; spilled his sand-box; in mending his pens, impatiently split them all to pieces, and threw them on the floor in a sudden passion; stood up, and leaned over his table, boxing his papers about in a most indecorous manner, very sad to behold in an elderly man like him. Nevertheless, as he was in many ways a most valuable person to me, and all the time before twelve o'clock, meridian, was the quickest, steadiest creature, too, accomplishing a great deal of work in a style not easily to be matched—for these reasons, I was willing to overlook his eccentricities, though, indeed, occasionally, I remonstrated with him. I did this very gently, however, because, though the civilest, nay, the blandest and most reverential of men in the morning, yet, in the afternoon, he was disposed, upon provocation, to be slightly rash with his tongue—in fact, insolent. Now, valuing his morning services as I did, and resolved not to lose them—yet, at the same time, made uncomfortable by his inflamed ways after twelve o'clock—and being a man of peace, unwilling by my admonitions to call forth unseemly retorts from him, I took upon me, one Saturday noon (he was always worse on Saturdays) to hint to him, very kindly, that, perhaps, now that he was growing old, it might be well to abridge his labors; in short, he need not come to my chambers after twelve o'clock, but, dinner over, had best go home to his lodgings, and rest himself till tea-time. But no; he insisted upon his afternoon devotions. His countenance became intolerably fervid, as he oratorically assured me—gesticulating with a long ruler at the other end of the room—that if his services in the morning were useful, how indispensable, then, in the afternoon?

"With submission, sir," said Turkey, on this occasion, "I consider myself your right-hand man. In the morning I but marshal and deploy my columns; but in the afternoon I put myself at their head, and gallantly charge the foe, thus"—and he made a violent thrust with the ruler.

"But the blots, Turkey," intimated I.

"True; but, with submission, sir, behold these hairs! I am getting old. Surely, sir, a blot or two of a warm afternoon is not to be severely urged against gray hairs. Old age—even if it blot the page—is honorable. With submission, sir, we *both* are getting old."

This appeal to my fellow-feeling was hardly to be resisted. At all events, I 10
saw that go he would not. So, I made up my mind to let him stay, resolving, nevertheless, to see to it that, during the afternoon, he had to do with my less important papers.

Nippers, the second on my list, was a whiskered, sallow, and, upon the whole, rather piratical-looking young man, of about five and twenty. I always deemed him the victim of two evil powers—ambition and indigestion. The ambition was evinced by a certain impatience of the duties of a mere copyist, an unwarrantable usurpation of strictly professional affairs, such as the original drawing up of legal documents. The indigestion seemed betokened in an occasional nervous testiness and grinning irritability, causing the teeth to audibly grind together over mistakes committed in copying; unnecessary maledictions, hissed, rather than spoken, in the heat of business; and especially by a continual discontent with the height of the table where he worked. Though of a very ingenious mechanical turn, Nippers could never get this table to suit him. He put chips under it, blocks of various sorts, bits of pasteboard, and at last went so far as to attempt an exquisite adjustment, by final pieces of folded blotting-paper. But no invention would answer. If, for the sake of easing his back, he brought the table lid at a sharp angle well up towards his chin, and wrote there like a man using the steep roof of a Dutch house for his desk, then he declared that it stopped the circulation in his arms. If now he lowered the table to his waistbands, and stooped over it in writing, then there was a sore aching in his back. In short, the truth of the matter was, Nippers knew not what he wanted. Or, if he wanted anything, it was to be rid of a scrivener's table altogether. Among the manifestations of his diseased ambition was a fondness he had for receiving visits from certain ambiguous-looking fellows in seedy coats, whom he called his clients. Indeed, I was aware that not only was he, at times, considerable of a ward-politician, but he occasionally did a little business at the Justices' courts, and was not unknown on the steps of the Tombs. I have good reason to believe, however, that one individual who called upon him at my chambers, and who, with a grand air, he insisted was his client, was no other than a dun, and the alleged title-deed, a bill. But, with all his failings, and the annoyances he caused me, Nippers, like his compatriot Turkey, was a very useful man to me; wrote a neat, swift hand; and, when he chose, was not deficient in a gentlemanly sort of deportment. Added to this, he always dressed in a gentlemanly sort of way; and so, incidentally, reflected credit upon my chambers. Whereas, with respect to Turkey, I had much ado to keep him from being a reproach to me. His clothes were apt to look oily, and smell of eating-houses. He wore his pantaloons very loose and baggy in summer. His coats were execrable; his hat not to be handled. But while the hat was a thing of indifference to me, inasmuch as his natural civility and deference, as a dependent Englishman, always led him to doff it the moment he entered the room, yet his coat was another matter. Concerning his coats, I reasoned with him; but with no effect. The truth was, I suppose, that a man with so small an income could not afford to sport such a lustrous face and a lustrous coat at one and the same time. As Nippers once observed, Turkey's money went chiefly for red ink. One winter day, I presented Turkey with a highly respectable-looking coat of my own—a padded gray coat, of a most comfortable warmth, and which buttoned straight up from the knee to the neck. I thought Turkey would appreciate the favor, and abate his rashness and obstreperousness of afternoons. But no; I verily believe that buttoning himself up in so downy and blanket-like a coat had a pernicious effect upon him—upon the same principle that too much oats are bad for horses. In fact, precisely as a rash, restive horse is said to feel his oats, so Turkey felt his coat. It made him insolent. He was a man whom prosperity harmed.

Though, concerning the self-indulgent habits of Turkey, I had my own private surmises, yet, touching Nippers, I was well persuaded that, whatever might be his faults in other respects, he was, at least, a temperate young man. But, indeed, nature herself seemed to have been his vintner, and, at his birth, charged him so thoroughly with an irritable, brandy-like disposition, that all subsequent potations were needless. When I consider how, amid the stillness of my chambers, Nippers would sometimes impatiently rise from his seat, and stooping over his table, spread his arms wide apart, seize the whole desk, and move it, and jerk it, with a grim, grinding motion on the floor, as if the table were a perverse voluntary agent, intent on thwarting and vexing him, I plainly perceive that, for Nippers, brandy-and-water were altogether superfluous.

It was fortunate for me that, owing to its peculiar cause—indigestion—the irritability and consequent nervousness of Nippers were mainly observable in the morning, while in the afternoon he was comparatively mild. So that, Turkey's paroxysms only coming on about twelve o'clock, I never had to do with their eccentricities at one time. Their fits relieved each other, like guards. When Nippers' was on, Turkey's was off; and *vice versa.* This was a good natural arrangement, under the circumstances.

Ginger Nut, the third on my list, was a lad, some twelve years old. His father was a car-man, ambitious of seeing his son on the bench instead of a cart, before he died. So he sent him to my office, as student at law, errand-boy, cleaner and sweeper, at the rate of one dollar a week. He had a little desk to himself, but he did not use it much. Upon inspection, the drawer exhibited a great array of the shells of various sorts of nuts. Indeed, to this quick-witted youth, the whole noble science of the law was contained in a nut-shell. Not the least among the employments of Ginger Nut, as well as one which he discharged with the most alacrity, was his duty as cake and apple purveyor for Turkey and Nippers. Copying law-papers being proverbially a dry, husky sort of business, my two scriveners were fain to moisten their mouths very often with Spitzenbergs, to be had at the numerous stalls nigh the Custom House and Post Office. Also, they sent Ginger Nut very frequently for that peculiar cake—small, flat, round, and very spicy—after which he had been named by them. Of a cold morning, when business was but dull, Turkey would gobble up scores of these cakes, as if they were mere wafers—indeed, they sell them at the rate of six or eight for a penny—the scrape of his pen blending with the crunching of the crisp particles in his mouth. Of all the fiery afternoon blunders and flurried rashnesses of Turkey, was his once moistening a ginger-cake between his lips, and clapping it on to a mortgage, for a seal. I came within an ace of dismissing him then. But he mollified me by making an oriental bow, and saying—

“With submission, sir, it was generous of me to find you in stationery on 15
my own account.”

Now my original business—that of a conveyancer and title hunter, and drawer-up of recondite documents of all sorts—was considerably increased by receiving the master's office. There was now great work for scriveners. Not only must I push the clerks already with me, but I must have additional help.

In answer to my advertisement, a motionless young man one morning stood upon my office threshold, the door being open, for it was summer. I can see that figure now—pallidly neat, pitiably respectable, incurably forlorn! It was Bartleby.

After a few words touching his qualifications, I engaged him, glad to have among my corps of copyists a man of so singularly sedate an aspect, which I thought might operate beneficially upon the flighty temper of Turkey, and the fiery one of Nippers.

I should have stated before that ground glass folding-doors divided my premises into two parts, one of which was occupied by my scriveners, the other by myself. According to my humor, I threw open these doors, or closed them. I resolved to assign Bartleby a corner by the folding-doors, but on my side of them, so as to have this quiet man within easy call, in case any trifling thing was to be done. I placed his desk close up to a small side-window in that part of the room, a window which originally had afforded a lateral view of certain grimy backyards and bricks, but which, owing to subsequent erections, commanded at present no view at all, though it gave some light. Within three feet of the panes was a wall, and the light came down from far above, between two lofty buildings, as from a very small opening in a dome. Still further to a satisfactory arrangement, I procured a high green folding screen, which might entirely isolate Bartleby from my sight, though not remove him from my voice. And thus, in a manner, privacy and society were conjoined.

At first, Bartleby did an extraordinary quantity of writing. As if long famishing for something to copy, he seemed to gorge himself on my documents. There was no pause for digestion. He ran a day and night line, copying by sun-light and by candle-light. I should have been quite delighted with his application, had he been cheerfully industrious. But he wrote on silently, palely, mechanically.

It is, of course, an indispensable part of a scrivener's business to verify the accuracy of his copy, word by word. Where there are two or more scriveners in an office, they assist each other in this examination, one reading from the copy, the other holding the original. It is a very dull, wearisome, and lethargic affair. I can readily imagine that, to some sanguine temperaments, it would be altogether intolerable. For example, I cannot credit that the mettlesome poet, Byron, would have contentedly sat down with Bartleby to examine a law document of, say five hundred pages, closely written in a crimpy hand.

Now and then, in the haste of business, it had been my habit to assist in comparing some brief document myself, calling Turkey or Nippers for this purpose. One object I had, in placing Bartleby so handy to me behind the screen, was, to avail myself of his services on such trivial occasions. It was on the third day, I think, of his being with me, and before any necessity had arisen for having his own writing examined, that, being much hurried to complete a small affair I had in hand, I abruptly called to Bartleby. In my haste and natural expectancy of instant compliance, I sat with my head bent over the original on my desk, and my right hand sideways, and somewhat nervously extended with the copy, so that, immediately upon emerging from his retreat, Bartleby might snatch it and proceed to business without the least delay.

In this very attitude did I sit when I called to him, rapidly stating what it was I wanted him to do—namely, to examine a small paper with me. Imagine my surprise, nay, my consternation, when, without moving from his privacy, Bartleby, in a singularly mild, firm voice, replied, "I would prefer not to."

I sat awhile in perfect silence, rallying my stunned faculties. Immediately it occurred to me that my ears had deceived me, or Bartleby had entirely misunderstood my meaning. I repeated my request in the clearest tone I could assume; but in quite as clear a one came the previous reply, "I would prefer not to."

"Prefer not to," echoed I, rising in high excitement, and crossing the 25
room with a stride. "What do you mean? Are you moon-struck? I want you to help me compare this sheet here—take it," and I thrust it towards him.

"I would prefer not to," said he.

I looked at him steadfastly. His face was leanly composed; his gray eye dimly calm. Not a wrinkle of agitation rippled him. Had there been the least uneasiness, anger, impatience or impertinence in his manner; in other words, had there been any thing ordinarily human about him, doubtless I should have violently dismissed him from the premises. But as it was, I should have as soon thought of turning my pale plaster-of-paris bust of Cicero out of doors. I stood gazing at him awhile, as he went on with his own writing, and then reseated myself at my desk. This is very strange, thought I. What had one best do? But my business hurried me. I concluded to forget the matter for the present, reserving it for my future leisure. So calling Nippers from the other room, the paper was speedily examined.

A few days after this, Bartleby concluded four lengthy documents, being quadruplicates of a week's testimony taken before me in my High Court of Chancery. It became necessary to examine them. It was an important suit, and great accuracy was imperative. Having all things arranged, I called Turkey, Nippers, and Ginger Nut, from the next room, meaning to place the four copies in the hands of my four clerks, while I should read from the original. Accordingly, Turkey, Nippers, and Ginger Nut had taken their seats in a row, each with his document in his hand, when I called to Bartleby to join this interesting group.

"Bartleby! quick, I am waiting."

I heard a slow scrape of his chair legs on the uncarpeted floor, and soon 30
he appeared standing at the entrance of his hermitage.

"What is wanted?" said he, mildly.

"The copies, the copies," said I, hurriedly. "We are going to examine them. There"—and I held towards him the fourth quadruplicate.

"I would prefer not to," he said, and gently disappeared behind the screen.

For a few moments I was turned into a pillar of salt, standing at the head of my seated column of clerks. Recovering myself, I advanced towards the screen, and demanded the reason for such extraordinary conduct.

"*Why* do you refuse?" 35

"I would prefer not to."

With any other man I should have flown outright into a dreadful passion, scorned all further words, and thrust him ignominiously from my presence. But there was something about Bartleby that not only strangely disarmed me, but, in a wonderful manner, touched and disconcerted me. I began to reason with him.

"These are your own copies we are about to examine. It is labor saving to you, because one examination will answer for your four papers. It is common usage. Every copyist is bound to help examine his copy. Is it not so? Will you not speak? Answer!"

"I prefer not to," he replied in a flutelike tone. It seemed to me that, while I had been addressing him, he carefully revolved every statement that I made; fully comprehended the meaning; could not gainsay the irresistible conclusion; but, at the same time, some paramount consideration prevailed with him to reply as he did.

"You are decided, then, not to comply with my request—a request made according to common usage and common sense?"

He briefly gave me to understand, that on that point my judgment was sound. Yes: his decision was irreversible.

It is not seldom the case that, when a man is browbeaten in some unprecedented and violently unreasonable way, he begins to stagger in his own plainest faith. He begins, as it were, vaguely to surmise that, wonderful as it may be, all the justice and all the reason is on the other side. Accordingly, if any disinterested persons are present, he turns to them for some reinforcement of his own faltering mind.

"Turkey," said I, "what do you think of this? Am I not right?"

"With submission, sir," said Turkey, in his blandest tone, "I think that you are."

"Nippers," said I, "what do *you* think of it?"

"I think I should kick him out of the office."

(The reader, of nice perceptions, will here perceive that, it being morning, Turkey's answer is couched in polite and tranquil terms, but Nippers' replies in ill-tempered ones. Or, to repeat a previous sentence, Nippers' ugly mood was on duty, and Turkey's off.)

"Ginger Nut," said I, willing to enlist the smallest suffrage in my behalf, "what do *you* think of it?"

"I think, sir, he's a little *luny*," replied Ginger Nut, with a grin.

"You hear what they say," said I, turning towards the screen, "come forth and do your duty."

But he vouchsafed no reply. I pondered a moment in sore perplexity. But once more business hurried me. I determined again to postpone the consideration of this dilemma to my future leisure. With a little trouble we made out to examine the papers without Bartleby, though at every page or two Turkey deferentially dropped his opinion, that this proceeding was quite out of the common; while Nippers, twitching in his chair with a dyspeptic nervousness, ground out, between his set teeth, occasional hissing maledictions against the stubborn oaf behind the screen. And for his (Nippers') part, this was the first and the last time he would do another man's business without pay.

Meanwhile Bartleby sat in his hermitage, oblivious to everything but his own peculiar business there.

Some days passed, the scrivener being employed upon another lengthy work. His late remarkable conduct led me to regard his ways narrowly. I observed that he never went to dinner; indeed, that he never went anywhere. As yet I had never, of my personal knowledge, known him to be outside of my office. He was a perpetual sentry in the corner. At about eleven o'clock though, in the morning, I noticed that Ginger Nut would advance toward the opening in Bartleby's screen, as if silently beckoned thither by a gesture invisible to me where I sat. The boy would then leave the office, jingling a few pence, and reappear with a handful of ginger-nuts, which he delivered in the hermitage, receiving two of the cakes for his trouble.

He lives, then, on ginger-nuts, thought I; never eats a dinner, properly speaking; he must be a vegetarian, then; but no; he never eats even vegetables, he eats nothing but ginger-nuts. My mind then ran on in reveries concerning the probable effects upon the human constitution of living entirely on ginger-nuts. Ginger-nuts are so called, because they contain ginger as one of their peculiar constituents, and the final flavoring one. Now, what was ginger? A hot, spicy thing. Was Bartleby hot and spicy? Not at all. Ginger, then, had no effect upon Bartleby. Probably he preferred it should have none.

55 Nothing so aggravates an earnest person as a passive resistance. If the individual so resisted be of a not inhumane temper, and the resisting one perfectly harmless in his passivity, then, in the better moods of the former, he will endeavor charitably to construe to his imagination what proves impossible to be solved by his judgment. Even so, for the most part, I regarded Bartleby and his ways. Poor fellow! thought I, he means no mischief; it is plain he intends no insolence; his aspect sufficiently evinces that his eccentricities are involuntary. He is useful to me. I can get along with him. If I turn him away, the chances are he will fall in with some less-indulgent employer, and then he will be rudely treated, and perhaps driven forth miserably to starve. Yes. Here I can cheaply purchase a delicious self-approval. To befriend Bartleby; to humor him in his strange willfulness, will cost me little or nothing, while I lay up in my soul what will eventually prove a sweet morsel for my conscience. But this mood was not invariable with me. The passiveness of Bartleby sometimes irritated me. I felt strangely goaded on to encounter him in new opposition—to elicit some angry spark from him answerable to my own. But, indeed, I might as well have essayed to strike fire with my knuckles against a bit of Windsor soap. But one afternoon the evil impulse in me mastered me, and the following little scene ensued:

"Bartleby," said I, "when those papers are all copied, I will compare them with you."

"I would prefer not to."

"How? Surely you do not mean to persist in that mulish vagary?"

No answer.

60 I threw open the folding-doors near by, and, turning upon Turkey and Nippers, exclaimed:

"Bartleby a second time says, he won't examine his papers. What do you think of it, Turkey?"

It was afternoon, be it remembered. Turkey sat glowing like a brass boiler; his bald head steaming; his hands reeling among his blotted papers.

"Think of it?" roared Turkey; "I think I'll just step behind his screen, and black his eyes for him!"

So saying, Turkey rose to his feet and threw his arms into a pugilistic position. He was hurrying away to make good his promise, when I detained him, alarmed at the effect of incautiously rousing Turkey's combativeness after dinner.

"Sit down, Turkey," said I, "and hear what Nippers has to say. What do 65
you think of it, Nippers? Would I not be justified in immediately dismissing Bartleby?"

"Excuse me, that is for you to decide, sir. I think his conduct quite unusual, and, indeed, unjust, as regards Turkey and myself. But it may only be a passing whim."

"Ah," exclaimed I, "you have strangely changed your mind, then—you speak very gently of him now."

"All beer," cried Turkey; "gentleness is effects of beer—Nippers and I dined together to-day. You see how gentle *I* am, sir. Shall I go and black his eyes?"

"You refer to Bartleby, I suppose. No, not to-day, Turkey," I replied; "pray, put up your fists."

I closed the doors, and again advanced towards Bartleby. I felt additional 70
incentives tempting me to my fate. I burned to be rebelled against again. I remember that Bartleby never left the office.

"Bartleby," said I, "Ginger Nut is away; just step around to the Post Office, won't you? (it was but a three minutes' walk), and see if there is anything for me."

"I would prefer not to."

"You *will* not?"

"I *prefer* not."

I staggered to my desk, and sat there in a deep study. My blind inveteracy 75
returned. Was there any other thing in which I could procure myself to be ignominiously repulsed by this lean, penniless wight?—my hired clerk? What added thing is there, perfectly reasonable, that he will be sure to refuse to do?

"Bartleby!"

No answer.

"Bartleby," in a louder tone.

No answer.

"Bartleby," I roared. 80

Like a very ghost, agreeably to the laws of magical invocation, at the third summons, he appeared at the entrance of his hermitage.

"Go to the next room, and tell Nippers to come to me."

"I prefer not to," he respectfully and slowly said, and mildly disappeared.

"Very good, Bartleby," said I, in a quiet sort of serenely-severe self-possessed tone, intimating the unalterable purpose of some terrible retribution very close at hand. But upon the whole, as it was drawing towards my dinner-hour, I thought it best to put on my hat and walk home for the day, suffering much from perplexity and distress of mind.

Shall I acknowledge it? The conclusion of this whole business was, that it 85
soon became a fixed fact of my chambers, that a pale young scrivener, by the name of Bartleby, had a desk there; that he copied for me at the usual rate of four cents a folio (one hundred words); but he was permanently exempt from

examining the work done by him, that duty being transferred to Turkey and Nippers, out of compliment, doubtless, to their superior acuteness; moreover, said Bartleby was never, on any account, to be dispatched on the most trivial errand of any sort; and that even if entreated to take upon him such a matter, it was generally understood that he would "prefer not to"—in other words, that he would refuse point-blank.

As days passed on, I became considerably reconciled to Bartleby. His steadiness, his freedom from all dissipation, his incessant industry (except when he chose to throw himself into a standing revery behind his screen), his great stillness, his unalterableness of demeanor under all circumstances, made him a valuable acquisition. One prime thing was this—*he was always there*—first in the morning, continually through the day, and the last at night. I had a singular confidence in his honesty. I felt my most precious papers perfectly safe in his hands. Sometimes, to be sure, I could not, for the very soul of me, avoid falling into sudden spasmodic passions with him. For it was exceeding difficult to bear in mind all the time those strange peculiarities, privileges, and unheard of exemptions, forming the tacit stipulations on Bartleby's part under which he remained in my office. Now and then, in the eagerness of dispatching pressing business, I would inadvertently summon Bartleby, in a short, rapid tone, to put his finger, say, on the incipient tie of a bit of red tape with which I was about compressing some papers. Of course, from behind the screen the usual answer, "I prefer not to," was sure to come; and then, how could a human creature, with the common infirmities of our nature, refrain from bitterly exclaiming upon such perverseness—such unreasonableness. However, every added repulse of this sort which I received only tended to lessen the probability of my repeating the inadvertence.

Here it must be said, that according to the custom of most legal gentlemen occupying chambers in densely-populated law buildings, there were several keys to my door. One was kept by a woman residing in the attic, which person weekly scrubbed and daily swept and dusted my apartments. Another was kept by Turkey for convenience sake. The third I sometimes carried in my own pocket. The fourth I knew not who had.

Now, one Sunday morning I happened to go to Trinity Church, to hear a celebrated preacher, and finding myself rather early on the ground I thought I would walk around to my chambers for a while. Luckily I had my key with me; but upon applying it to the lock, I found it resisted by something inserted from the inside. Quite surprised, I called out; when to my consternation a key was turned from within; and thrusting his lean visage at me, and holding the door ajar, the apparition of Bartleby appeared, in his shirt sleeves, and otherwise in a strangely tattered deshabille, saying quietly that he was sorry, but he was deeply engaged just then, and—preferred not admitting me at present. In a brief word or two, he moreover added, that perhaps I had better walk around the block two or three times, and by that time he would probably have concluded his affairs.

Now, the utterly unsurmised appearance of Bartleby, tenanting my law-chambers of a Sunday morning, with his cadaverously gentlemanly *nonchalance*, yet withal firm and self-possessed, had such a strange effect upon me, that incontinently I slunk away from my own door, and did as desired. But not without sundry twinges of impotent rebellion against the mild effrontery of this unaccountable scrivener. Indeed, it was his wonderful mildness chiefly, which not only disarmed me, but unmanned me as it were. For I consider that one, for the time, is somehow unmanned when he tranquilly permits his hired clerk to dictate to him, and order him away from his own premises. Furthermore, I was full of uneasiness as to what Bartleby could possibly be doing in my office in his shirt sleeves, and in an otherwise dismantled condition of a Sunday morning. Was anything amiss going on? Nay, that was out of the question. It was not to be thought of for a moment that Bartleby was an immoral person. But what could he be doing there?—copying? Nay again, whatever might be his eccentricities, Bartleby was an eminently decorous person. He would be the last man to sit down to his desk in any state approaching to nudity. Besides, it was Sunday; and there was something about Bartleby that forbade the supposition that he would by any secular occupation violate the proprieties of the day.

Nevertheless, my mind was not pacified; and full of a restless curiosity, at 90
last I returned to the door. Without hindrance I inserted my key, opened it, and entered. Bartleby was not to be seen. I looked round anxiously, peeped behind his screen; but it was very plain that he was gone. Upon more closely examining the place, I surmised that for an indefinite period Bartleby must have ate, dressed, and slept in my office, and that, too, without plate, mirror, or bed. The cushioned seat of a rickety old sofa in one corner bore the faint impression of a lean, reclining form. Rolled away under his desk, I found a blanket; on a chair, a tin basin, with soap and a ragged towel; in a newspaper a few crumbs of ginger-nuts and a morsel of cheese. Yes, thought I, it is evident enough that Bartleby has been making his home here, keeping bachelor's hall all by himself. Immediately then the thought came sweeping across me, what miserable friendlessness and loneliness are here revealed! His poverty is great; but his solitude, how horrible! Think of it. Of a Sunday, Wall Street is deserted as Petra; and every night of every day it is an emptiness. This building, too, which of week-days hums with industry and life, at nightfall echoes with sheer vacancy, and all through Sunday is forlorn. And here Bartleby makes his home; sole spectator of a solitude which he has seen all populous—a sort of innocent and transformed Marius brooding among the ruins of Carthage!

For the first time in my life a feeling of over-powering stinging melancholy seized me. Before, I had never experienced aught but a not unpleasing sadness. The bond of a common humanity now drew me irresistibly to gloom. A fraternal melancholy! For both I and Bartleby were sons of Adam. I remembered the bright silks and sparkling faces I had seen that day, in gala trim, swan-like sailing down the Mississippi of Broadway; and I contrasted them with the pallid copyist, and thought to myself, Ah, happiness courts the light, so we deem the world is gay; but misery hides aloof, so we deem that misery there is none. These sad fancyings—chimeras, doubtless, of a sick and silly brain—led on to other and more special thoughts, concerning the eccentricities of Bartleby. Presentiments of strange discoveries hovered round me. The scrivener's pale form appeared to me laid out, among uncaring strangers, in its shivering winding sheet.

Suddenly I was attracted by Bartleby's closed desk, the key in open sight left in the lock.

I mean no mischief, seek the gratification of no heartless curiosity, thought I; besides, the desk is mine, and its contents, too, so I will make bold to look within. Everything was methodically arranged, the papers smoothly placed. The pigeon holes were deep, and removing the files of documents, I groped into their recesses. Presently I felt something there, and dragged it out. It was an old bandanna handkerchief, heavy and knotted. I opened it, and saw it was a saving's bank.

I now recalled all the quiet mysteries which I had noted in the man. I remembered that he never spoke but to answer; that, though at intervals he had considerable time to himself, yet I had never seen him reading—no, not even a newspaper; that for long periods he would stand looking out, at his pale window behind the screen, upon the dead brick wall; I was quite sure he never visited any refectory or eating house; while his pale face clearly indicated that he never drank beer like Turkey, or tea and coffee even, like other men; that he never went anywhere in particular that I could learn; never went out for a walk, unless, indeed, that was the case at present; that he had declined telling who he was, or whence he came, or whether he had any relatives in the world; that though so thin and pale, he never complained of ill health. And more than all, I remembered a certain unconscious air of pallid—how shall I call it?—of pallid haughtiness, say, or rather an austere reserve about him, which had positively awed me into my tame compliance with his eccentricities, when I had feared to ask him to do the slightest incidental thing for me, even though I might know, from his long-continued motionlessness, that behind his screen he must be standing in one of those deadwall reveries of his.

95 Revolving all these things, and coupling them with the recently discovered fact, that he made my office his constant abiding place and home, and not forgetful of his morbid moodiness; revolving all these things, a prudential feeling began to steal over me. My first emotions had been those of pure melancholy and sincerest pity; but just in proportion as the forlornness of Bartleby grew and grew to my imagination, did that same melancholy merge into fear, that pity into repulsion. So true it is, and so terrible, too, that up to a certain point the thought or sight of misery enlists our best affections; but, in certain special cases, beyond that point it does not. They err who would assert that invariably this is owing to the inherent selfishness of the human heart. It rather proceeds from a certain hopelessness of remedying excessive and organic ill. To a sensitive being, pity is not seldom pain. And when at last it is perceived that such pity cannot lead to effectual succor, common sense bids the soul be rid of it. What I saw that morning persuaded me that the scrivener was the victim of inate and incurable disorder. I might give alms to his body; but his body did not pain him; it was his soul that suffered, and his soul I could not reach.

I did not accomplish the purpose of going to Trinity Church that morning. Somehow, the things I had seen disqualified me for the time from church-going. I walked homeward, thinking what I would do with Bartleby. Finally, I resolved upon this—I would put certain calm questions to him the next morning, touching his history, etc., and if he declined to answer them openly and unreservedly (and I supposed he would prefer not), then to give him a twenty dollar bill over and above whatever I might owe him, and tell him his services were no longer required; but that if in any other way I could assist him, I would be happy to do so, especially if he desired to return to his native place, wherever that might be, I would willingly help to defray the expenses. Moreover, if, after reaching home, he found himself at any time in want of aid, a letter from him would be sure of a reply.

The next morning came.

"Bartleby," said I, gently calling to him behind his screen.

No reply.

"Bartleby," said I, in a still gentler tone, "come here; I am not going to ask you to do anything you would prefer not to do—I simply wish to speak to you."

Upon this he noiselessly slid into view.

"Will you tell me, Bartleby, where you were born?"

"I would prefer not to."

"Will you tell me *anything* about yourself?"

"I would prefer not to."

"But what reasonable objection can you have to speak to me? I feel friendly towards you."

He did not look at me while I spoke, but kept his glance fixed upon my bust of Cicero, which, as I then sat, was directly behind me, some six inches above my head.

"What is your answer, Bartleby," said I, after waiting a considerable time for a reply, during which his countenance remained immovable, only there was the faintest conceivable tremor of the white attenuated mouth.

"At present I prefer to give no answer," he said, and retired into his hermitage.

It was rather weak in me I confess, but his manner, on this occasion, nettled me. Not only did there seem to lurk in it a certain calm disdain, but his perverseness seemed ungrateful, considering the undeniable good usage and indulgence he had received from me.

Again I sat ruminating what I should do. Mortified as I was at his behavior, and resolved as I had been to dismiss him when I entered my office, nevertheless I strangely felt something superstitious knocking at my heart, and forbidding me to carry out my purpose, and denouncing me for a villain if I dared to breathe one bitter word against this forlornest of mankind. At last, familiarly drawing my chair behind his screen, I sat down and said: "Bartleby, never mind, then, about revealing your history; but let me entreat you, as a friend, to comply as far as may be with the usages of this office. Say now, you will help to examine papers to-morrow or next day: in short, say now, that in a day or two you will begin to be a little reasonable:—say so, Bartleby."

"At present I would prefer not to be a little reasonable," was his mildly cadaverous reply.

Just then the folding-doors opened, and Nippers approached. He seemed suffering from an unusually bad night's rest, induced by severer indigestion than common. He overheard those final words of Bartleby.

"*Prefer not,* eh?" gritted Nippers—"I'd *prefer* him, if I were you, sir," addressing me—"I'd *prefer* him; I'd give him preferences, the stubborn mule! What is it, sir, pray, that he *prefers* not to do now?"

Bartleby moved not a limb. 115

"Mr. Nippers," said I, "I'd prefer that you would withdraw for the present."

Somehow, of late, I had got into the way of involuntarily using this word "prefer" upon all sorts of not exactly suitable occasions. And I trembled to think that my contact with the scrivener had already and seriously affected me in a mental way. And what further and deeper aberration might it not yet produce? This apprehension had not been without efficacy in determining me to summary measures.

As Nippers, looking very sour and sulky, was departing, Turkey blandly and deferentially approached.

"With submission, sir," said he, "yesterday I was thinking about Bartleby here, and I think that if he would but prefer to take a quart of good ale every day, it would do much towards mending him, and enabling him to assist in examining his papers."

"So you have got the word, too," said I, slightly excited. 120

"With submission, what word, sir," asked Turkey, respectfully crowding himself into the contracted space behind the screen, and by so doing, making me jostle the scrivener. "What word, sir?"

"I would prefer to be left alone here," said Bartleby, as if offended at being mobbed in his privacy.

"*That's* the word, Turkey," said I—"*that's* it."

"Oh, *prefer?* oh yes—queer word. I never use it myself. But, sir, as I was saying, if he would but prefer—"

"Turkey," interrupted I, "you will please withdraw." 125

"Oh, certainly, sir, if you prefer that I should."

As he opened the folding-door to retire, Nippers at his desk caught a glimpse of me, and asked whether I would prefer to have a certain paper copied on blue paper or white. He did not in the least roguishly accent the word prefer. It was plain that it involuntarily rolled from his tongue. I thought to myself, surely I must get rid of a demented man, who already has in some degree turned the tongues, if not the heads of myself and clerks. But I thought it prudent not to break the dismission at once.

The next day I noticed that Bartleby did nothing but stand at his window in his dead-wall revery. Upon asking him why he did not write, he said that he had decided upon doing no more writing.

"Why, how now? what next?" exclaimed I, "do no more writing?"

"No more." 130

"And what is the reason?"

"Do you not see the reason for yourself," he indifferently replied.

I looked steadfastly at him, and perceived that his eyes looked dull and glazed. Instantly it occurred to me, that his unexampled diligence in copying by his dim window for the first few weeks of his stay with me might have temporarily impaired his vision.

I was touched. I said something in condolence with him. I hinted that of course he did wisely in abstaining from writing for a while; and urged him to embrace that opportunity of taking wholesome exercise in the open air. This, however, he did not do. A few days after this, my other clerks being absent, and being in a great hurry to dispatch certain letters by the mail, I thought that, having nothing else earthly to do, Bartleby would surely be less inflexible than usual, and carry these letters to the post-office. But he blankly declined. So, much to my inconvenience, I went myself.

Still added days went by. Whether Bartleby's eyes improved or not, I 135
could not say. To all appearance, I thought they did. But when I asked him if they did, he vouchsafed no answer. At all events, he would do no copying. At last, in reply to my urgings, he informed me that he had permanently given up copying.

"What!" exclaimed I; "suppose your eyes should get entirely well—better than ever before—would you not copy then?"

"I have given up copying," he answered, and slid aside.

He remained as ever, a fixture in my chamber. Nay—if that were possible—he became still more of a fixture than before. What was to be done? He would do nothing in the office; why should he stay there? In plain fact, he had now become a millstone to me, not only useless as a necklace, but afflictive to bear. Yet I was sorry for him. I speak less than truth when I say that, on his own account, he occasioned me uneasiness. If he would but have named a single relative or friend, I would instantly have written, and urged their taking the poor fellow away to some convenient retreat. But he seemed alone, absolutely alone in the universe. A bit of wreck in the mid Atlantic. At length, necessities connected with my business tyrannized over all other considerations. Decently as I could, I told Bartleby that in six days time he must unconditionally leave the office. I warned him to take measures, in the interval, for procuring some other abode. I offered to assist him in this endeavor, if he himself would but take the first step towards a removal. "And when you finally quit me, Bartleby," added I, "I shall see that you go not away entirely unprovided. Six days from this hour, remember."

At the expiration of that period, I peeped behind the screen, and lo! Bartleby was there.

I buttoned up my coat, balanced myself; advanced slowly towards him, 140
touched his shoulder, and said, "The time has come; you must quit this place; I am sorry for you; here is money; but you must go."

"I would prefer not," he replied, with his back still towards me.

"You *must.*"

He remained silent.

Now I had an unbounded confidence in this man's common honesty. He had frequently restored to me sixpences and shillings carelessly dropped upon the floor, for I am apt to be very reckless in such shirt-button affairs. The proceeding, then, which followed will not be deemed extraordinary.

"Bartleby," said I, "I owe you twelve dollars on account; here are thirty- 145
two; the odd twenty are yours—Will you take it?" and I handed the bills towards him.

But he made no motion.

"I will leave them here, then," putting them under a weight on the table. Then taking my hat and cane and going to the door, I tranquilly turned and added—"After you have removed your things from these offices, Bartleby, you will of course lock the door—since every one is now gone for the day but you—and if you please, slip your key underneath the mat, so that I may have it in the morning. I shall not see you again; so good-by to you. If, hereafter, in your new place of abode, I can be of any service to you, do not fail to advise me by letter. Good-by, Bartleby, and fare you well."

But he answered not a word; like the last column of some ruined temple, he remained standing mute and solitary in the middle of the otherwise deserted room.

As I walked home in a pensive mood, my vanity got the better of my pity. I could not but highly plume myself on my masterly management in getting rid of Bartleby. Masterly I call it, and such it must appear to any dispassionate thinker. The beauty of my procedure seemed to consist in its perfect quietness. There was no vulgar bullying, no bravado of any sort, no choleric hectoring, and striding to and fro across the apartment, jerking out vehement commands for Bartleby to bundle himself off with his beggarly traps. Nothing of the kind. Without loudly bidding Bartleby depart—as an inferior genius might have done—I *assumed* the ground that depart he must; and upon that assumption built all I had to say. The more I thought over my procedure, the more I was charmed with it. Nevertheless, next morning, upon awakening, I had my doubts—I had somehow slept off the fumes of vanity. One of the coolest and wisest hours a man has, is just after he awakes in the morning. My procedure seemed as sagacious as ever—but only in theory. How it would prove in practice—there was the rub. It was truly a beautiful thought to have assumed Bartleby's departure; but, after all, that assumption was simply my own, and none of Bartleby's. The great point was, not whether I had assumed that he would quit me, but whether he would prefer so to do. He was more a man of preferences than assumptions.

After breakfast, I walked down town, arguing the probabilities *pro* and 150
con. One moment I thought it would prove a miserable failure, and Bartleby would be found all alive at my office as usual; the next moment it seemed certain that I should find his chair empty. And so I kept veering about. At the corner of Broadway and Canal Street, I saw quite an excited group of people standing in earnest conversation.

"I'll take odds he doesn't," said a voice as I passed.

"Doesn't go?—done!" said I, "put up your money."

I was instinctively putting my hand in my pocket to produce my own, when I remembered that this was an election day. The words I had overheard bore no reference to Bartleby, but to the success or nonsuccess of some candidate for the mayoralty. In my intent frame of mind, I had, as it were, imagined that all Broadway shared in my excitement, and were debating the same question with me. I passed on, very thankful that the uproar of the street screened my momentary absent-mindedness.

As I had intended, I was earlier than usual at my office door. I stood listening for a moment. All was still. He must be gone. I tried the knob. The door was locked. Yes, my procedure had worked to a charm; he indeed must be vanished. Yet a certain melancholy mixed with this: I was almost sorry for my brilliant success. I was fumbling under the door mat for the key, which Bartleby was to have left there for me, when accidentally my knee knocked against a panel, producing a summoning sound, and in response a voice came to me from within—"Not yet; I am occupied."

It was Bartleby. 155

I was thunderstruck. For an instant I stood like the man who, pipe in mouth, was killed one cloudless afternoon long ago in Virginia, by summer lightning; at his own warm open window he was killed, and remained leaning out there upon the dreamy afternoon, till some one touched him, when he fell.

"Not gone!" I murmured at last. But again obeying that wondrous ascendancy which the inscrutable scrivener had over me, and from which ascendancy, for all my chafing, I could not completely escape, I slowly went down stairs and out into the street, and while walking round the block, considered what I should next do in this unheard-of perplexity. Turn the man out by an actual thrusting I could not; to drive him away by calling him hard names would not do; calling in the police was an unpleasant idea; and yet, permit him to enjoy his cadaverous triumph over me—this, too, I could not think of. What was to be done? or, if nothing could be done, was there anything further that I could *assume* in the matter? Yes, as before I had prospectively assumed that Bartleby would depart, so now I might retrospectively assume that departed he was. In the legitimate carrying out of this assumption, I might enter my office in a great hurry, and pretending not to see Bartleby at all, walk straight against him as if he were air. Such a proceeding would in a singular degree have the appearance of a home-thrust. It was hardly possible that Bartleby could withstand such an application of the doctrine of assumptions. But upon second thoughts the success of the plan seemed rather dubious. I resolved to argue the matter over with him again.

"Bartleby," said I, entering the office, with a quietly severe expression, "I am seriously displeased. I am pained, Bartleby. I had thought better of you. I had imagined you of such a gentlemanly organization, that in any delicate dilemma a slight hint would suffice—in short, an assumption. But it appears I am deceived. Why," I added, unaffectedly starting, "you have not even touched that money yet," pointing to it, just where I had left it the evening previous.

He answered nothing.

"Will you, or will you not, quit me?" I now demanded in a sudden pas- 160
sion, advancing close to him.

"I would prefer *not* to quit you," he replied, gently emphasizing the *not.*

"What earthly right have you to stay here? Do you pay any rent? Do you pay my taxes? Or is this property yours?"

He answered nothing.

"Are you ready to go on and write now? Are your eyes recovered? Could you copy a small paper for me this morning? or help examine a few lines? or step round to the post-office? In a word, will you do anything at all, to give a coloring to your refusal to depart the premises?"

He silently retired into his hermitage.

I was now in such a state of nervous resentment that I thought it but prudent to check myself at present from further demonstrations. Bartleby and I were alone. I remembered the tragedy of the unfortunate Adams and the still more unfortunate Colt in the solitary office of the latter; and how poor Colt, being dreadfully incensed by Adams, and imprudently permitting himself to get wildly excited, was at unawares hurried into his fatal act—an act which certainly no man could possibly deplore more than the actor himself. Often it had occurred to me in my ponderings upon the subject, that had that altercation taken place in the public street, or at a private residence, it would not have terminated as it did. It was the circumstance of being alone in a solitary office, up stairs, of a building entirely unhallowed by humanizing domestic associations—an uncarpeted office, doubtless, of a dusty, haggard sort of appearance—this it must have been, which greatly helped to enhance the irritable desperation of the hapless Colt.

But when this old Adam of resentment rose in me and tempted me concerning Bartleby, I grappled him and threw him. How? Why, simply by recalling the divine injunction: "A new commandment give I unto you, that ye love one another." Yes, this it was that saved me. Aside from higher considerations, charity often operates as a vastly wise and prudent principle—a great safeguard to its possessor. Men have committed murder for jealousy's sake, and anger's sake, and hatred's sake, and selfishness' sake, and spiritual pride's sake; but no man, that ever I heard of, ever committed a diabolical murder for sweet charity's sake. Mere self-interest, then, if no better motive can be enlisted, should, especially with high-tempered men, prompt all beings to charity and philanthropy. At any rate, upon the occasion in question, I strove to drown my exasperated feelings towards the scrivener by benevolently construing his conduct. Poor fellow, poor fellow! thought I, he don't mean anything; and besides, he has seen hard times, and ought to be indulged.

I endeavored, also, immediately to occupy myself, and at the same time to comfort my despondency. I tried to fancy, that in the course of the morning, at such time as might prove agreeable to him, Bartleby, of his own free accord, would emerge from his hermitage and take up some decided line of march in the direction of the door. But no. Half-past twelve o'clock came; Turkey began to glow in the face, overturn his inkstand, and become generally obstreperous; Nippers abated down into quietude and courtesy; Ginger Nut munched his noon apple; and Bartleby remained standing at his window in one of his profoundest dead-wall reveries. Will it be credited? Ought I to acknowledge it? That afternoon I left the office without saying one further word to him.

Some days now passed, during which, at leisure intervals I looked a little into "Edwards on the Will," and "Priestly on Necessity." Under the circumstances, those books induced a salutary feeling. Gradually I slid into the persuasion that these troubles of mine, touching the scrivener, had been all predestinated from eternity, and Bartleby was billeted upon me for some mysterious purpose of an allwise Providence, which it was not for a mere mortal like me to fathom. Yes, Bartleby, stay there behind your screen, thought I; I shall persecute you no more; you are harmless and noiseless as any of these old chairs; in short, I never feel so private as when I know you are here. At last I see it, I feel it; I penetrate to the predestinated purpose of my life. I am content. Others may have loftier parts to enact; but my mission in this world, Bartleby, is to furnish you with office-room for such period as you may see fit to remain.

I believe that this wise and blessed frame of mind would have continued with me, had it not been for the unsolicited and uncharitable remarks obtruded upon me by my professional friends who visited the rooms. But thus it often is, that the constant friction of illiberal minds wears out at last the best resolves of the more generous. Though to be sure, when I reflected upon it, it was not strange that people entering my office should be struck by the peculiar aspect of the unaccountable Bartleby, and so be tempted to throw out some sinister observations concerning him. Sometimes an attorney, having business with me, and calling at my office, and finding no one but the scrivener there, would undertake to obtain some sort of precise information from him touching my whereabouts; but without heeding his idle talk, Bartleby would remain standing immovable in the middle of the room. So after contemplating him in that position for a time, the attorney would depart, no wiser than he came.

Also, when a reference was going on, and the room full of lawyers and witnesses, and business driving fast, some deeply-occupied legal gentleman present, seeing Bartleby wholly unemployed, would request him to run round to his (the legal gentleman's) office and fetch some papers for him. Thereupon, Bartleby would tranquilly decline, and yet remain idle as before. Then the lawyer would give a great stare, and turn to me. And what could I say? At last I was made aware that all through the circle of my professional acquaintance, a whisper of wonder was running round, having reference to the strange creature I kept at my office. This worried me very much. And as the idea came upon me of his possibly turning out a long-lived man, and keep occupying my chambers, and denying my authority; and perplexing my visitors; and scandalizing my professional reputation; and casting a general gloom over the premises; keeping soul and body together to the last upon his savings (for doubtless he spent but half a dime a day), and in the end perhaps outlive me, and claim possession of my office by right of his perpetual occupancy: as all these dark anticipations crowded upon me more and more, and my friends continually intruded their relentless remarks upon the apparition in my room;

a great change was wrought in me. I resolved to gather all my faculties together, and forever rid me of this intolerable incubus.

Ere revolving any complicated project, however, adapted to this end, I first simply suggested to Bartleby the propriety of his permanent departure. In a calm and serious tone, I commended the idea to his careful and mature consideration. But, having taken three days to meditate upon it, he apprised me, that his original determination remained the same; in short, that he still preferred to abide with me.

What shall I do? I now said to myself, buttoning up my coat to the last button. What shall I do? what ought I to do? what does conscience say I *should* do with this man, or, rather, ghost. Rid myself of him, I must; go, he shall. But how? You will not thrust him, the poor, pale, passive mortal—you will not thrust such a helpless creature out of your door? you will not dishonor yourself by such cruelty? No, I will not, I cannot do that. Rather would I let him live and die here, and then mason up his remains in the wall. What, then, will you do? For all your coaxing, he will not budge. Bribes he leaves under your own paper-weight on your table; in short, it is quite plain that he prefers to cling to you.

Then something severe, something unusual must be done. What! surely you will not have him collared by a constable, and commit his innocent pallor to the common jail? And upon what ground could you procure such a thing to be done?—a vagrant, is he? What! he a vagrant, a wanderer, who refuses to budge? It is because he will *not* be a vagrant, then, that you seek to count him *as* a vagrant. That is too absurd. No visible means of support: there I have him. Wrong again: for indubitably he *does* support himself, and that is the only unanswerable proof that any man can show of his possessing the means so to do. No more, then. Since he will not quit me, I must quit him. I will change my offices; I will move elsewhere, and give him fair notice, that if I find him on my new premises I will then proceed against him as a common trespasser.

Acting accordingly, next day I thus addressed him: "I find these chambers too far from the City Hall; the air is unwholesome. In a word, I propose to remove my offices next week, and shall no longer require your services. I tell you this now, in order that you may seek another place."

He made no reply, and nothing more was said.

On the appointed day I engaged carts and men, proceeded to my chambers, and, having but little furniture, everything was removed in a few hours. Throughout, the scrivener remained standing behind the screen, which I directed to be removed the last thing. It was withdrawn; and, being folded up like a huge folio, left him the motionless occupant of a naked room. I stood in the entry watching him a moment, while something from within me upbraided me.

I re-entered, with my hand in my pocket—and—and my heart in my mouth.

"Good-by, Bartleby; I am going—good-by, and God some way bless you; and take that," slipping something in his hand. But it dropped upon the floor, and then—strange to say—I tore myself from him whom I had so longed to be rid of.

Established in my new quarters, for a day or two I kept the door locked, 180
and started at every footfall in the passages. When I returned to my rooms, after any little absence, I would pause at the threshold for an instant, and attentively listen, ere applying my key. But these fears were needless. Bartleby never came nigh me.

I thought all was going well, when a perturbed-looking stranger visited me, inquiring whether I was the person who had recently occupied rooms at No.—Wall Street.

Full of forebodings, I replied that I was.

"Then, sir," said the stranger, who proved a lawyer, "you are responsible for the man you left there. He refuses to do any copying; he refuses to do anything; he says he prefers not to; and he refuses to quit the premises."

"I am very sorry, sir," said I, with assumed tranquillity, but an inward tremor, "but, really, the man you allude to is nothing to me—he is no relation or apprentice of mine, that you should hold me responsible for him."

"In mercy's name, who is he?" 185

"I certainly cannot inform you. I know nothing about him. Formerly I employed him as a copyist; but he has done nothing for me now for some time past."

"I shall settle him, then—good morning, sir."

Several days passed, and I heard nothing more; and, though I often felt a charitable prompting to call at the place and see poor Bartleby, yet a certain squeamishness, of I know not what, withheld me.

All is over with him, by this time, thought I, at last, when, through another week, no further intelligence reached me. But, coming to my room the day after, I found several persons waiting at my door in a high state of nervous excitement.

"That's the man—here he comes," cried the foremost one, whom I rec- 190
ognized as the lawyer who had previously called upon me alone.

"You must take him away, sir, at once," cried a portly person among them, advancing upon me, and whom I knew to be the landlord of No.—Wall Street. "These gentlemen, my tenants, cannot stand it any longer; Mr. B——," pointing to the lawyer, "has turned him out of his room, and he now persists in haunting the building generally, sitting upon the banisters of the stairs by day, and sleeping in the entry by night. Everybody is concerned; clients are leaving the offices; some fears are entertained of a mob; something you must do, and that without delay."

Aghast at this torrent, I fell back before it, and would fain have locked myself in my new quarters. In vain I persisted that Bartleby was nothing to me—no more than to any one else. In vain—I was the last person known to have anything to do with him, and they held me to the terrible account. Fearful, then, of being exposed in the papers (as one person present obscurely threatened), I considered the matter, and, at length, said, that if the lawyer would give me a confidential interview with the scrivener, in his (the lawyer's) own room, I would, that afternoon, strive my best to rid them of the nuisance they complained of.

Going up stairs to my old haunt, there was Bartleby silently sitting upon the banister at the landing.

"What are you doing here, Bartleby?" said I.

"Sitting upon the banister," he mildly replied.

I motioned him into the lawyer's room, who then left us.

"Bartleby," said I, "are you aware that you are the cause of great tribulation to me, by persisting in occupying entry after being dismissed from the office?"

No answer.

"Now one of two things must take place. Either you must do something, or something must be done to you. Now what sort of business would you like to engage in? Would you like to re-engage in copying for some one?"

"No; I would prefer not to make any change."

"Would you like a clerkship in a dry-goods store?"

"There is too much confinement about that. No, I would not like a clerkship; but I am not particular."

"Too much confinement," I cried, "why you keep yourself confined all the time!"

"I would prefer not to take a clerkship," he rejoined, as if to settle that little item at once.

"How would a bar-tender's business suit you? There is no trying of the eye-sight in that."

"I would not like it at all; though, as I said before, I am not particular."

His unwonted wordiness inspirited me. I returned to the charge.

"Well, then, would you like to travel through the country collecting bills for the merchants? That would improve your health."

"No, I would prefer to be doing something else."

"How, then, would going as a companion to Europe, to entertain some young gentleman with your conversation—how would that suit you?"

"Not at all. It does not strike me that there is anything definite about that. I like to be stationary. But I am not particular."

"Stationary you shall be, then," I cried, now losing all patience, and, for the first time in all my exasperating connection with him, fairly flying into a passion. "If you do not go away from these premises before night, I shall feel bound—indeed, I *am* bound—*to—to—to* quit the premises myself!" I rather absurdly concluded, knowing not with what possible threat to try to frighten his immobility into compliance. Despairing of all further efforts, I was precipitately leaving him, when a final thought occurred to me—one which had not been wholly unindulged before.

"Bartleby," said I, in the kindest tone I could assume under such exciting circumstances, "will you go home with me now—not to my office, but my dwelling—and remain there till we can conclude upon some convenient arrangement for you at our leisure? Come, let us start now, right away."

"No: at present I would prefer not to make any change at all."

I answered nothing; but, effectually dodging every one by the suddenness and rapidity of my flight, rushed from the building, ran up Wall Street towards Broadway, and, jumping into the first omnibus, was soon removed from pursuit. As soon as tranquillity returned, I distinctly perceived that I had now done all that I possibly could, both in respect to the demands of the landlord and his tenants, and with regard to my own desire and sense of duty, to benefit Bartleby, and shield him from rude persecution. I now strove to be entirely care-free and quiescent; and my conscience justified me in the attempt; though, indeed, it was not so successful as I could have wished. So fearful was I of being again hunted out by the incensed landlord and his exasperated tenants, that, surrendering my business to Nippers, for a few days, I drove about the upper part of the town and through the suburbs, in my rockaway; crossed over to Jersey City and Hoboken, and paid fugitive visits to Manhattanville and Astoria. In fact, I almost lived in my rockaway for the time.

When again I entered my office, lo, a note from the landlord lay upon the desk. I opened it with trembling hands. It informed me that the writer had sent to the police, and had Bartleby removed to the Tombs as a vagrant. Moreover, since I knew more about him than any one else, he wished me to appear at that place, and make a suitable statement of the facts. These tidings had a conflicting effect upon me. At first I was indignant; but, at last, almost approved. The landlord's energetic, summary disposition, had led him to adopt a procedure which I do not think I would have decided upon myself; and yet, as a last resort, under such peculiar circumstances, it seemed the only plan.

As I afterwards learned, the poor scrivener, when told that he must be conducted to the Tombs, offered not the slightest obstacle, but, in his pale, unmoving way, silently acquiesced.

Some of the compassionate and curious bystanders joined the party; and headed by one of the constables arm in arm with Bartleby, the silent procession filed its way through all the noise, and heat, and joy of the roaring thoroughfares at noon.

The same day I received the note, I went to the Tombs, or, to speak more properly, the Halls of Justice. Seeking the right officer, I stated the purpose of my call, and was informed that the individual I described was, indeed, within. I then assured the functionary that Bartleby was a perfectly honest man, and greatly to be compassionated, however unaccountably eccentric. I narrated all I knew, and closed by suggesting the idea of letting him remain in as indulgent confinement as possible, till something less harsh might be done—though, indeed, I hardly knew what. At all events, if nothing else could be decided upon, the almshouse must receive him. I then begged to have an interview.

Being under no disgraceful charge, and quite serene and harmless in all 220
his ways, they had permitted him freely to wander about the prison, and, especially, in the inclosed grass-platted yards thereof. And so I found him there, standing all alone in the quietest of the yards, his face towards a high wall, while all around, from the narrow slits of the jail windows, I thought I saw peering out upon him the eyes of murderers and thieves.

"Bartleby!"

"I know you," he said without looking round—"and I want nothing to say to you."

"It was not I that brought you here, Bartleby," said I, keenly pained at his implied suspicion. "And to you, this should not be so vile a place. Nothing reproachful attaches to you by being here. And see, it is not so sad a place as one might think. Look, there is the sky, and here is the grass."

"I know where I am," he replied, but would say nothing more, and so I left him.

As I entered the corridor again, a broad meat-like man, in an apron, accosted me, and, jerking his thumb over his shoulder, said—"Is that your friend?"

"Yes."

"Does he want to starve? If he does, let him live on the prison fare, that's all."

"Who are you?" asked I, not knowing what to make of such an unofficially speaking person in such a place.

"I am the grub-man. Such gentlemen as have friends here, hire me to provide them with something good to eat."

"Is this so?" said I, turning to the turnkey.

He said it was.

"Well, then," said I, slipping some silver into the grub-man's hands (for so they called him), "I want you to give particular attention to my friend there; let him have the best dinner you can get. And you must be as polite to him as possible."

"Introduce me, will you?" said the grub-man, looking at me with an expression which seemed to say he was all impatience for an opportunity to give a specimen of his breeding.

Thinking it would prove of benefit to the scrivener, I acquiesced; and, asking the grub-man his name, went up with him to Bartleby.

"Bartleby, this is a friend; you will find him very useful to you."

"Your sarvant, sir, your sarvant," said the grub-man, making a low salutation behind his apron. "Hope you find it pleasant here, sir; nice grounds—cool apartments—hope you'll stay with us sometime—try to make it agreeable. What will you have for dinner to-day?"

"I prefer not to dine to-day," said Bartleby, turning away. "It would disagree with me; I am unused to dinners." So saying, he slowly moved to the other side of the inclosure, and took up a position fronting the dead-wall.

"How's this?" said the grub-man, addressing me with a stare of astonishment, "He's odd, ain't he?"

"I think he is a little deranged," said I, sadly.

"Deranged? deranged is it? Well, now, upon my word, I thought that friend of yourn was a gentleman forger; they are always pale and genteel-like, them forgers. I can't help pity 'em—can't help it, sir. Did you know Monroe Edwards?" he added, touchingly, and paused. Then, laying his hand piteously on my shoulder, sighed, "he died of consumption at Sing-Sing. So you weren't acquainted with Monroe?"

"No, I was never socially acquainted with any forgers. But I cannot stop longer. Look to my friend yonder. You will not lose by it. I will see you again."

Some few days after this, I again obtained admission to the Tombs, and went through the corridors in quest of Bartleby; but without finding him.

"I saw him coming from his cell not long ago," said a turnkey, "may be he's gone to loiter in the yards."

So I went in that direction.

"Are you looking for the silent man?" said another turnkey, passing me. "Yonder he lies—sleeping in the yard there. 'Tis not twenty minutes since I saw him lie down."

The yard was entirely quiet. It was not accessible to the common prisoners. The surrounding walls, of amazing thickness, kept off all sounds behind them. The Egyptian character of the masonry weighed upon me with its gloom. But a soft imprisoned turf grew under foot. The heart of the eternal pyramids, it seemed, wherein, by some strange magic, through the clefts, grass-seed, dropped by birds, had sprung.

Strangely huddled at the base of the wall, his knees drawn up, and lying on his side, his head touching the cold stones, I saw the wasted Bartleby. But nothing stirred. I paused; then went close up to him; stooped over, and saw that his dim eyes were open; otherwise he seemed profoundly sleeping. Something prompted me to touch him. I felt his hand, when a tingling shiver ran up my arm and down my spine to my feet.

The round face of the grub-man peered upon me now. "His dinner is ready. Won't he dine to-day, either? Or does he live without dining?"

"Lives without dining," said I, and closed the eyes.

"Eh!—He's asleep, ain't he?"

"With kings and counselors," murmured I.

There would seem little need for proceeding further in this history. Imagination will readily supply the meagre recital of poor Bartleby's interment. But, ere parting with the reader, let me say, that if this little narrative has sufficiently interested him, to awaken curiosity as to who Bartleby was, and what manner of life he led prior to the present narrator's making his acquaintance, I can only reply, that in such curiosity I fully share, but am wholly unable to gratify it. Yet here I hardly know whether I should divulge one little item of rumor, which came to my ear a few months after the scrivener's decease. Upon what basis it rested, I could never ascertain; and hence, how true it is I cannot now tell. But, inasmuch as this vague report has not been without a certain suggestive interest to me, however sad, it may prove the same with some others; and so I will briefly mention it. The report was this: that Bartleby had been a subordinate clerk in the Dead Letter Office at Washington, from which he had been suddenly removed by a change in the administration. When I think over this rumor, hardly can I express the emotions which seize me. Dead letters! does it not sound like dead men? Conceive a man by nature and misfortune prone to a pallid hopelessness, can any business seem more fitted to heighten it than that of continually handling these dead letters, and assorting them for the flames? For by the cartload they are annually burned. Sometimes from out the folded paper the pale clerk takes a ring—the finger it was meant for, perhaps, moulders in the grave; a bank-note sent in swiftest charity—he whom it would relieve, nor eats nor hungers any more; pardon for those who died despairing; hope for those who died unhoping; good tidings for those who died stifled by unrelieved calamities. On errands of life, these letters speed to death.

Ah, Bartleby! Ah, humanity!

Herman Melville

www (1819–1891) Web

After having worked as a bank clerk, farm hand, store clerk, schoolmaster, surveyor, and sailor, Melville became a writer. He began his career writing novels about South Seas adventures and in 1851 published *Moby Dick*. Melville's writing did not please the taste of the times sufficiently to enable him to live by the pen, so like his predecessor Nathaniel Hawthorne, he got a job in a customs house. Late in his life he inherited enough money to devote himself to writing full time.

www *TOPICS FOR CRITICAL THINKING* Web

1. Who is the protagonist in this story?
2. How does having worked in a Dead Letter Office account for Bartleby's behavior?
3. Why does Bartleby die soon after he is removed from the offices?
4. What is the function of such minor characters as Turkey, Nippers, and Ginger Nut?

www *TOPICS FOR CRITICAL WRITING* Web

1. What is the relation between the narrator and Bartleby?
2. In what ways does the image of the Dead Letter Office pervade the story?

Sarah Orne Jewett

The Flight of Betsey Lane *(1893)*

I.

One windy morning in May, three old women sat together near an open window in the shed chamber of Byfleet Poor-house. The wind was from the northwest, but their window faced the southeast, and they were only visited by an occasional pleasant waft of fresh air. They were close together, knee to knee, picking over a bushel of beans, and commanding a view of the dandelion-starred, green yard below, and of the winding, sandy road that led to the village, two miles away. Some captive bees were scolding among the cobwebs of the rafters overhead, or thumping against the upper panes of glass;

two calves were bawling from the barnyard, where some of the men were at work loading a dump-cart and shouting as if every one were deaf. There was a cheerful feeling of activity, and even an air of comfort, about the Byfleet Poor-house. Almost every one was possessed of a most interesting past, though there was less to be said about the future. The inmates were by no means distressed or unhappy; many of them retired to this shelter only for the winter season, and would go out presently, some to begin such work as they could still do, others to live in their own small houses; old age had impoverished most of them by limiting their power of endurance; but far from lamenting the fact that they were town charges, they rather liked the change and excitement of a winter residence on the poor-farm. There was a sharp-faced, hard-worked young widow with seven children, who was an exception to the general level of society, because she deplored the change in her fortunes. The older women regarded her with suspicion, and were apt to talk about her in moments like this, when they happened to sit together at their work.

The three bean-pickers were dressed alike in stout brown ginghams, checked by a white line, and all wore great faded aprons of blue drilling, with sufficient pockets convenient to the right hand. Miss Peggy Bond was a very small, belligerent-looking person, who wore a huge pair of steel-bowed spectacles, holding her sharp chin well up in air, as if to supplement an inadequate nose. She was more than half blind, but the spectacles seemed to face upward instead of square ahead, as if their wearer were always on the sharp lookout for birds. Miss Bond had suffered much personal damage from time to time, because she never took heed where she planted her feet, and so was always tripping and stubbing her bruised way through the world. She had fallen down hatchways and cellarways, and stepped composedly into deep ditches and pasture brooks; but she was proud of stating that she was upsighted, and so was her father before her. At the poor-house, where an unusual malady was considered a distinction, upsightedness was looked upon as a most honorable infirmity. Plain rheumatism, such as afflicted Aunt Lavina Dow, whose twisted hands found even this light work difficult and tiresome,—plain rheumatism was something of every-day occurrence, and nobody cared to hear about it. Poor Peggy was a meek and friendly soul, who never put herself forward; she was just like other folks, as she always loved to say, but Mrs. Lavina Dow was a different sort of person altogether, of great dignity and, occasionally, almost aggressive behavior. The time had been when she could do a good day's work with anybody: but for many years now she had not left the town-farm, being too badly crippled to work; she had no relations or friends to visit, but from an innate love of authority she could not submit to being one of those who are forgotten by the world. Mrs. Dow was the hostess and social lawgiver here, where she remembered every inmate and every item of interest for nearly forty years, besides an immense amount of town history and biography for three or four generations back.

She was the dear friend of the third woman, Betsey Lane; together they led thought and opinion—chiefly opinion—and held sway, not only over Byfleet Poor-farm, but also the selectmen and all others in authority. Betsey Lane had spent most of her life as aid-in-general to the respected household of old General Thornton. She had been much trusted and valued, and, at the breaking up of that once large and flourishing family, she had been left in good circumstances, what with legacies and her own comfortable savings; but by sad misfortune and lavish generosity everything had been scattered, and after much illness, which ended in a stiffened arm and more uncertainty, the good soul had sensibly decided that it was easier for the whole town to support her than for a part of it. She had always hoped to see something of the world before she died; she came of an adventurous, seafaring stock, but had never made a longer journey than to the towns of Danby and Northville, thirty miles away.

They were all old women; but Betsey Lane, who was sixty-nine, and looked much older, was the youngest. Peggy Bond was far on in the seventies, and Mrs. Dow was at least ten years older. She made a great secret of her years; and as she sometimes spoke of events prior to the Revolution with the assertion of having been an eye-witness, she naturally wore an air of vast antiquity. Her tales were an inexpressible delight to Betsey Lane, who felt younger by twenty years because her friend and comrade was so unconscious of chronological limitations.

The bushel basket of cranberry beans was within easy reach, and each of 5
the pickers had filled her lap from it again and again. The shed chamber was not an unpleasant place in which to sit at work, with its traces of seed corn hanging from the brown crossbeams, its spare churns, and dusty loom, and rickety wool-wheels, and a few bits of old furniture. In one far corner was a wide board of dismal use and suggestion, and close beside it an old cradle. There was a battered chest of drawers where the keeper of the poor-house kept his garden-seeds, with the withered remains of three seed cucumbers ornamenting the top. Nothing beautiful could be discovered, nothing interesting, but there was something usable and homely about the place. It was the favorite and untroubled bower of the bean-pickers, to which they might retreat unmolested from the public apartments of this rustic institution.

Betsey Lane blew away the chaff from her handful of beans. The spring breeze blew the chaff back again, and sifted it over her face and shoulders. She rubbed it out of her eyes impatiently, and happened to notice old Peggy holding her own handful high, as if it were an oblation, and turning her queer, uptilted head this way and that, to look at the beans sharply, as if she were first cousin to a hen.

"There, Miss Bond, 't is kind of botherin' work for you, ain't it?" Betsey inquired compassionately.

"I feel to enjoy it, anything that I can do my own way so," responded Peggy. "I like to do my part. Ain't that old Mis' Fales comin' up the road? It sounds like her step."

The others looked, but they were not farsighted, and for a moment Peggy had the advantage. Mrs. Fales was not a favorite.

"I hope she ain't comin' here to put up this spring. I guess she won't now, 10
it 's gettin' so late," said Betsey Lane. "She likes to go rovin' soon as the roads is settled."

"'T is Mis' Fales!" said Peggy Bond, listening with solemn anxiety. "There, do let 's pray her by!"

"I guess she 's headin' for her cousin's folks up Beech Hill way," said Betsey presently. "If she 'd left her daughter's this mornin', she 'd have got just about as far as this. I kind o' wish she had stepped in just to pass the time o' day, long 's she wa'n't going to make no stop."

There was a silence as to further speech in the shed chamber; and even the calves were quiet in the barnyard. The men had all gone away to the field where corn-planting was going on. The beans clicked steadily into the wooden measure at the pickers' feet. Betsey Lane began to sing a hymn, and the others joined in as best they might, like autumnal crickets; their voices were sharp and cracked, with now and then a few low notes of plaintive tone. Betsey herself could sing pretty well, but the others could only make a kind of accompaniment. Their voices ceased altogether at the higher notes.

"Oh my! I wish I had the means to go to the Centennial," mourned Betsey Lane, stopping so suddenly that the others had to go on croaking and shrilling without her for a moment before they could stop. "It seems to me as if I can't die happy 'less I do," she added; "I ain't never seen nothin' of the world, an' here I be."

"What if you was as old as I be?" suggested Mrs. Dow pompously. "You 15
've got time enough yet, Betsey; don't you go an' despair. I knowed of a woman that went clean round the world four times when she was past eighty, an' enjoyed herself real well. Her folks followed the sea; she had three sons an' a daughter married,—all shipmasters, and she 'd been with her own husband when they was young. She was left a widder early, and fetched up her family herself,—a real stirrin', smart woman. After they 'd got married off, an' settled, an' was doing well, she come to be lonesome; and first she tried to stick it out alone, but she wa'n't one that could; an' she got a notion she had n't nothin' before her but her last sickness, and she wa'n't a person that enjoyed havin' other folks do for her. So one on her boys—I guess 't was the oldest—said he was going to take her to sea; there was ample room, an' he was sailin' a good time o' year for the Cape o' Good Hope an' way up to some o' them tea-ports in the Chiny Seas. She was all high to go, but it made a sight o' talk at her age; an' the minister made it a subject o' prayer the last Sunday, and all the folks took a last leave; but she said to some she'd fetch 'em home something real pritty, and so did. An' then they come home t' other way, round the Horn, an' she done so well, an' was such a sight o' company, the other child'n was jealous, an' she promised she 'd go a v'y'ge long o' each on 'em. She was as sprightly a person as ever I see; an' could speak well o' what she'd seen."

"Did she die to sea?" asked Peggy, with interest.

"No, she died to home between v'y'ges, or she 'd gone to sea again. I was to her funeral. She liked her son George's ship the best; 't was the one she was going on to Callao. They said the men aboard all called her 'gran'ma'am,' an' she kep' 'em mended up, an' would go below and tend to 'em if they was sick. She might 'a' been alive an' enjoyin' of herself a good many years but for the kick of a cow; 't was a new cow out of a drove, a dreadful unruly beast."

Mrs. Dow stopped for breath, and reached down for a new supply of beans; her empty apron was gray with soft chaff. Betsey Lane, still pondering on the Centennial, began to sing another verse of her hymn, and again the old women joined her. At this moment some strangers came driving round into the yard from the front of the house. The turf was soft, and our friends did not hear the horses' steps. Their voices cracked and quavered; it was a funny little concert, and a lady in an open carriage just below listened with sympathy and amusement.

II.

"Betsey! Betsey! Miss Lane!" a voice called eagerly at the foot of the stairs that led up from the shed. "Betsey! There 's a lady here wants to see you right away."

Betsey was dazed with excitement, like a country child who knows the rare pleasure of being called out of school. "Lor', I ain't fit to go down, be I?" she faltered, looking anxiously at her friends; but Peggy was gazing even nearer to the zenith than usual, in her excited effort to see down into the yard, and Mrs. Dow only nodded somewhat jealously, and said that she guessed 't was nobody would do her any harm. She rose ponderously, while Betsey hesitated, being, as they would have said, all of a twitter. "It is a lady, certain," Mrs. Dow assured her; " 't ain't often there 's a lady comes here."

"While there was any of Mis' Gen'ral Thornton's folks left, I wa'n't without visits from the gentry," said Betsey Lane, turning back proudly at the head of the stairs, with a touch of old-world pride and sense of high station. Then she disappeared, and closed the door behind her at the stair-foot with a decision quite unwelcome to the friends above.

"She need n't 'a' been so dreadful 'fraid anybody was goin' to listen. I guess we 've got folks to ride an' see us, or had once, if we hain 't now," said Miss Peggy Bond, plaintively.

"I expect 't was only the wind shoved it to," said Aunt Lavina. "Betsey is one that gits flustered easier than some. I wish 't was somebody to take her off an' give her a kind of a good time; she 's young to settle down 'long of old folks like us. Betsey 's got a notion o' rovin' such as ain't my natur', but I should like to see her satisfied. She 'd been a very understandin' person, if she had the advantages that some does."

" 'T is so," said Peggy Bond, tilting her chin high. "I suppose you can't hear nothin' they 're saying? I feel my hearin' ain't up to whar it was. I can hear things close to me well as ever; but there, hearin' ain't everything; 't ain't as if we lived where there was more goin' on to hear. Seems to me them folks is stoppin' a good while."

"They surely be," agreed Lavina Dow.

"I expect it 's somethin' particular. There ain't none of the Thornton folks left, except one o' the gran'darters, an' I 've often heard Betsey remark that she should never see her more, for she lives to London. Strange how folks feels contented in them strayaway places off to the ends of the airth."

The flies and bees were buzzing against the hot window-panes; the handfuls of beans were clicking into the brown wooden measure. A bird came and perched on the window-sill, and then flitted away toward the blue sky. Below, in the yard, Betsey Lane stood talking with the lady. She had put her blue drilling apron over her head, and her face was shining with delight.

"Lor', dear," she said, for at least the third time, "I remember ye when I first see ye; an awful pritty baby you was, an' they all said you looked just like the old gen'ral. Be you goin' back to foreign parts right away?"

"Yes, I'm going back; you know that all my children are there. I wish I could take you with me for a visit," said the charming young guest. "I 'm going to carry over some of the pictures and furniture from the old house; I did n't care half so much for them when I was younger as I do now. Perhaps next summer we shall all come over for a while. I should like to see my girls and boys playing under the pines."

"I wish you re'lly was livin' to the old place," said Betsey Lane. Her imagination was not swift; she needed time to think over all that was being told her, and she could not fancy the two strange houses across the sea. The old Thornton house was to her mind the most delightful and elegant in the world.

"Is there anything I can do for you ?" asked Mrs. Strafford kindly, — "anything that I can do for you myself, before I go away? I shall be writing to you, and sending some pictures of the children, and you must let me know how you are getting on."

"Yes, there is one thing, darlin'. If you could stop in the village an' pick me out a pritty, little, small lookin'-glass, that I can keep for my own an' have to remember you by. 'T ain't that I want to set me above the rest o' the folks, but I was always used to havin' my own when I was to your grandma's. There 's very nice folks here, some on 'em, and I 'm better off than if I was able to keep house; but sence you ask me, that's the only thing I feel cropin' about. What be you goin' right back for? ain't you goin' to see the great fair to Pheladelphy, that everybody talks about?"

"No," said Mrs. Strafford, laughing at this eager and almost convicting question. "No; I 'm going back next week. If I were, I believe that I should take you with me. Good-by, dear old Betsey; you make me feel as if I were a little girl again; you look just the same."

For full five minutes the old woman stood out in the sunshine, dazed with delight, and majestic with a sense of her own consequence. She held something tight in her hand, without thinking what it might be: but just as the friendly mistress of the poor-farm came out to hear the news, she tucked the roll of money into the bosom of her brown gingham dress. "'T was my dear Mis' Katy Strafford," she turned to say proudly. "She come way over from London; she 's been sick; they thought the voyage would do her good. She said most the first thing she had on her mind was to come an' find me, and see how I was, an' if I was comfortable; an' now she 's goin' right back. She 's got two splendid houses; an' said how she wished I was there to look after things,—she remembered I was always her gran'ma's right hand. Oh, it does so carry me back, to see her! Seems if all the rest on 'em must be there together to the old house. There, I must go up an' tell Mis' Dow an' Peggy."

"Dinner's all ready; I was just goin' to blow the horn for the men-folks," said the keeper's wife. "They'll be right down. I expect you 've got along smart with them beans,—all three of you together;" but Betsey's mind roved so high and so far at that moment that no achievements of bean-picking could lure it back.

III.

The long table in the great kitchen soon gathered its company of waifs and strays,—creatures of improvidence and misfortune, and the irreparable victims of old age. The dinner was satisfactory, and there was not much delay for conversation. Peggy Bond and Mrs. Dow and Betsey Lane always sat together at one end, with an air of putting the rest of the company below the salt. Betsey was still flushed with excitement; in fact, she could not eat as much as usual, and she looked up from time to time expectantly, as if she were likely to be asked to speak of her guest; but everybody was hungry, and even Mrs. Dow broke in upon some attempted confidences by asking inopportunely for a second potato. There were nearly twenty at the table, counting the keeper and his wife and two children, noisy little persons who had come from school with the small flock belonging to the poor widow, who sat just opposite our friends. She finished her dinner before any one else, and pushed her chair back; she always helped with the housework,—a thin, sorry, bad-tempered-looking poor soul, whom grief had sharpened instead of softening. "I expect you feel too fine to set with common folks," she said enviously to Betsey.

"Here I be a-settin'," responded Betsey calmly. "I don' know 's I behave more unbecomin' than usual." Betsey prided herself upon her good and proper manners; but the rest of the company, who would have like to hear the bit of morning news, were now defrauded of that pleasure. The wrong note had been struck; there was a silence after the clatter of knives and plates, and one by one the cheerful town charges disappeared. The bean-picking had been finished, and there was a call for any of the women who felt like planting corn; so Peggy Bond, who could follow the line of hills pretty fairly, and Betsey herself, who was still equal to anybody at that work, and Mrs. Dow, all went out to the field together. Aunt Lavina labored slowly up the yard, carrying a light splint-bottomed kitchen chair and her knitting-work, and sat near the stone wall on a gentle rise, where she could see the pond and the green country, and exchange a word with her friends as they came and went up and down the rows. Betsey vouchsafed a word now and then about Mrs. Strafford, but you would have thought that she had been suddenly elevated to Mrs. Strafford's own cares and the responsibilities attending them, and had little in common with her old associates. Mrs. Dow and Peggy knew well that these high-feeling times never lasted long, and so they waited with as much patience as they could muster. They were by no means without that true tact which is only another word for unselfish sympathy.

The strip of corn land ran along the side of a great field; at the upper end of it was a field-corner thicket of young maples and walnut saplings, the children of a great nut-tree that marked the boundary. Once, when Betsey Lane found herself alone near this shelter at the end of her row, the other planters having lagged behind beyond the rising ground, she looked stealthily about, and then put her hand inside her gown, and for the first time took out the money that Mrs. Strafford had given her. She turned it over and over with an astonished look: there were new bank-bills for a hundred dollars. Betsey gave a funny little shrug of her shoulders, came out of the bushes, and took a step or two on the narrow edge of turf, as if she were going to dance; then she hastily tucked away her treasure, and stepped discreetly down into the soft harrowed and hoed land, and began to drop corn again, five kernels to a hill. She had seen the top of Peggy Bond's head over the knoll, and now Peggy herself came entirely into view, gazing upward to the skies, and stumbling more or less, but counting the corn by touch and twisting her head about anxiously to gain advantage over her uncertain vision. Betsey made a friendly, inarticulate little sound as they passed; she was thinking that somebody said once that Peggy's eyesight might be remedied if she could go to Boston to the hospital; but that was so remote and impossible an undertaking that no one had ever taken the first step. Betsey Lane's brown old face suddenly worked with excitement, but in a moment more she regained her usual firm expression, and spoke carelessly to Peggy as she turned and came alongside.

The high spring wind of the morning had quite fallen; it was a lovely May afternoon. The woods about the field to the northward were full of birds, and the young leaves scarcely hid the solemn shapes of a company of crows that patiently attended the cornplanting. Two of the men had finished their hoeing, and were busy with the construction of a scarecrow; they knelt in the furrows, chuckling, and looking over some forlorn, discarded garments. It was a time-honored custom to make the scarecrow resemble one of the poor-house family; and this year they intended to have Mrs. Lavina Dow protect the field in effigy; last year it was the counterfeit of Betsey Lane who stood on guard, with an easily recognized quilted hood and the remains of a valued shawl that one of the calves had found airing on a fence and chewed to pieces. Behind the men was the foundation for this rustic attempt at statuary,—an upright stake and bar in the form of a cross. This stood on the highest part of the field; and as the men knelt near it, and the quaint figures of the corn-planters went and came, the scene gave a curious suggestion of foreign life. It was not like New England; the presence of the rude cross appealed strangely to the imagination.

IV.

Life flowed so smoothly, for the most part, at the Byfleet Poor-farm, that nobody knew what to make, later in the summer, of a strange disappearance. All the elder inmates were familiar with illness and death, and the poor pomp of a town-pauper's funeral. The comings and goings and the various misfortunes of those who composed this strange family, related only through its disasters, hardly served for the excitement and talk of a single day. Now that the June days were at their longest, the old people were sure to wake earlier than ever; but one morning, to the astonishment of everyone, Betsey Lane's bed was empty; the sheets and blankets, which were her own, and guarded with jealous care, were carefully folded and placed on a chair not too near the window, and Betsey had flown. Nobody had heard her go down the creaking stairs. The kitchen door was unlocked, and the old watch-dog lay on the step outside in the early sunshine, wagging his tail and looking wise, as if he were left on guard and meant to keep the fugitive's secret.

"Never knowed her to do nothin' afore 'thout talking it over a fortnight, and paradin' off when we could all see her," ventured a spiteful voice. "Guess we can wait till night to hear 'bout it."

Mrs. Dow looked sorrowful and shook her head. "Betsey had an aunt on her mother's side that went and drownded of herself; she was a pritty-appearing woman as ever you see."

"Perhaps she 's gone to spend the day with Decker's folks," suggested Peggy Bond. "She always takes an extra early start; she was speakin' lately o' going up their way;" but Mrs. Dow shook her head with a most melancholy look. "I 'm impressed that something 's befell her," she insisted. "I heard her a-groanin' in her sleep. I was wakeful for the forepart o' the night,—'t is very unusual with me, too."

" 'T wa'n't like Betsey not to leave us any word," said the other old friend, with more resentment than melancholy. They sat together almost in silence that morning in the shed chamber. Mrs. Dow was sorting and cutting rags, and Peggy braided them into long ropes, to be made into mats at a later date. If they had only known where Betsey Lane had gone, they might have talked about it until dinner-time at noon; but failing this new subject, they could take no interest in any of their old ones. Out in the field the corn was well up, and the men were hoeing. It was a hot morning in the shed chamber, and the woolen rags were dusty and hot to handle.

V.

Byfleet people knew each other well, and when this mysteriously absent 45
person did not return to the town-farm at the end of a week, public interest became much excited; and presently it was ascertained that Betsey Lane was neither making a visit to her friends the Deckers on Birch Hill, nor to any nearer acquaintances; in fact, she had disappeared altogether from her wonted haunts. Nobody remembered to have seen her pass, hers had been such an early flitting; and when somebody thought of her having gone away by train, he was laughed at for forgetting that the earliest morning train from South Byfleet, the nearest station, did not start until long after eight o'clock; and if Betsey had designed to be one of the passengers, she would have started along the road at seven, and been seen and known of all women. There was not a kitchen in that part of Byfleet that did not have windows toward the road. Conversation rarely left the level of the neighborhood gossip: to see Betsey Lane, in her best clothes, at that hour in the morning, would have been the signal for much exercise of imagination; but as day after day went by without news, the curiosity of those who knew her best turned slowly into fear, and at last Peggy Bond again gave utterance to the belief that Betsey had either gone out in the early morning and put an end to her life, or that she had gone to the Centennial. Some of the people at table were moved to loud

laughter,—it was at supper-time on a Sunday night,—but others listened with great interest.

"She never 'd put on her good clothes to drownd herself," said the widow. "She might have thought 't was good as takin' 'em with her, though. Old folks has wandered off an' got lost in the woods afore now."

Mrs. Dow and Peggy resented this impertinent remark, but deigned to take no notice of the speaker. "She would n't have wore her best clothes to the Centennial, would she?" mildly inquired Peggy, bobbing her head toward the ceiling. "'T would be a shame to spoil your best things in such a place. An' I don't know of her havin' any money; there 's the end o' that."

"You 're bad as old Mis' Bland, that used to live neighbor to our folks," said one of the old men. "She was dreadful precise; an' she so begretched to wear a good alapaca dress that was left to her, that it hung in a press forty year, an' baited the moths at last."

"I often seen Mis' Bland a-goin' in to meetin' when I was a young girl," said Peggy Bond approvingly. "She was a good-appearin' woman, an' she left property."

"Wish she'd left it to me, then," said the poor soul opposite, glancing at her pathetic row of children: but it was not good manners at the farm to deplore one's situation, and Mrs. Dow and Peggy only frowned. "Where do you suppose Betsey can be?" said Mrs. Dow, for the twentieth time. "She did n't have no money. I know she ain't gone far, if it 's so that she 's yet alive. She 's b'en real pinched all the spring."

"Perhaps that lady that come one day give her some," the keeper's wife suggested mildly.

"Then Betsey would have told me," said Mrs. Dow, with injured dignity.

VI.

On the morning of her disappearance, Betsey rose even before the pewee and the English sparrow, and dressed herself quietly, though with trembling hands, and stole out of the kitchen door like a plunderless thief. The old dog licked her hand and looked at her anxiously; the tortoise-shell cat rubbed against her best gown, and trotted away up the yard, then she turned anxiously and came after the old woman, following faithfully until she had to be driven back. Betsey was used to long country excursions afoot. She dearly loved the early morning; and finding that there was no dew to trouble her, she began to follow pasture paths and short cuts across the field, surprising here and there a flock of sleepy sheep, or a startled calf that rustled out from the bushes. The birds were pecking their breakfast from bush and turf; and hardly any of the wild inhabitants of that rural world were enough alarmed by her presence to do more than flutter away if they chanced to be in her path. She stepped along, light-footed and eager as a girl, dressed in her neat old straw bonnet and black gown, and carrying a few belongings in her best bundle-handkerchief, one that her only brother had brought home from the East Indies fifty years before. There was an old crow perched as sentinel on a small, dead pine-tree, where he could warn friends who were pulling up the sprouted corn in a field close by; but he only gave a contemptuous caw as the adventurer appeared, and she shook her bundle at him in revenge, and laughed to see him so clumsy as he tried to keep his footing on the twigs.

"Yes, I be," she assured him. "I 'm a-goin' to Pheladelphy, to the Centennial, same 's other folks. I 'd jest as soon tell ye 's not, old crow;" and Betsey laughed aloud in pleased content with herself and her daring, as she walked along. She had only two miles to go to the station at South Byfleet, and she felt for the money now and then, and found it safe enough. She took great pride in the success of her escape, and especially in the long concealment of her wealth. Not a night had passed since Mrs. Strafford's visit that she had not slept with the roll of money under her pillow by night, and buttoned safe inside her dress by day. She knew that everybody would offer advice and even commands about the spending or saving of it; and she brooked no interference.

The last mile of the foot-path to South Byfleet was along the railway track; and Betsey began to feel in haste, though it was still nearly two hours to train time. She looked anxiously forward and back along the rails every few minutes, for fear of being run over; and at last she caught sight of an engine that was apparently coming toward her, and took flight into the woods before she could gather courage to follow the path again. The freight train proved to be at a standstill, waiting at a turnout; and some of the men were straying about, eating their early breakfast comfortably in this time of leisure. As the old woman came up to them, she stopped too, for a moment of rest and conversation.

"Where be ye goin'?" she asked pleasantly; and they told her. It was to the town where she had to change cars and take the great through train; a point of geography which she had learned from evening talks between the men at the farm.

"What'll ye carry me there for?"

"We don't run no passenger cars," said one of the young fellows, laughing. "What makes you in such a hurry?"

"I 'm startin' for Pheladelphy, an' it 's a gre't ways to go."

"So 't is; but you 're consid'able early, if you 're makin' for the eight-forty train. See here! You have n't got a needle an' thread 'long of you in that bundle, have you? If you 'll sew me on a couple o' buttons, I 'll give ye a free ride. I'm in a sight o' distress, an' none o' the fellows is provided with as much as a bent pin."

"You poor boy! I'll have you seen to, in half a minute. I 'm troubled with a stiff arm, but I 'll do the best I can."

The obliging Betsey seated herself stiffly on the slope of the embankment, and found her thread and needle with utmost haste. Two of the trainmen stood by and watched the careful stitches, and even offered her a place as spare brakeman, so that they might keep her near; and Betsey took the offer with considerable seriousness, only thinking it necessary to assure them that she was getting most too old to be out in all weathers. An express went by like an earthquake, and she was presently hoisted on board an empty box-car by two of her new and flattering acquaintances, and found herself before noon at the end of the first stage of her journey, without having spent a cent, and furnished with any amount of thrifty advice. One of the young men, being compassionate of her unprotected state as a traveler, advised her to find out the widow of an uncle of his in Philadelphia, saying despairingly that he could n't tell her just how to find the house; but Miss Betsey Lane said that she had an English tongue in her head, and should be sure to find whatever she was looking for. This unexpected incident of the freight train was the reason why everybody about the South Byfleet station insisted that no such person had taken passage by the regular train that same morning, and why there were those who persuaded themselves that Miss Betsey Lane was probably lying at the bottom of the poor-farm pond.

VII.

"Land sakes!" said Miss Betsey Lane, as she watched a Turkish person parading by in his red fez, "I call the Centennial somethin' like the day o' judgment! I wish I was goin' to stop a month, but I dare say 't would be the death o' my poor old bones."

She was leaning against the barrier of a patent pop-corn establishment, which had given her a sudden reminder of home, and of the winter nights when the sharp-kerneled little red and yellow ears were brought out, and Old Uncle Eph Flanders sat by the kitchen stove, and solemnly filled a great wooden chopping-tray for the refreshment of the company. She had wandered and loitered and looked until her eyes and head had grown numb and unreceptive; but it is only unimaginative persons who can be really astonished. The imagination can always outrun the possible and actual sights and sounds of the world; and this plain old body from Byfleet rarely found anything rich and splendid enough to surprise her. She saw the wonders of the West and the splendors of the East with equal calmness and satisfaction; she had always known that there was an amazing world outside the boundaries of Byfleet. There was a piece of paper in her pocket on which was marked, in her clumsy handwriting, "If Betsey Lane should meet with accident, notify the selectmen of Byfleet;" but having made this slight provision for the future, she had thrown herself boldly into the sea of strangers, and then had made the joyful discovery that friends were to be found at every turn.

There was something delightfully companionable about Betsey; she had 65
a way of suddenly looking up over her big spectacles with a reassuring and expectant smile, as if you were going to speak to her, and you generally did. She must have found out where hundreds of people came from, and whom they had left at home, and what they thought of the great show, as she sat on a bench to rest, or leaned over the railings where free luncheons were afforded by the makers of hot waffles and molasses candy and fried potatoes; and there was not a night when she did not return to her lodgings with a pocket crammed with samples of spool cotton and nobody knows what. She had already collected small presents for almost everybody she knew at home, and she was such a pleasant, beaming old country body, so unmistakably appreciative and interested, that nobody ever thought of wishing that she would move

on. Nearly all the busy people of the Exhibition called her either Aunty or Grandma at once, and made little pleasures for her as best they could. She was a delightful contrast to the indifferent, stupid crowd that drifted along, with eyes fixed at the same level, and seeing, even on that level, nothing for fifty feet at a time. "What be you making here, dear?" Betsey Lane would ask joyfully, and the most perfunctory guardian hastened to explain. She squandered money as she had never had the pleasure of doing before, and this hastened the day when she must return to Byfleet. She was always inquiring if there were any spectacle-sellers at hand, and received occasional directions; but it was a difficult place for her to find her way about in, and the very last day of her stay arrived before she found an exhibitor of the desired sort, an oculist and instrument-maker.

"I called to get some specs for a friend that 's upsighted," she gravely informed the salesman, to his extreme amusement. "She 's dreadful troubled, and jerks her head up like a hen a-drinkin'. She 's got a blur agrowin' an' spreadin', an' sometimes she can see out to one side on 't, and more times she can't."

"Cataracts," said a middle-aged gentleman at her side; and Betsey Lane turned to regard him with approval and curiosity.

" 'T is Miss Peggy Bond I was mentioning, of Byfleet Poor-farm," she explained. "I count on gettin' some glasses to relieve her trouble, if there 's any to be found."

"Glasses won't do her any good," said the stranger. "Suppose you come and sit down on this bench, and tell me all about it. First, where is Byfleet?" and Betsey gave the directions at length.

"I thought so," said the surgeon. "How old is this friend of yours?" 70

Betsey cleared her throat decisively, and smoothed her gown over her knees as if it were an apron; then she turned to take a good look at her new acquaintance as they sat on the rustic bench together. "Who be you, sir, I should like to know?" she asked, in a friendly tone.

"My name 's Dunster."

"I take it you 're a doctor," continued Betsey, as if they had overtaken each other walking from Byfleet to South Byfleet on a summer morning.

"I'm a doctor; part of one at least," said he. "I know more or less about eyes; and I spend my summers down on the shore at the mouth of your river; some day I'll come up and look at this person. How old is she?"

"Peggy Bond is one that never tells her age; 't ain't come quite up to 75
where she 'll begin to brag of it, you see," explained Betsey reluctantly; "but I know her to be nigh to seventy-six, one way or t' other. Her an' Mrs. Mary Ann Chick was same year's child'n, and Peggy knows I know it, an' two or three times when we 've be'n in the buryin'-ground where Mary Ann lays an' has her dates right on her headstone, I could n't bring Peggy to take no sort o' notice. I will say she makes, at times, a convenience of being upsighted. But there, I feel for her,—everybody does; it keeps her stubbin' an' trippin' against everything, beakin' and gazin' up the way she has to."

"Yes, yes," said the doctor, whose eyes were twinkling. "I 'll come and look after her, with your town doctor, this summer,—some time in the last of July or first of August."

"You'll find occupation," said Betsey, not without an air of patronage. "Most of us to the Byfleet Farm has got our ails, now I tell ye. You ain't got no bitters that 'll take a dozen years right off an ol' lady's shoulders?"

The busy man smiled pleasantly, and shook his head as he went away. "Dunster," said Betsey to herself, soberly committing the new name to her sound memory. "Yes, I must n't forget to speak of him to the doctor, as he directed. I do' know now as Peggy would vally herself quite so much accordin' to, if she had her eyes fixed same as other folks. I expect there would n't been a smarter woman in town, though, if she 'd had a proper chance. Now I've done what I set to do for her, I do believe, an' 't wa'n't glasses, neither. I 'll git her a pritty little shawl with that money I laid aside. Peggy Bond ain't got a pritty shawl. I always wanted to have a real good time, an' now I'm havin' it."

VIII.

Two or three days later, two pathetic figures might have been seen crossing the slopes of the poor-farm field, toward the low shores of Byfield pond. It was early in the morning, and the stubble of the lately mown grass was wet with rain and hindering to old feet. Peggy Bond was more blundering and liable to stray in the wrong direction than usual; it was one of the days when she could hardly see at all. Aunt Lavina Dow was unusually clumsy of movement, and stiff in the joints; she had not been so far from the house for three years. The morning breeze filled the gathers of her wide gingham skirt, and aggravated the size of her unwieldy figure. She supported herself with a stick, and trusted beside to the fragile support of Peggy's arm. They were talking together in whispers.

"Oh, my sakes!" exclaimed Peggy, moving her small head from side to side. "Hear you wheeze, Mis' Dow! This may be the death o' you; there, do go slow! You set here on the side-hill, an' le' me go try if I can see."

"It needs more eyesight than you 've got," said Mrs. Dow, panting between the words. "Oh! to think how spry I was in my young days, an' here I be now, the full of a door, an' all my complaints so aggravated by my size. 'T is hard! 't is hard! But I'm a-doin' of all this for pore Betsey's sake. I know they've all laughed, but I look to see her ris' to the top o' the pond this day,—'t is just nine days since she departed; an' say what they may, I know she hove herself in. It run in her family; Betsey had an aunt that done just so, an' she ain't be'n like herself, a-broodin' an' hivin' away alone, an' nothin' to say to you an' me that was always sich good company all together. Somethin' sprung her mind, now I tell ye, Mis' Bond."

"I feel to hope we sha'n't find her, I must say," faltered Peggy. It was plain that Mrs. Dow was the captain of this doleful expedition. "I guess she ain't never thought o' drowndin' of herself, Mis' Dow; she 's gone off a-visitin' way over to the other side o' South Byfleet; some thinks she 's gone to the Centennial even now!"

"She had n't no proper means, I tell ye," wheezed Mrs. Dow indignantly; "an' if you prefer that others should find her floatin' to the top this day, instid of us that 's her best friends, you can step back to the house."

They walked on in aggrieved silence. Peggy Bond trembled with excitement, but her companion's firm grasp never wavered, and so they came to the narrow, gravelly margin and stood still. Peggy tried in vain to see the glittering water and the pond-lilies that starred it; she knew that they must be there; once, years ago, she had caught fleeting glimpses of them, and she never forgot what she had once seen. The clear blue sky overhead, the dark pine-woods beyond the pond, were all clearly pictured in her mind. "Can't you see nothin'?" she faltered; "I believe I'm wuss'n upsighted this day. I'm going to be blind."

"No," said Lavina Dow solemnly; "no, there ain't nothin' whatever, Peggy. I hope to mercy she ain't"—

"Why, whoever'd expected to find you 'way out here!" exclaimed a brisk and cheerful voice. There stood Betsey Lane herself, close behind them, having just emerged from a thicket of alders that grew close by. She was following the short way homeward from the railroad.

"Why, what's the matter, Mis' Dow? You ain't overdoin', be ye? an' Peggy 's all of a flutter. What in the name o' natur' ails ye?"

"There ain't nothin' the matter, as I knows on," responded the leader of this fruitless expedition. "We only thought we 'd take a stroll this pleasant mornin'," she added, with sublime self-possession. "Where 've you be'n, Betsey Lane?"

"To Pheladelphy, ma'am," said Betsey, looking quite young and gay, and wearing a townish and unfamiliar air that upheld her words. "All ought to go that can; why, you feel 's if you 'd be'n all round the world. I guess I 've got enough to think of and tell ye for the rest o' my days. I 've always wanted to go somewheres. I wish you 'd be'n there, I do so. I 've talked with folks from Chiny an' the back o' Pennsylvany: and I see folks way from Australy that 'peared as well as anybody; an' I see how they made spool cotton, an' sights o' other things; an' I spoke with a doctor that lives down to the beach in the summer, an' he offered to come up 'long in the first of August, an' see what he can do for Peggy's eyesight. There was di'monds there as big as pigeon's eggs; an' I met with Mis' Abby Fletcher from South Byfleet depot; an' there was hogs there that weighed risin' thirteen hunderd"—

"I want to know," said Mrs. Lavina Dow and Peggy Bond, together.

"Well, 't was a great exper'ence for a person," added Lavina, turning ponderously, in spite of herself, to give a last wistful look at the smiling waters of the pond.

"I don't know how soon I be goin' to settle down," proclaimed the rustic sister of Sindbad. "What's for the good o' one 's for the good of all. You just wait till we 're setting together up in the old shed chamber! You know, my dear Mis' Katy Strafford give me a han'some present o' money that day she come to see me; and I 'd be'n a-dreamin' by night an' day o' seein' that Centennial; and when I come to think on 't I felt sure somebody ought to go from this neighborhood, if 't was only for the good o' the rest; and I thought I'd better be the one. I wa'n't goin' to ask the selec'men neither. I've come back with one-thirty-five in money, and I see everything there, an' I fetched ye all a little somethin'; but I 'm full o' dust now, an' pretty nigh beat out. I never see a place more friendly than Pheladelphy; but 't ain't natural to a Byfleet person to be always walkin' on a level. There, now, Peggy, you take my bundle-handkercher and the basket, and let Mis' Dow sag on to me. I'll git her along twice as easy."

With this the small elderly company set forth triumphant toward the poor-house, across the wide green field.

SARAH ORNE JEWETT

(1849–1909) **Web** *www*

Like Melville descended from an old New England family, Sarah Orne Jewett grew up in Maine. Though she wanted to be a medical doctor like her father, poor health made her choose writing instead. She preferred writing short stories, though she also wrote novels—*A Country Doctor* (1884) and *The Country of the Pointed Firs* (1896). Her stories often focus on characters and settings rather than on more conventional plots. Jewett was a major influence on the generation of women writers to follow, particularly Willa Cather, who dedicated her first novel to her.

TOPICS FOR CRITICAL THINKING **Web** *www*

1. Why does Betsey Lane go to the Centennial?
2. What reevaluations of old age do Betsey's actions inspire?
3. How does the character of Betsey Lane make a bridge between the small town and the world?
4. What is the function of the story of the old woman who sailed around the world?

TOPICS FOR CRITICAL WRITING **Web** *www*

1. The story's characters are quite tolerant of their friends' pretensions. Describe the faults of the characters and show how these faults combine to produce a generous portrait of older women.
2. In what ways do the characters of this story overcome the limitations of age and gender?

4 Setting

Though we rarely think about it, **setting** is all around us. As in life, setting in fiction consists of the physical, environmental, social, historical, and cultural contexts described in a story as the scene of its action. Although in discussions of fiction, setting sometimes seems less important than character or plot, it has tremendous power. It can evoke atmosphere, mood, and circumstances. The eerie darkness of a graveyard, for example, conveys horror, fright, or unworldliness. The junkyard atmosphere of contemporary science fiction in such films as *The Matrix* conveys a feeling of outdated technology and a makeshift existence. Setting can provide both motivation and explanations for characters' actions and demonstrate the effects of characters' choices. A bad storm might account for a character's desperate need to survive, or a posh mansion might indicate success and wealth.

Settings sometimes are literal, historical, and realistic, or subjective, dreamlike, and full of symbolic suggestion, or all of these. They can reflect characters' feelings in the same way houses or cars reflect the personalities of their owners, or they can parallel and anticipate events. An excessively messy environment (like some dorm rooms), for example, might suggest a character who is disorganized or who likes to party. An excessively neat room might signal someone who is organized, compulsive, or straight-laced. Setting can even serve as a character itself; the sea, untamed lands, the weather, and even buildings sometimes provide formidable foes, for example, as the weather does in *The Perfect Storm* or the arctic environment does in Jack London's stories of *www* human struggles to survive. **Web**

The presentation of setting varies from story to story. In some stories, setting is barely evoked, present merely as a suggestion or stereotype. This is *www* the case in Kate Chopin's "The Story of an Hour." **Web** In other stories, setting reflects and undergirds the story in complex but nonobtrusive ways, as in *www* Ambrose Bierce's "An Occurrence at Owl Creek Bridge." **Web** Sometimes the setting is more social than physical; and some stories are so preoccupied *www* with setting, like Jack London's "The Law of Life," **Web** that setting becomes an active part of the narrative.

While setting may seem to be simple background—the frame or context for a story's actions—it more often works as a complicated part of a story's intricate whole. Although we can easily point to elements of story we might understand as setting, separating such elements from character and plot is more difficult. For this reason, paying deliberate attention to the details of setting sometimes complicates our reading of a story or even suggests an opposite interpretation.

Critical Perspective: New Historicism

Analyses that focus on the historical and cultural aspects of a story's action look to history as a way of explaining or illuminating some of the story's art. This mode of criticism is called **New Historicism.** **Web** New Historicist critics look at the larger context of a story, both in terms of what it is describing and the culture in which it was written. Seeing a literary work as a piece of the culture, New Historicist criticism combines many disciplines—literature, politics, sociology, art, economics, and anthropology—to understand how a story relates to the social and historical conditions of its time. *www*

Stories About Setting

While we often understand characters as agents whose actions drive the story, we tend to regard setting as the passive ground of their actions. We look for setting in a story's descriptive passages and expect it to be the production of the artful use of adjectives. However, in stories where setting is more of an active agent, its role becomes more dynamic. This is certainly the case in Edgar Allan Poe's "The Fall of the House of Usher" with its dreamlike gothic setting, which aggressively reflects the decadence of the house's aristocratic inhabitants. Poe wrote this story in 1839 while he was serving as the coeditor of *Burton's Magazine* in New York and busily writing book reviews and other essays. Later published in Poe's collection of tales, *Tales of the Grotesque and the Arabesque* (1840), "Usher" reflects admirably Poe's theory that short stories should have a "unity of effect."

Poe's macabre effect in "The Fall of the House of Usher" contrasts with "Paul's Mistress," Guy de Maupassant's 1881 story about the nightclub scene along the Seine. This narrative depicts a different kind of obsession, one hinted at as the river's locales twist among the complex romances of Paul's mistress.

EDGAR ALLAN POE

The Fall of the House of Usher *(1839)*

Son coeur est un luth suspendu;
Sitôt qu'on le touche il résonne.
—DE BÉRANGER

During the whole of a dull, dark, and soundless day in the autumn of the year, when the clouds hung oppressively low in the heavens, I had been passing alone, on horseback, through a singularly dreary tract of country; and at length found myself, as the shades of the evening drew on, within view of the melancholy House of Usher. I knew not how it was—but, with the first glimpse of the building, a sense of insufferable gloom pervaded my spirit. I say insufferable; for the feeling was unrelieved by any of that half-pleasurable, because poetic, sentiment with which the mind usually receives even the sternest natural images of the desolate or terrible. I looked upon the scene before me—upon the mere house, and the simple landscape features of the domain, upon the bleak walls, upon the vacant eyelike windows, upon a few rank sedges, and upon a few white trunks of decayed trees—with an utter depression of soul which I can compare to no earthly sensation more properly than to the after-dream of the reveler upon opium; the bitter lapse into everyday life, the hideous dropping off of the veil. There was an iciness, a sinking, a sickening of the heart, an unredeemed dreariness of thought which no goading of the imagination could torture into aught of the sublime. What was it—I paused to think—what was it that so unnerved me in the contemplation of the House of Usher? It was a mystery all insoluble; nor could I grapple with the shadowy fancies that crowded upon me as I pondered. I was forced to fall back upon the unsatisfactory conclusion, that while, beyond doubt, there *are* combinations of very simple natural objects which have the power of thus affecting us, still the analysis of this power lies among considerations beyond our depth. It was possible, I reflected, that a mere different arrangement of the particulars of the scene, of the details of the picture, would be sufficient to modify, or perhaps to annihilate, its capacity for sorrowful impression; and, acting upon this idea, I reined my horse to the precipitous brink of a black and lurid tarn that lay in unruffled luster by the dwelling, and gazed down—but with a shudder even more thrilling than before—upon the remodeled and inverted images of the gray sedge, and the ghastly tree stems, and the vacant and eye-like windows.

Nevertheless, in this mansion of gloom I now proposed to myself a sojourn of some weeks. Its proprietor, Roderick Usher, had been one of my boon companions in boyhood; but many years had elapsed since our last meeting. A letter, however, had lately reached me in a distant part of the country—a letter from him—which in its wildly importunate nature had admitted of no other than a personal reply. The MS. gave evidence of nervous agitation. The writer spoke of acute bodily illness, of a mental disorder which oppressed him, and of an earnest desire to see me, as his best and indeed his only personal friend, with a view of attempting, by the cheerfulness of my society, some alleviation of his malady. It was the manner in which all this, and much more, was said—it was the apparent *heart* that went with his request—which allowed me no room for hesitation; and I accordingly obeyed forthwith what I still considered a very singular summons.

Although as boys we had been even intimate associates, yet I really knew little of my friend. His reserve had been always excessive and habitual. I was aware, however, that his very ancient family had been noted, time out of mind, for a peculiar sensibility of temperament, displaying itself, through long ages, in many works of exalted art, and manifested of late in repeated deeds of munificent yet unobtrusive charity, as well as in a passionate devotion of the intricacies, perhaps even more than to the orthodox and easily recognizable beauties, of musical science. I had learned, too, the very remarkable fact that the stem of the Usher race, all time-honored as it was, had put forth at no period any enduring branch; in other words, that the entire family lay in the direct line of descent, and had always, with very trifling and very temporary variation, so lain. It was this deficiency, I considered, while running over in thought the perfect keeping of the character of the premises with the accredited character of the people, and while speculating upon the possible influence which the one, in the long lapse of centuries, might have exercised upon the other—it was this deficiency, perhaps, of collateral issue, and the consequent undeviating transmission from sire to son of the patrimony with the name, which had, at length, so identified the two as to merge the original title of the estate in the quaint and equivocal appellation of the "House of Usher"—an appellation which seemed to include, in the minds of the peasantry who used it, both the family and the family mansion.

I have said that the sole effect of my somewhat childish experiment, that of looking down within the tarn, had been to deepen the first singular impression. There can be no doubt that the consciousness of the rapid increase of my superstition—for why should I not so term it?—served mainly to accelerate the increase itself. Such, I have long known, is the paradoxical law of all sentiments having terror as a basis. And it might have been for this reason only, that, when I again uplifted my eyes to the house itself, from its image in the pool, there grew in my mind a strange fancy—a fancy so ridiculous, indeed, that I but mention it to show the vivid force of the sensations which oppressed me. I had so worked upon my imagination as really to believe that about the whole mansion and domain there hung an atmosphere peculiar to themselves and their immediate vicinity: an atmosphere which had no affinity with the air of heaven, but which had reeked up from the decayed trees, and the gray wall, and the silent tarn: a pestilent and mystic vapor, dull, sluggish, faintly discernible, and leaden-hued.

Shaking off from my spirit what *must* have been a dream, I scanned more 5
narrowly the real aspect of the building. Its principal feature seemed to be that of an excessive antiquity. The discoloration of ages had been great. Minute fungi overspread the whole exterior, hanging in a fine tangled webwork from the eaves. Yet all this was apart from any extraordinary dilapidation. No portion of the masonry had fallen; and there appeared to be a wild inconsistency between its still perfect adaptation of parts and the crumbling condition of the individual stones. In this there was much that reminded me of the specious totality of old woodwork which has rotted for long years in some neglected vault, with no disturbance from the breath of the external air. Beyond this indication of excessive decay, however, the fabric gave little token of instability. Perhaps the eye of a scrutinizing observer might have discovered a barely perceptible fissure, which, extending from the roof of the building in front, made its way down the wall in a zigzag direction, until it became lost in the sullen waters of the tarn.

Noticing these things, I rode over a short causeway to the house. A servant in waiting took my horse, and I entered the Gothic archway of the hall. A valet, of stealthy step, thence conducted me, in silence, through many dark and intricate passages in my progress to the studio of his master. Much that I encountered on the way contributed, I know not how, to heighten the vague sentiments of which I have already spoken. While the objects around me—while the carvings of the ceilings, the somber tapestries of the walls, the ebon blackness of the floors, and the phantasmagoric armorial trophies which rattled as I strode, were but matters to which, or to such as which, I had been accustomed from my infancy—while I hesitated not to acknowledge how familiar was all this—I still wondered to find how unfamiliar were the fancies which ordinary images were stirring up. On one of the staircases, I met the physician of the family. His countenance, I thought, wore a mingled expression of low cunning and perplexity. He accosted me with trepidation and passed on. The valet now threw open a door and ushered me into the presence of his master.

The room in which I found myself was very large and lofty. The windows were long, narrow, and pointed, and at so vast a distance from the black oaken floor as to be altogether inaccessible from within. Feeble gleams of encrimsoned light made their way through the trellised panes, and served to render sufficiently distinct the more prominent objects around; the eye, however, struggled in vain to reach the remoter angles of the chamber, or the recesses of the vaulted and fretted ceiling. Dark draperies hung upon the walls. The general furniture was profuse, comfortless, antique, and tattered. Many books and musical instruments lay scattered about, but failed to give any vitality to the scene. I felt that I breathed an atmosphere of sorrow. An air of stern, deep, and irredeemable gloom hung over and pervaded all.

Upon my entrance, Usher arose from a sofa on which he had been lying at full length, and greeted me with a vivacious warmth which had much in it, I at first thought, of an overdone cordiality—of the constrained effort of the *ennuyé* man of the world. A glance, however, at his countenance, convinced me of his perfect sincerity. We sat down; and for some moments, while he spoke not, I gazed upon him with a feeling half of pity, half of awe. Surely man had never before so terribly altered in so brief a period as had Roderick Usher! It was with difficulty that I could bring myself to admit the identity of the wan being before me with the companion of my boyhood. Yet the character of his face had been at all times remarkable. A cadaverousness of complexion; an eye large, liquid, and luminous beyond comparison; lips somewhat thin and very pallid, but of a surpassingly beautiful curve; a nose of a delicate Hebrew model, but with a breadth of nostril unusual in similar formations; a finely molded chin, speaking, in its want of prominence, of a want of moral energy; hair of a more than web-like softness and tenuity; these features, with an inordinate expansion above the regions of the temple, made up altogether a countenance not easily to be forgotten. And now in the mere exaggeration of the prevailing character of these features, and of the expression they were wont to convey, lay so much of change that I doubted to whom I spoke. The now ghostly pallor of the skin, and the now miraculous luster of the eye, above all things startled and even awed me. The silken hair, too, had been suffered to grow all unheeded, and as, in its wild gossamer texture, it floated rather than fell about the face, I could not, even with effort, connect its arabesque expression with any idea of simple humanity.

In the manner of my friend I was at once struck with an incoherence, an inconsistency; and I soon found this to arise from a series of feeble and futile struggles to overcome an habitual trepidancy, an excessive nervous agitation. For something of this nature I had indeed been prepared, no less by his letter than by reminiscences of certain boyish traits, and by conclusions deduced from his peculiar physical conformation and temperament. His action was alternatively vivacious and sullen. His voice varied rapidly from a tremulous indecision (when the animal spirits seemed utterly in abeyance) to that species of energetic concision—that abrupt, weighty, unhurried, and hollow-sounding enunciation—that leaden, self-balanced and perfectly modulated guttural utterance—which may be observed in the lost drunkard, or the irreclaimable eater of opium, during the periods of his most intense excitement.

It was thus that he spoke of the object of my visit, of his earnest desire to 10
see me, and of the solace he expected me to afford him. He entered, at some length, into what he conceived to be the nature of his malady. It was, he said, a constitutional and a family evil, and one for which he despaired to find a remedy—a mere nervous affection, he immediately added, which would undoubtedly soon pass off. It displayed itself in a host of unnatural sensations. Some of these, as he detailed them, interested and bewildered me: although, perhaps, the terms and the general manner of the narration had their weight. He suffered much from a morbid acuteness of the senses; the most insipid food was alone endurable; he could wear only garments of a certain texture; the odors of all flowers were oppressive; his eyes were tortured by even a faint light; and there were but peculiar sounds, and these from stringed instruments, which did not inspire him with horror.

To an anomalous species of terror I found him a bounden slave. "I shall perish," said he, "I *must* perish in this deplorable folly. Thus, thus, and not otherwise, shall I be lost. I dread the events of the future, not in themselves, but in their results. I shudder at the thought of any, even the most trivial, incident, which may operate upon this intolerable agitation of soul. I have, indeed, no abhorrence of danger, except in its absolute effect—in terror. In this unnerved—in this pitiable condition—I feel that the period will sooner or later arrive when I must abandon life and reason together, in some struggle with the grim phantasm, FEAR."

I learned moreover at intervals, and through broken and equivocal hints, another singular feature of his mental condition. He was enchained by certain superstitious impressions in regard to the dwelling which he tenanted, and whence, for many years, he had never ventured forth—in regard to an influence whose supposititious force was conveyed in terms too shadowy here to be restated—an influence which some peculiarities in the mere form and substance of his family mansion, had, by dint of long sufferance, he said, obtained over his spirit—an effect which the physique of the gray walls and turrets, and of the dim tarn into which they all looked down, had, at length, brought about upon the morale of his existence.

He admitted, however, although with hesitation, that much of the peculiar gloom which thus afflicted him could be traced to a more natural and far more palpable origin—to the severe and long-continued illness, indeed to the evidently approaching dissolution, of a tenderly beloved sister—his sole companion for long years, his last and only relative on earth. "Her decease," he said, with a bitterness which I can never forget, "would leave him (him the hopeless and the frail) the last of the ancient race of the Ushers." While he spoke, the lady Madeline (for so was she called) passed slowly through a remote portion of the apartment, and, without having noticed my presence, disappeared. I regarded her with an utter astonishment not unmingled with dread, and yet I found it impossible to account for such feelings. A sensation of stupor oppressed me, as my eyes followed her retreating steps. When a door, at length, closed upon her, my glance sought instinctively and eagerly the countenance of the brother, but he had buried his face in his hands, and I could only perceive that a far more than ordinary wanness had overspread the emaciated fingers through which trickled many passionate tears.

The disease of the lady Madeline had long baffled the skill of her physicians. A settled apathy, a gradual wasting away of the person, and frequent although transient affections of a partially cataleptical character, were the unusual diagnosis. Hitherto she had steadily borne up against the pressure of her malady, and had not betaken herself finally to bed; but, on the closing in of the evening of my arrival at the house, she succumbed (as her brother told me at night with inexpressible agitation) to the prostrating power of the destroyer; and I learned that the glimpse I had obtained of her person would thus probably be the last I should obtain—that the lady, at least while living, would be seen by me no more.

For several days ensuing, her name was unmentioned by either Usher or 15
myself; and during this period I was busied in earnest endeavors to alleviate the melancholy of my friend. We painted and read together; or I listened, as if in a dream, to the wild improvisation of his speaking guitar. And thus, as a closer and still closer intimacy admitted me more unreservedly into the recesses of his spirit, the more bitterly did I perceive the futility of all attempt at cheering a mind from which darkness, as if an inherent positive quality, poured forth upon all objects of the moral and physical universe, in one unceasing radiation of gloom.

I shall ever bear about me a memory of the many solemn hours I thus spent alone with the master of the House of Usher. Yet I should fail in any attempt to convey an idea of the exact character of the studies, or of the occupations, in which he involved me, or led me the way. An excited and highly distempered ideality threw a sulphurous luster over all. His long improvised dirges will ring forever in my ears. Among other things, I hold painfully in mind a certain singular perversion and amplification of the wild air of the last waltz of Von Weber. From the paintings over which his elaborate fancy brooded, and which grew, touch by touch, into vagueness at which I shuddered the more thrillingly because I shuddered knowing not why;—from these paintings (vivid as their images now are before me) I would in vain endeavor to educe more than a small portion which should lie within the compass of merely written words. By the utter simplicity, by the nakedness of his designs, he arrested and overawed attention. If ever mortal painted an idea, that mortal was Roderick Usher. For me at least, in the circumstances then surrounding me, there arose, out of the pure abstractions which the hypochondriac contrived to throw upon his canvas, an intensity of intolerable awe, no shadow of which felt I ever yet in the contemplation of the certainly glowing yet too concrete reveries of Fuseli.

One of the phantasmagoric conceptions of my friend, partaking not so rigidly of the spirit of abstraction, may be shadowed forth, although feebly, in words. A small picture presented the interior of an immensely long and rectangular vault or tunnel, with low walls, smooth, white, and without interruption or device. Certain accessory points of the design served well to convey the idea that this excavation lay at an exceeding depth below the surface of the earth. No outlet was observed in any portion of its vast extent, and no torch or other artificial source of light was discernible; yet a flood of intense rays rolled throughout, and bathed the whole in a ghastly and inappropriate splendor.

I have just spoken of that morbid condition of the auditory nerve which rendered all music intolerable to the sufferer, with the exception of certain effects of stringed instruments. It was, perhaps, the narrow limits to which he thus confined himself upon the guitar, which gave birth, in great measure, to the fantastic character of his performances. But the fervid *facility* of his *impromptus* could not be so accounted for. They must have been, and were, in the notes, as well as in the words of his wild fantasias (for he not unfrequently accompanied himself with rhymed verbal improvisations), the result of that intense mental collectedness and concentration to which I have previously alluded as observable only in particular moments of the highest artificial excitement. The words of one of these rhapsodies I have easily remembered. I was, perhaps, the more forcibly impressed with it, as he gave it, because, in the under or mystic current of its meaning, I fancied that I perceived, and for the first time, a full consciousness, on the part of Usher, of the tottering of his lofty reason upon her throne. The verses, which were entitled "The Haunted Palace," ran very nearly, if not accurately, thus:

I

In the greenest of our valleys,
    By good angels tenanted,
Once a fair and stately palace—
    Radiant palace—reared its head.
In the monarch Thought's dominion,
    It stood there!
Never seraph spread a pinion
    Over fabric half so fair.

II

Banners yellow, glorious, golden,
    On its roof did float and flow,
(This—all this—was in the olden
    Time long ago)
And every gentle air that dallied,
    In that sweet day,

Along the ramparts plumed and pallid,
    A wingèd odor went away.

III

Wanderers in that happy valley
    Through two luminous windows saw
Spirits moving musically
    To a lute's well-tunèd law,
Round about a throne where, sitting,
    (Porphyrogene!)
In state his glory well befitting,
    The ruler of the realm was seen.

IV

And all with pearl and ruby glowing
    Was the fair palace door,
Through which came flowing, flowing, flowing,
    And sparkling evermore,
A troop of Echoes whose sweet duty
    Was but to sing,
In voices of surpassing beauty,
    The wit and wisdom of their king.

V

But evil things, in robes of sorrow,
    Assailed the monarch's high estate;
(Ah, let us mourn, for never morrow
    Shall dawn upon him, desolate!)
And round about his home the glory
    That blushed and bloomed
Is but a dim-remembered story
    Of the old time entombed.

VI

And travellers now within that valley
    Through the red-litten windows see
Vast forms that move fantastically
    To a discordant melody;
While, like a rapid ghastly river,
    Through the pale door,
A hideous throng rush out forever,
    And laugh—but smile no more.

I well remember that suggestions arising from this ballad led us into a train of thought, wherein there became manifest an opinion of Usher's which I mention not so much on account of its novelty (for other men have thought thus) as on account of the pertinacity with which he maintained it. This opinion, in its general form, was that of the sentience of all vegetable things. But in his disordered fancy the idea had assumed a more daring character, and trespassed, under certain conditions, upon the kingdom of inorganization. I lack words to express the full extent, or the earnest *abandon* of his persuasion. The belief, however, was connected (as I have previously hinted) with the gray stones of the home of his forefathers. The conditions of the sentience had been here, he imagined, fulfilled in the method of collocation of these stones—in the order of their arrangement, as well as in that of the many fungi which overspread them, and of the decayed trees which stood around—above all, in the long undisturbed endurance of this arrangement, and in its reduplication in the still waters of the tarn. Its evidence—the evidence of the sentience—was to be seen, he said (and I here started as he spoke), in the gradual yet certain condensation of an atmosphere of their own about the waters and the walls. The result was discoverable, he added, in that silent, yet importunate and terrible influence which for centuries had molded the destinies of his family, and which made *him* what I now saw him—what he was. Such opinions need no comment, and I will make none.

20 Our books—the books which, for years, had formed no small portion of the mental existence of the invalid—were, as might be supposed, in strict keeping with this character of phantasm. We pored together over such works as the Ververt and Chartreuse of Gresset; the Belphegor of Machiavelli; the Heaven and Hell of Swedenborg; the Subterranean Voyage of Nicholas Klimm by Holberg; the Chiromancy of Robert Flud, of Jean D'Indaginé, and of De la Chambre; the Journey into the Blue Distance of Tieck; and the City of the Sun of Campanella. One favorite volume was a small octavo edition of the *Directorium Inquisitorium*, by the Dominican Eymeric de Gironne; and there were passages in Pomponius Mela, about the old African Satyrs and Ægipans, over which Usher would sit dreaming for hours. His chief delight, however, was found in the perusal of an exceedingly rare and curious book in quarto Gothic—the manual of a forgotten church—the *Vigiliæ Mortuorum Secundum Chorum Ecclesiæ Maguntinæ*.

I could not help thinking of the wild ritual of this work, and of its probable influence upon the hypochondriac, when one evening, having informed me abruptly that the lady Madeline was no more, he stated his intention of preserving her corpse for a fortnight (previously to its final interment) in one of the numerous vaults within the main walls of the building. The worldly reason, however, assigned for this singular proceeding was one which I did not feel at liberty to dispute. The brother had been led to his resolution (so he told me) by consideration of the unusual character of the malady of the deceased, of certain obtrusive and eager inquiries on the part of her medical men, and of the remote and exposed situation of the burial-ground of the family. I will not deny that when I called to mind the sinister countenance of the person whom I met upon the staircase, on the day of my arrival at the house, I had no desire to oppose what I regarded as at best but a harmless, and by no means an unnatural, precaution.

At the request of Usher, I personally aided him in the arrangements for the temporary entombment. The body having been encoffined, we two alone bore it to its rest. The vault in which we placed it (and which had been so long unopened that our torches, half smothered in its oppressive atmosphere, gave us little opportunity for investigation) was small, damp, and entirely without means of admission for light; lying, at great depth, immediately beneath that portion of the building in which was my own sleeping apartment. It had been used, apparently, in remote feudal times, for the worst purposes of a donjon-keep, and in later days as a place of deposit for powder, or some other highly combustible substance, as a portion of its floor, and the whole interior of a long archway through which we reached it, were carefully sheathed with copper. The door, of massive iron, had been also similarly protected. Its immense weight caused an unusually sharp grating sound, as it moved upon its hinges.

Having deposited our mournful burden upon trestles within this region of horror, we partially turned aside the yet unscrewed lid of the coffin, and looked upon the face of the tenant. A striking similitude between the brother and sister now first arrested my attention; and Usher divining, perhaps, my thoughts, murmured out some few words from which I learned that the deceased and himself had been twins, and that sympathies of a scarcely intelligible nature had always existed between them. Our glances, however, rested not long upon the dead—for we could not regard her unawed. The disease which had thus entombed the lady in the maturity of youth, had left, as usual in all maladies of a strictly cataleptical character, the mockery of a faint blush upon the bosom and the face, and that suspiciously lingering smile upon the lip which is so terrible in death. We replaced and screwed down the lid, and, having secured the door of iron, made our way, with toil, into the scarcely less gloomy apartments of the upper portion of the house.

And now, some days of bitter grief having elapsed, an observable change came over the features of the mental disorder of my friend. His ordinary manner had vanished. His ordinary occupations were neglected or forgotten. He roamed from chamber to chamber with hurried, unequal, and objectless step. The pallor of his countenance had assumed, if possible, a more ghastly hue—but the luminousness of his eye had utterly gone out. The once occasional huskiness of his tone was heard no more; and a tremulous quaver, as if of extreme terror, habitually characterized his utterance. There were times, indeed, when I thought his unceasingly agitated mind was laboring with some oppressive secret, to divulge which he struggled for the necessary courage. At times, again, I was obliged to resolve all into the mere inexplicable vagaries of madness, for I beheld him gazing upon vacancy for long hours, in an attitude of the profoundest attention, as if listening to some imaginary sound. It was no wonder that his condition terrified—that it infected me. I felt creeping upon me, by slow yet certain degrees, the wild influences of his own fantastic yet impressive superstitions.

25 It was, especially, upon retiring to bed late in the night of the seventh or eighth day after the placing of the lady Madeline within the donjon, that I experienced the full power of such feelings. Sleep came not near my couch, while the hours waned and waned away. I struggled to reason off the nervousness which had dominion over me. I endeavored to believe that much, if not all, of what I felt was due to the bewildering influence of the gloomy furniture of the room—of the dark and tattered draperies which, tortured into motion by the breath of a rising tempest, swayed fitfully to and fro upon the

walls, and rustled uneasily about the decorations of the bed. But my efforts were fruitless. An irrepressible tremor gradually pervaded my frame; and at length there sat upon my very heart an incubus of utterly causeless alarm. Shaking this off with a gasp and a struggle, I uplifted myself upon the pillows, and, peering earnestly within the intense darkness of the chamber, hearkened—I know not why, except that an instinctive spirit prompted me—to certain low and indefinite sounds which came, through the pauses of the storm, at long intervals, I knew not whence. Overpowered by an intense sentiment of horror, unaccountable yet unendurable, I threw on my clothes with haste (for I felt that I should sleep no more during the night) and endeavored to arouse myself from the pitiable condition into which I had fallen, by pacing rapidly to and fro through the apartment.

I had taken but few turns in this manner, when a light step on an adjoining staircase arrested my attention. I presently recognized it as that of Usher. In an instant afterward he rapped with a gentle touch at my door, and entered, bearing a lamp. His countenance was, as usual, cadaverously wan—but, moreover, there was a species of mad hilarity in his eyes—an evidently restrained *hysteria* in his whole demeanor. His air appalled me—but anything was preferable to the solitude which I had so long endured, and I even welcomed his presence as a relief.

"And you have not seen it?" he said abruptly, after having stared about him for some moments in silence—"you have not then seen it?—but, stay! you shall." Thus speaking, and having carefully shaded his lamp, he hurried to one of the casements, and threw it freely open to the storm.

The impetuous fury of the entering gust nearly lifted us from our feet. It was, indeed, a tempestuous yet sternly beautiful night, and one wildly singular in its terror and its beauty. A whirlwind had apparently collected its force in our vicinity; for there were frequent and violent alterations in the direction of the wind; and the exceeding density of the clouds (which hung so low as to press upon the turrets of the house) did not prevent our perceiving the lifelike velocity with which they flew careening from all points against each other, without passing away into the distance. I say that even their exceeding density did not prevent our perceiving this; yet we had no glimpse of the moon or stars, nor was there any flashing forth of the lightning. But the under surfaces of the huge masses of agitated vapor, as well as all terrestrial objects immediately around us, were glowing in the unnatural light of a faintly luminous and distinctly visible gaseous exhalation which hung about and enshrouded the mansion.

"You must not—you shall not behold this!" said I, shudderingly, to Usher, as I led him with a gentle violence from the window to a seat. "These appearances, which bewilder you, are merely electrical phenomena not uncommon—or it may be that they have their ghastly origin in the rank miasma of the tarn. Let us close this casement; the air is chilling and dangerous to your frame. Here is one of your favorite romances. I will read, and you shall listen;—and so we will pass away this terrible night together."

The antique volume which I had taken up was the *Mad Trist* of Sir Launcelot Canning; but I had called it a favorite of Usher's more in sad jest than in earnest; for, in truth, there is little in its uncouth and unimaginative prolixity which could have had interest for the lofty and spiritual ideality of my friend. It was, however, the only book immediately at hand; and I indulged a vague hope that the excitement which now agitated the hypochondriac might find relief (for the history of mental disorder is full of similar anomalies) even in the extremeness of the folly which I should read. Could I have judged, indeed, by the wild overstrained air of vivacity with which he hearkened, or apparently hearkened, to the words of the tale, I might well have congratulated myself upon the success of my design.

I had arrived at that well-known portion of the story where Ethelred, the hero of the Trist, having sought in vain for peaceable admission into the dwelling of the hermit, proceeds to make good an entrance by force. Here, it will be remembered, the words of the narrative run thus:

> "And Ethelred, who was by nature of a doughty heart, and who was now mighty withal, on account of the powerfulness of the wine which he had drunken, waited no longer to hold parley with the hermit, who, in sooth, was of an obstinate and maliceful turn, but, feeling the rain upon his shoulders, and fearing the rising of the tempest, uplifted his mace outright, and, with blows, made quickly room in the plankings of the door for his gauntleted hand; and now pulling therewith sturdily, he so cracked, and ripped, and tore all asunder, that the noise of the dry and hollow-sounding wood alarummed and reverberated throughout the forest."

At the termination of this sentence I started, and for a moment paused; for it appeared to me (although I at once concluded that my excited fancy had deceived me)—it appeared to me that from some very remote portion of the mansion there came, indistinctly, to my ears, what might have been, in its exact similarity of character, the echo (but a stifled and dull one certainly) of the very cracking and ripping sound which Sir Launcelot had so particularly described. It was, beyond doubt, the coincidence alone which had arrested my attention; for, amid the rattling of the sashes of the casements, and the ordinary commingled noises of the still increasing storm, the sound, in itself, had nothing, surely, which should have interested or disturbed me. I continued the story:

> "But the good champion Ethelred, now entering within the door, was sore enraged and amazed to perceive no signal of the maliceful hermit; but, in the stead thereof, a dragon of a scaly and prodigious demeanor, and of a fiery tongue, which sate in guard before a palace of gold, with a floor of silver; and upon the wall there hung a shield of shining brass with this legend enwritten—
>
> Who entereth herein, a conqueror hath bin;
> Who slayeth the dragon, the shield he shall win
>
> And Ethelred uplifted his mace, and struck upon the head of the dragon, which fell before him, and gave up his pesty breath, with a shriek so horrid and harsh, and withal so piercing, that Ethelred had fain to close his ears with his hands against the dreadful noise of it, the like whereof was never before heard."

Here again I paused abruptly, and now with a feeling of wild amazement; for there could be no doubt whatever that, in this instance, I did actually hear (although from what direction it proceeded I found it impossible to say) a low and apparently distant, but harsh, protracted, and most unusual screaming or grating sound—the exact counterpart of what my fancy had already conjured up for the dragon's unnatural shriek as described by the romancer.

Oppressed, as I certainly was, upon the occurrence of this second and most extraordinary coincidence, by a thousand conflicting sensations, in which wonder and extreme terror were predominant, I still retained sufficient presence of mind to avoid exciting, by any observation, the sensitive nervousness of my companion. I was by no means certain that he had noticed the sounds in question; although, assuredly, a strange alteration had during the last few minutes taken place in his demeanor. From a position fronting my own, he had gradually brought round his chair, so as to sit with his face to the door of the chamber; and thus I could but partially perceive his features, although I saw that his lips trembled as if he were murmuring inaudibly. His head had dropped upon his breast—yet I knew that he was not asleep, from the wide and rigid opening of the eye as I caught a glance of it in profile. The motion of his body, too, was at variance with this idea—for he rocked from side to side with a gentle yet constant and uniform sway. Having rapidly taken notice of all this, I resumed the narrative of Sir Launcelot, which thus proceeded:

> "And now, the champion having escaped from the terrible fury of the dragon, bethinking himself of the brazen shield, and of the breaking up of the enchantment which was upon it, removed the carcass from out of the way before him, and approached valorously over the silver pavement of the castle to where the shield was upon the wall; which in sooth tarried not for his full coming, but fell down at his feet upon the silver floor, with a mighty great and terrible ringing sound."

No sooner had these syllables passed my lips, than—as if a shield of brass 35
had indeed, at the moment, fallen heavily upon a floor of silver—I became aware of a distinct, hollow, metallic and clangorous, yet apparently muffled reverberation. Completely unnerved, I leaped to my feet; but the measured rocking movement of Usher was undisturbed. I rushed to the chair in which he sat. His eyes were bent fixedly before him, and throughout his whole countenance there reigned a stony rigidity. But, as I placed my hand upon his shoulder, there came a strong shudder over his whole person; a sickly smile quivered about his lips; and I saw that he spoke in a low, hurried, and gibbering murmur, as if unconscious of my presence. Bending closely over him, I at length drank in the hideous import of his words.

"Not hear it?—yes, I hear it, and *have* heard it. Long—long—long—many minutes, many hours, many days, have I heard it—yet I dared not—oh, pity me, miserable wretch that I am!—I dared not—*I dared not speak! We have put her living in the tomb!* Said I not that my senses were acute? I *now* tell you that I heard her first feeble movements in the hollow coffin. I heard them—many, many days ago—yet I dared not—*I dared not speak!* And now—tonight—Ethelred—ha! ha!—the breaking of the hermit's door, and the death-cry of the dragon, and the clangor of the shield!—say, rather, the rending of her coffin, and the grating of the iron hinges of her prison, and her struggles within the coppered archway of the vault! Oh, whither shall I fly? Will she not be here anon? Is she not hurrying to upbraid me for my haste?

Have I not heard her footsteps on the stair? Do I not distinguish that heavy and horrible beating of her heart? Madman!"—here he sprang furiously to his feet, and shrieked out his syllables, as if in the effort he were giving up his soul—"*Madman! I tell you that she now stands without the door!*"

As if in the superhuman energy of his utterance there had been found the potency of a spell, the huge antique panels to which the speaker pointed drew slowly back, upon the instant, their ponderous and ebony jaws. It was the work of the rushing gust—but then without the doors there *did* stand the lofty and enshrouded figure of the lady Madeline of Usher. There was blood upon her white robes, and the evidence of some bitter struggle upon every portion of her emaciated frame. For a moment she remained trembling and reeling to and fro upon the threshold—then, with a low moaning cry, fell heavily inward upon the person of her brother, and, in her violent and now final death-agonies, bore him to the floor a corpse, and a victim to the terrors he had anticipated.

From that chamber, and from that mansion, I fled aghast. The storm was still abroad in all its wrath as I found myself crossing the old causeway. Suddenly there shot along the path a wild light, and I turned to see whence a gleam so unusual could have issued; for the vast house and its shadows were alone behind me. The radiance was that of the full, setting, and blood-red moon, which now shone vividly through that once barely discernible fissure, of which I have before spoken as extending from the roof of the building, in a zigzag direction, to the base. While I gazed, this fissure rapidly widened—there came a fierce breath of the whirlwind—the entire orb of the satellite burst at once upon my sight—my brain reeled as I saw the mighty walls rushing asunder—there was a long tumultuous shouting sound like the voice of a thousand waters—and the deep and dank tarn at my feet closed sullenly and silently over the fragments of the House of Usher.

EDGAR ALLAN POE

www

(1809–1849) **Web**

A West Point graduate, Poe quit the army to become a professional editor and writer. Poe was a conscious and controlled artist who was best known for his criticism, but who strove to write stories that would appeal to popular audiences. Poe's fiction fascinated later writers, from Charles-Pierre Baudelaire to Vladimir Nabokov, who admired and developed his atmospheric rendering of effect and complex intellectual games.

www

TOPICS FOR CRITICAL THINKING **Web**

1. How does the story's emphasis on setting signal the way it should be read?
2. The narrator notices the similarities between the Ushers' property and their family history. What are his theories about the relation of the two? What are Roderick Usher's theories?
3. What are the parallels among the story's setting, Usher's paintings and ballad, his books, and the feeling that pervades the mansion?

4. If the setting doubles (reflects, parallels, provides another version of) both characters and events, how does the idea of the double govern this story?

TOPICS FOR CRITICAL WRITING Web

www

1. In what ways does the setting reflect the story's events?
2. What elements does Poe's tale have in common with contemporary horror stories?

Guy de Maupassant

Translated by Ernest Boyd

Paul's Mistress

(1881)

The Restaurant Grillon, a small commonwealth of boatmen, was slowly emptying. In front of the door all was tumult—cries and calls—and huge fellows in white jerseys gesticulated with oars on their shoulders.

The ladies in bright spring toilettes stepped aboard the skiffs with care, and seating themselves astern, arranged their dresses, while the landlord of the establishment, a mighty, red-bearded, self-possessed individual of renowned strength, offered his hand to the pretty creatures, and kept the frail crafts steady.

The rowers, bare-armed, with bulging chests, took their places in their turn, playing to the gallery as they did so—a gallery consisting of middle-class people dressed in their Sunday clothes, of workmen and soldiers leaning upon their elbows on the parapet of the bridge, all taking a great interest in the sight.

One by one the boats cast off from the landing stage. The oarsmen bent forward and then threw themselves backward with even swing, and under the impetus of the long curved oars, the swift skiffs glided along the river, grew smaller in the distance, and finally disappeared under the railway bridge, as they descended the stream toward La Grenouillère. One couple only remained behind. The young man, still almost beardless, slender, with a pale countenance, held his mistress, a thin little brunette with the air of a grasshopper, by the waist; and occasionally they gazed into each other's eyes. The landlord shouted

"Come, Mr. Paul, make haste," and they drew near. 5

Of all the guests of the house, Mr. Paul was the most liked and most respected. He paid well and punctually, while the others hung back for a long time if indeed they did not vanish without paying. Besides which he was a sort of walking advertisement for the establishment, inasmuch as his father was a senator. When a stranger would inquire: "Who on earth is that little chap who thinks so much of his girl?"some *habitué* would reply, half-aloud, with a mysterious and important air: "Don't you know? That is Paul Baron, a senator's son."

And invariably the other would exclaim:

"Poor devil! He has got it badly."

Mother Grillon, a good and worthy business woman, described the young man and his companion as "her two turtledoves," and appeared quite touched by this passion, which was profitable for her business.

The couple advanced at a slow pace. The skiff "Madeleine" was ready, 10
and at the moment of embarking they kissed each other, which caused the public collected on the bridge to laugh. Mr. Paul took the oars, and rowed away for La Grenouillère.

When they arrived it was just upon three o'clock and the large floating café overflowed with people.

The immense raft, sheltered by a tarpaulin roof, is joined to the charming island of Croissy by two narrow footbridges, one of which leads into the centre of the aquatic establishment, while the other unites with a tiny islet, planted with a tree and called "The Flower Pot," and thence leads to land near the bath office.

Mr. Paul made fast his boat alongside the establishment, climbed over the railing of the café, and then, grasping his mistress's hands, assisted her out of the boat. They both seated themselves at the end of a table opposite each other.

On the opposite side of the river along the towing-path, a long string of vehicles was drawn up. Cabs alternated with the fine carriages of the swells; the first, clumsy, with enormous bodies crushing the springs, drawn by broken-down hacks with hanging heads and broken knees; the second, slightly built on light wheels, with horses slender and straight, their heads well up, their bits snowy with foam, and with solemn coachmen in livery, heads erect in high collars, waiting bolt upright, with whips resting on their knees.

The bank was covered with people who came off in families, or in parties, 15
or in couples, or alone. They plucked at the blades of grass, went down to the water, ascended the path, and having reached the spot, stood still awaiting the ferryman. The clumsy punt plied incessantly from bank to bank, discharging its passengers upon the island. The arm of the river (called the Dead Arm) upon which this refreshment wharf lay, seemed asleep, so feeble was the current. Fleets of yawls, of skiffs, of canoes, of podoscaphs, of gigs, of craft of all forms and of all kinds, crept about upon the motionless stream, crossing each other, intermingling, running foul of one another, stopping abruptly under a jerk of the arms only to shoot off afresh under a sudden strain of the muscles and gliding swiftly along like great yellow or red fishes.

Others arrived continually; some from Chatou up the stream; others from Bougival down it; laughter crossed the water from one boat to another, calls, admonitions, or imprecations. The boatmen exposed the bronzed and knotted muscles of their biceps to the heat of the day; and like strange floating flowers, the silk parasols, red, green, blue, or yellow, of the ladies bloomed in the sterns of the boats.

A July sun flamed high in the heavens; the atmosphere seemed full of burning merriment; not a breath of air stirred the leaves of the willows or poplars.

In front, away in the distance, the inevitable Mont-Valérien reared its fortified ramparts, tier above tier, in the intense light; while on the right the divine slopes of Louveciennes, following the bend of the river, disposed themselves in a semicircle, displaying in turn across the rich and shady lawns of large gardens the white walls of country seats.

Upon the outskirts of La Grenouillère a crowd of pedestrians moved about beneath the giant trees which make this corner of the island one of the most delightful parks in the world.

Women and girls with yellow hair and breasts developed beyond all mea- 20
surement, with exaggerated hips, their complexions plastered with rouge, their eyes daubed with charcoal, their lips blood-red, laced up, rigged out in outrageous dresses, trailed the crying bad taste of their toilettes over the fresh green sward; while beside them young men posed in their fashion-plate garments with light gloves, patent leather boots, canes the size of a thread, and single eyeglasses emphasizing the insipidity of their smiles.

Opposite La Grenouillère the island is narrow, and on its other side, where also a ferryboat plies, bringing people unceasingly across from Croissy, the rapid branch of the river, full of whirlpools and eddies and foam, rushes along with the strength of a torrent. A detachment of pontoon-builders, in the uniform of artillerymen, was encamped upon this bank, and the soldiers seated in a row on a long beam watched the water flowing.

In the floating establishment there was a boisterous and uproarious crowd. The wooden tables upon which the spilt refreshments made little sticky streams were covered with half-empty glasses and surrounded by half-tipsy individuals. The crowd shouted, sang, and brawled. The men, their hats at the backs of their heads, their faces red, with the shining eyes of drunkards, moved about vociferating and evidently looking for the quarrels natural to brutes. The women, seeking their prey for the night, sought for free liquor in the meantime; and the unoccupied space between the tables was dominated by the customary local public, a whole regiment of rowdy boatmen, with their female companions in short flannel skirts.

One of them performed on the piano and appeared to play with his feet as well as his hands; four couples glided through a quadrille, and some young men watched them, polished and correct, men who would have looked respectable, did not their innate viciousness show in spite of everything.

For there you see all the scum of society, all its well-bred debauchery, all the seamy side of Parisian society—a mixture of counter-jumpers, of strolling players, of low journalists, of gentlemen in tutelage, of rotten stock-jobbers, of ill-famed debauchees, of old used-up fast men; a doubtful crowd of suspicious characters, half-known, half-sunk, half-recognized, half-criminal, pickpockets, rogues, procurers of women, sharpers with dignified manners, and a bragging air which seems to say: "I shall kill the first man who treats me as a scoundrel."

The place reeks of folly, and stinks of vulgarity and cheap gallantry. Male 25
and female are just as bad one as the other. There dwells an odour of so-called love, and there one fights for a yes, or for a no, in order to sustain a worm-eaten reputation, which a thrust of the sword or a pistol bullet only destroys further.

Some of the neighbouring inhabitants looked in out of curiosity every

Sunday; some young men, very young, appeared there every year to learn how to live, some promenaders lounging about showed themselves there; some greenhorns wandered thither. With good reason is it named La Grenouillère. At the side of the covered wharf where drink was served, and quite close to the Flower Pot, people bathed. Those among the women who possessed the requisite roundness of form came there to display their wares and to get clients. The rest, scornful, although well filled out with wadding, supported by springs, corrected here and altered there, watched their dabbling sisters with disdain.

The swimmers crowded on to a little platform to dive. Straight like vine poles, or round like pumpkins, gnarled like olive branches, bowed over in front, or thrown backward by the size of their stomachs, and invariably ugly, they leaped into the water, splashing it over the drinkers in the café.

Notwithstanding the great trees which overhang the floating-house, and notwithstanding the vicinity of the water, a suffocating heat filled the place. The fumes of the spilt liquors mingled with the effluvia of the bodies and with the strong perfumes with which the skin of the trader in love is saturated and which evaporate in this furnace. But beneath all these diverse scents a slight aroma of *poudre de riz* lingered, disappearing and reappearing, and perpetually encountered as though some concealed hand had shaken an invisible powder-puff in the air. The show was on the river, where the perpetual coming and going of the boats attracted the eyes. The girls in the boats sprawled upon their seats opposite their strong-wristed males, and scornfully contemplated the dinner-hunting females prowling about the island.

Sometimes when a crew in full swing passed at top speed, the friends who had gone ashore gave vent to shouts, and all the people as if suddenly seized with madness commenced to yell.

At the bend of the river toward Chatou fresh boats continually appeared. They came nearer and grew larger, and as faces became recognisable, the vociferations broke out anew.

A canoe covered with an awning and manned by four women came slowly down the current. She who rowed was petite, thin, faded, in a cabin-boy's costume, her hair drawn up under an oilskin hat. Opposite her, a lusty blonde, dressed as a man, with a white flannel jacket, lay upon her back at the bottom of the boat, her legs in the air, resting on the seat at each side of the rower. She smoked a cigarette, while at each stroke of the oars, her chest and stomach quivered, shaken by the stroke. At the back, under the awning, two handsome girls, tall and slender, one dark and the other fair, held each other by the waist as they watched their companions.

A cry arose from La Grenouillère, "There's Lesbos," and all at once a furious clamour, a terrifying scramble took place; the glasses were knocked down; people clambered on to the tables; all in a frenzy of noise bawled "Lesbos! Lesbos! Lesbos!" The shout rolled along, became indistinct, was no longer more than a kind of deafening howl, and then suddenly it seemed to start anew, to rise into space, to cover the plain, to fill the foliage of the great trees, to extend to the distant slopes, and reach even to the sun.

The rower, in the face of this ovation, had quietly stopped. The handsome blonde, stretched out upon the bottom of the boat, turned her head with a careless air, as she raised herself upon her elbows; and the two girls at the back commenced laughing as they saluted the crowd.

Then the hullabaloo redoubled, making the floating establishment tremble. The men took off their hats, the women waved their handkerchiefs, and all voices, shrill or deep, together cried:

"Lesbos."

It was as if these people, this collection of the corrupt, saluted their chiefs like the war-ships which fire guns when an admiral passes along the line.

The numerous fleet of boats also saluted the women's boat, which pushed along more quickly to land farther off.

Mr. Paul, contrary to the others, had drawn a key from his pocket and whistled with all his might. His nervous mistress grew paler, caught him by the arm to make him be quiet, and upon this occasion she looked at him with fury in her eyes. But he appeared exasperated, as though borne away by jealousy of some man or by deep anger, instinctive and ungovernable. He stammered, his lips quivering with indignation:

"It is shameful! They ought to be drowned like puppies with a stone about the neck."

But Madeleine instantly flew into a rage; her small and shrill voice became a hiss, and she spoke volubly, as though pleading her own cause:

"And what has it to do with you—you indeed? Are they not at liberty to do what they wish since they owe nobody anything? You shut up and mind your own business."

But he cut her speech short:

"It is the police whom it concerns, and I will have them marched off to St. Lazare; indeed I will."

She gave a start:

"You?"

"Yes, I! And in the meantime I forbid you to speak to them—you understand, I forbid you to do so."

Then she shrugged her shoulders and grew calm in a moment:

"My dear, I shall do as I please; if you are not satisfied, be off, and instantly. I am not your wife, am I? Very well then, hold your tongue."

He made no reply and they stood face to face, their lips tightly closed, breathing quickly.

At the other end of the great wooden café the four women made their entry. The two in men's costumes marched in front: the one thin like an oldish tomboy, with a yellow tinge on her temples; the other filling out her white flannel garments with her fat, swelling out her wide trousers with her buttocks and swaying about like a fat goose with enormous legs and yielding knees. Their two friends followed them, and the crowd of boatmen thronged about to shake their hands.

The four had hired a small cottage close to the water's edge, and lived there as two households would have lived.

Their vice was public, recognised, patent to all. People talked of it as a natural thing, which almost excited their sympathy, and whispered in very low tones strange stories of dramas begotten of furious feminine jealousies, of the stealthy visit of well-known women and of actresses to the little house close to the water's edge.

A neighbour, horrified by these scandalous rumours, notified the police, and the inspector, accompanied by a man, had come to make inquiry. The mission was a delicate one; it was impossible, in short, to accuse these women, who did not abandon themselves to prostitution, of any tangible crime. The inspector, very much puzzled, and, indeed, ignorant of the nature of the offences suspected, had asked questions at random, and made a lofty report conclusive of their innocence.

The joke spread as far as Saint Germain. They walked about the Grenouillère establishment with mincing steps like queens; and seemed to glory in their fame, rejoicing in the gaze that was fixed on them, so superior to this crowd, to this mob, to these plebeians.

Madeleine and her lover watched them approach, and the girl's eyes 55
lit up.

When the first two had reached the end of the table, Madeleine cried:

"Pauline!"

The large woman turned and stopped, continuing all the time to hold the arm of her feminine cabin-boy:

"Good gracious, Madeleine! Do come and talk to me, my dear."

Paul squeezed his fingers upon his mistress's wrist, but she said to him, 60
with such an air: "You know, my dear, you can clear out, if you like," that he said nothing and remained alone.

Then they chatted in low voices, all three of them standing. Many pleasant jests passed their lips, they spoke quickly; and Pauline now and then looked at Paul, by stealth, with a shrewd and malicious smile.

At last, unable to put up with it any longer, he suddenly rose and in a single bound was at their side, trembling in every limb. He seized Madeleine by the shoulders.

"Come, I wish it," said he; "I have forbidden you to speak to these sluts."

Whereupon Pauline raised her voice and set to work blackguarding him with her Billingsgate vocabulary. All the bystanders laughed; they drew near him; they raised themselves on tiptoe in order the better to see him. He remained dumb under this downpour of filthy abuse. It appeared to him that the words which came from that mouth and fell upon him defiled him like dirt, and, in presence of the row which was beginning, he fell back, retraced his steps, and rested his elbows on the railing toward the river, turning his back upon the victorious women.

There he stayed watching the water, and sometimes with rapid gesture, as 65
though he could pluck it out, he removed with his nervous fingers the tear which stood in his eye.

The fact was that he was hopelessly in love, without knowing why, notwithstanding his refined instincts, in spite of his reason, in spite, indeed, of his will. He had fallen into this love as one falls into a muddy hole. Of a tender and delicate disposition, he had dreamed of liaisons, exquisite, ideal, and impassioned, and there that little bit of a woman, stupid like all prostitutes, with an exasperating stupidity, not even pretty, but thin and a spitfire, had taken him prisoner, possessing him from head to foot, body and soul. He had submitted to this feminine witchery, mysterious and all powerful, this unknown power, this prodigious domination—arising no one knows whence, but from the demon of the flesh—which casts the most sensible man at the feet of some harlot or other without there being anything in her to explain her fatal and sovereign power.

And there at his back he felt that some infamous thing was brewing. Shouts of laughter cut him to the heart. What should he do? He knew well, but he could not do it.

He steadily watched an angler upon the bank opposite him, and his motionless line.

Suddenly, the worthy man jerked a little silver fish, which wriggled at the end of his line, out of the river. Then he endeavoured to extract his hook, pulled and turned it, but in vain. At last, losing patience, he commenced to tear it out, and all the bleeding gullet of the fish, with a portion of its intestines came out. Paul shuddered, rent to his heartstrings. It seemed to him that the hook was his love, and that if he should pluck it out, all that he had in his breast would come out in the same way at the end of a curved iron, fixed in the depths of his being, to which Madeleine held the line.

A hand was placed on his shoulder; he started and turned; his mistress was at his side. They did not speak to each other; and like him she rested her elbows upon the railing, and fixed her eyes upon the river.

He tried to speak to her and could find nothing. He could not even disentangle his own emotions; all that he was sensible of was joy at feeling her there close to him, come back again, as well as shameful cowardice, a craving to pardon everything, to allow everything, provided she never left him.

At last, after a few minutes, he asked her in a very gentle voice:

"Would you like to go? It will be nicer in the boat."

She answered: "Yes, darling."

And he assisted her into the skiff, pressing her hands, all softened, with some tears still in his eyes. Then she looked at him with a smile and they kissed each other again.

They reascended the river very slowly, skirting the willow-bordered, grass-covered bank, bathed and still in the afternoon warmth. When they had returned to the Restaurant Grillon, it was barely six o'clock. Then leaving their boat they set off on foot towards Bezons, across the fields and along the high poplars which bordered the river. The long grass ready to be mowed was full of flowers. The sinking sun glowed from beneath a sheet of red light, and in the tempered heat of the closing day the floating exhalations from the grass, mingled with the damp scents from the river, filled the air with a soft languor, with a happy light, with an atmosphere of blessing.

A soft weakness overtook his heart, a species of communion with this splendid calm of evening, with this vague and mysterious throb of teeming life, with the keen and melancholy poetry which seems to arise from flowers and things, and reveals itself to the senses at this sweet and pensive time.

Paul felt all that; but for her part she did not understand anything of it.

They walked side by side; and, suddenly, tired of being silent, she sang. She sang in her shrill, unmusical voice some street song, some catchy air, which jarred upon the profound and serene harmony of the evening.

Then he looked at her and felt an impassable abyss between them. She beat the grass with her parasol, her head slightly inclined, admiring her feet and singing, dwelling on the notes, attempting trills, and venturing on shakes. Her smooth little brow, of which he was so fond, was at that time absolutely empty! empty! There was nothing therein but this canary music; and the ideas which formed there by chance were like this music. She did not understand anything of him; they were now as separated as if they did not live together. Did his kisses never go any farther than her lips?

Then she raised her eyes to him and laughed again. He was moved to 80
the quick and, extending his arms in a paroxysm of love, he embraced her passionately.

As he was rumpling her dress she finally broke away from him, murmuring by way of compensation as she did so:

"That's enough. You know I love you, my darling."

But he clasped her around the waist and, seized by madness, he started to run with her. He kissed her on the cheek, on the temple, on the neck, all the while dancing with joy. They threw themselves down panting at the edge of a thicket, lit up by the rays of the setting sun, and before they had recovered breath they were in one another's arms without her understanding his transport.

They returned, holding each other by the hand, when, suddenly, through the trees, they perceived on the river the skiff manned by the four women. Fat Pauline also saw them, for she drew herself up and blew kisses to Madeleine. And then she cried:

"Until to-night!" 85

Madeleine replied: "Until to-night!"

Paul felt as if his heart had suddenly been frozen.

They re-entered the house for dinner and installed themselves in one of the arbours, close to the water. They began to eat in silence. When night arrived, the waiter brought a candle enclosed in a glass globe, which gave a feeble and glimmering light; and they heard every moment the bursts of shouting from the boatmen in the large room on the first floor.

Toward dessert, Paul, taking Madeleine's hand, tenderly said to her:

"I feel very tired, my darling; unless you have any objection, we will go to 90
bed early."

She, however, understood the ruse, and shot an enigmatical glance at him—that glance of treachery which so readily appears in the depths of a woman's eyes. Having reflected she answered:

"You can go to bed if you wish, but I have promised to go to the ball at La Grenouillère."

He smiled in a piteous manner, one of those smiles with which one veils the most horrible suffering, and replied in a coaxing but agonized tone:

"If you were really nice, we should remain here, both of us."

She indicated no with her head, without opening her mouth. 95

He insisted:

"I beg of you, my darling."

Then she roughly broke out:

"You know what I said to you. If you are not satisfied, the door is open. No one wishes to keep you. As for myself, I have promised; I shall go."

He placed his two elbows upon the table, covered his face with his hands, 100
and remained there pondering sorrowfully.

The boat people came down again, shouting as usual, and set off in their vessels for the ball at La Grenouillère.

Madeleine said to Paul:

"If you are not coming, say so, and I will ask one of these gentlemen to take me."

Paul rose:

"Let us go!" murmured he. 105

And they left.

The night was black, the sky full of stars, but the air was heat-laden by oppressive breaths of wind, burdened with emanations, and with living germs, which destroyed the freshness of the night. It offered a heated caress, made one breathe more quickly, gasp a little, so thick and heavy did it seem. The boats started on their way, bearing Venetian lanterns at the prow. It was not possible to distinguish the craft, but only the little coloured lights, swift and dancing up and down like frenzied glowworms, while voices sounded from all sides in the shadows. The young people's skiff glided gently along. Now and then, when a fast boat passed near them, they could, for a moment, see the white back of the rower, lit up by his lantern.

When they turned the elbow of the river, La Grenouillère appeared to them in the distance. The establishment *en fête*, was decorated with flags and garlands of coloured lights, in grape-like clusters. On the Seine some great barges moved about slowly, representing domes, pyramids, and elaborate monuments in fires of all colours. Illuminated festoons hung right down to the water, and sometimes a red or blue lantern, at the end of an immense invisible fishing-rod, seemed like a great swinging star.

All this illumination spread a light around the café, lit up the great trees on the bank, from top to bottom, the trunks standing out in pale gray and the leaves in milky green upon the deep black of the fields and the heavens. The orchestra, composed of five suburban artists, flung far its public-house dance-music, poor of its kind and jerky, inciting Madeleine to sing anew.

She wanted to go in at once. Paul wanted first to take a stroll on the island, 110
but he was obliged to give way. The attendance was now more select. The boatmen, almost alone, remained, with here and there some better class people, and young men escorted by girls. The director and organiser of this spree, looking majestic in a jaded black suit, walked about in every direction, bald-headed and worn by his old trade of purveyor of cheap public amusements.

Fat Pauline and her companions were not there; and Paul breathed again.

They danced; couples opposite each other capered in the maddest fashion, throwing their legs in the air, until they were upon a level with the noses of their partners.

The women, whose thighs seemed disjointed, pranced around with flying skirts which revealed their underclothing, wriggling their stomachs and hips, causing their breasts to shake, and spreading the powerful odour of perspiring female bodies.

The men squatted like toads, some making obscene gestures; some twisted and distorted themselves, grimacing and hideous; some turned cartwheels on their hands, or, perhaps, trying to be funny, posed with exaggerated gracefulness.

A fat servant-maid and two waiters served refreshments. 115

The café boat being only covered with a roof and having no wall whatever to shut it in, this hare-brained dance flaunted in the face of the peaceful night and of the firmament powdered with stars.

Suddenly, Mont-Valérien, opposite, appeared, illuminated, as if some conflagration had arisen behind it. The radiance spread and deepened upon the sky, describing a large luminous circle of white, wan light. Then something or other red appeared, grew greater, shining with a burning crimson, like that of hot metal upon the anvil. It gradually developed into a round body rising from the earth; and the moon, freeing herself from the horizon, rose slowly into space. As she ascended, the purple tint faded and became yellow, a shining bright yellow, and the satellite grew smaller in proportion as her distance increased.

Paul watched the moon for some time, lost in contemplation, forgetting his mistress; when he returned to himself the latter had vanished.

He sought her, but could not find her. He threw his anxious eye over table after table, going to and fro unceasingly, inquiring for her from one person and then another. No one had seen her. He was tormented with uneasiness, when one of the waiters said to him:

"You are looking for Madame Madeleine, are you not? She left a few mo- 120
ments ago, with Madame Pauline." And at the same instant, Paul perceived the cabin-boy and the two pretty girls standing at the other end of the café, all three holding each other's waists and lying in wait for him, whispering to one another. He understood, and like a madman, dashed off into the island.

He first ran toward Chatou, but having reached the plain, retraced his steps. Then he began to search the dense coppices, occasionally roaming about distractedly, or halting to listen.

The toads all about him poured out their short metallic notes.

From the direction of Bougival, some unknown bird warbled a song which reached him faintly from the distance.

Over the broad fields the moon shed a soft light, resembling powdered wool; it penetrated the foliage, silvered the bark of the poplars, and riddled with its brilliant rays the waving tops of the great trees. The entrancing poetry of this summer night had, in spite of himself, entered into Paul, athwart his infatuated anguish, stirring his heart with ferocious irony, and increasing even to madness his craving for an ideal tenderness, for passionate outpourings on the breast of an adored and faithful woman. He was compelled to stop, choked by hurried and rending sobs.

The convulsion over, he went on. 125

Suddenly, he received what resembled the stab of a dagger. There, behind that bush, some people were kissing. He ran thither; and found an amorous couple whose faces were united in a endless kiss.

He dared not call, knowing well that She would not respond, and he had a frightful dread of coming upon them suddenly.

The flourishes of the quadrilles, with the earsplitting solos of the cornet, the false shriek of the flute, the shrill squeaking of the violin, irritated his feelings, and increased his suffering. Wild and limping music was floating under the trees, now feeble, now stronger, wafted hither and thither by the breeze.

Suddenly he thought that possibly She had returned. Yes, she had returned! Why not? He had stupidly lost his head, without cause, carried away by his fears, by the inordinate suspicions which had for some time overwhelmed him. Seized by one of those singular calms which will sometimes occur in cases of the greatest despair, he returned toward the ball-room.

With a single glance of the eye, he took in the whole room. He made the 130
round of the tables, and abruptly again found himself face to face with the three women. He must have had a doleful and queer expression of countenance, for all three burst into laughter.

He made off, returned to the island, and threw himself into the coppice panting. He listened again, listened a long time, for his ears were singing. At last, however, he believed he heard farther off a little, sharp laugh, which he recognized at once; and he advanced very quietly, on his knees, removing the branches from his path, his heart beating so rapidly, that he could no longer breathe.

Two voices murmured some words, the meaning of which he did not understand, and then they were silent.

Then, he was possessed by a frightful longing to fly, to save himself, for ever, from this furious passion which threatened his existence. He was about to return to Chatou and take the train, resolved never to come back again, never again to see her. But her likeness suddenly rushed in upon him, and he mentally pictured the moment in the morning when she would awake in their warm bed, and would press coaxingly against him, throwing her arms around his neck, her hair dishevelled, and a little entangled on the forehead, her eyes still shut and her lips apart ready to receive the first kiss. The sudden recollection of this morning caress filled him with frantic recollections and the maddest desire.

The couple began to speak again; and he approached, stooping low. Then a faint cry rose from under the branches quite close to him. He advanced again, in spite of himself, irresistibly attracted, without being conscious of anything—and he saw them.

If her companion had only been a man. But that! that! He felt as though 135
he were spellbound by the very infamy of it. And he stood there astounded and overwhelmed, as if he had discovered the mutilated corpse of one dear to him, a crime against nature, a monstrous, disgusting profanation. Then, in an involuntary flash of thought, he remembered the little fish whose entrails he had felt being torn out! But Madeleine murmured: "Pauline!" in the same

tone in which she had often called him by name, and he was seized by such a fit of anguish that he turned and fled.

He struck against two trees, fell over a root, set off again, and suddenly found himself near the rapid branch of the river, which was lit up by the moon. The torrent-like current made great eddies where the light played upon it. The high bank dominated the stream like a cliff, leaving a wide obscure zone at its foot where the eddies could be heard swirling in the darkness.

On the other bank, the country seats of Croissy could be plainly seen.

Paul saw all this as though in a dream; he thought of nothing, understood nothing, and all things, even his very existence, appeared vague, far-off, forgotten, and closed.

The river was there. Did he know what he was doing? Did he wish to die? He was mad. He turned, however, toward the island, toward Her, and in the still air of the night, in which the faint and persistent burden of the music was borne up and down, he uttered, in a voice frantic with despair, bitter beyond measure, and superhumanly low, a frightful cry:

"Madeleine!"

His heartrending call shot across the great silence of the sky, and sped over the horizon. Then with a tremendous leap, with the bound of a wild animal, he jumped into the river. The water rushed on, closed over him, and from the place where he had disappeared a series of great circles started, enlarging their brilliant undulations, until they finally reached the other bank. The two women had heard the noise of the plunge. Madeleine drew herself up and exclaimed:

"It is Paul,"—a suspicion having arisen in her soul,—"he has drowned himself"; and she rushed toward the bank, where Pauline rejoined her.

A clumsy punt, propelled by two men, turned round and round on the spot. One of the men rowed, the other plunged into the water a great pole and appeared to be looking for something. Pauline cried:

"What are you doing? What is the matter?"

An unknown voice answered:

"It is a man who has just drowned himself."

The two haggard women, huddling close to each other, followed the manœuvres of the boat. The music of La Grenouillère continued to sound in the distance, seeming with its cadences to accompany the movements of the sombre fishermen; and the river which now concealed a corpse, whirled round and round, illuminated. The search was prolonged. The horrible suspense made Madeleine shiver all over. At last, after at least half an hour, one of the men announced:

"I have got him."

And he pulled up his long pole very gently, very gently. Then something large appeared upon the surface. The other boatman left his oars, and by uniting their strength and hauling upon the inert weight, they succeeded in getting it into their boat.

Then they made for land, seeking a place well lighted and low. At the moment they landed, the women also arrived. The moment she saw him,

Madeleine fell back with horror. In the moonlight he already appeared green, with his mouth, his eyes, his nose, his clothes full of slime. His fingers, closed and stiff, were hideous. A kind of black and liquid plaster covered his whole body. The face appeared swollen, and from his hair, plastered down by the ooze, there ran a stream of dirty water.

The two men examined him.

"Do you know him?" asked one.

The other, the Croissy ferryman, hesitated:

"Yes, it certainly seems to me that I have seen that head; but you know when a body is in that state one cannot recognize it easily." And then, suddenly:

"Why, it's Mr. Paul!"

"Who is Mr. Paul?" inquired his comrade.

The first answered:

"Why, Mr. Paul Baron, the son of the senator, the little chap who was so much in love."

The other added, philosophically:

"Well, his fun is ended now; it is a pity, all the same, when one is rich!"

Madeleine had fallen on the ground sobbing. Pauline approached the body and asked:

"Is he really quite dead?"

The men shrugged their shoulders.

"Oh! After that length of time, certainly."

Then one of them asked:

"Was it not at Grillon's that he lodged?"

"Yes," answered the other; "we had better take him back there, there will be something to be made out of it."

They embarked again in their boat and set out, moving off slowly on account of the rapid current. For a long time after they were out of sight of the place where the women remained, the regular splash of the oars in the water could be heard.

Then Pauline took the poor weeping Madeleine in her arms, petted her, embraced her for a long while, and consoled her.

"How can you help it? it is not your fault, is it? It is impossible to prevent men from doing silly things. He did it of his own free will; so much the worse for him, after all!"

And then lifting her up:

"Come, my dear, come and sleep at the house; it is impossible for you to go back to Grillon's to-night."

And she embraced her again, saying: "Come, we will cure you."

Madeleine arose, and weeping all the while but with fainter sobs, laid her head upon Pauline's shoulder, as though she had found a refuge in a closer and more certain affection, more familiar and more confiding, and she went off slowly.

Guy de Maupassant

www

(1850–1893) Web

Author of more than three hundred short stories in nineteenth-century France, de Maupassant was known for his combination of realism and naturalism. The simplicity of his portraits of French bourgeois futility made him an influential writer among foreigners.

www

TOPICS FOR CRITICAL THINKING Web

1. How does the riverscape parallel or reflect the story's complicated romance?
2. What does the story's setting tell us about how we should regard the four women in the boat?
3. Is there a relation between setting and social class? What purpose might such a parallel serve?

www

TOPICS FOR CRITICAL WRITING Web

1. How do the repeated elements of the setting produce a feeling of decadence? To answer this question, select an element that is repeated and trace its various appearances throughout the story's continued establishment of setting.
2. To what end does the story compare various versions of romance? To answer this question, you need to establish the various kinds of romance in the story.

5 Plot

Plot is an element of fiction that we know very well. We know the shapes of a variety of plots and how they should unfold: a young person overcomes adversity and finds success; the good guys win the war; love is found, then lost, then found. Instead of having surprise endings, most stories play out familiar plots. Part of our pleasure in reading these plots stems from anticipating the detail of these plots and knowing how events in a story will conclude. Notice, for example, the ways Mark Twain solicits our knowledge of plot in the following brief story.

MARK TWAIN

Story of the Bad Little Boy *(1865)*

Once there was a bad little boy whose name was Jim—though, if you will notice, you will find that bad little boys are nearly always called James in your Sunday-school books. It was strange, but still it was true that this one was called Jim.

He didn't have any sick mother either—a sick mother who was pious and had the consumption, and would be glad to lie down in the grave and be at rest but for the strong love she bore her boy, and the anxiety she felt that the world might be harsh and cold towards him when she was gone. Most bad boys in the Sunday-books are named James, and have sick mothers, who teach them to say, "Now, I lay me down," etc., and sing them to sleep with sweet, plaintive voices, and then kiss them good-night, and kneel down by the bedside and weep. But it was different with this fellow. He was named Jim, and there wasn't anything the matter with his mother—no consumption, nor anything of that kind. She was rather stout than otherwise, and she was not pious; moreover, she was not anxious on Jim's account. She said if he were to break his neck it wouldn't be much loss. She always spanked Jim to sleep, and she never kissed him good-night; on the contrary, she boxed his ears when she was ready to leave him.

Once this little bad boy stole the key of the pantry, and slipped in there and helped himself to some jam, and filled up the vessel with tar, so that his mother would never know; but all at once a terrible feeling didn't come over him, and something didn't seem to whisper to him, "Is it right to disobey my mother? Isn't it sinful to do this? Where do bad little boys go who gobble up their good kind mother's jam?" and then he didn't kneel down all alone and promise never to be wicked any more, and rise up with a light, happy heart, and go and tell his mother all about it, and beg her forgiveness, and be blessed by her with tears of pride and thankfulness in her eyes. No; that is just the way with all other bad boys in the books; but it happened otherwise with Jim, strangely enough. He ate that jam, and said it was bully, in his sinful, vulgar way; and he put in the tar, and said that was bully also, and laughed, and observed "that the old woman would get up and snort" when she found it out; and when she did find it out, he denied knowing anything about it, and she whipped him severely, and he did the crying himself. Everything about this boy was curious—everything turned out differently with him from the way it does to the bad Jameses in the books.

Once he climbed up in Farmer Acorn's apple-tree to steal, and the limb didn't break, and he didn't fall and break his arm, and get torn by the farmer's great dog, and then languish on a sick bed for weeks, and repent and become good. Oh! no; he stole as many apples as he wanted and came down all right; and he was all ready for the dog too, and knocked him endways with a brick when he came to tear him. It was very strange—nothing like it ever happened in those mild little books with marbled backs, and with pictures in them of men with swallow-tailed coats and bell-crowned hats, and pantaloons that are short in the legs, and women with the waists of their dresses under their arms, and no hoops on. Nothing like it in any of the Sunday-school books.

Once he stole the teacher's pen-knife, and, when he was afraid it would be 5
found out and he would get whipped, he slipped it into George Wilson's cap—poor Widow Wilson's son, the moral boy, the good little boy of the village, who always obeyed his mother, and never told an untruth, and was fond of his lessons, and infatuated with Sunday-school. And when the knife dropped from the cap, and poor George hung his head and blushed, as if in conscious guilt, and the grieved teacher charged the theft upon him, and was just in the very act of bringing the switch down upon his trembling shoulders, a white-haired, improbable justice of the peace did not suddenly appear in their midst, and strike an attitude and say, "Spare this noble boy—there stands the cowering culprit! I was passing the school-door at recess, and unseen myself, I saw the theft committed!" And then Jim didn't get whaled, and the venerable judge didn't read the tearful school a homily, and take George by the hand and say such a boy deserved to be exalted, and then tell him to come and make his home with him, and sweep out the office, and make fires, and run errands, and chop wood, and study law, and help his wife do household labors, and have all the balance of the time to play, and get forty cents a month, and be happy. No; it would have happened that way in the books, but it didn't happen that way to Jim. No meddling old clam of a justice dropped in to make trouble, and so the model boy George got thrashed, and Jim was glad of it because, you know, Jim hated moral boys. Jim said he was "down on them milksops." Such was the coarse language of this bad, neglected boy.

But the strangest thing that ever happened to Jim was the time he went boating on Sunday, and didn't get drowned, and that other time that he got caught out in the storm when he was fishing on Sunday, and didn't get struck by lightning. Why, you might look, and look, all through the Sunday-school books from now till next Christmas, and you would never come across anything like this. Oh no; you would find that all the bad boys who go boating on Sunday invariably get drowned; and all the bad boys who get caught out in storms when they are fishing on Sunday infallibly get struck by lightning. Boats with bad boys in them always upset on Sunday, and it always storms when bad boys go fishing on the Sabbath. How this Jim ever escaped is a mystery to me.

This Jim bore a charmed life—that must have been the way of it. Nothing could hurt him. He even gave the elephant in the menagerie a plug of tobacco, and the elephant didn't knock the top of his head off with his trunk. He browsed around the cupboard after essence of peppermint, and didn't make a mistake and drink *aqua fortis*. He stole his father's gun and went hunting on the Sabbath, and didn't shoot three or four of his fingers off. He struck his little sister on the temple with his fist when he was angry, and she didn't linger in pain through long summer days, and die with sweet words of forgiveness upon her lips that redoubled the anguish of his breaking heart. No; she got over it. He ran off and went to sea at last, and didn't come back and find himself sad and alone in the world, his loved ones sleeping in the quiet churchyard, and the vine-embowered home of his boyhood tumbled down and gone to decay. Ah! no; he came home as drunk as a piper, and got into the station-house the first thing.

And he grew up and married, and raised a large family, and brained them all with an axe one night, and got wealthy by all manner of cheating and rascality; and now he is the infernalist wickedest scoundrel in his native village, and is universally respected, and belongs to the Legislature.

So you can see there never was a bad James in the Sunday-school books that had such a streak of luck as this sinful Jim with the charmed life.

Twain's story presumes that we know how the story should turn out. It points out the ways plots are related to character types, our sense of morality and justice, and our feeling about the fitness of cause and effect. In telling a story with a plot that doesn't "fit," Twain's narrative draws attention to the ways we think plot ought to be. But what exactly is this notion of plot we know so well?

In narrative fiction, **plot** refers to the events in a story and the order in which they are presented. Plot conveys the sense of a logical progression of events where causes precede and are properly proportionate to their effects. We understand that plot has a beginning, a middle, and an end. We often like to begin our analysis of a story by recounting its plot or "what happens"; but what we find is that stories are much more complicated than their plots. We understand that plot is a story's scaffold around which are folded the draperies of character and setting. Like character and setting, plot is intertwined with the other formal elements of fiction.

The plots we expect to read give an artificial ordering of events arranged in the story so as to deliver a message. We see these plots so often that we understand them as describing the state of the natural world rather than embodying an ethical system. Twain's "Story of the Bad Little Boy" comments on the expectations we might have about the shape of plot. A cause—the boy's bad behavior—results in an effect—usually punishment—and the effect is a lesson in morality. Bad behavior results in a bad fate. Twain's story cynically alters the expected effect of the bad cause. No longer a "as you sow, so shall you reap" plot of poetic justice, the plot of Twain's story consists merely of a series of actions. The failure of just retribution in Twain's story draws attention to the ways plot has served as a means of delivering moral lessons.

Plot Versus Story

Comprised of the events actually narrated in a specific piece of fiction, plot differs from what we call "story." Plot refers only to those events present in the text, including events that may not be an explicit part of the story—details about the circumstances of the story's telling, for example, or elements of the process of narrating related within the story, or even the author's name listed at the beginning of the text. In the sitcom *Friends*, for example, plot includes the opening titles, what the characters actually do and say in the show's twenty-three minutes of scenes. All of this is what actually happens. **Story** includes all of the events that belong to the space and time of the world created by the text as well as events that are only suggested or implied in the text. In the sit-com *Friends*, story consists of all of the conditions and actions implied by the plot such as the fact that the characters have lives off-screen, they breath, eat, work (which we rarely see), have families, had childhoods, and so on. Story consists of the common range of events that we all understand happen, a total picture of a series of events, narrated or not, understood in chronological order. Story is all of the elements of the world in which we imagine the characters to live; but, unlike plot, it does not include extraneous matter such as a show's credits.

Often plot consists of significant events that occur within the larger context of story. The order in which significant events are narrated may be altered in plot; short stories very typically do not arrange their events in chronological order but leave it to the reader to reorder plot events in relation to what they know about story. A good example of this is when stories begin in the present, then recount events from the past. The distinction between story and plot is important because the selection of events to be included in a plot tells readers something about the art of the story. Why were these particular events selected? Why are they related in this order?

For example, the film *Star Wars* includes a number of actions and events in a certain order. We see Luke Skywalker on his home planet with his aunt and uncle, we see Princess Leia hide the important information in the droid R2D2, we see the droids in an escape pod that lands on Luke's planet, and so on. These are all elements of plot. Story consists of everything we see as well as events that are only implied by suggestion (showing a small part of the droids' trek to represent the whole of it), reference (someone in the film refers to other planets), or their belonging to the normal laws of human behavior:

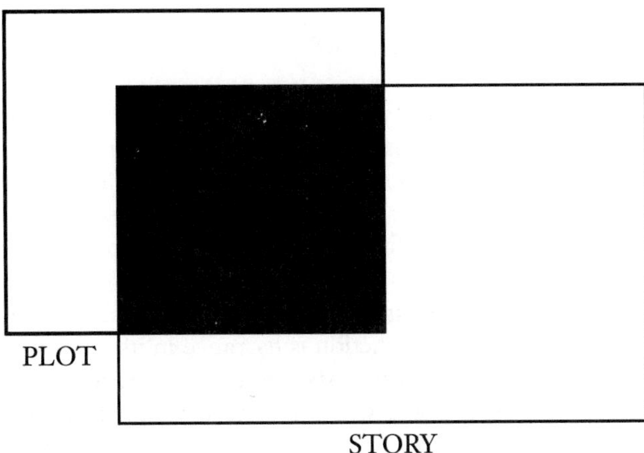

the existence of a larger galactic war, the entire sequence of the droids' trek across the planet, the actual murder of Luke's family, the methods of the imperial storm troopers. Together, plot and story give us an entire sense of the world of the narrative.

Plot and Chronology

Plots do not necessarily need to have a beginning, a middle, and an end, and certainly these elements do not need to be related in that order. Readers are quite capable of sorting out and rearranging chronologies of events from various flashbacks where events of the past are recounted after the story has begun in the present. A more precise literary term for flashback is **analepsis** or "leaping back." Analepses are often used to explain the current state of events or a character's motivations. Sometimes stories employ flash forwards when events from the future are recounted before their causes are presented. A more literary term for this is **prolepsis** or "leaping forward." Prolepses raise the question of how circumstances or characters will become what the future suggests. Both analepses and prolepses produce a desire to know by presenting elements of plot as mysteries to be explained. Thinking about the difference between the chronology of events in story and the order of their presentation as plot tells readers much about a **story's art**—the ways all of the material that makes up a story (plot, character, setting, image, symbol, theme, narrator, point of view, style, tone) work together to produce a set of effects that go beyond the simple recounting of a plot. What is the purpose of an analepsis? Prolepsis? What is the particular effect or strategy of ordering plot events in the way they are ordered?

Narrative

www Plot and story are parts of a way of ordering events called **narrative.** Web Narrative is our very idea of what might constitute a story in the first place. Narrative is a structure by which we make sense out of events by ordering them in a chain of cause/effect relations that play out in space and time. Causes, such as firing a gun, are linked to effects, such as someone being hit by a bullet. By associating gun and injury, we assume their connection as a relation of cause and effect. Seeing the gun as causing the injury makes sense of the two elements of the plot. Most prose fiction is narrative in its organization, as are most movies, television shows, newscasts, and even advertisements.

Narrative, however, is also a way for us to organize information into a coherent story. For example, we typically regard our lives as narratives, with beginnings, middles, and ends. This isn't necessarily because that is the shape of lives; it is more because this narrative shape is the way we make sense of things.

Types of Plot

Though strictly speaking, plot refers only to the order of specific events in a story, we use the term *plot* as a shorthand to refer both to the way events in a story are ordered and to the patterns that structure the arrangements of events in a story. There are only so many plot patterns; many story texts use the same general plot. We often understand that plot has a beginning or **exposition** in which the story introduces characters and circumstances. Occasionally stories begin in the middle of things, known as **in medias res**, without such exposition. The middle of a plot consists of a conflict or complication that is resolved ultimately in a story's **climax** and **dénouement**. Stories differ in the ways they define, arrange, and even omit the various parts of this pattern.

Patterns of events—such as those Twain makes fun of in "Story of the Bad Little Boy"—make up the trove of **paradigms**, the models or patterns, on which we depend for story material. There are also specific thematic patterns or paradigms of plot. There is, for example, a common plot based on the conflict between two opposing forces—a protagonist and an antagonist. There is a quest plot in which a protagonist searches for something or works to become something, as in the narrative of the young boxer discussed in the Introduction. Romance plots—two people who overcome obstacles to be together or tragically fail—may stand by themselves, combine with quest plots as in the young boxer's story, or be linked to coming-of-age plots that trace a young person's processes of learning and maturing. While these types of plot have a definite aim, some plots are structured more around subtle shifts in awareness or understanding. Some even seem to have no aim at all, focusing instead on acts of perception, irony, the absurdity of existence, or a critique of social customs.

Realism and Naturalism

Realist and naturalist writers of the nineteenth century turned the practices of everyday life into plot, though their stories ultimately focused on dramatic or humorous events. **Web** **Realism** and **naturalism** designate literary movements: a **literary movement** is a set of ideas formulated by authors and critics about what literature should do and how it should do it. Such movements account for why the work of authors who write during the same period in time often share the same sense of form and aesthetics. *www*

Twain's "Story of the Bad Little Boy" is one example of a realist story. The author's unveiling of the narrative's expected morality offers a far more realistic plot than would a sentimental lesson from a lesson book. The three stories that follow are realist stories: Each one presents a detailed account of the protagonist's experience rendered in such a way that the narrative conforms to the world as we sense it. Jack London's two tales of survival, "The Law of Life" and "To Build a Fire" render two incidents of a man's encounter with nature. "An Occurrence at Owl Creek Bridge" by satirist Ambrose Bierce more dramatically contrasts future and present, internal and external, while remaining realistic in its presentation of events.

JACK LONDON

The Law of Life *(1901)*

Old Koskoosh listened greedily. Though his sight had long since faded, his hearing was still acute, and the slightest sound penetrated to the glimmering intelligence which yet abode behind the withered forehead, but which no longer gazed forth upon the things of the world. Ah! that was Sit-cum-to-ha, shrilly anathematizing the dogs as she cuffed and beat them into the harnesses. Sit-cum-to-ha was his daughter's daughter, but she was too busy to waste a thought upon her broken grandfather, sitting alone there in the snow, forlorn and helpless. Camp must be broken. The long trail waited while the short day refused to linger. Life called her, and the duties of life, not death. And he was very close to death now.

The thought made the old man panicky for the moment, and he stretched forth a palsied hand which wandered tremblingly over the small heap of dry wood beside him. Reassured that it was indeed there, his hand returned to the shelter of his mangy furs, and he again fell to listening. The sulky crackling of half-frozen hides told him that the chief's moose-skin lodge had been struck, and even then was being rammed and jammed into portable compass. The chief was his son, stalwart and strong, head man of the tribesmen, and a mighty hunter. As the women toiled with the camp luggage, his voice rose, chiding them for their slowness. Old Koskoosh strained his ears. It was the last time he would hear that voice. There went Geehow's lodge! And Tusken's! Seven, eight, nine; only the shaman's could be still standing. There! They were at work upon it now. He could hear the shaman grunt as he piled it on the sled. A child whimpered, and a woman soothed it with soft, crooning gutturals. Little Koo-tee, the old man thought, a fretful child, and not overstrong. It would die soon, perhaps, and they would burn a hole through the frozen tundra and pile rocks above to keep the wolverines away. Well, what did it matter? A few years at best, and as many an empty belly as a full one. And in the end, Death waited, ever-hungry and hungriest of them all.

What was that? Oh, the men lashing the sleds and drawing tight the thongs. He listened, who would listen no more. The whip-lashes snarled and bit among the dogs. Hear them whine! How they hated the work and the trail! They were off! Sled after sled churned slowly away into the silence. They were gone. They had passed out of his life, and he faced the last bitter hour alone. No. The snow crunched beneath a moccasin; a man stood beside him; upon his head a hand rested gently. His son was good to do this thing. He remembered other old men whose sons had not waited after the tribe. But his son had. He wandered away into the past, till the young man's voice brought him back.

"Is it well with you?" he asked.

And the old man answered, "It is well." 5

"There be wood beside you," the younger man continued, "and the fire burns bright. The morning is gray, and the cold has broken. It will snow presently. Even now it is snowing."

"Ay, even now is it snowing."

"The tribesmen hurry. Their bales are heavy, and their bellies flat with lack of feasting. The trail is long and they travel fast. I go now. It is well?"

"It is well. I am as a last year's leaf, clinging lightly to the stem. The first breath that blows, and I fall. My voice is become like an old woman's. My eyes no longer show me the way of my feet, and my feet are heavy, and I am tired. It is well."

He bowed his head in content till the last noise of the complaining snow 10
had died away, and he knew his son was beyond recall. Then his hand crept out in haste to the wood. It alone stood between him and the eternity that yawned in upon him. At last the measure of his life was a handful of fagots. One by one they would go to feed the fire, and just so, step by step, death would creep upon him. When the last stick had surrendered up its heat, the frost would begin to gather strength. First his feet would yield, then his hands; and the numbness would travel, slowly, from the extremities to the body. His head would fall forward upon his knees, and he would rest. It was easy. All men must die.

He did not complain. It was the way of life, and it was just. He had been born close to the earth, close to the earth had he lived, and the law thereof was not new to him. It was the law of all flesh. Nature was not kindly to the flesh. She had no concern for that concrete thing called the individual. Her interest lay in the species, the race. This was the deepest abstraction old Koskoosh's barbaric mind was capable of, but he grasped it firmly. He saw it exemplified in all life. The rise of the sap, the bursting greenness of the willow bud, the fall of the yellow leaf—in this alone was told the whole history. But one task did Nature set the individual. Did he not perform it, he died. Did he perform it, it was all the same, he died. Nature did not care; there were plenty who were obedient, and it was only the obedience in this matter, not the obedient, which lived and lived always. The tribe of Koskoosh was very old. The old men he had known when a boy, had known old men before them. Therefore it was true that the tribe lived, that it stood for the obedience of all its members, way down into the forgotten past, whose very resting-places were unremembered. They did not count; they were episodes. They had passed away like clouds from a summer sky. He also was an episode, and would pass away. Nature did not care. To life she set one task, gave one law. To perpetuate was the task of life, its law was death. A maiden was a good creature to look upon, full-breasted and strong, with spring to her step and light in her eyes. But her task was yet before her. The light in her eyes brightened, her step quickened, she was now bold with the young men, now timid, and she gave them of her own unrest. And ever she grew fairer and yet fairer to look upon, till some hunter, able no longer to withhold himself, took her to his lodge to cook and toil for him and to become the mother of his children. And with the coming of her offspring her looks left her. Her limbs dragged and shuffled, her eyes dimmed and bleared, and only the little children found joy against the withered cheek of the old squaw by the fire. Her task was done. But a little while, on the first pinch of famine or the first long trail, and she would be left, even as he had been left, in the snow, with a little pile of wood. Such was the law.

He placed a stick carefully upon the fire and resumed his meditations. It was the same everywhere, with all things. The mosquitoes vanished with the first frost. The little tree-squirrel crawled away to die. When age settled upon the rabbit it became slow and heavy, and could no longer outfoot its enemies. Even the big bald-face grew clumsy and blind and quarrelsome, in the end to be dragged down by a handful of yelping huskies. He remembered how he had abandoned his own father on an upper reach of the Klondike one winter, the winter before the missionary came with his talk-books and his box of medicines. Many a time had Koskoosh smacked his lips over the recollection of that box, though now his mouth refused to moisten. The "painkiller" had been especially good. But the missionary was a bother after all, for he brought no meat into the camp, and he ate heartily, and the hunters grumbled. But he chilled his lungs on the divide by the Mayo, and the dogs afterwards nosed the stones away and fought over his bones.

Koskoosh placed another stick on the fire and harked back deeper into the past. There was the time of the Great Famine, when the old men crouched empty-bellied to the fire, and let fall from their lips dim traditions of the ancient day when the Yukon ran wide open for three winters, and then lay frozen for three summers. He had lost his mother in that famine. In the summer the salmon run had failed, and the tribe looked forward to the winter and the coming of the caribou. Then the winter came, but with it there were no caribou. Never had the like been known, not even in the lives of the old men. But the caribou did not come, and it was the seventh year, and the rabbits had not replenished, and the dogs were naught but bundles of bones. And through the long darkness the children wailed and died, and the women, and the old men; and not one in ten of the tribe lived to meet the sun when it came back in the spring. That *was* a famine!

But he had seen times of plenty, too, when the meat spoiled on their hands, and the dogs were fat and worthless with overeating—times when they let the game go unkilled, and the women were fertile, and the lodges were cluttered with sprawling men-children and women-children. Then it was the men became high-stomached, and revived ancient quarrels, and crossed the divides to the south to kill the Pellys, and to the west that they might sit by the dead fires of the Tananas. He remembered, when a boy, during a time of plenty, when he saw a moose pulled down by the wolves. Zing-ha lay with him in the snow and watched—Zing-ha, who later became the craftiest of hunters, and who, in the end, fell through an air-hole on the Yukon. They found him, a month afterward, just as he had crawled halfway out and frozen stiff to the ice.

But the moose. Zing-ha and he had gone out that day to play at hunting after the manner of their fathers. On the bed of the creek they struck the fresh track of a moose, and with it the tracks of many wolves. "An old one," Zing-ha, who was quicker at reading the sign, said—"an old one who cannot keep up with the herd. The wolves have cut him out from his brothers, and they will never leave him." And it was so. It was their way. By day and by night, never resting, snarling on his heels, snapping at his nose, they would stay by him to the end. How Zing-ha and he felt the blood-lust quicken! The finish would be a sight to see!

Eager-footed, they took the trail, and even he, Koskoosh, slow of sight and an unversed tracker, could have followed it blind, it was so wide. Hot were they on the heels of the chase, reading the grim tragedy, fresh-written, at every step. Now they came to where the moose had made a stand. Thrice the length of a grown man's body, in every direction, had the snow been stamped about and uptossed. In the midst were the deep impressions of the splay-hoofed game, and all about, everywhere, were the lighter footmarks of the wolves. Some, while their brothers harried the kill, had lain to one side and rested. The full-stretched impress of their bodies in the snow was as perfect as though made the moment before. One wolf had been caught in a wild lunge of the maddened victim and trampled to death. A few bones, well picked, bore witness.

Again, they ceased the uplift of their snowshoes at a second stand. Here the great animal had fought desperately. Twice had he been dragged down, as the snow attested, and twice had he shaken his assailants clear and gained footing once more. He had done his task long since, but none the less was life dear to him. Zing-ha said it was strange thing, a moose once down to get free again; but this one certainly had. The shaman would see signs and wonders in this when they told him.

And yet again, they come to where the moose had made to mount the bank and gain the timber. But his foes had laid on from behind, till he reared and fell back upon them, crushing two deep into the snow. It was plain the kill was at hand, for their brothers had left them untouched. Two more stands were hurried past, brief in time-length and very close together. The trail was red now, and the clean stride of the great beast had grown short and slovenly. Then they heard the first sounds of the battle—not the full-throated chorus of the chase, but the short, snappy bark which spoke of close quarters and teeth to flesh. Crawling up the wind, Zing-ha bellied it through the snow, and with him crept he, Koskoosh, who was to be chief of the tribesmen in the years to come. Together they shoved aside the under branches of a young spruce and peered forth. It was the end they saw.

The picture, like all of youth's impressions, was still strong with him, and his dim eyes watched the end played out as vividly as in that far-off time. Koskoosh marveled at this, for in the days which followed, when he was a leader of men and a head of councillors, he had done great deeds and made his name a curse in the mouths of the Pellys, to say naught of the strange white man he had killed, knife to knife, in open fight.

For long he pondered on the days of his youth, till the fire died down and the frost bit deeper. He replenished it with two sticks this time, and gauged his grip on life by what remained. If Sit-cum-to-ha had only remembered her grandfather, and gathered a larger armful, his hours would have been longer. It would have been easy. But she was ever a careless child, and honored not her ancestors from the time the Beaver, son of the son of Zing-ha, first cast eyes upon her. Well, what mattered it? Had he not done likewise in his own quick youth? For a while he listened to the silence. Perhaps the heart of his son might soften, and he would come back with the dogs to take his old father on with the tribe to where the caribou ran thick and the fat hung heavy upon them.

He strained his ears, his restless brain for the moment stilled. Not a stir, nothing. He alone took breath in the midst of the great silence. It was very lonely. Hark! What was that? A chill passed over his body. The familiar, long-drawn howl broke the void, and it was close at hand. Then on his darkened eyes was projected the vision of the moose—the old bull moose—the torn flanks and bloody sides, the riddled mane, and the great branching horns, down low and tossing to the last. He saw the flashing forms of gray, the gleaming eyes, the lolling tongues, the slavered fangs. And he saw the inexorable circle close in till it became a dark point in the midst of the stamped snow.

A cold muzzle thrust against his cheek, and at its touch his soul leaped back to the present. His hand shot into the fire and dragged out a burning faggot. Overcome for the nonce by his hereditary fear of man, the brute retreated, raising a prolonged call to his brothers; and greedily they answered, till a ring of crouching, jaw-slobbered gray was stretched round about. The old man listened to the drawing in of this circle. He waved his brand wildly, and sniffs turned to snarls; but the panting brutes refused to scatter. Now one wormed his chest forward, dragging his haunches after, now a second, now a third; but never a one drew back. Why should he cling to life? he asked, and dropped the blazing stick into the snow. It sizzled and went out. The circle grunted uneasily, but held its own. Again he saw the last stand of the old bull moose, and Koskoosh dropped his head wearily upon his knees. What did it matter after all? Was it not the law of life?

Jack London

www (1876–1916) **Web**

A jack of all trades, London finished high school after a stint in jail for vagrancy and became a successful and prolific writer who published more than fifty-one books before his early death at forty. Many of his stories involve the sea or adventures in the wild.

www *TOPICS FOR CRITICAL THINKING* **Web**

1. How is "the law of life" also the plot of the story?
2. What is the connection between Koskoosh's present circumstances and the story Koskoosh remembers?
3. How does this story's plot rely on character and setting?

www *TOPICS FOR CRITICAL WRITING* **Web**

1. What are the effects of narrating events out of their chronological order in this story?
2. How do the text's various stories parallel one another? To what end? To answer this question, you need to define the text's various stories.

To Build a Fire *(1902)*

For land travel or seafaring, the world over, a companion is usually considered desirable. In the Klondike, as Tom Vincent found out, such a companion is absolutely essential. But he found it out, not by precept, but through bitter experience.

"Never travel alone," is a precept of the north. He had heard it many times and laughed; for he was a strapping young fellow, big-boned and big-muscled, with faith in himself and in the strength of his head and hands.

It was on a bleak January day when the experience came that taught him respect for the frost, and for the wisdom of the men who had battled with it.

He had left Calumet Camp on the Yukon with a light pack on his back, to go up Paul Creek to the divide between it and Cherry Creek, where his party was prospecting and hunting moose.

5 The frost was sixty degrees below zero, and he had thirty miles of lonely trail to cover, but he did not mind. In fact, he enjoyed it, swinging along through the silence, his blood pounding warmly through his veins, and his mind carefree and happy. For he and his comrades were certain they had struck "pay" up there on the Cherry Creek Divide; and, further, he was returning to them from Dawson with cheery home letters from the States.

At seven o'clock, when he turned the heels of his moccasins toward Calumet Camp, it was still black night. And when day broke at half past nine he had made the four-mile cut-off across the flats and was six miles up Paul Creek. The trail, which had seen little travel, followed the bed of the creek, and there was no possibility of his getting lost. He had gone to Dawson by way of Cherry Creek and Indian River, so Paul Creek was new and strange. By half past eleven he was at the forks, which had been described to him, and he knew he had covered fifteen miles, half the distance.

He knew that in the nature of things the trail was bound to grow worse from there on, and thought that, considering the good time he had made, he merited lunch. Casting off his pack and taking a seat on a fallen tree, he unmittened his right hand, reached inside his shirt next to the skin, and fished out a couple of biscuits sandwiched with sliced bacon and wrapped in a handkerchief—the only way they could be carried without freezing solid.

He had barely chewed the first mouthful when his numbing fingers warned him to put his mitten on again. This he did, not without surprise at the bitter swiftness with which the frost bit in. Undoubtedly it was the coldest snap he had ever experienced, he thought.

He spat upon the snow,—a favorite northland trick,—and the sharp crackle of the instantly congealed spittle startled him. The spirit thermometer at Calumet had registered sixty below when he left, but he was certain it had grown much colder, how much colder he could not imagine.

Half of the first biscuit was yet untouched, but he could feel himself be- 10
ginning to chill—a thing most unusual for him. This would never do, he decided, and slipping the pack-straps across his shoulders, he leaped to his feet and ran briskly up the trail.

A few minutes of this made him warm again, and he settled down to a steady stride, munching the biscuits as he went along. The moisture that exhaled with his breath crusted his lips and mustache with pendent ice and formed a miniature glacier on his chin. Now and again sensation forsook his nose and cheeks, and he rubbed them till they burned with the returning blood.

Most men wore nose-straps; his partners did, but he had scorned such "feminine contraptions," and till now had never felt the need of them. Now he did feel the need, for he was rubbing constantly.

Nevertheless he was aware of a thrill of joy, of exultation. He was doing something, achieving something, mastering the elements. Once he laughed aloud in sheer strength of life, and with his clenched fist defied the frost. He was its master. What he did he did in spite of it. It could not stop him. He was going on to the Cherry Creek Divide.

Strong as were the elements, he was stronger. At such times animals crawled away into their holes and remained in hiding. But he did not hide. He was out in it, facing it, fighting it. He was a man, a master of things.

In such fashion, rejoicing proudly, he tramped on. After half an hour he 15
rounded a bend, where the creek ran close to the mountainside, and came upon one of the most insignificant-appearing but most formidable dangers in northern travel.

The creek itself was frozen solid to its rocky bottom, but from the mountain came the outflow of several springs. These springs never froze, and the only effect of the severest cold snaps was to lessen their discharge. Protected from the frost by the blanket of snow, the water of these springs seeped down into the creek, and, on top of the creek ice, formed shallow pools.

The surface of these pools, in turn, took on a skin of ice which grew thicker and thicker, until the water overran, and so formed a second ice-skinned pool above the first.

Thus at the bottom was the solid creek ice, then probably six to eight inches of water, then a thin ice-skin, then another six inches of water and another ice-skin. And on top of this last skin was about an inch of recent snow to make the trap complete.

To Tom Vincent's eye the unbroken snow surface gave no warning of the lurking danger. As the crust was thicker at the edge, he was well toward the middle before he broke through.

In itself it was a very insignificant mishap,—a man does not drown in twelve inches of water,—but in its consequences as serious an accident as could possibly befall him.

At the instant he broke through he felt the cold water strike his feet and ankles, and with half a dozen lunges he made the bank. He was quite cool and collected. The thing to do, and the only thing to do, was to build a fire. For another precept of the north runs: *Travel with wet socks down to twenty below zero; after that build a fire.* And it was three times twenty below and colder, and he knew it.

He knew, further, that great care must be exercised; that with failure at the first attempt, the chance was made greater for failure at the second attempt. In short, he knew that there must be no failure. The moment before a strong, exulting man, boastful of his mastery of the elements, he was now fighting for his life against those same elements—such was the difference caused by the injection of a quart of water into a northland traveller's calculations.

In a clump of pines on the rim of the bank the spring high-water had lodged many twigs and small branches. Thoroughly dried by the summer sun, they now waited the match.

It is impossible to build a fire with heavy Alaskan mittens on one's hands, so Vincent bared his, gathered a sufficient number of twigs, and knocking the snow from them, knelt down to kindle his fire. From an inside pocket he drew out his matches and a strip of thin birch bark. The matches were of the Klondike kind, sulphur matches, one hundred in a bunch.

He noticed how quickly his fingers had chilled as he separated one match from the bunch and scratched it on his trousers. The birch bark, like the dryest of paper, burst into bright flame. This he carefully fed with the smallest twigs and finest débris, cherishing the flame with the utmost care. It did not do to hurry things, as he well knew, and although his fingers were now quite stiff, he did not hurry.

After the first quick, biting sensation of cold, his feet had ached with a heavy, dull ache and were rapidly growing numb. But the fire, although a very young one, was now a success, and he knew that a little snow, briskly rubbed, would speedily cure his feet.

But at the moment he was adding the first thick twigs to the fire a grievous thing happened. The pine boughs above his head were burdened with a four months' snowfall, and so finely adjusted were the burdens that his slight movements in collecting the twigs had been sufficient to disturb the balance.

The snow from the topmost bough was the first to fall, striking and dislodging the snow on the boughs beneath. And all this snow, accumulating as it fell, smote Tom Vincent's head and shoulders and blotted out his fire.

He still kept his presence of mind, for he knew how great his danger was. He started at once to rebuild the fire, but his fingers were now so cold that he could not bend them, and he was forced to pick up each twig and splinter between the tips of the fingers of either hand.

30 When he came to the match he encountered great difficulty in separating one from the bunch. This he succeeded in managing, however, and also, by a great effort, in clutching the match between his thumb and forefinger. But in scratching it, he dropped it in the snow and could not pick it up again.

He stood up, desperate. He could not feel even his weight on his feet, although the ankles were aching painfully. Putting on his mittens, he stepped to one side, so that the snow would not fall upon the new fire he was to build, and beat his hands violently against a tree-trunk.

This enabled him to separate and strike a second match and to set fire to the remaining fragment of birch bark. But his body had now begun to chill and he was shivering, so that when he tried to add the first twigs his hand shook and the tiny flame was quenched.

The frost had beaten him. His hands were worthless. But he had the foresight to drop the bunch of matches into his wide-mouthed outside pocket before he slipped on his mittens in despair, and started to run up the trail. One cannot run the frost out of wet feet at sixty below and colder, however, as he quickly discovered.

He came round a sharp turn of the creek to where he could look ahead for a mile. But there was no help, no sign of help, only the white trees and the white hills, the quiet cold and the brazen silence! If only he had a comrade whose feet were not freezing, he thought, only such a comrade to start the fire that could save him!

35 Then his eyes chanced upon another high-water lodgment of twigs and leaves and branches. If he could strike a match, all might yet be well. With stiff fingers which he could not bend, he got out a bunch of matches, but found it impossible to separate them.

He sat down and awkwardly shuffled the bunch about on his knees, until he got it resting on his palm with the sulphur ends projecting, somewhat in the manner the blade of a hunting-knife would project when clutched in the fist.

But his fingers stood straight out. They could not clutch. This he overcame by pressing the wrist of the other hand against them, and so forcing them down upon the bunch. Time and again, holding thus by both hands, he scratched the bunch on his leg and finally ignited it. But the flame burned into the flesh of his hand, and he involuntarily relaxed his hold. The bunch fell into the snow, and while he tried vainly to pick it up, sizzled and went out.

Again he ran, by this time badly frightened. His feet were utterly devoid of sensation. He stubbed his toes once on a buried log, but beyond pitching him into the snow and wrenching his back, it gave him no feelings.

His fingers were helpless and his wrists were beginning to grow numb. His nose and cheeks he knew were freezing, but they did not count. It was his feet and hands that were to save him, if he was to be saved.

40 He recollected being told of a camp of moose-hunters somewhere above the forks of Paul Creek. He must be somewhere near it, he thought, and if he could find it he yet might be saved. Five minutes later he came upon it, lone and deserted, with drifted snow sprinkled inside the pine-bough shelter in which the hunters had slept. He sank down, sobbing. All was over. In an hour at best, in that terrific temperature, he would be an icy corpse.

But the love of life was strong in him, and he sprang again to his feet. He was thinking quickly. What if the matches did burn his hands? Burned hands were better than dead hands. No hands at all were better than death. He floundered along the trail till he came upon another high-water lodgment. There were twigs and branches, leaves and grasses, all dry and waiting the fire.

Again he sat down and shuffled the bunch of matches on his knees, got it into place on his palm, with the wrist of his other hand forced the nerveless fingers down against the bunch, and with the wrist kept them there. At the second scratch the bunch caught fire, and he knew that if he could stand the pain he was saved. He choked with the sulphur fumes, and the blue flame licked the flesh of his hands.

At first he could not feel it, but it burned quickly in through the frosted surface. The odor of the burning flesh—his flesh—was strong in his nostrils. He writhed about in his torment, yet held on. He set his teeth and swayed back and forth, until the clear white flame of the burning match shot up, and he had applied that flame to the leaves and grasses.

An anxious five minutes followed, but the fire gained steadily. Then he set to work to save himself. Heroic measures were necessary, such was his extremity, and he took them.

45 Alternately rubbing his hands with snow and thrusting them into the flames, and now and again beating them against the hard trees, he restored their circulation sufficiently for them to be of use to him. With his hunting-knife he slashed the straps from his pack, unrolled his blanket, and got out dry socks and foot-gear.

Then he cut away his moccasins and bared his feet. But while he had taken liberties with his hands, he kept his feet fairly away from the fire and rubbed them with snow. He rubbed till his hands grew numb, when he would cover his feet with the blanket, warm his hands by the fire, and return to the rubbing.

For three hours he worked, till the worst effects of the freezing had been counteracted. All that night he stayed by the fire, and it was late the next day when he limped pitifully into the camp on the Cherry Creek Divide.

In a month's time he was able to be about on his feet, although the toes were destined always after that to be very sensitive to frost. But the scars on his hands he knows he will carry to the grave. And—"*Never travel alone!*" he now lays down the precept of the north.

TOPICS FOR CRITICAL THINKING Web

www

1. Through what tactics does the story create a sense of urgency? For what purposes?
2. Why does this story reveal a moral lesson at the beginning?

TOPICS FOR CRITICAL WRITING Web

www

1. In what ways does the opening lesson affect the ways we read the story? What is the relation between the actual plot and the lesson with which the story begins?
2. What specific tactics does the story use to create a sense of doom? For what purposes does it create this sense?

AMBROSE BIERCE

An Occurrence at Owl Creek Bridge *(1891)*

I

A man stood upon a railroad bridge in northern Alabama, looking down into the swift water twenty feet below. The man's hands were behind his back, the wrists bound with a cord. A rope closely encircled his neck. It was attached to a stout cross-timber above his head and the slack fell to the level of his knees. Some loose boards laid upon the sleepers supporting the metals of the railway supplied a footing for him and his executioners—two private soldiers of the Federal army, directed by a sergeant who in civil life may have been a deputy sheriff. At a short remove upon the same temporary platform was an officer in the uniform of his rank, armed. He was a captain. A sentinel at each end of the bridge stood with his rifle in the position known as "support," that is to say, vertical in front of the left shoulder, the hammer resting on the forearm thrown straight across the chest—a formal and unnatural position, enforcing an erect carriage of the body. It did not appear to be the duty of these two men to know what was occurring at the center of the bridge; they merely blockaded the two ends of the foot planking that traversed it.

Beyond one of the sentinels nobody was in sight; the railroad ran straight away into a forest for a hundred yards, then, curving, was lost to view. Doubtless there was an outpost farther along. The other bank of the stream was open ground—a gentle acclivity topped with a stockade of vertical tree trunks, loopholed for rifles, with a single embrasure through which protruded the muzzle of a brass cannon commanding the bridge. Midway of the slope between bridge and fort were the spectators—a single company of infantry in line, at "parade rest," the butts of the rifles on the ground, the barrels inclining slightly backward against the right shoulder, the hands crossed upon the stock. A lieutenant stood at the right of the line, the point of his sword upon the ground, his left hand resting upon his right. Excepting the group of four at the center of the bridge, not a man moved. The company faced the bridge, staring stonily, motionless. The sentinels, facing the banks of the stream, might have been statues to adorn the bridge. The captain stood with folded arms, silent, observing the work of his subordinates, but making no sign. Death is a dignitary who when he comes announced is to be received with formal manifestations of respect, even by those most familiar with him. In the code of military etiquette silence and fixity are forms of deference.

The man who was engaged in being hanged was apparently about thirty-five years of age. He was a civilian, if one might judge from his habit, which was that of a planter. His features were good—a straight nose, firm mouth, broad forehead, from which his long, dark hair was combed straight back, falling behind his ears to the collar of his well-fitting frock coat. He wore a mustache and pointed beard, but no whiskers; his eyes were large and dark gray, and had a kindly expression which one would hardly have expected in one whose neck was in the hemp. Evidently this was no vulgar assassin. The liberal military code makes provision for hanging many kinds of persons, and gentlemen are not excluded.

The preparations being complete, the two private soldiers stepped aside and each drew away the plank upon which he had been standing. The sergeant turned to the captain, saluted, and placed himself immediately behind that officer, who in turn moved apart one pace. These movements left the condemned man and the sergeant standing on the two ends of the same plank, which spanned three of the cross-ties of the bridge. The end upon which the civilian stood almost, but not quite, reached a fourth. This plank had been held in place by the weight of the captain; it was now held by that of the sergeant. At a signal from the former the latter would step aside, the plank would tilt and the condemned man go down between two ties. The arrangement commended itself to his judgment as simple and effective. His face had not been covered nor his eyes bandaged. He looked a moment at his "unsteadfast footing," then let his gaze wander to the swirling water of the stream racing madly beneath his feet. A piece of dancing driftwood caught his attention and his eyes followed it down the current. How slowly it appeared to move! What a sluggish stream!

5 He closed his eyes in order to fix his last thoughts upon his wife and children. The water, touched to gold by the early sun, the brooding mists under the banks at some distance down the stream, the fort, the soldiers, the piece of drift—all had distracted him. And now he became conscious of a new disturbance. Striking through the thought of his dear ones was a sound which he could neither ignore nor understand, a sharp, distinct, metallic percussion like the stroke of a blacksmith's hammer upon the anvil; it had the same ringing quality. He wondered what it was, and whether immeasurably distant or nearby—it seemed both. Its recurrence was regular, but as slow as the tolling of a death knell. He awaited each stroke with impatience and—he knew not why—apprehension. The intervals of silence grew progressively longer; the delays became maddening. With their greater infrequency the sounds increased in strength and sharpness. They hurt his ear like the thrust of a knife; he feared he would shriek. What he heard was the ticking of his watch.

He unclosed his eyes and saw again the water below him. "If I could free my hands," he thought, "I might throw off the noose and spring into the stream. By diving I could evade the bullets and, swimming vigorously, reach the bank, take to the woods and get away home. My home, thank God, is as yet outside their lines; my wife and little ones are still beyond the invader's farthest advance."

As these thoughts, which have here to be set down in words, were flashed into the doomed man's brain rather than evolved from it the captain nodded to the sergeant. The sergeant stepped aside.

II

Peyton Farquhar was a well-to-do planter, of an old and highly respected Alabama family. Being a slave owner and like other slave owners a politician he was naturally an original secessionist and ardently devoted to the Southern cause. Circumstances of an imperious nature, which it is unnecessary to relate here, had prevented him from taking service with the gallant army that had fought the disastrous campaigns ending with the fall of Corinth, and he chafed under the inglorious restraint, longing for the release of his energies, the larger life of the soldier, the opportunity for distinction. That opportunity, he felt, would come, as it comes to all in wartime. Meanwhile he did what he could. No service was too humble for him to perform in aid of the South, no adventure too perilous for him to undertake if consistent with the character of a civilian who was at heart a soldier, and who in good faith and without too much qualification assented to at least a part of the frankly villainous dictum that all is fair in love and war.

One evening while Farquhar and his wife were sitting on a rustic bench near the entrance to his grounds, a gray-clad soldier rode up to the gate and asked for a drink of water. Mrs. Farquhar was only too happy to serve him with her own white hands. While she was fetching the water her husband approached the dusty horseman and inquired eagerly for news from the front.

10 "The Yanks are repairing the railroads," said the man, "and are getting ready for another advance. They have reached the Owl Creek bridge, put it in order, and built a stockade on the north bank. The commandant has issued an order, which is posted everywhere, declaring that any civilian caught interfering with the railroad, its bridges, tunnels or trains will be summarily hanged. I saw the order."

"How far is it to the Owl Creek bridge?" Farquhar asked.

"About thirty miles."

"Is there no force on this side the creek?"

"Only a picket post half a mile out, on the railroad, and a single sentinel at this end of the bridge."

15 "Suppose a man—a civilian and student of hanging—should elude the picket post and perhaps get the better of the sentinel," said Farquhar, smiling, "what could he accomplish?"

The soldier reflected. "I was there a month ago," he replied. "I observed that the flood of last winter had lodged a great quantity of driftwood against the wooden pier at this end of the bridge. It is now dry and would burn like tow."

The lady had now brought the water, which the soldier drank. He thanked her ceremoniously, bowed to her husband and rode away. An hour later, after nightfall, he repassed the plantation, going northward in the direction from which he had come. He was a Federal scout.

III

As Peyton Farquhar fell straight downward through the bridge he lost consciousness and was as one already dead. From this state he was awakened—ages later, it seemed to him—by the pain of a sharp pressure upon his throat, followed by a sense of suffocation. Keen, poignant agonies seemed to shoot from his neck downward through every fiber of his body and limbs. These pains appeared to flash along well-defined lines of ramification and to beat with an inconceivably rapid periodicity. They seemed like streams of pulsating fire heating him to an intolerable temperature. As to his head, he was conscious of nothing but a feeling of fullness—of congestion. These sensations were unaccompanied by thought. The intellectual part of his nature was already effaced; he had power only to feel, and feeling was torment. He was conscious of motion. Encompassed in a luminous cloud, of which he was now merely the fiery heart, without material substance, he swung through unthinkable arcs of oscillation, like a vast pendulum. Then all at once, with terrible suddenness, the light about him shot upward with the noise of a loud plash; a frightful roaring was in his ears, and all was cold and dark. The power of thought was restored; he knew that the rope had broken and he had fallen into the stream. There was no additional strangulation; the noose about his neck was already suffocating him and kept the water from his lungs. To die of hanging at the bottom of a river!—the idea seemed to him ludicrous. He opened his eyes in the darkness and saw above him a gleam of light, but how distant, how inaccessible! He was still sinking, for the light became fainter and fainter until it was a mere glimmer. Then it began to grow and brighten, and he knew that he was rising toward the surface—knew it with reluctance, for he was now very comfortable. "To be hanged and drowned," he thought, "that is not so bad, but I do not wish to be shot. No, I will not be shot. That is not fair."

He was not conscious of an effort, but a sharp pain in his wrist apprised him that he was trying to free his hands. He gave the struggle his attention, as an idler might observe the feat of a juggler, without interest in the outcome. What splendid effort! What magnificent, what superhuman strength! Ah, that was a fine endeavor! Bravo! The cord fell away; his arms parted and floated upward, the hands dimly seen on each side in the growing light. He watched them with a new interest as first one and then the other pounced upon the noose at his neck. They tore it away and thrust it fiercely aside, its undulations resembling those of a water snake. "Put it back, put it back!" He thought he shouted these words to his hands, for the undoing of the noose had been succeeded by the direst pang that he had yet experienced. His neck ached horribly; his brain was on fire; his heart, which had been fluttering faintly, gave a great leap, trying to force itself out at his mouth. His whole body was racked and wrenched with an insupportable anguish! But his disobedient hands gave no heed to the command. They beat the water vigorously with quick, downward strokes, forcing him to the surface. He felt his head emerge; his eyes were blinded by the sunlight; his chest expanded convulsively, and with a supreme and crowning agony his lungs engulfed a great draught of air, which instantly he expelled in a shriek!

He was now in full possession of his physical senses. They were, indeed, 20
preternaturally keen and alert. Something in the awful disturbance of his organic system had so exalted and defined them that they made record of things never before perceived. He felt the ripples upon his face and heard their separate sounds as they struck. He looked at the forest on the bank of the stream, saw the individual trees, the leaves and the veining of each leaf—saw the very insects upon them: the locusts, the brilliant-bodied flies, the gray spiders stretching their webs from twig to twig. He noted the prismatic colors in all the dewdrops upon a million blades of grass. The humming of the gnats that danced above the eddies of the stream, the beating of the dragonflies' wings, the strokes of the water spiders' legs, like oars which had lifted their boat—all these made audible music. A fish slid along beneath his eyes and he heard the rush of its body parting the water.

He had come to the surface facing down the stream; in a moment the visible world seemed to wheel slowly round, himself the pivotal point, and he saw the bridge, the fort, the soldiers upon the bridge, the captain, the sergeant, the two privates, his executioners. They were in silhouette against the blue sky. They shouted and gesticulated, pointing at him. The captain had drawn his pistol, but did not fire; the others were unarmed. Their movements were grotesque and horrible, their forms gigantic.

Suddenly he heard a sharp report and something struck the water smartly within a few inches of his head, spattering his face with spray. He heard a second report, and saw one of the sentinels with his rifle at his shoulder, a light cloud of blue smoke rising from the muzzle. The man in the water saw the eye of the man on the bridge gazing into his own through the sights of the rifle. He observed that it was a gray eye and remembered having read that gray eyes were keenest, and that all famous marksmen had them. Nevertheless, this one had missed.

A counterswirl had caught Farquhar and turned him half round; he was again looking into the forest on the bank opposite the fort. The sound of a clear, high voice in a monotonous singsong now rang out behind him and came across the water with a distinctness that pierced and subdued all other sounds, even the beating of the ripples in his ears. Although no soldier, he had frequented camps enough to know the dread significance of that deliberate, drawling aspirated chant; the lieutenant on shore was taking a part in the morning's work. How coldly and pitilessly—with what an even, calm intonation, presaging, and enforcing tranquillity in the men—with what accurately measured intervals fell those cruel words:

"Attention, company! . . . Shoulder arms! . . . Ready! . . . Aim! . . . Fire!"

Farquhar dived—dived as deeply as he could. The water roared in his ears 25
like the voice of Niagara, yet he heard the dulled thunder of the volley and, rising again toward the surface, met shining bits of metal, singularly flattened, oscillating slowly downward. Some of them touched him on the face and

hands, then fell away, continuing their descent. One lodged between his collar and neck; it was uncomfortably warm and he snatched it out.

As he rose to the surface, gasping for breath, he saw that he had been a long time under water; he was perceptibly farther downstream—nearer to safety. The soldiers had almost finished reloading; the metal ramrods flashed all at once in the sunshine as they were drawn from the barrels, turned in the air, and thrust into their sockets. The two sentinels fired again, independently and ineffectually.

The hunted man saw all this over his shoulder; he was now swimming vigorously with the current. His brain was as energetic as his arms and legs; he thought with the rapidity of lightning.

"The officer," he reasoned, "will not make that martinet's error a second time. It is as easy to dodge a volley as a single shot. He has probably already given the command to fire at will. God help me, I cannot dodge them all!"

An appalling plash within two yards of him was followed by a loud, rushing sound, diminuendo, which seemed to travel back through the air to the fort and died in an explosion which stirred the very river to its deeps! A rising sheet of water curved over him, fell down upon him, blinded him, strangled him! The cannon had taken a hand in the game. As he shook his head free from the commotion of the smitten water he heard the deflected shot humming through the air ahead, and in an instant it was cracking and smashing the branches in the forest beyond.

30 "They will not do that again," he thought. "The next time they will use a charge of grape. I must keep my eye upon the gun. The smoke will apprise me—the report arrives too late; it lags behind the missile. That is a good gun."

Suddenly he felt himself whirled round and round—spinning like a top. The water, the banks, the forests, the now distant bridge, fort and men—all were commingled and blurred. Objects were represented by their colors only; circular horizontal streaks of color—that was all he saw. He had been caught in a vortex and was being whirled on with a velocity of advance and gyration that made him giddy and sick. In a few moments he was flung upon the gravel at the foot of the left bank of the stream—the southern bank—and behind a projecting point which concealed him from his enemies. The sudden arrest of his motion, the abrasion of one of his hands on the gravel, restored him, and he wept with delight. He dug his fingers into the sand, threw it over himself in handfuls and audibly blessed it. It looked like diamonds, rubies, emeralds; he could think of nothing beautiful which it did not resemble. The trees upon the bank were giant garden plants; he noted a definite order in their arrangement, inhaled the fragrance of their blooms. A strange, roseate light shone through the spaces among their trunks and the wind made in their branches the music of aeolian harps. He had no wish to perfect his escape—was content to remain in that enchanting spot until retaken.

A whiz and rattle of grapeshot among the branches high above his head roused him from his dream. The baffled cannoneer had fired him a random farewell. He sprang to his feet, rushed up the sloping bank, and plunged into the forest.

All that day he traveled, laying his course by the rounding sun. The forest seemed interminable; nowhere did he discover a break in it, not even a woodman's road. He had not known that he lived in so wild a region. There was something uncanny in the revelation.

By nightfall he was fatigued, footsore, famishing. The thought of his wife and children urged him on. At last he found a road which led him in what he knew to be the right direction. It was as wide and straight as a city street, yet it seemed untraveled. No fields bordered it, no dwelling anywhere. Not so much as the barking of a dog suggested human habitation. The black bodies of the trees formed a straight wall on both sides, terminating on the horizon in a point, like a diagram in a lesson in perspective. Overhead, as he looked up through this rift in the wood, shone great golden stars looking unfamiliar and grouped in strange constellations. He was sure they were arranged in some order which had a secret and malign significance. The wood on either side was full of singular noises, among which—once, twice, and again—he distinctly heard whispers in an unknown tongue.

35 His neck was in pain and lifting his hand to it he found it horribly swollen. He knew that it had a circle of black where the rope had bruised it. His eyes felt congested; he could no longer close them. His tongue was swollen with thirst; he relieved its fever by thrusting it forward from between his teeth into the cold air. How softly the turf had carpeted the untraveled avenue—he could no longer feel the roadway beneath his feet!

Doubtless, despite his suffering, he had fallen asleep while walking, for now he sees another scene—perhaps he has merely recovered from a delirium. He stands at the gate of his own home. All is as he left it, and all bright and beautiful in the morning sunshine. He must have traveled the entire night. As he pushes open the gate and passes up the wide white walk, he sees a flutter of female garments; his wife, looking fresh and cool and sweet, steps down from the veranda to meet him. At the bottom of the steps she stands waiting, with a smile of ineffable joy, an attitude of matchless grace and dignity. Ah, how beautiful she is! He springs forward with extended arms. As he is about to clasp her he feels a stunning blow upon the back of the neck; a blinding white light blazes all about him with a sound like the shock of a cannon—then all is darkness and silence!

Peyton Farquhar was dead; his body, with a broken neck, swung gently from side to side beneath the timbers of the Owl Creek bridge.

AMBROSE BIERCE

(1842–1914?) **Web** *www*

A writer who fought for the Union in the Civil War, Bierce worked as a journalist in San Francisco until he disappeared while on a trip to Mexico. A satirist like Twain, Bierce often portrayed the ills of self-deception and the hypocrisies of bourgeois culture.

TOPICS FOR CRITICAL THINKING **Web** *www*

1. How does the story expand time?
2. What strategies make us believe Farquhar has escaped?

3. What clues suggest the unreality of Farquhar's experience after the hanging?
4. Why does the text describe the setting so carefully?

www

TOPICS FOR CRITICAL WRITING Web

1. Describe the ways "An Occurrence at Owl Creek Bridge" plays past against present and present against future. What tensions and desires does this intersection of times and plots create?
2. The story posits two potential endings to Farquhar's plight. Which is more just?

6 The Narrator and Point of View

Like character, setting, and plot, the narrator and point of view are formal elements of fiction. The **narrator** is a part of the story—the part that creates the sense of the scene of the story's telling. The narrator is also a part of what is *told*—what is conveyed or produced by the story. Although our notion of a narrator would seem to imply an agent who, existing somehow beyond the story, tells the story, any idea that the narrator exists separately from the story is an illusion produced by the story itself. The narrator can be a character, mind reader, and commentator, and at the same time function as an organizer, director, and lens. The kind of narrator a story has determines the choices of *point of view* available in a story. The narrator is not the author of the story. Rather, the narrator is a creation of an author, a formal element of a story that works in a dynamic relation with fiction's other elements. **Web** *www*

There are several different kinds of narrators. They are classified by two criteria: (1) whether the narrator is explicitly present in the world of the story (called its **diegesis**); and (2) the kind and extent of the narrator's knowledge. A **first-person narrator** is present in the story as a participating character and is identified as such through the narrator's use of *I*. Occasionally (but rarely), a first-person narrator is characterized through the use of *we* (as in William Faulkner's "A Rose for Emily"). First-person narrators know only what a single person (or group) would know. They cannot read other characters' minds, and they generally provide a source for any information they may convey about events they do not (or could not) witness. Thus, first-person narrators have only one point of view, although it is possible that such narrators will present their perceptions of what other characters are thinking or feeling.

We understand first-person narrators as necessarily **subjective;** that is, we do not expect their telling of events to be detached and unbiased. First-person narrators, however, may have different levels of **reliability.** Depending on how the narrator's speaking *I* is characterized in the story, we may be more or less likely to understand a narrator's account as generous, scrupulous, confused, mean-spirited, or motivated by psychological difficulties with other characters or events (such as the narrator in "Bartleby the Scrivener"). **Web** *www*

A **third-person narrator** is not explicitly present in the story's diegesis but appears to recount the story from a position outside of the story, which is not explained or accounted for by the story. Despite this illusion of outsidedness, third-person narrators are still present within the story and only exist as a part of the story. Because there need be no explanation of how third-person narrators get their information, they may have unlimited knowledge of events, histories, settings, and the thought-processes and feelings of all the other characters. Thus, third-person narrators provide a wide choice of points of view. Narrators who have a complete range of knowledge are referred to as **third-person omniscient narrators.** Because of this knowledge, third-person omniscient narrators sometimes present an appearance of great objectivity, detachment, and reliability (we have no reason not to believe that their account is in any way biased). However, it is important to consider why such a range of knowledge is necessary for the telling of the story and how such knowledge is used.

Often, third-person narrators present the knowledge and feelings of one or only a few (but not all) characters, even though they have an unlimited knowledge of events, histories, and settings. Since their implied knowledge is limited to the subjective experiences of only a few characters, these narrators are referred to as **third-person limited narrators.** Such narrators may create increased sympathy and understanding for those characters (see, for example, "The Flight of Betsey Lane" or "An Occurrence at Owl Creek Bridge"). Third-person narrators can present other characters' feelings as if they are separate from these characters (limited omniscience) or they can present characters' feelings from the point of view of the character—as if they are inside the character.

As with a third-person omniscient narrator, it is important to consider the relation between the narrator's range of knowledge and the other elements of the story. How does the story employ the kinds of knowledge a particular narrator can provide? How would the story look with a first-person as opposed to a third-person narrator? The narrator is a choice that relates to how the story works formally, aesthetically, and thematically.

Stories may also have more than one narrator. Stories may shift from one narrator to another, or they may present different narratives framed by one another. In this latter case, the story may begin with one narrator who describes another narrator telling the story. In this case, the first narrator is called a **frame narrator.** An example of a frame narrator is the first narrator in *Heart of Darkness* who introduces Marlow, who then tells the story of his African trip.

Point of View

When a third-person limited narrator narrates as if from the perspective of a single character, that perspective is referred to as point of view. **Point of view** is the sense that we are seeing events as if we are a particular character in a story. Although we might understand third-person omniscient narrators as having a wide perspective, they often do not have a specific point of view. Point of view, then, is a characteristic of narrators whose knowledge is limited to the experience of one or several characters. Not all narrators take the specific point of view of a character, and only first-person narrators automatically have a point of view. Some narrators present multiple points of view. If the narrator's function is to provide a sense of the scene of the story's telling, point of view contributes the additional lens or frame of a character's perceptions through which the story is filtered. This produces the illusion of subjectivity since the narrator provides only a partial view, one seemingly motivated by a particular character's desires and prejudices. It may also produce the illusion of greater **unreliability,** since characters often have biases, motivations, and interests that would logically sway their perception of events. Since the only way we can know those events is through a narration posed as limited, we must deduce that versions of events are unreliable based on our reading of character.

Although the kind of narrator may determine what points of view are possible in prose fiction, the choices and uses of point of view are still quite varied. Although a first-person narrator seems limited only to that character/narrator's perspective, it is possible for a first-person narrator to attempt to understand and produce another character's perspective. An example of this is when the narrator of "The Yellow Wall-Paper" presents what her husband thinks. A third-person narrator may narrate from the point of view of all characters, only a few, or none. The narrator of "The Story of an Hour" narrates only from the point of view of Louise Mallard, while the narrator of "The Birthmark" shifts point of view from Aylmer to Georgiana. The narrator of "The Horse-Dealer's Daughter" provides the point of view of both the young doctor and the young woman. The narrator of "Hills Like White Elephants" provides no specific point of view.

Although third-person omniscient narrators seemingly offer an objective point of view (but remember, even these narrators are constructions, and the elements narrated and the ways they are narrated are carefully chosen), third-person limited narrators may offer a number of different points of view with varying degrees of subjectivity. "Paul's Mistress," for example, presents several different points of view but develops most deeply Paul's. Although narrator and point of view might seem to be aspects of one another, they do represent an arsenal of different choices an author can make.

Point of view offers an additional frame through which the story is narrated. That frame itself becomes an object for inquiry and interpretation. Very often the biases and mental status of the character whose point of view we share are of prime importance in the story. Some stories are about contrasting points of view as enacted by narration from the points of view of different characters.

Point of view, like any other formal element of fiction (character, setting, plot, narrator) works in relation to the other elements. When interpreting prose fiction, readers need to consider point of view in relation to both the story's themes and its formal presentation. The purposes of employing subjective points of view in stories are many. Subjective point of view often elicits sympathy for the character whose perspective is shared, as in "The Story of an Hour." It can provide the impression of an unusual subjective experience, as in "The Fall of the House of Usher." It can also supply perspectives for a dialogue on various aspects of a particular issue or experience, as occurs in "The Garden-Party."

Critical Perspective: Gender and Point of View

Stories about the experience of minority or disenfranchised characters occasionally use point of view to convey the experience of individuals whose views traditionally have not been recognized as an intrinsic part of "official" or "dominant" culture (the culture that represents those who make decisions about proper aesthetics and subject matter). Since the Renaissance one function of literature has been to challenge the assumptions and dictates of dominant culture by portraying its oppressions (as in Harriet Beecher Stowe's *Uncle Tom's Cabin),* critiquing middle class values (for example, in "Paul's Mistress"), or presenting perspectives not typically acknowledged—those of women, people of color, and lower class citizens. The following three stories—Willa Cather's "Paul's Case," Charlotte Perkins Gilman's "The Yellow Wall-Paper," and Kate Chopin's "The Story of an Hour"—employ point of view as a prime strategy for conveying the experience of those often not permitted to speak for themselves. The experience presented in these stories is from the point of view of female and gay male protagonists and represents some of the complexities of the sex/gender system in a late-nineteenth- and early-twentieth-century culture that did not allow women or sexual minorities much individual freedom or choice. Their focus on questions of gender and sexuality makes the work of these writers extremely valuable to critics interested in the ways gender and sexuality define writing and individuals' experience in culture. Criticism that explores the many issues, relations, aesthetic practices, and problems of gender in literature and culture is called **feminist**
www **criticism.** Web

Critical Perspective: Secrets, Sexuality, and Interpretation

In many stories, narrators are the presenters and interpreters of secrets and mysteries. Sometimes these secrets are presented directly; sometimes they are hidden or encoded as part of what the narrator refers to but never addresses openly. One example of this is the way television shows aired before the late 1990s made a character's homosexuality a public secret. The character Ellen Morgan, for example, on *Ellen* was understood to be gay long before she actually announced the fact. Even an earlier show such as *Bewitched* had a gay character—Uncle Arthur (Paul Lynde)—who was never openly identified as such.

The audience knows the secret by interpreting the clues provided; this indirect approach was made necessary by the general lack of societal acceptance for homosexuality. While the notion of the secret does not refer necessarily to sexual orientations (it might refer to illness, for example), the necessity for protecting the secret or for using writing that has encoded meanings has long been a fact of existence for homosexuality in Western culture. That does not mean, however, that such sexualities were not present or represented in literature. The tactics of encodement and indirection often employed to present such characters are not simply reflections of cultural necessity; they also represent an aesthetic where desire is produced by the constant deferment of an answer or meaning.

Stories about sexuality may present the point of view of a character who views culture from the perspective of a sexual minority. Criticism that focuses on issues of sexuality, or on the politics and aesthetics of gay experience and representation, is called **gay and lesbian criticism** or **queer theory.** Web *www* The activities of such methods of criticism are closely allied with the insights of feminist criticism.

WILLA CATHER

Paul's Case (1905)

A Study in Temperament

It was Paul's afternoon to appear before the faculty of the Pittsburgh High School to account for his various misdemeanours. He had been suspended a week ago, and his father had called at the Principal's office and confessed his perplexity about his son. Paul entered the faculty room suave and smiling. His clothes were a trifle outgrown and the tan velvet on the collar of his open overcoat was frayed and worn; but for all that there was something of the dandy about him, and he wore an opal pin in his neatly knotted black four-in-hand, and a red carnation in his buttonhole. This latter adornment the faculty somehow felt was not properly significant of the contrite spirit befitting a boy under the ban of suspension.

Paul was tall for his age and very thin, with high, cramped shoulders and a narrow chest. His eyes were remarkable for a certain hysterical brilliancy and he continually used them in a conscious, theatrical sort of way, peculiarly offensive in a boy. The pupils were abnormally large, as though he were addicted to belladonna, but there was a glassy glitter about them which that drug does not produce.

When questioned by the Principal as to why he was there, Paul stated, politely enough, that he wanted to come back to school. This was a lie, but Paul was quite accustomed to lying; found it, indeed, indispensable for overcoming friction. His teachers were asked to state their respective charges against him, which they did with such a rancour and aggrievedness as evinced that this was not a usual case. Disorder and impertinence were among the offences named, yet each of his instructors felt that it was scarcely possible to put into words the real cause of the trouble, which lay in a sort of hysterically defiant manner of the boy's; in the contempt which they all knew he felt for them, and which he seemingly made not the least effort to conceal. Once, when he had been making a synopsis of a paragraph at the blackboard, his English teacher had stepped to his side and attempted to guide his hand. Paul had started back with a shudder and thrust his hands violently behind him. The astonished woman could scarcely have been more hurt and embarrassed had he struck at her. The insult was so involuntary and definitely personal as to be unforgettable. In one way and another, he had made all his teachers, men and women alike, conscious of the same feeling of physical aversion. In one class he habitually sat with his hand shading his eyes; in another he always looked out of the window during the recitation; in another he made a running commentary on the lecture, with humorous intention.

His teachers felt this afternoon that his whole attitude was symbolized by his shrug and his flippantly red carnation flower, and they fell upon him without mercy, his English teacher leading the pack. He stood through it smiling, his pale lips parted over his white teeth. (His lips were continually twitching, and he had a habit of raising his eyebrows that was contemptuous and irritating to the last degree.) Older boys than Paul had broken down and shed tears under that baptism of fire, but his set smile did not once desert him, and his only sign of discomfort was the nervous trembling of the fingers that toyed with the buttons of his overcoat, and an occasional jerking of the other hand that held his hat. Paul was always smiling, always glancing about him, seeming to feel that people might be watching him and trying to detect something. This conscious expression, since it was as far as possible from boyish mirthfulness, was usually attributed to insolence or "smartness."

5 As the inquisition proceeded, one of his instructors repeated an impertinent remark of the boy's, and the Principal asked him whether he thought that a courteous speech to have made a woman. Paul shrugged his shoulders slightly and his eyebrows twitched.

"I don't know," he replied. "I didn't mean to be polite or impolite, either. I guess it's a sort of way I have of saying things regardless."

The Principal, who was a sympathetic man, asked him whether he didn't think that a way it would be well to get rid of. Paul grinned and said he guessed so. When he was told that he could go, he bowed gracefully and went out. His bow was but a repetition of the scandalous red carnation.

His teachers were in despair, and his drawing master voiced the feeling of them all when he declared there was something about the boy which none of them understood. He added: " I don't really believe that smile of his comes altogether from insolence; there's something sort of haunted about it. The boy is not strong, for one thing. I happen to know that he was born in Colorado, only a few months before his mother died out there of a long illness. There is something wrong about the fellow."

The drawing master had come to realize that, in looking at Paul, one saw only his white teeth and the forced animation of his eyes. One warm afternoon the boy had gone to sleep at his drawing-board, and his master had noted with amazement what a white, blue-veined face it was; drawn and wrinkled like an old man's about the eyes, the lips twitching even in his sleep, and stiff with a nervous tension that drew them back from his teeth.

10 His teachers left the building dissatisfied and unhappy; humiliated to

have felt so vindictive toward a mere boy, to have uttered this feeling in cutting terms, and to have set each other on, as it were, in the grewsome game of intemperate reproach. Some of them remembered having seen a miserable street cat set at bay by a ring of tormentors.

As for Paul, he ran down the hill whistling the Soldiers' Chorus from *Faust* looking wildly behind him now and then to see whether some of his teachers were not there to writhe under his light-heartedness. As it was now late in the afternoon and Paul was on duty that evening as usher at Carnegie Hall, he decided that he would not go home to supper. When he reached the concert hall the doors were not yet open and, as it was chilly outside, he decided to go up into the picture gallery—always deserted at this hour—where there were some of Raffelli's gay studies of Paris streets and an airy blue Venetian scene or two that always exhilarated him. He was delighted to find no one in the gallery but the old guard, who sat in one corner, a newspaper on his knee, a black patch over one eye and the other closed. Paul possessed himself of the place and walked confidently up and down, whistling under his breath. After a while he sat down before a blue Rico and lost himself. When he bethought him to look at his watch, it was after seven o'clock, and he rose with a start and ran downstairs, making a face at Augustus, peering out from the castroom, and an evil gesture at the Venus of Milo as he passed her on the stairway.

When Paul reached the ushers' dressing-room half-a-dozen boys were there already, and he began excitedly to tumble into his uniform. It was one of the few that at all approached fitting, and Paul thought it very becoming—though he knew that the tight, straight coat accentuated his narrow chest, about which he was exceedingly sensitive. He was always considerably excited while he dressed, twanging all over to the tuning of the strings and the preliminary flourishes of the horns in the music-room; but to-night he seemed quite beside himself, and he teased and plagued the boys until, telling him that he was crazy, they put him down on the floor and sat on him.

Somewhat calmed by his suppression, Paul dashed out to the front of the house to seat the early comers. He was a model usher; gracious and smiling he ran up and down the aisles; nothing was too much trouble for him; he carried messages and brought programmes as though it were his greatest pleasure in life, and all the people in his section thought him a charming boy, feeling that he remembered and admired them. As the house filled, he grew more and more vivacious and animated, and the colour came to his cheeks and lips. It was very much as though this were a great reception and Paul were the host. Just as the musicians came out to take their places, his English teacher arrived with checks for the seats which a prominent manufacturer had taken for the season. She betrayed some embarrassment when she handed Paul the tickets, and a *hauteur* which subsequently made her feel very foolish. Paul was startled for a moment, and had the feeling of wanting to put her out; what business had she here among all these fine people and gay colours ? He looked her over and decided that she was not appropriately dressed and must be a fool to sit downstairs in such togs. The tickets had probably been sent her out of kindness, he reflected as he put down a seat for her, and she had about as much right to sit there as he had.

When the symphony began Paul sank into one of the rear seats with a long sigh of relief, and lost himself as he had done before the Rico. It was not that symphonies, as such, meant anything in particular to Paul, but the first sigh of the instruments seemed to free some hilarious and potent spirit within him; something that struggled there like the Genius in the bottle found by the Arab fisherman. He felt a sudden zest of life; the lights danced before his eyes and the concert hall blazed into unimaginable splendour. When the soprano soloist came on, Paul forgot even the nastiness of his teacher's being there and gave himself up to the peculiar stimulus such personages always had for him. The soloist chanced to be a German woman, by no means in her first youth, and the mother of many children; but she wore an elaborate gown and a tiara, and above all she had that indefinable air of achievement, that world-shine upon her which, in Paul's eyes, made her a veritable queen of Romance.

After a concert was over Paul was always irritable and wretched until he got to sleep, and to-night he was even more than usually restless. He had the feeling of not being able to let down, of its being impossible to give up this delicious excitement which was the only thing that could be called living at all. During the last number he withdrew and, after hastily changing his clothes in the dressing-room, slipped out to the side door where the soprano's carriage stood. Here he began pacing rapidly up and down the walk, waiting to see her come out.

Over yonder the Schenley, in its vacant stretch, loomed big and square through the fine rain, the windows of its twelve stories glowing like those of a lighted card-board house under a Christmas tree. All the actors and singers of the better class stayed there when they were in the city, and a number of the big manufacturers of the place lived there in the winter. Paul had often hung about the hotel, watching the people go in and out, longing to enter and leave school-masters and dull care behind him forever.

At last the singer came out, accompanied by the conductor, who helped her into her carriage and closed the door with a cordial *auf wiedersehen* which set Paul to wondering whether she were not an old sweetheart of his. Paul followed the carriage over to the hotel, walking so rapidly as not to be far from the entrance when the singer alighted and disappeared behind the swinging glass doors that were opened by a negro in a tall hat and a long coat. In the moment that the door was ajar it seemed to Paul that he, too, entered. He seemed to feel himself go after her up the steps, into the warm, lighted building, into an exotic, a tropical world of shiny, glistening surfaces and basking ease. He reflected upon the mysterious dishes that were brought into the dining-room, the green bottles in buckets of ice, as he had seen them in the supper party pictures of the *Sunday World* supplement. A quick gust of wind brought the rain down with sudden vehemence, and Paul was startled to find that he was still outside in the slush of the gravel driveway; that his boots were letting in the water and his scanty overcoat was clinging wet about him; that the lights in front of the concert hall were out, and that the rain was driving in sheets between him and the orange glow of the windows above him. There it was, what he wanted—tangibly before him, like the fairy world of a Christmas pantomime, but mocking spirits stood guard at the doors, and, as the rain beat in his face, Paul wondered whether he were destined always to shiver in the black night outside, looking up at it.

He turned and walked reluctantly toward the car tracks. The end had to come sometime; his father in his night-clothes at the top of the stairs, explanations that did not explain, hastily improvised fictions that were forever tripping him up, his upstairs room and its horrible yellow wall-paper, the creaking bureau with the greasy plush collar-box, and over his painted wooden bed the pictures of George Washington and John Calvin, and the framed motto, "Feed my Lambs," which had been worked in red worsted by his mother.

Half an hour later, Paul alighted from his car and went slowly down one of the side streets off the main thoroughfare. It was a highly respectable street, where all the houses were exactly alike, and where business men of moderate means begot and reared large families of children, all of whom went to Sabbath-school and learned the shorter catechism, and were interested in arithmetic; all of whom were as exactly alike as their homes, and of a piece with the monotony in which they lived. Paul never went up Cordelia Street without a shudder of loathing. His home was next to the house of the Cumberland minister. He approached it to-night with the nerveless sense of defeat, the hopeless feeling of sinking back forever into ugliness and commonness that he had always had when he came home. The moment he turned into Cordelia Street he felt the waters close above his head. After each of these orgies of living, he experienced all the physical depression which follows a debauch; the loathing of respectable beds, of common food, of a house penetrated by kitchen odours; a shuddering repulsion for the flavourless, colourless mass of every-day existence; a morbid desire for cool things and soft lights and fresh flowers.

The nearer he approached the house, the more absolutely unequal Paul 20
felt to the sight of it all; his ugly sleeping chamber; the cold bathroom with the grimy zinc tub, the cracked mirror, the dripping spiggots; his father, at the top of the stairs, his hairy legs sticking out from his night-shirt, his feet thrust into carpet slippers. He was so much later than usual that there would certainly be inquiries and reproaches. Paul stopped short before the door. He felt that he could not be accosted by his father to-night; that he could not toss again on that miserable bed. He would not go in. He would tell his father that he had no car fare, and it was raining so hard he had gone home with one of the boys and stayed all night.

Meanwhile, he was wet and cold. He went around to the back of the house and tried one of the basement windows, found it open, raised it cautiously, and scrambled down the cellar wall to the floor. There he stood, holding his breath, terrified by the noise he had made, but the floor above him was silent, and there was no creak on the stairs. He found a soap-box, and carried it over to the soft ring of light that streamed from the furnace door, and sat down. He was horribly afraid of rats, so he did not try to sleep, but sat looking distrustfully at the dark, still terrified lest he might have awakened his father. In such reactions, after one of the experiences which made days and nights out of the dreary blanks of the calendar, when his senses were deadened,

Paul's head was always singularly clear. Suppose his father had heard him getting in at the window and had come down and shot him for a burglar? Then, again, suppose his father had come down, pistol in hand, and he had cried out in time to save himself, and his father had been horrified to think how nearly he had killed him ? Then, again, suppose a day should come when his father would remember that night, and wish there had been no warning cry to stay his hand? With this last supposition Paul entertained himself until daybreak.

The following Sunday was fine; the sodden November chill was broken by the last flash of autumnal summer. In the morning Paul had to go to church and Sabbath-school, as always. On seasonable Sunday afternoons the burghers of Cordelia Street always sat out on their front "stoops," and talked to their neighbours on the next stoop, or called to those across the street in neighbourly fashion. The men usually sat on gay cushions placed upon the steps that led down to the sidewalk, while the women, in their Sunday "waists," sat in rockers on the cramped porches, pretending to be greatly at their ease. The children played in the streets; there were so many of them that the place resembled the recreation grounds of a kindergarten. The men on the steps—all in their shirt sleeves, their vests unbuttoned—sat with their legs well apart, their stomachs comfortably protruding, and talked of the prices of things, or told anecdotes of the sagacity of their various chiefs and overlords. They occasionally looked over the multitude of squabbling children, listened affectionately to their high-pitched, nasal voices, smiling to see their own proclivities reproduced in their offspring, and interspersed their legends of the iron kings with remarks about their sons' progress at school, their grades in arithmetic, and the amounts they had saved in their toy banks.

On this last Sunday of November, Paul sat all the afternoon on the lowest step of his "stoop," staring into the street, while his sisters, in their rockers, were talking to the minister's daughters next door about how many shirt-waists they had made in the last week, and how many waffles some one had eaten at the last church supper. When the weather was warm, and his father was in a particularly jovial frame of mind, the girls made lemonade, which was always brought out in a red-glass pitcher, ornamented with forget-me-nots in blue enamel. This the girls thought very fine, and the neighbours always joked about the suspicious colour of the pitcher.

To-day Paul's father sat on the top step, talking to a young man who shifted a restless baby from knee to knee. He happened to be the young man who was daily held up to Paul as a model, and after whom it was his father's dearest hope that he would pattern. This young man was of a ruddy complexion, with a compressed, red mouth, and faded, near-sighted eyes, over which he wore thick spectacles, with gold bows that curved about his ears. He was clerk to one of the magnates of a great steel corporation, and was looked upon in Cordelia Street as a young man with a future. There was a story that, some five years ago—he was now barely twenty-six—he had been a trifle dissipated but in order to curb his appetites and save the loss of time and strength that a sowing of wild oats might have entailed, he had taken his chief's advice, oft reiterated to his employees, and at twenty-one had married the first woman whom he could persuade to share his fortunes. She happened to be an angular schoolmistress, much older than he, who also wore thick glasses, and who had now borne him four children, all near-sighted, like herself.

The young man was relating how his chief, now cruising in the Mediterranean, kept in touch with all the details of the business, arranging his office hours on his yacht just as though he were at home, and "knocking off work enough to keep two stenographers busy." His father told, in turn, the plan his corporation was considering, of putting in an electric railway plant at Cairo. Paul snapped his teeth; he had an awful apprehension that they might spoil it all before he got there. Yet he rather liked to hear these legends of the iron kings, that were told and retold on Sundays and holidays; these stories of palaces in Venice, yachts on the Mediterranean, and high play at Monte Carlo appealed to his fancy, and he was interested in the triumphs of these cash boys who had become famous, though he had no mind for the cash-boy stage.

After supper was over, and he had helped to dry the dishes, Paul nervously asked his father whether he could go to George's to get some help in his geometry, and still more nervously asked for car fare. This latter request he had to repeat, as his father, on principle, did not like to hear requests for money, whether much or little. He asked Paul whether he could not go to some boy who lived nearer, and told him that he ought not to leave his school work until Sunday; but he gave him the dime. He was not a poor man, but he had a worthy ambition to come up in the world. His only reason for allowing Paul to usher was, that he thought a boy ought to be earning a little.

Paul bounded upstairs, scrubbed the greasy odour of the dish-water from his hands with the ill-smelling soap he hated, and then shook over his fingers a few drops of violet water from the bottle he kept hidden in his drawer. He left the house with his geometry conspicuously under his arm, and the moment he got out of Cordelia Street and boarded a downtown car, he shook off the lethargy of two deadening days, and began to live again.

The leading juvenile of the permanent stock company which played at one of the downtown theatres was an acquaintance of Paul's, and the boy had been invited to drop in at the Sunday-night rehearsals whenever he could. For more than a year Paul had spent every available moment loitering about Charley Edwards's dressing-room. He had won a place among Edwards's following not only because the young actor, who could not afford to employ a dresser, often found him useful, but because he recognized in Paul something akin to what churchmen term "vocation."

It was at the theatre and at Carnegie Hall that Paul really lived; the rest was but a sleep and a forgetting. This was Paul's fairy tale, and it had for him all the allurement of a secret love. The moment he inhaled the gassy, painty, dusty odour behind the scenes, he breathed like a prisoner set free, and felt within him the possibility of doing or saying splendid, brilliant, poetic things. The moment the cracked orchestra beat out the overture from *Martha*, or jerked at the serenade from *Rigoletto*, all stupid and ugly things slid from him, and his senses were deliciously, yet delicately fired.

Perhaps it was because, in Paul's world, the natural nearly always wore the guise of ugliness, that a certain element of artificiality seemed to him necessary in beauty. Perhaps it was because his experience of life elsewhere was so full of Sabbath-school picnics, petty economies, wholesome advice as to how to succeed in life, and the unescapable odours of cooking, that he found this existence so alluring, these smartly-clad men and women so attractive, that he was so moved by these starry apple orchards that bloomed perennially under the lime-light.

It would be difficult to put it strongly enough how convincingly the stage entrance of that theatre was for Paul the actual portal of Romance. Certainly none of the company ever suspected it, least of all Charley Edwards. It was very like the old stories that used to float about London of fabulously rich Jews, who had subterranean halls there, with palms, and fountains, and soft lamps and richly apparelled women who never saw the disenchanting light of London day. So, in the midst of that smoke-palled city, enamoured of figures and grimy toil, Paul had his secret temple, his wishing carpet, his bit of blue-and-white Mediterranean shore bathed in perpetual sunshine.

Several of Paul's teachers had a theory that his imagination had been perverted by garish fiction, but the truth was that he scarcely ever read at all. The books at home were not such as would either tempt or corrupt a youthful mind, and as for reading the novels that some of his friends urged upon him—well, he got what he wanted much more quickly from music; any sort of music, from an orchestra to a barrel organ. He needed only the spark, the indescribable thrill that made his imagination master of his senses, and he could make plots and pictures enough of his own. It was equally true that he was not stage struck—not, at any rate, in the usual acceptation of that expression. He had no desire to become an actor, any more than he had to become a musician. He felt no necessity to do any of these things; what he wanted was to see, to be in the atmosphere, float on the wave of it, to be carried out, blue league after blue league, away from everything.

After a night behind the scenes, Paul found the school-room more than ever repulsive; the bare floors and naked walls; the prosy men who never wore frock coats, or violets in their buttonholes; the women with their dull gowns, shrill voices, and pitiful seriousness about prepositions that govern the dative. He could not bear to have the other pupils think, for a moment, that he took these people seriously; he must convey to them that he considered it all trivial, and was there only by way of a jest, anyway. He had autographed pictures of all the members of the stock company which he showed his classmates, telling them the most incredible stories of his familiarity with these people, of his acquaintance with the soloists who came to Carnegie Hall, his suppers with them and the flowers he sent them. When these stories lost their effect, and his audience grew listless, he became desperate and would bid all the boys good-bye, announcing that he was going to travel for a while; going to Naples, to Venice, to Egypt. Then, next Monday, he would slip back, conscious and nervously smiling; his sister was ill, and he should have to defer his voyage until spring.

Matters went steadily worse with Paul at school. In the itch to let his instructors know how heartily he despised them and their homilies, and how thoroughly he was appreciated elsewhere, he mentioned once or twice that he had no time to fool with theorems; adding—with a twitch of the eyebrows and a touch of that nervous bravado which so perplexed them—that he was helping the people down at the stock company; they were old friends of his.

The upshot of the matter was that the Principal went to Paul's father, and 35
Paul was taken out of school and put to work. The manager at Carnegie Hall was told to get another usher in his stead; the doorkeeper at the theatre was warned not to admit him to the house; and Charley Edwards remorsefully promised the boy's father not to see him again.

The members of the stock company were vastly amused when some of Paul's stories reached them—especially the women. They were hardworking women, most of them supporting indigent husbands or brothers, and they laughed rather bitterly at having stirred the boy to such fervid and florid inventions. They agreed with the faculty and with his father that Paul's was a bad case.

The east-bound train was ploughing through a January snow-storm; the dull dawn was beginning to show grey when the engine whistled a mile out of Newark. Paul started up from the seat where he had lain curled in uneasy slumber, rubbed the breath-misted window glass with his hand, and peered out. The snow was whirling in curling eddies above the white bottom lands, and the drifts lay already deep in the fields and along the fences, while here and there the long dead grass and dried weed stalks protruded black above it. Lights shone from the scattered houses, and a gang of labourers who stood beside the track waved their lanterns.

Paul had slept very little, and he felt grimy and uncomfortable. He had made the all-night journey in a day coach, partly because he was ashamed, dressed as he was, to go into a Pullman, and partly because he was afraid of being seen there by some Pittsburgh business man, who might have noticed him in Denny & Carson's office. When the whistle awoke him, he clutched quickly at his breast pocket, glancing about him with an uncertain smile. But the little, clay-bespattered Italians were still sleeping, the slatternly women across the aisle were in open-mouthed oblivion, and even the crumby, crying babies were for the nonce stilled. Paul settled back to struggle with his impatience as best he could.

When he arrived at the Jersey City station, he hurried through his breakfast, manifestly ill at ease and keeping a sharp eye about him. After he reached the Twenty-third Street station, he consulted a cabman, and had himself driven to a men's furnishing establishment that was just opening for the day. He spent upward of two hours there, buying with endless reconsidering and great care. His new street suit he put on in the fitting-room; the frock coat and dress clothes he had bundled into the cab with his linen. Then he drove to a hatter's and a shoe house. His next errand was at Tiffany's, where he selected his silver and a new scarf-pin. He would not wait to have his silver marked, he said. Lastly, he stopped at a trunk shop on Broadway, and had his purchases packed into various travelling bags.

It was a little after one o'clock when he drove up to the Waldorf, and 40
after settling with the cabman, went into the office. He registered from

Washington; said his mother and father had been abroad, and that he had come down to await the arrival of their steamer. He told his story plausibly and had no trouble, since he volunteered to pay for them in advance, in engaging his rooms; a sleeping-room, sitting-room and bath.

Not once, but a hundred times Paul had planned this entry into New York. He had gone over every detail of it with Charley Edwards, and in his scrap book at home there were pages of description about New York hotels, cut from the Sunday papers. When he was shown to his sitting-room on the eighth floor, he saw at a glance that everything was as it should be; there was but one detail in his mental picture that the place did not realize, so he rang for the bell boy and sent him down for flowers. He moved about nervously until the boy returned, putting away his new linen and fingering it delightedly as he did so. When the flowers came, he put them hastily into water, and then tumbled into a hot bath. Presently he came out of his white bath-room, resplendent in his new silk underwear, and playing with the tassels of his red robe. The snow was whirling so fiercely outside his windows that he could scarcely see across the street, but within the air was deliciously soft and fragrant. He put the violets and jonquils on the taboret beside the couch, and threw himself down, with a long sigh, covering himself with a Roman blanket. He was thoroughly tired; he had been in such haste, he had stood up to such a strain, covered so much ground in the last twenty-four hours, that he wanted to think how it had all come about. Lulled by the sound of the wind, the warm air, and the cool fragrance of the flowers, he sank into deep, drowsy retrospection.

It had been wonderfully simple; when they had shut him out of the theatre and concert hall, when they had taken away his bone, the whole thing was virtually determined. The rest was a mere matter of opportunity. The only thing that at all surprised him was his own courage—for he realized well enough that he had always been tormented by fear, a sort of apprehensive dread that, of late years, as the meshes of the lies he had told closed about him, had been pulling the muscles of his body tighter and tighter. Until now, he could not remember the time when he had not been dreading something. Even when he was a little boy, it was always there—behind him, or before, or on either side. There had always been the shadowed corner, the dark place into which he dared not look, but from which something seemed always to be watching him—and Paul had done things that were not pretty to watch, he knew.

But now he had a curious sense of relief, as though he had at last thrown down the gauntlet to the thing in the corner.

Yet it was but a day since he had been sulking in the traces; but yesterday afternoon that he had been sent to the bank with Denny & Carson's deposit, as usual—but this time he was instructed to leave the book to be balanced. There was above two thousand dollars in checks, and nearly a thousand in the bank notes which he had taken from the book and quietly transferred to his pocket. At the bank he had made out a new deposit slip. His nerves had been steady enough to permit of his returning to the office, where he had finished his work and asked for a full day's holiday to-morrow, Saturday, giving a perfectly reasonable pretext. The bank book, he knew, would not be returned before Monday or Tuesday, and his father would be out of town for the next week. From the time he slipped the bank notes into his pocket until he boarded the night train for New York, he had not known a moment's hesitation. It was not the first time Paul had steered through treacherous waters.

How astonishingly easy it had all been; here he was, the thing done; and 45
this time there would be no awakening, no figure at the top of the stairs. He watched the snow flakes whirling by his window until he fell asleep.

When he awoke, it was three o'clock in the afternoon. He bounded up with a start; half of one of his precious days gone already! He spent more than an hour in dressing, watching every stage of his toilet carefully in the mirror. Everything was quite perfect; he was exactly the kind of boy he had always wanted to be.

When he went downstairs, Paul took a carriage and drove up Fifth Avenue toward the Park. The snow had somewhat abated; carriages and tradesmen's wagons were hurrying soundlessly to and fro in the winter twilight; boys in woollen mufflers were shovelling off the doorsteps; the avenue stages made fine spots of colour against the white street. Here and there on the corners were stands, with whole flower gardens blooming under glass cases, against the sides of which the snow flakes stuck and melted; violets, roses, carnations, lilies of the valley—somehow vastly more lovely and alluring that they blossomed thus unnaturally in the snow. The Park itself was a wonderful stage winterpiece.

When he returned, the pause of the twilight had ceased, and the tune of the streets had changed. The snow was falling faster, lights streamed from the hotels that reared their dozen stories fearlessly up into the storm, defying the raging Atlantic winds. A long, black stream of carriages poured down the avenue, intersected here and there by other streams, tending horizontally. There were a score of cabs about the entrance of his hotel, and his driver had to wait. Boys in livery were running in and out of the awning stretched across the sidewalk, up and down the red velvet carpet laid from the door to the street. Above, about, within it all was the rumble and roar, the hurry and toss of thousands of human beings as hot for pleasure as himself, and on every side of him towered the glaring affirmation of the omnipotence of wealth.

The boy set his teeth and drew his shoulders together in a spasm of realization; the plot of all dramas, the text of all romances, the nerve-stuff of all sensations was whirling about him like the snow flakes. He burnt like a faggot in a tempest.

When Paul went down to dinner, the music of the orchestra came float- 50
ing up the elevator shaft to greet him. His head whirled as he stepped into the thronged corridor, and he sank back into one of the chairs against the wall to get his breath. The lights, the chatter, the perfumes, the bewildering medley of colour—he had, for a moment, the feeling of not being able to stand it. But only for a moment; these were his own people, he told himself. He went slowly about the corridors, through the writing-rooms, smoking-rooms, reception-rooms, as though he were exploring the chambers of an enchanted palace, built and peopled for him alone.

When he reached the dining-room he sat down at a table near a window.

The flowers, the white linen, the many-coloured wine glasses, the gay toilettes of the women, the low popping of corks, the undulating repetitions of the *Blue Danube* from the orchestra, all flooded Paul's dream with bewildering radiance. When the roseate tinge of his champagne was added—that cold, precious, bubbling stuff that creamed and foamed in his glass—Paul wondered that there were honest men in the world at all. This was what all the world was fighting for, he reflected; this was what all the struggle was about. He doubted the reality of his past. Had he ever known a place called Cordelia Street, a place where fagged-looking businessmen got on the early car; mere rivets in a machine they seemed to Paul,—sickening men, with combings of children's hair always hanging to their coats, and the smell of cooking in their clothes. Cordelia Street—Ah! that belonged to another time and country; had he not always been thus, had he not sat here night after night, from as far back as he could remember, looking pensively over just such shimmering textures, and slowly twirling the stem of a glass like this one between his thumb and middle finger? He rather thought he had.

He was not in the least abashed or lonely. He had no especial desire to meet or to know any of these people; all he demanded was the right to look on and conjecture, to watch the pageant. The mere stage properties were all he contended for. Nor was he lonely later in the evening, in his loge at the Metropolitan. He was now entirely rid of his nervous misgivings, of his forced aggressiveness, of the imperative desire to show himself different from his surroundings. He felt now that his surroundings explained him. Nobody questioned the purple; he had only to wear it passively. He had only to glance down at his attire to reassure himself that here it would be impossible for anyone to humiliate him.

He found it hard to leave his beautiful sitting-room to go to bed that night, and sat long watching the raging storm from his turret window. When he went to sleep it was with the lights turned on in his bedroom; partly because of his old timidity, and partly so that, if he should wake in the night, there would be no wretched moment of doubt, no horrible suspicion of yellow wall-paper, or of Washington and Calvin above his bed.

Sunday morning the city was practically snow-bound. Paul breakfasted late, and in the afternoon he fell in with a wild San Francisco boy, a freshman at Yale, who said he had run down for a "little flyer" over Sunday. The young man offered to show Paul the night side of the town, and the two boys went out together after dinner, not returning to the hotel until seven o'clock the next morning. They had started out in the confiding warmth of a champagne friendship, but their parting in the elevator was singularly cool. The freshman pulled himself together to make his train, and Paul went to bed. He awoke at two o'clock in the afternoon, very thirsty and dizzy, and rang for ice-water, coffee, and the Pittsburgh papers.

On the part of the hotel management, Paul excited no suspicion. There was this to be said for him, that he wore his spoils with dignity and in no way made himself conspicuous. Even under the glow of his wine he was never boisterous, though he found the stuff like a magician's wand for wonder-building. His chief greediness lay in his ears and eyes, and his excesses were not offensive ones. His dearest pleasures were the grey winter twilights in his sitting-room; his quiet enjoyment of his flowers, his clothes, his wide divan, his cigarette and his sense of power. He could not remember a time when he had felt so at peace with himself. The mere release from the necessity of petty lying, lying every day and every day, restored his self-respect. He had never lied for pleasure, even at school; but to be noticed and admired, to assert his difference from other Cordelia Street boys; and he felt a good deal more manly, more honest, even, now that he had no need for boastful pretensions, now that he could, as his actor friends used to say, "dress the part." It was characteristic that remorse did not occur to him. His golden days went by without a shadow, and he made each as perfect as he could.

On the eighth day after his arrival in New York, he found the whole affair exploited in the Pittsburgh papers, exploited with a wealth of detail which indicated that local news of a sensational nature was at a low ebb. The firm of Denny & Carson announced that the boy's father had refunded the full amount of the theft, and that they had no intention of prosecuting. The Cumberland minister had been interviewed, and expressed his hope of yet reclaiming the motherless lad, and his Sabbath-school teacher declared that she would spare no effort to that end. The rumour had reached Pittsburgh that the boy had been seen in a New York hotel, and his father had gone East to find him and bring him home.

Paul had just come in to dress for dinner; he sank into a chair, weak to the knees, and clasped his head in his hands. It was to be worse than jail, even; the tepid waters of Cordelia Street were to close over him finally and forever. The grey monotony stretched before him in hopeless, unrelieved years; Sabbath-school, Young People's Meeting, the yellow-papered room, the damp dish-towels; it all rushed back upon him with a sickening vividness. He had the old feeling that the orchestra had suddenly stopped, the sinking sensation that the play was over. The sweat broke out on his face, and he sprang to his feet, looked about him with his white, conscious smile, and winked at himself in the mirror. With something of the old childish belief in miracles with which he had so often gone to class, all his lessons unlearned, Paul dressed and dashed whistling down the corridor to the elevator.

He had no sooner entered the dining-room and caught the measure of the music than his remembrance was lightened by his old elastic power of claiming the moment, mounting with it, and finding it all sufficient. The glare and glitter about him, the mere scenic accessories had again, and for the last time, their old potency. He would show himself that he was game, he would finish the thing splendidly. He doubted, more than ever, the existence of Cordelia Street, and for the first time he drank his wine recklessly. Was he not, after all, one of those fortunate beings born to the purple, was he not still himself and in his own place? He drummed a nervous accompaniment to the Pagliacci music and looked about him, telling himself over and over that it had paid.

He reflected drowsily, to the swell of the music and the chill sweetness of his wine, that he might have done it more wisely. He might have caught an outbound steamer and been well out of their clutches before now. But the other side of the world had seemed too far away and too uncertain then; he could not have waited for it; his need had been too sharp. If he had to choose over again, he would do the same thing tomorrow. He looked affectionately about the dining-room, now gilded with a soft mist. Ah, it had paid indeed!

Paul was awakened next morning by a painful throbbing in his head and feet. He had thrown himself across the bed without undressing, and had slept with his shoes on. His limbs and hands were lead heavy, and his tongue and throat were parched and burnt. There came upon him one of those fateful attacks of clear-headedness that never occurred except when he was physically exhausted and his nerves hung loose. He lay still and closed his eyes and let the tide of things wash over him.

His father was in New York; "stopping at some joint or other," he told himself. The memory of successive summers on the front stoop fell upon him like a weight of black water. He had not a hundred dollars left; and he knew now, more than ever, that money was everything, the wall that stood between all he loathed and all he wanted. The thing was winding itself up; he had thought of that on his first glorious day in New York, and had even provided a way to snap the thread. It lay on his dressing-table now; he had got it out last night when he came blindly up from dinner, but the shiny metal hurt his eyes, and he disliked the looks of it.

He rose and moved about with a painful effort, succumbing now and again to attacks of nausea. It was the old depression exaggerated; all the world had become Cordelia Street. Yet somehow he was not afraid of anything, was absolutely calm; perhaps because he had looked into the dark corner at last and knew. It was bad enough, what he saw there, but somehow not so bad as his long fear of it had been. He saw everything clearly now. He had a feeling that he had made the best of it, that he had lived the sort of life he was meant to live, and for half an hour he sat staring at the revolver. But he told himself that was not the way, so he went downstairs and took a cab to the ferry.

When Paul arrived at Newark, he got off the train and took another cab, directing the driver to follow the Pennsylvania tracks out of the town. The snow lay heavy on the roadways and had drifted deep in the open fields. Only here and there the dead grass or dried weed stalks projected, singularly black, above it. Once well into the country, Paul dismissed the carriage and walked, floundering along the tracks, his mind a medley of irrelevant things. He seemed to hold in his brain an actual picture of everything he had seen that morning. He remembered every feature of both his drivers, of the toothless old woman from whom he had bought the red flowers in his coat, the agent from whom he had got his ticket, and all of his fellow-passengers on the ferry. His mind, unable to cope with vital matters near at hand, worked feverishly and deftly at sorting and grouping these images. They made for him a part of the ugliness of the world, of the ache in his head, and the bitter burning on his tongue. He stooped and put a handful of snow into his mouth as he walked, but that, too, seemed hot. When he reached a little hillside, where the tracks ran through a cut some twenty feet below him, he stopped and sat down.

The carnations in his coat were drooping with the cold, he noticed; their red glory all over. It occurred to him that all the flowers he had seen in the glass cases that first night must have gone the same way, long before this. It was only one splendid breath they had, in spite of their brave mockery at the winter outside the glass; and it was a losing game in the end, it seemed, this revolt against the homilies by which the world is run. Paul took one of the blossoms carefully from his coat and scooped a little hole in the snow, where he covered it up. Then he dozed a while, from his weak condition, seemingly insensible to the cold.

The sound of an approaching train awoke him, and he started to his feet, 65
remembering only his resolution, and afraid lest he should be too late. He stood watching the approaching locomotive, his teeth chattering, his lips drawn away from them in a frightened smile; once or twice he glanced nervously sidewise, as though he were being watched. When the right moment came, he jumped. As he fell, the folly of his haste occurred to him with merciless clearness, the vastness of what he had left undone. There flashed through his brain, clearer than ever before, the blue of Adriatic water, the yellow of Algerian sands.

He felt something strike his chest, and that his body was being thrown swiftly through the air, on and on, immeasurably far and fast, while his limbs were gently relaxed. Then, because the picture making mechanism was crushed, the disturbing visions flashed into black, and Paul dropped back into the immense design of things.

WILLA CATHER

(1873–1947) **Web** *www*

Raised on the prairie, Cather moved to New York City. After working briefly for a magazine, Cather began writing short stories and novels. Cather's stories often focus on characters from the West like those with whom she grew up. The realism of her novels works toward exploring how people survive within cultural restrictions.

TOPICS FOR CRITICAL THINKING **Web** *www*

1. Through what strategies does the narrator present the character Paul?
2. What is the plot?
3. How and why does the narrator use both objective and subjective views of Paul to explain his character?
4. What is the relation between what Paul wants and the narrator's indirect descriptions of Paul's "problem"?
5. Why does Paul kill himself?

TOPICS FOR CRITICAL WRITING **Web** *www*

1. How does the narrator convey an understanding of Paul by not identifying his desires and problems directly?
2. Explain the title of the story.

Charlotte Perkins Gilman

The Yellow Wall-Paper *(1892)*

It is very seldom that mere ordinary people like John and myself secure ancestral halls for the summer.

A colonial mansion, a hereditary estate, I would say a haunted house, and reach the height of romantic felicity—but that would be asking too much of fate!

Still I will proudly declare that there is something queer about it.

Else, why should it be let so cheaply? And why have stood so long untenanted?

John laughs at me, of course, but one expects that in marriage. 5

John is practical in the extreme. He has no patience with faith, an intense horror of superstition, and he scoffs openly at any talk of things not to be felt and seen and put down in figures.

John is a physician, and *perhaps*—(I would not say it to a living soul, of course, but this is dead paper and a great relief to my mind)—*perhaps* that is one reason I do not get well faster.

You see he does not believe I am sick!

And what can one do?

If a physician of high standing, and one's own husband, assures friends 10 and relatives that there is really nothing the matter with one but temporary nervous depression—a slight hysterical tendency—what is one to do?

My brother is also a physician, and also of high standing, and he says the same thing.

So I take phosphates or phosphites—whichever it is, and tonics, and journeys, and air, and exercise, and am absolutely forbidden to "work" until I am well again.

Personally, I disagree with their ideas.

Personally, I believe that congenial work, with excitement and change, would do me good.

But what is one to do? 15

I did write for a while in spite of them; but it *does* exhaust me a good deal—having to be so sly about it, or else meet with heavy opposition.

I sometimes fancy that in my condition if I had less opposition and more society and stimulus—but John says the very worst thing I can do is to think about my condition, and I confess it always makes me feel bad.

So I will let it alone and talk about the house.

The most beautiful place! It is quite alone, standing well back from the road, quite three miles from the village. It makes me think of English places that you read about, for there are hedges and walls and gates that lock, and lots of separate little houses for the gardeners and people.

There is a *delicious* garden! I never saw such a garden—large and shady, 20 full of box-bordered paths, and lined with long grape-covered arbors with seats under them.

There were greenhouses, too, but they are all broken now.

There was some legal trouble, I believe, something about the heirs and co-heirs; anyhow, the place has been empty for years.

That spoils my ghostliness, I am afraid, but I don't care—there is something strange about the house—I can feel it.

I even said so to John one moonlight evening, but he said what I felt was a *draught*, and shut the window.

I get unreasonably angry with John sometimes. I'm sure I never used to 25
be so sensitive. I think it is due to this nervous condition.

But John says if I feel so, I shall neglect proper self-control; so I take pains to control myself—before him, at least, and that makes me very tired.

I don't like our room a bit. I wanted one downstairs that opened on the piazza and had roses all over the window, and such pretty old-fashioned chintz hangings! but John would not hear of it.

He said there was only one window and not room for two beds, and no near room for him if he took another.

He is very careful and loving, and hardly lets me stir without special direction.

I have a schedule prescription for each hour in the day; he takes all care 30
from me, and so I feel basely ungrateful not to value it more.

He said we came here solely on my account, that I was to have perfect rest and all the air I could get. "Your exercise depends on your strength, my dear," said he, "and your food somewhat on your appetite; but air you can absorb all the time." So we took the nursery at the top of the house.

It is a big, airy room, the whole floor nearly, with windows that look all ways, and air and sunshine galore. It was nursery first and then playroom and gymnasium, I should judge; for the windows are barred for little children, and there are rings and things in the walls.

The paint and paper look as if a boys' school had used it. It is stripped off—the paper—in great patches all around the head of my bed, about as far as I can reach, and in a great place on the other side of the room low down. I never saw a worse paper in my life.

One of those sprawling flamboyant patterns committing every artistic sin.

It is dull enough to confuse the eye in following, pronounced enough to 35
constantly irritate and provoke study, and when you follow the lame uncertain curves for a little distance they suddenly commit suicide—plunge off at outrageous angles, destroy themselves in unheard of contradictions.

The color is repellent, almost revolting; a smouldering unclean yellow, strangely faded by the slow-turning sunlight.

It is a dull yet lurid orange in some places, a sickly sulphur tint in others.

No wonder the children hated it! I should hate it myself if I had to live in this room long.

There comes John, and I must put this away,—he hates to have me write a word.

* * *

We have been here two weeks, and I haven't felt like writing before, since that first day.

I am sitting by the window now, up in this atrocious nursery, and there is nothing to hinder my writing as much as I please, save lack of strength.

John is away all day, and even some nights when his cases are serious.

I am glad my case is not serious!

But these nervous troubles are dreadfully depressing.

John does not know how much I really suffer. He knows there is no *reason* to suffer, and that satisfies him.

Of course it is only nervousness. It does weigh on me so not to do my duty in any way!

I meant to be such a help to John, such a real rest and comfort, and here I am a comparative burden already!

Nobody would believe what an effort it is to do what little I am able,—to dress and entertain, and order things.

It is fortunate Mary is so good with the baby. Such a dear baby!

And yet I *cannot* be with him, it makes me so nervous.

I suppose John never was nervous in his life. He laughs at me so about this wall-paper!

At first he meant to repaper the room, but afterwards he said that I was letting it get the better of me, and that nothing was worse for a nervous patient than to give way to such fancies.

He said that after the wall-paper was changed it would be the heavy bedstead, and then the barred windows, and then that gate at the head of the stairs, and so on.

"You know the place is doing you good," he said, "and really, dear, I don't care to renovate the house just for a three months' rental."

"Then do let us go downstairs," I said, "there are such pretty rooms there."

Then he took me in his arms and called me a blessed little goose, and said he would go down to the cellar, if I wished, and have it whitewashed into the bargain.

But he is right enough about the beds and windows and things.

It is an airy and comfortable room as any one need wish, and, of course, I would not be so silly as to make him uncomfortable just for a whim.

I'm really getting quite fond of the big room, all but that horrid paper.

Out of one window I can see the garden, those mysterious deep-shaded arbors, the riotous old-fashioned flowers, and bushes and gnarly trees.

Out of another I get a lovely view of the bay and a little private wharf belonging to the estate. There is a beautiful shaded lane that runs down there from the house. I always fancy I see people walking in these numerous paths and arbors, but John has cautioned me not to give way to fancy in the least. He says that with my imaginative power and habit of story-making, a nervous weakness like mine is sure to lead to all manner of excited fancies, and that I ought to use my will and good sense to check the tendency. So I try.

I think sometimes that if I were only well enough to write a little it would relieve the press of ideas and rest me.

But I find I get pretty tired when I try.

It is so discouraging not to have any advice and companionship about my work. When I get really well, John says we will ask Cousin Henry and Julia down for a long visit; but he says he would as soon put fireworks in my pillow-case as to let me have those stimulating people about now.

I wish I could get well faster.

But I must not think about that. This paper looks to me as if it *knew* what a vicious influence it had!

There is a recurrent spot where the pattern lolls like a broken neck and two bulbous eyes stare at you upside down.

I get positively angry with the impertinence of it and the everlastingness. Up and down and sideways they crawl, and those absurd, unblinking eyes are everywhere. There is one place where two breadths didn't match, and the eyes go all up and down the line, one a little higher than the other.

I never saw so much expression in an inanimate thing before, and we all know how much expression they have! I used to lie awake as a child and get more entertainment and terror out of blank walls and plain furniture than most children could find in a toy-store.

I remember what a kindly wink the knobs of our big, old bureau used to have, and there was one chair that always seemed like a strong friend.

I used to feel that if any of the other things looked too fierce I could always hop into that chair and be safe.

The furniture in this room is no worse than inharmonious, however, for we had to bring it all from downstairs. I suppose when this was used as a playroom they had to take the nursery things out, and no wonder! I never saw such ravages as the children have made here.

The wall-paper, as I said before, is torn off in spots, and it sticketh closer than a brother—they must have had perseverance as well as hatred.

Then the floor is scratched and gouged and splintered, the plaster itself is dug out here and there, and this great heavy bed which is all we found in the room, looks as if it had been through the wars.

But I don't mind it a bit—only the paper.

There comes John's sister. Such a dear girl as she is, and so careful of me! I must not let her find me writing.

She is a perfect and enthusiastic housekeeper, and hopes for no better profession. I verily believe she thinks it is the writing which made me sick!

But I can write when she is out, and see her a long way off from these windows.

There is one that commands the road, a lovely shaded winding road, and one that just looks off over the country. A lovely country, too, full of great elms and velvet meadows.

This wall-paper has a kind of sub-pattern in a different shade, a particularly irritating one, for you can only see it in certain lights, and not clearly then.

But in the places where it isn't faded and where the sun is just so—I can see a strange, provoking, formless sort of figure, that seems to skulk about behind that silly and conspicuous front design.

There's sister on the stairs!

Well, the Fourth of July is over! The people are all gone and I am tired out. John thought it might do me good to see a little company, so we just had mother and Nellie and the children down for a week.

Of course I didn't do a thing. Jennie sees to everything now.

But it tired me all the same. 85

John says if I don't pick up faster he shall send me to Weir Mitchell in the fall.

But I don't want to go there at all. I had a friend who was in his hands once, and she says he is just like John and my brother, only more so!

Besides, it is such an undertaking to go so far.

I don't feel as if it was worth while to turn my hand over for anything, and I'm getting dreadfully fretful and querulous.

I cry at nothing, and cry most of the time. 90

Of course I don't when John is here, or anybody else, but when I am alone.

And I am alone a good deal just now. John is kept in town very often by serious cases, and Jennie is good and lets me alone when I want her to.

So I walk a little in the garden or down that lovely lane, sit on the porch under the roses, and lie down up here a good deal.

I'm getting really fond of the room in spite of the wall-paper. Perhaps *because* of the wall-paper.

It dwells in my mind so! 95

I lie here on this great immovable bed—it is nailed down, I believe—and follow that pattern about by the hour. It is as good as gymnastics, I assure you. I start, we'll say, at the bottom, down in the corner over there where it has not been touched, and I determine for the thousandth time that I *will* follow that pointless pattern to some sort of a conclusion.

I know a little of the principle of design, and I know this thing was not arranged on any laws of radiation, or alternation, or repetition, or symmetry, or anything else that I ever heard of.

It is repeated, of course, by the breadths, but not otherwise.

Looked at in one way each breadth stands alone, the bloated curves and flourishes—a kind of "debased Romanesque" with *delirium tremens*—go waddling up and down in isolated columns of fatuity.

But, on the other hand, they connect diagonally, and the sprawling out- 100
lines run off in great slanting waves of optic horror, like a lot of wallowing seaweeds in full chase.

The whole thing goes horizontally, too, at least it seems so, and I exhaust myself in trying to distinguish the order of its going in that direction.

They have used a horizontal breadth for a frieze, and that adds wonderfully to the confusion.

There is one end of the room where it is almost intact, and there, when the crosslights fade and the low sun shines directly upon it, I can almost fancy radiation after all,—the interminable grotesques seem to form around a common centre and rush off in headlong plunges of equal distraction.

It makes me tired to follow it. I will take a nap I guess.

I don't know why I should write this.

I don't want to.

I don't feel able.

And I know John would think it absurd. But I *must* say what I feel and think in some way—it is such a relief!

But the effort is getting to be greater than the relief.

Half the time now I am awfully lazy, and lie down ever so much.

John says I mustn't lose my strength, and has me take cod liver oil and lots of tonics and things, to say nothing of ale and wine and rare meat.

Dear John! He loves me very dearly, and hates to have me sick. I tried to have a real earnest reasonable talk with him the other day, and tell him how I wish he would let me go and make a visit to Cousin Henry and Julia.

But he said I wasn't able to go, nor able to stand it after I got there; and I did not make out a very good case for myself, for I was crying before I had finished.

It is getting to be a great effort for me to think straight. Just this nervous weakness I suppose.

And dear John gathered me up in his arms, and just carried me upstairs and laid me on the bed, and sat by me and read to me till it tired my head.

He said I was his darling and his comfort and all he had, and that I must take care of myself for his sake, and keep well.

He says no one but myself can help me out of it, that I must use my will and self-control and not let any silly fancies run away with me.

There's one comfort, the baby is well and happy, and does not have to occupy this nursery with the horrid wall-paper.

If we had not used it, that blessed child would have! What a fortunate escape! Why, I wouldn't have a child of mine, an impressionable little thing, live in such a room for worlds.

I never thought of it before, but it is lucky that John kept me here after all, I can stand it so much easier than a baby, you see.

Of course I never mention it to them any more—I am too wise,—but I keep watch of it all the same.

There are things in that paper that nobody knows but me, or ever will.

Behind that outside pattern the dim shapes get clearer every day.

It is always the same shape, only very numerous.

And it is like a woman stooping down and creeping about behind that pattern. I don't like it a bit. I wonder—I begin to think—I wish John would take me away from here!

It is so hard to talk with John about my case, because he is so wise, and because he loves me so.

But I tried it last night.

It was moonlight. The moon shines in all around just as the sun does.

I hate to see it sometimes, it creeps so slowly, and always comes in by one window or another.

John was asleep and I hated to waken him, so I kept still and watched the moonlight on that undulating wall-paper till I felt creepy.

The faint figure behind seemed to shake the pattern, just as if she wanted to get out.

I got up softly and went to feel and see if the paper *did* move, and when I came back John was awake.

"What is it, little girl?" he said. "Don't go walking about like that—you'll get cold."

I thought it was a good time to talk, so I told him that I really was not gaining here, and that I wished he would take me away.

"Why darling!" said he, "our lease will be up in three weeks, and I can't see how to leave before."

"The repairs are not done at home, and I cannot possibly leave town just now. Of course if you were in any danger, I could and would, but you really are better, dear, whether you can see it or not. I am a doctor, dear, and I know. You are gaining flesh and color, your appetite is better, I feel really much easier about you."

"I don't weigh a bit more," said I, "nor as much; and my appetite may be better in the evening when you are here, but it is worse in the morning when you are away!"

"Bless her little heart!" said he with a big hug, "she shall be as sick as she pleases! But now let's improve the shining hours by going to sleep, and talk about it in the morning!"

"And you won't go away?" I asked gloomily.

"Why, how can I, dear? It is only three weeks more and then we will take a nice little trip of a few days while Jennie is getting the house ready. Really dear you are better!"

"Better in body perhaps—" I began, and stopped short, for he sat up straight and looked at me with such a stern, reproachful look that I could not say another word.

"My darling," said he, "I beg of you, for my sake and for our child's sake, as well as for your own, that you will never for one instant let that idea enter your mind! There is nothing so dangerous, so fascinating, to a temperament like yours. It is a false and foolish fancy. Can you not trust me as a physician when I tell you so?"

So of course I said no more on that score, and we went to sleep before long. He thought I was asleep first, but I wasn't, and lay there for hours trying to decide whether that front pattern and the back pattern really did move together or separately.

On a pattern like this, by daylight, there is a lack of sequence, a defiance of law, that is a constant irritant to a normal mind.

The color is hideous enough, and unreliable enough, and infuriating 145
enough, but the pattern is torturing.

You think you have mastered it, but just as you get well underway in following, it turns a back-somersault and there you are. It slaps you in the face, knocks you down, and tramples upon you. It is like a bad dream.

The outside pattern is a florid arabesque, reminding one of a fungus. If you can imagine a toadstool in joints, an interminable string of toadstools, budding and sprouting in endless convolutions—why, that is something like it.

That is, sometimes!

There is one marked peculiarity about this paper, a thing nobody seems to notice but myself, and that is that it changes as the light changes.

When the sun shoots in through the east window—I always watch for 150
that first long, straight ray—it changes so quickly that I never can quite believe it.

That is why I watch it always.

By moonlight—the moon shines in all night when there is a moon—I wouldn't know it was the same paper.

At night in any kind of light, in twilight, candle light, lamplight, and worst of all by moonlight, it becomes bars! The outside pattern I mean, and the woman behind it is as plain as can be.

I didn't realize for a long time what the thing was that showed behind, that dim sub-pattern, but now I am quite sure it is a woman.

By daylight she is subdued, quiet. I fancy it is the pattern that keeps her 155
so still. It is so puzzling. It keeps me quiet by the hour.

I lie down ever so much now. John says it is good for me, and to sleep all I can.

Indeed he started the habit by making me lie down for an hour after each meal.

It is a very bad habit I am convinced, for you see I don't sleep.

And that cultivates deceit, for I don't tell them I'm awake—O no!

The fact is I am getting a little afraid of John. 160

He seems very queer sometimes, and even Jennie has an inexplicable look.

It strikes me occasionally, just as a scientific hypothesis,—that perhaps it is the paper!

I have watched John when he did not know I was looking, and come into the room suddenly on the most innocent excuses, and I've caught him several times *looking at the paper!* And Jennie too. I caught Jennie with her hand on it once.

She didn't know I was in the room, and when I asked her in a quiet, a very quiet voice, with the most restrained manner possible, what she was doing with the paper—she turned around as if she had been caught stealing, and looked quite angry—asked me why I should frighten her so!

Then she said that the paper stained everything it touched, that she had 165
found yellow smooches on all my clothes and John's, and she wished we would be more careful!

Did not that sound innocent? But I know she was studying that pattern, and I am determined that nobody shall find it out but myself!

* * *

Life is very much more exciting now than it used to be. You see I have something more to expect, to look forward to, to watch. I really do eat better, and am more quiet than I was.

John is so pleased to see me improve! He laughed a little the other day, and said I seemed to be flourishing in spite of my wall-paper.

I turned it off with a laugh. I had no intention of telling him it was *because* of the wall-paper—he would make fun of me. He might even want to take me away.

I don't want to leave now until I have found it out. There is a week more, 170
and I think that will be enough.

I'm feeling ever so much better! I don't sleep much at night, for it is so interesting to watch developments; but I sleep a good deal in the daytime.

In the daytime it is tiresome and perplexing.

There are always new shoots on the fungus, and new shades of yellow all over it. I cannot keep count of them, though I have tried conscientiously.

It is the strangest yellow, that wall-paper! It makes me think of all the yellow things I ever saw—not beautiful ones like buttercups, but old foul, bad yellow things.

But there is something else about that paper—the smell! I noticed it the 175
moment we came into the room, but with so much air and sun it was not bad. Now we have had a week of fog and rain, and whether the windows are open or not, the smell is here.

It creeps all over the house.

I find it hovering in the dining-room, skulking in the parlor, hiding in the hall, lying in wait for me on the stairs.

It gets into my hair.

Even when I go to ride, if I turn my head suddenly and surprise it—there is that smell!

Such a peculiar odor, too! I have spent hours in trying to analyze it, to 180
find what it smelled like.

It is not bad—at first, and very gentle, but quite the subtlest, most enduring odor I ever met.

In this damp weather it is awful, I wake up in the night and find it hanging over me.

It used to disturb me at first. I thought seriously of burning the house—to reach the smell.

But now I am used to it. The only thing I can think of that it is like is the *color* of the paper! A yellow smell.

There is a very funny mark on this wall, low down, near the mopboard. 185
A streak that runs round the room. It goes behind every piece of furniture, except the bed, a long, straight, even *smooch*, as if it had been rubbed over and over.

I wonder how it was done and who did it, and what they did it for. Round and round and round—round and round and round—it makes me dizzy!

* * *

I really have discovered something at last.

Through watching so much at night, when it changes so, I have finally found out.

The front pattern *does* move—and no wonder! The woman behind shakes it!

Sometimes I think there are a great many women behind, and sometimes 190
only one, and she crawls around fast, and her crawling shakes it all over.

Then in the very bright spots she keeps still, and in the very shady spots she just takes hold of the bars and shakes them hard.

And she is all the time trying to climb through. But nobody could climb through that pattern—it strangles so; I think that is why it has so many heads.

They get through, and then the pattern strangles them off and turns them upside down, and makes their eyes white!

If those heads were covered or taken off it would not be half so bad.

I think that woman gets out in the daytime! 195

And I'll tell you why—privately—I've seen her!

I can see her out of every one of my windows!

It is the same woman, I know, for she is always creeping, and most women do not creep by daylight.

I see her on that long road under the trees, creeping along, and when a carriage comes she hides under the blackberry vines.

I don't blame her a bit. It must be very humiliating to be caught creeping 200
by daylight!

I always lock the door when I creep by daylight. I can't do it at night, for I know John would suspect something at once.

And John is so queer now, that I don't want to irritate him. I wish he would take another room! Besides, I don't want anybody to get that woman out at night but myself.

I often wonder if I could see her out of all the windows at once.

But, turn as fast as I can, I can only see out of one at one time.

And though I always see her, she *may* be able to creep faster than I 205
can turn!

I have watched her sometimes away off in the open country, creeping as fast as a cloud shadow in a high wind.

If only that top pattern could be gotten off from the under one! I mean to try it, little by little.

I have found out another funny thing, but I shan't tell it this time! It does not do to trust people too much.

There are only two more days to get this paper off, and I believe John is beginning to notice. I don't like the look in his eyes.

And I heard him ask Jennie a lot of professional questions about me. She 210
had a very good report to give.

She said I slept a good deal in the daytime.

John knows I don't sleep very well at night, for all I'm so quiet!

He asked me all sorts of questions, too, and pretended to be very loving and kind.

As if I couldn't see through him!

Still, I don't wonder he acts so, sleeping under this paper for three months.

It only interests me, but I feel sure John and Jennie are secretly affected by it.

Hurrah! This is the last day, but it is enough. John to stay in town over night, and won't be out until this evening.

Jennie wanted to sleep with me—the sly thing! but I told her I should undoubtedly rest better for a night all alone.

That was clever, for really I wasn't alone a bit! As soon as it was moonlight and that poor thing began to crawl and shake the pattern, I got up and ran to help her.

I pulled and she shook, I shook and she pulled, and before morning we had peeled off yards of that paper.

A strip about as high as my head and half around the room.

And then when the sun came and that awful pattern began to laugh at me, I declared I would finish it to-day!

We go away to-morrow, and they are moving all my furniture down again to leave things as they were before.

Jennie looked at the wall in amazement, but I told her merrily that I did it out of pure spite at the vicious thing.

She laughed and said she wouldn't mind doing it herself, but I must not get tired.

How she betrayed herself that time!

But I am here, and no person touches this paper but me,—not *alive!*

She tried to get me out of the room—it was too patent! But I said it was so quiet and empty and clean now that I believed I would lie down again and sleep all I could; and not to wake me even for dinner—I would call when I woke.

So now she is gone, and the servants are gone, and the things are gone, and there is nothing left but that great bedstead nailed down, with the canvas mattress we found on it.

We shall sleep downstairs to-night, and take the boat home tomorrow.

I quite enjoy the room, now it is bare again.

How those children did tear about here!

This bedstead is fairly gnawed!

But I must get to work.

I have locked the door and thrown the key down into the front path.

I don't want to go out, and I don't want to have anybody come in, till John comes.

I want to astonish him.

I've got a rope up here that even Jennie did not find. If that woman does get out, and tries to get away, I can tie her!

But I forgot I could not reach far without anything to stand on!

This bed will *not* move!

I tried to lift and push it until I was lame, and then I got so angry I bit off a little piece at one corner—but it hurt my teeth.

Then I peeled off all the paper I could reach standing on the floor. It sticks horribly and the pattern just enjoys it! All those strangled heads and bulbous eyes and waddling fungus growths just shriek with derision!

I am getting angry enough to do something desperate. To jump out of the window would be admirable exercise, but the bars are too strong even to try.

Besides I wouldn't do it. Of course not. I know well enough that a step like that is improper and might be misconstrued.

I don't like to *look* out of the windows even—there are so many of those creeping women, and they creep so fast.

I wonder if they all come out of that wall-paper as I did?

But I am securely fastened now by my well-hidden rope—you don't get *me* out in the road there!

I suppose I shall have to get back behind the pattern when it comes night, and that is hard!

It is so pleasant to be out in this great room and creep around as I please!

I don't want to go outside. I won't, even if Jennie asks me to.

For outside you have to creep on the ground, and everything is green instead of yellow.

But here I can creep smoothly on the floor, and my shoulder just fits in that long smooch around the wall, so I cannot lose my way.

Why there's John at the door!

It is no use, young man, you can't open it!

How he does call and pound!

Now he's crying for an axe.

It would be a shame to break down that beautiful door!

"John dear!" said I in the gentlest voice, "the key is down by the front steps, under a plantain leaf!"

That silenced him for a few moments.

Then he said—very quietly indeed, "Open the door, my darling!"

"I can't," said I. "The key is down by the front door under a plantain leaf!"

And then I said it again, several times, very gently and slowly, and said it so often that he had to go and see, and he got it of course, and came in. He stopped short by the door.

"What is the matter?" he cried. "For God's sake, what are you doing!"

I kept on creeping just the same, but I looked at him over my shoulder.

"I've got out at last," said I, "in spite of you and Jane. And I've pulled off most of the paper, so you can't put me back!"

Now why should that man have fainted? But he did, and right across my path by the wall, so that I had to creep over him every time!

CHARLOTTE PERKINS GILMAN

(1860–1935) **Web** *www*

Grand-niece of Harriet Beecher Stowe, Gilman wrote stories and prose essays on the plight of women. A social activist, Gilman published books and a monthly periodical, *The Forerunner*, in which she serialized several of her own novels.

www

TOPICS FOR CRITICAL THINKING Web

1. Why does the wallpaper captivate the narrator?
2. What various explanations are there for the narrator's interest in the wallpaper?
3. In what ways is the narrator conscious of contrary or differing opinions about the wallpaper?
4. What might the wallpaper represent other than itself?
5. What does the narrator's relation to the wallpaper say about the processes of reading and interpretation?
6. How do you understand the end of the story?

www

TOPICS FOR CRITICAL WRITING Web

1. How do the narrator's perceptions of the wallpaper shift your perceptions of the narrator?
2. In what ways does the narrator's relation to the wallpaper parallel the status of women in patriarchal society?

KATE CHOPIN

The Story of an Hour

(1894)

Knowing that Mrs. Mallard was afflicted with a heart trouble, great care was taken to break to her as gently as possible the news of her husband's death.

It was her sister Josephine who told her, in broken sentences, veiled hints that revealed in half concealing. Her husband's friend Richards was there, too, near her. It was he who had been in the newspaper office when intelligence of the railroad disaster was received, with Brently Mallard's name leading the list of "killed." He had only taken the time to assure himself of its truth by a second telegram, and had hastened to forestall any less careful, less tender friend in bearing the sad message.

She did not hear the story as many women have heard the same, with a paralyzed inability to accept its significance. She wept at once, with sudden, wild abandonment, in her sister's arms. When the storm of grief had spent itself she went away to her room alone. She would have no one follow her.

There stood, facing the open window, a comfortable, roomy armchair. Into this she sank, pressed down by a physical exhaustion that haunted her body and seemed to reach into her soul.

She could see in the open square before her house the tops of trees that 5
were all aquiver with the new spring life. The delicious breath of rain was in the air. In the street below a peddler was crying his wares. The notes of a distant song which some one was singing reached her faintly, and countless sparrows were twittering in the eaves.

There were patches of blue sky showing here and there through the clouds that had met and piled one above the other in the west facing her window.

She sat with her head thrown back upon the cushion of the chair, quite motionless, except when a sob came up into her throat and shook her, as a child who has cried itself to sleep continues to sob in its dreams.

She was young, with a fair, calm face, whose lines bespoke repression and even a certain strength. But now there was a dull stare in her eyes, whose gaze was fixed away off yonder on one of those patches of blue sky. It was not a glance of reflection, but rather indicated a suspension of intelligent thought.

There was something coming to her and she was waiting for it, fearfully. What was it? She did not know; it was too subtle and elusive to name. But she felt it, creeping out of the sky, reaching toward her through the sounds, the scents, the color that filled the air.

Now her bosom rose and fell tumultuously. She was beginning to recog- 10
nize this thing that was approaching to possess her, and she was striving to beat it back with her will—as powerless as her two white slender hands would have been.

When she abandoned herself a little whispered word escaped her slightly parted lips. She said it over and over under her breath: "Free, free, free!" The vacant stare and the look of terror that had followed it went from her eyes. They stayed keen and bright. Her pulses beat fast, and the coursing blood warmed and relaxed every inch of her body.

She did not stop to ask if it were or were not a monstrous joy that held her. A clear and exalted perception enabled her to dismiss the suggestion as trivial.

She knew that she would weep again when she saw the kind, tender hands folded in death; the face that had never looked save with love upon her, fixed and gray and dead. But she saw beyond that bitter moment a long procession of years to come that would belong to her absolutely. And she opened and spread her arms out to them in welcome.

There would be no one to live for during those coming years; she would live for herself. There would be no powerful will bending hers in that blind persistence with which men and women believe they have a right to impose a private will upon a fellow-creature. A kind intention or a cruel intention made the act seem no less a crime as she looked upon it in that brief moment of illumination.

And yet she had loved him—sometimes. Often she had not. What did it 15
matter! What could love, the unsolved mystery, count for in face of this possession of self-assertion which she suddenly recognized as the strongest impulse of her being!

"Free! Body and soul free!" she kept whispering.

Josephine was kneeling before the closed door with her lips to the keyhole, imploring for admission. "Louise, open the door! I beg, open the door—you will make yourself ill. What are you doing, Louise? For heaven's sake open the door."

"Go away. I am not making myself ill." No; she was drinking in a very elixir of life through that open window.

Her fancy was running riot along those days ahead of her. Spring days, and summer days, and all sorts of days that would be her own. She breathed a quick prayer that life might be long. It was only yesterday she had thought with a shudder that life might be long.

She arose at length and opened the door to her sister's importunities. 20
There was a feverish triumph in her eyes, and she carried herself unwittingly like a goddess of Victory. She clasped her sister's waist, and together they descended the stairs. Richards stood waiting for them at the bottom.

Some one was opening the front door with a latchkey. It was Brently Mallard who entered, a little travel-stained, composedly carrying his grip-sack and umbrella. He had been far from the scene of accident, and did not even know there had been one. He stood amazed at Josephine's piercing cry; at Richards' quick motion to screen him from the view of his wife.

But Richards was too late.

When the doctors came they said she had died of heart disease—of joy that kills.

KATE CHOPIN

www

(1851–1904) **Web**

Born in St. Louis and living in New Orleans, Chopin wrote stories that approached women's experiences from a woman's perspective. Chopin wrote stories about adultery, independence, miscegenation, and divorce, considered unwholesome subjects in the late nineteenth century.

www

TOPICS FOR CRITICAL WRITING **Web**

1. Does the point of view of the third-person narrator change during the course of the story? What is the purpose of this shift?
2. How does point of view produce double meanings in some of the story's key phrases (such as "a heart trouble" and "the joy that kills")?
3. How does this story take advantage of those double meanings to illustrate women's feelings about cultural roles?
4. What is "the joy that kills"?

www

TOPICS FOR CRITICAL WRITING **Web**

1. Define the relations between the story's third-person narrator and its point of view. How are the points of view constructed? How do we know they are differing points of view?
2. Trace the connections made between what Louise sees and her changing perspective on life.

7 Theme

Stories are generally about something (even if, as in the case of the television sitcom *Seinfeld*, they are about "nothing"). The ideas that organize stories—that tie together characters, settings, plots, narrators, and points of view—are called **themes**. Themes may be many different kinds of ideas or feelings. They might consist of a political concept such as democracy, freedom, or oppression.

Themes about interpersonal issues such as friendship, betrayal, sacrifice, or loyalty may tie stories together. Themes might focus on questions about art and culture, such as the possibility of communication, the passion of creativity, or the importance of intangible qualities in a materialist society. Stories may have a single dominant theme or several related themes. Like the other elements of fiction, theme does not function by itself; nor is it a more important consideration than other elements. Theme works in a cooperative relation with other elements of fiction, defining them and being defined by them.

Unlike character, setting, and plot, however, theme is not always immediately apparent. Some kinds of stories (such as fables) have a message—a clear directive about behavior or values such as the lesson of the fable about the tortoise and the hare. But not all stories have a message, and the message is not always the same as the theme. Messages tend to be clear and straightforward, while themes are ideas, questions, and issues that often appear in more than one guise in any given story. For example, commercials have messages; stories, novels, and films have themes. Stories such as "The Birthmark" have more than one theme—the relation of man to nature, the possibility of perfection. A story such as "Bartleby the Scrivener" presents the themes of inaction and passivity through both the narrator and Bartleby.

A story's themes frequently must be deduced from its events and the way they are presented. For example, a character's motives may relate to a story's themes. A character might be greedy in a story about the avaricious superficiality of the rich. Or several characters may encounter different versions of the same dilemma; for example, they may each experience some aspect of their parents aging. Theme may be deduced from a story's events (as in Peyton Farquhar's desperate fantasy of escape in "An Occurrence at Owl Creek Bridge"), the conditions a story describes (as in the harshness of nature in "The Law of Life"), or a preoccupation of the narrator (as in Marlow's fixation on Kurtz in *Heart of Darkness*). Often readers discern theme by noticing the ways ideas in a story repeat themselves through multiple characters, plots, points of view, and settings. A good example of this is the connection between the decadence of the Ushers' house, the deathlike nature of Roderick Usher's appearance, and the end of the family line in "The Fall of the House of Usher."

Critical Perspective: Race Criticism

In Chapter 6, we looked at criticism focused around the perspectives of gender and sexuality. Gender and sexuality may appear both as themes and as part of the very fabric of language and prose fiction. Like gender and sexuality, race is an intrinsic component of the way we understand the world. Gender, sexual, and racial issues are depicted as both personal and social; they all provide both points of view and themes in prose fiction. Often, issues of gender, sexuality, and race are combined. Interpretations of fiction that focus on race—whether black, white, Asian, or Native American, for example—either *www* as a theme or a perspective are called **race criticism.** Web

Critical Perspective: Marxist Criticism

Like gender, sexuality, and race, class is another lens through which experience is organized. Although Americans often believe that they live in a society without pronounced class differences, social class in part defines our use of language, our beliefs, and our possibilities. Some prose fiction focuses on class as a theme, portraying the effects of class differences or the experience of being a member of a particular class (particularly the lower class); stories about wealthy or upper class people tend not to see class as a problem. Other stories include class as an element defining character. Critics who study representations of class, the ways literature enacts the effects of economic disparity, and the material conditions and contexts within which stories are produced are *www* called **Marxist or materialist critics.** Web

Stories About Race and Class

The following five stories focus on the themes of race and class. The first three center on the experiences of African Americans in American culture. Alice Walker's "Everyday Use" shows the effects of change and bourgeois ambition within a rural African American family. Featured author James Baldwin's "Previous Condition" portrays the discrimination experienced by a young African American man struggling in New York City. "Sonny's Blues" contrasts two brothers, one who has learned to survive in the city and the other who turns to drugs and music as a way to bear his existence. The final story—Tillie Olsen's "I Stand Here Ironing" —portrays the effects of having to struggle in a poor economy. Olsen's reminiscence of her daughter's childhood reviews the hardships of being a single mother during the Depression.

ALICE WALKER

Everyday Use (1973)

For Your Grandmama

I will wait for her in the yard that Maggie and I made so clean and wavy yesterday afternoon. A yard like this is more comfortable than most people know. It is not just a yard. It is like an extended living room. When the hard clay is swept clean as a floor and the fine sand around the edges lined with tiny, irregular grooves, anyone can come and sit and look up into the elm tree and wait for the breezes that never come inside the house.

Maggie will be nervous until after her sister goes: she will stand hopelessly in corners, homely and ashamed of the burn scars down her arms and legs, eying her sister with a mixture of envy and awe. She thinks her sister has held life always in the palm of one hand, that "no" is a word the world never learned to say to her.

You've no doubt seen those TV shows where the child who has "made it" is confronted, as a surprise, by her own mother and father, tottering in weakly from backstage. (A pleasant surprise, of course: What would they do if parent and child came on the show only to curse out and insult each other?) On TV mother and child embrace and smile into each other's faces. Sometimes the mother and father weep, the child wraps them in her arms and leans across the table to tell how she would not have made it without their help. I have seen these programs.

Sometimes I dream a dream in which Dee and I are suddenly brought together on a TV program of this sort. Out of a dark and soft-seated limousine I am ushered into a bright room filled with many people. There I meet a smiling, gray, sporty man like Johnny Carson who shakes my hand and tells me what a fine girl I have. Then we are on the stage and Dee is embracing me with tears in her eyes. She pins on my dress a large orchid, even though she has told me once that she thinks orchids are tacky flowers.

In real life I am a large, big-boned woman with rough, man-working 5
hands. In the winter I wear flannel nightgowns to bed and overalls during the day. I can kill and clean a hog as mercilessly as a man. My fat keeps me hot in zero weather. I can work outside all day, breaking ice to get water for washing; I can eat pork liver cooked over the open fire minutes after it comes steaming from the hog. One winter I knocked a bull calf straight in the brain between the eyes with a sledge hammer and had the meat hung up to chill before nightfall. But of course all this does not show on television. I am the way my daughter would want me to be: a hundred pounds lighter, my skin like an uncooked barley pancake. My hair glistens in the hot bright lights. Johnny Carson has much to do to keep up with my quick and witty tongue.

But that is a mistake. I know even before I wake up. Who ever knew a

Johnson with a quick tongue? Who can even imagine me looking a strange white man in the eye? It seems to me I have talked to them always with one foot raised in flight, with my head turned in whichever way is farthest from them. Dee, though. She would always look anyone in the eye. Hesitation was no part of her nature.

"How do I look, Mama?" Maggie says, showing just enough of her thin body enveloped in pink skirt and red blouse for me to know she's there, almost hidden by the door.

"Come out into the yard," I say.

Have you ever seen a lame animal, perhaps a dog run over by some careless person rich enough to own a car, sidle up to someone who is ignorant enough to be kind to him? That is the way my Maggie walks. She has been like this, chin on chest, eyes on ground, feet in shuffle, ever since the fire that burned the other house to the ground.

Dee is lighter than Maggie, with nicer hair and a fuller figure. She's a 10
woman now, though sometimes I forget. How long ago was it that the other house burned? Ten, twelve years? Sometimes I can still hear the flames and feel Maggie's arms sticking to me, her hair smoking and her dress falling off her in little black papery flakes. Her eyes seemed stretched open, blazed open by the flames reflected in them. And Dee. I see her standing off under the sweet gum tree she used to dig gum out of; a look of concentration on her face as she watched the last dingy gray board of the house fall in toward the red-hot brick chimney. Why don't you do a dance around the ashes? I'd want to ask her. She had hated the house that much.

I used to think she hated Maggie, too. But that was before we raised the money, the church and me, to send her to Augusta to school. She used to read to us without pity; forcing words, lies, other folks' habits, whole lives upon us two, sitting trapped and ignorant underneath her voice. She washed us in a river of make-believe, burned us with a lot of knowledge we didn't necessarily need to know. Pressed us to her with the serious way she read, to shove us away at just the moment, like dimwits, we seemed about to understand.

Dee wanted nice things. A yellow organdy dress to wear to her graduation from high school; black pumps to match a green suit she'd made from an old suit somebody gave me. She was determined to stare down any disaster in her efforts. Her eyelids would not flicker for minutes at a time. Often I fought off the temptation to shake her. At sixteen she had a style of her own: and knew what style was.

I never had an education myself. After second grade the school was closed down. Don't ask me why: in 1927 colored asked fewer questions than they do now. Sometimes Maggie reads to me. She stumbles along good-naturedly but can't see well. She knows she is not bright. Like good looks and money, quickness passed her by. She will marry John Thomas (who has mossy teeth in an earnest face) and then I'll be free to sit here and I guess just sing church songs to myself. Although I never was a good singer. Never could carry a tune. I was always better at a man's job. I used to love to milk till I was hooked in the side in '49. Cows are soothing and slow and don't bother you, unless you try to milk them the wrong way.

I have deliberately turned my back on the house. It is three rooms, just like the one that burned, except the roof is tin; they don't make shingle roofs any more. There are no real windows, just some holes cut in the sides, like the portholes in a ship, but not round and not square, with rawhide holding the shutters up on the outside. This house is in a pasture, too, like the other one. No doubt when Dee sees it she will want to tear it down. She wrote me once that no matter where we "choose" to live, she will manage to come see us. But she will never bring her friends. Maggie and I thought about this and Maggie asked me, "Mama, when did Dee ever *have* any friends?"

15 She had a few. Furtive boys in pink shirts hanging about on washday after school. Nervous girls who never laughed. Impressed with her they worshipped the well-turned phrase, the cute shape, the scalding humor that erupted like bubbles in lye. She read to them.

When she was courting Jimmy T she didn't have much time to pay to us, but turned all her faultfinding power on him. He *flew* to marry a cheap city girl from a family of ignorant flashy people. She hardly had time to recompose herself.

When she comes I will meet—but there they are!

Maggie attempts to make a dash for the house, in her shuffling way, but I stay her with my hand. "Come back here," I say. And she stops and tries to dig a well in the sand with her toe.

It is hard to see them clearly through the strong sun. But even the first glimpse of leg out of the car tells me it is Dee. Her feet were always neat-looking, as if God himself had shaped them with a certain style. From the other side of the car comes a short, stocky man. Hair is all over his head a foot long and hanging from his chin like a kinky mule tail. I hear Maggie suck in her breath. "Uhnnnh," is what it sounds like. Like when you see the wriggling end of a snake just in front of your foot on the road. "Uhnnnh."

20 Dee next. A dress down to the ground, in this hot weather. A dress so loud it hurts my eyes. There are yellows and oranges enough to throw back the light of the sun. I feel my whole face warming from the heat waves it throws out. Earrings gold, too, and hanging down to her shoulders. Bracelets dangling and making noises when she moves her arm up to shake the folds of the dress out of her armpits. The dress is loose and flows, and as she walks closer, I like it. I hear Maggie go "Uhnnnh" again. It is her sister's hair. It stands straight up like the wool on a sheep. It is black as night and around the edges are two long pigtails that rope about like small lizards disappearing behind her ears.

"Wa-su-zo-Tean-o!" she says, coming on in that gliding way the dress makes her move. The short stocky fellow with the hair to his navel is all grinning and he follows up with "Asalamalakim, my mother and sister!" He moves to hug Maggie but she falls back, right up against the back of my chair.

I feel her trembling there and when I look up I see the perspiration falling off her chin.

"Don't get up," says Dee. Since I am stout it takes something of a push. You can see me trying to move a second or two before I make it. She turns, showing white heels through her sandals, and goes back to the car. Out she peeks next with a Polaroid. She stoops down quickly and lines up picture after picture of me sitting there in front of the house with Maggie cowering behind me. She never takes a shot without making sure the house is included. When a cow comes nibbling around the edge of the yard she snaps it and me and Maggie *and* the house. Then she puts the Polaroid in the back seat of the car, and comes up and kisses me on the forehead.

Meanwhile Asalamalakim is going through motions with Maggie's hand. Maggie's hand is as limp as a fish, and probably as cold, despite the sweat, and she keeps trying to pull it back. It looks like Asalamalakim wants to shake hands but wants to do it fancy. Or maybe he don't know how people shake hands. Anyhow, he soon gives up on Maggie.

"Well," I say. "Dee."

"No, Mama," she says. "Not 'Dee,' Wangero Leewanika Kemanjo!"

"What happened to 'Dee'?" I wanted to know.

"She's dead," Wangero said. "I couldn't bear it any longer, being named after the people who oppress me."

"You know as well as me you was named after your aunt Dicie," I said. Dicie is my sister. She named Dee. We called her "Big Dee" after Dee was born.

"But who was *she* named after?" asked Wangero.

"I guess after Grandma Dee," I said.

"And who was she named after?" asked Wangero.

"Her mother," I said, and saw Wangero was getting tired. "That's about as far back as I can trace it," I said. Though, in fact, I probably could have carried it back beyond the Civil War through the branches.

"Well," said Asalamalakim, "there you are."

"Uhnnnh," I heard Maggie say.

"There I was not," I said, "before 'Dicie' cropped up in our family, so why should I try to trace it that far back?"

He just stood there grinning, looking down on me like somebody inspecting a Model A car. Every once in a while he and Wangero sent eye signals over my head.

"How do you pronounce this name?" I asked.

"You don't have to call me by it if you don't want to," said Wangero.

"Why shouldn't I?" I asked. "If that's what you want us to call you, we'll call you."

"I know it might sound awkward at first," said Wangero.

"I'll get used to it," I said. "Ream it out again."

Well, soon we got the name out of the way. Asalamalakim had a name twice as long and three times as hard. After I tripped over it two or three times he told me to just call him Hakim-a-barber. I wanted to ask him was he a barber, but I didn't really think he was, so I didn't ask.

"You must belong to those beef-cattle peoples down the road," I said. They said "Asalamalakim" when they met you, too, but they didn't shake hands. Always too busy: feeding the cattle, fixing the fences, putting up salt-lick shelters, throwing down hay. When the white folks poisoned some of the herd the men stayed up all night with rifles in their hands. I walked a mile and a half just to see the sight.

Hakim-a-barber said, "I accept some of their doctrines, but farming and raising cattle is not my style." (They didn't tell me, and I didn't ask, whether Wangero (Dee) had really gone and married him.)

We sat down to eat and right away he said he didn't eat collards and pork 45
was unclean. Wangero, though, went on through the chitlins and corn bread, the greens and everything else. She talked a blue streak over the sweet potatoes. Everything delighted her. Even the fact that we still used the benches her daddy made for the table when we couldn't afford to buy chairs.

"Oh, Mama!" she cried. Then turned to Hakim-a-barber. "I never knew how lovely these benches are. You can feel the rump prints," she said, running her hands underneath her and long the bench. Then she gave a sigh and her hand closed over Grandma Dee's butter dish. "That's it!" she said. "I knew there was something I wanted to ask you if I could have." She jumped up from the table and went over in the corner where the churn stood, the milk in it clabber by now. She looked at the churn and looked at it.

"This churn top is what I need," she said. "Didn't Uncle Buddy whittle it out of a tree you all used to have?"

"Yes," I said.

"Uh huh," she said happily. "And I want the dasher, too."

"Uncle Buddy whittle that, too?" asked the barber. 50

Dee (Wangero) looked up at me.

"Aunt Dee's first husband whittled the dash," said Maggie so low you almost couldn't hear her. "His name was Henry, but they called him Stash."

"Maggie's brain is like an elephant's," Wangero said, laughing. "I can use the churn top as a centerpiece for the alcove table," she said, sliding a plate over the churn, "and I'll think of something artistic to do with the dasher."

When she finished wrapping the dasher the handle stuck out. I took it for a moment in my hands. You didn't even have to look close to see where hands pushing the dasher up and down to make butter had left a kind of sink in the wood. In fact, there were a lot of small sinks; you could see where thumbs and fingers had sunk into the wood. It was beautiful light yellow wood, from a tree that grew in the yard where Big Dee and Stash had lived.

After dinner Dee (Wangero) went to the trunk at the foot of my bed and 55
started rifling through it. Maggie hung back in the kitchen over the dishpan. Out came Wangero with two quilts. They had been pieced by Grandma Dee and then Big Dee and me had hung them on the quilt frames on the front porch and quilted them. One was in the Lone Star pattern. The other was Walk Around the Mountain. In both of them were scraps of dresses Grandma Dee had worn fifty and more years ago. Bits and pieces of Grandpa Jarrell's Paisley shirts. And one teeny faded blue piece, about the size of a penny

matchbox, that was from Great Grandpa Ezra's uniform that he wore in the Civil War.

"Mama," Wangero said sweet as a bird. "Can I have these old quilts?"

I heard something fall in the kitchen, and a minute later the kitchen door slammed.

"Why don't you take one or two of the others?" I asked. "These old things was just done by me and Big Dee from some tops your grandma pieced before she died."

"No," said Wangero. "I don't want those. They are stitched around the borders by machine."

"That'll make them last better," I said. 60

"That's not the point," said Wangero. "These are all pieces of dresses Grandma used to wear. She did all this stitching by hand. Imagine!" She held the quilts securely in her arms, stroking them.

"Some of the pieces, like those lavender ones, come from old clothes her mother handed down to her," I said, moving up to touch the quilts. Dee (Wangero) moved back just enough so that I couldn't reach the quilts. They already belonged to her.

"Imagine!" she breathed again, clutching them closely to her bosom.

"The truth is," I said, "I promised to give them quilts to Maggie, for when she marries John Thomas."

She gasped like a bee had stung her. 65

"Maggie can't appreciate these quilts!" she said. "She'd probably be backward enough to put them to everyday use."

"I reckon she would," I said. "God knows I been saving 'em for long enough with nobody using 'em. I hope she will!" I didn't want to bring up how I had offered Dee (Wangero) a quilt when she went away to college. Then she had told me they were old-fashioned, out of style.

"But they're *priceless!*" she was saying now, furiously; for she has a temper. "Maggie would put them on the bed and in five years they'd be in rags. Less than that!"

"She can always make some more," I said. "Maggie knows how to quilt."

Dee (Wangero) looked at me with hatred. "You just will not understand. 70
The point is these quilts, *these* quilts!"

"Well," I said, stumped. "What would *you* do with them?"

"Hang them," she said. As if that was the only thing you *could* do with quilts.

Maggie by now was standing in the door. I could almost hear the sound her feet made as they scraped over each other.

"She can have them, Mama," she said, like somebody used to never winning anything, or having anything reserved for her. "I can 'member Grandma Dee without the quilts."

I looked at her hard. She had filled her bottom lip with checkerberry 75
snuff and it gave her face a kind of dopey, hangdog look. It was Grandma Dee and Big Dee who taught her how to quilt herself. She stood there with her scarred hands hidden in the folds of her skirt. She looked at her sister with

something like fear but she wasn't mad at her. This was Maggie's portion. This was the way she knew God to work.

When I looked at her like that something hit me in the top of my head and ran down to the soles of my feet. Just like when I'm in church and the spirit of God touches me and I get happy and shout. I did something I never had done before: hugged Maggie to me, then dragged her on into the room, snatched the quilts out of Miss Wangero's hands and dumped them into Maggie's lap. Maggie just sat there on my bed with her mouth open.

"Take one or two of the others," I said to Dee.

But she turned without a word and went out to Hakim-a-barber.

"You just don't understand," she said, as Maggie and I came out to the car.

"What don't I understand?" I wanted to know. 80

"Your heritage," she said. And then she turned to Maggie, kissed her, and said, "You ought to try to make something of yourself, too, Maggie. It's really a new day for us. But from the way you and Mama still live you'd never know it."

She put on some sunglasses that hid everything above the tip of her nose and her chin.

Maggie smiled; maybe at the sunglasses. But a real smile, not scared. After we watched the car dust settle I asked Maggie to bring me a dip of snuff. And then the two of us sat there just enjoying, until it was time to go in the house and go to bed.

ALICE WALKER

(b. 1944) **Web** *www*

Winner of a Guggenheim Fellowship, Walker is the author of novels such as *The Color Purple* (1982), short stories, essays and poetry. She quit teaching to devote full-time to writing and activism, working for causes such as women's rights, anti-apartheid, and civil rights. Her work is both realist and mythical, the pragmatic reverberating meanings beyond its "everyday use."

TOPICS FOR CRITICAL THINKING **Web** *www*

1. Are differences in perception in the story merely a function of generation?
2. What does "heritage" mean?
3. How do objects in the story reflect the story's themes?

TOPICS FOR CRITICAL WRITING **Web** *www*

1. What might "everyday use" mean?
2. What different narratives of their history do the narrator and Dee have? What clues does the story provide about these narratives?

Featured Writer

James Baldwin CD-ROM

Previous Condition (1948)

I woke up shaking, alone in my room. I was clammy cold with sweat; under me the sheet and the mattress were soaked. The sheet was gray and twisted like a rope. I breathed like I had been running.

I couldn't move for the longest while. I just lay on my back, spread-eagled, looking up at the ceiling, listening to the sounds of people getting up in other parts of the house, alarm clocks ringing and water splashing and doors opening and shutting and feet on the stairs. I could tell when people left for work: the hall doorway downstairs whined and shuffled as it opened and gave a funny kind of double slam as it closed. One thud and then a louder thud and then a little final click. While the door was open I could hear the street sounds too, horses' hoofs and delivery wagons and people in the streets and big trucks and motor cars screaming on the asphalt.

I had been dreaming. At night I dreamt and woke up in the morning trembling, but not remembering the dream, except that in the dream I had been running. I could not remember when the dream—or dreams—had started; it had been long ago. For long periods maybe, I would have no dreams at all. And then they would come back, every night, I would try not to go to bed, I would go to sleep frightened and wake up frightened and have another day to get through with the nightmare at my shoulder. Now I was back from Chicago, busted, living off my friends in a dirty furnished room downtown. The show I had been with had folded in Chicago. It hadn't been much of a part—or much of a show either, to tell the truth. I played a kind of intellectual Uncle Tom, a young college student working for his race. The playwright had wanted to prove he was a liberal, I guess. But, as I say, the show had folded and here I was, back in New York and hating it. I knew that I should be getting another job, making the rounds, pounding the pavement. But I didn't. I couldn't face it. It was summer. I seemed to be fagged out. And every day I hated myself more. Acting's a rough life, even if you're white. I'm not tall and I'm not good looking and I can't sing or dance and I'm not white; so even at the best of times I wasn't in much demand.

The room I lived in was heavy ceilinged, perfectly square, with walls the color of chipped dry blood. Jules Weissman, a Jewboy, had got the room for me. It's a room to sleep in, he said, or maybe to die in but God knows it wasn't meant to live in. Perhaps because the room was so hideous it had a fantastic array of light fixtures: one on the ceiling, one on the left wall, two on the right wall, and a lamp on the table beside my bed. My bed was in front of the window through which nothing ever blew but dust. It was a furnished room and they'd thrown enough stuff in it to furnish three rooms its size. Two easy chairs and a desk, the bed, the table, a straight-backed chair, a bookcase, a cardboard wardrobe; and my books and my suitcase, both unpacked; and my dirty clothes flung in a corner. It was the kind of room that defeated you. It had a fireplace, too, and a heavy marble mantelpiece and a great gray mirror above the mantelpiece. It was hard to see anything in the mirror very clearly—which was perhaps just as well—and it would have been worth your life to have started a fire in the fireplace.

"Well, you won't have to stay here long," Jules told me the night I came. 5
Jules smuggled me in, sort of, after dark, when everyone had gone to bed.

"Christ, I hope not."

"I'll be moving to a big place soon," Jules said. "You can move in with me." He turned all the lights on. "Think it'll be all right for a while?" He sounded apologetic, as though he had designed the room himself.

"Oh, sure. D'you think I'll have any trouble?"

"I don't think so. The rent's paid. She can't put you out."

I didn't say anything to that. 10

"Sort of stay undercover," Jules said. "You know."

"Roger," I said.

I had been living there for three days, timing it so I left after everyone else had gone, coming back late at night when everyone else was asleep. But I knew it wouldn't work. A couple of the tenants had seen me on the stairs, a woman had surprised me coming out of the john. Every morning I waited for the landlady to come banging on the door. I didn't know what would happen. It might be all right. It might not be. But the waiting was getting me.

The sweat on my body was turning cold. Downstairs a radio was tuned in to the Breakfast Symphony. They were playing Beethoven. I sat up and lit a cigarette. "Peter," I said, "don't let them scare you to death. You're a man, too." I listened to Ludwig and I watched the smoke rise to the dirty ceiling. Under Ludwig's drums and horns I listened to hear footsteps on the stairs.

I'd done a lot of traveling in my time. I'd knocked about through St. 15
Louis, Frisco, Seattle, Detroit, New Orleans, worked at just about everything. I'd run away from my old lady when I was about sixteen. She'd never been able to handle me. You'll never be nothin' *but* a bum, she'd say. We lived in an old shack in a town in New Jersey in the nigger part of town, the kind of houses colored people live in all over the U.S. I hated my mother for living there. I hated all the people in my neighborhood. They went to church and they got drunk. They were nice to the white people. When the landlord came around they paid him and took his crap.

The first time I was ever called nigger I was seven years old. It was a little white girl with long black curls. I used to leave the front of my house and go wandering by myself through town. This little girl was playing ball alone and as I passed her the ball rolled out of her hands into the gutter.

I threw it back to her.

"Let's play catch," I said.

But she held the ball and made a face at me.

"My mother don't let me play with niggers," she told me. 20

I did not know what the word meant. But my skin grew warm. I stuck my tongue out at her.

"I don't care. Keep your old ball." I started down the street.

She screamed after me: "Nigger, nigger, nigger!"

I screamed back: "Your mother was a nigger!"

I asked my mother what a nigger was. 25

"Who called you that?"

"I heard somebody say it."

"Who?"

"Just somebody."

"Go wash your face," she said. "You dirty as sin. Your supper's on the 30
table."

I went to the bathroom and splashed water on my face and wiped my face and hands on the towel.

"You call that clean?" my mother cried. "Come here, boy!"

She dragged me back to the bathroom and began to soap my face and neck.

"You run around dirty like you do all the time, everybody'll call you a little nigger, you hear?" She rinsed my face and looked at my hands and dried me. "Now, go on and eat your supper."

I didn't say anything. I went to the kitchen and sat down at the table. I re- 35
member I wanted to cry. My mother sat down across from me.

"Mama," I said. She looked at me. I started to cry.

She came around to my side of the table and took me in her arms.

"Baby, don't fret. Next time somebody calls you nigger you tell them you'd rather be your color than be lowdown and nasty like some white folks is."

We formed gangs when I was older, my friends and I. We met white boys and their friends on the opposite sides of fences and we threw rocks and tin cans at each other.

I'd come home bleeding. My mother would slap me and scold me and cry. 40

"Boy, you wanna get killed? You wanna end up like your father?"

My father was a bum and I had never seen him. I was named for him: Peter.

I was always in trouble: truant officers, welfare workers, everybody else in town.

"You ain't never gonna be nothin' *but* a bum," my mother said.

By and by older kids I knew finished school and got jobs and got married 45
and settled down. They were going to settle down and bring more black babies into the world and pay the same rents for the same old shacks and it would go on and on—

When I was sixteen I ran away. I left a note and told Mama not to worry, I'd come back one day and I'd be all right. But when I was twenty-two she died. I came back and put my mother in the ground. Everything was like it had been. Our house had not been painted and the porch floor sagged and there was somebody's raincoat stuffed in the broken window. Another family was moving in.

Their furniture was stacked along the walls and their children were running through the house and laughing and somebody was frying pork chops in the kitchen. The oldest boy was tacking up a mirror.

Last year Ida took me driving in her big car and we passed through a couple of towns upstate. We passed some crumbling houses on the left. The clothes on the line were flying in the wind.

"Are people living there?" asked Ida.

"Just darkies," I said.

Ida passed the car ahead, banging angrily on the horn. "D'you know you're becoming paranoiac, Peter?"

"All right. All right. I know a lot of white people are starving too."

"You're damn right they are. I know a little about poverty myself."

Ida had come from the kind of family called shanty Irish. She was raised in Boston. She's a very beautiful woman who married young and married for money—so now I can afford to support attractive young men, she'd giggle. Her husband was a ballet dancer who was forever on the road. Ida suspected that he went with boys. Not that I give a damn, she said, as long as he leaves me alone. When we met last year she was thirty and I was twenty-five. We had a pretty stormy relationship but we stuck. Whenever I got to town I called her; whenever I was stranded out of town I'd let her know. We never let it get too serious. She went her way and I went mine.

In all this running around I'd learned a few things. Like a prizefighter learns to take a blow or a dancer learns to fall, I'd learned how to get by. I'd learned never to be belligerent with policemen, for instance. No matter who was right, I was certain to be wrong. What might be accepted as just good old American independence in someone else would be insufferable arrogance in me. After the first few times I realized that I had to play smart, to act out the role I was expected to play. I only had one head and it was too easy to get it broken. When I faced a policeman I acted like I didn't know a thing. I let my jaw drop and I let my eyes get big. I didn't give him any smart answers, none of the crap about my rights. I figured out what answers he wanted and I gave them to him. I never let him think he wasn't king. If it was more than routine, if I was picked up on suspicion of robbery or murder in the neighborhood, I looked as humble as I could and kept my mouth shut and prayed. I took a couple of beatings but I stayed out of prison and I stayed off chain gangs. That was also due to luck, Ida pointed out once. "Maybe it would've been better for you if you'd been a little less lucky. Worse things have happened than chain gangs. Some of them have happened to you."

There was something in her voice. "What are you talking about?" I asked.

"Don't lose your temper. I said maybe."

"You mean you think I'm a coward?"

"I didn't say that, Peter."

"But you meant that. Didn't you?"

"No. I didn't mean that. I didn't mean anything. Let's not fight."

There are times and places when a Negro can use his color like a shield. He can trade on the subterranean Anglo-Saxon guilt and get what he wants that way; or some of what he wants. He can trade on his nuisance value, his value as forbidden fruit; he can use it like a knife, he can twist it and get his vengeance that way. I knew these things long before I realized that I knew them and in the beginning I used them, not knowing what I was doing. Then when I began to see it, I felt betrayed. I felt beaten as a person. I had no honest place to stand.

This was the year before I met Ida. I'd been acting in stock companies and little theaters; sometimes fairly good parts. People were nice to me. They told me I had talent. They said it sadly, as though they were thinking, What a pity, he'll never get anywhere. I had got to the point where I resented praise and I resented pity and I wondered what people were thinking when they shook my hand. In New York I met some pretty fine people; easygoing, hard-drinking, flotsam and jetsam; and they liked me; and I wondered if I trusted them; if I was able any longer to trust anybody. Not on top, where all the world could see, but underneath where everybody lives.

Soon I would have to get up. I listened to Ludwig. He shook the little room like the footsteps of a giant marching miles away. On summer evenings (and maybe we would go this summer) Jules and Ida and I would go up to the Stadium and sit beneath the pillars on the cold stone steps. There it seemed to me the sky was far away; and I was not myself, I was high and lifted up. We never talked, the three of us. We sat and watched the blue smoke curl in the air and watched the orange tips of cigarettes. Every once in a while the boys who sold popcorn and soda pop and ice cream climbed the steep steps chattering; and Ida shifted slightly and touched her blue-black hair; and Jules scowled. I sat with my knee up watching the lighted half-moon below, the black-coated, straining conductor, the faceless men beneath him moving together in a rhythm like the sea. There were pauses in the music for the rushing, calling, halting piano. Everything would stop except the climbing soloist; he would reach a height and everything would join him, the violins first and then the horns; and then the deep blue bass and the flute and the bitter trampling drums; beating, beating and mounting together and stopping with a crash like daybreak. When I first heard the *Messiah* I was alone; my blood bubbled like fire and wine; I cried; like an infant crying for its mother's milk; or a sinner running to meet Jesus.

Now below the music I heard footsteps on the stairs. I put out my cigarette. My heart was beating so hard I thought it would tear my chest apart. Someone knocked on the door.

I thought: Don't answer. Maybe she'll go away.

But the knocking came again, harder this time.

Just a minute, I said. I sat on the edge of the bed and put on my bathrobe. I was trembling like a fool. For Christ's sake, Peter, you've been through this before. What's the worst thing that can happen? You won't have a room. The world's full of rooms.

When I opened the door the landlady stood there, red-and-whitefaced and hysterical.

"Who are you? I didn't rent this room to you." 70

My mouth was dry. I started to say something.

"I can't have no colored people here," she said. "All my tenants are complainin'. Women afraid to come home nights."

"They ain't gotta be afraid of me," I said. I couldn't get my voice up; it rasped and rattled in my throat; and I began to be angry. I wanted to kill her. "My friend rented this room for me," I said.

"Well, I'm sorry, he didn't have no right to do that, I don't have nothin' against you, but you gotta get out."

Her glasses blinked, opaque in the light on the landing. She was fright- 75
ened to death. She was afraid of me but she was more afraid of losing her tenants. Her face was mottled with rage and fear, her breath came rushed and little bits of spittle gathered at the edges of her mouth; her breath smelled bad, like rotting hamburger on a July day.

"You can't put me out," I said. "This room was rented in my name." I started to close the door, as though the matter was finished: "I live here, see, this is my room, you can't put me out."

"You get outa my house!" she screamed. "I got the right to know who's in my house! This is a white neighborhood, I don't rent to colored people. Why don't you go on uptown, like you belong?"

"I can't stand niggers," I told her. I started to close the door again but she moved and stuck her foot in the way. I wanted to kill her, I watched her stupid, wrinkled, frightened white face and I wanted to take a club, a hatchet, and bring it down with all my weight, splitting her skull down the middle where she parted her iron-grey hair.

"Get out of the door," I said. "I want to get dressed."

But I knew that she had won, that I was already on my way. We stared at 80
each other. Neither of us moved. From her came an emanation of fear and fury and something else. You maggot-eaten bitch, I thought. I said evilly, "You wanna come in and watch me?" Her face didn't change, she didn't take her foot away. My skin prickled, tiny hot needles punctured my flesh. I was aware of my body under the bathrobe; and it was as though I had done something wrong, something monstrous, years ago, which no one had forgotten and for which I would be killed.

"If you don't get out," she said, "I'll get a policeman to put you out."

I grabbed the door to keep from touching her. "All right. All right. You can have the goddamn room. Now get out and let me dress."

She turned away. I slammed the door. I heard her going down the stairs. I threw stuff into my suitcase. I tried to take as long as possible but I cut myself while shaving because I was afraid she would come back upstairs with a policeman.

Jules was making coffee when I walked in.

"Good morning, good morning! What happened to you?" 85

"No room at the inn," I said. "Pour a cup of coffee for the notorious son of man." I sat down and dropped my suitcase on the floor.

Jules looked at me. "Oh. Well. Coffee coming up."

He got out the coffee cups. I lit a cigarette and sat there. I couldn't think of anything to say. I knew that Jules felt bad and I wanted to tell him that it wasn't his fault.

He pushed coffee in front of me and sugar and cream.

"Cheer up, baby. The world's wide and life—life, she is very long."

"Shut up. I don't want to hear any of your bad philosophy."

"Sorry."

"I mean, let's not talk about the good, the true, and the beautiful."

"All right. But don't sit there holding onto your table manners. Scream if you want to."

"Screaming won't do any good. Besides I'm a big boy now."

I stirred my coffee. "Did you give her a fight?" Jules asked.

I shook my head. "No."

"Why the hell not?"

I shrugged; a little ashamed now. I couldn't have won it. What the hell.

"You might have won it. You might have given her a couple of bad moments."

"Goddamit to hell, I'm sick of it. Can't I get a place to sleep without dragging it through the courts? I'm goddamn tired of battling every Tom, Dick, and Harry for what everybody else takes for granted. I'm tired, man, tired! Have you ever been sick to death of something? Well, I'm sick to death. And I'm scared. I've been fighting so goddamn long I'm not a person any more. I'm not Booker T. Washington. I've got no vision of emancipating anybody. I want to emancipate myself. If this goes on much longer, they'll send me to Bellevue, I'll blow my top, I'll break somebody's head. I'm not worried about that miserable little room. I'm worried about what's happening to me, *to me*, inside. I don't walk the streets, I crawl. I've never been like this before. Now when I go to a strange place I wonder what will happen, will I be accepted, if I'm accepted, can I accept?—"

"Take it easy," Jules said.

"Jules, I'm beaten."

"I don't think you are. Drink your coffee."

"Oh," I cried, "I know you think I'm making it dramatic, that I'm paranoiac and just inventing trouble! Maybe I think so sometimes, how can I tell? You get so used to being hit you find you're always waiting for it. Oh, I know, you're Jewish, you get kicked around, too, but you can walk into a bar and nobody *knows* you're Jewish and if you go looking for a job you'll get a better job than mine! How can I say what it feels like? I don't know. I know everybody's in trouble and nothing is easy, but how can I explain to you what it feels like to be black when I don't understand it and don't want to and spend all my time trying to forget it? I don't want to hate anybody—but now maybe, I can't love anybody either—are we friends? Can we be really friends?"

"We're friends," Jules said, "don't worry about it." He scowled. "If I wasn't Jewish I'd ask you why you didn't live in Harlem." I looked at him. He raised his hand and smiled— "But I'm Jewish, so I didn't ask you. Ah Peter," he said, "I can't help you—take a walk, get drunk, we're all in this together."

I stood up. "I'll be around later. I'm sorry."

"Don't be sorry. I'll leave my door open. Bunk here for awhile."

"Thanks," I said.

I felt that I was drowning; that hatred had corrupted me like cancer in the bone.

I saw Ida for dinner. We met in a restaurant in the Village, an Italian place in a gloomy cellar with candles on the tables.

It was not a busy night, for which I was grateful. When I came in there were only two other couples on the other side of the room. No one looked at me. I sat down in a corner booth and ordered a Scotch old-fashioned. Ida was late and I had three of them before she came.

She was very fine in black, a high-necked dress with a pearl choker; and her hair was combed page-boy style, falling just below her ears.

"You look real sweet, baby."

"Thank you. It took fifteen extra minutes but I hoped it would be worth it."

"It was worth it. What're you drinking?"

"Oh—what're you drinking?"

"Old-fashioneds."

She sniffed and looked at me. "How many?"

I laughed. "Three."

"Well," she said, "I suppose you had to do something." The waiter came over. We decided on one Manhattan and one lasagna and one spaghetti with clam sauce and another old-fashioned for me.

"Did you have a constructive day, sweetheart? Find a job?"

"Not today," I said. I lit her cigarette. "Metro offered me a fortune to come to the coast and do the lead in *Native Son* but I turned it down. Type casting, you know. It's so difficult to find a decent part."

"Well, if they don't come up with a decent offer soon tell them you'll go back to Selznick. *He'll* find you a part with guts—the very *idea* of offering you *Native Son!* I wouldn't stand for it."

"You ain't gotta tell me. I told them if they didn't find me a decent script in two weeks I was through, that's all."

"Now that's talking, Peter my lad."

The drinks came and we sat in silence for a minute or two. I finished half of my drink at a swallow and played with the toothpicks on the table. I felt Ida watching me.

"Peter, you're going to be awfully drunk."

"Honeychile, the first thing a southern gentleman learns is how to hold his liquor."

"That myth is older than the rock of ages. And anyway you come from Jersey."

I finished my drink and snarled at her: "That's just as good as the South."

Across the table from me I could see that she was readying herself for trouble: her mouth tightened slightly, setting her chin so that the faint cleft showed: "What happened to you today?"

I resented her concern; I resented my need. "Nothing worth talking about," I muttered, "just a mood."

And I tried to smile at her, to wipe away the bitterness.

"Now I know something's the matter. Please tell me."

It sounded trivial as hell: "You know the room Jules found for me? Well, the landlady kicked me out of it today."

"God save the American republic," Ida said. "D'you want to waste some of my husband's money? We can sue her."

"Forget it. I'll end up with lawsuits in every state in the union."

"Still, as a gesture—"

"The devil with the gesture. I'll get by."

The food came. I didn't want to eat. The first mouthful hit my belly like a gong. Ida began cutting up lasagna.

"Peter," she said, "try not to feel so badly. We're all in this together, the whole world. Don't let it throw you. What can't be helped you have to learn to live with."

"That's easy for you to say," I told her.

She looked at me quickly and looked away. "I'm not pretending that it's easy to do," she said.

I didn't believe that she could really understand it; and there was nothing I could say. I sat like a child being scolded, looking down at my plate, not eating, not saying anything. I wanted her to stop talking, to stop being intelligent about it, to stop being calm and grown-up about it; good Lord, none of us has ever grown up, we never will.

"It's no better anywhere else," she was saying. "In all of Europe there's famine and disease, in France and England they hate the Jews—nothing's going to change, baby, people are too empty-headed, too empty-hearted—it's always been like that, people always try to destroy what they don't understand—and they hate almost everything because they understand so little—"

I began to sweat in my side of the booth. I wanted to stop her voice. I wanted her to eat and be quiet and leave me alone. I looked around for the waiter so I could order another drink. But he was on the far side of the restaurant, waiting on some people who had just come in; a lot of people had come in since we had been sitting there.

"Peter," Ida said, "Peter please don't look like that."

I grinned: the painted grin of the professional clown. "Don't worry, baby, I'm all right. I know what I'm going to do. I'm gonna go back to my people where I belong and find me a nice, black nigger wench and raise me a flock of babies."

Ida had an old maternal trick; the grin tricked her into using it now. She raised her fork and rapped me with it across the knuckles. "Now, stop that. You're too old for that."

I screamed and stood up screaming and knocked the candle over: "Don't *do* that, you bitch, don't *ever* do that!"

She grabbed the candle and set it up and glared at me. Her face had turned perfectly white: "Sit down! Sit *down!*"

I fell back into my seat. My stomach felt like water. Everyone was looking at us. I turned cold, seeing what they were seeing: a black boy and a white woman, alone together. I knew it would take nothing to have them at my throat.

"I'm sorry," I muttered, "I'm sorry, I'm sorry."

The waiter was at my elbow. "Is everything all right, miss?"

"Yes, quite, thank you." She sounded like a princess dismissing a slave. I didn't look up. The shadow of the waiter moved away from me.

"Baby," Ida said, "forgive me, please forgive me."

I stared at the tablecloth. She put her hand on mine, brightness and blackness.

"Let's go," I said, "I'm terribly sorry."

She motioned for the check. When it came she handed the I waiter a ten dollar bill without looking. She picked up her bag.

"Shall we go to a nightclub or a movie or something?"

"No, honey, not tonight." I looked at her. "I'm tired, I think I'll go on over to Jules's place. I'm gonna sleep on his floor for a while. Don't worry about me. I'm all right."

She looked at me steadily. She said: "I'll come see you tomorrow?"

"Yes, baby, please."

The waiter brought the change and she tipped him. We stood up; as we passed the tables (not looking at the people) the ground under me seemed falling, the doorway seemed impossibly far away. All my muscles tensed; I seemed ready to spring; I was waiting for the blow.

I put my hands in my pockets and we walked to the end of the block. The lights were green and red, the lights from the theater across the street exploded blue and yellow, off and on.

"Peter?"

"Yes?"

"I'll see you tomorrow?"

"Yeah. Come by Jules's. I'll wait for you."

"Goodnight, darling."

"Goodnight."

I started to walk away. I felt her eyes on my back. I kicked a bottle-top on the sidewalk.

God save the American republic.

I dropped into the subway and got on an uptown train, not knowing where it was going and not caring. Anonymous, islanded people surrounded me, behind newspapers, behind make-up, fat, fleshy masks and flat eyes. I watched the empty faces. (No one looked at me.) I looked at the ads, unreal women and pink-cheeked men selling cigarettes, candy, shaving cream, nightgowns, chewing gum, movies, sex; sex without organs, drier than sand and more secret than death. The train stopped. A white boy and a white girl got on. She was nice, short, svelte. Nice legs. She was hanging on his arm. He was the football type, blond, ruddy. They were dressed in summer clothes. The wind from the doors blew her print dress. She squealed, holding the dress at the knees and giggled and looked at him. He said something I didn't catch and she looked at me and the smile died. She stood so that she faced him and had her back to me. I looked back at the ads. Then I hated them. I wanted to do something to make them hurt, something that would crack the pink-cheeked mask. The white boy and I did not look at each other again. They got off at the next stop.

I wanted to keep on drinking. I got off in Harlem and went to a rundown bar on Seventh Avenue. My people, my people. Sharpies stood on the corner, waiting. Women in summer dresses pranced by on wavering heels. Click clack. Click clack. There were white mounted policemen in the streets. On every block there was another policeman on foot. I saw a black cop.

God save the American republic.

The juke box was letting loose with "Hamps' Boogie." The place was jumping, I walked over to the man.

"Rye," I said.

I was standing next to somebody's grandmother. "Hello, papa. What you 180
puttin' down?"

"Baby, you can't pick it up," I told her. My rye came and I drank.

"Nigger," she said, "you must think you's somebody."

I didn't answer. She turned away, back to her beer, keeping time to the juke box, her face sullen and heavy and aggrieved. I watched her out of the side of my eye. She had been good looking once, pretty even, before she hit the bottle and started crawling into too many beds. She was flabby now, flesh heaved all over in her thin dress. I wondered what she'd be like in bed; then I realized that I was a little excited by her; I laughed and set my glass down.

"The same," I said. "And a beer chaser."

The juke box was playing something else now, something brassy and 185
commercial which I didn't like. I kept on drinking, listening to the voices of my people, watching the faces of my people. (God pity us, the terrified republic.) Now I was sorry to have angered the woman who still sat next to me, now deep in conversation with another, younger woman. I longed for some opening, some sign, something to make me part of the life around me. But there was nothing except my color. A white outsider coming in would have seen a young Negro drinking in a Negro bar, perfectly in his element, in his place, as the saying goes. But the people here knew differently, as I did. I didn't seem to have a place.

So I kept on drinking by myself, saying to myself after each drink, Now I'll go. But I was afraid; I didn't want to sleep on Jules's floor; I didn't want to go to sleep. I kept on drinking and listening to the juke box. They were playing Ella Fitzgerald, "Cow-Cow Boogie."

"Let me buy you a drink," I said to the woman.

She looked at me, startled, suspicious, ready to blow her top.

"On the level," I said. I tried to smile. "Both of you."

"I'll take a beer," the young one said. 190

I was shaking like a baby. I finished my drink.
"Fine," I said. I turned to the bar.
"Baby," said the old one, "what's your story?"
The man put three beers on the counter.
"I got no story, Ma," I said.

JAMES BALDWIN

(1924–1987) **Web** *www*

Born in Harlem, Baldwin eventually moved to Paris, where he wrote novels, essays, and stories. In 1953 he published his first novel, *Go Tell It on a Mountain*, which enjoyed both popular and critical success. He won a prestigious Guggenheim Award and continued writing, publishing *Giovanni's Room*, a novel about a man's struggle with his sexuality, in 1955. Baldwin returned to New York in 1960, where he became active in the civil rights movement. From that point, much of his writing became more openly focused on racism in America. Baldwin's fiction combines the attentive realism traditional in America since the nineteenth century with a lyricism influenced by jazz and the blues. His characters are astute observers often caught in the chaos of warring truths.

TOPICS FOR CRITICAL THINKING **Web** *www*

1. Does sympathy for the protagonist help the reader understand the effects of racism?
2. What does it mean that this narrator feels that he doesn't belong anywhere?
3. What is the relation between the narrator's childhood experiences and his experiences as a man?
4. What is the relation between the story's themes and the choice of a first-person narrator?

TOPICS FOR CRITICAL WRITING **Web** *www*

1. What is the relation between acting and the narrator's experiences as a black man in America?
2. Why won't the narrator fight back?

Sonny's Blues *(1957)*

I read about it in the paper, in the subway, on my way to work. I read it, and I couldn't believe it, and I read it again. Then perhaps I just stared at it, at the newsprint spelling out his name, spelling out the story. I stared at it in the swinging lights of the subway car, and in the faces and bodies of the people, and in my own face, trapped in the darkness which roared outside.

It was not to be believed and I kept telling myself that as I walked from the subway station to the high school. And at the same time I couldn't doubt it. I was scared, scared for Sonny. He became real to me again. A great block of ice got settled in my belly and kept melting there slowly all day long, while I taught my classes algebra. It was a special kind of ice. It kept melting, sending trickles of ice water all up and down my veins, but it never got less. Sometimes it hardened and seemed to expand until I felt my guts were going to come spilling out or that I was going to choke or scream. This would always be at a moment when I was remembering some specific thing Sonny had once said or done.

When he was about as old as the boys in my classes his face had been bright and open, there was a lot of copper in it; and he'd had wonderfully direct brown eyes, and great gentleness and privacy. I wondered what he looked like now. He had been picked up, the evening before, in a raid on an apartment downtown, for peddling and using heroin.

I couldn't believe it: but what I mean by that is that I couldn't find any room for it anywhere inside me. I had kept it outside me for a long time. I hadn't wanted to know. I had had suspicions, but I didn't name them, I kept putting them away. I told myself that Sonny was wild, but he wasn't crazy. And he'd always been a good boy, he hadn't ever turned hard or evil or disrespectful, the way kids can, so quick, so quick, especially in Harlem. I didn't want to believe that I'd ever see my brother going down, coming to nothing, all that light in his face gone out, in the condition I'd already seen so many others. Yet it had happened and here I was, talking about algebra to a lot of boys who might, every one of them for all I knew, be popping off needles every time they went to the head. Maybe it did more for them than algebra could.

I was sure that the first time Sonny had ever had horse, he couldn't have 5
been much older than these boys were now. These boys, now, were living as we'd been living then, they were growing up with a rush and their heads bumped abruptly against the low ceiling of their actual possibilities. They were filled with rage. All they really knew were two darknesses, the darkness of their lives, which was now closing in on them, and the darkness of the movies, which had blinded them to that other darkness, and in which they now, vindictively, dreamed, at once more together than they were at any other time, and more alone.

When the last bell rang, the last class ended, I let out my breath. It seemed I'd been holding it for all that time. My clothes were wet—I may have looked as though I'd been sitting in a steam bath, all dressed up, all afternoon. I sat alone in the classroom a long time. I listened to the boys outside, downstairs, shouting and cursing and laughing. Their laughter struck me for perhaps the first time. It was not the joyous laughter which—God knows why—one associates with children. It was mocking and insular, its intent was to denigrate. It was disenchanted, and in this, also, lay the authority of their curses. Perhaps I was listening to them because I was thinking about my brother and in them I heard my brother. And myself.

One boy was whistling a tune, at once very complicated and very simple, it seemed to be pouring out of him as though he were a bird, and it sounded very cool and moving through all that harsh, bright air, only just holding its own through all those other sounds.

I stood up and walked over to the window and looked down into the courtyard. It was the beginning of the spring and the sap was rising in the boys. A teacher passed through them every now and again, quickly, as though he or she couldn't wait to get out of that courtyard, to get those boys out of their sight and off their minds. I started collecting my stuff. I thought I'd better get home and talk to Isabel.

The courtyard was almost deserted by the time I got downstairs. I saw this boy standing in the shadow of a doorway, looking just like Sonny. I almost called his name. Then I saw that it wasn't Sonny, but somebody we used to know, a boy from around our block. He'd been Sonny's friend. He'd never been mine, having been too young for me, and, anyway, I'd never liked him. And now, even though he was a grown-up man, he still hung around that block, still spent hours on the street corner, was always high and raggy. I used to run into him from time to time and he'd often work around to asking me for a quarter or fifty cents. He always had some real good excuse, too, and I always gave it to him, I don't know why.

But now, abruptly, I hated him. I couldn't stand the way he looked at me, 10
partly like a dog, partly like a cunning child. I wanted to ask him what the hell he was doing in the school courtyard.

He sort of shuffled over to me, and he said, "I see you got the papers. So you already know about it."

"You mean about Sonny? Yes, I already know about it. How come they didn't get you?"

He grinned. It made him repulsive and it also brought to mind what he'd looked like as a kid. "I wasn't there. I stay away from them people."

"Good for you." I offered him a cigarette and I watched him through the smoke. "You come all the way down here just to tell me about Sonny?"

"That's right." He was sort of shaking his head and his eyes looked 15
strange, as though they were about to cross. The bright sun deadened his damp dark brown skin and it made his eyes look yellow and showed up the dirt in his conked hair. He smelled funky. I moved a little away from him and I said, "Well, thanks. But I already know about it and I got to get home."

"I'll walk you a little ways," he said. We started walking. There were a couple of kids still loitering in the courtyard and one of them said good night to me and looked strangely at the boy beside me.

"What're you going to do?" he asked me. "I mean, about Sonny?"

"Look. I haven't seen Sonny for over a year, I'm not sure I'm going to do anything. Anyway, what the hell *can* I do?"

"That's right," he said quickly, "ain't nothing you can do. Can't much help old Sonny no more, I guess."

It was what I was thinking and so it seemed to me he had no right to 20
say it.

"I'm surprised at Sonny, though," he went on—he had a funny way of talking, he looked straight ahead as though he were talking to himself—"I thought Sonny was a smart boy, I thought he was too smart to get hung."

"I guess he thought so too," I said sharply, "and that's how he got hung. And how about you? You're pretty goddamn smart, I bet."

Then he looked directly at me, just for a minute. "I ain't smart," he said. "If I was smart, I'd have reached for a pistol a long time ago."

"Look. Don't tell *me* your sad story, if it was up to me, I'd give you one." Then I felt guilty—guilty, probably, for never having supposed that the poor bastard *had* a story of his own, much less a sad one, and I asked, quickly, "What's going to happen to him now?"

He didn't answer this. He was off by himself some place. "Funny thing," 25
he said, and from his tone we might have been discussing the quickest way to get to Brooklyn, "when I saw the papers this morning, the first thing I asked myself was if I had anything to do with it. I felt sort of responsible."

I began to listen more carefully. The subway station was on the corner, just before us, and I stopped. He stopped, too. We were in front of a bar and he ducked slightly, peering in, but whoever he was looking for didn't seem to be there. The juke box was blasting away with something black and bouncy and I half watched the barmaid as she danced her way from the juke box to her place behind the bar. And I watched her face as she laughingly responded to something someone said to her, still keeping time to the music. When she smiled one saw the little girl, one sensed the doomed, still-struggling woman beneath the battered face of the semi-whore.

"I never *give* Sonny nothing," the boy said finally, "but a long time ago I come to school high and Sonny asked me how it felt." He paused, I couldn't bear to watch him, I watched the barmaid, and I listened to the music which seemed to be causing the pavement to shake. "I told him it felt great." The music stopped, the barmaid paused and watched the juke box until the music began again. "It did."

All this was carrying me some place I didn't want to go. I certainly didn't want to know how it felt. It filled everything, the people, the houses, the music, the dark, quicksilver barmaid, with menace; and this menace was their reality.

"What's going to happen to him now?" I asked again.

"They'll send him away some place and they'll try to cure him." He shook 30
his head. "Maybe he'll even think he's kicked the habit. Then they'll let him loose"—he gestured, throwing his cigarette into the gutter. "That's all."

"What do you mean, that's *all?*"

But I knew what he meant.

"I *mean,* that's *all.*" He turned his head and looked at me, pulling down the corners of his mouth. "Don't you know what I mean?" he asked softly.

"How the hell *would* I know what you mean?" I almost whispered it, I don't know why.

"That's right," he said to the air, "how would *he* know what I mean?" He 35
turned toward me again, patient and calm, and yet I somehow felt him shaking, shaking as though he were going to fall apart. I felt that ice in my guts again, the dread I'd felt all afternoon; and again I watched the barmaid, moving about the bar, washing glasses, and singing. "Listen. They'll let him out and then it'll just start all over again. That's what I mean."

"You mean—they'll let him out. And then he'll just start working his way back in again. You mean he'll never kick the habit. Is that what you mean?"

"That's right," he said, cheerfully. "*You* see what I mean."

"Tell me," I said at last, "why does he want to die? He must want to die, he's killing himself, why does he want to die?"

He looked at me in surprise. He licked his lips. "He don't want to die. He wants to live. Don't nobody want to die, ever."

Then I wanted to ask him—too many things. He could not have an- 40
swered, or if he had, I could not have borne the answers. I started walking. "Well, I guess it's none of my business."

"It's going to be rough on old Sonny," he said. We reached the subway station. "This is your station?" he asked. I nodded. I took one step down. "Damn!" he said, suddenly. I looked up at him. He grinned again. "Damn if I didn't leave all my money home. You ain't got a dollar on you, have you? Just for a couple of days, is all."

All at once something inside gave and threatened to come pouring out of me. I didn't hate him any more. I felt that in another moment I'd start crying like a child.

"Sure," I said. "Don't sweat." I looked in my wallet and didn't have a dollar, I only had a five. "Here," I said. "That hold you?"

He didn't look at it—he didn't want to look at it. A terrible, closed look came over his face, as though he were keeping the number on the bill a secret from him and me. "Thanks," he said, and now he was dying to see me go. "Don't worry about Sonny. Maybe I'll write him or something."

"Sure," I said. "You do that. So long." 45

"Be seeing you," he said. I went on down the steps.

And I didn't write Sonny or send him anything for a long time. When I finally did, it was just after my little girl died, he wrote me back a letter which made me feel like a bastard.

Here's what he said:

DEAR BROTHER,

You don't know how much I needed to hear from you. I wanted to write you many a time but I dug how much I must have hurt you and so I didn't write. But now I feel like a man who's been trying to climb up out of some deep, real deep and funky hole and just saw the sun up there, outside. I got to get outside.

I can't tell you much about how I got here. I mean I don't know how to tell you. I guess I was afraid of something or I was trying to escape from something and you know I have never been very strong in the head (smile). I'm glad Mama and Daddy are dead and can't see what's happened to their son and I swear if I'd known what I was doing I would never have hurt you so, you and a lot of other fine people who were nice to me and who believed in me.

I don't want you to think it had anything to do with me being a musician. It's more than that. Or maybe less than that. I can't get anything straight in my head down here and I try not to think about what's going to happen to me when I get outside again. Sometime I think I'm going to flip and *never* get outside and sometime I think I'll come straight back. I tell you one thing, though, I'd rather blow my brains out than go through this again. But that's what they all say, so they tell me. If I tell you when I'm coming to New York and if you could meet me, I sure would appreciate it. Give my love to Isabel and the kids and I was sorry to hear about little Gracie.

I wish I could be like Mama and say the Lord's will be done, but I don't know it seems to me that trouble is the one thing that never does get stopped and I don't know what good it does to blame it on the Lord. But maybe it does some good if you believe it.

Your brother,
SONNY

Then I kept in constant touch with him and I sent him whatever I could and I went to meet him when he came back to New York. When I saw him many things I thought I had forgotten came flooding back to me. This was because I had begun, finally, to wonder about Sonny, about the life that Sonny lived inside. This life, whatever it was, had made him older and thinner and it had deepened the distant stillness in which he had always moved. He looked very unlike my baby brother. Yet, when he smiled, when we shook hands, the baby brother I'd never known looked out from the depths of his private life, like an animal waiting to be coaxed into the light.

"How you been keeping?" he asked me. 50

"All right. And you?"

"Just fine." He was smiling all over his face. "It's good to see you again."

"It's good to see you."

The seven years' difference in our ages lay between us like a chasm: I wondered if these years would ever operate between us as a bridge. I was remembering, and it made it hard to catch my breath, that I had been there when he was born; and I had heard the first words he had ever spoken. When he started to walk, he walked from our mother straight to me. I caught him just before he fell when he took the first steps he ever took in this world.

"How's Isabel?" 55

"Just fine. She's dying to see you."

"And the boys?"

"They're fine, too. They're anxious to see their uncle."

"Oh, come on. You know they don't remember me."

"Are you kidding? Of course they remember you." 60

He grinned again. We got into a taxi. We had a lot to say to each other, far too much to know how to begin.

As the taxi began to move, I asked, "You still want to go to India?"

He laughed. "You still remember that. Hell, no. This place is Indian enough for me."

"It used to belong to them," I said.

And he laughed again. "They damn sure knew what they were doing 65 when they got rid of it."

Years ago, when he was around fourteen, he'd been all hipped on the idea of going to India. He read books about people sitting on rocks, naked, in all kinds of weather, but mostly bad, naturally, and walking barefoot through hot coals and arriving at wisdom. I used to say that it sounded to me as though they were getting away from wisdom as fast as they could. I think he sort of looked down on me for that.

"Do you mind," he asked, "if we have the driver drive alongside the park? On the west side—I haven't seen the city in so long."

"Of course not," I said. I was afraid that I might sound as though I were humoring him, but I hoped he wouldn't take it that way.

So we drove along, between the green of the park and the stony, lifeless elegance of hotels and apartment buildings, toward the vivid, killing streets of our childhood. These streets hadn't changed, though housing projects jutted up out of them now like rocks in the middle of a boiling sea. Most of the houses in which we had grown up had vanished, as had the stores from which we had stolen, the basements in which we had first tried sex, the rooftops from which we had hurled tin cans and bricks. But houses exactly like the houses of our past yet dominated the landscape, boys exactly like the boys we once had been found themselves smothering in these houses, came down into the streets for light and air and found themselves encircled by disaster. Some escaped the trap, most didn't. Those who got out always left something of themselves behind, as some animals amputate a leg and leave it in the trap. It might be said, perhaps, that I had escaped, after all, I was a school teacher; or that Sonny had, he hadn't lived in Harlem for years. Yet, as the cab moved uptown through streets which seemed, with a rush, to darken with dark people, and as I covertly studied Sonny's face, it came to me that what we both were seeking through our separate cab windows was that part of ourselves which had been left behind. It's always at the hour of trouble and confrontation that the missing member aches.

70 We hit 110th Street and started rolling up Lenox Avenue. And I'd known this avenue all my life, but it seemed to me again, as it had seemed on the day I'd first heard about Sonny's trouble, filled with a hidden menace which was its very breath of life.

"We almost there," said Sonny.

"Almost." We were both too nervous to say anything more.

We live in a housing project. It hasn't been up long. A few days after it was up it seemed uninhabitably new, now, of course, it's already run-down. It looks like a parody of the good, clean, faceless life—God knows the people who live in it do their best to make it a parody. The beat-looking grass lying around isn't enough to make their lives green, the hedges will never hold out the streets, and they know it. The big windows fool no one, they aren't big enough to make space out of no space. They don't bother with the windows, they watch the TV screen instead. The playground is most popular with the children who don't play at jacks, or skip rope, or roller skate, or swing, and they can be found in it after dark. We moved in partly because it's not too far from where I teach, and partly for the kids; but it's really just like the houses in which Sonny and I grew up. The same things happen, they'll have the same things to remember. The moment Sonny and I started into the house I had the feeling that I was simply bringing him back into the danger he had almost died trying to escape.

Sonny has never been talkative. So I don't know why I was sure he'd be dying to talk to me when supper was over the first night. Everything went fine, the oldest boy remembered him, and the youngest boy liked him, and Sonny had remembered to bring something for each of them; and Isabel, who is really much nicer than I am, more open and giving, had gone to a lot of trouble about dinner and was genuinely glad to see him. And she's always been able to tease Sonny in a way that I haven't. It was nice to see her face so vivid again and to hear her laugh and watch her make Sonny laugh. She wasn't, or, anyway, she didn't seem to be, at all uneasy or embarrassed. She chatted as though there were no subject which had to be avoided and she got Sonny past his first, faint stiffness. And thank God she was there, for I was filled with that icy dread again. Everything I did seemed awkward to me, and everything I said sounded freighted with hidden meaning. I was trying to remember everything I'd heard about dope addiction and I couldn't help watching Sonny for signs. I wasn't doing it out of malice. I was trying to find out something about my brother. I was dying to hear him tell me he was safe.

"Safe!" my father grunted, whenever Mama suggested trying to move to 75
a neighborhood which might be safer for children. "Safe, hell! Ain't no place safe for kids, nor nobody."

He always went on like this, but he wasn't, ever, really as bad as he sounded, not even on weekends, when he got drunk. As a matter of fact, he was always on the lookout for "something a little better," but he died before he found it. He died suddenly, during a drunken weekend in the middle of the war, when Sonny was fifteen. He and Sonny hadn't ever got on too well. And this was partly because Sonny was the apple of his father's eye. It was because he loved Sonny so much and was frightened for him, that he was always fighting with him. It doesn't do any good to fight with Sonny. Sonny just moves back, inside himself, where he can't be reached. But the principal reason that they never hit it off is that they were so much alike. Daddy was big and rough and loud-talking, just the opposite of Sonny, but they both had—that same privacy.

Mama tried to tell me something about this, just after Daddy died. I was home on leave from the army.

This was the last time I ever saw my mother alive. Just the same, this picture gets all mixed up in my mind with pictures I had of her when she was younger. The way I always see her is the way she used to be on a Sunday afternoon, say, when the old folks were talking after the big Sunday dinner. I always see her wearing pale blue. She'd be sitting on the sofa. And my father would be sitting in the easy chair, not far from her. And the living room would be full of church folks and relatives. There they sit, in chairs all around the living room, and the night is creeping up outside, but nobody knows it yet. You can see the darkness growing against the window-panes and you hear the street noises every now and again, or maybe the jangling beat of a tambourine from one of the churches close by, but it's real quiet in the room. For a moment nobody's talking, but every face looks darkening, like the sky outside. And my mother rocks a little from the waist, and my father's eyes are closed. Everyone is looking at something a child can't see. For a minute they've forgotten the children. Maybe a kid is lying on the rug half asleep. Maybe somebody's got a kid on his lap and is absent-mindedly stroking the kid's head. Maybe there's a kid, quiet and big-eyed, curled up in a big chair in the corner. The silence, the darkness coming, and the darkness in the faces frightens the child obscurely. He hopes that the hand which strokes his forehead will never stop—will never die. He hopes that there will never come a time when the old folks won't be sitting around the living room, talking about where they've come from, and what they've seen, and what's happened to them and their kinfolk.

But something deep and watchful in the child knows that this is bound to end, is already ending. In a moment someone will get up and turn on the light. Then the old folks will remember the children and they won't talk any more that day. And when light fills the room, the child is filled with darkness. He knows that every time this happens he's moved just a little closer to that darkness outside. The darkness outside is what the old folks have been talking about. It's what they've come from. It's what they endure. The child knows that they won't talk any more because if he knows too much about what's happened to *them*, he'll know too much too soon, about what's going to happen to *him*.

The last time I talked to my mother, I remember I was restless. I wanted 80
to get out and see Isabel. We weren't married then and we had a lot to straighten out between us.

There Mama sat, in black, by the window. She was humming an old church song, *Lord, you brought me from a long ways off.* Sonny was out somewhere. Mama kept watching the streets.

"I don't know," she said, "if I'll ever see you again, after you go off from here. But I hope you'll remember the things I tried to teach you."

"Don't talk like that," I said, and smiled. "You'll be here a long time yet."

She smiled, too, but she said nothing. She was quiet for a long time. And I said, "Mama, don't you worry about nothing. I'll be writing all the time, and you be getting the checks. . . ."

"I want to talk to you about your brother," she said, suddenly. "If any- 85
thing happens to me he ain't going to have nobody to look out for him."

"Mama," I said, "ain't nothing going to happen to you *or* Sonny. Sonny's all right. He's a good boy and he's got good sense."

"It ain't a question of his being a good boy," Mama said, "nor of his having good sense. It ain't only the bad ones, nor yet the dumb ones that gets sucked under." She stopped, looking at me. "Your Daddy once had a brother," she said, and she smiled in a way that made me feel she was in pain. "You didn't never know that, did you?"

"No," I said, "I never knew that," and I watched her face.

"Oh, yes," she said, "your Daddy had a brother." She looked out of the window again. "I know you never saw your Daddy cry. But *I* did—many a time, through all these years."

I asked her, "What happened to his brother? How come nobody's ever 90
talked about him?"

This was the first time I ever saw my mother look old.

"His brother got killed," she said, "when he was just a little younger than you are now. I knew him. He was a fine boy. He was maybe a little full of the devil, but he didn't mean nobody no harm."

Then she stopped and the room was silent, exactly as it had sometimes been on those Sunday afternoons. Mama kept looking out into the streets.

"He used to have a job in the mill," she said, "and, like all young folks, he just liked to perform on Saturday nights. Saturday nights, him and your father would drift around to different places, go to dances and things like that, or just sit around with people they knew, and your father's brother would sing, he had a fine voice, and play along with himself on his guitar. Well, this particular Saturday night, him and your father was coming home from some place, and they were both a little drunk and there was a moon that night, it was bright like day. Your father's brother was feeling kind of good, and he was whistling to himself, and he had his guitar slung over his shoulder. They was coming down a hill and beneath them was a road that turned off from the highway. Well, your father's brother, being always kind of frisky, decided to run down this hill, and he did, with that guitar banging and clanging behind him, and he ran across the road, and he was making water behind a tree. And your father was sort of amused at him and he was still coming down the hill, kind of slow. Then he heard a car motor and that same minute his brother stepped from behind the tree, into the road, in the moonlight. And he started to cross the road. And your father started to run down the hill, he says he don't know why. This car was full of white men. They was all drunk, and when they seen your father's brother they let out a great whoop and holler and they aimed the car straight at him. They was having fun, they just wanted to scare him, the way they do sometimes, you know. But they was drunk. And I guess the boy, being drunk, too, and scared, kind of lost his head. By the time he jumped it was too late. Your father says he heard his brother scream when the car rolled over him, and he heard the wood of that guitar when it give, and he heard them strings go flying, and he heard them white men shouting, and the car kept on a-going and it ain't stopped till this day. And, time your father got down the hill, his brother weren't nothing but blood and pulp."

Tears were gleaming on my mother's face. There wasn't anything I could 95
say.

"He never mentioned it," she said, "because I never let him mention it before you children. Your Daddy was like a crazy man that night and for many a night thereafter. He says he never in his life seen anything as dark as that road after the lights of that car had gone away. Weren't nothing, weren't nobody on that road, just your Daddy and his brother and that busted guitar. Oh, yes. Your Daddy never did really get right again. Till the day he died he weren't sure but that every white man he saw was the man that killed his brother."

She stopped and took out her handkerchief and dried her eyes and looked at me.

"I ain't telling you all this," she said, "to make you scared or bitter or to make you hate nobody. I'm telling you this because you got a brother. And the world ain't changed."

I guess I didn't want to believe this. I guess she saw this in my face. She turned away from me, toward the window again, searching those streets.

"But I praise my Redeemer," she said at last, "that He called your Daddy 100
home before me. I ain't saying it to throw no flowers at myself, but, I declare, it keeps me from feeling too cast down to know I helped your father get safely through this world. Your father always acted like he was the roughest, strongest

man on earth. And everybody took him to be like that. But if he hadn't had *me* there—to see his tears!"

She was crying again. Still, I couldn't move. I said, "Lord, Lord, Mama, I didn't know it was like that."

"Oh, honey," she said, "there's a lot that you don't know. But you are going to find it out." She stood up from the window and came over to me. "You got to hold on to your brother," she said, "and don't let him fall, no matter what it looks like is happening to him and no matter how evil you gets with him. You going to be evil with him many a time. But don't you forget what I told you, you hear?"

"I won't forget," I said. "Don't you worry, I won't forget. I won't let nothing happen to Sonny."

My mother smiled as though she were amused at something she saw in my face. Then, "You may not be able to stop nothing from happening. But you got to let him know you's *there.*"

105 Two days later I was married, and then I was gone. And I had a lot of things on my mind and I pretty well forgot my promise to Mama until I got shipped home on a special furlough for her funeral.

And, after the funeral, with just Sonny and me alone in the empty kitchen, I tried to find out something about him.

"What do you want to do?" I asked him.

"I'm going to be a musician," he said.

For he had graduated, in the time I had been away, from dancing to the juke box to finding out who was playing what, and what they were doing with it, and he had bought himself a set of drums.

110 "You mean, you want to be a drummer?" I somehow had the feeling that being a drummer might be all right for other people but not for my brother Sonny.

"I don't think," he said, looking at me very gravely, "that I'll ever be a good drummer. But I think I can play a piano."

I frowned. I'd never played the role of the older brother quite so seriously before, had scarcely ever, in fact, *asked* Sonny a damn thing. I sensed myself in the presence of something I didn't really know how to handle, didn't understand. So I made my frown a little deeper as I asked: "What kind of musician do you want to be?"

He grinned. "How many kinds do you think there are?"

"Be *serious,*" I said.

115 He laughed, throwing his head back, and then looked at me. "I *am* serious."

"Well, then, for Christ's sake, stop kidding around and answer a serious question. I mean, do you want to be a concert pianist, you want to play classical music and all that, or—or what?" Long before I finished he was laughing again. "For Christ's *sake,* Sonny!"

He sobered, but with difficulty. "I'm sorry. But you sound so—*scared!*" and he was off again.

"Well, you may think it's funny now, baby, but it's not going to be so funny when you have to make your living at it, let me tell you *that.*" I was furious because I knew he was laughing at me and I didn't know why.

"No," he said, very sober now, and afraid, perhaps, that he'd hurt me, "I don't want to be a classical pianist. That isn't what interests me. I mean"—he paused, looking hard at me, as though his eyes would help me to understand, and then gestured helplessly, as though perhaps his hand would help—"I mean, I'll have a lot of studying to do, and I'll have to study *everything*, but I mean, I want to play *with*—jazz musicians." He stopped. "I want to play jazz," he said.

120 Well, the word had never before sounded as heavy, as real, as it sounded that afternoon in Sonny's mouth. I just looked at him and I was probably frowning a real frown by this time. I simply couldn't see why on earth he'd want to spend his time hanging around night clubs, clowning around on bandstands, while people pushed each other around a dance floor. It seemed—beneath him, somehow. I had never thought about it before, had never been forced to, but I suppose I had always put jazz musicians in a class with what Daddy called "good-time people."

"Are you *serious?*"

"Hell, *yes*, I'm serious."

He looked more helpless than ever, and annoyed, and deeply hurt.

I suggested, helpfully: "You mean—like Louis Armstrong?"

125 His face closed as though I'd struck him. "No. I'm not talking about none of that old-time, down home crap."

"Well, look, Sonny, I'm sorry, don't get mad. I just don't altogether get it, that's all. Name somebody—you know, a jazz musician you admire."

"Bird."

"Who?"

"Bird! Charlie Parker! Don't they teach you nothing in the goddamn army?"

130 I lit a cigarette. I was surprised and then a little amused to discover that I was trembling. "I've been out of touch," I said, "You'll have to be patient with me. Now. Who's this Parker character?"

"He's just one of the greatest jazz musicians alive," said Sonny, sullenly, his hands in his pockets, his back to me. "Maybe *the* greatest," he added, bitterly, "that's probably why *you* never heard of him."

"All right," I said. "I'm ignorant. I'm sorry. I'll go out and buy all the cat's records right away, all right?"

"It don't," said Sonny, with dignity, "make any difference to me. I don't care what you listen to. Don't do me no favors."

I was beginning to realize that I'd never seen him so upset before. With another part of my mind I was thinking that this would probably turn out to be one of those things kids go through and that I shouldn't make it seem important by pushing it too hard. Still, I didn't think it would do any harm to ask: "Doesn't all this take a lot of time? Can you make a living at it?"

135 He turned back to me and half leaned, half sat, on the kitchen table. "Everything takes time," he said, "and—well, yes, sure, I can make a living at it. But what I don't seem to be able to make you understand is that it's the only thing I want to do."

"Well Sonny," I said, gently, "you know people can't always do exactly what they *want* to do—"

"*No*, I don't know that," said Sonny, surprising me. "I think people *ought* to do what they want to do, what else are they alive for?"

"You getting to be a big boy," I said desperately, "it's time you started thinking about your future."

"I'm thinking about my future," said Sonny, grimly. "I think about it all the time."

I gave up. I decided, if he didn't change his mind, that we could always 140
talk about it later. "In the meantime," I said, "you got to finish school." We had already decided that he'd have to move in with Isabel and her folks. I knew this wasn't the ideal arrangement because Isabel's folks are inclined to be dicty and they hadn't especially wanted Isabel to marry me. But I didn't know what else to do. "And we have to get you fixed up at Isabel's."

There was a long silence. He moved from the kitchen table to the window. "That's a terrible idea. You know it yourself."

"Do you have a *better* idea?"

He just walked up and down the kitchen for a minute. He was as tall as I was. He had started to shave. I suddenly had the feeling that I didn't know him at all.

He stopped at the kitchen table and picked up my cigarettes. Looking at me with a kind of mocking, amused defiance, he put one between his lips. "You mind?"

"You smoking already?" 145

He lit the cigarette and nodded, watching me through the smoke. "I just wanted to see if I'd have the courage to smoke in front of you." He grinned and blew a great cloud of smoke to the ceiling. "It was easy." He looked at my face. "Come on, now. I bet you was smoking at my age, tell the truth."

I didn't say anything but the truth was on my face, and he laughed. But now there was something very strained in his laugh. "Sure. And I bet that ain't all you was doing."

He was frightening me a little. "Cut the crap," I said. "We already decided that you was going to go and live at Isabel's. Now what's got into you all of a sudden?"

"*You* decided it," he pointed out. "*I* didn't decide nothing." He stopped in front of me, leaning against the stove, arms loosely folded. "Look, brother. I don't want to stay in Harlem no more, I really don't." He was very earnest. He looked at me, then over toward the kitchen window. There was something in his eyes I'd never seen before, some thoughtfulness, some worry all his own. He rubbed the muscle of one arm. "It's time I was getting out of here."

"Where do you want to *go*, Sonny?" 150

"I want to join the army. Or the navy, I don't care. If I say I'm old enough they'll believe me."

Then I got mad. It was because I was so scared. "You must be crazy. You goddamn fool, what the hell do you want to go and join the *army* for?"

"I just told you. To get out of Harlem."

"Sonny, you haven't even finished *school.* And if you really want to be a musician, how do you expect to study if you're in the *army?*"

He looked at me, trapped, and in anguish. "There's ways. I might be able 155 to work out some kind of deal. Anyway, I'll have the G.I. Bill when I come out."

"*If* you come out." We stared at each other. "Sonny, please. Be reasonable. I know the setup is far from perfect. But we got to do the best we can."

"I ain't learning nothing in school," he said. "Even when I go." He turned away from me and opened the window and threw his cigarette out into the narrow alley. I watched his back. "At least, I ain't learning nothing you'd want me to learn." He slammed the window so hard I thought the glass would fly out, and turned back to me. "And I'm sick of the stink of these garbage cans!"

"Sonny," I said, "I know how you feel. But if you don't finish school now, you're going to be sorry later that you didn't." I grabbed him by the shoulders. "And you only got another year. It ain't so bad. And I'll come back and I swear I'll help you do *whatever* you want to do. Just try to put up with it till I come back. Will you please do that? For me?"

He didn't answer and he wouldn't look at me.

"Sonny. You hear me?" 160

He pulled away. "I hear you. But you never hear anything *I* say."

I didn't know what to say to that. He looked out of the window and then back at me. "OK," he said, and sighed. "I'll try."

Then I said, trying to cheer him up a little, "They got a piano at Isabel's. You can practice on it."

And as a matter of fact, it did cheer him up for a minute. "That's right," he said to himself. "I forgot that." His face relaxed a little. But the worry, the thoughtfulness, played on it still, the way shadows play on a face which is staring into the fire.

But I thought I'd never hear the end of that piano. At first, Isabel would 165 write me, saying how nice it was that Sonny was so serious about his music and how, as soon as he came in from school, or wherever he had been when he was supposed to be at school, he went straight to that piano and stayed there until suppertime. And, after supper, he went back to that piano and stayed there until everybody went to bed. He was at the piano all day Saturday and all day Sunday. Then he bought a record player and started playing records. He'd play one record over and over again, all day long sometimes, and he'd improvise along with it on the piano. Or he'd play one section of the record, one chord, one change, one progression, then he'd do it on the piano. Then back to the record. Then back to the piano.

Well, I really don't know how they stood it. Isabel finally confessed that it wasn't like living with a person at all, it was like living with sound. And the sound didn't make any sense to her, didn't make any sense to any of them—naturally. They began, in a way, to be afflicted by this presence that was living in their home. It was as though Sonny were some sort of god, or monster. He moved in an atmosphere which wasn't like theirs at all. They fed him and he ate, he washed himself, he walked in and out of their door; he certainly wasn't nasty or unpleasant or rude, Sonny isn't any of those things; but it was as though he were all wrapped up in some cloud, some fire, some vision all his own; and there wasn't any way to reach him.

At the same time, he wasn't really a man yet, he was still a child, and they had to watch out for him in all kinds of ways. They certainly couldn't throw him out. Neither did they dare to make a great scene about that piano because even they dimly sensed, as I sensed, from so many thousands of miles away, that Sonny was at that piano playing for his life.

But he hadn't been going to school. One day a letter came from the school board and Isabel's mother got it—there had, apparently, been other letters but Sonny had torn them up. This day, when Sonny came in, Isabel's mother showed him the letter and asked where he'd been spending his time. And she finally got it out of him that he'd been down in Greenwich Village, with musicians and other characters, in a white girl's apartment. And this scared her and she started to scream at him and what came up, once she began—though she denies it to this day—was what sacrifices they were making to give Sonny a decent home and how little he appreciated it.

Sonny didn't play the piano that day. By evening, Isabel's mother had calmed down but then there was the old man to deal with, and Isabel herself. Isabel says she did her best to be calm but she broke down and started crying. She says she just watched Sonny's face. She could tell, by watching him, what was happening with him. And what was happening was that they penetrated his cloud, they had reached him. Even if their fingers had been a thousand times more gentle than human fingers ever are, he could hardly help feeling that they had stripped him naked and were spitting on that nakedness. For he also had to see that his presence, that music, which was life or death to him, had been torture for them and that they had endured it, not at all for his sake, but only for mine. And Sonny couldn't take that. He can take it a little better today than he could then but he's still not very good at it and, frankly, I don't know anybody who is.

The silence of the next few days must have been louder than the sound of 170
all the music ever played since time began. One morning, before she went to work, Isabel was in his room for something and she suddenly realized that all of his records were gone. And she knew for certain that he was gone. And he was. He went as far as the navy would carry him. He finally sent me a postcard from some place in Greece and that was the first I knew that Sonny was still alive. I didn't see him any more until we were both back in New York and the war had long been over.

He was a man by then, of course, but I wasn't willing to see it. He came by the house from time to time, but we fought almost every time we met. I didn't like the way he carried himself, loose and dreamlike all the time, and I didn't like his friends, and his music seemed to be merely an excuse for the life he led. It sounded just that weird and disordered.

Then we had a fight, a pretty awful fight, and I didn't see him for months. By and by I looked him up, where he was living, in a furnished room in the Village, and I tried to make it up. But there were lots of other people in the room and Sonny just lay on his bed, and he wouldn't come downstairs with me, and he treated these other people as though they were his family and I weren't. So I got mad and then he got mad, and then I told him that he might just as well be dead as live the way he was living. Then he stood up and he told me not to worry about him any more in life, that he *was* dead as far as I was concerned. Then he pushed me to the door and the other people looked on as though nothing were happening, and he slammed the door behind me. I stood in the hallway, staring at the door. I heard somebody laugh in the room and then the tears came to my eyes. I started down the steps, whistling to keep from crying, I kept whistling to myself, *You going to need me, baby, one of these cold, rainy days.*

I read about Sonny's trouble in the spring. Little Grace died in the fall. She was a beautiful little girl. But she only lived a little over two years. She died of polio and she suffered. She had a slight fever for a couple of days, but it didn't seem like anything and we just kept her in bed. And we would certainly have called the doctor, but the fever dropped, she seemed to be all right. So we thought it had just been a cold. Then, one day, she was up, playing, Isabel was in the kitchen fixing lunch for the two boys when they'd come in from school, and she heard Grace fall down in the living room. When you have a lot of children you don't always start running when one of them falls, unless they start screaming or something. And, this time, Grace was quiet. Yet, Isabel says that when she heard that *thump* and then that silence, something happened in her to make her afraid. And she ran to the living room and there was little Grace on the floor, all twisted up and the reason she hadn't screamed was that she couldn't get her breath. And when she did scream, it was the worst sound, Isabel says, that she'd ever heard in all her life, and she still hears it sometimes in her dreams. Isabel will sometimes wake me up with a low, moaning, strangled sound and I have to be quick to awaken her and hold her to me and where Isabel is weeping against me seems a mortal wound.

I think I may have written Sonny the very day that little Grace was buried. I was sitting in the living room in the dark, by myself, and I suddenly thought of Sonny. My trouble made his real.

One Saturday afternoon, when Sonny had been living with us, or, anyway, 175
been in our house, for nearly two weeks, I found myself wandering aimlessly about the living room, drinking from a can of beer, and trying to work up the courage to search Sonny's room. He was out, he was usually out whenever I was home, and Isabel had taken the children to see their grandparents. Suddenly I was standing still in front of the living room window, watching Seventh Avenue. The idea of searching Sonny's room made me still. I scarcely dared to admit to myself what I'd be searching for. I didn't know what I'd do if I found it. Or if I didn't.

On the sidewalk across from me, near the entrance to a barbecue joint, some people were holding an old-fashioned revival meeting. The barbecue cook, wearing a dirty white apron, his conked hair reddish and metallic in the pale sun, and a cigarette between his lips, stood in the doorway, watching them. Kids and older people paused in their errands and stood there, along with some older men and a couple of very tough-looking women who watched everything that happened on the avenue, as though they owned it, or were maybe owned by it. Well, they were watching this, too. The revival was being carried on by three sisters in black, and a brother. All they had were their voices and their Bibles and a tambourine. The brother was testifying and while he testified two of the sisters stood together, seeming to say, Amen, and the third sister walked around with the tambourine outstretched and a couple of people dropped coins into it. Then the brother's testimony ended and the sister who had been taking up the collection dumped the coins into her palm and transferred them to the pocket of her long black robe. Then she raised both hands, striking the tambourine against the air, and then against one hand, and she started to sing. And the two other sisters and the brother joined in.

It was strange, suddenly, to watch, though I had been seeing these street meetings all my life. So, of course, had everybody else down there. Yet, they paused and watched and listened and I stood still at the window. *"Tis the old ship of Zion,"* they sang, and the sister with the tambourine kept a steady, jangling beat, *"It has rescued many a thousand!"* Not a soul under the sound of their voices was hearing this song for the first time, not one of them had been rescued. Nor had they seen much in the way of rescue work being done around them. Neither did they especially believe in the holiness of the three sisters and the brother, they knew too much about them, knew where they lived, and how. The woman with the tambourine, whose voice dominated the air, whose face was bright with joy, was divided by very little from the woman who stood watching her, a cigarette between her heavy, chapped lips, her hair a cuckoo's nest, her face scarred and swollen from many beatings, and her black eyes glittering like coal. Perhaps they both knew this, which was why, when, as rarely, they addressed each other, they addressed each other as Sister. As the singing filled the air the watching, listening faces underwent a change, the eyes focusing on something within; the music seemed to soothe a poison out of them; and time seemed, nearly, to fall away from the sullen, belligerent, battered faces, as though they were fleeing back to their first condition, while dreaming of their last. The barbecue cook half shook his head and smiled, and dropped his cigarette and disappeared into his joint. A man fumbled in his pockets for change and stood holding it in his hand impatiently, as though he had just remembered a pressing appointment further up the avenue. He looked furious. Then I saw Sonny, standing on the edge of the crowd. He was carrying a wide, flat notebook with a green cover, and it made him look, from where I was standing, almost like a schoolboy. The coppery sun brought out the copper in his skin, he was very faintly smiling, standing very still. Then the singing stopped, the tambourine turned into a collection plate again. The furious man dropped in his coins and vanished, so did a couple of the women, and Sonny dropped some change in the plate, looking directly at the woman with a little smile. He started across the avenue, toward the house. He has a slow, loping walk, something like the way Harlem hipsters walk, only he's imposed on this his own halfbeat. I had never really noticed it before.

I stayed at the window, both relieved and apprehensive. As Sonny disappeared from my sight, they began singing again. And they were still singing when his key turned in the lock.

"Hey," he said.

"Hey, yourself. You want some beer?"

"No. Well, maybe." But he came up to the window and stood beside me, looking out. "What a warm voice," he said.

They were singing *If I could only hear my mother pray again!*

"Yes," I said, "and she can sure beat that tambourine."

"But what a terrible song," he said, and laughed. He dropped his notebook on the sofa and disappeared into the kitchen. "Where's Isabel and the kids?"

"I think they went to see their grandparents. You hungry?"

"No." He came back into the living room with his can of beer. "You want to come some place with me tonight?"

I sensed, I don't know how, that I couldn't possibly say No. "Sure. Where?"

He sat down on the sofa and picked up his notebook and started leafing through it. "I'm going to sit in with some fellows in a joint in the Village."

"You mean, you're going to play, tonight?"

"That's right." He took a swallow of his beer and moved back to the window. He gave me a sidelong look. "If you can stand it."

"I'll try," I said.

He smiled to himself and we both watched as the meeting across the way broke up. The three sisters and the brother, heads bowed, were singing *God be with you till we meet again.* The faces around them were very quiet. Then the song ended. The small crowd dispersed. We watched the three women and the lone man walk slowly up the avenue.

"When she was singing before," said Sonny, abruptly, "her voice reminded me for a minute of what heroin feels like sometimes—when it's in your veins. It makes you feel sort of warm and cool at the same time. And distant. And—and sure." He sipped his beer, very deliberately not looking at me. I watched his face. "It makes you feel—in control. Sometimes you've got to have that feeling."

"Do you?" I sat down slowly in the easy chair.

"Sometimes." He went to the sofa and picked up his notebook again. "Some people do."

"In order," I asked, "to play?" And my voice was very ugly, full of contempt and anger.

"Well"—he looked at me with great, troubled eyes, as though, in fact, he hoped his eyes would tell me things he could never otherwise say—"they *think* so. And *if* they think so—!"

"And what do *you* think?" I asked.

He sat on the sofa and put his can of beer on the floor. "I don't know," he said, and I couldn't be sure if he were answering my question or pursuing his thoughts. His face didn't tell me. "It's not so much to *play*. It's to *stand* it, to be able to make it at all. On any level." He frowned and smiled: "In order to keep from shaking to pieces."

"But these friends of yours," I said, "they seem to shake themselves to pieces pretty goddamn fast." 200

"Maybe." He played with the notebook. And something told me that I should curb my tongue, that Sonny was doing his best to talk, that I should listen. "But of course you only know the ones that've gone to pieces. Some don't—or at least they haven't *yet* and that's just about all *any* of us can say." He paused. "And then there are some who just live, really, in hell, and they know it and they see what's happening and they go right on. I don't know." He sighed, dropped the notebook, folded his arms. "Some guys, you can tell from the way they play, they on something *all* the time. And you can see that, well, it makes something real for them. But of course," he picked up his beer from the floor and sipped it and put the can down again, "they *want* to, too, you've got to see that. Even some of them that say they don't—*some*, not all."

"And what about you?" I asked—I couldn't help it. "What about you? Do *you* want to?"

He stood up and walked to the window and remained silent for a long time. Then he sighed. "Me," he said. Then: "While I was downstairs before, on my way here, listening to that woman sing, it struck me all of a sudden how much suffering she must have had to go through—to sing like that. It's *repulsive* to think you have to suffer that much."

I said: "But there's no way not to suffer—is there, Sonny?"

"I believe not," he said, and smiled, "but that's never stopped anyone from trying." He looked at me. "Has it?" I realized, with this mocking look, that there stood between us, forever, beyond the power of time or forgiveness, the fact that I had held silence—so long!— when he had needed human speech to help him. He turned back to the window. "No, there's no way not to suffer. But you try all kinds of ways to keep from drowning in it, to keep on top of it, and to make it seem—well, like *you*. Like you did something, all right, and now you're suffering for it. You know?" I said nothing. "Well you know," he said, impatiently, "why *do* people suffer? Maybe it's better to do something to give it a reason, *any* reason." 205

"But we just agreed," I said, "that there's no way not to suffer. Isn't it better, then, just to—take it?"

"But nobody just takes it," Sonny cried, "that's what I'm telling you! *Everybody* tries not to. You're just hung up on the *way* some people try—it's not *your* way!"

The hair on my face began to itch, my face felt wet. "That's not true," I said, "that's not true. I don't give a damn what other people do, I don't even care how they suffer. I just care how *you* suffer." And he looked at me. "Please believe me," I said, "I don't want to see you—die—trying not to suffer."

"I won't," he said, flatly, "die trying not to suffer. At least, not any faster than anybody else."

"But there's no need," I said, trying to laugh, "is there? in killing yourself." 210

I wanted to say more, but I couldn't. I wanted to talk about will power and how life could be—well, beautiful. I wanted to say that it was all within; but was it? or, rather, wasn't that exactly the trouble? And I wanted to promise that I would never fail him again. But it would all have sounded—empty words and lies.

So I made the promise to myself and prayed that I would keep it.

"It's terrible sometimes, inside," he said, "that's what's the trouble. You walk these streets, black and funky and cold, and there's not really a living ass to talk to, and there's nothing shaking, and there's no way of getting it out—that storm inside. You can't talk it and you can't make love with it, and when you finally try to get with it and play it, you realize *nobody's* listening. So *you've* got to listen. You got to find a way to listen."

And then he walked away from the window and sat on the sofa again, as though all the wind had suddenly been knocked out of him. "Sometimes you'll do *anything* to play, even cut your mother's throat." He laughed and looked at me. "Or your brother's." Then he sobered. "Or your own." Then: "Don't worry. I'm all right now and I think I'll *be* all right. But I can't forget—where I've been. I don't mean just the physical place I've been, I mean where I've *been*. And *what* I've been."

"What have you been, Sonny?" I asked.

He smiled—but sat sideways on the sofa, his elbow resting on the back, his fingers playing with his mouth and chin, not looking at me. "I've been something I didn't recognize, didn't know I could be. Didn't know anybody could be." He stopped, looking inward, looking helplessly young, looking old. "I'm not talking about it now because I feel *guilty* or anything like that—maybe it would be better if I did, I don't know. Anyway, I can't really talk about it. Not to you, not to anybody," and now he turned and faced me. "Sometimes, you know, and it was actually when I was most *out* of the world, I felt that I was in it, and that I was *with* it, really, and I could play or I didn't really have to *play*, it just came out of me, it was there. And I don't know how I played, thinking about it now, but I know I did awful things, those times, sometimes, to people. Or it wasn't that I *did* anything to them—it was that they weren't real." He picked up the beer can; it was empty; he rolled it between his palms: "And other times—well, I needed a fix, I needed to find a place to lean, I needed to clear a space to *listen*—and I couldn't find it, and I—went crazy, I did terrible things to *me*, I was terrible *for* me." He began pressing the beer can between his hands, I watched the metal begin to give. It glittered, as he played with it, like a knife, and I was afraid he would cut himself, but I said nothing. "Oh well. I can never tell you. I was all by myself at the bottom of something, stinking and sweating and crying and shaking, and I smelled it, you know? *my* stink, and I thought I'd die if I couldn't get away from it and yet, all the same, I knew that everything I was doing was just locking me in with it. And I didn't know," he paused, still flattening the beer can, "I didn't know, I still *don't* know, something kept telling me that maybe it was good to smell your own stink, but I didn't think that *that* was what I'd been trying to do—and—who can stand it?" and he abruptly dropped the ruined beer can, looking at me with a small, still smile, and then rose, walking to the window as though it were the lodestone rock. I watched his face, he watched the avenue. "I couldn't tell you when Mama died—but the reason I wanted to leave Harlem so bad was to get away from drugs. And then, when I ran away, that's what I was running from—really. When I came back, nothing had changed, *I* hadn't changed, I was just—older." And he stopped, drumming with his fingers on the windowpane. The sun had vanished, soon darkness would fall. I watched his face. "It can come again," he said, almost as though speaking to himself. Then he turned to me. "It can come again," he repeated. "I just want you to know that."

"All right," I said, at last. "So it can come again. All right."

He smiled, but the smile was sorrowful. "I had to try to tell you," he said.

"Yes," I said. "I understand that."

"You're my brother," he said, looking straight at me, and not smiling 220
at all.

"Yes," I repeated, "yes. I understand that."

He turned back to the window, looking out. "All that hatred down there," he said, "all that hatred and misery and love. It's a wonder it doesn't blow the avenue apart."

We went to the only night club on a short, dark street, downtown. We squeezed through the narrow, chattering, jam-packed bar to the entrance of the big room, where the bandstand was. And we stood there for a moment, for the lights were very dim in this room and we couldn't see. Then, "Hello, boy," said a voice and an enormous black man, much older than Sonny or myself, erupted out of all that atmospheric lighting and put an arm around Sonny's shoulder. "I been sitting right here," he said, "waiting for you."

He had a big voice, too, and heads in the darkness turned toward us.

Sonny grinned and pulled a little away, and said, "Creole, this is my 225
brother. I told you about him."

Creole shook my hand. "I'm glad to meet you, son," he said, and it was clear that he was glad to meet me *there*, for Sonny's sake. And he smiled, "You got a real musician in *your* family," and he took his arm from Sonny's shoulder and slapped him, lightly, affectionately, with the back of his hand.

"Well. Now I've heard it all," said a voice behind us. This was another musician, and a friend of Sonny's, a coal-black, cheerful-looking man, built close to the ground. He immediately began confiding to me, at the top of his lungs, the most terrible things about Sonny, his teeth gleaming like a lighthouse and his laugh coming up out of him like the beginning of an earthquake. And it turned out that everyone at the bar knew Sonny, or almost everyone; some were musicians, working there, or nearby, or not working, some were simply hangers-on, and some were there to hear Sonny play. I was introduced to all of them and they were all very polite to me. Yet, it was clear that, for them, I was only Sonny's brother. Here, I was in Sonny's world. Or, rather: his kingdom. Here, it was not even a question that his veins bore royal blood.

They were going to play soon and Creole installed me, by myself, at a table in a dark corner. Then I watched them, Creole, and the little black man, and Sonny, and the others, while they horsed around, standing just below the bandstand. The light from the bandstand spilled just a little short of them and, watching them laughing and gesturing and moving about, I had the feeling that they, nevertheless, were being most careful not to step into that circle of light too suddenly: that if they moved into the light too suddenly, without thinking, they would perish in flame. Then, while I watched, one of them, the small, black man, moved into the light and crossed the bandstand and started fooling around with his drums. Then—being funny and being, also, extremely ceremonious—Creole took Sonny by the arm and led him to the piano. A woman's voice called Sonny's name and a few hands started clapping. And Sonny, also being funny and being ceremonious, and so touched, I think, that he could have cried, but neither hiding it nor showing it, riding it like a man, grinned, and put both hands to his heart and bowed from the waist.

Creole then went to the bass fiddle and a lean, very bright-skinned brown man jumped up on the bandstand and picked up his horn. So there they were, and the atmosphere on the bandstand and in the room began to change and tighten. Someone stepped up to the microphone and announced them. Then there were all kinds of murmurs. Some people at the bar shushed others. The waitress ran around, frantically getting in the last orders, guys and chicks got closer to each other, and the lights on the bandstand, on the quartet, turned to a kind of indigo. Then they all looked different there. Creole looked about him for the last time, as though he were making certain that all his chickens were in the coop, and then he—jumped and struck the fiddle. And there they were.

All I know about music is that not many people ever really hear it. And 230
even then, on the rare occasions when something opens within, and the music enters, what we mainly hear, or hear corroborated, are personal private, vanishing evocations. But the man who creates the music is hearing something else, is dealing with the roar rising from the void and imposing order on it as it hits the air. What is evoked in him, then, is of another order, more terrible because it has no words, and triumphant, too, for that same reason. And his triumph, when he triumphs, is ours. I just watched Sonny's face. His face was troubled, he was working hard, but he wasn't with it. And I had the feeling that, in a way, everyone on the bandstand was waiting for him, both waiting for him and pushing him along. But as I began to watch Creole, I realized that it was Creole who held them all back. He had them on a short rein. Up there, keeping the beat with his whole body, wailing on the fiddle, with his eyes half closed, he was listening to everything, but he was listening to Sonny. He was having a dialogue with Sonny. He wanted Sonny to leave the shore line and strike out for the deep water. He was Sonny's witness that deep water and drowning were not the same thing—he had been there, and he knew. And he wanted Sonny to know. He was waiting for Sonny to do the things on the keys which would let Creole know that Sonny was in the water.

And, while Creole listened, Sonny moved, deep within, exactly like someone in torment. I had never before thought of how awful the relationship must be between the musician and his instrument. He has to fill it, this instrument, with the breath of life, his own. He has to make it do what he wants it to do. And a piano is just a piano. It's made out of so much wood and wires and little hammers and big ones, and ivory. While there's only so much you can do with it, the only way to find this out is to try and make it do everything.

And Sonny hadn't been near a piano for over a year. And he wasn't on much better terms with his life, not the life that stretched before him now. He and the piano stammered, started one way, got scared, stopped; started another way, panicked, marked time, started again; then seemed to have found a direction, panicked again, got stuck. And the face I saw on Sonny I'd never seen before. Everything had been burned out of it, and, at the same time, things usually hidden were being burned in, by the fire and fury of the battle which was occurring in him up there.

Yet, watching Creole's face as they neared the end of the first set, I had the feeling that something had happened, something I hadn't heard. Then they finished, there was scattered applause, and then, without an instant's warning, Creole started into something else, it was almost sardonic, it was *Am I Blue*. And, as though he commanded, Sonny began to play. Something began to happen. And Creole let out the reins. The dry, low, black man said something awful on the drums, Creole answered, and the drums talked back. Then the horn insisted, sweet and high, slightly detached perhaps, and Creole listened, commenting now and then, dry, and driving, beautiful and calm and old. Then they all came together again, and Sonny was part of the family again. I could tell this from his face. He seemed to have found, right there beneath his fingers, a damn brand-new piano. It seemed that he couldn't get over it. Then, for awhile, just being happy with Sonny, they seemed to be agreeing with him that brand-new pianos certainly were a gas.

Then Creole stepped forward to remind them that what they were playing was the blues. He hit something in all of them, he hit something in me, myself, and the music tightened and deepened, apprehension began to beat the air. Creole began to tell us what the blues were all about. They were not about anything very new. He and his boys up there were keeping it new, at the risk of ruin, destruction, madness, and death, in order to find new ways to make us listen. For, while the tale of how we suffer, and how we are delighted, and how we may triumph is never new, it always must be heard. There isn't any other tale to tell, it's the only light we've got in all this darkness.

And this tale, according to that face, that body, those strong hands on 235
those strings, has another aspect in every country, and a new depth in every generation. Listen, Creole seemed to be saying, listen. Now these are Sonny's blues. He made the little black man on the drums know it, and the bright, brown man on the horn. Creole wasn't trying any longer to get Sonny in the water. He was wishing him Godspeed. Then he stepped back, very slowly, filling the air with the immense suggestion that Sonny speak for himself.

Then they all gathered around Sonny and Sonny played. Every now and again one of them seemed to say, Amen. Sonny's fingers filled the air with life, his life. But that life contained so many others. And Sonny went all the way back, he really began with the spare, flat statement of the opening phrase of the song. Then he began to make it his. It was very beautiful because it wasn't hurried and it was no longer a lament. I seemed to hear with what burning he had made it his, with what burning we had yet to make it ours, how we could cease lamenting. Freedom lurked around us and I understood, at last, that he could help us to be free if we would listen, that he would never be free until we did. Yet, there was no battle in his face now. I heard what he had gone through, and would continue to go through until he came to rest in earth. He had made it his: that long line, of which we knew only Mama and Daddy. And he was giving it back, as everything must be given back, so that, passing through death, it can live forever. I saw my mother's face again, and felt, for the first time, how the stones of the road she had walked on must have bruised her feet. I saw the moonlit road where my father's brother died. And it brought something else back to me, and carried me past it, I saw my little girl again and felt Isabel's tears again, and I felt my own tears begin to rise. And I was yet aware that this was only a moment, that the world waited outside, as hungry as a tiger, and that trouble stretched above us, longer than the sky.

Then it was over. Creole and Sonny let out their breath, both soaking wet, and grinning. There was a lot of applause and some of it was real. In the dark, the girl came by and I asked her to take drinks to the bandstand. There was a long pause, while they talked up there in the indigo light and after awhile I saw the girl put a Scotch and milk on top of the piano for Sonny. He didn't seem to notice it, but just before they started playing again, he sipped from it and looked toward me, and nodded. Then he put it back on top of the piano. For me, then, as they began to play again, it glowed and shook above my brother's head like the very cup of trembling.

www

TOPICS FOR CRITICAL THINKING Web

1. What kinds of darkness surround the narrator?
2. In what ways is this story itself like the blues?
3. How are drugs and music alike?
4. How does the narrator envision the possibilities for social change?

www

TOPICS FOR CRITICAL WRITING Web

1. How are modes of escape in this story also methods of coping? Where is the line between self-destruction and salvation?
2. How does this story represent the world of urban African Americans and for what purposes?

Issues of Class

TILLIE OLSEN

I Stand Here Ironing

(1953–1954)

I stand here ironing, and what you asked me moves tormented back and forth with the iron.

"I wish you would manage the time to come in and talk with me about your daughter. I'm sure you can help me understand her. She's a youngster who needs help and whom I'm deeply interested in helping."

"Who needs help." Even if I came, what good would it do? You think because I am her mother I have a key, or that in some way you could use me as a key? She has lived for nineteen years. There is all that life that has happened outside of me, beyond me.

And when is there time to remember, to sift, to weigh, to estimate, to total? I will start and there will be an interruption and I will have to gather it all together again. Or I will become engulfed with all I did or did not do, with what should have been and what cannot be helped.

5 She was a beautiful baby. The first and only one of our five that was beautiful at birth. You do not guess how new and uneasy her tenancy in her now-loveliness. You did not know her all those years she was thought homely, or see her poring over her baby pictures, making me tell her over and over how beautiful she had been—and would be, I would tell her—and was now, to the seeing eye. But the seeing eyes were few or nonexistent. Including mine.

I nursed her. They feel that's important nowadays. I nursed all the children, but with her, with all the fierce rigidity of first motherhood, I did like the books then said. Though her cries battered me to trembling and my breasts ached with swollenness, I waited till the clock decreed.

Why do I put that first? I do not even know if it matters, or if it explains anything.

She was a beautiful baby. She blew shining bubbles of sound. She loved motion, loved light, loved color and music and textures. She would lie on the floor in her blue overalls patting the surface so hard in ecstasy her hands and feet would blur. She was a miracle to me, but when she was eight months old I had to leave her daytimes with the woman downstairs to whom she was no miracle at all, for I worked or looked for work and for Emily's father, who "could no longer endure" (he wrote in his good-bye note) "sharing want with us."

I was nineteen. It was the pre-relief, pre-WPA world of the depression. I would start running as soon as I got off the streetcar, running up the stairs, the place smelling sour, and awake or asleep to startle awake, when she saw me she would break into a clogged weeping that could not be comforted, a weeping I can hear yet.

10 After a while I found a job hashing at night so I could be with her days, and it was better. But it came to where I had to bring her to his family and leave her.

It took a long time to raise the money for her fare back. Then she got chicken pox and I had to wait longer. When she finally came, I hardly knew her, walking quick and nervous like her father, looking like her father, thin, and dressed in a shoddy red that yellowed her skin and glared at the pockmarks. All the baby loveliness gone.

She was two. Old enough for nursery school they said, and I did not know then what I know now—the fatigue of the long day, and the lacerations of group life in nurseries that are only parking places for children.

Except that it would have made no difference if I had known. It was the only place there was. It was the only way we could be together, the only way I could hold a job.

And even without knowing, I knew. I knew the teacher that was evil because all these years it has curdled into my memory, the little boy hunched in the corner, her rasp, "why aren't you outside, because Alvin hits you? that's no reason, go out, scaredy." I knew Emily hated it even if she did not clutch and implore "don't go Mommy" like the other children, mornings.

She always had a reason why we should stay home. Momma, you look 15
sick. Momma, I feel sick. Momma, the teachers aren't there today, they're sick. Momma, we can't go, there was a fire there last night. Momma, it's a holiday today, no school, they told me.

But never a direct protest, never rebellion. I think of our others in their three-, four-year-oldness—the explosions, the tempers, the denunciations, the demands—and I feel suddenly ill. I put the iron down. What in me demanded that goodness in her? And what was the cost, the cost to her of such goodness?

The old man living in the back once said in his gentle way: "You should smile at Emily more when you look at her." What *was* in my face when I looked at her? I loved her. There were all the acts of love.

It was only with the others I remembered what he said, and it was the face of joy, and not of care or tightness or worry I turned to them—too late for Emily. She does not smile easily, let alone almost always as her brothers and sisters do. Her face is closed and sombre, but when she wants, how fluid. You must have seen it in her pantomimes, you spoke of her rare gift for comedy on the stage that rouses a laughter out of the audience so dear they applaud and applaud and do not want to let her go.

Where does it come from, that comedy? There was none of it in her when she came back to me that second time, after I had had to send her away again. She had a new daddy now to learn to love, and I think perhaps it was a better time.

Except when we left her alone nights, telling ourselves she was old 20
enough.

"Can't you go some other time, Mommy, like tomorrow?" she would ask. "Will it be just a little while you'll be gone? Do you promise?"

The time we came back, the front door open, the clock on the floor in the hall. She rigid awake. "It wasn't just a little while. I didn't cry. Three times I called you, just three times, and then I ran downstairs to open the door so you could come faster. The clock talked loud. I threw it away, it scared me what it talked."

She said the clock talked loud again that night I went to the hospital to have Susan. She was delirious with the fever that comes before red measles, but she was fully conscious all the week I was gone and the week after we were home when she could not come near the new baby or me.

She did not get well. She stayed skeleton thin, not wanting to eat, and night after night she had nightmares. She would call for me, and I would rouse from exhaustion to sleepily call back: "You're all right, darling, go to sleep, it's just a dream," and if she still called, in a sterner voice, "now go to sleep, Emily, there's nothing to hurt you." Twice, only twice, when I had to get up for Susan anyhow, I went in to sit with her.

Now when it is too late (as if she would let me hold and comfort her like 25

I do the others) I get up and go to her at once at her moan or restless stirring. "Are you awake, Emily? Can I get you something?" And the answer is always the same: "No, I'm all right, go back to sleep, Mother."

They persuaded me at the clinic to send her away to a convalescent home in the country where "she can have the kind of food and care you can't manage for her, and you'll be free to concentrate on the new baby." They still send children to that place. I see pictures on the society page of sleek young women planning affairs to raise money for it, or dancing at the affairs, or decorating Easter eggs or filling Christmas stockings for the children.

They never have a picture of the children so I do not know if the girls still wear those gigantic red bows and the ravaged looks on the every other Sunday when parents can come to visit "unless otherwise notified"—as we were notified the first six weeks.

Oh it is a handsome place, green lawns and tall trees and fluted flower beds. High up on the balconies of each cottage the children stand, the girls in their red bows and white dresses, the boys in white suits and giant red ties. The parents stand below shrieking up to be heard and the children shriek down to be heard, and between them the invisible wall "Not To Be Contaminated by Parental Germs or Physical Affection."

There was a tiny girl who always stood hand in hand with Emily. Her parents never came. One visit she was gone. "They moved her to Rose College," Emily shouted in explanation. "They don't like you to love anybody here."

She wrote once a week, the labored writing of a seven-year-old. "I am fine. How is the baby. If I write my leter nicly I will have a star. Love." There never was a star. We wrote every other day, letters she could never hold or keep but only hear read—once. "We simply do not have room for children to keep any personal possessions," they patiently explained when we pieced one Sunday's shrieking together to plead how much it would mean to Emily, who loved so to keep things, to be allowed to keep her letters and cards.

Each visit she looked frailer. "She isn't eating," they told us.

(They had runny eggs for breakfast or mush with lumps, Emily said later, I'd hold it in my mouth and not swallow. Nothing ever tasted good, just when they had chicken.)

It took us eight months to get her released home, and only the fact that she gained back so little of her seven lost pounds convinced the social worker.

I used to try to hold and love her after she came back, but her body would stay stiff, and after a while she'd push away. She ate little. Food sickened her, and I think much of life too. Oh she had physical lightness and brightness, twinkling by on skates, bouncing like a ball up and down up and down over the jump rope, skimming over the hill; but these were momentary.

She fretted about her appearance, thin and dark and foreign-looking at a time when every little girl was supposed to look or thought she should look a chubby blonde replica of Shirley Temple. The doorbell sometimes rang for her, but no one seemed to come and play in the house or be a best friend. Maybe because we moved so much.

There was a boy she loved painfully through two school semesters. Months later she told me how she had taken pennies from my purse to buy him candy. "Licorice was his favorite and I brought him some every day, but he still liked Jennifer better'n me. Why, Mommy?" The kind of question for which there is no answer.

School was a worry to her. She was not glib or quick in a world where glibness and quickness were easily confused with ability to learn. To her overworked and exasperated teachers she was an over-conscientious "slow learner" who kept trying to catch up and was absent entirely too often.

I let her be absent, though sometimes the illness was imaginary. How different from my now-strictness about attendance with the others. I wasn't working. We had a new baby, I was home anyhow. Sometimes, after Susan grew old enough, I would keep her home from school, too, to have them all together.

Mostly Emily had asthma, and her breathing, harsh and labored, would fill the house with a curiously tranquil sound. I would bring the two old dresser mirrors and her boxes of collections to her bed. She would select beads and single earrings, bottle tops and shells, dried flowers and pebbles, old postcards and scraps, all sorts of oddments; then she and Susan would play Kingdom, setting up landscapes and furniture, peopling them with action.

Those were the only times of peaceful companionship between her and Susan. I have edged away from it, that poisonous feeling between them, that terrible balancing of hurts and needs I had to do between the two, and did so badly, those earlier years.

Oh there are conflicts between the others too, each one human, needing, demanding, hurting, taking—but only between Emily and Susan, no, Emily toward Susan that corroding resentment. It seems so obvious on the surface, yet it is not obvious. Susan, the second child, Susan, golden- and curly-haired and chubby, quick and articulate and assured, everything in appearance and manner Emily was not; Susan, not able to resist Emily's precious things, losing or sometimes clumsily breaking them; Susan telling jokes and riddles to company for applause while Emily sat silent (to say to me later: that was *my* riddle, Mother, I told it to Susan); Susan, who for all the five years' difference in age was just a year behind Emily in developing physically.

I am glad for that slow physical development that widened the difference between her and her contemporaries, though she suffered over it. She was too vulnerable for that terrible world of youthful competition, of preening and parading, of constant measuring of yourself against every other, of envy, "If I had that copper hair," "If I had that skin. . . ." She tormented herself enough about not looking like the others, there was enough of the unsureness, the having to be conscious of words before you speak, the constant caring—what are they thinking of me? without having it all magnified by the merciless physical drives.

Ronnie is calling. He is wet and I change him. It is rare there is such a cry now. That time of motherhood is almost behind me when the ear is not one's own but must always be racked and listening for the child cry, the child call. We sit for a while and I hold him, looking out over the city spread in charcoal with its soft aisles of light. "*Shoogily,*" he breathes and curls closer. I carry him back to bed, asleep. *Shoogily.* A funny word, a family word, inherited from Emily, invented by her to say: *comfort.*

In this and other ways she leaves her seal, I say aloud. And startle at my saying it. What do I mean? What did I start to gather together, to try and make coherent? I was at the terrible, growing years. War years. I do not remember them well. I was working, there were four smaller ones now, there was not time for her. She had to help be a mother, and housekeeper, and shopper. She had to set her seal. Mornings of crisis and near hysteria trying to get lunches packed, hair combed, coats and shoes found, everyone to school or Child Care on time, the baby ready for transportation. And always the paper scribbled on by a smaller one, the book looked at by Susan then mislaid, the homework not done. Running out to that huge school where she was one, she was lost, she was a drop; suffering over the unpreparedness, stammering and unsure in her classes.

There was so little time left at night after the kids were bedded down. She 45
would struggle over books, always eating (it was in those years she developed her enormous appetite that is legendary in our family) and I would be ironing, or preparing food for the next day, or writing V-mail to Bill, or tending the baby. Sometimes, to make me laugh, or out of her despair, she would imitate happenings or types at school.

I think I said once: "Why don't you do something like this in the school amateur show?" One morning she phoned me at work, hardly understandable through the weeping: "Mother, I did it. I won, I won; they gave me first prize; they clapped and clapped and wouldn't let me go."

Now suddenly she was Somebody, and as imprisoned in her difference as she had been in anonymity.

She began to be asked to perform at other high schools, even in colleges, then at city and statewide affairs. The first one we went to, I only recognized her that first moment when thin, shy, she almost drowned herself into the curtains. Then: Was this Emily? The control, the command, the convulsing and deadly clowning, the spell, then the roaring, stamping audience, unwilling to let this rare and precious laughter out of their lives.

Afterwards: You ought to do something about her with a gift like that— but without money or knowing how, what does one do? We have left it all to her, and the gift has as often eddied inside, clogged and clotted, as been used and growing.

She is coming. She runs up the stairs two at a time with her light graceful 50
step, and I know she is happy tonight. Whatever it was that occasioned your call did not happen today.

"Aren't you ever going to finish the ironing, Mother? Whistler painted his mother in a rocker. I'd have to paint mine standing over an ironing board." This is one of her communicative nights and she tells me everything and nothing as she fixes herself a plate of food out of the icebox.

She is so lovely. Why did you want me to come in at all? Why were you concerned? She will find her way.

She starts up the stairs to bed. "Don't get me up with the rest in the morning." "But I thought you were having midterms." "Oh, those," she comes back in, kisses me, and says quite lightly, "in a couple of years when we'll all be atom-dead they won't matter a bit."

She has said it before. She *believes* it. But because I have been dredging the past, and all that compounds a human being is so heavy and meaningful in me, I cannot endure it tonight.

55 I will never total it all. I will never come in to say: She was a child seldom smiled at. Her father left me before she was a year old. I had to work her first six years when there was work, or I sent her home and to his relatives. There were years she had care she hated. She was dark and thin and foreign-looking in a world where the prestige went to blondeness and curly hair and dimples, she was slow where glibness was prized. She was a child of anxious, not proud, love. We were poor and could not afford for her the soil of easy growth. I was a young mother, I was a distracted mother. There were the other children pushing up, demanding. Her younger sister seemed all that she was not. There were years she did not want me to touch her. She kept too much in herself, her life was such she had to keep too much in herself. My wisdom came too late. She has much to her and probably nothing will come of it. She is a child of her age, of depression, of war, of fear.

Let her be. So all that is in her will not bloom—but in how many does it? There is still enough left to live by. Only help her to know—help make it so there is cause for her to know—that she is more than this dress on the ironing board, helpless before the iron.

TILLIE OLSEN

www

(b. 1913?) **Web**

A single mother with four children, Olsen began to write in the 1930s. She was awarded a Guggenheim Fellowship.

www

TOPICS FOR CRITICAL THINKING **Web**

1. Why is this story framed with a request that the narrator come in and discuss the daughter?
2. In what ways does this story question mainstream ideas about hard work and family?
3. What alternative possibilities to middle class notions of parenting does the narrator offer?

www

TOPICS FOR CRITICAL WRITING **Web**

1. What are the connections between ironing and storytelling?
2. What norms does the story bring into question? How does it accomplish this questioning?

Part II
Image, Style, Structure

8 Reading Image and Style Closely

"Sarrasine," a story written by Honoré de Balzac, is one of the most closely analyzed stories in the history of literary criticism. Full of rich, enigmatic images and puzzles about gender and history, "Sarrasine" is the focus of Roland
www Barthes's comprehensive analysis in *S/Z* (1970). Web Barthes, an influential critic and literary theorist, helped enlist new ways of analyzing both literature and culture. The thoroughness of Barthes's reading (which does not even pretend to be complete) illustrates how stories are comprised of many interconnected and elaborate sign systems (systems such as fashion, food, social customs, and courtesy, in addition to language and literary conventions).

Analyzing the formal elements of fiction (character, setting, plot, narrator, point of view, and theme) helps readers understand what a story is "about." But studying a story's use of images and style increases our understanding of the story's *art*—what it says, how it says it, and how form and content relate to one another. Studying imagery and style often engages readers in a more detailed examination of a story. This might make the task of interpretation more complicated, but it also shows how intricate and complex stories really are. To understand how image, language, and structure work together with a story's other formal elements requires a painstaking scrutiny of the text. It also requires a more sophisticated understanding of language. The purpose of such an analysis is to discover how all the elements of a text work together *as a story*.

Much of what Barthes discerns in his study of "Sarrasine" is based on the connotative qualities of the words that appear in the text. Words both refer to something specific (they denote) and suggest associations, contexts, or shades of meaning (they connote). For example, the word *tycoon* denotes a very rich man, while it connotes a specific kind of rich man who has accumulated vast wealth through corporate dealings. Because all of the words in a story both denote and connote, a story's language is a rich site of multiple and often ambivalent and conflicting meanings. While Barthes demonstrates how this happens in "Sarrasine," it happens in all fiction. In Nathaniel Hawthorne's "The Birthmark," for example, the narrator refers to the birthmark as a "mark," an "impress," and a "stain." Though they all denote the same thing, each of these words connotes something slightly different—"mark" connoting the addition of a spot, "impress" connoting that the spot had been formed by something touching the heroine's cheek, and "stain" suggesting something slightly shameful or dirty. In "The Birthmark," these differing connotations represent different opinions about the birthmark's beauty.

Studying the shades of meaning in a story's language in relation to its images and ideas helps critics and readers define subsystems within the story. **Subsystems** are a way of understanding how different aspects of a story both break down into coherent groups and fit together. They are different for every story. For example, in the young boxer's story presented in the Introduction, the politics and rules of boxing might form one subsystem, while the racial and class positions of the various characters might form another. These subsystems come together in the boxing match, which gains part of its impact from the clash of underdog and champion, black man and white man. A primary subsystem in "The Birthmark" is the many interpretations of the birthmark itself. When the birthmark comes up against the story's subsystem of science, both the birthmark and its bearer are destroyed. Subsystems combine with the story's obvious or surface elements of plot, characterization, and setting to reveal the larger system of the story—its preoccupations, conflicts, issues, and the ways it represents them. What Barthes's analysis of "Sarrasine" shows is that the choices that make up the story are not at all random. Rather, they constitute a multilayered architecture constructed with the balanced tensions characteristic of a gothic arch or an extension bridge.

Critical Perspective: Semiotics Web

www

The method Barthes uses to analyze stories is known as *semiotics*. **Semiotics** is the study of how various signs (or signifiers) relate to one another in complex webs of meaning. Semiotics is the study of both what signs are and how they work together. Signs consist of anything from words, names, and road signs to gestures, objects, and social conventions. A simple example of a sign system is how the shapes of road signs tell us what the sign says—the triangular yield sign, octagonal stop sign, shield-like route sign, and so on. A more complex example is the system of signs that signal ways to understand a movie—for example, camera angles and methods of editing. We understand that when an image fades out, time passes; when the camera focuses on a detail, this detail will play an important role in the story.

Written in 1830, Balzac's "Sarrasine" is part of his large series of stories and novels called *La Comédie Humaine*. Like the American authors who would follow him, Balzac was a realist, describing with unsentimental detail the more than two thousand named characters that appear throughout his work.

HONORÉ DE BALZAC

Translated by Richard Miller

Sarrasine *(1830)*

I was deep in one of those daydreams which overtake even the shallowest of men, in the midst of the most tumultuous parties. Midnight had just sounded from the clock of the Elysée-Bourbon. Seated in a window recess and hidden behind the sinuous folds of a silk curtain, I could contemplate at my leisure the garden of the mansion where I was spending the evening. The trees, partially covered with snow, stood out dimly against the grayish background of a cloudy sky, barely whitened by the moon. Seen amid these fantastic surroundings, they vaguely resembled ghosts half out of their shrouds, a gigantic representation of the famous Dance of the Dead. Then, turning in the other direction, I could admire the Dance of the Living! a splendid salon decorated in silver and gold, with glittering chandeliers, sparkling with candles. There, milling about, whirling around, flitting here and there, were the most beautiful women of Paris, the richest, the noblest, dazzling, stately, resplendent with diamonds, flowers in their hair, on their bosoms, on their heads, strewn over dresses or in garlands at their feet. Light, rustling movements, voluptuous steps, made the laces, the silk brocades, the gauzes, float around their delicate forms. Here and there, some overly animated glances darted forth, eclipsing the lights, the fire of the diamonds, and stimulated anew some too-ardent hearts. One might also catch movements of the head meaningful to lovers, and negative gestures for husbands. The sudden outburst of the gamblers' voices at each unexpected turn of the dice, the clink of gold, mingled with the music and the murmur of conversation, and to complete the giddiness of this mass of people intoxicated by everything seductive the world can hold, a haze of perfume and general inebriation played upon the fevered mind. Thus, on my right, the dark and silent image of death; on my left, the seemly bacchanalias of life: here, cold nature, dull, in mourning; there, human beings enjoying themselves. On the borderline between these two so different scenes, which, a thousand times repeated in various guises, make Paris the world's most amusing and most philosophical city, I was making for myself a moral macédoine, half pleasant, half funereal. With my left foot I beat time, and I felt as though the other were in the grave. My leg was in fact chilled by one of those insidious drafts which freeze half our bodies while the other half feels the humid heat of rooms, an occurrence rather frequent at balls.

"Monsieur de Lanty hasn't owned this house for very long, has he?"

"Oh yes. Maréchal Carigliano sold it to him nearly ten years ago."

"Ah!"

"These people must have a huge fortune." 5

"They must have."

"What a party! It's shockingly elegant."

"Do you think they're as rich as M. de Nucingen or M. de Gondreville?"

"You mean you don't know?" . . .

I stuck my head out and recognized the two speakers as members of that 10
strange race which, in Paris, deals exclusively with "whys" and "hows," with "Where did they come from?" "What's happening?" "What has she done?" They lowered their voices and walked off to talk in greater comfort on some isolated sofa. Never had a richer vein been offered to seekers after mystery. Nobody knew what country the Lanty family came from, or from what business, what plunder, what piratical activity, or what inheritance derived a fortune estimated at several millions. All the members of the family spoke Italian,

French, Spanish, English, and German perfectly enough to create the belief that they must have spent a long time among these various peoples. Were they gypsies? Were they freebooters?

"Even if it's the devil," some young politicians said, "they give a marvelous party."

"Even if the Count de Lanty had robbed a bank, I'd marry his daughter any time!" cried a philosopher.

Who wouldn't have married Marianina, a girl of sixteen whose beauty embodied the fabled imaginings of the Eastern poets! Like the sultan's daughter, in the story of the Magic Lamp, she should have been kept veiled. Her singing put into the shade the partial talents of Malibran, Sontag, and Fodor, in whom one dominant quality has always excluded over-all perfection; whereas Marianina was able to bring to the same level purity of sound, sensibility, rightness of movement and pitch, soul and science, correctness and feeling. This girl was the embodiment of that secret poetry, the common bond among all the arts, which always eludes those who search for it. Sweet and modest, educated and witty, no one could eclipse Marianina, save her mother.

Have you ever encountered one of those women whose striking beauty defies the inroads of age and who seem at thirty-six more desirable than they could have been fifteen years earlier? Their visage is a vibrant soul, it glows; each feature sparkles with intelligence; each pore has a special brilliance, especially in artificial light. Their seductive eyes refuse, attract, speak or remain silent; their walk is innocently knowledgeable; their voices employ the melodious wealth of the most coquettishly soft and tender notes. Based on comparisons, their praises flatter the self-love of the most sentient. A movement of their eyebrows, the least glance, their pursed lips, fill with a kind of terror those whose life and happiness depend upon them. Inexperienced in love and influenced by words, a young girl can be seduced; for this kind of woman, however, a man must know, like M. de Jaucourt, not to cry out when he is hiding in a closet and the maid breaks two of his fingers as she shuts the door on them. In loving these powerful sirens, one gambles with one's life. And this, perhaps, is why we love them so passionately. Such was the Countess de Lanty.

Filippo, Marianina's brother, shared with his sister in the Countess's mar- 15
velous beauty. To be brief, this young man was a living image of Antinous, even more slender. Yet how well these thin, delicate proportions are suited to young people when an olive complexion, strongly defined eyebrows, and the fire of velvet eyes give promise of future male passion, of brave thoughts! If Filippo resided in every girl's heart as an ideal, he also resided in the memory of every mother as the best catch in France.

The beauty, the fortune, the wit, the charms of these two children, came solely from their mother. The Count de Lanty was small, ugly, and pockmarked; dark as a Spaniard, dull as a banker. However, he was taken to be a deep politician, perhaps because he rarely laughed, and was always quoting Metternich or Wellington.

This mysterious family had all the appeal of one of Lord Byron's poems, whose difficulties each person in the fashionable world interpreted in a different way: an obscure and sublime song in every strophe. The reserve maintained by M. and Mme de Lanty about their origin, their past life, and their relationship with the four corners of the globe had not lasted long as a subject of astonishment in Paris. Nowhere perhaps is Vespasian's axiom better understood. There, even bloodstained or filthy money betrays nothing and stands for everything. So long as high society knows the amount of your fortune, you are classed among those having an equal amount, and no one asks to see your family tree, because everyone knows how much it cost. In a city where social problems are solved like algebraic equations, adventurers have every opportunity in their favor. Even supposing this family were of gypsy origin, it was so wealthy, so attractive, that society had no trouble in forgiving its little secrets. Unfortunately, however, the mystery of the Lantys presented a continuing source of curiosity, rather like that contained in the novels of Ann Radcliffe.

Observers, people who make it a point to know in what shop you buy your candlesticks, or who ask the amount of your rent when they find your apartment attractive, had noticed, now and then, in the midst of the Countess's parties, concerts, balls, and routs, the appearance of a strange personage. It was a man. The first time he had appeared in the mansion was during a concert, when he seemed to have been drawn to the salon by Marianina's enchanting voice.

"All of a sudden, I'm cold," a lady had said who was standing with a friend by the door.

The stranger, who was standing next to the women, went away. 20

"That's odd! I'm warm now," she said, after the stranger had gone. "And you'll say I'm mad, but I can't help thinking that my neighbor, the man dressed in black who just left, was the cause of my chill."

Before long, the exaggeration native to those in high society gave birth to and accumulated the most amusing ideas, the most outrageous expressions, the most ridiculous anecdotes about this mysterious personage. Although not a vampire, a ghoul, or an artificial man, a kind of Faust or Robin Goodfellow, people fond of fantasy said he had something of all these anthropomorphic natures about him. Here and there, one came across some Germans who accepted as fact these clever witticisms of Parisian scandal-mongering. The stranger was merely an old man. Many of the young men who were in the habit of settling the future of Europe every morning in a few elegant phrases would have liked to see in this stranger some great criminal, the possessor of vast wealth. Some storytellers recounted the life of this old man and provided really curious details about the atrocities he had committed while in the service of the Maharaja of Mysore. Some bankers more positive by nature, invented a fable about money. "Bah," they said, shrugging their shoulders in pity, "this poor old man is a *tête génoise!*"

"Sir, without being indiscreet, could you please tell me what you mean by a *tête génoise?*"

"A man, sir, with an enormous lifetime capital and whose family's income doubtless depends on his good health."

I remember having heard at Mme d'Espard's a hypnotist proving on 25
highly suspect historical data that this old man, preserved under glass, was the famous Balsamo, known as Cagliostro. According to this contemporary al-

chemist, the Sicilian adventurer had escaped death and passed his time fabricating gold for his grandchildren. Last, the bailiff of Ferette maintained that he had recognized this odd personage as the Count of Saint-Germain. These stupidities, spoken in witty accents, with the mocking air characteristic of atheistic society in our day, kept alive vague suspicions about the Lanty family. Finally, through a strange combination of circumstances, the members of this family justified everyone's conjectures by behaving somewhat mysteriously toward this old man, whose life was somehow hidden from all investigation.

Whenever this person crossed the threshold of the room he was supposed to inhabit in the Lanty mansion, his appearance always created a great sensation among the family. One might have called it an event of great importance. Filippo, Marianina, Mme de Lanty, and an old servant were the only persons privileged to assist the old man in walking, arising, sitting down. Each of them watched over his slightest movement. It seemed that he was an enchanted being upon whom depended the happiness, the life, or the fortune of them all. Was it affection or fear? Those in society were unable to discover any clue to help them solve this problem. Hidden for whole months in the depths of a secret sanctuary, this family genie would suddenly come forth, unexpectedly, and would appear in the midst of the salons like those fairies of bygone days who descended from flying dragons to interrupt the rites to which they had not been invited. Only the most avid onlookers were then able to perceive the uneasiness of the heads of the house, who could conceal their feelings with unusual skill. Sometimes, however, while dancing a quadrille, Marianina, naïve as she was, would cast a terrified glance at the old man when she spied him among the crowd. Or else Filippo would slip quickly through the throng to his side and would stay near him, tender and attentive, as though contact with others or the slightest breath would destroy this strange creature. The Countess would make a point of drawing near, without seeming to have any intention of joining them; then, assuming a manner and expression of servitude mixed with tenderness, submission, and power, she would say a few words, to which the old man nearly always deferred, and he would disappear, led off, or, more precisely, carried off, by her. If Mme de Lanty were not present, the Count used a thousand stratagems to reach his side; however, he seemed to have difficulty making himself heard, and treated him like a spoiled child whose mother gives in to his whims in order to avoid a scene. Some bolder persons having thoughtlessly ventured to question the Count de Lanty, this cold, reserved man had appeared never to understand them. And so, after many tries, all futile because of the circumspection of the entire family, everyone stopped trying to fathom such a well-kept secret. Weary of trying, the companionable spies, the idly curious, and the politic all gave up bothering about this mystery.

However, even now perhaps in these glittering salons there were some philosophers who, while eating an ice or a sherbert, or placing their empty punch glass on a side table, were saying to each other: "It wouldn't surprise me to learn that those people are crooks. The old man who hides and only makes his appearance on the first day of spring or winter, or at the solstices, looks to me like a killer . . ."

"Or a confidence man . . ."

"It's almost the same thing. Killing a man's fortune is sometimes worse than killing the man."

"Sir, I have bet twenty louis, I should get back forty."

"But, sir, there are only thirty on the table."

"Ah well, you see how mixed the crowd is, here. It's impossible to play."

"True . . . But it's now nearly six months since we've seen the Spirit. Do you think he's really alive?"

"Hah! at best . . ."

These last words were spoken near me by people I did not know, as they were moving off, and as I was resuming, in an afterthought, my mixed thoughts of white and black, life and death. My vivid imagination as well as my eyes looked back and forth from the party, which had reached the height of its splendor, and the somber scene in the gardens. I do not know how long I meditated on these two faces of the human coin; but all at once I was awakened by the stifled laugh of a young woman. I was stunned by the appearance of the image which arose before me. By one of those tricks of nature, the half-mournful thought turning in my mind had emerged, and it appeared living before me, it had sprung like Minerva from the head of Jove, tall and strong, it was at once a hundred years old and twenty-two years old; it was alive and dead. Escaped from his room like a lunatic from his cell, the little old man had obviously slipped behind a hedge of people who were listening to Marianina's voice, finishing the cavatina from *Tancredi.* He seemed to have come out from underground, impelled by some piece of stage machinery. Motionless and somber, he stood for a moment gazing at the party, the noises of which had perhaps reached his ears. His almost somnambulatory preoccupation was so concentrated on things that he was in the world without seeing it. He had unceremoniously sprung up next to one of the most ravishing women in Paris, a young and elegant dancer, delicately formed, with one of those faces as fresh as that of a child, pink and white, so frail and transparent that a man's glance seems to penetrate it like a ray of sunlight going through ice. They were both there before me, together, united, and so close that the stranger brushed against her, her gauzy dress, her garlands of flowers, her softly curled hair, her floating sash.

I had brought this young woman to Mme de Lanty's ball. Since this was her first visit to the house, I forgave her her stifled laugh, but I quickly gave her a signal which completely silenced her and filled her with awe for her neighbor. She sat down next to me. The old man did not want to leave this lovely creature, to whom he had attached himself with that silent and seemingly baseless stubbornness to which the extremely old are prone, and which makes them appear childish. In order to sit near her, he had to take a folding chair. His slightest movements were full of that cold heaviness, the stupid indecision, characteristic of the gestures of a paralytic. He sat slowly down on his seat, with circumspection, muttering some unintelligible words. His worn-out voice was like the sound made by a stone falling down a well. The young woman held my hand tightly, as if seeking protection on some precipice, and she shivered when this man at whom she was looking turned upon her two eyes without warmth, glaucous eyes which could only be compared to dull mother-of-pearl.

"I'm afraid," she said, leaning toward my ear.

"You can talk," I answered. "He is very hard of hearing."

"Do you know him?"

"Yes."

Thereupon, she gathered up enough courage to look for a moment at this creature for which the human language had no name, a form without substance, a being without life, or a life without action. She was under the spell of that timorous curiosity which leads women to seek out dangerous emotions, to go see chained tigers, to look at boa constrictors, frightening themselves because they are separated from them only by weak fences. Although the little old man's back was stooped like a laborer's, one could easily tell that he must have had at one time a normal shape. His excessive thinness, the delicacy of his limbs, proved that he had always been slender. He was dressed in black silk trousers which fell about his bony thighs in folds, like an empty sail. An anatomist would have promptly recognized the symptoms of galloping consumption by looking at the skinny legs supporting this strange body. You would have said they were two bones crossed on a tombstone.

A feeling of profound horror for mankind gripped the heart when one saw the marks that decrepitude had left on this fragile machine. The stranger was wearing an old-fashioned gold-embroidered white waistcoat, and his linen was dazzlingly white. A frill of somewhat yellowed lace, rich enough for a queen's envy, fell into ruffles on his breast. On him, however, this lace seemed more like a rag than like an ornament. Centered on it was a fabulous diamond which glittered like the sun. This outmoded luxury, this particular and tasteless jewel, made the strange creature's face even more striking. The setting was worthy of the portrait. This dark face was angular and all sunk in. The chin was sunken, the temples were sunken; the eyes were lost in yellowish sockets. The jawbones stood out because of his indescribable thinness, creating cavities in the center of each cheek. These deformations, more or less illuminated by the candles, produced shadows and strange reflections which succeeded in erasing any human characteristics from his face. And the years had glued the thin, yellow skin of his face so closely to his skull that it was covered all over with a multitude of circular wrinkles, like the ripples on a pond into which a child has thrown a pebble, or star-shaped, like a cracked windowpane, but everywhere deep and close-set as the edges of pages in a closed book. Some old people have presented more hideous portraits; what contributed the most, however, in lending the appearance of an artificial creature to the specter which had risen up before us was the red and white with which he glistened. The eyebrows of his mask took from the light a luster which revealed that they were painted on. Fortunately for the eye depressed by the sight of such ruin, his cadaverous skull was covered by a blond wig whose innumerable curls were evidence of an extraordinary pretension. For the rest, the feminine coquetry of this phantasmagorical personage was rather strongly emphasized by the gold ornaments hanging from his ears, by the rings whose fine stones glittered on his bony fingers, and by a watch chain which shimmered like the brilliants of a choker around a woman's neck. Finally, this sort of Japanese idol had on his bluish lips a fixed and frozen smile, implacable and mocking, like a skull. Silent and motionless as a statue, it exuded the musty odor of old clothes which the heirs of some duchess take out for inventory. Although the old man turned his eyes toward the crowd, it seemed that the movements of those orbs, incapable of sight, were accomplished only by means of some imperceptible artifice; and when the eyes came to rest on something, anyone looking at them would have concluded that they had not moved at all. To see, next to this human wreckage, a young woman whose neck, bosom, and arms were bare and white, whose figure was in the full bloom of its beauty, whose hair rose from her alabaster forehead and inspired love, whose eyes did not receive but gave off light, who was soft, fresh, and whose floating curls and sweet breath seemed too heavy, too hard, too powerful for this shadow, for this man of dust: ah! here were death and life indeed, I thought, in a fantastic arabesque, half hideous chimera, divinely feminine from the waist up.

"Yet there are marriages like that often enough in the world," I said to myself.

"He smells like a graveyard," cried the terrified young woman, pressing against me for protection, and whose uneasy movements told me she was frightened. "What a horrible sight," she went on. "I can't stay here any longer. If I look at him again, I shall believe that death itself has come looking for me. Is he alive?"

She reached out to the phenomenon with that boldness women can sum- 45
mon up out of the strength of their desires; but she broke into a cold sweat, for no sooner had she touched the old man than she heard a cry like a rattle. This sharp voice, if voice it was, issued from a nearly dried up throat. Then the sound was quickly followed by a little, convulsive, childish cough of a peculiar sonorousness. At this sound, Marianina, Filippo, and Mme de Lanty looked in our direction, and their glances were like bolts of lightning. The young woman wished she were at the bottom of the Seine. She took my arm and led me into a side room. Men, women, everyone made way for us. At the end of the public rooms, we came into a small, semicircular chamber. My companion threw herself onto a divan, trembling with fright, oblivious to her surroundings.

"Madame, you are mad," I said to her.

"But," she replied, after a moment's silence, during which I gazed at her in admiration, "is it my fault? Why does Mme de Lanty allow ghosts to wander about in her house?"

"Come," I replied, "you are being ridiculous, taking a little old man for a ghost."

"Be still," she said, with that forceful and mocking air all women so easily assume when they want to be in the right. "What a pretty room!" she cried, looking around. "Blue satin always makes such wonderful wall hangings. How refreshing it is! Oh! what a beautiful painting!" she went on, getting up and going to stand before a painting in a magnificent frame.

We stood for a moment in contemplation of this marvel, which seemed to 50
have been painted by some supernatural brush. The picture was of Adonis lying on a lion's skin. The lamp hanging from the ceiling of the room in an al-

abaster globe illuminated this canvas with a soft glow which enabled us to make out all the beauties of the painting.

"Does such a perfect creature exist?" she asked me, after having, with a soft smile of contentment, examined the exquisite grace of the contours, the pose, the color, the hair; in short, the entire picture.

"He is too beautiful for a man," she added, after an examination such as she might have made of some rival.

Oh! how jealous I then felt: something in which a poet had vainly tried to make me believe, the jealousy of engravings, of pictures, wherein artists exaggerate human beauty according to the doctrine which leads them to idealize everything.

"It's a portrait," I replied, "the product of the talent of Vien. But that great painter never saw the original and maybe you'd admire it less if you knew that this daub was copied from the statue of a woman."

"But who is it?" 55

I hesitated.

"I want to know," she added, impetuously.

"I believe," I replied, "that this Adonis is a . . . a relative of Mme de Lanty."

I had the pain of seeing her rapt in the contemplation of this figure. She sat in silence; I sat down next to her and took her hand without her being aware of it! Forgotten for a painting! At this moment, the light footsteps of a woman in a rustling dress broke the silence. Young Marianina came in, and her innocent expression made her even more alluring than did her grace and her lovely dress; she was walking slowly and escorting with maternal care, with filial solicitude, the costumed specter who had made us flee from the music room and whom she was leading, watching with what seemed to be concern as he slowly advanced on his feeble feet. They went together with some difficulty to a door hidden behind a tapestry. There, Marianina knocked softly. At once, as if by magic, a tall, stern man, a kind of family genie, appeared. Before entrusting the old man to the care of his mysterious guardian, the child respectfully kissed the walking corpse, and her chaste caress was not devoid of that graceful cajolery of which some privileged women possess the secret.

"Addio, addio," she said, with the prettiest inflection in her youthful 60
voice.

She added to the final syllable a marvelously well-executed trill, but in a soft voice, as if to give poetic expression to the emotions in her heart. Suddenly struck by some memory, the old man stood on the threshold of this secret hideaway. Then, through the silence, we heard the heavy sigh that came from his chest: he took the most beautiful of the rings which adorned his skeletal fingers, and placed it in Marianina's bosom. The young girl broke into laughter, took the ring, and slipped it onto her finger over her glove; then she walked quickly toward the salon, from which there could be heard the opening measures of a quadrille. She saw us:

"Ah, you were here," she said, blushing.

After having seemed as if about to question us, she ran to her partner with the careless petulance of youth.

"What did that mean?" my young companion asked me. "Is he her husband? I must be dreaming. Where am I?"

"You," I replied, "you, madame, superior as you are, you who understand so well the most hidden feelings, who know how to inspire in a man's heart the most delicate of feelings without blighting it, without breaking it at the outset, you who pity heartache and who combine the wit of a Parisienne with a passionate soul worthy of Italy or Spain—"

She perceived the bitter irony in my speech; then, without seeming to have heard, she interrupted me: "Oh, you fashion me to your own taste. What tyranny! You don't want me for myself!"

"Ah, I want nothing," I cried, taken aback by her severity. "Is it true, at least, that you enjoy hearing stories of those vivid passions that ravishing Southern women inspire in our hearts?"

"Yes, so?"

"So, I'll call tomorrow around nine and reveal this mystery to you."

"No," she replied, "I want to know now."

"You haven't yet given me the right to obey you when you say: I want to."

"At this moment," she replied with maddening coquetry, "I have the most burning desire to know the secret. Tomorrow, I might not even listen to you . . ."

She smiled and we parted; she just as proud, just as forbidding, and I just as ridiculous as ever. She had the audacity to waltz with a young aide-de-camp; and I was left in turn angry, pouting, admiring, loving, jealous.

"Till tomorrow," she said, around two in the morning, as she left the ball.

"I won't go," I thought to myself. "I'll give you up. You are more capricious, perhaps a thousand times more fanciful . . . than my imagination."

The next evening, we were both seated before a good fire in a small, elegant salon, she on a low sofa, I on cushions almost at her feet, and my eyes below hers. The street was quiet. The lamp shed a soft light. It was one of those evenings pleasing to the soul, one of those never-to-be-forgotten moments, one of those hours spent in peace and desire whose charm, later on, is a matter for constant regret, even when we may be happier. Who can erase the vivid imprint of the first feelings of love?

"Well," she said, "I'm listening."

"I don't dare begin. The story has some dangerous passages for its teller. If I become too moved, you must stop me."

"Tell."

"I will obey."

Ernest-Jean Sarrasine was the only son of a lawyer in the Franche-Comté, I went on, after a pause. His father had amassed six or eight thousand livres of income honestly enough, a professional's fortune which at that time in the provinces, was considered to be colossal. The elder Sarrasine, having but one child and anxious to overlook nothing where his education was concerned, hoped to make a magistrate of him, and to live long enough to see, in his old age, the grandson of Matthieu Sarrasine, farmer of Saint-Dié, seated beneath the lilies and napping through some trial for the greater glory of the law; however, heaven did not hold this pleasure in store for the lawyer.

The younger Sarrasine, entrusted to the Jesuits at an early age, evidenced an unusual turbulence. He had the childhood of a man of talent. He would study only what pleased him, frequently rebelled, and sometimes spent hours on end plunged in confused thought, occupied at times in watching his comrades at play, at times dreaming of Homeric heroes. Then, if he made up his mind to amuse himself, he threw himself into games with an extraordinary ardor. When a fight broke out between him and a friend, the battle rarely ended without bloodshed. If he was the weaker of the two, he would bite. Both active and passive by turns, without aptitude and not overly intelligent, his bizarre character made his teachers as wary of him as were his classmates. Instead of learning the elements of Greek, he drew the Reverend Father as he explained a passage in Thucydides to them, sketched the mathematics teacher, the tutors, the Father in charge of discipline, and he scribbled shapeless designs on the walls. Instead of singing the Lord's praises in church, he distracted himself during services by whittling on a pew; or when he had stolen a piece of wood, he carved some holy figure. If he had no wood, paper, or pencil, he reproduced his ideas with bread crumbs. Whether copying the characters in the pictures that decorated the choir, or improvising, he always left behind him some gross sketches whose licentiousness shocked the youngest Fathers; evil tongues maintained that the older Jesuits were amused by them. Finally, if we are to believe school gossip, he was expelled for having, while awaiting his turn at the confessional on Good Friday, shaped a big stick of wood into the form of Christ. The impiety with which this statue was endowed was too blatant not to have merited punishment of the artist. Had he not had the audacity to place this somewhat cynical figure on top of the tabernacle!

Sarrasine sought in Paris a refuge from the effects of a father's curse. Having one of those strong wills that brook no obstacle, he obeyed the commands of his genius and entered Bouchardon's studio. He worked all day, and in the evening went out to beg for his living. Astonished at the young artist's progress and intelligence, Bouchardon soon became aware of his pupil's poverty; he helped him, grew fond of him, and treated him like his own son. Then, when Sarrasine's genius was revealed in one of those works in which future talent struggles with the effervescence of youth, the warmhearted Bouchardon endeavored to restore him to the old lawyer's good graces. Before the authority of the famous sculptor, the parental anger subsided. All Besançon rejoiced at having given birth to a great man of the future. In the first throes of the ecstasy produced by his flattered vanity, the miserly lawyer gave his son the means to cut a good figure in society. For a long time, the lengthy and laborious studies demanded by sculpture tamed Sarrasine's impetuous nature and wild genius. Bouchardon, foreseeing the violence with which the passions would erupt in this young soul, which was perhaps as predisposed to them as Michelangelo's had been, channeled his energy into constant labor. He succeeded in keeping Sarrasine's extraordinary impetuosity within limits by forbidding him to work; by suggesting distractions when he saw him being carried away by the fury of some idea, or by entrusting him with important work when he seemed on the point of abandoning himself to dissipation. However, gentleness was always the most powerful of weapons where this passionate soul was concerned, and the master had no greater control over his student than when he inspired his gratitude through paternal kindness.

At twenty-two, Sarrasine was necessarily removed from the salutary influence Bouchardon had exercised over his morals and his habits. He reaped the fruits of his genius by winning the sculpture prize established by the Marquis de Marigny, the brother of Mme de Pompadour, who did so much for the arts. Diderot hailed the statue by Bouchardon's pupil as a masterpiece. The King's sculptor, not without great sorrow, saw off to Italy a young man whom he had kept, as a matter of principle, in total ignorance of the facts of life.

For six years, Sarrasine had boarded with Bouchardon. As fanatic in his 85
art as Canova was later to be, he arose at dawn, went to the studio, did not emerge until nightfall, and lived only with his Muse. If he went to the Comédie-Française, he was taken by his master. He felt so out of place at Mme Geoffrin's and in high society, into which Bouchardon tried to introduce him, that he preferred to be alone, and shunned the pleasures of that licentious era. He had no other mistress but sculpture and Clotilde, one of the luminaries of the Opéra. And even this affair did not last. Sarrasine was rather ugly, always badly dressed, and so free in his nature, so irregular in his private life, that the celebrated nymph, fearing some catastrophe, soon relinquished the sculptor to his love of the Arts. Sophie Arnould made one of her witticisms on this subject. She confessed her surprise, I believe, that her friend had managed to triumph over statuary.

Sarrasine left for Italy in 1758. During the journey, his vivid imagination caught fire beneath a brilliant sky and at the sight of the wonderful monuments which are to be found in the birthplace of the Arts. He admired the statues, the frescoes, the paintings, and thus inspired, he came to Rome, filled with desire to carve his name between Michelangelo's and M. Bouchardon's. Accordingly, at the beginning, he divided his time between studio tasks and examining the works of art in which Rome abounds. He had already spent two weeks in the ecstatic state which overwhelms young minds at the sight of the queen of ruins, when he went one evening to the Teatro Argentina, before which a huge crowd was assembled. He inquired as to the causes of this gathering and everyone answered with two names: Zambinella! Jomelli! He entered and took a seat in the orchestra, squeezed between two notably fat *abbati;* however, he was lucky enough to be fairly close to the stage. The curtain rose. For the first time in his life, he heard that music whose delights M. Jean-Jacques Rousseau had so eloquently praised to him at one of Baron d'Holbach's evenings. The young sculptor's senses were, so to speak, lubricated by the accents of Jomelli's sublime harmony. The languorous novelties of these skillfully mingled Italian voices plunged him into a delicious ecstasy. He remained speechless, motionless, not even feeling crowded by the two priests. His soul passed into his ears and eyes. He seemed to hear through every pore. Suddenly a burst of applause which shook the house greeted the prima donna's entrance. She came coquettishly to the front of the stage and greeted the audience with infinite grace. The lights, the general enthusiasm, the theatrical illusion, the glamour of a style of dress which in those days was quite attractive, all conspired in favor of this woman. Sarrasine cried out with pleasure.

At that instant he marveled at the ideal beauty he had hitherto sought in life, seeking in one often unworthy model the roundness of a perfect leg; in another, the curve of a breast; in another, white shoulders; finally taking some girl's neck, some woman's hands, and some child's smooth knees, without ever having encountered under the cold Parisian sky the rich, sweet creations of ancient Greece. La Zambinella displayed to him, united, living, and delicate, those exquisite female forms he so ardently desired, of which a sculptor is at once the severest and the most passionate judge. Her mouth was expressive, her eyes loving, her complexion dazzlingly white. And along with these details, which would have enraptured a painter, were all the wonders of those images of Venus revered and rendered by the chisels of the Greeks. The artist never wearied of admiring the inimitable grace with which the arms were attached to the torso, the marvelous roundness of the neck, the harmonious lines drawn by the eyebrows, the nose, and the perfect oval of the face, the purity of its vivid contours and the effect of the thick, curved lashes which lined her heavy and voluptuous eyelids. This was more than a woman, this was a masterpiece! In this unhoped-for creation could be found a love to enrapture any man, and beauties worthy of satisfying a critic. With his eyes, Sarrasine devoured Pygmalion's statue, come down from its pedestal. When La Zambinella sang, the effect was delirium. The artist felt cold; then he felt a heat which suddenly began to prickle in the innermost depth of his being, in what we call the heart, for lack of any other word! He did not applaud, he said nothing, he experienced an impulse of madness, a kind of frenzy which overcomes us only when we are at the age when desire has something frightening and infernal about it. Sarrasine wanted to leap onto the stage and take possession of this woman: his strength, increased a hundredfold by a moral depression impossible to explain, since these phenomena occur in an area hidden from human observation, seemed to manifest itself with painful violence. Looking at him, one would have thought him a cold and senseless man. Fame, knowledge, future, existence, laurels, everything collapsed.

"To be loved by her, or die!" Such was the decree Sarrasine passed upon himself. He was so utterly intoxicated that he no longer saw the theater, the spectators, the actors, or heard the music. Moreover, the distance between himself and La Zambinella had ceased to exist, he possessed her, his eyes were riveted upon her, he took her for his own. An almost diabolical power enabled him to feel the breath of this voice, to smell the scented powder covering her hair, to see the planes of her face, to count the blue veins shadowing her satin skin. Last, this agile voice, fresh and silvery in timbre, supple as a thread shaped by the slightest breath of air, rolling and unrolling, cascading and scattering, this voice attacked his soul so vividly that several times he gave vent to involuntary cries torn from him by convulsive feelings of pleasure which are all too rarely vouchsafed by human passions. He was presently obliged to leave the theater. His trembling legs almost refused to support him. He was limp, weak as a sensitive man who has given way to overwhelming anger. He had experienced such pleasure, or perhaps he had suffered so keenly, that his life had drained away like water from a broken vase. He felt empty inside, a prostration similar to the debilitation that overcomes those convalescing from serious illness.

Overcome by an inexplicable sadness, he sat down on the steps of a church. There, leaning back against a pillar, he fell into a confused meditation, as in a dream. He had been smitten by passion. Upon returning to his lodgings, he fell into one of those frenzies of activity which disclose to us the presence of new elements in our lives. A prey to this first fever of love derived equally from both pleasure and pain, he tried to appease his impatience and his delirium by drawing La Zambinella from memory. It was a kind of embodied meditation. On one page, La Zambinella appeared in that apparently calm and cool pose favored by Raphael, Giorgione, and every great painter. On another, she was delicately turning her head after having finished a trill, and appeared to be listening to herself. Sarrasine sketched his mistress in every pose: he drew her unveiled, seated, standing, lying down, chaste or amorous, embodying through the delirium of his pencils every capricious notion that can enter our heads when we think intently about a mistress. However, his fevered thoughts went beyond drawing. He saw La Zambinella, spoke to her, beseeched her, he passed a thousand years of life and happiness with her by placing her in every imaginable position; in short, by sampling the future with her. On the following day, he sent his valet to rent a box next to the stage for the entire season. Then, like all young people with lusty souls, he exaggerated to himself the difficulties of his undertaking and first fed his passion with the pleasure of being able to admire his mistress without obstruction. This golden age of love, during which we take pleasure in our own feeling and in which we are happy almost by ourselves, was not destined to last long in Sarrasine's case. Nevertheless, events took him by surprise while he was still under the spell of this vernal hallucination, as naïve as it was voluptuous. In a week he lived a lifetime, spending the mornings kneading the clay by which he would copy La Zambinella, despite the veils, skirts, corsets, and ribbons which concealed her from him. In the evenings, installed in his box early, alone, lying on a sofa like a Turk under the influence of opium, he created for himself a pleasure as rich and varied as he wished it to be. First, he gradually familiarized himself with the overly vivid emotions his mistress's singing afforded him; he then trained his eyes to see her, and finally he could contemplate her without fearing an outburst of the wild frenzy which had seized him on the first day. As his passion became calmer, it grew deeper. For the rest, the unsociable sculptor did not allow his friends to intrude upon his solitude, which was peopled with images, adorned with fantasies of hope, and filled with happiness. His love was so strong, so naïve, that he experienced all the innocent scruples that assail us when we love for the first time. As he began to realize that he would soon have to act, to plot, to inquire where La Zambinella lived, whether she had a mother, uncle, teacher, family, to ponder, in short, on ways to see her, speak to her, these great, ambitious thoughts made his heart swell so painfully that he put them off until later, deriving as much satisfaction from his physical suffering as he did from his intellectual pleasures.

"But," Mme de Rochefide interrupted me, "I still don't see anything 90
about either Marianina or her little old man."

"You are seeing nothing but him!" I cried impatiently, like an author who is being forced to spoil a theatrical effect.

For several days, I resumed after a pause, Sarrasine had reappeared so faithfully in his box and his eyes had expressed such love that his passion for La Zambinella's voice would have been common knowledge throughout Paris, had this adventure happened there; however, in Italy, madame, everyone goes to the theater for himself, with his own passions, and with a heartfelt interest which precludes spying through opera glasses. Nevertheless, the sculptor's enthusiasm did not escape the attention of the singers for long. One evening, the Frenchman saw that they were laughing at him in the wings. It is hard to know what extreme actions he might not have taken had La Zambinella not come onto the stage. She gave Sarrasine one of those eloquent glances which often reveal much more than women intend them to. This glance was a total revelation. Sarrasine was loved!

"If it's only a caprice," he thought, already accusing his mistress of excessive ardor, "she doesn't know what she is subjecting herself to. I am hoping her caprice will last my whole life."

At that moment, the artist's attention was distracted by three soft knocks on the door of his box. He opened it. An old woman entered with an air of mystery.

"Young man," she said, "if you want to be happy, be prudent. Put on a 95
cape, wear a hat drawn down over your eyes; then, around ten in the evening, be in the Via del Corso in front of the Hotel di Spagna."

"I'll be there," he replied, placing two louis in the duenna's wrinkled hand.

He left his box after having given a signal to La Zambinella, who timidly lowered her heavy eyelids, like a woman pleased to be understood at last. Then he ran home to dress himself as seductively as he could. As he was leaving the theater, a strange man took his arm.

"Be on your guard, Frenchman," he whispered in his ear. "This is a matter of life and death. Cardinal Cicognara is her protector and doesn't trifle."

At that moment, had some demon set the pit of hell between Sarrasine and La Zambinella, he would have crossed it with one leap. Like the horses of the gods described by Homer, the sculptor's love had traversed vast distances in the twinkling of an eye.

"If death itself were waiting for me outside the house, I would go even 100
faster," he replied.

"*Poverino!*" the stranger cried as he disappeared.

Speaking of danger to a lover is tantamount to selling him pleasure, is it not? Sarrasine's valet had never seen his master take so much care over his toilette. His finest sword, a gift from Bouchardon, the sash Clotilde had given him, his embroidered coat, his silver-brocade waistcoat, his gold snuffbox, his jeweled watches, were all taken from their coffers, and he adorned himself like a girl about to appear before her first love. At the appointed hour, drunk with love and seething with hope, Sarrasine, concealed in his cape, sped to the rendezvous the old woman had given him. The duenna was waiting for him.

"You took a long time," she said. "Come."

She led the Frenchman along several back streets and stopped before a rather handsome mansion. She knocked. The door opened. She led Sarrasine along a labyrinth of stairways, galleries, and rooms which were lit only by the feeble light of the moon, and soon came to a door through whose cracks gleamed bright lights and from behind which came the joyful sounds of several voices. When at a word from the old woman he was admitted to this mysterious room, Sarrasine was suddenly dazzled at finding himself in a salon as brilliantly lighted as it was sumptuously furnished, in the center of which stood a table laden with venerable bottles and flashing flagons sparkling with ruby facets. He recognized the singers from the theater, along with some charming women, all ready to begin an artists' orgy as soon as he was among them. Sarrasine suppressed a feeling of disappointment and put on a good face. He had expected a dim room, his mistress seated by the fire, some jealous person nearby, death and love, an exchange of confidences in low voices, heart to heart, dangerous kisses and faces so close that La Zambinella's hair would have caressed his forehead throbbing with desire, feverish with happiness.

"*Vive la folie!*" he cried. "*Signori e belle donne*, you will allow me to take my 105
revenge later and to show you my gratitude for the way you have welcomed a poor sculptor."

Having been greeted warmly enough by most of those present, whom he knew by sight, he sought to approach the armchair on which La Zambinella was casually reclining. Ah! how his heart beat when he spied a delicate foot shod in one of those slippers which in those days, may I say, madame, gave women's feet such a coquettish and voluptuous look that I don't know how men were able to resist them. The well-fitting white stockings with green clocks, the short skirts, the slippers with pointed toes, and the high heels of Louis XV's reign may have contributed something to the demoralization of Europe and the clergy.

"Something?" the Marquise replied. "Have you read nothing?"

La Zambinella, I continued, smiling, had impudently crossed her legs and was gently swinging the upper one with a certain attractive indolence which suited her capricious sort of beauty. She had removed her costume and was wearing a bodice that accentuated her narrow waist and set off the satin panniers of her dress, which was embroidered with blue flowers. Her bosom, the treasures of which were concealed, in an excess of coquetry, by a covering of lace, was dazzlingly white. Her hair arranged something like that of Mme du Barry, her face, though it was partially hidden under a full bonnet, appeared only the more delicate, and powder suited her. To see her thus was to adore her. She gave the sculptor a graceful smile. Unhappy at not being able to speak to her without witnesses present, Sarrasine politely sat down next to her and talked about music, praising her extraordinary talent; but his voice trembled with love, with fear and hope.

"What are you afraid of?" asked Vitagliani, the company's most famous singer. "Go ahead; you need fear no rivals here." Having said this, the tenor smiled without another word. This smile was repeated on the lips of all the guests, whose attention contained a hidden malice a lover would not have noticed. Such openness was like a dagger thrust in Sarrasine's heart. Although endowed with a certain strength of character, and although nothing could change his love, it had perhaps not yet occurred to him that La Zambinella was virtually a courtesan, and that he could not have both the pure pleasures that make a young girl's love so delicious and the tempestuous transports by which the hazardous possession of an actress must be purchased. He reflected and resigned himself. Supper was served. Sarrasine and La Zambinella sat down informally side by side. For the first half of the meal, the artists preserved some decorum, and the sculptor was able to chat with the singer. He found her witty, acute, but astonishingly ignorant, and she revealed herself to be weak and superstitious. The delicacy of her organs was reflected in her understanding. When Vitagliani uncorked the first bottle of champagne, Sarrasine read in his companion's eyes a start of terror at the tiny explosion caused by the escaping gas. The love-stricken artist interpreted the involuntary shudder of this feminine constitution as the sign of an excessive sensitivity. The Frenchman was charmed by this weakness. How much is protective in a man's love!

"My strength your shield!" Is this not written at the heart of all declara- 110
tions of love? Too excited to shower the beautiful Italian with compliments, Sarrasine, like all lovers, was by turns serious, laughing, or reflective. Although he seemed to be listening to the other guests, he did not hear a word they were saying, so absorbed was he in the pleasure of finding himself beside her, touching her hand as he served her. He bathed in a secret joy. Despite the eloquence of a few mutual glances, he was astonished at the reserve La Zambinella maintained toward him. Indeed, she had begun by pressing his foot and teasing him with the flirtatiousness of a woman in love and free to show it; but she suddenly wrapped herself in the modesty of a young girl, after hearing Sarrasine describe a trait which revealed the excessive violence of his character. When the supper became an orgy, the guests broke into song under the influence of the Peralta and the Pedro-Ximenes. There were ravishing duets, songs from Calabria, Spanish seguidillas, Neapolitan canzonettas. Intoxication was in every eye, in the music, in hearts and voices alike. Suddenly an enchanting vivacity welled up, a gay abandon, and Italian warmth of feeling inconceivable to those acquainted only with Parisian gatherings, London routs, or Viennese circles. Jokes and words of love flew like bullets in a battle through laughter, profanities, and invocations to the Holy Virgin or *il Bambino*. Someone lay down on a sofa and fell asleep. A girl was listening to a declaration of love unaware that she was spilling sherry on the tablecloth. In the midst of this disorder, La Zambinella remained thoughtful, as though terror-struck.

She refused to drink, perhaps she ate a bit too much; however, it is said that greediness in a woman is a charming quality. Admiring his mistress's modesty, Sarrasine thought seriously about the future.

"She probably wants to be married," he thought. He then turned his thoughts to the delights of this marriage. His whole life seemed too short to exhaust the springs of happiness he found in the depths of his soul. Vitagliani, who was sitting next to him, refilled his glass so often that, toward three in the morning, without being totally drunk, Sarrasine could no longer control his delirium. Impetuously, he picked up the woman, escaping into a kind of boudoir next to the salon, toward the door of which he had glanced more than once. The Italian woman was armed with a dagger.

"If you come any closer," she said, "I will be forced to plunge this weapon into your heart. Let me go! You would despise me. I have conceived too much respect for your character to surrender in this fashion. I don't want to betray the feeling you have for me."

"Oh no!" cried Sarrasine. "You cannot stifle a passion by stimulating it! Are you already so corrupt that, old in heart, you would act like a young courtesan who whets the emotions by which she plies her trade?"

"But today is Friday," she replied, frightened at the Frenchman's violence.

Sarrasine, who was not devout, broke into laughter. La Zambinella 115
jumped up like a young deer and ran toward the salon. When Sarrasine appeared in her pursuit, he was greeted by an infernal burst of laughter.

He saw La Zambinella lying in a swoon upon a sofa. She was pale and drained by the extraordinary effort she had just made. Although Sarrasine knew little Italian, he heard his mistress saying in a low voice to Vitagliani: "But he will kill me!"

The sculptor was utterly confounded by this strange scene. He regained his senses. At first he stood motionless; then he found his voice, sat down next to his mistress, and assured her of his respect. He was able to divert his passion by addressing the most high-minded phrases to this woman; and in depicting his love, he used all the resources of that magical eloquence, that inspired intermediary which women rarely refuse to believe. When the guests were surprised by the first gleams of morning light, a woman suggested they go to Frascati. Everyone enthusiastically fell in with the idea of spending the day at the Villa Ludovisi. Vitagliani went down to hire some carriages. Sarrasine had the pleasure of leading La Zambinella to a phaeton. Once outside Rome, the gaiety which had been momentarily repressed by each person's battle with sleepiness suddenly revived. Men and women alike seemed used to this strange life, these ceaseless pleasures, this artist's impulsiveness which turns life into a perpetual party at which one laughed unreservedly. The sculptor's companion was the only one who seemed downcast.

"Are you ill?" Sarrasine asked her. "Would you rather go home?"

"I'm not strong enough to stand all these excesses," she replied. "I must be very careful; but with you I feel so well! Had it not been for you, I would never have stayed for supper; a sleepless night and I lose whatever bloom I have."

"You are so delicate," Sarrasine said, looking at the charming creature's 120
pretty face.

"Orgies ruin the voice."

"Now that we're alone," the artist cried, "and you no longer need fear the outbursts of my passion, tell me that you love me."

"Why?" she replied. "What would be the use? I seemed pretty to you. But you are French and your feelings will pass. Ah, you would not love me as I long to be loved."

"How can you say that?"

"Not to satisfy any vulgar passion; purely. I abhor men perhaps even more 125
than I hate women. I need to seek refuge in friendship. For me, the world is a desert. I am an accursed creature, condemned to understand happiness, to feel it, to desire it, and, like many others, forced to see it flee from me continually. Remember, sir, that I will not have deceived you. I forbid you to love me. I can be your devoted friend, for I admire your strength and your character. I need a brother, a protector. Be all that for me, but no more."

"Not love you!" Sarrasine cried. "But my dearest angel, you are my life, my happiness!"

"If I were to say one word, you would repulse me with horror."

"Coquette! Nothing can frighten me. Tell me you will cost my future, that I will die in two months, that I will be damned merely for having kissed you."

He kissed her, despite La Zambinella's efforts to resist this passionate embrace.

"Tell me you are a devil, that you want my money, my name, all my fame! 130
Do you want me to give up being a sculptor? Tell me."

"And if I were not a woman?" La Zambinella asked in a soft silvery voice.

"What a joke!" Sarrasine cried. "Do you think you can deceive an artist's eye? Haven't I spent ten days devouring, scrutinizing, admiring your perfection? Only a woman could have this round, soft arm, these elegant curves. Oh, you want compliments."

She smiled at him sadly, and raising her eyes heavenward, she murmured: "Fatal beauty!"

At that moment her gaze had an indescribable expression of horror, so powerful and vivid that Sarrasine shuddered.

"Frenchman," she went on, "forget this moment of madness forever. I re- 135
spect you, but as for love, do not ask it of me; that feeling is smothered in my heart. I have no heart!" she cried, weeping. "The stage where you saw me, that applause, that music, that fame I am condemned to, such is my life, I have no other. In a few hours you will not see me in the same way, the woman you love will be dead."

The sculptor made no reply. He was overcome with a dumb rage which oppressed his heart. He could only gaze with enflamed, burning eyes at this extraordinary woman. La Zambinella's weak voice, her manner, her movements and gestures marked with sorrow, melancholy, and discouragement, awakened all the wealth of passion in his soul. Each word was a goad. At that moment they reached Frascati. As the artist offered his mistress his arm to assist her in alighting, he felt her shiver.

"What is wrong? You would kill me," he cried, seeing her grow pale, "if I were even an innocent cause of your slightest unhappiness."

"A snake," she said, pointing to a grass snake which was sliding along a ditch. "I am afraid of those horrid creatures." Sarrasine crushed the snake's head with his heel.

"How can you be so brave?" La Zambinella continued, looking with visible horror at the dead reptile.

"Ah," the artist replied, smiling, "now do you dare deny you are a woman?" 140

They rejoined their companions and strolled through the woods of the Villa Ludovisi, which in those days belonged to Cardinal Cicognara. That morning fled too quickly for the enamored sculptor, but it was filled with a host of incidents which revealed to him the coquetry, the weakness, and the delicacy of this soft and enervated being. This was woman herself, with her sudden fears, her irrational whims, her instinctive worries, her impetuous boldness, her fussings, and her delicious sensibility. It happened that as they were wandering in the open countryside, the little group of merry singers saw in the distance some heavily armed men whose manner of dress was far from reassuring. Someone said, "They must be highwaymen," and everyone quickened his pace toward the refuge of the Cardinal's grounds. At this critical moment, Sarrasine saw from La Zambinella's pallor that she no longer had the strength to walk; he took her up in his arms and carried her for a while, running. When he came to a nearby arbor, he put her down.

"Explain to me," he said, "how this extreme weakness, which I would find hideous in any other woman, which would displease me and whose slightest indication would be almost enough to choke my love, pleases and charms me in you? Ah, how I love you," he went on. "All your faults, your terrors, your resentments, add an indefinable grace to your soul. I think I would detest a strong woman, a Sappho, a courageous creature, full of energy and passion. Oh, soft, frail creature, how could you be otherwise? That angelic voice, that delicate voice would be an anomaly coming from any body but yours."

"I cannot give you any hope," she said. "Stop speaking to me in this way, because they will make a fool of you. I cannot stop you from coming to the theater; but if you love me or if you are wise, you will come there no more. Listen, monsieur," she said in a low voice.

"Oh, be still," the impassioned artist said. "Obstacles make my love more ardent."

La Zambinella's graceful and modest attitude did not change, but she fell 145
silent as though a terrible thought had revealed some misfortune to her. When it came time to return to Rome, she got into the four-seated coach, ordering the sculptor with imperious cruelty to return to Rome alone in the carriage. During the journey, Sarrasine resolved to kidnap La Zambinella. He spent the entire day making plans, each more outrageous than the other. At nightfall, as he was going out to inquire where his mistress's palazzo was located, he met one of his friends on the threshold.

"My dear fellow," he said, "our ambassador has asked me to invite you to his house tonight. He is giving a magnificent concert, and when I tell you that Zambinella will be there . . ."

"Zambinella," cried Sarrasine, intoxicated by the name, "I'm mad about her!"

"You're like everyone else," his friend replied.

"If you are my friends, you, Vien, Lauterbourg, and Allegrain, will you help me do something after the party?" Sarrasine asked.

"It's not some cardinal to be killed? . . . not . . . ?" 150

"No, no," Sarrasine said, "I'm not asking you to do anything an honest person couldn't do."

In a short time, the sculptor had arranged everything for the success of his undertaking. He was one of the last to arrive at the ambassador's, but he had come in a traveling carriage drawn by powerful horses and driven by one of the most enterprising *veturini* of Rome. The ambassador's palazzo was crowded; not without some difficulty, the sculptor, who was a stranger to everyone present, made his way to the salon where Zambinella was singing at that very moment.

"Is it out of consideration for the cardinals, bishops, and abbés present," Sarrasine asked, "that *she* is dressed like a man, that she is wearing a snood, kinky hair, and a sword?"

"She? What she?" asked the old nobleman to whom Sarrasine had been speaking. "La Zambinella." "La Zambinella!" the Roman prince replied. "Are you joking? Where are you from? Has there ever been a woman on the Roman stage? And don't you know about the creatures who sing female roles in the Papal States? I am the one, monsieur, who gave Zambinella his voice. I paid for everything that scamp ever had, even his singing teacher. Well, he has so little gratitude for the service I rendered him that he has never consented to set foot in my house. And yet, if he makes a fortune, he will owe it all to me."

Prince Chigi may well have gone on talking for some time; Sarrasine was 155
not listening to him. A horrid truth had crept into his soul. It was as though he had been struck by lightning. He stood motionless, his eyes fixed on the false singer. His fiery gaze exerted a sort of magnetic influence on Zambinella, for the *musico* finally turned to look at Sarrasine, and at that moment his heavenly voice faltered. He trembled! An involuntary murmur escaping from the audience he had kept hanging on his lips completed his discomfiture; he sat down and cut short his aria. Cardinal Cicognara, who had glanced out the corner of his eye to see what had attracted his protégé's attention, then saw the Frenchman: he leaned over to one of his ecclesiastical aides-de-camp and appeared to be asking the sculptor's name. Having obtained the answer he sought, he regarded the artist with great attention and gave an order to an abbé, who quickly disappeared.

During this time, Zambinella, having recovered himself, once more began the piece he had so capriciously interrupted; but he sang it badly, and despite all the requests made to him, he refused to sing anything else. This was the first time he displayed that capricious tyranny for which he would later be as celebrated as for his talent and his vast fortune, due, as they said, no less to his voice than to his beauty.

"It is a woman," Sarrasine said, believing himself alone. "There is some hidden intrigue here. Cardinal Cicognara is deceiving the Pope and the whole city of Rome!"

The sculptor thereupon left the salon, gathered his friends together, and posted them out of sight in the courtyard of the palazzo. When Zambinella was confident that Sarrasine had departed, he appeared to regain his composure. Around midnight, having wandered through the rooms like a man seeking some enemy, the *musico* departed. As soon as he crossed the threshold of the palazzo, he was adroitly seized by men who gagged him with a handkerchief and drew him into the carriage Sarrasine had hired. Frozen with horror, Zambinella remained in a corner, not daring to move. He saw before him the terrible face of the artist, who was silent as death.

The journey was brief. Carried in Sarrasine's arms, Zambinella soon found himself in a dark, empty studio. Half dead, the singer remained in a chair, without daring to examine the statue of a woman in which he recognized his own features. He made no attempt to speak, but his teeth chattered. Sarrasine paced up and down the room. Suddenly he stopped in front of Zambinella.

"Tell me the truth," he pleaded in a low, altered voice. "You are a woman? 160
Cardinal Cicognara . . ."

Zambinella fell to his knees, and in reply lowered his head.

"Ah, you are a woman," the artist cried in a delirium, "for even a . . ." He broke off. "No," he continued, "*he* would not be so cowardly."

"Ah, do not kill me," cried Zambinella, bursting into tears. "I only agreed to trick you to please my friends, who wanted to laugh."

"Laugh!" the sculptor replied in an infernal tone. "Laugh! Laugh! You dared play with a man's feelings, you?"

"Oh, have mercy!" Zambinella replied. 165

"I ought to kill you," Sarrasine cried, drawing his sword with a violent gesture. "However," he went on, in cold disdain, "were I to scour your body with this blade, would I find there one feeling to stifle, one vengeance to satisfy? You are nothing. If you were a man or a woman, I would kill you, but . . ."

Sarrasine made a gesture of disgust which forced him to turn away, whereupon he saw the statue.

"And it's an illusion," he cried. Then, turning to Zambinella: "A woman's heart was a refuge for me, a home. Have you any sisters who resemble you? Then die! But no, you shall live. Isn't leaving you alive condemning you to something worse than death? It is neither my blood nor my existence that I regret, but the future and my heart's fortune. Your feeble hand has destroyed my happiness. What hope can I strip from you for all those you have blighted? You have dragged me down to your level. *To love, to be loved!* are henceforth meaningless words for me, as they are for you. I shall forever think of this imaginary woman when I see a real woman." He indicated the statue with a gesture of despair. "I shall always have the memory of a celestial harpy who thrusts its talons into all my manly feelings, and who will stamp all other women with a seal of imperfection! Monster! You who can give life to nothing. For me, you have wiped women from the earth."

Sarrasine sat down before the terrified singer. Two huge tears welled from his dry eyes, rolled down his manly cheeks, and fell to the ground: two tears of rage, two bitter and burning tears.

"No more love! I am dead to all pleasure, to every human emotion." 170

So saying, he seized a hammer and hurled it at the statue with such extraordinary force that he missed it. He thought he had destroyed this monument to his folly, and then took up his sword and brandished it to kill the singer. Zambinella uttered piercing screams. At that moment, three men entered and at once the sculptor fell, stabbed by three stiletto thrusts.

"On behalf of Cardinal Cicognara," one of them said.

"It is a good deed worthy of a Christian," replied the Frenchman as he died. These sinister messengers informed Zambinella of the concern of his protector, who was waiting at the door in a closed carriage, to take him away as soon as he had been rescued.

"But," Mme de Rochefide asked me, "what connection is there between this story and the little old man we saw at the Lantys'?"

"Madame, Cardinal Cicognara took possession of Zambinella's statue and 175
had it executed in marble; today it is in the Albani Museum. There, in 1791, the Lanty family found it and asked Vien to copy it. The portrait in which you saw Zambinella at twenty, a second after having seen him at one hundred, later served for Girodet's *Endymion;* you will have recognized its type in the Adonis."

"But this Zambinella—he or she?"

"He, madame, is none other than Marianina's great-uncle. Now you can readily see what interest Mme de Lanty has in hiding the source of a fortune which comes from—"

"Enough!" she said, gesturing to me imperiously. We sat for a moment plunged in the deepest silence.

"Well?" I said to her.

"Ah," she exclaimed, standing up and pacing up and down the room. She 180
looked at me and spoke in an altered voice. "You have given me a disgust for life and for passions that will last a long time. Excepting for monsters, don't all human feelings come down to the same thing, to horrible disappointments? Mothers, our children kill us either by their bad behavior or by their lack of affection. Wives, we are deceived. Mistresses, we are forsaken, abandoned. Does friendship even exist? I would become a nun tomorrow did I not know that I can remain unmoved as a rock amid the storms of life. If the Christian's future is also an illusion, at least it is not destroyed until after death. Leave me."

"Ah," I said, "you know how to punish."

"Am I wrong?'

"Yes," I replied, with a kind of courage. "In telling this story, which is fairly well known in Italy, I have been able to give you a fine example of the progress made by civilization today. They no longer create these unfortunate creatures."

"Paris is a very hospitable place," she said. "It accepts everything, shameful fortunes and bloodstained fortunes. Crime and infamy can find asylum here; only virtue has no altars here. Yes, pure souls have their home in heaven! No one will have known me. I am proud of that!"

And the Marquise remained pensive. 185

Honoré de Balzac

www

(1799–1850) Web

A prolific author, Balzac wrote to pay his business debts. Addicted to coffee, he got up in the middle of the night to write, and for nineteen years he wrote an average of thirty-eight pages per week. He produced a vast array of characters, all of whom are described in the realistic style that made them come alive.

www

TOPICS FOR CRITICAL THINKING Web

1. What are the relations between beauty and gender in the story?
2. In what various ways does the story present a spot "in between"?
3. What is the role of painting in the story?
4. How does castration figure as a metaphor in the story?
5. What are the relations between the frame narrative (the party) and the embedded story (the narrative of Sarrasine)?

www

TOPICS FOR CRITICAL WRITING Web

1. Read closely a single line or paragraph of "Sarrasine." What patterns, motifs, and connotations structure the passage?
2. Read closely a single line or paragraph of "Sarrasine." How does this passage relate to the rest of the work? You might want to consider how its images repeat images from the rest of the text, or the ways it varies or modifies your understanding of character through its use of language.

9 Image, Motif, and Symbol

Image, *motif*, and *symbol* are three terms describing different ways language evokes complex and multilayered meanings in prose fiction. The terms *image*, *motif*, and *symbol* actually refer to three different but related uses of images. Confusing them is a common mistake, one that not only limits the tools and concepts you might use to analyze a text, but one that also might confuse those who read your work. **Image** refers to the way words create or suggest sensory phenomena: what we see, hear, smell, feel, or even taste. **Motif** refers to images, words, or ideas that recur in a story; it is a way stories organize images or themes through repetition. A **symbol** is an image that always refers to the same thing.

Image and Motif

Images are crucial components of stories. Rather than being mere decoration or elaboration, images are often the means through which a story comes alive, especially in **modernist** literature, discussed below. In appealing to the reader's senses, images evoke the feel and impression of the world of the story; they portray experience and feelings in a vivid and immediate way. Almost everything in a story is an image produced in the way language creates the scene and action of a story. Although the visual image is the prototype—so much so that twenty-first-century readers think of texts in cinematic terms—images may refer to sounds, smells, tactile sensations, and even taste.

In stories, images are produced by language. Sometimes images are simply descriptions of places or things—"stony hills ablaze with heat" (*Heart of Darkness*) or "Outside, the fire-red, gas-blue, ghost-green signs shone smokily through the tranquil rain" ("Babylon Revisited"). The sense of an image can be created through the artful use of detail—"his starched collars and got-up shirtfronts were achievements of character" (*Heart of Darkness*). "The wild garden behind the house contained a central apple tree and a few straggling bushes, under one of which I found the late tenant's rusty bicycle pump" ("Araby"). Image is also produced by sketching the broad outlines of familiar objects—"The sun set" (*Heart of Darkness*) or "The girl stood up and walked to the end of the station" ("Hills Like White Elephants"). Sometimes an image is evoked through suggestion by using elements of common knowledge to suggest a place, thing, or sensation—"I had a cup of tea—the last decent cup of tea for many days" (*Heart of Darkness*) or "Then the breeze stirred rather more briskly overhead" ("Kew Gardens"). Images can be things we all see every day or they may be subjective or dreamlike.

The exact language and details used to create images are important. Details often link one image to another or connect images to actions or impressions (as we saw in the discussion of Roland Barthes's analysis of "Sarrasine" in Chapter 8). It is by means of imagery that the sense of the story's world—its **diegesis**—is produced. This sense of a world is what Marlow creates in Joseph Conrad's novella *Heart of Darkness*. A story about a story told by the seaman Marlow on a ship waiting for the tide on the Thames, *Heart of Darkness* explores the image of the colonial ivory agent, Kurtz, and the practices of colonial rule through Marlow's impressions of his journey to Brussels and Africa. (See Colonial and Postcolonial Criticism. **Web**) In this narrative, images are Marlow's most profound impressions and his primary way of recounting his experience. Images of the jungle, the river, Kurtz, and even the sunset on the Thames convey Marlow's feelings about his journey into the heart of Africa.

www

Critical Perspective: On Imagery

"Some of the images in [*Heart of Darkness*] are representative in a limited and mainly pictorial way; the older knitter, for example, with her wart and her flat cloth slippers, becomes a stark visual image of physical and spiritual deformity combined with imperturbable self-complacence. But there is another, larger, and to some extent contrary, tendency, where the extreme selectivity of Marlow's memory draws our attention to his state of mind at the time. For instance, when Marlow comments about the tycoon: 'He shook hands, I fancy,' his uncertainty suggests that his consciousness was occupied with other matters. Marlow omits much that would certainly be mentioned in an autobiography, or a naturalist novel; we are not, for instance, given the details of Marlow's contract, or the name of the people. This omission of proper names is a particularly symbolist procedure—in Maeterlinck, for instance, or in Kafka. The general reason for this strategy is clear: most of the details about the narrative object are omitted, so that what details remain, liberated from the bonds and irrelevancies of the purely circumstantial and contingent, can be recognized as representatives of larger ideas and attitudes."

—Ian Watt, "Impressionism and Symbolism in *Heart of Darkness*," in Joseph Conrad, *Heart of Darkness* (3rd ed.), ed. Robert Kimbrough (1988), p. 326.

In this brief consideration of the ways Conrad uses images and symbols in *Heart of Darkness*, Watt focuses on the ways the novella employs imagery to convey images and states of mind and uses selected details as a way of conveying larger ideas and attitudes.

JOSEPH CONRAD

Heart of Darkness

(1899)

I

The *Nellie*, a cruising yawl, swung to her anchor without a flutter of the sails, and was at rest. The flood had made, the wind was nearly calm, and being bound down the river, the only thing for it was to come to and wait for the turn of the tide.

The sea-reach of the Thames stretched before us like the beginning of an interminable waterway. In the offing the sea and the sky were welded together without a joint, and in the luminous space the tanned sails of the barges drifting up with the tide seemed to stand still in red clusters of canvas sharply peaked, with gleams of varnished sprits. A haze rested on the low shores that ran out to sea in vanishing flatness. The air was dark above Gravesend, and farther back still seemed condensed into a mournful gloom, brooding motionless over the biggest, and the greatest, town on earth.

The director of Companies was our captain and our host. We four affectionately watched his back as he stood in the bows looking to seaward. On the whole river there was nothing that looked half so nautical. He resembled a pilot, which to a seaman is trustworthiness personified. It was difficult to realize his work was not out there in the luminous estuary, but behind him, within the brooding gloom.

Between us there was, as I have already said somewhere, the bond of the sea. Besides holding our hearts together through long periods of separation, it had the effect of making us tolerant of each other's yarns—and even convictions. The Lawyer—the best of old fellows—had, because of his many years and many virtues, the only cushion on deck, and was lying on the only rug. The Accountant had brought out already a box of dominoes, and was toying architecturally with the bones. Marlow sat cross-legged right aft, leaning against the mizzen-mast. He had sunken cheeks, a yellow complexion, a straight back, an ascetic aspect, and, with his arms dropped, the palms of hands outwards, resembled an idol. The Director, satisfied the anchor had good hold, made his way aft and sat down amongst us. We exchanged a few words lazily. Afterwards there was silence on board the yacht. For some reason or other we did not begin that game of dominoes. We felt meditative, and fit for nothing but placid staring. The day was ending in a serenity of still and exquisite brilliance. The water shone pacifically; the sky, without a speck, was a benign immensity of unstained light; the very mist on the Essex marshes was like a gauzy and radiant fabric, hung from the wooded rises inland, and draping the low shores in diaphanous folds. Only the gloom to the west, brooding over the upper reaches, became more somber every minute, as if angered by the approach of the sun.

And at last, in its curved and imperceptible fall, the sun sank low, and from glowing white changed to a dull red without rays and without heat, as if about to go out suddenly, stricken to death by the touch of that gloom brooding over a crowd of men.

Forthwith a change came over the waters, and the serenity became less brilliant but more profound. The old river in its broad reach rested unruffled at the decline of day, after ages of good service done to the race that peopled its banks, spread out in the tranquil dignity of a waterway leading to the uttermost ends of the earth. We looked at the venerable stream not in the vivid flush of a short day that comes and departs for ever, but in the august light of abiding memories. And indeed nothing is easier for a man who has, as the phrase goes, "followed the sea" with reverence and affection, than to evoke the great spirit of the past upon the lower reaches of the Thames. The tidal current runs to and fro in its unceasing service, crowded with memories of men and ships it had borne to the rest of home or to the battles of the sea. It had known and served all the men of whom the nation is proud, from Sir Francis Drake to Sir John Franklin, knights all, titled and untitled—the great knights-errant of the sea. It had borne all the ships whose names are like jewels flashing in the night of time, from the *Golden Hind* returning with her round flanks full of treasure, to be visited by the Queen's Highness and thus pass out of the gigantic tale, to the *Erebus* and *Terror*, bound on other conquests—and that never returned. It had known the ships and the men. They had sailed from Deptford, from Greenwich, from Erith—the adventurers and the settlers; kings' ships and the ships of men on 'Change; captains, admirals, the dark "interlopers" of the Eastern trade, and the commissioned "generals" of East India fleets. Hunters for gold or pursuers of fame, they all had gone out on that stream, bearing the sword, and often the torch, messengers of the might within the land, bearers of a spark from the sacred fire. What greatness had not floated on the ebb of that river into the mystery of an unknown earth! . . . The dreams of men, the seed of commonwealths, the germs of empires.

The sun set; the dusk fell on the stream, and lights began to appear along the shore. The Chapman lighthouse, a three-legged thing erect on a mud-flat, shone strongly. Lights of ships moved in the fairway—a great stir of lights going up and going down. And farther west on the upper reaches the place of the monstrous town was still marked ominously on the sky, a brooding gloom in sunshine, a lurid glare under the stars.

"And this also," said Marlow suddenly, "has been one of the dark places of the earth."

He was the only man of us who still "followed the sea." The worst that could be said of him was that he did not represent his class. He was a seaman, but he was a wanderer too, while most seamen lead, if one may so express it, a sedentary life. Their minds are of the stay-at-home order, and their home is always with them—the ship; and so is their country—the sea. One ship is very much like another, and the sea is always the same. In the immutability of their surroundings the foreign shores, the foreign faces, the changing immensity of life, glide past, veiled not by a sense of mystery but by a slightly disdainful ignorance; for there is nothing mysterious to a seaman unless it be the sea itself, which is the mistress of his existence and as inscrutable as Destiny. For the rest, after his hours of work, a casual stroll or a casual spree on shore suffices to unfold for him the secret of a whole continent, and generally he finds the secret not worth knowing. The yarns of seamen have a direct simplicity, the whole meaning of which lies within the shell of a cracked nut. But Marlow was not typical (if his propensity to spin yarns be excepted), and to him the meaning of an episode was not inside like a kernel but outside, enveloping the tale which brought it out only as a glow brings out a haze, in the likeness of one of these misty halos that sometimes are made visible by the spectral illumination of moonshine.

10 His remark did not seem at all surprising. It was just like Marlow. It was accepted in silence. No one took the trouble to grunt even; and presently he said, very slow—

"I was thinking of very old times, when the Romans first came here, nineteen hundred years ago—the other day. . . . Light came out of this river since—you say Knights? Yes; but it is like a running blaze on a plain, like a flash of lightning in the clouds. We live in the flicker—may it last as long as the old earth keeps rolling! But darkness was here yesterday. Imagine the feelings of a commander of a fine—what d'ye call 'em?—trireme in the Mediterranean, ordered suddenly to the north; run overland across the Gauls in a hurry; put in charge of one of these craft the legionaries,—a wonderful lot of handy men they must have been too—used to build, apparently by the hundred, in a month or two, if we may believe what we read. Imagine him here—the very end of the world, a sea the color of lead, a sky the color of smoke, a kind of ship about as rigid as a concertina—and going up this river with stores, or orders, or what you like. Sandbanks, marshes, forests, savages,—precious little to eat fit for a civilized man, nothing but Thames water to drink. No Falernian wine here, no going ashore. Here and there a military camp lost in a wilderness, like a needle in a bundle of hay—cold, fog, tempests, disease, exile, and death,—death skulking in the air, in the water, in the bush. They must have been dying like flies here. Oh yes—he did it. Did it very well, too, no doubt, and without thinking much about it either, except afterwards to brag of what he had gone through in his time, perhaps. They were men enough to face the darkness. And perhaps he was cheered by keeping his eye on a chance of promotion to the fleet at Ravenna by-and-by, if he had good friends in Rome and survived the awful climate. Or think of a decent young citizen in a toga—perhaps too much dice, you know—coming out here in the train of some prefect, or tax-gatherer, or trader even, to mend his fortunes. Land in a swamp, march through the woods, and in some inland post feel the savagery, the utter savagery, had closed round him,—all that mysterious life of the wilderness that stirs in the forest, in the jungles, in the hearts of wild men. There's no initiation either into such mysteries. He has to live in the midst of the incomprehensible, which is also detestable. And it has a fascination, too, that goes to work upon him. The fascination of the abomination—you know. Imagine the growing regrets, the longing to escape, the powerless disgust, the surrender, the hate."

He paused.

"Mind," he began again, lifting one arm from the elbow, the palm of the hand outwards, so that, with his legs folded before him, he had the pose of a Buddha preaching in European clothes and without a lotus-flower—"Mind, none of us would feel exactly like this. What saves us is efficiency—the devotion to efficiency. But these chaps were not much account, really. They were no colonists; their administration was merely a squeeze, and nothing more, I suspect. They were conquerors, and for that you want only brute force—nothing to boast of, when you have it, since your strength is just an accident arising from the weakness of others. They grabbed what they could get for the sake of what was to be got. It was just robbery with violence, aggravated murder on a great scale, and men going at it blind—as is very proper for those who tackle a darkness. The conquest of the earth, which mostly means the taking it away from those who have a different complexion or slightly flatter noses than ourselves, is not a pretty thing when you look into it too much. What redeems it is the idea only. An idea at the back of it; not a sentimental pretense but an idea; and an unselfish belief in the idea—something you can set up, and bow down before, and offer a sacrifice to. . . ."

He broke off. Flames glided in the river, small green flames, red flames, white flames, pursuing, overtaking, joining, crossing each other—then separating slowly or hastily. The traffic of the great city went on in the deepening night upon the sleepless river. We looked on, waiting patiently—there was nothing else to do till the end of the flood; but it was only after a long silence, when he said, in a hesitating voice, "I suppose you fellows remember I did once turn fresh-water sailor for a bit," that we knew we were fated, before the ebb began to run, to hear about one of Marlow's inconclusive experiences.

"I don't want to bother you much with what happened to me personally," 15
he began, showing in this remark the weakness of many tellers of tales who seem so often unaware of what their audience would best like to hear: "yet to understand the effect of it on me you ought to know how I got out there, what I saw, how I went up that river to the place where I first met the poor chap. It was the farthest point of navigation and the culminating point of my experience. It seemed somehow to throw a kind of light on everything about me—and into my thoughts. It was somber enough too—and pitiful—not ex-

traordinary in any way—not very clear either. No, not very clear. And yet it seemed to throw a kind of light.

"I had then, as you remember, just returned to London after a lot of Indian Ocean, Pacific, China Seas—a regular dose of the East—six years or so, and I was loafing about, hindering you fellows in your work and invading your homes, just as though I had got a heavenly mission to civilize you. It was very fine for a time, but after a bit I did get tired of resting. Then I began to look for a ship—I should think the hardest work on earth. But the ships wouldn't even look at me. And I got tired of that game too.

"Now when I was a little chap I had a passion for maps. I would look for hours at South America, or Africa, or Australia, and lose myself in all the glories of exploration. At that time there were many blank spaces on the earth, and when I saw one that looked particularly inviting on a map (but they all look that) I would put my finger on it and say, When I grow up I will go there. The North Pole was one of these places, I remember. Well, I haven't been there yet, and shall not try now. The glamour's off. Other places were scattered about the Equator, and in every sort of latitude all over the two hemispheres. I have been in some of them, . . . well, we won't talk about that. But there was one yet—the biggest, the most blank, so to speak—that I had a hankering after.

"True, by this time it was not a blank space any more. It had got filled since my boyhood with rivers and lakes and names. It had ceased to be a blank space of delightful mystery—a white patch for a boy to dream gloriously over. It had become a place of darkness. But there was in it one river especially, a mighty big river, that you could see on the map, resembling an immense snake uncoiled, with its head in the sea, its body at rest curving afar over a vast country, and its tail lost in the depths of the land. And as I looked at the map of it in a shop-window, it fascinated me as a snake would a bird—a silly little bird. Then I remembered there was a big concern, a Company for trade on that river. Dash it all! I thought to myself, they can't trade without using some kind of craft on that lot of fresh water—steamboats! Why shouldn't I try to get charge of one. I went on along Fleet Street, but could not shake off the idea. The snake had charmed me.

"You understand it was a Continental concern, that Trading society; but I have a lot of relations living on the Continent, because it's cheap and not so nasty as it looks, they say.

"I am sorry to own I began to worry them. This was already a fresh de- 20
parture for me. I was not used to get things that way, you know. I always went my own road and on my own legs where I had a mind to go. I wouldn't have believed it of myself; but, then—you see—I felt somehow I must get there by hook or by crook. So I worried them. The men said 'My dear fellow,' and did nothing. Then—would you believe it?—I tried the women. I, Charlie Marlow, set the women to work—to get a job. Heavens! Well, you see, the notion

drove me. I had an aunt, a dear enthusiastic soul. She wrote: 'It will be delightful. I am ready to do anything, anything for you. It is a glorious idea. I know the wife of a very high personage in the Administration, and also a man who has lots of influence with,' &c., &c. She was determined to make no end of fuss to get me appointed skipper of a river steamboat, if such was my fancy.

"I got my appointment—of course; and I got it very quick. It appears the Company had received news that one of their captains had been killed in a scuffle with the natives. This was my chance, and it made me the more anxious to go. It was only months and months afterwards, when I made the attempt to recover what was left of the body, that I heard the original quarrel arose from a misunderstanding about some hens. Yes, two black hens. Fresleven—that was the fellow's name, a Dane—thought himself wronged somehow in the bargain, so he went ashore and started to hammer the chief of the village with a stick. Oh, it didn't surprise me in the least to hear this, and at the same time to be told that Fresleven was the gentlest, quietest creature that ever walked on two legs. No doubt he was; but he had been a couple of years already out there engaged in the noble cause, you know, and he probably felt the need at last of asserting his self-respect in some way. Therefore he whacked the old nigger mercilessly, while a big crowd of his people watched him, thunderstruck, till some man,—I was told the chief's son,—in desperation at hearing the old chap yell, made a tentative jab with a spear at the white man—and of course it went quite easy between the shoulder-blades. Then the whole population cleared into the forest, expecting all kinds of calamities to happen, while, on the other hand, the steamer Fresleven commanded left also in a bad panic, in charge of the engineer, I believe. Afterwards nobody seemed to trouble much about Fresleven's remains, till I got out and stepped into his shoes. I couldn't let it rest, though; but when an opportunity offered at last to meet my predecessor, the grass growing through his ribs was tall enough to hide his bones. They were all there. The supernatural being had not been touched after he fell. And the village was deserted, the huts gaped black, rotting, all askew within the fallen enclosures. A calamity had come to it, sure enough. The people had vanished. Mad terror had scattered them, men, women, and children, through the bush, and they had never returned. What became of the hens I don't know either. I should think the cause of progress got them, anyhow. However, through this glorious affair I got my appointment, before I had fairly begun to hope for it.

"I flew around like mad to get ready, and before forty-eight hours I was crossing the Channel to show myself to my employers, and sign the contract. In a very few hours I arrived in a city that always makes me think of a whited sepulcher. Prejudice no doubt. I had no difficulty in finding the Company's offices. It was the biggest thing in the town, and everybody I met was full of it. They were going to run an over-sea empire, and make no end of coin by trade.

"A narrow and deserted street in deep shadow, high houses, innumerable windows with venetian blinds, a dead silence, grass sprouting between the stones, imposing carriage archways right and left, immense double doors standing ponderously ajar. I slipped through one of these cracks, went up a swept and ungarnished staircase, as arid as a desert, and opened the first door I came to. Two women, one fat and the other slim, sat on straw-bottomed chairs, knitting black wool. The slim one got up and walked straight at me—still knitting with downcast eyes—and only just as I began to think of getting out of her way, as you would for a somnambulist, stood still, and looked up. Her dress was as plain as an umbrella-cover, and she turned round without a word and preceded me into a waiting-room. I gave my name, and looked about. Deal table in the middle, plain chairs all round the walls, on one end a large shining map, marked with all the colors of a rainbow. There was a vast amount of red—good to see at any time, because one knows that some real work is done in there, a deuce of a lot of blue, a little green, smears of orange, and, on the East Coast, a purple patch, to show where the jolly pioneers of progress drink the jolly lager-beer. However, I wasn't going into any of these. I was going into the yellow. Dead in the center. And the river was there—fascinating—deadly—like a snake. Ough! A door opened, a white-haired secretarial head, but wearing a compassionate expression, appeared, and a skinny forefinger beckoned me into the sanctuary. Its light was dim, and a heavy writing-desk squatted in the middle. From behind that structure came out an impression of pale plumpness in a frock-coat. The great man himself. He was five feet six, I should judge, and had his grip on the handle-end of ever so many millions. He shook hands, I fancy, murmured vaguely, was satisfied with my French. *Bon voyage.*

"In about forty-five seconds I found myself again in the waiting-room with the compassionate secretary, who, full of desolation and sympathy, made me sign some document. I believe I undertook amongst other things not to disclose any trade secrets. Well, I am not going to.

"I began to feel slightly uneasy. You know I am not used to such ceremonies, and there was something ominous in the atmosphere. It was just as though I had been let into some conspiracy—I don't know—something not quite right; and I was glad to get out. In the other room the two women knitted black wool feverishly. People were arriving, and the younger one was walking back and forth introducing them. The old one sat on her chair. Her flat cloth slippers were propped up on a foot-warmer, and a cat reposed on her lap. She wore a starched white affair on her head, had a wart on one cheek, and silver-rimmed spectacles hung on the tip of her nose. She glanced at me above the glasses. The swift and indifferent placidity of that look troubled me. Two youths with foolish and cheery countenances were being piloted over, and she threw at them the same quick glance of unconcerned wisdom. She seemed to know all about them and about me too. An eerie feeling came over me. She seemed uncanny and fateful. Often far away there I thought of these two, guarding the door of Darkness, knitting black wool as for a warm pall, one introducing, introducing continuously to the unknown, the other scrutinizing the cheery and foolish faces with unconcerned old eyes. *Ave!* Old knitter of black wool. *Morituri te salutant.* Not many of those she looked at ever saw her again—not half, by a long way.

"There was yet a visit to the doctor. 'A simple formality,' assured me the secretary, with an air of taking an immense part in all my sorrows. Accordingly a young chap wearing his hat over the left eyebrow, some clerk I suppose,—there must have been clerks in the business, though the house was as still as a house in a city of the dead,—came from somewhere up-stairs, and led me forth. He was shabby and careless, with ink-stains on the sleeves of his jacket, and his cravat was large and billowy, under a chin shaped like the toe of an old boot. It was a little too early for the doctor, so I proposed a drink, and thereupon he developed a vein of joviality. As we sat over our vermouths he glorified the Company's business, and by-and-by I expressed casually my surprise at him not going out there. He became very cool and collected all at once. 'I am not such a fool as I look, quoth Plato to his disciples,' he said sententiously, emptied his glass with great resolution, and we rose.

"The old doctor felt my pulse, evidently thinking of something else the while. 'Good, good for there,' he mumbled, and then with a certain eagerness asked me whether I would let him measure my head. Rather surprised, I said Yes, when he produced a thing like calipers and got the dimensions back and front and every way, taking notes carefully. He was an unshaven little man in a threadbare coat like a gabardine, with his feet in slippers, and I thought him a harmless fool. 'I always ask leave, in the interests of science, to measure the crania of those going out there,' he said. 'And when they come back too?' I asked. 'Oh, I never see them,' he remarked; 'and, moreover, the changes take place inside, you know.' He smiled, as if at some quiet joke. 'So you are going out there. Famous. Interesting too.' He gave me a searching glance, and made another note. 'Ever any madness in your family?' he asked, in a matter-of-fact tone. I felt very annoyed. 'Is that question in the interests of science too?' 'It would be,' he said, without taking notice of my irritation, 'interesting for science to watch the mental changes of individuals, on the spot, but . . .' 'Are you an alienist?' I interrupted. 'Every doctor should be—a little,' answered that original, imperturbably. 'I have a little theory which you Messieurs who go out there must help me to prove. This is my share in the advantages my country shall reap from the possession of such a magnificent dependency. The mere wealth I leave to others. Pardon my questions, but you are the first Englishman coming under my observation. . . .' I hastened to assure him I was not in the least typical. 'If I were,' said I, 'I wouldn't be talking like this with you.' 'What you say is rather profound, and probably erroneous,' he said, with a laugh. 'Avoid irritation more than exposure to the sun. Adieu. How do you English say, eh? Good-by. Ah! Good-by. Adieu. In the tropics one must before everything keep calm.' . . . He lifted a warning forefinger. . . . '*Du calme, du calme. Adieu.*'

"One thing more remained to do—say good-by to my excellent aunt. I found her triumphant. I had a cup of tea—the last decent cup of tea for many days—and in a room that most soothingly looked just as you would expect a lady's drawing-room to look, we had a long quiet chat by the fireside. In the course of these confidences it became quite plain to me I had been represented to the wife of the high dignitary, and goodness knows to how many more people besides, as an exceptional and gifted creature—a piece of good fortune for the Company—a man you don't get hold of every day. Good heavens! and I was going to take charge of a two-penny-halfpenny river-steamboat with a penny whistle attached! It appeared, however, I was also one of the Workers, with a capital—you know. Something like an emissary of light, something like a lower sort of apostle. There had been a lot of such rot let loose in print and talk just about that time, and the excellent woman, living right in the rush of all that humbug, got carried off her feet. She talked about 'weaning those ignorant millions from their horrid ways,' till, upon my word, she made me quite uncomfortable. I ventured to hint that the Company was run for profit.

"'You forget, dear Charlie, that the laborer is worthy of his hire,' she said, brightly. It's queer how out of touch with truth women are. They live in a world of their own, and there had never been anything like it, and never can be. It is too beautiful altogether, and if they were to set it up it would go to pieces before the first sunset. Some confounded fact we men have been living contentedly with ever since the day of creation would start up and knock the whole thing over.

"After this I got embraced, told to wear flannel, be sure to write often, and so on—and I left. In the street—I don't know why—a queer feeling came to me that I was an imposter. Odd thing that I, who used to clear out for any part of the world at twenty-four hours' notice, with less thought than most men give to the crossing of a street, had a moment—I won't say of hesitation, but of startled pause, before this commonplace affair. The best way I can explain it to you is by saying that, for a second or two, I felt as though, instead of going to the center of a continent, I were about to set off for the center of the earth.

"I left in a French steamer, and she called in every blamed port they have out there, for, as far as I could see, the sole purpose of landing soldiers and custom-house officers. I watched the coast. Watching a coast as it slips by the ship is like thinking about an enigma. There it is before you—smiling, frowning, inviting, grand, mean, insipid, or savage, and always mute with an air of whispering, Come and find out. This one was almost featureless, as if still in the making, with an aspect of monotonous grimness. The edge of a colossal jungle, so dark-green as to be almost black, fringed with white surf, ran straight, like a ruled line, far, far away along a blue sea whose glitter was blurred by a creeping mist. The sun was fierce, the land seemed to glisten and drip with steam. Here and there grayish-whitish specks showed up, clustered inside the white surf, with a flag flying above them perhaps. Settlements some centuries old, and still no bigger than pin-heads on the untouched expanse of their background. We pounded along, stopped, landed soldiers; went on, landed custom-house clerks to levy toll in what looked like a God-forsaken wilderness, with a tin shed and a flag-pole lost in it; landed more soldiers—to take care of the custom-house clerks, presumably. Some, I heard, got drowned in the surf; but whether they did or not, nobody seemed particularly to care. They were just flung out there, and on we went. Every day the coast looked the same, as though we had not moved; but we passed various places—trading places—with names like Gran' Bassam Little Popo; names that seemed to belong to some sordid farce acted in front of a sinister backcloth. The idleness of a passenger, my isolation amongst all these men with whom I had no point of contact, the oily and languid sea, the uniform somberness of the coast, seemed to keep me away from the truth of things, within the toil of a mournful and senseless delusion. The voice of the surf heard now and then was a positive pleasure, like the speech of a brother. It was something natural, that had its reason, that had a meaning. Now and then a boat from the shore gave one a momentary contact with reality. It was paddled by black fellows. You could see from afar the white of their eyeballs glistening. They shouted, sang; their bodies streamed with perspiration; they had faces like grotesque masks—these chaps; but they had bone, muscle, a wild vitality, an intense energy of movement, that was as natural and true as the surf along their coast. They wanted no excuse for being there. They were a great comfort to look at. For a time I would feel I belonged still to a world of straightforward facts; but the feeling would not last long. Something would turn up to scare it away. Once, I remember, we came upon a man-of-war anchored off the coast. There wasn't even a shed there, and she was shelling the bush. It appears the French had one of their wars going on thereabouts. Her ensign dropped limp like a rag; the muzzles of the long six-inch guns stuck out all over the low hull; the greasy, slimy swell swung her up lazily and let her down, swaying her thin masts. In the empty immensity of earth, sky, and water, there she was, incomprehensible, firing into a continent. Pop, would go one of the six-inch guns; a small flame would dart and vanish, a little white smoke would disappear, a tiny projectile would give a feeble screech—and nothing happened. Nothing could happen. There was a touch of insanity in the proceeding, a sense of lugubrious drollery in the sight; and it was not dissipated by somebody on board assuring me earnestly there was a camp of natives—he called them enemies!—hidden out of sight somewhere.

"We gave her her letters (I heard the men in that lonely ship were dying of fever at the rate of three a day) and went on. We called at some more places with farcical names, where the merry dance of death and trade goes on in a still and earthy atmosphere as of an overheated catacomb; all along the formless coast bordered by dangerous surf, as if Nature herself had tried to ward off intruders; in and out of rivers, streams of death in life, whose banks were rotting into mud, whose waters, thickened into slime, invaded the contorted mangroves, that seemed to writhe at us in the extremity of an impotent despair. Nowhere did we stop long enough to get a particularized impression, but the general sense of vague and oppressive wonder grew upon me. It was like a weary pilgrimage amongst hints for nightmares.

"It was upward of thirty days before I saw the mouth of the big river. We anchored off the seat of the government. But my work would not begin till some two hundred miles farther on. So as soon as I could I made a start for a place thirty miles higher up.

"I had my passage on a little sea-going steamer. Her captain was a Swede, and knowing me for a seaman, invited me on the bridge. He was a young man, lean, fair, and morose, with lanky hair and a shuffling gait. As we left the miserable little wharf, he tossed his head contemptuously at the shore. 'Been living there?' he asked. I said, 'Yes.' 'Fine lot these government chaps—are they not?' he went on, speaking English with great precision and considerable bitterness. 'It is funny what some people will do for a few francs a month. I wonder what becomes of that kind when it goes up country?' I said to him I expected to see that soon. 'So-o-o!' he exclaimed. He shuffled athwart, keeping one eye ahead vigilantly. 'Don't be too sure,' he continued. 'The other day I took up a man who hanged himself on the road. He was a Swede, too.' 'Hanged himself! Why, in God's name?' I cried. He kept on looking out watchfully. 'Who knows? The sun too much for him, or the country perhaps.'

"At last we opened a reach. A rocky cliff appeared, mounds of turned-up earth by the shore, houses on a hill, others, with iron roofs, amongst a waste of excavations, or hanging to the declivity. A continuous noise of the rapids above hovered over this scene of inhabited devastation. A lot of people, mostly black and naked, moved about like ants. A jetty projected into the river. A blinding sunlight drowned all this at times in a sudden recrudescence of glare. 'There's your Company's station,' said the Swede, pointing to three wooden barrack-like structures on the rocky slope. 'I will send your things up. Four boxes did you say? So. Farewell.'

"I came upon a boiler wallowing in the grass, then found a path leading up the hill. It turned aside for the bowlders, and also for an undersized railway-truck lying there on its back with its wheels in the air. One was off. The thing looked as dead as the carcass of some animal. I came upon more pieces of decaying machinery, a stack of rusty nails. To the left a clump of trees made a shady spot, where dark things seemed to stir feebly. I blinked, the path was steep. A horn tooted to the right, and I saw the black people run. A heavy and dull detonation shook the ground, a puff of smoke came out of the cliff, and that was all. No change appeared on the face of the rock. They were building a railway. The cliff was not in the way or anything; but this objectless blasting was all the work going on.

"A slight clinking behind me made me turn my head. Six black men advanced in a file, toiling up the path. They walked erect and slow, balancing small baskets full of earth on their heads, and the clink kept time with their footsteps. Black rags were wound round their loins, and the short ends behind waggled to and fro like tails. I could see every rib, the joints of their limbs were like knots in a rope; each had an iron collar on his neck, and all were connected together with a chain whose bights swung between them, rhythmically clinking. Another report from the cliff made me think suddenly of that ship of war I had seen firing into a continent. It was the same kind of ominous voice; but these men could by no stretch of imagination be called enemies. They were called criminals, and the outraged law, like the bursting shells, had come to them, an insoluble mystery from the sea. All their meager breasts panted together, the violently dilated nostrils quivered, the eyes stared stonily uphill. They passed me within six inches, without a glance, with that complete, deathlike indifference of unhappy savages. Behind this raw matter one of the reclaimed, the product of the new forces at work, strolled despondently, carrying a rifle by its middle. He had a uniform jacket with one button off, and seeing a white man on the path, hoisted his weapon to his shoulder with alacrity. This was simple prudence, white men being so much alike at a distance that he could not tell who I might be. He was speedily reassured, and with a large, white, rascally grin, and a glance at his charge, seemed to take me into partnership in his exalted trust. After all, I also was a part of the great cause of these high and just proceedings.

"Instead of going up, I turned and descended to the left. My idea was to let that chain-gang get out of sight before I climbed the hill. You know I am not particularly tender; I've had to strike and to fend off. I've had to resist and to attack sometimes—that's only one way of resisting—without counting the exact cost, according to the demands of such sort of life as I had blundered into. I've seen the devil of violence, and the devil of greed, and the devil of hot desire; but, by all the stars! these were strong, lusty, red-eyed devils, that swayed and drove men—men, I tell you. But as I stood on this hillside, I foresaw that in the blinding sunshine of that land I would become acquainted with a flabby, pretending, weak-eyed devil of a rapacious and pitiless folly. How insidious he could be, too, I was only to find out several months later and a thousand miles farther. For a moment I stood appalled, as though by a warning. Finally I descended the hill, obliquely, towards the trees I had seen.

"I avoided a vast artificial hole somebody had been digging on the slope, the purpose of which I found it impossible to divine. It wasn't a quarry or a sandpit, anyhow. It was just a hole. It might have been connected with the philanthropic desire of giving the criminals something to do. I don't know. Then I nearly fell into a very narrow ravine, almost no more than a scar in the hillside. I discovered that a lot of imported drainage-pipes for the settlement had been tumbled in there. There wasn't one that was not broken. It was a wanton smash-up. At last I got under the trees. My purpose was to stroll into the shade for a moment; but no sooner within than it seemed to me I had stepped into a gloomy circle of some Inferno. The rapids were near, and an uninterrupted, uniform, headlong, rushing noise filled the mournful stillness of the grove, where not a breath stirred, not a leaf moved, with a mysterious sound—as though the tearing pace of the launched earth had suddenly become audible.

"Black shapes crouched, lay, sat between the trees, leaning against the 40
trunks, clinging to the earth, half coming out, half effaced within the dim light, in all the attitudes of pain, abandonment, and despair. Another mine on the cliff went off, followed by a slight shudder of the soil under my feet. The work was going on. The work! And this was the place where some of the helpers had withdrawn to die.

"They were dying slowly—it was very clear. They were not enemies, they were not criminals, they were nothing earthly now,—nothing but black shadows of disease and starvation, lying confusedly in the greenish gloom. Brought from all the recesses of the coast in all the legality of time contracts, lost in uncongenial surroundings, fed on unfamiliar food, they sickened, became inefficient, and were then allowed to crawl away and rest. These moribund shapes were free as air—and nearly as thin. I began to distinguish the gleam of the eyes under the trees. Then, glancing down, I saw a face near my hand. The black bones reclined at full length with one shoulder against the tree, and slowly the eyelids rose and the sunken eyes looked up at me, enormous and vacant, a kind of blind, white flicker in the depths of the orbs, which died out slowly. The man seemed young—almost a boy—but you know with them it's hard to tell. I found nothing else to do but to offer him one of my good Swede's ship's biscuits I had in my pocket. The fingers closed slowly on it and held—there was no other movement and no other glance. He had tied a bit of white worsted round his neck—Why? Where did he get it? Was it a badge—an ornament—a charm—a propitiatory act? Was there any idea at all connected with it? It looked startling round his black neck, this bit of white thread from beyond the seas.

"Near the same tree two more bundles of acute angles sat with their legs drawn up. One, with his chin propped on his knees, stared at nothing, in an intolerable and appalling manner: his brother phantom rested its forehead, as if overcome with a great weariness; and all about others scattered in every pose of contorted collapse, as in some picture of a massacre or a pestilence. While I stood horror-struck, one of these creatures rose to his hands and knees, and went off on all-fours towards the river to drink. He lapped out of his hand, then sat up in the sunlight, crossing his shins in front of him, and after a time let his woolly head fall on his breastbone.

"I didn't want any more loitering in the shade, and I made haste towards the station. When near the buildings I met a white man, in such an unexpected elegance of get-up that in the first moment I took him for a sort of vision. I saw a high starched collar, white cuffs, a light alpaca jacket, snowy trousers, a clean necktie, and varnished boots. No hat. Hair parted, brushed, oiled, under a green-lined parasol held in a big white hand. He was amazing, and had a penholder behind his ear.

"I shook hands with this miracle, and I learned he was the Company's chief accountant, and that all the bookkeeping was done at this station. He had come out for a moment, he said, 'to get a breath of fresh air.' The expression sounded wonderfully odd, with its suggestion of sedentary desk-life. I wouldn't have mentioned the fellow to you at all, only it was from his lips that I first heard the name of the man who is so indissolubly connected with the memories of that time. Moreover, I respected the fellow. Yes; I respected his collars, his vast cuffs, his brushed hair. His appearance was certainly that of a hairdresser's dummy; but in the great demoralization of the land he kept up his appearance. That's backbone. His starched collars and got-up shirtfronts were achievements of character. He had been out nearly three years; and, later on, I could not help asking him how he managed to sport such linen. He had just the faintest blush, and said modestly, 'I've been teaching one of the native women about the station. It was difficult. She had a distaste for the work.' Thus this man had verily accomplished something. And he was devoted to his books, which were in apple-pie order.

"Everything else in the station was in a muddle,—heads, things, build- 45
ings. Strings of dusty niggers with splay feet arrived and departed; a stream of manufactured goods, rubbishy cottons, beads, and brass-wire sent into the depths of darkness, and in the return came a precious trickle of ivory.

"I had to wait in the station for ten days—an eternity. I lived in a hut in the yard, but to be out of the chaos I would sometimes get into the accountant's office. It was built of horizontal planks, and so badly put together that, as he bent over his desk, he was barred from neck to heels with narrow strips of sunlight. There was no need to open the big shutter to see. It was hot there too; big flies buzzed fiendishly, and did not sting, but stabbed. I sat generally on the floor, while, of faultless appearance (and even slightly scented), perching on a high stool, he wrote, he wrote. Sometimes he stood up for exercise. When a truckle-bed with a sick man (some invalided agent from up-country) was put in there, he exhibited a gentle annoyance. 'The groans of this sick person,' he said, 'distract my attention. And without that it is extremely difficult to guard against clerical errors in this climate.'

"One day he remarked, without lifting his head, 'In the interior you will no doubt meet Mr. Kurtz.' On my asking who Mr. Kurtz was, he said he was a first-class agent; and seeing my disappointment at this information, he added slowly, laying down his pen, 'He is a very remarkable person.' Further questions elicited from him that Mr. Kurtz was at present in charge of a trading post, a very important one, in the true ivory-country, at 'the very bottom of there. Sends in as much ivory as all the others put together. . . .' He began to write again. The sick man was too ill to groan. The flies buzzed in a great peace.

"Suddenly there was a growing murmur of voices and a great tramping of feet. A caravan had come in. A violent babble of uncouth sounds burst out on the other side of the planks. All the carriers were speaking together, and in the midst of the uproar the lamentable voice of the chief agent was heard 'giving it up' tearfully for the twentieth time that day. . . . He rose slowly. 'What a frightful row,' he said. He crossed the room gently to look at the sick man, and returning, said to me, 'He does not hear.' 'What! Dead?' I asked, startled.

'No, not yet,' he answered, with great composure. Then, alluding with a toss of the head to the tumult in the station-yard, 'When one has got to make correct entries, one comes to hate those savages—hate them to the death.' He remained thoughtful for a moment. 'When you see Mr. Kurtz,' he went on, 'tell him from me that everything here'—he glanced at the desk—'is very satisfactory. I don't like to write to him—with those messengers of ours you never know who may get hold of your letter—at that Central Station.' He stared at me for a moment with his mild, bulging eyes. 'Oh, he will go far, very far,' he began again. 'He will be a somebody in the Administration before long. They, above—the Council in Europe, you know—mean him to be.'

"He turned to his work. The noise outside had ceased, and presently in going out I stopped at the door. In the steady buzz of flies the homeward-bound agent was lying flushed and insensible; the other, bent over his books, was making correct entries of perfectly correct transactions; and fifty feet below the doorstep I could see the still tree-tops of the grove of death.

"Next day I left that station at last, with a caravan of sixty men, for a two- 50
hundred-mile tramp.

"No use telling you much about that. Paths, paths, everywhere; a stamped-in network of paths spreading over the empty land, through long grass, through burnt grass, through thickets, down and up chilly ravines, up and down stony hills ablaze with heat; and a solitude, nobody, not a hut. The population had cleared out a long time ago. Well, if a lot of mysterious niggers armed with all kinds of fearful weapons suddenly took to traveling on the road between Deal and Gravesend, catching the yokels right and left to carry heavy loads for them, I fancy every farm and cottage thereabouts would get empty very soon. Only here the dwellings were gone too. Still I passed through several abandoned villages. There's something pathetically childish in the ruins of grass walls. Day after day, with the stamp and shuffle of sixty pair of bare feet behind me, each pair under a 60-lb. load. Camp, cook, sleep, strike camp, march. Now and then a carrier dead in harness, at rest in the long grass near the path, with an empty water-gourd and his long staff lying by his side. A great silence around and above. Perhaps on some quiet night the tremor of far-off drums, sinking, swelling, a tremor vast, faint; a sound weird, appealing, suggestive, and wild—and perhaps with as profound a meaning as the sound of bells in a Christian country. Once a white man in an unbuttoned uniform, camping on the path with an armed escort of lank Zanzibaris, very hospitable and festive—not to say drunk. Was looking after the upkeep of the road, he declared. Can't say I saw any road or any upkeep, unless the body of a middle-aged negro, with a bullet-hole in the forehead, upon which I absolutely stumbled three miles farther on, may be considered as a permanent improvement. I had a white companion too, not a bad chap, but rather too fleshy and with the exasperating habit of fainting on the hot hillsides, miles away from the least bit of shade and water. Annoying, you know, to hold your own coat like a parasol over a man's head while he is coming-to. I couldn't help asking him once what he meant by coming there at all. 'To make money, of course. What do you think?' he said, scornfully. Then he got fever, and had to be carried in a hammock slung under a pole. As he weighed sixteen stone I had no end of rows with the carriers. They jibbed, ran away, sneaked off with their loads in the night—quite a mutiny. So, one evening, I made a speech in English with gestures, not one of which was lost to the sixty pairs of eyes before me, and the next morning I started the hammock off in front all right. An hour afterwards I came upon the whole concern wrecked in a bush—man, hammock, groans, blankets, horrors. The heavy pole had skinned his poor nose. He was very anxious for me to kill somebody, but there wasn't the shadow of a carrier near. I remembered the old doctor,—'It would be interesting for science to watch the mental changes of individuals, on the spot.' I felt I was becoming scientifically interesting. However, all that is to no purpose. On the fifteenth day I came in sight of the big river again, and hobbled into the Central Station. It was on a back water surrounded by scrub and forest, with a pretty border of smelly mud on one side, and on the three others inclosed by a crazy fence of rushes. A neglected gap was all the gate it had, and the first glance at the place was enough to let you see the flabby devil was running that show. White men with long staves in their hands appeared languidly from amongst the buildings, strolling up to take a look at me, and then retired out of sight somewhere. One of them, a stout, excitable chap with black mustaches, informed me with great volubility and many digressions, as soon as I told him who I was, that my steamer was at the bottom of the river. I was thunderstruck. What, how, why? Oh, it was 'all right.' The 'manager himself' was there. All quite correct. 'Everybody had behaved splendidly! splendidly!'—'you must,' he said in agitation, 'go and see the general manager at once. He is waiting!'

"I did not see the real significance of that wreck at once. I fancy I see it now, but I am not sure—not at all. Certainly the affair was too stupid—when I think of it—to be altogether natural. Still. . . . But at the moment it presented itself simply as a confounded nuisance. The steamer was sunk. They had started two days before in a sudden hurry up the river with the manager on board, in charge of some volunteer skipper, and before they had been out three hours they tore the bottom out of her on stones, and she sank near the south bank. I asked myself what I was to do there, now my boat was lost. As a matter of fact, I had plenty to do in fishing my command out of the river. I had to set about it the very next day. That, and the repairs when I brought the pieces to the station, took some months.

"My first interview with the manager was curious. He did not ask me to sit down after my twenty-mile walk that morning. He was commonplace in complexion, in feature, in manners, and in voice. He was of middle size and of ordinary build. His eyes, of the usual blue, were perhaps remarkably cold, and he certainly could make his glance fall on one as trenchant and heavy as an ax. But even at these times the rest of his person seemed to disclaim the intention. Otherwise there was only an indefinable, faint expression of his lips, something stealthy—a smile—not a smile—I remember it, but I can't explain. It was unconscious, this smile was, though just after he had said something it got intensified for an instant. It came at the end of his speeches like a seal applied on the words to make the meaning of the commonest phrase appear absolutely inscrutable. He was a common trader, from his youth up employed in these parts—nothing more. He was obeyed, yet he inspired neither love nor fear, nor even respect. He inspired uneasiness. That was it! Uneasiness. Not a definite mistrust—just uneasiness—nothing more. You have no idea how effective such a . . . a . . . faculty can be. He had no genius for organizing, for initiative, or for order even. That was evident in such things as the deplorable state of the station. He had no learning, and no intelligence. His position had come to him—why? Perhaps because he was never ill . . . He had served three terms of three years out there . . . Because triumphant health in the general rout of constitutions is a kind of power in itself. When he went home on leave he rioted on a large scale—pompously. Jack ashore—with a difference—in externals only. This one could gather from his casual talk. He originated nothing, he could keep the routine going—that's all. But he was great. He was great by this little thing that it was impossible to tell what could control such a man. He never gave that secret away. Perhaps there was nothing within him. Such a suspicion made one pause—for out there there were no external checks. Once when various tropical diseases had laid low almost every 'agent' in the station, he was heard to say, 'Men who come out here should have no entrails.' He sealed the utterance with that smile of his, as though it had been a door opening into a darkness he had in his keeping. You fancied you had seen things—but the seal was on. When annoyed at meal-times by the constant quarrels of the white men about precedence, he ordered an immense round table to be made, for which a special house had to be built. This was the station's mess-room. Where he sat was the first place—the rest were nowhere. One felt this to be his unalterable conviction. He was neither civil nor uncivil. He was quiet. He allowed his 'boy'—an overfed young negro from the coast—to treat the white men, under his very eyes, with provoking insolence.

"He began to speak as soon as he saw me. I had been very long on the road. He could not wait. Had to start without me. The up-river stations had to be relieved. There had been so many delays already that he did not know who was dead and who was alive, and how they got on—and so on, and so on. He paid no attention to my explanations, and, playing with a stick of sealing-wax, repeated several times that the situation was 'very grave, very grave.' There were rumors that a very important station was in jeopardy, and its chief, Mr. Kurtz, was ill. Hoped it was not true. Mr. Kurtz was . . . I felt weary and irritable. Hang Kurtz, I thought. I interrupted him by saying I had heard of Mr. Kurtz on the coast. 'Ah! So they talk of him down there,' he murmured to himself. Then he began again, assuring me Mr. Kurtz was the best agent he had, an exceptional man, of the greatest importance to the Company; therefore I could understand his anxiety. He was, he said, 'very, very uneasy.' Certainly he fidgeted on his chair a good deal, exclaimed, 'Ah, Mr. Kurtz!' broke the stick of sealing-wax and seemed dumbfounded by the accident. Next thing he wanted to know 'how long it would take to' . . . I interrupted him again. Being hungry, you know, and kept on my feet too, I was getting savage. 'How could I tell,' I said. 'I hadn't even seen the wreck yet—some months, no doubt! All this talk seemed to me so futile. 'Some months,' he said. 'Well, let us say three months before we can make a start. Yes. That ought to do the affair.' I flung out of his hut (he lived all alone in a clay hut with a sort of veranda) muttering to myself my opinion of him. He was a chattering idiot. Afterwards I took it back when it was borne in upon me startlingly with what extreme nicety he had estimated the time requisite for the 'affair.'

55 "I went to work the next day, turning, so to speak, my back on that station. In that way only it seemed to me I could keep my hold on the redeeming facts of life. Still, one must look about sometimes; and then I saw this station, these men strolling aimlessly about in the sunshine of the yard. I asked myself sometimes what it all meant. They wandered here and there with their absurd long staves in their hands, like a lot of faithless pilgrims bewitched inside a rotten fence. The word 'ivory' rang in the air, was whispered, was sighed. You would think they were praying to it. A taint of imbecile rapacity blew through it all, like a whiff from some corpse. By Jove! I've never seen anything so unreal in my life. And outside, the silent wilderness surrounding this cleared speck on the earth struck me as something great and invincible, like evil or truth, waiting patiently for the passing away of this fantastic invasion.

"Oh, these months! well, never mind. Various things happened. One evening a grass shed full of calico, cotton prints, beads, and I don't know what else, burst into a blaze so suddenly that you would have thought the earth had opened to let an avenging fire consume all that trash. I was smoking my pipe quietly by my dismantled steamer, and saw them all cutting capers in the light, with their arms lifted high, when the stout man with mustaches came tearing down to the river, a tin pail in his hand, assured me that everybody was 'behaving splendidly, splendidly,' dipped about a quart of water and tore back again. I noticed there was a hole in the bottom of his pail.

"I strolled up. There was no hurry. You see the thing had gone off like a box of matches. It had been hopeless from the very first. The flame had leaped high, driven everybody back, lighted up everything—and collapsed. The shed was already a heap of embers glowing fiercely. A nigger was being beaten near by. They said he had caused the fire in some way; be that as it may, he was screeching most horribly. I saw him, later on, for several days, sitting in a bit of shade looking very sick and trying to recover himself: afterwards he arose and went out—and the wilderness without a sound took him into its bosom again. As I approached the glow from the dark I found myself at the back of two men, talking. I heard the name of Kurtz pronounced, then the words, 'take advantage of this unfortunate accident.' One of the men was the manager. I wished him a good evening. 'Did you ever see anything like it—eh? it is incredible,' he said and walked off. The other man remained. He was a first-class agent, young, gentlemanly, a bit reserved, with a forked little beard and a hooked nose. He was standoffish with the other agents, and they on their side said he was the manager's spy upon them. As to me, I had hardly ever spoken to him before. We got into talk, and by-and-by we strolled away from the hissing ruins. Then he asked me to his room, which was in the main building of the station. He struck a match, and I perceived that this young aristocrat had only a silver-mounted dressing-case but also a whole candle all to himself. Just at that time the manager was the only man supposed to have any right to candles. Native mats covered the clay walls; a collection of spears, assegais, shields, knives was hung up in trophies. The business intrusted to this fellow was the making of bricks—so I had been informed; but there wasn't a fragment of a brick anywhere in the station, and he had been there more than a year—waiting. It seems he could not make bricks without something, I don't know what—straw maybe. Anyways, it could not be found there, and as it was not likely to be sent from Europe, it did not appear clear to me what he was waiting for. An act of special creation perhaps. However, they were all waiting—all the sixteen or twenty pilgrims of them—for something; and upon my word it did not seem an uncongenial occupation, from the way they took it, though the only thing that ever came to them was disease—as far as I could see. They beguiled the time by backbiting and intriguing against each other in a foolish kind of way. There was an air of plotting about that station, but nothing came of it, of course. It was as unreal as everything else—as the philanthropic pretense of the whole concern, as their talk, as their government, as their show of work. The only real feeling was a desire to get appointed to a trading-post where ivory was to be had, so that they could earn percentages. They intrigued and slandered and hated each other only on that account,—but as to effectually lifting a little finger—oh, no. By heavens! there is something after all in the world allowing one man to steal a horse while another must not look at a halter. Steal a horse straight out. Very well. He has done it. Perhaps he can ride. But there is a way of looking at a halter that would provoke the most charitable of saints into a kick.

"I had no idea why he wanted to be sociable, but as we chatted in there it suddenly occurred to me the fellow was trying to get at something—in fact, pumping me. He alluded constantly to Europe, to the people I was supposed to know there—putting leading questions as to my acquaintances in the sepulchral city, and so on. His little eyes glittered like mica discs—with curiosity,—though he tried to keep up a bit of superciliousness. At first I was astonished, but very soon I became awfully curious to see what he would find out from me. I couldn't possibly imagine what I had in me to make it worth his while. It was very pretty to see how he baffled himself, for in truth my body was full of chills, and my head had nothing in it but that wretched steamboat business. It was evident he took me for a perfectly shameless prevaricator. At last he got angry, and, to conceal a movement of furious annoyance, he yawned. I rose. Then I noticed a small sketch in oils, on a panel, representing a woman, draped and blindfolded, carrying a lighted torch. The background was somber—almost black. The movement of the woman was stately, and the effect of the torchlight on the face was sinister.

"It arrested me, and he stood by civilly, holding an empty half-pint champagne bottle (medical comforts) with the candle stuck in it. To my question he said Mr. Kurtz had painted this—in this very station more than a year ago—while waiting for means to go to his trading-post. 'Tell me, pray,' said I, 'who is this Mr. Kurtz?'

"'The chief of the Inner Station,' he answered in a short tone, looking 60 away. 'Much obliged,' I said, laughing. 'And you are the brickmaker of the Central Station. Everyone knows that.' He was silent for a while. 'He is a prodigy,' he said at last. 'He is an emissary of pity, and science, and progress, and devil knows what else. We want,' he began to declaim suddenly, 'for the guidance of the cause intrusted to us by Europe, so to speak, higher intelligence, wide sympathies, a singleness of purpose.' 'Who says that?' I asked. 'Lots of them,' he replied. 'Some even write that; and so *he* comes here, a special being, as you ought to know.' 'Why ought I to know?' I interrupted, really surprised. He paid no attention. 'Yes. To-day he is chief of the best station, next year he will be assistant-manager, two years more and . . . but I dare say you know what he will be in two years' time. You are the new gang—the gang of virtue. The same people who sent him specially also recommended you. Oh, don't say no. I've my own eyes to trust.' Light dawned upon me. My dear aunt's influential acquaintances were producing an unexpected effect upon that young man. I nearly burst into a laugh. 'Do you read the Company's confidential correspondence?' I asked. He hadn't a word to say. It was great fun. 'When Mr. Kurtz,' I continued severely, 'is General Manager, you won't have the opportunity.'

"He blew the candle out suddenly, and we went outside. The moon had risen. Black figures strolled about listlessly, pouring water on the glow, whence proceeded a sound of hissing; steam ascended in the moonlight, the beaten nigger groaned somewhere. 'What a row the brute makes!' said the indefatigable man with the mustaches, appearing near us. 'Serve him right. Transgression—punishment—bang! Pitiless, pitiless. That's the only way. This will prevent all conflagration for the future. I was just telling the manager . . .' He noticed my companion, and became crestfallen all at once. 'Not in bed yet,' he said, with a kind of servile heartiness; 'it's so natural. Ha! Danger-agitation.' He vanished. I went on to the river-side, and the other followed me. I heard a scathing murmur at my ear. 'Heap of muffs—go to.' The pilgrims could be seen in knots gesticulating, discussing. Several had still their staves in their hands. I verily believe they took these sticks to bed with them. Beyond the fence the forest stood up spectrally in the moonlight, and through the dim stir, through the faint sounds of that lamentable courtyard, the silence of the land when home to one's very heart,—its mystery, its greatness, the amazing reality of its concealed life. The hurt nigger moaned feebly somewhere near by, and then fetched a deep sigh that made me mend my pace away from there. I felt a hand introducing itself under my arm. 'My dear sir,' said the fellow, 'I don't want to be misunderstood, and especially by you, who will see Mr. Kurtz long before I can have that pleasure. I wouldn't like him to get a false idea of my disposition. . . .'

"I let him run on, this papier-maché Mephistopheles, and it seemed to me that if I tried I could poke my forefinger through him, and would find nothing inside but a little loose dirt, maybe. He, don't you see, had been planning to be assistant-manager by-and-by under the present man, and I could see that the coming of that Kurtz had upset them both not a little. He talked precipitately, and I did not try to stop him. I had my shoulders against the wreck of my steamer, hauled up on the slope like a carcass of some big river animal.

The smell of mud, of primeval mud, by Jove! was in my nostrils, the high stillness of primeval forest was before my eyes; there were shiny patches on the black creek. The moon had spread over everything a thin layer of silver—over the rank grass, over the mud, upon the wall of matted vegetation standing higher than the wall of a temple, over the great river I could see through a somber gap glittering, glittering, as it flowed broadly by without a murmur. All this was great, expectant, mute, while the man jabbered about himself. I wondered whether the stillness on the face of the immensity looking at us two were meant as an appeal or as a menace. What were we who had strayed in here? Could we handle that dumb thing, or would it handle us? I felt how big, how confoundedly big, was that thing that couldn't talk, and perhaps was deaf as well. What was in there? I could see a little ivory coming out from there, and I had heard Mr. Kurtz was in there. I had heard enough about it too—God knows! Yet somehow it didn't bring any image with it—no more than if I had been told an angel or a fiend was in there. I believed it in the same way one of you might believe there are inhabitants in the planet Mars. I knew once a Scotch sailmaker who was certain, dead sure, there were people in Mars. If you asked him for some idea how they looked and behaved, he would get shy and mutter something about 'walking on all-fours.' If you as much as smiled, he would—though a man of sixty—offer to fight you. I would not have gone so far as to fight for Kurtz, but I went for him near enough to a lie. You know I hate, detest, and can't bear a lie, not because I am straighter than the rest of us, but simply because it appalls me. There is a taint of death, a flavor of mortality in lies,—which is exactly what I hate and detest in the world—what I want to forget. It makes me miserable and sick, like biting something rotten would do. Temperament, I suppose. Well, I went near enough to it by letting the young fool there believe anything he liked to imagine as to my influence in Europe. I became in an instant as much of a pretense as the rest of the bewitched pilgrims. This simply because I had a notion it somehow would be of help to that Kurtz whom at the time I did not see—you understand. He was just a word for me. I did not see the man in the name any more than you do. Do you see him? Do you see the story? Do you see anything? It seems to me I am trying to tell you a dream—making a vain attempt, because no relation of a dream can convey the dream-sensation, that commingling of absurdity, surprise, and bewilderment in a tremor of struggling revolt, that notion of being captured by the incredible which is of the very essence of dreams. . . ."

He was silent for a while.

". . . No, it is impossible; it is impossible to convey the life-sensation of any given epoch of one's existence,—that which makes its truth, its meaning—its subtle and penetrating essence. It is impossible. We live, as we dream—alone. . . ."

He paused again as if reflecting, then added— 65

"Of course in this you fellows see more than I could then. You see me, whom you know. . . ."

It had become so pitch dark that we listeners could hardly see one another. For a long time already he, sitting apart, had been no more to us than a voice. There was not a word from anybody. The others might have been asleep, but I was awake. I listened, I listened on the watch for the sentence, for the word, that would give me the clew to the faint uneasiness inspired by this narrative that seemed to shape itself without human lips in the heavy night-air of the river.

"... Yes—I let him run on," Marlow began again, "and think what he pleased about the powers that were behind me. I did! And there was nothing behind me! There was nothing but that wretched, old, mangled steamboat I was leaning against, while he talked fluently about 'the necessity for every man to get on.' 'And when one comes out here, you conceive, it is not to gaze at the moon.' Mr. Kurtz was a 'universal genius,' but even a genius would find it easier to work with 'adequate tools—intelligent men.' He did not make bricks—why, there was a physical impossibility in the way—as I was well aware; and if he did secretarial work for the manager, it was because 'no sensible man rejects wantonly the confidence of his superiors.' Did I see it? I saw it. What more did I want? What I really wanted was rivets, by heaven! Rivets. To get on with the work—to stop the hole. Rivets I wanted. There were cases of them down at the coast—cases—piled up—burst—split! You kicked a loose rivet at every second step in that station yard on the hillside. Rivets had rolled into the grove of death. You could fill your pockets with rivets for the trouble of stooping down—and there wasn't one rivet to be found where it was wanted. We had plates that would do, but nothing to fasten them with. And every week the messenger, a lone negro, letter-bag on shoulder and staff in hand, left our station for the coast. And several times a week a coast caravan came in with trade goods,—ghastly glazed calico that made you shudder only to look at it, glass beads value about a penny a quart, confounded spotted cotton handkerchiefs. And no rivets. Three carriers could have brought all that was wanted to set that steamboat afloat.

"He was becoming confidential now, but I fancy my unresponsive attitude must have exasperated him at last, for he judged it necessary to inform me he feared neither God nor devil, let alone any mere man. I said I could see that very well, but what I wanted was a certain quantity of rivets—and rivets were what really Mr. Kurtz wanted, if he had only known it. Now letters went to the coast every week.... 'My dear sir,' he cried, 'I write from dictation.' I demanded rivets. There was a way—for an intelligent man. He changed his manner; became very cold, and suddenly began to talk about a hippopotamus; wondered whether sleeping on board the steamer (I stuck to my salvage night and day) I wasn't disturbed. There was an old hippo that had the bad habit of getting out on the bank and roaming at night over the station grounds. The pilgrims use to turn out in a body and empty every rifle they could lay hands on at him. Some even had sat up o' nights for him. All this energy was wasted, though. 'That animal has a charmed life,' he said; 'but you can say this only of brutes in this country. No man—you apprehend me?—no man here bears a charmed life.' He stood there for a moment in the moonlight with his delicate hooked nose set a little askew, and his mica eyes glittering without a wink, then, with a curt Good night, he strode off. I could see he was disturbed and considerably puzzled, which made me feel more hopeful than I had been for days. It was a great comfort to turn from that chap to my influential friend, the battered, twisted, ruined, tin-pot steamboat. I clambered on board. She rang under my feet like an empty Huntley & Palmer biscuit-tin kicked along a gutter; she was nothing so solid in make, and rather less pretty in shape, but I had expended enough hard work on her to make me love her. No influential friend would have served me better. She had given me a chance to come out a bit—to find out what I could do. No, I don't like work. I had rather laze about and think of all the fine things that can be done. I don't like work—no man does—but I like what is in the work,—the chance to find yourself. Your own reality—for yourself, not for others—what no other man can ever know. They can only see the mere show, and never can tell what it really means.

"I was not surprised to see somebody sitting aft, on the deck, with his legs dangling over the mud. You see I rather chummed with the few mechanics there were in that station, whom the other pilgrims naturally despised—on account of their imperfect manners, I suppose. This was the foreman—a boiler-maker by trade—a good worker. He was a lank, bony, yellow-faced man, with big intense eyes. His aspect was worried, and his head was as bald as the palm of my hand; but his hair in falling seemed to have stuck to his chin, and had prospered in the new locality, for his beard hung down to his waist. He was a widower with six young children (he had left them in charge of a sister of his to come out there), and the passion of his life was pigeon-flying. He was an enthusiast and a connoisseur. He would rave about pigeons. After work hours he used sometimes to come over from his hut for a talk about his children and his pigeons; at work, when he had to crawl in the mud under the bottom of the steamboat, he would tie up that beard of his in a kind of white serviette he brought for the purpose. It had loops to go over his ears. In the evening he could be seen squatted on the bank rinsing that wrapper in the creek with great care, then spreading it solemnly on a bush to dry.

"I slapped him on the back and shouted 'We shall have rivets!' He scrambled to his feet exclaiming 'No! Rivets!' as though he couldn't believe his ears. Then in a low voice, 'You . . . eh?' I don't know why we behaved like lunatics. I put my finger to the side of my nose and nodded mysteriously. 'Good for you!' he cried, snapped his fingers above his head, lifting one foot. I tried a jig. We capered on the iron deck. A frightful clatter came out of that hulk, and the virgin forest on the other bank of the creek sent it back in a thundering roll upon the sleeping station. It must have made some of the pilgrims sit up in their hovels. A dark figure obscured the lighted doorway of the manager's hut, vanished, then, a second or so after, the doorway itself vanished too. We stopped, and the silence driven away by the stamping of our feet flowed back again from the recesses of the land. The great wall of vegetation, an exuberant and entangled mass of trunks branches, leaves, boughs, festoons, motionless in the moonlight, was like a rioting invasion of soundless life, a rolling wave of plants piled up, crested, ready to topple over the creek, to sweep every little man of us out of his little existence. And it moved not. A deadened burst of mighty splashes and snorts reached us from afar, as though an ichthyosaurus had been taking a bath of glitter in that great river. 'After all,' said the boiler-maker in a reasonable tone, 'why shouldn't we get the rivets?' Why not, indeed! I did not know of any reason why we shouldn't. 'They'll come in three weeks,' I said, confidently.

“But they didn’t. Instead of rivets there came an invasion, an infliction, a visitation. It came in sections during the next three weeks, each section headed by a donkey carrying a white man in new clothes and tan shoes, bowing from that elevation right and left to the impressed pilgrims. A quarrelsome band of footsore sulky niggers trod on the heels of the donkey; a lot of tents, camp-stools, tin boxes, white cases, brown bales would be shot down in the courtyard, and the air of mystery would deepen a little over the muddle of the station. Five such installments came, with their absurd air of disorderly flight with the loot of innumerable outfit shops and provision stores, that, one would think, they were lugging, after a raid, into the wilderness for equitable division. It was an inextricable mess of things decent in themselves but that human folly made look like the spoils of thieving.

“This devoted band called itself the Eldorado Exploring Expedition, and I believe they were sworn to secrecy. Their talk, however, was the talk of sordid buccaneers: it was reckless without hardihood, greedy without audacity, and cruel without courage; there was not an atom of foresight or of serious intention in the whole batch of them, and they did not seem aware these things are wanted for the work of the world. To tear treasure out of the bowels of the land was their desire, with no more moral purpose at the back of it than there is in burglars breaking into a safe. Who paid the expenses of the noble enterprise I don’t know; but the uncle of our manager was leader of that lot.

“In exterior he resembled a butcher in a poor neighborhood, and his eyes had a look of sleepy cunning. He carried his fat paunch with ostentation on his short legs, and during the time his gang infested the station spoke to no one but his nephew. You could see these two roaming about all day long with their heads close together in an everlasting confab.

“I had given up worrying myself about the rivets. One’s capacity for that 75
kind of folly is more limited than you would suppose. I said Hang!—and let things slide. I had plenty of time for meditation, and now and then I would give some thought to Kurtz. I wasn’t very interested in him. No. Still, I was curious to see whether this man, who had come out equipped with moral ideas of some sort, would climb to the top after all, and how he would set about his work when there.”

II

“One evening as I was lying flat on the deck of my steamboat, I heard voices approaching—and there were the nephew and the uncle strolling along the bank. I laid my head on my arm again, and had nearly lost myself in a doze, when somebody said in my ear, as it were: ‘I am as harmless as a little child, but I don’t like to be dictated to. Am I the manager—or am I not? I was ordered to send him there. It’s incredible.’ . . . I became aware that the two were standing on the shore alongside the forepart of the steamboat, just below my head. I did not move; it did not occur to me to move: I was sleepy. ‘It *is* unpleasant,” grunted the uncle. ‘He asked the Administration to be sent there,’ said the other, ‘with the idea of showing what he could do; and I was instructed accordingly. Look at the influence that man must have. Is it not frightful?' They both agreed it was frightful, then made several bizarre remarks: 'Make rain and fine weather—one man—the Council—by the nose'—bits of absurd sentences that got the better of my drowsiness, so that I had pretty near the whole of my wits about me when the uncle said, 'The climate may do away with this difficulty for you. Is he alone there?' 'Yes,' answered the manager; 'he sent his assistant down the river with a note to me in these terms: "Clear this poor devil out of the country, and don't bother sending more of that sort. I had rather be alone than have the kind of men you can dispose of with me." It was more than a year ago. Can you imagine such impudence!' 'Anything since then?' asked the other, hoarsely. 'Ivory,' jerked the nephew; "lots of it—prime sort—lots—most annoying, from him. 'And with that?' questioned the heavy rumble. 'Invoice,' was the reply fired out, so to speak. Then silence. They had been talking about Kurtz.

"I was broad awake by this time, but, lying perfectly at ease, remained still, having no inducement to change my position. 'How did that ivory come all this way?' growled the elder man, who seemed very vexed. The other explained that it had come with a fleet of canoes in charge of an English half-caste clerk Kurtz had with him; that Kurtz had apparently intended to return himself, the station being by that time bare of goods and stores, but after coming three hundred miles, had suddenly decided to go back, which he started to do alone in a small dug-out with four paddlers, leaving the half-caste to continue down the river with the ivory. The two fellows there seemed astounded at anybody attempting such a thing. They were at a loss for an adequate motive. As to me, I seemed to see Kurtz for the first time. It was a distinct glimpse: the dug-out, four paddling savages, and the lone white man turning his back suddenly on the headquarters, on relief, on thoughts of home—perhaps; setting his face towards the depths of the wilderness, towards his empty and desolate station. I did not know the motive. Perhaps he was just simply a fine fellow who stuck to his work for its own sake. His name, you understand, had not been pronounced once. He was 'that man.' The half-caste, who, as far as I could see, had conducted a difficult trip with great prudence and pluck, was invariably alluded to as 'that scoundrel.' The 'scoundrel' had reported that the 'man' had been very ill—had recovered imperfectly. . . . The two below me moved away then a few paces, and strolled back and forth at some little distance. I heard: 'Military post—doctor—two hundred miles—quite alone now—unavoidable delays—nine months—no news—strange rumors.' They approached again, just as the manager was saying, 'No one, as far as I know, unless a species of wandering trader—a pestilential fellow, snapping ivory from the natives.' Who was it they were talking about now? I gathered in snatches that this was some man supposed to be in Kurtz's district, and of whom the manager did not approve. 'We will not be free from unfair competition till one of these fellows is hanged for an example,' he said. 'Certainly,' grunted the other; 'get him hanged! Why not? Anything—anything can be done in this country. That's what I say; nobody here, you understand, *here*, can endanger your position. And why? You stand the climate—you outlast them all. The danger is in Europe; but there before I left I took care to—' They moved off and whispered, then their voices rose again. 'The extraordinary series of delays is not my fault. I did my possible." The fat man sighed, 'Very sad.' 'And the pestiferous absurdity of his talk,' continued the other; 'he bothered me enough when he was here. "Each station should be like a beacon on the road towards better things, a center for trade of course, but also for humanizing, improving, instructing." Conceive you—that ass! And he wants to be manager! No, it's—' Here he got choked by excessive indignation, and I lifted my head the least bit. I was surprised to see how near they were—right under me. I could have spat upon their hats. They were looking on the ground, absorbed in thought. The manager was switching his leg with a slender twig: his sagacious relative lifted his head. 'You have been well since you came out this time?' he asked. The other gave a start. 'Who? I? Oh! Like a charm—like a charm. But the rest—oh, my goodness! All sick. They die so quick, too, that I haven't the time to send them out of the country—it's incredible!' 'H'm. Just so,' grunted the uncle. 'Ah! my boy, trust to this—I say, trust to this.' I saw him extend his short flipper of an arm for a gesture that took in the forest, the creek, the mud, the river,—seemed to beckon with a dishonoring flourish before the sunlit face of the land a treacherous appeal to the lurking death, to the hidden evil, to the profound darkness of its heart. It was so startling that I leaped to my feet and looked back at the edge of the forest, as though I had expected an answer of some sort to that black display of confidence. You know the foolish notions that come to one sometimes. The high stillness confronted these two figures with its ominous patience, waiting for the passing away of a fantastic invasion.

"They swore aloud together—out of sheer fright, I believe—then pretending not to know anything of my existence, turned back to the station. The sun was low; and leaning forward side by side, they seemed to be tugging painfully uphill their two ridiculous shadows of unequal length, that trailed behind them slowly over the tall grass without bending a single blade.

"In a few days the Eldorado Expedition went into the patient wilderness, that closed upon it as the sea closes over a diver. Long afterwards the news came that all the donkeys were dead. I know nothing as to the fate of the less valuable animals. They, no doubt, like the rest of us, found what they deserved. I did not inquire. I was then rather excited at the prospect of meeting Kurtz very soon. When I say very soon I mean it comparatively. It was just two months from the day we left the creek when we came to the bank below Kurtz's station.

"Going up that river was like traveling back to the earliest beginnings of 80
the world, when vegetation rioted on the earth and the big trees were kings. An empty stream, a great silence, and impenetrable forest. The air was warm, thick, heavy, sluggish. There was no joy in the brilliance of sunshine. The long stretches of the waterway ran on, deserted, into the gloom of over-shadowed distances. On silvery sandbanks hippos and alligators sunned themselves side by side. The broadening waters flowed through a mob of wooded islands; you lost your way on that river as you would in a desert, and butted all day long against shoals, trying to find the channel, till you thought yourself bewitched and cut off for ever from everything you had known once—somewhere—far away—in another existence perhaps. There were moments when one's past

came back to one, as it will sometimes when you have not a moment to spare to yourself; but it came in the shape of an unrestful and noisy dream, remembered with wonder amongst the overwhelming realities of this strange world of plants, and water, and silence. And this stillness of life did not in the least resemble a peace. It was the stillness of an implacable force brooding over an inscrutable intention. It looked at you with a vengeful aspect. I got used to it afterwards; I did not see it any more; I had no time. I had to keep guessing at the channel; I had to discern, mostly by inspiration, the signs of hidden banks; I watched for sunken stones; I was learning to clap my teeth smartly before my heart flew out, when I shaved by a fluke some infernal sly old snag that would have ripped the life out of the tin-pot steamboat and drowned all the pilgrims; I had to keep a look-out for the signs of dead wood we could cut up in the night for next day's steaming. When you have to attend to things of that sort, to the mere incidents of the surface, the reality—the reality, I tell you—fades. The inner truth is hidden—luckily, luckily. But I felt it all the same; I felt often its mysterious stillness watching me at my monkey tricks, just as it watches you fellows performing on your respective tight-ropes for—what is it? half-a-crown a tumble—"

"Try to be civil, Marlow," growled a voice, and I knew there was at least one listener awake besides myself.

"I beg your pardon. I forgot the heartache which makes up the rest of the price. And indeed what does the price matter, if the trick be well done? You do your tricks very well. And I didn't do badly either, since I managed not to sink that steamboat on my first trip. It's a wonder to me yet. Imagine a blindfolded man set to drive a van over a bad road. I sweated and shivered over that business considerably, I can tell you. After all, for a seaman, to scrape the bottom of the thing that's supposed to float all the time under his care is the unpardonable sin. No one may know of it, but you never forget the thump—eh? A blow on the very heart. You remember it, you dream of it, you wake up at night and think of it—years after—and go hot and cold all over. I don't pretend to say that steamboat floated all the time. More than once she had to wade for a bit, with twenty cannibals splashing around and pushing. We had enlisted some of these chaps on the way for a crew. Fine fellows—cannibals—in their place. They were men one could work with, and I am grateful to them. And, after all, they did not eat each other before my face: they had brought along a provision of hippo-meat which went rotten, and made the mystery of the wilderness stink in my nostrils. Phoo! I can sniff it now. I had the manager on board and three or four pilgrims with their staves—all complete. Sometimes we came upon a station close by the bank, clinging to the skirts of the unknown, and the white men rushing out of a tumble-down hovel, with great gestures of joy and surprise and welcome, seemed very strange,—had the appearance of being held there captive by a spell. The word ivory would ring in the air for a while—and on we went again into the silence, along empty reaches, round the still bends, between the high walls of our winding way, reverberating in hollow claps the ponderous beat of the sternwheel. Trees, trees, millions of trees, massive, immense, running up high; and at their foot, hugging the bank against the stream, crept the little begrimed steamboat, like a sluggish beetle crawling on the floor of a lofty portico. It made you feel very small, very lost, and yet it was not altogether depressing that feeling. After all, if you were small, the grimy beetle crawled on—which was just what you wanted it to do. Where the pilgrims imagined it crawled to I don't know. To some place where they expected to get something, I bet! For me it crawled toward Kurtz—exclusively; but when the steam-pipes started leaking we crawled very slow. The reaches opened before us and closed behind, as if the forest had stepped leisurely across the water to bar the way for our return. We penetrated deeper and deeper into the heart of darkness. It was very quiet there. At night sometimes the roll of drums behind the curtain of trees would run up the river and remain sustained faintly, as if hovering in the air high over our heads, till the first break of day. Whether it meant war, peace, or prayer we could not tell. The dawns were heralded by the descent of a chill stillness; the woodcutters slept, their fires burned low; the snapping of a twig would make you start. We were wanderers in a prehistoric earth, on an earth that wore the aspect of an unknown planet. We could have fancied ourselves the first of men taking possession of an accursed inheritance, to be subdued at the cost of profound anguish and of excessive toil. But suddenly, as we struggled round a bend, there would be a glimpse of rush walls, of peaked grass-roofs, a burst of yells, a whirl of black limbs, a mass of hands clapping, of feet stamping, of bodies swaying, of eyes rolling, under the droop of heavy and motionless foliage. The steamer toiled along slowly on the edge of a black and incomprehensible frenzy. The prehistoric man was cursing us, praying to us, welcoming us—who could tell? We were cut off from the comprehension of our surroundings; we glided past like phantoms, wondering and secretly appalled, as sane men would be before an enthusiastic outbreak in a madhouse. We could not understand, because we were too far and could not remember, because we were traveling in the night of first ages, of those ages that are gone, leaving hardly a sign—and no memories.

"The earth seemed unearthly. We are accustomed to look upon the shackled form of a conquered monster, but there—there you could look at a thing monstrous and free. It was unearthly, and the men were—No, they were not inhuman. Well, you know, that was the worst of it—this suspicion of their not being inhuman. It would come slowly to one. They howled, and leaped, and spun, and made horrid faces; but what thrilled you was just the thought of their humanity—like yours—the thought of your remote kinship with this wild and passionate uproar. Ugly. Yes, it was ugly enough; but if you were man enough you would admit to yourself that there was in you just the faintest trace of a response to the terrible frankness of that noise, a dim suspicion of there being a meaning in which you—you so remote from the night of first ages—could comprehend. And why not? The mind of a man is capable of anything—because everything is in it, all the past as well as all the future. What was there after all? Joy, fear, sorrow, devotion, valor, rage—who can tell?—but truth—truth stripped of its cloak of time. Let the fool gape and shudder—the man knows, and can look on without a wink. But he must at least be as much of a man as these on the shore. He must meet that truth with his own true stuff—with his own inborn strength. Principles? Principles won't do. Acquisitions, clothes, pretty rags—rags that would fly off at the first good shake. No; you want a deliberate belief. An appeal to me in this fiendish row—is there? Very well; I hear; I admit, but I have a voice, too, and for good or evil mine is the speech that cannot be silenced. Of course, a fool, what with sheer fright and fine sentiments, is always safe. Who's that grunting? You wonder I didn't go ashore for a howl and a dance? Well, no—I didn't. Fine sentiments, you say? Fine sentiments, be hanged! I had no time. I had to mess about with white-lead and strips of woolen blanket helping to put bandages on those leaky steam-pipes—I tell you. I had to watch the steering, and circumvent those snags, and get the tin-pot along by hook or by crook. There was surface-truth enough in these things to save a wiser man. And between whiles I had to look after the savage who was fireman. He was an improved specimen; he could fire up a vertical boiler. He was there below me, and, upon my word, to look at him was as edifying as seeing a dog in a parody of breeches and a feather hat, walking on his hindlegs. A few months of training had done for that really fine chap. He squinted at the steam-gauge and at the water-gauge with an evident effort of intrepidity—and he had filed teeth too, the poor devil, and the wool of his pate shaved into queer patterns, and three ornamental scars on each of his cheeks. He ought to have been clapping his hands and stamping his feet on the bank, instead of which he was hard at work, a thrall to strange witchcraft, full of improving knowledge. He was useful because he had been instructed; and what he knew was this—that should the water in that transparent thing disappear, the evil spirit inside the boiler would get angry through the greatness of his thirst, and take a terrible vengeance. So he sweated and fired up and watched the glass fearfully (with an impromptu charm, made of rags, tied to his arm, and a piece of polished bone, as big as a watch, stuck flatways through his lower lip), while the wooded banks slipped past us slowly, the short noise was left behind the interminable miles of silence—and we crept on, towards Kurtz. But the snags were thick, the water was treacherous and shallow, the boiler seemed indeed to have a sulky devil in it, and thus neither that fireman nor I had any time to peer into our creepy thoughts.

"Some fifty miles below the Inner Station we came upon a hut of reeds, an inclined and melancholy pole, with the unrecognizable tatters of what had been a flag of some sort flying from it, and a neatly stacked wood-pile. This was unexpected. We came to the bank, and on the stack of firewood found a flat piece of board with some faded pencil-writing on it. When deciphered it said: 'Wood for you. Hurry up. Approach cautiously.' There was a signature, but it was illegible—not Kurtz—a much longer word. Hurry up. Where? Up the river? 'Approach cautiously.' We had not done so. But the warning could not have been meant for the place where it could be only found after approach. Something was wrong above. But what—and how much? That was the question. We commented adversely upon the imbecility of that telegraphic style. The bush around said nothing, and would not let us look very far, either. A torn curtain of red twill hung in the doorway of the hut, and flapped sadly in our faces. The dwelling was dismantled; but we could see a white man had lived there not very long ago. There remained a rude table—

a plank on two posts; a heap of rubbish reposed in a dark corner, and by the door I picked up a book. It had lost its covers, and the pages had been thumbed into a state of extremely dirty softness; but the back had been lovingly stitched afresh with white cotton thread, which looked clean yet. It was an extraordinary find. Its title was, 'An Inquiry into some Points of Seamanship,' by a man Tower, Towson—some such name—Master in his Majesty's Navy. The matter looked dreary reading enough, with illustrative diagrams and repulsive tables of figures, and the copy was sixty years old. I handled this amazing antiquity with the greatest possible tenderness, lest it should dissolve in my hands. Within, Towson or Towser was inquiring earnestly into the breaking strain of ships' chains and tackle, and other such matters. Not a very enthralling book; but at the first glance you could see there a singleness of intention, an honest concern for the right way of going to work, which made these humble pages, thought out so many years ago, luminous with another than a professional light. The simple old sailor, with his talk of chains and purchases, made me forget the jungle and the pilgrims in a delicious sensation of having come upon something unmistakably real. Such a book being there was wonderful enough; but still more astounding were the notes penciled in the margin, and plainly referring to the text. I couldn't believe my eyes! They were in cipher! Yes, it looked like cipher. Fancy a man lugging with him a book of that description into this nowhere and studying it—and making notes—in cipher at that! It was an extravagant mystery.

"I had been dimly aware for some time of a worrying noise, and when I 85
lifted my eyes I saw the wood-pile was gone, and the manager, aided by all the pilgrims, was shouting at me from the river-side. I slipped the book into my pocket. I assure you to leave off reading was like tearing myself away from the shelter of an old and solid friendship.

"I started the lame engine ahead. 'It must be this miserable trader—this intruder,' exclaimed the manager, looking back malevolently at the place we had left. 'He must be English,' I said. 'It will not save him from getting into trouble if he is not careful,' muttered the manager darkly. I observed with assumed innocence that no man was safe from trouble in this world.

"The current was more rapid now, the steamer seemed at her last gasp, the stern-wheel flopped languidly, and I caught myself listening on tiptoe for the next beat of the float, for in sober truth I expected the wretched thing to give up every moment. It was like watching the last flickers of life. But still we crawled. Sometimes I would pick out a tree a little way ahead to measure our progress towards Kurtz by, but I lost it invariably before we got abreast. To keep the eyes so long on one thing was too much for human patience. The manager displayed a beautiful resignation. I fretted and fumed and took to arguing with myself whether or no I would talk openly with Kurtz; but before I could come to any conclusion it occurred to me that my speech or my silence, indeed any action of mine, would be a mere futility. What did it matter what anyone knew or ignored? What did it matter who was manager? One gets sometimes such a flash of insight. The essentials of this affair lay deep under the surface, beyond my reach, and beyond my power of meddling.

"Towards the evening of the second day we judged ourselves about eight miles from Kurtz's station. I wanted to push on; but the manager looked grave, and told me the navigation up there was so dangerous that it would be advisable, the sun being very low already, to wait where we were till next morning. Moreover, he pointed out that if the warning to approach cautiously were to be followed, we must approach in daylight—not at dusk, or in the dark. This was sensible enough. Eight miles meant nearly three hours' steaming for us, and I could also see suspicious ripples at the upper end of the reach. Nevertheless, I was annoyed beyond expression at the delay, and most unreasonably too, since one night more could not matter much after so many months. As we had plenty of wood, and caution was the word, I brought up in the middle of the stream. The reach was narrow, straight, with high sides like a railway cutting. The dusk came gliding into it long before the sun had set. The current ran smooth and swift, but a dumb immobility sat on the banks. The living trees, lashed together by the creepers and every living bush of the undergrowth, might have been changed into stone, even to the slenderest twig, to the lightest leaf. It was not sleep—it seemed unnatural, like a state of trance. Not the faintest sound of any kind could be heard. You looked on amazed, and began to suspect yourself of being deaf—then the night came suddenly, and struck you blind as well. About three in the morning some large fish leaped, and the loud splash made me jump as though a gun had been fired. When the sun rose there was a white fog, very warm and clammy, and more blinding than the night. It did not shift or drive; it was just there, standing all round you like something solid. At eight or nine, perhaps, it lifted as a shutter lifts. We had a glimpse of the towering multitude of trees, of the immense matted jungle, with the blazing little ball of the sun hanging over it—all perfectly still—and then the white shutter came down again, smoothly, as if sliding in greased grooves. I ordered the chain, which we had begun to heave in, to be paid out again. Before it stopped running with a muffled rattle, a cry, a very loud cry, as of infinite desolation, soared slowly in the opaque air. It ceased. A complaining clamor, modulated in savage discords, filled our ears. The sheer unexpectedness of it made my hair stir under my cap. I don't know how it struck the others: to me it seemed as though the mist itself had screamed, so suddenly, and apparently from all sides at once, did this tumultuous and mournful uproar arise. It culminated in a hurried outbreak of almost intolerably excessive shrieking, which stopped short, leaving us stiffened in a variety of silly attitudes, and obstinately listening to the nearly as appalling and excessive silence. 'Good God! What is the meaning—?' stammered at my elbow one of the pilgrims,—a little fat man, with sandy hair and red whiskers, who wore side-spring boots, and pink pyjamas tucked into his socks. Two others remained open-mouthed a whole minute, then dashed into the little cabin, to rush out incontinently and stand darting scared glances, with Winchesters at 'ready' in their hands. What we could see was just the steamer we were on, her outlines blurred as though she had been on the point of dissolving, and a misty strip of water, perhaps two feet broad, around her—and that was all. The rest of the world was nowhere, as far as our eyes and ears were concerned. Just nowhere. Gone, disappeared; swept off without leaving a whisper or a shadow behind.

"I went forward, and ordering the chain to be hauled in short, so as to be ready to trip the anchor and move the steamboat at once if necessary. 'Will they attack?' whispered an awed voice. 'We will be butchered in this fog,' murmured another. The faces twitched with the strain, the hands trembled slightly, the eyes forgot to wink. It was very curious to see the contrast of expressions of the white men and of the black fellows of our crew, who were as much strangers to that part of the river as we, though their homes were only eight hundred miles away. The whites, of course greatly discomposed, had besides a curious look of being painfully shocked by such an outrageous row. The others had an alert, naturally interested expression; but their faces were essentially quiet, even those of the one or two who grinned as they hauled at the chain. Several exchanged short, grunting phrases, which seemed to settle the matter to their satisfaction. Their headman, a young, broad-chested black, severely draped in dark-blue fringed cloths, with fierce nostrils and his hair all done up artfully in oily ringlets, stood near me. 'Aha!' I said, just for good fellowship's sake. 'Catch 'im,' he snapped, with a bloodshot widening of his eyes and a flash of sharp teeth—'catch 'im. Give 'im to us.' 'To you, eh?' I asked; 'what would you do with them?' 'Eat 'im!' he said curtly, and, leaning his elbow on the rail, looked out into the fog in a dignified and profoundly pensive attitude. I would no doubt have been properly horrified, had it not occurred to me that he and his chaps must be very hungry: that they must have been growing increasingly hungry for at least this month past. They had been engaged for six months (I don't think a single one of them had any clear idea of time, as we at the end of countless ages have. They still belonged to the beginnings of time—had no inherited experience to teach them as it were), and of course, as long as there was a piece of paper written over in accordance with some farcical law or other made down the river, it didn't enter anybody's head to trouble how they would live. Certainly they had brought with them some rotten hippo-meat, which couldn't have lasted very long, anyway, even if the pilgrims hadn't, in the midst of a shocking hullabaloo, thrown a considerable quantity of it overboard. It looked like a high-handed proceeding; but it was really a case of legitimate self-defense. You can't breathe dead hippo waking, sleeping, and eating, and at the same time keep your precarious grip on existence. Besides that, they had given them every week three pieces of brass wire, each about nine inches long; and the theory was they were to buy their provisions with that currency in river-side villages. You can see how *that* worked. There were either no villages, or the people were hostile, or the director, who like the rest of us fed out of tins, with an occasional old he-goat thrown in, didn't want to stop the steamer for some more or less recondite reason. So, unless they swallowed the wire itself, or made loops of it to snare the fishes with, I don't see what good their extravagant salary could be to them. I must say it was paid with a regularity worthy of a large and honorable trading company. For the rest, the only thing to eat—though it didn't look eatable in the least—I saw in their possession was a few lumps of some stuff like half-cooked dough, of a dirty lavender color, they kept wrapped in leaves, and now and then swallowed a piece of, but so small that it seemed done for more for the looks of the thing than for any serious purpose of sustenance. Why in the name of all the gnawing devils of hunger they didn't go for us—they were thirty to five—and have a good tuck in for once, amazes me now when I think of it. They were big powerful men, with not much capacity to weigh the consequences, with courage, with strength, even yet, though their skins were no longer glossy and their muscles no longer hard. And I saw that something restraining, one of those human secrets that baffle probability, had come into play there. I looked at them with a swift quickening of interest—not because it occurred to me I might be eaten by them before very long, though I own to you that just then I perceived—in a new light, as it were—how unwholesome the pilgrims looked, and I hoped, yes, I positively hoped, that my aspect was not so—what shall I say?—so—unappetizing: a touch of fantastic vanity which fitted well with the dream-sensation that pervaded all my days at that time. Perhaps I had a little fever too. One can't live with one's finger everlastingly on one's pulse. I had often 'a little fever,' or a little touch of other things—the playful paw-strokes of the wilderness, the preliminary trifling before the more serious onslaught which came in due course. Yes; I looked at them as you would on any human being, with a curiosity of their impulses, motives, capacities, weaknesses, when brought to the test of an inexorable physical necessity. Restraint! What possible restraint? Was it superstition, disgust, patience, fear—or some kind of primitive honor? No fear can stand up to hunger, no patience can wear it out, disgust simply does not exist where hunger is; and as to superstition, beliefs, and what you may call principles, they are less than chaff in a breeze. Don't you know the devilry of lingering starvation, its exasperating torment, its black thoughts, its somber and brooding ferocity? Well, I do. It takes a man all his inborn strength to fight hunger properly. It's really easier to face bereavement, dishonor, and the perdition of one's soul—than this kind of prolonged hunger. Sad, but true. And these chaps too had no earthly reason for any kind of scruple. Restraint! I would just as soon have expected restraint from a hyena prowling amongst the corpses of a battlefield. But there was the fact facing me—the fact dazzling, to be seen, like the foam on the depths of the sea, like a ripple on a unfathomable enigma, a mystery greater—when I thought of it—than the curious, inexplicable note of desperate grief in this savage clamor that had swept by us on the river-bank, behind the blind whiteness of the fog.

"Two pilgrims were quarreling in hurried whispers as to which bank. 90
'Left.' 'No, no; how can you? Right, right, of course.' 'It is very serious,' said the manager's voice behind me; 'I would be desolated if anything should happen to Mr. Kurtz before we came up.' I looked at him, and had not the slightest doubt he was sincere. He was just the kind of man who would wish to preserve appearances. That was his restraint. But when he muttered something about going on at once, I did not even take the trouble to answer him. I knew, and he knew, that it was impossible. Were we to let go our hold of the bottom, we would be absolutely in the air—in space. We wouldn't be able to tell where we were going to—whether up or down stream, or across—till we fetched against one bank or the other,—and then we wouldn't know at first

which it was. Of course I made no move. I had no mind for a smash-up. You couldn't imagine a more deadly place for a shipwreck. Whether drowned at once or not, we were sure to perish speedily in one way or another. 'I authorize you to take all the risks,' he said, after a short silence. 'I refuse to take any,' I said shortly; which was just the answer he expected, though its tone might have surprised him. 'Well, I must defer to your judgment. You are captain,' he said, with marked civility. I turned my shoulder to him in sign of my appreciation, and looked into the fog. How long would it last? It was the most hopeless look-out. The approach to this Kurtz grubbing for ivory in the wretched bush was beset by as many dangers as though he had been an enchanted princess sleeping in a fabulous castle. 'Will they attack, do you think?' asked the manager, in a confidential tone.

"I did not think they would attack, for several obvious reasons. The thick fog was one. If they left the bank in their canoes they would get lost in it, as we would be if we attempted to move. Still, I had also judged the jungle of both banks quite impenetrable—and yet eyes were in it, eyes that had seen us. The river-side bushes were certainly thick; but the undergrowth behind was evidently penetrable. However, during the short lift I had seen no canoes anywhere in the reach—certainly not abreast of the steamer. But what made the idea of attack inconceivable to me was the nature of the noise—of the cries we had heard. They had not the fierce character boding of immediate hostile intention. Unexpected, wild, and violent as they had been, they had given me an irresistible impression of sorrow. The glimpse of the steamboat had for some reason filled those savages with unrestrained grief. The danger, if any, I expounded, was from our proximity to a great human passion let loose. Even extreme grief may ultimately vent itself in violence—but more generally takes the form of apathy. . . .

"You should have seen the pilgrims stare! They had no heart to grin, or even to revile me; but I believe they thought me gone mad—with fright, maybe. I delivered a regular lecture. My dear boys, it was no good bothering. Keep a look-out? Well, you may guess I watched the fog for the signs of lifting as a cat watches a mouse; but for anything else our eyes were of no more use to us than if we had been buried miles deep in a heap of cotton-wool. It felt like it too—choking, warm, stifling. Besides, all I said, though it sounded extravagant, was absolutely true to fact. What we afterwards alluded to as an attack was really an attempt at repulse. The action was very far from being aggressive—it was not even defensive, in the usual sense: it was undertaken under the stress of desperation, and in its essence was purely protective.

"It developed itself, I should say, two hours after the fog lifted, and its commencement was at a spot, roughly speaking, about a mile and a half below Kurtz's station. We had just floundered and flopped round a bend, when I saw an islet, a mere grassy hummock of bright green, in the middle of the stream. It was the only thing of the kind; but as we opened the reach more, I perceived it was the head of a long sandbank, or rather a chain of shallow patches stretching down the middle of the river. They were discolored, just awash, and the whole lot was seen just under the water, exactly as a man's backbone is seen running down the middle of his back under the skin. Now, as far as I did see, I could go to the right or to the left of this. I didn't know either channel, of course. The banks looked pretty well alike, the depth appeared the same; but as I had been informed the station was on the west side, I naturally headed for the western passage.

"No sooner had we fairly entered it than I became aware it was much narrower than I had supposed. To the left of us there was the long uninterrupted shoal, and to the right a high, steep bank heavily overgrown with bushes. Above the bush the trees stood in serried ranks. The twigs overhung the current thickly, and from distance to distance a large limb of some tree projected rigidly over the stream. It was then well on in the afternoon, the face of the forest was gloomy, and a broad strip of shadow had already fallen on the water. In this shadow we steamed up—very slowly, as you may imagine. I sheered her well inshore—the water being deepest near the bank, as the sounding-pole informed me.

95 "One of my hungry and forbearing friends was sounding in the bows just below me. This steamboat was exactly like a decked scow. On the deck there were two little teak-wood houses, with doors and windows. The boiler was in the fore-end, and the machinery right astern. Over the whole there was a light roof, supported on stanchions. The funnel projected through that roof, and in front of the funnel a small cabin built of light planks served for a pilot-house. It contained a couch, two campstools, a loaded Martini-Henry leaning in one corner, a tiny table, and the steering-wheel. It had a wide door in front and a broad shutter at each side. All these were always thrown open, of course. I spent my days perched up there on the extreme fore-end of that roof, before the door. At night I slept, or tried to, on the couch. An athletic black belonging to some coast tribe, and educated by my poor predecessor, was the helmsman. He sported a pair of brass earrings, wore a blue cloth wrapper from the waist to the ankles, and thought all the world of himself. He was the most unstable kind of fool I had ever seen. He steered with no end of a swagger while you were by; but if he lost sight of you, he became instantly the prey of an abject funk, and would let that cripple of a steamboat get the upper hand of him in a minute.

"I was looking down at the sounding-pole, and feeling much annoyed to see at each try a little more of it stick out of that river, when I saw my poleman give up the business suddenly, and stretch himself flat on the deck, without even taking the trouble to haul his pole in. He kept hold on it though, and it trailed in the water. At the same time the fireman, whom I could also see below me, sat down abruptly before his furnace and ducked his head. I was amazed. Then I had to look at the river mighty quick, because there was a snag in the fairway. Sticks, little sticks, were flying about—thick: they were whizzing before my nose, dropping below me, striking behind me against my pilot-house. All this time the river, the shore, the woods, were very quiet—perfectly quiet. I could only hear the heavy splashing thump of the stern-wheel and the patter of these things. We cleared the snag clumsily. Arrows, by Jove! We were being shot at! I stepped in quickly to close the shutter on the land side. That fool-helmsman, his hands on the spokes, was lifting his knees high, stamping his feet, champing his mouth, like a reined-in horse. Confound him! And we were staggering within ten feet of the bank. I had to lean right out to swing the heavy shutter, and I saw a face amongst the leaves on the level with my own, looking at me very fierce and steady; and then suddenly, as though a veil had been removed from my eyes, I made out, deep in the tangled gloom, naked breasts, arms, legs, glaring eyes,—the bush was swarming with human limbs in movement, glistening, of bronze color. The twigs shook, swayed, and rustled, the arrows flew out of them, and then the shutter came to. 'Steer her straight,' I said to the helmsman. He held his head rigid, face forward; but his eyes rolled, he kept lifting and setting down his feet gently, his mouth foamed a little. 'Keep quiet!' I said in a fury. I might just as well have ordered a tree not to sway in the wind. I darted out. Below me there was a great scuffle of feet on the iron deck; confused exclamations; a voice screamed, 'Can you turn back?' I caught sight of a V-shaped ripple on the water ahead. What? Another snag! A fusillade burst out under my feet. The pilgrims had opened their little Winchesters, and were simply squirting lead into that bush. A deuce of a lot of smoke came up and drove slowly forward. I swore at it. Now I couldn't see the ripple or the snag either. I stood in the doorway, peering, and the arrows came in swarms. They might have been poisoned, but they looked as though they wouldn't kill a cat. The bush began to howl. Our wood-cutters raised a warlike whoop; the report of a rifle just at my back deafened me. I glanced over my shoulder, and the pilot-house was yet full of noise and smoke when I made a dash at the wheel. The fool-nigger had dropped everything, to throw the shutter open and let off that Martini-Henry. He stood before the wide opening, glaring, and I yelled at him to come back, while I straightened the sudden twist out of that steamboat. There was no room to turn even if I had wanted to, the snag was somewhere very near ahead in that confounded smoke, there was no time to lose, so I just crowded her into the bank—right into the bank, where I knew the water was deep.

"We tore slowly along the overhanging bushes in a whirl of broken twigs and flying leaves. The fusillade below stopped short, as I had foreseen it would when the squirts got empty. I threw my head back to a glinting whizz that traversed the pilot-house, in at one shutter-hole and out at the other. Looking past that mad helmsman, who was shaking the empty rifle and yelling at the shore, I saw vague forms of men running bent double, leaping, gliding, distinct, incomplete, evanescent. Something big appeared in the air before the shutter, the rifle went overboard, and the man stepped back swiftly, looked at me over his shoulder in an extraordinary, profound, familiar manner, and fell upon my feet. The side of his head hit the wheel twice, and the end of what appeared a long cane clattered round and knocked over a little camp-stool. It looked as though after wrenching that thing from somebody ashore he had lost his balance in the effort. The thin smoke had blown away, we were clear of the snag, and looking ahead I could see that in another hundred yards or so I would be free to sheer off, away from the bank; but my feet felt so very warm and wet that I had to look down. The man had rolled on his back and stared straight up at me; both his hands clutched that cane. It was the shaft of a spear that, either thrown or lunged through the opening, had caught him in the side just below the ribs; the blade had gone in out of sight, after making a frightful gash; my shoes were full; a pool of blood lay very still, gleaming dark-red under the wheel; his eyes shone with an amazing luster. The fusillade burst out again. He looked at me anxiously, gripping the spear like something precious, with an air of being afraid I would try to take it away from him. I had to make an effort to free my eyes from his gaze and attend to the steering. With one hand I felt above my head for the line of the steam-whistle, and jerked out screech after screech hurriedly. The tumult of angry and warlike yells was checked instantly, and then from the depths of the woods went out such a tremulous and prolonged wail of mournful fear and utter despair as may be imagined to follow the flight of the last hope from the earth. There was a great commotion in the bush; the shower of arrows stopped, a few dropping shots rang out sharply—then silence, in which the languid beat of the stern-wheel came plainly to my ears. I put the helm hard a-starboard at the moment when the pilgrim in pink pyjamas, very hot and agitated, appeared in the doorway. 'The manager sends me—' he began in an official tone, and stopped short. 'Good God!' he said, glaring at the wounded man.

"We two whites stood over him, and his lustrous and inquiring glance enveloped us both. I declare it looked as though he would presently put to us some question in an understandable language; but he died without uttering a sound, without moving a limb, without twitching a muscle. Only in the very last moment, as though in response to some sign we could not see, to some whisper we could not hear, he frowned heavily, and that frown gave to his black death-mask an inconceivably somber, brooding, and menacing expression. The luster of inquiring glance faded swiftly into vacant glassiness. 'Can you steer?' I asked the agent eagerly. He looked very dubious; but I made a grab at his arm, and he understood at once I meant him to steer whether or no. To tell you the truth, I was morbidly anxious to change my shoes and socks. 'He is dead,' murmured the fellow, immensely impressed. 'No doubt about it,' said I, tugging like mad at the shoe-laces. 'And, by the way, I suppose Mr. Kurtz is dead as well by this time.'

"For the moment that was the dominant thought. There was a sense of extreme disappointment, as though I had found out I had been striving after something altogether without a substance. I couldn't have been more disgusted if I had traveled all this way for the sole purpose of talking with Mr. Kurtz. Talking with . . . I flung one shoe overboard, and became aware that was exactly what I had been looking forward to—a talk with Kurtz. I made the strange discovery that I had never imagined him as doing, you know, but as discoursing. I didn't say to myself, 'Now I will never see him,' or 'Now I will never shake him by the hand,' but, 'Now I will never hear him.' The man presented himself as a voice. Not of course that I did not connect him with some sort of action. Hadn't I been told in all the tones of jealousy and admiration that he had collected, bartered, swindled, or stolen more ivory than all the other agents together? That was not the point. The point was in his being a gifted creature, and that of all his gifts the one that stood out preeminently, that carried with it a sense of real presence, was his ability to talk, his words—

the gift of expression, the bewildering, the illuminating, the most exalted and the most contemptible, the pulsating stream of light, or the deceitful flow from the heart of an impenetrable darkness.

"The other shoe went flying unto the devil-god of that river. I thought, By Jove! it's all over. We are too late; he has vanished—the gift has vanished, by means of some spear, arrow, or club. I will never hear that chap speak after all,—and my sorrow had a startling extravagance of emotion, even such as I had noticed in the howling sorrow of these savages in the bush. I couldn't have felt more of lonely desolation somehow, had I been robbed of a belief or had missed my destiny in life. . . . Why do you sigh in this beastly way, somebody? Absurd? Well, absurd. Good Lord! mustn't a man ever—Here, give me some tobacco."

There was a pause of profound stillness, then a match flared, and Marlow's lean face appeared, worn, hollow, with downward folds and dropped eyelids, with an aspect of concentrated attention; and as he took vigorous draws at his pipe, it seemed to retreat and advance out of the night in the regular flicker of the tiny flame. The match went out.

"Absurd!" he cried. "This is the worst of trying to tell. . . . Here you all are, each moored with two good addresses, like a hulk with two anchors, a butcher round one corner, a policeman round another, excellent appetites, and temperature normal—you hear—normal from year's end to year's end. And you say, Absurd! Absurd be—exploded! Absurd! My dear boys, what can you expect from a man who out of sheer nervousness had just flung overboard a pair of new shoes. Now I think of it, it is amazing I did not shed tears. I am, upon the whole, proud of my fortitude. I was cut to the quick at the idea of having lost the inestimable privilege of listening to the gifted Kurtz. Of course I was wrong. The privilege was waiting for me. Oh yes, I heard more than enough. And I was right, too. A voice. He was very little more than a voice. And I heard—him—it—this voice—other voices—all of them were so little more than voices—and the memory of that time itself lingers around me, impalpable, like a dying vibration of one immense jabber, silly, atrocious, sordid, savage, or simply mean, without any kind of sense. Voices, voices—even the girl herself—now—"

He was silent for a long time.

"I laid the ghost of his gifts at last with a lie," he began suddenly. "Girl! What? Did I mention a girl? Oh, she is out of it—completely. They—the women I mean—are out of it—should be out of it. We must help them to stay in that beautiful world of their own, lest ours gets worse. Oh, she had to be out of it. You should have heard the disinterred body of Mr. Kurtz saying, 'My Intended.' You would have perceived directly then how completely she was out of it. And the lofty frontal bone of Mr. Kurtz! They say the hair goes on growing sometimes, but this—ah—specimen, was impressively bald. The wilderness had patted him on the head, and, behold, it was like a ball—an ivory ball; it had caressed him, and—lo!—he had withered; it had taken him, loved him, embraced him, got into his veins, consumed his flesh, and sealed his soul to its own by the inconceivable ceremonies of some devilish initiation. He was its spoiled and pampered favorite. Ivory? I should think so. Heaps of it, stacks of it. The old mud shanty was bursting with it. You would think there was not a single tusk left either above or below the ground in the whole country. 'Mostly fossil,' the manager had remarked disparagingly. It was no more fossil than I am; but they call it fossil when it is dug up. It appears these niggers do bury the tusks sometimes—but evidently they couldn't bury this parcel deep enough to save the gifted Mr. Kurtz from his fate. We filled the steamboat with it, and had to pile a lot on the deck. Thus he could see and enjoy as long as he could see, because the appreciation of this favor had remained with him to the last. You should have heard him say, 'My ivory.' Oh yes, I heard him. 'My Intended, my ivory, my station, my river, my—' everything belonged to him. It made me hold my breath in expectation of hearing the wilderness burst in to a prodigious peal of laughter that would shake the fixed stars in their places. Everything belonged to him—but that was a trifle. The thing was to know what he belonged to, how many powers of darkness claimed him for their own. That was the reflection that made you creepy all over. It was impossible—it was not good for one either—trying to imagine. He had taken a high seat amongst the devils of the land—I mean literally. You can't understand. How could you?—with solid pavement under your feet, surrounded by kind neighbors ready to cheer you or to fall on you, stepping delicately between the butcher and the policeman, in the holy terror of scandal and gallows and lunatic asylums—how can you imagine what particular region of the first ages a man's untrammeled feet may take him into by the way of solitude—utter solitude without a policeman—by the way of silence—utter silence, where no warning voice of a kind neighbor can be heard whispering of public opinion? These little things make all the great difference. When they are gone you must fall back upon your own innate strength, upon your own capacity for faithfulness. Of course you may be too much of a fool to go wrong—too dull even to know you are being assaulted by the powers of darkness. I take it, no fool ever made a bargain for this soul with the devil: the fool is too much of a fool, or the devil too much of a devil—I don't know which. Or you may be such a thunderingly exalted creature as to be altogether deaf and blind to anything but heavenly sights and sounds. Then the earth for you is only a standing place—and whether to be like this is your loss or your gain I won't pretend to say. But most of us are neither one nor the other. The earth for us is a place to live in, where we must put up with sights, with sounds, with smells too, by Jove!—breathe dead hippo, so to speak, and not be contaminated. And there, don't you see? your strength comes in, the faith in your ability for the digging of unostentatious holes to bury the stuff in—your power of devotion, not to yourself, but to an obscure, back-breaking business. And that's difficult enough. Mind, I am not trying to excuse or even explain—I am trying to account to myself for—for—Mr. Kurtz—for the shade of Mr. Kurtz. This initiated wraith from the back of Nowhere honored me with its amazing confidence before it vanished altogether. This was because it could speak English to me. The original Kurtz had been educated partly in England, and—

as he was good enough to say himself—his sympathies were in the right place. His mother was half-English, his father was half-French. All Europe contributed to the making of Kurtz; and by-and-by I learned that, most appropriately, the International Society for the Suppression of Savage Customs had entrusted him with the making of a report, for its future guidance. And he had written it too. I've seen it. I've read it. It was eloquent, vibrating with eloquence, but too high-strung, I think. Seventeen pages of close writing he had found time for! But this must have been before his—let us say—nerves, went wrong, and caused him to preside at certain midnight dances ending with unspeakable rites, which—as far as I reluctantly gathered from what I heard at various times—were offered up to him—do you understand?—to Mr. Kurtz himself. But it was a beautiful piece of writing. The opening paragraph, however, in the light of later information, strikes me now as ominous. He began with the argument that we whites, from the point of development we had arrived at, 'must necessarily appear to them [savages] in the nature of supernatural beings—we approach them with the might as of a deity,' and so on, and so on. 'By the simple exercise of our will we can exert a power for good practically unbounded,' &c., &c. From that point he soared and took me with him. The peroration was magnificent, though difficult to remember, you know. It gave me the notion of an exotic Immensity ruled by an august Benevolence. It made me tingle with enthusiasm. This was the unbounded power of eloquence—of words—of burning noble words. There were no practical hints to interrupt the magic current of phrases, unless a kind of note at the foot of the last page, scrawled evidently much later, in an unsteady hand, may be regarded as the exposition of a method. It was very simple, and at the end of that moving appeal to every altruistic sentiment it blazed at you, luminous and terrifying, like a flash of lightning in a serene sky: 'Exterminate all the brutes!' The curious part was that he had apparently forgotten all about that valuable postscriptum, because, later on, when he in a sense came to himself, he repeatedly entreated me to take good care of 'my pamphlet' (he called it), as it was sure to have in the future a good influence upon his career. I had full information about all these things, and, besides, as it turned out, I was to have the care of his memory. I've done enough for it to give me the indisputable right to lay it, if I choose, for an everlasting rest in the dust-bin of progress, amongst all the sweepings and, figuratively speaking, all the dead cats of civilization. But then, you see, I can't choose. He wouldn't be forgotten. Whatever he was, he was not common. He had the power to charm or frighten rudimentary souls into an aggravated witch-dance in his honor; he could also fill the small souls of the pilgrims with bitter misgivings: he had one devoted friend at least, and he had conquered one soul in the world that was neither rudimentary nor tainted with self-seeking. No; I can't forget him, though I am not prepared to affirm the fellow was exactly worth the life we lost in getting to him. I missed my late helmsman awfully,—I missed him even while his body was still lying in the pilot-house. Perhaps you will think it passing strange this regret for a savage who was no more account than a grain of sand in a black Sahara. Well, don't you see, he had done something, he had steered; for months I had him at my back—a help—an instrument. It was a kind of partnership. He steered for me—I had to look after him, I worried about his deficiencies, and thus a subtle bond had been created, of which I only became aware when it was suddenly broken. And the intimate profundity of that look he gave me when he received his hurt remains to this day in my memory—like a claim of distant kinship affirmed in a supreme moment.

"Poor fool! If he had only left that shutter alone. He had no restraint, no 105
restraint—just like Kurtz—a tree swayed in the wind. As soon as I had put on a dry pair of slippers, I dragged him out, after first jerking the spear out of his side, which operation I confess I performed with my eyes shut tight. His heels leaped together over the little door-step; his shoulders were pressed to my breast; I hugged him from behind desperately. Oh! he was heavy, heavy; heavier than any man on earth, I should imagine. Then without more ado I tipped him overboard. The current snatched him as though he had been a wisp of grass, and I saw the body roll over twice before I lost sight of it for ever. All the pilgrims and the manager were then congregated on the awning-deck about the pilot-house, chattering at each other like a flock of excited magpies, and there was a scandalized murmur at my heartless promptitude. What they wanted to keep that body hanging about for I can't guess. Embalm it, maybe. But I had also heard another, and a very ominous, murmur on the deck below. My friends the wood-cutters were likewise scandalized, and with a better show of reason—though I admit that the reason itself was quite inadmissible. Oh, quite! I had made up my mind that if my late helmsman was to be eaten, the fishes alone should have him. He had been a very second-rate helmsman while alive, but now he was dead he might have become a first-class temptation, and possibly cause some startling trouble. Besides, I was anxious to take the wheel, the man in pink pyjamas showing himself a hopeless duffer at the business.

"This I did directly the simple funeral was over. We were going half-speed, keeping right in the middle of the stream, and I listened to the talk about me. They had given up Kurtz, they had given up the station; Kurtz was dead, and the station had been burnt—and so on—and so on. The red-haired pilgrim was beside himself with the thought that at least this poor Kurtz had been properly revenged. 'Say! We must have made a glorious slaughter of them in the bush. Eh? What do you think? Say?' He positively danced, the bloodthirsty little gingery beggar. And he had nearly fainted when he saw the wounded man! I could not help saying, 'You made a glorious lot of smoke, anyhow.' I had seen, from the way the tops of the bushes rustled and flew, that almost all the shots had gone too high. You can't hit anything unless you take aim and fire from the shoulder; but these chaps fired from the hip with their eyes shut. The retreat, I maintained—and I was right—was caused by the screeching of the steam-whistle. Upon this they forgot Kurtz, and began to howl at me with indignant protests.

"The manager stood by the wheel murmuring confidentially about the necessity of getting well away down the river before dark at all events, when I saw in the distance a clearing on the river-side and the outlines of some sort of building. 'What's this?' I asked. He clapped his hands in wonder. 'The station!' he cried. I edged in at once, still going half-speed.

"Through my glasses I saw the slope of a hill interspersed with rare trees and perfectly free from undergrowth. A long decaying building on the summit was half buried in the high grass; the large holes in the peaked roof gaped back from afar; the jungle and the woods made a background. There was no inclosure or fence of any kind; but there had been one apparently, for near the house half-a-dozen slim posts remained in a row, roughly trimmed, and with their upper ends ornamented with round curved balls. The rails, or whatever there had been between, had disappeared. Of course the forest surrounded all that. The river-bank was clear, and on the water-side I saw a white man under a hat like a cart-wheel beckoning persistently with his whole arm. Examining the edge of the forest above and below, I was almost certain I could see movements—human forms gliding here and there. I steamed past prudently, then stopped the engines and let her drift down. The man on the shore began to shout, urging us to land. 'We have been attacked,' screamed the manager. 'I know—I know. It's all right,' yelled back the other, as cheerful as you please. 'Come along. It's all right. I am glad.'

"His aspect reminded me of something I had seen—something funny I had seen somewhere. As I maneuvered to get alongside, I was asking myself, 'What does this fellow look like?' Suddenly I got it. He looked like a harlequin. His clothes had been made of some stuff that was brown holland probably, but it was covered with patches all over, with bright patches, blue, red, and yellow,—patches on the back, patches on front, patches on elbows, on knees; colored binding round his jacket, scarlet edging at the bottom of his trousers; and the sunshine made him look extremely gay and wonderfully neat withal, because you could see how beautifully all this patching had been done. A beardless, boyish face, very fair, no features to speak of, nose peeling, little blue eyes, smiles and frowns chasing each other over that open countenance like sunshine and shadow on a wind-swept plain. 'Look out, captain!' he cried; 'there's a snag lodged in here last night.' What! Another snag? I confess I swore shamefully. I had nearly holed my cripple, to finish off that charming trip. The harlequin on the bank turned his little pug nose up to me. 'You English?' he asked, all smiles. 'Are you?' I shouted from the wheel. The smiles vanished, and he shook his head as if sorry for my disappointment. Then he brightened up. 'Never mind!' he cried encouragingly. 'Are we in time?' I asked. 'He is up there,' he replied, with a toss of the head up the hill, and becoming gloomy all of a sudden. His face was like the autumn sky, overcast one moment and bright the next.

"When the manager, escorted by the pilgrims, all of them armed to the 110
teeth, had gone to the house, this chap came on board. 'I say, I don't like this. These natives are in the bush,' I said. He assured me earnestly it was all right. 'They are simple people,' he added; 'well, I am glad you came. It took me all my time to keep them off.' 'But you said it was all right,' I cried. 'Oh, they

meant no harm,' he said; and as I stared he corrected himself, 'Not exactly.' Then vivaciously, 'My faith, your pilot-house wants a clean up!' In the next breath he advised me to keep enough steam on the boiler to blow the whistle in case of any trouble. 'One good screech will do more for you than all your rifles. They are simple people,' he repeated. He rattled away at such a rate he quite overwhelmed me. He seemed to be trying to make up for lots of silence, and actually hinted, laughing, that such was the case. 'Don't you talk with Mr. Kurtz?' I said. 'You don't talk with that man—you listen to him,' he exclaimed with severe exaltation. 'But now—' He waved his arm, and in the twinkling of an eye was in the uttermost depths of despondency. In a moment he came up again with a jump, possessed himself of both my hands, shook them continuously, while he gabbed: 'Brother sailor . . . honor . . . pleasure . . . delight . . . introduce myself . . . Russian . . . son of an archpriest . . . Government of Tambov . . . What? Tobacco! English tobacco; the excellent English tobacco! Now, that's brotherly. Smoke? Where's a sailor that does not smoke?"

"The pipe soothed him, and gradually I made out he had run away from school, had gone to sea in a Russian ship; ran away again; served some time in English ships; was now reconciled with the arch-priest. He made a point of that. 'But when one is young one must see things, gather experience, ideas; enlarge the mind.' 'Here!' I interrupted. 'You can never tell! Here I have met Mr. Kurtz,' he said, youthfully solemn and reproachful. I held my tongue after that. It appears he had persuaded a Dutch trading-house on the coast to fit him out with stores and goods, and had started for the interior with a light heart, and no more idea of what would happen to him than a baby. He had been wandering about that river for nearly two years alone, cut off from everybody and everything. 'I am not so young as I look. I am twenty-five,' he said. 'At first old Van Shuyten would tell me to go to the devil,' he narrated with keen enjoyment; 'but I stuck to him, and talked and talked, till at last he got afraid I would talk the hind-leg off his favorite dog, so he gave me some cheap things and a few guns, and told me he hoped he would never see my face again. Good old Dutchman, Van Shuyten. I've sent him one small lot of ivory a year ago, so that he can't call me a little thief when I get back. I hope he got it. And for the rest I don't care. I had some wood stacked for you. That was my old house. Did you see?

"I gave him Towson's book. He made as though he would kiss me, but restrained himself. 'The only book I had left, and I thought I had lost it,' he said, looking at it ecstatically. 'So many accidents happen to a man going about alone, you know. Canoes get upset sometimes—and sometimes you've got to clear out so quick when the people get angry.' He thumbed the pages. 'You made notes in Russian?' I asked. He nodded. 'I thought they were written in cipher,' I said. He laughed, then became serious. 'I had lots of trouble to keep these people off,' he said. 'Did they want to kill you?' I asked. 'Oh no!' he cried, and checked himself. 'Why did they attack us?' I pursued. He hesitated, then said shamefacedly, 'They don't want him to go.' 'Don't they?' I said, curiously. He nodded a nod full of mystery and wisdom. 'I tell you,' he cried, 'this man has enlarged my mind.' He opened his arms wide, staring at me with his little blue eyes that were perfectly round."

III

"I looked at him, lost in astonishment. There he was before me, in motley, as though he had absconded from a troupe of mimes, enthusiastic, fabulous. His very existence was improbable, inexplicable, and altogether bewildering. He was an insoluble problem. It was inconceivable how he had existed, how he had succeeded in getting so far, how he had managed to remain—why he did not instantly disappear. 'I went a little farther,' he said, 'then still a little farther—till I had gone so far that I don't know how I'll ever get back. Never mind. Plenty time. I can manage. You take Kurtz away quick—quick—I tell you.' The glamour of youth enveloped his particolored rags, his destitution, his loneliness, the essential desolation of his futile wanderings. For months—for years—his life hadn't been worth a day's purchase; and there he was gallantly, thoughtlessly alive, to all appearance indestructible solely by the virtue of his few years and of his unreflecting audacity. I was seduced into something like admiration—like envy. Glamour urged him on, glamour kept him unscathed. He surely wanted nothing from the wilderness but space to breathe in and to push on through. His need was to exist, and to move onwards at the greatest possible risk, and with a maximum of privation. If the absolutely pure, uncalculating, unpractical spirit of adventure had ever ruled a human being, it ruled this be-patched youth. I almost envied him the possession of this modest and clear flame. It seemed to have consumed all thought of self so completely, that, even while he was talking to you, you forgot that it was he—the man before your eyes—who had gone through these things. I did not envy him his devotion to Kurtz, though. He had not meditated over it. It came to him, and he accepted it with a sort of eager fatalism. I must say that to me it appeared about the most dangerous thing in every way he had come upon so far.

"They had come together unavoidably, like two ships becalmed near each other, and lay rubbing sides at last. I suppose Kurtz wanted an audience, because on a certain occasion, when encamped in the forest, they had talked all night, or more probably Kurtz had talked. 'We talked of everything,' he said, quite transported at the recollection. 'I forgot there was such a thing as sleep. The night did not seem to last an hour. Everything! Everything! . . . Of love too.' 'Ah, he talked to you of love!' I said, much amused, 'It isn't what you think,' he cried, almost passionately. 'It was in general. He made me see things—things.'

"He threw his arms up. We were on deck at the time, and the headman of 115
my wood-cutters, lounging near by, turned upon him his heavy and glittering eyes. I looked around, and I don't know why, but I assure you that never, never before, did this land, this river, this jungle, the very arch of this blazing sky, appear to me so hopeless and so dark, so impenetrable to human thought, so pitiless to human weakness. 'And, ever since, you have been with him, of course?' I said.

"On the contrary. It appears their intercourse had been very much broken by various causes. He had, as he informed me proudly, managed to nurse Kurtz through two illnesses (he alluded to it as you would to some risky feat), but as a rule Kurtz wandered alone, far in the depths of the forest. 'Very often coming to this station, I had to wait days and days before he would turn up,' he said. 'Ah, it was worth waiting for!—sometimes.' 'What was he doing? exploring or what?' I asked. 'Oh yes, of course'; he had discovered lots of villages, a lake too—he did not know exactly in what direction, it was dangerous to inquire too much—but mostly his expeditions had been for ivory. 'But he had no goods to trade with by that time,' I objected. 'There's a good lot of cartridges left even yet,' he answered, looking away. 'To speak plainly, he raided the country,' I said. He nodded. 'Not alone, surely!' He muttered something about the villages round that lake. 'Kurtz got the tribe to follow him, did he?' I suggested. He fidgeted a little. 'They adored him,' he said. The tone of these words was so extraordinary that I looked at him searchingly. It was curious to see his mingled eagerness and reluctance to speak of Kurtz. The man filled his life, occupied his thoughts, swayed his emotions. 'What can you expect?' he burst out; 'he came to them with thunder and lightning, you know—and they had never seen anything like it—and very terrible. He could be very terrible. You can't judge Mr. Kurtz as you would an ordinary man. No, no, no! Now—just to give you an idea—I don't mind telling you, he wanted to shoot me too one day—but I don't judge him.' 'Shoot you!' I cried. 'What for?' 'Well, I had a small lot of ivory the chief of that village near my house gave me. You see I used to shoot game for them. Well, he wanted it, and wouldn't hear reason. He declared he would shoot me unless I gave him the ivory and then cleared out of the country, because he could do so, and had a fancy for it, and there was nothing on earth to prevent him killing whom he jolly well pleased. And it was true too. I gave him the ivory. What did I care! But I didn't clear out. No, no. I couldn't leave him. I had to be careful, of course, till we got friendly again for a time. He had his second illness then. Afterwards I had to keep out of the way; but I don't mind. He was living for the most part in those villages on the lake. When he came down to the river, sometimes he would take me, and sometimes it was better for me to be careful. This man suffered too much. He hated all this, and somehow he couldn't get away. When I had a chance I begged him to try and leave while there was time; I offered to go back with him. And he would say yes, and then he would remain; go off on another ivory hunt; disappear for weeks; forget himself amongst these people—forget himself—you know.' 'Why! he's mad,' I said. He protested indignantly. Mr. Kurtz couldn't be mad. If I had heard him talk, only two days ago, I wouldn't dare hint at such a thing. . . . I had taken up my binoculars while we talked and was looking at the shore, sweeping the limit of the forest at each side and at the back of the house. The consciousness of there being people in that bush, so silent, so quiet—as silent and quiet as the ruined house on the hill—made me uneasy. There was no sign on the face of nature of this amazing tale that was not so much told as suggested to me in desolate exclamations, completed by shrugs, in interrupted phrases, in hints ending in deep sighs. The woods were unmoved, like a mask—heavy, like the closed door of a prison—they looked with their air of hidden knowledge, of patient expectation, of unapproachable silence. The Russian was explaining to me that it was only lately that Mr. Kurtz had come down to the river, bringing along with him all the fighting men of that lake tribe. He had been absent for several months—getting himself adored, I suppose—and had come down unexpectedly, with the intention to all appearance of making a raid either across the river or down stream. Evidently the appetite for more ivory had got the better of the—what shall I say?—less material aspirations. However he had got much worse suddenly. 'I heard he was lying helpless, and so I came up—took my chance,' said the Russian. 'Oh, he is bad, very bad.' I directed my glass to the house. There were no signs of life, but there was the ruined roof, the long mud wall peeping above the grass, with three little square window-holes, no two of the same size; all this brought within reach of my hand, as it were. And then I made a brusque movement, and one of the remaining posts of that vanished fence leaped up in the field of my glass. You remember I told you I had been struck at the distance by certain attempts at ornamentation, rather remarkable in the ruinous aspect of the place. Now I had suddenly a nearer view, and its first result was to make me throw my head back as if before a blow. Then I went carefully from post to post with my glass, and I saw my mistake. These round knobs were not ornamental but symbolic; they were expressive and puzzling, striking and disturbing—food for thought and also for the vultures if there had been any looking down from the sky; but at all events for such ants as were industrious enough to ascend the pole. They would have been even more impressive, those heads on the stakes, if their faces had not been turned to the house. Only one, the first I had made out, was facing my way. I was not so shocked as you may think. The start back I had given was really nothing but a movement of surprise. I had expected to see a knob of wood there, you know. I returned deliberately to the first I had seen—and there it was, black, dried, sunken, with closed eyelids—a head that seemed to sleep at the top of that pole, and, with the shrunken dry lips showing a narrow white line of the teeth, was smiling too, smiling continuously at some endless and jocose dream of that eternal slumber.

"I am not disclosing any trade secrets. In fact the manager said afterwards that Mr. Kurtz's methods had ruined the district. I have no opinion on that point, but I want you clearly to understand that there was nothing exactly profitable in these heads being there. They only showed that Mr. Kurtz lacked restraint in the gratification of his various lusts, that there was something wanting in him—some small matter which, when the pressing need arose, could not be found under his magnificent eloquence. Whether he knew of this deficiency himself I can't say. I think the knowledge came to him at last—only at the very last. But the wilderness had found him out early, and had taken on him a terrible vengeance for the fantastic invasion. I think it had whispered to him things about himself which he did not know, things of which he had no conception till he took counsel with this great solitude—and the whisper had proved irresistibly fascinating. It echoed loudly within him because he was hollow at the core. . . . I put down the glass, and the head that had appeared near enough to be spoken to seemed at once to have leaped away from me into inaccessible distance.

"The admirer of Mr. Kurtz was a bit crestfallen. In a hurried, indistinct voice he began to assure me he had not dared to take these—say, symbols—down. He was not afraid of the natives; they would not stir till Mr. Kurtz gave the word. His ascendancy was extraordinary. The camps of these people surrounded the place, and the chiefs came every day to see him. They would crawl. . . . 'I don't want to know anything of the ceremonies used when approaching Mr. Kurtz,' I shouted. Curious, this feeling that came over me that such details would be more intolerable than those heads drying on the stakes under Mr. Kurtz's windows. After all, that was only a savage sight, while I seemed at one bound to have been transported into some lightless region of subtle horrors, where pure, uncomplicated savagery was a positive relief, being something that had a right to exist—obviously—in the sunshine. The young man looked at me with surprise. I suppose it did not occur to him that Mr. Kurtz was no idol of mine. He forgot I hadn't heard any of these splendid monologues on, what was it? on love, justice, conduct of life—or what not. If it had come to crawling before Mr. Kurtz, he crawled as much as the veriest savage of them all. I had no idea of the conditions, he said: these heads were the heads of rebels. I shocked him excessively by laughing. Rebels! What would be the next definition I was to hear? There had been enemies, criminals, workers—and these were rebels. Those rebellious heads looked very subdued to me on their sticks. 'You don't know how such a life tries a man like Kurtz,' cried Kurtz's last disciple. 'Well, and you?' I said. 'I! I! I am a simple man. I have no great thoughts. I want nothing from anybody. How can you compare me to . . . ?' His feelings were too much for speech, and suddenly he broke down. 'I don't understand,' he groaned. 'I've been doing my best to keep him alive, and that's enough. I had no hand in all this. I have no abilities. There hasn't been a drop of medicine or a mouthful of invalid food for months here. He was shamefully abandoned. A man like this, with such ideas. Shamefully! Shamefully! I—I—haven't slept for the last ten nights. . . .'

"His voice lost itself in the calm of the evening. The long shadows of the forest had slipped down hill while we talked, had gone far beyond the ruined hovel, beyond the symbolic row of stakes. All this was in the gloom, while we down there were yet in the sunshine, and the stretch of the river abreast of the clearing glittered in a still and dazzling splendor, with a murky and overshadowed bend above and below. Not a living soul was seen on the shore. The bushes did not rustle.

"Suddenly round the corner of the house a group of men appeared, as 120
though they had come up from the ground. They waded waist-deep in the grass, in a compact body, bearing an improvised stretcher in their midst. Instantly, in the emptiness of the landscape, a cry arose whose shrillness pierced the still air like a sharp arrow flying straight to the very heart of the land; and, as if by enchantment, streams of human beings—of naked human beings—with spears in their hands, with bows, with shields, with wild glances and savage movements, were poured into the clearing by the dark-faced and pensive forest. The bushes shook, the grass swayed for a time, and then everything stood still in attentive immobility.

"'Now, if he does not say the right thing to them we are all done for,' said the Russian at my elbow. The knot of men with the stretcher had stopped too, halfway to the steamer, as if petrified. I saw the man on the stretcher sit up, lank and with an uplifted arm, above the shoulders of the bearers. 'Let us hope that the man who can talk so well of love in general will find some particular reason to spare us this time,' I said. I resented bitterly the absurd danger of our situation, as if to be at the mercy of that atrocious phantom had been a dishonoring necessity. I could not hear a sound, but through my glasses I saw the thin arm extended commandingly, the lower jaw moving, the eyes of that apparition shining darkly far in its bony head that nodded with grotesque jerks. Kurtz—Kurtz—that means short in German—don't it? Well, the name was as true as everything else in his life—and death. He looked at least seven feet long. His covering had fallen off, and his body emerged from it pitiful and appalling as from a winding-sheet. I would see the cage of his ribs all astir, the bones of his arm waving. It was as though an animated image of death carved out of old ivory had been shaking its hand with menaces at a motionless crowd of men made of dark and glittering bronze. I saw him open his mouth wide—it gave him a weirdly voracious aspect, as though he had wanted to swallow all the air, all the earth, all the men before him. A deep voice reached me faintly. He must have been shouting. He fell back suddenly. The stretcher shook as the bearers staggered forward again, and almost at the same time I noticed that the crowd of savages was vanishing without any perceptible movement of retreat, as if the forest that had ejected these beings so suddenly had drawn them in again as the breath is drawn in a long aspiration.

"Some of the pilgrims behind the stretcher carried his arms—two shot-guns, a heavy rifle, and a light revolver-carbine—the thunderbolts of that pitiful Jupiter. The manager bent over him murmuring as he walked beside his head. They laid him down in one of the little cabins—just a room for a bed-place and a camp-stool or two, you know. We had brought his belated correspondence, and a lot of torn envelopes and open letters littered his bed. His hand roamed feebly amongst these papers. I was struck by the fire of his eyes and the composed languor of his expression. It was not so much the exhaustion of disease. He did not seem in pain. This shadow looked satiated and calm, as though for the moment it had had its fill of all the emotions.

"He rustled one of the letters, and looking straight in my face said, 'I am glad.' Somebody had been writing to him about me. These special recommendations were turning up again. The volume of tone he emitted without effort, almost without the trouble of moving his lips, amazed me. A voice! a voice! It was grave, profound, vibrating, while the man did not seem capable of a whisper. However, he had enough strength in him—factitious no doubt—to very nearly make an end of us, as you shall hear directly.

"The manager appeared silently in the doorway; I stepped out at once and he drew the curtain after me. The Russian, eyed curiously by the pilgrims, was staring at the shore. I followed the direction of his glance.

"Dark human shapes could be made out in the distance, flitting in- 125
distinctly against the gloomy border of the forest, and near the river two

bronze figures, leaning on tall spears, stood in the sunlight under fantastic head-dresses of spotted skins, warlike and still in statuesque repose. And from right to left along the lighted shore moved a wild and gorgeous apparition of a woman.

“She walked with measured steps, draped in striped and fringed cloths, treading the earth proudly, with a slight jingle and flash of barbarous ornaments. She carried her head high; her hair was done in the shape of a helmet; she had brass leggings to the knee, brass wire gauntlets to the elbow, a crimson spot on her tawny cheek, innumerable necklaces of glass beads on her neck; bizarre things, charms, gifts of witch-men, that hung about her, glittered and trembled at every step. She must have had the value of several elephant tusks upon her. She was savage and superb, wild-eyed and magnificent; there was something ominous and stately in her deliberate progress. And in the hush that had fallen suddenly upon the whole sorrowful land, the immense wilderness, the colossal body of the fecund and mysterious life seemed to look at her, pensive, as though it had been looking at the image of its own tenebrous and passionate soul.

“She came abreast of the steamer, stood still, and faced us. Her long shadow fell to the water's edge. Her face had a tragic and fierce aspect of wild sorrow and of dumb pain mingled with the fear of some struggling, half-shaped resolve. She stood looking at us without a stir and like the wilderness itself, with an air of brooding over an inscrutable purpose. A whole minute passed, and then she made a step forward. There was a low jingle, a glint of yellow metal, a sway of fringed draperies, and she stopped as if her heart had failed her. The young fellow by my side growled. The pilgrims murmured at my back. She looked at us all as if her life had depended upon the unswerving steadiness of her glance. Suddenly she opened her bared arms and threw them up rigid above her head, as though in an uncontrollable desire to touch the sky, and at the same time the swift shadows darted out on the earth, swept around on the river, gathering the steamer into a shadowy embrace. A formidable silence hung over the scene.

“She turned away slowly, walked on, following the bank, and passed into the bushes to the left. Once only her eyes gleamed back at us in the dusk of the thickets before she disappeared.

“‘If she had offered to come aboard I really think I would have tried to shoot her,’ said the man of patches, nervously. ‘I had been risking my life every day for the last fortnight to keep her out of the house. She got in one day and kicked up a row about those miserable rags I picked up in the storeroom to mend my clothes with. I wasn't decent. At least it must have been that, for she talked like a fury to Kurtz for an hour, pointing at me now and then. I don't understand the dialect of this tribe. Luckily for me, I fancy Kurtz felt too ill that day to care, or there would have been mischief. I don't understand. . . . No—it's too much for me. Ah, well, it's all over now.’

“At this moment I heard Kurtz's deep voice behind the curtain, ‘Save 130
me!—save the ivory, you mean. Don't tell me. Save *me!* Why, I've had to save you. You are interrupting my plans now. Sick! Sick! Not so sick as you would like to believe. Never mind. I'll carry my ideas out yet—I will return. I'll show

you what can be done. You with your little peddling notions—you are interfering with me. I will return. I . . .'

"The manager came out. He did me the honor to take me under the arm and lead me aside. 'He is very low, very low,' he said. He considered it necessary to sigh, but neglected to be consistently sorrowful. 'We have done all we could for him—haven't we? But there is no disguising the fact, Mr. Kurtz has done more harm than good to the Company. He did not see the time was not ripe for vigorous action. Cautiously, cautiously—that's my principle. We must be cautious yet. The district is closed to us for a time. Deplorable! Upon the whole, the trade will suffer. I don't deny there is a remarkable quantity of ivory—mostly fossil. We must save it, at all events—but look how precarious the position is—and why? Because the method is unsound.' 'Do you,' said I, looking at the shore, 'call it "unsound method"?' 'Without doubt,' he exclaimed, hotly. 'Don't you?' . . . 'No method at all,' I murmured after a while. 'Exactly,' he exulted. 'I anticipated this. Shows a complete want of judgment. It is my duty to point it out in the proper quarter.' 'Oh,' said I, 'that fellow—what's his name?—the brickmaker, will make a readable report for you.' He appeared confounded for a moment. It seemed to me I had never breathed an atmosphere so vile, and I turned mentally to Kurtz for relief—positively for relief. 'Nevertheless I think Mr. Kurtz is a remarkable man,' I said with emphasis. He started, dropped on me a cold heavy glance, said very quietly, 'He *was,*' and turned his back on me. My hour of favor was over; I found myself lumped along with Kurtz as a partisan of methods for which the time was not ripe: I was unsound! Ah! but it was something to have at least a choice of nightmares.

"I had turned to the wilderness really, not to Mr. Kurtz, who, I was ready to admit, was as good as buried. And for a moment it seemed to me as if I also were buried in a vast grave full of unspeakable secrets. I felt an intolerable weight oppressing my breast, the smell of the damp earth, the unseen presence of victorious corruption, the darkness of an impenetrable night. . . . The Russian tapped me on the shoulder. I heard him mumbling and stammering something about 'brother seaman—couldn't conceal—knowledge of matters that would affect Mr. Kurtz's reputation.' I waited. For him evidently Mr. Kurtz was not in his grave; I suspect that for him Mr. Kurtz was one of the immortals. 'Well!' said I at last, 'speak out. As it happens, I am Mr. Kurtz's friend—in a way.'

"He stated with a good deal of formality that had we not been 'of the same profession,' he would have kept the matter to himself without regard to consequences. 'He suspected there was an active ill-will towards him on the part of these white men that—' 'You are right,' I said, remembering a certain conversation I had overheard. 'The manager thinks you ought to be hanged.' He showed a concern at this intelligence which amused me at first. 'I had better get out of the way quietly,' he said, earnestly. 'I can do no more for Kurtz now, and they would soon find some excuse. What's to stop them? There's a military post three hundred miles from here.' 'Well, upon my word,' said I, 'perhaps you had better go if you have any friends amongst the savages near by.' 'Plenty,' he said. 'They are simple people—and I want nothing, you know.' He stood biting his lip, then: 'I don't want any harm to happen to these whites here, but of course I was thinking of Mr. Kurtz's reputation—but you are a brother seaman and—' 'All right,' said I, after a time. 'Mr. Kurtz's reputation is safe with me.' I did not know how truly I spoke.

"He informed me, lowering his voice, that it was Kurtz who had ordered the attack to be made on the steamer. 'He hated sometimes the idea of being taken away—and then again. . . . But I don't understand these matters. I am a simple man. He thought it would scare you away—that you would give it up, thinking him dead. I could not stop him. Oh, I had an awful time of it this last month.' 'Very well,' I said. 'He is all right now.' 'Ye-e-es,' he muttered, not very convinced apparently. 'Thanks,' said I; 'I shall keep my eyes open.' 'But quiet—eh?' he urged, anxiously. 'It would be awful for his reputation if anybody here—' I promised a complete discretion with great gravity. 'I have a canoe and three black fellows waiting not very far. I am off. Could you give me a few Martini-Henry cartridges?' I could, and did, with proper secrecy. He helped himself, with a wink at me, to a handful of my tobacco. 'Between sailors—you know—good English tobacco.' At the door of the pilot-house he turned round—'I say, haven't you a pair of shoes you could spare?' He raised one leg. 'Look.' The soles were tied with knotted strings sandal-wise under his bare feet. I rooted out an old pair, at which he looked with admiration before tucking it under his left arm. One of his pockets (bright red) was bulging with cartridges, from the other (dark blue) peeped 'Towson's Inquiry,' &c., &c. He seemed to think himself excellently well equipped for a renewed encounter with the wilderness. 'Ah! I'll never, never meet such a man again. You ought to have heard him recite poetry—his own too it was, he told me. Poetry!' He rolled his eyes at the recollection of these delights. 'Oh, he enlarged my mind!' 'Good-by,' said I. He shook hands and vanished in the night. Sometimes I ask myself whether I had ever really seen him—whether it was possible to meet such a phenomenon! . . .

"When I woke up shortly after midnight his warning came to mind with 135
its hint of danger that seemed, in the starred darkness, real enough to make me get up for the purpose of having a look round. On the hill a big fire burned, illuminating fitfully a crooked corner of the station-house. One of the agents with a picket of a few of our blacks, armed for the purpose, was keeping guard over the ivory; but deep within the forest, red gleams that wavered, that seemed to sink and rise from the ground amongst confused columnar shapes of intense blackness, showed the exact position of the camp where Mr. Kurtz's adorers were keeping their uneasy vigil. The monotonous beating of a big drum filled the air with muffled shocks and a lingering vibration. A steady droning sound of many men chanting each to himself some weird incantation came out from the black, flat wall of the woods as the humming of bees comes out of a hive, and had a strange narcotic effect upon my half-awake senses. I believe I dozed off leaning over the rail, till an abrupt burst of yells, an overwhelming outbreak of a pent-up and mysterious frenzy, woke me up in a bewildered wonder. It was cut short all at once, and the low droning went on with an effect of audible and soothing silence. I glanced casually into the little cabin. A light was burning within, but Mr. Kurtz was not there.

"I think I would have raised an outcry if I had believed my eyes. But I didn't believe them at first—the thing seemed so impossible. The fact is I was completely unnerved by a sheer blank fright, pure abstract terror, unconnected with any distinct shape of physical danger. What made this emotion so overpowering was—how shall I define it?—the moral shock I received, as if something altogether monstrous, intolerable to thought and odious to the soul, had been thrust upon me unexpectedly. This lasted of course the merest fraction of a second, and then the usual sense of commonplace, deadly danger, the possibility of a sudden onslaught and massacre, or something of the kind, which I saw impending, was positively welcome and composing. It pacified me, in fact, so much, that I did not raise an alarm.

"There was an agent buttoned up inside an ulster and sleeping on a chair on deck within three feet of me. The yells had not awakened him; he snored very slightly; I left him to his slumbers and leaped shore. I did not betray Mr. Kurtz—it was ordered I should never betray him—it was written I should be loyal to the nightmare of my choice. I was anxious to deal with this shadow by myself alone,—and to this day I don't know why I was so jealous of sharing with anyone the peculiar blackness of that experience.

"As soon as I got on the bank I saw a trail—a broad trail through the grass. I remember the exultation with which I said to myself, 'He can't walk—he is crawling on all-fours—I've got him.' The grass was wet with dew. I strode rapidly with clenched fists. I fancy I had some vague notion of falling upon him and giving him a drubbing. I don't know. I had some imbecile thoughts. The knitting old woman with the cat obtruded herself upon my memory as a most improper person to be sitting at the other end of such an affair. I saw a row of pilgrims squirting lead in the air out of Winchesters held to the hip. I thought I would never get back to the steamer, and imagined myself living alone and unarmed in the woods to an advanced age. Such silly things—you know. And I remember I confounded the beat of the drum with the beating of my heart, and was pleased at its calm regularity.

"I kept to the track though—then stopped to listen. The night was very clear: a dark blue space, sparkling with dew and starlight, in which black things stood very still. I thought I could see a kind of motion ahead of me. I was strangely cocksure of everything that night. I actually left the track and ran in a wide semicircle (I verily believe chuckling to myself) so as to get in front of that stir, of that motion I had seen—if indeed I had seen anything. I was circumventing Kurtz as though it had been a boyish game.

"I came upon him, and, if he had not heard me coming, I would have 140
fallen over him too, but he got up in time. He rose, unsteady, long, pale, indistinct, like a vapor exhaled by the earth, and swayed slightly, misty and silent before me; while at my back the fires loomed between the trees, and the murmur of many voices issued from the forest. I had cut him off cleverly; but when actually confronting him I seemed to come to my senses, I saw the danger in its right proportion. It was by no means over yet. Suppose he began to shout? Though he could hardly stand, there was still plenty of vigor in his voice. 'Go away—hide yourself,' he said, in that profound tone. It was very awful. I glanced back. We were within thirty yards from the nearest fire. A

black figure stood up, strode on long black legs, waving long black arms, across the glow. It had horns—antelope horns, I think—on its head. Some sorcerer, some witch-man, no doubt; it looked fiend-like enough. 'Do you know what you are doing?' I whispered. 'Perfectly,' he answered, raising his voice for that single word: it sounded to me far off and yet loud, like a hail through a speaking-trumpet. If he makes a row we are lost, I thought to myself. This clearly was not a case for fisticuffs, even apart from the very natural aversion I had to beat that Shadow—this wandering and tormented thing. 'You will be lost.' I said—'utterly lost.' One gets sometimes such a flash of inspiration, you know. I did say the right thing, though indeed he could not have been more irretrievably lost than he was at this very moment, when the foundations of our intimacy were being laid—to endure—to endure—even to the end—even beyond.

"'I had immense plans,' he muttered irresolutely. 'Yes,' said I; 'but if you try to shout I'll smash your head with—' there was not a stick or a stone near. 'I will throttle you for good,' I corrected myself. 'I was on the threshold of great things,' he pleaded, in a voice of longing, with a wistfulness of tone that made my blood run cold. 'And now for this stupid scoundrel—' 'Your success in Europe is assured in any case,' I affirmed, steadily. I did not want to have the throttling of him, you understand—and indeed it would have been very little use for any practical purpose. I tried to break the spell—the heavy, mute spell of the wilderness—that seemed to draw him to its pitiless breast by the awakening of forgotten and brutal instincts, by the memory of gratified and monstrous passions. This alone, I was convinced, had driven him out to the edge of the forest, to the bush, towards the gleam of fires, the throb of drums, the drone of weird incantations; this alone had beguiled his unlawful soul beyond the bounds of permitted aspirations. And, don't you see, the terror of the position was not in being knocked on the head—though I had a very lively sense of that danger too—but in this, that I had to deal with a being to whom I could not appeal in the name of anything high or low. I had, even like the niggers, to invoke him—himself—his own exalted and incredible degradation. There was nothing either above or below him, and I knew it. He had kicked himself loose of the earth. Confound the man! he had kicked the very earth to pieces. He was alone, and I before him did not know whether I stood on the ground or floated in the air. I've been telling you what we said—repeating the phrases we pronounced,—but what's the good? They were common everyday words,—the familiar, vague sounds exchanged on every waking day of life. But what of that? They had behind them, to my mind, the terrific suggestiveness of words heard in dreams, of phrases spoken in nightmares. Soul! If anybody had ever struggled with a soul, I am the man. And I wasn't arguing with a lunatic either. Believe me or not, his intelligence was perfectly clear—concentrated, it is true, upon himself with horrible intensity, yet clear; and therein was my only chance—barring, of course, the killing him there and then, which wasn't so good, on account of unavoidable noise. But his soul was mad. Being alone in the wilderness, it had looked within itself, and, by heavens! I tell you, it had gone mad. I had—for my sins, I suppose—to go through the ordeal of looking into it myself. No eloquence could have been so withering to one's belief in mankind as his final burst of sincerity. He struggled with himself, too. I saw it,—I heard it. I saw the inconceivable mystery of a soul that knew no restraint, no faith, and no fear, yet struggling blindly with itself. I kept my head pretty well; but when I had him at last stretched on the couch, I wiped my forehead, while my legs shook under me as though I had carried half a ton on my back down that hill. And yet I had only supported him, his bony arm clasped around my neck—and he was not much heavier than a child.

"When next day we left at noon, the crowd, of whose presence behind the curtain of trees I had been acutely conscious all the time, flowed out of the woods again, filled the clearing, covered the slope with a mass of naked, breathing, quivering, bronze bodies. I steamed up a bit, then swung downstream, and two thousand eyes followed the evolutions of the splashing, thumping, fierce river-demon beating the water with its terrible tail and breathing black smoke into the air. In front of the first rank, along the river, three men, plastered with bright red earth from head to foot, strutted to and fro restlessly. When we came abreast again, they faced the river, stamped their feet, nodded their horned heads, swayed their scarlet bodies; they shook towards the fierce river-demon a bunch of black feathers, a mangy skin with a pendent tail—something that looked like a dried gourd; they shouted periodically together strings of amazing words that resembled no sounds of human language; and the deep murmurs of the crowd, interrupted suddenly, were like the response of some satanic litany.

"We had carried Kurtz into the pilot-house: there was more air there. Lying on the couch, he stared through the open shutter. There was an eddy in the mass of human bodies, and the woman with helmeted head and tawny cheeks rushed out to the very brink of the stream. She put out her hands, shouted something, and all that wild mob took up the shout in a roaring chorus of articulated, rapid, breathless utterance.

"'Do you understand this?' I asked.

"He kept on looking out past me with fiery, longing eyes, with a mingled 145
expression of wistfulness and hate. He made no answer, but I saw a smile, a smile of indefinable meaning, appear on his colorless lips that a moment after twitched convulsively. 'Do I not?' he said slowly, gasping, as if the words had been torn out of him by a supernatural power.

"I pulled the string of the whistle, and I did this because I saw the pilgrims on deck getting out their rifles with an air of anticipating a jolly lark. At the sudden screech there was a movement of abject terror through that wedged mass of bodies. 'Don't! don't! you frighten them away,' cried someone on deck disconsolately. I pulled the string time after time. They broke and ran, they leaped, they crouched, they swerved, they dodged the flying terror of the sound. The three red chaps had fallen flat, face down on the shore, as though they had been shot dead. Only the barbarous and superb woman did not so much as flinch, and stretched tragically her bare arms after us over the somber and glittering river.

"And then that imbecile crowd down on the deck started their little fun, and I could see nothing more for smoke.

"The brown current ran swiftly out of the heart of darkness, bearing us down towards the sea with twice the speed of our upward progress; and Kurtz's life was running swiftly too, ebbing, ebbing out of his heart into the sea of inexorable time. The manager was very placid, he had no vital anxieties now, he took us both in with a comprehensive and satisfied glance: the 'affair' had come off as well as could be wished. I saw the time approaching when I would be left alone of the party of 'unsound method.' The pilgrims looked upon me with disfavor. I was, so to speak, numbered with the dead. It is strange how I accepted this unforeseen partnership, this choice of nightmares forced upon me in the tenebrous land invaded by these mean and greedy phantoms.

"Kurtz discoursed. A voice! a voice! It rang deep to the very last. It survived his strength to hide in the magnificent folds of eloquence the barren darkness of his heart. Oh, he struggled! he struggled! The wastes of his weary brain were haunted by shadowy images now—images of wealth and fame revolving obsequiously round his unextinguishable gift of noble and lofty expression. My Intended, my station, my career, my ideas—these were the subjects for the occasional utterances of elevated sentiments. The shade of the original Kurtz frequented the bedside of the hollow sham, whose fate it was to be buried presently in the mold of primeval earth. But both the diabolic love and the unearthly hate of the mysteries it had penetrated fought for the possession of that soul satiated with primitive emotions, avid of lying fame, of sham distinction, of all the appearances of success and power.

"Sometimes he was contemptibly childish. He desired to have kings meet 150
him at railway-stations on his return from some ghastly Nowhere, where he intended to accomplish great things. 'You show them you have in you something that is really profitable, and then there will be no limits to the recognition of your ability,' he would say. 'Of course you must take care of the motives—right motives—always.' The long reaches that were like one and the same reach, monotonous bends that were exactly alike, slipped past the steamer with their multitude of secular trees looking patiently after this grimy fragment of another world, the forerunner of change, of conquest, of trade, of massacres, of blessings. I looked ahead—piloting. 'Close the shutter,' said Kurtz suddenly one day; 'I can't bear to look at this.' I did so. There was a silence. 'Oh, but I will wring your heart yet!' he cried at the invisible wilderness.

"We broke down—as I had expected—and had to lie up for repairs at the head of an island. This delay was the first thing that shook Kurtz's confidence. One morning he gave me a packet of papers and a photograph,—the lot tied together with a shoestring. 'Keep this for me,' he said. 'This noxious fool' (meaning the manager) 'is capable of prying into my boxes when I am not looking.' In the afternoon I saw him. He was lying on his back with closed eyes, and I withdrew quietly, but I heard him mutter, 'Live rightly, die, die . . .' I listened. There was nothing more. Was he rehearsing some speech in his sleep, or was it a fragment of a phrase from some newspaper article? He had been writing for the papers and meant to do so again, 'for the furthering of my ideas. It's a duty.'

"His was an impenetrable darkness. I looked at him as you peer down at a man who is lying at the bottom of a precipice where the sun never shines. But I had not much time to give him, because I was helping the engine-driver to take to pieces the leaky cylinders, to straighten a bent connecting-rod, and in other such matters. I lived in an infernal mess of rust, filings, nuts, bolts, spanners, hammers, ratchet-drills—things I abominate, because I don't get on with them. I tended the little forge we fortunately had aboard; I toiled wearily in a wretched scrap-heap—unless I had the shakes too bad to stand.

"One evening coming in with a candle I was startled to hear him say a little tremulously, 'I am lying here in the dark waiting for death.' The light was within a foot of his eyes. I forced myself to murmur. 'Oh, nonsense!' and stood over him as if transfixed.

"Anything approaching the change that came over his features I have never seen before, and hope never to see again. Oh, I wasn't touched. I was fascinated. It was as though a veil had been rent. I saw on that ivory face the expression of somber pride, of ruthless power, of craven terror—of an intense and hopeless despair. Did he live his life again in every detail of desire, temptation, and surrender during that supreme moment of complete knowledge? He cried in a whisper at some image, at some vision,—he cried out twice, a cry that was no more than a breath—

"'The horror! The horror!' 155

"I blew the candle out and left the cabin. The pilgrims were dining in the mess-room, and I took my place opposite the manager, who lifted his eyes to give me a questioning glance, which I successfully ignored. He leaned back, serene, with that peculiar smile of his sealing the unexpressed depths of his meanness. A continuous shower of small flies streamed upon the lamp, upon the cloth, upon our hands and faces. Suddenly the manager's boy put his insolent black head in the doorway, and said in a tone of scathing contempt—

"'Mistah Kurtz—he dead.'

"All the pilgrims rushed out to see. I remained, and went on with my dinner. I believe I was considered brutally callous. However, I did not eat much. There was a lamp in there—light, don't you know—and outside it was so beastly, beastly dark. I went no more near the remarkable man who had pronounced a judgment upon the adventures of his soul on this earth. The voice was gone. What else had been there? But I am of course aware that next day the pilgrims buried something in a muddy hole.

"And then they very nearly buried me.

"However, as you see, I did not go to join Kurtz there and then. I did not. 160
I remained to dream the nightmare out to the end, and to show my loyalty to Kurtz once more. Destiny. My destiny! Droll thing life is—that mysterious arrangement of merciless logic for a futile purpose. The most you can hope from it is some knowledge of yourself—that comes too late—a crop of unextinguishable regrets. I have wrestled with death. It is the most unexciting contest you can imagine. It takes place in an impalpable grayness, with nothing underfoot, with nothing around, without spectators, without clamor, without glory, without the great desire of victory, without the great fear of defeat, in a sickly atmosphere of tepid skepticism, without much belief in your own right, and still less in that of your adversary. If such is the form of ultimate wisdom, then life is a greater riddle than some of us think it to be. I was within a hair's-breadth of the last opportunity for pronouncement, and I found with humili-

ation that probably I would have nothing to say. This is the reason why I affirm that Kurtz was a remarkable man. He had something to say. He said it. Since I had peeped over the edge myself, I understand better the meaning of his stare, that could not see the flame of the candle, but was wide enough to embrace the whole universe, piercing enough to penetrate all the hearts that beat in the darkness. He had summed up—he had judged. 'The horror!' He was a remarkable man. After all, this was the expression of some sort of belief; it had candor, it had conviction, it had a vibrating note of revolt in its whisper, it had the appalling face of a glimpsed truth—the strange commingling of desire and hate. And it is not my own extremity I remember best—a vision of grayness without form filled with physical pain, and a careless contempt for the evanescence of all things—even of this pain itself. No! It is his extremity that I seem to have lived through. True, he had made that last stride, he had stepped over the edge, while I had been permitted to draw back my hesitating foot. And perhaps in this is the whole difference; perhaps all the wisdom, and all truth, and all sincerity, are just compressed into the inappreciable moment of time in which we step over the threshold of the invisible. Perhaps! I like to think my summing-up would not have been a world of careless contempt. Better his cry—much better. It was an affirmation, a moral victory paid for by innumerable defeats, by abominable terrors, by abominable satisfactions. But it was a victory! That is why I have remained loyal to Kurtz to the last, and even beyond, when a long time after I heard once more, not his own voice, but the echo of his magnificent eloquence thrown to me from a soul as translucently pure as a cliff of crystal.

"No, they did not bury me, though there is a period of time which I remember mistily, with a shuddering wonder, like a passage through some inconceivable world that had no hope in it and no desire. I found myself back in the sepulchral city resenting the sight of people hurrying through the streets to filch a little money from each other, to devour their infamous cookery, to gulp their unwholesome beer, to dream their insignificant and silly dreams. They trespassed upon my thoughts. They were intruders whose knowledge of life was to me an irritating pretense, because I felt so sure they could not possibly know the things I knew. Their bearing, which was simply the bearing of commonplace individuals going about their business in the assurance of perfect safety, was offensive to me like the outrageous flauntings of folly in the face of a danger it is unable to comprehend. I had no particular desire to enlighten them, but I had some difficulty in restraining myself from laughing in their faces, so full of stupid importance. I dare say I was not very well at that time. I tottered about the streets—there were various affairs to settle—grinning bitterly at perfectly respectable persons. I admit my behavior was inexcusable, but then my temperature was seldom normal in these days. My dear aunt's endeavors to 'nurse up my strength' seemed altogether beside the mark. It was not my strength that wanted nursing, it was my imagination that wanted soothing. I kept the bundle of papers given me by Kurtz, not knowing exactly what to do with it. His mother had died lately, watched over, as I was told, by his Intended. A clean-shaved man, with an official manner and wearing gold-rimmed spectacles, called on me one day and made inquiries, at first circuitous, afterwards suavely pressing, about what he was pleased to denominate certain 'documents.' I was not surprised, because I had had two rows with the manager on the subject out there. I had refused to give up the smallest scrap out of that package, and I took the same attitude with the spectacled man. He became darkly menacing at last, and with much heat argued that the Company had the right to every bit of information about its 'territories.' And, said he, 'Mr. Kurtz's knowledge of unexplored regions must have been necessarily extensive and peculiar—owing to his great abilities and to the deplorable circumstances in which he had been placed: therefore'—I assured him Mr. Kurtz's knowledge, however extensive, did not bear upon the problems of commerce or administration. He invoked then the name of science. 'It would be an incalculable loss if,' &c., &c. I offered him the report on the 'Suppression of Savage Customs,' with the postscriptum torn off. He took it up eagerly, but ended by sniffing at it with an air of contempt. 'This is not what we had a right to expect,' he remarked. 'Expect nothing else,' I said. 'There are only private letters.' He withdrew upon some threat of legal proceedings, and I saw him no more; but another fellow, calling himself Kurtz's cousin, appeared two days later, and was anxious to hear all the details about his dear relative's last moments. Incidentally he gave me to understand that Kurtz had been essentially a great musician. 'There was the making of an immense success,' said the man, who was an organist, I believe, with lank gray hair flowing over a greasy coat-collar. I had no reason to doubt his statement; and to this day I am unable to say what was Kurtz's profession, whether he ever had any—which was the greatest of his talents. I had taken him for a painter who wrote for the papers, or else for a journalist who could print—but even the cousin (who took snuff during the interview) could not tell me what he had been—exactly. He was a universal genius—on that point I agreed with the old chap, who thereupon blew his nose noisily into a large cotton handkerchief and withdrew in senile agitation, bearing off some family letters and memoranda without importance. Ultimately a journalist anxious to know something of the fate of his 'dear colleague' turned up. This visitor informed me Kurtz's proper sphere ought to have been politics 'on the popular side.' He had furry straight eyebrows, bristly hair cropped short, an eye-glass on a broad ribbon, and, becoming expansive, confessed his opinion that Kurtz really couldn't write a bit—'but heavens! how that man could talk! He electrified large meetings. He had faith—don't you see?—he had the faith. He could get himself to believe anything—anything. He would have been a splendid leader of an extreme party.' 'What party?' I asked. 'Any party,' answered the other. 'He was an—an—extremist.' Did I not think so? I assented. Did I know, he asked, with a sudden flash of curiosity, 'what it was that had induced him to go out there?' 'Yes,' said I, and forthwith handed him the famous Report for publication, if he thought fit. He glanced through it hurriedly, mumbling all the time, judged 'it would do,' and took himself off with this plunder.

"Thus I was left at last with a slim packet of letters and the girl's portrait. She struck me as beautiful—I mean she had a beautiful expression. I know that the sunlight can be made to lie too, yet one felt that no manipulation of light and pose could have conveyed the delicate shade of truthfulness upon those features. She seemed ready to listen without mental reservation, without suspicion, without a thought for herself. I concluded I would go and give her back her portrait and those letters myself. Curiosity? Yes; and also some other feeling perhaps. All that had been Kurtz's had passed out of my hands: his soul, his body, his station, his plans, his ivory, his career. There remained only his memory and his Intended—and I wanted to give that up too to the past, in a way,—to surrender personally all that remained of him with me to that oblivion which is the last word of our common fate. I don't defend myself. I had no clear perception of what it was I really wanted. Perhaps it was an impulse of unconscious loyalty, or the fulfillment of one of these ironic necessities that lurk in the facts of human existence. I don't know. I can't tell. But I went.

"I thought his memory was like the other memories of the dead that accumulate in every man's life—a vague impress on the brain of shadows that had fallen on it in their swift and final passage; but before the high and ponderous door, between the tall houses of a street as still and decorous as a well-kept alley in a cemetery, I had a vision of him on the stretcher, opening his mouth voraciously, as if to devour all the earth with all its mankind. He lived then before me; he lived as much as he had ever lived—a shadow insatiable of splendid appearances, of frightful realities; a shadow darker than the shadow of the night, and draped nobly in the folds of a gorgeous eloquence. The vision seemed to enter the house with me—the stretcher, the phantom-bearers, the wild crowd of obedient worshipers, the gloom of the forests, the glitter of the reach between the murky bends, the beat of the drum, regular and muffled like the beating of a heart—the heart of a conquering darkness. It was a moment of triumph for the wilderness, an invading and vengeful rush which, it seemed to me, I would have to keep back alone for the salvation of another soul. And the memory of what I had heard him say afar there, with the horned shapes stirring at my back, in the glow of fires, within the patient woods, those broken phrases came back to me, were heard again in their ominous and terrifying simplicity. I remembered his abject pleading, his abject threats, the colossal scale of his vile desires, the meanness, the torment, the tempestuous anguish of his soul. And later on I seemed to see his collected languid manner, when he said one day, 'This lot of ivory now is really mine. The Company did not pay for it. I collected it myself at a very great personal risk. I am afraid they will try to claim it as theirs though. H'm. It is a difficult case. What do you think I ought to do—resist? Eh? I want no more than justice.' . . . He wanted no more than justice—no more than justice. I rang the bell before a mahogany door on the first floor, and while I waited he seemed to stare at me out of the glassy panel—stare with that wide and immense stare embracing, condemning, loathing all the universe. I seemed to hear the whispered cry, 'The horror! The horror!'

"The dusk was falling. I had to wait in a lofty drawing-room with three long windows from floor to ceiling that were like three luminous and bedraped columns. The bent gilt legs and backs of the furniture shone in indistinct curves. The tall marble fireplace had a cold and monumental whiteness. A grand piano stood massively in a corner, with dark gleams on the flat surfaces like a somber and polished sarcophagus. A high door opened—closed. I rose.

"She came forward, all in black, with a pale head, floating towards me in 165
the dusk. She was in mourning. It was more than a year since his death, more than a year since the news came; she seemed as though she would remember and mourn for ever. She took both my hands in hers and murmured, 'I had heard you were coming.' I noticed she was not very young—I mean not girlish. She had a mature capacity for fidelity, for belief, for suffering. The room seemed to have grown darker, as if all the sad light of the cloudy evening had taken refuge on her forehead. This fair hair, this pale visage, this pure brow, seemed surrounded by an ashy halo from which the dark eyes looked out at me. Their glance was guileless, profound, confident, and trustful. She carried her sorrowful head as though she were proud of that sorrow, as though she would say, I—I alone know how to mourn for him as he deserves. But while we were shaking hands, such a look of awful desolation came upon her face that I perceived she was one of those creatures that are not the playthings of Time. For her he had died only yesterday. And, by Jove! The impression was so powerful that for me too he seemed to have died only yesterday—nay, this very minute. I saw her and him in the same instant of time—his death and her sorrow—I saw her sorrow in the very moment of his death. Do you understand? I saw them together—I heard them together. She had said, with a deep catch of the breath, 'I have survived;' while my strained ears seemed to hear distinctly, mingled with her tone of despairing regret, the summing-up whisper of his eternal condemnation. I asked myself what I was doing there, with a sensation of panic in my heart as though I had blundered into a place of cruel and absurd mysteries not fit for a human being to behold. She motioned me to a chair. We sat down, I laid the packet gently on the little table, and she put her hand over it . . . 'You knew him well,' she murmured, after a moment of mourning silence.

"'Intimacy grows quick out there,' I said. 'I knew him as well as it is possible for one man to know another.'

"'And you admired him,' she said. 'It was impossible to know him and not to admire him. Was it?'

"'He was a remarkable man,' I said, unsteadily. Then before the appealing fixity of her gaze, that seemed to watch for more words on my lips, I went on, 'It was impossible not to—'

"'Love him,' she finished eagerly, silencing me into an appalled dumbness. 'How true! how true! But when you think that no one knew him so well as I! I had all his noble confidence. I knew him best.'

"'You knew him best,' I repeated. And perhaps she did. But with every 170
word spoken the room was growing darker, and only her forehead, smooth and white, remained illumined by the unextinguishable light of belief and love.

"'You were his friend,' she went on. 'His friend,' she repeated, a little louder. 'You must have been, if he had given you this, and sent you to me. I feel I can speak to you—and oh! I must speak. I want you—you who have heard his last words—to know I have been worthy of him. . . . It is not pride. . . . Yes! I am proud to know I understood him better than anyone on earth—he told me so himself. And since his mother died I have had no one—no one—to—to—'

"I listened. The darkness deepened. I was not even sure whether he had given me the right bundle. I rather suspect he wanted me to take care of another batch of his papers which, after his death, I saw the manager examining under the lamp. And the girl talked, easing her pain in the certitude of my sympathy; she talked as thirsty men drink. I had heard that her engagement with Kurtz had been disapproved by her people. He wasn't rich enough or something. And indeed I don't know whether he had not been a pauper all his life. He had given me some reason to infer that it was his impatience of comparative poverty that drove him out there.

"'. . . Who was not his friend who had heard him speak once?' she was saying. 'He drew men towards him by what was best in them.' She looked at me with intensity. 'It is the gift of the great,' she went on, and the sound of her low voice seemed to have the accompaniment of all the other sounds, full of mystery, desolation, and sorrow, I had ever heard—the ripple of the river, the soughing of the trees swayed by the wind, the murmurs of wild crows, the faint ring of incomprehensible words cried from afar, the whisper of a voice speaking from beyond the threshold of an eternal darkness. 'But you have heard him! You know!' she cried.

"'Yes, I know,' I said with something like despair in my heart, but bowing my head before the faith that was in her, before that great and saving illusion that shone with an unearthly glow in the darkness, in the triumphant darkness from which I could not have defended her—from which I could not even defend myself.

"'What a loss to me—to us!'—she corrected herself with beautiful gen- 175
erosity; then added in a murmur, 'To the world.' By the last gleams of twilight I could see the glitter of her eyes, full of tears—of tears that would not fall.

"'I have been very happy—very fortunate—very proud,' she went on. 'Too fortunate. Too happy for a little while. And now I am unhappy—for life.'

"She stood up; her fair hair seemed to catch all the remaining light in a glimmer of gold. I rose too.

"'And of all this,' she went on, mournfully, 'of all his promise, and of all his greatness, of his generous mind, of his noble heart, nothing remains—nothing but a memory. You and I—'

"'We shall always remember him,' I said, hastily.

"'No!' she cried. 'It is impossible that all this should be lost—that such a 180
life should be sacrificed to leave nothing—but sorrow. You know what vast plans he had. I knew of them too—I could not perhaps understand,—but others knew of them. Something must remain. His words, at least, have not died.'

"'His words will remain,' I said.

"'And his example,' she whispered to herself. 'Men looked up to him,—his goodness shone in every act. His example—'

"'True,' I said; 'his example too. Yes, his example. I forgot that.'

"'But I do not. I cannot—I cannot believe—not yet. I cannot believe that I shall never see him again, that nobody will see him again, never, never, never.'

"She put out her arms as if after a retreating figure, stretching them back 185 and with clasped pale hands across the fading and narrow sheen of the window. Never see him! I saw him clearly enough then. I shall see this eloquent phantom as long as I live, and I shall see her too, a tragic and familiar Shade, resembling in this gesture another one, tragic also, and bedecked with powerless charms, stretching bare brown arms over the glitter of the infernal stream, the stream of darkness. She said suddenly very low, 'He died as he lived.'

"'His end,' said I, with dull anger stirring in me, 'was in every way worthy of his life.'

"'And I was not with him,' she murmured. My anger subsided before a feeling of infinite pity.

"'Everything that could be done—' I mumbled.

"'Ah, but I believed in him more than anyone on earth—more than his own mother, more than—himself. He needed me! Me! I would have treasured every sigh, every word, every sign, every glance.'

"I felt like a chill grip on my chest. 'Don't,' I said, in a muffled voice. 190

"'Forgive me. I—I—have mourned so long in silence—in silence. . . . You were with him—to the last? I think of his loneliness. Nobody near to understand him as I would have understood. Perhaps no one to hear. . . .'

"'To the very end,' I said, shakily. 'I heard his very last words. . . .' I stopped in a fright.

"'Repeat them,' she murmured in a heart-broken tone. 'I want—I want—something—something—to—to live with.'

"I was on the point of crying at her, 'Don't you hear them?' The dusk was repeating them in a persistent whisper all around us, in a whisper that seemed to swell menacingly like the first whisper of a rising wind. 'The horror! The horror!'

"'His last word—to live with,' she insisted. 'Don't you understand I loved 195
him—I loved him—I loved him!'

"I pulled myself together and spoke slowly.

"'The last word he pronounced was—your name.'

"I heard a light sigh, and then my heart stood still, stopped dead short by an exulting and terrible cry, by the cry of inconceivable triumph and of unspeakable pain. 'I knew it—I was sure!' . . . She knew. She was sure. I heard her weeping; she had hidden her face in her hands. It seemed to me that the house would collapse before I could escape, that the heavens would fall upon my head. But nothing happened. The heavens do not fall for such a trifle. Would they have fallen, I wonder, if I had rendered Kurtz that justice which was his due? Hadn't he said he wanted only justice? But I couldn't. I could not tell her. It would have been too dark—too dark altogether. . . ."

Marlow ceased, and sat apart, indistinct and silent, in the pose of a meditating Buddha. Nobody moved for a time. "We have lost the first of the ebb," said the Director, suddenly. I raised my head. The offing was barred by a black bank of clouds, and the tranquil waterway leading to the uttermost ends of the earth flowed somber under an overcast sky—seemed to lead into the heart of an immense darkness.

Joseph Conrad

(1857–1924) Web www

Born in Poland, Conrad became a sailor on English ships and retired to become a writer, penning more than eighteen novels and novellas. Many of them involve the sea; many focus on characters who must make choices in ambiguous circumstances. Conrad's command of language is so masterful that it is difficult to believe that his writing is the work of someone for whom English is a third language.

TOPICS FOR CRITICAL THINKING Web www

1. Who is the story's narrator?
2. What does it mean that the tall, elegant African woman defies the boat whistle as they take Kurtz away?
3. Why is Marlow compared to a Buddha? How does this image relate to the story's other images?
4. What does Kurtz mean by "The horror, the horror"?
5. Why does Marlow lie to Kurtz's intended?

TOPICS FOR CRITICAL WRITING Web www

1. Select a recurrent image and trace it through the story. What various objects and ideas does this image describe? How does it link these various objects and ideas together?
2. In what ways is *Heart of Darkness* not like the "kernel" but like the haze outside?

Modernism

Modernism in literature refers to the gradual shift from the realist, almost empirically-based literature of the nineteenth century to a more subjective, impressionistic literature. Fueled by nineteenth-century critic Matthew Arnold's aesthetic "art-for-art's-sake" movement and avant-garde movements such as Symbolism, modernism focuses on representing impression and individual consciousness and questions both literary form and the reliability of language. The evolution of this shift is traced in the paintings included on the first page of color inserts. Web Modernist fiction represents the subjective perception of temporality, the vagaries of human consciousness ("stream of consciousness"), the loss of shared cultural values, and the sensitivity of the artist in a culture increasingly dulled by technology and mass media. In other words, modernist fiction often describes the ways individuals (often sensitive or artistic people) perceive their world and see that others perceive it completely differently. www

As contemporary fiction writer John Barth describes in it "The Literature of Replenishment," modernism is characterized by

> [t]he radical disruption of linear flow of narrative; the frustration of conventional expectations concerning unity and coherence of plot and character and the cause

> and effect development thereof; the deployment of ironic and ambiguous juxtapositions to call into question the moral and philosophical meaning of literary action; the adoption of a tone of epistemological self-mockery aimed at naive pretensions of bourgeois rationality; the opposition of inward consciousness to rational, public, objective discourse; and an inclination to subjective distortion to point up the evanescence of the social world of the nineteenth-century bourgeoisie.

Many early-twentieth-century writers from both the United Kingdom and the United States wrote in a modernist style, though the writings of authors such as E. M. Forster, Katherine Mansfield, D. H. Lawrence, James Joyce, Virginia Woolf, Ernest Hemingway, Gertrude Stein, F. Scott Fitzgerald, and William Faulkner differ greatly. All of these modernist writers depend on the power of the image as a way to convey complex ideas. All focus on the subjective experience of the characters as they encounter the ambiguities of modern existence. Many are ironic in their observation of character. E. M. Forster's "The Road from Colonus" describes an old man's epiphany while on a trip to Greece and how he subsequently forgets it. An **epiphany,** a term first used by James Joyce, describes a sudden transcendent insight, the sense that one sees the truth one has been seeking. Katherine Mansfield's "The Garden-Party" depicts a young girl's perception of class differences. D. H. Lawrence's "The Horse-Dealer's Daughter" portrays an accidental but inevitable falling in love. James Joyce's "Araby" from *Dubliners* tracks the ironies of a young man's first love. All employ images as the primary medium for presenting characters and focusing on characters' perceptions.

E. M. Forster

The Road from Colonus *(1903)*

I

For no very intelligible reason, Mr. Lucas had hurried ahead of his party. He was perhaps reaching the age at which independence becomes valuable, because it is so soon to be lost. Tired of attention and consideration, he liked breaking away from the younger members, to ride by himself, and to dismount unassisted. Perhaps he also relished that more subtle pleasure of being kept waiting for lunch, and of telling the others on their arrival that it was of no consequence.

So, with childish impatience, he battered the animal's sides with his heels, and made the muleteer bang it with a thick stick and prick it with a sharp one, and jolted down the hill sides through clumps of flowering shrubs and stretches of anemones and asphodel, till he heard the sound of running water, and came in sight of the group of plane trees where they were to have their meal.

Even in England those trees would have been remarkable, so huge were they, so interlaced, so magnificently clothed in quivering green. And here in Greece they were unique, the one cool spot in that hard brilliant landscape, already scorched by the heat of an April sun. In their midst was hidden a tiny

Khan or country inn, a frail mud building with a broad wooden balcony in which sat an old woman spinning, while a small brown pig, eating orange peel, stood beside her. On the wet earth below squatted two children, playing some primeval game with their fingers; and their mother, none too clean either, was messing with some rice inside. As Mrs. Forman would have said, it was all very Greek, and the fastidious Mr. Lucas felt thankful that they were bringing their own food with them, and should eat it in the open air.

Still, he was glad to be there—the muleteer had helped him off—and glad that Mrs. Forman was not there to forestall his opinions—glad even that he should not see Ethel for quite half an hour. Ethel was his youngest daughter, still unmarried. She was unselfish and affectionate, and it was generally understood that she was to devote her life to her father, and be the comfort of his old age. Mrs. Forman always referred to her as Antigone, and Mr. Lucas tried to settle down to the role of Oedipus, which seemed the only one that public opinion allowed him.

5 He had this in common with Oedipus, that he was growing old. Even to himself it had become obvious. He had lost interest in other people's affairs, and seldom attended when they spoke to him. He was fond of talking himself but often forgot what he was going to say, and even when he succeeded, it seldom seemed worth the effort. His phrases and gestures had become stiff and set, his anecdotes, once so successful, fell flat, his silence was as meaningless as his speech. Yet he had led a healthy, active life, had worked steadily, made money, educated his children. There was nothing and no one to blame: he was simply growing old.

At the present moment, here he was in Greece, and one of the dreams of his life was realized. Forty years ago he had caught the fever of Hellenism, and all his life he had felt that could he but visit that land, he would not have lived in vain. But Athens had been dusty, Delphi wet, Thermopylae flat, and he had listened with amazement and cynicism to the rapturous exclamations of his companions. Greece was like England: it was a man who was growing old, and it made no difference whether that man looked at the Thames or the Eurotas. It was his last hope of contradicting that logic of experience, and it was failing.

Yet Greece had done something for him, though he did not know it. It had made him discontented, and there are stirrings of life in discontent. He knew that he was not the victim of continual ill-luck. Something great was wrong, and he was pitted against no mediocre or accidental enemy. For the last month a strange desire had possessed him to die fighting.

"Greece is the land for young people," he said to himself as he stood under the plane trees, "but I will enter into it, I will possess it. Leaves shall be green again, water shall be sweet, the sky shall be blue. They were so forty years ago, and I will win them back. I do mind being old, and I will pretend no longer."

He took two steps forward, and immediately cold waters were gurgling over his ankle.

10 "Where does the water come from?" he asked himself. "I do not even know that." He remembered that all the hill sides were dry; yet here the road was suddenly covered with flowing streams.

He stopped still in amazement, saying: "Water out of a tree—out of a hollow tree? I never saw nor thought of that before."

For the enormous plane that leant towards the Khan was hollow—it had been burnt out for charcoal—and from its living trunk there gushed an impetuous spring, coating the bark with fern and moss, and flowing over the mule track to create fertile meadows beyond. The simple country folk had paid to beauty and mystery such tribute as they could, for in the rind of the tree a shrine was cut, holding a lamp and a little picture of the Virgin, inheritor of the Naiad's and Dryad's joint abode.

"I never saw anything so marvellous before," said Mr. Lucas. "I could even step inside the trunk and see where the water comes from."

For a moment he hesitated to violate the shrine. Then he remembered with a smile his own thought—"the place shall be mine; I will enter it and possess it"—and leapt almost aggressively on to a stone within.

The water pressed up steadily and noiselessly from the hollow roots and 15
hidden crevices of the plane, forming a wonderful amber pool ere it spilt over the lip of bark on to the earth outside. Mr. Lucas tasted it and it was sweet, and when he looked up the black funnel of the trunk he saw sky which was blue, and some leaves which were green; and he remembered, without smiling, another of his thoughts.

Others had been before him—indeed he had a curious sense of companionship. Little votive offerings to the presiding Power were fastened on to the bark—tiny arms and legs and eyes in tin, grotesque models of the brain or the heart—all tokens of some recovery of strength or wisdom or love. There was no such thing as the solitude of nature, for the sorrows and joys of humanity had pressed even into the bosom of a tree. He spread out his arms and steadied himself against the soft charred wood, and then slowly leant back, till his body was resting on the trunk behind. His eyes closed, and he had the strange feeling of one who is moving, yet at peace—the feeling of the swimmer, who, after long struggling with chopping seas, finds that after all the tide will sweep him to his goal.

So he lay motionless, conscious only of the stream below his feet, and that all things were a stream, in which he was moving.

He was aroused at last by a shock—the shock of an arrival perhaps, for when he opened his eyes, something unimagined, indefinable, had passed over all things, and made them intelligible and good.

There was meaning in the stoop of the old woman over her work, and in the quick motions of the little pig, and in her diminishing globe of wool. A young man came singing over the streams on a mule, and there was beauty in his pose and sincerity in his greeting. The sun made no accidental patterns upon the spreading roots of the trees, and there was intention in the nodding clumps of asphodel, and in the music of the water. To Mr. Lucas, who, in a brief space of time, had discovered not only Greece, but England and all the world and life, there seemed nothing ludicrous in the desire to hang within the tree another votive offering—a little model of an entire man.

"Why, here's papa, playing at being Merlin." 20

All unnoticed they had arrived—Ethel, Mrs. Forman, Mr. Graham, and the English-speaking dragoman. Mr. Lucas peered out at them suspiciously. They had suddenly become unfamiliar, and all that they did seemed strained and coarse.

"Allow me to give you a hand," said Mr. Graham, a young man who was always polite to his elders.

Mr. Lucas felt annoyed. "Thank you, I can manage perfectly well by myself," he replied. His foot slipped as he stepped out of the tree, and went into the spring.

"Oh papa, my papa!" said Ethel, "what are you doing? Thank goodness I have got a change for you on the mule."

She tended him carefully, giving him clean socks and dry boots, and then sat him down on the rug beside the lunch basket, while she went with the others to explore the grove.

They came back in ecstasies, in which Mr. Lucas tried to join. But he found them intolerable. Their enthusiasm was superficial, commonplace, and spasmodic. They had no perception of the coherent beauty that was flowering around them. He tried at least to explain his feelings, and what he said was:

"I am altogether pleased with the appearance of this place. It impresses me very favourably. The trees are fine, remarkably fine for Greece, and there is something very poetic in the spring of clear running water. The people too seem kindly and civil. It is decidedly an attractive place."

Mrs. Forman upbraided him for his tepid praise.

"Oh, it is a place in a thousand!" she cried. "I could live and die here! I really would stop if I had not to be back at Athens! It reminds me of the Colonus of Sophocles."

"Well, *I* must stop," said Ethel. "I positively must."

"Yes, do! You and your father! Antigone and Oedipus. Of course you must stop at Colonus!"

Mr. Lucas was almost breathless with excitement. When he stood within the tree, he had believed that his happiness would be independent of locality. But these few minutes' conversation had undeceived him. He no longer trusted himself to journey through the world, for old thoughts, old wearinesses might be waiting to rejoin him as soon as he left the shade of the planes, and the music of the virgin water. To sleep in the Khan with the gracious, kind-eyed country people, to watch the bats flit about within the globe of shade, and see the moon turn the golden patterns into silver—one such night would place him beyond relapse, and confirm him for ever in the kingdom he had regained. But all his lips could say was: "I should be willing to put in a night here."

"You mean a week, papa! It would be sacrilege to put in less."

"A week then, a week," said his lips, irritated at being corrected, while his heart was leaping with joy. All through lunch he spoke to them no more, but watched the place he should know so well, and the people who would so soon be his companions and friends. The inmates of the Khan only consisted of an old woman, a middle-aged woman, a young man and two children, and to none of them had he spoken, yet he loved them as he loved everything that moved or breathed or existed beneath the benedictory shade of the planes.

"*En route!*" said the shrill voice of Mrs. Forman. "Ethel! Mr. Graham! The best of things must end."

"To-night," thought Mr. Lucas, "they will light the little lamp by the shrine. And when we all sit together on the balcony, perhaps they will tell me which offerings they put up."

"I beg your pardon, Mr. Lucas," said Graham, "but they want to fold up the rug you are sitting on."

Mr. Lucas got up, saying to himself: "Ethel shall go to bed first, and then I will try to tell them about my offering too—for it is a thing I must do. I think they will understand if I am left with them alone."

Ethel touched him on the cheek. "Papa! I've called you three times. All the mules are here."

"Mules? What mules?"

"Our mules. We're all waiting. Oh, Mr. Graham, do help my father on."

"I don't know what you're talking about, Ethel."

"My dearest papa, we must start. You know we have to get to Olympia to-night."

Mr. Lucas in pompous, confident tones replied: "I always did wish, Ethel, that you had a better head for plans. You know perfectly well that we are putting in a week here. It is your own suggestion."

Ethel was startled into impoliteness. "What a perfectly ridiculous idea. You must have known I was joking. Of course I meant I wished we could."

"Ah! if we could only do what we wished!" sighed Mrs. Forman, already seated on her mule.

"Surely," Ethel continued in calmer tones, "you didn't think I meant it."

"Most certainly I did. I have made all my plans on the supposition that we are stopping here, and it will be extremely inconvenient, indeed, impossible for me to start."

He delivered this remark with an air of great conviction, and Mrs. Forman and Mr. Graham had to turn away to hide their smiles.

"I am sorry I spoke so carelessly; it was wrong of me. But, you know, we can't break up our party, and even one night here would make us miss the boat at Patras."

Mrs. Forman, in an aside, called Mr. Graham's attention to the excellent way in which Ethel managed her father.

"I don't mind about the Patras boat. You said that we should stop here, and we are stopping."

It seemed as if the inhabitants of the Khan had divined in some mysterious way that the altercation touched them. The old woman stopped her spinning, while the young man and the two children stood behind Mr. Lucas, as if supporting him.

Neither arguments nor entreaties moved him. He said little, but he was absolutely determined, because for the first time he saw his daily life aright. What need had he to return to England? Who would miss him? His friends were dead or cold. Ethel loved him in a way, but, as was right, she had other interests. His other children he seldom saw. He had only one other relative, his sister Julia, whom he both feared and hated. It was no effort to struggle. He would be a fool as well as a coward if he stirred from the place which brought him happiness and peace.

At last Ethel, to humour him, and not disinclined to air her modern

Greek, went into the Khan with the astonished dragoman to look at the rooms. The woman inside received them with loud welcomes, and the young man, when no one was looking, began to lead Mr. Lucas' mule to the stable.

"Drop it, you brigand!" shouted Graham, who always declared that foreigners could understand English if they chose. He was right, for the man obeyed, and they all stood waiting for Ethel's return.

She emerged at last, with close-gathered skirts, followed by the dragoman bearing the little pig, which he had bought at a bargain.

"My dear papa, I will do all I can for you, but stop in that Khan—no."

"Are there—fleas?" asked Mrs. Forman.

Ethel intimated that "fleas" was not the word.

"Well, I am afraid that settles it," said Mrs. Forman, "I know how particular Mr. Lucas is."

"It does not settle it," said Mr. Lucas. "Ethel, you go on. I do not want you. I don't know why I ever consulted you. I shall stop here alone."

"That is absolute nonsense," said Ethel, losing her temper. "How can you be left alone at your age? How would you get your meals or your bath? All your letters are waiting for you at Patras. You'll miss the boat. That means missing the London operas, and upsetting all your engagements for the month. And as if you could travel by yourself!"

"They might knife you," was Mr. Graham's contribution.

The Greeks said nothing; but whenever Mr. Lucas looked their way, they beckoned him towards the Khan. The children would even have drawn him by the coat, and the old woman on the balcony stopped her almost completed spinning, and fixed him with mysterious appealing eyes. As he fought, the issue assumed gigantic proportions, and he believed that he was not merely stopping because he had regained youth or seen beauty or found happiness, but because in that place and with those people a supreme event was awaiting him which would transfigure the face of the world. The moment was so tremendous that he abandoned words and arguments as useless, and rested on the strength of his mighty unrevealed allies: silent men, murmuring water, and whispering trees. For the whole place called with one voice, articulate to him, and his garrulous opponents became every minute more meaningless and absurd. Soon they would be tired and go chattering away into the sun, leaving him to the cool grove and the moonlight and the destiny he foresaw.

Mrs. Forman and the dragoman had indeed already started, amid the piercing screams of the little pig, and the struggle might have gone on indefinitely if Ethel had not called in Mr. Graham.

"Can you help me?" she whispered. "He is absolutely unmanageable."

"I'm no good at arguing—but if I could help you in any other way——" and he looked down complacently at his well-made figure.

Ethel hesitated. Then she said: "Help me in any way you can. After all, it is for his good that we do it."

"Then have his mule led up behind him."

So when Mr. Lucas thought he had gained the day, he suddenly felt himself lifted off the ground, and sat sideways on the saddle, and at the same time the mule started off at a trot. He said nothing, for he had nothing to say, and even his face showed little emotion as he felt the shade pass and heard the sound of the water cease. Mr. Graham was running at his side, hat in hand, apologizing.

"I know I had no business to do it, and I do beg your pardon awfully. But I do hope that some day you too will feel that I was—damn!"

A stone had caught him in the middle of the back. It was thrown by the little boy, who was pursuing them along the mule track. He was followed by his sister, also throwing stones.

Ethel screamed to the dragoman, who was some way ahead with Mrs. Forman, but before he could rejoin them, another adversary appeared. It was the young Greek, who had cut them off in front, and now dashed down at Mr. Lucas' bridle. Fortunately Graham was an expert boxer, and it did not take him a moment to beat down the youth's feeble defence, and to send him sprawling with a bleeding mouth into the asphodel. By this time the dragoman had arrived, the children, alarmed at the fate of their brother, had desisted, and the rescue party, if such it is to be considered, retired in disorder to the trees.

"Little devils!" said Graham, laughing with triumph. "That's the modern Greek all over. Your father meant money if he stopped, and they consider we were taking it out of their pocket."

"Oh, they are terrible—simple savages! I don't know how I shall ever thank you. You've saved my father."

"I only hope you didn't think me brutal."

"No," replied Ethel with a little sigh. "I admire strength."

Meanwhile the cavalcade reformed, and Mr. Lucas, who, as Mrs. Forman said, bore his disappointment wonderfully well, was put comfortably on to his mule. They hurried up the opposite hillside, fearful of another attack, and it was not until they had left the eventful place far behind that Ethel found an opportunity to speak to her father and ask his pardon for the way she had treated him.

"You seemed so different, dear father, and you quite frightened me. Now I feel that you are your old self again."

He did not answer, and she concluded that he was not unnaturally offended at her behaviour.

By one of those curious tricks of mountain scenery, the place they had left an hour before suddenly reappeared far below them. The Khan was hidden under the green dome, but in the open there still stood three figures, and through the pure air rose up a faint cry of defiance or farewell.

Mr. Lucas stopped irresolutely, and let the reins fall from his hand.

"Come, father dear," said Ethel gently.

He obeyed, and in another moment a spur of the hill hid the dangerous scene for ever.

II

It was breakfast time, but the gas was alight, owing to the fog. Mr. Lucas was in the middle of an account of a bad night he had spent. Ethel, who was to be married in a few weeks, had her arms on the table, listening.

"First the door bell rang, then you came back from the theatre. Then the dog started, and after the dog the cat. And at three in the morning a young hooligan passed by singing. Oh yes: then there was the water gurgling in the pipe above my head."

"I think that was only the bath water running away," said Ethel, looking rather worn.

"Well, there's nothing I dislike more than running water. It's perfectly impossible to sleep in the house. I shall give it up. I shall give notice next quarter. I shall tell the landlord plainly, 'The reason I am giving up the house is this: it is perfectly impossible to sleep in it.' If he says—says—well, what has he got to say?"

"Some more toast, father?"

"Thank you, my dear." He took it, and there was an interval of peace.

But he soon recommenced. "I'm not going to submit to the practising next door as tamely as they think. I wrote and told them so—didn't I?"

"Yes," said Ethel, who had taken care that the letter should not reach. "I have seen the governess, and she has promised to arrange it differently. And Aunt Julia hates noise. It will sure to be all right."

Her aunt, being the only unattached member of the family, was coming to keep house for her father when she left him. The reference was not a happy one, and Mr. Lucas commenced a series of half articulate sighs, which was only stopped by the arrival of the post.

"Oh, what a parcel!" cried Ethel. "For me! What can it be! Greek stamps. This is most exciting!"

It proved to be some asphodel bulbs, sent by Mrs. Forman from Athens for planting in the conservatory.

"Doesn't it bring it all back! You remember the asphodels, father. And all wrapped up in Greek newspapers. I wonder if I can read them still. I used to be able to, you know."

She rattled on, hoping to conceal the laughter of the children next door—a favourite source of querulousness at breakfast time.

"Listen to me! 'A rural disaster.' Oh, I've hit on something sad. But never mind. 'Last Tuesday at Plataniste, in the province of Messenia, a shocking tragedy occurred. A large tree'—aren't I getting on well?—'blew down in the night and'—wait a minute—oh, dear! 'crushed to death the five occupants of the little Khan there, who had apparently been sitting in the balcony. The bodies of Maria Rhomaides, the aged proprietress, and of her daughter, aged forty-six, were easily recognizable, whereas that of her grandson'—oh, the rest is really too horrid; I wish I had never tried it, and what's more I feel to have heard the name Plataniste before. We didn't stop there, did we, in the spring?"

"We had lunch," said Mr. Lucas, with a faint expression of trouble on his vacant face. "Perhaps it was where the dragoman bought the pig."

"Of course," said Ethel in a nervous voice. "Where the dragoman bought the little pig. How terrible!"

"Very terrible!" said her father, whose attention was wandering to the noisy children next door. Ethel suddenly started to her feet with genuine interest.

"Good gracious!" she exclaimed. "This is an old paper. It happened not lately but in April—the night of Tuesday the eighteenth—and we—we must have been there in the afternoon."

"So we were," said Mr. Lucas. She put her hand to her heart, scarcely able to speak.

"Father, dear father, I must say it: you wanted to stop there. All those 105
people, those poor half-savage people, tried to keep you, and they're dead. The whole place, it says, is in ruins, and even the stream has changed its course. Father, dear, if it had not been for me, and if Arthur had not helped me, you must have been killed."

Mr. Lucas waved his hand irritably. "It is not a bit of good speaking to the governess, I shall write to the landlord and say, 'The reason I am giving up the house is this: the dog barks, the children next door are intolerable, and I cannot stand the noise of running water.'"

Ethel did not check his babbling. She was aghast at the narrowness of the escape, and for a long time kept silence. At last she said: "Such a marvellous deliverance does make one believe in Providence."

Mr. Lucas, who was still composing his letter to the landlord, did not reply.

EDWARD MORGAN FORSTER

www *(1879–1970)* Web

www A part of the Bloomsbury Group Web, Forster wrote novels and stories that often focus on failures of communication among people of different classes and aspirations. His work often conveys the drabness of middle class existence, comparing it to the more spontaneous life in such Mediterranean countries as Italy and Greece. Five of his novels have been adapted to film.

www *TOPICS FOR CRITICAL THINKING* Web

1. In what ways is "The Road from Colonus" a retelling of the Oedipus myth? (See **myth criticism** and the discussion in Chapter 43.
2. How does Mr. Lucas change when he enters the plane tree? What insight does he gain?
3. Why does Mr. Lucas detest the sound of water at the story's end?
4. Is this story ironic? In what ways?

www *TOPICS FOR CRITICAL WRITING* Web

1. Select one recurrent image or motif and discuss how it functions through the story.
2. How does setting convey entirely different ways of seeing the world?

KATHERINE MANSFIELD

The Garden-Party

(1924)

And after all the weather was ideal. They could not have had a more perfect day for a garden-party if they had ordered it. Windless, warm, the sky without a cloud. Only the blue was veiled with a haze of light gold, as it is sometimes in early summer. The gardener had been up since dawn, mowing the lawns and sweeping them, until the grass and the dark flat rosettes where the daisy plants had been seemed to shine. As for the roses, you could not help feeling they understood that roses are the only flowers that impress people at garden-parties; the only flowers that everybody is certain of knowing. Hundreds, yes, literally hundreds, had come out in a single night; the green bushes bowed down as though they had been visited by archangels.

Breakfast was not yet over before the men came to put up the marquee.

"Where do you want the marquee put, mother?"

"My dear child, it's no use asking me. I'm determined to leave everything to you children this year. Forget I am your mother. Treat me as an honoured guest."

But Meg could not possibly go and supervise the men. She had washed her hair before breakfast, and she sat drinking her coffee in a green turban, with a dark wet curl stamped on each cheek. Jose, the butterfly, always came down in a silk petticoat and a kimono jacket. 5

"You'll have to go, Laura; you're the artistic one."

Away Laura flew, still holding her piece of bread-and butter. It's so delicious to have an excuse for eating out of doors, and besides, she loved having to arrange things; she always felt she could do it so much better than anybody else.

Four men in their shirt-sleeves stood grouped together on the garden path. They carried staves covered with rolls of canvas, and they had big tool-bags slung on their backs. They looked impressive. Laura wished now that she had not got the bread-and-butter, but there was nowhere to put it, and she couldn't possibly throw it away. She blushed and tried to look severe and even a little bit short-sighted as she came up to them.

"Good morning," she said, copying her mother's voice. But that sounded so fearfully affected that she was ashamed, and stammered like a little girl, "Oh—er—have you come—is it about the marquee?"

"That's right, miss," said the tallest of the men, a lanky, freckled fellow, and he shifted his tool-bag, knocked back his straw hat and smiled down at her. "That's about it." 10

His smile was so easy, so friendly that Laura recovered. What nice eyes he had, small, but such a dark blue! And now she looked at the others, they were smiling too. "Cheer-up, we won't bite," their smile seemed to say. How very nice workmen were! And what a beautiful morning! She mustn't mention the morning; she must be business like. The marquee.

"Well, what about the lily-lawn? Would that do?"

And she pointed to the lily-lawn with the hand that didn't hold the bread-and-butter. They turned, they stared in the direction. A little fat chap thrust out his under-lip, and the tall fellow frowned.

"I don't fancy it," said he. "Not conspicuous enough. You see, with a thing like a marquee," and he turned to Laura in his easy way, "you want to put it somewhere where it'll give you a bang slap in the eye, if you follow me."

Laura's upbringing made her wonder for a moment whether it was quite respectful of a workman to talk to her of bangs slap in the eye. But she did quite follow him.

"A corner of the tennis-court," she suggested. "But the band's going to be in one corner."

"H'm, going to have a band, are you?" said another of the workmen. He was pale. He had a haggard look as his dark eyes scanned the tennis-court. What was he thinking?

"Only a very small band," said Laura gently. Perhaps he wouldn't mind so much if the band was quite small. But the tall fellow interrupted.

"Look here, miss, that's the place. Against those trees. Over there. That'll do fine."

Against the karakas. Then the karaka trees would be hidden. And they were so lovely, with their broad, gleaming leaves, and their clusters of yellow fruit. They were like trees you imagined growing on a desert island, proud, solitary, lifting their leaves and fruits to the sun in a kind of silent splendour. Must they be hidden by a marquee?

They must. Already the men had shouldered their staves and were making for the place. Only the tall fellow was left. He bent down, pinched a sprig of lavender, put his thumb and forefinger to his nose and snuffed up the smell. When Laura saw that gesture she forgot all about the karakas in her wonder at him caring for things like that—caring for the smell of lavender. How many men that she knew would have done such a thing? Oh, how extraordinarily nice workmen were, she thought. Why couldn't she have workmen for friends rather than the silly boys she danced with and who came to Sunday night supper? She would get on much better with men like these.

It's all the fault, she decided, as the tall fellow drew something on the back of an envelope, something that was to be looped up or left to hang, of these absurd class distinctions. Well, for her part, she didn't feel them. Not a bit, not an atom. . . . And now there came the chock-chock of wooden hammers. Some one whistled, some one sang out, "Are you right there, matey?" "Matey!" The friendliness of it, the—the— Just to prove how happy she was, just to show the tall fellow how at home she felt, and how she despised stupid conventions, Laura took a big bite of her bread-and-butter as she stared at the little drawing. She felt just like a work-girl.

"Laura, Laura, where are you? Telephone, Laura!" a voice cried from the house.

"Coming!" Away she skimmed, over the lawn, up the path, up the steps, across the verandah, and into the porch. In the hall her father and Laurie were brushing their hats ready to go to the office.

25 "I say, Laura," said Laurie very fast, "you might just give a squiz at my coat before this afternoon. See if it wants pressing."

"I will," she said. Suddenly she couldn't stop herself. She ran at Laurie and gave him a small, quick squeeze. "Oh, I do love parties, don't you?" gasped Laura.

"Rather," said Laurie's warm, boyish voice, and he squeezed his sister too, and gave her a gentle push. "Dash off to the telephone, old girl."

The telephone. "Yes, yes; oh yes. Kitty? Good morning, dear. Come to lunch? Do, dear. Delighted of course. It will only be a very scratch meal—just the sandwich crusts and broken meringue-shells and what's left over. Yes, isn't it a perfect morning? Your white? Oh, I certainly should. One moment—hold the line. Mother's calling." And Laura sat back. "What, mother? Can't hear."

Mrs. Sheridan's voice floated down the stairs. "Tell her to wear that sweet hat she had on last Sunday."

30 "Mother says you're to wear that *sweet* hat you had on last Sunday. Good. One o'clock. Bye-bye."

Laura put back the receiver, flung her arms over her head, took a deep breath, stretched and let them fall. "Huh," she sighed, and the moment after the sigh she sat up quickly. She was still, listening. All the doors in the house seemed to open. The house was alive with soft, quick steps and running voices. The green baize door that led to the kitchen regions swung open and shut with a muffled thud. And now there came a long, chuckling absurd sound. It was the heavy piano being moved on its stiff castors. But the air! If you stopped to notice, was the air always like this? Little faint winds were playing chase, in at the tops of the windows, out at the doors. And there were two tiny spots of sun, one on the inkpot, one on a silver photograph frame, playing too. Darling little spots. Especially the one on the inkpot lid. It was quite warm. A warm little silver star. She could have kissed it.

The front door bell pealed, and there sounded the rustle of Sadie's print skirt on the stairs. A man's voice murmured; Sadie answered, careless, "I'm sure I don't know. Wait. I'll ask Mrs. Sheridan."

"What is it, Sadie?" Laura came into the hall.

"It's the florist, Miss Laura."

35 It was, indeed. There, just inside the door, stood a wide, shallow tray full of pots of pink lilies. No other kind. Nothing but lilies—canna lilies, big pink flowers, wide open, radiant, almost frighteningly alive on bright crimson stems.

"O-oh, Sadie!" said Laura, and the sound was like a little moan. She crouched down as if to warm herself at that blaze of lilies; she felt they were in her fingers, on her lips, growing in her breast.

"It's some mistake," she said faintly. "Nobody ever ordered so many. Sadie, go and find mother."

But at that moment Mrs. Sheridan joined them.

"It's quite right," she said calmly. "Yes, I ordered them. Aren't they lovely?" She pressed Laura's arm. "I was passing the shop yesterday, and I saw them in the window. And I suddenly thought for once in my life I shall have enough canna lilies. The garden-party will be a good excuse."

"But I thought you said you didn't mean to interfere," said Laura. Sadie had gone. The florist's man was still outside at his van. She put her arm round her mother's neck and gently, very gently, she bit her mother's ear.

"My darling child, you wouldn't like a logical mother, would you? Don't do that. Here's the man."

He carried more lilies still, another whole tray.

"Bank them up, just inside the door, on both sides of the porch, please," said Mrs. Sheridan. "Don't you agree, Laura?"

"Oh, I *do* mother."

In the drawing-room, Meg, Jose and good little Hans had at last succeeded in moving the piano.

"Now, if we put this chesterfield against the wall and move everything out of the room except the chairs, don't you think?"

"Quite."

"Hans, move these tables into the smoking-room, and bring a sweeper to take these marks off the carpet and—one moment, Hans—" Jose loved giving orders to the servants, and they loved obeying her. She always made them feel they were taking part in some drama. "Tell mother and Miss Laura to come here at once."

"Very good, Miss Jose."

She turned to Meg. "I want to hear what the piano sounds like, just in case I'm asked to sing this afternoon. Let's try over 'This life is Weary.'"

Pom! Ta-ta-ta *Tee*-ta! The piano burst out so passionately that Jose's face changed. She clasped her hands. She looked mournfully and enigmatically at her mother and Laura as they came in.

This Life is *Wee*-ary,
A Tear—a Sigh.
A Love that *Chan*-ges,
  This life is *Wee*-ary,
A Tear—a Sigh.
A Love that *Chan*-ges,
And then . . . Good-bye!

But at the word "Good-bye," and although the piano sounded more desperate than ever, her face broke into a brilliant, dreadfully unsympathetic smile.

"Aren't I in good voice, mummy?" she beamed.

This Life is *Wee*-ary,
Hope come to Die.
A Dream—a *Wa*-kening.

But now Sadie interrupted them. "What is it, Sadie?"

"If you please, m'm, cook says have you got the flags for the sandwiches?"

"The flags for the sandwiches, Sadie?" echoed Mrs. Sheridan dreamily. And the children knew by her face that she hadn't got them. "Let me see." And she said to Sadie firmly, "Tell cook I'll let her have them in ten minutes."

Sadie went.

"Now, Laura," said her mother quickly. "Come with me into the smoking-room. I've got the names somewhere on the back of an envelope. You'll have to write them out for me. Meg, go upstairs this minute and take that wet thing off your head. Jose, run and finish dressing this instant. Do you hear me, children, or shall I have to tell your father when he comes home to-night? And—and, Jose, pacify cook if you do go into the kitchen, will you? I'm terrified of her this morning."

The envelope was found at last behind the dining-room clock, though how it had got there Mrs. Sheridan could not imagine.

"One of you children must have stolen it out of my bag, because I remember vividly—cream cheese and lemon-curd. Have you done that?"

"Yes."

"Egg and—" Mrs. Sheridan held the envelope away from her. "It looks like mice. It can't be mice, can it?"

"Olive, pet," said Laura, looking over her shoulder.

"Yes, of course, olive. What a horrible combination it sounds. Egg and olive."

They were finished at last, and Laura took them off to the kitchen. She found Jose there pacifying the cook, who did not look at all terrifying.

"I have never seen such exquisite sandwiches," said Jose's rapturous voice. "How many kinds did you say there were, cook? Fifteen?"

"Fifteen, Miss Jose."

"Well, cook, I congratulate you."

Cook swept up crusts with the long sandwich knife, and smiled broadly.

"Godber's has come," announced Sadie, issuing out of the pantry. She had seen the man pass the window.

That meant the cream puffs had come. Godber's were famous for their cream puffs. Nobody ever thought of making them at home.

"Bring them in and put them on the table, my girl," ordered cook.

Sadie brought them in and went back to the door. Of course Laura and Jose were far too grown-up to really care about such things. All the same, they couldn't help agreeing that the puffs looked very attractive. Very. Cook began arranging them, shaking off the extra icing sugar.

"Don't they carry one back to all one's parties?" said Laura.

"I suppose they do," said practical Jose, who never liked to be carried back. "They look beautifully light and feathery, I must say."

"Have one each, my dears," said cook in her comfortable voice. "Yer ma won't know."

Oh, impossible. Fancy cream puffs so soon after breakfast. The very idea made one shudder. All the same, two minutes later Jose and Laura were licking their fingers with that absorbed inward look that only comes from whipped cream.

"Let's go into the garden, out by the back way," suggested Laura. "I want to see how the men are getting on with the marquee. They're such awfully nice men."

But the back door was blocked by cook, Sadie, Godber's man and Hans.

Something had happened. 80

"Tuk-tuk-tuk," clucked cook like an agitated hen. Sadie had her hand clapped to her cheek as though she had toothache. Hans' face was screwed up in the effort to understand. Only Godber's man seemed to be enjoying himself; it was his story.

"What's the matter? What's happened?"

"There's been a horrible accident," said cook. "A man killed."

"A man killed! Where? How? When?"

But Godber's man wasn't going to have his story snatched from under his 85
very nose.

"Know those little cottages just below here, miss?" Know them? Of course, she knew them. "Well, there's a young chap living there, name of Scott, a carter. His horse shied at a traction-engine, corner of Hawke Street this morning, and he was thrown out on the back of his head. Killed."

"Dead!" Laura stared at Godber's man.

"Dead when they picked him up," said Godber's man with relish. "They were taking the body home as I come up here." And he said to the cook, "He's left a wife and five little ones."

"Jose, come here." Laura caught hold of her sister's sleeve and dragged her through the kitchen to the other side of the green baize door. There she paused and leaned against it. "Jose!" she said, horrified, "however are we going to stop everything?"

"Stop everything, Laura!" cried Jose in astonishment. "What do you mean?" 90

"Stop the garden-party, of course." Why did Jose pretend?

But Jose was still more amazed. "Stop the garden-party? My dear Laura, don't be so absurd. Of course we can't do anything of the kind. Nobody expects us to. Don't be so extravagant."

"But we can't possibly have a garden-party with a man dead just outside the front gate."

That really was extravagant, for the little cottages were in a lane to themselves at the very bottom of a steep rise that led up to the house. A broad road ran between. True, they were far too near. They were the greatest possible eyesore, and they had no right to be in that neighbourhood at all. They were little mean dwellings painted a chocolate brown. In the garden patches there was nothing but cabbage stalks, sick hens and tomato cans. The very smoke coming out of their chimneys was poverty-stricken. Little rags and shreds of smoke, so unlike the great silvery plumes that uncurled from the Sheridans' chimneys. Washerwomen lived in the lane and sweeps and a cobbler, and a man whose house-front was studded all over with minute bird-cages. Children swarmed. When the Sheridans were little they were forbidden to set foot there because of the revolting language and of what they might catch. But since they were grown up, Laura and Laurie on their prowls sometimes walked through. It was disgusting and sordid. They came out with a shudder. But still one must go everywhere; one must see everything. So through they went.

"And just think of what the band would sound like to that poor woman," 95
said Laura.

"Oh, Laura!" Jose began to be seriously annoyed. "If you're going to stop a band playing every time some one has an accident, you'll lead a very strenuous life. I'm every bit as sorry about it as you. I feel just as sympathetic." Her eyes hardened. She looked at her sister just as she used to when they were little and fighting together. "You won't bring a drunken workman back to life by being sentimental," she said softly.

"Drunk! Who said he was drunk?" Laura turned furiously on Jose. She said, just as they had used to say on those occasions, "I'm going straight up to tell mother."

"Do, dear," cooed Jose.

"Mother, can I come into your room?" Laura turned the big glass doorknob.

"Of course, child. Why, what's the matter? What's given you such a 100
colour?" And Mrs. Sheridan turned round from her dressing table. She was trying on a new hat.

"Mother, a man's been killed," began Laura.

"*Not* in the garden?" interrupted her mother.

"No, no!"

"Oh, what a fright you gave me!" Mrs. Sheridan sighed with relief, and took off the big hat and held it on her knees.

"But listen, mother," said Laura. Breathless, half-choking, she told the 105
dreadful story. "Of course, we can't have our party, can we?" she pleaded. "The band and everybody arriving. They'd hear us, mother, they're nearly neighbours!"

To Laura's astonishment her mother behaved just like Jose; it was harder to bear because she seemed amused. She refused to take Laura seriously.

"But, my dear child, use your common sense. It's only by accident we've heard of it. If some one had died there normally—and I can't understand how they keep alive in those poky little holes—we should still be having our party, shouldn't we?"

Laura had to say "yes" to that, but she felt it was all wrong. She sat down on her mother's sofa and pinched the cushion frill.

"Mother, isn't it really terribly heartless of us?" she asked.

"Darling!" Mrs. Sheridan got up and came over to her, carrying the hat. 110
Before Laura could stop her she had popped it on. "My child," said her mother, "the hat is yours. It's made for you. It's much too young for me. I have never seen you look such a picture. Look at yourself!" And she held up her hand-mirror.

"But, mother," Laura began again. She couldn't look at herself; she turned aside.

This time Mrs. Sheridan lost patience just as Jose had done.

"You are being very absurd, Laura," she said coldly. "People like that don't expect sacrifices from us. And it's not very sympathetic to spoil everybody's enjoyment as you're doing now."

"I don't understand," said Laura, and she walked quickly out of the room into her own bedroom. There, quite by chance, the first thing she saw was this charming girl in the mirror, in her black hat trimmed with gold daisies, and a long black velvet ribbon. Never had she imagined she could look like that. Is mother right? she thought. And now she hoped her mother was right. Am I being extravagant? Perhaps it was extravagant. Just for a moment she had another glimpse of that poor woman and those little children, and the body being carried into the house. But it all seemed blurred, unreal, like a picture in the newspaper. I'll remember it again after the party's over, she decided. And somehow that seemed quite the best plan. . . .

Lunch was over by half past one. By half past two they were all ready for 115
the fray. The green-coated band had arrived and was established in a corner of the tennis-court.

"My dear!" trilled Kitty Maitland, "aren't they too like frogs for words? You ought to have arranged them round the pond with the conductor in the middle on a leaf."

Laurie arrived and hailed them on his way to dress. At the sight of him Laura remembered the accident again. She wanted to tell him. If Laurie agreed with the others, then it was bound to be all right. And she followed him into the hall.

"Laurie!" "Hallo!" He was half-way upstairs, but when he turned around and saw Laura he suddenly puffed out his cheeks and goggled his eyes at her. "My word, Laura; you do look stunning," said Laurie. "What an absolutely topping hat!"

Laura said faintly "Is it?" and smiled up at Laurie, and didn't tell him after all.

Soon after that people began coming in streams. The band struck up; the 120
hired waiters ran from the house to the marquee. Wherever you looked there were couples strolling, bending to the flowers, greeting, moving on over the lawn. They were like bright birds that had alighted in the Sheridans' garden for this one afternoon, on their way to—where? Ah, what happiness it is to be with people who all are happy, to press hands, press cheeks, smile into eyes.

"Darling Laura, how well you look!"

"What a becoming hat, child!"

"Laura, you look quite Spanish. I've never seen you look so striking."

And Laura, glowing, answered softly, "Have you had tea? Won't you have an ice? The passion-fruit ices really are rather special." She ran to her father and begged him. "Daddy darling, can't the band have something to drink?"

And the perfect afternoon slowly ripened, slowly faded, slowly its petals 125
closed.

"Never a more delightful garden-party . . ." "The greatest success . . ." "Quite the most . . ."

Laura helped her mother with the good-byes. They stood side by side in the porch till it was all over.

"All over, all over, thank heaven," said Mrs. Sheridan. "Round in the others, Laura. Let's go and have some fresh coffee. I'm exhausted. Yes, it's been very successful. But oh, these parties, these parties! Why will you children insist on giving parties!" And they all of them sat down in the deserted marquee.

"Have a sandwich, daddy dear. I wrote the flag."

"Thanks." Mr. Sheridan took a bite and the sandwich was gone. He took 130 another. "I suppose you didn't hear of a beastly accident that happened to-day?" he said.

"My dear," said Mrs. Sheridan, holding up her hand, "we did. It nearly ruined the party. Laura insisted we should put it off."

"Oh, mother!" Laura didn't want to be teased about it.

"It was a horrible affair all the same," said Mr. Sheridan. "The chap was married too. Lived just below in the lane, and leaves a wife and half a dozen kiddies, so they say."

An awkward little silence fell. Mrs. Sheridan fidgeted with her cup. Really, it was very tactless of father . . .

Suddenly she looked up. There on the table were all those sandwiches, 135
cakes, puffs, all uneaten, all going to be wasted. She had one of her brilliant ideas.

"I know," she said. "Let's make up a basket. Let's send that poor creature some of this perfectly good food. At any rate, it will be the greatest treat for the children. Don't you agree? And she's sure to have neighbours calling in and so on. What a point to have it all ready prepared. Laura!" She jumped up. "Get me the big basket out of the stairs cupboard."

"But, mother, do you really think it's a good idea?" said Laura.

Again, how curious, she seemed to be different from them all. To take scraps from their party. Would the poor woman really like that?

"Of course!" What's the matter with you to-day? An hour or two ago you were insisting on us being sympathetic, and now—"

Oh, well! Laura ran for the basket. It was filled, it was heaped by her mother. 140

"Take it yourself, darling," said she. "Run down just as you are. No, wait, take the arum lilies too. People of that class are so impressed by arum lilies."

"The stems will ruin her lace frock," said practical Jose.

So they would. Just in time. "Only the basket, then. And, Laura!"—her mother followed her out of the marquee—"don't on any account—"

"What, mother?"

No, better not put such ideas into the child's head! "Nothing! Run along." 145

It was just growing dusky as Laura shut their garden gates. A big dog ran by like a shadow. The road gleamed white, and down below in the hollow the little cottages were in deep shade. How quiet it seemed after the afternoon. Here she was going down the hill to somewhere where a man lay dead, and she couldn't realize it. Why couldn't she? She stopped a minute. And it seemed to her that kisses, voices, tinkling spoons, laughter, the smell of crushed grass were somehow inside her. She had no room for anything else. How strange! She looked up at the pale sky, and all she thought was, "Yes, it was the most successful party."

Now the broad road was crossed. The lane began, smoky and dark. Women in shawls and men's tweed caps hurried by. Men hung over the palings; the children played in the doorways. A low hum came from the mean little cottages. In some of them there was a flicker of light, and a shadow, crab-like, moved across the window. Laura bent her head and hurried on. She wished now she had put on a coat. How her frock shone! And the big hat with the velvet streamer—if only it was another hat! Were the people looking at her? They must be. It was a mistake to have come; she knew all along it was a mistake. Should she go back even now?

No, too late. This was the house. It must be. A dark knot of people stood outside. Beside the gate an old, old woman with a crutch sat in a chair, watching. She had her feet on a newspaper. The voices stopped as Laura drew near. The group parted. It was as though she was expected, as though they had known she was coming here.

Laura was terribly nervous. Tossing the velvet ribbon over her shoulder, she said to a woman standing by, "Is this Mrs. Scott's house?" and the woman, smiling queerly, said, "It is, my lass."

Oh, to be away from this! She actually said, "Help me, God," as she 150
walked up the tiny path and knocked. To be away from those staring eyes, or to be covered up in anything, one of those women's shawls even. I'll just leave the basket and go, she decided. I shan't even wait for it to be emptied.

Then the door opened. A little woman in black showed in the gloom.

Laura said, "Are you Mrs. Scott?" But to her horror the woman answered, "Walk in please, miss," and she was shut in the passage.

"No," said Laura, "I don't want to come in. I only want to leave this basket. Mother sent—"

The little woman in the gloomy passage seemed not to have heard her. "Step this way, please, miss," she said in an oily voice, and Laura followed her.

She found herself in a wretched little low kitchen, lighted by a smoky 155
lamp. There was a woman sitting before the fire.

"Em," said the little creature who had let her in. "Em! It's a young lady." She turned to Laura. She said meaningly, "I'm 'er sister, miss. You'll excuse 'er, won't you?"

"Oh, but of course!" said Laura. "Please, don't disturb her. I—I only want to leave—"

But at that moment the woman at the fire turned round. Her face, puffed up, red, with swollen eyes and swollen lips, looked terrible. She seemed as though she couldn't understand why Laura was there. What did it mean? Why was this stranger standing in the kitchen with a basket? What was it all about? And the poor face puckered up again.

"All right, my dear," said the other. "I'll thank the young lady."

And again she began, "You'll excuse her, miss, I'm sure," and her face, 160
swollen too, tried an oily smile.

Laura only wanted to get out, to get away. She was back in the passage. The door opened. She walked straight through into the bedroom, where the dead was lying.

"You'd like a look at 'im, wouldn't you?" said Em's sister, and she brushed past Laura over to the bed. "Don't be afraid, my lass,—" and now her voice sounded fond and sly, and fondly she drew down the sheet—" 'e looks a picture. There's nothing to show. Come along, my dear."

Laura came.

There lay a young man, fast asleep—sleeping so soundly, so deeply, that he was far, far away from them both. Oh, so remote, so peaceful. He was dreaming. Never wake him up again. His head was sunk in the pillow, his eyes were closed; they were blind under the closed eyelids. He was given up to his dream. What did garden-parties and baskets and lace frocks matter to him? He was far from all those things. He was wonderful, beautiful. While they were laughing and while the band was playing, this marvel had come to the lane. Happy . . . happy. . . . All is well, said that sleeping face. This is just as it should be. I am content.

But all the same you had to cry, and she couldn't go out of the room without saying something to him. Laura gave a loud childish sob.

"Forgive my hat," she said.

And this time she didn't wait for Em's sister. She found her way out of the door, down the path, past all those dark people. At the corner of the lane she met Laurie.

He stepped out of the shadow. "Is that you, Laura?"

"Yes."

"Mother was getting anxious. Was it all right?"

"Yes, quite. Oh, Laurie!" She took his arm, she pressed up against him.

"I say, you're not crying, are you?" asked her brother.

Laura shook her head. She was.

Laurie put his arm round her shoulder. "Don't cry," he said in his warm, loving voice. "Was it awful?"

"No," sobbed Laura. "It was simply marvelous. But. Laurie—" She stopped, she looked at her brother. "Isn't life," she stammered, "Isn't life—" But what life was she couldn't explain. No matter. He quite understood.

"*Isn't* it, darling?" said Laurie.

KATHERINE MANSFIELD

(1888–1923) **Web** *www*

Born in New Zealand, Katherine Mansfield Beauchamp attended college in London. Mansfield's métier was the short story, and she wrote stories for magazines and published collections of stories with Hogarth Press. Mansfield had the ability to capture atmosphere and dilemma through the strategic use of imagery and detail. She died of tuberculosis at the age of thirty-four.

TOPICS FOR CRITICAL THINKING **Web** *www*

1. In what ways does this story approach the question of class?
2. What are the functions of the hat motif?
3. Through what devices does this story show the shallowness of the Sheridans?
4. Why does Laura say, "Excuse my hat"?

TOPICS FOR CRITICAL WRITING **Web** *www*

1. In what ways does this story portray Laura's search for identity?
2. What indications are there that the story's narrator takes a slightly ironic view of the Sheridans? To what end?

D. H. Lawrence

The Horse-Dealer's Daughter *(1922)*

'Well, Mabel, and what are you going to do with yourself?' asked Joe, with foolish flippancy. He felt quite safe himself. Without listening for an answer, he turned aside, worked a grain of tobacco to the tip of his tongue, and spat it out. He did not care about anything, since he felt safe himself.

The three brothers and the sister sat round the desolate breakfast-table, attempting some sort of desultory consultation. The morning's post had given the final tap to the family fortunes, and all was over. The dreary dining-room itself, with its heavy mahogany furniture, looked as if it were waiting to be done away with.

But the consultation amounted to nothing. There was a strange air of ineffectuality about the three men, as they sprawled at table, smoking and reflecting vaguely on their own condition. The girl was alone, a rather short, sullen-looking young woman of twenty-seven. She did not share the same life as her brothers. She would have been good-looking, save for the impressive fixity of her face, 'bull-dog', as her brothers called it.

There was a confused tramping of horses' feet outside. The three men all sprawled round in their chairs to watch. Beyond the dark holly bushes that separated the strip of lawn from the high-road, they could see a cavalcade of shire horses swinging out of their own yard, being taken for exercise. This was the last time. These were the last horses that would go through their hands. The young men watched with critical, callous look. They were all frightened at the collapse of their lives, and the sense of disaster in which they were involved left them no inner freedom.

Yet they were three fine, well-set fellows enough. Joe, the eldest, was a 5
man of thirty-three, broad and handsome in a hot, flushed way. His face was red, he twisted his black moustache over a thick finger, his eyes were shallow and restless. He had a sensual way of uncovering his teeth when he laughed, and his bearing was stupid. Now he watched the horses with a glazed look of helplessness in his eyes, a certain stupor of downfall.

The great draught-horses swung past. They were tied head to tail, four of them, and they heaved along to where a lane branched off from the high-road, planting their great hoofs floutingly in the fine black mud, swinging their great rounded haunches sumptuously, and trotting a few sudden steps as they were led into the lane, round the corner. Every movement showed a massive, slumbrous strength, and a stupidity which held them in subjection. The groom at the head looked back, jerking the leading rope. And the cavalcade moved out of sight up the lane, the tail of the last horse, bobbed up tight and stiff, held out taut from the swinging great haunches as they rocked behind the hedges in a motion-like sleep.

Joe watched with glazed hopeless eyes. The horses were almost like his own body to him. He felt he was done for now. Luckily he was engaged to a woman as old as himself, and therefore her father, who was steward of a neighbouring estate, would provide him with a job. He would marry and go into harness. His life was over, he would be a subject animal now.

He turned uneasily aside, the retreating steps of the horses echoing in his ears. Then, with foolish restlessness, he reached for the scraps of bacon-rind from the plates, and making a faint whistling sound, flung them to the terrier that lay against the fender. He watched the dog swallow them, and waited till the creature looked into his eyes. Then a faint grin came on his face, and in a high, foolish voice he said:

'You won't get much more bacon, shall you, you little b——?'

The dog faintly and dismally wagged its tail, the lowered its haunches, 10
circled round, and lay down again.

There was another helpless silence at the table. Joe sprawled uneasily in his seat, not willing to go till the family conclave was dissolved. Fred Henry, the second brother, was erect, clean-limbed, alert. He had watched the passing of the horses with more sang-froid. If he was an animal, like Joe, he was an animal which controls, not one which is controlled. He was master of any horse, and he carried himself with a well-tempered air of mastery. But he was not master of the situations of life. He pushed his coarse brown moustache upwards, off his lip, and glanced irritably at his sister, who sat impassive and inscrutable.

'You'll go and stop with Lucy for a bit, shan't you?' he asked. The girl did not answer.

'I don't see what else you can do,' persisted Fred Henry.

'Go as a skivvy,' Joe interpolated laconically.

The girl did not move a muscle. 15

'If I was her, I should go in for training for a nurse,' said Malcolm, the youngest of them all. He was the baby of the family, a young man of twenty-two, with a fresh, jaunty *museau*.

But Mabel did not take any notice of him. They had talked at her and round her for so many years, that she hardly heard them at all.

The marble clock on the mantelpiece softly chimed the half-hour, the dog rose uneasily from the hearth-rug and looked at the party at the breakfast-table. But still they sat on in ineffectual conclave.

'Oh, all right,' said Joe suddenly, apropos of nothing. 'I'll get a move on.'

He pushed back his chair, straddled his knees with a downward jerk, to 20
get them free, in horsey fashion, and went to the fire. Still, he did not go out of the room; he was curious to know what the others would do or say. He began to charge his pipe, looking down at the dog and saying in a high, affected voice:

'Going wi' me? Going wi' me are ter? Tha'rt goin' further than tha counts on just now, dost hear?'

The dog faintly wagged its tail, the man stuck out his jaw and covered his pipe with his hands, and puffed intently, losing himself in the tobacco, looking down all the while at the dog with an absent brown eye. The dog looked up at him in mournful distrust. Joe stood with his knees stuck out, in real horsey fashion.

'Have you had a letter from Lucy?' Fred Henry asked of his sister.

'Last week,' came the neutral reply.

'And what does she say?'

There was no answer.

'Does she *ask* you to go and stop there?' persisted Fred Henry.

'She says I can if I like.'

'Well, then, you'd better. Tell her you'll come on Monday.'

This was received in silence.

'That's what you'll do then, is it?' said Fred Henry, in some exasperation.

But she made no answer. There was a silence of futility and irritation in the room. Malcolm grinned fatuously.

'You'll have to make up your mind between now and next Wednesday,' said Joe loudly, 'or else find yourself lodgings on the kerbstone.'

The face of the young woman darkened, but she sat on immutable.

'Here's Jack Fergusson!' exclaimed Malcolm, who was looking aimlessly out of the window.

'Where?' exclaimed Joe loudly.

'Just gone past.'

'Coming in?'

Malcolm craned his neck to see the gate.

'Yes,' he said.

There was a silence. Mabel sat on like one condemned, at the head of the table. Then a whistle was heard from the kitchen. The dog got up and barked sharply. Joe opened the door and shouted:

'Come on.'

After a moment a young man entered. He was muffled up in overcoat and a purple woollen scarf, and his tweed cap, which he did not remove, was pulled down on his head. He was of medium height, his face was rather long and pale, his eyes looked tired.

'Hello, Jack! Well, Jack!' exclaimed Malcolm and Joe. Fred Henry merely said: 'Jack.'

'What's doing?' asked the newcomer, evidently addressing Fred Henry.

'Same. We've got to be out by Wednesday. Got a cold?'

'I have—got it bad, too.'

'Why don't you stop in?'

'*Me* stop in? When I can't stand on my legs, perhaps I shall have a chance.' The young man spoke huskily. He had a slight Scotch accent.

'It's a knock-out, isn't it,' said Joe, boisterously, 'if a doctor goes round croaking with a cold. Looks bad for the patients, doesn't it?'

The young doctor looked at him slowly.

'Anything the matter with *you*, then?' he asked sarcastically.

'Not as I know of. Damn your eyes, I hope not. Why?'

'I thought you were very concerned about the patients, wondered if you might be one yourself.'

'Damn it, no, I've never been patient to no flaming doctor, and hope I never shall be,' returned Joe.

At this point Mabel rose from the table, and they all seemed to become aware of her existence. She began putting the dishes together. The young doctor looked at her, but did not address her. He had not greeted her. She went out of the room with the tray, her face impassive and unchanged.

'When are you off then, all of you?' asked the doctor.

'I'm catching the eleven-forty,' replied Malcolm. 'Are you goin' down wi' th' trap, Joe?'

'Yes, I've told you I'm going down wi' th' trap, haven't I?'

'We'd better be getting her in then. So long, Jack, if I don't see you before I go,' said Malcolm, shaking hands.

He went out, followed by Joe, who seemed to have his tail between his legs.

'Well, this is the devil's own,' exclaimed the doctor, when he was left alone with Fred Henry. 'Going before Wednesday, are you?'

'That's the orders,' replied the other.

'Where, to Northampton?'

'That's it.'

'The devil!' exclaimed Fergusson, with quiet chagrin.

And there was silence between the two.

'All settled up, are you?' asked Fergusson.

'About.'

There was another pause.

'Well, I shall miss yer, Freddy, boy,' said the young doctor.

'And I shall miss thee, Jack,' returned the other.

'Miss you like hell,' mused the doctor.

Fred Henry turned aside. There was nothing to say. Mabel came in again, to finish clearing the table.

'What are *you* going to do, then, Miss Pervin?' asked Fergusson. 'Going to your sister's, are you?'

Mabel looked at him with her steady, dangerous eyes, that always made him uncomfortable, unsettling his superficial ease.

'No,' she said.

'Well, what in the name of fortune *are* you going to do? Say what you mean to do,' cried Fred Henry, with futile intensity.

But she only averted her head, and continued her work. She folded the white table-cloth, and put on the chenille cloth.

'The sulkiest bitch that ever trod!' muttered her brother.

But she finished her task with perfectly impassive face, the young doctor watching her interestedly all the while. Then she went out.

Fred Henry stared after her, clenching his lips, his blue eyes fixing in sharp antagonism, as he made a grimace of sour exasperation.

'You could bray her into bits, and that's all you'd get out of her,' he said, in a small, narrowed tone.

The doctor smiled faintly.

'What's she *going* to do, then?' he asked.

'Strike me if *I* know!' returned the other.

There was a pause. Then the doctor stirred.

'I'll be seeing you to-night, shall I?' he said to his friend.

'Ay—where's it to be? Are we going over to Jessdale?'

'I don't know. I've got such a cold on me. I'll come round to the "Moon and Stars", anyway.'

'Let Lizzie and May miss their night for once, eh?'

'That's it—if I feel as I do now.'

'All's one—'

The two young men went through the passage and down to the back door together. The house was large, but it was servantless now, and desolate. At the back was a small bricked house-yard and beyond that a big square, gravelled fine and red, and having stables on two sides. Sloping, dank, winter-dark fields stretched away on the open sides.

But the stables were empty. Joseph Pervin, the father of the family, had been a man of no education, who had become a fairly large horse dealer. The stables had been full of horses, there was a great turmoil and come-and-go of horses and of dealers and grooms. Then the kitchen was full of servants. But of late things had declined. The old man had married a second time, to retrieve his fortunes. Now he was dead and everything was gone to the dogs, there was nothing but debt and threatening.

For months, Mabel had been servantless in the big house, keeping the home together in penury for her ineffectual brothers. She had kept house for ten years. But previously it was with unstinted means. Then, however brutal and coarse everything was, the sense of money had kept her proud, confident. The men might be foul-mouthed, the women in the kitchen might have bad reputations, her brothers might have illegitimate children. But so long as there was money, the girl felt herself established, and brutally proud, reserved.

No company came to the house, save dealers and coarse men. Mabel had no associates of her own sex, after her sister went away. But she did not mind. She went regularly to church, she attended to her father. And she lived in the memory of her mother, who had died when she was fourteen, and whom she had loved. She had loved her father, too, in a different way, depending upon him, and feeling secure in him, until at the age of fifty-four he married again. And then she had set hard against him. Now he had died and left them all hopelessly in debt.

She had suffered badly during the period of poverty. Nothing, however, could shake the curious, sullen, animal pride that dominated each member of the family. Now, for Mabel, the end had come. Still she would not cast about her. She would follow her own way just the same. She would always hold the keys of her own situation. Mindless and persistent, she endured from day to day. Why should she think? Why should she answer anybody? It was enough that this was the end, and there was no way out. She need not pass any more darkly along the main street of the small town, avoiding every eye. She need not demean herself any more, going into the shops and buying the cheapest food. This was at an end. She thought of nobody, not even of herself. Mindless and persistent, she seemed in a sort of ecstasy to be coming nearer to her fulfilment, her own glorification, approaching her dead mother, who was glorified.

In the afternoon she took a little bag, with shears and sponge and a small scrubbing-brush, and went out. It was a grey, wintry day, with saddened, dark green fields and an atmosphere blackened by the smoke of foundries not far off. She went quickly, darkly along the causeway, heeding nobody, through the town to the churchyard.

There she always felt secure, as if no one could see her, although as a mat- 100
ter of fact she was exposed to the stare of everyone who passed along under the churchyard wall. Nevertheless, once under the shadow of the great looming church, among the graves, she felt immune from the world, reserved within the thick churchyard wall as in another country.

Carefully she clipped the grass from the grave, and arranged the pinky white, small chrysanthemums in the tin cross. When this was done, she took an empty jar from a neighbouring grave, brought water, and carefully, most scrupulously sponged the marble headstone and the coping-stone.

It gave her sincere satisfaction to do this. She felt in immediate contact with the world of her mother. She took minute pains, went through the park in a state bordering on pure happiness, as if in performing this task she came into a subtle, intimate connection with her mother. For the life she followed here in the world was far less real than the world of death she inherited from her mother.

The doctor's house was just by the church. Fergusson, being a mere hired assistant, was slave to the country-side. As he hurried now to attend to the out-patients in the surgery, glancing across the graveyard with his quick eye, he saw the girl at her task at the grave. She seemed so intent and remote, it was like looking into another world. Some mystical element was touched in him. He slowed down as he walked, watching her as if spellbound.

She lifted her eyes, feeling him looking. Their eyes met. And each looked again at once, each feeling, in some way, found out by the other. He lifted his cap and passed on down the road. There remained distinct in his consciousness, like a vision, the memory of her face, lifted from the tombstone in the churchyard, and looking at him with slow, large, portentous eyes. It *was* portentous, her face. It seemed to mesmerise him. There was a heavy power in her eyes which laid hold of his whole being, as if he had drunk some powerful drug. He had been feeling weak and done before. Now the life came back into him, he felt delivered from his own fretted, daily self.

He finished his duties at the surgery as quickly as might be, hastily filling 105
up the bottles of the waiting people with cheap drugs. Then, in perpetual haste, he set off again to visit several cases in another part of his round, before tea-time. At all times he preferred to walk if he could, but particularly when he was not well. He fancied the motion restored him.

The afternoon was falling. It was grey, deadened, and wintry, with a slow, moist, heavy coldness sinking in and deadening all the faculties. But why should he think or notice? He hastily climbed the hill and turned across the dark green fields, following the black cinder-track. In the distance, across a shallow dip in the country, the small town was clustered like smouldering ash, a tower, a spire, a heap of low, raw, extinct houses. And on the nearest fringe of the town, sloping into the dip, was Oldmeadow, the Pervins' house. He could see the stables and the outbuildings distinctly, as they lay towards him on the slope. Well, he would not go there many more times! Another resource would be lost to him, another place gone: the only company he cared for in the alien, ugly little town he was losing. Nothing but work, drudgery, constant hastening from dwelling to dwelling among the colliers and the iron-workers. It wore him out, but at the same time he had a craving for it. It was a stimulant to him to be in the homes of the working people, moving, as it were, through the innermost body of their life. His nerves were excited and gratified. He could come so near, into the very lives of the rough, inarticulate, powerfully emotional men and women. He grumbled, he said he hated the hellish hole. But as a matter of fact it excited him, the contact with the rough, strongly-feeling people was a stimulant applied direct to his nerves.

Below Oldmeadow, in the green, shallow, soddened hollow of fields, lay a square, deep pond. Roving across the landscape, the doctor's quick eye detected a figure in black passing through the gate of the field, down towards the pond. He looked again. It would be Mabel Pervin. His mind suddenly became alive and attentive.

Why was she going down there? He pulled up on the path on the slope above, and stood staring. He could just make sure of the small black figure moving in the hollow of the failing day. He seemed to see her in the midst of such obscurity, that he was like a clairvoyant, seeing rather with the mind's eye than with ordinary sight. Yet he could see her positively enough, whilst he kept his eye attentive. He felt, if he looked away from her, in the thick, ugly falling dusk, he would lose her altogether.

He followed her minutely as she moved, direct and intent, like something transmitted rather than stirring in voluntary activity, straight down the field towards the pond. There she stood on the bank for a moment. She never raised her head. Then she waded slowly into the water.

110 He stood motionless as the small black figure walked slowly and deliberately towards the centre of the pond, very slowly, gradually moving deeper into the motionless water, and still moving forward as the water got up to her breast. Then he could see her no more in the dusk of the dead afternoon.

'There!' he exclaimed. 'Would you believe it?'

And he hastened straight down, running over the wet, soddened fields, pushing through the hedges, down into the depression of callous wintry obscurity. It took him several minutes to come to the pond. He stood on the bank, breathing heavily. He could see nothing. His eyes seemed to penetrate the dead water. Yes, perhaps that was the dark shadow of her black clothing beneath the surface of the water.

He slowly ventured into the pond. The bottom was deep, soft clay, he sank in, and the water clasped dead cold round his legs. As he stirred he could smell the cold, rotten clay that fouled up into the water. It was objectionable in his lungs. Still, repelled and yet not heeding, he moved deeper into the pond. The cold water rose over his thighs, over his loins, upon his abdomen. The lower part of his body was all sunk in the hideous cold element. And the bottom was so deeply soft and uncertain, he was afraid of pitching with his mouth underneath. He could not swim, and was afraid.

He crouched a little, spreading his hands under the water and moving them round, trying to feel for her. The dead cold pond swayed upon his chest. He moved again, a little deeper, and again, with his hands underneath, he felt all around under the water. And he touched her clothing. But it evaded his fingers. He made a desperate effort to grasp it.

And so doing he lost his balance and went under, horribly, suffocating in 115
the foul earthy water, struggling madly for a few moments. At last, after what seemed an eternity, he got his footing, rose again into the air and looked around. He gasped, and knew he was in the world. Then he looked at the water. She had risen near him. He grasped her clothing, and drawing her nearer, turned to take his way to land again.

He went very slowly, carefully, absorbed in the slow process. He rose higher, climbing out of the pond. The water was now only about his legs; he was thankful, full of relief to be out of the clutches of the pond. He lifted her and staggered on to the bank, out of the horror of wet, grey clay.

He laid her down on the bank. She was quite unconscious and running with water. He made the water come from her mouth, he worked to restore her. He did not have to work very long before he could feel the breathing begin again in her; she was breathing naturally. He worked a little longer. He could feel her live beneath his hands; she was coming back. He wiped her face, wrapped her in his overcoat, looked round into the dim, dark grey world, then lifted her and staggered down the bank and across the fields.

It seemed an unthinkably long way, and his burden so heavy he felt he would never get to the house. But at last he was in the stable-yard, and then in the house-yard. He opened the door and went into the house. In the kitchen he laid her down on the hearth-rug and called. The house was empty. But the fire was burning in the grate.

Then again he kneeled to attend to her. She was breathing regularly, her eyes were wide open and as if conscious, but there seemed something missing in her look. She was conscious in herself, but unconscious of her surroundings.

He ran upstairs, took blankets from a bed, and put them before the fire to 120
warm. Then he removed her saturated, earthy-smelling clothing, rubbed her dry with a towel, and wrapped her naked in the blankets. Then he went into the dining-room, to look for spirits. There was a little whisky. He drank a gulp himself, and put some into her mouth.

The effect was instantaneous. She looked full into his face, as if she had been seeing him for some time, and yet had only just become conscious of him.

'Dr. Fergusson?' she said.

'What?' he answered.

He was divesting himself of his coat, intending to find some dry clothing upstairs. He could not bear the smell of the dead, clayey water, and he was mortally afraid for his own health.

'What did I do?' she asked. 125

'Walked into the pond,' he replied. He had begun to shudder like one sick, and could hardly attend to her. Her eyes remained full on him, he seemed to be going dark in his mind, looking back at her helplessly. The shuddering became quieter in him, his life came back to him, dark and unknowing, but strong again.

'Was I out of my mind?' she asked, while her eyes were fixed on him all the time.

'Maybe, for the moment,' he replied. He felt quiet, because his strength had come back. The strange fretful strain had left him.

'Am I out of my mind now?' she asked.

'Are you?' he reflected a moment. 'No,' he answered truthfully, 'I don't 130
see that you are.' He turned his face aside. He was afraid now, because he felt dazed, and felt dimly that her power was stronger than his, in this issue. And she continued to look at him fixedly all the time. 'Can you tell me where I shall find some dry things to put on?' he asked.

'Did you dive into the pond for me?' she asked.

'No,' he answered. 'I walked in. But I went in overhead as well.'

There was silence for a moment. He hesitated. He very much wanted to go upstairs to get into dry clothing. But there was another desire in him. And she seemed to hold him. His will seemed to have gone to sleep, and left him, standing there slack before her. But he felt warm inside himself. He did not shudder at all, though his clothes were sodden on him.

'Why did you?' she asked.

'Because I didn't want you to do such a foolish thing,' he said. 135

'It wasn't foolish,' she said, still gazing at him as she lay on the floor, with a sofa cushion under her head. 'It was the right thing to do. *I* knew best, then.'

'I'll go and shift these wet things,' he said. But still he had not the power to move out of her presence, until she sent him. It was as if she had the life of his body in her hands, and he could not extricate himself. Or perhaps he did not want to.

Suddenly she sat up. Then she became aware of her own immediate condition. She felt the blankets about her, she knew her own limbs. For a moment it seemed as if her reason were going. She looked round, with wild eye, as if seeking something. He stood still with fear. She saw her clothing lying scattered.

'Who undressed me?' she asked, her eyes resting full and inevitable on his face.

'I did,' he replied, 'to bring you round.' 140

For some moments she sat and gazed at him awfully, her lips parted.

'Do you love me, then?' she asked.

He only stood and stared at her, fascinated. His soul seemed to melt.

She shuffled forward on her knees, and put her arms round him, round his legs, as he stood there, pressing her breasts against his knees and thighs, clutching him with strange, convulsive certainty, pressing his thighs against her, drawing him to her face, her throat, as she looked up at him with flaring, humble eyes and transfiguration, triumphant in first possession.

'You love me,' she murmured, in strange transport, yearning and tri- 145
umphant and confident. 'You love me. I know you love me, I know.'

And she was passionately kissing his knees, through the wet clothing, passionately and indiscriminately kissing his knees, his legs, as if unaware of everything.

He looked down at the tangled wet hair, the wild, bare, animal shoulders. He was amazed, bewildered, and afraid. He had never thought of loving her. He had never wanted to love her. When he rescued her and restored her, he was a doctor, and she was a patient. He had had no single personal thought of her. Nay, this introduction of the personal element was very distasteful to him, a violation of his professional honour. It was horrible to have her there embracing his knees. It was horrible. He revolted from it, violently. And yet—and yet—he had not the power to break away.

She looked at him again, with the same supplication of powerful love, and that same transcendent, frightening light of triumph. In view of the delicate flame which seemed to come from her face like a light, he was powerless. And yet he had never intended to love her. He had never intended. And something stubborn in him could not give way.

'You love me,' she repeated, in a murmur of deep, rhapsodic assurance. 'You love me.'

150 Her hands were drawing him, drawing him down to her. He was afraid, even a little horrified. For he had, really, no intention of loving her. Yet her hands were drawing him towards her. He put out his hand quickly to steady himself, and grasped her bare shoulder. A flame seemed to burn the hand that grasped her soft shoulder. He had no intention of loving her: his whole will was against his yielding. It was horrible. And yet wonderful was the touch of her shoulders, beautiful the shining of her face. Was she perhaps mad? He had a horror of yielding to her. Yet something in him ached also.

He had been staring away at the door, away from her. But his hand remained on her shoulder. She had gone suddenly very still. He looked down at her. Her eyes were now wide with fear, with doubt, the light was dying from her face, a shadow of terrible greyness was returning. He could not bear the touch of her eyes' question upon him, and the look of death behind the question.

With an inward groan he gave way, and let his heart yield towards her. A sudden gentle smile came on his face. And her eyes, which never left his face, slowly, slowly filled with tears. He watched the strange water rise in her eyes, like some slow fountain coming up. And his heart seemed to burn and melt away in his breast.

He could not bear to look at her any more. He dropped on his knees and caught her head with his arms and pressed her face against his throat. She was very still. His heart, which seemed to have broken, was burning with a kind of agony in his breast. And he felt her slow, hot tears wetting his throat. But he could not move.

He felt the hot tears wet his neck and the hollows of his neck, and he remained motionless, suspended through one of man's eternities. Only now it had become indispensable to him to have her face pressed close to him; he could never let her go again. He could never let her head go away from the close clutch of his arm. He wanted to remain like that for ever, with his heart hurting him in a pain that was also life to him. Without knowing, he was looking down on her damp, soft brown hair.

155 Then, as it were suddenly, he smelt the horrid stagnant smell of that water. And at the same moment she drew away from him and looked at him. Her eyes were wistful and unfathomable. He was afraid of them, and he fell to kissing her, not knowing what he was doing. He wanted her eyes not to have that terrible, wistful, unfathomable look.

When she turned her face to him again, a faint delicate flush was glowing, and there was again dawning that terrible shining of joy in her eyes, which really terrified him, and yet which he now wanted to see, because he feared the look of doubt still more.

'You love me?' she said, rather faltering.

'Yes.' The word cost him a painful effort. Not because it wasn't true. But because it was too newly true, the *saying* seemed to tear open again his newly-torn heart. And he hardly wanted it to be true, even now.

She lifted her face to him, and he bent forward and kissed her on the mouth, gently, with the one kiss that is an eternal pledge. And as he kissed her his heart strained again in his breast. He never intended to love her. But now it was over. He had crossed over the gulf to her, and all that he had left behind had shrivelled and become void.

160 After the kiss, her eyes again slowly filled with tears. She sat still, away from him, with her face drooped aside, and her hands folded in her lap. The tears fell very slowly. There was complete silence. He too sat there motionless and silent on the hearth-rug. The strange pain of his heart that was broken seemed to consume him. That he should love her? That this was love! That he should be ripped open in this way! Him, a doctor! How they would all jeer if they knew! It was agony to him to think they might know.

In the curious naked pain of the thought he looked again to her. She was sitting there drooped into a muse. He saw a tear fall, and his heart flared hot. He saw for the first time that one of her shoulders was quite uncovered, one arm bare, he could see one of her small breasts; dimly, because it had become almost dark in the room.

'Why are you crying?' he asked, in an altered voice.

She looked up at him, and behind her tears the consciousness of her situation for the first time brought a dark look of shame to her eyes.

'I'm not crying, really,' she said, watching him, half frightened.

165 He reached his hand, and softly closed it on her bare arm.

'I love you! I love you!' he said in a soft, low vibrating voice, unlike himself.

She shrank, and dropped her head. The soft, penetrating grip of his hand on her arm distressed her. She looked up at him.

'I want to go,' she said. 'I want to go and get you some dry things.'

'Why?' he said. 'I'm all right.'

170 'But I want to go,' she said. 'And I want you to change your things.'

He released her arm, and she wrapped herself in the blanket, looking at him rather frightened. And still she did not rise.

'Kiss me,' she said wistfully.

He kissed her, but briefly, half in anger.

Then, after a second, she rose nervously, all mixed up in the blanket. He watched her in her confusion as she tried to extricate herself and wrap herself up so that she could walk. He watched her relentlessly, as she knew. And as she went, the blanket trailing, and as he saw a glimpse of her feet and her white leg, he tried to remember her as she was when he had wrapped her in the blanket. But then he didn't want to remember, because she had been nothing to him then, and his nature revolted from remembering her as she was when she was nothing to him.

A tumbling, muffled noise from within the dark house startled him. Then 175
he heard her voice: 'There are clothes.' He rose and went to the foot of the stairs, and gathered up the garments she had thrown down. Then he came back to the fire, to rub himself down and dress. He grinned at his own appearance when he had finished.

The fire was sinking, so he put on coal. The house was now quite dark, save for the light of a street-lamp that shone in faintly from beyond the holly trees. He lit the gas with matches he found on the mantelpiece. Then he emptied the pockets of his own clothes, and threw all his wet things in a heap into the scullery. After which he gathered up her sodden clothes, gently, and put them in a separate heap on the copper-top in the scullery.

It was six o'clock on the clock. His own watch had stopped. He ought to go back to the surgery. He waited, and still she did not come down. So he went to the foot of the stairs and called:

'I shall have to go.'

Almost immediately he heard her coming down. She had on her best dress of black voile, and her hair was tidy, but still damp. She looked at him—and in spite of herself, smiled.

'I don't like you in those clothes,' she said. 180

'Do I look a sight?' he answered.

They were shy of one another.

'I'll make you some tea,' she said.

'No, I must go.'

'Must you?' And she looked at him again with the wide, strained, doubt- 185
ful eyes. And again, from the pain of his breast, he knew how he loved her. He went and bent to kiss her, gently, passionately, with his heart's painful kiss.

'And my hair smells so horrible,' she murmured in distraction. 'And I'm so awful, I'm so awful! Oh no, I'm too awful.' And she broke into bitter, heartbroken sobbing. 'You can't want to love me, I'm horrible.'

'Don't be silly, don't be silly,' he said, trying to comfort her, kissing her, holding her in his arms. 'I want you, I want to marry you, we're going to be married, quickly, quickly—to-morrow if I can.'

But she only sobbed terribly, and cried:

'I feel awful. I feel awful. I feel I'm horrible to you.'

'No, I want you, I want you,' was all he answered, blindly, with that terri- 190
ble intonation which frightened her almost more than her horror lest he should *not* want her.

D. H. LAWRENCE

(1885–1930) **Web** *www*

Son of a coal miner and a schoolteacher, D. H. Lawrence became a schoolteacher and finally a writer. Lawrence's fiction deploys the significant events and details about the physical environment as ways to work through the conflicts that beset modern humanity: humanity versus nature, humanity versus technology, man versus woman, soul versus matter. Always, Lawrence wrote against the constricting norms of conventional society.

www

TOPICS FOR CRITICAL THINKING Web

1. What kind of narrator does this story have, and what points of view does this narrator assume?
2. What clues are there that there will be a romantic relation between the Doctor and Mabel?
3. What observations about class and love does the story make?
4. What does the pond stand for?

www

TOPICS FOR CRITICAL WRITING Web

1. Trace the ways the story uses animal imagery. What do these animal motifs tell us about what is happening in the story?
2. What is the future of this couple? What clues does the story offer about the possibilities of relations between men and women?

JAMES JOYCE

Araby

(1904–1905)

North Richmond Street, being blind, was a quiet street except at the hour when the Christian Brothers' School set the boys free. An uninhabited house of two stories stood at the blind end, detached from its neighbours in a square ground. The other houses of the street, conscious of decent lives within them, gazed at one another with brown imperturbable faces.

The former tenant of our house, a priest, had died in the back drawing-room. Air, musty from having been long enclosed, hung in all the rooms, and the waste room behind the kitchen was littered with old useless papers. Among these I found a few paper-covered books, the pages of which were curled and damp: *The Abbot*, by Walter Scott, *The Devout Communicant*, and *The Memoirs of Vidocq*. I liked the last best because its leaves were yellow. The wild garden behind the house contained a central apple tree and a few straggling bushes under one of which I found the late tenant's rusty bicycle pump. He had been a very charitable priest; in his will he had left all his money to institutions and the furniture of his house to his sister.

When the short days of winter came dusk fell before we had well eaten our dinners. When we met in the street the houses had grown sombre. The space of sky above us was the colour of ever-changing violet and towards it the lamps of the street lifted their feeble lanterns. The cold air stung us and we played till our bodies glowed. Our shouts echoed in the silent street. The career of our play brought us through the dark muddy lanes behind the houses where we ran the gauntlet of the rough tribes from the cottages, to the back doors of the dark dripping gardens where odours arose from the ash-pits, to the dark odorous stables where a coachman smoothed and combed the horse or shook music from the buckled harness. When we returned to the street, light from the kitchen windows had filled the areas. If my uncle was seen turning the corner we hid in the shadow until we had seen him safely housed. Or if Mangan's sister came out on the doorstep to call her brother in to his tea we watched her from our shadow peer up and down the street. We waited to see whether she would remain or go in and, if she remained, we left our shadow and walked up to Mangan's steps resignedly. She was waiting for us, her figure defined by the light from the half-opened door. Her brother always teased her before he obeyed and I stood by the railings looking at her. Her dress swung as she moved her body and the soft rope of her hair tossed from side to side.

Every morning I lay on the floor in the front parlour watching her door. The blind was pulled down to within an inch of the sash so that I could not be seen. When she came out on the doorstep my heart leaped. I ran to the hall, seized my books and followed her. I kept her brown figure always in my eye and, when we came near the point at which our ways diverged, I quickened my pace and passed her. This happened morning after morning. I had never spoken to her, except for a few casual words, and yet her name was like a summons to all my foolish blood.

Her image accompanied me even in places the most hostile to romance. 5
On Saturday evenings when my aunt went marketing I had to go to carry some of the parcels. We walked through the flaring streets, jostled by drunken men and bargaining women, amid the curses of labourers, the shrill litanies of shop-boys who stood on guard by the barrels of pigs' cheeks, the nasal chanting of street-singers, who sang a *come-all-you* about O'Donovan Rossa, or a ballad about the troubles in our native land. These noises converged in a single sensation of life for me: I imagined that I bore my chalice safely through a throng of foes. Her name sprang to my lips at moments in strange prayers and praises which I myself did not understand. My eyes were often full of tears (I could not tell why) and at times a flood from my heart seemed to pour itself out into my bosom. I thought little of the future. I did not know whether I would ever speak to her or not or, if I spoke to her, how I could tell her of my confused adoration. But my body was like a harp and her words and gestures were like fingers running upon the wires.

One evening I went into the back drawing-room in which the priest had died. It was a dark rainy evening and there was no sound in the house. Through one of the broken panes I heard the rain impinge upon the earth, the fine incessant needles of water playing in the sodden beds. Some distant lamp or lighted window gleamed below me. I was thankful that I could see so little. All my senses seemed to desire to veil themselves and, feeling that I was about to slip from them, I pressed the palms of my hands together until they trembled, murmuring: *"O love! O love!"* many times.

At last she spoke to me. When she addressed the first words to me I was so confused that I did not know what to answer. She asked me was I going to

Araby. I forgot whether I answered yes or no. It would be a splendid bazaar, she said she would love to go.

"And why can't you?" I asked.

While she spoke she turned a silver bracelet round and round her wrist. She could not go, she said, because there would be a retreat that week in her convent. Her brother and two other boys were fighting for their caps and I was alone at the railings. She held one of the spikes, bowing her head towards me. The light from the lamp opposite our door caught the white curve of her neck, lit up her hair that rested there and, falling, lit up the hand upon the railing. It fell over one side of her dress and caught the white border of a petticoat, just visible as she stood at ease.

"It's well for you," she said. 10

"If I go," I said, "I will bring you something."

What innumerable follies laid waste my waking and sleeping thoughts after the evening! I wished to annihilate the tedious intervening days. I chafed against the work of school. At night in my bedroom and by day in the classroom her image came between me and the page I strove to read. The syllables of the word *Araby* were called to me through the silence in which my soul luxuriated and cast an Eastern enchantment over me. I asked for leave to go to the bazaar on Saturday night. My aunt was surprised and hoped it was not some Freemason affair. I answered few questions in class. I watched my master's face pass from amiability to sternness; he hoped I was not beginning to idle, I could not call my wandering thoughts together. I had hardly any patience with the serious work of life which, now that it stood between me and my desire, seemed to me child's play, ugly monotonous child's play.

On Saturday morning I reminded my uncle that I wished to go to the bazaar in the evening. He was fussing at the hall-stand, looking for the hat brush, and answered me curtly:

"Yes, boy, I know."

As he was in the hall I could not go into the front parlour and lie at the 15
window. I left the house in bad humour and walked slowly towards the school. The air was pitilessly raw and already my heart misgave me.

When I came home to dinner my uncle had not yet been home. Still it was early. I sat staring at the clock for some time and, when its ticking began to irritate me, I left the room. I mounted the staircase and gained the upper part of the house. The high cold empty gloomy rooms liberated me and I went from room to room singing. From the front window I saw my companions playing below in the street. Their cries reached me weakened and indistinct and, leaning my forehead against the cool glass, I looked over at the dark house where she lived. I may have stood there for an hour, seeing nothing but the brown-clad figure cast by my imagination, touched discreetly by the lamplight at the curved neck, at the hand upon the railings and at the border below the dress.

When I came downstairs again I found Mrs. Mercer sitting at the fire. She was an old garrulous woman, a pawnbroker's widow, who collected used stamps for some pious purpose. I had to endure the gossip of the tea-table. The meal was prolonged beyond an hour and still my uncle did not come. Mrs. Mercer stood up to go: she was sorry she couldn't wait any longer, but it was after eight o'clock and she did not like to be out late, as the night air was bad for her. When she had gone I began to walk up and down the room, clenching my fists. My aunt said:

"I'm afraid you may put off your bazaar for this night of Our Lord."

At nine o'clock I heard my uncle's latchkey in the hall-door. I heard him talking to himself and heard the hall-stand rocking when it had received the weight of his overcoat. I could interpret these signs. When he was midway through his dinner I asked him to give me the money to go to the bazaar. He had forgotten.

"The people are in bed and after their first sleep now," he said. 20

I did not smile. My aunt said to him energetically:

"Can't you give him the money and let him go? You've kept him late enough as it is."

My uncle said he was very sorry he had forgotten. He said he believed in the old saying: "All work and no play makes Jack a dull boy." He asked me where I was going and, when I had told him a second time, he asked me did I know *The Arab's Farewell to his Steed.* When I left the kitchen he was about to recite the opening lines of the piece to my aunt.

I held a florin tightly in my hand as I strode down Buckingham Street towards the station. The sight of the streets thronged with buyers and glaring with gas recalled to me the purpose of my journey. I took my seat in a third-class carriage of a deserted train. After an intolerable delay the train moved out of the station slowly. It crept onward among ruinous houses and over the twinkling river. At Westland Row Station a crowd of people pressed to the carriage doors; but the porters moved them back, saying that it was a special train for the bazaar. I remained alone in the bare carriage. In a few minutes the train drew up beside an improvised wooden platform. I passed out on the road and saw by the lighted dial of a clock that it was ten minutes to ten. In front of me was a large building which displayed the magical name.

I could not find any sixpenny entrance and, fearing that the bazaar would 25
be closed, I passed in quickly through a turnstile, handing a shilling to a weary-looking man. I found myself in a big hall girdled at half its height by a gallery. Nearly all the stalls were closed and the greater part of the hall was in darkness. I recognized a silence like that which pervades a church after a service. I walked into the center of the bazaar timidly. A few people were gathered about the stalls which were still open. Before a curtain, over which the words *Café Chantant* were written in coloured lamps, two men were counting money on a salver. I listened to the fall of the coins.

Remembering with difficulty why I had come I went over to one of the stalls and examined porcelain vases and flowered tea-sets. At the door of the stall a young lady was talking and laughing with two young gentlemen. I remarked their English accents and listened vaguely to their conversation.

"O, I never said such a thing!"

"O, but you did!"

"O, but I didn't!"

"Didn't she say that?" 30

"Yes. I heard her."

"O, there's a . . . fib!"

Observing me, the young lady came over and asked me did I wish to buy anything. The tone of her voice was not encouraging; she seemed to have spoken to me out of a sense of duty. I looked humbly at the great jars that stood like eastern guards at either side of the dark entrance to the stall and murmured:

"No, thank you."

The young lady changed the position of one of the vases and went back 35
to the two young men. They began to talk of the same subject. Once or twice the young lady glanced at me over her shoulder.

I lingered before her stall, though I knew my stay was useless, to make my interest in her wares seem the more real. Then I turned away slowly and walked down the middle of the bazaar. I allowed the two pennies to fall against the sixpence in my pocket. I heard a voice call from one end of the gallery that the light was out. The upper part of the hall was now completely dark.

Gazing up into the darkness I saw myself as a creature driven and derided by vanity; and my eyes burned with anguish and anger.

James Joyce

www *(1882–1941)* **Web**

Born in Dublin to a middle-class Catholic family, Joyce moved to Europe as a young man, living in Paris, Italy, and Switzerland. From his more distanced vantage point on the continent, Joyce wrote about Irish characters. His novels and short stories are multilayered, presenting the lively detail of a Dublin existence in concert with the psychological experience of insight and awareness.

www *TOPICS FOR CRITICAL THINKING* **Web**

1. Trace the text's use of light and dark imagery.
2. What various things might "Araby" represent?
3. Why did the narrator's eyes burn "with anguish and anger" at the end?

www *TOPICS FOR CRITICAL WRITING* **Web**

1. On one level, "Araby" is about a young man's insight. What else might this story be about?
2. From what vantage does the narrator see himself? What does the narration tell us about the narrator who sees himself as he was as a child?

Symbols

Images that refer to the same set of ideas are **symbols.** Culturally, we understand images such as the clock face, the flag, a stop sign, a crucifix, the mountain peak, or even a lighthouse, which has come to stand as a beacon of hope and salvation, as symbols. Prose fiction can employ these standard cultural symbols or it can establish its own by always linking a particular image to a particular idea or set of ideas. In Virginia Woolf's short story "The Symbol," consider the ways in which the image of the mountain becomes a symbol.

Featured Writer

VIRGINIA WOOLF

The Symbol *(1941)*

There was a little dent on the top of the mountain like a crater on the moon. It was filled with snow, iridescent like a pigeon's breast, or dead white. There was a scurry of dry particles now and again, covering nothing. It was too high for breathing flesh or fur covered life. All the same the snow was iridescent one moment; and blood red; and pure white, according to the day.

The graves in the valley—for there was a vast descent on either side; first pure rock; snow silted; lower a pine tree gripped a crag; then a solitary hut; then a saucer of pure green; then a cluster of eggshell roofs; at last, at the bottom, a village, an hotel, a cinema, and a graveyard—the graves in the churchyard near the hotel recorded the names of several men who had fallen climbing.

'The mountain,' the lady wrote, sitting on the balcony of the hotel, 'is a symbol . . .' She paused. She could see the topmost height through her glasses. She focussed the lens, as if to see what the symbol was. She was writing to her elder sister at Birmingham.

The balcony overlooked the main street of the Alpine summer resort, like a box at a theatre. There were very few private sitting rooms, and so the plays—such as they were—the curtain raisers—were acted in public. They were always a little provisional; preludes, curtain raisers. Entertainments to pass the time; seldom leading to any conclusion, such as marriage; or even lasting friendship. There was something fantastic about them, airy, inconclusive. So little that was solid could be dragged to this height. Even the houses looked gimcrack. By the time the voice of the English Announcer had reached the village it too became unreal.

Lowering her glasses, she nodded at the young men who in the street be- 5
low were making ready to start. With one of them she had a certain connection—that is, an Aunt of his had been Mistress of her daughter's school.

Still holding the pen, still tipped with a drop of ink, she waved down at the climbers. She had written the mountain was a symbol. But of what? In the forties of the last century two men, in the sixties four men had perished; the first party when a rope broke; the second when night fell and froze them to death. We are always climbing to some height; that was the cliché. But it did not represent what was in her mind's eye; after seeing through her glasses the virgin height.

She continued, inconsequently. 'I wonder why it makes me think of the Isle of Wight? You remember when Mama was dying, we took her there. And

I would stand on the balcony, when the boat came in and describe the passengers. I would say, I think that must be Mr Edwardes . . . He has just come off the gangway. Then, now all the passengers have landed. Now they have turned the boat . . . I never told you, naturally not—you were in India; you were going to have Lucy—how I longed when the doctor came, that he should say, quite definitely, She cannot live another week. It was very prolonged; she lived eighteen months. The mountain just now reminded me how when I was alone, I would fix my eyes upon her death, as a symbol. I would think if I could reach that point—when I should be free—we could not marry as you remember until she died—A cloud then would do instead of the mountain. I thought, when I reach that point—I have never told anyone; for it seemed so heartless; I shall be at the top. And I could imagine so many sides. We come of course of an Anglo Indian family. I can still imagine, from hearing stories told, how people live in other parts of the world. I can see mud huts; and savages; I can see elephants drinking at pools. So many of our uncles and cousins were explorers. I have always had a great desire to explore for myself. But of course, when the time came it seemed more sensible, considering our long engagement, to marry.'

She looked across the street at a woman shaking a mat on another balcony. Every morning at the same time she came out. You could have thrown a pebble into her balcony. They had indeed come to the point of smiling at each other across the street.

'The little villas,' she added, taking up her pen, 'are much the same here as in Birmingham. Every house takes in lodgers. The hotel is quite full. Though monotonous, the food is not what you would call bad. And of course the hotel has a splendid view. One can see the mountain from every window. But then that's true of the whole place. I can assure you, I could shriek sometimes coming out of the one shop where they sell papers—we get them a week late—always to see that mountain. Sometimes it looks just across the way. At others, like a cloud; only it never moves. Somehow the talk, even among the invalids, who are every where, is always about the mountain. Either, how clear it is today, it might be across the street; or, how far away it looks; it might be a cloud. That is the usual cliché. In the storm last night, I hoped for once it was hidden. But just as they brought in the anchovies, The Rev. W. Bishop said, "Look there's the mountain!"

Am I being selfish? Ought I not to be ashamed of myself, when there is so much suffering? It is not confined to the visitors. The natives suffer dreadfully from goitre. Of course it could be stopped, if any one had enterprise, and money. Ought one not to be ashamed of dwelling upon what after all can't be cured? It would need an earthquake to destroy that mountain, just as, I suppose, it was made by an earthquake. I asked the Proprietor, Herr Melchior, the other day, if there were ever earthquakes now? No, he said, only landslides and avalanches. They have been known he said to blot out a whole village. But he added quickly, there's no danger here.

As I write these words, I can see the young men quite plainly on the slopes of the mountain. They are roped together. One I think I told you was at the same school with Margaret. They are now crossing a crevasse. . . .'

The pen fell from her hand, and the drop of ink straggled in a zig zag line down the page. The young men had disappeared.

It was only late that night when the search party had recovered the bodies that she found the unfinished letter on the table on the balcony. She dipped her pen once more; and added, 'The old clichés will come in very handy. They died trying to climb the mountain . . . And the peasants brought spring flowers to lay upon their graves. They died in an attempt to discover . . .'

There seemed no fitting conclusion. And she added, 'Love to the children,' and then her pet name.

In her short story "The Symbol," Virginia Woolf depicts how a letter-writing vacationer takes a particular mountain in the Swiss landscape as a symbol. In the course of the woman's day, the mountain changes appearance and prominence. The woman's search for the meaning of the mountain leads her to a series of associations and observations about her mother's dying (which the mountain reminds her of), life in the Alpine village where she is staying, her wish to have been an explorer, and her desire that the mountain might disappear. During these ruminations, the woman sees the mountain, oppressive and mysterious in its changing appearances, as a symbol of dying and of freedom. At the end of the day (and the story), the mountain claims the lives of more climbers. The mountain retains its complex but stable symbolic significance.

Woolf's story illustrates the difference between image and symbol. Images include the letter-writer's different accounts of the mountain's appearances as well as her descriptions of the Alpine village, and her imagined portraits of India. Symbols include the mountain itself. Its persistent presence, like the graves below, consistently reminds the letter-writer of death. Images are impressions that evoke the senses and that might refer to a number of different phenomena in any given story. Symbols are objects which, throughout a story, always refer to the same complex meaning. In *Heart of Darkness* for example, imagery includes descriptions of the jungle, but the jungle itself is a complex symbol of ignorance, greed, the resilience of nature, and the forbidden. Symbols are, in fact, like mountains in that they tend to be broodingly present throughout a story. They often connote (suggest) a meaning that is associated with them in the culture at large, as Woolf's protagonist demonstrates in her struggle with the mountain's significance.

VIRGINIA WOOLF

(1882–1941) **Web** *www*

Co-owner of the Hogarth Press in the Bloomsbury section of London, Woolf wrote novels that helped define modernism with their prose that shifts rapidly and fluidly among present events and memory and one person's thoughts and another's, and that weaves imagery and rhythm to produce a sense of the richness of moments of being. The daughter of Sir Leslie Stephen, a noted British intellectual, Woolf and her husband Leonard became the center of the Bloomsbury Group, a group of artists, writers, and thinkers who helped www formulate concepts of literary modernism **Web** (see Bell painting in first color insert). From 1913 until 1941, Woolf was busy as a writer, critic, and publisher, publishing seven novels as well as stories and extended essays such as *A Room of One's Own* (1929) and *Three Guineas* (1938). Dreading another World War and worried about her tendency towards nervous breakdowns, Woolf committed suicide in March 1941.

www

Kew Gardens **Web** *(1917–1921)*

From the oval-shaped flower-bed there rose perhaps a hundred stalks spreading into heart-shaped or tongue-shaped leaves half way up and unfurling at the tip red or blue or yellow petals marked with spots of colour raised upon the surface; and from the red, blue or yellow gloom of the throat emerged a straight bar, rough with gold dust and slightly clubbed at the end. The petals were voluminous enough to be stirred by the summer breeze, and when they moved, the red, blue and yellow lights passed one over the other, staining an inch of the brown earth beneath with a spot of the most intricate colour. The light fell either upon the smooth grey back of a pebble, or the shell of a snail with its brown circular veins, or, falling into a raindrop, it expanded with such intensity of red, blue and yellow the thin walls of water that one expected them to burst and disappear. Instead, the drop was left in a second silver grey once more, and the light now settled upon the flesh of a leaf, revealing the branching thread of fibre beneath the surface, and again it moved on and spread its illumination in the vast green spaces beneath the dome of the heart-shaped and tongue-shaped leaves. Then the breeze stirred rather more briskly overhead and the colour was flashed into the air above, into the eyes of the men and women who walk in Kew Gardens in July.

The figures of these men and women straggled past the flower-bed with a curiously irregular movement not unlike that of the white and blue butterflies who crossed the turf in zig-zag flights from bed to bed. The man was about six inches in front of the woman, strolling carelessly, while she bore on with greater purpose, only turning her head now and then to see that the children were not too far behind. The man kept this distance in front of the woman purposely, though perhaps unconsciously, for he wanted to go on with his thoughts.

"Fifteen years ago I came here with Lily," he thought. "We sat somewhere over there by a lake, and I begged her to marry me all through the hot afternoon. How the dragon-fly kept circling round us: how clearly I see the dragon-fly and her shoe with the square silver buckle at the toe. All the time I spoke I saw her shoe and when it moved impatiently I knew without looking up what she was going to say: the whole of her seemed to be in her shoe. And my love, my desire, were in the dragon-fly; for some reason I thought that if it settled there, on that leaf, the broad one with the red flower in the middle of it, if the dragon-fly settled on the leaf she would say 'Yes' at once. But the dragon-fly went round and round: it never settled anywhere—of course not, happily not, or I shouldn't be walking here with Eleanor and the children—Tell me, Eleanor, d'you ever think of the past?"

"Why do you ask, Simon?"

"Because I've been thinking of the past. I've been thinking of Lily, the 5 woman I might have married . . . Well, why are you silent? Do you mind my thinking of the past?"

"Why should I mind, Simon? Doesn't one always think of the past, in a garden with men and women lying under the trees? Aren't they one's past, all that remains of it, those men and women, those ghosts lying under the trees, . . . one's happiness, one's reality?"

"For me, a square silver shoe-buckle and a dragon-fly—"

"For me, a kiss. Imagine six little girls sitting before their easels twenty years ago, down by the side of a lake, painting the water-lilies, the first red water-lilies I'd ever seen. And suddenly a kiss, there on the back of my neck. And my hand shook all the afternoon so that I couldn't paint. I took out my watch and marked the hour when I would allow myself to think of the kiss for five minutes only—it was so precious—the kiss of an old grey-haired woman with a wart on her nose, the mother of all my kisses all my life. Come Caroline, come Hubert."

They walked on past the flower-bed, now walking four abreast, and soon diminished in size among the trees and looked half transparent as the sunlight and shade swam over their backs in large trembling irregular patches.

10 In the oval flower-bed the snail, whose shell had been stained red, blue and yellow for the space of two minutes or so, now appeared to be moving very slightly in its shell, and next began to labour over the crumbs of loose earth which broke away and rolled down as it passed over them. It appeared to have a definite goal in front of it, differing in this respect from the singular high-stepping angular green insect who attempted to cross in front of it, and waited for a second with its antennae trembling as if in deliberation, and then stepped off as rapidly and strangely in the opposite direction. Brown cliffs with deep green lakes in the hollows, flat blade-like trees that waved from root to tip, round boulders of grey stone, vast crumpled surfaces of a thin crackling texture—all these objects lay across the snail's progress between one stalk and another to his goal. Before he decided whether to circumvent the arched tent of a dead leaf or to breast it there came past the bed the feet of other human beings.

This time they were both men. The younger of the two wore an expression of perhaps unnatural calm; he raised his eyes and fixed them very steadily in front of him while his companion spoke, and directly his companion had done speaking he looked on the ground again and sometimes opened his lips only after a long pause and sometimes did not open them at all. The elder man had a curiously uneven and shaky method of walking, jerking his hand forward and throwing up his head abruptly, rather in the manner of an impatient carriage horse tired of waiting outside a house; but in the man these gestures were irresolute and pointless. He talked almost incessantly; he smiled to himself and again began to talk, as if the smile had been an answer. He was talking about spirits—the spirits of the dead, who, according to him, were even now telling him all sorts of odd things about their experiences in Heaven.

"Heaven was known to the ancients as Thessaly, William, and now, with this war, the spirit matter is rolling between the hills like thunder." He paused, seemed to listen, smiled, jerked his head and continued:—

"You have a small electric battery and a piece of rubber to insulate the wire—isolate?—insulate?—well, we'll skip the details, no good going into details that wouldn't be understood—and in short the little machine stands in any convenient position by the head of the bed, we will say, on a neat mahogany stand. All arrangements being properly fixed by workmen under my direction, the widow applies her ear and summons the spirit by sign as agreed. Women! Widows! Women in black—"

Here he seemed to have caught sight of a woman's dress in the distance, which in the shade looked a purple black. He took off his hat, placed his hand upon his heart, and hurried towards her muttering and gesticulating feverishly. But William caught him by the sleeve and touched a flower with the tip of his walking-stick in order to divert the old man's attention. After looking at it for a moment in some confusion the old man bent his ear to it and seemed to answer a voice speaking from it, for he began talking about the forests of Uruguay which he had visited hundreds of years ago in company with the most beautiful young woman in Europe. He could be heard murmuring about forests of Uruguay blanketed with the wax petals of tropical roses, nightingales, sea beaches, mermaids and women drowned at sea, as he suffered himself to be moved on by William, upon whose face the look of stoical patience grew slowly deeper and deeper.

Following his steps so closely as to be slightly puzzled by his gestures 15
came two elderly women of the lower middle class, one stout and ponderous, the other rosy-cheeked and nimble. Like most people of their station they were frankly fascinated by any signs of eccentricity betokening a disordered brain, especially in the well-to-do; but they were too far off to be certain whether the gestures were merely eccentric or genuinely mad. After they had scrutinised the old man's back in silence for a moment and given each other a queer, sly look, they went on energetically piecing together their very complicated dialogue:

"Nell, Bert, Lot, Cess, Phil, Pa, he says, I says, she says, I says, I says, I says—"

"My Bert, Sis, Bill, Grandad, the old man, sugar,
Sugar, flour, kippers, greens
Sugar, sugar, sugar."

The ponderous woman looked through the pattern of falling words at the flowers standing cool, firm and upright in the earth, with a curious expression. She saw them as a sleeper waking from a heavy sleep sees a brass candlestick reflecting the light in an unfamiliar way, and closes his eyes and opens them, and seeing the brass candlestick again, finally starts broad awake and stares at the candlestick with all his powers. So the heavy woman came to a standstill opposite the oval-shaped flower-bed, and ceased even to pretend to listen to what the other woman was saying. She stood there letting the words fall over her, swaying the top part of her body slowly backwards and forwards, looking at the flowers. Then she suggested that they should find a seat and have their tea.

The snail had now considered every possible method of reaching his goal without going round the dead leaf or climbing over it. Let alone the effort needed for climbing a leaf, he was doubtful whether the thin texture which vibrated with such an alarming crackle when touched even by the tip of his horns would bear his weight; and this determined him finally to creep beneath it, for there was a point where the leaf curved high enough from the ground to admit him. He had just inserted his head in the opening and was taking stock of the high brown roof and was getting used to the cool brown light when two other people came past outside on the turf. This time they were both young, a young man and a young woman. They were both in the prime of youth, or even in that season which precedes the prime of youth, the season before the smooth pink folds of the flower have burst their gummy case, when the wings of the butterfly, though fully grown, are motionless in the sun.

"Lucky it isn't Friday," he observed.

"Why? D'you believe in luck?"

"They make you pay sixpence on Friday." 20

"What's sixpence anyway? Isn't it worth sixpence?"

"What's 'it'—what do you mean by 'it'?"

"O anything—I mean—you know what I mean."

Long pauses came between each of these remarks: they were uttered in toneless and monotonous voices. The couple stood still on the edge of the flower-bed, and together pressed the end of her parasol deep down into the soft earth. The action and the fact that this hand rested on the top of hers expressed their feelings in a strange way, as these short insignificant words also expressed something, words with short wings for their heavy body of meaning, inadequate to carry them far and thus alighting awkwardly upon the very common objects that surrounded them and were to their inexperienced touch so massive: but who knows (so they thought as they pressed the parasol into the earth) what precipices aren't concealed in them, or what slopes of ice don't shine in the sun on the other side? Who knows? Who has ever seen this before? Even when she wondered what sort of tea they gave you at Kew, he felt that something loomed up behind her words, and stood vast and solid behind them; and the mist very slowly rose and uncovered—O Heavens,—what were those shapes?—little white tables, and waitresses who looked first at her and then at him; and there was a bill that he would pay with a real two shilling piece, and it was real, all real, he assured himself, fingering the coin in his pocket, real to everyone except to him and to her; even to him it began to seem real and then—but it was too exciting to stand and think any longer, and he pulled the parasol out of the earth with a jerk and was impatient to find the place where one had tea with other people, like other people.

"Come along, Trissie; it's time we had our tea." 25

"Wherever *does* one have one's tea?" she asked with the oddest thrill of excitement in her voice, looking vaguely round and letting herself be drawn on down the grass path, trailing her parasol, turning her head this way and that way, forgetting her tea, wishing to go down there and then down there, remembering orchids and cranes among wild flowers, a Chinese pagoda and a crimson-crested bird; but he bore her on.

Thus one couple after another with much the same irregular and aimless movement passed the flower-bed and were enveloped in layer after layer of green-blue vapour, in which at first their bodies had substance and a dash of colour, but later both substance and colour dissolved in the green-blue atmosphere. How hot it was! So hot that even the thrush chose to hop, like a mechanical bird, in the shadow of the flowers, with long pauses between one movement and the next; instead of rambling vaguely the white butterflies danced once above another, making with their white shifting flakes the outline of a shattered marble column above the tallest flowers; the glass roofs of the palm house shone as if a whole market full of shiny green umbrellas had opened in the sun; and in the drone of the aeroplane the voice of the summer sky murmured its fierce soul. Yellow and black, pink and snow white, shapes of all these colours, men, women and children, were spotted for a second upon the horizon, and then, seeing the breadth of yellow that lay upon the grass, they wavered and sought shade beneath the trees, dissolving like drops of water in the yellow and green atmosphere, staining it faintly with red and blue. It seemed as if all gross and heavy bodies had sunk down in the heat motionless and lay huddled upon the ground, but their voices went wavering from them as if they were flames lolling from the thick waxen bodies of candles. Voices, yes, voices, wordless voices, breaking the silence suddenly with such depth of contentment, such passion of desire, or, in the voices of children, such freshness of surprise; breaking the silence? But there was no silence; all the time the motor omnibuses were turning their wheels and changing their gear; like a vast nest of Chinese boxes all of wrought steel turning ceaselessly one within another the city murmured; on the top of which the voices cried aloud and the petals of myriads of flowers flashed their colours into the air.

www *TOPICS FOR CRITICAL THINKING* **Web**

1. In what ways does the story convey the sense of simultaneous action?
2. How does that simultaneity relate to the story's views of different stages in life?
3. How does the past relate to the present in this story?
4. What does the story illustrate about the connectedness (or lack) among human beings?

www *TOPICS FOR CRITICAL WRITING* **Web**

1. How does the image of the Chinese box describe the story itself?
2. In what ways is this story like a painting?

The Introduction

(1922–1925)

Lily Everit saw Mrs Dalloway bearing down on her from the other side of the room, and could have prayed her not to come and disturb her; and yet, as Mrs Dalloway approached with her right hand raised and a smile which Lily knew (though this was her first party) meant: 'But you've got to come out of your corner and talk,' a smile at once benevolent and drastic, commanding, she felt the strangest mixture of excitement and fear, of desire to be left alone and of longing to be taken out and thrown down, down into the boiling depths. But

Mrs Dalloway was intercepted; caught by an old gentleman with white moustaches, and thus Lily Everit had two minutes respite in which to hug to herself, like a spar in the sea, to sip, like a glass of wine, the thought of her essay upon the character of Dean Swift which Professor Miller had marked that morning with three red stars; First rate. First rate; she repeated that to herself, but the cordial was ever so much weaker now than it had been when she stood before the long glass being finished off (a pat here, a dab there) by her sister and Mildred, the housemaid. For as their hands moved about her, she felt that they were fidgeting agreeably on the surface but beneath lay untouched like a lump of glowing metal her essay on the character of Dean Swift, and all their praises when she came downstairs and stood in the hall waiting for a cab—Rupert had come out of his room and said what a swell she looked—ruffled the surface, went like a breeze among ribbons, but no more. One divided life (she felt sure of it) into fact, this essay, and into fiction, this going out, into rock and into wave, she thought, driving along and seeing things with such intensity that for ever she would see the truth and herself, a white reflection in the driver's dark back inextricably mixed: the moment of vision. Then as she came into the house, at the very first sight of people moving up stairs, down stairs, this hard lump (her essay on the character of Swift) wobbled, began melting, she could not keep hold of it, and all her being (no longer sharp as a diamond cleaving the heart of life asunder) turned to a mist of alarm, apprehension, and defence as she stood at bay in her corner. This was the famous place: the world.

Looking out, Lily Everit instinctively hid that essay of hers, so ashamed was she now, so bewildered too, and on tiptoe nevertheless to adjust her focus and get into right proportions (the old having been shamefully wrong) these diminishing and expanding things (what could one call them? people—impressions of people's lives?) which seemed to menace her and mount over her, to turn everything to water, leaving her only—for that she would not resign—the power to stand at bay.

Now Mrs Dalloway, who had never quite dropped her arm, had shown by the way she moved it while she stood talking that she remembered, was only interrupted by the old soldier with the white moustaches, raised it again definitely and came straight down on her, and said to the shy charming girl, with her pale skin, her bright eyes, the dark hair which clustered poetically round her head and the thin body in a dress which seemed slipping off,

'Come and let me introduce you,' and there Mrs Dalloway hesitated, and then remembering that Lily was the clever one, who read poetry, looked about for some young man, some young man just down from Oxford, who would have read everything and could talk about Shelley. And holding Lily Everit's hand [she] led her towards a group where there were young people talking, and Bob Brinsley.

Lily Everit hung back a little, might have been the wayward sailing boat 5
curtseying in the wake of a steamer, and felt as Mrs Dalloway led her on, that it was now going to happen; that nothing could prevent it now; or save her (and she only wanted it to be over now) from being flung into a whirlpool where either she would perish or be saved. But what was the whirlpool?

Oh it was made of a million things and each was distinct to her;

Westminster Abbey; the sense of enormously high solemn buildings surrounding them; being a woman. Perhaps that was the thing that came out, that remained, it was partly the dress, but all the little chivalries and respects of the drawing-room—all made her feel that she had come out of her chrysalis and was being proclaimed what in the comfortable darkness of childhood she had never been—this frail and beautiful creature, before whom men bowed, this limited and circumscribed creature who could not do what she liked, this butterfly with a thousand facets to its eyes and delicate fine plumage, and difficulties and sensibilities and sadnesses innumerable; a woman.

As she walked with Mrs Dalloway across the room she accepted the part which was now laid on her and, naturally, overdid it a little as a soldier, proud of the traditions of an old and famous uniform might overdo it, feeling conscious as she walked, of her finery; of her tight shoes; of her coiled and twisted hair; and how if she dropped a handkerchief (this had happened) a man would stoop precipitately and give it her; thus accentuating the delicacy, the artificiality of her bearing unnaturally, for they were not hers after all.

Hers it was, rather, to run and hurry and ponder on long solitary walks, climbing gates, stepping through the mud, and through the blur, the dream, the ecstasy of loneliness, to see the plover's wheel and surprise the rabbits, and come in the hearts of woods or wide lonely moors upon little ceremonies which had no audience, private rites, pure beauty offered by beetles and lilies of the valley and dead leaves and still pools, without any care whatever what human beings thought of them, which filled her mind with rapture and wonder and held her there till she must touch the gate post to recollect herself—all this was, until tonight her ordinary being, by which she knew and liked herself and crept into the heart of mother and father and brothers and sisters; and this other was a flower which had opened in ten minutes. As the flower opened so too [came], incontrovertibly, the flower's world, so different, so strange; the towers of Westminster; the high and formal buildings; talk; this civilisation, she felt, hanging back, as Mrs Dalloway led her on, this regulated way of life, which fell like a yoke about her neck, softly, indomitably, from the skies, a statement which there was no gainsaying. Glancing at her essay, the three red stars dulled to obscurity, but peacefully, pensively, as if yielding to the pressure of unquestionable might, that is the conviction that it was not hers to dominate, or to assert; rather to air and embellish this orderly life where all was done already; high towers, solemn bells, flats built every brick of them by men's toil, churches built by men's toil, parliaments too; and even the criss-cross of telegraph wires she thought looking at the window as she walked. What had she to oppose to this massive masculine achievement? An essay on the character of Dean Swift! And as she came up to the group, which Bob Brinsley dominated, (with his heel on the fender, and his head back), with his great honest forehead, and his self-assurance, and his delicacy, and honour and robust physical well being, and sunburn, and airiness and direct descent from Shakespeare, what could she do but lay her essay, oh and the whole of her being, on the floor as a cloak for him to trample on, as a rose for him to rifle. Which she did, emphatically, when Mrs Dalloway said, still holding her hand as if she would run away from this supreme trial, this introduction, 'Mr

Brinsley—Miss Everit. Both of you love Shelley.' But hers was not love compared with his.

Saying this, Mrs Dalloway felt, as she always felt remembering her youth, absurdly moved; youth meeting youth at her hands, and there flashing, as at the concussion of steel upon flint (both stiffened to her feeling perceptibly) the loveliest and most ancient of all fires as she saw in Bob Brinsley's change of expression from carelessness to conformity, to formality, as he shook hands, which foreboded Clarissa thought, the tenderness, the goodness, the carefulness of women latent in all men, to her a sight to bring tears to the eyes, as it moved her even more intimately, to see in Lily herself the shy look, the startled look, surely the loveliest of all looks on a girl's face; and man feeling this for woman, and woman that for man, and there flowing from that contact all those homes, trials, sorrows, profound joy and ultimate staunchness in the face of catastrophe, humanity was sweet at its heart, thought Clarissa, and her own life (to introduce a couple made her think of meeting Richard for the first time!) infinitely blessed. And on she went.

But, thought Lily Everit. But—but—but what?

Oh nothing, she thought hastily smothering down softly her sharp instinct. Yes, she said. She did like reading.

'And I suppose you write?' he said, 'poems presumably?'

'Essays,' she said. And she would not let this horror get possession of her. Churches and parliaments, flats, even the telegraph wires—all, she told herself, made by men's toil, and this young man, she told herself, is in direct descent from Shakespeare, so she would not let this terror, this suspicion of something different, get hold of her and shrivel up her wings and drive her out into loneliness. But as she said this, she saw him—how else could she describe it—kill a fly. He tore the wings off a fly, standing with his foot on the fender his head thrown back, talking insolently about himself, arrogantly, but she didn't mind how insolent and arrogant he was to her, if only he had not been brutal to flies.

But she said, fidgeting as she smothered down that idea, why not, since he is the greatest of all worldly objects? And to worship, to adorn, to embellish was her task, and to be worshipped, her wings were for that. But he talked; but he looked; but he laughed; he tore the wings off a fly. He pulled the wings off its back with his clever strong hands, and she saw him do it; and she could not hide the knowledge from herself. But it is necessary that it should be so, she argued, thinking of the churches, of the parliaments and the blocks of flats, and so tried to crouch and cower and fold the wings down flat on her back. But—but, what was it why was it? In spite of all she could do her essay upon the character of Swift became more and more obtrusive and the three stars burnt quite bright again, only no longer clear and brilliant, but troubled and bloodstained as if this man, this great Mr Brinsley, had just by pulling the wings off a fly as he talked (about his essay, about himself and once laughing, about a girl there) charged her light being with cloud, and confused her for ever and ever and shrivelled her wings on her back, and, as he turned away from her, he made her think of the towers of civilisation with horror, and the yoke that had fallen from the skies onto her neck crushed her, and she felt like a naked wretch who having sought shelter in some shady garden is turned out and told—no, that there are no sanctuaries, or butterflies, in this world, and this civilisation, churches, parliaments and flats—this civilisation, said Lily Everit to herself, as she accepted the kind compliments of old Mrs Bromley on her appearance[, depends upon me,] and Mrs Bromley said later that like all the Everits Lily looked 'as if she had the weight of the world upon her shoulders'.

www

TOPICS FOR CRITICAL THINKING **Web**

1. What does Lily come to understand about gender?
2. For what purposes does the story shift points of view?
3. What does Lily understand through her evocation of Mr. Brinsley tearing the wings off of flies?
4. How does this short scene embody the complex issues of a girl becoming a woman?

www

TOPICS FOR CRITICAL WRITING **Web**

1. To what does the story's title refer?
2. How does this story use the contrast between images of the city and the country?

10 Language and Style

Prose fiction is made up of words. The ways these words are arranged is called **style**. Web The study of style is called **stylistics** Web. Style involves many choices on the part of the writer about the language of the piece—diction, sentence length, the rhythm of the words, a predominance of action or imagery, and the repetition of words or phrases. **Diction** refers to the choice of words. If, for example, a writer chooses to use the word *prevaricate* instead of *lie*, the writer is selecting a word that connotes a level of sophistication and seriousness that is not implied by the use of the plainer term *lie*. Or a writer might use the word *luscious* instead of *delicious*. Though the words mean the same thing, they have different **connotations**. In prose fiction, diction is used as a way to set tone (see Chapter 11); to aid characterization (see Chapter 3); to convey social class, age, gender, and race; and to help constitute the rhythm, sound, and patterns of language (or *motifs*) that constitute the art of the prose. *www*

Georgia O'Keeffe, *Black Abstraction* (1927)

Style also involves how sentence grammar is used. Sentences may be long and complex (as they are in the writings of Nathaniel Hawthorne, Virginia Woolf, James Joyce, and D. H. Lawrence) or shorter and simpler (as in the work of Jack London, Mark Twain, Tillie Olsen, Alice Walker, Ernest Hemingway, and Gertrude Stein). Compare, for example, these two sentences. The first is from Joyce's "Araby," and the second is from Hemingway's "Hills Like White Elephants."

> I may have stood there for an hour, seeing nothing but a brown-clad figure cast by my imagination, touched discreetly by the lamplight at the curved neck, at the hand upon the railings and at the border below the dress.

> The Hills across the valley of the Ebro were long and white.

Sentence length and complexity might vary in relation to the actions described as in Kate Chopin's, James Baldwin's, or Joyce's stories, or as a way of establishing mood or atmosphere, as in Edgar Allan Poe's stories. For example, the impact of the news of Mr. Mallard's death in Chopin's "The Story of an Hour" tends to produce a series of accumulating emotions in Mrs. Mallard. These emotions are conveyed by sentences in which feelings and events gather in extended phrases: "She was young, with a fair, calm face, whose lines bespoke repression and even a certain strength." In Baldwin's "Sonny's Blues," sentences sometimes imitate the music they describe: "One boy was whistling a tune, at once very complicated and very simple, it seemed to be pouring out of him as though he were a bird, and it sounded very cool and moving through all that harsh, bright air, only just holding its own through all those other sounds."

Style also consists of how much of a story's prose focuses on images, describes actions, or presents dialogue. Some stories rely on imagery and suggestion; these use many adjectives and often linger over descriptions of people and places. "The Birthmark" and "Kew Gardens" are such stories. London's story "The Law of Life" concentrates on the character's actions. Other stories present the more staccato rhythms of dialogue. "Hills Like White Elephants" is almost entirely dialogue: "Four reales." "We want two Anis del Toro." "With water?" "I don't know." John Updike's "A & P" tells its story through the running interior monologue of the main character: "I thought and said 'No' but it wasn't about that I was thinking."

www Style is intimately linked to *image* **Web**, conveying via language impressions that match or complement a story's imagery. Images are partly an effect of style. The sentences from Joyce and Hemingway above both demonstrate how diction and grammar combine to produce both an image and an atmosphere. Joyce's sentence ruminates, lingering on detail and the effects of light on the person the character is in love with, while Hemingway's sentence is as straightforward as the hills it describes.

Critical Perspective: On Style

"In a large studio in Paris, hung with paintings by Renoir, Matisse and Picasso, Gertrude Stein is doing with words what Picasso is doing with paint. She is impelling language to induce new states of consciousness, and in doing so language becomes with her a creative art rather than a mirror of history. In her impressionistic writing she uses familiar words to create perceptions, conditions, and states of being, never before quite consciously experienced. She does this by using words that appeal to her as having the meaning that they seem to have. She has taken the English language and, according to many people, has misused it, or has used it roughly, uncouthly and brutally, or madly, stupidly and hideously, but by her method she is finding the hidden and inner nature of nature. . . .

"In Gertrude Stein's writing every word lives and, apart from the concept, it is so exquisitely rhythmical and cadenced, that when read aloud and received as pure sound, it is like a kind of sensuous music. Just as one may stop, for once in a way, before a canvas of Picasso, and, letting one's reason sleep for an instant, may exclaim: 'It is a fine pattern!'—so listening to Gertrude Stein's words and forgetting to try to understand what they mean, one submits to their gradual charm. Huntley Carter, of the *New Age*, says that her use of language has a curious hypnotic effect when read aloud. In one part of her writing she made use of repetition and the rearranging of certain words over and over, so that they became adjusted into a kind of incantation, and in listening one feels that from the combination of repeated sounds, varied ever so little, that there emerges gradually a perception of some meaning quite other than that of the contents of the phrases. Many people have experienced this magical evocation, but have been unable to explain in what way it came to pass, but though they did not know what meaning the words were bearing, nor how they were affected by them, yet they had begun to know what it all meant, because they were not indifferent."

—Mabel Dodge, "Speculations, or Post-Impressionism in Prose," *Arts and Decoration* (March 1913).

Mabel Dodge, a friend of Stein's, analyzes Stein's style—the ways she uses language—as a way of explaining what Stein's work achieves. Describing what the rhythms and sounds of Stein's language evokes, Dodge conveys how Stein's writing depends on the effects of style.

Critical Perspectives: Close Readings and Deconstructive Readings

Analyzing how language and image might match or work in tension with one another is a task of both close reading **Web** and deconstruction **Web**. **Close readings** investigate the ways language and image work together. Both **New** *www*

Criticism Web and **semiotics** Web affirm the idea that insights about the ways texts work can be gained from looking at the relationships among their various elements. Building on the practice of close reading, **deconstructive readings** focus on the precariousness of a story's elements, looking at the ways language in a story might work against itself or against its imagery, producing tensions, contradictions, and enigmas that partly account for a story's complexity and richness.

Style is almost always in line with a story's atmosphere—the combination of setting, plot, and tone that indicates whether a story is comic, tragic, ironic, cynical, or romantic. Style provides clues about how a story should be read: whether it is serious or lighthearted, everyday or unusual. Style also plays a large part in defining literary movements such as **realism** Web, **naturalism** Web, and **modernism** Web, so much so that these movements are also sometimes called *styles*.

Stories About Language and Style

The stories that follow are all examples of stories that develop the style of American modernism. The authors—F. Scott Fitzgerald, Ernest Hemingway, and Gertrude Stein—experiment with language and style. Hemingway and Stein were influenced by *cubist* painters Web (see cubist paintings in first color insert), and their styles are often lean, but musical. Along with Fitzgerald, Hemingway and Stein were part of the rich and lively culture of a *transatlantic modernism* Web that mingled the work of European writers and innovations in the plastic arts (such as *cubism* and *surrealism* Web with fresh ideas from the *Harlem Renaissance* Web and the elegant discipline of an American vision.

F. Scott Fitzgerald

Babylon Revisited

(1941)

I

"And where's Mr. Campbell?" Charlie asked.

"Gone to Switzerland. Mr. Campbell's a pretty sick man, Mr. Wales."

"I'm sorry to hear that. And George Hardt?" Charlie inquired.

"Back in America, gone to work."

"And where is the Snow Bird?"

"He was in here last week. Anyway, his friend, Mr. Schaeffer, is in Paris."

Two familiar names from the long list of a year and a half ago. Charlie scribbled an address in his notebook and tore out the page.

"If you see Mr. Schaeffer, give him this," he said. "It's my brother-in-law's address. I haven't settled on a hotel yet."

He was not really disappointed to find Paris was so empty. But the stillness in the Ritz bar was strange and portentous. It was not an American bar any more—he felt polite in it, and not as if he owned it. It had gone back into France. He felt the stillness from the moment he got out of the taxi and saw the doorman, usually in a frenzy of activity at this hour, gossiping with a *chasseur* by the servants' entrance.

Passing through the corridor, he heard only a single, bored voice in the once-clamorous women's room. When he turned into the bar he traveled the twenty feet of green carpet with his eyes fixed straight ahead by old habit; and then, with his foot firmly on the rail, he turned and surveyed the room, encountering only a single pair of eyes that fluttered up from a newspaper in the corner. Charlie asked for the head barman, Paul, who in the latter days of the bull market had come to work in his own custom-built car—disembarking, however, with due nicety at the nearest corner. But Paul was at his country house today and Alix giving him information.

"No, no more," Charlie said, "I'm going slow these days."

Alix congratulated him: "You were going pretty strong a couple of years ago."

"I'll stick to it all right," Charlie assured him. "I've stuck to it for over a year and a half now."

"How do you find conditions in America?"

"I haven't been to America for months. I'm in business in Prague, representing a couple of concerns there. They don't know about me down there."

Alix smiled.

"Remember the night of George Hardt's bachelor dinner here?" said Charlie. "By the way, what's become of Claude Fessenden?"

Alix lowered his voice confidentially: "He's in Paris, but he doesn't come here any more. Paul doesn't allow it. He ran up a bill of thirty thousand francs, charging all his drinks and his lunches, and usually his dinner, for more than a year. And when Paul finally told him he had to pay, he gave him a bad check."

Alix shook his head sadly.

"I don't understand it, such a dandy fellow. Now he's all bloated up—" He made a plump apple of his hands.

Charlie watched a group of strident queens installing themselves in a corner.

"Nothing affects them," he thought. "Stocks rise and fall, people loaf or work, but they go on forever." The place oppressed him. He called for the dice and shook with Alix for the drink.

"Here for long, Mr. Wales?"

"I'm here for four or five days to see my little girl."

"Oh-h! You have a little girl?"

Outside, the fire-red, gas-blue, ghost-green signs shone smokily through the tranquil rain. It was late afternoon and the streets were in movement; the bistros gleamed. At the corner of the Boulevard des Capucines he took a taxi.

The Place de la Concorde moved by in pink majesty; they crossed the logical Seine, and Charlie felt the sudden provincial quality of the Left Bank.

Charlie directed his taxi to the Avenue de l'Opéra, which was out of his way. But he wanted to see the blue hour spread over the magnificent façade, and imagine that the cab horns, playing endlessly the first few bars of *Le Plus que Lent,* were the trumpets of the Second Empire. They were closing the iron grill in front of Brentano's Bookstore, and people were already at dinner behind the trim little bourgeois hedge of Duval's. He had never eaten at a really cheap restaurant in Paris. Five-course dinner, four francs fifty, eighteen cents, wine included. For some odd reason he wished that he had.

As they rolled on to the Left Bank, and he felt its sudden provincialism, he thought, "I spoiled this city for myself. I didn't realize it, but the days came along one after another, and then two years were gone, and everything was gone, and I was gone."

He was thirty-five, and good to look at. The Irish mobility of his face was sobered by a deep wrinkle between his eyes. As he rang his brother-in-law's bell in the Rue Palatine, the wrinkle deepened till it pulled down his brows; he felt a cramping sensation in his belly. From behind the maid who opened the door darted a lovely little girl of nine who shrieked "Daddy!" and flew up, struggling like a fish, into his arms. She pulled his head around by one ear and set her cheek against his.

"My old pie," he said. 30

"Oh, daddy, daddy, daddy, daddy, dads, dads, dads!"

She drew him into the salon, where the family waited, a boy and a girl his daughter's age, his sister-in-law and her husband. He greeted Marion with his voice pitched carefully to avoid either feigned enthusiasm or dislike, but her response was more frankly tepid, though she minimized her expression of unalterable distrust by directing her regard toward his child. The two men clasped hands in a friendly way and Lincoln Peters rested his for a moment on Charlie's shoulder.

The room was warm and comfortably American. The three children moved intimately about, playing through the yellow oblongs that led to other rooms; the cheer of six o'clock spoke in the eager smacks of the fire and the sounds of French activity in the kitchen. But Charlie did not relax; his heart sat up rigidly in his body and he drew confidence from his daughter, who from time to time came close to him, holding in her arms the doll he had brought.

"Really extremely well," he declared in answer to Lincoln's question. "There's a lot of business there that isn't moving at all, but we're doing even better than ever. In fact, damn well. I'm bringing my sister over from America next month to keep house for me. My income last year was bigger than it was when I had money. You see, the Czechs—"

His boasting was for a specific purpose; but after a moment, seeing a faint 35
restiveness in Lincoln's eye, he changed the subject:

"Those are fine children of yours, well brought up, good manners."

"We think Honoria's a great little girl too."

Marion Peters came back from the kitchen. She was a tall woman with worried eyes, who had once possessed a fresh American loveliness. Charlie had never been sensitive to it and was always surprised when people spoke of how pretty she had been. From the first there had been an instinctive antipathy between them.

"Well, how do you find Honoria?" she asked.

"Wonderful. I was astonished how much she's grown in ten months. All the children are looking well."

"We haven't had a doctor for a year. How do you like being back in Paris?"

"It seems very funny to see so few Americans around."

"I'm delighted," Marion said vehemently. "Now at least you can go into a store without their assuming you're a millionaire. We've suffered like everybody, but on the whole it's a good deal pleasanter."

"But it was nice while it lasted," Charlie said. "We were a sort of royalty, almost infallible, with a sort of magic around us. In the bar this afternoon"—he stumbled, seeing his mistake—"there wasn't a man I knew."

She looked at him keenly. "I should think you'd have had enough of bars."

"I only stayed a minute. I take one drink every afternoon, and no more."

"Don't you want a cocktail before dinner?" Lincoln asked.

"I take only one drink every afternoon, and I've had that."

"I hope you keep to it," said Marion.

Her dislike was evident in the coldness with which she spoke, but Charlie only smiled; he had larger plans. Her very aggressiveness gave him an advantage, and he knew enough to wait. He wanted them to initiate the discussion of what they knew had brought him to Paris.

At dinner he couldn't decide whether Honoria was most like him or her mother. Fortunate if she didn't combine the traits of both that had brought them to disaster. A great wave of protectiveness went over him. He thought he knew what to do for her. He believed in character; he wanted to jump back a whole generation and trust in character again as the eternally valuable element. Everything else wore out.

He left soon after dinner, but not to go home. He was curious to see Paris by night with clearer and more judicious eyes than those of other days. He bought a *strapontin* for the Casino and watched Josephine Baker go through her chocolate arabesques.

After an hour he left and strolled toward Montmartre, up the Rue Pigalle into the Place Blanche. The rain had stopped and there were a few people in evening clothes disembarking from taxis in front of cabarets, and *cocottes* prowling singly or in pairs, and many Negroes. He passed a lighted door from which issued music, and stopped with the sense of familiarity; it was Bricktop's, where he had parted with so many hours and so much money. A few doors farther on he found another ancient rendezvous and incautiously put his head inside. Immediately an eager orchestra burst into sound, a pair of professional dancers leaped to their feet and a maitre d'hôtel swooped toward him, crying, "Crowd just arriving, sir!" But he withdrew quickly.

"You have to be damn drunk," he thought.

Zelli's was closed, the bleak and sinister cheap hotels surrounding it were 55
dark; up in the Rue Blanche there was more light and a local, colloquial French crowd. The Poet's Cave had disappeared, but the two great mouths of the Café of Heaven and the Café of Hell still yawned—even devoured, as he watched, the meager contents of a tourist bus—a German, a Japanese, and an American couple who glanced at him with frightened eyes.

So much for the effort and ingenuity of Montmartre. All the catering to vice and waste was on an utterly childish scale, and he suddenly realized the meaning of the word "dissipate"—to dissipate into thin air; to make nothing out of something. In the little hours of the night every move from place to place was an enormous human jump, an increase of paying for the privilege of slower and slower motion.

He remembered thousand-franc notes given to an orchestra for playing a single number, hundred-franc notes tossed to a doorman for calling a cab.

But it hadn't been given for nothing.

It had been given, even the most wildly squandered sum, as an offering to destiny that he might not remember the things most worth remembering, the things that now he would always remember—his child taken from his control, his wife escaped to a grave in Vermont.

In the glare of a *brasserie* a woman spoke to him. He bought her some 60
eggs and coffee, and then, eluding her encouraging stare, gave her a twenty-franc note and took a taxi to his hotel.

II

He woke upon a fine fall day—football weather. The depression of yesterday was gone and he liked the people on the streets. At noon he sat opposite Honoria at Le Grand Vatel, the only restaurant he could think of not reminiscent of champagne dinners and long luncheons that began at two and ended in a blurred and vague twilight.

"Now, how about vegetables? Oughtn't you to have some vegetables?"

"Well, yes."

"Here's *épinards* and *chou-fleur* and carrots and *haricots*."

"I'd like *chou-fleur*." 65

"Wouldn't you like to have two vegetables?"

"I usually only have one at lunch."

The waiter was pretending to be inordinately fond of children. *"Qu'elle est mignonne la petite! Elle parle exactement comme une française."*

"How about dessert? Shall we wait and see?"

The waiter disappeared. Honoria looked at her father expectantly. 70

"What are we going to do?"

"First, we're going to that toy store in the Rue Saint-Honoré and buy you anything you like. And then we're going to the vaudeville at the Empire."

She hesitated. "I like it about the vaudeville, but not the toy store."

"Why not?"

"Well, you brought me this doll." She had it with her. "And I've got lots of things. And we're not rich any more, are we?" 75

"We never were. But today you are to have anything you want."

"All right," she agreed resignedly.

When there had been her mother and a French nurse he had been inclined to be strict; now he extended himself, reached out for a new tolerance; he must be both parents to her and not shut any of her out of communication.

"I want to get to know you," he said gravely. "First let me introduce myself. My name is Charles J. Wales, of Prague."

"Oh, daddy!" her voice cracked with laughter. 80

"And who are you, please?" he persisted, and she accepted a role immediately: "Honoria Wales, Rue Palatine, Paris."

"Married or single?"

"No, not married. Single."

He indicated the doll. "But I see you have a child, madame."

Unwilling to disinherit it, she took it to her heart and thought quickly: "Yes, I've been married, but I'm not married now. My husband is dead." 85

He went on quickly, "And the child's name?"

"Simone. That's after my best friend at school."

"I'm very pleased that you're doing so well at school."

"I'm third this month," she boasted. "Elsie"—that was her cousin—"is only about eighteenth, and Richard is about at the bottom."

"You like Richard and Elsie, don't you?" 90

"Oh, yes. I like Richard quite well and I like her all right."

Cautiously and casually he asked: "And Aunt Marion and Uncle Lincoln—which do you like best?"

"Oh, Uncle Lincoln, I guess."

He was increasingly aware of her presence. As they came in, a murmur of ". . . adorable" followed them, and now the people at the next table bent all their silences upon her, staring as if she were something no more conscious than a flower.

"Why don't I live with you?" she asked suddenly. "Because mamma's dead?" 95

"You must stay here and learn more French. It would have been hard for daddy to take care of you so well."

"I don't really need much taking care of any more. I do everything for myself."

Going out of the restaurant, a man and a woman unexpectedly hailed him. "Well, the old Wales!"

"Hello there, Lorraine. . . . Dunc."

Sudden ghosts out of the past: Duncan Schaeffer, a friend from college. Lorraine Quarrles, a lovely, pale blonde of thirty; one of a crowd who had helped him make months into days in the lavish times of three years ago.

"My husband couldn't come this year," she said, in answer to his question. "We're poor as hell. So he gave me two hundred a month and told me I could do my worst on that. . . . This your little girl?"

"What about coming back and sitting down?" Duncan asked.

"Can't do it." He was glad for an excuse. As always, he felt Lorraine's passionate, provocative attraction, but his own rhythm was different now.

"Well, how about dinner?" she asked.

"I'm not free. Give me your address and let me call you."

"Charlie, I believe you're sober," she said judicially. "I honestly believe he's sober, Dunc. Pinch him and see if he's sober."

Charlie indicated Honoria with his head. They both laughed.

"What's your address?" said Duncan skeptically.

He hesitated, unwilling to give the name of his hotel.

"I'm not settled yet. I'd better call you. We're going to see the vaudeville at the Empire."

"There! That's what I want to do," Lorraine said. "I want to see some clowns and acrobats and jugglers. That's just what we'll do, Dunc."

"We've got to do an errand first," said Charlie. "Perhaps we'll see you there."

"All right, you snob. . . . Good-by, beautiful little girl."

"Good-by."

Honoria bobbed politely.

Somehow, an unwelcome encounter. They liked him because he was functioning, because he was serious; they wanted to see him, because he was stronger than they were now, because they wanted to draw a certain sustenance from his strength.

At the Empire, Honoria proudly refused to sit upon her father's folded coat. She was already an individual with a code of her own, and Charlie was more and more absorbed by the desire of putting a little of himself into her before she crystallized utterly. It was hopeless to try to know her in so short a time.

Between the acts they came upon Duncan and Lorraine in the lobby where the band was playing.

"Have a drink?"

"All right, but not up at the bar. We'll take a table."

"The perfect father."

Listening abstractedly to Lorraine, Charlie watched Honoria's eyes leave their table, and he followed them wistfully about the room, wondering what they saw. He met her glance and she smiled.

"I liked that lemonade," she said.

What had she said? What had he expected? Going home in a taxi afterward, he pulled her over until her head rested against his chest.

"Darling, do you ever think about your mother?"

"Yes, sometimes," she answered vaguely.

"I don't want you to forget her. Have you got a picture of her?"

"Yes, I think so. Anyhow, Aunt Marion has. Why don't you want me to forget her?"

"She loved you very much."

"I loved her too." 130

They were silent for a moment.

"Daddy, I want to come and live with you," she said suddenly.

His heart leaped; he had wanted it to come like this.

"Aren't you perfectly happy?"

"Yes, but I love you better than anybody. And you love me better than 135 anybody, don't you, now that mummy's dead?"

"Of course I do. But you won't always like me best, honey. You'll grow up and meet somebody your own age and go marry him and forget you ever had a daddy."

"Yes, that's true," she agreed tranquilly.

He didn't go in. He was coming back at nine o'clock and he wanted to keep himself fresh and new for the thing he must say then.

"When you're safe inside, just show yourself in that window."

"All right. Good-by, dads, dads, dads, dads." 140

He waited in the dark street until she appeared, all warm and glowing, in the window above and kissed her fingers out into the night.

III

They were waiting. Marion sat behind the coffee service in a dignified black dinner dress that just faintly suggested mourning. Lincoln was walking up and down with the animation of one who had already been talking. They were as anxious as he was to get into the question. He opened it almost immediately:

"I suppose you know what I want to see you about—why I really came to Paris."

Marion played with the black stars on her necklace and frowned.

"I'm awfully anxious to have a home," he continued. "And I'm awfully 145 anxious to have Honoria in it. I appreciate your taking in Honoria for her mother's sake, but things have changed now"—he hesitated and then continued more forcibly—"changed radically with me, and I want to ask you to reconsider the matter. It would be silly for me to deny that about three years ago I was acting badly—"

Marion looked up at him with hard eyes.

"—but all that's over. As I told you, I haven't had more than a drink a day for over a year, and I take that drink deliberately, so that the idea of alcohol won't get too big in my imagination. You see the idea?"

"No," said Marion succinctly.

"It's a sort of stunt I set myself. It keeps the matter in proportion."

"I get you," said Lincoln. "You don't want to admit it's got any attraction 150 for you."

"Something like that. Sometimes I forget and don't take it. But I try to take it. Anyhow, I couldn't afford to drink in my position. The people I represent are more than satisfied with what I've done, and I'm bringing my sister over from Burlington to keep house for me, and I want awfully to have Honoria too. You know that even when her mother and I weren't getting along well we never let anything that happened touch Honoria. I know she's fond of me and I know I'm able to take care of her and—well, there you are. How do you feel about it?"

He knew that now he would have to take a beating. It would last an hour or two hours, and it would be difficult, but if he modulated his inevitable resentment to the chastened attitude of the reformed sinner, he might win his point in the end.

Keep your temper, he told himself. You don't want to be justified. You want Honoria.

Lincoln spoke first: "We've been talking it over ever since we got your letter last month. We're happy to have Honoria here. She's a dear little thing, and we're glad to be able to help her, but of course that isn't the question—"

Marion interrupted suddenly. "How long are you going to stay sober, Charlie?" she asked.

"Permanently, I hope."

"How can anybody count on that?"

"You know I never did drink heavily until I gave up business and came over here with nothing to do. Then Helen and I began to run around with—"

"Please leave Helen out of it. I can't bear to hear you talk about her like that."

He stared at her grimly; he had never been certain how fond of each other the sisters were in life.

"My drinking only lasted about a year and a half—from the time we came over until I—collapsed."

"It was time enough."

"It was time enough," he agreed.

"My duty is entirely to Helen," she said. "I try to think what she would have wanted me to do. Frankly, from the night you did that terrible thing you haven't really existed for me. I can't help that. She was my sister."

"Yes."

"When she was dying she asked me to look out for Honoria. If you hadn't been in a sanitarium then, it might have helped matters."

He had no answer.

"I'll never in my life be able to forget the morning when Helen knocked at my door, soaked to the skin and shivering, and said you'd locked her out."

Charlie gripped the sides of the chair. This was more difficult than he expected; he wanted to launch out into a long expostulation and explanation, but he only said: "The night I locked her out—" and she interrupted, "I don't feel up to going over that again."

After a moment's silence Lincoln said: "We're getting off the subject. You want Marion to set aside her legal guardianship and give you Honoria. I think the main point for her is whether she has confidence in you or not."

"I don't blame Marion," Charlie said slowly, "but I think she can have entire confidence in me. I had a good record up to three years ago. Of course, it's within human possibilities I might go wrong any time. But if we wait much longer I'll lose Honoria's childhood and my chance for a home." He shook his head. "I'll simply lose her, don't you see?"

"Yes, I see," said Lincoln.

"Why didn't you think of all this before?" Marion asked.

"I suppose I did, from time to time, but Helen and I were getting along badly. When I consented to the guardianship, I was flat on my back in a sanitarium and the market had cleaned me out. I knew I'd acted badly, and I thought if it would bring any peace to Helen, I'd agree to anything. But now it's different. I'm functioning, I'm behaving damn well, so far as—"

"Please don't swear at me," Marion said. 175

He looked at her, startled. With each remark the force of her dislike became more and more apparent. She had built up all her fear of life into one wall and faced it toward him. This trivial reproof was possibly the result of some trouble with the cook several hours before. Charlie became increasingly alarmed at leaving Honoria in this atmosphere of hostility against himself; sooner or later it would come out, in a word here, a shake of the head there, and some of that distrust would be irrevocably implanted in Honoria. But he pulled his temper down out of his face and shut it up inside him; he had won a point, for Lincoln realized the absurdity of Marion's remark and asked her lightly since when she had objected to the word "damn."

"Another thing," Charlie said: "I'm able to give her certain advantages now. I'm going to take a French governess to Prague with me. I've got a lease on a new apartment—"

He stopped, realizing that he was blundering. They couldn't be expected to accept with equanimity the fact that his income was again twice as large as their own.

"I suppose you can give her more luxuries than we can," said Marion. "When you were throwing away money we were living along watching every ten francs. . . . I suppose you'll start doing it again."

"Oh, no," he said. "I've learned. I worked hard for ten years, you know— 180
until I got lucky in the market, like so many people. Terribly lucky. It won't happen again."

There was a long silence. All of them felt their nerves straining, and for the first time in a year Charlie wanted a drink. He was sure now that Lincoln Peters wanted him to have his child.

Marion shuddered suddenly; part of her saw that Charlie's feet were planted on the earth now, and her own maternal feeling recognized the naturalness of his desire; but she had lived for a long time with a prejudice—a prejudice founded on a curious disbelief in her sister's happiness, which, in the shock of one terrible night, had turned to hatred for him. It had all happened at a point in her life where the discouragement of ill health and adverse circumstances made it necessary for her to believe in tangible villainy and a tangible villain.

"I can't help what I think!" she cried out suddenly. "How much you were responsible for Helen's death, I don't know. It's something you'll have to square with your own conscience."

An electric current of agony surged through him; for a moment he was almost on his feet, an unuttered sound echoing in his throat. He hung on to himself for a moment, another moment.

"Hold on there," said Lincoln uncomfortably. "I never thought you were responsible for that."

"Helen died of heart trouble," Charlie said dully.

"Yes, heart trouble." Marion spoke as if the phrase had another meaning for her. Then, in the flatness that followed her outburst, she saw him plainly and she knew he had somehow arrived at control over the situation. Glancing at her husband, she found no help from him, and as abruptly as if it were a matter of no importance, she threw up the sponge.

"Do what you like!" she cried, springing up from her chair. "She's your child. I'm not the person to stand in your way. I think if it were my child I'd rather see her—" She managed to check herself. "You two decide it. I can't stand this. I'm sick. I'm going to bed."

She hurried from the room; after a moment Lincoln said:

"This has been a hard day for her. You know how strongly she feels—" His voice was almost apologetic: "When a woman gets an idea in her head."

"Of course."

"It's going to be all right. I think she sees now that you—can provide for the child, and so we can't very well stand in your way or Honoria's way."

"Thank you, Lincoln."

"I'd better go along and see how she is."

"I'm going."

He was still trembling when he reached the street, but a walk down the Rue Bonaparte to the *quais* set him up, and as he crossed the Seine, fresh and new by the *quai* lamps, he felt exultant. But back in his room he couldn't sleep. The image of Helen haunted him. Helen whom he had loved so until they had senselessly begun to abuse each other's love, tear it into shreds. On that terrible February night that Marion remembered so vividly, a slow quarrel had gone on for hours. There was a scene at the Florida, and then he attempted to take her home, and then she kissed young Webb at a table; after that there was what she had hysterically said. When he arrived home alone he turned the key in the lock in wild anger. How could he know she would arrive an hour later alone, that there would be a snow storm in which she wandered about in slippers, too confused to find a taxi? Then the aftermath, her escaping pneumonia by a miracle, and all the attendant horror. They were "reconciled," but that was the beginning of the end, and Marion, who had seen with her own eyes and who imagined it to be one of many scenes from her sister's martyrdom, never forgot.

Going over it again brought Helen nearer, and in the white, soft light that steals upon half sleep near morning he found himself talking to her again. She said that he was perfectly right about Honoria and that she wanted Honoria to be with him. She said she was glad he was being good and doing better. She said a lot of other things—very friendly things—but she was in a swing in a white dress, and swinging faster and faster all the time, so that at the end he could not hear clearly all that she said.

IV

He woke up feeling happy. The door of the world was open again. He made plans, vistas, futures for Honoria and himself, but suddenly he grew sad, remembering all the plans he and Helen had made. She had not planned to die. The present was the thing—work to do and someone to love. But not to love too much, for he knew the injury that a father can do to a daughter or a mother to a son by attaching them too closely: afterward, out in the world, the child would seek in the marriage partner the same blind tenderness and, failing probably to find it, turn against love and life.

It was another bright, crisp day. He called Lincoln Peters at the bank where he worked and asked if he could count on taking Honoria when he left for Prague. Lincoln agreed that there was no reason for delay. One thing—the legal guardianship. Marion wanted to retain that awhile longer. She was upset by the whole matter, and it would oil things if she felt that the situation was still in her control for another year. Charlie agreed, wanting only the tangible, visible child.

Then the question of a governess. Charlie sat in a gloomy agency and talked to a cross Béarnaise and to a buxom Breton peasant, neither of whom he could have endured. There were others whom he would see tomorrow.

He lunched with Lincoln Peters at Griffons, trying to keep down his exultation.

"There's nothing quite like your own child," Lincoln said. "But you understand how Marion feels too."

"She's forgotten how hard I worked for seven years there," Charlie said. "She just remembers one night."

"There's another thing," Lincoln hesitated. "While you and Helen were tearing around Europe throwing money away, we were just getting along. I didn't touch any of the prosperity because I never got ahead enough to carry anything but my insurance. I think Marion felt there was some kind of injustice in it—you not even working toward the end, and getting richer and richer."

"It went just as quick as it came," said Charlie.

"Yes, a lot of it stayed in the hands of *chasseurs* and saxaphone players and maitres d'hôtel—well, the big party's over now. I just said that to explain Marion's feeling about those crazy years. If you drop in about six o'clock tonight before Marion's too tired, we'll settle the details on the spot."

Back at his hotel, Charlie found a *pneumatique* that had been redirected from the Ritz bar, where Charlie had left his address for the purpose of a certain man.

Dear Charlie:

You were so strange when we saw you the other day that I wondered if I did something to offend you. If so, I'm not conscious of it. In fact, I have thought about you too much for the last year, and it's always been in the back of my mind that I might see you if I came over here. We *did* have such good times that crazy spring, like the night you and I stole the butcher's tricycle, and the time we tried to call on the president and you had the old derby rim and the wire cane. Everybody seems so old lately, but I don't feel old a bit. Couldn't we get together some time today for old time's sake? I've got a vile hangover for the moment, but will be feeling better this afternoon and will look for you about five in the sweatshop at the Ritz.

Always devotedly,
Lorraine

His first feeling was one of awe that he had actually, in his mature years, stolen a tricycle and pedaled Lorraine all over the Étoile between the small hours and dawn. In retrospect it was a nightmare. Locking out Helen didn't fit in with any other act of his life, but the tricycle incident did—it was one of many. How many weeks or months of dissipation to arrive at that condition of utter irresponsibility?

He tried to picture how Lorraine had appeared to him then—very attractive; Helen was unhappy about it, though she said nothing. Yesterday, in the restaurant, Lorraine had seemed trite, blurred, worn away. He emphatically did not want to see her, and he was glad Alix had not given away his hotel address. It was a relief to think, instead, of Honoria, to think of Sundays spent with her and of saying good morning to her and knowing she was there in his house at night, drawing her breath in the darkness.

At five he took a taxi and bought presents for all the Peterses—a piquant cloth doll, a box of Roman soldiers, flowers for Marion, big linen handkerchiefs for Lincoln.

He saw, when he arrived in the apartment, that Marion had accepted the inevitable. She greeted him now as though he were a recalcitrant member of the family, rather than a menacing outsider. Honoria had been told she was going; Charlie was glad to see that her tact made her conceal her excessive happiness. Only on his lap did she whisper her delight and the question "When?" before she slipped away with the other children.

He and Marion were alone for a minute in the room, and on an impulse he spoke out boldly:

"Family quarrels are bitter things. They don't go according to any rules. They're not like aches or wounds; they're more like splits in the skin that won't heal because there's not enough material. I wish you and I could be on better terms."

"Some things are hard to forget," she answered. "It's a question of confidence." There was no answer to this and presently she asked, "When do you propose to take her?"

"As soon as I can get a governess. I hoped the day after tomorrow."

"That's impossible. I've got to get her things in shape. Not before Saturday."

He yielded. Coming back into the room, Lincoln offered him a drink.

"I'll take my daily whisky," he said.

It was warm here, it was a home, people together by a fire. The children felt very safe and important; the mother and father were serious, watchful. They had things to do for the children more important than his visit here. A spoonful of medicine was, after all, more important than the strained relations between Marion and himself. They were not dull people, but they were very much in the grip of life and circumstances. He wondered if he couldn't do something to get Lincoln out of his rut at the bank.

220 A long peal at the doorbell; the *bonne à tout faire* passed through and went down the corridor. The door opened upon another long ring, and then voices, and the three in the salon looked up expectantly; Richard moved to bring the corridor within his range of vision, and Marion rose. Then the maid came back along the corridor, closely followed by the voices, which developed under the light into Duncan Schaeffer and Lorraine Quarrles.

They were gay, they were hilarious, they were roaring with laughter. For a moment Charlie was astounded; unable to understand how they ferreted out the Peterses' address.

"Ah-h-h!" Duncan wagged his finger roguishly at Charlie, "Ah-h-h!"

They both slid down another cascade of laughter. Anxious and at a loss, Charlie shook hands with them quickly and presented them to Lincoln and Marion. Marion nodded, scarcely speaking. She had drawn back a step toward the fire; her little girl stood beside her, and Marion put an arm about her shoulder.

With growing annoyance at the intrusion, Charlie waited for them to explain themselves. After some concentration Duncan said:

225 "We came to invite you out to dinner. Lorraine and I insist that all this shishi, cagy business 'bout your address got to stop."

Charlie came closer to them, as if to force them backward down the corridor.

"Sorry, but I can't. Tell me where you'll be and I'll phone you in half an hour."

This made no impression. Lorraine sat down suddenly on the side of a chair, and focusing her eyes on Richard, cried, "Oh, what a nice little boy! Come here, little boy." Richard glanced at his mother, but did not move. With a perceptible shrug of her shoulder, Lorraine turned back to Charlie:

"Come and dine. Sure your cousins won' mine. See you so sel'om. Or solemn."

230 "I can't," said Charlie sharply. "You two have dinner and I'll phone you."

Her voice became suddenly unpleasant. "All right, we'll go. But I remember once when you hammered on my door at four A.M. I was enough of a good sport to give you a drink. Come on, Dunc."

Still in slow motion, with blurred, angry faces, with uncertain feet, they retired along the corridor.

"Good night," Charlie said.

"Good night!" responded Lorraine emphatically.

235 When he went back into the salon Marion had not moved, only now her

son was standing in the circle of her other arm. Lincoln was still swinging Honoria back and forth like a pendulum from side to side.

"What an outrage!" Charlie broke out. "What an absolute outrage!"

Neither of them answered. Charlie dropped into an armchair, picked up his drink, set it down again and said:

"People I haven't seen for two years having the colossal nerve—"

He broke off. Marion had made the sound "Oh!" in one swift, furious breath, turned her body from him with a jerk and left the room.

Lincoln set down Honoria carefully.

"You children go in and start your soup," he said, and when they obeyed, he said to Charlie:

"Marion's not well and she can't stand shocks. That kind of people make her really physically sick."

"I didn't tell them to come here. They wormed your name out of somebody. They deliberately—"

"Well, it's too bad. It doesn't help matters. Excuse me a minute."

Left alone, Charlie sat tense in his chair. In the next room he could hear the children eating, talking in monosyllables, already oblivious to the scene between their elders. He heard a murmur of conversation from a farther room and then the ticking bell of a telephone receiver picked up, and in a panic he moved to the other side of the room and out of earshot.

In a minute Lincoln came back. "Look here, Charlie. I think we'd better call off dinner for tonight. Marion's in bad shape."

"Is she angry with me?"

"Sort of," he said, almost roughly. "She's not strong and—"

"You mean she's changed her mind about Honoria?"

"She's pretty bitter right now. I don't know. You phone me at the bank tomorrow."

"I wish you'd explain to her I never dreamed these people would come here. I'm just as sore as you are."

"I couldn't explain anything to her now."

Charlie got up. He took his coat and hat and started down the corridor. Then he opened the door of the dining room and said in a strange voice, "Good night, children."

Honoria rose and ran around the table to hug him.

"Good night, sweetheart," he said vaguely, and then trying to make his voice more tender, trying to conciliate something. "Good night, dear children."

V

Charlie went directly to the Ritz bar with the furious idea of finding Lorraine and Duncan, but they were not there, and he realized that in any case there was nothing he could do. He had not touched his drink at the Peterses, and now he ordered a whisky-and-soda. Paul came over to say hello.

"It's a great change," he said sadly. "We do about half the business we did. So many fellows I hear about back in the States lost everything, maybe not in the first crash, but then in the second. Your friend George Hardt lost every cent, I hear. Are you back in the States?"

"No, I'm in business in Prague."

"I heard that you lost a lot in the crash."

"I did," and he added grimly, "but I lost everything I wanted in the boom."

"Selling short."

"Something like that."

Again the memory of those days swept over him like a nightmare—the people they had met traveling; then people who couldn't add a row of figures or speak a coherent sentence. The little man Helen had consented to dance with at the ship's party, who had insulted her ten feet from the table; the women and girls carried screaming with drink or drugs out of public places—

The men who locked their wives out in the snow, because the snow of twenty-nine wasn't real snow. If you didn't want it to be snow, you just paid some money.

He went to the phone and called the Peterses' apartment; Lincoln answered.

"I called up because this thing is on my mind. Has Marion said anything definite?"

"Marion's sick," Lincoln answered shortly. "I know this thing isn't altogether your fault, but I can't have her go to pieces about it. I'm afraid we'll have to let it slide for six months; I can't take the chance of working her up to this state again."

"I see."

"I'm sorry, Charlie."

He went back to his table. His whisky glass was empty, but he shook his head when Alix looked at it questioningly. There wasn't much he could do now except send Honoria some things; he would send her a lot of things tomorrow. He thought rather angrily that this was just money—he had given so many people money. . . .

"No, no more," he said to another waiter. "What do I owe you?"

He would come back some day; they couldn't make him pay forever. But he wanted his child, and nothing was much good now, beside that fact. He wasn't young any more, with a lot of nice thoughts and dreams to have by himself. He was absolutely sure Helen wouldn't have wanted him to be so alone.

F. Scott Fitzgerald

(1896–1940) **Web** *www*

A successful writer from the Midwest, Fitzgerald lived and worked for a while in Paris, then returned to America and wrote for Hollywood. His most famous novel is *The Great Gatsby* (1925).

TOPICS FOR CRITICAL THINKING **Web** *www*

1. What are the functions of the snow image?
2. What feelings, events, and images are linked to alcohol in this story?
3. Why does Charlie take a drink each day? How does that practice relate to his dealing with the past?
4. What does the story's title mean?
5. Why does the story end with Charlie evoking Helen?

www

TOPICS FOR CRITICAL WRITING Web

1. Does Charlie unconsciously want his past to catch up to him? Support your position with details from the story.
2. In what ways is "Babylon Revisited" about loss?

Ernest Hemingway

Hills Like White Elephants *(1927)*

The Hills across the valley of the Ebro were long and white. On this side there was no shade and no trees and the station was between two lines of rails in the sun. Close against the side of the station there was the warm shadow of the building and a curtain, made of strings of bamboo beads, hung across the open door into the bar, to keep out flies. The American and the girl with him sat at a table in the shade, outside the building. It was very hot and the express from Barcelona would come in forty minutes. It stopped at this junction for two minutes and went on to Madrid.

"What should we drink?" the girl asked. She had taken off her hat and put it on the table.

"It's pretty hot," the man said.

"Let's drink beer."

"Dos cervezas," the man said into the curtain. 5

"Big ones?" a woman asked from the doorway.

"Yes. Two big ones."

The woman brought two glasses of beer and two felt pads. She put the felt pads and the beer glasses on the table and looked at the man and the girl. The girl was looking off at the line of hills. They were white in the sun and the country was brown and dry.

"They look like white elephants," she said.

"I've never seen one," the man drank his beer. 10

"No, you wouldn't have."

"I might have," the man said. "Just because you say I wouldn't have doesn't prove anything."

The girl looked at the bead curtain. "They've painted something on it," she said. "What does it say?"

"Anis del Toro. It's a drink."

"Could we try it?" 15

The man called "Listen" through the curtain. The woman came out from the bar.

"Four reales."

"We want two Anis del Toro."

"With water?"

"Do you want it with water?" 20

"I don't know," the girl said. "Is it good with water?"

"It's all right."

"You want them with water?" asked the woman.

"Yes, with water."

"It tastes like licorice," the girl said and put the glass down. 25

"That's the way with everything."

"Yes," said the girl. "Everything tastes of licorice. Especially all the things you've waited so long for, like absinthe."

"Oh, cut it out."

"You started it," the girl said. "I was being amused. I was having a fine time."

"Well, let's try and have a fine time." 30

"All right. I was trying. I said the mountains looked like white elephants. Wasn't that bright?"

"That was bright."

"I wanted to try this new drink. That's all we do, isn't it—look at things and try new drinks?"

"I guess so."

The girl looked across at the hills. 35

"They're lovely hills," she said. "They don't really look like white elephants. I just meant the coloring of their skin through the trees."

"Should we have another drink?"

"All right."

The warm wind blew the bead curtain against the table.

"The beer's nice and cool," the man said. 40

"It's lovely," the girl said.

"It's really an awfully simple operation, Jig," the man said. "It's not really an operation at all."

The girl looked at the ground the table legs rested on.

"I know you wouldn't mind it, Jig. It's really not anything. It's just to let the air in."

The girl did not say anything. 45

"I'll go with you and I'll stay with you all the time. They just let the air in and then it's all perfectly natural."

"Then what will we do afterward?"

"We'll be fine afterward. Just like we were before."

"What makes you think so?"

"That's the only thing that bothers us. It's the only thing that's made us unhappy." 50

The girl looked at the bead curtain, put her hand out and took hold of two of the strings of beads.

"And you think then we'll be all right and be happy."

"I know we will. You don't have to be afraid. I've known lots of people that have done it."

"So have I," said the girl. "And afterward they were all so happy."

"Well," the man said, "if you don't want to you don't have to. I wouldn't have you do it if you didn't want to. But I know it's perfectly simple." 55

"And you really want to?"

"I think it's the best thing to do. But I don't want you to do it if you don't really want to."

"And if I do it you'll be happy and things will be like they were and you'll love me?"

"I love you now. You know I love you."

"I know. But if I do it, then it will be nice again if I say things are like white elephants, and you'll like it?"

"I'll love it. I love it now but I just can't think about it. You know how I get when I worry."

"If I do it you won't ever worry?"

"I won't worry about that because it's perfectly simple."

"Then I'll do it. Because I don't care about me."

"What do you mean?"

"I don't care about me."

"Well, I care about you."

"Oh, yes. But I don't care about me. And I'll do it and then everything will be fine."

"I don't want you to do it if you feel that way."

The girl stood up and walked to the end of the station. Across, on the other side, were fields of grain and trees along the banks of the Ebro. Far away, beyond the river, were mountains. The shadow of a cloud moved across the field of grain and she saw the river through the trees.

"And we could have all this," she said. "And we could have everything and every day we make it more impossible."

"What did you say?"

"I said we could have everything."

"We can have everything."

"No, we can't."

"We can have the whole world."

"No, we can't."

"We can go everywhere."

"No, we can't. It isn't ours any more."

"It's ours."

"No, it isn't. And once they take it away, you never get it back."

"But they haven't taken it away."

"We'll wait and see."

"Come on back in the shade," he said. "You mustn't feel that way."

"I don't feel any way," the girl said. "I just know things."

"I don't want you to do anything that you don't want to do——"

"Nor that isn't good for me," she said. "I know. Could we have another beer?"

"All right. But you've got to realize——"

"I realize," the girl said. "Can't we maybe stop talking?"

They sat down at the table and the girl looked across at the hills on the dry side of the valley and the man looked at her and at the table.

"You've got to realize," he said, "that I don't want you to do it if you don't want to. I'm perfectly willing to go through with it if it means anything to you."

"Doesn't it mean anything to you? We could get along."

"Of course it does. But I don't want anybody but you. I don't want any one else. And I know it's perfectly simple."

"Yes, you know it's perfectly simple."

"It's all right for you to say that, but I do know it." 95

"Would you do something for me now?"

"I'd do anything for you."

"Would you please please please please please please please stop talking?"

He did not say anything but looked at the bags against the wall of the station. There were labels on them from all the hotels where they had spent nights.

"But I don't want you to," he said, "I don't care anything about it." 100

"I'll scream," the girl said.

The woman came out through the curtains with two glasses of beer and put them down on the damp felt pads. "The train comes in five minutes," she said.

"What did she say?" asked the girl.

"That the train is coming in five minutes."

The girl smiled brightly at the woman, to thank her. 105

"I'd better take the bags over to the other side of the station," the man said. She smiled at him.

"All right. Then come back and we'll finish the beer."

He picked up the two heavy bags and carried them around the station to the other tracks. He looked up the tracks but could not see the train. Coming back, he walked through the barroom, where people waiting for the train were drinking. He drank an Anis at the bar and looked at the people. They were all waiting reasonably for the train. He went out through the bead curtain. She was sitting at the table and smiled at him.

"Do you feel better?" he asked.

"I feel fine," she said. "There's nothing wrong with me. I feel fine." 110

ERNEST HEMINGWAY

(1899–1961) **Web** ***www***

An outdoorsman and journalist, Nobel Laureate Hemingway began writing serious fiction in Paris. Associated with fishing and bullfights, Hemingway perfected a style based on verbal economy.

TOPICS FOR CRITICAL THINKING **Web** ***www***

1. Does the woman always mean what she says? The man?
2. Pinpoint moments in the conversation when the characters might be speaking ironically.
3. How would you describe the style of the story?
4. Does this story show an insensitivity toward the woman's feelings or an understanding of her plight?
5. What is the relation between their drinking and their talking?
6. Can things ever be the same again for them?

www

TOPICS FOR CRITICAL WRITING Web

1. What various elements of the story might the metaphor of the hills stand for?
2. What does the woman mean at the end of the story when she says, "There's nothing wrong with me. I feel fine."?

Gertrude Stein

Miss Furr and Miss Skeene *(1922)*

Helen Furr had quite a pleasant home. Mrs. Furr was quite a pleasant woman. Mr. Furr was quite a pleasant man. Helen Furr had quite a pleasant voice quite worth cultivating. She did not mind working. She worked to cultivate her voice. She did not find it gay living in the same place where she had always been living. She went to a place where some were cultivating something, voices and other things needing cultivating. She met Georgine Skeene there who was cultivating her voice which some thought was quite a pleasant one. Helen Furr and Georgine Skeene lived together then. Georgine Skeene liked travelling. Helen Furr did not care about travelling, she liked to stay in one place and be gay there. They were together then and travelled to another place and stayed there and were gay there.

They stayed there and were gay there, not very gay there, just gay there. They were both gay there, they were regularly working there both of them cultivating their voices there, they were both gay there. Georgine Skeene was gay there and she was regular, regular in being gay, regular in not being gay, regular in being a gay one who was not being gay longer than was needed to be one being quite a gay one. They were both gay then there and both working there then.

They were in a way both gay there where there were many cultivating something. They were both regular in being gay there. Helen Furr was gay there, she was gayer and gayer there and really she was just gay there, she was gayer and gayer there, that is to say she found ways of being gay there that she was using in being gay there. She was gay there, not gayer and gayer, just gay there, that is to say she was not gayer by using the things she found there that were gay things, she was gay there.

They were quite regularly gay there, Helen Furr and Georgine Skeene, they were regularly gay there where they were gay. They were very regularly gay.

To be regularly gay was to do every day the gay thing that they did every 5
day. To be regularly gay was to end every day at the same time after they had been regularly gay. They were regularly gay. They were gay every day. They ended every day in the same way, at the same time, and they had been every day regularly gay.

The voice Helen Furr was cultivating was quite a pleasant one. The voice Georgine Skeene was cultivating was, some said, a better one. The voice Helen Furr was cultivating she cultivated and it was quite completely a pleasant enough one then, a cultivated enough one then. The voice Georgine Skeene was cultivating she did not cultivate too much. She cultivated it quite some. She cultivated and she would sometime go on cultivating it and it was not then an unpleasant one, it would not be then an unpleasant one, it would be a quite richly cultivated one, it would be quite richly enough to be a pleasant enough one.

They were gay where there were many cultivating something. The two were gay there, were regularly gay there. Georgine Skeene would have liked to do more travelling. They did some travelling, not very much travelling, Georgine Skeene would have liked to do more travelling, Helen Furr did not care about doing travelling, she liked to stay in a place and be gay there.

They stayed in a place and were gay there, both of them stayed there, they stayed together there, they were gay there, they were regularly gay there.

They went quite often, not very often, but they did go back to where Helen Furr had a pleasant enough home and then Georgine Skeene went to a place where her brother had quite some distinction. They both went, every few years, went visiting to where Helen Furr had quite a pleasant home. Certainly Helen Furr would not find it gay to stay, she did not find it gay, she said she would not stay, she said she did not find it gay, she said she would not stay where she did not find it gay, she said she found it gay where she did stay and she did stay there where very many were cultivating something. She did stay there. She always did find it gay there.

She went to see them where she had always been living and where she did not find it gay. She had a pleasant home there, Mrs. Furr was a pleasant enough woman, Mr. Furr was a pleasant enough man, Helen told them and they were not worrying, that she did not find it gay living where she had always been living.

Georgine Skeene and Helen Furr were living where they were both cultivating their voices and they were gay there. They visited where Helen Furr had come from and then they went to where they were living where they were then regularly living.

There were some dark and heavy men there then. There were some who were not so heavy and some who were not so dark. Helen Furr and Georgine Skeene sat regularly with them. They sat regularly with the ones who were dark and heavy. They sat regularly with the ones who were not so dark. They sat regularly with the ones that were not so heavy. They sat with them regularly, sat with some of them. They went with them regularly went with them. They were regular then, they were gay then, they were where they wanted to be then where it was gay to be then, they were regularly gay then. There were men there then who were dark and heavy and they sat with them with Helen Furr and Georgine Skeene and they went with them with Miss Furr and Miss Skeene, and they went with the heavy and dark men Miss Furr and Miss Skeene went with them, and they sat with them, Miss Furr and Miss Skeene sat with them, and there were other men, some were not heavy men and they sat with Miss Furr and Miss Skeene and Miss Furr and Miss Skeene sat with them, and there were other men who were not dark men and they sat with Miss Furr and Miss Skeene and Miss Furr and Miss Skeene sat with them. Miss

Furr and Miss Skeene went with them and they went with Miss Furr and Miss Skeene, some who were not heavy men, some who were not dark men. Miss Furr and Miss Skeene sat regularly, they sat with some men. Miss Furr and Miss Skeene went and there were some men with them. There were men and Miss Furr and Miss Skeene went with them, went somewhere with them, went with some of them.

Helen Furr and Georgine Skeene were regularly living where very many were living and cultivating in themselves something. Helen Furr and Georgine Skeene were living very regularly then, being very regular then in being gay then. They did then learn many ways to be gay and they were then being gay being quite regular in being gay, being gay and they were learning little things, little things in ways of being gay, they were very regular then, they were learning very many little things in ways of being gay, they were being gay and using these little things they were learning to have to be gay with regularly gay with then and they were gay the same amount they had been gay. They were quite gay, they were quite regular, they were learning little things, gay little things, they were gay inside them the same amount they had been gay, they were gay the same length of time they had been gay every day.

They were regular in being gay, they learned little things that are things in being gay, they learned many little things that are things in being gay, they were gay every day, they were regular, they were gay, they were gay the same length of time every day, they were gay, they were quite regularly gay.

Georgine Skeene went away to stay two months with her brother. Helen Furr did not go then to stay with her father and her mother. Helen Furr stayed there where they had been regularly living the two of them and she would then certainly not be lonesome, she would go on being gay. She did go on being gay. She was not any more gay but she was gay longer every day than they had been being gay when they were together being gay. She was gay then quite exactly the same way. She learned a few more little ways of being gay. She was quite gay and in the same way, the same way she had been gay and she was gay a little longer in the day, more of each day she was gay. She was gay longer every day than when the two of them had been being gay. She was gay quite in the way they had been gay, quite in the same way.

She was not lonesome then, she was not at all feeling any need of having Georgine Skeene. She was not astonished at this thing. She would have been a little astonished by this thing but she knew she was not astonished at anything and so she was not astonished at this thing not astonished at not feeling any need of having Georgine Skeene.

Helen Furr had quite a completely pleasant voice and it was quite well enough cultivated and she could use it and she did use it but then there was not any way of working at cultivating a completely pleasant voice when it has become a quite completely well enough cultivated one, and there was not much use in using it when one was not wanting it to be helping to make one a gay one. Helen Furr was not needing using her voice to be a gay one. She was gay then and sometimes she used her voice and she was not using it very often. It was quite completely enough cultivated and it was quite completely a pleasant one and she did not use it very often. She was then, she was quite exactly as gay as she had been, she was gay a little longer in the day than she had been.

She was gay exactly the same way. She was never tired of being gay that way. She had learned very many little ways to use in being gay. Very many were telling about using other ways in being gay. She was gay enough, she was always gay exactly the same way, she was always learning little things to use in being gay, she was telling about using other ways in being gay, she was telling about learning other ways in being gay, she was learning other ways in being gay, she would be using other ways in being gay, she would always be gay in the same way, when Georgine Skeene was there not so long each day as when Georgine Skeene was away.

She came to using many ways in being gay, she came to use every way in being gay. She went on living where many were cultivating something and she was gay, she had used every way to be gay.

They did not live together then Helen Furr and Georgine Skeene. Helen 20
Furr lived there the longer where they had been living regularly together. Then neither of them were living there any longer. Helen Furr was living somewhere else then and telling some about being gay and she was gay then and she was living quite regularly then. She was regularly gay then. She was quite regular in being gay then. She remembered all the little ways of being gay. She used all the little ways of being gay. She was quite regularly gay. She told many then the way of being gay, she taught very many then little ways they could use in being gay. She was living very well, she was gay then, she went on living then, she was regular in being gay, she always was living very well and was gay very well and was telling about little ways one could be learning to use in being gay, and later was telling them quite often, telling them again and again.

GERTRUDE STEIN

(1874–1946) **Web** *www*

Originally a medical student and later a patron of the arts, Stein provided a center for innovative artistic activity in Paris. Befriending artists Pablo Picasso and Henri Matisse and young writers such as Ernest Hemingway and Sherwood Anderson, Stein developed a writing style in tune with cubism and verbal economy.

TOPICS FOR CRITICAL THINKING **Web** *www*

1. What are the relations between style and character in this story?
2. In what ways does the style of the story relate to the ideas of cubism? (For a discussion of cubism, see **Web**.) *www*
3. Through what strategies does the story convey the quality of the relationship between the two main characters?

TOPICS FOR CRITICAL WRITING **Web** *www*

1. Analyze the story's use of repetition. Link repetition to characterization, plot, and setting.
2. Define Stein's style and its relation to narrative.

Style as Substance

The complexities of style make it a crucial element of prose fiction, and yet because of the number and subtleties of the elements that comprise style, it is often difficult to describe. For this reason, style will often seem to be more a feeling or presence in the text. Just as Gertrude Stein's style might evoke the geometries of cubism, so also it conjures a particular presence—the substantial sense of a narrator who is guiding the telling. In the writing of William Faulkner, style contributes to the feeling that the narrator speaks from a position of wisdom that comes from a sense of the mythical patterns (life, death, renewal) that govern people and events: "When Miss Emily Grierson died, our whole town went to her funeral: the men through a sort of respectful attention for a fallen monument, the women mostly out of curiosity to see the inside of her house." Part of this effect is created through tone, which we will examine in greater depth in Chapter 11. Much of it, however, is created through such elements of style as the strategic use of adjectives ("respectful") and Faulkner's drawing attention to the differences in men's and women's motivations. This combination of wisdom and detail creates a feeling of simultaneously being close and distant from events. Style, in other words, can convey the sense of presence within a text as well as its perspective and range of knowledge.

Faulkner, a writer who produced prose invested with a strong sense of regional flavor, often wove tales of mythic proportion that focused on moments in the lives of individuals. His epic tale of generations of families in mythical Yoknapatawpha County, Mississippi, provides both a privileged view of history and the meaning of generations as well as an often sympathetic portrayal of the peculiarities and experiences of specific characters. (Note, for example, the way "A Rose for Emily" combines a historical view with the description of Emily's odd behaviors.) In drawing together the breadth of life with the idiosyncrasy of event, Faulkner's work produces a sustained portrait of the human comedy.

Featured Writer

WILLIAM FAULKNER

A Rose for Emily *(1930)*

I

When Miss Emily Grierson died, our whole town went to her funeral: the men through a sort of respectful affection for a fallen monument, the women mostly out of curiosity to see the inside of her house, which no one save an old man-servant—a combined gardener and cook—had seen in at least ten years.

It was a big, squarish frame house that had once been white, decorated with cupolas and spires, and scrolled balconies in the heavily lightsome style of the seventies, set on what had once been our most select street. But garages and cotton gins had encroached and obliterated even the august names of that neighborhood; only Miss Emily's house was left, lifting its stubborn and coquettish decay above the cotton wagons and the gasoline pumps—an eyesore among eyesores. And now Miss Emily had gone to join the representatives of those august names where they lay in the cedar-bemused cemetery among the ranked and anonymous graves of Union and Confederate soldiers who fell at the battle of Jefferson.

Alive, Miss Emily had been a tradition, a duty, and a care; a sort of hereditary obligation upon the town, dating from that day in 1894 when Colonel Sartoris, the mayor—he who fathered the edict that no Negro woman should appear on the street without an apron—remitted her taxes, the dispensation dating from the death of her father on into perpetuity. Not that Miss Emily would have accepted charity. Colonel Sartoris invented an involved tale to the effect that Miss Emily's father had loaned money to the town, which the town, as a matter of business, preferred this way of repaying. Only a man of Colonel Sartoris' generation and thought could have invented it, and only a woman could have believed it.

When the next generation, with its more modern ideas, became mayors and aldermen, this arrangement created some little dissatisfaction. On the first of the year they mailed her a tax notice. February came, and there was no reply. They wrote her a formal letter, asking her to call at the sheriff's office at her convenience. A week later the mayor wrote her himself, offering to call or to send his car for her, and received in reply a note on paper of an archaic shape, in a thin, flowing calligraphy in faded ink, to the effect that she no longer went out at all. The tax notice was also enclosed, without comment.

They called a special meeting of the Board of Aldermen. A deputation 5
waited upon her, knocked at the door through which no visitor had passed

since she ceased giving china-painting lessons eight or ten years earlier. They were admitted by the old Negro into a dim hall from which a stairway mounted into still more shadow. It smelled of dust and disuse—a close, dank smell. The Negro led them into the parlor. It was furnished in heavy, leather-covered furniture. When the Negro opened the blinds of one window, they could see that the leather was cracked; and when they sat down, a faint dust rose sluggishly about their thighs, spinning with slow motes in the single sun-ray. On a tarnished gilt easel before the fireplace stood a crayon portrait of Miss Emily's father.

They rose when she entered—a small, fat woman in black, with a thin gold chain descending to her waist and vanishing into her belt, leaning on an ebony cane with a tarnished gold head. Her skeleton was small and spare; perhaps that was why what would have been merely plumpness in another was obesity in her. She looked bloated, like a body long submerged in motionless water, and of that pallid hue. Her eyes, lost in the fatty ridges of her face, looked like two small pieces of coal pressed into a lump of dough as they moved from one face to another while the visitors stated their errand.

She did not ask them to sit. She just stood in the door and listened quietly until the spokesman came to a stumbling halt. Then they could hear the invisible watch ticking at the end of the gold chain.

Her voice was dry and cold. "I have no taxes in Jefferson. Colonel Sartoris explained it to me. Perhaps one of you can gain access to the city records and satisfy yourselves."

"But we have. We are the city authorities, Miss Emily. Didn't you get a notice from the sheriff, signed by him?"

"I received a paper, yes," Miss Emily said. "Perhaps he considers himself 10
the sheriff . . . I have no taxes in Jefferson."

"But there is nothing on the books to show that, you see. We must go by the—"

"See Colonel Sartoris. I have no taxes in Jefferson."

"But Miss Emily—"

"See Colonel Sartoris." (Colonel Sartoris had been dead almost ten years.) "I have no taxes in Jefferson. Tobe!" The Negro appeared. "Show these gentlemen out."

II

So she vanquished them, horse and foot, just as she had vanquished their 15
fathers thirty years before about the smell. That was two years after her father's death and a short time after her sweetheart—the one we believed would marry her—had deserted her. After her father's death she went out very little; after her sweetheart went away, people hardly saw her at all. A few of the ladies had the temerity to call, but were not received, and the only sign of life about the place was the Negro man—a young man then—going in and out with a market basket.

"Just as if a man—any man—could keep a kitchen properly," the ladies said; so they were not surprised when the smell developed. It was another link between the gross, teeming world and the high and mighty Griersons.

Edward Steichen, *Heavy Roses* (1914)

A neighbor, a woman, complained to the mayor, Judge Stevens, eighty years old.

"But what will you have me do about it, madam?" he said.

"Why, send her word to stop it," the woman said. "Isn't there a law?"

"I'm sure that won't be necessary," Judge Stevens said. "It's probably 20
just a snake or a rat that nigger of hers killed in the yard. I'll speak to him about it."

The next day he received two more complaints, one from a man who came in diffident deprecation. "We really must do something about it, Judge. I'd be the last one in the world to bother Miss Emily, but we've got to do something." That night the Board of Aldermen met—three graybeards and one younger man, a member of the rising generation.

"It's simple enough," he said. "Send her word to have her place cleaned up. Give her a certain time do it in, and if she don't . . ."

"Dammit, sir," Judge Stevens said, "will you accuse a lady to her face of smelling bad?"

So the next night, after midnight, four men crossed Miss Emily's lawn and slunk about the house like burglars, sniffing along the base of the brick-work and at the cellar openings while one of them performed a regular sowing motion with his hand out of a sack slung from his shoulder. They broke open the cellar door and sprinkled lime there, and in all the outbuildings. As they recrossed the lawn, a window that had been dark was lighted and Miss Emily sat in it, the light behind her, and her upright torso motionless as that of an idol. They crept quietly across the lawn and into the shadow of the locusts that lined the street. After a week or two the smell went away.

That was when people had begun to feel really sorry for her. People in 25
our town, remembering how old lady Wyatt, her great-aunt, had gone completely crazy at last, believed that the Griersons held themselves a little too high for what they really were. None of the young men were quite good enough for Miss Emily and such. We had long thought of them as a tableau, Miss Emily a slender figure in white in the background, her father a spraddled silhouette in the foreground, his back to her and clutching a horsewhip, the two of them framed by the backflung front door. When she got to be thirty and was still single, we were not pleased exactly, but vindicated; even with insanity in the family she wouldn't have turned down all of her chances if they had really materialized.

When her father died, it got about that the house was all that was left to her; and in a way, people were glad. At last they could pity Miss Emily. Being left alone, and a pauper, she had become humanized. Now she too would know the old thrill and the old despair of a penny more or less.

The day after his death all the ladies prepared to call at the house and offer condolence and aid, as is our custom. Miss Emily met them at the door, dressed as usual and with no trace of grief on her face. She told them that her father was not dead. She did that for three days, with the ministers calling on her, and the doctors, trying to persuade her to let them dispose of the body. Just as they were about to resort to law and force, she broke down, and they buried her father quickly.

We did not say she was crazy then. We believed she had to do that. We remembered all the young men her father had driven away, and we knew that with nothing left, she would have to cling to that which had robbed her, as people will.

III

She was sick for a long time. When we saw her again, her hair was cut short, making her look like a girl, with a vague resemblance to those angels in colored church windows—sort of tragic and serene.

The town had just let the contracts for paving the sidewalks, and in the 30
summer after her father's death they began the work. The construction company came with niggers and mules and machinery, and a foreman named Homer Barron, a Yankee—a big, dark, ready man, with a big voice and eyes lighter than his face. The little boys would follow in groups to hear him cuss the niggers, and the niggers singing in time to the rise and fall of picks. Pretty soon he knew everybody in town. Whenever you heard a lot of laughing anywhere about the square, Homer Barron would be in the center of the group. Presently we began to see him and Miss Emily on Sunday afternoons driving in the yellow-wheeled buggy and the matched team of bays from the livery stable.

At first we were glad that Miss Emily would have an interest, because the ladies all said, "Of course a Grierson would not think seriously of a Northerner, a day laborer." But there were still others, older people, who said that even grief could not cause a real lady to forget *noblesse oblige*—without calling it *noblesse oblige*. They just said, "Poor Emily. Her kinsfolk should come to her." She had some kin in Alabama; but years ago her father had fallen out with them over the estate of old Lady Wyatt, the crazy woman, and there was no communication between the two families. They had not even been represented at the funeral.

And as soon as the old people said, "Poor Emily," the whispering began. "Do you suppose it's really so?" they said to one another. "Of course it is. What else could . . ." This behind their hands; rustling of craned silk and satin behind jalousies closed upon the sun of Sunday afternoon as the thin, swift clop-clop-clop of the matched team passed: "Poor Emily."

She carried her head high enough—even when we believed that she was fallen. It was as if she demanded more than ever the recognition of her dignity as the last Grierson; as if it had wanted that touch of earthiness to reaffirm her imperviousness. Like when she bought the rat poison, the arsenic. That was over a year after they had begun to say "Poor Emily," and while the two female cousins were visiting her.

"I want some poison," she said to the druggist. She was over thirty then, still a slight woman, though thinner than usual, with cold, haughty black eyes in a face the flesh of which was strained across the temples and about the eyesockets as you imagine a lighthousekeeper's face ought to look. "I want some poison," she said.

"Yes, Miss Emily. What kind? For rats and such? I'd recom—" 35

"I want the best you have. I don't care what kind."

The druggist named several. "They'll kill anything up to an elephant. But what you want is—"

"Arsenic," Miss Emily said. "Is that a good one?"

"Is . . . arsenic? Yes, ma'am. But what you want—"

"I want arsenic." 40

The druggist looked down at her. She looked back at him, erect, her face like a strained flag. "Why, of course," the druggist said. "If that's what you want. But the law requires you to tell what you are going to use it for."

Miss Emily just stared at him, her head tilted back in order to look him eye for eye, until he looked away and went and got the arsenic and wrapped it up. The Negro delivery boy brought her the package; the druggist didn't come back. When she opened the package at home there was written on the box, under the skull and bones: "For rats."

IV

So the next day we all said, "She will kill herself"; and we said it would be the best thing. When she had first begun to be seen with Homer Barron, we had said, "She will marry him." Then we said, "She will persuade him yet," because Homer himself had remarked—he liked men, and it was known that he drank with the younger men in the Elks' Club—that he was not a marrying man. Later we said, "Poor Emily" behind the jalousies as they passed on

Sunday afternoon in the glittering buggy, Miss Emily with her head high and Homer Barron with his hat cocked and cigar in his teeth, reins and whip in a yellow glove.

Then some of the ladies began to say that it was a disgrace to the town and a bad example to the young people. The men did not want to interfere, but at last the ladies forced the Baptist minister—Miss Emily's people were Episcopal—to call upon her. He would never divulge what happened during that interview, but he refused to go back again. The next Sunday they again drove about the streets, and the following day the minister's wife wrote to Miss Emily's relations in Alabama.

So she had blood-kin under her roof again and we sat back to watch de- 45
velopments. At first nothing happened. Then we were sure that they were to be married. We learned that Miss Emily had been to the jeweler's and ordered a man's toilet set in silver, with the letters H. B. on each piece. Two days later we learned that she had bought a complete outfit of men's clothing, including a nightshirt, and we said, "They are married." We were really glad. We were glad because the two female cousins were even more Grierson than Miss Emily had ever been.

So we were not surprised when Homer Barron—the streets had been finished some time since—was gone. We were a little disappointed that there was not a public blowing-off, but we believed that he had gone on to prepare for Miss Emily's coming, or to give her a chance to get rid of the cousins. (By that time it was a cabal, and we were all Miss Emily's allies to help circumvent the cousins.) Sure enough, after another week they departed. And, as we had expected all along, within three days Homer Barron was back in town. A neighbor saw the Negro man admit him at the kitchen door at dusk one evening.

And that was the last we saw of Homer Barron. And of Miss Emily for some time. The Negro man went in and out with the market basket, but the front door remained closed. Now and then we would see her at a window for a moment, as the men did that night when they sprinkled the lime, but for almost six months she did not appear on the streets. Then we knew that this was to be expected too; as if that quality of her father which had thwarted her woman's life so many times had been too virulent and too furious to die.

When we next saw Miss Emily, she had grown fat and her hair was turning gray. During the next few years it grew grayer and grayer until it attained an even pepper-and-salt iron-gray, when it ceased turning. Up to the day of her death at seventy-four it was still that vigorous iron-gray, like the hair of an active man.

From that time on her front door remained closed, save for a period of six or seven years, when she was about forty, during which she gave lessons in china-painting. She fitted up a studio in one of the downstairs rooms, where the daughters and granddaughters of Colonel Sartoris' contemporaries were sent to her with the same regularity and in the same spirit that they were sent to church on Sunday with a twenty-five-cent piece for the collection plate. Meanwhile her taxes had been remitted.

Then the newer generation became the backbone and the spirit of the 50 town, and the painting pupils grew up and fell away and did not send their children to her with boxes of color and tedious brushes and pictures cut from the ladies' magazines. The front door closed upon the last one and remained closed for good. When the town got free postal delivery, Miss Emily alone refused to let them fasten the metal numbers above her door and attach a mailbox to it. She would not listen to them.

Daily, monthly, yearly we watched the Negro grow grayer and more stooped, going in and out with the market basket. Each December we sent her a tax notice, which would be returned by the post office a week later, unclaimed. Now and then we would see her in one of the downstairs windows—she had evidently shut up the top floor of the house—like the carven torso of an idol in a niche, looking or not looking at us, we could never tell which. Thus she passed from generation to generation—dear, inescapable, impervious, tranquil, and perverse.

And so she died. Fell ill in the house filled with dust and shadows, with only a doddering Negro man to wait on her. We did not even know she was sick; we had long since given up trying to get any information from the Negro. He talked to no one, probably not even to her, for his voice had grown harsh and rusty, as if from disuse.

She died in one of the downstairs rooms, in a heavy walnut bed with a curtain, her gray head propped on a pillow yellow and moldy with age and lack of sunlight.

V

The Negro met the first of the ladies at the front door and let them in, with their hushed, sibilant voices and their quick, curious glances, and then he disappeared. He walked right through the house and out the back and was not seen again.

55 The two female cousins came at once. They held the funeral on the second day, with the town coming to look at Miss Emily beneath a mass of bought flowers, with the crayon face of her father musing profoundly above the bier and the ladies sibilant and macabre; and the very old men—some in their brushed Confederate uniforms—on the porch and the lawn, talking of Miss Emily as if she had been a contemporary of theirs, believing that they had danced with her and courted her perhaps, confusing time with its mathematical progression, as the old do, to whom all the past is not a diminishing road but, instead, a huge meadow which no winter ever quite touches, divided from them now by the narrow bottle-neck of the most recent decade of years.

Already we knew that there was one room in that region above stairs which no one had seen in forty years, and which would have to be forced. They waited until Miss Emily was decently in the ground before they opened it.

The violence of breaking down the door seemed to fill this room with pervading dust. A thin, acrid pall of the tomb seemed to lie everywhere upon this room decked and furnished as for a bridal: upon the valance curtains of faded rose color, upon the rose-shaded lights, upon the dressing table, upon the delicate array of crystal and the man's toilet things backed with tarnished silver, silver so tarnished that the monogram was obscured. Among them lay a collar and tie, as if they had just been removed, which, lifted, left upon the surface a pale crescent in the dust. Upon a chair hung the suit, carefully folded; beneath it the two mute shoes and the discarded socks.

The man himself lay in the bed.

For a long while we just stood there, looking down at the profound and fleshless grin. The body had apparently once lain in the attitude of an embrace, but now the long sleep that outlasts love, that conquers even the grimace of love, had cuckolded him. What was left of him, rotted beneath what was left of the nightshirt, had become inextricable from the bed in which he lay; and upon him and upon the pillow beside him lay that even coating of the patient and biding dust.

Then we noticed that in the second pillow was the indentation of a head. One of us lifted something from it, and leaning forward, that faint and invisible dust dry and acrid in the nostrils, we saw a long strand of iron-gray hair.

WILLIAM FAULKNER

www

(1897–1962) **Web**

An airman in the Royal Air Force, William Faulkner was another writer who sought a Parisian atmosphere in which to write. Unlike Fitzgerald and Hemingway, however, Faulkner's writing was best nourished by his Mississippi home, about which he wrote for the rest of his life. After marrying his childhood sweetheart in 1929, Faulkner wrote *The Sound and the Fury* and *As I Lay Dying*, beginning a major body of work that would eventually win him the Nobel Prize (1949). From 1932 and through the 1940s, Faulkner worked on and off as a Hollywood screenwriter, collaborating with directors Howard Hawks and Jean Renoir and garnering six screenwriting credits for films, most notably for the film *To Have and Have Not* staring Humphrey Bogart and Lauren Bacall. Spinning out the intertwined histories of several families, Faulkner's novels have an epic quality derived from their sense of generations and the mythical play of sin, debt, and legacy that haunts the present from the past.

www

TOPICS FOR CRITICAL THINKING **Web**

1. Through the use of which specific words does the story change the feeling of distance and proximity from point to point in the story?
2. What purpose does the narrator's flexible distance serve in relation to the narrative of Miss Emily?
3. At what point in the story does the reader begin to suspect what has happened in Miss Emily's life? What are the functions of the dramatic irony that ensues?
4. What is the meaning of the gray hair on the pillow?
5. Explain the story's title.

www

TOPICS FOR CRITICAL WRITING **Web**

1. Explain the various social and personal relations "taxes" might represent in this story.
2. In what ways is the story about community?

Golden Land

(1935)

If he had been thirty, he would not have needed the two aspirin tablets and the half glass of raw gin before he could bear the shower's needling on his body and steady his hands to shave. But then when he had been thirty neither could he have afforded to drink as much each evening as he now drank; certainly he would not have done it in the company of the men and the women in which, at forty-eight, he did each evening, even though knowing during the very final hours filled with the breaking of glass and the shrill cries of drunken women above the drums and saxophones—the hours during which he carried a little better than his weight both in the amount of liquor consumed and in the number and sum of checks paid—that six or eight hours later he would rouse from what had not been sleep at all but instead that dreamless stupefaction of alcohol out of which last night's turgid and licensed uproar would die, as though without any interval for rest or recuperation, into the familiar shape of his bedroom—the bed's foot silhouetted by the morning light which entered the bougainvillaea-bound windows beyond which his painful and almost unbearable eyes could see the view which might be called the monument to almost twenty-five years of industry and desire, of shrewdness and luck and even fortitude—the opposite canyonflank dotted with the white villas halfhidden in imported olive groves or friezed by the sombre spaced columns of cypress like the façades of eastern temples, whose owners' names and faces and even voices were glib and familiar in back corners of the United States and of America and of the world where those of Einstein and Rousseau and Esculapius had never sounded.

He didn't waken sick. He never wakened ill nor became ill from drinking, not only because he had drunk too long and too steadily for that, but because he was too tough even after the thirty soft years; he came from too tough stock on that day thirty-four years ago when at fourteen he had fled, on the brakebeam of a westbound freight, the little lost Nebraska town named for, permeated with, his father's history and existence—a town to be sure, but only in the sense that any shadow is larger than the object which casts it. It was still frontier even as he remembered it at five and six—the projected and increased shadow of a small outpost of sodroofed dugouts on the immense desolation of the plains where his father, Ira Ewing too, had been first to essay to wring wheat during the six days between those when, outdoors in spring and summer and in the fetid halfdark of a snowbound dugout in the winter and fall, he preached. The second Ira Ewing had come a long way since then, from that barren and treeless village which he had fled by a night freight to where he now lay in a hundred-thousand-dollar house, waiting until he knew that he could rise and go to the bath and put the two aspirin tablets into his mouth. They—his mother and father—had tried to explain it to him—something about fortitude, the will to endure. At fourteen he could neither answer them with logic and reason nor explain what he wanted: he could only flee. Nor was he fleeing his father's harshness and wrath. He was fleeing the scene itself—the treeless immensity in the lost center of which he seemed to see the sum of his father's and mother's dead youth and bartered lives as a tiny forlorn spot which nature permitted to green into brief and niggard wheat for a season's moment before blotting it all with the primal and invincible snow as though (not even promise, not even threat) in grim and almost playful augury of the final doom of all life. And it was not even this that he was fleeing because he was not fleeing: it was only that absence, removal, was the only argument which fourteen knew how to employ against adults with any hope of success. He spent the next ten years half tramp half casual laborer as he drifted down the Pacific Coast to Los Angeles; at thirty he was married, to a Los Angeles girl, daughter of a carpenter, and father of a son and a daughter and with a foothold in real estate; at forty-eight he spent fifty thousand dollars a year, owning a business which he had built up unaided and preserved intact through nineteen-twenty-nine; he had given to his children luxuries and advantages which his own father not only could not have conceived in fact but would have condemned completely in theory—as it proved, as the paper which the Filipino chauffeur, who each morning carried him into the house and undressed him and put him to bed, had removed from the pocket of his topcoat and laid on the reading table proved, with reason. On the death of his father twenty years ago he had returned to Nebraska, for the first time, and fetched his mother back with him, and she was now established in a home of her own only the less sumptuous because she refused (with a kind of abashed and thoughtful unshakability which he did not remark) anything finer or more elaborate. It was the house in which they had all lived at first, though he and his wife and children had moved within the year. Three years ago they had moved again, into the house where he now waked in a select residential section of Beverley Hills, but not once in the nineteen years had he failed to stop (not even during the last five, when to move at all in the mornings required a terrific drain on that character or strength which the elder Ira had bequeathed him, which had enabled the other Ira to pause on the Nebraska plain and dig a hole for his wife to bear children in while he planted wheat) on his way to the office (twenty miles out of his way to the office) and spend ten minutes with her. She lived in as complete physical ease and peace as he could devise. He had arranged her affairs so that she did not even need to bother with money, cash, in order to live; he had arranged credit for her with a neighboring market and butcher so that the Japanese gardener who came each day to water and tend the flowers could do her shopping for her; she never even saw the bills. And the only reason she had no servant was that even at seventy she apparently clung stubbornly to the old habit of doing her own cooking and housework. So it would seem that he had been right. Perhaps there were times when, lying in bed like this and waiting for the will to rise and take the aspirin and the gin (mornings perhaps following evenings when he had drunk more than ordinarily and when even the six or seven hours of oblivion had not been sufficient to enable him to distinguish between reality and illusion) something of the old strong harsh Campbellite blood which the elder Ira must have bequeathed him might have caused him to see or feel or imagine his father looking down from somewhere upon him, the prodigal, and what he had accomplished. If this were so, then surely the elder Ira, looking down for the last two mornings upon the two tabloid papers which the Filipino removed from his master's topcoat and laid on the reading table, might have taken advantage of that old blood and taken his revenge, not just for that afternoon thirty-four years ago but for the entire thirty-four years.

When he gathered himself, his will, his body, at last and rose from the bed he struck the paper so that it fell to the floor and lay open at his feet, but he did not look at it. He just stood so, tall in silk pajamas, thin where his father had been gaunt with the years of hard work and unceasing struggle with the unpredictable and implacable earth (even now, despite the life which he had led, he had very little paunch) looking at nothing while at his feet the black headline flared above the row of five or six tabloid photographs from which his daughter alternately stared back or flaunted long pale shins: APRIL LALEAR BARES ORGY SECRETS. When he moved at last he stepped on the paper, walking on his bare feet into the bath; now it was his trembling and jerking hands that he watched as he shook the two tablets onto the glass shelf and set the tumbler into the rack and unstoppered the gin bottle and braced his knuckles against the wall in order to pour into the tumbler. But he did not look at the paper, not even when, shaved, he re-entered the bedroom and went to the bed beside which his slippers sat and shoved the paper aside with his foot in order to step into them. Perhaps, doubtless, he did not need to. The trial was but entering its third tabloidal day now, and so for two days his daughter's face had sprung out at him, hard, blonde and inscrutable, from every paper he opened; doubtless he had never forgot her while he slept even, that he had waked into thinking about remembering her as he had waked into the dying drunken uproar of the evening eight hours behind him without any interval between for rest or forgetting.

Nevertheless as, dressed, in a burnt orange turtleneck sweater beneath his gray flannels, he descended the Spanish staircase, he was outwardly calm and possessed. The delicate iron balustrade and the marble steps coiled down to the tile-floored and barnlike living room beyond which he could hear his wife and son talking on the breakfast terrace. The son's name was Voyd. He and his wife had named the two children by what might have been called mutual contemptuous armistice—his wife called the boy Voyd, for what reason he never knew; he in his turn named the girl (the child whose woman's face had met him from every paper he touched for two days now beneath or above the name, April Lalear) Samantha, after his own mother. He could hear them talking—the wife between whom and himself there had been nothing save civility, and not always a great deal of that, for ten years now; and the son who one afternoon two years ago had been delivered at the door drunk and insensible by a car whose occupants he did not see and, it devolving upon him to undress the son and put him to bed, whom he discovered to be wearing, in place of underclothes, a woman's brassière and step-ins. A few minutes later, hearing the blows perhaps, Voyd's mother ran in and found her husband beating the still unconscious son with a series of towels which a servant was steeping in rotation in a basin of ice-water. He was beating the son hard, with grim and deliberate fury. Whether he was trying to sober the son up or was merely beating him, possibly he himself did not know. His wife though jumped to the latter conclusion. In his raging disillusionment he tried to tell her about the woman's garments but she refused to listen; she assailed him in turn with virago fury. Since that day the son had contrived to see his father only in his mother's presence (which neither the son nor the mother found very difficult, by the way) and at which times the son treated his father with a blend of cringing spite and vindictive insolence half a cat's and half a woman's.

5 He emerged onto the terrace; the voices ceased. The sun, strained by the vague high soft almost nebulous California haze, fell upon the terrace with a kind of treacherous unbrightness. The terrace, the sundrenched terra cotta tiles, butted into a rough and savage shear of canyonwall bare yet without dust, on or against which a solid mat of flowers bloomed in fierce lush myriad-colored paradox as though in place of being rooted into and drawing from the soil they lived upon air alone and had been merely leaned intact against the sustenanceless lavawall by someone who would later return and take them away. The son, Voyd, apparently naked save for a pair of straw-colored shorts, his body brown with sun and scented faintly by the depilatory which he used on arms, chest and legs, lay in a wicker chair, his feet in straw beach shoes, an open newspaper across his brown legs. The paper was the highest class one of the city, yet there was a black headline across half of it too, and even without pausing, without even being aware that he had looked, Ira saw there too the name which he recognized. He went on to his place; the Filipino who put him to bed each night, in a white service jacket now, drew his chair. Beside the glass of orange juice and the waiting cup lay a neat pile of mail topped by a telegram. He sat down and took up the telegram; he had not glanced at his wife until she spoke:

"Mrs. Ewing telephoned. She says for you to stop in there on your way to town."

He stopped; his hands opening the telegram stopped. Still blinking a little against the sun he looked at the face opposite him across the table—the smooth dead makeup, the thin lips and the thin nostrils and the pale blue unforgiving eyes, the meticulous platinum hair which looked as though it had been transferred to her skull with a brush from a book of silver leaf such as window painters use. "What?" he said. "Telephoned? Here?"

"Why not? Have I ever objected to any of your women telephoning you here?"

The unopened telegram crumpled suddenly in his hand. "You know what I mean," he said harshly. "She never telephoned me in her life. She don't have to. Not that message. When have I ever failed to go by there on my way to town?"

10 "How do I know?" she said. "Or are you the same model son you have been a husband and seem to be a father?" Her voice was not shrill yet, nor even very loud, and none could have told how fast her breathing was because she sat so still, rigid beneath the impeccable and unbelievable hair, looking at him with that pale and outraged unforgiveness. They both looked at each other across the luxurious table—the two people who at one time twenty years ago would have turned as immediately and naturally and unthinkingly to one another in trouble, who even ten years ago might have done so.

"You know what I mean," he said, harshly again, holding himself too against the trembling which he doubtless believed was from last night's drinking, from the spent alcohol. "She don't read papers. She never even sees one. Did you send it to her?"

"I?" she said. "Send what?"

"Damnation!" he cried. "A paper! Did you send it to her? Don't lie to me."

"What if I did?" she cried. "Who is she, that she must not know about it? Who is she, that you should shield her from knowing it? Did you make any effort to keep me from knowing it? Did you make any effort to keep it from happening? Why didn't you think about that all those years while you were too drunk, too besotted with drink, to know or notice or care what Samantha was—"

"Miss April Lalear of the cinema, if you please," Voyd said. They paid no attention to him; they glared at one another across the table.

"Ah," he said, quiet and rigid, his lips scarcely moving. "So I am to blame for this too, am I? I made my daughter a bitch, did I? Maybe you will tell me next that I made my son a f—"

"Stop!" she cried. She was panting now; they glared at one another across the suave table, across the five feet of irrevocable division.

"Now, now," Voyd said. "Don't interfere with the girl's career. After all these years, when at last she seems to have found a part that she can—" He ceased; his father had turned and was looking at him. Voyd lay in his chair, looking at his father with that veiled insolence that was almost feminine. Suddenly it became completely feminine; with a muffled halfscream he swung his legs out to spring up and flee but it was too late; Ira stood above him, gripping him not by the throat but by the face with one hand, so that Voyd's mouth puckered and slobbered in his father's hard, shaking hand. Then the mother sprang forward and tried to break Ira's grip but he flung her away and then caught and held her, struggling too, with the other hand when she sprang in again.

"Go on," he said. "Say it." But Voyd could say nothing because of his father's hand gripping his jaws open, or more than likely because of terror. His body was free of the chair now, writhing and thrashing while he made his slobbering, moaning sound of terror while his father held him with one hand and held his screaming mother with the other one. Then Ira flung Voyd free, onto the terrace; Voyd rolled once and came onto his feet, crouching, retreating toward the French windows with one arm flung up before his face while he cursed his father. Then he was gone. Ira faced his wife, holding her quiet too at last, panting too, the skillful map of makeup standing into relief now like a paper mask trimmed smoothly and pasted onto her skull. He released her.

"You sot," she said. "You drunken sot. And yet you wonder why your children—"

"Yes," he said quietly. "All right. That's not the question. That's all done. The question is, what to do about it. My father would have known. He did it once." He spoke in a dry light pleasant voice: so much so that she stood, panting still but quiet, watching him. "I remember. I was about ten. We had rats in the barn. We tried everything. Terriers. Poison. Then one day father said, 'Come.' We went to the barn and stopped all the cracks, the holes. Then we set fire to it. What do you think of that?" Then she was gone too. He stood for a moment, blinking a little, his eyeballs beating faintly and steadily in his skull with the impact of the soft unchanging sunlight, the fierce innocent mass of the flowers. "Philip!" he called. The Filipino appeared, brownfaced, impassive, with a pot of hot coffee, and set it beside the empty cup and the icebedded glass of orange juice. "Get me a drink," Ira said. The Filipino glanced at him, then he became busy at the table, shifting the cup and setting the pot down and shifting the cup again while Ira watched him. "Did you hear me?" Ira said. The Filipino stood erect and looked at him.

"You told me not to give it to you until you had your orange juice and coffee."

"Will you or won't you get me a drink?" Ira shouted.

"Very good, sir," the Filipino said. He went out. Ira looked after him; this had happened before: he knew well that the brandy would not appear until he had finished the orange juice and the coffee, though just where the Filipino lurked to watch him he never knew. He sat again and opened the crumpled telegram and read it, the glass of orange juice in the other hand. It was from his secretary: MADE SETUP BEFORE I BROKE STORY LAST NIGHT STOP THIRTY PERCENT FRONT PAGE STOP MADE APPOINTMENT FOR YOU COURTHOUSE THIS P.M. STOP WILL YOU COME TO OFFICE OR CALL ME. He read the telegram again, the glass of orange juice still poised. Then he put both down and rose and went and lifted the paper from the terrace where Voyd had flung it, and read the half headline: LALEAR WOMAN DAUGHTER OF PROMINENT LOCAL FAMILY. Admits Real Name Is Samantha Ewing, Daughter of Ira Ewing, Local Realtor. He read it quietly; he said quietly, aloud:

"It was that Jap that showed her the paper. It was that damned gardener." He returned to the table. After a while the Filipino came, with the brandy-and-soda, and wearing now a jacket of bright imitation tweed, telling him that the car was ready.

II

His mother lived in Glendale; it was the house which he had taken when he married and later bought, in which his son and daughter had been born—a bungalow in a cul-de-sac of pepper trees and flowering shrubs and vines which the Japanese tended, backed into a barren foothill combed and curried into a cypress-and-marble cemetery dramatic as a stage set and topped by an electric sign in red bulbs which, in the San Fernando valley fog, glared in broad sourceless ruby as though just beyond the crest lay not heaven but hell. The length of his sports model car in which the Filipino sat reading a paper dwarfed it. But she would have no other, just as she would have neither servant, car, nor telephone—a gaunt spare slightly stooped woman upon whom even California and ease had put no flesh, sitting in one of the chairs which she had insisted on bringing all the way from Nebraska. At first she had been content to allow the Nebraska furniture to remain in storage, since it had not been needed (when Ira moved his wife and family out of the house and into the second one, the intermediate one, they had bought new furniture too, leaving the first house furnished complete for his mother) but one day, he could not recall just when, he discovered that she had taken the one chair out of storage and was using it in the house. Later, after he began to sense that quality of unrest in her, he had suggested that she let him clear the house of its present furniture and take all of hers out of storage but she declined, apparently preferring or desiring to leave the Nebraska furniture where it was. Sitting so, a knitted shawl about her shoulders, she looked less like she lived in or belonged to the house, the room, than the son with his beach burn and his faintly theatrical gray temples and his bright expensive suavely antiphonal garments did. She had changed hardly at all in the thirty-four years; she and the older Ira Ewing too, as the son remembered him, who, dead, had suffered as little of alteration as while he had been alive. As the sod Nebraska outpost had grown into a village and then into a town, his father's aura alone had increased, growing into the proportions of a giant who at some irrevocable yet recent time had engaged barehanded in some titanic struggle with the pitiless earth and endured and in a sense conquered—it too, like the town, a shadow out of all proportion to the gaunt gnarled figure of the actual man. And the actual woman too as the son remembered them back in that time. Two people who drank air and who required to eat and sleep as he did and who had brought him into the world, yet were strangers as though of another race, who stood side by side in an irrevocable loneliness as though strayed from another planet, not as husband and wife but as blood brother and sister, even twins, of the same travail because they had gained a strange peace through fortitude and the will and strength to endure.

"Tell me again what it is," she said. "I'll try to understand."

"So it was Kazimura that showed you the damned paper," he said. She didn't answer this; she was not looking at him.

"You tell me she has been in the pictures before, for two years. That that was why she had to change her name, that they all have to change their names."

"Yes. They call them extra parts. For about two years, God knows why."

"And then you tell me that this—that all this was so she could get into the pictures—"

He started to speak, then he caught himself back out of some quick impatience, some impatience perhaps of grief or despair or at least rage, holding his voice, his tone, quiet: "I said that that was one possible reason. All I know is that the man has something to do with pictures, giving out the parts. And that the police caught him and Samantha and the other girl in an apartment with the doors all locked and that Samantha and the other woman were naked. They say that he was naked too and he says he was not. He says in the trial that he was framed—tricked; that they were trying to blackmail him into giving them parts in a picture; that they fooled him into coming there and arranged for the police to break in just after they had taken off their clothes; that one of them made a signal from the window. Maybe so. Or maybe they were all just having a good time and were innocently caught." Unmoving, rigid, his face broke, wrung with faint bitter smiling as though with indomitable and impassive suffering, or maybe just smiling, just rage. Still his mother did not look at him.

"But you told me she was already in the pictures. That that was why she had to change her—"

"I said, extra parts," he said. He had to catch himself again, out of his jangled and outraged nerves, back from the fierce fury of the impatience. "Can't you understand that you don't get into the pictures just by changing your name? and that you don't even stay there when you get in? that you can't even stay there by being female? that they come here in droves on every train—girls younger and prettier than Samantha and who will do anything to get into the pictures? So will she, apparently; but who know or are willing to learn to do more things than even she seems to have thought of? But let's don't talk about it. She has made her bed; all I can do is to help her up: I can't wash the sheets. Nobody can. I must go, anyway; I'm late." He rose, looking down at her. "They said you telephoned me this morning. Is this what it was?"

"No," she said. Now she looked up at him; now her gnarled hands began to pick faintly at one another. "You offered me a servant once."

"Yes. I thought fifteen years ago that you ought to have one. Have you changed your mind? Do you want me to—"

Now she stopped looking at him again, though her hands did not cease. "That was fifteen years ago. It would have cost at least five hundred dollars a year. That would be—"

He laughed, short and harsh. "I'd like to see the Los Angeles servant you could get for five hundred dollars a year. But what—" He stopped laughing, looking down at her.

"That would be at least five thousand dollars," she said.

He looked down at her. After a while he said, "Are you asking me again for money?" She didn't answer nor move her hands picking slowly and quietly at one another. "Ah," he said. "You want to go away. You want to run from it. So do I!" he cried, before he could catch himself this time; "so do I! But you did not choose me when you elected a child; neither did I choose my two. But I shall have to bear them and you will have to bear all of us. There is no help for it." He caught himself now, panting, quieting himself by will as when he would rise from bed, though his voice was still harsh: "Where would you go? Where would you hide from it?"

"Home," she said.

"Home?" he repeated; he repeated in a kind of amazement: "home?" before he understood. "You would go back there? with those winters, that snow and all? Why, you wouldn't live to see the first Christmas: don't you know that?" She didn't move nor look up at him. "Nonsense," he said. "This will blow over. In a month there will be two others and nobody except us will even remember it. And you don't need money. You have been asking me for money for years, but you don't need it. I had to worry about money so much at one time myself that I swore that the least I could do was to arrange your affairs so you would never even have to look at the stuff. I must go; there is something at the office today. I'll see you tomorrow."

It was already one o'clock. "Courthouse," he told the Filipino, settling back into the car. "My God, I want a drink." He rode with his eyes closed against the sun; the secretary had already sprung onto the runningboard before he realized that they had reached the courthouse. The secretary, bareheaded too, wore a jacket of authentic tweed; his turtleneck sweater was dead black, his hair was black too, varnished smooth to his skull; he spread before Ira a dummy newspaper page laid out to embrace the blank space for the photograph beneath the caption: APRIL LALEAR'S FATHER. Beneath the space was the legend: IRA EWING, PRESIDENT OF THE EWING REALTY CO.,—WILSHIRE BOULEVARD, BEVERLY HILLS.

"Is thirty percent all you could get?" Ira said. The secretary was young; he glared at Ira for an instant in vague impatient fury.

"Jesus, thirty percent is thirty percent. They are going to print a thousand 45
extra copies and use our mailing list. It will be spread all up and down the Coast and as far East as Reno. What do you want? We can't expect them to put under your picture, 'Turn to page fourteen for halfpage ad,' can we?" Ira sat again with his eyes closed, waiting for his head to stop.

"All right," he said. "Are they ready now?"

"All set. You will have to go inside. They insisted it be inside, so everybody that sees it will know it is the courthouse."

"All right," Ira said. He got out; with his eyes half closed and the secretary at his elbow he mounted the steps and entered the courthouse. The reporter and the photographer were waiting but he did not see them yet; he was aware only of being enclosed in a gaping crowd which he knew would be mostly women, hearing the secretary and a policeman clearing the way in the corridor outside the courtroom door.

"This is O.K.," the secretary said. Ira stopped; the darkness was easier on his eyes though he did not open them yet; he just stood, hearing the secretary and the policeman herding the women, the faces, back; someone took him by the arm and turned him; he stood obediently; the magnesium flashed and glared, striking against his painful eyeballs like blows; he had a vision of wan faces craned to look at him from either side of a narrow human lane; with his eyes shut tight now he turned, blundering until the reporter in charge spoke to him:

"Just a minute, chief. We better get another one just in case." This time 50
his eyes were tightly closed; the magnesium flashed, washed over them; in the thin acrid smell of it he turned and with the secretary again at his elbow he moved blindly back and into the sunlight and into his car. He gave no order this time, he just said, "Get me a drink." He rode with his eyes closed again while the car cleared the downtown traffic and then began to move quiet, powerful and fast under him; he rode so for a long while before he felt the car swing into the palmbordered drive, slowing. It stopped; the doorman opened the door for him, speaking to him by name. The elevator boy called him by name too, stopping at the right floor without direction; he followed the corridor and knocked at a door and was fumbling for the key when the door opened upon a woman in a bathing suit beneath a loose beach cloak—a woman with treated hair also and brown eyes, who swung the door back for him to enter and then to behind him, looking at him with the quick bright

faint serene smiling which only a woman nearing forty can give to a man to whom she is not married and from whom she has had no secrets physical and few mental over a long time of pleasant and absolute intimacy. She had been married though and divorced; she had a child, a daughter of fourteen, whom he was now keeping in boarding school. He looked at her, blinking, as she closed the door.

"You saw the papers," he said. She kissed him, not suddenly, without heat, in a continuation of the movement which closed the door, with a sort of warm envelopment; suddenly he cried, "I can't understand it! After all the advantages that . . . after all I tried to do for them—"

"Hush," she said. "Hush, now. Get into your trunks; I'll have a drink ready for you when you have changed. Will you eat some lunch if I have it sent up?"

"No. I don't want any lunch. —after all I have tried to give—"

"Hush, now. Get into your trunks while I fix you a drink. It's going to be swell at the beach." In the bedroom his bathing trunks and robe were laid out on the bed. He changed, hanging his suit in the closet where her clothes hung, where there hung already another suit of his and clothes for the evening. When he returned to the sitting room she had fixed the drink for him; she held the match to his cigarette and watched him sit down and take up the glass, watching him still with that serene impersonal smiling. Now he watched her slip off the cape and kneel at the cellarette, filling a silver flask, in the bathing costume of the moment, such as ten thousand wax female dummies wore in ten thousand shop windows that summer, such as a hundred thousand young girls wore on California beaches; he looked at her, kneeling—back, buttocks and flanks trim enough, even firm enough (so firm in fact as to be a little on the muscular side, what with unremitting and perhaps even rigorous care) but still those of forty. But I don't want a young girl, he thought. Would to God that all young girls, all young female flesh, were removed, blasted even, from the earth. He finished the drink before she had filled the flask.

"I want another one," he said.

"All right," she said. "As soon as we get to the beach."

"No. Now."

"Let's go on to the beach first. It's almost three o'clock. Won't that be better?"

"Just so you are not trying to tell me I can't have another drink now."

"Of course not," she said, slipping the flask into the cape's pocket and looking at him again with that warm, faint, inscrutable smiling. "I just want to have a dip before the water gets too cold." They went down to the car; the Filipino knew this too: he held the door for her to slip under the wheel, then he got himself into the back. The car moved on; she drove well. "Why not lean back and shut your eyes," she told Ira, "and rest until we get to the beach? Then we will have a dip and a drink."

"I don't want to rest," he said. "I'm all right." But he did close his eyes again and again the car ran powerful, smooth, and fast beneath him, performing its afternoon's jaunt over the incredible distances of which the city was composed; from time to time, had he looked, he could have seen the city in the bright soft vague hazy sunlight, random, scattered about the arid earth like so many gay scraps of paper blown without order, with its curious air of being rootless—of houses bright beautiful and gay, without basements or foundations, lightly attached to a few inches of light penetrable earth, lighter even than dust and laid lightly in turn upon the profound and primeval lava, which one good hard rain would wash forever from the sight and memory of man as a firehose flushes down a gutter—that city of almost incalculable wealth whose queerly appropriate fate it is to be erected upon a few spools of a substance whose value is computed in billions and which may be completely destroyed in that second's instant of a careless match between the moment of striking and the moment when the striker might have sprung and stamped it out.

"You saw your mother today," she said. "Has she—"

"Yes." He didn't open his eyes. "That damned Jap gave it to her. She asked me for money again. I found out what she wants with it. She wants to run, to go back to Nebraska. I told her, so did I. . . . If she went back there, she would not live until Christmas. The first month of winter would kill her. Maybe it wouldn't even take winter to do it."

She still drove, she still watched the road, yet somehow she had contrived to become completely immobile. "So that's what it is," she said.

He did not open his eyes. "What what is?" 65

"The reason she has been after you all this time to give her money, cash. Why, even when you won't do it, every now and then she asks you again."

"What what . . ." He opened his eyes, looking at her profile; he sat up suddenly. "You mean, she's been wanting to go back there all the time? That all these years she has been asking me for money, that that was what she wanted with it?"

She glanced at him swiftly, then back to the road. "What else can it be? What else could she use money for?"

"Back there?" he said. "To those winters, that town, that way of living, where she's bound to know that the first winter would . . . You'd almost think she wanted to die, wouldn't you?"

70 "Hush," she said quickly. "Shhhhh. Don't say that. Don't say that about anybody." Already they could smell the sea; now they swung down toward it; the bright salt wind blew upon them, with the long-spaced sound of the rollers; now they could see it—the dark blue of water creaming into the blanched curve of beach dotted with bathers. "We won't go through the club," she said. "I'll park in here and we can go straight to the water." They left the Filipino in the car and descended to the beach. It was already crowded, bright and gay with movement. She chose a vacant space and spread her cape.

"Now that drink," he said.

"Have your dip first," she said. He looked at her. Then he slipped his robe off slowly; she took it and spread it beside her own; he looked down at her.

"Which is it? Will you always be too clever for me, or is it that every time I will always believe you again?"

She looked at him, bright, warm, fond and inscrutable. "Maybe both. Maybe neither. Have your dip; I will have the flask and a cigarette ready when you come out." When he came back from the water, wet, panting, his heart a little too hard and fast, she had the towel ready, and she lit the cigarette and uncapped the flask as he lay on the spread robes. She lay too, lifted to one elbow, smiling down at him, smoothing the water from his hair with the towel while he panted, waiting for his heart to slow and quiet. Steadily between them and the water, and as far up and down the beach as they could see, the bathers passed—young people, young men in trunks, and young girls in little more, with bronzed, unselfconscious bodies. Lying so, they seemed to him to walk along the rim of the world as though they and their kind alone inhabited it, and he with his forty-eight years were the forgotten last survivor of another race and kind, and they in turn precursors of a new race not yet seen on the earth: of men and women without age, beautiful as gods and goddesses, and with the minds of infants. He turned quickly and looked at the woman beside him—at the quiet face, the wise, smiling eyes, the grained skin and temples, the hairroots showing where the dye had grown out, the legs veined faint and blue and myriad beneath the skin. "You look better than any of them!" he cried. "You look better to me than any of them!"

III

The Japanese gardener, with his hat on, stood tapping on the glass and 75
beckoning and grimacing until old Mrs. Ewing went out to him. He had the afternoon's paper with its black headline: LALEAR WOMAN CREATES SCENE IN COURTROOM. "You take," the Japanese said. "Read while I catch water." But she declined; she just stood in the soft halcyon sunlight, surrounded by the myriad and almost fierce blooming of flowers, and looked quietly at the headline without even taking the paper, and that was all.

"I guess I won't look at the paper today," she said. "Thank you just the same." She returned to the living room. Save for the chair, it was exactly as it had been when she first saw it that day when her son brought her into it and told her that it was now her home and that her daughter-in-law and her grandchildren were now her family. It had changed very little, and that which had altered was the part which her son knew nothing about, and that too had changed not at all in so long that she could not even remember now when she had added the last coin to the hoard. This was in a china vase on the mantel. She knew what was in it to the penny; nevertheless, she took it down and sat in the chair which she had brought all the way from Nebraska and emptied the coins and the worn timetable into her lap. The timetable was folded back at the page on which she had folded it the day she walked downtown to the ticket office and got it fifteen years ago, though that was so long ago now that the pencil circle about the name of the nearest junction point to Ewing, Nebraska, had faded away. But she did not need that either; she knew the distance to the exact halfmile, just as she knew the fare to the penny, and back in the early twenties when the railroads began to become worried and passenger fares began to drop, no broker ever watched the grain and utilities market any closer than she watched the railroad advertisements and quotations. Then at last the fares became stabilized with the fare back to Ewing thirteen dollars more than she had been able to save, and at a time when her source of income had ceased. This was the two grandchildren. When she entered the house that day twenty years ago and looked at the two babies for the first time, it was with diffidence and eagerness both. She would be dependent for the rest of her life, but she would give something in return for it. It was not that she would attempt to make another Ira and Samantha Ewing of them; she had made that mistake with her own son and had driven him from home. She was wiser now; she saw now that it was not the repetition of hardship: she would merely take what had been of value in hers and her husband's hard lives—that which they had learned through hardship and endurance of honor and courage and pride—and transmit it to the children without their having to suffer the hardship at all, the travail and the despairs. She had expected that there would be some friction between her and the young daughter-in-law, but she had believed that her son, the actual Ewing, would be her ally; she had even reconciled herself after a year to waiting, since the children were still but babies; she was not alarmed, since they were Ewings too: after she had looked that first searching time at the two puttysoft little faces feature by feature, she had said it was because they were babies yet and so looked like no one. So she was content to bide and wait; she did not even know that her son was planning to move until he told her that the other house was bought and that the present one was to be hers until she died. She watched them go; she said nothing; it was not to begin then. It did not begin for five years, during which she watched her son making money faster and faster and easier and easier, gaining with apparent contemptible and contemptuous ease that substance for which in niggard amounts her husband had striven while still clinging with undeviating incorruptibility to honor and dignity and pride, and spending it, squandering it, in the same way. By that time she had given up the son and she had long since learned that she and her daughter-in-law were irrevocable and implacable moral enemies. It was in the fifth year. One day in her son's home she saw the two children take money from their mother's purse lying on a table. The mother did not even know how much she had in the purse; when the grandmother told her about it she became angry and dared the older woman to put it to the test. The grandmother accused the children, who denied the whole affair with perfectly straight faces. That was the actual break between herself and her son's family; after that she saw the two children only when the son would bring them with him occasionally on his unfailing daily visits. She had a few broken dollars which she had brought from Nebraska and had kept intact for five years, since she had no need for money here; one day she planted one of the coins while the children were there, and when she went back to look, it was gone too. The next morning she tried to talk to her son about the children, remembering her experience with the daughter-in-law and approaching the matter indirectly, speaking generally of money. "Yes," the son said. "I'm making money. I'm making it fast while I can. I'm going to make a lot of it. I'm going to give my children luxuries and advantages that my father never dreamed a child might have."

"That's it," she said. "You make money too easy. This whole country is too easy for us Ewings. It may be all right for them that have been born here for generations; I don't know about that. But not for us."

"But these children were born here."

"Just one generation. The generation before that they were born in a sodroofed dugout on the Nebraska wheat frontier. And the one before that in a log house in Missouri. And the one before that in a Kentucky blockhouse with Indians around it. This world has never been easy for Ewings. Maybe the Lord never intended it to be."

"But it is from now on," he said; he spoke with a kind of triumph. "For you and me too. But mostly for them."

And that was all. When he was gone she sat quietly in the single Nebraska chair which she had taken out of storage—the first chair which the older Ira Ewing had bought for her after he built a house and in which she had rocked the younger Ira to sleep before he could walk, while the older Ira himself sat in the chair which he had made out of a flour barrel, grim, quiet and incorruptible, taking his earned twilight ease between a day and a day—telling herself quietly that that was all. Her next move was curiously direct; there was something in it of the actual pioneer's opportunism, of taking immediate and cold advantage of Spartan circumstance; it was as though for the first time in her life she was able to use something, anything, which she had gained by bartering her youth and strong maturity against the Nebraska immensity, and this not in order to live further but in order to die; apparently she saw neither paradox in it nor dishonesty. She began to make candy and cake of the materials which her son bought for her on credit, and to sell them to the two grandchildren for the coins which their father gave them or which they perhaps purloined also from their mother's purse, hiding the coins in the vase with the timetable, watching the niggard hoard grow. But after a few years the children outgrew candy and cake, and then she had watched railroad fares go down and down and then stop thirteen dollars away. But she did not give up, even then. Her son had tried to give her a servant years ago and she had refused; she believed that when the time came, the right moment, he would not refuse to give her at least thirteen dollars of the money which she had saved him. Then this had failed. "Maybe it wasn't the right time," she thought. "Maybe I tried it too quick. I was surprised into it," she told herself, looking down at the heap of small coins in her lap. "Or maybe he was surprised into saying No. Maybe when he has had time . . ." She roused; she put the coins back into the vase and set it on the mantel again, looking at the clock as she did so. It was just four, two hours yet until time to start supper. The sun was high; she could see the water from the sprinkler flashing and glinting in it as she went to the window. It was still high, still afternoon; the mountains stood serene and drab against it; the city, the land, lay sprawled and myriad beneath it—the land, the earth which spawned a thousand new faiths, nostrums and cures each year but no disease to even disprove them on—beneath the golden days unmarred by rain or weather, the changeless monotonous beautiful days without end countless out of the halcyon past and endless into the halcyon future.

"I will stay here and live forever," she said to herself.

Jacques-Louis David, *Madame Recamier* (1800)

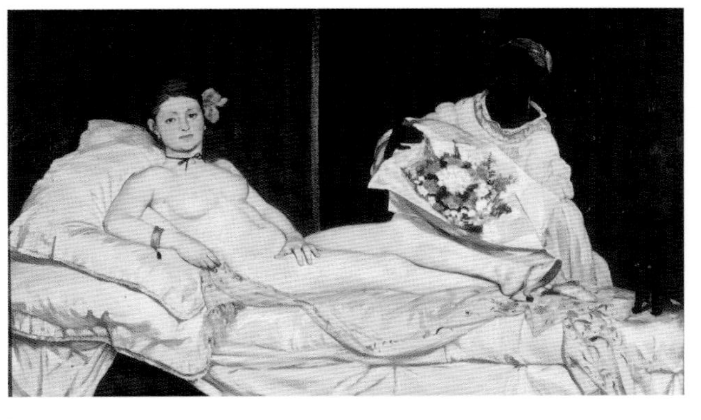

Edouard Manet, *Olympia* (1863)

Henri Matisse, *Odalisque* (1923–1924)

Amadeo Modigliani, *Reclining Nude from the Back* (1917)

Vanessa Bell, *The Memoir Club* (c. 1943) Figures in the picture, from left to right: Duncan Grant, Leonard Woolf, Vanessa and Clive Bell, David Garnett, Maynard and Lydia Keynes, Desmond and Millie MacCarthy, Quentin Bell and E. M. Forster. Portraits on the wall of Woolf by Duncan Grant, Lytton Strachey by Grant, and Roger Fry by Vanessa Bell.

Paul Cézanne, *Mont Sainte-Victoire* (1900)

Pablo Picasso, *Les demoiselles d'Avignon* (1907)

Georges Braque, *The Bather* (1907)

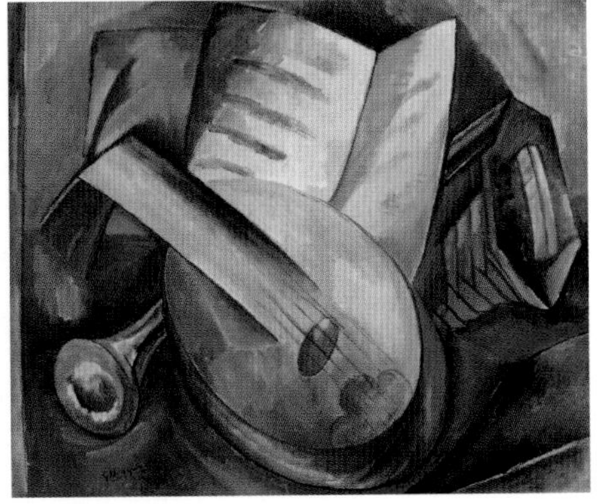

Georges Braque, *Musical Instruments* (1908)

Pablo Picasso, *The Aficionado* (1912)

Umberto Boccioni, *The Dynamism of a Soccer Player* (1913)

TOPICS FOR CRITICAL THINKING Web

www

1. In what ways do the children embody the attitudes of the "golden land"?
2. In terms of the question of values, what does it mean that Ira's son is gay?
3. What is the connection between sex and success?
4. Why does Ira keep his mother prisoner?
5. What is the relation between the beauty of the golden land and the events that transpire in it?

TOPICS FOR CRITICAL WRITING Web

www

1. In what ways does "Golden Land" unravel the relations between material and emotional success?
2. In what ways is "Golden Land" a critique of American society?"

11 Tone

Most of us have ideas about how a story sounds. The literary concept of **tone** is analogous to the tone of voice in spoken language. It is an attitude conveyed through inflection, **diction** (word choice), sentence structure, the speaker's character, the distribution of knowledge among characters within the text, and the information shared between the story and the reader. Inflection relates to various qualities added to words when they are spoken. One can emphasize words for the sake of explanation, humor, or even out of exasperation. One can say words snidely, sarcastically, ironically, caressingly, tauntingly, interrogatively, mockingly, curtly, angrily, or any way that conveys an attitude. For example, imagine the differences in tone of voice if the word *honey* is said in any of the ways listed above. By simply altering the attitude conveyed by the voice, very different scenarios are conjured. Since written texts cannot directly convey the quality of a voice, vocal inflections are signaled in other ways. One way is simply through the use of adverbs. "Honey," he said caressingly. "Honey," she said, exasperated. "Honey?" Another way to imply inflection in written texts is through circumstances. The word *honey* spoken at a romantic luncheon has a different inflection than if the word is used by one gang member to refer to another.

Diction is another means through which written texts produce tone. Diction may be employed by a narrator to convey an attitude. Compare for example, the tone conveyed by the following two lines:

> "As always, he was unfailingly polite to women."
>
> "As usual, he didn't fail to make use of the opportunity to impress women with his manners."

The tone of the first sentence suggests a straightforward, admirably earnest man. The second conveys sarcasm in its description of an opportunist. The first is Beaver Cleaver, the second, Eddie Haskell. The narrator's tone is produced in this case by a combination of word choice ("as always" instead "as usual," the more sarcastic selection) and through sentence structure. The first sentence is a positive declaration. The second sentence employs a negative to produce a positive ("didn't fail to make use"), which suggests snideness or sarcasm in the negative's understatement of the man's avid use of opportunity.

Occasionally, tone is conveyed by a story's characters or setting. Some characters are portrayed as having an attitude (as does the husband in "Sweat"); this attitude contributes to the story's tone. A setting may evoke a gloomy feeling that sets its tone. This atmosphere or feeling defines its **mood**. *www* **Web**

Tone is also an effect of differences between what the readers, the narrator, and various characters know. When the readers know more than the characters, such a disparity is called **dramatic irony**. While this irony is not quite the same as knowing that narrators or characters actually mean the opposite of what they say (as in **irony**), it does produce a tone or attitude in the story.

Critical Perspective: On Tone

The first paragraph of Flannery O'Connor's "A Good Man Is Hard to Find" displays the essence of irony both in its complex playful/authoritative tone and in the way it signals the inevitability of the fate to be avoided. The story takes irony apart, exhibiting on the one hand the sense of a controlling voice typical of irony and on the other the innocent lack of awareness on the part of those whose lives are narrated. The difference in feel between narrator and narrated is a difference in knowledge and attitude. The narrator seems to know far more than the characters, who because of a lack of foresight, can be no more than the dupes of fate or of their own unconscious. At the same time, the narrator's tone indicates that the narrator knows fate but for the sake of the story will only hint at the outcome. The trick or talent of irony is the way its tone stealthily and irresistibly seduces readers to the side of knowledge. When, for example, the narrator states in the story's first line, "The grandmother didn't want to go to Florida," it appears to convey a simple fact about the grandmother's desires, but it also and at the same time conveys the sense that despite what the grandmother wants, something else is in store for her. The next sentence elaborates the grandmother's wishes but in so doing increases the sense readers might have that the narrator in fact knows better than the grandmother both what she wants and what will happen anyway. This duplicity, produced through tone, defines the story that follows in which some force, other than the characters' wishes or conscious desires, determines where the characters will go. It is as if the narrator, representing the inevitable, pushes the characters against their wishes, and we readers watch it all, privy to the duplicities of fate, the unconscious, and bad luck. Irony is, in fact, a "misfit," present in the difference between what the narrator says and what it conveys that it knows, which matches the difference in the story between what the characters think they are doing and where they inevitably end up.

Stories About Tone

The three stories that follow all employ tone as a central element of their telling. Zora Neale Hurston's "Sweat" takes a studied detached tone to offset the story's ironies. Flannery O'Connor's "A Good Man Is Hard to Find" depends heavily on both dramatic irony and the narrator's ironic tone. W. S. Penn's "In Dreams Begins Reality" plays with the ambiguities of tone as the narrator tries to understand the women he encounters.

Zora Neale Hurston

Sweat

(1926)

It was eleven o'clock of a Spring night in Florida. It was Sunday. Any other night, Delia Jones would have been in bed for two hours by this time. But she was a washwoman, and Monday morning meant a great deal to her. So she collected the soiled clothes on Saturday when she returned the clean things. Sunday night after church, she sorted them and put the white things to soak. It saved her almost a half day's start. A great hamper in the bedroom held the clothes that she brought home. It was so much neater than a number of bundles lying around.

She squatted on the kitchen floor beside the great pile of clothes, sorting them into small heaps according to color, and humming a song in a mournful key, but wondering through it all where Sykes, her husband, had gone with her horse and buckboard.

Just then something long, round, limp and black fell upon her shoulders and slithered to the floor beside her. A great terror took hold of her. It softened her knees and dried her mouth so that it was a full minute before she could cry out or move. Then she saw that it was the big bull whip her husband liked to carry when he drove.

She lifted her eyes to the door and saw him standing there bent over with laughter at her fright. She screamed at him.

"Sykes, what you throw dat whip on me like dat? You know it would skeer 5
me—looks just like a snake, an' you knows how skeered Ah is of snakes."

"Course Ah knowed it! That's how come Ah done it." He slapped his leg with his hand and almost rolled on the ground in his mirth. "If you such a big fool dat you got to have a fit over a earth worm or a string, Ah don't keer how bad Ah skeer you."

"You aint got no business doing it. Gawd knows it's a sin. Some day Ah'm gointuh drop dead from some of yo' foolishness. 'Nother thing, where you been wid mah rig? Ah feeds dat pony. He aint fuh you to be drivin' wid no bull whip."

"You sho is one aggravatin' nigger woman!" he declared and stepped into the room. She resumed her work and did not answer him at once. "Ah done tole you time and again to keep them white folks' clothes outa dis house."

He picked up the whip and glared down at her. Delia went on with her work. She went out into the yard and returned with a galvanized tub and set it on the washbench. She saw that Sykes kicked all of the clothes together again, and now stood in her way truculently, his whole manner hoping, *praying*, for an argument. But she walked calmly around him and commenced to re-sort the things.

"Next time, Ah'm gointer kick 'em outdoors," he threatened as he struck 10
a match along the leg of his corduroy breeches.

Delia never looked up from her work, and her thin, stooped shoulders sagged further.

"Ah aint for no fuss t'night, Sykes. Ah just come from taking sacrament at the church house."

Two months after the wedding, he had given her the first brutal beating. She had the memory of his numerous trips to Orlando with all of his wages when he had returned to her penniless, even before the first year had passed. She was young and soft then, but now she thought of her knotty, muscled limbs, her harsh, knuckly hands, and drew herself up into an unhappy little ball in the middle of the big feather bed. Too late now to hope for love, even if it were not Bertha it could be someone else. This case differed from the others only in that she was bolder than the others. Too late for everything except her little home. She had built it for her old days, and planted one by one the trees and flowers there. It was lovely to her, lovely.

Somehow, before sleep came, she found herself saying aloud: "Oh well, whatever goes over the Devil's back, is got to come under his belly. Sometime or ruther, Sykes, like everybody else, is gointer reap his sowing." After that she was able to build a spiritual earthworks against her husband. His shells could no longer reach her. *Amen.* She went to sleep and slept until he announced his presence in bed by kicking her feet and rudely snatching the covers away.

"Gimme some kivah heah, an' git yo' damn foots over on yo' own side! 15
Ah oughter mash you in yo' mouf fuh drawing dat skillet on me."

Delia went clear to the rail without answering him. A triumphant indifference to all that he was or did.

The week was as full of work for Delia as all other weeks, and Saturday found her behind her little pony, collecting and delivering clothes.

It was a hot, hot day near the end of July. The village men on Joe Clarke's porch even chewed cane listlessly. They did not hurl the caneknots as usual. They let them dribble over the edge of the porch. Even conversation had collapsed under the heat.

"Heah come Delia Jones," Jim Merchant said, as the shaggy pony came 'round the bend of the road toward them. The rusty buckboard was heaped with baskets of crisp, clean laundry.

"Yep," Joe Lindsay agreed. "Hot or col', rain or shine, jes ez reg'lar ez de 20
weeks roll roun' Delia carries 'em an' fetches 'em on Sat'day."

"She better if she wanter eat," said Moss. "Syke Jones aint wuth de shot an' powder hit would tek tuh kill 'em. Not to *huh* he aint."

"He sho' aint," Walter Thomas chimed in. "It's too bad, too, cause she wuz a right pritty lil trick when he got huh. Ah'd uh mah'ied huh mahseff if he hadnter beat me to it."

Delia nodded briefly at the men as she drove past.

"Too much knockin' will ruin *any* 'oman. He done beat huh 'nough tuh kill three women, let 'lone change they looks," said Elijah Moseley. "How Syke kin stommuck dat big black greasy Mogul he's layin' roun' wid, gits me. Ah swear dat eight-rock couldn't kiss a sardine can Ah done thowed out de back do' 'way las' yeah."

"Aw, she's fat, thass how come. He's allus been crazy 'bout fat women," put in Merchant. "He'd a' been tied up wid one long time ago if he could a' found one tuh have him. Did Ah tell yuh 'bout him come sidlin' roun' *mah* wife—bringin' her a basket uh peecans outa his yard fuh a present? Yessir, mah wife! She tol' him tuh take em right straight back home, cause Delia works so hard ovah dat wash tub she reckon everything on de place taste lak sweat an' soapsuds. Ah jus' wisht Ah'd a caught 'im 'roun' dere! Ah'd a' made his hips ketch on fiah down dat shell road."

"Ah know he done it, too. Ah sees 'im grinnin' at every 'oman dat passes," Walter Thomas said. "But even so, he useter eat some mighty big hunks uh humble pie tuh git dat lil' 'oman he got. She wuz ez pritty ez a speckled pup! Dat wuz fifteen yeahs ago. He useter be so skeered uh losin' huh, she could make him do some parts of a husband's duty. Dey never wuz de same in de mind."

"There oughter be a law about him," said Lindsay. "He aint fit tuh carry guts tuh a bear."

Clarke spoke for the first time. "Taint no law on earth dat kin make a man be decent if it aint in 'im. There's plenty men dat takes a wife lak dey do a joint uh sugar-cane. It's round, juicy an' sweet when dey gits it. But dey squeeze an' grind, squeeze an' grind an' wring tell dey wring every drop uh pleasure dat's in 'em out. When dey's satisfied dat dey is wrung dry, dey treats 'em jes lak dey do a cane-chew. Dey thows 'em away. Dey knows whut dey is doin' while dey is at it, an' hates theirselves fuh it but they keeps on hangin' after huh tell she's empty. Den dey hates huh fuh bein' a cane-chew an' in de way."

"We oughter take Syke an' dat stray 'oman uh his'n down in Lake Howell swamp an' lay on de rawhide till they cain't say Lawd a' mussy.' He allus wuz uh ovahbearin' niggah, but since dat white 'oman from up north done teached 'im how to run a automobile, he done got too biggety to live—an' we oughter kill 'im." Old Man Anderson advised.

A grunt of approval went around the porch. But the heat was melting their civic virtue and Elijah Moseley began to bait Joe Clarke.

"Come on, Joe, git a melon outa dere an' slice it up for yo' customers. We'se all sufferin' wid de heat. De bear's done got *me!*"

"Thass right, Joe, a watermelon is jes' whut Ah needs tuh cure de eppizudicks," Walter Thomas joined forces with Moseley. "Come on dere, Joe. We all is steady customers an' you aint set us up in a long time. Ah chooses dat long, bowlegged Floridy favorite."

"A god, an' be dough. You all gimme twenty cents and slice way," Clarke retorted. “Ah needs a col’ slice m’self. Heah, everybody chip in. Ah’ll lend y’ll mah meat knife.”

The money was quickly subscribed and the huge melon brought forth. At that moment, Sykes and Bertha arrived. A determined silence fell on the porch and the melon was put away again.

35 Merchant snapped down the blade of his jacknife and moved toward the store door.

“Come on in, Joe, an’ gimme a slab uh sow belly an’ uh pound uh coffee—almost fuhgot ’twas Sat’day. Got to git on home.” Most of the men left also.

Just then Delia drove past on her way home, as Sykes was ordering magnificently for Bertha. It pleased him for Delia to see.

“Git whutsoever yo’ heart desires, Honey. Wait a minute, Joe. Give huh two bottles uh strawberry soda-water, uh quart uh parched ground-peas, an’ a block uh chewin’ gum.”

With all this they left the store, with Sykes reminding Bertha that this was his town and she could have it if she wanted it.

40 The men returned soon after they left, and held their watermelon feast.

“Where did Syke Jones git da ’oman from nohow?” Lindsay asked.

“Ovah Apopka. Guess dey musta been cleanin’ out de town when she lef’. She don’t look lak a thing but a hunk uh liver wid hair on it.”

“Well, she sho’ kin squall,” Dave Carter contributed. “When she gits ready tuh laff, she jes’ opens huh mouf an’ latches it back tuh de las’ notch. No ole grandpa alligator down in Lake Bell ain’t got nothin’ on huh.”

Bertha had been in town three months now. Sykes was still paying her room rent at Della Lewis’—the only house in town that would have taken her in. Sykes took her frequently to Winter Park to “stomps.” He still assured her that he was the swellest man in the state.

45 “Sho’ you kin have dat lil’ ole house soon’s Ah kin git dat ’oman outa dere. Everything b’longs tuh me an’ you sho’ kin have it. Ah sho’ ’bominates uh skinny ’oman. Lawdy, you sho’ is got one portly shape on you! You kin git *anything* you wants. Dis is *mah* town an’ you sho’ kin have it.”

Delia’s work-worn knees crawled over the earth in Gethsemane and up the rocks of Calvary many, many times during these months. She avoided the villagers and meeting places in her efforts to be blind and deaf. But Bertha nullified this to a degree, by coming to Delia’s house to call Sykes out to her at the gate.

Delia and Sykes fought all the time now with no peaceful interludes. They slept and ate in silence. Two or three times Delia had attempted a timid friendliness, but she was repulsed each time. It was plain that the breaches must remain agape.

The sun had burned July to August. The heat streamed down like a million hot arrows, smiting all things living upon the earth. Grass withered, leaves browned, snakes went blind in shedding and men and dogs went mad. Dog days!

Delia came home one day and found Sykes there before her. She wondered, but started to go on into the house without speaking, even though he was standing in the kitchen door and she must either stoop under his arm or ask him to move. He made no room for her. She noticed a soap box beside the steps, but paid no particular attention to it, knowing that he must have brought it there. As she was stooping to pass under his outstretched arm, he suddenly pushed her backward, laughingly.

"Look in de box dere Delia, Ah done brung yuh somethin'!"

She nearly fell upon the box in her stumbling, and when she saw what it held, she all but fainted outright.

"Syke! Syke, mah Gawd! You take dat rattlesnake 'way from heah! You *gottuh*. Oh, Jesus, have mussy!"

"Ah aint gut tuh do nuthin' uh de kin'—fact is Ah aint got tuh do nothin' but die. Taint no use uh you puttin' on airs makin' out lak you skeered uh dat snake—he's gointer stay right heah tell he die. He wouldn't bite me cause Ah knows how tuh handle 'im. Nohow he wouldn't risk breakin' out his fangs 'gin *yo'* skinny laigs."

"Naw, now Syke, don't keep dat thing 'roun' heah tuh skeer me tuh death. You knows Ah'm even feared uh earth worms. Thass de biggest snake Ah evah did see. Kill 'im Syke, please."

"Doan ast me tuh do nothin' fuh yuh. Goin' 'roun' tryin' tuh be so damn asterperious. Naw, Ah aint gonna kill it. Ah think uh damn sight mo' uh him dan you! Dat's a nice snake an' anybody doan lak 'im kin jes' hit de grit."

The village soon heard that Sykes had the snake, and came to see and ask questions.

"How de hen-fire did you ketch dat six-foot rattler, Syke?" Thomas asked.

"He's full uh frogs so he caint hardly move, thass how Ah eased up on 'm. But Ah'm a snake charmer an' knows how tuh handle 'em. Shux, dat aint nothin'. Ah could ketch one eve'y day if Ah so wanted tuh."

"Whut he needs is a heavy hick'ry club leaned real heavy on his head. Dat's de bes 'way tuh charm a rattlesnake."

"Naw, Walt, y'll jes' don't understand dese diamon' backs lak Ah do," said Sykes in a superior tone of voice.

The village agreed with Walter, but the snake stayed on. His box remained by the kitchen door with its screen wire covering. Two or three days later it had digested its meal of frogs and literally came to life. It rattled at every movement in the kitchen or the yard. One day as Delia came down the kitchen steps she saw his chalky-white fangs curved like scimitars hung in the wire meshes. This time she did not run away with averted eyes as usual. She stood for a long time in the doorway in a red fury that grew bloodier for every second that she regarded the creature that was her torment.

That night she broached the subject as soon as Sykes sat down to the table.

"Syke, Ah wants you tuh take dat snake 'way fum heah. You done starved me an' Ah put up widcher, you done beat me an Ah took dat, but you done kilt all mah insides bringin' dat varmint heah."

Sykes poured out a saucer full of coffee and drank it deliberately before he answered her.

65 "A whole lot Ah keer 'bout how you feels inside uh out. Dat snake aint goin' no damn wheah till Ah gits ready fuh 'im tuh go. So fur as beatin' is concerned, yuh aint took near all dat you gointer take ef you stay 'roun' *me*."

Delia pushed back her plate and got up from the table. "Ah hates you, Sykes," she said calmly. "Ah hates you tuh de same degree dat Ah useter love yuh. Ah done took an' took till mah belly is full up tuh mah neck. Dat's de reason Ah got mah letter fum de church an' moved mah membership tuh Woodbridge—so Ah don't haftuh take no sacrament wid yuh. Ah don't wantuh see yuh 'roun' me atall. Lay 'roun' wid dat 'oman all yuh wants tuh, but gwan 'way fum me an' mah house. Ah hates yuh lak uh suck-egg dog."

Sykes almost let the huge wad of corn bread and collard greens he was chewing fall out of his mouth in amazement. He had a hard time whipping himself up to the proper fury to try to answer Delia.

"Well, Ah'm glad you does hate me. Ah'm sho' tiahed uh you hangin' ontuh me. Ah don't want yuh. Look at yuh stringey ole neck! Yo' rawbony laigs an' arms is enough tuh cut uh man tuh death. You looks jes' lak de devvul's doll-baby tuh *me*. You cain't hate me no worse dan Ah hates you. Ah been hatin' *you* fuh years."

"Yo' ole black hide don't look lak nothin' tuh me, but uh passle uh wrinkled up rubber, wid yo' big ole yeahs flappin' on each side lak uh paih uh buzzard wings. Don't think Ah'm gointuh be run 'way fum mah house neither. Ah'm goin' tuh de white folks bout *you*, mah young man, de very nex' time you lay yo' han's on me. Mah cup is done run ovah."

70 Delia said this with no signs of fear and Sykes departed from the house, threatening her, but made not the slightest move to carry out any of them.

That night he did not return at all, and the next day being Sunday, Delia was glad she did not have to quarrel before she hitched up her pony and drove the four miles to Woodbridge.

She stayed to the night service—"love feast"—which was very warm and full of spirit. In the emotional winds her domestic trials were borne far and wide so that she sang as she drove homeward,

> "Jurden water, black an' col'
> Chills de body, not de soul
> An' Ah wantah cross Jurden in uh calm time."

She came from the barn to the kitchen door and stopped.

"Whut's de mattah, ol' satan, you aint kickin' up yo' racket?" She addressed the snake's box. Complete silence. She went on into the house with a new hope in its birth struggles. Perhaps her threat to go to the white folks had frightened Sykes! Perhaps he was sorry! Fifteen years of misery and suppression had brought Delia to the place where she would hope *anything* that looked towards a way over or through her wall of inhibitions.

She felt in the match safe behind the stove at once for a match. There was 75
only one there.

"Dat niggah wouldn't fetch nothin' heah tuh save his rotten neck, but he kin run thew whut Ah brings quick enough. Now he done toted off nigh on tuh haff uh box uh matches. He done had dat 'oman heah in mah house too."

Nobody but a woman could tell how she knew this even before she struck the match. But she did and it put her into a new fury.

Presently she brought in the tubs to put the white things to soak. This time she decided she need not bring the hamper out of the bedroom: she would go in there and do the sorting. She picked up the pot-bellied lamp and went in. The room was small and the hamper stood hard by the foot of the white iron bed. She could sit and reach through the bedposts—resting as she worked.

"Ah wantah cross Jurden in uh calm time." She was singing again. The mood of the "love feast" had returned. She threw back the lid of the basket almost gaily. Then, moved by both horror and terror, she sprang back toward the door. *There lay the snake in the basket!* He moved sluggishly at first, but even as she turned round and round, jumped up and down in an insanity of fear, he began to stir vigorously. She saw him pouring his awful beauty from the basket upon the bed, then she seized the lamp and ran as fast as she could to the kitchen. The wind from the open door blew out the light and the darkness added to her terror. She sped to the darkness of the yard, slamming the door after her before she thought to set down the lamp. She did not feel safe even on the ground, so she climbed up in the hay barn.

There for an hour or more she lay sprawled upon the hay a gibbering 80
wreck.

Finally she grew quiet, and after that, coherent thought. With this, stalked through her a cold, bloody rage. Hours of this. A period of introspection, a space of retrospection, then a mixture of both. Out of this an awful calm.

"Well, Ah done de bes' Ah could. If things aint right, Gawd knows taint mah fault."

She went to sleep—a twitch sleep—and woke up to a faint gray sky. There was a loud hollow sound below. She peered out. Sykes was at the wood-pile, demolishing a wire-covered box.

He hurried to the kitchen door, but hung outside there some minutes before he entered, and stood some minutes more inside before he closed it after him.

The gray in the sky was spreading. Delia descended without fear now, and 85
crouched beneath the low bedroom window. The drawn shade shut out the dawn, shut in the night. But the thin walls held back no sound.

"Dat ol' scratch is woke up now!" She mused at the tremendous whirr inside, which every woodsman knows, is one of the sound illusions. The rattler is a ventriloquist. His whirr sounds to the right, to the left, straight ahead, behind, close under foot—everywhere but where it is. Woe to him who guesses wrong unless he is prepared to hold up his end of the argument! Sometimes he strikes without rattling at all.

Inside, Sykes heard nothing until he knocked a pot lid off the stove while trying to reach the match safe in the dark. He had emptied his pockets at Bertha's.

The snake seemed to wake up under the stove and Sykes made a quick leap into the bedroom. In spite of the gin he had had, his head was clearing now.

"Mah Gawd!" he chattered, "ef Ah could on'y strack uh light!"

The rattling ceased for a moment as he stood paralyzed. He waited. It 90
seemed that the snake waited also.

"Oh, fuh de light! Ah thought he'd be too sick"—Sykes was muttering to himself when the whirr began again, closer, right underfoot this time. Long before this, Sykes' ability to think had been flattened down to primitive instinct and he leaped—onto the bed.

Outside Delia heard a cry that might have come from a maddened chimpanzee, a stricken gorilla. All the terror, all the horror, all the rage that man possibly could express, without a recognizable human sound.

A tremendous stir inside there, another series of animal screams, the intermittent whirr of the reptile. The shade torn violently down from the window, letting in the red dawn, a huge brown hand seizing the window stick, great dull blows upon the wooden floor punctuating the gibberish of sound long after the rattle of the snake had abruptly subsided. All this Delia could see and hear from her place beneath the window, and it made her ill. She crept over to the four-o'clocks and stretched herself on the cool earth to recover.

She lay there. "Delia, Delia!" She could hear Sykes calling in a most despairing tone as one who expected no answer. The sun crept on up, and he called. Delia could not move—her legs were gone flabby. She never moved, he called, and the sun kept rising.

"Mah Gawd!" She heard him moan, "Mah Gawd fum Heben!" She heard 95
him stumbling about and got up from her flower-bed. The sun was growing warm. As she approached the door she heard him call out hopefully, "Delia, is dat you Ah heah?"

She saw him on his hands and knees as soon as she reached the door. He crept an inch or two toward her—all that he was able, and she saw his horribly swollen neck and his one open eye shining with hope. A surge of pity too strong to support bore her away from that eye that must, could not, fail to see the tubs. He would see the lamp. Orlando with its doctors was too far. She could scarcely reach the Chinaberry tree, where she waited in the growing heat while inside she knew the cold river was creeping up and up to extinguish that eye which must know by now that she knew.

ZORA NEALE HURSTON

(1891–1960) Web www

Educated at Howard University, Hurston worked both as a writer and an anthropologist, published the novel *Their Eyes Were Watching God* in 1937, and collected folktales in Florida. She was part of the Harlem Renaissance. Web www

She published nothing after 1948 and died penniless twelve years later. In the 1970s, both African American and feminist critics renewed interest in her work.

www

TOPICS FOR CRITICAL THINKING Web

1. What effect does the narrator's tone have on the ways we might sympathize with Delia?
2. Why is this story told primarily through dialogue?
3. What relations between the genders does this story present?
4. Is Delia right?
5. What is the story's mood?

www

TOPICS FOR CRITICAL WRITING Web

1. In what specific ways does the snake function in the story?
2. Why is the story titled "Sweat"?

FLANNERY O'CONNOR

A Good Man Is Hard to Find

(1955)

The grandmother didn't want to go to Florida. She wanted to visit some of her connections in east Tennessee and she was seizing at every chance to change Bailey's mind. Bailey was the son she lived with, her only boy. He was sitting on the edge of his chair at the table, bent over the orange sports section of the *Journal.* "Now look here, Bailey," she said, "see here, read this," and she stood with one hand on her thin hip and the other rattling the newspaper at his bald head. "Here this fellow that calls himself The Misfit is aloose from the Federal Pen and headed toward Florida and you read here what it says he did to these people. Just you read it. I wouldn't take my children in any direction with a criminal like that aloose in it. I couldn't answer to my conscience if I did."

Bailey didn't look up from his reading so she wheeled around then and faced the children's mother, a young woman in slacks, whose face was as broad and innocent as a cabbage and was tied round with a green head-kerchief that had two points on the top like rabbit's ears. She was sitting on the sofa, feeding the baby his apricots out of a jar. "The children have been to Florida before," the old lady said. "You all ought to take them somewhere else for a change so they would see different parts of the world and be broad. They never have been to east Tennessee."

The children's mother didn't seem to hear her but the eight-year-old boy, John Wesley, a stocky child with glasses, said, "If you don't want to go to Florida, why dontcha stay at home?" He and the little girl, June Star, were reading the funny papers on the floor.

"She wouldn't stay at home to be queen for a day," June Star said without raising her yellow head.

“Yes and what would you do if this fellow, The Misfit, caught you?” the 5
grandmother asked.

“I'd smack his face,” John Wesley said.

“She wouldn't stay at home for a million bucks,” June Star said. “Afraid she'd miss something. She has to go everywhere we go.”

“All right, Miss,” the grandmother said. “Just remember that the next time you want me to curl your hair.”

June Star said her hair was naturally curly.

The next morning the grandmother was the first one in the car, ready to 10
go. She had her big black valise that looked like the head of a hippopotamus in one corner, and underneath it she was hiding a basket with Pitty Sing, the cat, in it. She didn't intend for the cat to be left alone in the house for three days because he would miss her too much and she was afraid he might brush against one of the gas burners and accidentally asphyxiate himself. Her son, Bailey, didn't like to arrive at a motel with a cat.

She sat in the middle of the back seat with John Wesley and June Star on either side of her. Bailey and the children's mother and the baby sat in the front and they left Atlanta at eight forty-five with the mileage on the car at 55890. The grandmother wrote this down because she thought it would be interesting to say how many miles they had been when they got back. It took them twenty minutes to reach the outskirts of the city.

The old lady settled herself comfortably, removing her white cotton gloves and putting them up with her purse on the shelf in front of the back window. The children's mother still had on slacks and still had her head tied up in a green kerchief, but the grandmother had on a navy blue straw sailor hat with a bunch of white violets on the brim and a navy blue dress with a small white dot in the print. Her collar and cuffs were white organdy trimmed with lace and at her neckline she had pinned a purple spray of cloth violets containing a sachet. In case of an accident, anyone seeing her dead on the highway would know at once that she was a lady.

She said she thought it was going to be a good day for driving, neither too hot nor too cold, and she cautioned Bailey that the speed limit was fifty-five miles an hour and that the patrolmen hid themselves behind billboards and small clumps of trees and sped out after you before you had a chance to slow down. She pointed out interesting details of the scenery: Stone Mountain; the blue granite that in some places came up to both sides of the highway; the brilliant red clay banks slightly streaked with purple; and the various crops that made rows of green lace-work on the ground. The trees were full of silver-white sunlight and the meanest of them sparkled. The children were reading comic magazines and their mother had gone back to sleep.

“Let's go through Georgia fast so we won't have to look at it much,” John Wesley said.

“If I were a little boy,” said the grandmother, “I wouldn't talk about my 15
native state that way. Tennessee has the mountains and Georgia has the hills.”

“Tennessee is just a hillbilly dumping ground,” John Wesley said, “and Georgia is a lousy state too.”

“You said it,” June Star said.

“In my time,” said the grandmother, folding her thin veined fingers, "children were more respectful of their native states and their parents and everything else. People did right then. Oh look at the cute little pickaninny!" she said and pointed to a Negro child standing in the door of a shack. "Wouldn't that make a picture, now?" she asked and they all turned and looked at the little Negro out of the back window. He waved.

"He didn't have any britches on," June said.

"He probably didn't have any," the grandmother explained. "Little nig- 20
gers in the country don't have things like we do. If I could paint, I'd paint that picture," she said.

The children exchanged comic books.

The grandmother offered to hold the baby and the children's mother passed him over the front seat to her. She set him on her knee and bounced him and told him about the things they were passing. She rolled her eyes and screwed up her mouth and stuck her leathery thin face into his smooth bland one. Occasionally he gave her a faraway smile. They passed a large cotton field with five or six graves fenced in the middle of it, like a small island. "Look at the graveyard!" the grandmother said, pointing it out. "That was the old family burying ground. That belonged to the plantation."

"Where's the plantation?" John Wesley asked.

"Gone With the Wind," said the grandmother. "Ha. Ha."

When the children finished all the comic books they had brought, they 25
opened the lunch and ate it. The grandmother ate a peanut butter sandwich and an olive and would not let the children throw the box and the paper napkins out the window. When there was nothing else to do they played a game by choosing a cloud and making the other two guess what shape it suggested. John Wesley took one the shape of a cow and June Star guessed a cow and John Wesley said, no, an automobile, and June Star said he didn't play fair, and they began to slap each other over the grandmother.

The grandmother said she would tell them a story if they would keep quiet. When she told a story, she rolled her eyes and waved her head and was very dramatic. She said once when she was a maiden lady she had been courted by a Mr. Edgar Atkins Teagarden from Jasper, Georgia. She said he was a very good-looking man and a gentleman and that he brought her a watermelon every Saturday afternoon with his initials cut in it, E. A. T. Well, one Saturday, she said, Mr. Teagarden brought the watermelon and there was nobody at home and he left it on the front porch and returned in his buggy to Jasper, but she never got the watermelon, she said, because a nigger boy ate it when he saw the initials, E. A. T.! This story tickled John Wesley's funny bone and he giggled and giggled but June Star didn't think it was any good. She said she wouldn't marry a man that just brought her a watermelon on Saturday. The grandmother said she would have done well to marry Mr. Teagarden because he was a gentleman and had bought Coca-Cola stock when it first came out and that he had died only a few years ago, a very wealthy man.

They stopped at The Tower for barbecued sandwiches. The Tower was a part stucco and part wood filling station and dance hall set in a clearing outside of Timothy. A fat man named Red Sammy Butts ran it and there were signs stuck here and there on the building and for miles up and down the highway saying, TRY RED SAMMY'S FAMOUS BARBEQUE, NONE LIKE FAMOUS RED SAMMY'S! RED SAM! THE FAT BOY WITH THE HAPPY LAUGH. A VETERAN! SAMMY'S YOUR MAN!

Red Sammy was lying on the bare ground outside The Tower with his head under a truck while a gray monkey about a foot high, chained to a small chinaberry tree, chattered nearby. The monkey sprang back into the tree and got on the highest limb as soon as he saw the children jump out of the car and run toward him.

Inside, The Tower was a long dark room with a counter at one end and tables at the other and dancing space in the middle. They all sat down at a broad table next to the nickelodeon and Red Sam's wife, a tall burnt-brown woman with hair and eyes lighter than her skin, came and took their order. The children's mother put a dime in the machine and played "The Tennessee Waltz," and the grandmother said that tune always made her want to dance. She asked Bailey if he would like to dance but he only glared at her. He didn't have a naturally sunny disposition like she did and trips made him nervous. The grandmother's brown eyes were very bright. She swayed her head from side to side and pretended she was dancing in her chair. June Star said play something she could tap to so the children's mother put in another dime and played a fast number and June Star stepped out onto the dance floor and did her tap routine.

"Ain't she cute?" Red Sam's wife said, leaning over the counter. "Would 30
you like to come be my little girl?"

"No I certainly wouldn't," June Star said. "I wouldn't live in a broken-down place like this for a million bucks!" and she ran back to the table.

"Ain't she cute?" the woman repeated, stretching her mouth politely.

"Aren't you ashamed?" hissed the grandmother.

Red Sam came in and told his wife to quit lounging on the counter and hurry with these people's order. His khaki trousers reached just to his hip bones and his stomach hung over them like a sack of meal swaying under his shirt. He came over and sat down at a table nearby and let out a combination sigh and yodel. "You can't win," he said. "You can't win," and he wiped his sweating red face off with a gray handkerchief. "These days you don't know who to trust," he said. "Ain't that the truth?"

"People are certainly not nice like they used to be," said the grandmother. 35

"Two fellers come in here last week," Red Sammy said, "driving a Chrysler. It was a old beat-up car but it was a good one and these boys looked all right to me. Said they worked at the mill and you know I let them fellers charge the gas they bought? Now why did I do that?"

"Because you're a good man!" the grandmother said at once.

"Yes'm, I suppose so," Red Sam said as if he were struck with the answer.

His wife brought the orders, carrying the five plates all at once without a tray, two in each hand and one balanced on her arm. "It isn't a soul in this green world of God's that you can trust," she said. "And I don't count anybody out of that, not nobody," she repeated, looking at Red Sammy.

"Did you read about that criminal, The Misfit, that's escaped?" asked the 40
grandmother.

"I wouldn't be a bit surprised if he didn't attact this place right here," said the woman. "If he hears about it being here, I wouldn't be none surprised to see him. If he hears it's two cent in the cash register, I wouldn't be a tall surprised if he . . ."

"That'll do," Red Sam said. "Go bring these people their Co'Colas," and the woman went off to get the rest of the order.

"A good man is hard to find," Red Sammy said. "Everything is getting terrible. I remember the day you could go off and leave your screen door unlatched. Not no more."

He and the grandmother discussed better times. The old lady said that in her opinion Europe was entirely to blame for the way things were now. She said the way Europe acted you would think we were made of money and Red Sam said it was no use talking about it, she was exactly right. The children ran outside into the white sunlight and looked at the monkey in the lacy chinaberry tree. He was busy catching fleas on himself and biting each one carefully between his teeth as if it were a delicacy.

They drove off again into the hot afternoon. The grandmother took cat 45
naps and woke up every few minutes with her own snoring. Outside of Toombsboro she woke up and recalled an old plantation that she had visited in this neighborhood once when she was a young lady. She said the house had six white columns across the front and that there was an avenue of oaks leading up to it and two little wooden trellis arbors on either side in front where you sat down with your suitor after a stroll in the garden. She recalled exactly which road to turn off to get to it. She knew that Bailey would not be willing to lose any time looking at an old house, but the more she talked about it, the more she wanted to see it once again and find out if the little twin arbors were still standing. "There was a secret panel in this house," she said craftily, not telling the truth but wishing that she were, "and the story went that all the family silver was hidden in it when Sherman came through but it was never found . . ."

"Hey!" John Wesley said. "Let's go see it! We'll find it! We'll poke all the woodwork and find it! Who lives there? Where do you turn off at? Hey Pop, can't we turn off there?"

"We never have seen a house with a secret panel!" June Star shrieked. "Let's go to the house with the secret panel! Hey, Pop, can't we go see the house with the secret panel!"

"It's not far from here, I know," the grandmother said. "It wouldn't take over twenty minutes."

Bailey was looking straight ahead. His jaw was as rigid as a horseshoe. "No," he said.

The children began to yell and scream that they wanted to see the house 50
with the secret panel. John Wesley kicked the back of the front seat and June Star hung over her mother's shoulder and whined desperately into her ear that they never had any fun even on their vacation, and that they could never do what they wanted to do. The baby began to scream and John Wesley kicked the back of the seat so hard that his father could feel the blows in his kidney.

"All right!" he shouted, and drew the car to a stop at the side of the road. "Will you all shut up? Will you all just shut up for one second? If you don't shut up, we won't go anywhere."

"It would be very educational for them," the grandmother murmured.

"All right," Bailey said, "but get this: this is the only time we're going to stop for anything like this. This is the one and only time."

"The dirt road that you have to turn down is about a mile back," the grandmother directed. "I marked it when we passed."

"A dirt road," Bailey groaned. 55

After they had turned around and were headed toward the dirt road, the grandmother recalled other points about the house, the beautiful glass over the front doorway and the candle-lamp in the hall. John Wesley said that the secret panel was probably in the fireplace.

"You can't go inside this house," Bailey said. "You don't know who lives there."

"While you all talk to the people in front, I'll run around behind and get in a window," John Wesley suggested.

"We'll all stay in the car," his mother said.

They turned onto the dirt road and the car raced roughly along in a swirl 60
of pink dust. The grandmother recalled the times when there were no paved roads and thirty miles was a day's journey. The dirt road was hilly and there were sudden washes in it and sharp curves on dangerous embankments. All at once they would be on a hill, looking down over the blue tops of trees for miles around, then the next minute, they would be in a red depression with the dust-coated trees looking down on them.

"This place had better turn up in a minute," Bailey said, "or I'm going to turn around."

The road looked as if no one had traveled on it in months.

"It's not much farther," the grandmother said and just as she said it, a horrible thought came to her. The thought was so embarrassing that she turned red in the face and her eyes dilated and her feet jumped up, upsetting her valise in the corner. The instant the valise moved, the newspaper top she had over the basket under it rose with a snarl and Pitty Sing, the cat, sprang onto Bailey's shoulder.

The children were thrown to the floor and their mother, clutching the baby, was thrown out the door onto the ground, the old lady was thrown into the front seat. The car turned over once and landed right-side-up in a gulch on the side of the road. Bailey remained in the driver's seat with the cat—gray-striped with a broad white face and an orange nose—clinging to his neck like a caterpillar.

As soon as the children saw they could move their arms and legs, they 65
scrambled out of the car, shouting. "We've had an ACCIDENT!" The grandmother was curled up under the dashboard, hoping she was injured so that Bailey's wrath would not come down on her all at once. The horrible thought she had had before the accident was that the house she had remembered so vividly was not in Georgia but in Tennessee.

Bailey removed the cat from his neck with both hands and flung it out the window against the side of a pine tree. Then he got out of the car and started looking for the children's mother. She was sitting against the side of the red gutted ditch, holding the screaming baby, but she only had a cut down her face and a broken shoulder. "We've had an ACCIDENT!" the children screamed in a frenzy of delight.

"But nobody's killed," June Star said with disappointment as the grandmother limped out of the car, her hat still pinned to her head but the broken front brim standing up at a jaunty angle and the violet spray hanging off the side. They all sat down in the ditch, except the children, to recover from the shock. They were all shaking.

"Maybe a car will come along," said the children's mother hoarsely.

"I believe I have injured an organ," said the grandmother, pressing her side, but no one answered her. Bailey's teeth were clattering. He had on a yellow sport shirt with bright blue parrots designed in it and his face was as yellow as the shirt. The grandmother decided that she would not mention that the house was in Tennessee.

The road was about ten feet above and they could see only the tops of the 70
trees on the other side of it. Behind the ditch they were sitting in there were more woods, tall and dark and deep. In a few minutes they saw a car some distance away on top of a hill, coming slowly as if the occupants were watching them. The grandmother stood up and waved both arms dramatically to attract their attention. The car continued to come on slowly, disappeared around a bend and appeared again, moving even slower, on top of the hill they had gone over. It was a big black battered hearse-like automobile. There were three men in it.

It came to a stop just over them and for some minutes, the driver looked down with a steady expressionless gaze to where they were sitting, and didn't speak. Then he turned his head and muttered something to the other two and they got out. One was a fat boy in black trousers and a red sweat shirt with a silver stallion embossed on the front of it. He moved around on the right side of them and stood staring, his mouth partly open in a kind of loose grin. The other had on khaki pants and a blue striped coat and a gray hat pulled down very low, hiding most of his face. He came around slowly on the left side. Neither spoke.

The driver got out of the car and stood by the side of it, looking down at them. He was an older man than the other two. His hair was just beginning to gray and he wore silver-rimmed spectacles that gave him a scholarly look. He had a long creased face and didn't have on any shirt or undershirt. He had on blue jeans that were too tight for him and was holding a black hat and a gun. The two boys also had guns.

"We've had an ACCIDENT!" the children screamed.

The grandmother had the peculiar feeling that the bespectacled man was someone she knew. His face was as familiar to her as if she had known him all her life but she could not recall who he was. He moved away from the car and began to come down the embankment, placing his feet carefully so that he wouldn't slip. He had on tan and white shoes and no socks, and his ankles were red and thin. "Good afternoon," he said. "I see you all had you a little spill."

"We turned over twice!" said the grandmother. 75

"Oncet," he corrected. "We seen it happen. Try their car and see will it run, Hiram," he said quietly to the boy with the gray hat.

"What you got that gun for?" John Wesley asked. "Whatcha gonna do with that gun?"

"Lady," the man said to the children's mother, "would you mind calling them children to sit down by you? Children make me nervous. I want all you all to sit down right together there where you're at."

"What are you telling us what to do for?" June Star asked.

80 Behind them the line of woods gaped like a dark open mouth. "Come here," said their mother.

"Look here now," Bailey began suddenly, "we're in a predicament! We're in . . ."

The grandmother shrieked. She scrambled to her feet and stood staring. "You're The Misfit!" she said. "I recognized you at once."

"Yes'm," the man said, smiling slightly as if he were pleased in spite of himself to be known, "but it would have been better for all of you, lady, if you hadn't of reckernized me."

Bailey turned his head sharply and said something to his mother that shocked even the children. The old lady began to cry and The Misfit reddened.

85 "Lady," he said, "don't you get upset. Sometimes a man says things he don't mean. I don't reckon he meant to talk to you thataway."

"You wouldn't shoot a lady, would you?" the grandmother said and removed a clean handkerchief from her cuff and began to slap at her eyes with it.

The Misfit pointed the toe of his shoe into the ground and made a little hole and then covered it up again. "I would hate to have to," he said.

"Listen," the grandmother almost screamed, "I know you're a good man. You don't look a bit like you have common blood. I know you must come from nice people!"

"Yes mam," he said, "finest people in the world." When he smiled he showed a row of strong white teeth. "God never made a finer woman than my mother and my daddy's heart was pure gold," he said. The boy with the red sweat shirt had come around behind them and was standing with his gun at his hip. The Misfit squatted down on the ground. "Watch them children, Bobby Lee," he said. "You know they make me nervous." He looked at the six of them huddled together in front of him and he seemed to be embarrassed as if he couldn't think of anything to say. "Ain't a cloud in the sky," he remarked, looking up at it. "Don't see no sun but don't see no cloud neither."

90 "Yes, it's a beautiful day," said the grandmother. "Listen," she said, "you shouldn't call yourself The Misfit because I know you're a good man at heart. I can just look at you and tell."

"Hush!" Bailey yelled. "Hush! Everybody shut up and let me handle this!" He was squatting in the position of a runner about to sprint forward but he didn't move.

"I pre-chate that, lady," The Misfit said and drew a little circle in the ground with the butt of his gun.

"It'll take a half a hour to fix this here car," Hiram called, looking over the raised hood of it.

"Well, first you and Bobby Lee get him and that little boy to step over yonder with you," The Misfit said, pointing to Bailey and John Wesley. "The boys want to ask you something," he said to Bailey. "Would you mind stepping back in them woods there with them?"

95 “Listen,” Bailey began, “we’re in a terrible predicament. Nobody realizes what this is,” and his voice cracked. His eyes were as blue and intense as the parrots in his shirt and he remained perfectly still.

The grandmother reached up to adjust her hat brim as if she were going to the woods with him but it came off in her hand. She stood staring at it and after a second she let it fall on the ground. Hiram pulled Bailey up by the arm as if he were assisting an old man. John Wesley caught hold of his father’s hand and Bobby Lee followed. They went off toward the woods and just as they reached the dark edge, Bailey turned and supporting himself against a gray naked pine trunk, he shouted, “I’ll be back in a minute, Mamma, wait on me!”

“Come back this instant!” his mother shrilled but they all disappeared into the woods.

“Bailey Boy!” the grandmother called in a tragic voice but she found she was looking at The Misfit squatting on the ground in front of her. “I just know you’re a good man,” she said desperately. “You’re not a bit common!”

“Nome, I ain’t a good man,” The Misfit said after a second as if he had considered her statement carefully, “but I ain’t the worst in the world neither. My daddy said I was different breed of dog from my brothers and sisters. ‘You know,’ Daddy said, ‘it’s some that can live their whole life out without asking about it and it’s others has to know why it is, and this boy is one of the latters. He’s going to be into everything!’” He put on his black hat and looked up suddenly and then away deep into the woods as if he were embarrassed again. “I’m sorry I don’t have on a shirt before you ladies,” he said, hunching his shoulders slightly. “We buried our clothes that we had on when we escaped and we’re just making do until we can get better. We borrowed these from some folks we met,” he explained.

100 “That’s perfectly all right,” the grandmother said. “Maybe Bailey has an extra shirt in his suitcase.”

“I’ll look and see terrectly,” The Misfit said.

“Where are they taking him?” the children’s mother screamed.

“Daddy was a card himself,” the Misfit said. “You couldn’t put anything over on him. He never got in trouble with the Authorities though. Just had the knack of handling them.”

“You could be honest too if you’d only try,” said the grandmother. “Think how wonderful it would be to settle down and live a comfortable life and not have to think about somebody chasing you all the time.”

105 The Misfit kept scratching in the ground with the butt of his gun as if he were thinking about it. “Yes’m, somebody is always after you,” he murmured.

The grandmother noticed how thin his shoulder blades were just behind his hat because she was standing up looking down on him. “Do you ever pray?” she asked.

He shook his head. All she saw was the black hat wiggle between his shoulder blades. “Nome,” he said.

There was a pistol shot from the woods, followed closely by another. Then silence. The old lady’s head jerked around. She could hear the wind move through the tree tops like a long satisfied insuck of breath. “Bailey Boy!” she called.

"I was a gospel singer for a while," The Misfit said. "I been most everything. Been in the arm service, both land and sea, at home and abroad, been twict married, been an undertaker, been with the railroads, plowed Mother Earth, been in a tornado, seen a man burnt alive oncet," and he looked up at the children's mother and the little girl who were sitting close together, their faces white and their eyes glassy; "I even seen a woman flogged," he said.

"Pray, pray," the grandmother began, "pray, pray . . ." 110

"I never was a bad boy that I remember of," The Misfit said in an almost dreamy voice, "but somewheres along the line I done something wrong and got sent to the penitentiary. I was buried alive," and he looked up and held her attention to him by a steady stare.

"That's when you should have started to pray," she said. "What did you do to get sent to the penitentiary that first time?"

"Turn to the right, it was a wall," The Misfit said, looking up again at the cloudless sky. "Turn to the left, it was a wall. Look up it was a ceiling, look down it was a floor. I forgot what I done, lady. I set there and set there, trying to remember what it was I done and I ain't recalled it to this day. Oncet in a while, I would think it was coming to me, but it never come."

"Maybe they put you in by mistake," the old lady said vaguely.

"Nome," he said. "It wasn't no mistake. They had the papers on me." 115

"You must have stolen something," she said.

The Misfit sneered slightly. "Nobody had nothing I wanted," he said. "It was a head-doctor at the penitentiary said what I had done was kill my daddy but I know that for a lie. My daddy died in nineteen ought nineteen of the epidemic flu and I never had a thing to do with it. He was buried in the Mount Hopewell Baptist churchyard and you can go there and see for yourself."

"If you would pray," the old lady said, "Jesus would help you."

"That's right," The Misfit said.

"Well then, why don't you pray?" she asked trembling with delight 120
suddenly.

"I don't want no hep," he said. "I'm doing all right by myself."

Bobby Lee and Hiram came ambling back from the woods. Bobby Lee was dragging a yellow shirt with bright blue parrots in it.

"Throw me that shirt, Bobby Lee," The Misfit said. The shirt came flying at him and landed on his shoulder and he put it on. The grandmother couldn't name what the shirt reminded her of. "No, lady," The Misfit said while he was buttoning it up. "I found out the crime don't matter. You can do one thing or you can do another, kill a man or take a tire off his car, because sooner or later you're going to forget what it was you done and just be punished for it."

The children's mother had begun to make heaving noises as if she couldn't get her breath. "Lady," he asked, "would you and that little girl like to step off yonder with Bobby Lee and Hiram and join your husband?"

"Yes, thank you," the mother said faintly. Her left arm dangled helplessly 125
and she was holding the baby, who had gone to sleep, in the other. "Hep that lady up, Hiram," The Misfit said as she struggled to climb out of the ditch, "and Bobby Lee, you hold onto that little girl's hand."

"I don't want to hold hands with him," June Star said. "He reminds me of a pig."

The fat boy blushed and laughed and caught her by the arm and pulled her off into the woods after Hiram and her mother.

Alone with The Misfit, the grandmother found that she had lost her voice. There was not a cloud in the sky nor any sun. There was nothing around her but woods. She wanted to tell him that he must pray. She opened and closed her mouth several times before anything came out. Finally she found herself saying, "Jesus, Jesus," meaning Jesus will help you, but the way she was saying it, it sounded as if she might be cursing.

"Yes'm," The Misfit said as if he agreed. "Jesus thown everything off balance. It was the same case with Him as with me except He hadn't committed any crime and they could prove I had committed one because they had the papers on me. Of course," he said, "they never shown me any papers. That's why I sign myself now. I said long ago, you get you a signature and sign everything you do and keep a copy of it. Then you'll know what you done and you can hold up the crime to the punishment and see do they match and in the end you'll have something to prove you ain't been treated right. I call myself The Misfit," he said, "because I can't make what all I done wrong fit what all I gone through in punishment."

There was a piercing scream from the woods, followed closely by a pistol 130
report. "Does it seem right to you, lady, that one is punished a heap and another ain't punished at all?"

"Jesus!" the old lady cried. "You've got good blood! I know you wouldn't shoot a lady! I know you come from nice people! Pray! Jesus, you ought not to shoot a lady. I'll give you all the money I've got!"

"Lady," The Misfit said, looking beyond her far into the woods, "there never was a body that give the undertaker a tip."

There were two more pistol reports and the grandmother raised her head like a parched old turkey hen crying for water and called, "Bailey Boy, Bailey Boy!" as if her heart would break.

"Jesus was the only One that ever raised the dead," The Misfit continued, "and He shouldn't have done it. He thown everything off balance. If He did what He said, then it's nothing for you to do but thow away everything and follow Him, and if He didn't, then it's nothing for you to do but enjoy the few minutes you got left the best way you can—by killing somebody or burning down his house or doing some other meanness to him. No pleasure but meanness," he said and his voice had become almost a snarl.

"Maybe He didn't raise the dead," the old lady mumbled, not knowing 135
what she was saying and feeling so dizzy that she sank down in the ditch with her legs twisted under her.

"I wasn't there so I can't say He didn't," The Misfit said. "I wisht I had of been there," he said, hitting the ground with his fist. "It ain't right I wasn't there because if I had of been there I would of known. Listen lady," he said in a high voice, "if I had of been there I would of known and I wouldn't be like I am now." His voice seemed about to crack and the grandmother's head cleared for an instant. She saw the man's face twisted close to her own as if he were going to cry and she murmured, "Why you're one of my babies. You're one of my own children!" She reached out and touched him on the shoulder. The Misfit sprang back as if a snake had bitten him and shot her three times through the chest. Then he put his gun down on the ground and took off his glasses and began to clean them.

Hiram and Bobby Lee returned from the woods and stood over the ditch, looking down at the grandmother who half sat and half lay in a puddle of blood with her legs crossed under her like a child's and her face smiling up at the cloudless sky.

Without his glasses, The Misfit's eyes were red-rimmed and pale and defenseless-looking. "Take her off and thow her where you thown the others," he said, picking up the cat that was rubbing itself against his leg.

"She was a talker, wasn't she?" Bobby Lee said, sliding down the ditch with a yodel.

"She would of been a good woman," The Misfit said, "if it had been 140
somebody there to shoot her every minute of her life."

"Some fun!" Bobby Lee said.

"Shut up, Bobby Lee," The Misfit said. "It's no real pleasure in life."

FLANNERY O'CONNOR

(1925–1964) **Web** *www*

A Depression-era child, O'Connor earned an MFA from the University of Iowa, worked briefly in New York, and then returned to Georgia to write. A winner of the National Book Award for her collected stories, O'Connor died of lupus when she was only thirty-nine. Her stories and novels are all set in the American South; she found in Georgia a "collection of goods and evils which are intensely stimulating to the imagination."

TOPICS FOR CRITICAL THINKING **Web** *www*

1. At what point in the story do you know that the family will meet The Misfit? What are the clues?
2. How does this knowledge produce tension when reading the story?
3. What does The Misfit mean when he says, "She would of been a good woman if it had been somebody there to shoot her every minute of her life"?
4. How does the end of the story both meet and defy the reader's expectations?

TOPICS FOR CRITICAL WRITING **Web** *www*

1. What does the phrase "a good man is hard to find" mean?
2. What is the relation between the story and the story about the watermelon the grandmother tells?

W. S. Penn

In Dreams Begins Reality

(2000)

My first wife was mad. Or so my sister said. "She was crazy as a loon, Albert," she'd say. She never said it while we were happily married, but waited until things had fallen apart. I think of the times we visited my sister and I came out of the shower in the morning to find my wife hunched on the edge of the makeshift bed in her hot-pink flannels, eating her breakfast with the door closed, and I wish my sister had said something earlier. But when I remember the look on my wife's face as she explained why she was eating in the bedroom instead of with my sister and her husband, I am unconvinced. She didn't sound like a madwoman.

"They either sit there reading and ignoring me," she said, "or she berates him for keeping her awake all night with his snoring. It makes me uncomfortable."

"That's just the way she is," I'd say.

The second wife, my sister said, was dull as brass. "She's a very nice person, Albert. But what do you have in common?"

Again she waited until I was alone, nightly trying to find a way to make 5
the king-sized bed seem less like the Wallowa Valley. It was comforting to know I hadn't made a mistake. That's what sisters were for, I figured, like codeine. And I was grateful.

My sister never met the hat-trick wife. She was a hinter. You know the type, the woman who warns you a hundred times a day in small unnoticeable ways that something is wrong. She hints so much that your only recourse is to mistake her meaning. When she came home and said, What did I want for dinner, pork? Or just the fat? I pretended she was being humorous.

When she asked the same question about lamb—"You want some lamb? Or you just want me to slice off the fat and heat it up in the micro?"—I took her seriously and weighed my choices.

"Lamb would be fine," I said. "Thank you very much. Dear." She was dressed in a gregarious sheath of red. "Nice dress," I said.

"I'm going out later," she replied.

Sometimes, I'd try to participate in the hinting, make it fun. Like when 10
we went to her sister's to look at wedding pictures and generally gush and glow over her sister's actually getting married. There was a picture of the rear of me, my feet and head lopped off by the viewfinder.

"Is it the same on a tug? Is port left and starboard right?" the wife asked her sister as they looked at the picture. Her sister squirmed. So as not to embarrass her, I joined in.

"That's not a tugboat," I said, grinning.

The wife gave me a piercing look.

"More like Moby-Dick with a tie."

The wife didn't laugh. 15

"Put cameras and 'Goodyear' on it and run it up in the air and it'll shoot the Super Bowl," I said.

The wife shot me a look that felt like the searing flames of hatred.

We divorced. "Three's the charm," I said, and decided that I was through with women. A hat trick's enough by anyone's measure. I have made an effort to remain friends with her, mostly for the sake of our love's by-product, Alicia, who is six.

She's still a hinter. Talking with her on the phone just now, I was regaling her with my theory that the president we see giving a prepared speech is really the brilliant artistry of an automatist, the careful modulations of the recorded voice the secret of Dolby. "That's why the real man seems so stupid at press conferences. It's not just that he is virtually incapable of a solitary logical thought. It's the contrast between art and life that really brings it home."

"Still as much fun as always," the ex-wife hinted.

"That a question or a statement?" I asked. "How's my little girl, anyway?"

"She's right here. Want to speak to her? Alicia," I could hear the ex-wife say, "come listen to your father. Yes, *now*."

"Hello, Father," Alicia said.

"Hi, precious. How's my little pumpkin?"

"Father!" Alicia complained. She doesn't like these affectionate nicknames. Thinks she's outgrown them. I try not to use them, but I can't help myself. As with a full half of what I say, the words just slip out when I'm not looking.

"When are you going to come up for a visit?" I asked.

"Don't know. It's so far."

"Maybe that's true, honeybunch. But I'd be happy to come down and get you, if your mother is afraid of the subway." Alicia lives with her mother in the East Village. I live at the far reaches of the Upper West Side. "Or I'll send you cab fare."

"Maybe after the Bahamas. Richard's taking Mommy and me to the Bahamas next month."

"I know," I said.

"Richard bought me a new bathing suit just for the trip. It's red. He's gonna teach me to scuba-dive."

"That Richard sounds like quite a guy. By the way, do you know what the letters in 'scuba' stand for?"

"Do I have to?" Alicia sighed.

"No. No, Richard will probably tell you anyway. 'Self-contained underwater breathing apparatus' people are like that. They like you to know the rituals and symbols of their sport. They're like sailors. Like dieters or people into meditation. . . ."

"Father," Alicia interrupted. "What's a wonk?"

"Why, sweetcakes? Where'd you hear that word?"

"Richard."

"Yeah?" I wasn't sure I liked Richard teaching my babydoll such language. Where did it lead?

"Yeah. He says you're a real—"

"So Albert," the ex-wife's voice said after a scuffle over the receiver.

"We've got to run along. The Bottom Line is playing Trump's Trumps this afternoon."

"What in the world is 'the bottom line'?"

"Richard's softball team," the ex-wife said. "Talk to you later. Maybe you should get out and join a softball team. Be good for you. And you could supply the team with chatter."

I can take a hint. "If I do, will you come back to me? Would you love me again?"

"I'll make Alicia send you a postcard from the Bahamas," she said. She hung up.

Normally I keep Sundays to myself, reserving time to browse through the 45
Times and time to think up letters to the editor of the book review section. These letters range from chilling attacks on the entire section to letters with specific focus. I never send these letters, at least in part because I never write them. I think them. Taking the time to write them would waste precious Sunday minutes.

After shaming the book review editor, I stroll down to Zabar's and buy fresh bagels, then cut over to Columbus and stop by the deli to pick up chopped Nova lox, then home again to eat them both with cream cheese, while I decide what to do with the rest of the day. Most Sundays, this deciding takes me into late afternoon, at which point I allow myself to look through the television section and start thinking about having a drink before dinner. With mixed emotions, I decide this Sunday to get out and get some exercise. By the boat pond in the park, radio-controlled sailboats compete for attention with radio-controlled roller skaters. In a vee of grass among the trees, the pitched laughter of twelve Asians playing volleyball sounds like the delicate and oddly beautiful plink of Eastern music. A girl on the frontier of womanhood and leaning to tart buys ice cream from a vendor's cart, her red nylon stretch pants drawing L's—from lust and longing to leers and leaving. Her pants are so revealing that she almost achieves the nun-like innocence of the over-clothed. The feeling of her as I walk away stays with me like the sunrise over Makrialos.

I sit on a bench and watch sides being chosen for a pickup softball game, imaginatively penning another letter to the *Times*. A woman comes over and asks me if I want to play. Her name is Gail. Even with her dirty blond hair held back by a headband you can tell Gail has what can only be called big hair.

"No. Thank you."

"We can use another player," she says.

"You've got a backstop," I say. She just looks perplexed. "Well, what the 50
heck. Okay." I figured I'd play catcher.

Gail borrows a glove for me from the other team and assigns me third base, a position I want about as much as another divorce. I'm no better at third base than I am at marriage or poker, preferring low-risk bets like catcher to the high stakes of double plays and charging grounders.

Gail takes shortstop. In all my years of watching softball, this hasn't happened often, but Gail looks as though she can handle the job. Indeed, Gail seems eager, ready, willing, and able to field grounders, pop-ups, and line drives, as well as to egg on those of us less eager or able. As the first baseman lobs grounders at us and warms us up she moves with grace and not a little strength. Her chatter as the game begins sounds like any shortstop's chatter. Except for the pitch of her voice and the fact that despite her big hair Gail is pretty, she could be Phil Rizzuto. Pee Wee Reese. The girl in red comes over and stands there, tongue licking about the rim of her ice cream cone, watching. She suddenly takes me back to days when little boys played softball and little girls looked appealingly on the sidelines, careful not to show too much calf between their bobby socks and the hems of their full skirts.

Days of an uneasy détente when our mothers apprenticed us to the world of action by telling us to stop moping around the house and go out and kill off a tribe or two of Indians. (Moping was for girls and when Mother's friends heard that I liked books more than ball, they coughed.) Days of a recurring boyhood dream: I'm at third base, a huge white softball bouncing ten feet in front of me and beginning to spin. With the instinct of Brooks Robinson, I understood that the second bounce would send the ball kicking over my head, so I charged it and knocked it down heroically. Feeling the little girls smile from the sidelines, I concentrated on keeping my wits about me. I picked up the ball and looked toward first. "I'm making a play," I thought, and realizing that I was making a play, I threw the ball hard at the first baseman.

The ball orbited over first base, returned to earth a good forty feet beyond, and rolled white and solitary for a decade. Long enough for the shortstop to stroll over and force himself to say, "It's all right. We'll get the next batter." Long enough for the sidelined girls to giggle and twitter and point, and for me to hate their twittering. I'd awaken, swearing off softball, swearing that I would show those girls, that I'd never let this happen again.

But it did. It happened again, again and again, over thirty-odd years. 55
Crouching there beside Gail, I see how I'm a sucker for games. How if there was one to be played, I played it.

I come to life like the stone guest in *Don Giovanni* as a hard-hit grounder—mine—skips to my left. Gail slides deep into the hole behind me, knocks the ball down, and, despite the thrill of making the play, decides against throwing to first. The men on the opposing team's bench smile secretly. Chagrined, I look away and see the girl in nylon pants poke the last of her ice cream cone through her lips and smirk.

"Sorry," I mutter to Gail. "Daydreaming."

"S'okay," Gail says. "We'll get the next batter." She smiles and slaps me on the rear end, coach-like, and for a moment I feel, deep down, an awakening of the simple innocence of my boyish heart. I believe we will get the next batter, Gail and I, if only I can pay attention. I crouch, eye on the next batter and ready for the pitch, determined not to let Gail down, marveling at the way things change. Had little girls giggled and twittered not at me but because they were denied the chance to make the same errors? I was grateful for the way some of them had grown up, giving up limp-wristed dainty flings, learning to throw from the shoulder.

I was grateful for Gail and I was amused by the antics of the men on the other team, celebrating their victory with lots of expensive-looking beer. "If only I'd caught that pop-up," I said.

"What the hell," Gail said. "It's only a game. See you next week?" 60

"Maybe," I said.

"Maybe we'll try you at catcher."

"Sure. Whatever. Even backstop." Gail didn't get it and I let it go. We said goodbye.

Heading past the boat pond out of the park, the roller skaters had been replaced by a bunch of boys bouncing like popcorn to the dulcet strains of their rap music on a ghetto blaster. "Ghetto-blasting their way right out of the power structure," I think. "Right out of time." I think about the girl in red pants. She, too, seems out of time, like an illusion from the past which has become a present anachronism. Maybe she would grow up like Gail. Then again, maybe she wouldn't.

"Anything's possible," I think, and then I say it, out loud, making a pret- 65
zel vendor wonder if I am speaking to him or, like so many in this city, simply speaking to anyone who might be listening. For the first time in years, I know what to do with the rest of my Sunday. Go downtown and buy Alicia a softball glove. Maybe some sweatpants. Some loose blue sweatpants.

W. S. PENN

www

(b. 1949) **Web**

An urban mixed-blood Nez Perce, W. S. Penn is the author of *The Absence of Angels* (1994) and *All My Sins Are Relatives* (1995). A writer of both fiction and nonfictional essays, he has been named Writer of the Year and Editor of the Year by the Woodcraft Circle of Native Writers and Storytellers.

www

TOPICS FOR CRITICAL THINKING **Web**

1. In what ways does the narrator interpret his first wife's tone?
2. In what ways is the narrator's tone related to what he knows or understands?
3. Does the narrator's tone shift? If so, when and why?
4. In what ways does tone indicate class tensions?
5. What is the relation between daydreaming and tone?

www

TOPICS FOR CRITICAL WRITING **Web**

1. How do the two parts of the story relate to shifts in the story's tone?
2. What are the dreams in the story?

12 Structure

All of the elements that make up a story do not occur randomly, but rather are arranged to work together. The ways a story organizes its elements is called **structure.** Structure is the difference between a rambling recital of events as might happen in a personal conversation and the tightly organized telling that occurs in prose fiction. Structure refers to the way a story's various elements work together to produce patterns of meaning. As discussed in Chapter 6, the primary structure that organizes stories is **narrative.** Narrative refers both to the act of telling a story and to our sense of what makes something a story (as opposed to a list or an argument) in the first place. **Plot** is the ordering of events, while structure includes the ways *plot*, *imagery*, *motifs*, and *character* are organized as repetitions, variations, or a series of oppositions. Although stories all have a narrative structure—that is, they consist of a series of events related through cause and effect and they have a beginning, a middle, and an end—they also each have their own particular structure that relates to both the ways the story is told (style, tone, narrator, point of view) and its themes.

Structure is often *conventional;* that is, it consists of a familiar pattern (like the story of the conquering hero or the young person who is growing up) repeated throughout culture. Stories borrow structures from tradition, as in the folktale or joke, or from other stories deeply embedded in culture, such as the success narrative attached to the American dream where the young, poor person grows up, works hard, and achieves wealth. Sometimes structure is very simple—a repetition of the same event or image, an inevitable moving towards what one is trying to avoid, or a simple conflict of human and nature. Occasionally structure seems quite complex, as in stories with multiple plots or elaborate chronologies or stories with very intricate imagery and characterization. Often stories contain a series of oppositions—between characters, images, ideas—that organize its themes within its plot. At the same time, however, stories are quite economical, consisting of very few elements or actions. The structure of economical stories often uses all details and events for multiple purposes. An example of this is the way Ernest Hemingway's "Hills Like White Elephants" uses only conversation and drinking to convey the couple's larger dilemma and the character of their relationship.

Discerning a story's structure is sometimes the beginning of analysis, sometimes the end. In some stories, parts of structure are evident, marked by dates, subtitles, or divisions in the text. Other ways of determining structure are to see what elements are repeated or form systems of opposition in which the same ideas are contrasted in many different ways throughout the story in its events, imagery, and characterization. Another way to see structure is to see how ideas or themes vary or change throughout a story.

The overall effect of some stories is in their structure. The surprise ending, for example, is partly the effect of a story's structure, which plays on the reader's expectations about the patterns of narrative that seem to lead another direction. In other stories, structure is a corollary of style or tone. In ironic stories, structure often conforms to, helps produce, and reaffirms a sense of **dramatic irony**. In Flannery O'Connor's "A Good Man Is Hard to Find," for example, our sense that the family will meet The Misfit is encouraged both by the narrator's tone and by the series of events, which inevitably lead to an encounter with the man who is feared from the beginning. Sometimes structure provides a platform for other kinds of expression such as description, characterization, or tone. Stories that focus on a single character, for example, provide ample opportunity for describing the character. Structure is a combination of elements that itself works with other elements to produce a story's aesthetic or its **art**—the particular ways a story is more than simply the events it describes.

Critical Perspectives: Structuralism and Psychoanalytic Criticism

Criticism that studies what a story's structure tells us about how it works as *www* a story is called **structuralist criticism**. **Web** Building on structure, criticism that looks at the ways a story's structures (repetitions, oppositions, appearances of what is avoided) reveal a story's preoccupations is called **psychoanalytic criticism**. *www* **Web** Based on the ways psychoanalysts analyze their patients' narratives, psychoanalytic critics treat stories as if they were patients who have symptoms and an unconscious that is revealed in the ways stories structure events. Another mode of criticism that considers these structural elements is **deconstruction,** which looks at how structures as well as language and imagery might work against or contradict themselves or other aspects of a story's *www* expression. **Web**

Stories About Structure

The stories that follow illustrate various structural possibilities and conventions from the folktale to the romance. Chinua Achebe's "The Sacrificial Egg" is a modern folktale. Anita Desai's "Studies in the Park" is structured around repeated actions and the opposition between parental expectations and youthful rebellion. Hanif Kureishi's "Blue, Blue Pictures of You" is a variation on the structure of the romance. All illustrate in some way the clash of cultures, conventions, and perspectives occurring when writers from colonized areas such as Africa and the Indian Subcontinent write about the experiences of colonization, oppression, and the problems of shifting from one culture to another.

CHINUA ACHEBE

The Sacrificial Egg

(1959)

Julius Obi sat gazing at his typewriter. The fat Chief Clerk, his boss, was snoring at his table. Outside, the gatekeeper in his green uniform was sleeping at his post. You couldn't blame him; no customer had passed through the gate for nearly a week. There was an empty basket on the giant weighing machine. A few palm-kernels lay desolately in the dust around the machine. Only the flies remained in strength.

Julius went to the window that overlooked the great market on the bank of the River Niger. The market, though still called Nkwo, had long spilled over into Eke, Oye, and Afọ with the coming of civilization and the growth of the town into a big palm-oil port. In spite of this encroachment, however, it was still busiest on its original Nkwo day, because the deity who had presided over it from antiquity still cast her spell only on her own day—let men in their greed spill over themselves. It was said that she appeared in the form of an old woman in the centre of the market just before cock-crow and waved her magic fan in the four directions of the earth—in front of her, behind her, to the right and to the left—to draw to the market men and women from distant places. And they came bringing the produce of their lands—palm-oil and kernels, kola nuts, cassava, mats, baskets and earthenware pots; and took home many-coloured cloths, smoked fish, iron pots and plates. These were the forest peoples. The other half of the world who lived by the great rivers came down also—by canoe, bringing yams and fish. Sometimes it was a big canoe with a dozen or more people in it; sometimes it was a lone fisherman and his wife in a small vessel from the swift-flowing Anambara. They moored their canoe on the bank and sold their fish, after much haggling. The woman then walked up the steep banks of the river to the heart of the market to buy salt and oil and, if the sales had been very good, even a length of cloth. And for her children at home she bought bean cakes and mai-mai which the Igara women cooked. As evening approached, they took up their paddles again and paddled away, the water shimmering in the sunset and their canoe becoming smaller and smaller in the distance until it was just a dark crescent on the water's face and two dark bodies swaying forwards and backwards in it. Umuru then was the meeting place of the forest people who were called Igbo and the alien riverain folk whom the Igbo called Olu and beyond whom the world stretched in indefiniteness.

Julius Obi was not a native of Umuru. He had come like countless others from some bush village inland. Having passed his Standard Six in a mission school he had come to Umuru to work as a clerk in the offices of the all-powerful European trading company which bought palm-kernels at its own price and sold cloth and metalware, also at its own price. The offices were situated beside the famous market so that in his first two or three weeks Julius had to learn to work within its huge enveloping hum. Sometimes when the Chief Clerk was away he walked to the window and looked down on the vast anthill activity. Most of these people were not there yesterday, he thought, and yet the market had been just as full. There must be many, many people in the world to be able to fill the market day after day like this. Of course they say not all who came to the great market were real people. Janet's mother, Ma, had said so.

"Some of the beautiful young women you see squeezing through the crowds are not people like you or me but mammy-wota who have their town in the depths of the river," she said. "You can always tell them, because they are beautiful with a beauty that is too perfect and too cold. You catch a glimpse of her with the tail of your eye, then you blink and look properly, but she has already vanished in the crowd."

Julius thought about these things as he now stood at the window looking down on the silent, empty market. Who would have believed that the great boisterous market could ever be quenched like this? But such was the strength of Kitikpa, the incarnate power of smallpox. Only he could drive away all those people and leave the market to the flies.

When Umuru was a little village, there was an age-grade who swept its market-square every Nkwo day. But progress had turned it into a busy, sprawling, crowded and dirty river port, a no-man's-land where strangers outnumbered by far the sons of the soil, who could do nothing about it except shake their heads at this gross perversion of their prayer. For indeed they had prayed—who will blame them—for their town to grow and prosper. And it had grown. But there is good growth and there is bad growth. The belly does not bulge out only with food and drink; it might be the abominable disease which would end by sending its sufferer out of the house even before he was fully dead.

The strangers who came to Umuru came for trade and money, not in search of duties to perform, for they had those in plenty back home in their village which was real home.

And as if this did not suffice, the young sons and daughters of Umuru soil, encouraged by schools and churches were behaving no better than the strangers. They neglected all their old tasks and kept only the revelries.

Such was the state of the town when Kitikpa came to see it and to demand the sacrifice the inhabitants owed the gods of the soil. He came in confident knowledge of the terror he held over the people. He was an evil deity, and boasted it. Lest he be offended those he killed were not killed but decorated, and no one dared weep for them. He put an end to the coming and going between neighbours and between villages. They said, "Kitikpa is in that village," and immediately it was cut off by its neighbours.

Julius was sad and worried because it was almost a week since he had seen

Janet, the girl he was going to marry. Ma had explained to him very gently that he should no longer go to see them "until this thing is over, by the power of Jehovah." (Ma was a very devout Christian convert and one reason why she approved of Julius for her only daughter was that he sang in the choir of the CMS church.)

"You must keep to your rooms," she had said in hushed tones, for Kitikpa strictly forbade any noise or boisterousness. "You never know whom you might meet on the streets. That family has got it." She lowered her voice even more and pointed surreptitiously at the house across the road whose doorway was barred with a yellow palm-frond. "He has decorated one of them already and the rest were moved away today in a big government lorry."

Janet walked a short way with Julius and stopped; so he stopped too. They seemed to have nothing to say to each other yet they lingered on. Then she said goodnight and he said goodnight. And they shook hands, which was very odd, as though parting for the night were something new and grave.

He did not go straight home, because he wanted desperately to cling, even alone, to this strange parting. Being educated he was not afraid of whom he might meet, so he went to the bank of the river and just walked up and down it. He must have been there a long time because he was still there when the wooden gong of the night-mask sounded. He immediately set out for home, half-walking and half-running, for night-masks were not a matter of superstition; they were real. They chose the night for their revelry because like the bat's their ugliness was great.

In his hurry he stepped on something that broke with a slight liquid explosion. He stopped and peeped down at the footpath. The moon was not up yet but there was a faint light in the sky which showed that it would not be long delayed. In this half-light he saw that he had stepped on an egg offered in sacrifice. Someone oppressed by misfortune had brought the offering to the crossroads in the dusk. And he had stepped on it. There were the usual young palm-fronds around it. But Julius saw it differently as a house where the terrible artist was at work. He wiped the sole of his foot on the sandy path and hurried away, carrying another vague worry in his mind. But hurrying was no use now; the fleet-footed mask was already abroad. Perhaps it was impelled to hurry by the threatening imminence of the moon. Its voice rose high and clear in the still night air like a flaming sword. It was yet a long way away, but Julius knew that distances vanished before it. So he made straight for the cocoyam farm beside the road and threw himself on his belly, in the shelter of the broad leaves. He had hardly done this when he heard the rattling staff of the spirit and a thundering stream of esoteric speech. He shook all over. The sounds came bearing down on him, almost pressing his face into the moist earth. And now he could hear the footsteps. It was as if twenty evil men were running together. Panic sweat broke all over him and he was nearly impelled to get up and run. Fortunately he kept a firm hold on himself . . . In no time at all the commotion in the air and on the earth—the thunder and torrential rain, the earthquake and flood—passed and disappeared in the distance on the other side of the road.

The next morning, at the office the Chief Clerk, a son of the soil spoke 15 bitterly about last night's provocation of Kitikpa by the headstrong youngsters who had launched the noisy fleet-footed mask in defiance of their elders, who knew that Kitikpa would be enraged, and then . . .

The trouble was that the disobedient youths had never yet experienced the power of Kitikpa themselves; they had only heard of it. But soon they would learn.

As Julius stood at the window looking out on the emptied market he lived through the terror of that night again. It was barely a week ago but already it seemed like another life, separated from the present by a vast emptiness. This emptiness deepened with every passing day. On this side of it stood Julius, and on the other Ma and Janet whom the dread artist decorated.

Chinua Achebe

www *(b. 1930)* **Web**

Born in Nigeria and educated in English, Achebe writes about the tensions between African traditions and folk ways and the effects of Westernization. Considered by many to be Africa's premier novelist, Achebe is currently the Charles P. Stevenson Jr. Professor of Languages and Literature at Bard College in New York State.

www *TOPICS FOR CRITICAL THINKING* **Web**

1. What elements in the story represent traditional African culture?
2. What elements represent Western culture?
3. Which elements are divine? Which are mundane?
4. What are the connections among time, geography, tradition, Westernization, and death?

www *TOPICS FOR CRITICAL WRITING* **Web**

1. What are the different meanings of Julius stepping on the sacrificial egg?
2. In what ways does this story represent the difficulties of change?

Anita Desai

Studies in the Park *(1978)*

—Turn it off, turn it off, turn it off! First he listens to the news in Hindi. Directly after, in English. Broom—brrroom—brrrroom—the voice of doom roars. Next, in Tamil. Then in Punjabi. In Gujarati. What next, my god, what next? Turn it off before I smash it onto his head, fling it out of the window, do nothing of the sort of course, nothing of the sort.

—And my mother. She cuts and fries, cuts and fries. All day I hear her chopping and slicing and the pan of oil hissing. What all does she find to fry and feed us on, for God's sake? Eggplants, potatoes, spinach, shoe soles, newspapers, finally she'll slice me and feed me to my brothers and sisters. Ah, now she's turned on the tap. It's roaring and pouring, pouring and roaring into a bucket without a bottom.

—The bell rings. Voices clash, clatter and break. The tin-and-bottle man? The neighbours? The police? The Help-the-Blind man? Thieves and burglars? All of them, all of them, ten or twenty or a hundred of them, marching up the stairs, hammering at the door, breaking in and climbing over me—ten, twenty or a hundred of them.

—Then, worst of all, the milk arrives. In the tallest glass in the house. 'Suno, drink your milk. Good for you, Suno. You need it. Now, before the exams. Must have it, Suno. Drink.' The voice wheedles its way into my ear like a worm. I shudder. The table tips over. The milk runs. The tumbler clangs on the floor. 'Suno, Suno, how will you do your exams?'

—That is precisely what I ask myself. All very well to give me a room— 5
Uncle's been pushed off on a pilgrimage to Hardwar to clear a room for me—and to bring me milk and say, 'Study, Suno, study for your exam.' What about the uproar around me? These people don't know the meaning of the word Quiet. When my mother fills buckets, sloshes the kitchen floor, fries and sizzles things in the pan, she thinks she is being Quiet. The children have never even heard the word, it amazes and puzzles them. On their way back from school they fling their satchels in at my door, then tear in to snatch them back before I tear them to bits. Bawl when I pull their ears, screech when mother whacks them. Stuff themselves with her fries and then smear the grease on my books.

So I raced out of my room, with my fingers in my ears, to scream till the roof fell down about their ears. But the radio suddenly went off, the door to my parents' room suddenly opened and my father appeared, bathed and shaven, stuffed and set up with the news of the world in six different languages—his white *dhoti* blazing, his white shirt crackling, his patent leather pumps glittering. He stopped in the doorway and I stopped on the balls of my feet and wavered. My fingers came out of my ears, my hair came down over my eyes. Then he looked away from me, took his watch out of his pocket and enquired, 'Is the food ready?' in a voice that came out of his nose like the whistle of a punctual train. He skated off towards his meal, I turned and slouched back to my room. On his way to work, he looked in to say, 'Remember, Suno, I expect good results from you. Study hard, Suno.' Just behind him, I saw all the rest of them standing, peering in, silently. All of them stared at me, at the exam I was to take. At the degree I was to get. Or not get. Horrifying thought. Oh study, study, study, they all breathed at me while my father's footsteps went down the stairs, crushing each underfoot in turn. I felt their eyes on me, goggling, and their breath on me, hot with earnestness. I looked back at them, into their open mouths and staring eyes.

'Study,' I said, and found I croaked. 'I know I ought to study. And how do you expect me to study—in this madhouse? You run wild, *wild.* I'm getting out,' I screamed, leaping up and grabbing my books, 'I'm going to study outside. Even the street is quieter,' I screeched and threw myself past them and down the stairs that my father had just cowed and subjugated so that they still lay quivering, and paid no attention to the howls that broke out behind me of 'Suno, Suno, listen. Your milk—your studies—your exams, Suno!'

At first I tried the tea shop at the corner. In my reading I had often come across men who wrote at café tables—letters, verse, whole novels—over a cup of coffee or a glass of absinthe. I thought it would be simple to read a chapter of history over a cup of tea. There was no crowd in the mornings, none of my friends would be there. But the proprietor would not leave me alone. Bored, picking his nose, he wandered down from behind the counter to my table by the weighing machine and tried to pass the time of day by complaining about his piles, the new waiter and the high prices. 'And sugar,' he whined. 'How can I give you anything to put in your tea with sugar at four rupees a kilo? There's rationed sugar, I know, at two rupees, but that's not enough to feed even an ant. And the way you all sugar your tea—*hai, hai*,' he sighed, worse than my mother. I didn't answer. I frowned at my book and looked stubborn. But when I got rid of him, the waiter arrived. 'Have a biscuit?' he murmured, flicking at my table and chair with his filthy duster. 'A bun? Fritters? Make you some hot fritters?' I snarled at him but he only smiled, determined to be friendly. Just a boy, really, in a pink shirt with purple circles stamped all over it—he thought he looked so smart. He was growing sideburns, he kept fingering them. 'I'm a student, too,' he said, 'sixth class, fail. My mother wanted me to go back and try again, but I didn't like the teacher—he beat me. So I came here to look for a job. Lala-*ji* had just thrown out a boy called Hari for selling lottery tickets to the clients so he took me on. I can make out a bill . . .' He would have babbled on if Lala-*ji* had not come and shoved him into the kitchen with an oath. So it went on. I didn't read more than half a chapter that whole morning. I didn't want to go home either. I walked along the street, staring at my shoes, with my shoulders slumped in the way that makes my father scream, 'What's the matter? Haven't you bones? A spine?' I kicked some rubble along the pavement, down the drain, then stopped at the iron gates of King Edward's Park.

'Exam troubles?' asked a *gram* vendor who sat outside it, in a friendly voice. Not insinuating, but low, pleasant. 'The park's full of boys like you,' he continued in that sympathetic voice. 'I see them walk up and down, up and down with their books, like mad poets. Then I'm glad I was never sent to school,' and he began to whistle, not impertinently but so cheerfully that I stopped and stared at him. He had a crippled arm that hung out of his shirt sleeve like a leg of mutton dangling on a hook. His face was scarred as though he had been dragged out of some terrible accident. But he was shuffling hot *gram* into paper cones with his one hand and whistling like a bird, whistling the tune of, 'We are the *bul-buls* of our land, our land is Paradise.' Nodding at the greenery beyond the gates, he said, 'The park's a good place to study in,' and, taking his hint, I went in.

I wonder how it is I never thought of the park before. It isn't far from our 10
house and I sometimes went there as a boy, if I managed to run away from

school, to lie on a bench, eat peanuts, shy stones at the chipmunks that came for the shells, and drink from the fountain. But then it was not as exciting as playing marbles in the street or stoning rats with my school friends in the vacant lot behind the cinema. It had straight paths, beds of flapping red flowers—cannas, I think—rows of palm trees like limp flags, a dry fountain and some green benches. Old men sat on them with their legs far apart, heads drooping over the tops of sticks, mumbling through their dentures or cackling with that mad, ripping laughter that makes children think of old men as wizards and bogey-men. Bag-like women in grey and fawn *saris* or black *borkhas* screamed, just as grey and fawn and black birds do, at children falling into the fountain or racing on rickety legs after the chipmunks and pigeons. A madman or two, prancing around in paper caps and bits of rags, munching banana peels and scratching like monkeys. Corners behind hibiscus bushes stinking of piss. Iron rails with rows of beggars contentedly dozing, scratching, gambling, with their sackcloth backs to the rails. A city park.

What I hadn't noticed, or thought of, were all the students who escaped from their city flats and families like mine to come and study here. Now, walking down a path with my history book tucked under my arm, I felt like a gatecrasher at a party or a visitor to a public library trying to control a sneeze. They all seemed to belong here, to be at home here. Dressed in loose pyjamas, they strolled up and down under the palms, books open in their hands, heads lowered into them. Or they sat in twos and threes on the grass, reading aloud in turns. Or lay full length under the trees, books spread out across their faces—sleeping, or else imbibing information through the subconscious. Opening out my book, I too strolled up and down, reading to myself in a low murmur.

In the beginning, when I first started studying in the park, I couldn't concentrate on my studies. I'd keep looking up at the boy strolling in front of me, reciting poetry in a kind of thundering whisper, waving his arms about and running his bony fingers through his hair till it stood up like a thorn bush. Or at the chipmunks that fought and played and chased each other all over the park, now and then joining forces against the sparrows over a nest or a paper cone of *gram.* Or at the madman going through the rubble at the bottom of the dry fountain and coming up with a rubber shoe, a banana peel or a piece of glittering tin that he appreciated so much that he put it in his mouth and chewed it till blood ran in strings from his mouth.

It took me time to get accustomed to the ways of the park. I went there daily, for the whole day, and soon I got to know it as well as my own room at home and found I could study there, or sleep, or daydream, as I chose. Then I fell into its routine, its rhythm, and my time moved in accordance with its time. We were like a house-owner and his house, or a turtle and its shell, or a river and its bank—so close. I resented everyone else who came to the park—I thought they couldn't possibly share my feeling for it. Except, perhaps, the students.

The park was like an hotel, or an hospital, belonging to the city but with its own order and routine, enclosed by iron rails, laid out according to prescription in rows of palms, benches and paths. If I went there very early in the morning, I'd come upon a yoga class. It consisted of young bodybuilders rippling their muscles like snakes as well as old crack-pots determined to keep up with the youngest and fittest, all sitting cross-legged on the grass and displaying *hus-mukh* to the sun just rising over the palms: the Laughing Face pose it was called, but they looked like gargoyles with their mouths torn open and their thick, discoloured tongues sticking out. If I were the sun, I'd feel so disgusted by such a reception I'd just turn around and go back. And that was the simplest of their poses—after that they'd go into contortions that would embarrass an ape. Once their leader, a black and hirsute man like an aborigine, saw me watching and called me to join them. I shook my head and ducked behind an oleander. You won't catch me making an ass of myself in public. And I despise all that body-beautiful worship anyway. What's the body compared to the soul, the mind?

I'd stroll under the palms, breathing in the cool of the early morning, feeling it drive out, or wash clean, the stifling dark of the night, and try to avoid bumping into all the other early morning visitors to the park—mostly aged men sent by their wives to fetch the milk from the Government dairy booth just outside the gates. Their bottles clinking in green cloth bags and newspapers rolled up and tucked under their arms, they strutted along like stiff puppets and mostly they would be discussing philosophy. 'Ah but in Vedanta it is a different matter,' one would say, his eyes gleaming fanatically, and another would announce, 'The sage Shanakaracharya showed the way,' and some would refer to the Upanishads or the Bhagavad Puranas, but in such argumentative, hacking tones that you could see they were quite capable of coming to blows over some theological argument. Certainly it was the mind above the body for these old coots but I found nothing to admire in them either. I particularly resented it when one of them disengaged himself from the discussion long enough to notice me and throw me a gentle look of commiseration. As if he'd been through exams, too, long long ago, and knew all about them. So what?

Worst of all were the athletes, wrestlers, Mr Indias and others who lay on their backs and were massaged with oil till every muscle shone and glittered. The men who massaged them huffed and puffed and cursed as they climbed up and down the supine bodies, pounding and pummelling the men who lay there wearing nothing but little greasy clouts, groaning and panting in a way I found obscene and disgusting. They never looked up at me or at anyone. They lived in a meaty, sweating world of their own—massages, oils, the body, a match to be fought and won—I kicked up dust in their direction but never went too close.

The afternoon would be quiet, almost empty. I would sit under a tree and read, stroll and study, doze too. Then, in the evening, as the sky softened from its blank white glare and took on shades of pink and orange and the palm trees rustled a little in an invisible breeze, the crowds would begin to pour out of Darya Ganj, Mori Gate, Chandni Chowk and the Jama Masjid bazaars and slums. Large families would come to sit about on the grass, eating peanuts and listening to a transistor radio placed in the center of the circle. Mothers would sit together in flocks like screeching birds while children jumped into the dry fountains, broke flowers and terrorized each other. There would be a few young men moaning at the corners, waiting for a girl to roll her hips and dart her fish eyes in their direction, and then start the exciting adventure of pursuit. The children's cries would grow more piercing with the dark; frightened, shrill and exalted with mystery and farewell. I would wander back to the flat.

The exams drew nearer. Not three, not two, but only one month to go. I had to stop daydreaming and set myself tasks for every day and remind myself constantly to complete them. It grew so hot I had to give up strolling on the paths and staked out a private place for myself under a tree. I noticed the tension tightening the eyes and mouths of other students—they applied themselves more diligently to their books, talked less, slept less. Everyone looked a little demented from lack of sleep. Our books seemed attached to our hands as though by roots, they were a part of us, they lived because we fed them. They were parasites and, like parasites, were sucking us dry. We mumbled to ourselves, not always consciously. Chipmunks jumped over our feet, mocking us. The *gram* seller down at the gate whistled softly 'I'm glad I never went to school, I am a *bul-bul*, I live in Paradise . . .'

My brains began to jam up. I could feel it happening, slowly. As if the oil were all used up. As if everything was getting locked together, rusted. The white cells, the grey matter, the springs and nuts and bolts. I yelled at my mother—I think it was my mother—'What do you think I am? What do you want of me?' and crushed a glass of milk between my hands. It was sticky. She had put sugar in my milk. As if I were a baby. I wanted to cry. They wouldn't let me sleep, they wanted to see my light on all night, they made sure I never stopped studying. Then they brought me milk and sugar and made clicking sounds with their tongues. I raced out to the park. I think I sobbed as I paced up and down, up and down, in the corner that stank of piss. My head ached worse than ever. I slept all day under the tree and had to work all night.

My father laid his hand on my shoulder. I knew I was not to fling it off. So 20
I sat still, slouching, ready to spring aside if he lifted it only slightly. 'You must get a first, Suno,' he said through his nose, 'must get a first, or else you won't get a job. Must get a job, Suno,' he sighed and wiped his nose and went off, his patent leather pumps squealing like mice. I flung myself back in my chair and howled. Get a first, get a first, get a first—like a railway engine, it went charging over me, grinding me down, and left me dead and mangled on the tracks.

Everything hung still and yellow in the park. I lay sluggishly on a heap of waste paper under my tree and read without seeing, slept without sleeping. Sometimes I went to the water tap that leaked and drank the leak. It tasted of brass. I spat out a mouthful. It nearly went over the feet of the student waiting for his turn at that dripping tap. I stepped aside for him. He swilled the water around his mouth and spat, too, carefully missing my feet. Wiping his mouth, he asked, 'B.A.?'

'No, Inter.'

'Hu,' he burped. 'Wait till you do your B.A. Then you'll get to know.' His face was like a grey bone. It was not unkind, it simply had no expression. 'Another two weeks,' he sighed and slouched off to his own lair.

I touched my face. I thought it would be all bone, like his. I was surprised to find a bit of skin still covering it. I felt as if we were all dying in the park, that when we entered the examination hall it would be to be declared officially dead. That's what the degree was about. What else was it all about? Why were we creeping around here, hiding from the city, from teachers and parents, pretending to study and prepare? Prepare for what? We hadn't been told. Inter, they said, or B.A., or M.A. These were like official stamps—they would declare us dead. Ready for a dead world. A world in which ghosts went about, squeaking or whining, rattling or rustling. Slowly, slowly we were killing ourselves in order to join them. The ball-point pen in my pocket was the only thing that still lived, that still worked. I didn't work myself any more—I mean physically, my body no longer functioned. I was constipated, I was dying. I was lying under a yellow tree, feeling the dust sift through the leaves to cover me. It was filling my eyes, my throat. I could barely walk. I never strolled. Only on the way out of the park, late in the evening, I crept down the path under the palms, past the benches.

Then I saw the scene that stopped it all, stopped me just before I died.

Hidden behind an oleander was a bench. A woman lay on it, stretched out. She was a Muslim, wrapped in a black *borkha.* I hesitated when I saw this straight, still figure in black on the bench. Just then she lifted a pale, thin hand and lifted her veil. I saw her face. It lay bared, in the black folds of her *borkha,* like a flower, wax-white and composed, like a Persian lily or a tobacco flower at night. She was young. Very young, very pale, beautiful with a beauty I had never come across even in a dream. It caught me and held me tight, tight till I couldn't breathe and couldn't move. She was so white, so still, I saw she was very ill—with anaemia, perhaps, or t.b. Too pale, too white—I could see she was dying. Her head—so still and white it might have been carved if it weren't for this softness, this softness of a flower at night—lay in the lap of a very old man. Very much older than her. With spectacles and a long grey beard like a goat's, or a scholar's. He was looking down at her and caressing her face—so tenderly, so tenderly, I had never seen a hand move so gently and tenderly. Beside them, on the ground, two little girls were playing. Round little girls, rather dirty, drawing lines in the gravel. They stared at me but the man and the woman did not notice me. They never looked at anyone else, only at each other, with an expression that halted me. It was tender, loving, yes, but in an inhuman way, so intense. Divine, I felt, or insane. I stood, half-hidden by the bush, holding my book, and wondered at them. She was ill, I could see, dying. Perhaps she had only a short time to live. Why didn't he take her to the Victoria Zenana Hospital, so close to the park? Who was this man—her husband, her father, a lover? I couldn't make out although I watched them without moving, without breathing. I felt not as if I were staring rudely at strangers, but as if I were gazing at a painting or a sculpture, some work of art. Or seeing a vision. They were still and I stood still and the children stared. Then she lifted her arms above her head and laughed. Very quietly.

I broke away and hurried down the path, in order to leave them alone, in privacy. They weren't a work of art, or a vision, but real, human and alive as no one else in my life had been real and alive. I had only that glimpse of them. But I felt I could never open my books and study or take degrees after that. They belonged to the dead, and now I had seen what being alive meant. The vision burnt the surfaces of my eyes so that they watered as I groped my way up the stairs to the flat. I could hardly find my way to the bed.

It was not just the examination but everything else had suddenly withered and died, gone lifeless and purposeless when compared with this vision. My studies, my family, my life—they all belonged to the dead and only what I had seen in the park had any meaning.

Since I did not know how to span the distance between that beautiful ideal and my stupid, dull existence, I simply lay still and shut my eyes. I kept them shut so as not to see all the puzzled, pleading, indignant faces of my family around me, but I could not shut out their voices.

'Suno, Suno,' I heard them croon and coax and mourn.

'Suno, drink milk.'

'Suno, study.'

'Suno, take the exam.'

And when they tired of being so patient with me and I still would not get up, they began to crackle and spit and storm.

'Get up, Suno.'

'Study, Suno.'

'At once, Suno'

Only my mother became resigned and gentle. She must have seen something quite out of the ordinary on my face to make her so. I felt her hand on my forehead and heard her say, 'Leave him alone. Let him sleep tonight. He is tired out, that is what it is—he has driven himself too much and now he must sleep.'

Then I heard all of them leave the room. Her hand stayed on my forehead, wet and smelling of onions, and after a bit my tears began to flow from under my lids.

'Poor Suno, sleep,' she murmured.

I went back to the park of course. But now I was changed. I had stopped being a student—I was a 'professional'. My life was dictated by the rules and routine of the park. I still had my book open on the palms of my hands as I strolled but now my eyes strayed without guilt, darting at the young girls walking in pairs, their arms linked, giggling and bumping into each other. Sometimes I stopped to rest on a bench and conversed with one of the old men, told him who my father was and what examination I was preparing for, and allowing him to tell me about his youth, his politics, his philosophy, his youth and again his youth. Or I joked with the other students, sitting on the grass and throwing peanut shells at the chipmunks, and shocking them, I could see, with my irreverence and cynicism about the school, the exam, the system. Once I even nodded at the yoga teacher and exchanged a few words with him. He suggested I join his class and I nodded vaguely and said I would think it over. It might help. My father says I need help. He says I am hopeless but that I need help. I just laugh but I know that he knows I will never appear for the examination, I will never come up to that hurdle or cross it—life has taken a different path for me, in the form of a search, not a race as it is for him, for them.

Yes, it is a search, a kind of perpetual search for me and now that I have accepted it and don't struggle, I find it satisfies me entirely, and I wander about the park as freely as a prince in his palace garden. I look over the benches, I glance behind the bushes, and wonder if I shall ever get another glimpse of that strange vision that set me free. I never have but I keep hoping, wishing.

Anita Desai

www

(b. 1937) Web

An Indian writer who writes in English, Desai focuses on changes in Indian culture and the plight of women in a society still heavily invested in family tradition. Because in India written literature was less the custom than recited stories, Desai's writing belongs to a newer tradition of Indian literature that dates only to the 1930s. She has taught at universities in England and America, including Mt. Holyoke College, Smith College, and Cambridge University.

www

TOPICS FOR CRITICAL THINKING Web

1. From the story's first five paragraphs, what can you discern about the probable outcome of Suno's studies? What are the clues?
2. What kinds of actions are repeated in the story?
3. What oppositions (or alternatives) does Suno create in his world?
4. In what ways does every distraction repeat Suno's alternatives?
5. What does this pattern (or structure) suggest about what Suno really desires?

www

TOPICS FOR CRITICAL WRITING Web

1. What does Suno study in the park?
2. How does the image of the woman reflect the themes and structure of the story?

Hanif Kureishi

Blue, Blue Pictures of You *(1997)*

I used to like talking about sex. All of life, I imagined—from politics to aesthetics—merged in passionate human conjunctions. A caress, not to speak of a kiss, could transport you from longing to Russia, on to Velazquez and ahead to anarchism. To illustrate this fancy, I did, at one time, consider collecting a 'book of desire,' an anthology of outlandish, melancholy and droll stories about the subject. This particular story was one, had the project been finished—or even started—I would have included. It was an odd story. Eshan, the photographer who told it to me, used the word himself. At least he said it was the oddest request he'd had. When it was put to him by his pub companion, his first response was embarrassment and perplexity. But of course he was fascinated too.

At the end of the street where Eshan had a tiny office and small dark room, there was a pub where he'd go at half past six or seven, most days. He liked to work office hours, believing much discipline was required to do what he did, as if without it he would fly off into madness—though he had, in fact, never flown anywhere near madness, except to sit in the pub.

Eshan thought he liked routine, and for weeks would do exactly the same thing every day, while frequently loathing this decline into habit. In the pub he would smoke, drink and read the paper for an hour or longer, depending on his mood and on whether he felt sentimental, guilty or plain affectionate towards his wife and two children. Sometimes he'd get home before the children were asleep, and carry them around on his back, kick balls with them, and tell them stories of pigs with spiders on their heads. Other times he would turn up late so he could have his wife make supper, and be free of the feeling that the kids were devouring his life.

Daily, there were many hapless people in that bar: somnolent junkies from the local rehab, the unemployed and unemployable, pinball pillocks. Eshan nodded at many of them, but if one sat at his table without asking, he could become truculent. Often, however, he would chat to people as he passed to and fro, being more grateful than he knew for distracting conversation. He had become, without meaning to, one of the bar's characters.

5 Eshan's passion was to photograph people who had produced something of significance, whose work had 'meaning.' These were philosophers, novelists, painters, film and theatre directors. He used only minimal props and hard, direct lighting. The idea wasn't to conceal but to expose. The spectator could relate the face to what the subject did. He called it the moment of truth in the features of people seeking the truth.

He photographed 'artists' but also considered himself, in private only, to be 'some sort' of an artist. To represent oneself—a changing being, alive with virtues and idiocies—was, for Eshan, the task that entailed the most honesty and fulfillment. But although his work had been published and exhibited, he still had to send out his portfolio with introductory letters, and harass people about his abilities. This was demeaning. By now he should, he reckoned, have got further. But he accepted his condition, imagining that overall he possessed most of what he required to live a simple but not complacent life. His wife illustrated children's books, and could earn decent money, so they got by. To earn a reasonable living himself, Eshan photographed new groups for the pop press—not that he was stimulated by these callow faces, though occasionally he was moved by their ugliness, the stupidity of their innocence, and their crass hopes. But they wanted only clichés.

A young man called Brian, who always wore pink shades, started to join Eshan regularly. The pub was his first stop of the day after breakfast. He was vague about what he did, though it seemed to involve trying to manage bands and set up businesses around music. His main occupation was dealing drugs, and he liked supplying Eshan with different kinds of grass that he claimed would make him 'creative.' Eshan replied that he took drugs in the evenings to stop himself getting creative. When Eshan talked about surrealism, or the great photographers, Brian listened with innocent enthusiasm, as if these were things he could get interested in were he a different person. It turned out that he did know a little about the music that Eshan particularly liked, West Coast psychedelic music of the mid-sixties, and the films, writing and politics that accompanied it. Eshan talked of the dream of freedom, rebellion and irresponsibility it had represented, and how he wished he'd had the courage to go there and join in.

'You make it sound like the past few years in London,' Brian said. 'Except the music is faster.'

A couple of months after Eshan started seeing him in the pub, Brian parted from his casual girlfriends. He went out regularly—it was like a job; and he was the sort of man that women were attracted to in pubic places. There was hope; every night could take you somewhere new. But Brian was nearly thirty; for a long time he had been part of everything new, living not for the present but for the next thing. He was beginning to see how little it had left him, and he was afraid.

One day he met a girl who used to play the drums in a trip-hop group. Any subject—the economy, the comparative merits of Paris, Rome or Berlin—would return him to this woman. Every day he went to some trouble to buy her something, even if it was only a pencil. Other times it might be a first-edition Elizabeth David, an art deco lamp from Prague, a tape of Five Easy Pieces, a bootleg of Lennon singing 'On the Road to Rishikesh.' These things he would anxiously bring to the pub to ask Eshan's opinion of. Eshan wondered if Brian imagined that because he was a photographer he had taste and judgement, and, being married, had some knowledge of romance.

After a few drinks Eshan would go home and Brian would start phoning to make his plans for the night ahead. In what Eshan considered to be the middle of the night, Brian and Laura would go to a club, to someone's house, and then on to another club. Eshan learned that there were some places that only opened at nine on Sunday morning.

Lying in bed with his wife as they watched TV and read nineteenth-century novels while drinking camomile tea, Eshan found himself trying to picture what Brian and Laura were doing, what sort of good time they were having. He looked forward to hearing next day where they'd been, what drugs they'd taken, what they wore and how the conversation had gone. He was particularly curious about her reaction to each gift; he wanted to know whether she was demanding more and better gifts, or if she appreciated the merits of each one. And what, Eshan inquired with some concern, was Brian getting in return?

'Enough,' Brian inevitably replied.

'So she's good to you?'

Unusually, Brian replied that no lover had ever shown him what she had. Then he leaned forward, glanced left and right, and felt compelled to say, despite his loving loyalty, what this was. Her touch, her words, her sensual art, not to mention her murmurs, gasps, cries; and her fine wrists, long fingers and dark fine-haired bush that stood out like a punk's back-combed mohican—all were an incomparable rapture. Only the previous evening she had taken him by the shoulders and said—

'Yes?' Eshan asked.

'Your face, your hands, you, all of you, you . . .'

Eshan dried his palms on his trousers. Sighing inwardly, he listened, while signalling a detached approval. He encouraged Brian to repeat everything, like a much-loved story, and Brian was delighted to do so, until they were no longer sure of the facts.

Perhaps Eshan envied Brian his lover and their pleasure, and Brian was beginning to envy Eshan his stability. Whatever it was between them, Brian involved Eshan in his new love. It was, Eshan was pleased to see, agonising. Laura drew out Brian's best impulses; tenderness, kindness, generosity. He became more fervent as a dealer so as to take her to restaurants most nights; he borrowed money and took her to Budapest for a week.

20 But in love each moment is magnified, and every gesture, word and syllable is examined like a speech by the President. Solid expectation, unfurled hope, immeasurable disappointment—all are hurled together like a cocktail of random drugs that, quaffed within the hour, make both lovers reel. If she dressed up and went to a party with a male friend, he spent the night catatonic with paranoia; if he saw an old girlfriend, she assumed they would never speak again. And surely she was seeing someone else, someone better in every way? Did she feel about him as he did her? To love her was to fear losing her. Brian would have locked her in a bare room to have everything hold still a minute.

One day when Eshan went to the bar he returned to see that Brian had picked up a folder Eshan had left on the table, opened it, and was holding up the photographs. Brian could be impudent, which was his charm, and Eshan liked charm, because it was rare and good to watch as a talent. But it also exposed Brian as a man who was afraid; his charm was charged with the task of disarming people before they damaged him.

'Hey,' said Eshan.

Brian placed his finger on a picture of Doris Lessing. Laura was reading *The Golden Notebook;* could he buy it for her? Eshan said, yes, and he wouldn't charge. But Brian insisted. They agreed on a price and on a black frame. They drank more and wondered what Laura would think. A few days later Brian reported that though Laura would never finish the book—she never finished any book, the satisfaction was too diffuse—she had been delighted by the picture. Could she visit his studio?

'Studio? If only it was. But yes, bring her over—it's time we met.'

25 'Tomorrow, then.'

They were more than two hours late. Eshan had been meditating, which he did whenever he was tense or angry. You couldn't beat those Eastern religions for putting the wet blanket on desire. When he was turning out the lights and ready to leave, Brian and Laura arrived at the door with wine. Eshan put out his work for Laura. She looked closely at everything. They smoked the dope he had grown on his balcony from Brian's seeds, lay on the floor with the tops of their heads touching, and watched a Kenneth Anger film. Brian and Laura rang some people and said they were going out. Would he like to come? Eshan almost agreed. He said he would like to have joined them, but that he got up early to work. And the music, an electronic blizzard of squeaks, bleeps and beats, had nothing human in it.

'Yes, that's right,' Laura said. 'Nothing human there. A bunch of robots on drugs.'

'You don't mean that,' said Brian.

A few days after the visit Brian made the strange request.

'She enjoyed meeting you,' he was saying, as Eshan read his newspaper in the pub.

'And me her,' Eshan murmured without raising his eyes. 'Anyone would.'

It cheered Brian to hear her praised. 'She's pretty, eh?'

'No, beautiful.'

'Yes, that's it, you've got the right word.'

He picked up his phone. 'She wants to ask you a favour. Can she join us?'

'I've got to go.'

'Of course, you've got to put the kids to bed, but I think you'll find it an interesting favour.'

Laura arrived within fifteen minutes. She sat down at their table and began.

'What we want is for you to photograph us.'

Eshan nodded. Laura glanced at Brian. 'Naked. Or we could wear things. Rings through our belly buttons or something. But anyway—making love.' Eshan looked at her. 'You photograph us fucking,' she concluded. 'Do you see?'

Eshan didn't know what to say.

She asked, 'What about it?'

'I am not a pornographer.'

It must have sounded pompous. She gave him an amused look.

'I've seen your stuff, and we haven't the nerve for pornography. It isn't even beauty we want. And I know you don't go for that.'

'No. What is it?'

'You see, we go to bed and eat crackers and drink wine and caress one another and chatter all day. We've both been through terrible things in our lives, you see. Now we want to capture this summer moment—I mean we want you to capture it for us.'

'To look back on?'

She said, 'I suppose that is it. We all know love doesn't last.'

'Is that right?' said Eshan.

Brian added, 'It might be replaced by something else.'

'But this terrible passion and suspicion . . . and the intensity of it . . . will get domesticated.' She went on, 'I think that when one has an idea, even if it is a queer one, one should follow it through, don't you?'

Eshan supposed he agreed with this.

Laura kissed Brian and said to him, 'Eshan's up for it.'

'I'm not sure,' said Brian.

Eshan had picked up his things, said goodbye and reached the door, before he returned.

'Why me?'

She was looking up at him.

'Why? Brian has run into you with your children. You're a kind father, a normal man, and you will surely understand what we want.' Eshan looked at Brian, who had maintained a neutral expression. She said, 'But . . . if it's all too much, let's forget it.'

It was an idea they'd conceived frivolously. He would give her the chance to drop the whole thing. She should call in the morning.

He thought it over in bed. When Laura made the request, though excited, she hadn't seemed mad or over-ebullient. It was vanity, of course, but a touching, naive vanity, not a grand one; and he was, more than ever, all for naivety. Laura was, too, a woman anyone would want to look at.

An old upright piano and guitar; painted canvases leaning against the wall; club fliers, rolling papers, pills, a razor blade, beer bottles empty and full, standing on a chest of drawers. Leaning against this, a long mirror. The bed, its linen white, was in the center of the room.

Laura pulled the curtains, and then half-opened them again.

'Will you have enough light?'

'I'll manage,' Eshan whispered 65

Brian went to shave. Then, while Eshan unpacked his things, he plucked at the guitar with his mouth open, and drank beer. The three of them spoke in low voices and were solicitous of one another, as if they were about to do something dangerous but delicate, like planting a bomb.

A young man, covered in spots, wandered into the room.

'Get out now and go to bed,' Laura said. 'You've got chickenpox. Everyone here had it?' she asked.

They all laughed. It was better then. She put a chair against the door. They watched her arrange herself on the bed. Eshan photographed her back; he photographed her face. She took her clothes off. The breeze from the open window caressed her. She stretched out her fingers to Brian.

He walked over to her and they pressed their faces together. Eshan pho- 70
tographed that. She undressed him. Eshan shot his discomfort.

Soon they were taking up different positions, adjusting their heads, putting their hands here and there for each shot. Brian began to smile as if he fancied himself as a model.

'It's very sweet, but it ain't going to work,' Eshan told them. 'There's nothing there. It's dead.'

'He might be right,' Laura told Brian. 'We're going to have to pretend he's not here.'

Eshan said, "I'll put film in the camera now, then.'

Eshan didn't go to bed but carried his things through the dark city back 75
to his studio. He developed the material as quickly as he could and when it was done went home. His wife and children were having breakfast, laughing and arguing as usual. He walked in and his children kept asking him to take off his coat. He felt like a criminal, though the only laws he'd broken were his own, and he wasn't sure which ones they were.

Unusually he had the pictures with him and he went through them several times as he ate his toast, keeping them away from the children.

'Please, can I see?' His wife put her hand on his shoulder. 'Don't hide them. It's a long time since you've shown me your work. You live such a secret life.'

'Do I?'

'Sometimes I think you're not doing anything at all over there but just sitting.'

She looked at the photographs and then closed the folder. 80

'You stayed out all night without getting in touch. What have you been doing?'

'Taking pictures.'

'Don't talk to me like that. Who are these people, Eshan?'

'People I met in the pub. They asked me to photograph them.'

They went into the kitchen and she closed the door. She could be very disapproving, and she didn't like mysteries.

'And you did this?'

'You know I like to start somewhere and finish somewhere else. It wasn't an orgy.'

'Are you going to publish or sell them?'

'No. They paid me. And that's it.'

He got up.

'Where are you going?'

'Back to work.'

'If this the same kind of thing you'll be doing today?'

'Ha ha ha.'

He tried to resume his routine but couldn't work, or even listen to music or read the papers. He could only look at the pictures. They were not pornography, being too crude and unembellished for that. He had omitted nothing human. All the same, the images gave him a dry mouth, exciting and distressing him at the same time. He wouldn't be able to start anything else until the material was out of the studio.

He thought Brian would have gone back to his place, but wasn't certain. However, he couldn't persuade himself to ring first. He took a chance and walked all the way back there again. He was exhausted but was careful to cross the road where he crossed it before.

She came to the door in her dressing gown, and was surprised to see him. He said he'd brought the stuff round, and proffered the folder as evidence.

He went past her and up the stairs. She tugged her dressing gown around herself, as if he hadn't seen her body before. Upstairs they sat on the broken sofa. She was reluctant to look at the stuff, but knew she had to. She held up the contact sheets, turning them this way and that, repeatedly.

'Is that what you wanted?' he asked.

'I don't know.'

'Is that what you do on a good day?'

'I should thank you for the lovely job you've done. I don't know what I can do in return.' He looked at her. She said, 'How about a drum lesson?'

'Why not?'

She took him into a larger room, where he noticed some of Brian's gifts. Set before a big window, with a view of the street and the square, was her red spangled kit. She showed him how she played, and demonstrated how he could. Soon this bored her and she made lunch. As he ate she returned to the photographs, glanced through them without comment, and went back to the table. He wasn't certain that she wanted him there. But she didn't ask him to go away and seemed to assume that he had nothing better to do. He didn't know what else he would do anyway, as if something had come to an end.

They started to watch television, but suddenly she switched it off and stood up and sat down. She started agitatedly asking him questions about the people he knew, how many friends he had, what he liked about them, and what they said to one another. At first he answered abruptly, afraid of boring her. But she said she'd never had any guidance, and for the past few years, like everyone else, had only wanted a good time. Now she wanted to find something important to do, wanted a reason to get out of bed before four. He murmured that fucking might be a good excuse for staying in bed, just as the need to wash was an excuse for lying in the bath. She understood that, she said. She hardly knew anyone with a job; London was full of drugged, useless people who didn't listen to one another but merely thought all the time of how to distract themselves and never spoke of anything serious. She was tired of it; she was even tired of being in love; it had become another narcotic. Now she wanted interesting difficulty, not pleasure or even ease.

'And look, look at the pictures . . .'

'What do they say?'

'Too much, my friend.'

She hurried from the room. After a time she returned with a bucket which she set down on the carpet. She held the photographs over it and invited him to set fire to them.

'Are you sure?' he said.

'Oh yes.'

They singed the carpet and burned their fingers, and then they threw handfuls of ash out of the window and cheered.

'Are you going to the pub now?' she asked as he said goodbye.

'I don't think I'll be going there for a while.'

He told her that the next day he was going to photograph a painter who had also done record covers. He asked her to come along, 'to have a look.' She said she would.

Leaving the house he crossed the street. He could see her sitting in the window playing. When he walked away he could hear her all the way to the end of the road.

HANIF KUREISHI

(b. 1954) **Web** *www*

Kureishi, the son of a Pakistani father and English mother, grew up in England. After attending the University of London, he began writing plays, screenplays, stories, and novels dealing with the experiences of young immigrants in London. He wrote the screenplays for *My Beautiful Laundrette* and *Sammy and Rosie Get Laid.*

TOPICS FOR CRITICAL THINKING **Web** *www*

1. How many different versions of love does the story suggest?
2. How many frame narrators does this story have?
3. What kind of structure does a frame narrator create?

4. What narrative of art or being an artist does the story recount? Is that narrative repeated?
5. What oppositions do the various layers of this story set up around art and love?
6. How do those oppositions structure the story?
7. What is the function of image in the story?

www

TOPICS FOR CRITICAL WRITING Web

1. How does this story compare the writer to the photographer? What does this comparison tell us about art or love?
2. Why did Laura burn the pictures? What is Laura's and Brian's future, and why?

Part III
Reading and Interpreting

13 The Perils of Interpretation

Interpretation is generally understood to be the art of drawing conclusions from a series of clues offered by a text. The activity of interpreting a literary text is not unlike the activity of interpreting any set of circumstances. Readers gather clues about character, plot, circumstance, and motivation, and from these clues they deduce (or make conclusions) based on how these details fit into patterns with which they are familiar. For example, in a detective story, a detective gathers clues about how a crime was committed. Based on how those clues fit into a sensible plan of behavior, which explains how a crime was accomplished, the detective determines the identity of a malefactor (thief, murderer, and so on) as the only one whose circumstances fit the crime. Interpreting literature is not unlike this process, except that the questions a reader attempts to answer are questions not only about plot and character motivation, but also those about how the various elements of a story work together in relation to what happens.

Interpreting, however, also has dangers. One danger, of course, is drawing the wrong conclusion. That is easily corrected, generally by the story itself. If we think, for example, that Charlie in "Babylon Revisited" is going to regain custody of his daughter based on our (and Charlie's own) astute reading of the clues, we realize that conclusion is no longer possible once Charlie's friends show up. Another danger is that our process of interpretation will be clouded by what we want to see happen. This has a tendency to skew the ways

we understand and interpret the clues offered by stories. One of the best examples about the way our own desires cloud our ability to interpret is Edgar Allan Poe's "The Purloined Letter." Consider the ways the story brings processes of interpretation into question.

EDGAR ALLAN POE

The Purloined Letter *(1844)*

Nil sapientae odiosius acumine nimio.
—SENECA

At Paris, just after dark one gusty evening in the autumn of 18——, I was enjoying the twofold luxury of meditation and a meerschaum, in company with my friend C. Auguste Dupin, in his little back library, or book-closet, *au troisième, No. 33, Rue Dunôt, Faubourg St. Germain.* For one hour at least we had maintained a profound silence; while each, to any casual observer, might have seemed intently and exclusively occupied with the curling eddies of smoke that oppressed the atmosphere of the chamber. For myself, however, I was mentally discussing certain topics which had formed matter for conversation between us at an earlier period of the evening; I mean the affair of the Rue Morgue, and the mystery attending the murder of Marie Rogêt. I looked upon it, therefore, as something of a coincidence, when the door of our apartment was thrown open and admitted our old acquaintance, Monsieur G——, the Prefect of the Parisian police.

We gave him a hearty welcome; for there was nearly half as much of the entertaining as of the contemptible about the man, and we had not seen him for several years. We had been sitting in the dark, and Dupin now arose for the purpose of lighting a lamp, but sat down again, without doing so, upon G.'s saying that he had called to consult us, or rather to ask the opinion of my friend, about some official business which had occasioned a great deal of trouble.

"If it is any point requiring reflection," observed Dupin, as he forbore to enkindle the wick, "we shall examine it to better purpose in the dark."

"That is another of your odd notions," said the Prefect, who had a fashion of calling every thing "odd" that was beyond his comprehension, and thus lived amid an absolute legion of "oddities."

"Very true," said Dupin, as he supplied his visitor with a pipe, and rolled 5
towards him a comfortable chair.

"And what is the difficulty now?" I asked. "Nothing more in the assassination way, I hope?"

"Oh no; nothing of that nature. The fact is, the business is *very* simple indeed, and I make no doubt that we can manage it sufficiently well ourselves; but then I thought Dupin would like to hear the details of it, because it is so excessively *odd.*"

"Simple and odd," said Dupin.

"Why, yes; and not exactly that either. The fact is, we have all been a good deal puzzled because the affair *is* so simple, and yet baffles us altogether."

"Perhaps it is the very simplicity of the thing which puts you at fault," said 10
my friend.

"What nonsense you *do* talk!" replied the Prefect, laughing heartily.

"Perhaps the mystery is a little *too* plain," said Dupin.

"Oh, good heavens! who ever heard of such an idea?"

"A little *too* self-evident."

"Ha! ha! ha!—ha! ha! ha!—ho! ho! ho!"—roared our visitor, profoundly 15
amused, "oh, Dupin, you will be the death of me yet!"

"And what, after all, *is* the matter on hand?" I asked.

"Why, I will tell you," replied the Prefect, as he gave a long, steady, and contemplative puff, and settled himself in his chair. "I will tell you in a few words; but, before I begin, let me caution you that this is an affair demanding the greatest secrecy, and that I should most probably lose the position I now hold, were it known that I confided it to any one."

"Proceed," said I.

"Or not," said Dupin.

"Well, then; I have received personal information, from a very high quarter, 20
that a certain document of the last importance has been purloined from the royal apartments. The individual who purloined it is known; this beyond a doubt; he was seen to take it. It is known, also, that it still remains in his possession."

"How is this known?" asked Dupin.

"It is clearly inferred," replied the Prefect, "from the nature of the document, and from the non-appearance of certain results which would at once arise from its passing *out* of the robber's possession;—that is to say, from his employing it as he must design in the end to employ it."

"Be a little more explicit," I said.

"Well, I may venture so far as to say that the paper gives its holder a certain power in a certain quarter where such power is immensely valuable." The Prefect was fond of the cant of diplomacy.

"Still I do not quite understand," said Dupin. 25

"No? Well; the disclosure of the document to a third person, who shall be nameless, would bring in question the honour of a personage of most exalted station; and this fact gives the holder of the document an ascendancy over the illustrious personage whose honour and peace are so jeopardized."

"But this ascendancy," I interposed, "would depend upon the robber's knowledge of the loser's knowledge of the robber. Who would dare—"

"The thief," said G., "is the Minister D——, who dares all things, those unbecoming as well as those becoming a man. The method of the theft was not less ingenious than bold. The document in question—a letter, to be frank—had been received by the personage robbed while alone in the royal *boudoir*. During its perusal she was suddenly interrupted by the entrance of the other exalted personage from whom especially it was her wish to conceal it. After a hurried and vain endeavour to thrust it in a drawer, she was forced to place it, open it was, upon a table. The address, however, was uppermost, and, the contents thus unexposed, the letter escaped notice. At this juncture enters the Minister D——. His lynx eye immediately perceives the paper, recognizes the handwriting of the address, observes the confusion of the personage addressed, and fathoms her secret. After some business transactions, hurried through in his ordinary manner, he produces a letter somewhat similar to the one in question, opens it, pretends to read it, and then places it in close juxtaposition to the other. Again he converses, for some fifteen minutes, upon the public affairs. At length, in taking leave, he takes also from the table the letter to which he had no claim. Its rightful owner saw, but, of course, dared not call attention to the act, in the presence of the third personage who stood at her elbow. The minister decamped; leaving his own letter—one of no importance—upon the table."

"Here, then," said Dupin to me, "you have precisely what you demand to make the ascendancy complete—the robber's knowledge of the loser's knowledge of the robber."

"Yes," replied the Prefect; "and the power thus attained has, for some 30
months past, been wielded, for political purposes, to a very dangerous extent. The personage robbed is more thoroughly convinced, every day, of the necessity of reclaiming her letter. But this, of course, cannot be done openly. In fine, driven to despair, she has committed the matter to me."

"Than whom," said Dupin, amid a perfect whirlwind of smoke, "no more sagacious agent could, I suppose, be desired, or even imagined."

"You flatter me," replied the Prefect; "but it is possible that some such opinion may have been entertained."

"It is clear," said I, "as you observe, that the letter is still in the possession of the minister; since it is this possession, and not any employment of the letter, which bestows the power. With the employment the power departs."

"True," said G.; "and upon this conviction I proceeded. My first care was to make thorough search of the minister's hotel; and here my chief embarrassment lay in the necessity of searching without his knowledge. Beyond all things, I have been warned of the danger which would result from giving him reason to suspect our design."

"But," said I, "you are quite *au fait* in these investigations. The Parisian 35
police have done this thing often before."

"O yes; and for this reason I did not despair. The habits of the minister gave me, too, a great advantage. He is frequently absent from home all night. His servants are by no means numerous. They sleep at a distance from their master's apartment, and being chiefly Neapolitans, are readily made drunk. I have keys, as you know, with which I can open any chamber or cabinet in Paris. For three months a night has not passed, during the greater part of which I have not been engaged, personally, in ransacking the D—— Hôtel. My honour is interested, and, to mention a great secret, the reward is enormous. So I did not abandon the search until I had become fully satisfied that the thief is a more astute man than myself. I fancy that I have investigated every nook and corner of the premises in which it is possible that the paper can be concealed."

"But is it not possible," I suggested, "that although the letter may be in the possession of the minister, as it unquestionably is, he may have concealed it elsewhere than upon his own premises?"

"This is barely possible," said Dupin. "The present peculiar condition of affairs at court, and especially of those intrigues in which D—— is known to be involved, would render the instant availability of the document—its susceptibility of being produced at a moment's notice—a point of nearly equal importance with its possession."

"Its susceptibility of being produced?" said I.

"That is to say, of being *destroyed*," said Dupin.

"True," I observed; "the paper is clearly then upon the premises. As for its being upon the person of the minister, we may consider that as out of the question."

"Entirely," said the Prefect. "He had been twice waylaid, as if by footpads, and his person rigorously searched under my own inspection."

"You might have spared yourself this trouble," said Dupin. "D——, I presume, is not altogether a fool, and, if not, must have anticipated these waylayings, as a matter of course."

"Not *altogether* a fool," said G., "but then he is a poet, which I take to be only one remove from a fool."

"True," said Dupin, after a long and thoughtful whiff from his meerschaum, "although I have been guilty of certain doggerel myself."

"Suppose you detail," said I, "the particulars of your search."

"Why the fact is, we took our time, and we searched *every where*. I have had long experience in these affairs. I took the entire building, room by room; devoting the nights of a whole week to each. We examined, first, the furniture of each apartment. We opened every possible drawer; and I presume you know that, to a properly trained police agent, such a thing as a *secret* drawer is impossible. Any man is a dolt who permits a 'secret' drawer to escape him in a search of this kind. The thing is *so* plain. There is a certain amount of bulk—of space—to be accounted for in every cabinet. Then we have accurate rules. The fiftieth part of a line could not escape us. After the cabinets we took the chairs. The cushions we probed with the fine long needles you have seen me employ. From the tables we removed the tops."

"Why so?"

"Sometimes the top of a table, or other similarly arranged piece of furniture, is removed by the person wishing to conceal an article; then the leg is excavated, the article deposited within the cavity, and the top replaced. The bottoms and tops of bedposts are employed in the same way."

"But could not the cavity be detected by sounding?" I asked.

"By no means, if, when the article is deposited, a sufficient wadding of cotton be placed around it. Besides, in our case, we were obliged to proceed without noise."

"But you could not have removed—you could not have taken to pieces *all* articles of furniture in which it would have been possible to make a deposit in the manner you mention. A letter may be compressed into a thin spiral roll, not differing much in shape or bulk from a large knitting-needle, and in this form it might be inserted into the rung of a chair, for example. You did not take to pieces all the chairs?"

"Certainly not; but we did better—we examined the rungs of every chair in the hotel, and indeed the jointings of every description of furniture, by the aid of a most powerful microscope. Had there been any traces of recent disturbance we should not have failed to detect it instantly. A single grain of gimlet-dust, for example, would have been as obvious as an apple. Any disorder in the glueing—any unusual gaping in the joints—would have sufficed to insure detection."

"I presume you looked to the mirrors, between the boards and the plates, and you probed the beds and the bed-clothes, as well as the curtains and carpets."

"That of course; and when we had absolutely completed every particle of the furniture in this way, then we examined the house itself. We divided its entire surface into compartments, which we numbered, so that none might be missed; then we scrutinized each individual square inch throughout the premises, including the two houses immediately adjoining, with the microscope as before."

"The two houses adjoining!" I exclaimed; "you must have had a great deal of trouble."

"We had; but the reward offered is prodigious."

"You include the *grounds* about the houses?"

"All the grounds are paved with brick. They gave us comparatively little trouble. We examined the moss between the bricks, and found it undisturbed."

"You looked among D——'s papers, of course, and into the books of the library?"

"Certainly; we opened every package and parcel; we not only opened every book, but we turned over every leaf in each volume, not contenting ourselves with a mere shake, according to the fashion of some of our police officers. We also measured the thickness of every book-*cover*, with the most accurate admeasurement, and applied to each the most jealous scrutiny of the microscope. Had any of the bindings been recently meddled with, it would have been utterly impossible that the fact should have escaped observation. Some five or six volumes, just from the hands of the binder, we carefully probed, longitudinally, with the needles."

"You explored the floors beneath the carpets?"

"Beyond doubt. We removed every carpet, and examined the boards with the microscope."

"And the paper on the walls?"

"Yes."

"You looked into the cellars?"

"We did."

"Then," I said, "you have been making a miscalculation, and the letter is *not* upon the premises as you suppose."

"I fear you are right there," said the Prefect. "And now, Dupin, what would you advise me to do?"

"To make a thorough re-search of the premises."

"That is absolutely needless," replied G——. "I am not more sure that I breathe than I am that the letter is not at the Hôtel."

"I have no better advice to give you," said Dupin. "You have, of course, an accurate description of the letter?"

"Oh, yes!"—And here the Prefect, producing a memorandum-book, proceeded to read aloud a minute account of the internal, and especially of the external, appearance of the missing document. Soon after finishing the perusal of this description, he took his departure, more entirely depressed in spirits than I had ever known the good gentleman before.

In about a month afterward he paid us another visit, and found us occupied very nearly as before. He took a pipe and a chair and entered into some ordinary conversation. At length I said;—

"Well, but G——, what of the purloined letter? I presume you have at last made up your mind that there is no such thing as overreaching the Minister?"

"Confound him, say I—yes; I made the re-examination, however, as Dupin suggested—but it was all labour lost, as I knew it would be."

"How much was the reward offered, did you say?" asked Dupin.

"Why, a very great deal—a *very* liberal reward—I don't like to say how much, precisely; but one thing I *will* say, that I wouldn't mind giving my individual check for fifty thousand francs to any one who could obtain me that letter. The fact is, it is becoming of more and more importance every day; and the reward has been lately doubled. If it were trebled, however, I could do no more than I have done."

"Why, yes," said Dupin, drawlingly, between the whiffs of his meerschaum, "I really—think, G——, you have not exerted yourself—to the utmost in this matter. You might—do a little more, I think, eh?"

"How?—in what way?"

"Why—puff, puff,—you might—puff, puff—employ counsel in the matter, eh?—puff, puff, puff. Do you remember the story they tell of Abernethy?"

"No; hang Abernethy!"

"To be sure! hang him and welcome. But, once upon a time, a certain rich miser conceived the design of spunging upon this Abernethy for a medical opinion. Getting up, for this purpose, an ordinary conversation in a private company, he insinuated his case to the physician, as that of an imaginary individual."

" 'We will suppose,' said the miser, 'that his symptoms are such and such; now, doctor, what would *you* have directed him to take?' "

" 'Take!' said Abernethy, 'why, take *advice*, to be sure.' "

"But," said the Prefect, a little discomposed, "I am *perfectly* willing to take advice, and to pay for it. I would *really* give fifty thousand francs to any one who would aid me in the matter."

"In that case," replied Dupin, opening a drawer, and producing a check-book, "you may as well fill me up a check for the amount you mentioned. When you have signed it, I will hand you the letter."

I was astounded. The Prefect appeared absolutely thunderstricken. For some minutes he remained speechless and motionless, looking incredulously at my friend with open mouth, and eyes that seemed starting from their sockets;

then, apparently recovering himself in some measure, he seized a pen, and after several pauses and vacant stares, finally filled up and signed a check for fifty thousand francs, and handed it across the table to Dupin. The latter examined it carefully and deposited it in his pocket-book; then, unlocking an *escritoire*, took thence a letter and gave it to the Prefect. This functionary grasped it in a perfect agony of joy, opened it with a trembling hand, cast a rapid glance at its contents, and then, scrambling and struggling to the door, rushed at length unceremoniously from the room and from the house, without having uttered a syllable since Dupin had requested him to fill up the check.

When he had gone, my friend entered into some explanations.

90 "The Parisian police," he said, "are exceedingly able in their way. They are persevering, ingenious, cunning, and thoroughly versed in the knowledge which their duties seem chiefly to demand. Thus, when G—— detailed to us his mode of searching the premises at the Hôtel D——, I felt entire confidence in his having made a satisfactory investigation—so far as his labours extended."

"So far as his labours extended?" said I.

"Yes," said Dupin. "The measures adopted were not only the best of their kind, but carried out to absolute perfection. Had the letter been deposited within the range of their search, these fellows would, beyond a question, have found it."

I merely laughed—but he seemed quite serious in all that he said.

"The measures, then," he continued, "were good in their kind, and well executed; their defect lay in their being inapplicable to the case, and to the man. A certain set of highly ingenious resources are, with the Prefect, a sort of Procrustean bed, to which he forcibly adapts his designs. But he perpetually errs by being too deep or too shallow, for the matter in hand; and many a schoolboy is a better reasoner than he. I knew one about eight years of age, whose success at guessing in the game of 'even and odd' attracted universal admiration. This game is simple, and is played with marbles. One player holds in his hand a number of these toys, and demands of another whether that number is even or odd. If the guess is right, the guesser wins one; if wrong, he loses one. The boy to whom I allude won all the marbles of the school. Of course he had some principle of guessing; and this lay in mere observation and admeasurement of the astuteness of his opponents. For example, an arrant simpleton is his opponent, and, holding up his closed hand, asks: 'Are they even or odd?' Our schoolboy replies, 'Odd,' and loses; but upon the second trial he wins, for he then says to himself, 'The simpleton had them even upon the first trial, and his amount of cunning is just sufficient to make him have them odd upon the second; I will therefore guess odd';—he guesses odd, and wins. Now, with a simpleton a degree above the first, he would have reasoned thus: 'This fellow finds that in the first instance I guessed odd, and, in the second, he will propose to himself upon the first impulse, a simple variation from even to odd, as did the first simpleton; but then a second thought will suggest that this is too simple a variation, and finally he will decide upon putting it even as before. I will therefore guess even';—he guesses even, and wins. Now this mode of reasoning in the schoolboy, whom his fellows termed 'lucky,'—what, in its last analysis, is it?"

"It is merely," I said, "an identification of the reasoner's intellect with that 95
of his opponent."

"It is," said Dupin; "and, upon inquiring of the boy by what means he effected the *thorough* identification in which his success consisted, I received answer as follows: 'When I wish to find out how wise, or how stupid, or how good, or how wicked is any one, or what are his thoughts at the moment, I fashion the expression on my face, as accurately as possible, in accordance with the expression of his, and then wait to see what thoughts or sentiments arise in my mind or heart, as if to match or correspond with the expression.' This response of the schoolboy lies at the bottom of all the spurious profundity which has been attributed to Rochefoucault, to La Bougive, to Machiavelli, and to Campanella."

"And the identification," I said, "of the reasoner's intellect with that of his opponent, depends, if I understand you aright, upon the accuracy with which the opponent's intellect is admeasured."

"For its practical value it depends upon this," replied Dupin; "and the Prefect and his cohort fail so frequently, first, by default of this identification, and secondly, by ill-admeasurement, or rather through non-admeasurement, of the intellect with which they are engaged. They consider only their *own* ideas of ingenuity; and, in searching for anything hidden, advert only to the modes in which *they* would have hidden it. They are right in this much—that their own ingenuity is a faithful representative of that of *the mass;* but when the cunning of the individual felon is diverse in character from their own, the felon foils them, of course. This always happens when it is above their own, and very usually when it is below. They have no variation of principle in their investigations; at best, when urged by some unusual emergency—by some extraordinary reward—they extend or exaggerate their old modes of *practice,* without touching their principles. What, for example, in this case of D——, has been done to vary the principle of action? What is all this boring, and probing, and sounding, and scrutinizing with the microscope, and dividing the surface of the building into registered square inches—what is it all but an exaggeration *of the application* of one principle or set of principles of search, which are based upon the one set of notions regarding human ingenuity, to which the Prefect, in the long routine of his duty, has been accustomed? Do you not see he has taken it for granted that *all* men proceed to conceal a letter,—not exactly in a gimlet-hole bored in a chair-leg—but, at least, in *some* out-of-the-way hole or corner suggested by the same tenor or thought which would urge a man to secret a letter in a gimlet-hole bored in a chair-leg? And do you not see also, that such *recherchés* nooks for concealment are adapted only for ordinary occasions, and would be adopted only by ordinary intellects; for, in all cases of concealment, a disposal of the article concealed—a disposal of it in this *recherché* manner—is, in the very first instance, presumable and presumed; and thus its discovery depends, not at all upon the acumen, but altogether upon the mere care, patience, and determination of the seekers; and where the case is of importance—or, what amounts to the same thing in the political eyes, when the reward is of magnitude,—the qualities in question have *never* been known to fail. You will now understand what I meant in suggesting that, had the purloined letter been hidden anywhere within the limits of the Prefect's examination—in other words, had the principle of its concealment been comprehended within the principles of the Prefect—its discovery would have been a matter altogether beyond question. This functionary, however, has been thoroughly mystified; and the remote source of his defeat lies in the supposition that the Minister is a fool, because he has acquired renown as a poet. All fools are poets; this the Prefect *feels;* and he is merely guilty of a *non distributio medii* in thence inferring that all poets are fools."

"But is this really the poet?" I asked. "There are two brothers, I know; and both have attained reputation in letters. The Minister I believe has written learnedly on the Differential Calculus. He is a mathematician, and no poet."

"You are mistaken; I know him well: he is both. As poet *and* mathematician, he would reason well; as mere mathematician, he could not have reasoned at all, and thus would have been at the mercy of the Prefect."

"You surprise me," I said, "by these opinions, which have been contradicted by the voice of the world. You do not mean to set at naught the well-digested idea of centuries. The mathematical reason has long been regarded as *the* reason *par excellence.*"

"'*Il y a à parier,*'" replied Dupin, quoting from Chamfort, "'*que toute idée publique, toute convention reçue, est une sottise, car elle a convenu au plus grand nombre.*' The mathematicians, I grant you, have done their best to promulgate the popular error to which you allude, and which is none the less an error for its promulgation as truth. With an art worthy a better cause, for example, they have insinuated the term 'analysis' into application to algebra. The French are the originators of this particular deception; but if a term is of any importance—if words derive any value from applicability—then 'analysis' conveys 'algebra' about as much as, in Latin, '*ambitus*' implies 'ambition,' '*religio*' 'religion,' or '*homines honesti,*' a set of *honourable* men."

"You have a quarrel on hand, I see," said I, "with some of the algebraists of Paris; but proceed."

"I dispute the availability, and thus the value, of that reason which is cultivated in any especial form other than the abstractly logical. I dispute, in particular, the reason educed by mathematical study. The mathematics are the science of form and quantity; mathematical reasoning is merely logic applied to observation upon form and quantity. The great error lies in supposing that even the truths of what is called *pure* algebra, are abstract or general truths. And this error is so egregious that I am confounded at the universality with which it has been received. Mathematical axioms are *not* axioms of general truth. What is true of *relation*—of form and quantity—is often grossly false in regard to morals, for example. In this latter science it is very usually *un*true that the aggregated parts are equal to the whole. In chemistry also the axiom fails. In the consideration of motive it fails; for two motives, each of a given value, have not, necessarily, a value when united, equal to the sum of their values apart. There are numerous other mathematical truths which are only truths within the limits of *relation.* But the mathematician argues from his *finite truths*, through habit, as if they were of an absolutely general applicability—as the world indeed imagines them to be. Bryant, in his very learned 'Mythology,' mentions an analogous source of error, when he says that 'although the Pagan fables are not believed, yet we forget ourselves continually, and make inferences from them as existing realities.' With the algebraists, however, who are Pagans themselves, the 'Pagan fables' *are* believed, and the inferences are made, not so much through lapse of memory as through an unaccountable addling of the brains. In short, I never yet encountered the mere mathematician who could be trusted out of equal roots, or one who did not clandestinely hold it as a point of his faith that $x^2 + px$ was absolutely and unconditionally equal to q. Say to one of these gentlemen, by way of experiment, if you please, that you believe occasions may occur where $x^2 + px$ is *not* altogether equal to q, and having made him understand what you mean, get out of his reach as speedily as convenient, for, beyond doubt, he will endeavour to knock you down."

"I mean to say," continued Dupin, while I merely laughed at his last ob- 105
servations, "that if the Minister had been no more than a mathematician, the Prefect would have been under no necessity of giving me this check. I knew him, however, as both mathematician and poet, and my measures were adapted to his capacity, with reference to the circumstances by which he was surrounded. I knew him as a courtier, too, and as a bold *intriguant.* Such a man, I considered, could not fail to be aware of the ordinary political modes of action. He could not have failed to anticipate—and events have proved that he did not fail to anticipate—the waylayings to which he was subjected. He must have foreseen, I reflected, the secret investigations of his premises. His frequent absences from home at night, which were hailed by the Prefect as certain aids to his success, I regarded only as *ruses,* to afford opportunity for thorough search to the police, and thus the sooner to impress them with the conviction to which G——, in fact, did finally arrive—the conviction that the letter was not upon the premises. I felt, also, that the whole train of thought, which I was at some pains in detailing to you just now, concerning the invariable principle of political action in searches for articles concealed—I felt that this whole train of thought would necessarily pass through the mind of the Minister. It would imperatively lead him to despise all the ordinary *nooks* of concealment. *He* could not, I reflected, be so weak as not to see that the most intricate and remote recess of his hotel would be as open as his commonest closets to the eyes, to the probes, to the gimlets, and to the microscopes of the Prefect. I saw, in fine, that he would be driven, as a matter of course, to simplicity, if not deliberately induced to it as a matter of choice. You will remember, perhaps, how desperately the Prefect laughed when I suggested, upon our first interview, that it was just possible this mystery troubled him so much on account of its being so *very* self-evident."

"Yes," said I, "I remember his merriment well. I really thought he would have fallen into convulsions."

"The material world," continued Dupin, "abounds with very strict analogies to the immaterial; and thus some color of truth has been given to the rhetorical dogma, that metaphor, or simile, may be made to strengthen an argument as well as to embellish a description. The principle of the *vis inertiae,* for example, seems to be identical in physics and metaphysics. It is not more true in the former, that a large body is with more difficulty set in motion than a smaller one, and that its subsequent *momentum* is commensurate with this difficulty, than it is, in the latter, that intellects of the vaster capacity, while more forcible, more constant, and more eventful in their movements than those of inferior grade, are yet the less readily moved, and more embarrassed and full of hesitation in the first few steps of their progress. Again: have you ever noticed which of the street signs, over the shop doors, are the most attractive of attention?"

"I have never given the matter a thought," I said.

"There is a game of puzzles," he resumed, "which is played upon a map. One party playing requires another to find a given word—the name of town, river, state, or empire—any word, in short, upon the motley and perplexed surface of the chart. A novice in the game generally seeks to embarrass his opponents by giving them the most minutely lettered names; but the adept selects such words as stretch, in large characters, from one end of the chart to the other. These, like the over-largely lettered signs and placards of the street, escape observation by the dint of being excessively obvious; and here the physical oversight is precisely analogous with the moral inapprehension by which the intellect suffers to pass unnoticed those considerations which are too obtrusively and too palpably self-evident. But this is a point, it appears, somewhat above or beneath the understanding of the Prefect. He never once thought it probable, or possible, that the Minister had deposited the letter immediately beneath the nose of the whole world, by way of best preventing any portion of that world from perceiving it."

110 "But the more I reflected upon the daring, dashing, and discriminating ingenuity of D——; upon the fact that the document must always have been *at hand*, if he intended to use it to good purpose; and upon the decisive evidence, obtained by the Prefect, that it was not hidden within the limits of that dignitary's ordinary search—the more satisfied I became that, to conceal this letter, the Minister had resorted to the comprehensive and sagacious expedient of not attempting to conceal it at all."

"Full of these ideas, I prepared myself with a pair of green spectacles, and called one fine morning, quite by accident, at the Ministerial hotel. I found D—— at home, yawning, lounging, and dawdling, as usual, and pretending to be in the last extremity of *ennui*. He is, perhaps, the most really energetic human being now alive—but that is only when nobody sees him."

"To be even with him, I complained of my weak eyes, and lamented the necessity of the spectacles, under cover of which I cautiously and thoroughly surveyed the whole apartment, while seemingly intent only upon the conversation of my host."

"I paid especial attention to a large writing-table near which he sat, and upon which lay confusedly, some miscellaneous letters and other papers, with one or two musical instruments and a few books. Here, however, after a long and very deliberate scrutiny, I saw nothing to excite particular suspicion."

"At length my eyes, in going the circuit of the room, fell upon a trumpery filigree card-rack of pasteboard, that hung dangling by a dirty blue ribbon, from a little brass knob just beneath the middle of the mantel-piece. In this rack, which had three or four compartments, were five or six visiting cards and a solitary letter. This last was much soiled and crumpled. It was torn nearly in two, across the middle—as if a design, in the first instance, to tear it entirely up as worthless, had been altered, or stayed, in the second. It had a large black seal, bearing the D—— cipher *very* conspicuously, and was addressed, in a diminutive female hand, to D——, the minister, himself. It was thrust carelessly, and even, as it seemed, contemptuously, into one of the upper divisions of the rack."

"No sooner had I glanced at this letter than I concluded it to be that of 115
which I was in search. To be sure, it was, to all appearance, radically different from the one of which the Prefect had read us so minute a description. Here the seal was large and black, with the D—— cipher; there it was small and red, with the ducal arms of the S—— family. Here, the address, to the Minister, was diminutive and feminine; there the superscription, to a certain royal personage, was markedly bold and decided; the size alone formed a point of correspondence. But, then, the *radicalness* of these differences, which was excessive; the dirt; the soiled and torn condition of the paper, so inconsistent with the *true* methodical habits of D——, and so suggestive of a design to delude the beholder into an idea of the worthlessness of the document; these things, together with the hyperobtrusive situation of this document, full in the view of every visitor, and thus exactly in accordance with the conclusions to which I had previously arrived; these things, I say, were strongly corroborative of suspicion, in one who came with the intention to suspect."

"I protracted my visit as long as possible, and, while I maintained a most animated discussion with the Minister, upon a topic which I knew well had never failed to interest and excite him, I kept my attention really riveted upon the letter. In this examination, I committed to memory its external appearance and arrangement in the rack; and also fell, at length, upon a discovery which set at rest whatever trivial doubt I might have entertained. In scrutinizing the edges of the paper, I observed them to be more *chafed* than seemed necessary. They presented the *broken* appearance which is manifested when a stiff paper, having been once folded and pressed with a folder, is refolded in a reversed direction, in the same creases or edges which had formed the original fold. This discovery was sufficient. It was clear to me that the letter had been turned, as a glove, inside out, re-directed, and re-sealed. I bade the Minister good morning, and took my departure at once, leaving a gold snuff-box upon the table."

"The next morning I called for the snuff-box, when we resumed, quite eagerly, the conversation of the preceding day. While thus engaged, however, a loud report, as if of a pistol, was heard immediately beneath the windows of the hotel, and was succeeded by a series of fearful screams, and the shoutings of a mob. D—— rushed to a casement, threw it open, and looked out. In the meantime I stepped to the card-rack, took the letter, put it in my pocket, and replaced it by a *facsimile*, (so far as regards externals) which I had carefully prepared at my lodgings; imitating the D—— cipher, very readily, by means of a seal formed of bread."

"The disturbance in the street had been occasioned by the frantic behaviour of a man with a musket. He had fired it among a crowd of women and children. It proved, however, to have been without ball, and the fellow was suffered to go his way as a lunatic or a drunkard. When he had gone, D—— came from the window, whither I had followed him immediately upon securing the object in view. Soon afterward I bade him farewell. The pretended lunatic was a man in my own pay."

"But what purpose had you," I asked, "in replacing the letter by a *facsimile?* Would it not have been better, at the first visit, to have seized it openly, and departed?"

"D——," replied Dupin, "is a desperate man, and a man of nerve. His ho- 120
tel, too, is not without attendants devoted to his interests. Had I made the wild attempt you suggest, I might never have left the Ministerial presence alive. The good people of Paris might have heard of me no more. But I had an object apart from these considerations. You know my political prepossessions. In this matter, I act as a partisan of the lady concerned. For eighteen months the Minister has had her in his power. She has now him in hers; since, being unaware that the letter is not in his possession, he will proceed with his exactions as if it was. Thus will he inevitably commit himself, at once, to his political destruction. His downfall, too, will not be more precipitate than awkward. It is all very well to talk about the *facilis descensus Averni;* but in all kinds of climbing, as Catalani said of singing, it is far more easy to get up than to come down. In the present instance I have no sympathy—at least no pity—for him who descends. He is that *monstrum horrendum*, an unprincipled man of genius. I confess, however, that I should like very well to know the precise character of his thoughts, when, being defied by her whom the Prefect terms 'a certain personage,' he is reduced to opening the letter which I left for him in the card-rack."

"How? did you put any thing particular in it?"

"Why—it did not seem altogether right to leave the interior blank—that would have been insulting. D——, at Vienna once, did me an evil turn, which I told him, quite good-humouredly, that I should remember. So, as I knew he would feel some curiosity in regard to the identity of the person who had outwitted him, I thought it a pity not to give him a clue. He is well acquainted with my MS., and I just copied into the middle of the blank sheet the words—

> ——Un dessein si funeste,
> S'il n'est digne d'Atrée, est digne
> de Thyeste.

They are to be found in Crébillon's 'Atrée.'"

Edgar Allan Poe

(1809–1849) Web www

A West Point graduate, Poe quit the army to become a professional editor and writer. Poe was a conscious and controlled artist who was best known for his criticism, but who strove to write stories that would appeal to popular audiences. His fiction fascinated later writers from Charles-Pierre Baudelaire to Vladimir Nabokov, who admired and developed Poe's atmospheric rendering of effect and his complex intellectual games.

www *TOPICS FOR CRITICAL THINKING* **Web**

1. Why can't the Inspector find the letter?
2. What methods and assumptions make Dupin successful?
3. Who is the story's narrator?
4. How do the layers of the story relate to the layers of deception around the letter?
5. How might the processes of detection in the story relate to processes of literary interpretation?

www *TOPICS FOR CRITICAL WRITING* **Web**

1. In what ways does the circulation of the letter parallel the ways a story might circulate in processes of interpretation?
2. In what ways do the characters reveal their own desires in the ways they search for the letter? How is this an analogy for the process of reading?

Desire and Interpretation

Poe's detective, Monsieur Dupin, is able to see the forest for the trees. He can do this because, unlike the Inspector, he seems to have freed himself from presuppositions about the proper places to hide purloined documents. The Inspector doggedly persists in his "close" reading, examining details and deducing the presence of a foreign object through calculations about space. In contrast, Dupin's method consists of identifying with (putting himself in the place of) the various figures—the Queen, the Minister—who have tried to hide the letter. Like a good critic (or at least a canny one), Dupin sees the same trick repeated. Both the Queen and the Minister hide the letter by leaving it in clear sight, assuming that the presumptions others make about hiding things will blind them to the object's blatant presence.

If Poe's story on one level is about competing modes of interpretation, on another level it shows some of the dangers of interpretation. In committing herself to one tactic, the Queen exposes herself to the mercy of the savvy "reader," the Minister. In the same way, the Minister exposes himself to the canny Dupin. To whom might Dupin finally expose himself? In interpreting others (or texts), one always leaves oneself open to critique—to being read. And one always reveals a blind spot—the element one cannot see because of the positions one occupies and assumptions one makes.

Those who write about literature know that they inevitably choose certain approaches from which to interpret a text and not others. (One cannot possibly undertake them all at the same time.) Some of what a critic chooses to do is suggested by the text, but some is unconscious and reveals the desires of the critic. Not only does this selection determine the kinds of interpretations that will be possible, it also reveals something about the critic. In any case, interpretation produces another text, which in its turn can become the subject of another interpretation. The perils of interpretation are thus twofold: The choice of subject and approach exposes the desires of the critic; and the critic produces another text that itself becomes subject of another interpretation, one that inevitably will find a blind spot. Students find this out when their interpretations are scrutinized by a teacher just as they have attempted to scrutinize a text. Like Dupin, teachers always find the blind spot.

Critical Perspective: Reader Response Criticism

Because reading is never passive but is influenced by the dynamics of the story and the reader's desires, how readers read and respond to a story provides valuable insights about how a story works. Criticism that focuses on processes of reading and the readers' responses is called **reader response criticism** Web. Instead of focusing on the text itself, as does **New Criticism**, reader re- *www*
sponse criticism emphasizes the role of the reader in a process of interpretation. But such criticism is not simply the collection of individual responses to a text. Rather, many different critics who emphasize the role of the reader use different methodologies (**formalism, psychoanalysis, Marxism, feminism, historicism** Web) to account for the ways thinking about how one reads a *www*
text might illuminate the text one reads.

Parables of Reading and Desire, or Seeing What You Want to See

The following stories—Franz Kafka's "A Hunger Artist," Jorge Luis Borges's "The Shape of the Sword," and Gabriel García Márquez's "The Handsomest Drowned Man in the World"—all illustrate the ways people interpret events according to what they want to see. These interpretations are as much about the desires of those who are interpreting as they are about the phenomena they interpret.

FRANZ KAFKA

Translated by Willa and Edwin Muir

A Hunger Artist *(1922)*

During these last decades the interest in professional fasting has markedly diminished. It used to pay very well to stage such great performances under one's own management, but today that is quite impossible. We live in a different world now. At one time the whole town took a lively interest in the hunger artist; from day to day of his fast the excitement mounted; everybody wanted to see him at least once a day; there were people who bought season tickets for the last few days and sat from morning till night in front of his small barred cage; even in the nighttime there were visiting hours, when the whole effect was heightened by torch flares; on fine days the cage was set out in the open air, and then it was the children's special treat to see the hunger artist; for their elders he was often just a joke that happened to be in fashion, but the children stood open-mouthed, holding each other's hands for greater security, marvelling at him as he sat there pallid in black tights, with his ribs sticking out so prominently, not even on a seat but down among straw on the ground, sometimes giving a courteous nod, answering questions with a constrained smile, or perhaps stretching an arm through the bars so that one might feel how thin it was, and then again withdrawing deep into himself, paying no attention to anyone or anything, not even to the all-important striking of the clock that was the only piece of furniture in his cage, but merely staring into vacancy with half-shut eyes, now and then taking a sip from a tiny glass of water to moisten his lips.

Besides casual onlookers there were also relays of permanent watchers selected by the public, usually butchers, strangely enough, and it was their task to watch the hunger artist day and night, three of them at a time, in case he should have some secret recourse to nourishment. This was nothing but a formality, instituted to reassure the masses, for the initiates knew well enough that during his fast the artist would never in any circumstances, not even under forcible compulsion, swallow the smallest morsel of food; the honor of his profession forbade it. Not every watcher, of course, was capable of understanding this, there were often groups of night watchers who were very lax in carrying out their duties and deliberately huddled together in a retired corner to play cards with great absorption, obviously intending to give the hunger artist the chance of a little refreshment, which they supposed he could draw from some private hoard. Nothing annoyed the artist more than such watchers; they made him miserable; they made his fast seem unendurable; sometimes he mastered his feebleness sufficiently to sing during their watch for as long as he could keep going, to show them how unjust their suspicions were. But that was of little use; they only wondered at his cleverness in being able to fill his mouth even while singing. Much more to his taste were the watchers who sat close up to the bars, who were not content with the dim night lighting of the hall but focused him in the full glare of the electric pocket torch given them by the impresario. The harsh light did not trouble him at all. In any case he could never sleep properly, and he could always drowse a little, whatever the light, at any hour, even when the hall was thronged with noisy onlookers. He was quite happy at the prospect of spending a sleepless night with such watchers; he was ready to exchange jokes with them, to tell them stories out of his nomadic life, anything at all to keep them awake and demonstrate to them again that he had no eatables in his cage and that he was fasting as not one of them could fast. But his happiest moment was when the morning came and an enormous breakfast was brought them, at his expense, on which they flung themselves with the keen appetite of healthy men after a weary night of wakefulness. Of course there were people who argued that this breakfast was an unfair attempt to bribe the watchers, but that was going rather too far, and when they were invited to take on a night's vigil without a breakfast, merely for the sake of the cause, they made themselves scarce, although they stuck stubbornly to their suspicions.

Such suspicions, anyhow, were a necessary accompaniment to the profession of fasting. No one could possibly watch the hunger artist continuously, day and night, and so no one could produce first-hand evidence that the fast had really been rigorous and continuous; only the artist himself could know that; he was therefore bound to be the sole completely satisfied spectator of his own fast. Yet for other reasons he was never satisfied; it was not perhaps mere fasting that had brought him to such skeleton thinness that many people had regretfully to keep away from his exhibitions, because the sight of him was too much for them, perhaps it was dissatisfaction with himself that had worn him down. For he alone knew, what no other initiate knew, how easy it was to fast. It was the easiest thing in the world. He made no secret of this, yet people did not believe him; at the best they set him down as modest, most of them, however, thought he was out for publicity or else was some kind of cheat who found it easy to fast because he had discovered a way of making it easy, and then had the impudence to admit the fact, more or less. He had to put up with all that, and in the course of time had got used to it, but his inner dissatisfaction always rankled, and never yet, after any term of fasting—this must be granted to his credit—had he left the cage of his own free will. The longest period of fasting was fixed by his impresario at forty days, beyond that term he was not allowed to go, not even in great cities, and there was good reason for it, too. Experience had proved that for about forty days the interest of the public could be stimulated by a steadily increasing pressure of advertisement, but after that the town began to lose interest, sympathetic support began notably to fall off; there were of course local variations as between one town and another or one country and another, but as a general rule forty days marked the limit. So on the fortieth day the flower-bedecked cage was opened, enthusiastic spectators filled the hall, a military band played, two doctors entered the cage to measure the results of the fast, which were announced through a megaphone, and finally two young ladies appeared, blissful at having been selected for the honor, to help the hunger artist down the few steps leading to a small table on which was spread a carefully chosen invalid repast. And at this very moment the artist always turned stubborn. True, he would entrust his bony arms to the outstretched helping hands of the ladies bending over him, but stand up he would not. Why stop fasting at this particular moment, after forty days of it? He had held out for a long time, an illimitably long time; why stop now, when he was in his best fasting form, or rather, not yet quite in his best fasting form? Why should he be cheated of the fame he would get for fasting longer, for being not only the record hunger artist of all time, which presumably he was already, but for beating his own record by a performance beyond human imagination, since he felt that there were no limits to his capacity for fasting? His public pretended to admire him so much, why should it have so little patience with him; if he could endure fasting longer, why shouldn't the public endure it? Besides, he was tired, he was comfortable sitting in the straw, and now he was supposed to lift himself to his full height and go down to a meal the very thought of which gave him a nausea that only the presence of the ladies kept him from betraying, and even that with an effort. And he looked up into the eyes of the ladies who were apparently so friendly and in reality so cruel, and shook his head, which felt too heavy on its strengthless neck. But then there happened yet again what always happened. The impresario came forward, without a word—for the band made speech impossible—lifted his arms in the air above the artist, as if inviting Heaven to look down upon its creature here in the straw, this suffering martyr, which indeed he was, although in quite another sense; grasped him round the emaciated waist, with exaggerated caution, so that the frail condition he was in might be appreciated; and committed him to the care of the blenching ladies, not without secretly giving him a shaking so that his legs and body tottered and swayed. The artist now submitted completely; his head lolled on his breast as if it had landed there by chance; his body was hollowed out; his legs in a spasm of self-preservation clung close to each other at the knees, yet scraped on the ground as if it were not really solid ground, as if they were only trying to find solid ground; and the whole weight of his body, a featherweight after all, relapsed onto one of the ladies, who, looking round for help and panting a little—this post of honor was not at all what she had expected it to be—first stretched her neck as far as she could to keep her face at least free from contact with the artist, then finding this impossible, and her more fortunate companion not coming to her aid but merely holding extended on her own trembling hand the little bunch of knucklebones that was the artist's, to the great delight of the spectators burst into tears and had to be replaced by an attendant who had long been stationed in readiness. Then came the food, a little of which the impresario managed to get between the artist's lips, while he sat in a kind of half-fainting trance, to the accompaniment of cheerful patter designed to distract the public's attention from the artist's condition; after that, a toast was drunk to the public, supposedly prompted by a whisper from the artist in the impresario's ear; the band confirmed it with a mighty flourish, the spectators melted away, and no one had any cause to be dissatisfied with the proceedings, no one except the hunger artist himself, he only, as always.

So he lived for many years, with small regular intervals of recuperation, in visible glory, honored by the world, yet in spite of that troubled in spirit, and all the more troubled because no one would take his trouble seriously. What comfort could he possibly need? What more could he possibly wish for? And if some good-natured person, feeling sorry for him, tried to console him by pointing out that his melancholy was probably caused by fasting, it could happen, especially when he had been fasting for some time, that he reacted with an outburst of fury and to the general alarm began to shake the bars of his cage like a wild animal. Yet the impresario had a way of punishing these outbreaks which he rather enjoyed putting into operation. He would apologize publicly for the artist's behavior, which was only to be excused, he admitted, because of the irritability caused by fasting; a condition hardly to be understood by well-fed people; then by natural transition he went on to mention the artist's equally incomprehensible boast that he could fast for much longer than he was doing; he praised the high ambition, the good will, the great self-denial undoubtedly implicit in such a statement; and then quite simply countered it by bringing out photographs, which were also on sale to the public, showing the artist on the fortieth day of a fast lying in bed almost dead from exhaustion. This perversion of the truth, familiar to the artist though it was, always unnerved him afresh and proved too much for him. What was a consequence of the premature ending of his fast was here presented as the cause of it! To fight against this lack of understanding, against a whole world of non-understanding, was impossible. Time and again in good faith he stood by the bars listening to the impresario, but as soon as the photographs appeared he always let go and sank with a groan back on to his straw, and the reassured public could once more come close and gaze at him.

A few years later when the witnesses of such scenes called them to mind, 5
they often failed to understand themselves at all. For meanwhile the aforementioned change in public interest had set in; it seemed to happen almost overnight; there may have been profound causes for it, but who was going to bother about that; at any rate the pampered hunger artist suddenly found himself deserted one fine day by the amusement seekers, who went streaming past him to other more favored attractions. For the last time the impresario hurried him over half Europe to discover whether the old interest might still survive here and there; all in vain; everywhere, as if by secret agreement, a positive revulsion from professional fasting was in evidence. Of course it could not really have sprung up so suddenly as all that, and many premonitory symptoms which had not been sufficiently remarked or suppressed during the rush and glitter of success now came retrospectively to mind, but it was now too late to take any countermeasures. Fasting would surely come into fashion again at some future date, yet that was no comfort for those living in the present. What, then, was the hunger artist to do? He had been applauded by thousands in his time and could hardly come down to showing himself in a street booth at village fairs, and as for adopting another profession, he was not only too old for that but too fanatically devoted to fasting. So he took leave of the impresario, his partner in an unparalleled career, and hired himself to a large circus; in order to spare his own feelings he avoided reading the conditions of his contract.

A large circus with its enormous traffic in replacing and recruiting men, animals and apparatus can always find a use for people at any time, even for a hunger artist, provided of course that he does not ask too much, and in this particular case anyhow it was not only the artist who was taken on but his famous and long-known name as well; indeed considering the peculiar nature of his performance, which was not impaired by advancing age, it could not be objected that here was an artist past his prime, no longer at the height of his professional skill, seeking a refuge in some quiet corner of a circus; on the contrary, the hunger artist averred that he could fast as well as ever, which was entirely credible; he even alleged that if he were allowed to fast as he liked, and this was at once promised him without more ado, he could astound the world by establishing a record never yet achieved, a statement which certainly provoked a smile among the other professionals, since it left out of account the change in public opinion, which the hunger artist in his zeal conveniently forgot.

He had not, however, actually lost his sense of the real situation and took it as a matter of course that he and his cage should be stationed, not in the middle of the ring as a main attraction, but outside, near the animal cages, on a site that was after all easily accessible. Large and gaily painted placards made a frame for the cage and announced what was to be seen inside it. When the public came thronging out in the intervals to see the animals, they could hardly avoid passing the hunger artist's cage and stopping there for a moment, perhaps they might even have stayed longer had not those pressing behind them in the narrow gangway, who did not understand why they should be held up on their way towards the excitements of the menagerie, made it impossible for anyone to stand gazing quietly for any length of time. And that was the reason why the hunger artist, who had of course been looking forward to these visiting hours as the main achievement of his life, began instead to shrink from them. At first he could hardly wait for the intervals; it was exhilarating to watch the crowds come streaming his way, until only too soon—not even the most obstinate self-deception, clung to almost consciously, could hold out against the fact—the conviction was borne in upon him that these people, most of them, to judge from their actions, again and again, without exception, were all on their way to the menagerie. And the first sight of them from the distance remained the best. For when they reached his cage he was at once deafened by the storm of shouting and abuse that arose from the two contending factions, which renewed themselves continuously, of those who wanted to stop and stare at him—he soon began to dislike them more than the others—not out of real interest but only out of obstinate self-assertiveness, and those who wanted to go straight on to the animals. When the first great rush was past, the stragglers came along, and these, whom nothing could have prevented from stopping to look at him as long as they had breath, raced past with long strides, hardly even glancing at him, in their haste to get to the menagerie in time. And all too rarely did it happen that he had a stroke of luck, when some father of a family fetched up before him with his children, pointed a finger at the hunger artist and explained at length what the phenomenon meant, telling stories of earlier years when he himself had watched similar but much more thrilling performances, and the children, still rather uncomprehending, since neither inside nor outside school had they been sufficiently prepared for this lesson—what did they care about fasting?—yet showed by the brightness of their intent eyes that new and better times might be coming. Perhaps, said the hunger artist to himself many a time, things would be a little better if his cage were set not quite so near the menagerie. That made it too easy for people to make their choice, to say nothing of what he suffered from the stench of the menagerie, the animals' restlessness by night, the carrying past of raw lumps of flesh for the beasts of prey, the roaring at feeding times, which depressed him continually. But he did not dare to lodge a complaint with the management; after all, he had the animals to thank for the troops of people who passed his cage, among whom there might always be one here and there to take an interest in him, and who could tell where they might seclude him if he called attention to his existence and thereby to the fact that, strictly speaking, he was only an impediment on the way to the menagerie.

A small impediment, to be sure, one that grew steadily less. People grew familiar with the strange idea that they could be expected, in times like these, to take an interest in a hunger artist, and with this familiarity the verdict went out against him. He might fast as much as he could, and he did so; but nothing could save him now, people passed him by. Just try to explain to anyone the art of fasting! Anyone who has no feeling for it cannot be made to understand it. The fine placards grew dirty and illegible, they were torn down; the little notice board telling the number of fast days achieved, which at first was changed carefully every day, had long stayed at the same figure, for after the first few weeks even this small task seemed pointless to the staff; and so the artist simply fasted on and on, as he had once dreamed of doing, and it was no trouble to him, just as he had always foretold, but no one counted the days, no one, not even the artist himself, knew what records he was already breaking, and his heart grew heavy. And when once in a time some leisurely passer-by stopped, made merry over the old figure on the board and spoke of swindling, that was in its way the stupidest lie ever invented by indifference and inborn malice, since it was not the hunger artist who was cheating; he was working honestly, but the world was cheating him of his reward.

Many more days went by, however, and that too came to an end. An overseer's eye fell on the cage one day and he asked the attendants why this perfectly good stage should be left standing there unused with dirty straw inside it; nobody knew, until one man, helped out by the notice board, remembered about the hunger artist. They poked into the straw with sticks and found him in it. "Are you still fasting?" asked the overseer. "When on earth do you mean to stop?" "Forgive me, everybody," whispered the hunger artist; only the overseer, who had his ear to the bars, understood him. "Of course," said the overseer, and tapped his forehead with a finger to let the attendants know what state the man was in, "we forgive you." "I always wanted you to admire my fasting," said the hunger artist. "We do admire it," said the overseer, affably. "But you shouldn't admire it," said the hunger artist. "Well, then we don't admire it," said the overseer, "but why shouldn't we admire it?" "Because I have to fast, I can't help it," said the hunger artist. "What a fellow you are," said the overseer, "and why can't you help it?" "Because," said the hunger artist, lifting his head a little and speaking, with his lips pursed, as if for a kiss, right into the overseer's ear, so that no syllable might be lost, "because I couldn't find the food I liked. If I had found it, believe me, I should have made no fuss and stuffed myself like you or anyone else." These were his last words, but in his dimming eyes remained the firm though no longer proud persuasion that he was still continuing to fast.

"Well, clear this out now!" said the overseer, and they buried the hunger 10
artist, straw and all. Into the cage they put a young panther. Even the most insensitive felt it refreshing to see this wild creature leaping around the cage that had so long been dreary. The panther was all right. The food he liked was brought him without hesitation by the attendants; he seemed not even to miss

his freedom; his noble body, furnished almost to the bursting point with all that it needed, seemed to carry freedom around with it too; somewhere in his jaws it seemed to lurk; and the joy of life streamed with such ardent passion from his throat that for the onlookers it was not easy to stand the shock of it. But they braced themselves, crowded round the cage, and did not want ever to move away.

FRANZ KAFKA

www *(1883–1924)* **Web**

A lawyer who worked for an insurance company, Kafka lived in Czechoslovakia and wrote in German. Never famous in his own lifetime, his vision of culture seemed more in tune with post-World War II horrors such as recognition of Nazi genocide and the terrors of the atomic bomb.

www *TOPICS FOR CRITICAL THINKING* **Web**

1. In what ways does the hunger artist's performance require the active involvement of his audience?
2. What various interpretations of the hunger artist's practices do spectators offer?
3. In what ways is the hunger artist an artist?
4. How does context change the way spectators view the hunger artist?
5. If "The Hunger Artist" comments on how spectators interpret the artist's performance, what kinds of interpretation are possible for the story's readers?
6. What comments does this story make about the desires of the audience/reader?

www *TOPICS FOR CRITICAL WRITING* **Web**

1. What does "The Hunger Artist" suggest about the relation between art and interpretation?
2. The artist suggests that photos taken at the end of the fast are evidence of the damage done by ending the fast rather than evidence that the fast should be ended. What does this reversal of cause and effect suggest about the relations between art, interpretation, and truth?

JORGE LUIS BORGES

Translated by Donald A. Yates

The Shape of the Sword *(1944)*

A spiteful scar crossed his face: an ash-colored and nearly perfect arc that creased his temple at one tip and his cheek at the other. His real name is of no importance; everyone in Tacuarembó called him the "Englishman from La Colorada." Cardoso, the owner of those fields, refused to sell them: I understand that the Englishman resorted to an unexpected argument: he confided to Cardoso the secret of the scar. The Englishman came from the border, from Río Grande Del Sur; there are many who say that in Brazil he had been a smuggler. The fields were overgrown with grass, the waterholes brackish; the Englishman, in order to correct those deficiencies, worked fully as hard as his laborers. They say that he was severe to the point of cruelty, but scrupulously just. They say also that he drank: a few times a year he locked himself into an upper room, not to emerge until two or three days later as if from a battle or from vertigo, pale, trembling, confused and as authoritarian as ever. I remember the glacial eyes, the energetic leanness, the gray mustache. He had no dealings with anyone; it is a fact that his Spanish was rudimentary and cluttered with Brazilian. Aside from a business letter or some pamphlet, he received no mail.

The last time I passed through the northern provinces, a sudden overflowing of the Caraguatá stream compelled me to spend the night at La Colorada. Within a few moments, I seemed to sense that my appearance was inopportune; I tried to ingratiate myself with the Englishman; I resorted to the least discerning of passions: patriotism. I claimed as invincible a country with such a spirit as England's. My companion agreed, but added with a smile that he was not English. He was Irish, from Dungarvan. Having said this, he stopped short, as if he had revealed a secret.

After dinner we went outside to look at the sky. It had cleared up, but beyond the low hills the southern sky, streaked and gashed by lightning, was conceiving another storm. Into the cleared up dining room the boy who had served dinner brought a bottle of rum. We drank for some time, in silence.

I don't know what time it must have been when I observed that I was drunk; I don't know what inspiration or what exultation or tedium made me mention the scar. The Englishman's face changed its expression; for a few seconds I thought he was going to throw me out of the house. At length he said in his normal voice:

"I'll tell you the history of my scar under one condition: that of not miti- 5
gating one bit of the opprobrium, of the infamous circumstances."

I agreed. This is the story that he told me, mixing his English with Spanish, and even with Portuguese:

"Around 1922, in one of the cities of Connaught, I was one of the many who were conspiring for the independence of Ireland. Of my comrades, some are still living, dedicated to peaceful pursuits; others, paradoxically, are fighting on desert and sea under the English flag; another, the most worthy, died in the courtyard of a barracks, at dawn, shot by men filled with sleep; still others (not the most unfortunate) met their destiny in the anonymous and almost secret battles of the civil war. We were Republicans, Catholics; we were, I suspect, Romantics. Ireland was for us not only the utopian future and the intolerable present; it was a bitter and cherished mythology, it was the circular towers and the red marshes, it was the repudiation of Parnell and the enormous epic poems which sang of the robbing of bulls which in another incarnation were heroes and in others fish and mountains . . . One afternoon I will never forget, an affiliate from Munster joined us: one John Vincent Moon.

"He was scarcely twenty years old. He was slender and flaccid at the same time; he gave the uncomfortable impression of being invertebrate. He had studied with fervor and with vanity nearly every page of Lord knows what Communist manual; he made use of dialectical materialism to put an end to any discussion whatever. The reasons one can have for hating another man, or for loving him, are infinite: Moon reduced the history of the universe to a sordid economic conflict. He affirmed that the revolution was predestined to succeed. I told him that for a gentleman only lost causes should be attractive . . . Night had already fallen; we continued our disagreement in the hall, on the stairs, then along the vague streets. The judgments Moon emitted impressed me less than his irrefutable, apodictic note. The new comrade did not discuss: he dictated opinions with scorn and with a certain anger.

"As we were arriving at the outlying houses, a sudden burst of gunfire stunned us. (Either before or afterwards we skirted the blank wall of a factory or barracks.) We moved into an unpaved street; a soldier, huge in the firelight, came out of a burning hut. Crying out, he ordered us to stop. I quickened my pace; my companion did not follow. I turned around: John Vincent Moon was motionless, fascinated, as if eternized by fear. I then ran back and knocked the soldier to the ground with one blow, shook Vincent Moon, insulted him and ordered him to follow. I had to take him by the arm; the passion of fear had rendered him helpless. We fled, into the night pierced by flames. A rifle volley reached out for us, and a bullet nicked Moon's right shoulder; as we were fleeing amid pines, he broke out in weak sobbing.

"In that fall of 1923 I had taken shelter in General Berkeley's country 10
house. The general (whom I had never seen) was carrying out some administrative assignment or other in Bengal; the house was less than a century old, but it was decayed and shadowy and flourished in puzzling corridors and in pointless antechambers. The museum and the huge library usurped the first floor: controversial and uncongenial books which in some manner are the history of the nineteenth century; scimitars from Nishapur, along whose captured arcs there seemed to persist still the wind and violence of battle. We entered (I seem to recall) through the rear. Moon, trembling, his mouth parched, murmured that the events of the night were interesting; I dressed his wound and brought him a cup of tea; I was able to determine that his 'wound' was superficial. Suddenly he stammered in bewilderment:

"'You know, you ran a terrible risk.'

"I told him not to worry about it. (The habit of the civil war had incited me to act as I did; besides, the capture of a single member could endanger our cause.)

"By the following day Moon had recovered his poise. He accepted a cigarette and subjected me to a severe interrogation on the 'economic resources of our revolutionary party.' His questions were very lucid; I told him (truthfully) that the situation was serious. Deep bursts of rifle fire agitated the south. I told Moon our comrades were waiting for us. My overcoat and my revolver were in my room; when I returned, I found Moon stretched out on the sofa, his eyes closed. He imagined he had a fever; he invoked a painful spasm in his shoulder.

"At that moment I understood that his cowardice was irreparable. I clumsily entreated him to take care of himself and went out. This frightened man mortified me, as if I were the coward, not Vincent Moon. Whatever one man does, it is as if all men did it. For that reason it is not unfair that one disobedience in a garden should contaminate all humanity; for that reason it is not unjust that the crucifixion of a single Jew should be sufficient to save it. Perhaps Schopenhauer was right: I am all other men, any man is all men, Shakespeare is in some manner the miserable John Vincent Moon.

"Nine days we spent in the general's enormous house. Of the agonies and the successes of the war I shall not speak: I propose to relate the history of the scar that insults me. In my memory, those nine days form only a single day, save for the next to the last, when our men broke into a barracks and we were able to avenge precisely the sixteen comrades who had been machine-gunned in Elphin. I slipped out of the house towards dawn, in the confusion of daybreak. At nightfall I was back. My companion was waiting for me upstairs: his wound did not permit him to descend to the ground floor. I recall him having some volume of strategy in his hand, F. N. Maude or Clausewitz. 'The weapon I prefer is the artillery,' he confessed to me one night. He inquired into our plans; he liked to censure them or revise them. He also was accustomed to denouncing 'our deplorable economic basis'; dogmatic and gloomy, he predicted the disastrous end. *'C'est une affaire flambée,'* he murmured. In order to show that he was indifferent to being a physical coward, he magnified his mental arrogance. In this way, for good or for bad, nine days elapsed.

"On the tenth day the city fell definitely to the Black and Tans. Tall, silent horsemen patrolled the roads; ashes and smoke rode on the wind; on the corner I saw a corpse thrown to the ground, an impression less firm in my memory than that of a dummy on which the soldiers endlessly practiced their marksmanship, in the middle of the square . . . I had left when dawn was in the sky; before noon I returned. Moon, in the library, was speaking with someone; the tone of his voice told me he was talking on the telephone. Then I heard my name; then, that I would return at seven; then, the suggestion that they should arrest me as I was crossing the garden. My reasonable friend was reasonably selling me out. I heard him demand guarantees of personal safety.

"Here my story is confused and becomes lost. I know that I pursued the informer along the black, nightmarish halls and along deep stairways of dizziness. Moon knew the house very well, much better than I. One or two times I lost him. I cornered him before the soldiers stopped me. From one of the general's collections of arms I tore a cutlass: with that half moon I carved into his face forever a half moon of blood. Borges, to you, a stranger, I have made this confession. Your contempt does not grieve me so much."

Here the narrator stopped. I noticed that his hands were shaking.

"And Moon?" I asked him.

"He collected his Judas money and fled to Brazil. That afternoon, in the square, he saw a dummy shot up by some drunken men."

I waited in vain for the rest of the story. Finally I told him to go on.

Then a sob went through his body; and with a weak gentleness he pointed to the whitish curved scar.

"You don't believe me?" he stammered. "Don't you see that I carry written on my face the mark of my infamy? I have told you the story thus so that you would hear me to the end. I denounced the man who protected me: I am Vincent Moon. Now despise me."

Jorge Luis Borges

www

(1899–1986) **Web**

Argentinian Borges was brought up speaking both Spanish and English. Educated in Europe, Borges returned to Argentina to pursue a lengthy and innovative literary career. Beginning to go blind in his thirties, Borges began writing in earnest, developing the metafictional style that would become his legacy.

www

TOPICS FOR CRITICAL THINKING Web

1. In what ways does the narrator try to read or interpret the "Englishman from Colorado"?
2. When are his readings wrong, and why?
3. What clues enable the reader to recognize who the real narrator of the enframed story is?
4. How does our interpretation of the "Englishman's" story change when we learn who is narrating?
5. How does the shift in the identity of the narrator invite a rereading of the entire story?
6. In what different ways are we likely to understand the "Englishman's" behaviors before and after he tells the story?

www

TOPICS FOR CRITICAL WRITING Web

1. In what different ways can one interpret the scar?
2. What does the story say about the assumptions of readers?

Gabriel García Márquez

Translated by Gregory Rebassa

The Handsomest Drowned Man in the World *(1970)*

A Tale for Children

The first children who saw the dark and slinky bulge approaching through the sea let themselves think it was an empty ship. Then they saw it had no flags or masts and they thought it was a whale. But when it washed up on the beach, they removed the clumps of seaweed, the jellyfish tentacles, and the remains of fish and flotsam, and only then did they see that it was a drowned man.

They had been playing with him all afternoon, burying him in the sand and digging him up again, when someone chanced to see them and spread the alarm in the village. The men who carried him to the nearest house noticed the he weighed more than any dead man they had ever known, almost as much as a horse, and they said to each other that maybe he'd been floating too long and the water had got into his bones. When they laid him on the floor they said he'd been taller than all other men because there was barely enough room for him in the house, but they thought that maybe the ability to keep on growing after death was part of the nature of certain drowned men. He had the smell of the sea about him and only his shape gave one to suppose that it was the corpse of a human being, because the skin was covered with a crust of mud and scales.

They did not even have to clean off his face to know that the dead man was a stranger. The village was made up of only twenty-odd wooden houses that had stone courtyards with no flowers and which were spread about on the end of a desertlike cape. There was so little land that mothers always went about with the fear that the wind would carry off their children and the few dead that the years had caused among them had to be thrown off the cliffs. But the sea was calm and bountiful and all the men fit into seven boats. So when they found the drowned man they simply had to look at one another to see that they were all there. That night they did not go out to work at sea. While the men went to find out if anyone was missing in neighboring villages, the women stayed behind to care for the drowned man. They took the mud off with grass swabs, they removed the underwater stones entangled in his hair, and they scraped the crust off with tools used for scaling fish. As they were doing that they noticed that the vegetation on him came from faraway oceans and deep water and that his clothes were in tatters, as if he had sailed through labyrinths of coral. They noticed too that he bore his death with pride, for he did not have the lonely look of other drowned men who came out of the sea or that haggard, needy look of men who drowned in rivers. But only when they finished cleaning him off did they become aware of the kind of man he was and it left them breathless. Not only was he the tallest, strongest, most virile, and best built man they had ever seen, but even though they were looking at him there was no room for him in their imagination.

They could not find a bed in the village large enough to lay him on nor was there a table solid enough to use for his wake. The tallest men's holiday pants would not fit him, nor the fattest ones' Sunday shirts, nor the shoes of the one with the biggest feet. Fascinated by his huge size and his beauty, the women then decided to make him some pants from a large piece of sail and a shirt from some bridal brabant linen so that he could continue through his death with dignity. As they sewed, sitting in a circle and gazing at the corpse between stitches, it seemed to them that the wind had never been so steady nor the sea so restless as on that night and they supposed that the change had something to do with the dead man. They thought that if that magnificent man had lived in the village, his house would have had the widest doors, the highest ceiling, and the strongest floor, his bedstead would have been made from a midship frame held together by iron bolts, and his wife would have been the happiest woman. They thought that he would have had so much authority that he could have drawn fish out of the sea simply by calling their names and that he would have put so much work into his land that springs would have burst forth from among the rocks so that he would have been able to plant flowers on the cliffs. They secretly compared him to their own men, thinking that for all their lives theirs were incapable of doing what he could do in one night, and they ended up dismissing them deep in their hearts as the weakest, meanest, and most useless creatures on earth. They were wandering through that maze of fantasy when the oldest woman, who as the oldest had looked upon the drowned man with more compassion than passion, sighed:

"He has the face of someone called Esteban." 5

It was true. Most of them had only to take another look at him to see that he could not have any other name. The more stubborn among them, who were the youngest, still lived for a few hours with the illusion that when they put his clothes on and he lay among the flowers in patent leather shoes his name might be Lautaro. But it was a vain illusion. There had not been enough canvas, the poorly cut and worse sewn pants were too tight, and the hidden strength of his heart popped the buttons on his shirt. After midnight the whistling of the wind died down and the sea fell into its Wednesday drowsiness. The silence put an end to any last doubts: he was Esteban. The women who had dressed him, who had combed his hair, had cut his nails and shaved him were unable to hold back a shudder of pity when they had to resign themselves to his being dragged along the ground. It was then that they understood how unhappy he must have been with that huge body since it bothered him even after death. They could see him in life, condemned to go through doors sideways, cracking his head on crossbeams, remaining on his feet during visits, not knowing what to do with his soft, pink, sea lion hands while the lady of the house looked for her most resistant chair and begged him, frightened to death, sit here, Esteban, please, and he, leaning against the wall, smiling, don't bother, ma'am, I'm fine where I am, his heels raw and his back roasted from having done the same thing so many times whenever he paid a visit, don't bother, ma'am, I'm fine where I am, just to avoid the embarrassment of breaking up the chair, and never knowing perhaps that the ones who said don't go, Esteban, at least wait till the coffee's ready, where the ones who later on would whisper the big boob finally left, how nice, the handsome fool has gone. That was what the women were thinking beside the body a little before dawn. Later, when they covered his face with a handkerchief so that the light would not bother him, he looked so forever dead, so defenseless, so much like their men that the first furrows of tears opened in their hearts. It was one of the younger ones who began the weeping. The others, coming to, went from sighs to wails, and the more they sobbed the more they felt like weeping, because the drowned man was becoming all the more Esteban for them, and so they wept so much, for he was the most destitute, most peaceful, and most obliging man on earth, poor Esteban. So when the men returned with the news that the drowned man was not from the neighboring villages either, the women felt an opening of jubilation in the midst of their tears.

"Praise the Lord," they sighed, "he's ours!"

The men thought the fuss was only womanish frivolity. Fatigued because of the difficult nighttime inquiries, all they wanted was to get rid of the bother of the newcomer once and for all before the sun grew strong on that arid, windless day. They improvised a litter with the remains of foremasts and gaffs, tying it together with rigging so that it would bear the weight of the body until they reached the cliffs. They wanted to tie the anchor from a cargo ship to him so that he would sink easily into the deepest waves, where fish are blind and divers die of nostalgia, and bad currents would not bring him back to shore, as had happened with other bodies. But the more they hurried, the more the women thought of ways to waste time. They walked about like startled hens, pecking with the sea charms on their breasts, some interfering on one side to put a scapular of the good wind on the drowned man, some on the other side to put a wrist compass on him, and after a great deal of *get away from there, woman, stay out of the way, look, you almost made me fall on top of the dead man*, the men began to feel mistrust in their livers and started grumbling about why so many main-altar decorations for a stranger, because no matter how many nails and holy-water jars he had on him, the sharks would chew him all the same, but the women kept piling on their junk relics, running back and forth, stumbling, while they released in sighs what they did not in tears, so that the men finally exploded with *since when has there ever been such a fuss over a drifting corpse, a drowned nobody, a piece of cold Wednesday meat.* One of the women, mortified by so much lack of care, then removed the handkerchief from the dead man's face and the men were left breathless too.

He was Esteban. It was not necessary to repeat it for them to recognize him. If they had been told Sir Walter Raleigh, even they might have been impressed with his gringo accent, the macaw on his shoulder, his cannibal-killing blunderbuss, but there could be only one Esteban in the world and there he was, stretched out like a sperm whale, shoeless, wearing the pants of an undersized child, and with those stony nails that had to be cut with a knife. They only had to take the handkerchief off his face to see that he was ashamed, that it was not his fault that he was so big or so heavy or so handsome, and if he had known that this was going to happen, he would have looked for a more discreet place to drown in, seriously, I even would have tied the anchor off a galleon around my neck and staggered off a cliff like someone who doesn't like things in order not to be upsetting people now with this Wednesday dead body, as you people say, in order not to be bothering anyone with this filthy piece of cold meat that doesn't have anything to do with me. There was so much truth in his manner that even the most mistrustful men, the ones who felt the bitterness of endless nights at sea fearing that their women would tire of dreaming about them and begin to dream of drowned men, even they and others who were harder still shuddered in the marrow of their bones at Esteban's sincerity.

That was how they came to hold the most splendid funeral they could 10
conceive of for an abandoned drowned man. Some women who had gone to get flowers in the neighboring villages returned with other women who could not believe what they had been told, and those women went back for more flowers when they saw the dead man, and they brought more and more until there were so many flowers and so many people that it was hard to walk about. At the final moment it pained them to return him to the waters as an orphan and they chose a father and mother from among the best people, and aunts

and uncles and cousins, so that through him all the inhabitants of the village became kinsmen. Some sailors who heard weeping from a distance went off course and people heard of one who had himself tied to the mainmast, remembering ancient fables about sirens. While they fought for the privilege of carrying him on their shoulders along the steep escarpment by the cliffs, men and women became aware for the first time of the desolation of their streets, the dryness of their courtyards, the narrowness of their dreams as they faced the splendor and beauty of their drowned man. They let him go without an anchor so that he could come back if he wished and whenever he wished, and they all held their breath for the fraction of centuries the body took to fall into the abyss. They did not need to look at one another to realize that they were no longer all present, that they would never be. But they also knew that everything would be different from then on, that their houses would have wider doors, higher ceilings, and stronger floors so that Esteben's memory could go everywhere without bumping into beams and so that no one in the future would dare whisper the big boob finally died, too bad, the handsome fool has finally died, because they were going to paint their house fronts gay colors to make Esteban's memory eternal and they were going to break their backs digging for springs among the stones and planting flowers on the cliffs so that in future years at dawn the passengers on great liners would awaken, suffocated by the smell of gardens on the high seas, and the captain would have to come down from the bridge in his dress uniform, with his astrolabe, his pole star, and his row of war medals and, pointing to the promontory of roses on the horizon, he would say in fourteen languages, look there, where the wind is so peaceful now that it's gone to sleep beneath the beds, over there, where the sun's so bright that the sunflowers don't know which way to turn, yes, that's Esteban's village.

Gabriel García Márquez

www

(b. 1928) **Web**

Educated in law and influenced by Franz Kafka and William Faulkner, García Márquez worked as a journalist and became a writer who continued the development of magical realism. Always interested in politics, García Márquez worked as a leftist journalist while writing the novels that resulted in his winning the Nobel Prize in literature in 1982.

www

TOPICS FOR CRITICAL THINKING **Web**

1. How does the description of the drowned man change through the course of the story?
2. What do changes in the drowned man tell us about the villagers themselves?
3. What changes in the village come about through the villagers' interpretations of the drowned man?
4. What is the significance of the fact that the drowned man is very large?
5. Why is this story subtitled "A Tale for Children"?

TOPIC FOR CRITICAL WRITING Web

www

What does "The Handsomest Drowned Man in the World" suggest about the relations between perception and interpretation? Desire and interpretation?

Reading and Misreading

The effect of some stories relies on revealing how characters' desires produce interpretations, making the readers of the story the wise and masterful consumers of such events. Some stories show how characters within stories rely on the misreadings that a character assumes other characters will make. Other stories work by catching up readers in their own desires and then revealing their mistakes at the end.

While the processes of reading and interpretation are bound up with the reader's desire, they are also products of cultural assumptions (ideologies) of race, gender, and class. Notions about how people of different races, genders, classes, and sexual orientations look and act often determine how we identify and relate to people we don't know. Stories that feature such misinterpretations illustrate the extent to which preconceptions and essentialized ideas about such categories shape the ways certain characters are treated. In other words, reading is not always something that must occur in relation to a text.

Often a story's examination of the biases of reading provides a necessary commentary on various kinds of social and cultural oppression. For this reason the problems of reading become one way to examine larger assumptions about others—such as stereotypes and the causes of miscommunication and misunderstanding. Stories treating issues of race, gender, and sexuality often bring the acts of reading, interpreting, and misreading into question. These readings or misreadings based on cultural stereotypes may suggest entire histories, as in María Cristina Mena's "The Vine-Leaf" (1914), which asks readers to follow sets of assumptions made by an enframed narrator about the identity and motives of a female character. Misreadings may enable characters to fool other characters by taking advantage of their misinterpretations or might provide the basis for ironic commentary on the misreading characters' investments and assumptions about gender and sexuality, as in Colette's "The Hidden Woman" (1924) and Dorothy Parker's "The Waltz" (1933).

María Cristina Mena

The Vine-Leaf

(1914)

It is a saying in the capital of Mexico that Dr. Malsufrido carries more family secrets under his hat than any archbishop, which applies, of course, to family secrets of the rich. The poor have no family secrets, or none that Dr. Malsufrido would trouble to carry under his hat.

The doctor's hat is, appropriately enough, uncommonly capacious, rising very high, and sinking so low that it seems to be supported by his ears and eyebrows, and it has a furry look, as if it had been brushed the wrong way, which is perhaps what happens to it if it is ever brushed at all. When the doctor takes it off, the family secrets do not fly out like a flock of parrots, but remain nicely bottled up beneath a dome of old and highly polished ivory, which, with its unbroken fringe of dyed black hair, has the effect of a tonsure; and then Dr. Malsufrido looks like one of the early saints. I've forgotten which one.

So edifying is his personality that, when he marches into a sick-room, the forces of disease and infirmity march out of it, and do not dare to return until he has taken his leave. In fact, it is well known that none of his patients has ever had the bad manners to die in his presence.

If you will believe him, he is almost ninety years old, and everybody knows that he has been dosing good Mexicans for half a century. He is forgiven for being a Spaniard on account of a legend that he physicked royalty in his time, and that a certain princess—but that has nothing to do with this story.

It is sure he has a courtly way with him that captivates his female patients, 5
of whom he speaks as his *penitentes*, insisting on confession as a prerequisite of diagnosis, and declaring that the physician who undertakes to cure a woman's body without reference to her soul is a more abominable kill-healthy than the famous *Dr. Sangrado*, who taught medicine to *Gil Blas*.

"Describe me the symptoms of your conscience, *Señora*," he will say. "Fix yourself that I shall forget one tenth of what you tell me."

"But what of the other nine tenths, Doctor?" the troubled lady will exclaim.

"The other nine tenths I shall take care not to believe," Dr. Malsufrido will reply, with a roar of laughter. And sometimes he will add:

"Do not confess your neighbor's sins; the doctor will have enough with your own."

When an inexperienced one fears to become a *penitente* lest that terrible 10
old doctor betray her confidence, he reassures her as to his discretion, and at the same time takes her mind off her anxieties by telling her the story of his first patient.

"Figure you my prudence, *Señora*," he begins, "that, although she was my patient, I did not so much as see her face."

And then, having enjoyed the startled curiosity of his hearer, he continues:

"On that day of two crosses when I first undertook the mending of mortals, she arrived to me beneath a veil as impenetrable as that of a nun, saying:

"'To you I come, *Señor* Doctor, because no one knows you.'

"'Who would care for fame, *Señorita*,' said I, 'when obscurity bring such 15
excellent fortune?'

"And the lady, in a voice which trembled slightly, returned:

"'If your knife is as apt as your tongue, and your discretion equal to both, I shall not regret my choice of a surgeon.'

"With suitable gravity I reassured her, and inquired how I might be privileged to serve her. She replied:

"'By ridding me of a blemish, if you are skillful enough to leave no trace on the skin.'

"'Of that I will judge, with the help of God, when the *señorita* shall have 20
removed her veil.'

"'No, no; you shall not see my face. Praise the saints the blemish is not there!'

"'Wherever it be,' said I, resolutely, 'my science tells me that it must be seen before it can be well removed.'

"The lady answered with great simplicity that she had no anxiety on that account, but that, as she had neither duena nor servant with her, I must help her. I had no objection, for a surgeon must needs be something of a lady's maid. I judged from the quality of her garments that she was of an excellent family, and I was ashamed of my clumsy fingers; but she was as patient as marble, caring only to keep her face closely covered. When at last I saw the blemish she had complained of, I was astonished, and said:

"'But it seems to me a blessed stigma, *Señorita*, this delicate, wine-red vine-leaf, staining a surface as pure as the petal of any magnolia. With permission, I should say that the god Bacchus himself painted it here in the arch of this chaste back, where only the eyes of Cupid could find it; for it is safely below the line of the most fashionable gown.'

"But she replied: 25

"'I have my reasons. Fix yourself that I am superstitious.'

"I tried to reason with her on that, but she lost her patience, and cried:

"'For favor, good surgeon, your knife!'

"Even in those days I had much sensibility, *Señora*, and I swear that my heart received more pain from the knife than did she. Neither the cutting nor the stitching brought a murmur from her. Only some strong ulterior thought could have armed a delicate woman with such valor. I beat my brains to construe the case, but without success. A caprice took me to refuse the fee she offered me.

"'No, *Señorita*,' I said, 'I have not seen your face, and if I were to take 30
your money, it might pass that I should not see the face of a second patient, which would be a great misfortune. You are my first, and I am as superstitious as you.'

"I would have added that I had fallen in love with her, but I feared to appear ridiculous, having seen no more than her back.

"'You would place me under an obligation,' she said. I felt that her eyes studied me attentively through her veil. 'Very well, I can trust you the better for that. *Adiós*, *Señor* Surgeon.'

"She came once more to have me remove the stitches, as I had told her, and again her face was concealed, and again I refused payment; but I think she knew that the secret of the vine-leaf was buried in my heart."

"But that secret, what was it, Doctor? Did you ever see the mysterious lady again?"

"*¡Chist!* Little by little one arrives to the *rancho, Señora.* Five years passed, 35
and many patients arrived to me, but, although all showed me their faces, I loved none of them better than the first one. Partly through family influence, partly through well-chosen friendships, and perhaps a little through that diligence in the art of Hippocrates for which in my old age I am favored by the most charming of Mexicans, I had prospered, and was no longer unknown.

"At a meeting of a learned society I became known to a certain *marqués* who had been a great traveler in his younger days. We had a discussion on a point of anthropology, and he invited me to his house, to see the curiosities he had collected in various countries. Most of them recalled scenes of horror, for he had a morbid fancy.

"Having taken from my hand the sword with which he had seen five Chinese pirates sliced into small pieces, he led me toward a little door, saying:

"'Now you shall see the most mysterious and beautiful of my mementos, one which recalls a singular event in our own peaceful Madrid.'

"We entered a room lighted by a skylight, and containing little but an easel on which rested a large canvas. The *marqués* led me where the most auspicious light fell upon it. It was a nude, beautifully painted. The model stood poised divinely, with her back to the beholder, twisting flowers in her hair before a mirror. And there, in the arch of that chaste back, staining a surface as pure as the petal of any magnolia, what did my eyes see? Can you possibly imagine, *Señora?*"

"*¡Válgame Dios!* The vine-leaf, Doctor!" 40

"What penetration of yours, *Señora!* It was veritably the vine-leaf, wine-red, as it had appeared to me before my knife barbarously extirpated it from the living flesh; but in the picture it seemed unduly conspicuous, as if Bacchus had been angry when he kissed. You may imagine how the sight startled me. But those who know Dr. Malsufrido need no assurance that even in those early days he never permitted himself one imprudent word. No, *Señora;* I only remarked, after praising the picture in proper terms:

"'What an interesting moon is that upon the divine creature's back!'

"'Does it not resemble a young vine-leaf in early spring?' said the *marqués,* who contemplated the picture with the ardor of a connoisseur. I agreed politely, saying:

"'Now that you suggest it, *Marqués,* it has some of the form and color of a tender vine-leaf. But I could dispense me a better vine-leaf, with many bunches of grapes, to satisfy the curiosity I have to see such a well-formed lady's face. What a misfortune that it does not appear in that mirror, as the artist doubtless intended! The picture was never finished, then?'

"'I have reason to believe that it was finished,' he replied, 'but that the 45
face painted in the mirror was obliterated. Observe that its surface is an opaque and disordered smudge of many pigments, showing no brush-work, but only marks of a rude rubbing that in some places has overlapped the justly painted frame of the mirror.'

"'This promises an excellent mystery,' I commented lightly. 'Was it the artist or his model who was dissatisfied with the likeness, *Marqués?*'

"'I suspect that the likeness was more probably too good than not good enough,' returned the *marqués*. 'Unfortunately, poor Andrade is not here to tell us.'

"'Andrade! The picture was his work?'

"'The last his hand touched. Do you remember when he was found murdered in his studio?'

"'With a knife sticking between his shoulders. I remember it very well.' 50

"The *marqués* continued:

"'I had asked him to let me have this picture. He was then working on that rich but subdued background. The figure was finished, but there was no vine-leaf, and the mirror was empty of all but a groundwork of paint, with a mere luminous suggestion of a face.

"'Andrade, however, refused to name me a price, and tried to put me off with excuses. His friends were jesting about the unknown model, whom no one had managed to see, and all suspected that he designed to keep the picture for himself. That made me the more determined to possess it. I wished to make it a betrothal gift to the beautiful *Señorita* Lisarda Monte Alegre, who had then accepted the offer of my hand, and who is now the *marquesa*. When I have a desire, Doctor, it bites me, and I make it bite others. That poor Andrade, I gave him no peace.

"'He fell into one of his solitary fits, shutting himself in his studio, and seeing no one; but that did not prevent me from knocking at his door whenever I had nothing else to do. Well, one morning the door was open.'

"'Yes, yes!' I exclaimed. 'I remember now, *Marqués*, that it was you who 55
found the body.'

"'You have said it. He was lying in front of this picture, having dragged himself across the studio. After assuring myself that he was beyond help, and while awaiting the police, I made certain observations. The first thing to strike my attention was this vine-leaf. The paint was fresh, whereas the rest of the figure was comparatively dry. Moreover, its color had not been mixed with Andrade's usual skill. Observe you, Doctor, that the blemish is not of the texture of the skin, or bathed in its admirable atmosphere. It presents itself as an excrescence. And why? Because that color had been mixed and applied with feverish haste by the hand of a dying man, whose one thought was to denounce his assassin—she who undoubtedly bore such a mark on her body, and who had left him for dead, after carefully obliterating the portrait of herself which he had painted in the mirror.'

"'*¡Ay Dios!* But the police, *Marqués*—they never reported these details so significant?'

"'Our admirable police are not connoisseurs of the painter's art, my friend. Moreover, I had taken the precaution to remove from the dead man's fingers the empurpled brush with which he had traced that accusing symbol.'

"'You wished to be the accomplice of an unknown assassin?'

"'Inevitably, *Señor*, rather than deliver that lovely body to the hands of the 60
public executioner.'

"The *marqués* raised his lorgnette and gazed at the picture. And I—I was recovering from my agitation, *Señora*. I said:

"'It seems to me, *Marqués*, that if I were a woman and loved you, I should be jealous of that picture.'

"He smiled and replied:

"'It is true that the *marquesa* affects some jealousy on that account, and will not look at the picture. However, she is one who errs on the side of modesty, and prefers more austere objects of contemplation. She is excessively religious.'

"'I have been called superstitious,' pronounced a voice behind me.

"It was a voice that I had heard before. I turned, *Señora*, and I ask you to try to conceive whose face I now beheld."

"*Válgame la Virgen*, Dr. Malsufrido, was it not the face of the good *marquesa*, and did she not happen to have been also your first patient?"

"Again such penetration, *Señora*, confounds me. It was she. The *marqués* did me the honor to present me to her.

"'I have heard of your talents, *Señor* Surgeon,' she said.

"'And I of your beauty, *marquesa*,' I hastened to reply; 'but that tale was not well told.' And I added, 'If you are superstitious, I will be, too.'

"With one look from her beautiful and devout eyes she thanked me for that prudence which to this day, *Señora*, is at the service of my *penitentes*, little daughters of my affections and my prayers; and then she sighed and said:

"'Can you blame me for not loving this questionable lady of the vine-leaf, of whom my husband is such a gallant accomplice?'

"'Not for a moment,' I replied, 'for I am persuaded, *marquesa*, that a lady of rare qualities may have power to bewitch an unfortunate man without showing him the light of her face.'"

María Cristina Mena

www

(1893–1965) **Web**

Born in Mexico, Mena was sent to the United States before the Mexican Revolution. She published short stories in American magazines and befriended D. H. Lawrence.

TOPICS FOR CRITICAL THINKING

1. What various clues does the Doctor use to establish identity? Are these reliable?
2. Why does the patient have the birthmark removed?
3. What story is implied by the text but not told?
4. What various meanings might the vine-leaf have?

TOPIC FOR CRITICAL WRITING

Compare the functions of the birthmark in this story to the functions of the birthmark in "The Birthmark."

Sidonie-Gabrielle Colette

Translated by Matthew Ward

The Hidden Woman *(1924)*

He had been looking at the swirl of masks in front of him for a long time, suffering vaguely from the intermingling of their colors and the synchronized sound of two orchestras too close together. His cowl pressed his temples; a nervous headache was building between his eyes. But he savored, without impatience, a mixture of malaise and pleasure which allowed the hours to fly by unnoticed. He had wandered down all the corridors of the Opéra, had drunk in the silvery dust of the dance floor, recognized bored friends, and wrapped around his neck the indifferent arms of a very fat girl humorously disguised as a sylph. Though embarrassed by his long domino, tripping over it like a man in skirts, the cowled doctor did not dare take off either the domino or the hood, because of his schoolboy lie.

"I'll be spending tomorrow night in Nogent," he had told his wife the evening before. "They just telephoned and I'm afraid that my patient, you know, that poor old lady . . . Can you imagine? And I was looking forward to this ball like a kid. It's ridiculous, isn't it, a man my age who's never been to the Opéra Ball?"

"Very, darling, very ridiculous! If I had known I might never have married you . . ."

She laughed, and he admired her narrow face, pink, matte, and long, like a thin sugared almond.

"But . . . don't you want to go to the Green and Purple Ball? You know 5
you can go without me if you want, darling."

She trembled with one of those long shivers of disgust which made her hair, her delicate hands, and her chest in her white dress shudder at the sight of a slug or some filthy passer-by.

"Oh, no! Can you see me in a crowd, all those hands . . . What can I do? It's not that I'm a prude, it's . . . it makes my skin crawl. There's nothing I can do about it."

Leaning against the balustrade of the loggia, above the main staircase, he thought about this trembling hand, as he contemplated, directly in front of him, on the bare back of a sultana, the grasp of two enormous square hands with black nails. Bursting out of the braid-trimmed sleeves of a Venetian lord, they sank into the white female flesh as if it were dough. Because he was thinking about her, it gave him quite a start to hear, next to him, a little "ahem," a little cough typical of his wife. He turned around and saw someone in a long and impenetrable disguise, sitting sidesaddle on the balustrade, Pierrot by the looks of the huge-sleeved tunic, the loose-fitting pantaloons, the skullcap, the plaster-like whiteness coating the little bit of skin visible above the half-mask bearded with lace. The fabric of the costume and skullcap, woven of dark violet and silver, glistened like a conger eel fished for by night with iron hooks, in boats with resin lanterns. Overcome with surprise, he waited to hear the little "ahem," which did not come again. The Pierrot-Eel, seated, casual, tapped the marble balusters with a dangling heel, revealing only its two satin slippers and a black-gloved hand bent back against one hip. The two oblique slits in the mask, carefully covered over with a tulle mesh, allowed only a smothered fire of indeterminate color to pass through.

He almost called out, "Irene!" but held back, remembering his own lie. Not good at playacting, he also decided against disguising his voice. The Pierrot scratched its thigh, with a free and uninhibited gesture, and the anxious husband sighed in relief.

"Ah! It's not her." 10

But out of a pocket the Pierrot pulled a flat gold box, opened it to take out a lipstick, and the anxious husband recognized an antique snuffbox, fitted with a mirror inside, the last birthday present . . . He put his left hand on the pain in his chest with so brusque and so involuntarily theatrical a motion that the Pierrot-Eel noticed him.

"Is that a declaration, Purple Domino?"

He did not answer, half choked with surprise, anticipating, as in a bad dream, and listened for a long moment to the thinly disguised voice—the voice of his wife. The Eel, sitting there cavalierly, its head tilted like a bird's, looked at him; she shrugged her shoulders, hopped down, and walked away. Her movement freed the distraught husband, who, restored to an active and normal jealousy, started to think clearly again, and calmly rose to follow his wife.

"She's here for someone, with someone. In less than an hour I'll know everything."

A hundred other purple or green cowls guaranteed that he would be nei- 15
ther noticed nor recognized. Irene walked ahead of him nonchalantly. He was amazed to see her roll her hips softly and drag her feet a little as if she were wearing Turkish slippers. A Byzantine, in embroidered emerald green and gold, grabbed her as she passed, and she bent back, grown thinner in his arms, as if his grasp were going to cut her in half. Her husband ran a few steps forward and reached the couple as Irene cried out flatteringly, "You big brute, you!"

She walked away, with the same relaxed and calm step, stopping often, musing at the open doors of the boxes, almost never turning around. She hesitated at the bottom of a staircase, turned aside, came back toward the entrance to the orchestra stalls, slid into a noisy, dense group with slippery skillfulness, the exact movement of a knife blade sliding into its sheath. Ten arms imprisoned her, an almost naked wrestler roughly pinned her up against the edge of the boxes on the main floor and held her there. She yielded under the weight of the naked man, threw back her head with a laugh that was drowned out by other laughter, and the man in the purple cowl saw her teeth flash beneath the mask's lacy beard. Then she slipped away again with ease and sat down on the steps which led to the dance floor. Her husband, standing two steps behind, watched her. She readjusted her mask, and her crumpled tunic, and tightened the roll of her headband. She seemed calm, as though alone, and walked away again after a few minutes' rest. She went down the steps, and put her arms on the shoulders of a warrior who invited her, without speaking, to dance, and she danced, clinging to him.

"That's him," the husband said to himself.

But she did not say a word to the dancer, clad in iron and moist skin, and left him quietly, when the dance ended. She went off to have a glass of champagne at the buffet, and then a second glass, paid, and then watched, motionless and curious, as two men began scuffling, surrounded by screaming women. Then she amused herself by placing her little satanic hands, all black, on the white throat of a Dutch girl with golden hair, who cried out nervously. At last the anxious man who was following her saw her stop as she bumped up against a young man collapsed on a banquette, out of breath, fanning himself with his mask. She leaned over, disdainfully took his handsome face, rugged and fresh, by the chin, and kissed the panting, half-open mouth . . .

But her husband, instead of rushing forward and tearing the two joined mouths away from each other, disappeared into the crowd. Dismayed, he no longer feared, he no longer hoped for betrayal. He was sure now that Irene did not know the adolescent, drunk with dancing, whom she was kissing, or the Hercules. He was sure that she was not waiting or looking for anyone, that the lips she held beneath her own like a crushed grape, she would abandon, leave again the next minute, then wander about again, gather up some other passer-by, forget him, until she felt tired and it was time to go back home, tasting only the monstrous pleasure of being alone, free, honest, in her native brutality, of being the one who is unknown, forever solitary and without shame, whom a little mask and a hermetic costume had restored to her irremediable solitude and her immodest innocence.

SIDONIE-GABRIELLE COLETTE

(1873–1954) **Web** ***www***

One of the most esteemed women writers of twentieth century France, Colette enjoyed careers as writer and music hall performer. Popular in her time, she is now best known for her novels *Chéri* and *Gigi*. Many of her novels and short stories treat the dilemmas of female independence.

TOPICS FOR CRITICAL THINKING

1. What clues about the identity of the Pierrot does the husband's close reading of the Pierrot provide?
2. How might the story's point-of-view relate to different ways of understanding the Pierrot's actions?
3. What do the husband's interpretations of the Pierrot tell us about the husband?
4. What might we understand about the reliability of our own readings when we see the reliability of the husband's readings?
5. What insight does the husband gain?

TOPICS FOR CRITICAL WRITING

1. On what various levels and in what ways do characters and readers engage in a process of interpretation? (See also sample student essay in Chapter 53.)
2. In what ways is this story about the husband's desire?

DOROTHY PARKER

The Waltz *(1933)*

Why, thank you so much, I'd adore to.

I don't want to dance with him. I don't want to dance with anybody. And even if I did, it wouldn't be him. He'd be well down among the last ten. I've seen the way he dances; it looks like something you do on Saint Walpurgis Night. Just think, not a quarter of an hour ago, here I was sitting, feeling so sorry for the poor girl he was dancing with. And now *I'm* going to be the poor girl. Well, well. Isn't it a small world?

And a peach of a world, too. A true little corker. It's events are so fascinatingly unpredictable, are not they? Here I was, minding my own business, not doing a stitch of harm to any living soul. And then he comes into my life, all smiles and city manners, to sue me for the favor of one memorable mazurka. Why, he scarcely knows my name, let alone what it stands for. It stands for Despair, Bewilderment, Futility, Degradation, and Premeditated Murder, but little does he wot. I don't wot his name, either; I haven't any idea what it is. Jukes, would be my guess from the look in his eyes. How do you do, Mr. Jukes? And how is that dear little brother of yours, with the two heads?

Ah, now why did he have to come around me, with his low requests? Why can't he let me lead my own life? I ask so little—just to be left alone in my quiet corner of the table, to do my evening brooding over all my sorrows. And he must come, with his bows and his scrapes and his may-I-have-this-ones. And I had to go and tell him that I'd adore to dance with him. I cannot understand why I wasn't struck right down dead. Yes, and being struck dead would look like a day in the country, compared to struggling out a dance with this boy. But what could I do? Everyone else at the table had got up to dance, except him and me. There was I, trapped. Trapped like a trap in a trap.

What can you say, when a man asks you to dance with him? I most cer- 5
tainly will *not* dance with you, I'll see you in hell first. Why, thank you, I'd like to awfully, but I'm having labor pains. Oh, yes, *do* let's dance together—it's so nice to meet a man who isn't a scaredy-cat about catching my beri-beri. No. There was nothing for me to do, but say I'd adore to. Well, we might as well get it over with. All right, Cannonball, let's run out on the field. You won the toss; you can lead.

Why, I think it's more of a waltz, really. Isn't it? We might just listen to the music a second. Shall we? Oh, yes, it's a waltz. Mind? Why, I'm simply thrilled. I'd love to waltz with you.

I'd love to waltz with you. I'd love to waltz with you. I'd love to have my tonsils out, I'd love to be in a midnight fire at sea. Well, it's too late now. We're getting under way. *Oh.* Oh, dear. Oh, dear, dear, dear. Oh, this is even worse than I thought it would be. I suppose that's the one dependable law of life—everything is always worse than you thought it was going to be. Oh, if I had any real grasp of what this dance would be like, I'd have held out for sitting it out. Well, it will probably amount to the same thing in the end. We'll be sitting it out on the floor in a minute, if he keeps this up.

I'm so glad I brought it to his attention that this is a waltz they're playing. Heaven knows what might have happened, if he had thought it was something fast; we'd have blown the sides right out of the building. Why does he always want to be somewhere that he isn't? Why can't we stay in one place just long enough to get acclimated? It's this constant rush, rush, rush, that's the curse of American life. That's the reason that we're all of us so—*Ow!* For God's sake, don't *kick*, you idiot; this is only second down. Oh, my shin. My poor, poor shin, that I've had ever since I was a little girl!

Oh, no, no, no. Goodness, no. It didn't hurt the least little bit. And anyway it was my fault. Really it was. Truly. Well, you're just being sweet, to say that. It really was all my fault.

I wonder what I'd better do—kill him this instant, with my naked hands, 10
or wait and let him drop in his traces. Maybe it's best not to make a scene. I guess I'll just lie low, and watch the pace get him. He can't keep this up indefinitely—he's only flesh and blood. Die he must, and die he shall, for what he did to me. I don't want to be of the oversensitive type, but you can't tell me that kick was unpremeditated. Freud says there are no accidents. I've led no cloistered life, I've known dancing partners who have spoiled my slippers and torn my dress; but when it comes to kicking, I am Outraged Womanhood. When you kick me in the shin, *smile.*

Maybe he didn't do it maliciously. Maybe it's just his way of showing his high spirits. I suppose I ought to be glad that one of us is having such a good time. I suppose I ought to think myself lucky if he brings me back alive. Maybe it's captious to demand of a practically strange man that he leave your shins as he found them. After all, the poor boy's doing the best he can. Probably he grew up in the hill country, and never had no larnin'. I bet they had to throw him on his back to get shoes on him.

Yes, it's lovely, isn't it? It's simply lovely. It's the loveliest waltz. Isn't it? Oh, I think it's lovely, too.

Why, I'm getting positively drawn to the Triple Threat here. He's my hero. He has the heart of a lion, and the sinews of a buffalo. Look at him—never a thought of the consequences, never afraid of his face, hurling himself into every scrimmage, eyes shining, cheeks ablaze. And shall it be said that I hung back? No, a thousand times no. What's it to me if I have to spend the next couple of years in a plaster cast? Come on, Butch, right through them! Who wants to live forever?

Oh. Oh, dear. Oh, he's all right, thank goodness. For a while I thought they'd have to carry him off the field. Ah, I couldn't bear to have anything happen to him. I love him. I love him better than anybody in the world. Look at the spirit he gets into a dreary, commonplace waltz; how effete the other dancers seem, beside him. He is youth and vigor and courage, he is strength and gaiety and—*Ow!* Get off my instep, you hulking peasant! What do you think I am, anyway—a gangplank? *Ow!*

15 *No, of course it didn't hurt. Why, it didn't a bit. Honestly. And it was all my fault. You see, that little step of yours—well, it's perfectly lovely, but it's just a tiny bit tricky to follow at first. Oh, did you work it up yourself? You really did? Well, aren't you amazing! Oh, now I think I've got it. Oh, I think it's lovely. I was watching you do it when you were dancing before. It's awfully effective when you look at it.*

It's awfully effective when you look at it. I bet I'm awfully effective when you look at me. My hair is hanging along my cheeks, my skirt is swaddled about me, I can feel the cold damp of my brow. I must look like something out of "The Fall of the House of Usher." This sort of thing takes a fearful toll of a woman my age. And he worked up his little step himself, he with his degenerate cunning. And it was just a tiny bit tricky at first, but now I think I've got it. Two stumbles, slip, and a twenty-yard dash; yes. I've got it. I've got several other things, too, including a split shin and a bitter heart. I hate this creature I'm chained to. I hated him the moment I saw his leering, bestial face. And here I've been locked in his noxious embrace for the thirty-five years this waltz has lasted. Is that orchestra never going to stop playing? Or must this obscene travesty of a dance go on until hell burns out?

Oh, they're going to play another encore. Oh, goody. Oh, that's lovely. Tired? I should say I'm not tired. I'd like to go on like this forever.

I should say I'm not tired. I'm dead, that's all I am. Dead, and in what a cause! And the music is never going to stop playing, and we're going on like this, Double-Time Charlie and I, throughout eternity. I suppose I won't care any more, after the first hundred thousand years. I suppose nothing will matter then, not heat nor pain nor broken heart nor cruel, aching weariness. Well. It can't come too soon for me.

I wonder why I didn't tell him I was tired. I wonder why I didn't suggest going back to the table. I could have said let's just listen to the music. Yes, and if he would, that would be the first bit of attention he has given it all evening. George Jean Nathan said that the lovely rhythms of the waltz should be listened to in stillness and not be accompanied by strange gyrations of the human body. I think that's what he said. I think it was George Jean Nathan. Anyhow, whatever he said and whoever he was and whatever he's doing now, he's better off than I am. That's safe. Anybody who isn't waltzing with this Mrs. O'Leary's cow I've got here is having a good time.

20 Still if we were back at the table, I'd probably have to talk to him. Look at him—what could you say to a thing like that! Did you go to the circus this year, what's your favorite kind of ice cream, how do you spell cat? I guess I'm as well off here. As well off as if I were in a cement mixer in full action.

I'm past all feeling now. The only way I can tell when he steps on me is that I can hear the splintering of bones. And all the events of my life are passing before my eyes. There was the time I was in a hurricane in the West Indies, there was the day I got my head cut open in the taxi smash, there was the night the drunken lady threw a bronze ash-tray at her own true love and got me instead, there was that summer that the sailboat kept capsizing. Ah, what an easy, peaceful time was mine, until I fell in with Swifty, here. I didn't know what trouble was, before I got drawn into this *danse macabre.* I think my mind is beginning to wander. It almost seems to me as if the orchestra were stopping. It couldn't be, of course; it could never, never be. And yet in my ears there is a silence like the sound of angel voices. . . .

Oh, they've stopped, the mean things. They're not going to play any more. Oh, darn. Oh, do you think they would? Do you really think so, if you gave them fifty dollars? Oh, that would be lovely. And look, do tell them to play this same thing. I'd simply adore to go on waltzing.

DOROTHY PARKER

(1893–1967) **Web** ***www***

Noted journalist and wit, Dorothy Parker wrote short stories, poetry, screenplays, reviews, criticism, and newspaper columns. A member of the noted New York Algonquin Round Table **Web**, Parker exemplified the cosmopolitan genius of the self-made woman of the twentieth century. ***www***

TOPICS FOR CRITICAL THINKING

1. In what ways does "The Waltz" enact the differences between what one says and what one means?
2. How do those differences illustrate gender politics?
3. Are we to take the narrator's commentary literally? If not, how do we know what is happening?
4. How should the story's readers understand the narrator's tone?
5. Is it likely that the gentleman waltzer is aware of his partner's feelings?

TOPIC FOR CRITICAL WRITING

Is "The Waltz" about only a dance?

Questions of Perception and Representation: Postmodernism

What happens when we can no longer trust our eyes to see or our language to convey what we mean? Writers of the first part of the twentieth century such as Franz Kafka wrote about the difference between an individual's experience and how the individual perceives that experience. Some writers in the later twentieth century bring even a character's perceptions into doubt—not in the way Colette does by showing the way characters perceive the same event differently, but instead by showing how perception itself is unreliable. While early twentieth-century writers brought language into question as a reliable medium for expressing meaning, later twentieth-century writers question whether we can communicate at all via language and show the ways our perceptions themselves are unreliable.

Postmodernism

This doubt about the reliability of perception and representation is a part of a *www* larger philosophical and aesthetic attitude called **postmodernism**. **Web** Coming from the disparate realms of architecture, literature, art, and philosophy, postmodernists question whether there can be a universal truth or narratives about truth that can produce and sustain any belief in singular meaning (that is, that everything has only one definite, locatable truth). Postmodernism even challenges an individual's belief in his or her own unified singular and stable identity, over which he or she has complete control.

Postmodernism is characterized by its attention to the making of art as the subject of art, a focus on process rather than product, and concern about the ways we think and the assumptions and premises we hold rather than the validity or truth of our conclusions. Postmodernism brings meaning into question while producing artistic works that explore whether anything can really be represented at all.

Postmodernist literature is characterized by some of the following qualities.

- It is often fragmented or nonsense narrative. See the film *Memento*, for an example.
- It often disrupts our sense of spatial or temporal continuity. Again, the film *Memento* is a good example.

- It often makes use of pastiche or the combination of different styles and elements. Web (See Mark Leyner's *My Cousin, My Gastroenterologist* in Chapter 16 for an example of pastiche.) *www*
- It includes characters who do not seem to be in command of themselves or their motives. These characters are called *split* or *disunified subjects*. An example is the protagonist of "How I Contemplated the World from the Detroit House of Correction and Began My Life Over Again" in Chapter 15.
- It has a consciousness of the processes of representation, for example, stories about writing stories or *metanarrative* Web (see Chapter 15 for a discussion about metanarrative). Examples of this include "A Story," "How I Contemplated the World from the Detroit House of Correction and Began My Life Over Again," and "The Calmative," all in Chapter 15. *www*
- It distrusts such institutions as government, religion, and capitalism and questions the possibility of any single, transcendent truth. Featured writer Salman Rushdie's story "The Free Radio" and this chapter's story "Blow Up" exemplify this distrust, as does much of the work of Beat writers such as Allen Ginsberg and Jack Kerouac. See Chapter 19 for a discussion of the Beats. Web *www*
- It embodies a sense of the failure of language as a mode of communication.

Not all postmodern works demonstrate all of these characteristics, but all manifest one or more. Some prose fiction is a combination of modernist and postmodernist elements. (For the difference between these, see Web.) What is ultimately important to an understanding of postmodernism in writing is the way a story regards the possibilities of truth and certainty. *www*

The following stories—Julio Cortázar's "Blow-Up," Italo Calvino's "Mr. Palomar on the Beach," and Michelle Cliff's "The Store of a Million Items"—all raise questions about the reliability of perception, not only as it reflects the perceiver's desires, but as it is inherently unreliable. Bringing perception into question also brings the perceiver into question and, with this, any narrative he or she might construct.

Critical Perspective: On Postmodernism

"To come now to the last of these parallels: Both Jorge Luis Borges and Italo Calvino managed marvelously to combine in their fiction the values that I call Algebra and Fire (I'm borrowing those terms here, as I have done elsewhere, from Borges's *First Encyclopedia of Tlon*, a realm complete, he reports, "with its emperors and its seas, with its minerals and its birds and its fish, with its algebra and its fire"). Let "algebra" stand for formal ingenuity and "fire" for what touches our emotions (it's tempting to borrow instead Calvino's alternative values of "crystal" and "flame," from his lecture on exactitude, but he happens not to mean by those terms what I'm referring to here). Formal virtuosity itself can of course be breathtaking, but much algebra and little or no fire makes for mere gee-whizzery, like Queneau's *Exercises in Style* and *One Hundred Thousand Billion Sonnets*. Much fire and little or no algebra, on the other hand, makes for heartfelt muddles—no examples needed. What most of us want from literature most of the time is what has been called passionate virtuosity, and both Borges and Calvino deliver it. Although I find both writers indispensable and would never presume to rank them as literary artists, by my lights Calvino perhaps comes closer to being the very model of a modern major Postmodernist—not that that very much matters, and whatever the capacious bag is that can contain such otherwise dissimilar spirits as Donald Barthelme, Samuel Beckett, J. L. Borges, Italo Calvino, Angela Carter, Robert Coover, Gabriel García Márquez, Elsa Morante, Vladimir Nabokov, Grace Paley, Thomas Pychon, et al. . . . What I mean is not only the fusion of algebra and fire, the great (and in Calvino's case high-spirited) virtuosity, the massive acquaintance with and respectfully ironic recycling of what Umberto Eco calls "the already said," and the combination of storytelling charm with zero naiveté, but also the keeping of one authorial foot in narrative antiquity while the other rests firmly in the high-tech (in Calvino's case, the Parisian "structuralist") narrative present. Add to this what I have cited as our chap's perhaps larger humanity and in-the-worldness, and you have my reasons."

—John Barth, "The Parallels! Italo Calvino and Jorge Luis Borges," in *Context: A Forum for Literary Arts and Culture*, (1999), p. 1.

In this passage, author John Barth analyzes the ways in which he understands the work of Italo Calvino to be postmodernist. In so doing, he also defines what he considers to be postmodernist writing.

JULIO CORTÁZAR

Translated by Paul Blackburn

Blow-Up

(1951)

It'll never be known how this has to be told, in the first person or in the second, using the third person plural or continually inventing modes that will serve for nothing. If one might say: I will see the moon rose, or: we hurt me at the back of my eyes, and especially: you the blond woman was the clouds that race before my your his our yours their faces. What the hell.

Seated ready to tell it, if one might go to drink a bock over there, and the typewriter continue by itself (because I use the machine), that would be perfection. And that's not just a manner of speaking. Perfection, yes, because here is the aperture which must be counted also as a machine (of another sort, a Contax 1.1.2) and it is possible that one machine may know more about another machine than I, you, she—the blond—and the clouds. But I have the dumb luck to know that if I go this Remington will sit turned to stone on top of the table with the air of being twice as quiet that mobile things have when they are not moving. So, I have to write. One of us all has to write, if this is going to get told. Better that it be me who am dead, for I'm less compromised than the rest; I who see only the clouds and can think without being distracted, write without being distracted (there goes another, with a grey edge) and remember without being distracted, I who am dead (and I'm alive, I'm not trying to fool anybody, you'll see when we get to the moment, because I have to begin some way and I've begun with this period, the last one back, the one at the beginning, which in the end is the best of the periods when you want to tell something).

All of a sudden I wonder why I have to tell this, but if one begins to wonder why he does all he does do, if one wonders why he accepts an invitation to lunch (now a pigeon's flying by and it seems to me a sparrow), or why when someone has told us a good joke immediately there starts up something like a tickling in the stomach and we are not at peace until we've gone into the office across the hall and told the joke over again; then it feels good immediately, one is fine, happy, and can get back to work. For I imagine that no one has explained this, that really the best thing is to put aside all decorum and tell it, because, after all's done, nobody is ashamed of breathing or of putting on his shoes; they're things that you do, and when something weird happens, when you find a spider in your shoe or if you take a breath and feel like a broken window, then you have to tell what's happening, tell it to the guys at the office or to the doctor. Oh, doctor, every time I take a breath . . . Always tell it, always get rid of that tickle in the stomach that bothers you.

And now that we're finally going to tell it, let's put things a little bit in order, we'd be walking down the staircase in this house as far as Sunday, November 7, just a month back. One goes down five floors and stands then in the Sunday in the sun one would not have suspected of Paris in November, with a large appetite to walk around, to see things, to take photos (because we were photographers, I'm a photographer). I know that the most difficult thing is going to be finding a way to tell it, and I'm not afraid of repeating myself. It's going to be difficult because nobody really knows who it is telling it, if I am I or what actually occurred or what I'm seeing (clouds, and once in a while a pigeon) or if, simply, I'm telling a truth which is only my truth, and then is the truth only for my stomach, for this impulse to go running out and to finish up in some manner with, this, whatever it is.

We're going to tell it slowly, what happens in the middle of what I'm writ- 5
ing is coming already. If they replace me, if, so soon, I don't know what to say, if the clouds stop coming and something else starts (because it's impossible that this keep coming, clouds passing continually and occasionally a pigeon), if something out of all this . . . And after the "if" what am I going to put if I'm going to close the sentence structure correctly? But if I begin to ask questions, I'll never tell anything, maybe to tell would be like an answer, at least for someone who's reading it.

Roberto Michel, French-Chilean, translator and in his spare time an amateur photographer, left number 11, rue Monsieur-le-Prince Sunday November 7 of the current year (now they're two small ones passing, with silver linings). He had spent three weeks working on the French version of a treatise on challenges and appeals by José Norberto Allende, professor at the University of Santiago. It's rare that there's wind in Paris, and even less seldom a wind like this that swirled around corners and rose up to whip at old wooden venetian blinds behind which astonished ladies commented variously on how unreliable the weather had been these last few years. But the sun was out also, riding the wind and friend of the cats, so there was nothing that would keep me from taking a walk along the docks of the Seine and taking photos of the Conservatoire and Sainte-Chapelle. It was hardly ten o'clock, and I figured that by eleven the light would be good, the best you can get in the fall; to kill some time I detoured around by the Isle Saint-Louis and started to walk along the quai d'Anjou, I stared for a bit at the hôtel de Lauzun, I recited bits from Apollinaire which always get into my head whenever I pass in front of the hôtel de Lauzun (and at that I ought to be remembering the other poet, but Michel is an obstinate beggar), and when the wind stopped all at once and the sun came out at least twice as hard (I mean warmer, but really it's the same thing), I sat down on the parapet and felt terribly happy in the Sunday morning.

One of the many ways of contesting level-zero, and one of the best, is to take photographs, an activity in which one should start becoming an adept very early in life, teach it to children since it requires discipline, aesthetic education, a good eye and steady fingers. I'm not talking about waylaying the lie like any old reporter, snapping the stupid silhouette of the VIP leaving number 10 Downing Street, but in all ways when one is walking about with a camera, one has almost a duty to be attentive, to not lose that abrupt and happy rebound of sun's rays off an old stone, or the pigtails-flying run of a small girl going home with a loaf of bread or a bottle of milk. Michel knew that the photographer always worked as a permutation of his personal way of seeing the world as other than the camera insidiously imposed upon it (now a large cloud is going by, almost black), but he lacked no confidence in himself, knowing that he had only to go out without the Contax to recover the keynote of distraction, the sight without a frame around it, light without the diaphragm aperture or 1/250 sec. Right now (what a word, *now*, what a dumb lie) I was able to sit quietly on the railing overlooking the river watching the red and black motorboats passing below without it occurring to me to think photographically of the scenes, nothing more than letting myself go in the letting go of objects, running immobile in the stream of time. And then the wind was not blowing.

After, I wandered down the quai de Bourbon until getting to the end of the isle where the intimate square was (intimate because it was small, not that it was hidden, it offered its whole breast to the river and the sky), I enjoyed it, a lot. Nothing there but a couple and, of course, pigeons; maybe even some of those which are flying past now so that I'm seeing them. A leap up and I settled on the wall, and let myself turn about and be caught and fixed by the sun, giving it my face and ears and hands (I kept my gloves in my pocket). I had no desire to shoot pictures, and lit a cigarette to be doing something; I think it was that moment when the match was about to touch the tobacco that I saw the young boy for the first time.

What I'd thought was a couple seemed much more now a boy with his mother, although at the same time I realized that it was not a kid and his mother, and that it was a couple in the sense that we always allegate to couples when we see them leaning up against the parapets or embracing on the benches in the squares. As I had nothing else to do, I had more than enough time to wonder why the boy was so nervous, like a young colt or a hare, sticking his hands into his pockets, taking them out immediately, one after the other, running his fingers through his hair, changing his stance, and especially why was he afraid, well, you could guess that from every gesture, a fear suffocated by his shyness, an impulse to step backwards which he telegraphed, his body standing as if it were on the edge of flight, holding itself back in a final, pitiful decorum.

10 All this was so clear, ten feet away—and we were alone against the parapet at the tip of the island—that at the beginning the boy's fright didn't let me see the blond very well. Now, thinking back on it, I see her much better at that first second when I read her face (she'd turned around suddenly, swinging like a metal weathercock, and the eyes, the eyes were there), when I vaguely understood what might have been occurring to the boy and figured it would be worth the trouble to stay and watch (the wind was blowing their words away and they were speaking in a low murmur). I think that I know how to look, if it's something I know, and also that every looking oozes with mendacity, because it's that which expels us furthest outside ourselves, without the least guarantee, whereas to smell, or (but Michel rambles on to himself easily enough, there's no need to let him harangue on this way). In any case, if the likely inaccuracy can be seen beforehand, it becomes possible again to look; perhaps it suffices to choose between looking and the reality looked at, to strip things of all their unnecessary clothing. And surely all that is difficult besides.

As for the boy I remember the image before his actual body (that will clear itself up later), while now I am sure that I remember the woman's body much better than the image. She was thin and willowy, two unfair words to describe what she was, and was wearing an almost-black fur coat, almost long, almost handsome. All the morning's wind (now it was hardly a breeze and it wasn't cold) had blown through her blond hair which pared away her white, bleak face—two unfair words—and put the world at her feet and horribly alone in front of her dark eyes, her eyes fell on things like two eagles, two leaps into nothingness, two puffs of green slime. I'm not describing anything, it's more a matter of trying to understand it. And I said two puffs of green slime.

Let's be fair, the boy was well enough dressed and was sporting yellow gloves which I would have sworn belonged to his older brother, a student of law or sociology; it was pleasant to see the fingers of the gloves sticking out of his jacket pocket. For a long time I didn't see his face, barely a profile, not stupid—a terrified bird, a Fra Filippo angel, rice pudding with milk—and the back of an adolescent who wants to take up judo and has had a scuffle or two in defense of an idea or his sister. Turning fourteen, perhaps fifteen, one would guess that he was dressed and fed by his parents but without a nickel in his pocket, having to debate with his buddies before making up his mind to buy a coffee, a cognac, a pack of cigarettes. He'd walk through the streets thinking of the girls in his class, about how good it would be to go to the movies and see the latest film, or to buy novels or neckties or bottles of liquor with green and white labels on them. At home (it would be a respectable home, lunch at noon and romantic landscapes on the walls, with a dark entryway and a mahogany umbrella stand inside the door) there'd be the slow rain of time, for studying, for being mama's hope, for looking like dad, for writing to his aunt in Avignon. So that there was a lot of walking the streets, the whole of the river for him (but without a nickel) and the mysterious city of fifteen-year-olds with its signs in doorways, its terrifying cats, a paper of fried potatoes for thirty francs, the pornographic magazine folded four ways, a solitude like the emptiness of his pockets, the eagerness for so much that was incomprehensible but illumined by a total love, by the availability analogous to the wind and the streets.

This biography was of the boy and of any boy whatsoever, but this particular one now, you could see he was insular, surrounded solely by the blond's presence as she continued talking with him. (I'm tired of insisting, but two long ragged ones just went by. That morning I don't think I looked at the sky once, because what was happening with the boy and the woman appeared so soon I could do nothing but look at them and wait, look at them and . . .) To cut it short, the boy was agitated and one could guess without too much trouble what had just occurred a few minutes before, at most half-an-hour. The boy had come onto the tip of the island, seen the woman and thought her marvelous. The woman was waiting for that because she was there waiting for that, or maybe the boy arrived before her and she saw him from one of the balconies or from a car and got out to meet him, starting the conversation with whatever, from the beginning she was sure that he was going to be afraid and want to run off, and that, naturally, he'd stay, stiff and sullen, pretending experience and the pleasure of the adventure. The rest was easy because it was happening ten feet away from me, and anyone could have gauged the stages of the game, the derisive, competitive fencing; its major attraction was not that it was happening but in foreseeing its denouement. The boy would try to end it by pretending a date, an obligation, whatever, and would go stumbling off disconcerted, wishing he were walking with some assurance, but naked under the mocking glance which would follow him until he was out of sight. Or rather, he would stay there, fascinated or simply incapable of taking the initiative, and the woman would begin to touch his face gently, muss his hair, still talking to him voicelessly, and soon would take him by the arm to lead him off, unless he, with an uneasiness beginning to tinge the edge of desire, even his stake in the adventure, would rouse himself to put his arm around her waist and to kiss her. Any of this could have happened, though it did not, and perversely Michel waited, sitting on the railing, making the settings almost without looking at the camera, ready to take a picturesque shot of a corner of the island with an uncommon couple talking and looking at one another.

Strange how the scene (almost nothing: two figures there mismatched in their youth) was taking on a disquieting aura. I thought it was I imposing it, and that my photo, if I shot it, would reconstitute things in their true stupidity. I would have liked to know what he was thinking, a man in a grey hat sitting at the wheel of a car parked on the dock which led up to the footbridge, and whether he was reading the paper or asleep. I had just discovered him because people inside a parked car have a tendency to disappear, they get lost in that wretched, private cage stripped of the beauty that motion and danger give it. And nevertheless, the car had been there the whole time, forming part (or deforming that part) of the isle. A car: like saying a lighted streetlamp, a park bench. Never like saying wind, sunlight, those elements always new to the skin and the eyes, and also the boy and the woman, unique, put there to change the island, to show it to me in another way. Finally, it may have been that the man with the newspaper also became aware of what was happening and would, like me, feel that malicious sensation of waiting for everything to happen. Now the woman had swung around smoothly, putting the young boy between herself and the wall, I saw them almost in profile, and he was tall, though not much taller, and yet she dominated him, it seemed like she was hovering over him (her laugh, all at once, a whip of feathers), crushing him just by being there, smiling, one hand taking a stroll through the air. Why wait any longer? Aperture at sixteen, a sighting which would not include the horrible black car, but yes, that tree, necessary to break up too much grey space . . .

I raised the camera, pretended to study a focus which did not include 15
them, and waited and watched closely, sure that I would finally catch the revealing expression, one that would sum it all up, life that is rhythmed by movement but which a stiff image destroys, taking time in cross section, if we do not choose the essential imperceptible fraction of it. I did not have to wait long. The woman was getting on with the job of handcuffing the boy smoothly, stripping from him what was left of his freedom a hair at a time, in an incredibly slow and delicious torture. I imagined the possible endings (now a small fluffy cloud appears, almost alone in the sky), I saw their arrival at the house (a basement apartment probably, which she would have filled with large cushions and cats) and conjectured the boy's terror and his desperate decision to play it cool and to be led off pretending there was nothing new in it for

him. Closing my eyes, if I did in fact close my eyes, I set the scene: the teasing kisses, the woman mildly repelling the hands which were trying to undress her, like in novels, on a bed that would have a lilac-colored comforter, on the other hand she taking off his clothes, plainly mother and son under a milky yellow light, and everything would end up as usual, perhaps, but maybe everything would go otherwise, and the initiation of the adolescent would not happen, she would not let it happen, after a long prologue wherein the awkwardnesses, the exasperating caresses, the running of hands over bodies would be resolved in who knows what, in a separate and solitary pleasure, in a petulant denial mixed with the art of tiring and disconcerting so much poor innocence. It might go like that, it might very well go like that; that woman was not looking for the boy as a lover, and at the same time she was dominating him toward some end impossible to understand if you do not imagine it as a cruel game, the desire to desire without satisfaction, to excite herself for someone else, someone who in no way could be that kid.

Michel is guilty of making literature, of indulging in fabricated unrealities. Nothing pleases him more than to imagine exceptions to the rule, individuals outside the species, not-always-repugnant monsters. But that woman invited speculation, perhaps giving clues enough for the fantasy to hit the bullseye. Before she left, and now that she would fill my imaginings for several days, for I'm given to ruminating, I decided not to lose a moment more. I got it all into the view-finder (with the tree, the railing, the eleven-o'clock sun) and took the shot. In time to realize that they both had noticed and stood there looking at me, the boy surprised and as though questioning, but she was irritated, her face and body flat-footedly hostile, feeling robbed, ignominiously recorded on a small chemical image.

I might be able to tell it in much greater detail but it's not worth the trouble. The woman said that no one had the right to take a picture without permission, and demanded that I hand her over the film. All this in a dry, clear voice with a good Parisian accent, which rose in color and tone with every phrase. For my part, it hardly mattered whether she got the roll of film or not, but anyone who knows me will tell you, if you want anything from me, ask nicely. With the result that I restricted myself to formulating the opinion that not only was photography in public places not prohibited, but it was looked upon with decided favor, both private and official. And while that was getting said, I noticed on the sly how the boy was falling back, sort of actively backing up though without moving, and all at once (it seemed almost incredible) he turned and broke into a run, the poor kid, thinking that he was walking off and in fact in full flight, running past the side of the car, disappearing like a gossamer filament of angel-spit in the morning air.

But filaments of angel-spittle are also called devil-spit, and Michel had to endure rather particular curses, to hear himself called meddler and imbecile, taking great pains meanwhile to smile and to abate with simple movements of his head such a hard sell. As I was beginning to get tired, I heard the car door slam. The man in the grey hat was there, looking at us. It was only at that point that I realized he was playing a part in the comedy.

He began to walk toward us, carrying in his hand the paper he had been pretending to read. What I remember best is the grimace that twisted his mouth askew, it covered his face with wrinkles, changed somewhat both in location and shape because his lips trembled and the grimace went from one side of his mouth to the other as though it were on wheels, independent and involuntary. But the rest stayed fixed, a flour-powdered clown or bloodless man, dull dry skin, eyes deepset, the nostrils black and prominently visible, blacker than the eyebrows or hair or the black necktie. Walking cautiously as though the pavement hurt his feet; I saw patent-leather shoes with such thin soles that he must have felt every roughness in the pavement. I don't know why I got down off the railing, nor very well why I decided to not give them the photo, to refuse that demand in which I guessed at their fear and cowardice. The clown and the woman consulted one another in silence: we made a perfect and unbearable triangle, something I felt compelled to break with a crack of a whip. I laughed in their faces and began to walk off, a little more slowly, I imagine, than the boy. At the level of the first houses, beside the iron footbridge, I turned around to look at them. They were not moving, but the man had dropped his newspaper; it seemed to me that the woman, her back to the parapet, ran her hands over the stone with the classical and absurd gesture of someone pursued looking for a way out.

What happened after that happened here, almost just now, in a room on the fifth floor. Several days went by before Michel developed the photos he'd taken on Sunday; his shots of the Conservatoire and of Sainte-Chapelle were all they should be. Then he found two or three proof-shots he'd forgotten, a poor attempt to catch a cat perched astonishingly on the roof of a rambling public urinal, and also the shot of the blond and the kid. The negative was so good that he made an enlargement; the enlargement was so good that he made one very much larger, almost the size of a poster. It did not occur to him (now one wonders and wonders) that only the shots of the Conservatoire were worth so much work. Of the whole series, the snapshot of the tip of the island was the only one which interested him; he tacked up the enlargement on one wall of the room, and the first day he spent some time looking at it and remembering, that gloomy operation of comparing the memory with the gone reality; a frozen memory, like any photo, where nothing is missing, not even, and especially, nothingness, the true solidifier of the scene. There was the woman, there was the boy, the tree rigid above their heads, the sky as sharp as the stone of the parapet, clouds and stones melded into a single substance and inseparable (now one with sharp edges is going by, like a thunderhead). The first two days I accepted what I had done, from the photo itself to the enlargement on the wall, and didn't even question that every once in a while I would interrupt my translation of José Norberto Allende's treatise to encounter once more the woman's face, the dark splotches on the railing. I'm such a jerk; it had never occurred to me that when we look at a photo from the front, the eyes reproduce exactly the position and the vision of the lens; it's these things that are taken for granted and it never occurs to anyone to think about them. From my chair, with the typewriter directly in front of me, I looked at the photo ten feet away, and then it occurred to me that I had hung it exactly at the point of view of the lens. It looked very good that way; no doubt, it was the best way to appreciate a photo, though the angle from the diagonal doubtless has its pleasures and might even divulge different aspects.

Every few minutes, for example when I was unable to find the way to say in good French what José Norberto Allende was saying in very good Spanish, I raised my eyes and looked at the photo; sometimes the woman would catch my eye, sometimes the boy, sometimes the pavement where a dry leaf had fallen admirably situated to heighten a lateral section. Then I rested a bit from my labors, and I enclosed myself again happily in that morning in which the photo was drenched, I recalled ironically the angry picture of the woman demanding I give her the photograph, the boy's pathetic and ridiculous flight, the entrance on the scene of the man with the white face. Basically, I was satisfied with myself; my part had not been too brilliant, and since the French have been given the gift of the sharp response, I did not see very well why I'd chosen to leave without a complete demonstration of the rights, privileges and prerogatives of citizens. The important thing, the really important thing was having helped the kid to escape in time (this in case my theorizing was correct, which was not sufficiently proven, but the running away itself seemed to show it so). Out of plain meddling, I had given him the opportunity finally to take advantage of his fright to do something useful; now he would be regretting it, feeling his honor impaired, his manhood diminished. That was better than the attentions of a woman capable of looking as she had looked at him on that island. Michel is something of a puritan at times, he believes that one should not seduce someone from a position of strength. In the last analysis, taking that photo had been a good act.

Well, it wasn't because of the good act that I looked at it between paragraphs while I was working. At that moment I didn't know the reason, the reason I had tacked the enlargement onto the wall; maybe all fatal acts happen that way, and that is the condition of their fulfillment. I don't think the almost-furtive trembling of the leaves on the tree alarmed me, I was working on a sentence and rounded it out successfully. Habits are like immense herbariums, in the end an enlargement of 32 x 28 looks like a movie screen, where, on the tip of the island, a woman is speaking with a boy and a tree is shaking its dry leaves over their heads.

But her hands were just too much. I had just translated: "In that case, the second key resides in the intrinsic nature of difficulties which societies . . ."—when I saw the woman's hand beginning to stir slowly, finger by finger. There was nothing left of me, a phrase in French which I would never have to finish, a typewriter on the floor, a chair that squeaked and shook, fog. The kid had ducked his head like boxers do when they've done all they can and are waiting for the final blow to fall; he had turned up the collar of his overcoat and seemed more a prisoner than ever, the perfect victim helping promote the catastrophe. Now the woman was talking into his ear, and her hand opened again to lay itself against his cheekbone, to caress and caress it, burning it, taking her time. The kid was less startled than he was suspicious, once or twice he poked his head over the woman's shoulder and she continued talking, saying something that made him look back every few minutes toward that area where Michel knew the car was parked and the man in the grey hat, carefully eliminated from the photo but present in the boy's eyes (how doubt that now) in the words of the woman, in the woman's hands, in the vicarious presence of the woman. When I saw the man come up, stop near them and look at them, his hands in his pockets and a stance somewhere between disgusted and demanding, the master who is about to whistle in his dog after a frolic in the square, I understood, if that was to understand, what had to happen now, what had to have happened then, what would have to happen at that moment, among these people, just where I had poked my nose in to upset an established order, interfering innocently in that which had not happened, but which was now going to happen, now was going to be fulfilled. And what I had imagined earlier was much less horrible than the reality, that woman, who was not there by herself, she was not caressing or propositioning or encouraging for her own pleasure, to lead the angel away with his tousled hair and play the tease with his terror and eager grace. The real boss was waiting there, smiling petulantly, already certain of the business; he was not the first to send a woman in the vanguard, to bring him the prisoners manacled with flowers. The rest of it would be so simple, the car, some house or another, drinks, stimulating engravings, tardy tears, the awakening in hell. And there was nothing I could do, this time I could do absolutely nothing. My strength had been a photograph, that, there, where they were taking their revenge on me, demonstrating clearly what was going to happen. The photo had been taken, the time had run out, gone; we were so far from one another, the abusive act had certainly already taken place, the tears already shed, and the rest conjecture and sorrow. All at once the order was inverted, they were alive, moving, they were deciding and had decided, they were going to their future; and I on this side, prisoner of another time, in a room on the fifth floor, to not know who they were, that woman, that man, and that boy, to be only the lens of my camera, something fixed, rigid, incapable of intervention. It was horrible, their mocking me, deciding it before my impotent eye, mocking me, for the boy again was looking at the flour-faced clown and I had to accept the fact that he was going to say yes, that the proposition carried money with it or a gimmick, and I couldn't yell for him to run, or even open the road to him again with a new photo, a small and almost meek intervention which would ruin the framework of drool and perfume. Everything was going to resolve itself right there, at that moment; there was like an immense silence which had nothing to do with physical silence. It was stretching it out, setting itself up. I think I screamed, I screamed terribly, and that at that exact second I realized that I was beginning to move toward them, four inches, a step, another step, the tree swung its branches rhythmically in the foreground, a place where the railing was tarnished emerged from the frame, the woman's face turned toward me as though surprised, was enlarging, and then I turned a bit, I mean that the camera turned a little, and without losing sight of the woman, I began to close in on the man who was looking at me with the black holes he had in the place of eyes, surprised and angered both, he looked, wanting to nail me onto the air, and at that instant I happened to see something like a large bird outside the focus that was flying in a single swoop in front of the picture, and I leaned up against the wall of my room and was happy because the boy had just managed to escape, I saw him running off, in focus again, sprinting with his hair flying in the wind, learning finally to fly across the island, to arrive at the footbridge, return to the city. For the second time he'd escaped them, for the second time I was helping him to escape, returning him to his precarious paradise. Out of breath, I stood in front of them; no need to step closer, the game was played out. Of the woman you could see just maybe a shoulder and a bit of the hair, brutally cut off by the frame of the picture; but the man was directly center, his mouth half open, you could see a shaking black tongue, and he lifted his hands slowly, bringing them into the foreground, an instant still in perfect focus, and then all of him a lump that blotted out the island, the tree, and I shut my eyes, I didn't want to see any more, and I covered my face and broke into tears like an idiot.

Now there's a big white cloud, as on all these days, all this untellable time. What remains to be said is always a cloud, two clouds, or long hours of a sky perfectly clear, a very clean, clear rectangle tacked up with pins on the wall of my room. That was what I saw when I opened my eyes and dried them with my fingers: the clear sky, and then a cloud that drifted in from the left, passed gracefully and slowly across and disappeared on the right. And then another, and for a change sometimes, everything gets grey, all one enormous cloud, and suddenly the splotches of rain cracking down, for a long spell you can see it raining over the picture, like a spell of weeping reversed, and little by little, the frame becomes clear, perhaps the sun comes out, and again the clouds begin to come, two at a time, three at a time. And the pigeons once in a while, and a sparrow or two.

JULIO CORTÁZAR

www *(1914–1984)* **Web**

Trained as a teacher, Cortázar moved from Argentina to France. Politically active, he contributed the prize money from one of his novels to the United Chilean Front. Cortázar is best known for his novel *Hopscotch* (1963) and the short story "Blow-Up," made into a film with the same name by Michelangelo Antonioni.

www *TOPICS FOR CRITICAL THINKING* **Web**

1. How many different times are combined in this narrative and how are they introduced?
2. In what ways is this story conscious of the process of its own writing?
3. How does this story illustrate the ways knowledge might be an illusion?
4. Does reading "Blow-Up" repeat in any way the photographer's experience?
5. What conclusions might we make about the nature of perception based on the narrator's experience?

www *TOPICS FOR CRITICAL WRITING* **Web**

1. In what ways is the narrator like the man in the car?
2. What is the role of the machine?

Italo Calvino

Translated by William Weaver

Mr. Palomar on the Beach *(1983)*

Reading a Wave

The sea is barely wrinkled, and little waves strike the sandy shore. Mr. Palomar is standing on the shore, looking at a wave. Not that he is lost in contemplation of the waves. He is not lost, because he is quite aware of what he is doing: he wants to look at a wave and he is looking at it. He is not contemplating, because for contemplation you need the right temperament, the right mood, and the right combination of exterior circumstances; and though Mr. Palomar has nothing against contemplation in principle, none of these three conditions applies to him. Finally, it is not "the waves" that he means to look at, but just one individual wave: in his desire to avoid vague sensations, he establishes for his every action a limited and precise object.

Mr. Palomar sees a wave rise in the distance, grow, approach, change form and color, fold over itself, break, vanish, and flow again. At this point he could convince himself that he has concluded the operation he had set out to achieve, and he could go away. But isolating one wave is not easy, separating it from the wave immediately following, which seems to push it and at times overtakes it and sweeps it away; and it is no easier to separate that one wave from the preceding wave, which seems to drag it toward the shore, unless it turns against the following wave, as if to arrest it. Then, if you consider the breadth of the wave, parallel to the shore, it is hard to decide where the advancing front extends regularly and where it is separated and segmented into independent waves, distinguished by their speed, shape, force, direction.

In other words, you cannot observe a wave without bearing in mind the complex features that concur in shaping it and the other, equally complex ones that the wave itself originates. These aspects vary constantly, so each wave is different from another wave, even if not immediately adjacent or successive; in other words, there are some forms and sequences that are repeated, though irregularly distributed in space and time. Since what Mr. Palomar means to do at this moment is simply *see* a wave—that is, to perceive all its simultaneous components without overlooking any of them—his gaze will dwell on the movement of the wave that strikes the shore until it can record aspects not previously perceived; as soon as he notices that the images are being repeated, he will know he has seen everything he wanted to see and he will be able to stop.

A nervous man who lives in a frenzied and congested world, Mr. Palomar tends to reduce his relations with the outside world; and, to defend himself against the general neurasthenia, he tries to keep his sensations under control insofar as possible.

The hump of the advancing wave rises more at one point than at any 5
other, and it is here that it becomes hemmed in white. If this occurs at some

distance from the shore, there is time for the foam to fold over upon itself and vanish again, as if swallowed, and at the same moment invade the whole, but this time emerging again from below, like a white carpet rising from the bank to welcome the wave that is arriving. But just when you expect that wave to roll over the carpet, you realize it is no longer wave but only carpet, and this also rapidly disappears, to become a glinting of wet sand that quickly withdraws, as if driven back by the expansion of the dry, opaque sand that moves its jagged edge forward.

At this same time, the indentations in the brow of the wave must be considered, where it splits into two wings, one stretching toward the shore from right to left and the other from left to right, and the departure point or the destination of their divergence or convergence is this negative tip, which follows the advance of the wings but is always held back, subject to their alternate overlapping until another wave, a stronger wave, overtakes it, with the same problem of divergence-convergence, and then a wave stronger still, which resolves the knot by shattering it.

Taking the pattern of the waves as model, the beach thrusts into the water some faintly hinted points, prolonged in submerged sandy shoals, shaped and destroyed by the currents at every tide. Mr. Palomar has chosen one of these low tongues of sand as his observation point, because the waves strike it on either side, obliquely, and, overrunning the half-submerged surface, they meet their opposites. So, to understand the composition of a wave, you have to consider these opposing thrusts, which are to some extent counterbalanced and to some extent added together, to produce a general shattering of thrusts and counterthrusts in the usual spreading of foam.

Mr. Palomar now tries to limit his field of observation; if he bears in mind a square zone of, say, ten meters of shore by ten meters of sea, he can carry out an inventory of all the wave movements that are repeated with varying frequency within a given time interval. The hard thing is to fix the boundaries of this zone, because if, for example, he considers as the side farthest from him the outstanding line of an advancing wave, as this line approaches him and rises it hides from his eyes everything behind it, and thus the space under examination is overturned and at the same time crushed.

In any case, Mr. Palomar does not lose heart and at each moment he thinks he has managed to see everything to be seen from his observation point, but then something always crops up that he had not borne in mind. If it were not for his impatience to reach a complete, definitive conclusion of his visual operation, looking at waves would be a very restful exercise for him and could save him from neurasthenia, heart attack, and gastric ulcer. And it could perhaps be the key to mastering the world's complexity by reducing it to its simplest mechanism.

But every attempt to define this model must take into account a long 10
wave that is arriving in a direction perpendicular to the breakers and parallel to the shore, creating the flow of a constant, barely surfacing crest. The shifts of the waves that ruffle toward the shore do not disturb the steady impulse of this compact crest that slices them at a right angle, and there is no knowing where it comes from or where it then goes. Perhaps it is a breath of east wind

that stirs the sea's surface against the deep drive that comes from the mass of water far out to sea, but this wave born of air, in passing, receives also the oblique thrusts from the water's depth and redirects them, straightening them in its own direction and bearing them along. And so the wave continues to grow and gain strength until the clash with contrary waves gradually dulls it and makes it disappear, or else twists it until it is confused in one of the many dynasties of oblique waves slammed against the shore.

Concentrating the attention on one aspect makes it leap into the foreground and occupy the square, just as, with certain drawings, you have only to close your eyes and when you open them the perspective has changed. Now, in the overlapping of crests moving in various directions, the general pattern seems broken down into sections that rise and vanish. In addition, the reflux of every wave also has a power of its own that hinders the oncoming waves. And if you concentrate your attention on these backward thrusts, it seems that the true movement is the one that begins from the shore and goes out to sea. Is this perhaps the real result that Mr. Palomar is about to achieve? To make the waves run in the opposite direction, to overturn time, to perceive the true substance of the world beyond sensory and mental habits? No, he feels a slight dizziness, but it goes no further than that. The stubbornness that drives the waves toward the shore wins the match: in fact, the waves have swelled considerably. Is the wind about to change? It would be disastrous if the image that Mr. Palomar has succeeded painstakingly in putting together were to shatter and be lost. Only if he manages to bear all the aspects in mind at once can he begin the second phase of the operation: extending this knowledge to the entire universe.

It would suffice not to lose patience, as he soon does. Mr. Palomar goes off along the beach, tense and nervous as when he came, and even more unsure about everything.

ITALO CALVINO

(1923–1984) **Web** *www*

Like many authors, Calvino moved to Paris to write. He found that the distance from his homeland made him more perceptive about his own experiences and processes of perception. Born in Italy and influenced by the work of Jorge Luis Borges, Calvino mastered the art of metafiction. He published numerous novels, including *Cosmicomics* (1968) and *If on a Winter's Night a Traveler* (1981).

TOPICS FOR CRITICAL THINKING **Web** *www*

1. What does watching the wave indicate about the reliability of perception?
2. Why is Mr. Palomar "tense and nervous" after watching the wave?
3. Is objectivity possible?
4. What aspects of this story, if any, are postmodern?

TOPIC FOR CRITICAL WRITING **Web** *www*

In what ways is the wave like writing?

MICHELLE CLIFF

The Store of a Million Items *(1998)*

As children we had our seasons, apart from growing up, growing seasons. Our own ways of dividing time, managing the elliptical motion of the Earth, life on a spinning planet. Our ways were grounded, uncelestial. Light years were beyond us; black holes not yet imagined. Our idea of matter-destroying entity was the sewer under the city, stygian, dripping, where Floridian Godzillas survived on Norwegian rats.

No, our seasons were set by the appearance of something in The Store of a Million Items, on Victory Boulevard between the Mercury Cleaners and the Mill End Shop. The store was a postwar phenomenon, promising a bounty only available in America. Everything we loved was there; there we flocked. As close to infinity as we dared.

The first Duncan yo-yo—the first to catch the eye, splendid, gold-flecked, *deluxe*, guaranteed to go around the world, without end, singing all the while—usually appeared sometime in March, brought by common carrier from the Midwest. It led the way, grand marshal of a parade of yo-yos, lined up in a corner of the store window, as less *deluxe*, less articulate yo-yos followed, right down to the 29¢ model, thick wood and flaccid kitchen string, unable to sleep or sing, promising no momentum at all. Its brand-new cherry-red face was deceptively bright, for the paint would soon enough crack, strip, even run in the rain, dyeing its master, mistress red-handed. Stamped MADE IN JAPAN, which phrase then signified nothing so much as inferiority, cheapness. The work of the un-American.

But—and this is important, the teacher stressed—you couldn't trust MADE IN USA either, for right after Hiroshima, a Japanese town had changed its name to USA (pronounced you-sah) and therefore MADE IN USA was suspect. The un-American was crafty.

"Too many people don't understand Hiroshima," Miss Clausen contin- 5
ued. "Make sure it's U-period, S-period, A-period," she cautioned.

Yet the child who couldn't afford a grander, made in U-period, S-period, A-period yo-yo (and was too chicken, or good, to lift one) would treasure even the Japanese version, determined to overcome its birthright and teach it to sleep. Fingering the wood in his pants pocket, rubbing it along the wale of her corduroy skirt, you could hear the call of the schoolyard, while the teacher's voice became white noise.

We stood in clusters on the concrete, surrounded by the whirr of yo-yos sleeping. In the shape of the world, the world on a string.

We were truly blessed, the principal assured us.

Behind the Iron Curtain were streets of empty markets, with nothing but shelf after shelf of noodles. That's what happened when people lived on handouts. Everybody had cardboard in their shoes, not just the poor kids or the kids whose parents had better use for their money. Behind the Iron Curtain they sold *Uncle Tom's Cabin*, stamped 1955, with the words "first edition" on the title page.

We knew better. 10

On August 28, 1955, Emmett Till's body was dredged from the River Pearl. But teachers weren't responsible for telling us about things that happened in summer.

Behind the Iron Curtain everything was gray—people, cities, skies. The sun didn't shine there. They were deprived of Happy Tooth, while Mr. Tooth Decay dogged their tracks, like a villain in a silent two-reeler. Even the children had false teeth, if they were lucky.

In 1956 we passed around a special edition of *Life* devoted to the Hungarian Revolution. We were about to receive a refugee classmate. Some of us were foreign-born, but he would be our first refugee. Gray tanks rumbled through streets page after page. People were squashed. For some reason the refugee went to Chicago instead.

The years moved on. Jacks. Marbles. Jump ropes. Pea shooters.

Water pistols. My personal favorite. Coming at the end of spring, the 15
verge of summer vacation, when we watched the green canvas shade, drawn down against the sun and against our eyes, drawn by the warmth of the outdoors, trained on long evenings. The shade flapped gently, but any breeze was trapped.

Black lugers. Silver derringers. Translucent ray guns. One blast and your enemy would disintegrate before your very eyes. We'd all seen *The Day the Earth Stood Still. The Thing. It Came from Outer Space.* Pods landing in a California valley.

Earth Versus the Flying Saucers.

"Will they be back, Brad?"

"Not as long as we're here, Sally."

Saturday mornings in the children's pit of the local movie house, the ma- 20
tron, whom some of us would come to remember as a stone butch, patrolled the aisles during the show. She collected water pistols at the door, those she could detect, or tried to remember the children who were likely to be armed.

We hated her with a feeling as natural as what we felt for Messala in *Ben Hur.*

"C'mon, Ben!" we cheered during the chariot race and thrilled as Ben's nemesis was dragged bloody through the sand of the Circus Maximus.

Of course some of us eluded the matron's once-over and we blasted her again and again, water running over her ducktail, droplets bouncing off her Vitalis'ed strands, soaking the nurse's uniform they dressed her in.

"Bas-tuds!" She swore at us, calling us chicken, threatening to stop the picture and raise the lights.

When the water ran out, we pelted her with Goobers and Raisinets, 25
Good-and-Plenty, and Milk Duds.

Then she brought out the heavy artillery, the ticket-taker, for one final warning: "Now, boys and girls." To which we either feigned good behavior or began a rampage, depending on whether we knew the ending of the movie or cared. We were in that dark pit gloriously leaderless. Anarchy for the most part prevailed.

In school we declared War! (what else?) on each other. The-girls-against-the-boys, the-boys-against-the-girls, ancient compound nouns, spoken in one rapid breath, running back and forth during recess, reloading our side-arms in the girls' room, the boys' room. There was a rumor a boy in 5-3 peed in his.

Even Gerald O'Brien who draped pop beads from The Store of a Million Items around his waist and pretended he was a mermaid—like Ann Blyth, he said—armed himself. Gerald wouldn't have been caught dead at the movies on Saturday morning. He said he preferred solitude, hated crowds, and watched his movies in peace on *The Early Show*, in the time between the end of school and his parents' return from work. He drank tap water from a stemmed glass he'd bought in The Store of a Million Items, into which he dropped two cocktail onions, calling himself a Gibson Girl. He would have preferred to have used his water pistol as a prop in high drama or melodrama, *The Letter* or *Deception*, the first frames of *Mildred Pierce*, the final scene of *Duel in the Sun*, not as the rest of us did, in gross displays of force.

"Boys and girls, boys and girls, hold your partner's hand," we were told, as we were marched from one place to another, to the schoolyard, gym, auditorium for assembly on Friday mornings, to the lunchroom, which always smelled of alphabet soup no matter the entree of the day.

Seated in front of a plate on which sugary Franco-American ravioli and sauce has congealed, a girl suddenly pulls a derringer from a pleat in her plaid skirt and lays waste to her lunch partner.

"Drop it!" The lunch marshal swoops into action, confiscating the gun, huge tins (fallout shelter size) of cling peaches bearing witness on a shelf behind her, SCIENTIA EST POTENTIA etched in tile above her head.

A visit to the Brooklyn Botanical Gardens, where exotica have been gathered, labeled, staked. Where armed children descend in the glass-enclosed re-creation of a tropical rain forest, heavy mist thickening with their excited breath, the City's rising humidity. We are running, tripping over metal stakes, tags identifying tree ferns, bromeliads, orchids, flesh wet with scent, the place as lush as the Hanging Gardens of Babylon, which we've memorized as one of the Seven Wonders of the Ancient World and can only imagine.

The tropics have seized us. The teachers have not seen anything like it since some seventh-graders escaped from the star show at the Hayden Planetarium and occupied the war canoe at the Museum of Natural History.

They scream for order.

"Hey, Jesse, this make you homesick for Puerto Rico?"

Does he mean the chaos or the foliage?

"Man, you don't know nothing."

"I like to be in America . . ."

The guerrillas are swarming. Thin streams from our pistols whip the mist further. We have created our own fog. A wall lies ahead of us.

Someone, off by himself, hidden, is tracing in the glass of the greenhouse: VITO WAS HERE.

The steam will dissipate, the letters disappear.

* * *

"Death doesn't make sense in summer," one girl tells another. "Last summer, when Marilyn Monroe died, I just didn't get it."

"Yeah."

"Maybe it's not summer. Maybe it is being at camp. You don't expect bad things to happen."

"Yeah."

There was a vacant lot about two blocks up the hill from school. Traces of a former structure could be detected in the ground, but what dominated the lot and drew some of us into it were several huge boulders we named the Mexican Rocks, lending the exotic, the untamed, to a common urban terrain, making it strange.

One day Gerald O'Brien is taking a shortcut from school to *The Early Show* through the vacant lot. He hears a moan, then the sound of something scraping against rock, the granite which is the bedrock of the island. He looks into the bushes. Suddenly he is afraid of what he will find. He sees the thin arm of a girl, charm bracelet dragging in the dirt. Zodiacal fishes, Eiffel Tower, Statue of Liberty, Sacred Heart, each displayed in clear plastic trays at The Store of a Million Items, are visible, beside the bulk of a man in a business suit, who is moaning. Gerald wishes he were in The Store of a Million Items right now, browsing.

Or at home, in front of his flickering images, hearing "The Syncopated Clock," heralding *The Early Show*.

"Hey, mister! Quit it, mister! Quit it!" He screams at the back of the man. "You wanna crush her?!"

The man doesn't seem to hear him.

Gerald picks up a discarded Pepsi bottle and, knowing only he wants this to stop, shuts his eyes and cracks the man on the back of the head.

"What the fuck?!"

Gerald has the man's attention. He moves back a few steps, afraid of what is coming next. "Oh, shit," the man says, under his breath, as if this were nothing.

He gets up and begins to walk away, down the hill toward the schoolyard, brushing his suit as he goes.

The girl just lies there, uncovered, her plaid skirt up, bright red stains her upper leg. Gerald is afraid to touch her. He lays his pullover over her. The wool scratches her. She starts; cries. "Stay here," he says.

"Please; don't leave me."

He sits with her until another grown-up comes by, a woman loaded down with groceries. He does his best to tell the woman what happened. He stares at the ACME stamped on her bags as he speaks.

"Why, you're a little hero," she says.

Gerald is commended at the next assembly. He never sees the girl again. No one does. She disappears down the Jersey shore with her mother and father, who pray it will not follow them. Gerald's father tries to reconcile his pansy of a son with the hero of the Mexican Rocks.

The PTA chips in and buys Gerald a glove embossed with Mickey Mantle's signature.

* * *

At The Store of a Million Items baseball gloves, cards, bats, balls, caps give way. School approaches. Marbled notebooks, Crayolas, pencil cases, rulers, erasers, compasses, protractors, things vital and unnecessary lie side by side under BACK TO SCHOOL.

Time passes. Seasons change.

Soon enough it is nearing Christmas and "Silver Bells" is piped to the sidewalk from The Store of a Million Items. We're getting in the mood. We watch as a whole window is cleared for the Flexible Flyers—surely the most beautiful name anything was ever given. They are arranged like fallen dominoes, one resting against the next, Eagle trademark echoing behind the glass.

There is a loud explosion. A huge clap over the City.

A fireball follows, rolling in the early dark of the December afternoon, above the last-minute shoppers, the schoolchildren looking to the holiday. Some of us think: "Russia," "Communism," "Sneak attack." We duck and cover and wait for the all-clear.

There is no sound.

Outside it begins to rain people. Arms and legs catch in the ailanthus, the ginkgo trees. Torsos bounce from awnings. Scraps of metal shine through the slush. Airsick bags dissolve in the streets. Samsonite jams a storm drain. It's unbelievable.

No one will forget it. Nobody doesn't talk about it. I heard this, I heard that. In the halls, on the line in the lunchroom, over trays heavy with Weissglass milk and Dinty Moore beef stew. "I seen a head rolling to the Colonial Lanes."

"You're full of it."

"My mom's a nurse. You probably wouldn't believe her neither. She said they had to put the pieces together, just so's they could bury them. There must have been millions of pieces, she said."

"I bet."

"She said you couldn't tell if they were a man or a woman, or colored neither."

That gets someone's attention.

"Isn't that a sin?"

"What?"

"To bury people all mixed up."

"I guess."

A woman on the radio says she dreamed it before it happened. "That's right. I dreamed there were sugar packets falling from the sky. Some said TWA, some said United. That's when I knew. I just didn't have the flight numbers."

"Have you had this . . ."

"Kind of experience before? You bet."

"They didn't know what hit them," is spoken all over the City as benediction.

The Store of a Million Items shifts the display of Flexible Flyers, moves the mechanical Santa bowing to passers-by, cuts off "Silver Bells," and on snow made from Ivory flakes, sets two black-shrouded model planes, assembled by the owner's grandson.

The collision, the crash, the manmade thunder and lightning, the rain of people, this was horrible enough, and then came the news that a kid had caused it.

A girl and her father are sitting at a kitchen table. The tabletop is Formica, gray with pink flamingos, covered with a striped tablecloth. The table is a gift from generous in-laws; the mother prefers the table covered. "No taste," her rationale.

The man is wearing a freshly laundered breakneck shirt, his name embroidered over his left nipple. It's his bowling night. He's taking time out to talk to his daughter.

"You know why those planes collided and all those people died?"

"No," she responds; but she does. The teacher told them during current events that morning. Finding irresistible the news that a boy playing with his transistor interfered with the planes' communication with the tower at Idlewild and BOOM!

"What does that tell us, boys and girls?"

The girl knows her father wants to be the first to tell her; so she lies, and feigns surprise as he gets to the point.

"A kid."

"I didn't know that." The woman at the sink, carefully soaping the dinner plates, comments.

"Didn't you hear me?"

"Yes, Dad."

"Well?"

"You need help, Mom?"

"Stay put, young lady."

"Okay."

"Don't 'okay' me. I want you to hear this. A kid caused the whole thing."

"How?" She plays along.

"He was playing with his transistor, that's how."

Maybe it was hearing it a second time, being weary of the adult version, the blame attached to this dead boy. Maybe it was remembering Jesse Moreno whispering in her ear, "Better he shoulda been playing with himself." But a smile was starting and she was desperate to erase it.

Too late.

"You think that's funny?"

"No, Dad."

"Well, then. That's not all. You know what happened to him?"

"No."

"He landed a few blocks from his grandparents' house in Bay Ridge. He was visiting them for the holidays."

She is biting her bottom lip, hoping to bring on tears, avoid laughter. She hates crying in front of her parents but would welcome the embarrassment right now.

Her mother only makes it worse.

"What were his grandparents?"

"Catholic." He is adamant in his knowledge of these strangers.

"From Naples, originally."
"Poor things."
"Irony is what you call that."
"Honey?"
"What?"
"If they're all dead, how come we know this?"
"Know what?"
"That the boy caused the crash."
"The papers said he confessed before he died. Said he didn't listen to the stewardess when she asked him to stop. It was in all the papers."
"Poor thing."
"What poor thing? He took all those people with him. All because he wouldn't listen."
"Imagine how his people feel."

When we went with our mothers to buy shoes, in the back of The Store of a Million Items, the shoe salesman had us stand on a pair of metal feet and we were x-rayed. They thought they saw right through us, tissue, muscle, tendon became transparent and the bones beneath the skin, the skeleton of our feet was bared, cast in negative, like the Mr. Boneses hanging in the window around Halloween time.

MICHELLE CLIFF

www *(b. 1946)* **Web**

The author of short stories, poetry, and novels, Cliff was born in Jamaica and lives in New York. Her writing retells stories of the colonized and enslaved.

www *TOPICS FOR CRITICAL THINKING* **Web**

1. How does the narrator understand the passage of time?
2. (www) In what ways does the story engage the notion of commodity culture? **Web** Does it critique such a culture?
3. In what ways does the story bring to light the increasing globalization of commerce?
4. How does this story contrast disparate items and places, and to what ends?
5. In what ways is this story postmodern?

www *TOPIC FOR CRITICAL WRITING* **Web**

Discuss the ironies of "The Store of a Million Items."

15 Metanarrative

An important part of postmodernism is the way it focuses on the processes of writing and telling. Stories that draw attention to the mechanisms of telling stories are called **metanarratives,** Web and stories about stories are called *www* **metafiction.** Metanarrative is narrative that is in some way conscious of itself as narrative. Although metanarrative certainly exists in fiction from all periods (storytellers are often concerned about the art of telling stories), it is a prominent feature of postmodern literature. This is partly because postmodern tellers no longer trust either language or story to convey meaning. Meaning (if there is any) thus resides in the act of telling itself—or in telling about the uncertainties of telling.

Metanarrative takes several forms. One form is to tell a story about telling a story, as in Rudolfo Anaya's "A Story." Joyce Carol Oates's "How I Contemplated the World from the Detroit House of Correction and Began My Life Over Again" invites the reader to become part of the storytelling process as the story presents a series of fragments in a portrait of a young writer's struggles. Salman Rushdie's short stories, "The Free Radio" and "At the Auction of the Ruby Slippers," draw attention to the act of narration; the narrator often interrupts the stories to point out his stratagems. In addition, these stories play on the power of stories in culture—how stories shape our perceptions of events, the ways we value commodities (objects we desire and purchase), and the identities we adopt. Samuel Beckett's "The Calmative" demonstrates the ways narratives are a conscious way of passing time and distracting attention; his fiction depicts the minute difficulties of making meaning in any form.

Critical Perspective: On Metanarrative

"Once reading has become a questioning, rather than a finding of thematic and discursive answers, it shows itself as coinciding with, rather than simply reflecting, the human experience of life, our basic 'reading' of the world. . . .

"By exceeding the self-reflective quality of the most sophisticated modern artifacts, Beckett's texts create the awareness of their self-reflexive (i.e., critical, not only self-reflective), procedural occurrence.

"Beckett makes us aware of this textual economy because he 'hampers' the realization of meaning, and by suspending reference, by withholding referential meanings (which are themselves the result of interpretation), connotes reading as a matter of interpretation rather than as a simple referential recognition."

—Carla Locatelli, "My Life Natural Order More or Less," in Lois Oppenheim and Marius Buning (eds.), *Beckett On and On* . . . (1996), pp. 135, 139.

In these excerpts, Carla Locatelli considers the ways Beckett's fiction both reflects on itself as fiction and invites us to reflect on the processes of reading. Suggesting that Beckett's fiction draws attention to what we do when we read, the essay argues that all reading is interpreting. It also suggests that by frustrating the reader, Beckett's fiction draws attention to the ways it reflects on itself.

RUDOLFO ANAYA

A Story

(1982)

Cast of Characters as created by the writer:
The Writer: myself
My Wife: herself
Sabrina: Grandpa's daughter
Sabrina's Husband: a foreigner
Federico: Grandpa's son
Federico's wife
Grandpa: Don Francisco Gomez
Alfredo: Grandpa's nephew
Don Cosme del Rincón: My dead uncle who wants to be a character
Others: Characters on the periphery who also want to get into the story

TIME: It is late New Year's morning.

PLACE: My writing room.

SITUATION: I am trying to cure a hangover with a dose of New Year's football games and left over, stale beer that tastes like sudsy water. I belch. Dandy Don smiles at me and reminds me the eyes of Texas are upon me. I remember a hangover remedy my uncle Cosme used to concoct when he was alive.

"Poke a hole in one side of the egg, put some salt and tabasco sauce in it, and stir it with a toothpick," he says from somewhere over my shoulder.

5 "It's not your story, uncle," I remind him and frown. He's been trying to get into a story since last week, when I remembered the story my father told me about my uncle Cosme's death. But my head is too full of cobwebs to remember the details.

"Who are you talking to?" my wife calls from upstairs.

"The TV," I answer.

"I can't write today," I mumble to myself as I drag into the kitchen. "I need another situation. Real characters. . . ." I find a nice lopsided, speckled egg in the frig, poke a hole in it, pour in salt and tabasco sauce and mix. The phone rings.

"Phone's ringing," I call to my wife, then suck at the egg. Only the hot sauce keeps me from emptying my queasy stomach.

"Damn, uncle, I don't know what's worse, the hangover or the cure. . . ." I shudder and return to my room to sit at my typewriter. My uncle smiles. The paper stares at me.

Menudo, the Breakfast of Champions, I write, is a sure cure for a hangover.

"It's Sabrina!" my wife calls. "She wants us to come over for menudo!"

Great, I think, the situation is improving. It's just what I needed, a new situation for a story. Then I remember last night's party. Slinky Sabrina kept throwing herself all over me, swearing I was the best writer she ever knew. The situation became, uh, sticky, uncomfortable. I erase quickly with Liquid Paper Correction Fluid and I shout "No!" but it's too late. MENUDO, THE BREAKFAST OF CHAMPIONS has already become **A STORY.**

"We'll be right over, Sabrina," my wife says into the phone, "as soon as we can get ready."

"I don't want to go!" I shout. Sabrina and her husband live across the street in an old, rambling adobe house. He's a foreigner, a German, I think. He's the quiet type; he likes to pierce you with his cold, analytic eyes. Sabrina grew up in my hometown, left, some say, because she got pregnant, wandered around the world and found the German. They're both okay, but what I can't stand is her family. They are the greatest liars in the world. They love to make up stories. Awful stories! I can never think when I'm around people who tell stories.

"Ready," my wife smiles.

"What happened at the party last night?"

"You should know; you were there."

Perhaps it wasn't as bad as I thought, I reassure myself. I drank one too many, I remember. We lean into the cold, January wind. It comes down like, like, a wolf on the fold. . . .

"That's awful!" my wife says.

"It's cold," I answer lamely and stumble across the road to Sabrina's house. It's a large house, and it's always full of relatives. Everyone who comes from the llano, that strange ocean of plain which keeps haunting me, stops to visit us. There's already a whiff on the llano that I'm a writer, so people poke around to see where they fit into my stories. Sabrina has many visitors because her family is large. And each one of them is an obsessive storyteller. Gaunt people with dark eyes set in deep sockets, they brood with their dark secrets. But they're lousy storytellers, I think, a bunch of liars.

"Don't talk nasty about people," my wife says over my shoulder.

I have to in order to write stories, I think. Who wants to read about saints. I remember my uncle Cosme del Rincón. What's the story he's trying to tell me? The wind moans and swirls dust. Suddenly Sabrina's house looms before us. The curtains are pulled and eyes stare at me from the windows. I have the feeling that I shouldn't have come. Perhaps I should go back and start all over.

"No," my wife says and knocks. Sabrina opens the door. She's dressed in a dark, revealing morning gown. "I'm so glad you came!" She smiles and throws her arms around me. “Happy New Year! Happy New Year!” I glance at my wife. What a character, she’s thinking.

“We’re glad we came, too,” my wife smiles. There’s a hug for her. 25

“Yes, so glad . . . come in, come in. Everything’s fine. Oh, that was a great party last night!”

“Yes, it was nice. . . .”

“Come in. . . .”

“Yes.”

We enter and Sabrina leads us to the den. It’s a dark, subterranean room. 30
Sabrina stumbles in the dark. She’s already been nipping, I think. I take off my sheepskin jacket and look around. Good place for a scene. There are shadows wandering around the dark corners of the room, lurking at the story’s edge. Sabrina reaches for two and brings them into the light.

“This is my brother, Federico, and his wife . . . they just came in from Tucumcari last night, well you know, they were at the party!”

There are greetings and abrazos for everyone as we’re introduced. I remember somewhere I wrote: . . . there’s something rotten in Tucumcari. I look closely at Federico, but I can’t remember him from anywhere. Federico looks closely at me. Sabrina’s husband serves us sherry. “Want to play a game of billiards?” he asks and stares at me.

“No, thanks.” I refuse and pick a chair where I can observe all the action. A writer always sits where he can observe the action. “Want to arm wrestle?” he asks, and I refuse again. He draws back into the shadows; I know he’ll keep his eyes on me, though. I look at Federico.

“Good party last night,” he nods, “but I think this neighborhood is going to the dogs.”

“Someone threw a rock at him last night,” his wife explains. 35

“It’s my story!” he growls at her. “I’ll tell it!” He moves dramatically to the middle of the circle. Center stage. Even the shadows that circle around us turn to listen. I nod and Federico begins his story.

“I was driving home from the party last night,” he begins. I don’t remember him from the party.

“Alone?” I ask.

“That’s what I’d like to know!” He glares at me and sips his beer. His drooping mustache glistens with droplets of beer. The dim, overhead light makes his eyes look menacing. “That rock hit my window like an explosion!” he shouts. “There was flying glass all over!”

“Did you call the police?” Sabrina asks. She sips her sherry and swings a 40
long, sleek leg for attention. I think she wants to get into the storytelling. Her husband clears his throat and leans over to whisper in my ear, “Federico thinks his wife was out with someone last night . . . he came from the party and didn’t find her home.”

“There were two cops just down the street!” Federico struggles to retain my interest in his story. “They were waiting for me! But I was drunk, so. . . .”

“Was it a real rock?” I ask.

“You should know!” he answers sharply. “It was thrown so hard it shattered the entire window! There was glass all over! It could’ve killed me,” he whispers soto voce, for dramatic emphasis, but I'm not interested. It's a dull story. I know Sabrina's kin, they're all exaggerators, liars, storytellers.

"He could've been killed!" Sabrina gasps.

"He's too mean to kill," Federico's wife snickers.

"She's got a big insurance policy on him," Sabrina whispers to my wife, "he drinks a lot. . . ."

Sabrina's husband serves more sherry. Federico stalks off for a beer. Sabrina looks at me; she wants to begin her story.

"I wrecked my car before the party," she laughs. "I was at the beauty shop, getting all dolled up for that wild party last night, when who do you suppose called me and wanted a ride?" Her legs swing with mean intent. She looks at me. Don't look at me, I think.

Federico returns and fights to keep his position at the center of the stage. "I jumped out of the truck and looked around, but it was too dark. I couldn't see anything except the two cops down the street, drinking coffee while innocent drunk people are getting their windows smashed! Oh, I got madder than hell! I'm going to go home and get my guns and kill this sonofabeech that's throwing rocks, I said to myself!" He looks at me.

"He's got a lot of guns," his wife nods at me.

"I jumped out of my chair at the beauty shop and ran to my car to pick up whoever called me!" Sabrina says. They're both working with a mystery element which keeps us listening, but the stories aren't very interesting. Soap opera, I think. Who threw the rock that bopped Federico? Who called Sabrina for a ride just before the party started? For these and more answers, tune in tomorrow for another exciting episode in AS THE SPIRIT MOVES US! Organ music. Fade out.

"I'm going home," I say. My wife agrees.

"Stay for menudo!" Sabrina insists. "Grandpa's coming soon. Stay and meet him! I know he wants to meet you. He's a great storyteller! I swear, you won't believe a word he says!"

"Is Grandpa coming?" Federico asks. He peers into the shadows.

Grandpa, Don Francisco Gomez, was in the story we began at the party last night, I remember. That's where all this started.

"Yes," Grandpa speaks from the shadows, "and I have a story to tell. . . ."

I feel goose pimples spread along my back. "Not yet, Grandpa," I say and turn to Federico. "Did you save the rock for fingerprints?" I ask.

"Yes, I saved the rock!" Federico nods and juts his face in front of mine. "I'm not dumb!" He spews beer-breath all over me. "I saved that rock, and I'm goin' to find out who threw it, an', an' in case you don't know it," he said threateningly, "there's a dead cat on the street!" He nods for emphasis and staggers a little.

"Federico ran over a cat last week," his wife explains. "Maybe that's why someone is throwing rocks at you!" Sabrina laughs. We all laugh.

"Yeah, dead pussy!" Federico exclaims.

"There's a lot of stories been told about dead pussy," Grandpa adds as he enters. "But jours is by far dee worse one I eber hear!" he says with his fake accent.

Grandpa is a small, wiry man. He wears boots, a leather jacket and a cowboy hat. There's a twinkle in his eyes that can suddenly turn into a threatening flash. I feel uncomfortable with him, but it's too late to do anything about it; he's pushed his way in. Alfredo, his nephew, follows him.

"Grandpa!" Sabrina jumps up to greet her father. "When did you get there? Never mind, we're glad you're here." She hugs him. "You're just in time for a drink, then we're going to eat menudo. . . ."

I remember that it was menudo that got me into this situation. Everyone rises to greet Grandpa. Sabrina introduces me as a writer.

65 "Don Francisco Gomez, a sus ordenes," Grandpa says and shakes my hand. I wince under the grip of a man who has chopped a lot of wood in his time. I feel the bones in my hand cracking. Grandpa looks into my eyes; he recognizes me from somewhere.

"My writing hand. . . ." I smile weakly and withdraw it from his grip.

"So jew are a righter, huh?" He smiles. He has yellow teeth stained from tobacco. He wears a red kerchief tied around his neck. When he greets my wife he bows low and says, "Enchanted, miss. . . ." He kisses her hand. A real ham, I think. But then I've met enough of Sabrina's family to know they're all like that. Now I know they got it from the old man.

"I'm glad to meet you," my wife smiles. Grandpa winks.

Federico continues with his story. He's desperate now. "I ran ober dat cat a week ago," he slurs his words. "So last night they were waiting for me, right? I killed their pussy so they wanted to get even. . . ."

70 "Federico, jew neber deed know how to tell a story. Dat dead pussy story, eet stink!" Grandpa says and moves towards center stage, threatening Federico; it's obvious Grandpa came to tell a story.

It's then that I remember Federico from the party. He came late. Stayed in a corner and drank to himself. But did he come before or after the rock-throwing incident? And was he looking for me? I look at his wife. She smiles.

"Let me tell jew a real story," Grandpa smiles, a cold glint in his eyes. He looks at me for approval. He sips his bourbon.

"Grandpa, we were talking about you last night, at the party!" Sabrina exclaims. "About the time you saw Don Cosme del Rincón murdered! Don Cosme was. . . ." She points at me but Federico interrupts.

"I know the pussy was dead. I ran over it. I whammed it myself!" he shouts. "But I don't know who that pussy belongs to. I was too drunk," he admits and looks at his wife. "Maybe I was just thinking about dead pussy. . . . but I could smell it." He shakes his head sadly. "But why did the rock hit my window at that exact spot? At that exact time?"

75 "It always happens like that," Sabrina insists. "The right situation requires the right time, that's what Grandpa always said." Grandpa nods. He's still looking at me. "Look what happened to me when I'm driving to meet my friend!" She emphasizes my friend and swings her legs. "I'm driving down Central, and I know it's very crowded at 5 o'clock, so I decide to take Lomas, and it's exactly at the moment that I decide to change streets that the other car hits me! Wham, just like that! Has that ever happened to you?" she asks.

"No," I answer. "So you never got to your friend, the one who called for a ride?"

"No," she pouts and downs the remainder of her sherry. I feel easier.

"So I decided to take the law into my own hands!" Federico continues. "I went home to get my guns."

"He's got a closet full of guns," his wife nods.

Sabrina whispers to my wife: "Federico shot a man once. He's very jealous. He came home late from work one night and found a man leaving his house, so he shot him. Turned out to be a poor telegraph boy just delivering a telegram." She laughs. My wife looks at me as if to say be careful with these characters. I shrug.

"I know who murder' Don Cosme del Rincón," Grandpa nods and begins his story. "I hab dee gun dat kill heem. . . ."

Cut the cheap theatrics, I think. Grandpa grins and drops his accent. "The first gun I ever owned was an old Smith and Wesson .38. I was just a kid, 1914, and I was herding sheep on the Rincón llano when three men who had just escaped from the Santa Fe Prison rode into our camp. . . ."

Sabrina claps her hands. "But he's from that llano, from the Rincón!" She points at me. "He's a writer! He writes stories! And Don Cosme was his uncle!"

"Ah, I thought so," Grandpa nods. The twinkle in his eyes has changed to a cold, piercing stare. "I thought I recognized you," he says, "the chin, the nose."

"Jew right books, huh?" Federico asks. He has acquired Grandpa's accent; he thinks I'm interested in the accent instead of the story.

"Yes," I say and stand to leave. "But I'm tired, I think we should leave." I look at my wife. She nods agreement. It's hard to observe a potential story if the characters know the writer is present; it causes too many interferences. The characters start acting and hamming it up, looking for a part.

"You can't go until I show you the pistol," Grandpa says sternly. "Go get the pistol, Alfredo!" he orders and Alfredo disappears into the shadows. "You know, they're writing a book about me, too," he says. His eyes bore into mine. "All those years I spent working on the llano, I saw a lot, there's a lot of stories I can tell. . . ." He turns and walks to center stage. His presence holds our attention. The room grows silent. This is the silence before the story begins, the most challenging part of the story. The silence is ominous. From it will come the words that will affect all of us. I shiver, lean forward and wait. Alfredo returns with the pistol. The small Smith and Wesson curls like a black snake into Grandpa's hand.

"Three men escaped from prison," Grandpa begins. His words hypnotize us, rivet us to our spots. I have to give Grandpa credit, when he drops the cheap theatrics he's a real story teller. There's an aura around him, as if he's infused with the spirit of the past. "One of the escaped prisoners was a Mexican nationalist, and he was shot and killed by a deputy sheriff from Pastura. That man's family later sent many sons across the border to avenge the death, and for years the llano was filled with bloodshed . . . but that's another story. The other man was a dirt farmer who didn't know his way in the llano, so there's no need to speak of him. The third man. . . ."

"The third man was the man who killed my uncle Cosme," I interrupt. I feel a cold sweat on my forehead. So this is what my uncle Cosme was trying to warn me about! That's why he keeps appearing at the edges of the story!

But what were the details of that story? I ask myself. Why am I on dangerous ground with Grandpa?

"Uncle?" I say.

My uncle Cosme struggles forward. He is a terrible sight. He has been dead for half a century. He is moldy from the grave, but I can still make out the bullet hole in his forehead. He wants to speak, he wants to warn me, but there is only a dry, raspy rattle as Grandpa pushes him back into the shadows.

"It's my story," Grandpa insists, "and I haven't finished it yet!" He has grown very strong. His knuckles are white around the pistol as he points it my way. He grins. "The third man was my brother," he says, "and he returned to kill your uncle who had stolen his woman. I was herding sheep for your uncle when they rode in. At first I didn't recognize my older brother. Then he shot Don Cosme del Rincón, and he gave me the pistol and he told me to hide it. I've kept it ever since. I needed to keep it because after that killing a war broke out on the llano. There was no mercy when the family honor was violated. Blood called for blood. . . ."

"So, you deserve what you get," Federico nods drunkenly.

I know, I think. I had been told that story a hundred times, but I had forgotten it. I thought I had left the past behind. I thought I had left the family feuds of the llano behind me, and now they had returned to trap me, perhaps to kill me. My legs feel weak. I look at Grandpa pointing the pistol at me.

"It must have been you who called," Sabrina says, "you're the only one I could tell my story to. . . ."

Over my shoulder I hear Sabrina's husband whisper, "You would have been better off playing cards with me, a simple game to pass the time. Now look at the situation you've gotten yourself into."

It was a situation I was looking for, I think. I needed a story, I needed to create a situation. I see the typewriter paper in front of me and secretly yearn to recreate the past. I wish I could undo what I have done. I look at Grandpa. I know I've created my own destruction. He's an old man, and he's still avenging the old feud. I can see blood in his narrow eyes.

"Grandpa, don't point the gun!" Federico's wife cries nervously.

"Don't, Grandpa!" Sabrina cries.

"No!" my wife shouts and jumps between Grandpa at me.

There is a profound silence; the cold wind whistles around the edges of the house. The shadows shrink back into the dark corners. Then Grandpa smiles. He tosses the small pistol at me and I catch it. "It's not loaded," he says, "I just wanted you to see it. It's a beauty, isn't it? And it did so much killing in its time. But that's over now. . . ."

Yes, I nod and look at the small, black pistol nestled in my hand, that's over now. My wife slips her arm around my waist. I look at her. Her presence is reassuring. I think she's the only one who understands what I go through with my crazy characters.

"Oh, Grandpa, you're such a joker," Federico's wife smiles.

"It's not fair to use stuff like that when you tell a story," Federico says lamely.

"Okay, enough of this nonsense, enough of this story telling!" Sabrina announces. "It's time to eat menudo! That's why all of you were invited, for a good meal of spicy menudo! And I've got hot chile and beans. . . ." She takes her husband's arm and leads us into the kitchen.

I feel my wife take my hand. "You ready to eat?" she asks.

"Yeah," I nod.

"How's the situation?" she smiles back.

"I think I've got it under control," I say. I look at Grandpa. "That was a good story," I tell him.

His eyes twinkle. "There's a lot of stories that happened on the llano," he 110
says. "I never told too many of them, but now one of my grand-daughters has gotten her college degree, and she wants to write down my stories. So why not," he chuckles.

"Hey," Federico asks as we enter the kitchen, "maybe someday you'll want to write down my story, huh? I could tell you about the time we went hunting up in the Pecos. . . ."

RUDOLFO ANAYA

(b. 1937) **Web** *www*

Rudolfo Anaya is an award-winning southwestern writer, whose work focuses on the experiences of Chicano people caught between folk culture and the changes forced by modernization and population movement. Raised in rural New Mexico, Anaya grew up in a bilingual home steeped in the traditions of Catholicism and folk medicine.

TOPICS FOR CRITICAL THINKING **Web** *www*

1. In what ways does this story make evident its status as a story?
2. What constitutes a good story in "A Story"?
3. In what ways is "A Story" an example of postmodernism?
4. In what ways is Anaya's story part of the tradition of folk storytelling?
5. How can folk tradition and postmodernism be mixed?

TOPIC FOR CRITICAL WRITING **Web** *www*

What does this story's rendition of the processes of writing a story reveal about the story "A Story"?

JOYCE CAROL OATES

How I Contemplated the World from the Detroit House of Correction and Began My Life Over Again

(1971)

Notes for an Essay for an English Class at Baldwin Country Day School; Poking Around in Debris; Disgust and Curiosity; A Revelation of the Meaning of Life; A Happy Ending . . .

I Events

1. The girl (myself) is walking through Branden's, that excellent store. Suburb of a large famous city that is a symbol for large famous American cities. The event sneaks up on the girl, who believes she is herding it along with a small fixed smile, a girl of fifteen, innocently experienced. She dawdles in a certain style by a counter of costume jewellery. Rings, earrings, necklaces. Prices from $5 to $50, all within reach. All ugly. She eases over to the glove counter, where everything is ugly too. In her close-fitted coat with its black fur collar she contemplates the luxury of Branden's, which she has known for many years: its many mild pale lights, easy on the eye and the soul, its elaborate tinkly decorations, its women shoppers with their excellent shoes and coats and hairdos, all dawdling gracefully, in no hurry.

Who was ever in a hurry here?

2. The girl seated at home. A small library, panelled walls of oak. Someone is talking to me. An earnest, husky, female voice drives itself against my ears, nervous, frightened, groping around my heart, saying, 'If you wanted gloves, why didn't you say so? Why didn't you ask for them?' That store, Branden's, is owned by Raymond Forrest who lives on Du Maurier Drive. We live on Sioux Drive. Raymond Forrest. A handsome man? An ugly man? A man of fifty or sixty, with grey hair, or a man of forty with earnest, courteous eyes, a good golf game; who is Raymond Forrest, this man who is my salvation? Father has been talking to him. Father is not his physician; Dr Berg is his physician. Father and Dr Berg refer patients to each other. There is a connection. Mother plays bridge with . . . On Mondays and Wednesdays our maid Billie works at . . . The strings draw together in a cat's cradle, making a net to save you when you fall. . . .

3. *Harriet Arnold's.* A small shop, better than Branden's. Mother in her black coat, I in my close-fitted blue coat. Shopping. Now look at this, isn't this cute, do you want this, why don't you want this, try this on, take this with you to the fitting room, take this also, what's wrong with you, what can I do for you, why are you so strange . . . ? 'I wanted to steal but not to buy,' I don't tell her. The girl droops along in her coat and gloves and leather boots, her eyes

scan the horizon, which is pastel pink and decorated like Branden's, tasteful walls and modern ceilings with graceful glimmering lights.

4. Weeks later, the girl at a bus stop. Two o'clock in the afternoon, a 5
Tuesday; obviously she has walked out of school.

5. The girl stepping down from a bus. Afternoon, weather changing to colder. Detroit. Pavement and closed-up stores; grill-work over the windows of a pawnshop. What is a pawnshop, exactly?

II Characters

1. The girl stands five feet five inches tall. An ordinary height. Baldwin Country Day School draws them up to that height. She dreams along the corridors and presses her face against the Thermoplex glass. No frost or steam can ever form on that glass. A smudge of grease from her forehead . . . could she be boiled down to grease? She wears her hair loose and long and straight in suburban teen-age style, 1968. Eyes smudged with pencil, dark brown. Brown hair. Vague green eyes. A pretty girl? An ugly girl? She sings to herself under her breath, idling in the corridor, thinking of her many secrets (the thirty dollars she once took from the purse of a friend's mother, just for fun, the basement window she smashed in her own house just for fun) and thinking of her brother who is at Susquehanna Boys' Academy, an excellent preparatory school in Maine, remembering him unclearly . . . he has long manic hair and a squeaking voice and he looks like one of the popular teenage singers of 1968, one of those in a group, *The Certain Forces*, *The Way Out*, *The Maniacs Responsible*. The girl in her turn looks like one of those fieldsful of girls who listen to the boys' singing, dreaming and mooning restlessly, breaking into high sullen laughter, innocently experienced.

2. The mother. A Midwestern woman of Detroit and suburbs. Belongs to the Detroit Athletic Club. Also the Detroit Golf Club. Also the Bloomfield Hills Country Club. The Village Women's Club at which lectures are given each winter on Genet and Sartre and James Baldwin, by the Director of the Adult Education Program at Wayne State University. . . . The Bloomfield Art Association. Also the Founders Society of the Detroit Institute of Arts. Also . . . Oh, she is in perpetual motion, this lady, hair like blown-up gold and finer than gold, hair and fingers and body of inestimable grace. Heavy weighs the gold on the back of her hairbrush and hand mirror. Heavy heavy the candlesticks in the dining room. Very heavy is the big car, a Lincoln, long and black, that on one cool autumn day split a squirrel's body in two unequal parts.

3. The father. Dr——. He belongs to the same clubs as ——2. A player of squash and golf; he has a golfer's umbrella of stripes. Candy stripes. In his mouth nothing turns to sugar, however; saliva works no miracles here. His doctoring is of the slightly sick. The sick are sent elsewhere (to Dr Berg?), the deathly sick are sent back for more tests and their bills are sent to their homes,

the unsick are sent to Dr Coronet (Isabel, a lady), an excellent psychiatrist for unsick people who angrily believe they are sick and want to do something about it. If they demand a male psychiatrist, the unsick are sent by Dr (my father) to Dr Lowenstein, a male psychiatrist, excellent and expensive, with a limited practice.

4. Clarita. She is twenty, twenty-five, she is thirty or more? Pretty, ugly, what? She is a woman lounging by the side of a road, in jeans and a sweater, hitchhiking, or she is slouched on a stool at a counter in some roadside diner. A hard line of jaw. Curious eyes. Amused eyes. Behind her eyes processions move, funeral pageants, cartoons. She says, 'I never can figure out why girls like you bum around down here. What are you looking for anyway?' An odour of tobacco about her. Unwashed underclothes, or no underclothes, unwashed skin, gritty toes, hair long and falling into strands, not recently washed.

5. Simon. In this city the weather changes abruptly, so Simon's weather changes abruptly. He sleeps through the afternoon. He sleeps through the morning. Rising, he gropes around for something to get him going, for a cigarette or a pill to drive him out to the street, where the temperature is hovering around 35°. Why doesn't it drop? Why, why doesn't the cold clean air come down from Canada; will he have to go up into Canada to get it? will he have to leave the Country of his Birth and sink into Canada's frosty fields . . . ? Will the F.B.I. (which he dreams about constantly) chase him over the Canadian border on foot, hounded out in a blizzard of broken glass and horns . . . ?

'Once I was Huckleberry Finn,' Simon says, 'but now I am Roderick Usher.' Beset by frenzies and fears, this man who makes my spine go cold, he takes green pills, yellow pills, pills of white and capsules of dark blue and green . . . he takes other things I may not mention, for what if Simon seeks me out and climbs into my girl's bedroom here in Bloomfield Hills and strangles me, what then . . . ? (As I write this I begin to shiver. Why do I shiver? I am now sixteen and sixteen is not an age for shivering.) It comes from Simon, who is always cold.

III World Events

Nothing.

IV People & Circumstances Contributing to This Delinquency

Nothing.

V Sioux Drive

George, Clyde G. 240 Sioux. A manufacturer's representative; children, a dog, a wife. Georgian with the usual columns. You think of the White House, then of Thomas Jefferson, then your mind goes blank on the white pillars and you think of nothing. Norris, Ralph W. 246 Sioux. Public relations. Colonial. Bay window, brick, stone, concrete, wood, green shutters, sidewalk, lantern, grass, trees, blacktop drive, two children, one of them my classmate Esther (Esther Norris) at Baldwin. Wife, cars. Ramsey, Michael D. 250 Sioux. Colonial. Big living room, thirty by twenty-five, fireplaces in living room, library, recreation room, panelled walls wet bar five bathrooms five bedrooms two lavatories central air conditioning automatic sprinkler automatic garage door three children one wife two cars a breakfast room a patio a large fenced lot fourteen trees a front door with a brass knocker never knocked. Next is our house. Classic contemporary. Traditional modern. Attached garage, attached Florida room, attached patio, attached pool and cabana, attached roof. A front door mail slot through which pour *Time Magazine*, *Fortune*, *Life*, *Business Week*, the *Wall Street Journal*, the *New York Times*, the *New Yorker*, the *Saturday Review*, *M.D.*, *Modern Medicine*, *Disease of the Month* . . . and also. . . . And in addition to all this, a quiet sealed letter from Baldwin saying: *Your daughter is not doing work compatible with her performance on the Stanford-Binet*. . . . And your son is not doing well, not well at all, very sad. Where is your son anyway? Once he stole trick-and-treat candy from some six-year-old kids, he himself being a robust ten. The beginning. Now your daughter steals. In the Village Pharmacy she made off with, yes she did, don't deny it, she made off with a copy of *Pageant Magazine* for no reason, she swiped a roll of Life Savers in a green wrapper and was in no need of saving her life or even in need of sucking candy; when she was no more than eight years old she stole, don't blush, she stole a package of Tums only because it was out on the counter and available, and the nice lady behind the counter (now dead) said nothing. . . . Sioux Drive. Maples, oaks, elms. Diseased elms cut down. Sioux Drive runs into Roosevelt Drive. Slow, turning lanes, not streets, all drives and lanes and ways and passes. A private police force. Quiet private police, in unmarked cars. Cruising on Saturday evenings with paternal smiles for the residents who are streaming in and out of houses, going to and from parties, a thousand parties, slightly staggering, the women in their furs alighting from automobiles bought of Ford and General Motors and Chrysler, very heavy automobiles. No foreign cars. Detroit. In 275 Sioux, down the block in that magnificent French-Normandy mansion, lives——himself, who has the C—— account itself, imagine that! Look at where he lives and look at the enormous trees and chimneys, imagine his many fireplaces, imagine his wife and children, imagine his wife's hair, imagine her fingernails, imagine her bathtub of smooth clean glowing pink, imagine their embraces, his trouser pockets filled with odd coins and keys and dust and peanuts, imagine their ecstasy on Sioux Drive, imagine their income tax returns, imagine their little boy's pride in his experimental car, a scaled-down C——, as he roars around the neighborhood on the sidewalks frightening dogs and Negro maids, oh imagine all these things, imagine everything, let your mind roar out all over Sioux Drive and Du Maurier Drive and Roosevelt Drive and Ticonderoga Pass and Burning Bush Way and Lincolnshire Pass and Lois Lane.

When spring comes, its winds blow nothing to Sioux Drive, no odours of hollyhocks or forsythia, nothing Sioux Drive doesn't already possess, everything is planted and performing. The weather vanes, had they weather vanes, don't have to turn with the wind, don't have to contend with the weather. There is no weather.

VI Detroit

There is always weather in Detroit. Detroit's temperature is always 32°. Fast-falling temperatures. Slow-rising temperatures. Wind from the north-northeast four to forty miles an hour, small-craft warnings, partly cloudy today and Wednesday changing to partly sunny through Thursday . . . small warnings of frost, soot warnings, traffic warnings, hazardous lake conditions for small craft and swimmers, restless Negro gangs, restless cloud formations, restless temperatures aching to fall out the very bottom of the thermometer or shoot up over the top and boil everything over in red mercury.

Detroit's temperature is 32°. Fast-falling temperatures. Slow-rising temperatures. Wind from the north-northeast four to forty miles an hour. . . .

VII Events

1. The girl's heart is pounding. In her pocket is a pair of gloves! In a plastic bag! Airproof breathproof plastic bag, gloves selling for twenty-five dollars on Branden's counter! In her pocket! Shoplifted! . . . In her purse is a blue comb, not very clean. In her purse is a leather billfold (a birthday present from her grandmother in Philadelphia) with snapshots of the family in clean plastic windows, in the billfold are bills, she doesn't know how many bills. . . . In her purse is an ominous note from her friend Tykie *What's this about Joe H. and the kids hanging around at Louise's Sat. night? You heard anything?* . . . passed in French class. In her purse is a lot of dirty yellow Kleenex, her mother's heart would break to see such very dirty Kleenex, and at the bottom of her purse are brown hairpins and safety pins and a broken pencil and a ballpoint pen (blue) stolen from somewhere forgotten and a purse-size compact of Cover Girl Make-Up, Ivory Rose. . . . Her lipstick is Broken Heart, a corrupt pink; her fingers are trembling like crazy; her teeth are beginning to chatter; her insides are alive; her eyes glow in her head; she is saying to her mother's astonished face *I want to steal but not to buy.*

2. At Clarita's. Day or night? What room is this? A bed, a regular bed, 20
and a mattress on the floor nearby. Wallpaper hanging in strips. Clarita says she tore it like that with her teeth. She was fighting a barbaric tribe that night, high from some pills; she was battling for her life with men wearing helmets of heavy iron and their faces no more than Christian crosses to breathe through, every one of those bastards looking like her lover Simon, who seems to breathe with great difficulty through the slits of mouth and nostrils in his face. Clarita has never heard of Sioux Drive. Raymond Forrest cuts no ice with her, nor does the C—— account and its millions; Harvard Business School could be at the corner of Vernor and 12th Street for all she cares, and Vietnam might have sunk by now into the Dead Sea under its ton of debris,

for all the amazement she could show . . . her face is overworked, overwrought, at the age of twenty (thirty?) it is already exhausted but fanciful and ready for a laugh. Clarita says mournfully to me *Honey somebody is going to turn you out let me give you warning.* In a movie shown on late television Clarita is not a mess like this but a nurse, with short neat hair and a dedicated look, in love with her doctor and her doctor's patients and their diseases, enamoured of needles and sponges and rubbing alcohol. . . . Or no: she is a private secretary. Robert Cummings is her boss. She helps him with fantastic plots, the canned audience laughs, no, the audience doesn't laugh because nothing is funny, instead her boss is Robert Taylor and they are not boss and secretary but husband and wife, she is threatened by a young starlet, she is grim, handsome, wifely, a good companion for a good man. . . . She is Claudette Colbert. Her sister too is Claudette Colbert. They are twins, identical. Her husband Charles Boyer is a very rich handsome man and her sister, Claudette Colbert, is plotting her death in order to take her place as the rich man's wife, no one will know because they are *twins*. . . . All these marvellous lives Clarita might have lived, but she fell out the bottom at the age of thirteen. At the age when I was packing my overnight case for a slumber party at Toni Deshield's she was tearing filthy sheets off a bed and scratching up a rash on her arms. . . . Thirteen is uncommonly young for a white girl in Detroit, Miss Brock of the Detroit House of Correction said in a sad newspaper interview for the *Detroit News;* fifteen and sixteen are more likely. Eleven, twelve, thirteen are not surprising in coloured . . . they are more precocious. What can we do? Taxes are rising and the tax base is falling. The temperature rises slowly but falls rapidly. Everything is falling out the bottom, Woodward Avenue is filthy, Livernois Avenue is filthy! Scraps of paper flutter in the air like pigeons, dirt flies up and hits you right in the eye, oh Detroit is breaking up into dangerous bits of newspaper and dirt, watch out. . . .

Clarita's apartment is over a restaurant. Simon her lover emerges from the cracks at dark. Mrs Olesko, a neighbour of Clarita's, an aged white wisp of a woman, doesn't complain but sniffs with contentment at Clarita's noisy life and doesn't tell the cops, hating cops, when the cops arrive. I should give more fake names, more blanks, instead of telling all these secrets. I myself am a secret; I am a minor.

3. My father reads a paper at a medical convention in Los Angeles. There he is, on the edge of the North American continent, when the unmarked detective put his hand so gently on my arm in the aisle of Branden's and said, 'Miss, would you like to step over here for a minute?'

And where was he when Clarita put her hand on my arm, that wintry dark sulphurous aching day in Detroit, in the company of closed-down barber shops, closed-down diners, closed-down movie houses, homes, windows, basements, faces . . . she put her hand on my arm and said, 'Honey, are you looking for somebody down here?'

And was he home worrying about me, gone for two weeks solid, when they carried me off . . . ? It took three of them to get me in the police cruiser, so they said, and they put more than their hands on my arm.

4. I work on this lesson. My English teacher is Mr Forest, who is from 25
Michigan State. Not handsome, Mr Forest, and his name is plain, unlike Raymond Forrest's, but he is sweet and rodentlike, he has conferred with the principal and my parents, and everything is fixed . . . treat her as if nothing has happened, a new start, begin again, only sixteen years old, what a shame, how did it happen?—nothing happened, nothing could have happened, a slight physiological modification known only to a gynecologist or to Dr Coronet. I work on my lesson. I sit in my pink room. I look around the room with my sad pink eyes. I sigh, I dawdle, I pause, I eat up time, I am limp and happy to be home, I am sixteen years old suddenly, my head hangs heavy as a pumpkin on my shoulders, and my hair has just been cut by Mr Faye at the Crystal Salon and is said to be very becoming.

(Simon too put his hand on my arm and said, 'Honey, you have got to come with me,' and in his six-by-six room we got to know each other. Would I go back to Simon again? Would I lie down with him in all that filth and craziness? Over and over again.

a Clarita is being
betrayed as in front of a Cunningham Drug Store she is nervously eying a coloured man who may or may not have money, or a nervous white boy of twenty with sideburns and an Appalachian look, who may or may not have a knife hidden in his jacket pocket, or a husky red-faced man of friendly countenance who may or may not be a member of the Vice Squad out for an early twilight walk.)

I work on my lesson for Mr Forest. I have filled up eleven pages. Words pour out of me and won't stop. I want to tell everything . . . what was the song Simon was always humming, and who was Simon's friend in a very new trench coat with an old high school graduation ring on his finger . . . ? Simon's bearded friend? When I was down too low for him, Simon kicked me out and gave me to him for three days, I think, on Fourteenth Street in Detroit, an airy room of cold cruel drafts with newspapers on the floor. . . . Do I really remember that or am I piecing it together from what they told me? Did they tell the truth? Did they know much of the truth?

VIII Characters

1. Wednesdays after school, at four; Saturday mornings at ten. Mother drives me to Dr Coronet. Ferns in the office, plastic or real, they look the same. Dr Coronet is queenly, an elegant nicotine-stained lady who would have studied with Freud had circumstances not prevented it, a bit of a Catholic, ready to offer you some mystery if your teeth will ache too much without it. Highly recommended by Father! Forty dollars an hour, Father's forty dollars! Progress! Looking up! Looking better! That new haircut is so becoming, says Dr Coronet herself, showing how normal she is for a woman with an I.Q. of 180 and many advanced degrees.

2. Mother. A lady in a brown suede coat. Boots of shiny black material, black gloves, a black fur hat. She would be humiliated could she know that of

all the people in the world it is my ex-lover Simon who walks most like her . . . self-conscious and unreal, listening to distant music, a little bowlegged with craftiness. . . .

3. Father. Tying a necktie. In a hurry. On my first evening home he put 30
his hand on my arm and said, 'Honey, we're going to forget all about this.'

4. Simon. Outside, a plane is crossing the sky, in here we're in a hurry. Morning. It must be morning. The girl is half out of her mind, whimpering and vague; Simon her dear friend is wretched this morning . . . he is wretched with morning itself . . . he forces her to give him an injection with that needle she knows is filthy, she has a dread of needles and surgical instruments and the odour of things that are to be sent into the blood, thinking somehow of her father. . . . This is a bad morning, Simon says that his mind is being twisted out of shape, and so he submits to the needle that he usually scorns and bites his lip with his yellowish teeth, his face going very pale. *Ah baby!* he says in his soft mocking voice, which with all women is a mockery of love, *do it like this—Slowly*—And the girl, terrified, almost drops the precious needle but manages to turn it up to the light from the window . . . is it an extension of herself then? She can give him this gift then? *I wish you wouldn't do this to me*, she says, wise in her terror, because it seems to her that Simon's danger—in a few minutes he may be dead—is a way of pressing her against him that is more powerful than any other embrace. She has to work over his arm, the knotted corded veins of his arm, her forehead wet with perspiration as she pushes and releases the needle, staring at that mixture of liquid now stained with Simon's bright blood. . . . When the drug hits him she can feel it herself, she feels that magic that is more than any woman can give him, striking the back of his head and making his face stretch as if with the impact of a terrible sun. . . . She tries to embrace him but he pushes her aside and stumbles to his feet. *Jesus Christ*, he says. . . .

5. Princess, a Negro girl of eighteen. What is her charge? She is closed-mouthed about it, shrewd and silent, you know that no one had to wrestle her to the sidewalk to get her in here; she came with dignity. In the recreation room she sits reading *Nancy Drew and the Jewel Box Mystery*, which inspires in her face tiny wrinkles of alarm and interest: what a face! Light brown skin, heavy shaded eyes, heavy eyelashes, a serious sinister dark brow, graceful fingers, graceful wristbones, graceful legs, lips, tongue, a sugar-sweet voice, a leggy stride more masculine than Simon's and my mother's, decked out in a dirty white blouse and dirty white slacks; vaguely nautical is Princess' style. . . . At breakfast she is in charge of clearing the table and leans over me, saying, *Honey you sure you ate enough?*

6. The girl lies sleepless, wondering. Why here, why not there? Why Bloomfield Hills and not jail? Why jail and not her pink room? Why downtown Detroit and not Sioux Drive? What is the difference? Is Simon all the difference? The girl's head is a parade of wonders. She is nearly sixteen, her breath is marvellous with wonders, not long ago she was colouring with crayons and now she is smearing the landscape with paints that won't come off

and won't come off her fingers either. She says to the matron *I am not talking about anything*, not because everyone has warned her not to talk but because, because she will not talk; because she won't say anything about Simon, who is her secret. And she says to the matron, *I won't go home*, up until that night in the lavatory when everything was changed. . . . 'No, I won't go home I want to stay here,' she says, listening to her own words with amazement, thinking that weeds might climb everywhere over that marvellous $180,000 house and dinosaurs might return to muddy the beige carpeting, but never never will she reconcile four o'clock in the morning in Detroit with eight o'clock breakfasts in Bloomfield Hills. . . . oh, she aches still for Simon's hands and his caressing breath, though he gave her little pleasure, he took everything from her (five-dollar bills, ten-dollar bills, passed into her numb hands by men and taken out of her hands by Simon) until she herself was passed into the hands of other men, police, when Simon evidently got tired of her and her hysteria. . . . *No, I won't go home, I don't want to be bailed out.* The girl thinks as a *Stubborn and Wayward Child* (one of several charges lodged against her), and the matron understands her crazy white-rimmed eyes that are seeking out some new violence that will keep her in jail, should someone threaten to let her out. Such children try to strangle the matrons, the attendants, or one another . . . they want the locks locked forever, the doors nailed shut . . . and this girl is no different up until that night her mind is changed for her. . . .

IX That Night

Princess and Dolly, a little white girl of maybe fifteen, hardy however as a sergeant and in the House of Correction for armed robbery, corner her in the lavatory at the farthest sink and the other girls look away and file out to bed, leaving her. God, how she is beaten up! Why is she beaten up? Why do they pound her, why such hatred? Princess vents all the hatred of a thousand silent Detroit winters on her body, this girl whose body belongs to me, fiercely she rides across the Midwestern plains on this girl's tender bruised body . . . revenge on the oppressed minorities of America! revenge on the slaughtered Indians! revenge on the female sex, on the male sex, revenge on Bloomfield Hills, revenge revenge. . . .

X Detroit

In Detroit, weather weighs heavily upon everyone. The sky looms large. The horizon shimmers in smoke. Downtown the buildings are imprecise in the haze. Perpetual haze. Perpetual motion inside the haze. Across the choppy river is the city of Windsor, in Canada. Part of the continent has bunched up here and is bulging outward, at the tip of Detroit; a cold hard rain is forever falling on the expressways. . . . Shoppers shop grimly, their cars are not parked in safe places, their windshields may be smashed and graceful ebony hands may drag them out through their shatterproof smashed windshields, crying, *Revenge for the Indians!* Ah, they all fear leaving Hudson's and being dragged to the very tip of the city and thrown off the parking roof of Cobo Hall, that expensive tomb, into the river. . . .

XI Characters We Are Forever Entwined With

1. Simon drew me into his tender rotting arms and breathed gravity into me. Then I came to earth, weighed down. He said, *You are such a little girl,* and he weighed me down with his delight. In the palms of his hands were teeth marks from his previous life experiences. He was thirty-five, they said. Imagine Simon in this room, in my pink room: he is about six feet tall and stoops slightly, in a feline cautious way, always thinking, always on guard, with his scuffed light suede shoes and his clothes that are anyone's clothes, slightly rumpled ordinary clothes that ordinary men might wear to not-bad jobs. Simon has fair long hair, curly hair, spent languid curls that are like . . . exactly like the curls of wood shavings to the touch, I am trying to be exact . . . and he smells of unheated mornings and coffee and too many pills coating his tongue with a faint green-white scum. . . . Dear Simon, who would be panicked in this room and in this house (right now Billie is vacuuming next door in my parents' room; a vacuum cleaner's roar is a sign of all good things), Simon who is said to have come from a home not much different from this, years ago, fleeing all the carpeting and the polished banisters . . . Simon has a deathly face, only desperate people fall in love with it. His face is bony and cautious, the bones of his cheeks prominent as if with the rigidity of his ceaseless thinking, plotting, for he has to make money out of girls to whom money means nothing, they're so far gone they can hardly count it, and in a sense money means nothing to him either except as a way of keeping on with his life. *Each Day's Proud Struggle,* the title of a novel we could read at jail. . . . Each day he needs a certain amount of money. He devours it. It wasn't love he uncoiled in me with his hollowed-out eyes and his courteous smile, that remnant of a prosperous past, but a dark terror that needed to press itself flat against him, or against another man . . . but he was the first, he came over to me and took my arm, a claim. We struggled on the stairs and I said, *Let me loose, you're hurting my neck, my face,* it was such a surprise that my skin hurt where he rubbed it, and afterward we lay face to face and he breathed everything into me. In the end I think he turned me in.

2. Raymond Forrest. I just read this morning that Raymond Forrest's father, the chairman of the board at , died of a heart attack on a plane bound for London. I would like to write Raymond Forrest a note of sympathy. I would like to thank him for not pressing charges against me one hundred years ago, saving me, being so generous . . . well, men like Raymond Forrest are generous men, not like Simon. I would like to write him a letter telling of my love, or of some other emotion that is positive and healthy. Not like Simon and his poetry, which he scrawled down when he was high and never changed a word . . . but when I try to think of something to say, it is Simon's language that comes back to me, caught in my head like a bad song, it is always Simon's language:

> There is no reality only dreams
> Your neck may get snapped when you wake

My love is drawn to some violent end
She keeps wanting to get away
My love is heading downward
And I am heading upward
She is going to crash on the sidewalk
And I am going to dissolve into the clouds

XII Events

1. Out of the hospital, bruised and saddened and converted, with Princess' grunts still tangled in my hair . . . and Father in his overcoat looking like a prince himself, come to carry me off. Up the expressway and out north to home. Jesus Christ, but the air is thinner and cleaner here. Monumental houses. Heartbreaking sidewalks, so clean.

2. Weeping in the living room. The ceiling is two stories high and two chandeliers hang from it. Weeping, weeping, though Billie the maid is *probably listening.* I will never leave home again. Never. Never leave home. Never leave this home again, never.

3. Sugar doughnuts for breakfast. The toaster is very shiny and my face is distorted in it. Is that my face?

4. The car is turning in the driveway. Father brings me home. Mother embraces me. Sunlight breaks in movieland patches on the roof of our traditional-contemporary home, which was designed for the famous automotive stylist whose identity, if I told you the name of the famous car he designed, you would all know, so I can't tell you because my teeth chatter at the thought of being sued . . . or having someone climb into my bedroom window with a rope to strangle me. . . . The car turns up the blacktop drive. The house opens to me like a doll's house, so lovely in the sunlight, the big living room beckons to me with its walls falling away in a delirium of joy at my return, Billie the maid is *no doubt* listening from the kitchen as I burst into tears and the hysteria Simon got so sick of. Convulsed in Father's arms, I say I will never leave again, never, why did I leave, where did I go, what happened, my mind is gone wrong, my body is one big bruise, my backbone was sucked dry, it wasn't the men who hurt me and Simon never hurt me but only those girls . . . my God, how they hurt me . . . I will never leave home again. . . . The car is perpetually turning up the drive and I am perpetually taking the right exit from the expressway (Lahser Road) and the wall of the rest room is perpetually banging against my head and perpetually are Simon's hands moving across my body and adding everything up and so too are Father's hands on my shaking bruised back, far from the surface of my skin on the surface of my good blue cashmere coat (dry-cleaned for my release). . . . I weep for all the money here, for God in gold and beige carpeting, for the beauty of chandeliers and the miracle of a clean polished gleaming toaster and faucets that run

both hot and cold water, and I tell them, *I will never leave home, this is my home, I love everything here, I am in love with everything here. . . .*

I am home.

JOYCE CAROL OATES

(b. 1938) **Web** *www*

A prolific portrayer of contemporary American life, Oates is the author of more than forty novels. Oates's work details realistic portraits of human nature within the specific environments produced by rapid social change. She currently teaches at Princeton University.

TOPICS FOR CRITICAL THINKING **Web** *www*

1. Assemble a chronological narrative from the pieces the narrator has provided.
2. What are the effects of breaking the story into its various elements?
3. Is this story an example of metafiction? Of metanarrative? In what ways?
4. Is there any relation between the narrator's fragmentation of experience and the nature and quality of her experience?
5. What commentary does this story make on suburbia?

TOPIC FOR CRITICAL WRITING **Web** *www*

In what ways does this story bring larger metanarratives underwriting American culture into question?

SAMUEL BECKETT

The Calmative

(1967)

I don't know when I died. It always seemed to me I died old, about ninety years old, and what years, and that my body bore it out, from head to foot. But this evening, alone in my icy bed, I have the feeling I'll be older than the day, the night, when the sky with all its lights fell upon me, the same I had so often gazed on since my first stumblings on the distant earth. For I'm too frightened this evening to listen to myself rot, waiting for the great red lapses of the heart, the tearings at the caecal walls, and for the slow killings to finish in my skull, the assaults on unshakable pillars, the fornications with corpses. So I'll tell myself a story, I'll try and tell myself another story, to try and calm myself, and it's there I feel I'll be old, old, even older than the day I fell, calling for help, and it came. Or is it possible that in this story I have come back to life, after my death? No, it's not like me to come back to life, after my death.

What possessed me to stir when I wasn't with anybody? Was I being thrown out? No, I wasn't with anybody. I see a kind of den littered with empty tins. And yet we are not in the country. Perhaps it's just ruins, a ruined folly, on the skirts of the town, in a field, for the fields come right up to our walls, their walls, and the cows lie down at night in the lee of the ramparts. I have changed refuge so often, in the course of my rout, that now I can't tell between dens and ruins. But there was never any city but the one. It is true you often move along in a dream, houses and factories darken the air, trams go by, and under your feet wet from the grass there are suddenly cobbles. I only know the city of my childhood, I must have seen the other, but unbelieving. All I say cancels out, I'll have said nothing. Was I hungry itself? Did the weather tempt me? It was cloudy and cool, I insist, but not to the extent of luring me out. I couldn't get up at the first attempt, nor let us say at the second, and once up, propped against the wall, I wondered if I could go on, I mean up, propped against the wall. Impossible to go out and walk. I speak as though it all happened yesterday. Yesterday indeed is recent, but not enough. For what I tell this evening is passing this evening, at this passing hour. I'm no longer with these assassins, in this bed of terror, but in my distant refuge, my hands twined together, my head bowed, weak, breathless, calm, free, and older than I'll have ever been, if my calculations are correct. I'll tell my story in the past none the less, as though it were a myth, or an old fable, for this evening I need another age, that age to become another age in which I became what I was.

But little by little I got myself out and started walking with short steps among the trees, oh look, trees! The paths of other days were rank with tangled growth. I leaned against the trunks to get my breath and pulled myself forward with the help of boughs. Of my last passage no trace remained. They were the perishing oaks immortalized by d'Aubigné. It was only a grove. The fringe was near, a light less green and kind of tattered told me so, in a whisper. Yes, no matter where you stood, in this little wood, and were it in the furthest recess of its poor secrecies, you saw on every hand the gleam of this pale light, promise of God knows what fatuous eternity. Die without too much pain, a little, that's worth your while. Under the blind sky close with your own hands the eyes soon sockets, then quick into carrion not to mislead the crows. That's the advantage of death by drowning, one of the advantages, the crabs never get there too soon. But here a strange thing, I was no sooner free of the wood at last, having crossed unminding the ditch that girdles it, than thoughts came to me of cruelty, the kind that smiles. A lush pasture lay before me, nonsuch perhaps, who cares, drenched in evening dew or recent rain. Beyond this meadow to my certain knowledge a path, then a field and finally the ramparts, closing the prospect. Cyclopean and crenellated, standing out faintly against a sky scarcely less sombre, they did not seem in ruins, viewed from mine, but were, to my certain knowledge. Such was the scene offered to me, in vain, for I knew it well and loathed it. What I saw was a bald man in a brown suit, a comedian. He was telling a funny story about a fiasco. Its point escaped me. He used the word snail, or slug, to the delight of all present. The women seemed even more entertained than their escorts, if that were possible. Their shrill laughter pierced the clapping and, when this had subsided, broke out still here and there in sudden peals even after the next story had begun, so that part of it was lost. Perhaps they had in mind the reigning penis sitting who knows by their side and from that sweet shore launched their cries of joy towards the comic vast, what a talent. But it's to me this evening something has to happen, to my body as in myth and metamorphosis, this old body to which nothing ever happened, or so little, which never met with anything, loved anything, wished for anything, in its tarnished universe, except for the mirrors to shatter, the plane, the curved, the magnifying, the minifying, and to vanish in the havoc of its images. Yes, this evening it has to be as in the story my father used to read to me, evening after evening, when I was small, and he had all his health, to calm me, evening after evening, year after year it seems to me this evening, which I don't remember much about, except that it was the adventure of one Joe Breem, or Breen, the son of a lighthouse-keeper, a strong muscular lad of fifteen, those were the words, who swam for miles in the night, a knife between his teeth, after a shark, I forget why, out of sheer heroism. He might have simply told me the story, he knew it by heart, so did I, but that wouldn't have calmed me, he had to read it to me, evening after evening, or pretend to read it to me, turning the pages and explaining the pictures that were of me already, evening after evening the same pictures, till I dozed off on his shoulder. If he had skipped a single word I would have hit him, with my little fist, in his big belly bursting out of the old cardigan and unbuttoned trousers that rested him from his office canonicals. For me now the setting forth, the struggle and perhaps the return, for the old man I am this evening, older than my father ever was, older than I shall ever be. I crossed the meadow with little stiff steps at the same time limp, the best I could manage. Of my last passage no trace remained, it was long ago. And the little bruised stems soon straighten up again, having need of air and light, and as for the broken their place is soon taken. I entered the town by what they call the Shepherds' Gate without having seen a soul, only the first bats like flying crucifixions, nor heard a sound except my steps, my heart in my breast and then, as I went under the arch, the hoot of an owl, that cry at once so soft and fierce which in the night, calling, answering, through my little wood and those nearby, sounded in my shelter like a tocsin. The further I went into the city the more I was struck by its deserted air. It was lit as usual, brighter than usual, although the shops were shut. But the lights were on in their windows with the object no doubt of attracting customers and prompting them to say, I say, I like that, not dear either, I'll come back tomorrow, if I'm still alive. I nearly said, Good God it's Sunday. The trams were running, the buses too, but few, slow, empty, noiseless, as if under water. I didn't see a single horse! I was wearing my long green greatcoat with the velvet collar, such as motorists wore about 1900, my father's, but that day it was sleeveless, a vast cloak. But on me it was still the same great dead weight, with no warmth to it, and the tails swept the ground, scraped it rather, they had grown so stiff, and I so shrunken. What would, what could happen to me in this empty place? But I felt the houses packed with people, lurking behind the curtains they looked out into the street or, crouched far back in the depths of the room, head in hands, were sunk in dream. Up aloft my hat, the same as always, I reached no further. I went right across the city and came to the sea, having followed the river to its mouth. I kept saying, I'll go back, unbelieving. The boats at anchor in the harbour, tied up to the jetty, seemed no less numerous than usual, as if I knew anything about what was usual. But the quays were deserted and there was no sign or stir of arrival or departure. But all might change from one moment to the next and be transformed like magic before my eyes. Then all the bustle of the people and things of the sea, the masts of the big craft gravely rocking and of the small more jauntily, I insist, and I'd hear the gulls' terrible cry and perhaps the sailors' cry. And I might slip unnoticed aboard a freighter outward bound and get far away and spend far away a few good months, perhaps even a year or two, in the sun, in peace, before I died. And without going that far it would be a sad state of affairs if in that unscandalizable throng I couldn't achieve a little encounter that would calm me a little, or exchange a few words with a navigator for example, words to carry away with me to my refuge, to add to my collection. I waited sitting on a kind of topless capstan, saying, The very capstans this evening are out of order. And I gazed out to sea, out beyond the breakwaters, without sighting the least vessel. I could see lights flush with the water. And the pretty beacons at the harbour mouth I could see too, and others in the distance, flashing from the coast, the islands, the headlands. But seeing still no sign or stir I made ready to go, to turn away sadly from this dead haven, for there are scenes that call for strange farewells. I had merely to bow my head and look down at my feet, for it is in this attitude I always drew the strength to, how shall I say, I don't know, and it was always from the earth, rather than from the sky, notwithstanding its reputation, that my help came in time of trouble. And there, on the flagstone, which I was not focussing, for why focus it, I saw haven afar, where the black swell was most perilous, and all about me storm and wreck. I'll never come back here, I said. But when with a thrust of both hands against the rim of the capstan I heaved myself up I found facing me a young boy holding a goat by a horn. I sat down again. He stood there silent looking at me without visible fear or revulsion. Admittedly the light was poor. His silence seemed natural to me, it befitted me as the elder to speak first. He was barefoot and in rags. Haunter of the waterfront he had stepped aside to see what the dark hulk could be abandoned on the quayside. Such was my train of thought. Close up to me now with his little guttersnipe's eye there could be no doubt left in his mind. And yet he stayed. Can this base thought be mine? Moved, for after all that is what I must have come out for, in a way, and with little expectation of advantage from what might follow, I resolved to speak to him. So I marshalled the words and opened my mouth, thinking I would hear them. But all I heard was a kind of rattle, unintelligible even to me who knew what was intended. But it was nothing, mere speechlessness due to long silence, as in the wood that darkens the mouth of hell, do you remember, I only just. Without letting go of his goat he moved right up against me and offered me a sweet out of a twist of paper such as you could buy for a penny. I hadn't been offered a sweet for eighty years at least, but I took it eagerly and put it in my mouth, the old gesture came back to me, more and more moved since that is what I wanted. The sweets were stuck together and I had my work cut out to separate the top one, a green one, from the others, but he helped me and his hand brushed mine. And a moment later as he made to move away, hauling his goat after him, with a great gesticulation of my whole body I motioned him to stay and I said, in an impetuous murmur, Where are you off to, my little man, with your nanny? The words were hardly out of my mouth when for shame I covered my face. And yet they were the same I had tried to utter but a moment before. Where are you off to, my little man, with your nanny! If I could have blushed I would have, but there was not enough blood left in my extremities. If I had had a penny in my pocket I would have given it to him, for him to forgive me, but I did not have a penny in my pocket, nor anything resembling it. Nothing that could give pleasure to a little unfortunate at the mouth of life. I suspect I had nothing with me but my stone, that day, having gone out as it were without premeditation. Of his little person I was fated to see no more than the black curly hair and the pretty curve of the long bare legs all muscle and dirt. And the hand, so fresh and keen, I would not forget in a hurry either. I looked for better words to say to him, I found them too late, he was gone, oh not far, but far. Out of my life too he went without a care, not one of his thoughts would ever be for me again, unless perhaps when he was old and, delving in his boyhood, would come upon that gallows night and hold the goat by the horn again and linger again a moment by my side, with who knows perhaps a touch of tenderness, even of envy, but I have my doubts. Poor dear dumb beasts, how you will have helped me. What does your daddy do? that's what I would have said to him if he had given me the chance. Soon they were no more than a single blur which if I hadn't known I might have taken for a young centaur. I was nearly going to have the goat dung, then pick up a handful of the pellets so soon cold and hard, sniff and even taste them, no, that would not help me this evening. I say this evening as if it were always the same evening, but are there two evenings? I went, intending to get back as fast as I could, but it would not be quite empty-handed, repeating, I'll never come back here. My legs were paining me, every step would gladly have been the last, but the glances I darted towards the windows, stealthily, showed me a great cylinder sweeping past as though on rollers on the asphalt. I must indeed have been moving fast, for I overhauled more than one pedestrian, there are the first men, without extending myself, I who in the normal way was left standing by cripples, and then I seemed to hear the footfalls die behind me. And yet each little step would gladly have been the last. So much so that when I emerged on a square I hadn't noticed on the way out, with a cathedral looming on the far side, I decided to go in, if it was open, and hide, as in the Middle Ages, for a space. I say cathedral, it may not have been, I don't know, all I know is it would vex me in this story that aspires to be the last, to have taken refuge in a common church. I remarked the Saxon Stützenwechsel. Charming effect, but it didn't charm me. The brilliantly lit nave appeared deserted. I walked round it several times without seeing a soul. They were hiding perhaps, under the choirstalls, or dodging behind the pillars, like woodpeckers. Suddenly close to where I was, and without my having heard the long preliminary rumblings, the organ began to boom. I sprang up from the mat on which I lay before the altar and hastened to the far end of the nave as if on my way out. But it was a side aisle and the door I disappeared through was not the exit. For instead of being restored to the night I found myself at the foot of a spiral staircase which I began to climb at top speed, mindless of my heart, like one hotly pursued by a homicidal maniac. This staircase faintly lit by I know not what means, slits perhaps, I mounted panting as far as the projecting gallery in which it culminated and which, separated from the void by a cynical parapet, encompassed a smooth round wall capped by a little dome covered with lead or verdigrised copper, phew, if that's not clear. People must have come here for the view, those who fall die on the way. Flattening myself against the wall I started round, clockwise. But I had hardly gone a few steps when I met a man revolving in the other direction, with the utmost circumspection. How I'd love to push him, or him to push me, over the edge. He gazed at me wild-eyed for a moment and then, not daring to pass me on the parapet side and surmising correctly that I would not relinquish the wall just to oblige him, abruptly turned his back on me, his head rather, for his back remained glued to the wall, and went back the way he had come so that soon there was nothing left of him but a left hand. It lingered a moment, then slid out of sight. All that remained to me was the vision of two burning eyes starting out of their sockets under a check cap. Into what nightmare thingness am I fallen? My hat flew off, but did not get far thanks to the string. I turned my head towards the staircase and lent an eye. Nothing. Then a little girl came into view followed by a man holding her by the hand, both pressed against the wall. He pushed her into the stairway, disappeared after her, turned and raised towards me a face that made me recoil. I could only see his bare head above the top step. When they were gone I called. I completed in haste the round of the gallery. No one. I saw on the horizon, where sky, sea, plain and mountain meet, a few low stars, not to be confused with the fires men light, at night, or that go alight alone. Enough. Back in the street I tried to find my way in the sky, where I knew the Bears so well. If I had seen someone I would have stopped him to ask, the most ferocious aspect would not have daunted me. I would have said, touching my hat, Pardon me your honour, the Shepherds' Gate for the love of God. I thought I could go no further, but no sooner had the impetus reached my legs than on I went, believe it or not, at a very fair pace. I wasn't returning empty-handed, not quite, I was taking back with me the virtual certainty that I was still of this world, of that world too, in a way. But I was paying the price. I would have done better to spend the night in the cathedral, on the mat before the altar, I would have continued on my way at first light, or they would have found me stretched out in the rigor of death, the genuine bodily article, under the blue eyes fount of so much hope, and put me in the evening papers. But suddenly I was descending a wide street, vaguely familiar, but in which I could never have set foot, in my lifetime. But soon realizing I was going downhill I turned about and set off in the other direction. For I was afraid if I went downhill of returning to the sea where I had sworn never to return. When I say I turned about I mean I wheeled round in a wide semi-circle without slowing down, for I was afraid if I stopped of not being able to start again, yes, I was afraid of that too. And this evening too I dare not stop. I was struck more and more by the contrast between the brightly lit streets and their deserted air. To say it distressed me, no, but I say it all the same, in the hope of calming myself. To say there was no one abroad, no, I would not go that far, for I remarked a number of shapes, male and female, strange shapes, but not more so than usual. As to what hour it might have been I had no idea, except that it must have been some hour of the night. But it might have been three or four in the morning just as it might have been ten or eleven in the evening, depending no doubt on whether one wondered at the scarcity of passers-by or at the extraordinary radiance shed by the street-lamps and traffic-lights. For at one or other of these no one could fail to wonder, unless he was out of his mind. Not a single private car, but admittedly from time to time a public vehicle, slow sweep of light silent and empty. It is not my wish to labour these antinomies, for we are needless to say in a skull, but I have no choice but to add the following few remarks. All the mortals I saw were alone and as if sunk in themselves. It must be a common sight, but mixed with something else I imagine. The only couple was two men grappling, their legs intertwined. I only saw one cyclist! He was going the same way as I was. All were going the same way as I was, vehicles too, I have only just realized it. He was pedalling slowly in the middle of the street, reading a newspaper which he held with both hands spread open before his eyes. Every now and then he rang his bell without interrupting his reading. I watched him recede till he was no more than a dot on the horizon. Suddenly a young woman perhaps of easy virtue, dishevelled and her dress in disarray, darted across the street like a rabbit. That is all I had to add. But here a strange thing, yet another, I had no pain whatever, not even in my legs. Weakness. A good night's nightmare and a tin of sardines would restore my sensitivity. My shadow, one of my shadows, flew before me, dwindled, slid under my feet, trailed behind me the way shadows will. This degree of opacity appeared to me conclusive. But suddenly ahead of me a man on the same side of the street and going the same way, to keep harping on the same thing lest I forget. The distance between us was considerable, seventy paces at least, and fearing he might escape me I quickened my step with the result I swept forward as if on rollers. This is not me, I said, let us make the most of it. Finding myself in an instant a bare ten paces in his rear I slowed down so as not to burst in on him and so heighten the aversion my person inspired even in its most abject and obsequious attitudes. And a moment later, keeping humbly in step with him, Excuse me your honour, the Shepherds' Gate for the love of God! At close quarters he appeared normal apart from that air already noted of ebbing inward. I drew a few steps ahead, turned, cringed, touched my hat and said, The right time for mercy's sake! I might as well not have existed. But what about the sweet? A light! I cried. Given my need of help I can't think why I did not bar his path. I couldn't have, that's all, I couldn't have touched him. Seeing a stone seat by the kerb I sat down and crossed my legs, like Walther. I must have dozed off, for the next thing was a man sitting beside me. I was still taking him in when he opened his eyes and set them on me, as if for the first time, for he shrank back unaffectedly. Where did you spring from? he said. To hear myself addressed again so soon impressed me greatly. What's the matter with you? he said. I tried to look like one with whom that only is the matter which is native to him. Forgive me your honour, I said, gingerly lifting my hat and rising a fraction from the seat, the right time for the love of God! He said a time, I don't remember which, a time that explained nothing, that's all I remember, and did not calm me. But what time could have done that? Oh I know, I know, one will come that will. But in the meantime? What's that you said? he said. Unfortunately I had said nothing. But I wriggled out of it by asking him if he could help me find my way which I had lost. No, he said, for I am not from these parts and if I am sitting on this slab it is because the hotels were full or would not let me in, I have no opinion. But tell me the story of your life, then we'll see. My life! I cried. Why yes, he said, you know, that kind of—what shall I say? He brooded for a time, no doubt trying to think of what life could well be said to be a kind. In the end he went on, testily, Come now, everyone knows that. He jogged me in the ribs. No details, he said, the main drift, the main drift. But as I remained silent he said, Shall I tell you mine, then you'll see what I mean. The account he then gave was brief and dense, facts, without comment. That's what I call a life, he said, do you follow me now? It wasn't bad, his story, positively fairy-like in places. But that Pauline, I said, are you still with her? I am, he said, but I'm going to leave her and set up with another, younger and plumper. You travel a lot, I said. Oh widely, widely, he said. Words were coming back to me, and the way to make them sound. All that's a thing of the past for you no doubt, he said. Do you think of spending some time among us? I said. This sentence struck me as particularly well turned. If it's not a rude question, he said, how old are you? I don't know, I said. You don't know! he cried. Not exactly, I said. Are thighs much in your thoughts, he said, arses, cunts and environs. I didn't follow. No more erections naturally, he said. Erections? I said. The penis, he said, you know what the penis is, there, between the legs. Ah that, I said. It thickens, lengthens, stiffens and rises, he said, does it not? I assented, though they were not the terms I would have used. That is what we call an erection, he said. He pondered, then exclaimed, Phenomenal! No? Strange right enough, I said. And there you have it all, he said. But what will become of her? I said. Who? he said. Pauline, I said. She will grow old, he said with tranquil assurance, slowly at first, then faster and faster, in pain and bitterness, pulling the devil by the tail. The face was not full, but I eyed it in vain, it remained clothed in its flesh instead of turning all chalky and channelled as with a gouge. The very vomer kept its cushion. It is true discussion was always bad for me. I longed for the tender nonsuch, I would have trodden it gently, with my boots in my hand, and for the shade of my wood, far from this terrible light. What are you grinning and bearing? he said. He held on his knees a big black bag, like a midwife's I imagine. It was full of glittering phials. I asked him if they were all alike. Oho no, he said, for every taste. He took one and held it out to me, saying, One and six. What did he want? To sell it to me? Proceeding on this hypothesis I told him I had no money. No money! he cried. All of a sudden his hand came down on the back of my neck, his sinewy fingers closed and with a jerk and a twist he had me up against him. But instead of dispatching me he began to murmur words so sweet that I went limp and my head fell forward in his lap. Between the caressing voice and the fingers rowelling my neck the contrast was striking. But gradually the two things merged in a devastating hope, if I dare say so, and I dare. For this evening I have nothing to lose that I can discern. And if I have reached this point (in my story) without anything having changed, for if anything had changed I think I'd know, the fact remains I have reached it, and that's something, and with nothing changed, and that's something too. It's no excuse for rushing matters. No, it must cease gently, as gently cease on the stairs the steps of the loved one, who could not love and will not come back, and whose steps say so, that she could not love and will not come back. He suddenly shoved me away and showed me the phial again. There you have it all, he said. It can't have been the same all as before. Want it? he said. No, but I said yes, so as not to vex him. He proposed an exchange. Give me your hat, he said. I refused. What vehemence! he said. I haven't a thing, I said. Try in your pockets, he said. I haven't a thing, I said, I came out without a thing. Give me a lace, he said. I refused. Long silence. And if you gave me a kiss, he said finally. I knew there were kisses in the air. Can you take off your hat? he said. I took it off. Put it back, he said, you look nicer with it on. I put it on. Come on, he said, give me a kiss and let there be an end to it. Did it not occur to him I might turn him down? No, a kiss is not a bootlace, he must have seen from my face that all passion was not quite spent. Come, he said. I wiped my mouth in its tod of hair and advanced it towards his. Just a moment, he said. My mouth stood still. You know what a kiss is? he said. Yes yes, I said? If it's not a rude question, he said, when was your last? Some time ago, I said, but I can still do them. He took off his hat, a bowler, and tapped the middle of his forehead. There, he said, and there only. He had a noble brow, white and high. He leaned forward, closing his eyes. Quick, he said? I pursed up my lips as mother had taught me and brought them down where he had said. Enough, he said. He raised his hand towards the spot, but left the gesture unfinished and put on his hat. I turned away and looked across the street. It was then I noticed we were sitting opposite a horse-butcher's. Here, he said, take it. I had forgotten. He rose. Standing he was quite short. One good turn, he said, with radiant smile. His teeth shone. I listened to his steps die away. How tell what remains. But it's the end. Or have I been dreaming, am I dreaming? No, no, none of that, for dream is nothing, a joke, and significant what is worse. I said, Stay where you are till day breaks, wait sleeping till the lamps go out and the streets come to life. But I stood up and moved off. My pains were back, but with something untoward which prevented my wrapping them round me. But I said, Little by little you are coming to. From my gait alone, slow, stiff and which seemed at every step to solve a statodynamic problem never posed before, I would have been known again, if I had been known. I crossed over and stopped before the butcher's. Behind the grille the curtains were drawn, rough canvas curtains striped blue and white, colours of the Virgin, and stained with great pink stains. They did not quite meet in the middle, and through the chink I could make out the dim carcasses of the gutted horses hanging from hooks head downwards. I hugged the walls, famished for shadow. To think that in a moment all will be said, all to do again. And the city clocks, what was wrong with them, whose great chill clang even in my wood fell on me from the air? What else? Ah yes, my spoils. I tried to think of Pauline, but she eluded me, gleamed an instant and was gone, like the young woman in the street. So I went in the atrocious brightness, buried in my old flesh, straining towards an issue and passing them by to left and right, and my mind panting after this and that and always flung back to where there was nothing. I succeeded however in fastening briefly on the little girl, long enough to see her a little more clearly than before, so that she wore a kind of bonnet and clasped in her hand a book, of common prayer perhaps, and to try and have her smile, but she did not smile, but vanished down the staircase without having yielded me her little face. I had to stop. At first nothing, then little by little, I mean rising up out of the silence till suddenly no higher, a kind of massive murmur coming perhaps from the house that was propping me up. That reminded me that the houses were full of people, besieged, no, I don't know. When I stepped back to look at the windows I could see, in spite of shutters, blinds and muslins, that many of the rooms were lit. The light was so dimmed by the brilliancy flooding the boulevard that short of knowing or suspecting it was not so one might have supposed everyone sleeping. The sound was not continuous, but broken by silences possibly of consternation. I thought of ringing at the door and asking for shelter and protection till morning. But suddenly I was on my way again. But little by little, in a slow swoon, darkness fell about me. I saw a mass of bright flowers fade in an exquisite cascade of paling colours. I found myself admiring, all along the housefronts, the gradual blossoming of squares and rectangles, casement and sash, yellow, green, pink, according to the curtains and blinds, finding that pretty. Then at last, before I fell, first to my knees, as cattle do, then on my face, I was in a throng. I didn't lose consciousness, when I lose consciousness it will not be to recover it. They paid no heed to me, though careful not to walk on me, a courtesy that must have touched me, it was what I had come out for. It was well with me, sated with dark and calm, lying at the feet of mortals, fathom deep in the grey of dawn, if it was dawn. But reality, too tired to look for the right word, was soon restored, the throng fell away, the light came back and I had no need to raise my head from the ground to know I was back in the same blinding void as before. I said, Stay where you are, down on the friendly stone, or at least indifferent, don't open your eyes, wait for morning. But up with me again and back on the way that was not mine, on uphill along the boulevard. A blessing he was not waiting for me, poor old Breem, or Breen. I said, The sea is east, it's west I must go, to the left of north. But in vain I raised without hope my eyes to the sky to look for the Bears. For the light I steeped in put out the stars, assuming they were there, which I doubted, remembering the clouds.

Samuel Beckett

www

(1906–1989) **Web**

Nobel Prize-winning author of such plays as *Waiting for Godot* and *Krapp's Last Tape,* Beckett is known for his minimalist style, innovative use of the stage, and self-conscious narratives. Born in Foxcroft, a suburb of Dublin, of Protestant Irish parents, Samuel Beckett went to private school and then to Trinity College. After graduate study, Beckett moved to Paris, where he became friends with James Joyce. During World War II, Beckett worked as a member of the French Resistance.

www

TOPICS FOR CRITICAL THINKING **Web**

1. Is there a distinction between story and action?
2. How many stories does the story the narrator tells contain?

3. Is the story "The Calmative" the story the narrator tells?
4. How is a story a "calmative"?
5. In what ways is this story conscious of its telling?
6. Why does this story have only three paragraphs?

TOPICS FOR CRITICAL WRITING Web

www

1. Select an episode in the narrator's story and consider how that episode relates to the whole story. Are there ways it doesn't relate?
2. How does this story deviate from the typical narrative structure we have seen in most stories? In what ways is that deviation itself a commentary on the idea of a story?

Featured Writer

Salman Rushdie

The Free Radio *(1994)*

We all knew nothing good would happen to him while the thief's widow had her claws dug into his flesh, but the boy was an innocent, a real donkey's child, you can't teach such people.

That boy could have had a good life. God had blessed him with God's own looks, and his father had gone to the grave for him, but didn't he leave the boy a brand-new first-class cycle rickshaw with plastic covered seats and all? So: looks he had, his own trade he had, there would have been a good wife in time, he should just have taken out some years to save some rupees; but no, he must fall for a thief's widow before the hairs had time to come out on his chin, before his milk-teeth had split, one might say.

We felt bad for him, but who listens to the wisdom of the old today?

I say: who listens?

Exactly; nobody, certainly not a stone-head like Ramani the rickshaw-wallah. But I blame the widow. I saw it happen, you know, I saw most of it until I couldn't stand any more. I sat under this very banyan, smoking this selfsame hookah, and not much escaped my notice.

And at one time I tried to save him from his fate, but it was no go . . .

The widow was certainly attractive, no point denying, in a sort of hard vicious way she was all right, but it is her mentality that was rotten. Ten years older than Ramani she must have been, five children alive and two dead, what that thief did besides robbing and making babies God only knows, but he left her not one new paisa, so of course she would be interested in Ramani. I'm not saying a rickshaw-wallah makes much in this town but two mouthfuls are better to eat than wind. And not many people will look twice at the widow of a good-for-nothing.

They met right here.

One day Ramani rode into town without a passenger, but grinning as usual as if someone had given him a ten-chip tip, singing some playback music from the radio, his hair greased like for a wedding. He was not such a fool that he didn't know how the girls watched him all the time and passed remarks about his long and well-muscled legs.

The thief's widow had gone to the bania stop to buy some three grains of dal and I won't say where the money came from, but people saw men at night near her rutputty shack, even the bania himself they were telling me but I personally will not comment.

She had all her five brats with her and then and there, cool as a fan, she called out: '*Hey! Rickshaaa!*' Loud, you know, like a truly cheap type. Showing us she can afford to ride in rickshaws, as if anyone was interested. Her children must have gone hungry to pay for the ride but in my opinion it was an investment for her, because must-be she had decided already to put her hooks into Ramani. So they all poured into the rickshaw and he took her away, and with the five kiddies as well as the widow there was quite a weight, so he was puffing hard, and the veins were standing out on his legs, and I thought, careful, my son, or you will have this burden to pull for all of your life.

But after that Ramani and the thief's widow were seen everywhere, shamelessly, in public places, and I was glad his mother was dead because if she had lived to see this her face would have fallen off from shame.

Sometimes in those days Ramani came into this street in the evenings to meet some friends, and they thought they were very smart because they would go into the back room of the Irani's canteen and drink illegal liquor, only of course everybody knew, but who would do anything, if boys ruin their lives let their relations worry.

I was sad to see Ramani fall into this bad company. His parents were known to me when alive. But when I told Ramani to keep away from those hot-shots he grinned like a sheep and said I was wrong, nothing bad was taking place.

Let it go, I thought.

I knew those cronies of his. They all wore the armbands of the new Youth Movement. This was the time of the State of Emergency, and these friends were not peaceful persons, there were stories of beatings-up, so I sat quiet under my tree. Ramani wore no armband but he went with them because they impressed him, the fool.

These armband youths were always flattering Ramani. Such a handsome chap, they told him, compared to you Shashi Kapoor and Amitabh are like lepers only, you should go to Bombay and be put in the motion pictures.

They flattered him with dreams because they knew they could take money from him at cards and he would buy them drink while they did it, though he was no richer than they. So now Ramani's head became filled with these movie dreams, because there was nothing else inside to take up any space, and this is another reason why I blame the widow woman, because she had more years and should have had more sense. In two ticks she could have made him forget all about it, but no, I heard her telling him one day for all to hear, 'Truly you have the looks of Lord Krishna himself, except you are not blue all over.' In the street! So all would know they were lovers! From that day on I was sure a disaster would happen.

The next time the thief's widow came into the street to visit the bania shop I decided to act. Not for my own sake but for the boy's dead parents I risked being shamed by a . . . no, I will not call her the name, she is elsewhere now and they will know what she is like.

'Thief's widow!' I called out. 20

She stopped dead, jerking her face in an ugly way, as if I had hit her with a whip.

'Come here and speak,' I told her.

Now she could not refuse because I am not without importance in the town and maybe she calculated that if people saw us talking they would stop ignoring her when she passed, so she came as I knew she would.

'I have to say this thing only,' I told her with dignity. 'Ramani the rickshaw boy is dear to me, and you must find some person of your own age, or, better still, go to the widows' ashrams in Benares and spend the rest of your life there in holy prayer, thanking God that widow-burning is now illegal.'

So at this point she tried to shame me by screaming out and calling me 25
curses and saying that I was a poisonous old man who should have died years ago, and then she said, 'Let me tell you, mister teacher sahib *retired*, that your Ramani has asked to marry me and I have said no, because I wish no more children, and he is a young man and should have his own. So tell that to the whole world and stop your cobra poison.'

For a time after that I closed my eyes to this affair of Ramani and the thief's widow, because I had done all I could and there were many other things in the town to interest a person like myself. For instance, the local health officer had brought a big white caravan into the street and was given permission to park it out of the way under the banyan tree; and every night men were taken into this van for a while and things were done to them.

I did not care to be in the vicinity at these times, because the youths with armbands were always in attendance, so I took my hookah and sat in another place. I heard rumours of what was happening in the caravan but I closed my ears.

But it was while this caravan, which smelled of ether, was in town that the extent of the widow's wickedness became plain; because at this time Ramani suddenly began to talk about his new fantasy, telling everyone he could find that very shortly he was to receive a highly special and personalised gift from the Central Government in Delhi itself, and this gift was to be a brand-new first-class battery-operated transistor radio.

Now then: we had always believed that our Ramani was a little soft in the head, with his notions of being a film star and what all; so most of us just nodded tolerantly and said, 'Yes, Ram, that is nice for you,' and, 'What a fine, generous Government it is that gives radios to persons who are so keen on popular music.'

But Ramani insisted it was true, and seemed happier than at any time in 30
his life, a happiness which could not be explained simply by the supposed imminence of the transistor.

Soon after the dream-radio was first mentioned, Ramani and the thief's widow were married, and then I understood everything. I did not attend the nuptials—it was a poor affair by all accounts—but not long afterwards I spoke to Ram when he came past the banyan with an empty rickshaw one day.

He came to sit by me and I asked, 'My child, did you go to the caravan? What have you let them do to you?'

'Don't worry,' he replied. 'Everything is tremendously wonderful. I am in love, teacher sahib, and I have made it possible for me to marry my woman.'

I confess I became angry; indeed, I almost wept as I realised that Ramani had gone voluntarily to subject himself to a humiliation which was being forced upon the other men who were taken to the caravan. I reproved him bitterly. 'My idiot child, you have let that woman deprive you of your manhood!'

'It is not so bad,' Ram said, meaning the *nasbandi*. 'It does not stop love-making or anything, excuse me, teacher sahib, for speaking of such a thing. It stops babies only and my woman did not want children any more, so now all is hundred per cent OK. Also it is in national interest,' he pointed out. 'And soon the free radio will arrive.'

'The free radio,' I repeated.

'Yes, remember, teacher sahib,' Ram said confidentially, 'some years back, in my kiddie days, when Laxman the tailor had this operation? In no time the radio came and from all over town people gathered to listen to it. It is how the Government says thank you. It will be excellent to have.'

'Go away, get away from me,' I cried out in despair, and did not have the heart to tell him what everyone else in the country already knew, which was that the free radio scheme was a dead duck, long gone, long forgotten. It had been over—*funtoosh!*—for years.

After these events the thief's widow, who was now Ram's wife, did not come into town very often, no doubt being too ashamed of what she had made him do, but Ramani worked longer hours than ever before, and every time he saw any of the dozens of people he'd told about the radio he would put one hand up to his ear as if he were already holding the blasted machine in it, and he would mimic broadcasts with a certain energetic skill.

'*Yé Akashvani hai*,' he announced to the streets. 'This is All-India Radio. Here is the news. A Government spokesman today announced that Ramani rickshaw-wallah's radio was on its way and would be delivered at any moment. And now some playback music.' After which he would sing songs by Asha Bhonsle or Lata Mangeshkar in a high, ridiculous falsetto.

Ram always had the rare quality of total belief in his dreams, and there were times when his faith in the imaginary radio almost took us in, so that we half-believed it was really on its way, or even that it was already there, cupped invisibly against his ear as he rode his rickshaw around the streets of the town. We began to expect to hear Ramani, around a corner or at the far end of a lane, ringing his bell and yelling cheerfully:

'All-India Radio! This is All-India Radio!'

Time passed. Ram continued to carry the invisible radio around town. One year passed. Still his caricatures of the radio channel filled the air in the streets. But when I saw him now, there was a new thing in his face, a strained thing, as if he were having to make a phenomenal effort, which was much more tiring than driving a rickshaw, more tiring even than pulling a rickshaw containing a thief's widow and her five living children and the ghosts of two dead ones; as if all the energy of his young body was being poured into that fictional space between his ear and his hand, and he was trying to bring the radio into existence by a mighty, and possibly fatal, act of will.

I felt most helpless, I can tell you, because I had divined that Ram had poured into the idea of the radio all his worries and regrets about what he had done, and that if the dream were to die he would be forced to face the full gravity of his crime against his own body, to understand that the thief's widow had turned him, before she married him, into a thief of a stupid and terrible kind, because she had made him rob himself.

And then the white caravan came back to its place under the banyan tree 45
and I knew there was nothing to be done, because Ram would certainly come to get his gift.

He did not come for one day, then for two, and I learned afterwards that he had not wished to seem greedy; he didn't want the health officer to think he was desperate for the radio. Besides, he was half hoping they would come over and give it to him at his place, perhaps with some kind of small, formal presentation ceremony. A fool is a fool and there is no accounting for his notions.

On the third day he came. Ringing his bicycle-bell and imitating weather forecasts, ear cupped as usual, he arrived at the caravan. And in the rickshaw behind him sat the thief's widow, the witch, who had not been able to resist coming along to watch her companion's destruction.

It did not take very long.

Ram went into the caravan gaily, waving at his arm-banded cronies who were guarding it against the anger of the people, and I am told—for I had left the scene to spare myself the pain—that his hair was well-oiled and his clothes were freshly starched. The thief's widow did not move from the rickshaw, but sat there with a black sari pulled over her head, clutching at her children as if they were straws.

After a short time there were sounds of disagreement inside the caravan, 50
and then louder noises still, and finally the youths in armbands went in to see what was becoming, and soon after that Ram was frogmarched out by his drinking-chums, and his hair-grease was smudged on to his face and there was blood coming from his mouth. His hand was no longer cupped by his ear.

And still—they tell me—the thief's black widow did not move from her place in the rickshaw, although they dumped her husband in the dust.

Yes, I know, I'm an old man, my ideas are wrinkled with age, and these days they tell me sterilisation and God knows what is necessary, and maybe I'm wrong to blame the widow as well—why not? Maybe all the views of the old can be discounted now, and if that's so, let it be. But I'm telling this story and I haven't finished yet.

Some days after the incident at the caravan I saw Ramani selling his rickshaw to the old Muslim crook who runs the bicycle-repair shop. When he saw me watching, Ram came to me and said, 'Goodbye, teacher sahib, I am off to Bombay, where I will become a bigger film star than Shashi Kapoor or Amitabh Bachchan even.'

'"*I* am off," you say?' I asked him. 'Are you perhaps travelling alone?'

He stiffened. The thief's widow had already taught him not to be humble in the presence of elders.

'My wife and children will come also,' he said. It was the last time we spoke. They left that same day on the down train.

After some months had passed I got his first letter, which was not written by himself, of course, since in spite of all my long-ago efforts he barely knew how to write. He had paid a professional letter-writer, which must have cost him many rupees, because everything in life costs money and in Bombay it costs twice as much. Don't ask me why he wrote to me, but he did. I have the letters and can give you proof positive, so maybe there are some uses for old people still, or maybe he knew I was the only one who would be interested in his news.

Anyhow: the letters were full of his new career, they told me how he'd been discovered at once, a big studio had given him a test, now they were grooming him for stardom, he spent his days at the Sun'n'Sand Hotel at Juhu beach in the company of top lady artistes, he was buying a big house at Pali Hill, built in the split-level mode and incorporating the latest security equipment to protect him from the movie fans, the thief's widow was well and happy and getting fat, and life was filled with light and success and no-questions-asked alcohol.

They were wonderful letters, brimming with confidence, but whenever I read them, and sometimes I read them still, I remember the expression which came over his face in the days just before he learned the truth about his radio, and the huge mad energy which he had poured into the act of conjuring reality, by an act of magnificent faith, out of the hot thin air between his cupped hand and his ear.

SALMAN RUSHDIE

(b. 1947) **Web** *www*

Rushdie was born in India, moved to Pakistan, educated in England, and now writes novels in English. His work is renowned for its mixture of magical realism (writing that presents fantastic or impossible events as if they were a part of everyday life), self-reflexive narrative, and comic portrayals of people caught in the shifts of postcolonial cultures. He was sentenced to death by Iran's Ayatollah Khomeini for his novel *The Satanic Verses* (1988).

TOPICS FOR CRITICAL THINKING **Web** *www*

1. What different kinds of narrative does this story include?
2. What is the relation between fate, dream, and narrative?

3. In what ways is this story conscious of its own process of being told?
4. In what ways is this story conscious of the various shapes stories can take?
5. In what ways does faith in a story prove to be misleading?
6. What comment does this story make on the power of stories?
7. In what ways is "reality" conjured by stories, and to what ends?

www *TOPIC FOR CRITICAL WRITING* **Web**

What does the radio represent? Why a radio?

At the Auction of the Ruby Slippers *(1994)*

The bidders who have assembled for the auction of the magic slippers bear little resemblance to your usual saleroom crowd. The Auctioneers have publicised the event widely and are prepared for all comers. People venture out but rarely nowadays; nevertheless, and rightly, the Auctioneers believed this prize would tempt us from our bunkers. High feelings are anticipated. Accordingly, in addition to the standard facilities provided for the comfort and security of the more notable personages, extra-large bronze cupsidors have been placed in the vestibules and toilets, for the use of the physically sick; teams of psychiatrists of varying disciplines have been installed in strategically located neo-Gothic confessional booths, to counsel the sick at heart.

Most of us nowadays are sick.

There are no priests. The Auctioneers have drawn a line. The priests remain in other, nearby buildings, buildings with which they are familiar, hoping to deal with any psychic fall-out, any insanity overspill.

Units of obstetricians and helmeted police SWAT teams wait out of sight in side alleys in case the excitement leads to unexpected births or deaths. Lists of next of kin have been drawn up and their contact numbers recorded. A supply of strait-jackets has been laid in.

See: behind bullet-proof glass, the ruby slippers sparkle. We do not know 5
the limits of their powers. We suspect that these limits may not exist.

Movie stars are here, among the bidders, bringing their glossy, spangled auras to the saleroom. Movie-star auras, developed in collaboration with masters of Applied Psychics, are platinum, golden, silver, bronze. Certain genre actors specialising in villainous rôles are surrounded by auras of evil—livid green, mustard yellow, inky red. When one of us collides with a star's priceless (and fragile) aura, he or she is instantly knocked to the floor by a security team and hustled out to the waiting paddy-wagons. Such incidents slightly reduce the crush in the Grand Saleroom.

The memorabilia junkies are out in predictable force, and now with a ducking movement of the head one of them applies her desperate lips to the slippers' transparent cage, setting off the state-of-the-art defence system whose programmers have neglected to teach it about the relative harmlessness of such a gesture of adoration. The system pumps a hundred thousand volts of electricity into the collagen-implanted lips of the glass-kisser, terminating her interest in the proceedings.

It is an unpleasantly whiffy moment, but it fails to deter a second *aficionado* from the same suicidal act of devotion. When we learn that this moron was the lover of the first fatality, we rather wonder at the mysteries of love, whilst reaching once again for our perfumed handkerchiefs.

The cult of the ruby slippers is at its height. A fancy dress party is in full swing. Wizards, Lions, Scarecrows are in plentiful supply. They jostle crossly for position, stamping on one another's feet. There is a scarcity of Tin Men on account of the particular discomfort of the costume. Witches bide their time on the *balcons* and *galeries* of the Grand Saleroom, living gargoyles with, in many cases, high credit ratings. One corner is occupied entirely by Totos, several of whom are copulating enthusiastically, obliging a rubber-gloved janitor to separate them so as to avoid giving public offence. He does this with great delicacy and taste.

We, the public, are easily, lethally offended. We have come to think of 10
taking offence as a fundamental right. We value very little more highly than our rage, which gives us, in our opinion, the moral high ground. From this high ground we can shoot down at our enemies and inflict heavy fatalities. We take pride in our short fuses. Our anger elevates, transcends.

Around the—let us say—shrine of the ruby-sequinned slippers, pools of saliva have been forming. There are those of us who lack restraint, who drool. The jump-suited Latino janitor moves amongst us, a pail in one hand and a squeegee mop in the other. We admire and are grateful for his talent for self-effacement. He removes our mouth waters from the floor without causing any loss of face on our part.

Opportunities for encountering the truly miraculous are limited in our Nietzschean, relativistic universe. Behaviourist philosophers and quantum scientists crowd around the magic shoes. They make indecipherable notes.

Exiles, displaced persons of all sorts, even homeless tramps have turned up for a glimpse of the impossible. They have emerged from their subterranean hollows and braved the bazookas, the Uzi-armed gangs high on crack or smack or ice, the smugglers, the emptiers of houses. The tramps wear stenchy jute ponchos and hawk noisily into the giant potted yuccas. They grab fistfuls of canapés from trays borne upon the superb palms of A-list caterers. Sushi is eaten by them with impressive quantities of *wasabi* sauce, to whose inflammatory powers the hoboes' innards seem impervious. SWAT teams are summoned and after a brief battle involving the use of rubber bullets and sedative darts the tramps are removed, clubbed into unconsciousness and driven away. They will be deposited some distance beyond the city limits, out there in that smoking no-man's-land surrounded by giant advertising hoardings into which we venture no more. Wild dogs will gather around them, eager for luncheon. These are uncompromising times.

Political refugees are at the auction: conspirators, deposed monarchs, defeated factions, poets, bandit chieftains. Such figures no longer wear the black berets, the pebble-lensed spectacles and enveloping greatcoats of yesteryear, but strike resplendent attitudes in boxy silken jackets and high-waisted Japanese couture pantaloons. The women sport toreador jackets bearing sequinned representations of great works of art. One beauty parades *Guernica* on her back, while several others wear glittering scenes from the *Disasters of War* sequence by Francisco Goya.

Incandescent as they are in their suits of lights, the female political refugees fail to eclipse the ruby slippers, and huddle with their male comrades in small hissing bunches, periodically hurling imprecations, ink-pellets, spitballs and paper darts across the salon at rival clusters of *émigrés*. The guards at the exits crack their bullwhips idly and the politicals control themselves.

We revere the ruby slippers because we believe they can make us invulnerable to witches (and there are so many sorcerers pursuing us nowadays); because of their powers of reverse metamorphosis, their affirmation of a lost state of normalcy in which we have almost ceased to believe and to which the slippers promise us we can return; and because they shine like the footwear of the gods.

Disapproving critiques of the fetishing of the slippers are offered by religious fundamentalists, who have been allowed to gain entry by virtue of the extreme liberalism of some of the Auctioneers, who argue that a civilised saleroom must be a broad church, open, tolerant. The fundamentalists have openly stated that they are interested in buying the magic footwear only in order to burn it, and this is not, in the view of the liberal Auctioneers, a reprehensible programme. What price tolerance if the intolerant are not tolerated also? 'Money insists on democracy,' the liberal Auctioneers insist. 'Anyone's cash is as good as anyone else's.' The fundamentalists fulminate from soapboxes constructed of special, sanctified wood. They are ignored, but some senior figures present speak ominously of the thin end of the wedge.

Orphans arrive, hoping that the ruby slippers might transport them back through time as well as space (for, as our equations prove, all space machines are time machines as well): they hope to be reunited with their deceased parents by the famous shoes.

Men and women of dubious character are present—untouchables, outcasts. The security forces deal brusquely with many of these.

'Home' has become such a scattered, damaged, various concept in our present travails. There is no much to yearn for. There are so few rainbows any more. How hard can we expect even a pair of magic shoes to work? They promised to take us *home*, but are metaphors of homeliness comprehensible to them, are abstractions permissible? Are they literalists, or will they permit us to redefine the blessed word?

Are we asking, hoping for, too much?

As our numberless needs emerge from their redoubts and press in upon the electrified glass, will the shoes, like the Grimms' ancient flatfish, lose patience with our ever-growing demands and return us to the hovels of our discontents?

The presence of imaginary beings in the Saleroom may be the last straw. Children from nineteenth-century Australian paintings are here, whining from their ornate, gilded frames about being lost in the immensity of the Outback. In blue smocks and ankle socks they gaze into rain forests and red deserts, and tremble.

A literary character, condemned to an eternity of reading the works of Dickens to an armed madman in a jungle, has sent in a written bid.

On a television monitor, I notice the frail figure of an alien creature with 25
an illuminated fingertip.

This permeation of the real world by the fictional is a symptom of the moral decay of our post-millennial culture. Heroes step down off cinema screens and marry members of the audience. Will there be no end to it? Should there be more rigorous controls? Is the State employing insufficient violence? We debate such questions often. There can be little doubt that a large majority of us opposes the free, unrestricted migration of imaginary beings into an already damaged reality, whose resources diminish by the day. After all, few of us would choose to travel in the opposite direction (though there are persuasive reports of an increase in such migrations latterly).

I shelve such disputes for the moment. The Auction is about to begin.

It is necessary that I speak about my cousin Gale, and her habit of moaning loudly while making love. Let me be frank: my cousin Gale was and is the love of my life, and even now that we have parted I am easily aroused by the mere memory of her erotic noisiness. I hasten to add that except for this volubility there was nothing abnormal about our love-making, nothing, if I may put it thus, *fictional.* Yet it satisfied me deeply, deeply, especially when she chose to cry out at the moment of penetration: 'Home, boy! Home, baby, yes—you've come home!'

One day, sad to relate, I came home to find her in the arms of a hairy escapee from a caveman movie. I moved out the same day, weeping my way down the street with my portrait of Gale in the guise of a tornado cradled in my arms and my collection of old Pat Boone 78 r.p.m. records in a rucksack on my back.

This happened many years ago. 30

For a time after Gale dumped me I was bitter and would reveal to our social circle that she had lost her virginity at the age of fourteen in an accident involving a defective shooting-stick; but vindictiveness did not satisfy me for long.

Since those days I have dedicated myself to her memory. I have made of myself a candle at her temple.

I am aware that, after all these years of separation and non-communication, the Gale I adore is not entirely a real person. The real Gale has become confused with my re-imagining of her, with my private elaboration of our continuing life together in an alternative universe devoid of ape-men. The real Gale may by now be beyond our grasp, ineffable.

I caught a glimpse of her recently. She was at the far end of a long, dark, subterranean bar-room guarded by freelance commandos bearing battlefield nuclear weapons. There were Polynesian snacks on the counter and beers from the Pacific rim on tap: Kirin, Tsingtao, Swan.

At that time many television channels were devoted to the sad case of the 35
astronaut stranded on Mars without hope of rescue, and with diminishing supplies of food and breathable air. Official spokesmen told us of the persuasive arguments for the abrupt cancellation of the space exploration budget. We found these arguments powerful; influential voices complained of the sentimentality of the images of the dying spaceman. Nevertheless, the cameras inside his marooned craft continued to send us poignant pictures of his slow descent into despair, his low-gravity, weight-reduced death.

I watched my cousin Gale as she watched the bar's TV. She did not see me watching her, did not know that she had become my chosen programme.

The condemned man on another planet—the condemned man *on* TV—began to sing a squawky medley of half-remembered songs. I was reminded of the dying computer, Hal, in the old film *2001: A Space Odyssey.* Hal sang 'Daisy, Daisy' as it was being unplugged.

The Martian—for he was now a permanent resident of that planet—offered us his spaced-out renditions of 'Swanee', 'Show Me the Way to Go Home' and several numbers from *The Wizard of Oz;* and Gale's shoulders began to shake. She was crying.

I did not go across to comfort her.

I first heard about the upcoming auction of the ruby slippers the very next 40
morning, and resolved at once to buy them, whatever the cost. My plan was simple: I would offer the miracle-shoes to Gale in all humility. If she wished, I would say, she could use them to travel to Mars and bring the spaceman back to Earth.

Perhaps I might even click the heels together three times, and win back her heart by murmuring, in soft reminder of our wasted love, *There's no place like home.*

You laugh at my desperation. Ha! Go tell a drowning man not to clutch at straws. Go ask a dying astronaut not to sing. Come here and stand in my shoes. What was it the Cowardly Lion said? Put 'em up. Put 'em uuuuup. I'll fight you with one hand tied behind my back. I'll fight you with my eyes closed.

Scared, huh? Scared?

* * *

The Grand Saleroom of the Auctioneers is the beating heart of the earth. If you stand here for long enough all the wonders of the world will pass by. In the Grand Saleroom, in recent years, we have witnessed the auction of the Taj Mahal, the Statue of Liberty, the Alps, the Sphinx. We have assisted at the sale of wives and the purchase of husbands. State secrets have been sold here, openly, to the highest bidder. On one very special occasion, the Auctioneers presided over the sale, to an overheated and inter-denominational bunch of smouldering red demons, of a wide selection of human souls of all classes, qualities, ages, races and creeds.

Everything is for sale, and under the firm yet essentially benevolent supervision of the Auctioneers, their security dogs and SWAT teams, we engage in a battle of wits and wallets, a war of nerves.

There is a purity about our actions here, and also an aesthetically pleasing tension between the vast complexity of the life that turns up, packaged into lots, to go under the hammer, and the equally immense simplicity of our manner of dealing with this life.

We bid, the Auctioneers knock a lot down, we pass on.

All are equal before the justice of the gavels: the pavement artist and Michelangelo, the slave girl and the Queen.

This is the courtroom of demand.

They are bidding for the slippers now. As the price rises, so does my gorge. Panic clutches at me, pulling me down, drowning me. I think of Gale—sweet coz!—and fight back fear, and bid.

Once I was asked by the widower of a world-famous and much-loved pop singer to attend an auction of rock memorabilia on his behalf. He was the sole trustee of her estate, which was worth tens of millions. I treated him with respect.

'There's only one lot I want,' he said. 'Spend whatever you have to spend.'

It was an article of clothing, a pair of edible rice-paper panties in peppermint flavour, purchased long ago in a store on (I think this was the name) Rodeo Drive. My employer's late wife's stage act had included the public removal and consumption of several such pairs. More panties, in a variety of flavours—chocolate chip, knickerbocker glory, cassata—were hurled into the crowd. These, too, were gobbled up in the general excitement of the concert, the lucky recipients being too carried away to consider the future value of what they had caught. Undergarments that had actually been worn by the lady were therefore in short supply, and presently in great demand.

During that auction, bids came in across the video links with Tokyo, Los Angeles, Paris and Milan, bids so rapid and of such size that I lost my nerve. However, when I telephoned my employer to confess my failure he was quite unperturbed, interested only in the final price. I mentioned a five-figure sum, and he laughed. It was the first genuinely joyful laugh I had heard from him since the day his wife died.

'That's all right then,' he said. 'I've got three hundred thousand of those.'

* * *

It is to the Auctioneers we go to establish the value of our pasts, of our futures, of our lives.

The price for the ruby slippers is rising ever higher. Many of the bidders would appear to be proxies, as I was on the day of the underpants; as I am so often, in so many ways.

Today, however, I am bidding—perhaps literally—for myself.

There's an explosion in the street outside. We hear running feet, sirens, screams. Such things have become commonplace. We stay where we are, absorbed by a higher drama.

60 The cuspidors are in full employment. Witches keen, movie stars flounce off with tarnished auras. Queues of the disconsolate form at the psychiatrists' booths. There is work for the club-wielding guards, though not, as yet, for the obstetricians. Order is maintained. I am the only person in the Saleroom still in the bidding. My rivals are disembodied heads on video screens, and unheard voices on telephone links. I am doing battle with an invisible world of demons and ghosts, and the prize is my lady's hand.

At the height of an auction, when the money has become no more than a way of keeping score, a thing happens which I am reluctant to admit: one becomes detached from the earth.

There is a loss of gravity, a reduction in weight, a floating in the capsule of the struggle. The ultimate goal crosses a delirious frontier. Its achievement and our own survival becomes—yes!—fictions.

And fictions, as I have come close to suggesting before, are dangerous.

In fiction's grip, we may mortgage our homes, sell our children, to have whatever it is we crave. Alternatively, in that miasmal ocean, we may simply float away from our desires, and see them anew, from a distance, so that they seem weightless, trivial. We let them go. Like men dying in a blizzard, we lie down in the snow to rest.

65 So it is that my cousin Gale loses her hold over me in the crucible of the auction. So it is that I drop out of the bidding, go home, and fall asleep.

When I awake I feel refreshed, and free.

Next week there is another auction. Family trees, coats of arms, royal lineages will be up for sale, and into any of these one may insert any name one chooses, one's own, or one's beloved's. Canine and feline pedigrees will be on offer, too: Alsatian, Burmese, saluki, Siamese, cairn terrier.

Thanks to the infinite bounty of the Auctioneers, any of us, cat, dog, man, woman, child, can be a blue-blood; can be—as we long to be; and as, cowering in our shelters, we fear we are not—*somebody.*

www

TOPICS FOR CRITICAL THINKING **Web**

1. What elements of style work in this story to produce a consciousness of narrative?
2. What do the ruby slippers stand for?

3. What are the connections among the auction, the narrator's love for Gale, and the dying astronaut?
4. In what ways is this story connected to the *Wizard of Oz?*
5. What commentary does this story make about commodity culture? **Web** *www*

TOPIC FOR CRITICAL WRITING **Web** *www*

What does this story suggest about the power (for good or bad) of fiction?

16 Intertextuality

Every literary text bears within it a sense of its place in the history of literature, the evolution of genres, the legacies of style, and the politics of its themes. Not only are stories produced within a cultural context, which they inevitably reflect (even if the story is about another time and place); they also exist in relation to all other stories we have read—that is, to a tradition of literature. The
www various ways literary texts refer to other texts is called **intertextuality**. **Web** Intertextuality exists within individual texts and among texts. It consists of such practices as citing and alluding to other texts (or to other parts of itself); employing structures and conventions common to many texts; writing about other texts using parody, satire, and burlesque; and employing the methods of
www **collage** and **pastiche.** **Web** (see examples of collage in first color insert).

The question postmodern intertextuality raises is not necessarily one of reference but more one of how multiple texts do or do not work together. Reading literature that employs intertextuality does not mean looking up every allusion to another text or knowing the reference for every style, but rather involves the constant acknowledgment of all texts together as a teeming body. Intertextual reading means enjoying the interplay of multiple texts and styles in works that mesmerize through their ability to manage the disparate multitudes of representations bombarding contemporary culture. While intertextuality deploys familiar modes of narrative and organization such as the frame narrator and the embedded narrative (see Chapter 6), it uses them in a manner somewhat different from the ways in which Joseph Conrad and other modernist writers use them, producing a sense of distance, alienation, and intimacy all at the same time.

Collage and Pastiche

Collage and pastiche are the intertextual methods most often associated with postmodern literature, though postmodern texts may also be intertextual in other ways. Collage, which was used widely by early twentieth-century avant-garde artists, involves cutting and pasting parts from different texts together to make a single ensemble. **Dada** poets such as Tristan Tzara, for example, composed poems by randomly picking out of a hat words cut from a newspa-
www per. **Web** The method of collage used by postmodern writers is not so random. Postmodern intertextuality may emphasize the similarities among disparate texts, as in Mark Leyner's juxtaposition of advertising language with the claims of science in *My Cousin, My Gastroenterologist*. Literary collage may

take the form of framing, where one narrative encompasses multiple other stories. It may consist of the swift cutting and combination that occurs in Leyner's stories where sentences shift rapidly through vocabularies from many different contexts, or it may quickly range, as *Ghosts* does, through allusions to many different texts. Intertextuality is one way postmodern texts bring together material from high (literary and intellectual) and low (popular) culture and from many different genres and vocabularies. For some idea of the range of intertextual references in the texts below, see **Web**. *www*

Critical Perspective: An Example of Criticism Focused on Intertextuality

"For the postmodern detective this anxiety increases in correlation to the poststructuralist questions concerning language and subjectivity, along with the increase in unstable home-lives, overcrowded cities, and high-speed technologies—postmodern 'realities' for which Wakefield functions as the perfect embodiment. The detective's present condition is nowhere more evident than in Paul Auster's *The New York Trilogy*, possibly the best example of Wakefield parody and appropriation in postmodern detective fictions. Auster's trilogy concerns itself primarily with problems of language and identity. The detective in those novels 'becomes a pilgrim searching for correspondence between signifiers and signifieds,' a search that becomes 'a quest for his own identity' (Russell 72–3). But those are impossible tasks for the detective, for in the world of these novels signifiers have divorced themselves from signifieds, while the distinction between self and other has conflated. To further complicate matters, in all three narratives the detective, the high priest of logic, in his attempt to locate missing persons becomes himself the missing person, a Wakefield who can no longer return home.

"Not only does Auster's trilogy share similar themes with 'Wakefield,' but more significantly the trilogy itself refers us directly to 'Wakefield' as a significant intratext for the perplexities of subjectivity involved in postmodern experience. In the second book of the trilogy, *Ghosts*, Black, the man Blue has been hired to watch, at one point actually tells Blue the story of Wakefield. By the end of the novel we realize that the Wakefield story is not only relevant to *Ghosts* but actually functions as a mise-en-abyme for the larger narrative—and for the entire trilogy. *Ghosts* is riddled with mise-en-abymes functioning at various fictional or metafictional levels, but at all levels those reflections of the larger text point back to 'Wakefield.' For example, Blue's history of detective work includes a case concerning a man named Gray who has disappeared, but just when Gray's wife concedes his death, Blue finds an amnesiac Gray, now Green, working in a bar not two blocks from his old home, echoing Hawthorne (166–67).

"In light of those intratexts, it should come as no surprise that Blue himself comes to resemble Wakefield, as does Black for that matter."

—Richard Swope, "Approaching the Threshold(s) in Postmodern Detective Fiction: Hawthorne's Wakefield and Other Missing Persons," *Critique* 39:3 (Spring: 1998)

In this passage, critic Richard Swope investigates the relation between one of *Ghosts*'s intertexts, Nathaniel Hawthorne's story "Wakefield" and the themes and behaviors of the characters in *Ghosts*.

PAUL AUSTER

Ghosts

(1983)

First of all there is Blue. Later there is White, and then there is Black, and before the beginning there is Brown. Brown broke him in, Brown taught him the ropes, and when Brown grew old, Blue took over. That is how it begins. The place is New York, the time is the present, and neither one will ever change. Blue goes to his office every day and sits at his desk, waiting for something to happen. For a long time nothing does, and then a man named White walks through the door, and that is how it begins.

The case seems simple enough. White wants Blue to follow a man named Black and to keep an eye on him for as long as necessary. While working for Brown, Blue did many tail jobs, and this one seems no different, perhaps even easier than most.

Blue needs the work, and so he listens to White and doesn't ask many questions. He assumes it's a marriage case and that White is a jealous husband. White doesn't elaborate. He wants a weekly report, he says, sent to such and such a postbox number, typed out in duplicate on pages so long and so wide. A check will be sent each week to Blue in the mail. White then tells Blue where Black lives, what he looks like, and so on. When Blue asks White how long he thinks the case will last, White says he doesn't know. Just keep sending the reports, he says, until further notice.

To be fair to Blue, he finds it all a little strange. But to say that he has misgivings at this point would be going too far. Still, it's impossible for him not to notice certain things about White. The black beard, for example, and the overly bushy eyebrows. And then there is the skin, which seems inordinately white, as though covered with powder. Blue is no amateur in the art of disguise, and it's not difficult for him to see through this one. Brown was his teacher, after all, and in his day Brown was the best in the business. So Blue begins to think he was wrong, that the case has nothing to do with marriage. But he gets no farther than this, for White is still speaking to him, and Blue must concentrate on following his words.

Everything has been arranged, White says. There's a small apartment di- 5
rectly across the street from Black's. I've already rented it, and you can move in there today. The rent will be paid for until the case is over.

Good idea, says Blue, taking the key from White. That will eliminate the legwork.

Exactly, White answers, stroking his beard.

And so it's settled. Blue agrees to take the job, and they shake hands on it. To show his good faith, White even gives Blue an advance of ten fifty-dollar bills.

That is how it begins, then. The young Blue and a man named White, who is obviously not the man he appears to be. It doesn't matter, Blue says to himself after White has left. I'm sure he has his reasons. And besides, it's not my problem. The only thing I have to worry about is doing my job.

10 It is February 3, 1947. Little does Blue know, of course, that the case will go on for years. But the present is no less dark than the past, and its mystery is equal to anything the future might hold. Such is the way of the world: one step at a time, one word and then the next. There are certain things that Blue cannot possibly know at this point. For knowledge comes slowly, and when it comes, it is often at great personal expense.

White leaves the office, and a moment later Blue picks up the phone and calls the future Mrs. Blue. I'm going under cover, he tells his sweetheart. Don't worry if I'm out of touch for a little while. I'll be thinking of you the whole time.

Blue takes a small gray satchel down from the shelf and packs it with his thirty-eight, a pair of binoculars, a notebook, and other tools of the trade. Then he tidies his desk, puts his papers in order, and locks up the office. From there he goes to the apartment that White has rented for him. The address is unimportant. But let's say Brooklyn Heights, for the sake of argument. Some quiet, rarely traveled street not far from the bridge—Orange Street perhaps. Walt Whitman handset the first edition of Leaves of Grass on this street in 1855, and it was here that Henry Ward Beecher railed against slavery from the pulpit of his red-brick church. So much for local color.

It's a small studio apartment on the third floor of a four-story brownstone. Blue is happy to see that it's fully equipped, and as he walks around the room inspecting the furnishings, he discovers that everything in the place is new: the bed, the table, the chair, the rug, the linens, the kitchen supplies, everything. There is a complete set of clothes hanging in the closet, and Blue, wondering if the clothes are meant for him, tries them on and sees that they fit. It's not the biggest place I've ever been in, he says to himself, pacing from one end of the room to the other, but it's cozy enough, cozy enough.

He goes back outside, crosses the street, and enters the opposite building. In the entryway he searches for Black's name on one of the mailboxes and finds it: Black—3rd floor. So far so good. Then he returns to his room and gets down to business.

15 Parting the curtains of the window, he looks out and sees Black sitting at a table in his room across the street. To the extent that Blue can make out what is happening, he gathers that Black is writing. A look through the binoculars confirms that he is. The lenses, however, are not powerful enough to pick up the writing itself, and even if they were, Blue doubts that he would be able to read the handwriting upside down. All he can say for certain, therefore, is that Black is writing in a notebook with a red fountain pen. Blue takes out his own notebook and writes: Feb. 3, 3 P.M. Black writing at his desk.

Now and then Black pauses in his work and gazes out the window. At one point, Blue thinks that he is looking directly at him and ducks out of the way. But on closer inspection he realizes that it is merely a blank stare, signifying thought rather than seeing, a look that makes things invisible, that does not let them in. Black gets up from his chair every once in a while and disappears to a hidden spot in the room, a corner Blue supposes, or perhaps the bathroom, but he is never gone for very long, always returning promptly to the desk. This goes on for several hours, and Blue is none the wiser for his efforts At six o'clock he writes the second sentence in his notebook: This goes on for several hours.

It's not so much that Blue is bored, but that he feels thwarted. Without being able to read what Black has written, everything is a blank so far. Perhaps he's a madman, Blue thinks, plotting to blow up the world. Perhaps that writing has something to do with his secret formula. But Blue is immediately embarrassed by such a childish notion. It's too early to know anything, he says to himself, and for the time being he decides to suspend judgment.

His mind wanders from one small thing to another, eventually settling on the future Mrs. Blue. They were planning to go out tonight, he remembers, and if it hadn't been for White showing up at the office today and this new case, he would be with her now. First the Chinese restaurant on 39th Street, where they would have wrestled with the chopsticks and held hands under the table, and then the double feature at the Paramount. For a brief moment he has a startlingly clear picture of her face in his mind (laughing with lowered eyes, feigning embarrassment), and he realizes that he would much rather be with her than sitting in this little room for God knows how long. He thinks about calling her up on the phone for a chat, hesitates, and then decides against it. He doesn't want to seem weak. If she knew how much he needed her, he would begin to lose his advantage, and that wouldn't be good. The man must always be the stronger one.

Black has now cleared his table and replaced the writing materials with dinner. He sits there chewing slowly, staring out the window in that abstracted way of his. At the sight of food, Blue realizes that he is hungry and hunts through the kitchen cabinet for something to eat. He settles on a meal of canned stew and soaks up the gravy with a slice of white bread. After dinner he has some hope that Black will be going outside, and he is encouraged when he sees a sudden flurry or activity in Black's room. But all comes to nothing. Fifteen minutes later, Black is sitting at his desk again, this time reading a book. A lamp is on beside him, and Blue has a clearer view of Black's face than before. Blue estimates Black's age to be the same as his, give or take a year or two. That is to say, somewhere in his late twenties or early thirties. He finds Black's face pleasant enough, with nothing to distinguish it from a thousand other faces one sees every day. This is a disappointment to Blue, for he is still secretly hoping to discover that Black is a madman. Blue looks through the binoculars and reads the title of the book that Black is reading. Walden, by Henry David Thoreau. Blue has never heard of it before and writes it down carefully in his notebook.

So it goes for the rest of the evening, with Black reading and Blue watch- 20
ing him read. As time passes, Blue grows more and more discouraged. He's not used to sitting around like this, and with the darkness closing in on him now, it's beginning to get on his nerves. He likes to be up and about, moving from one place to another, doing things. I'm not the Sherlock Holmes type,

he would say to Brown, whenever the boss gave him a particularly sedentary task. Give me something I can sink my teeth into. Now, when he himself is the boss, this is what he gets: a case with nothing to do. For to watch someone read and write is in effect to do nothing. The only way for Blue to have a sense of what is happening is to be inside Black's mind, to see what he is thinking, and that of course is impossible. Little by little, therefore, Blue lets his own mind drift back to the old days. He thinks of Brown and some of the cases they worked on together, savoring the memory of their triumphs. There was the Redman Affair, for example, in which they tracked down the bank teller who had embezzled a quarter of a million dollars. For that one Blue pretended to be a bookie and lured Redman into placing a bet with him. The money was traced back to the bills missing from the bank, and the man got what was coming to him. Even better was the Gray Case. Gray had been missing for over a year, and his wife was ready to give him up for dead. Blue searched through all the normal channels and came up empty. Then, one day, as he was about to file his final report, he stumbled on Gray in a bar, not two blocks from where the wife was sitting, convinced he would never return. Gray's name was now Green, but Blue knew it was Gray in spite of this, for he had been carrying around a photograph of the man for the past three months and knew his face by heart. It turned out to be amnesia. Blue took Gray back to his wife, and although he didn't remember her and continued to call himself Green, he found her to his liking and some days later proposed marriage. So Mrs. Gray became Mrs. Green, married to the same man a second time, and while Gray never remembered the past—and stubbornly refused to admit that he had forgotten anything—that did not seem to stop him from living comfortably in the present. Whereas Gray had worked as an engineer in his former life, as Green he now kept the job as bartender in the bar two blocks away. He liked mixing drinks, he said, and talking to the people who came in, and he couldn't imagine doing anything else. I was born to be a bartender, he announced to Brown and Blue at the wedding party, and who were they to object to what a man chose to do with his life?

Those were the good old days, Blue says to himself now, as he watches Black turn off the light in his room across the street. Full of strange twists and amusing coincidences. Well, not every case can be exciting. You've got to take the good with the bad.

Blue, ever the optimist, wakes up the next morning in a cheerful mood. Outside, snow is falling on the quiet street, and everything has turned white. After watching Black eat his breakfast at the table by the window and read a few more pages of Walden, Blue sees him retreat to the back of the room and then return to the window dressed in his overcoat. The time is shortly after eight o'clock. Blue reaches for his hat, his coat, his muffler, and boots, hastily scrambles into them, and gets downstairs to the street less than a minute after Black. It is a windless morning, so still that he can hear the snow falling on the branches of the trees. No one else is about, and Black's shoes have made a perfect set of tracks on the white pavement. Blue follows the tracks around the corner and then sees Black ambling down the next street, as if enjoying the weather. Not the behavior of a man about to escape, Blue thinks, and accordingly he slows his pace. Two streets later, Black enters a small grocery store, stays ten or twelve minutes, and then comes out with two heavily loaded brown paper bags. Without noticing Blue, who is standing in a doorway across the street, he begins retracing his steps towards Orange Street. Stocking up for the storm, Blue says to himself. Blue then decides to risk losing contact with Black and goes into the store himself to do the same. Unless it's a decoy, he thinks, and Black is planning to dump the groceries and take off, it's fairly certain that he's on his way home. Blue therefore does his own shopping, stops in next door to buy a newspaper and several magazines, and then returns to his room on Orange Street. Sure enough, Black is already at his desk by the window, writing in the same notebook as the day before.

Because of the snow, visibility is poor, and Blue has trouble deciphering what is happening in Black's room. Even the binoculars don't help much. The day remains dark, and through the endlessly falling snow, Black appears to be no more than a shadow. Blue resigns himself to a long wait and then settles down with his newspapers and magazines. He is a devoted reader of True Detective and tries never to miss a month. Now, with time on his hands, he reads the new issue thoroughly, even pausing to read the little notices and ads on the back pages. Buried among the feature stories on gangbusters and secret agents, there is one short article that strikes a chord in Blue, and even after he finishes the magazine, he finds it difficult not to keep thinking about it. Twenty-five years ago, it seems, in a patch of woods outside Philadelphia, a little boy was found murdered. Although the police promptly began work on the case, they never managed to come up with any clues. Not only did they have no suspects, they could not even identify the boy. Who he was, where he had come from, why he was there—all these questions remained unanswered. Eventually, the case was dropped from the active file, and if not for the coroner who had been assigned to do the autopsy on the boy, it would have been forgotten altogether. This man, whose name was Gold, became obsessed by the murder. Before the child was buried, he made a death mask of his face, and from then on devoted whatever time he could to the mystery. After twenty years, he reached retirement age, left his job, and began spending every moment on the case. But things did not go well. He made no headway, came not one step closer to solving the crime. The article in True Detective describes how he is now offering a reward of two thousand dollars to anyone who can provide information about the little boy. It also includes a grainy, retouched photograph of the man holding the death mask in his hands. The look in his eyes is so haunted and imploring that Blue can scarcely turn his own eyes away. Gold is growing old now, and he is afraid that he will die before he solves the case. Blue is deeply moved by this. If it were possible, he would like nothing better than to drop what he's doing and try to help Gold. There aren't enough men like that, he thinks. If the boy were Gold's son, then it would make sense: revenge, pure and simple, and anyone can understand that. But the boy was a complete stranger to him, and so there's nothing personal about it, no hint of a secret motive. It is this thought that so affects Blue. Gold refuses to accept a world in which the murderer of a child can go unpunished, even if the murderer himself is now dead, and he is willing to sacrifice his own life and happiness to right the wrong. Blue then thinks about the little boy for a while, trying to imagine what really happened, trying to feel what the boy must have felt, and then it dawns on him that the murderer must have been one of the parents, for otherwise the boy would have been reported as missing. That only makes it worse, Blue thinks, and as he begins to grow sick at the thought of it, fully understanding now what Gold must feel all the time, he realizes that twenty-five years ago he too was a little boy and that had the boy lived he would be Blue's age now. It could have been me, Blue thinks. I could have been that little boy. Not knowing what else to do, he cuts out the picture from the magazine and tacks it onto the wall above his bed.

So it goes for the first days. Blue watches Black, and little of anything happens. Black writes, reads, eats, takes brief strolls through the neighborhood, seems not to notice that Blue is there. As for Blue, he tries not to worry. He assumes that Black is lying low, biding his time until the right moment comes. Since Blue is only one man, he realizes that constant vigilance is not expected of him. After all, you can't watch someone twenty-four hours a day. There has to be time for you to sleep, to eat, to do your laundry, and so on. If White wanted Black to be watched around the clock, he would have hired two or three men, not one. But Blue is only one, and more than what is possible he cannot do.

Still, he does begin to worry, in spite of what he tells himself. For if Black must be watched, then it would follow that he must be watched every hour of every day. Anything less than constant surveillance would be as no surveillance at all. It would not take much, Blue reasons, for the entire picture to change. A single moment's inattention—a glance to the side of him, a pause to scratch his head, the merest yawn—and presto, Black slips away and commits whatever heinous act he is planning to commit. And yet, there will necessarily be such moments, hundreds and even thousands of them every day. Blue finds this troubling, for no matter how often he turns this problem over inside himself, he gets no closer to solving it. But that is not the only thing that troubles him.

Until now, Blue has not had much chance for sitting still, and this new idleness has left him at something of a loss. For the first time in his life, he finds that he has been thrown back on himself, with nothing to grab hold of, nothing to distinguish one moment from the next. He has never given much thought to the world inside him, and though he always knew it was there, it has remained an unknown quantity, unexplored and therefore dark, even to himself. He has moved rapidly along the surface of things for as long as he can remember, fixing his attention on these surfaces only in order to perceive them, sizing up one and then passing on to the next, and he has always taken pleasure in the world as such, asking no more of things than that they be there. And until now they have been, etched vividly against the daylight, distinctly telling him what they are, so perfectly themselves and nothing else that he has never had to pause before them or look twice. Now, suddenly, with the world as it were removed from him, with nothing much to see but a vague shadow by the name of Black, he finds himself thinking about things that have never occurred to him before, and this, too, has begun to trouble him. If thinking is perhaps too strong a word at this point, a slightly more modest term—speculation, for example—would not be far from the mark. To speculate, from the Latin speculatus, meaning to spy out, to observe, and linked to the word speculum, meaning mirror or looking glass. For in spying out at Black across the street, it is as though Blue were looking into a mirror, and instead of merely watching another, he finds that he is also watching himself. Life has slowed down so drastically for him that Blue is now able to see things that have previously escaped his attention. The trajectory of the light that passes through the room each day, for example, and the way the sun at certain hours will reflect the snow on the far corner of the ceiling in his room. The beating of his heart, the sound of his breath, the blinking of his eyes—Blue is now aware of these tiny events, and try as he might to ignore them, they persist in his mind like a nonsensical phrase repeated over and over again. He knows it cannot be true, and yet little by little this phrase seems to be taking on a meaning.

Of Black, of White, of the job he has been hired to do, Blue now begins to advance certain theories. More than just helping to pass the time, he discovers that making up stories can be a pleasure in itself. He thinks that perhaps White and Black are brothers and that a large sum of money is at stake—an inheritance, for example, or the capital invested in a partnership. Perhaps White wants to prove that Black is incompetent, have him committed to an institution, and take control of the family fortune himself. But Black is too clever for that and has gone into hiding, waiting for the pressure to ease up. Another theory that Blue puts forward has White and Black as rivals, both of them racing toward the same goal—the solution to a scientific problem, for example—and White wants Black watched in order to be sure he isn't outsmarted. Still another story has it that White is a renegade agent from the F.B.I. or some espionage organization, perhaps foreign, and has struck out on his own to conduct some peripheral investigation not necessarily sanctioned by his superiors. By hiring Blue to do his work for him, he can keep the surveillance of Black a secret and at the same time continue to perform his normal duties. Day by day, the list of these stories grows, with Blue sometimes returning in his mind to an early story to add certain flourishes and details and at other times starting over again with something new. Murder plots, for instance, and kidnapping schemes for giant ransoms. As the days go on, Blue realizes there is no end to the stories he can tell. For Black is no more than a kind of blankness, a hold in the texture of things, and one story can fill this hold as well as any other.

Blue does not mince words, however. He knows that more than anything else he would like to learn the real story. But at this early stage he also knows that patience is called for. Bit by bit, therefore, he begins to dig in, and with each day that passes he finds himself a little more comfortable with his situation, a little more resigned to the fact that he is in for the long haul.

Unfortunately, thoughts of the future Mrs. Blue occasionally disturb his growing peace of mind. Blue misses her more than ever, but he also senses somehow that things will never be the same again. Where this feeling comes from he cannot tell. But while he feels reasonably content whenever he confines his thoughts to Black, to his room, to the case he is working on, whenever the future Mrs. Blue enters his consciousness, he is seized by a kind of panic. All of a sudden, his calm turns to anguish, and he feels as though he is falling into some dark, cave-like place, with no hope of finding a way out. Nearly every day he has been tempted to pick up the phone and call her, thinking that perhaps a moment of real contact would break the spell. But the days pass, and still he doesn't call. This, too, is troubling to him, for he cannot remember a time in his life when he has been so reluctant to do a thing he so clearly wants to do. I'm changing, he says to himself. Little by little, I'm no longer the same. This interpretation reassures him somewhat, at least for a while, but in the end it only leaves him feeling stranger than before. The days pass, and it becomes difficult for him not to keep seeing pictures of the future Mrs. Blue in his head, especially at night, and there in the darkness of his room, lying on his back with his eyes open, he reconstructs her body piece by piece, beginning with her feet and ankles, working his way up her legs and along her thighs, climbing from her belly toward her breasts, and then, roaming happily among the softness, dipping down to her buttocks and then up again along her back, at last finding her neck and curling forward to her round and smiling face. What is she doing now? he sometimes asks himself. And what does she think of all this? But he can never come up with a satisfactory answer. If he is able to invent a multitude of stories to fit the facts concerning Black, with the future Mrs. Blue all is silence, confusion, and emptiness.

The day comes for him to write his final report. Blue is an old hand at such compositions and has never had any trouble with them. His method is to stick to outward facts, describing events as though each word tallied exactly with the thing described, and to question the matter no further. Words are transparent for him, great windows that stand between him and the world, and until now they have never impeded his view, have never even seemed to be there. Oh, there are moments when the glass gets a trifle smudged and Blue has to polish it in one spot or another, but once he finds the right word, everything clears up. Drawing on the entries he has made previously in his notebook, sifting through them to refresh his memory and to underscore pertinent remarks, he tries to fashion a coherent whole, discarding the slack and embellishing the gist. In every report he has written so far, action holds forth over interpretation. For example: The subject walked from Columbus Circle to Carnegie Hall. No references to the weather, no mention of the traffic, no stab at trying to guess what the subject might be thinking. The report confines itself to known and verifiable facts, and beyond this limit it does not try to go.

Faced with the facts of the Black case, however, Blue grows aware of his predicament. There is the notebook, of course, but when he looks through it to see what he has written, he is disappointed to find such paucity of detail. It's as though his words, instead of drawing out the facts and making them sit palpably in the world, have induced them to disappear. This has never happened to Blue before. He looks out across the street and sees Black sitting at his desk as usual. Black, too, is looking through the window at that moment, and it suddenly occurs to Blue that he can no longer depend on the old procedures. Clues, legwork, investigative routine—none of this is going to matter anymore. But then, when he tries to imagine what will replace these things, he gets nowhere. At this point, Blue can only surmise what the case is not. To say what it is, however, is completely beyond him.

Blue sets his typewriter on the table and casts about for ideas, trying to apply himself to the task at hand. He thinks that perhaps a truthful account of the past week would include the various stories he has made up for himself concerning Black. With so little else to report, these excursions into the make-believe would at least give some flavor of what has happened. But Blue brings himself up short, realizing that they have nothing really to do with Black. This isn't the story of my life, after all, he says. I'm supposed to be writing about him, not myself.

Still, it looms as a perverse temptation, and Blue must struggle with himself for some time before fighting it off. He goes back to the beginning and works his way through the case, step by step. Determined to do exactly what has been asked of him, he painstakingly composes the report in the old style, tackling each detail with such care and aggravating precision that many hours go by before he manages to finish. As he reads over the results, he is forced to admit that everything seems accurate. But then why does he feel so dissatisfied, so troubled by what he has written? He says to himself: what happened is not really what happened. For the first time in his experience of writing reports, he discovers that words do not necessarily work, that it is possible for them to obscure the things they are trying to say. Blue looks around the room and fixes his attention on various objects, one after another. He sees the lamp and says to himself, lamp. He sees the bed and says to himself, bed. He sees the notebook and says to himself, notebook. It will not do to call the lamp a bed, he thinks, or the bed a lamp. No, these words fit snugly around the things they stand for, and the moment Blue speaks them, he feels a deep satisfaction, as though he has just proved the existence of the world. Then he looks out across the street and sees Black's window. It is dark now, and Black is asleep. That's the problem, Blue says to himself, trying to find a little courage. That and nothing else. He's there, but it's impossible to see him. And even when I do see him it's as though the lights are out.

He seals up his report in an envelope and goes outside, walks to the corner, and drops it into the mailbox. I may not be the smartest person in the world, he says to himself, but I'm doing my best, I'm doing my best.

After that, the snow begins to melt. The next morning, the sun is shining brightly, clusters of sparrows are chirping in the trees, and Blue can hear the pleasant dripping of water from the edge of the roof, the branches, the lampposts. Spring suddenly does not seem far away. Another few weeks, he says to himself, and every morning will be like this one.

Black takes advantage of the weather to wander farther afield than previously, and Blue follows. Blue is relieved to be moving again, and as Black continues on his way, Blue hopes the journey will not end before he's had a chance to work out the kinks. As one would imagine, he has always been an ardent walker, and to feel his legs striding along through the morning air fills him with happiness. As they move through the narrow streets of Brooklyn Heights, Blue is encouraged to see that Black keeps increasing his distance from home. But then, his mood suddenly darkens. Black begins to climb the staircase that leads to the walkway across the Brooklyn Bridge, and Blue gets it into his head that he's planning to jump. Such things happen, he tells himself. A man goes to the top of the bridge, gives a last look to the world through the wind and the clouds, and then leaps out over the water, bones cracking on impact, his body broken apart. Blue gags on the image, tells himself to stay alert. If anything starts to happen, he decides, he will step out from his role as neutral bystander and intervene. For he does not want Black to be dead—at least not yet.

It has been many years since Blue crossed the Brooklyn Bridge on foot. The last time was with his father when he was a boy, and the memory of that day comes back to him now. He can see himself holding his father's hand and walking at his side, and as he hears the traffic moving along the steel bridge-road below, he can remember telling his father that this noise sounded like the buzzing of an enormous swarm of bees. To his left is the Statue of Liberty; to his right is Manhattan, the buildings so tall in the morning sun they seem to be figments. His father was a great one for facts, and he told Blue the stories of all the monuments and skyscrapers, vast litanies of detail—the architects, the dates, the political intrigues—and how at one time the Brooklyn Bridge was the tallest structure in America. The old man was born the same year the bridge was finished, and there was always that link in Blue's mind, as though the bridge were somehow a monument to his father. He liked the story he was told that day as he and Blue Senior walked home over the same wooden planks he was walking on now, and for some reason he never forgot it. How John Roebling, the designer of the bridge, got his foot crushed between the dock pilings and a ferry boat just days after finishing the plans and died from gangrene in less than three weeks. He didn't have to die, Blue's father said, but the only treatment he would accept was hydrotherapy, and that proved useless, and Blue was struck that a man who had spent his life building bridges over bodies of water so that people wouldn't get wet should believe that the only true medicine consisted in immersing oneself in water. After John Roebling's death, his son Washington took over as chief engineer, and that was another curious story. Washington Roebling was just thirty-one at the time, with no building experience except for the wooden bridges he designed during the Civil War, but he proved to be even more brilliant than his father. Not long after construction began on the Brooklyn Bridge, however, he was trapped for several hours during a fire in one of the underwater caissons and came out of it with a severe case of the bends, an excruciating disease in which nitrogen bubbles gather in the bloodstream. Nearly killed by the attack, he was thereafter an invalid, unable to leave the top floor room where he and his wife set up house in Brooklyn Heights. There Washington Roebling sat every day for many years, watching the progress of the bridge through a telescope, sending his wife down every morning with his instructions, drawing elaborate color pictures for the foreign workers who spoke no English so they would understand what to do next, and the remarkable thing was that the whole bridge was literally in his head: every piece of it had been memorized, down to the tiniest bits of steel and stone, and though Washington Roebling never set foot on the bridge, it was totally present inside him, as though by the end of all those years it had somehow grown into his body.

Blue thinks of this now as he makes his way across the river, watching Black ahead of him and remembering his father and his boyhood out in Gravesend. The old man was a cop, later a detective at the 77th precinct, and life would have been good, Blue thinks, if it hadn't been for the Russo Case and the bullet that went through his father's brain in 1927. Twenty years ago, he says to himself, suddenly appalled by the time that has passed, wondering if there is a heaven, and if so whether or not he will get to see his father again after he dies. He remembers a story from one of the endless magazines he has read this week, a new monthly called Stranger than Fiction, and it seems somehow to follow from all the other thoughts that have just come to him. Somewhere in the French Alps, he recalls, a man was lost skiing twenty or twenty-five years ago, swallowed up by an avalanche, and his body was never recovered. His son, who was a little boy at the time, grew up and also became a skier. One day in the past year he went skiing, not far from the spot where his father was lost—although he did not know this. Through the minute and persistent displacements of the ice over the decades since his father's death, the terrain was now completely different from what it had been. All alone there in the mountains, miles away from any other human being, the son chanced upon a body in the ice—a dead body, perfectly intact, as though preserved in suspended animation. Needless to say, the young man stopped to examine it, and as he bent down and looked at the face of the corpse, he had the distinct and terrifying impression that he was looking at himself. Trembling with fear, as the article put it, he inspected the body more closely, all sealed away as it was in the ice, like someone on the other side of a thick window, and saw that it was his father. The dead man was still young, even younger than his son was now, and there was something awesome about it, Blue felt, something so odd and terrible about being older than your own father, that he actually had to fight back tears as he read the article. Now, as he nears the end of the bridge, these same feelings come back to him, and he wishes to God that his father could be there, walking over the river and telling him stories. Then, suddenly aware of what his mind is doing, he wonders why he has turned so sentimental, why all these thoughts keep coming to him, when for so many years they have never even occurred to him. It's all part of it, he thinks, embarrassed at himself for being like this. That's what happens when you have no one to talk to.

He comes to the end and sees that he was wrong about Black. There will be no suicides today, no jumping from bridges, no leaps into the unknown. For there goes his man, as blithe and unperturbed as anyone can be, descending the stairs of the walkway and traveling along the street that curves around City Hall, then moving north along Centre Street past the courthouse and other municipal buildings, never once slackening his pace, continuing on through Chinatown and beyond. These divagations last several hours, and at no point does Blue have the sense that Black is walking to any purpose. He seems rather to be airing his lungs, walking for the pure pleasure of walking, and as the journey goes on Blue confesses to himself for the first time that he is developing a certain fondness for Black.

At one point Black enters a bookstore and Blue follows him in. There Black browses for half an hour or so, accumulating a small pile of books in the process, and Blue, with nothing better to do, browses as well, all the while trying to keep his face hidden from Black. The little glances he takes when Black seems not to be looking give him the feeling that he has seen Black before, but he can't remember where. There's something about the eyes, he says to himself, but that's as far as he gets, not wanting to call attention to himself and not really sure if there's anything to it.

A minute later, Blue comes across a copy of Walden by Henry David Thoreau. Flipping through the pages, he is surprised to discover that the name of the publisher is Black: "Published for the Classics Club by Walter J. Black, Inc., Copyright 1942." Blue is momentarily jarred by this coincidence, thinking that perhaps there is some message in it for him, some glimpse of meaning that could make a difference. But then, recovering from the jolt, he begins to think not. It's a common enough name, he says to himself—and besides, he knows for a fact that Black's name is not Walter. Could be a relative though, he adds, or maybe even his father. Still turning this last point over in his mind, Blue decides to buy the book. If he can't read what Black writes, at least he can read what he reads. A long shot, he says to himself, but who knows that it won't give some hint of what the man is up to.

So far so good. Black pays for his books, Blue pays for his book, and the walk continues. Blue keeps looking for some pattern to emerge, for some clue to drop in his path that will lead him to Black's secret. But Blue is too honest a man to delude himself, and he knows that no rhyme or reason can be read into anything that's happened so far. For once, he is not discouraged by this. In fact, as he probes more deeply into himself, he realizes that on the whole he feels rather invigorated by it. There is something nice about being in the dark, he discovers, something thrilling about not knowing what is going to happen next. It keeps you alert, he thinks, and there's no harm in that, is there? Wide awake and on your toes, taking it all in, ready for anything.

A few moments after thinking this thought, Blue is finally offered a new development, and the case takes on its first twist. Black turns a corner in midtown, walks halfway down the block, hesitates briefly, as if searching for an address, backtracks a few paces, moves on again, and several seconds later enters a restaurant. Blue follows him in, thinking nothing much of it, since it's lunchtime after all, and people have to eat, but it does not escape him that Black's hesitation seems to indicate that he's never been here before, which in turn might mean that Black has an appointment. It's a dark place inside, fairly crowded, with a group of people clustered around the bar in front, lots of chatter and the clinking of silverware and plates in the background. It looks expensive, Blue thinks, with wood paneling on the walls and white tablecloths, and he decides to keep his bill as low as he can. Tables are available, and Blue takes it as a good omen when he is seated within eyeshot of Black, not obtrusively close, but not so far as not to be able to watch what he does. Black tips his hand by asking for two menus, and three or four minutes later breaks into a smile when a woman walks across the room, approaches Black's table, and kisses him on the cheek before sitting down. The woman's not bad, Blue thinks. A bit on the lean side for his taste, but not bad at all. Then he thinks: now the interesting part begins.

Unfortunately, the woman's back is turned to Blue, so he can't watch her face as the meal progresses. As he sits there eating his Salisbury steak, he thinks that maybe his first hunch was the right one, that it's a marriage case after all. Blue is already imagining the kinds of things he will write in his next report, and it gives him pleasure to contemplate the phrases he will use to describe what he is seeing now. By having another person in the case, he knows that certain decisions have to be made. For example: should he stick with Black or divert his attention to the woman? This could possibly accelerate matters a bit, but at the same time it could mean that Black would be given the chance to slip away from him, perhaps for good. In other words, is the meeting with the woman a smoke-screen or the real thing? Is it a part of the case or not, is it an essential or contingent fact? Blue ponders these questions for a while and concludes that it's too early to tell. Yes, it could be one thing, he tells himself. But it could be another.

About midway through the meal, things seem to take a turn for the worse. Blue detects a look of great sadness in Black's face, and before he knows it the woman seems to be crying. At least that is what he can gather from the sudden change in the position of her body: her shoulders slumped, her head leaning forward, her face perhaps covered by her hands, the slight shuddering along her back. It could be a fit of laughter, Blue reasons, but then why would Black be so miserable? It looks as though the ground has just been cut out from under him. A moment later, the woman turns her face away from Black, and Blue gets a glimpse of her profile: tears without question, he thinks, as he watches her dab her eyes with a napkin and sees a smudge of wet mascara glistening on her cheek. She stands up abruptly and walks off in the direction of the ladies' room. Again Blue has an unobstructed view of Black, and seeing the sadness in his face, that look of absolute dejection, he almost begins to feel sorry for him. Black glances in Blue's direction, but clearly he's not seeing anything, and then, an instant later, he buries his face in his hands. Blue tries to guess what is happening, but it's impossible to know. It looks like it's over between them, he thinks, it has the feeling of something that's come to an end. And yet, for all that, it could be just a tiff.

The woman returns to the table looking a little better, and then the two of them sit there for a few minutes without saying anything, leaving their food untouched. Black sighs once or twice, looking off into the distance, and finally calls for the check. Blue does the same and then follows the two of them out of the restaurant. He notes that Black has his hand on her elbow, but that could just be a reflex he tells himself, and probably means nothing. They walk down the street in silence, and at the corner Black waves down a cab. He opens the door for the woman, and before she climbs in he touches her very gently on the cheek. She gives him a brave little smile in return, but still they don't say a word. Then she sits down in the back seat, Black shuts the door, and the cab takes off.

Black walks around for a few minutes, pausing briefly in front of a travel agency window to study a poster of the White Mountains, and then climbs into a cab himself. Blue gets lucky again and manages to find another cab just seconds later. He tells the driver to follow Black's cab and then sits back as the two yellow cars make their way slowly through the traffic downtown, across the Brooklyn Bridge, and finally to Orange Street. Blue is shocked by the fare and kicks himself mentally for not following the woman instead. He should have known that Black was going home.

His mood brightens considerably when he enters his building and finds a letter in his mailbox. It can only be one thing, he tells himself, and sure enough as he walks upstairs and opens the envelope, there it is: the first check, a postal money order for the exact amount settled on with White. He finds it a bit perplexing, however, that the method of payment should be so anonymous. Why not a personal check from White? This leads Blue to toy with the thought that White is a renegade agent after all, eager to cover his tracks and therefore making sure there will be no record of the payments. Then, removing his hat and overcoat and stretching out on the bed, Blue realizes that he's a little disappointed not to have had some comment about the report. Considering how hard he struggled to get it right, a word of encouragement would have been welcomed. The fact that the money was sent means that White was not dissatisfied. But still—silence is not a rewarding response, no matter what it means. If that's the way it is, Blue says to himself, I'll just have to get used it.

The days go by, and once again things settle down to the barest of routines. Black writes, reads, shops in the neighborhood, visits the post office, takes an occasional stroll. The woman does not reappear, and Black makes no further excursions to Manhattan. Blue begins to think that any day he will get a letter telling him the case is closed. The woman is gone, he reasons, and that could be the end of it. But nothing of the sort happens. Blue's meticulous description of the scene in restaurant draws no special response from White, and week after week the checks continue to arrive on time. So much for love, Blue says to himself. The woman never meant anything. She was just a diversion.

In this early period, Blue's state of mind can best be described as one of ambivalence and conflict. There are moments when he feels so completely in harmony with Black, so naturally at one with the other man, that to anticipate what Black is going to do, to know when he will stay in his room and when he will go out, he need merely look into himself. Whole days go by when he doesn't even bother to look through the window or follow Black onto the street. Now and then, he even allows himself to make solo expeditions, knowing full well that during the time he is gone Black will not have budged from his spot. How he knows this remains something of a mystery to him, but the fact is that he is never wrong, and when the feeling comes over him, he is beyond all doubt and hesitation. On the other hand, not all moments are like these. There are times when he feels totally removed from Black, cut off from him in a way that is so stark and absolute that he begins to lose the sense of who he is. Loneliness envelopes him, sits him in, and with it comes a terror worse than anything he has ever known. It puzzles him that he should switch so rapidly from one state to another, and for a long time he goes back and forth between extremes, not knowing which one is true and which one is false.

After a stretch of particularly bad days, he begins to long for some companionship. He sits down and writes a detailed letter to Brown, outlining the case and asking for his advice. Brown has retired to Florida, where he spends most of his time fishing, and Blue knows that it will take quite a while before he receives an answer. Still, the day after he mails the letter, he begins looking forward to the reply with an eagerness that soon grows to obsession. Each morning, about an hour before the mail is delivered, he plants himself by the window, watching for the postman to round the corner and come into view, pinning all his hopes on what Brown will say to him. What he is expecting from this letter is not certain. Blue does not even ask the question, but surely it is something monumental, some luminous and extraordinary words that will bring him back to the world of the living.

As the days and weeks go by without any letter from Brown, Blue's disappointment grows into aching, irrational desperation. But that is nothing compared to what he feels when the letter finally comes. For Brown does not even address himself to what Blue wrote. It's good to hear from you, the letter begins, and good to know you're working so hard. Sounds like an interesting case. Can't say I miss any of it, though. Here it's the good life for me—get up early and fish, spend some time with my wife, read a little, sleep in the sun, nothing to complain about. The only thing I don't understand is why I didn't move down here years ago.

The letter goes on in that vein for several pages, never once broaching the subject of Blue's torments and anxieties. Blue feels betrayed by the man who was once like a father to him, and when he finishes the letter he feels empty, the stuffing all knocked out of him. I'm on my own, he thinks, there's no one to turn to anymore. This is followed by several hours of despondency and self-pity, with Blue thinking once or twice that maybe he'd be better off dead. But eventually he works his way out of the gloom. For Blue is a solid character on the whole, less given to dark thoughts than most, and if there are moments when he feels the world is a foul place, who are we to blame him for it? By the time supper rolls around, he has even begun to look on the bright side. This is perhaps his greatest talent: not that he does not despair, but that he never despairs for very long. It might be a good thing after all, he says to himself. It might be better to stand alone than to depend on anyone else. Blue thinks about this for a while and decides there is something to be said for it. He is no longer an apprentice. There is no master above him anymore. I'm my own man, he says to himself. I'm my own man, accountable to no one but myself.

Inspired by this new approach to things, he discovers that he has at last found the courage to contact the future Mrs. Blue. But when he picks up the phone and dials her number, there is no answer. This is a disappointment, but he remains undaunted. I'll try again some other time, he says. Some time soon.

The days continue to pass. Once again, Blue falls into step with Black, per- 55
haps even more harmoniously than before. In doing so, he discovers the in-

herent paradox of his situation. For the closer he feels to Black, the less he finds it necessary to think about him. In other words, the more deeply entangled he becomes, the freer he is. What bogs him down is not involvement but separation. For it is only when Black seems to drift away from him that he must go out looking for him, and this takes time and effort, not to speak of struggle. At those moments when he feels closest to Black, however, he can even begin to lead the semblance of an independent life. At first he is not very daring in what he allows himself to do, but even so he considers it a kind of triumph, almost an act of bravery. Going outside, for example, and walking up and down the block. Small as it might be, this gesture fills him with happiness, and as he moves back and forth along Orange Street in the lovely spring weather, he is glad to be alive in a way he has not felt in years. At one end there is a view of the river, the harbor, the Manhattan skyline, the bridges. Blue finds all this beautiful, and on some days he even allows himself to sit for several minutes on one of the benches and look out at the boats. In the other direction there is the church, and sometimes Blue goes to the small grassy yard to sit for a while, studying the bronze statue of Henry Ward Beecher. Two slaves are holding on to Beecher's legs, as though begging him to help them, to make them free at last, and in the brick wall behind there is a porcelain relief of Abraham Lincoln. Blue cannot help but feel inspired by these images, and each time he comes to the churchyard his head fills with noble thoughts about the dignity of man.

Little by little, he becomes more bold in his strayings from Black. It is 1947, the year that Jackie Robinson breaks in with the Dodgers, and Blue follows in his progress closely, remembering the churchyard and knowing there is more to it than just baseball. One bright Tuesday afternoon in May, he decides to make an excursion to Ebbetts Field, and as he leaves Black behind in his room on Orange Street, hunched over his desk as usual with his pen and papers, he feels no cause for worry, secure in the fact that everything will be exactly the same when he returns. He rides the subway, rubs shoulders with the crowd, feels himself lunging towards a sense of the moment. As he takes his seat at the ball park, he is struck by the sharp clarity of the colors around him: the green grass, the brown dirt, the white ball, the blue sky above. Each thing is distinct from every other thing, wholly separate and defined, and the geometric simplicity for the pattern impresses Blue with its force. Watching the game, he finds it difficult to take his eyes off Robinson, lured constantly by the blackness of the man's face, and he thinks it must take courage to do what he is doing, to be alone like that in front of so many strangers, with half of them no doubt wishing him to be dead. As the game moves along, Blue finds himself cheering whatever Robinson does, and when the black man steals a base in the third inning he rises to his feet, and later, in the seventh, when Robinson doubles off the wall in left, he actually pounds the back of the man next to him for joy. The Dodgers pull it out in the ninth with a sacrifice fly, and as Blue shuffles off with the rest of the crowd and makes his way home, it occurs to him that Black did not cross his mind even once.

But the ball games are only the beginning. On certain nights, when it is clear to Blue that Black will not be going anywhere, he slips out to a bar not far away for a beer or two, enjoying the conversations he sometimes has with the bartender, whose name is Red, and who bears an uncanny resemblance to Green, the bartender from the Gray Case so long ago. A blowsy tart named Violet is often there, and once or twice Blue gets her tipsy enough to get invited back to her place around the corner. He knows that she likes him well enough because she never makes him pay for it, but he also knows that it has nothing to do with love. She calls him honey and her flesh is soft and ample, but whenever she has one drink too many she begins to cry, and then Blue has to console her, and he secretly wonders if it's worth the trouble. His guilt towards the future Mrs. Blue is scant, however, for he justifies these sessions with Violet by comparing himself to a soldier at war in another country. Every man needs a little comfort, especially when his number could be up tomorrow. And besides, he isn't made of stone, he says to himself.

More often than not, however, Blue will bypass the bar and go to the movie theatre several blocks away. With summer coming on now and the heat beginning to hover uncomfortably in his little room, it's refreshing to be able to sit in the cool theater and watch the feature show. Blue is fond of the movies, not only for the stories they tell and the beautiful women he can see in them, but for the darkness of the theater itself, the way the pictures on the screen are somehow like the thoughts inside his head whenever he closes his eyes. He is more or less indifferent to the kinds of movies he sees, whether comedies or dramas, for example, or whether the film is shot in black and white or color, but he has a particular weakness for movies about detectives, since there is a natural connection, and he is always gripped by these stories more than by others. During this period he sees a number of such movies and enjoys them all: Lady in the Lake, Fallen Angel, Dark Passage, Body and Soul, Ride the Pink Horse, Desperate, and so on. But for Blue there is one that stands out from the rest, and he likes it so much that he actually goes back the next night to see it again.

It's called Out of the Past, and it stars Robert Mitchum as an ex-private eye who is trying to build a new life for himself in a small town under an assumed name. He has a girl friend, a sweet country girl named Ann, and runs a gas station with the help of a deaf-and-dumb boy, Jimmy, who is firmly devoted to him. But the past catches up with Mitchum, and there's little he can do about it. Years ago, he had been hired to look for Jane Greer, the mistress of gangster Kirk Douglas, but once he found her they fell in love and ran off together to live in secret. One thing led to another—money was stolen, a murder was committed—and eventually Mitchum came to his senses and left Greer, finally understanding the depth of her corruption. Now he is being blackmailed by Douglas and Greer into committing a crime, which itself is merely a set-up, for once he figures out what is happening, he sees that they are planning to frame him for another murder. A complicated story unfolds, with Mitchum desperately trying to extricate himself from the trap. At one point, he returns to the small town where he lives, tells Ann that he's innocent, and again persuades her of his love. But it's really too late, and Mitchum knows it. Towards the end, he manages to convince Douglas to turn in Greer for the murder she committed, but at that moment Greer enters the room, calmly takes out a gun, and kills Douglas. She tells Mitchum that they belong to each other, and he, fatalistic to the last, appears to go along. They decide to escape the country together, but as Greer goes to pack her bag, Mitchum picks up the phone and calls the police. They get into the car and drive off, but soon they come to a police roadblock. Greer, seeing that she's been double-crossed, pulls a gun from her bag and shoots Mitchum. The police then open fire on the car and Greer is killed as well. After that, there's one last scene—the next morning, back in the small town of Bridgeport. Jimmy is sitting on a bench outside the gas station, and Ann walks over and sits down beside him. Tell me one thing, Jimmy, she says, I've got to know this one thing: was he running away with her or not? The boy thinks for a moment, trying to decide between truth and kindness. Is it more important to preserve a friend's good name or to spare the girl? All this happens in no more than an instant. Looking into the girl's eyes, he nods his head, as if to say yes, he was in love with Greer after all. Ann pats Jimmy's arm and thanks him, then walks off to her former boyfriend, a straight-arrow local policeman who always despised Mitchum. Jimmy looks up at the gas station sign with Mitchum's name on it, gives a little salute of friendship, and then turns away and walks down the road. He is the only one who knows the truth, and he will never tell.

For the next few days, Blue goes over this story many times in his head. 60
It's a good thing, he decides, that the movie ends with the deaf mute boy. The secret is buried, and Mitchum will remain an outsider, even in death. His ambition was simple enough: to become a normal citizen in a normal American town, to marry the girl next door, to live a quiet life. It's strange, Blue thinks, that the new name Mitchum chooses for himself is Jeff Bailey. This is remarkably close to the name of another character in a movie he saw the previous year with the future Mrs. Blue—George Bailey, played by James Stewart in It's a Wonderful Life. That story was also about small town America, but from the opposite point of view: the frustrations of a man who spends his whole life trying to escape. But in the end he comes to understand that his life has been a good one, that he has done the right thing all along. Mitchum's Bailey would no doubt like to be the same man as Stewart's Bailey. But in his case the name is Markham—or, as Blue sounds it out to himself, mark him—and that is the whole point. He has been marked by the past, and once that happens, nothing can be done about it. Something happens, Blue thinks, and then it goes on happening forever. It can never be changed, can never be otherwise. Blue begins to be haunted by this thought, for he sees it as a kind of warning, a message delivered up from within himself, and try as he does to push it away, the darkness of this thought does not leave him.

One night, therefore, Blue finally turns to his copy of Walden. The time has come, he says to himself, and if he doesn't make an effort now, he knows that he never will. But the book is not a simple business. As Blue begins to read, he feels as though he is entering an alien world. Trudging through swamps and brambles, hoisting himself up gloomy screes and treacherous cliffs, he feels like a prisoner on a forced march, and his only thought is to escape. He is bored by Thoreau's words and finds it difficult to concentrate. Whole chapters go by, and when he comes to the end of them he realizes that he has not retained a thing. Why would anyone want to go off and live alone in the woods? What's all this about planting beans and not drinking coffee or eating meat? Why all these interminable descriptions of birds? Blue thought that he was going to get a story, or at least something like a story, but this is no more than blather, an endless harangue about nothing at all.

It would be unfair to blame him, however. Blue has never read much of anything except newspapers and magazines, and an occasional adventure novel when he was a boy. Even experienced and sophisticated readers have been known to have trouble with Walden, and no less a figure than Emerson once wrote in his journal that reading Thoreau made him feel nervous and wretched. To Blue's credit, he does not give up. The next day he begins again, and this second go-through is somewhat less rocky than the first. In the third chapter he comes across a sentence that finally says something to him—Books must be read as deliberately and reservedly as they were written—and suddenly he understands that the trick is to go slowly, more slowly than he has ever gone with words before. This helps to some extent, and certain passages begin to grow clear: the business about clothes in the beginning, the battle between the red ants and the black ants, the argument against work. But Blue still finds it painful, and though he grudgingly admits that Thoreau is perhaps not as stupid as he thought, he begins to resent Black for putting him through this torture. What he does not know is that were he to find the patience to read the book in the spirit in which it asks to be read, his entire life would begin to change, and little by little he would come to a full understanding to his situation—that is to say, of Black, of White, of the case, of everything that concerns him. But lost chances are as much a part of life as chances taken, and a story cannot dwell on what might have been. Throwing the book aside in disgust, Blue puts on his coat (for it is fall now) and goes out for a breath of air. Little does he realize that this is the beginning of the end. For something is about to happen, and once it happens, nothing will ever be the same again.

He goes to Manhattan, wandering farther from Black than at any time before, venting his frustration in movement, hoping to calm himself down by exhausting his body. He walks north, alone in his thoughts, not bothering to take in the things around him. On East 26th Street his left shoelace comes undone, and it is precisely then, as he bends down to tie it, crouching on one knee, that the sky falls on top of him. For who should he glimpse at just that moment but the future Mrs. Blue. She is coming up the street with her two arms linked through the right arm of a man Blue has never seen before, and she is smiling radiantly, engrossed in what the man is saying to her. For several moments Blue is so at a loss that he doesn't know whether to bend his head farther down and hide his face or stand up and greet the woman whom he now understands—with a knowledge as sudden and irrevocable as the slamming of a door—will never be his wife. As it turns out, he manages neither—first ducking his head, but then discovering a second later that he wants her to recognize him, and when he sees she will not, being so wrapped up in her companion's talk, Blue abruptly rises from the pavement when they are no more than six feet away from him. It is as though some spectre has suddenly materialized in front of her, and the ex–future Mrs. Blue gives out a little gasp, even before she sees who the spectre is. Blue speaks her name, in a voice that seems strange to him, and she stops dead in her tracks, her expression turns to one of anger.

You! she says to him. You!

Before he has a chance to say a word, she disentangles herself from her 65
companion's arm and begins pounding Blue's chest with her fists, screaming insanely at him, accusing him of one foul crime after another. It is all Blue can do to repeat her name over and over, as though trying desperately to distinguish between the woman he loves and the wild beast who is now attacking him. He feels totally defenseless, and as the onslaught continues, he begins to welcome each new blow as just punishment for his behavior. The other man soon puts a stop to it, however, and though Blue is tempted to take a swing at him, he is too stunned to act quickly enough, and before he knows it the man has led away the weeping ex-future Mrs. Blue down the street and around the corner, and that's the end of it.

This brief scene, so unexpected and devastating, turns Blue inside out. By the time he regains his composure and manages to return home, he realizes that he has thrown away his life. It's not her fault, he says to himself, wanting to blame her but knowing he can't. He might have been dead for all she knew, and how can he hold it against her for wanting to live? Blue feels tears forming in his eyes, but more than grief he feels anger at himself for being such a fool. He has lost whatever chance he might have had for happiness, and if that is the case, then it would not be wrong to say that this is truly the beginning of the end.

Blue gets back to his room on Orange Street, lies down on his bed, and tries to weigh the possibilities. Eventually, he turns his face to the wall and encounters the photograph of the coroner from Philadelphia, Gold. He thinks of the sad blankness of the unsolved case, the child lying in his grave with no name, and as he studies the death mask of the little boy, he begins to turn an idea over in his mind. Perhaps there are ways of getting close to Black, he thinks, ways that need not give him away. God knows there must be. Moves that can be made, plans that can be set in motion—perhaps two or three at the same time. Never mind the rest, he tells himself. It's time to turn the page.

His next report is due the day after tomorrow, and so he sits down to it now in order to get it mailed off on schedule. For the past few months his reports have been exceedingly cryptic, no more than a paragraph or two, giving the bare bones and nothing else, and this time he does not depart from the pattern. However, at the bottom of the page he interjects an obscure comment as a kind of test, hoping to elicit something more than silence from White: Black seems ill. I'm afraid he might be dying. Then he seals up the report, saying to himself that this is only the beginning.

Two days hence, Blue hastens early in the morning to the Brooklyn Post Office, a great castle of a building within eyeshot of the Manhattan Bridge. All of Blue's reports have been addressed to box number one thousand and one, and he walks over to it now as though by accident, sauntering past it and unobtrusively peeking inside to see if the report has come. It has. Or at least a letter is there—a solitary white envelope tilted at a forty-five degree angle in the narrow cubby—and Blue has no reason to suspect it's any letter other than his own. He then begins a slow circular walk around the area, determined to remain until White or someone working for White appears, his eyes fixed on the huge wall of numbered boxes, each box with a different combination, each one holding a different secret. People come and go, open boxes and close them, and Blue keeps wandering in his circle, pausing every now and then in some random spot and then moving on. Everything seems brown to him, as though the fall weather outside has penetrated the room, and the place smells pleasantly of cigar smoke. After several hours he begins to get hungry, but he does not give in to the call of his stomach, telling himself it's now or never and therefore holding his ground. Blue watches everyone who approaches the bank of post boxes, zeroing in on each person who skirts the vicinity of one thousand and one, aware of the fact that if it's not White who comes for the reports it could be anyone—an old woman, a young child, and consequently he must take nothing for granted. But none of these possibilities comes to anything, for the box remains untouched throughout, and though Blue momentarily and successively spins a story for each candidate who comes near, trying to imagine how that person might be connected to White and or Black, what role he or she might play in the case, and so on, one by one he is forced to diminish them from his mind, casting them back into the oblivion from which they have come.

70 Just past noon, at a moment when the post office begins to get crowded—an influx of people on their lunch break rushing through to mail letters, buy stamps, attend to business of one sort or another—a man with a mask on his face walks through the door. Blue doesn't notice him at first, what with so many others coming through the door at the same time, but as the man separates himself from the crowd and begins walking toward the numbered post boxes, Blue finally catches sight of the mask—a mask of the sort that children wear on Halloween, made of rubber and portraying some hideous monster with gashes in his forehead and bleeding eyeballs and fangs for teeth. The rest of him is perfectly ordinary (gray tweed overcoat, red scarf wrapped around his neck), and Blue senses in this first moment that the man behind the mask is White. As the man continues walking toward the area of box one thousand and one, this sense grows to conviction. At the same time, Blue also feels that the man is not really there, that even though he knows he is seeing him, it is more than likely that he is the only one who can. On this point, however, Blue is wrong, for as the masked man continues moving across the vast marble floor, Blue sees a number of people laughing and pointing at him—but whether this is better or worse he cannot say. The masked man reaches box one thousand and one, spins the combination wheel back and forth and back again, and opens the box. As soon as Blue sees that this is definitely his man, he begins making a move toward him, not really sure of what he is planning to do, but in the back of his mind no doubt intending to grab hold of him and tear the mask off his face. But the man is too alert, and once he has pocketed the envelope and locked the box, he gives a quick glance around the room, sees Blue approaching, and makes a dash for it, heading for the door as fast as he can. Blue runs after him, hoping to catch him from behind and tackle him, but he gets tangled momentarily in a crowd of people at the door, and by the

time he manages to get through it, the masked man is bounding down the stairs, landing on the sidewalk, and running down the street. Blue continues in pursuit, even feels he is gaining ground, but then the man reaches the corner, where a bus just happens to be pulling out from a stop, and so he conveniently leaps aboard, and Blue is left in the lurch, all out of breath and standing there like an idiot.

Two days later, when Blue receives his check in the mail, there is finally a word from White. No more funny business, it says, and though it's not much of a word, for all that Blue is glad to have received it, happy to have cracked White's wall of silence at last. It's not clear to him, however, whether the message refers to the last report or to the incident in the post office. After thinking it over for a while, he decides that it makes no difference. One way or another, the key to the case is action. He must go on disrupting things wherever he can, a little here, a little there, chipping away at each conundrum until the whole structure begins to weaken, until one day the whole rotten business comes toppling to the ground.

Over the next few weeks, Blue returns to the post office several times, hoping to catch another glimpse of White. But nothing comes of it. Either the report is already gone from the box when he gets there, or White does not show up. The fact that this area of the post office is open twenty-four hours a day leaves Blue with few options. White is on to him now, and he will not make the same mistake twice. He will simply wait until Blue is gone before going to the box, and unless Blue is willing to spend his entire life in the post office, there's no way he can expect to sneak up on White again.

The picture is far more complicated than Blue ever imagined. For almost a year now, he has thought of himself as essentially free. For better or worse he has been doing his job, looking straight ahead of him and studying Black, waiting for a possible opening, trying to stick with it, but through it all he has not given a single thought to what might be going on behind him. Now, after the incident with the masked man and the further obstacles that have ensued, Blue no longer knows what to think. It seems perfectly plausible to him that he is also being watched, observed by another in the same way that he has been observing Black. If that is the case, then he has never been free. From the very start he has been the man in the middle, thwarted in front and hemmed in on the rear. Oddly enough, this thought reminds him of some sentences from Walden, and he searches through his notebook for the exact phrasing, fairly certain that he has written them down. We are not where we are, he finds, but in a false position Through an infirmity of our natures, we suppose a case, and put ourselves into it, and hence are in two cases at the same time, and it is doubly difficult to get out. This makes sense to Blue, and though he is beginning to feel a little frightened, he thinks that perhaps it is not too late for him to do something about it.

The real problem boils down to identifying the nature of the problem itself. To start with, who poses the greater threat to him, White or Black? White has kept up his end of the bargain: the checks have come on time every week, and to turn against him now, Blue knows, would be to bite the hand that feeds him. And yet White is the one who set the case in motion—thrusting Blue into an empty room, as it were, and then turning off the light and locking the door. Ever since, Blue has been groping about in the darkness, feeling blindly for the light switch, a prisoner of the case itself. All well and good, but why would White want to do such a thing? When Blue comes up against this question, he can no longer think. His brain stops working, he can get no farther than this.

75 Take Black, then. Until now he has been the entire case, the apparent cause of all his troubles. But if White is really out to get Blue and not Black, then perhaps Black has nothing to do with it, perhaps he is no more than an innocent bystander. In that case, it is Black who occupies the position Blue has assumed all along to be his, and Blue who takes the role of Black. There is something to be said for this. On the other hand, it is also possible that Black is somehow working in league with White and that together they have conspired to do Blue in.

If so, what are they doing to him? Nothing very terrible, finally—at least not in any absolute sense. They have trapped Blue into doing nothing, into being so inactive as to reduce his life to almost no life at all. Yes, says Blue to himself, that's what it feels like: like nothing at all. He feels like a man who has been condemned to sit in a room and go on reading a book for the rest of his life. This is strange enough—to be only half alive at best, seeing the world only through words, living only through the lives of others. But if the book were an interesting one, perhaps it wouldn't be so bad. He could get caught up in the story, so to speak, and little by little begin to forget himself. But this book offers him nothing. There is no story, no plot, no action—nothing but a man sitting alone in a room and writing a book. That's all there is, Blue realizes, and he no longer wants any part of it. But how to get out? How to get out of the room that is the book that will go on being written for as long as he stays in the room?

As for Black, the so-called writer of this book, Blue can no longer trust what he sees. Is it possible that there really is such a man—who does nothing, who merely sits in his room and writes? Blue has followed him everywhere, has tracked him down into the remotest corners, has watched him so hard that his eyes seem to be failing him. Even when he does leave his room, Black never goes anywhere, never does much of anything: grocery shopping, an occasional haircut, a trip to the movies, and so on. But mostly he just wanders around the streets, looking at odd bits of scenery, clusters of random data, and even this happens only in spurts. For a while it will be buildings—craning his neck to catch a glimpse of the roofs, inspecting doorways, running his hands slowly over the stone facades. And then, for a week or two, it will be public statues, or the boats in the river, or the signs in the street. Nothing more than that, with scarcely a word to anyone, and no meetings with others except for that one lunch with the woman in tears by now so long ago. In one sense, Blue knows everything there is to know about Black: what kind of soap he buys, what newspapers he reads, what clothes he wears, and each of these things he has faithfully recorded in his notebook. He has learned a thousand facts, but the only thing they have taught him is that he knows nothing. For the fact remains that none of this is possible. It is not possible for such a man as Black to exist.

Consequently, Blue begins to suspect that Black is no more than a ruse, another one of White's hirelings, paid by the week to sit in that room and do nothing. Perhaps all that writing is merely a sham—page after page of it: a list of every name in the phone book, for example, or each word from the dictionary in alphabetical order, or a handwritten copy of Walden. Or perhaps they are not even words, but senseless scribbles, random marks of a pen, a growing heap of nonsense and confusion. This would make White the real writer then—and Black no more than his stand-in, a fake, an actor with no substance of his own. Then there are the times, following through with this thought, that Blue believes the only logical explanation is that Black is not one man but several. Two, three, four look-alikes who play the role of Black for Blue's benefit, each one putting in his allotted time and then going back to the comforts of hearth and home. But this is a thought too monstrous for Blue to contemplate for very long. Months go by, and at last he says to himself out loud: I can't breathe anymore. This is the end. I'm dying.

It is midsummer, 1948. Finally mustering the courage to act, Blue reaches into his bag of disguises and casts about for a new identity. After dismissing several possibilities, he settles on an old man who used to beg on the corners of his neighborhood when he was a boy—a local character by the name of Jimmy Rose—and decks himself out in the garb of tramphood: tattered woolen clothes, shoes held together with string to prevent the soles from flapping, a weathered carpetbag to hold his belongings, and then, last of all, a flowing white beard and long white hair. These final details give him the look of an Old Testament prophet. Blue as Jimmy Rose is not a scrofulous down-and-outer so much as a wise fool, a saint of penury living in the margins of society. A trifle daft perhaps, but harmless: he exudes a sweet indifference to the world around him, for since everything has happened to him already, nothing can disturb him anymore.

Blue posts himself in a suitable spot across the street, takes a fragment of a broken magnifying glass from his pocket, and begins reading a crumpled day-old newspaper that he has salvaged from one of the nearby garbage cans. Two hours later, Black appears, walking down the steps of his house and then turning in Blue's direction. Black pays no attention to the bum—either lost in his own thoughts or ignoring him on purpose—and so as he begins to approach, Blue addresses him in a pleasant voice.

Can you spare some change, mister?

Black stops, looks over the disheveled creature who has just spoken, and gradually relaxes into a smile as he realizes he is not in danger. Then he reaches into his pocket, pulls out a coin, and puts it in Blue's hand.

Here you are, he says.

God bless you, says Blue.

Thank you, answers Black, touched by the sentiment.

Never fear, says Blue. God blesses all.

And with that word of reassurance, Black tips his hat to Blue and continues on his way.

The next afternoon, once again in bum's regalia, Blue waits for Black in the same spot. Determined to keep the conversation going a little longer this time, now that he has won Black's confidence, Blue finds that the problem is taken out of his hands when Black himself shows an eagerness to linger. It is late in the day by now, not yet dusk but no longer afternoon, the twilight hour of slow changes, of glowing bricks and shadows. After greeting the bum cordially and giving him another coin, Black hesitates a moment, as though debating whether to take the plunge, and then says:

Has anyone ever told you that you look just like Walt Whitman?

Walt who? answers Blue, remembering to play his part. 90

Walt Whitman. A famous poet.

No, says Blue. I can't say I know him.

You wouldn't know him, says Black. He's not alive anymore. But the resemblance is remarkable.

Well, you know what they say, says Blue. Every man has his double somewhere. I don't see why mine can't be a dead man.

The funny thing, continues Black, is that Walt Whitman used to work on 95
this street. He printed his first book right here, not far from where we're standing.

You don't say, says Blue, shaking his head pensively. It makes you stop and think, doesn't it?

There are some odd stories about Whitman, Black says, gesturing to Blue to sit down on the stoop of the building behind them, which he does, and then Black does the same, and suddenly it's just the two of them out there in the summer light together, chatting away like two old friends about this and that.

Yes, says Black, settling in comfortably to the languor of the moment, a number of very curious stories. The one about Whitman's brain, for example. All his life Whitman believed in the science of phrenology—you know, reading the bumps on the skull. It was very popular at the time.

Can't say I've ever heard of it, replies Blue.

Well, that doesn't much matter, says Black. The main thing is that Whit- 100
man was interested in brains and skulls—thought they could tell you everything about a man's character. Anyway, when Whitman lay dying over there in New Jersey about fifty or sixty years ago, he agreed to let them perform an autopsy on him after he was dead.

How could he agree to it after he was dead?

Ah, good point. I didn't say it right. He was still alive when he agreed. He just wanted them to know that he didn't mind if they opened him up later. What you might call his dying wish.

Famous last words.

That's right. A lot of people thought he was a genius, you see, and they wanted to take a look at his brain to find out if there was anything special about it. So, the day after he died, a doctor removed Whitman's brain—cut it right out of his head—and had it sent to the American Anthropometric Society to be measured and weighed.

Like a giant cauliflower, interjects Blue. 105

Exactly. Like a big gray vegetable. But this is where the story gets interesting. The brain arrives at the laboratory, and just as they're about to get to work on it, one of the assistants drops it on the floor.

Did it break?

Of course it broke. A brain isn't very tough, you know. It splattered all over the place, and that was that. The brain of America's greatest poet got swept up and thrown out with the garbage.

Blue, remembering to respond in character, emits several wheezing laughs—a good imitation of an old codger's mirth. Black laughs, too, and by now the atmosphere has thawed to such an extent that no one could ever know they were not lifelong chums.

It's sad to think of poor Walt lying in his grave, though, says Black. All alone and without any brains.

Just like that scarecrow, says Blue.

Sure enough, says Black. Just like the scarecrow in the land of Oz.

After another good laugh, Black says: And then there's the story of the time Thoreau came to visit Whitman. That's a good one, too.

Was he another poet?

Not exactly. But a great writer just the same. He's the one who lived alone in the woods.

Oh yes, says Blue, not wanting to carry his ignorance too far. Someone once told me about him. Very fond of nature he was. Is that the man you mean?

Precisely, answers Black. Henry David Thoreau. He came down from Massachusetts for a little while and paid a call on Whitman in Brooklyn. But the day before that he came right here to Orange Street.

Any particular reason?

Plymouth Church. He wanted to hear Henry Ward Beecher's sermon.

A lovely spot, says Blue, thinking of the pleasant hours he has spent in the grassy yard. I like to go there myself.

Many great men have gone there, says Black. Abraham Lincoln, Charles Dickens—they all walked down this street and went into the church.

Ghosts.

Yes, there are ghosts all around us.

And the story?

It's really very simple. Thoreau and Bronson Alcott, a friend of his, arrived at Whitman's house on Myrtle Avenue, and Walt's mother sent them up to the attic bedroom he shared with his mentally retarded brother, Eddy. Everything was just fine. They shook hands, exchanged greetings, and so on. But then, when they sat down to discuss their views of life, Thoreau and Alcott noticed a full chamber pot right in the middle of the floor. Walt was of course an expansive fellow and paid no attention, but the two New Englanders found it hard to keep talking with a bucket of excrement in front of them. So eventually they went downstairs to the parlor and continued the conversation there. It's a minor detail, I realize. But still, when two great writers meet, history is made, and it's important to get all the facts straight. That chamber pot, you see, somehow reminds me of the brains on the floor. And when you stop to think about it, there's a certain similarity of form. The bumps and convolutions, I mean. There's a definite connection. Brains and guts, the insides of a man. We always talk about trying to get inside a writer to understand his work better. But when you get right down to it, there's not much to find in there—at least not much that's different from what you'd find in anyone else.

You seem to know a lot about these things, says Blue, who's beginning to lose the thread of Black's argument.

It's my hobby, says Black. I like to know how writers live, especially American writers. It helps me to understand things.

I see, says Blue, who sees nothing at all, for with each word Black speaks, he finds himself understanding less and less.

Take Hawthorne, says Black. A good friend of Thoreau's, and probably the first real writer America ever had. After he graduated from college, he went back to his mother's house in Salem, shut himself up in his room, and didn't come out for twelve years.

What did he do in there? 130

He wrote stories.

Is that all? He just wrote?

Writing is a solitary business. It takes over your life. In some sense, a writer has no life of his own. Even when he's there, he's not really there.

Another ghost.

Exactly. 135

Sounds mysterious.

It is. But Hawthorne wrote great stories, you see, and we still read them now, more than a hundred years later. In one of them, a man named Wakefield decides to play a joke on his wife. He tells her that he has to go away on a business trip for a few days, but instead of leaving the city, he goes around the corner, rents a room, and just waits to see what will happen. He can't say for sure why he's doing it, but he does it just the same. Three or four days go by, but he doesn't feel ready to return home yet, and so he stays on in the rented room. The days turn into weeks, the weeks turn into months. One day Wakefield walks down his old street and sees his house decked out in mourning. It's his own funeral, and his wife has become a lonely widow. Years go by. Every now and then he crosses paths with his wife in town, and once, in the middle of a large crowd, he actually brushes up against her. But she doesn't recognize him. More years pass, more than twenty years, and little by little Wakefield has become an old man. One rainy night in autumn, as he's taking a walk through the empty streets, he happens to pass by his old house and peeks through the window. There's a nice warm fire burning in the fireplace, and he thinks to himself: how pleasant it would be if I were in there right now, sitting in one of those cozy chairs by the hearth, instead of standing out here in the rain. And so, without giving it any more thought than that, he walks up the steps of the house and knocks on the door.

And then?

That's it. That's the end of the story. The last thing we see is the door opening and Wakefield going inside with a crafty smile on his face.

And we never know what he says to his wife? 140

No. That's the end. Not another word. But he moved in again, we know that much, and remained a loving spouse until death.

By now the sky has begun to darken overhead, and night is fast approaching.

A last glimmer of pink remains in the west, but the day is as good as done. Black, taking his cue from the darkness, stands up from his spot and extends his hand to Blue.

It's been a pleasure talking to you, he says. I had no idea we'd been sitting here so long.

The pleasure's been mine, says Blue, relieved that the conversation is over, for he knows that it won't be long now before his beard begins to slip, what with the summer heat and his nerves making him perspire into the glue.

My name is Black, says Black, shaking Blue's hand.

Mine's Jimmy, says Blue. Jimmy Rose.

I'll remember this little talk of ours for a long time, Jimmy, says Black.

I will, too, says Blue. You've given me a lot to think about.

God bless you, Jimmy Rose, says Black.

And God bless you, sir, says Blue.

And then, with one last handshake, they walk off in opposite directions, each one accompanied by his own thoughts.

Later that night, when Blue returns to his room, he decides that he had best bury Jimmy Rose now, get rid of him for good. The old tramp has served his purpose, but beyond this point it would not be wise to go.

Blue is glad to have made this initial contact with Black, but the encounter did not quite have its desired effect, and all in all he feels rather shaken by it. For even though the talk had nothing to do with the case, Blue cannot help feeling that Black was actually referring to it all along—talking in riddles, so to speak, as though trying to tell Blue something, but not daring to say it out loud. Yes, Black was more than friendly, his manner was altogether pleasant, but still Blue cannot get rid of the thought that the man was on to him from the start. If so, then Black is surely one of the conspirators—for why else would he have gone on talking to Blue as he did? Not from loneliness, certainly. Assuming that Black is for real, then loneliness cannot be an issue. Everything about his life to this point has been part of a determined plan to remain alone, and it would be absurd to read his willingness to talk as an effort to escape the throes of solitude. Not at this late date, not after more than a year of avoiding all human contact. If Black is finally resolved to break out of his hermetic routine, then why would he begin by talking to a broken-down old man on a street corner? No, Black knew that he was talking to Blue. And if he knew that, then he knows who Blue is. No two ways about it, Blue says to himself: he knows everything.

When the time comes for him to write his next report, Blue is forced to confront this dilemma. White never said anything about making contact with Black. Blue was to watch him, no more, no less, and he wonders now if he has not in fact broken the rules of his assignment. If he includes the conversation in his report, then White might object. On the other hand, if he does not put it in, and if Black is indeed working with White, then White will know immediately that Blue is lying. Blue mulls this over for a long time, but for all that he gets no closer to finding a solution. He's stuck, one way or the other, and he knows it. In the end, he decides to leave it out, but only because he still puts some meager hope in the fact that he has guessed wrong and that White and Black are not in it together. But this last little stab at optimism soon comes to naught. Three days after sending in the sanitized report, his weekly check comes in the mail, and inside the envelope there is also a note that says, Why do you lie?, and then Blue has proof beyond any shadow of a doubt. And from that moment on, Blue lives with the knowledge that he is drowning.

155 The next night he follows Black into Manhattan on the subway, dressed in his normal clothes, no longer feeling he has to hide anything. Black gets off at Times Square and wanders around for a while in the bright lights, the noise, the crowds of people surging this way and that. Blue, watching him as though his life depended on it, is never more than three or four steps behind him. At nine o'clock, Black enters the lobby of the Algonquin Hotel, and Blue follows him in. There's quite a crowd milling about, and tables are scarce, so when Black sits down in a corner nook that just that moment has become free, it seems perfectly natural for Blue to approach and politely ask if he can join him. Black has no objection and gestures with an indifferent shrug of the shoulders for Blue to take the chair opposite. For several minutes they say nothing to each other, waiting for someone to take their orders, in the meantime watching the women walk by in their summer dresses, inhaling the different perfumes that flit behind them in the air, and Blue feels no rush to jump into things, content to bide his time and let the business take its course. When the waiter at last comes to ask their pleasure, Black orders a Black and White on the rocks, and Blue cannot help but take this as a secret message that the fun is about to begin, all the while marveling at Black's effrontery, his crassness, his vulgar obsession. For the sake of symmetry, Blue orders the same drink. As he does so, he looks Black in the eyes, but Black gives nothing away, looking back at Blue with utter blankness, dead eyes that seem to say there is nothing behind them and that no matter how hard Blue looks, he will never find a thing.

This gambit nevertheless breaks the ice, and they begin by discussing the merits of various brands of scotch. Plausibly enough, one thing leads to another, and as they sit there chatting about the inconveniences of the New York summer season, the decor of the hotel, the Algonquin Indians who lived in the city long ago when it was all woods and fields, Blue slowly evolves into the character he wants to play for the night, settling on a jovial blowhard by the name of Snow, a life insurance salesman from Kenosha, Wisconsin. Play dumb, Blue tells himself, for he knows that it would make no sense to reveal who he is, even though he knows that Black knows. It's got to be hide and seek, he says, hide and seek to the end.

They finish their first drink and order another round, followed by yet another, and as the talk ambles from actuarial tables to the life expectancies of men in different professions, Black lets fall a remark that turns the conversation in another direction.

I suppose I wouldn't be very high up on your list, he says.

Oh? says Blue, having no idea what to expect. What kind of work do you do?

160 I'm a private detective, says Black, point blank, all cool and collected, and for a brief moment Blue is tempted to throw his drink in Black's face, he's that peeved, that burned at the man's gall.

You don't say! Blue exclaims, quickly recovering and managing to feign a bumpkin's surprise. A private detective. Imagine that. In the flesh. Just think of what the wife will says when I tell her. Me in New York having drinks with a private eye. She'll never believe it.

What I'm trying to say, says Black rather abruptly, is that I don't imagine my life expectancy is very great. At least not according to your statistics.

Probably not, Blue blusters on. But think of the excitement! There's more to life than living a long time, you know. Half the men in America would give ten years off their retirement to live the way you do. Cracking cases, living by your wits, seducing women, pumping bad guys full of lead—God, there's a lot to be said for it.

That's all make-believe, says Black. Real detective work can be pretty dull.

Well, every job has its routines, Blue continues. But in your case at least you know that all the hard work will eventually lead to something out of the ordinary.

Sometimes yes, sometimes no. But most of the time it's no. Take the case I'm working on now. I've been at it for more than a year already, and nothing could be more boring. I'm so bored that sometimes I think I'm losing my mind.

How so?

Well, figure it out for yourself. My job is to watch someone, no one in particular as far as I can tell, and send in a report about him every week. Just that. Watch this guy and write about it. Not one damned thing more.

What's so terrible about that?

He doesn't do anything, that's what. He just sits in his room all day and writes. It's enough to drive you crazy.

It could be that he's leading you along. You know, lulling you to sleep before springing into action.

That's what I thought at first. But now I'm sure that nothing's going to happen—not ever. I can feel it in my bones.

That's too bad, says Blue sympathetically. Maybe you should resign from the case.

I'm thinking about it. I'm also thinking that maybe I should just chuck the whole business and go into something else. Some other line of work. Sell insurance, maybe, or run off to join the circus.

I never realized it could get as bad as that, says Blue, shaking his head. But tell me, why aren't you watching your man now? Shouldn't you be keeping an eye on him?

That's just the point, answers Black. I don't even have to bother anymore. I've been watching him for so long now that I know him better than I know myself. All I have to do is think about him, and I know what he's doing, I know where he is, I know everything. It's come to the point that I can watch him with my eyes closed.

Do you know where he is now?

At home. The same as usual. Sitting in his room and writing.

What's he writing about?

I'm not sure, but I have a pretty good idea. I think he's writing about himself. The story of his life. That's the only possible answer. Nothing else would fit.

So why all the mystery?

I don't know, says Black, and for the first time his voice betrays some emotion, catching ever so slightly on the words.

It all boils down to one question, then, doesn't it? says Blue, forgetting all about Snow now and looking Black straight in the eyes. Does he know you're watching him or not?

Black turns away, unable to look at Blue anymore, and says with a suddenly trembling voice: Of course he knows. That's the whole point, isn't it? He's got to know, or else nothing makes sense.

Why? 185

Because he needs me, says Black, still looking away. He needs my eyes looking at him. He needs me to prove he's alive.

Blue sees a tear fall down Black's cheek, but before he can say anything, before he can begin to press home his advantage, Black stands up hastily and excuses himself, saying that he has to make a telephone call. Blue waits in his chair for ten or fifteen minutes, but he knows that he's wasting his time. Black won't be back. The conversation is over, and no matter how long he sits there, nothing more will happen tonight.

Blue pays for the drinks and then heads back to Brooklyn. As he turns down Orange Street, he looks up at Black's window and sees that everything is dark. No matter, says Blue, he'll return before long. We haven't come to the end yet. The party is only beginning. Wait until the champagne is opened, and then we'll see what's what.

Once inside, Blue paces back and forth, trying to plot his next move. It seems to him that Black has finally made a mistake, but he is not quite certain. For in spite of the evidence, Blue cannot shrug the feeling that it was all done on purpose, and that Black has now begun to call out to him, leading him along, so to speak, urging him on towards whatever end he is planning.

Still, he has broken through to something, and for the first time since the 190
case began he is no longer standing where he was. Ordinarily, Blue would be celebrating this little triumph of his, but it turns out that he is in no mood for patting himself on the back tonight. More than anything else, he feels sad, he feels drained of enthusiasm, he feels disappointed in the world. Somehow, the facts have finally let him down, and he finds it hard not to take it personally, knowing full well that however he might present the case to himself, he is a part of it, too. Then he walks to the window, looks out across the street, and sees that the lights are now on in Black's room.

He lies down on his bed and thinks: good-bye, Mr. White. You were never really there, were you? There never was such a man as White. And then: poor Black. Poor soul. Poor blighted no one. And then, as his eyes grow heavy and sleep begins to wash over him, he thinks how strange it is that everything has its own color. Everything we see, everything we touch—everything in the world has its own color. Struggling to stay awake a little longer, he begins to make a list. Take blue for example, he says. There are bluebirds and blue jays and blue herons. There are cornflowers and periwinkles. There is noon over New York. There are blueberries, huckleberries, and the Pacific Ocean.

There are blue devils and blue ribbons and blue bloods. There is a voice singing the blues. There is my father's police uniform. There are blue laws and blue movies. There are my eyes and my name. He pauses, suddenly at a loss for more blue things, and then moves on to white. There are seagulls, he says, and terns and storks and cockatoos. There are the walls of this room and the sheets on my bed. There are lilies-of-the-valley, carnations, and the petals of daisies. There is the flag of peace and Chinese death. There is mother's milk and semen. There are my teeth. There are the whites of my eyes. There are white bass and white pines and white ants. There is the President's house and white rot. There are white lies and white heat. Then, without hesitating, he moves on to black, beginning with black books, the black market, and the Black Hand. There is night over New York, he says. There are the Chicago Black Sox. There are blackberries and crows, blackouts and black marks, Black Tuesday and the Black Death. There is blackmail. There is my hair. There is the ink that comes out of a pen. There is the world a blind man sees. Then, finally growing tired of the game, he begins to drift, saying to himself that there is no end to it. He falls asleep, dreams of things that happened long ago, and then, in the middle of the night, wakes up suddenly and begins pacing the room again, thinking about what he will do next.

Morning comes, and Blue starts busying himself with another disguise. This time it's the Fuller brush man, a trick he has used before, and for the next two hours he patiently goes about giving himself a bald head, a moustache, and age lines around his eyes and mouth, sitting in front of his little mirror like an old-time vaudevillian on tour. Shortly after eleven o'clock, he gathers up his case of brushes and walks across the street to Black's building. Picking the lock on the front door is child's play for Blue, no more than a matter of seconds, and as he slips into the hallway he can't help feeling something of the old thrill. No tough stuff, he reminds himself, as he starts climbing the stairs to Black's floor. This visit is only to get a look inside, to stake out the room for future reference. Still, there's an excitement to the moment that Blue can't quite suppress. For it's more than just seeing the room, he knows—it's the thought of being there himself, of standing inside those four walls, of breathing the same air as Black. From now on, he thinks, everything that happens will affect everything else. The door will open, and after that Black will be inside of him forever.

He knocks, the door opens, and suddenly there is no more distance, the thing and the thought of the thing are one and the same. Then it's Black who is there, standing in the doorway with an uncapped fountain pen in his right hand, as though interrupted in his work, and yet with a look in his eyes that tells Blue he's been expecting him, resigned to the hard truth, but no longer seeming to care.

Blue launches into his patter about the brushes, pointing to the case, offering apologies, asking admittance, all in the same breath, with that rapid salesman's pitch he's done a thousand times before. Black calmly lets him in, saying he might be interested in a toothbrush, and as Blue steps across the sill, he goes rattling on about hair brushes and clothes brushes, anything to keep the words flowing, for in that way he can leave the rest of himself free to take in the room, observe the observable, think, all the while diverting Black from his true purpose.

The room is much as he imagined it would be, though perhaps even more 195
austere. Nothing on the walls, for example, which surprises him a little, since he always thought there would be a picture or two, an image of some kind just to break the monotony, a nature scene perhaps, or else a portrait of someone Black might once have loved. Blue was always curious to know what the picture would be, thinking it might be a valuable clue, but now that he sees there is nothing, he understands that this is what he should have expected all along. Other than that, there's precious little to contradict his former notions. It's the same monk's cell he saw in his mind: the small, neatly made bed in one corner, the kitchenette in another corner, everything spotless, not a crumb to be seen. Then, in the center of the room facing the window, the wooden table with a single stiff-backed wooden chair. Pencils, pens, a typewriter. A bureau, a night table, a lamp. A bookcase on the north wall, but no more than several books in it: Walden, Leaves of Grass, Twice-Told Tales, a few others. No telephone, no radio, no magazines. On the table, neatly stacked around the edges, piles of paper: some blank, some written on, some typed, some in longhand. Hundreds of pages, perhaps thousands. But you can't call this a life, thinks Blue. You can't really call it anything. It's a no man's land, the place you come to at the end of the world.

They look through the toothbrushes, and Black finally chooses a red one. From there they start examining the various clothes brushes, with Blue giving demonstrations on his own suit. For a man as neat as yourself, says Blue, I should think you'd find it indispensable. But Black says he's managed so far without one. On the other hand, maybe he'd like to consider a hair brush, and so they go through the possibilities in the sample case, discussing the different sizes and shapes, the different kinds of bristles, and so on. Blue is already done with his real business, of course, but he goes through the motions nevertheless, wanting to do the things right, even if it doesn't matter. Still, after Black has paid for the brushes and Blue is packing up his case to go, he can't resist making one little remark. You seem to be a writer, he says, gesturing to the table, and Black says yes, that's right, he's a writer.

It looks like a big book, Blue continues.

Yes, says Black. I've been working on it for many years.

Are you almost finished?

I'm getting there, Black says thoughtfully. But sometimes it's hard to 200
know where you are. I think I'm almost done, and then I realize I've left out something important, and so I have to go back to the beginning again. But yes, I do dream of finishing it one day. One day soon, perhaps.

I hope I get a chance to read it, says Blue.

Anything is possible, says Black. But first of all, I've got to finish it. There are days when I don't even know if I'll live that long.

Well, we never know, do we? says Blue, nodding philosophically. One day we're alive, and the next day we're dead. It happens to all of us.

Very true, says Black. It happens to all of us.

They're standing by the door now, and something in Blue wants to go on 205
making inane remarks of this sort. Playing the buffoon is enjoyable, he realizes, but at the same time there's an urge to toy with Black, to prove that nothing has escaped him—for deep down Blue wants Black to know that he's just as smart as he is, that he can match wits with him every step of the way. But Blue manages to fight back the impulse and hold his tongue, nodding politely in thanks for the sales, and then makes his exit. That's the end of the Fuller brush man, and less than an hour later he is discarded into the same bag that holds the remains of Jimmy Rose. Blue knows that no more disguises will be needed. The next step is inevitable, and the only thing that matters now is to choose the right moment.

But three nights later, when he finally gets his chance, Blue realizes that he's scared. Black goes out at nine o'clock, walks down the street, and vanishes around the corner. Although Blue knows that this is a direct signal, that Black is practically begging him to make his move, he also feels that it could be a set-up, and now, at the last possible moment, when only just before he was filled with confidence, almost swaggering with a sense of his own power, he sinks into a fresh torment of self-doubt. Why should he suddenly begin to trust Black? What earthly cause could there be for him to think they are both working on the same side now? How has this happened, and why does he find himself so obsequiously at Black's bidding once again? Then, from out of the blue, he begins to consider another possibility. What if he just simply left? What if he stood up, went out the door, and walked away from the whole business? He ponders this thought for a while, testing it out in his mind, and little by little he begins to tremble, overcome by terror and happiness, like a slave stumbling onto a vision of his own freedom. He imagines himself somewhere else, far away from here, walking through the woods and swinging an axe over his shoulder. Alone and free, his own man at last. He would build his life from the bottom up, an exile, a pioneer, a pilgrim in the new world. But that is as far as he gets. For no sooner does he begin to walk through these woods in the middle of nowhere than he feels that Black is there, too, hiding behind some tree, stalking invisibly through some thicket, waiting for Blue to lie down and close his eyes before sneaking up on him and slitting his throat. It goes on and on, Blue thinks. If he doesn't take care of Black now, there will never be any end to it. This is what the ancients called fate, and every hero must submit to it. There is no choice, and if there is anything to be done, it is only the one thing that leaves no choice. But Blue is loathe to acknowledge it. He struggles against it, he rejects it, he grows sick at heart. But that is only because he already knows, and to fight it is already to have accepted it, to want to say no is already to have said yes. And so Blue gradually comes round, at last giving in to the necessity of the thing to be done. But that is not to say he does not feel afraid. From this moment on, there is only one word that speaks for Blue, and that word is fear.

He has wasted valuable time, and now he must rush forth onto the street, hoping feverishly it is not too late. Black will not be gone forever, and who knows if he is not lurking around the corner, just waiting for the moment to pounce? Blue races up the steps of Black's building, fumbles awkwardly as he picks the front door lock, continually glancing over his shoulder, and then goes up the stairs to Black's floor. The second lock gives him more trouble than the first, though theoretically it should be simpler, an easy job even for the rawest beginner. This clumsiness tells Blue that he's losing control, letting it all get the better of him; but even though he knows it, there's little he can do but ride it out and hope that his hands will stop shaking. But it goes from bad to worse, and the moment he sets foot in Black's room, he feels everything go dark inside him, as though the night were pressing through his pores, sitting on top of him with a tremendous weight, and at the same time his head seems to be growing, filling with air as though about to detach itself from his body and float away. He takes one more step into the room and then blacks out, collapsing to the floor like a dead man.

His watch stops with the fall, and when he comes to he doesn't know how long he's been out. Dimly at first, he regains consciousness with a sense of having been here before, perhaps long ago, and as he sees the curtains fluttering by the open window and the shadows moving strangely on the ceiling, he thinks that he is lying in bed at home, back when he was a little boy, unable to sleep during the hot summer nights, and he imagines that if he listens hard enough he will be able to hear the voices of his mother and father talking quietly in the next room. But this lasts only a moment. He begins to feel the ache in his head, to register the disturbing queasiness in his stomach, and then, finally seeing where he is, to relive the panic that gripped him the moment he entered the room. He scrambles shakily to his feet, stumbling once or twice in the process, and tells himself he can't stay here, he's got to be going, yes, and right away. He grabs hold of the doorknob, but then, remembering suddenly why he came here in the first place, snatches the flashlight from his pocket and turns it on, waving it fitfully around the room until the light falls by chance on a pile of papers stacked neatly at the edge of Black's desk. Without thinking twice, Blue gathers up the papers with his free hand, saying to himself it doesn't matter, this will be a start, and then makes his way to the door.

Back in his room across the street, Blue pours himself a glass of brandy, sits down on his bed, and tells himself to be calm. He drinks off the brandy sip by sip and then pours himself another glass. As his panic begins to subside, he is left with a feeling of shame. He's botched it, he tells himself, and that's the long and the short of it. For the first time in his life he has not been equal to the moment, and it comes as a shock to him—to see himself as a failure, to realize that at bottom he's a coward.

He picks up the papers he has stolen, hoping to distract himself from 210
these thoughts. But this only compounds the problem, for once he begins to read them, he sees they are nothing more than his own reports. There they are, one after the other, the weekly accounts, all spelled out in black and white, meaning nothing, saying nothing, as far from the truth of the case as silence would have been. Blue groans when he sees them, sinking down deep within himself, and then, in the face of what he finds there, begins to laugh, at first faintly, but with growing force, louder and louder, until he is gasping for breath, almost choking on it, as though trying to obliterate himself once and for all. Taking the papers firmly in his hand, he flings them up to the ceiling

and watches the pile break apart, scatter, and come fluttering to the ground, page by miserable page.

It is not certain that Blue ever really recovers from the events of this night. And even if he does, it must be noted that several days go by before he returns to a semblance of his former self. In that time he does not shave, he does not change his clothes, he does not even contemplate stirring from his room. When the day comes for him to write his next report, he does not bother. It's finished now, he says, kicking one of the old reports on the floor, and I'll be damned if I ever write one of those again.

For the most part, he either lies on his bed or paces back and forth in his room. He looks at the various pictures he has tacked onto the walls since starting the case, studying each one in its turn, thinking about it for as long as he can, and then passing on to the next. There is the coroner from Philadelphia, Gold, with the death mask of the little boy. There is a snow-covered mountain, and in the upper right hand corner of the photograph, an inset of the French skier, his face enclosed in a small box. There is the Brooklyn Bridge, and next to it the two Roeblings, father and son. There is Blue's father, dressed in his police uniform and receiving a medal from the mayor of New York, Jimmy Walker. Again there is Blue's father, this time in his street clothes, standing with his arm around Blue's mother in the early days of their marriage, the two of them smiling brightly into the camera. There is a picture of Brown with his arm around Blue, taken in front of their office on the day Blue was made a partner. Below it there is an action shot of Jackie Robinson sliding into second base. Next to that there is a portrait of Walt Whitman. And finally, directly to the poet's left, there is a movie still of Robert Mitchum from one of the fan magazines: gun in hand, looking as though the world is about to cave in on him. There is no picture of the ex–future Mrs. Blue, but each time Blue makes a tour of his little gallery, he pauses in front of a certain blank spot on the wall and pretends that she, too, is there.

For several days, Blue does not bother to look out the window. He has enclosed himself so thoroughly in his own thoughts that Black no longer seems to be there. The drama is Blue's alone, and if Black is in some sense the cause of it, it's as though he has already played his part, spoken his lines, and made his exit from the stage. For Blue at this point can no longer accept Black's existence, and therefore he denies it. Having penetrated Black's room and stood there alone, having been, so to speak, in the sanctum of Black's solitude, he cannot respond to the darkness of that moment except by replacing it with a solitude of his own. To enter Black, then, was the equivalent of entering himself, and once inside himself, he can no longer conceive of being anywhere else. But this is precisely where Black is, even though Blue does not know it.

One afternoon, therefore, as if by chance, Blue comes closer to the window than he has in many days, happens to pause in front of it, and then as if for old times' sake, parts the curtains and looks outside. The first thing he sees is Black—not inside his room, but sitting on the stoop of his building across the street, looking up at Blue's window. Is he finished, then? Blue wonders. Does this mean it's over?

Blue retrieves his binoculars from the back of the room and returns to the 215 window. Bringing them into focus on Black, he studies the man's face for several minutes, first one feature and then another, the eyes, the lips, the nose, and so on, taking the face apart and then putting it back together. He is moved by the depth of Black's sadness, the way the eyes looking up at him seem so devoid of hope, and in spite of himself, caught unawares by this image, Blue feels compassion rising up in him, a rush of pity for that forlorn figure across the street. He wishes it were not so, however, wishes he had the courage to load his gun, take aim at Black, and fire a bullet through his head. He'd never know what hit him, Blue thinks, he'd be in heaven before he touched the ground. But as soon as he has played out this little scene in his mind, he begins to recoil from it. No, he realizes, that's not what he wishes at all. If not that, then—what? Still struggling against the surge of tender feelings, saying to himself that he wants to be left alone, that all he wants is peace and quiet, it gradually dawns on him that he has in fact been standing there for several minutes wondering if there is not some way that he might help Black, if it would not be possible for him to offer his hand in friendship. That would certainly turn the tables, Blue thinks, that would certainly stand the whole business on its head. But why not? Why not do the unexpected? To knock on the door, to erase the whole story—it's no less absurd than anything else. For the fact of the matter is, all the fight has been taken out of Blue. He no longer has the stomach for it. And, to all appearances, neither does Black. Just look at him, Blue says to himself. He's the saddest creature in the world. And then, the moment he says these words, he understands that he's also talking about himself.

Long after Black leaves the steps, therefore, turning around and reentering the building, Blue goes on staring at the vacant spot. An hour or two before dusk, he finally turns from the window, sees the disorder he has allowed his room to fall into, and spends the next hour straightening up—washing the dishes, making the bed, putting away his clothes, removing the old reports from the floor. Then he goes into the bathroom, takes a long shower, shaves, and puts on fresh clothes, selecting his best blue suit for the occasion. Everything is different for him now, suddenly and irrevocably different. There is no more dread, no more trembling. Nothing but a calm assurance, a sense of rightness in the thing he is about to do.

Shortly after nightfall, he adjusts his tie one last time before the mirror and then leaves the room, going outside, crossing the street, and entering Black's building. He knows that Black is there, since a small lamp is on in his room, and as he walks up the stairs he tries to imagine the expression that will come over Black's face when he tells him what he has in mind. He knocks twice on the door, very politely, and then hears Black's voice from within: The door's open. Come in.

It is difficult to say exactly what Blue was expecting to find—but in all events, it was not this, not the thing that confronts him the moment he steps into the room. Black is there, sitting on his bed, and he's wearing the mask again, the same one Blue saw on the man in the post office, and in his right hand he's holding a gun, a thirty-eight revolver, enough to blow a man apart at such close range, and he's pointing it directly at Blue. Blue stops in his tracks, says nothing. So much for burying the hatchet, he thinks. So much for turning the tables.

Sit down in the chair, Blue, says Black, gesturing with the gun to the wooden desk chair. Blue has no choice, and so he sits—now facing Black, but too far away to make a lunge at him, too awkwardly positioned to do anything about the gun.

I've been waiting for you, says Black. I'm glad you finally made it.

I figured as much, answers Blue.

Are you surprised?

Not really. At least not at you. Myself maybe—but only because I'm so stupid. You see, I came here tonight in friendship.

But of course you did, says Black, in a slightly mocking voice. Of course we're friends. We've been friends from the beginning, haven't we? The very best of friends.

If this is how you treat your friends, says Blue, then lucky for me I'm not one of your enemies.

Very funny.

That's right, I'm the original funny man. You can always count on a lot of laughs when I'm around.

And the mask—aren't you going to ask me about the mask?

I don't see why. If you want to wear that thing, it's not my problem.

But you have to look at it, don't you?

Why ask questions when you already know the answer?

It's grotesque, isn't it?

Of course it's grotesque.

And frightening to look at.

Yes, very frightening.

Good. I like you, Blue. I always knew you were the right one for me. A man after my own heart.

If you stopped waving that gun around, maybe I'd start feeling the same about you.

I'm sorry, I can't do that. It's too late now.

Which means?

I don't need you anymore, Blue.

It might not be so easy to get rid of me, you know. You got me into this, and now you're stuck with me.

No, Blue, you're wrong. Everything is over now.

Stop the doubletalk.

It's finished. The whole thing is played out. There's nothing more to be done.

Since when?

Since now. Since this moment.

You're out of your mind.

No, Blue. If anything, I'm in my mind, too much in my mind. It's used me up, and now there's nothing left. But you know that, Blue, you know that better than anyone.

So why don't you just pull the trigger?

When I'm ready, I will.

And then walk out of here leaving my body on the floor? Fat chance.

Oh no, Blue. You don't understand. It's going to be the two of us together, just like always.

But you're forgetting something, aren't you?

Forgetting what?

You're supposed to tell me the story. Isn't that how it's supposed to end? You tell me the story, and then we say good-bye.

You know it already, Blue. Don't you understand that? You know the story by heart.

Then why did you bother in the first place?

Don't ask stupid questions.

And me—what was I there for? Comic relief?

No, Blue, I've needed you from the beginning. If it hadn't been for you, I couldn't have done it.

Needed me for what?

To remind me of what I was supposed to be doing. Every time I looked up, you were there, watching me, following me, always in sight, boring into me with your eyes. You were the whole world to me, Blue, and I turned you into my death. You're the one thing that doesn't change, the one thing that turns everything inside out.

And now there's nothing left. You've written your suicide note, and that's the end of it.

Exactly.

You're a fool. You're a goddamned, miserable fool.

I know that. But no more than anyone else. Are you going to sit there and tell me that you're smarter than I am? At least I know what I've been doing. I've had my job to do, and I've done it. But you're nowhere, Blue. You've been lost from the first day.

Why don't you pull the trigger, then, you bastard? says Blue, suddenly standing up and pounding his chest in anger, daring Black to kill him. Why don't you shoot me now and get it over with?

Blue then takes a step towards Black, and when the bullet doesn't come, he takes another, and then another, screaming at the masked man to shoot, no longer caring if he lives or dies. A moment later, he's right up against him. Without hesitating he swats the gun out of Black's hand, grabs him by the collar, and yanks him to his feet. Black tries to resist, tries to struggle against Blue, but Blue is too strong for him, all crazy with the passion of his anger, as though turned into someone else, and as the first blows begin to land on Black's face and groin and stomach, the man can do nothing, and not long after that he's out cold on the floor. But that does not prevent Blue from continuing the assault, battering the unconscious Black with his feet, picking him up and banging his head on the floor, pelting his body with one punch after another. Eventually, when Blue's fury begins to abate and he sees what he has done, he cannot say for certain whether Black is alive or dead. He removes the mask from Black's face and puts his ear against his mouth, listening for the sound of Black's breath. There seems to be something, but he can't tell if it's coming from Black or himself. If he's alive now, Blue thinks, it won't be for long. And if he's dead, then so be it.

Blue stands up, his suit all in tatters, and begins collecting the pages of Black's manuscript from the desk. This takes several minutes. When he has all of them, he turns off the lamp in the corner and leaves the room, not even bothering to give Black a last look.

It's past midnight when Blue gets back to his room across the street. He puts the manuscript down on the table, goes into the bathroom, and washes the blood off his hands. Then he changes his clothes, pours himself a glass of scotch, and sits down at the table with Black's book. Time is short. They'll be coming before he knows it, and then there will be hell to pay. Still, he does not let this interfere with the business at hand.

He reads the story right through, every word of it from beginning to end. By the time he finishes, dawn has come, and the room has begun to brighten. He hears a bird sing, he hears footsteps going down the street, he hears a car driving across the Brooklyn Bridge. Black was right, he says to himself. I knew it all by heart.

But the story is not yet over. There is still the final moment, and that will not come until Blue leaves the room. Such is the way of the world: not one moment more, not one moment less. When Blue stands up from his chair, puts on his hat, and walks through the door, that will be the end of it.

Where he goes after that is not important. For we must remember that all this took place more than thirty years ago, back in the days of our earliest childhood. Anything is possible, therefore. I myself prefer to think that he went far away, boarding a train that morning and going out West to start a new life. It is even possible that America was not the end of it. In my secret dreams, I like to think of Blue booking passage on some ship and sailing to China. Let it be China, then, and we'll leave it at that. For now is the moment that Blue stands up from his chair, puts on his hat, and walks through the door. And from this moment on, we know nothing.

PAUL AUSTER

(b. 1947) **Web** *www*

A translator and student of French, Paul Auster has written poetry, novels, and screenplays. He lives in Brooklyn.

TOPICS FOR CRITICAL THINKING **Web** *www*

1. What embedded narratives does the novella include?
2. Are there similarities in theme or subject among these embedded narratives?
3. In what ways do the embedded narratives reflect the larger themes of the novella?
4. What other kinds of intertextuality does *Ghosts* employ?
5. In what ways is intertextuality itself the subject of the novella?
6. In what ways does *Ghosts* use or alter the conventions of detective fiction?
7. Why make all proper names references to colors?

www

TOPIC FOR CRITICAL WRITING Web

Select one of the many embedded stories, and show how it connects to the larger narrative.

Mark Leyner

Selections from *My Cousin, My Gastroenterologist* (1990)

i was an infinitely hot and dense dot
idyll
the suggestiveness of one stray hair in an otherwise perfect coiffure

1. *i was an infinitely hot and dense dot*

I was driving to Las Vegas to tell my sister that I'd had Mother's respirator unplugged. Four bald men in the convertible in front of me were picking the scabs off their sunburnt heads and flicking them onto the road. I had to swerve to avoid riding over one of the oozy crusts of blood and going into an uncontrollable skid. I maneuvered the best I could in my boxy Korean import but my mind was elsewhere. I hadn't eaten for days. I was famished. Suddenly as I reached the crest of a hill, emerging from the fog, there was a bright neon sign flashing on and off that read: . . . FOIE GRAS AND HARICOTS VERTS NEXT EXIT. I checked the guidebook and it said: *Excellent food, malevolent ambience.* I'd been habitually abusing an illegal growth hormone extracted from the pituitary glands of human corpses and I felt as if I were drowning in excremental filthiness but the prospect of having something good to eat cheered me up. I asked the waitress about the soup du jour and she said that it was primordial soup—which is ammonia and methane mixed with ocean water in the presence of lightning. Oh I'll take a tureen of that embryonic broth, I say, constraint giving way to exuberance—but as soon as she vanishes my spirit immediately sags because the ambience is so malevolent. The bouncers are hassling some youngsters who want drinks—instead of simply carding the kids, they give them radiocarbon tests, using traces of carbon 14 to determine how old they are—and also there's a young wise guy from Texas A&M at a table near mine who asks for freshly ground Rolaids on his fettuccine and two waiters viciously work him over with heavy bludgeon-sized pepper mills, so I get right back into my car and narcissistically comb my thick jet-black hair in the rearview mirror and I check the guidebook. There's an inn nearby—it's called Little Bo Peep's—its habitués are shepherds. And after a long day of herding, shearing, panpipe playing, muse invoking, and conversing in eclogues, it's Miller time, and Bo Peep's is packed with rustic swains who've left their flocks and sunlit, idealized arcadia behind for the more pungent charms of hard-core social intercourse. Everyone's favorite waitress is Kikugoro. She wears a pale-blue silk kimono and a brocade obi of gold and silver chrysanthemums with a small fan tucked into its folds, her face is painted and powdered to a porcelain white. A cowboy from south of the border orders a "Biggu Makku." But Kikugoro says, "This is not Makudonarudo." She takes a long cylinder of gallium arsenide crystal and slices him a thin wafer which she serves with soy sauce, wasabi, picked ginger, and daikon. "Conducts electrons ten times faster than silicon . . . taste good, gaucho-*san*, you eat," she says, bowing.

My sister is the beautiful day. Oh beautiful day, my sister, wipe my nose, swaddle me in fresh-smelling garments. I nurse at the adamantine nipple of the beautiful day. I quaff the milk of the beautiful day, and for the first time since 1956, I cheese on the shoulder of the beautiful day. Oh beautiful day, wash me in your lake of cloudless azure. I have overdosed on television, I am unresponsive and cyanotic, revive me in your shower of gelid light and walk me through your piazza which is made of elegant slabs of time. Oh beautiful day, kiss me. Your mouth is like Columbus Day. You are the menthol of autumn. My lungs cannot quench their thirst for you. Resuscitate me—I will never exhale your tonic gasses. Inflate me so that I may rise into the sky and mourn the monotonous topography of my life. Oh beautiful day, my sister, wipe my nose and adorn me in your finery. Let us lunch alfresco. Your club sandwiches are made of mulch and wind perfumed with newsprint. Your frilly toothpicks are the deciduous trees of school days.

I was an infinitely hot and dense dot. So begins the autobiography of a feral child who was raised by huge and lurid puppets. An autobiography written wearing wrist weights. It ends with these words: A car drives through a puddle of sperm, sweat, and contraceptive jelly, splattering the great chopsocky vigilante from Hong Kong. Inside, two acephalic sardines in mustard sauce are asleep in the rank darkness of their tin container. Suddenly, the swinging doors burst open and a mesomorphic cyborg walks in and whips out a 35-lb. phallus made of corrosion-resistant nickel-base alloy and he begins to stroke it sullenly, his eyes half shut. It's got a metal-oxide membrane for absolute submicron filtration of petrochemical fluids. It can ejaculate herbicides, sulfuric acid, tar glue, you name it. At the end of the bar, a woman whose album-length poem about temporomandibular joint dysfunction (TMJ) had won a Grammy for best spoken word recording is gently slowly ritually rubbing copper hexafluoroacetylacetone into her clitoris as she watches the hunk with the non-Euclidian features shoot a gob of dehydrogenated ethylbenzene 3,900 miles towards the Arctic archipelago, eventually raining down upon a fiord on Baffin Bay. Outside, a basketball plunges from the sky, killing a dog. At a county fair, a huge and hairy man in mud-caked blue overalls, surrounded by a crowd of retarded teenagers, swings a sledgehammer above his head with brawny keloidal arms and then brings it down with all his brute force on a tofu-burger on a flowery paper plate. A lizard licks the dew from the stamen of a stunted crocus. Rivets and girders float above the telekinetic construction workers. The testicular voice of Barry White emanates from some occult source within the laundry room. As I chugalug a glass of tap water milky with contaminants, I realize that my mind is being drained of its contents and refilled with the beliefs of the most mission-oriented, can-do feral child ever raised by huge and lurid puppets. I am the voice . . . the voice from beyond and the voice from within—can you hear me? Yes. I speak to you and you only—is that clear? Yes, master. To whom do I speak? To me and me only. Is "happy" the appropriate epithet for someone who experiences each moment as if he were being alternately flayed alive and tickled to death? No, master.

In addition to the growth hormone extracted from the glands of human corpses, I was using anabolic steroids, tissue regeneration compounds, granulocyte-macrophage colony-stimulating factor (GM-CSF)—a substance used to stimulate growth of certain vital blood cells in radiation victims—and a nasal spray of neuropeptides that accelerates the release of pituitary hormones and I was getting larger and larger and my food bills were becoming enormous. So I went on a TV game show in the hopes of raising cash. This was my question, for $250,000 in cash and prizes: If the Pacific Ocean were filled with gin, what would be, in terms of proportionate volume, the proper lake of vermouth necessary to achieve a dry martini? I said Lake Ontario—but the answer was the Caspian Sea which is called a sea but is a lake by definition. I had failed. I had humiliated my family and disgraced the king fu masters of the Shaolin temple. I stared balefully out into the studio audience which was chanting something that sounded like "dork." I'm in my car. I'm high on Sinutab. And I'm driving anywhere. The vector of my movement from a given point is isotropic—meaning that all possible directions are equally probable. I end up at a squalid little dive somewhere in Vegas maybe Reno maybe Tahoe. I don't know . . . but there she is. I can't tell if she's a human or a fifth-generation gynemorphic android and I don't care. I crack open an ampule of mating pheromone and let it waft across the bar, as I sip my drink, a methyl isocyanate on the rocks—methyl isocyanate is the substance which killed more than 2,000 people when it leaked in Bhopal, India, but thanks to my weight training, aerobic workouts, and a low-fat fiber-rich diet, the stuff has no effect on me. Sure enough she strolls over and occupies the stool next to mine. After a few moments of silence, I make the first move: We're all larval psychotics and have been since the age of two, I say, spitting an ice cube back into my glass. She moves closer to me. At this range, the downy cilia-like hairs that trickle from her navel remind me of the fractal ferns produced by injecting dyed water into an aqueous polymer solution, and I tell her so. She looks into my eyes: You have the glibness, superficial charm, grandiosity, lack of guilt, shallow feelings, impulsiveness, and lack of realistic long-term plans that excite me right now, she says, moving even closer. We feed on the same prey species, I growl. My lips are now one angstrom unit from her lips, which is one ten-billionth of a meter. I begin to kiss her but she turns her head away. Don't good little boys who finish all their vegetables get dessert? I ask. I can't kiss you, we're monozygotic replicants—we share 100% of our genetic material. My head spins. You are the beautiful day, I exclaim, your breath is a zephyr of eucalyptus that does a pas de bourrée across the Sea of Galilee. Thanks, she says, but we can't go back to my house and make love because monozygotic incest is forbidden by the elders. What if I said I could change all that . . . What if I said that I had a miniature shotgun that blasts gene fragments into the cells of living organisms, altering their genetic matrices so that a monozygotic replicant would no longer be a monozygotic replicant and she could then make love to a muscleman without transgressing the incest taboo, I say, opening my shirt and exposing the device which I had stuck in the waistband of my black jeans. How'd you get that thing? she gasps, ogling its thick fiber-reinforced plastic barrel and the Uzi-Biotech logo embossed on the magazine which held two cartridges of gelated recombinant DNA. I got it for Christmas. . . . Do you have any last words before I scramble your chromosomes, I say, taking aim. Yes, she says, you first. I put the barrel to my heart. These are my last words: When I emerged from my mother's uterus I was the size of a chicken bouillon cube and Father said to the obstetrician: I realize that at this stage it's difficult to prognosticate his chances for a productive future, but if he's going to remain six-sided and 0.4 grams for the rest of his life, then euthanasia's our best bet. But Mother, who only milliseconds before was in the very throes of labor, had already slipped on her muumuu and espadrilles and was puffing on a Marlboro: No pimple-faced simp two months out of Guadalajara is going to dissolve this helpless little hexahedron in a mug of boiling water, she said, as a nurse managed with acrobatic desperation to slide a suture basin under the long ash of her cigarette which she'd consumed in one furiously deep drag. These are my last words: My fear of being bullied and humiliated stems from an incident that occurred many years ago in a diner. A 500-lb. man seated next to me at the counter was proving that one particular paper towel was more absorbent than another brand. His face was swollen and covered with patches of hectic red. He spilled my glass of chocolate milk on the counter and then sopped it up with one paper towel and then with the other. With each wipe of the counter the sweep of his huge dimpled arm became wider and wider until he was repeatedly smashing his flattened hand and the saturated towel into my chest. There was an interminable cadence to the blows I endured. And instead of assistance from other patrons at the counter, I received their derision, their sneering laughter. But now look at me! I am a terrible god. When I enter the forest the mightiest oaks blanch and tremble. All rustling, chirping, growling, and buzzing cease, purling brooks become still. This is all because of my tremendous muscularity . . . which is the result of the hours of hard work that I put in at the gym and the strict dietary regimen to which I adhere. When I enter the forest the birds become incontinent with fear so there's this torrential downpour of shit from the trees. And I stride through—my whistle is like an ear-splitting fife being played by a lunatic with a bloody bandage around his head. And the sunlight, rent into an incoherence of blazing vectors, illuminates me: a shimmering, serrated monster!

2. *idyll*

I was reading an article that contained the words "vineyards, orchards, and fields bountiful with fruits and vegetables; sheeps and goats graze on hillsides of lush greenery" and I realized that in five months none of these things would exist and I realized that as the last sheep on earth is skinned, boned, filleted, and flash-frozen, Arleen and I would probably be making love for the last time, mingling—for the last time—the sweet smell of her flesh which is like hyacinths and narcissus with the virile tang of my own which is like pond scum and headcheese and then I realized that the only thing that would distinguish me in the eyes of posterity from—for instance—those three sullen Chinese yuppies slumped over in their bentwood chairs at the most elegant McDonald's in the world is that I wrote the ads that go: "Suddenly There's Vancouver!" . . .

6. *the suggestiveness of one stray hair in an otherwise perfect coiffure*

He's got a car bomb. He puts the key in the ignition and turns it—the car blows up. He gets out. He opens the hood and makes a cursory inspection. He closes the hood and gets back in. He turns the key in the ignition. The car blows up. He gets out and slams the door shut disgustedly. He kicks the tire. He takes off his jacket and shimmies under the chassis. He pokes around. He slides back out and wipes the grease off his shirt. He puts his jacket back on. He gets in. He turns the key in the ignition. The car blows up, sending debris into the air and shattering windows for blocks. He gets out and says, Damn it! He calls a tow truck. He gives them his AAA membership number. They tow the car to an Exxon station. The mechanic gets in and turns the key in the ignition. The car explodes, demolishing the gas pumps, the red-and-blue Exxon logo high atop its pole bursting like a balloon on a string. The mechanic steps out. You got a car bomb, he says. The man rolls his eyes. I know that, he says.

MARK LEYNER

www

(b. 1956) **Web**

Referred to as an "avant-pop" writer, Leyner, from Hoboken, New Jersey, writes a poetic prose that is as dense and frenetic as the multitasked layers of culture that blanket the world.

www

TOPICS FOR CRITICAL THINKING **Web**

1. Language from how many different contexts appears in Leyner's stories?
2. What is the effect of the juxtaposition of languages from different contexts?
3. What various aspects of the stories unify them, both individually and as a group?
4. In what ways is Leyner's writing like collage? Pastiche?
5. What commentary on contemporary culture does Leyner's writing make?
6. How do Leyner's stories imagine a transglobal world, one in which national boundaries no longer make much difference?

www

TOPICS FOR CRITICAL WRITING **Web**

1. Consider the various ways one of Leyner's stories disrupts traditional notions of the story. What are the effects of that disruption? Do Leyner's stories present a new idea of what a story can be?
2. In what ways is Leyner's writing like commodity culture?

17 Fiction Across Media: Film

Fiction is not limited to stories written to be read. The characteristics of prose fiction—character, setting, plot, narrator, point of view, theme, image, motif, style, tone, and structure—are also attributes of narrative fiction produced in such other media as film, television, comic books, and computer games. It is tempting to think of these media as interchangeable, especially if we only focus on plot, character, and setting. We might make little distinction, for example, among Ian Fleming's novel *Diamonds Are Forever*, the movie *Diamonds Are Forever*, and a computer game based on James Bond's exploits (such as *007 Nightfire*). Any comparison of the three would probably focus on differences in plot and characterization—the kind of critique we often hear when seeing a movie made from a book.

Although all of these stories about James Bond are fictional, they cannot be treated as if they are the same. The medium through which a story is presented, whether print, film, computer, or picture, makes a difference in what is told and how actions, characters, settings, and stories are rendered. It also makes a difference in the ways we consume, understand, enjoy, and evaluate it. We must understand and take account of the differences among media when we look at the film version of a story, such as the short film *An Occurrence at Owl Creek Bridge* filmed for the television show *The Twilight Zone* in 1962, or Francis Ford Coppola's *Apocalypse Now* (1979), adapted from Joseph Conrad's *Heart of Darkness* (1902). Movies based on stories written to be read are never simply "adaptations," or filmed versions, of a story. They are instead new interpretations that might be based on a specific story, but which are rendered into the terms of another medium. The complexity of this process and the differences in the media make the film text another story altogether. (See **CD-ROM**.)

There are several stories included in this collection that have been made into movies. Some, such as Julio Cortázar's "Blow-Up" (1963), are better known in the film versions—Michelangelo Antonioni's *Blow Up* (1966) and the later *Blow Out* (1981), which transforms the photographer protagonist of "Blow-Up" (and *Blow Up*) into a sound technician (see the case study of Antonioni's *Blow Up*, below). Some stories, such as Edgar Allen Poe's "The Fall of the House of Usher" (1839), have inspired multiple film versions. "Usher" has provided material for at least seven screen versions, beginning with two silent films made in 1928. There have been five film versions of Herman Melville's "Bartleby the Scrivener" and even a version of Guy de Maupassant's "Paul's Mistress," transformed by avant-garde filmmaker Jean-Luc Godard in *Masculin/Féminin* (1966). (For an extended list, see **CD-ROM**.)

Fiction Film

But what exactly is different in a filmic rendering of a prose fiction story? What should we take account of when thinking about fiction in film? Thinking about film fiction is never simply a matter of comparing how a film treats or changes a prose fiction story's plot, character, and setting; nor is it a matter of tracking what the film omits or judging its casting decisions. Rather, when looking at fiction in the medium of film, one needs to take account of the ways the film medium works as art, just as in looking at fiction we consider how language produces the art of prose fiction. This means understanding the ways film arranges events, relates character, establishes setting, conveys the passage of time, signals subjective experience (those wavy lines, for example), and produces the implication of a narrator. Though some aspects of film fiction correlate to the formal categories through which we begin our analysis of fiction (plot, character, setting, narrative, structure, and motif), film's set of tools also differs from that of prose fiction. When looking at film fiction, the action of the camera—of filming itself—is an integral part of the art of film. Film art is not merely a transparent mode of storytelling; it adds and shapes the meanings, impressions, and moods of a story. It addresses its consumer differently than prose fiction, appearing to provide a view of events instead of a description, seeming to have a window into a world of actual people and at the same time subtly directing and controlling viewer perspective and attention.

As a visual and aural medium, film differs from prose fiction in three major ways:

- It tells stories through realistic images and sounds (after the sound era).
- It combines images through a process called editing.
- It has no specific narrator.

Each of these aspects of film has its own vocabulary (see "Film Concepts," below). This vocabulary is useful because it represents concepts that ground the art of the cinema. Being familiar with the concepts and terms used in studying cinema makes it easier to think specifically about film art as well as about the differences between filmic and literary texts.

Films also often combine the ideas, characters, or plots from stories and novels with other issues, arguments, and approaches. For example, Coppola's *Apocalypse Now* borrows the idea of finding a mysterious charismatic figure in a jungle from Conrad's *Heart of Darkness* and combines it with a commentary about the problems of the Viet Nam War. The film's setting in southeast Asia, and the different cast of characters serve the film's different emphasis.

Adaptation, Translation, Transliteration

Although many people think of films based on novels as "adaptations," it is sometimes more enlightening to think of these films as new texts. A prose fiction story and a film based on that story may indeed have much in common, but thinking of a film only as an "adaptation" makes us miss much that is interesting and innovative about it. In other words, we tend to think of the film precisely as an adaptation—as the product of adjusting the very same story to the specific circumstances of film's visual and aural technologies.

Part of the ease with which we equate print and visual texts comes from our familiarity with narrative. For most viewers, films are about stories and characterizations, aspects of film that often do seem to be simple translations of a story. If we focus on comparing the differences between a prose story and the film that tells the same story, our understanding of the film version consists of the ways the film has "changed" the story—that is, the ways the film has in some way altered the order of events, omitting and adding actions and characters, and changing settings. Thinking of films as translations also encourages us to measure the effects of casting decisions to the point that discussing any film based on a novel becomes a matter of discussing whether or not Marlon Brando was a good choice to play Mr. Kurtz. These conversations can be interesting, but they tend not to tell us much about how a film text itself works as an integrated work of art.

For these reasons, it is most profitable to consider any film a text that stands alone with its own system and integrity. Thinking of films as standalone texts encourages us to see how the various elements of a film work together rather than only in reference to a print story. Films perceived as separate texts are at best "transliterations" of print stories—renderings of material made in a completely different "alphabet" and "language," and hence barely the same thing at all.

Of course, the relation between films and the stories that inspired them varies from film to film. Films are conceived in many different relations to stories. Some films are made for the express purpose of making a specific text consumable under different circumstances. This is true, for example, of many films made of Shakespeare's plays. Films made expressly for showing in literature classes, such as the film version of "A Rose for Emily," bear a close relation to the stories they present. Viewers are most often aware of the prose and perhaps the dramatic renditions upon which these kinds of films are based. Watching these films becomes a matter of mentally comparing the film to the story. Even if such films are intended to be simple adaptations, however, they still have their own system and art.

Other films have a more distant relation to the prose texts upon which they are only loosely based. These films—*Blow Up*, for example, or *Apocalypse Now*—capitalize and elaborate on particular aspects and relationships within a story. Such films do not worry about reproducing other aspects of the stories that have offered only a suggestion and often change settings, characters, historical era, and even the focus of the story. Viewers often consume these films without necessarily knowing the stories upon which they are roughly based.

Case Study: *Blow Up**

A fashion photographer who is also in the process of producing an artistic coffee-table book takes pictures of an unwary couple in a London park. He has been accompanied in his journey to the park by a group of reveling mimes. The woman in the couple notices him taking pictures and demands the roll of film. Thomas, the photographer, gives her his address and rushes off to photograph a fashion spread. Later, the woman appears in his apartment and he gives her the wrong roll of film. Curious, he develops his park pictures and, fascinated by something he sees, begins blowing up portions of a picture. He hangs these in the living room of his loft, and looking at them closely, sees what looks like the barrel of a gun poking through the bushes. He concludes that his photography has interrupted a murder and goes to a restaurant to tell his agent about his fabulous coup. He returns to his loft, is accosted by teenage groupies with whom he frolics, and while on the floor, sees a body lying on the ground in one of the pictures. He rushes back to the park and finds a body. He tries to get someone to go to the park, but everyone is busy partying. When he returns to his loft, the pictures are all gone, except one. He returns to the park, finds that the body has also disappeared, and begins to play mime tennis with the revelers.

What is it about Michelangelo Antonioni's film, *Blow Up* (1966), other than its title, that would suggest that it has any connection to Julio Cortázar's short story "Blow-Up" (1963)? On the surface, it seems quite different:

"Blow-Up" (story)	*Blow Up (film)*
Protagonist is a writer.	Protagonist is a photographer.
Set in Paris	Set in London
Protagonist enjoys photography.	Protagonist aggressively seeks to photograph.
Initial situation involves a woman and a teenage boy.	Initial situation involves a woman and an older man.
Third party is a man in a car.	Third party is a man in bushes with a gun.
Situation photographed involves a woman's attempt to seduce the boy on behalf of the waiting man in the car.	Situation photographed involves a woman's attempt to seduce a man to his death.
Both the woman and man in the car confront the protagonist.	Woman confronts the protagonist, visits his studio. Murderous third party remains a mystery.
Protagonist returns to his apartment with no further attempts to intercede.	Protagonist actively tries to solve the mystery of the park.

Blow Up* is available on VHS, as is *Apocalypse Now*. For a complete list of stories in this volume that have been made into films, see **CD-ROM.

Story is written in a self-conscious, self-reflective manner.	Film has no consciousness of itself as a film.
Traces modest thoughts of the protagonist as he understands that the position from which one sees affects the story one contrives to account for events.	Traces the conceited heroism of the protagonist, who thinks he has prevented a murder and then thinks he has recorded one.
Story is framed by images of birds.	Film is framed by images of mimes and revelers.

Although these differences may seem to be substantial, producing what is in effect a completely different story, what is perhaps more interesting are the ideas the print and filmic texts share. Looking at similarities helps us see what differences a medium itself makes. The texts share three central ideas:

- The position from which one views an event influences how one sees the event.
- Observers inevitably produce stories to account for what they see.
- Art necessarily engages with life.

Both protagonists experience a revelation about the nature of seeing as they study the photograph they have blown up. Both attempt to account for the events they have caught on film by contriving stories to explain the relations among the characters. Those stories change, of course, when the protagonists change their positions in relation to the images. In both cases, the seemingly detached activity of taking pictures embroils the protagonists in a real-life dispute in which they reflect on their solitary pursuit of their respective arts.

How, then, to account for the differences between the texts? One way is to consider the ways in which the differences in details relate to the media through which the texts are presented. Cortázar's story is partly about writing. The medium reflects upon itself. (When a story is about writing, a play is about a play, or a film is about filmmaking, we call this preoccupation with the medium *self-reflective*). If that is the case in a print story, then we might expect that a self-reflective film would reflect upon modes of seeing. This is a way of matching the story to the medium. Both the story and the film are in some way about how we contrive stories to explain what we see, but because the story cannot reproduce the actual experience of seeing, it focuses much more on understanding how changing the position of the viewer changes the viewer's perspective. The film, on the other hand, because it can reproduce the experience of seeing, focuses more on the protagonist's study of the blowups. It also makes more central and complex the moment during which his literal change of position (he views the photos from the floor) changes what he sees.

Another way to account for differences (or really to account for how the same idea appears slightly differently in two different media) is to consider the scope and capabilities of the medium. Short stories can present interior thoughts and can move around in time much more easily than films, which are limited to some degree to the need to make thoughts and feelings visible in some way.

Blow Up's protagonist, however, must act out his insights, not only by looking like he has them, but by acting on them. Cortázar's story has an understated, self-reflective quality that, in focusing on the process of writing, partially obscures the moment of the writer's insight, even though the story moves toward such insight. To conform to the expectations of mainstream cinema, *Blow Up* makes the photographer's dilemma larger than life—a murder instead of a paltry attempt at seduction, action instead of reflection. In addition, the film adds several encounters with groupies not enjoyed by the modest writer.

Although "Blow-Up" and *Blow Up* are completely different texts, one can see that their differences depend partly upon the dictates of their media. For this reason, it is useful to consider the ways each works as a complete and artful text in itself. Just as it is necessary to understand something about the various elements of fiction to analyze it, so it is useful to understand the various elements of film. Although film is a complex topic that is itself the subject of an entire textbook, the following sets out some of the basic concepts to take into account when thinking about film as texts.

Film Concepts

Concepts Relating to Film

The shot Film consists of recorded image and sound contained in units called shots. A shot consists of the length of film from the point where the camera is turned on to the point where it is turned off. Some shots may be as short as several *frames;* others may run as long as the roll of film. In the wisdom that declares that a picture is worth 1,000 words, film shots contain far more information than a verbal description in a story.

A frame A frame is a single image. Each frame consists of a still photograph. Films consist of a series of frames that run through both camera and projector at the rate of twenty-four frames per second. A frame is also a basic rectangular shape of the film's image.

Mise en scène (put in the scene) Each film shot conveys information about what is in the scene. Everything in front of the camera is called the mise en scène. Mise en scène includes not only characters, settings, actions, costumes, makeup, and some special effects, but also the effects of lighting.

The camera Everything we see in a film we see from the point of view of the camera. Each shot conveys information about where the camera was situated when the scene was photographed:

- *Height:* the camera's height from the ground in relation to the subject being filmed.
- *Angle:* the angle from which the camera views the subject. If the camera is below the subject looking up, it produces a *low angle* shot.
- *Distance:* the distance from which a scene is photographed measured by how

much of the human figure the image includes (for example, head only, as in a *close-up*, or a *long shot*, which includes the entire human figure).

- *Level:* whether or not the camera was parallel to the ground while shooting. If the camera is not level, the shot is *canted*. Cameras may moved while shooting, producing a *pan* (turning in a "no" motion, or along a vertical axis) or a *tilt* (turning in a "yes" motion, or along a horizontal axis), moving along a track or *dolly*, or sitting on a *crane*.
- *Filters:* may distort or soften shots, and lenses (wide angle, telephoto) may change our perspective.

In film studies there are sets of specific terms for each of these categories—height, angle, distance, and others. What is important is that all of this information is a part of what films display, and all is material not conveyed in prose except through description. Prose fiction could not possibly describe the detail film can present, which indicates one reason film and prose approach the telling of their stories differently.

Editing Shots are combined with one another through a practice called editing or montage. Film editing follows certain conventions by which the sense of continuous space and time is preserved. Sometimes films combine shots to produce certain effects: rhythm (as in MTV), disturbance, comparisons, and tension. Editing, like the camera's view, directs viewer attention to certain scenes and parts of scenes while at the same time seeming invisible.

Narrator and Point of View

In film, the camera automatically provides a point of view. This point of view is sometimes aligned with a particular character (that is, it seems to reproduce what a particular character would see). An example of this is when the camera peers through Thomas's camera lense in *Blow Up*. More often, a film is presented from a seemingly omniscient site we rarely think about. This gives us the sense that the world of the film is given for us to see and that we have the best view in the house.

The fact that we have such a view, however, does create difficulty in identifying any specific narrator like that which functions in prose fiction. Like the prose narrator, the camera provides our view to action, but the camera has no persona and is not, like the narrator, quite as much a character or presence. Sometimes films provide a *voice-over* narrator—the voice of someone who seems to be seeing or experiencing what the film presents (though very often such a person could not possibly see what the camera presents). Usually, however, the camera's operations seem almost invisible, or at least we pay little attention to them.

Sound

Film sound is an important element in the ways films provide information and render atmosphere. Dialogue not only relates plot and feelings, it also characterizes the players. Music, often unnoticed, evokes emotion, sets tone, and creates tension. To see exactly how much, try watching a horror movie without the sound. How scary is it? As mentioned above, voice-overs add the illusion of a narrator, who describes the film's action as an expert (as in documentaries) or as a point of subjective experience (as when the narrator is a character). Sound contributes to the film's illusion that we are present and that the scenes it portrays are real.

TOPICS FOR CRITICAL THINKING

1. What elements of fiction cannot be rendered in film and why?
2. What can film do that prose cannot?
3. What are the differences in the ways readers consume a printed text and viewers consume a visual text?
4. What are the purposes of comparing a prose fiction story with a film that borrows its ideas?

TOPICS FOR CRITICAL WRITING

1. Produce a "treatment," or outline, of how you would make a film from a particular short story.
2. Use the mode of analysis employed here to compare *Blow Up* with "Blow-Up" or to analyze another film derived from a story. (For a list of such films, see CD-ROM.)

18 The Limits of Fiction: Autobiography

Fiction and Nonfiction

The line between fiction, or writing that presents events that are not considered to be a rendition of historical fact, and nonfiction, or writing that presents historical fact, is a very blurry one. We all know that events and impressions presented in fictional stories may be "true" in the deepest sense. Human beings may be selfish, desperate, guilty, loving, kind, and generous, for example. The difference between prose fiction and prose nonfiction is that prose nonfiction presents a specific human being or event that existed at some point in history as a deliberate rendition of that history. Forms of nonfiction such as history, biography, and journalism attempt to portray what we know of the historical facts of this specific individual or incident. Prose fiction may take up incidents and types of characters that we know have existed and may even base itself on a "real-life event," but its portrayal is interested in elaborating, dramatizing, and embroidering events toward the kinds of fictional art we have studied in the previous seventeen chapters.

Autobiography is often considered a form of nonfiction since it describes historical people and events rendered as a kind of history. While those who write nonfiction generally have an interest in presenting an "unbiased" view of facts, the authors of autobiographies are writing about themselves. Although they may wish to be objective it is difficult for anyone to write about him- or herself in an unbiased fashion. Because autobiography is a form of self-presentation, autobiographers also tend to pay attention to the artfulness of their writing. For this reason, autobiographies often seem similar to prose fiction in the formal elements of plot, character, setting, and narrator, as well as in their style, structure, and use of imagery and motifs. The most significant differences between autobiography and prose fiction are that we imagine that the events of autobiography happened and that the narrator of autobiography is the same as the author.

Although autobiography presents what are presumably factual events, many times it is difficult to confirm whether the events, characters, feelings, and perceptions described are indeed fact or the product of memory and retrospection. For this reason, it is wise to study the art of autobiography rather than the history it describes. This does not mean that autobiography's narrative did

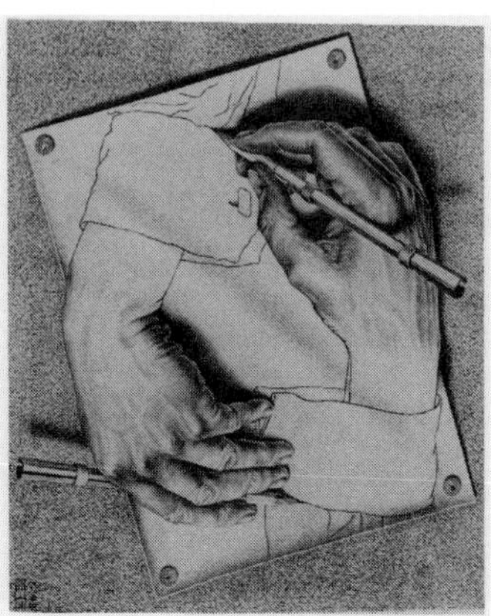

M. C. Escher "Drawing Hands" 1948

not happen or isn't "true," but that the processes of memory and writing tend to "fictionalize" accounts, rendering them with the formal and poetic qualities of fiction, such as imagery, style, and tone.

Thinking of the narrator as the author provides readers with the illusion that we are reading the words of a real person. But it is also wise to be aware that all narrators, even those purporting to be real people, are constructions. No narrator can ever present all aspects of a complex human being, and most authors have a stake in presenting only their best and cleverest side. Like fiction, autobiography has a style; it can be serious writing (Maya Angelou's *I Know Why the Caged Bird Sings*) or simply fodder for the popular market (Roseanne Barr's *Roseanne*). Autobiography can be realist, modernist, or postmodern.

Autobiography, which, like historical writing, predates the emergence of the short story, has several purposes. Most obviously, it preserves firsthand descriptions of people and events, some famous, some not. Second, it serves as a record of the author. Third, writing autobiography may be a way for individuals to explore the meaning of their experiences or work out problems. This is why autobiography is sometimes referred to as "life writing." Fourth, autobiography may help individuals work through traumatic memories such as the Holocaust or violent crime.

Many different kinds of people write autobiographies. Today, celebrities, notorious figures (such as Monica Lewinsky), politicians, and athletes all publish autobiographies, often with the help of ghostwriters. Collaboration with another writer poses interesting questions about the relation between an autobiography's author and its narrator. Some autobiographies, such as those that follow, are written by fiction writers. It is interesting to compare the ways in which authors write fiction with the ways they write their autobiographies. Note, for example, the ways in which Mark Twain's humorous anecdotal style appears equally well in a chapter from his autobiography, while Chester Himes's account presents a very different tone from his short story. W. S. Penn's ironic style carries into his autobiographical essays but changes its targets. The other three selections are also the work of writers. Carl Van Vechten and Jean Rhys are writers of the modernist period who recount their experiences from various perspectives, Van Vechten from the vantage point of breakfast and Rhys from her experiences as an immigrant chorus girl in England. The excerpt from Nicole Brossard's *Surfaces of Sense* represents the limits of fiction in its weaving of life, art, and experiment.

MARK TWAIN

from *The Autobiography of Mark Twain* (1906)

Chapter 10

In Hannibal when I was about fifteen I was for a short time a Cadet of Temperance, an organization which probably covered the whole United States during as much as a year—possibly even longer. It consisted in a pledge to refrain, during membership, from the use of tobacco; I mean it consisted partly in that pledge and partly in a red merino sash, but the red merino sash was the main part. The boys joined in order to be privileged to wear it—the pledge part of the matter was of no consequence. It was so small in importance that, contrasted with the sash, it was in effect nonexistent. The organization was weak and impermanent because there were not enough holidays to support it. We could turn out and march and show the red sashes on May Day with the Sunday schools and on the Fourth of July with the Sunday schools, the independent fire company and the militia company. But you can't keep a juvenile moral institution alive on two displays of its sash per year. As a private I could not have held out beyond one procession but I was Illustrious Grand Worthy Secretary and Royal Inside Sentinel and had the privilege of inventing the passwords and of wearing a rosette on my sash. Under these conditions I was enabled to remain steadfast until I had gathered the glory of two displays—May Day and the Fourth of July. Then I resigned straightway and straightway left the lodge.

I had not smoked for three full months and no words can adequately describe the smoke appetite that was consuming me. I had been a smoker from my ninth year—a private one during the first two years but a public one after that—that is to say, after my father's death. I was smoking and utterly happy before I was thirty steps from the lodge door. I do not now know what the brand of the cigar was. It was probably not choice, or the previous smoker would not have thrown it away so soon. But I realized that it was the best cigar that was ever made. The previous smoker would have thought the same if he had been without a smoke for three months. I smoked that stub without shame. I could not do it now without shame, because now I am more refined than I was then. But I would smoke it just the same. I know myself and I know the human race well enough to know that.

In those days the native cigar was so cheap that a person who could afford anything could afford cigars. Mr. Garth had a great tobacco factory and he also had a small shop in the village for the retail sale of his products. He had one brand of cigars which even poverty itself was able to buy. He had had these in stock a good many years and although they looked well enough on the outside, their insides had decayed to dust and would fly out like a puff of vapor when they were broken in two. This brand was very popular on account of its extreme cheapness. Mr. Garth had other brands which were cheap and some that were bad, but the supremacy over them enjoyed by this brand was indicated by its name. It was called "Garth's damnedest." We used to trade old newspapers (exchanges) for that brand.

There was another shop in the village where the conditions were friendly to penniless boys. It was kept by a lonely and melancholy little hunchback and we could always get a supply of cigars by fetching a bucket of water for him from the village pump, whether he needed water or not. One day we found him asleep in his chair—a custom of his—and we waited patiently for him to wake up, which was a custom of ours. But he slept so long this time that at last our patience was exhausted and we tried to wake him—but he was dead. I remember the shock of it yet.

In my early manhood and in middle life I used to vex myself with reforms every now and then. And I never had occasion to regret these divergencies for, whether the resulting deprivations were long or short, the rewarding pleasure which I got out of the vice when I returned to it always paid me for all that it cost.

It was back in those far-distant days that Jim Wolf came to us. He was from Shelbyville, a hamlet thirty or forty miles back in the country, and he brought all his native sweetness and gentlenesses and simplicities with him. He was approaching seventeen, a grave and slender lad, trustful, honest, honorable, a creature to love and cling to. And he was incredibly bashful. He was with us a good while but he could never conquer that peculiarity; he could not be at ease in the presence of any woman, not even in my good and gentle mother's; and as to speaking to any girl, it was wholly impossible.

It is to this kind that untoward things happen. My sister gave a "candy-pull" on a winter's night. I was too young to be of the company and Jim was too diffident. I was sent up to bed early and Jim followed of his own motion. His room was in the new part of the house and his window looked out on the roof of the L annex. That roof was six inches deep in snow and the snow had an ice crust upon it which was as slick as glass. Out of the comb of the roof projected a short chimney, a common resort for sentimental cats on moonlight nights—and this was a moonlight night. Down at the eaves, below the chimney, a canopy of dead vines spread away to some posts, making a cozy shelter, and after an hour or two the rollicking crowd of young ladies and gentlemen grouped themselves in its shade, with their saucers of liquid and piping-hot candy disposed about them on the frozen ground to cool. There was joyous chaffing and joking and laughter—peal upon peal of it.

About this time a couple of old, disreputable tomcats got up on the chimney and started a heated argument about something; also about this time I gave up trying to get to sleep and went visiting to Jim's room. He was awake and fuming about the cats and their intolerable yowling. I asked him, mockingly, why he didn't climb out and drive them away. He was nettled and said overboldly that for two cents he *would*.

It was a rash remark and was probably repented of before it was fairly out of his mouth. But it was too late—he was committed. I knew him; and I knew he would rather break his neck than back down, if I egged him on judiciously.

"Oh, of course you would! Who's doubting it?"

It galled him and he burst out, with sharp irritation, "Maybe *you* doubt it!"

"I? Oh no! I shouldn't think of such a thing. You are always doing wonderful things, with your mouth."

He was in a passion now. He snatched on his yarn socks and began to raise the window, saying in a voice quivering with anger:

"*You* think I dasn't—you do! Think what you blame please. *I* don't care what you think. I'll show you!"

The window made him rage; it wouldn't stay up.

I said, "Never mind, I'll hold it."

Indeed, I would have done anything to help. I was only a boy and was already in a radiant heaven of anticipation. He climbed carefully out, clung to the window sill until his feet were safely placed, then began to pick his perilous way on all-fours along the glassy comb, a foot and a hand on each side of it. I believe I enjoy it now as much as I did then; yet it is nearly fifty years ago. The frosty breeze flapped his short shirt about his lean legs; the crystal roof shone like polished marble in the intense glory of the moon; the unconscious cats sat erect upon the chimney, alertly watching each other, lashing their tails and pouring out their hollow grievances; and slowly and cautiously Jim crept on, flapping as he went, the gay and frolicsome young creatures under the vine canopy unaware, and outraging these solemnities with their misplaced laughter. Every time Jim slipped I had a hope; but always on he crept and disappointed it. At last he was within reaching distance. He paused, raised himself carefully up, measured his distance deliberately, then made a frantic grab at the nearest cat—and missed it. Of course he lost his balance. His heels flew up, he struck on his back, and like a rocket he darted down the roof feet first, crashed through the dead vines and landed in a sitting position in fourteen saucers of red-hot candy in the midst of all that party—and dressed as *he* was—this lad who could not look a girl in the face with his clothes on. There was a wild scramble and a storm of shrieks and Jim fled up the stairs, dripping broken crockery all the way.

The incident was ended. But I was not done with it yet, though I supposed I was. Eighteen or twenty years later I arrived in New York from California, and by that time I had failed in all my other undertakings and had stumbled into literature without intending it. This was early in 1867. I was offered a large sum to write something for the *Sunday Mercury* and I answered with the tale of "Jim Wolf and the Cats." I also collected the money for it—twenty-five dollars. It seemed over-pay but I did not say anything about that, for I was not so scrupulous then as I am now.

A year or two later "Jim Wolf and the Cats" appeared in a Tennessee paper in a new dress—as to spelling; it was masquerading in a Southern dialect.

The appropriator of the tale had a wide reputation in the West and was exceedingly popular. Deservedly so, I think. He wrote some of the breeziest and funniest things I have ever read and did his work with distinguished ease and fluency. His name has passed out of my memory.

A couple of years went by; then the original story cropped up again and went floating around in the original spelling and with my name to it. Soon, first one paper and then another fell upon me vigorously for "stealing" "Jim Wolf and the Cats" from the Tennessee man. I got a merciless basting but I did not mind it. It's all in the game. Besides, I had learned, a good while before that, that it is not wise to keep the fires going under a slander unless you can get some large advantage out of keeping it alive. Few slanders can stand the wear of silence.

Uncle Remus still lives, and must be over a thousand years old. Indeed I know that this must be so, because I have seen a new photograph of him in the public prints within the last month or so[1] and in that picture his aspects are distinctly and strikingly geological and one can see that he is thinking about the mastodons and the plesiosaurs that he used to play with when he was young.

It is just a quarter of a century since I have seen Uncle Remus. He visited us in our home in Hartford and was reverently devoured by the big eyes of Susy and Clara, for I made a deep and awful impression upon the little creatures—who knew his book by heart through my nightly declamation of its tales to them—by revealing to them privately that he was the real Uncle Remus whitewashed so that he could come into people's houses the front way.

He was the bashfulest grown person I have ever met. When there were people about he stayed silent and seemed to suffer until they were gone. But he was lovely nevertheless, for the sweetness and benignity of the immortal Remus looked out from his eyes and the graces and sincerities of his character shone in his face.

It may be that Jim Wolf was as bashful as Harris. It hardly seems possible, yet as I look back fifty-six years and consider Jim Wolf I am almost persuaded that he was. He was seventeen and yet he was as much as four times as bashful as I was, though I was only fourteen. He boarded and slept in the house but he was always tongue-tied in the presence of my sister, and when even my gentle mother spoke to him he could not answer save in frightened monosyllables. He would not enter a room where a girl was; nothing could persuade him to do such a thing.

Once when he was in our small parlor alone, two majestic old maids entered and seated themselves in such a way that Jim could not escape without passing by them. He would as soon have thought of passing by one of Harris's plesiosaurs, ninety feet long. I came in presently, was charmed with the situation and sat down in a corner to watch Jim suffer and to enjoy it. My mother followed a minute later and sat down with the visitors and began to talk. Jim sat upright in his chair, and during a quarter of an hour he did not change his

[1]Written October 16, 1906

position by a shade—neither General Grant nor a bronze image could have maintained that immovable pose more successfully. I mean as to body and limbs; with the face there was a difference. By fleeting revealments of the face I saw that something was happening—something out of the common. There would be a sudden twitch of the muscles of the face, an instant distortion which in the next instant had passed and left no trace. These twitches gradually grew in frequency but no muscle outside of the face lost any of its rigidity or betrayed any interest in what was happening to Jim. I mean if something *was* happening to him, and I knew perfectly well that that was the case. At last a pair of tears began to swim slowly down his cheeks amongst the twitchings, but Jim sat still and let them run; then I saw his right hand steal along his thigh until halfway to his knee, then take a vigorous grip upon the cloth.

That was a wasp that he was grabbing. A colony of them were climbing up his legs and prospecting around, and every time he winced they stabbed him to the hilt—so for a quarter of an hour one group of excursionists after another climbed up Jim's legs and resented even the slightest wince or squirm that he indulged himself with in his misery. When the entertainment had become nearly unbearable he conceived the idea of gripping them between his fingers and putting them out of commission. He succeeded with many of them but at great cost, for as he couldn't see the wasp he was as likely to take hold of the wrong end of him as he was the right; then the dying wasp gave him a punch to remember the incident by.

If those ladies had stayed all day and if all the wasps in Missouri had come and climbed up Jim's legs nobody there would ever have known it but Jim and the wasps and me. There he would have sat until the ladies left. When they were gone we went upstairs and he took his clothes off and his legs were a picture to look at. They looked as if they were mailed all over with shirt buttons, each with a single red hole in the center. The pain was intolerable—no, would have been intolerable, but the pain of the presence of those ladies had been so much harder to bear that the pain of the wasps' stings was quite pleasant and enjoyable by comparison.

Jim never could enjoy wasps. I remember a circumstance in support of this conviction of mine; it preceded the episode which I have just recorded. In those extremely youthful days I was not aware that practical joking was a thing which, aside from being as a rule witless, is a base pastime and disreputable. In those early days I gave the matter no thought but indulged freely in practical joking without stopping to consider its moral aspects. During three-fourths of my life I have held the practical joker in limitless contempt and detestation; I have despised him as I have despised no other criminal, and when I am delivering my opinion about him the reflection that I have been a practical joker myself seems to increase my bitterness rather than to modify it.

One afternoon I found the upper part of the window in Jim's bedroom thickly cushioned with wasps. Jim always slept on the side of his bed that was against the window. I had what seemed to me a happy inspiration: I turned back the bedclothes and, at cost of one or two stings, brushed the wasps down and collected a few hundred of them on the sheet on that side of the bed, then turned the covers over them and made prisoners of them. I made a deep crease down the center of the bed to protect the front side from invasion by them and then at night I offered to sleep with Jim. He was willing.

I made it a point to be in bed first to see if my side of it was still a safe place to rest in. It was. None of the wasps had passed the frontier. As soon as Jim was ready for bed I blew out the candle and let him climb in in the dark. He was talking as usual but I couldn't answer, because by anticipation I was suffocating with laughter, and although I gagged myself with a hatful of the sheet, I was on the point of exploding all the time. Jim stretched himself out comfortably, still pleasantly chatting; then his talk began to break and become disjointed; separations intervened between his words, and each separation was emphasized by a more or less sudden and violent twitch of his body, and I knew that the immigrants were getting in their work. I knew I ought to evince some sympathy and ask what was the matter but I couldn't do it because I should laugh if I tried. Presently he stopped talking altogether—that is, on the subject which he had been pursuing, and he said, "There is something in this bed."

I knew it but held my peace.

He said, "There's thousands of them."

Then he said he was going to find out what it was. He reached down and began to explore. The wasps resented this intrusion and began to stab him all over and everywhere. Then he said he had captured one of them and asked me to strike a light. I did it and when he climbed out of bed his shirt was black with half crushed wasps dangling by one hind leg, and in his two hands he held a dozen prisoners that were stinging and stabbing him with energy, but his grit was good and he held them fast. By the light of the candle he identified them and said, "Wasps!"

It was his last remark for the night. He added nothing to it. In silence he uncovered his side of the bed and, dozen by dozen, he removed the wasps to the floor and beat them to a pulp with the bootjack, with earnest and vindictive satisfaction, while I shook the bed with mute laughter—laughter which was not all a pleasure to me, for I had the sense that his silence was ominous. The work of extermination being finally completed, he blew out the light and returned to bed and seemed to compose himself to sleep—in fact he did lie stiller than anybody else could have done in the circumstances.

I remained awake as long as I could and did what I could to keep my laughter from shaking the bed and provoking suspicion, but even my fears could not keep me awake forever and finally fell asleep and presently woke again—under persuasion of circumstances. Jim was kneeling on my breast and pounding me in the face with both fists. It hurt—but he was knocking all the restraints of my laughter loose; I could not contain it any longer and I laughed until all my body was exhausted and my face, as I believed, battered to a pulp.

Jim never afterward referred to that episode and I had better judgment than to do it myself, for he was a third longer than I was, although not any wider.

I played many practical jokes upon him but they were all cruel and all barren of wit. Any brainless swindler could have invented them. When a person of mature age perpetrates a practical joke it is fair evidence, I think, that he is weak in the head and hasn't enough heart to signify.

Mark Twain

(1835–1910)

A popular and successful writer, Samuel Clemens **Web** wrote novels, including *Huckleberry Finn*, and satires such as *A Connecticut Yankee in King Arthur's Court.* Known as a humorist, Twain often used dialects in writing his stories. Twain traveled widely and worked as everything from a printer's apprentice to a steamboat pilot before becoming a writer. ***www***

TOPICS FOR CRITICAL THINKING

1. What elements does this autobiographical passage have in common with prose fiction?
2. What clues are there that this episode is shaped as a coherent story?
3. Do we read this differently if we believe the author and the narrator are the same? How does this change the way we read?
4. Compare the style of this selection with the style of Twain's "The Story of the Bad Little Boy" (Chapter 5). Is there any difference in style that would suggest that the autobiography is nonfiction?

TOPICS FOR CRITICAL WRITING

1. Consider the ways in which the notion of the "story" shapes the ways in which this anecdote is told.
2. What are the connections between not smoking and walking on roofs?

Carl Van Vechten

A Note on Breakfasts *(1925)*

Breakfast is the most personal meal of the day. It requires, therefore, the most careful consideration. Luncheon, in the city at any rate, is a hasty, chatty meal, shared with intimates. At dinner it is possible that one may sit down with comparative strangers—comparative in the sense that you have been introduced to them in the drawing-room only a moment before—provided the cocktails have been sufficiently powerful. Assuredly, overlooking the idiosyncrasies of personal taste, it is a matter of indifference what one eats at these later repasts. At breakfast, on the contrary, the nature of food and of companions is of paramount importance.

Everything depends, of course, on the habitual mood of your awakening. There are those who bound out of bed whistling, or singing lustily, the latest popular tune. This sort of person demands a cold shower and indulges in chamber-athletics. To him, a heavy breakfast with several courses will not seem abhorrent. To him, who imbibes cheer and health and life from the morning air, it will not be unpleasing to share the table with friends or relatives. This fellow is an excellent choice for a week-end house-party, provided it is convenient to offer him a room and bath to himself.

The individual who awakes with a bad taste in his mouth and no conversation is indubitably more prevalent. He turns over several times and rearranges the sheets and pillows before he is able to invoke even enough energy to press a button on his bed-table. When his coffee is brought to him on a tray he regards it languidly. The first sip, he endures; the second is slightly more agreeable; in time, he drains the cup and pours out another. At the end of half-an-hour, he feels sufficiently human to read his morning mail or to scan the headlines of his newspaper.

Between these two extreme types there lie, naturally, many variations. For myself, I may confess that I never take cold baths and I never sing. It is equally true that I never sing before dinner. Nevertheless, my breakfast manners are by no means steadfast. I have discovered them to be prescribed by environment.

In my home in the Middle West it was the unhappy custom to serve breakfast for all the members of the family, fully dressed, at seven-thirty. I conformed to this custom, although not without hearty protest, until, at the age of nineteen, I went away to college. To approach the table at that hour properly clad, for dressing-gowns were forbidden, demanded rising a full thirty minutes earlier. In a futile attempt to bring about this desirable end, my mother used to call me when she herself arose. This warning was usually unavailing. I found myself able to reply to the call in my sleep and then to doze more deeply again, with the result that frequently the family were half through their rations before I made an appearance in the dining-room. To miss the whole of this meal was not a simple feat, as the summons was repeated at intervals and breakfast at our house continued for nearly an hour. First, there was fruit, preserved or fresh, then a breakfast food, usually oatmeal, for this was before the day when it became fashionable to christen cereal foods after Pullman cars, then the principal course, sausage, or bacon and eggs, or fried steak, together with potatoes, often boiled and smothered in cream. An extraordinary collection of pots appeared on the table in front of my mother: a pot of coffee, a pot of tea, and a pot of postum, to satisfy the diversity in taste for beverages on the part of the several members of my family. Until I was fifteen I added to the confusion by drinking hot milk. After, or during the meat course, pancakes, buckwheat, corn, or wheat, were served, although occasionally popovers, or Sally Lunns, or doughnuts were substituted for these. Such were the breakfasts I was brought up on and which I have never eaten since, save when I have revisited my birthplace.

On my first morning at the University of Chicago I lonelily awoke to realize the fact that I must forage for my breakfast, as no meals were served in the hall where I slept. After dressing, therefore, I emerged to walk several blocks before I discovered an eating-house. Precisely the foods I was accustomed to at home were on the bill of fare, but the prices alarmed me. How could I afford to pay thirty-five cents for bacon and eggs and then lay out an additional twenty cents for pancakes? My modest alllowance did not seem to warrant such extravagance. I compromised on rolls, two fried eggs, and coffee. A few days later, after I had accumulated an acquaintance or two, I learned that it was the thing to sit on a stool in a snug little cabin near the athletic field and crack jokes with the untidy old woman who prepared the rude fare. It was here that I first consumed sinkers and, curiously enough, from that moment on, I never again suffered from the indigestion which had caused me so much pain in my extreme youth. Thereafter, my college breakfasts varied. On bright, spring mornings it was pleasant to sit before a table in the pavilion in Jackson Park. Later, in my fraternity house we demanded what we wanted when we wanted it from Desdemona Sublett, who sold bricks for the projected new African M. E. Church for four or five years.

I began my newspaper days with an early shift. Working on an afternoon paper, I was obliged to report at four in the morning to clip the rival papers and arrange the strings of stories in a convenient manner to meet the eye of the city editor, who arrived at seven. To prepare myself for this task, at three-forty-five I hied myself to one of the few restaurants in the loop open so early. There each morning I munched two large pieces of apple pie and drank a great cup of worse coffee than any I have ever sampled before or since. I could, I believe, eat anything in those days, and often did.

Three years later, at the age of twenty-six, I was discharged from the Chicago American for "lowering the tone of the Hearst newspapers"—I am quoting from the managing editor's note to me. Feeling certain that I had accomplished all that was possible in the West, I took a train for New York where, almost immediately, I found employment on the Times. Here, I was not obliged to report for duty until eleven. For the first time in my life, therefore, I enjoyed the luxury of lying in bed in the morning. During my second year in New York I moved into the Maison Favre on Seventh Avenue, where Madame Favre, often in a dressing-sacque, presided in the evening over a good, old-fashioned table d'hôte. Bottles of wine, furnished free with the dinner—and the dinner in those days cost seventy-five cents—stood on the tables and the conversation was coevally referred to as bohemian. The phrase went that you could cut the smoke with a knife. It was also considered clever to remark from time to time, So this is Paris! Occasionally Lotta Faust, the famous half-back of her time, or some minor opera singer from the Metropolitan, enlivened the evening for me merely by her presence. Well, at the Maison Favre—which deserves a whole story to itself; some day I may take the trouble to write down—as I have said, I lay in bed until late in the morning, when good old Annie, incongruously Irish, at a certain set hour brought up my breakfast, consisting invariably of shirred eggs, chocolate, and croissants. She rapped gently before she deposited the tray on the floor outside my door. If I did not heed the tap immediately, ten to one Madame's little black-and-tan, Fifi, ate the breakfast and another had to be provided for me.

Petit déjeuner at the Maison Favre served to prepare me for Paris where it is the excellent tradition to sip chocolate or coffee and crunch croissants in bed, but, inexplicably, when I went to London, I began, quite avidly, to enjoy English breakfasts. In the public dining-room of my hotel I ate kippers or bloaters and followed them up with a healthy helping of meat and eggs, accompanied by orange marmalade, a conserve I cannot even look at anywhere else. This benign adaptability is a quality I still possess. Invariably, in London, I wake up in the morning with a good appetite. In a Munich pension, discovering the coffee and chocolate to be indifferent and the beer heavenly, it occurred to me to sample Münchener as a breakfast beverage, and thereafter I followed this system with regularity. I did not, reflection informs me, invent this plan. Some years earlier, in Chicago, I had been assigned in my capacity as reporter to meet Sarah Bernhardt at the railway station. The actress, fresh—or weary—from a South American tour, had disembarked in New York and caught a train leaving directly for the West, where she proposed to open one of her farewell American tours. If memory serves, she undertook five more. I still recall the crowd in the station, the diva's exit from her private car, all velvets and furs and carnations. Leaning on the arm of one of her comrades, she bestowed on the bystanders her alarming smile with the gums exposed, at the same time seductive and repulsive, and then tottered up the platform to clasp the hand of the engineer who had driven her safely to her destination, all this to the accompaniment of innumerable flashlight explosions. Then, entering a vehicle, Madame was borne to the Auditorium, a hotel erected in the purest Style Benjamin Harrison, where I, together with a half-dozen other newspaper men, rejoined her. How do you like America? What is your favourite city in the United States? All the usual questions were asked and answered in the usual way. Now, her manager entered, breathless. The theatre, at which she was announced to appear in a different play each night, and for two matinees, was sold out for the week. Would Madame consent to play matinees on the five remaining afternoons? . . . But yes, was her reply. You know my terms, so much a performance—in advance . . . Splendid! cried the impresario. We shall endeavour to make it easy for Madame. What would Madame wish to play? Some lighter piece, perhaps, on these extra days? . . . Sarah, the divine, shrugged her shoulders. Don't annoy me with business details, she urged. You know I have a repertory of fifty dramas. Announce anything you like and let me know in time to get my dresses to the theatre. . . . During this conversation and the ensuing interviews with the journalists, Madame consumed her breakfast: two poached eggs, a porterhouse steak, fried potatoes, and *two bottles of Budweiser.*

I have a vague memory of having sampled Edam cheese at eight A.M. in Amsterdam some fifteen years ago but continental breakfasts in later years have left a more enduring and a more æsthetic impression. It is pleasant to recall the breakfasts at the Villa Allegra outside of Florence, where I rose at my desire and strolled out into the garden to gaze over the balustrade towards the lovely hills, given form and colour by the gnarled olive-trees with their sage-green foliage, and the funereal heaven-pointing cypresses—I am reminded, with some amusement, of the fact recorded by Bernard Shaw that a scene-painter for Augustin Daly painted these trees a lettuce-green for a production of The Two Gentlemen of Verona. I listened to the bells tolling softly from the invisible campanili in the city below. In the garden itself, where daphnes and oleanders and gardenias blossomed, a white peacock strutted and a monkey screamed. Presently, my morning revery was interrupted by the appearance of Vittorio, obsequious and sardonic, bearing a tray and demanding where I would have it placed. Quite alone, I sat on a marble bench to enjoy my drip coffee, honey, and rolls in this curious confusion of nature and artifice, so like a stage-setting for an Oscar Wilde comedy. In English and American country-houses I have since frequently experienced a similar decorative solitude. I recall too an amusing episode in the garden of an inn on the mountain above Heidelberg where I was forced to compete with a swarm of bees for my food and, finally vanquished, ran laughing down the mountainside.

Perhaps the most titillating breakfasts of all are those of which one partakes before going to bed, the early dawn breakfasts at Pré Catalan in the Bois of Paris where it formerly was the fashion—and possibly still is: I have not been there at the proper hour for many years—to actually milk the cow to the astonishment of the intoxicated customers, or the breakfasts one eats at some hole in the wall off the Place Pigalle where sleepy women of the streets share snacks with their souteneurs before officially retiring. In New York, in the days before the war, unless one modestly repaired to Childs' for butter-cakes, Jack's was the rendezvous for all the delightful people who like to stay up all night. Jack's did as flourishing a business at six in the morning as any other successful restaurant does at seven-thirty in the evening. Here newspaper men and actresses gobbled platters of scrambled eggs and tomatoes, garnished with Irish bacon, and washed down with good beer or Scotch highballs—unless they had acquired a taste for Bushnell's Irish whisky, which has an aroma like that of apple-blossoms. The stragglers from smart East Side parties also wandered in and, as people who stay up all night form a kind of club, and as no one who eats breakfast before he goes to bed objects to sharing it, there was a good deal of visiting from table to table. It was here that Vernon Castle, then engaged in "feeding" Lew Fields in The Girl Behind the Counter at the old Herald Square Theatre, executed amusing slight-of-hand tricks with table-knives. It was here that Monsieur de Max, remembering, perhaps, the tribulations of Œdipus Rex, glowered saturninely from a corner table. It was here that Frank O'Malley, who had recently created that masterpiece of journalistic spoofing, The Good Ship Wobble, in the Sun, was an inevitable figure. One night a soldier from one of the armouries rode his bewildered stallion into the rooms. One night Donald Evans, requisitioning a bowl of fresh blood, employed it to indite a sonnet on the table-cloth. Donald invariably breakfasted on six raw eggs and six cups of black coffee, as strong as he could get it made, which reminds me that Edgar Saltus has described another poet who breakfasted on foie gras and curaçao. Jack himself, grey-haired and grey-moustached, always immaculate in his evening clothes, a scarlet carnation in his button-hole, wandered about like the host of a yachting party, while the Irish waiters exchanged questionable pleasantries with the customers or occasionally formed a flying-wedge to bounce an obstreperous guest. Jack's only recently closed its doors for ever, but long ago prohibition and the passage of time had changed the character of the place, although many of the identical waiters remained to the end to remind us that some things in life are stable. They became sadder eyed and less spry of limb, however, and it was a melancholy experience to observe their faces brighten whenever chance brought an old habitué back to his table.

Carl Van Vechten

(1880–1964)

www Journalist and critic Carl Van Vechten **Web** was born in Iowa, studied at the University of Chicago, and became associated with America's expatriate culture in Europe. A promoter of the Harlem Renaissance, Van Vechten became known as a portrait photographer.

TOPICS FOR CRITICAL THINKING

1. What do breakfasts reveal about the narrator? About the places he visits?
2. Does this chapter have a plot? Characters? A setting?
3. What is the purpose of mentioning so many places, times, and people?

TOPICS FOR CRITICAL WRITING

1. Is this review of breakfasts a "sacred" or a "profane" memory? What is at stake in thinking of life events in this way?
2. Analyze the portrait of one figure in this selection. How does the selection employ detail and breakfast?

Jean Rhys

Chorus Girls

I was a year and a half to two years in *Our Miss Gibbs.* In the winter we toured small towns in the north, and in the summer the seaside places. The chorus girls' wages were thirty-five shillings a week and extra for every matinée. When you signed the contract you gave them the option for the next tour so long as it was work you were capable of doing. It was a steady job. There was, however, a dreadful gap after the winter tour finished and before the summer tour started. It was impossible to save enough to tide you over this gap, so most of the girls lived at home for those two or three months. The few who, like myself, had no home tried to get a job in what were known as music-hall sketches, which went on all the year round.

In one of the gaps I managed to be taken on in the chorus of a music-hall sketch called *Chanticleer.* The name was taken from a Paris revue that was a great success at that time. Ours was an appalling show. The biggest joke in it was a girl in tights walking across the stage, dropping an egg and clucking loudly. Only one or two of the girls were at all attractive and we were hardly rehearsed. However, we opened at a town in the north and there we were, waiting in the wings, ready to go on. It was cold and I was shivering. We heard a loud tramping noise and somebody said, 'What on earth's that?' The answer was: 'That's the gallery walking out.' The gallery didn't hiss or boo if they disliked a show, they simply walked out, making as much noise as possible. When it was our turn to go on with our very amateurish dance I was shivering with fear as well as with cold.

As soon as we began I felt the mockery and scorn coming up from the audience like smoke. I was at the end of the line, near the wings, and after a bit of this I simply left the line and went off stage. Before I left I looked at the girl next to me. Her face was grim. She felt it as much as I did but bravely she went on dancing. I took my make-up off and went back to my lodgings feeling very unhappy at being so cowardly. I kept thinking, 'She stuck it, why couldn't I?' I made up my mind that on the next night I would stick it whatever they did, whether they hissed, booed or even threw things.

I was in the dressing-room with the other girls, making up, when the call-boy knocked and said, 'Will Miss Gray please go to Mr. Peterman's office at once.' Gray was the name I was using then. Mr. Peterman was the owner and manager of the show. As soon as I got into the room I saw he was in a towering rage. As he glared at me with a tight mouth he looked terrifying. 'Why,' he said, 'did you walk off stage in the middle of the act last night? Were you ill?'

'No, I wasn't ill,' I said. 'I was frightened.'

'And what were you frightened of?'

I said that I was frightened of the audience.

He said: 'And what the hell are you doing on the stage, may I ask, if you are frightened of an audience? You can take off your make-up and go home. I don't want to have anything to do with you, letting down the show like that.'

I said: 'Well, I shouldn't have run away I know, but I think you ought to give me my fare back to London.'

'And why should I give you your fare? I'll do nothing of the sort.'

I had no money at all, so—as always when I am desperate—I was able to fight.

There was a society called, I think, 'for the Protection of Chorus Girls'. I knew the address and I said: 'Mr. Peterman, if you don't give me my fare back to London I will write to the society and complain about you.' He growled. I had never before heard a man growl like a dog, but he did. He said: 'There's an excursion train to London tomorrow. I'll give you the money for that, nothing else.'

When I returned to the dressing-room to take my make-up off the girl next to me said: 'Peterman's in an awful rage because I think he's got hardly any bookings for this show.'

'I don't wonder,' I said.

I was used to sleeping late and the excursion train left at some abnormally early hour. I was so afraid of missing it that I stayed up all night, suitcase at my feet, waiting. When I got to London and to my aunt, who was there at the time, she said: 'Whatever have you been doing with yourself? You look shocking. You'd better go and have a bath at once, you're so dirty.'

I have forgotten how I got over the rest of the gap, I suppose my aunt helped me. Later I went back to *Our Miss Gibbs.*

* * *

There was an elaborate dancer in the show, what they called a speciality dancer, and the speciality dancer and the chorus girls were at daggers drawn. She would seldom have anything to do with us; the chorus, in retaliation, responded by attacking her appearance, her manners, her morals. Every possible vice was piled on the poor girl. She had a little dog with her, and the sort of thing the chorus girls said was that she kept the dog to make love to her. I used to watch her from the wings because I loved her dance, and I didn't think she was bad, though rather haughty and touch-me-not. I knew the things said about her were unfair.

People talk about chorus girls as if they were all exactly alike, all immoral, all silly, all on the make. As a matter of fact, far from being all alike they were rather a strange mixture. One of them was the daughter of a well-known Labour leader and we noticed that whenever a Conservative victory had been won and we all cheered (for we were all Conservatives), she cheered more than any of us. We decided she hated her father. Another girl was the daughter of a woman who stood up for Oscar Wilde. There were chorus girls of sixteen and chorus girls of nearly forty; the contract signed with George Dance for *Our Miss Gibbs* enabled you to stay forever if you liked, until you were old and grey. Besides, the older ones often had good voices and were very useful. Some, though not many, were married. Some were engaged to be married and looking forward to their marriages like any other girl. Some were very ambitious, determined to make a good marriage (which was quite possible), and if you imagine they ever did anything which might interfere with that you don't know the type. Some were ambitious to get on in the theatre. These were rather few and far between and I noticed that nearly all of them came from theatrical families.

There was always the company tart but no one ever called her a tart. They just said, 'So-and-so has a lot of friends.' She would seldom turn up for the train calls, for someone would be sure to take her by car from one town to the next. I will never forget the face of the stage manager when a girl called Nancy was missing for the rehearsal call on a Monday. A telegram was brought in to him, he opened it and said in a bewildered voice: '*Contretemps*—what the devil does she mean, *contretemps?*' I think it was a day or two before Nancy turned up and somebody else had to be taught her dance.

We travelled with theatrical baskets which were collected by the theatrical baggage man every Thursday and went with the scenery. So we were left with small suitcases with washing things, toothbrush and very minimal make-up. Sunday was travelling day. The classic joke about travelling was two railway men talking. 'What have you got there, Bill?'—'Fish and actors.'—'Oh, shove them on a siding.'

Everybody knew the good theatrical lodgings, and everyone knew they were taken in advance. We had to do the best we could. Sometimes we struck lucky, sometimes not. You could save a bit if you lived with another girl, more if you lived with two. The food was always the same. We would get to the new lodgings after our Sunday train journey to a large joint of beef, usually very tough. On Monday we had it warmed up. On Tuesday minced. On Wednesday shepherd's pie or stew. On Thursday something exotic like eggs and bacon or liver. On Friday it was go as you can. On Saturday we were much too busy packing. On Sunday we left for another town which was exactly like the last one, or so I thought. All this was in the winter, in the North.

I never liked our landladies, but one I hated. I was living with a girl called Billie, and we were waiting upstairs with our suitcases packed when the landlady came in and presented us with her bill. It was enormous, about three times what we were expecting. Billie gave one look at it and said, 'We're not going to pay this!' The landlady said, 'Oh yes you will, or you won't leave here.' She left the room and locked the door. Billie and I emptied our purses and there wasn't nearly enough to pay her, nor to pay the fare to the next town if we missed our train. Billie said, 'There's only one thing to do about this,' and opened the window. We were on the second floor but the snow was very thick on the ground down below. Billie said: 'Well here's to it.' She threw her suitcase out and jumped after it. She lay still on the ground and I was frightened. After a while she looked up and said, 'Come on,' I wondered if it was awful but I didn't ask her. I threw my suitcase out too, and jumped. It was an awful bump in spite of the snow and for a while I lay still, wondering if I was dead. Then Billie said, 'Come on' so I got up, and we were running out of the garden gate with our suitcases when we saw the landlady looking after us and frowning. Billie said, 'One word to you!' and together we ran out of the gate, laughing. From this time dated my irrevocable hatred of landladies.

In England my love and longing for books completely left me. I never felt the least desire to read anything, not even a newspaper, and I think this indifference lasted a long time. Years. I don't remember reading anything on tour except *Forest Lovers. Forest Lovers* was a book set in the Middle Ages, about a man and a girl who loved each other very much and who escaped into the forest to hide, but they always slept with a sword between them. All the girls in the dressing-room had read the book and the conversation about the sword was endless. 'What did they have to do that for? Why? Besides, you could easily get over the sword.'—'No you couldn't, you'd get cut.'—'Of course you wouldn't.' The company tart, whom I liked very much, would sometimes lend me a book. I wouldn't really read it and sometimes forgot it, and she would embarrass me at train calls by shouting down the platform: 'Now then, Verney, what've you done with my book?' However abominable and dull my life was, it never occurred to me to buy a book or even a newspaper, which now seems very strange to me.

Going from room to room in this cold dark country, England, I never knew what it was that spurred me on and gave me an absolute certainty that there would be something else for me before long. Now I think the 'something else' was something small and limited. I realise that I was no good on the stage, forgot my lines, didn't thirst for the theatre as some of the girls did, yet I was so sure.

I got sick of being in *Our Miss Gibbs*, sick of wearing old Gaiety dresses cleaned. So we left—who was the girl I left with? I have forgotten—and got a job in the chorus of a pantomime at the Old Lyceum Theatre. The Tiller girls used to dance in it. I remember the song they sang.

Away down
In jungle town
Honeymoon
Is coming soon
And we hear the serenade
To a pretty monkey maid
And now in jungle town
The moon shines down
Without a frown
I'll be true
To monkey doodle-doo.

Then the Tiller girls danced, their heels clacking.

I'll be true
To monkey doodle-doo.

There were supposed to be rats in the dressing-room but I never saw one. By now my first real affair with a man had started. The pantomime didn't run for long and I didn't try for anything afterwards. I knew that however crudely Mr. Peterman had spoken when he asked what the hell I was doing on the stage, he had spoken the truth, but my lover imagined that I could get on in the theatre and insisted that I should have singing and dancing lessons. Dutifully I attended them. The rest of my time I spent looking out of the window for the messenger boy, because he always sent his letters by messenger.

Jean Rhys

(1894–1979)

www Ella Gwendolyn Rees Williams **Web** was born in Dominica, West Indies. Rhys was educated in England, worked as a chorus girl, and moved to the Continent with her first husband. She began writing novels in the late 1920s, quit writing for twenty years, and began again in the 1960s. She is most famous for her novel *The Wide Sargasso Sea* (1966), which traces the history of Rochester's first wife, Bertha, in *Jane Eyre.*

TOPICS FOR CRITICAL THINKING

1. In what ways does the passage's ending invite us to reconsider the experience?
2. What is the purpose of the excerpt's series of brief character sketches?
3. What does this passage tell us about the narrator?

TOPICS FOR CRITICAL WRITING

1. Through what specific tactics does the narrator hint that she is a different person than she describes at the time she wrote this?
2. How does the image of a "backstage" figure in other aspects of the girl's life?

Chester Himes

from *The Quality of Hurt* *(1971)*

I suppose there were many reasons for my coming to Europe, but I don't remember them clearly. It was very like the many impressions my seven and one half prison years had made on me: I knew that my long prison term had left its scars, I knew that many aspects of prison life had made deep impressions on my subconscious, but now I cannot distinctly recall what they are or should have been. I find it necessary to read what I have written in the past about my prison experiences to recall any part of them. I have almost completely forgotten prison, what it was like and what I was like while there. The only impression it left absolutely and irrevocably is that human beings—all human beings, of whatever race or nationality or religious belief or ideology—will do anything and everything. And I think it has partly convinced me—at least I have tried to convince myself that it has convinced me—that I can never again be hurt as much as I have already been hurt, even though I should live one hundred thousand years.

It is like that with my reasons for coming to Europe. I am not certain that I remember clearly what they were. Race prejudice, of course. I know that was one even though I don't remember it. I am black and I was born and raised and lived in America, and the fact that race prejudice was one of my reasons for leaving it is inescapable. But I know there were many others as well. Perhaps one is that I had the money for it. Another is that I came very close to killing the white woman, Vandi Haygood, with whom I had lived; and I was both shocked and frightened. I suppose murder, and more, given America's sex and racism syndrome, when the potential murderer is a black male and his potential victim a white female. I had always believed that to defend my life or my honor I would kill a white man without a second thought. But when I discovered that this applied to white women too, I was profoundly shaken. Because by then, white women were all I had left.

I begin to realize I must tell you more of my life in the U.S.A.

I was born July 29, 1909 in Jefferson City, Missouri, the state capital, across the street from the entrance to Lincoln Institute, where my father, Professor Joseph Sandy Himes, taught blacksmithing and wheelwrighting as the head of the Mechanical Department. Most Negro colleges in the South were known as "A. & M." colleges—agricultural and mechanical—in the Booker T. Washington tradition. As a child I often heard my father quote the famous saying of the great educator: "Let down your buckets where you are."

I was the youngest of three children, all boys. The only memory I have of my life in Jefferson City is of my brother Joseph and myself painting our hair with green paint left by the house painters. I also vaguely remember our mother instructing us to squeeze the bridges of our noses to keep them from becoming flat. My mother was an octoroon, or perhaps whiter. I remember her as looking like a white woman who had suffered a long siege of illness; she had hazel eyes, a sallow complexion, and auburn hair. Her family, the Bomars, were descended on their father's side from their white slaveowner and a slave, and on their mother's side from an Indian slave. I remember once seeing Grandmother Bomar when I was a child; she looked like a lithograph of an old, deeply wrinkled, pipe-smoking squaw from a Hollywood film. I saw only a picture of my grandfather; he was a tall fair white-looking man with a long blond beard, holding the reins of the horse of a Confederate cavalryman who was his master, and his half-brother, according to my mother. He was his master's body-servant and followed him to war.

My mother claimed that my grandfather's father was a direct descendant from an English noble family, and she was very proud of it. Much of her nagging and scolding and punishing and pushing us stemmed from her desire for us to live up to our "heritage."

All of the Bomars I ever saw were very fair, and some had moved into the white race. The only two I remember well were my mother's cousins, Mabel and Margaret Bomar, who had taught at Haines Institute in Augusta, Georgia, the year my mother went there to teach and took my brother Joseph and me. I remember them as being very animated and pretty; I was eight years old and I fell in love with them.

By then we had moved to Mississippi, where my father had taken a post as the head of the Mechanical Department of Alcorn A. & M., the Mississippi state college for blacks. Alcorn, formerly the white state school, named after Governor Alcorn, had been handed down to blacks when the white college moved to Oxford—the "Ole Miss" made famous by William Faulkner and James Meredith.

My father was the exact opposite of my mother. He was a short black man with bowed legs, a perfect ellipsoidal skull, and an Arabic face with a big hooked nose.

Now you can imagine what I look like. We all looked like that—like what you are imagining would be the combination of our mother and our father. Only I look more so. My hair is kinky, my complexion sepia, my features might be handsome were my nose not so tiny, and my skull is so flat and misshapen the students of my father used to say he had made it in the blacksmith shop.

My father's father was the slave blacksmith of a Jewish slaveowner, probably named Heinz, whose name he took when he was freed. That's how I came by the name Himes. I do not remember ever having heard any reference to his mother. He had two sisters, Fanny and Leah, who migrated to Cleveland, Ohio, with their husbands, and one brother, Andrew, whom I knew, although I seem to remember hearing that he had another brother, named Tom, whom I never met. "Uncle Tom" was a joke of my generation.

Aunt Fanny was married to a "stationary engineer" who tended a boiler for the Standard Oil refinery in Cleveland; he was a huge, rawboned dark-brown man who would eat great quantities of food—he didn't care what, as long as there was plenty. I have seen Uncle Wade eat a platter of boiled rice, a dishpanful of boiled beef lungs ("lights"), a gallon can of string beans, and a loaf of white bread for one meal. They had a son, Gerald, a few years younger than me, a fat boy whom they spoiled by overindulgence because he was their only child. Uncle Wade was operated on for gallbladder trouble, and enough gallstones the size of marbles were taken from his gallbladder to fill a Bull Durham sack; he never recovered. Aunt Fanny died a couple of years later from cancer. And a short time afterward my cousin Gerald shot his sweetheart twice in the head and himself once; she lived and he died.

Aunt Leah married a former teacher, Rodney Moon, who became a federal meat inspector after they emigrated to Cleveland. When I knew them they were the only black family in a white neighborhood in the 105th Street–Superior Avenue district (which has since become a ghetto), and as a consequence had great social status. They had two children, both considerably older than myself. One, Henry Lee, graduated from Howard University in Washington, D.C., I believe, and became a journalist-cum-schoolteacher of a sort; and his sister Ella, who had also been a schoolteacher. To my knowledge Henry taught at Talladega University in Alabama, was city editor of the Harlem newspaper the *Amsterdam News*, an executive of Sidney Hillman's Political Action Committee when Franklin Roosevelt ran for his last term in office, and was one of the group of black writers and intellectuals who were invited to Russia by the Russian government in the 1930s to make a film about Lincoln freeing the slaves. These brothers and sisters, among whom were Ted Poston, Langston Hughes, Loren Miller, Arabel Thompson, Molly Lewis, one of the founders of the Urban League Guild and now my cousin Henry's wife, quarreled among themselves and were sent home, it may now be said. Henry Moon, along with Ted Poston, now a reporter for the New York *Post*, Robert Weaver, former executive director of H.U.D., and other soul brothers, were members of President Roosevelt's "Black Cabinet," a group of visible black faces in federal jobs. Now Henry is a member of the national executive board of the NAACP and editor of *The Crisis*.

My father's generation are all dead as far as I know: Uncle Roddy and Aunt Leah, Uncle Andrew and perhaps Uncle Tom, and my father. We three brothers are still alive, but none of us has any children, so the Himes family will die with us. Joseph is an internationally known sociologist, a professor in the North Carolina College in Durham, North Carolina, and Edward, my eldest brother, was a waiter at a chichi restaurant on midtown Lexington Avenue, the last I heard, and an executive of the waiters union. I've heard black waiters in Harlem address him as "Mister Himes" with great respect, which they never did for either Joe or me, so he must be important. The fact that he lives in Harlem doesn't have anything to do with it.

I can't say that I remember very much of Eddie from childhood. He is about nine or ten years older than me, and I don't remember seeing too much of him. I was too young to remember him from Jefferson City, Missouri, and for most of the time we lived at Alcorn, Mississippi, he was away—first at school at Atlanta University and later on the road as a dining-car waiter.

But Joe and I were inseparable, despite the year's difference in our ages. Our mother was horrified by the elementary schools for blacks in Mississippi, and she taught Joe and me herself, in our living room, year in and year out, until we finished the seventh grade, or its equivalent in the Southern black school system. Haines Institute in Augusta was the first school we attended; I was eight or nine years old, and we were enrolled in the eighth grade. We were so far ahead in our studies that from the start we were always in classes with students twice our age.

Aside from Miss Lucy Laney, the big black woman founder and principal of Haines, whipping my bare bottom with an inch-thick pine board, latticed by a number of dollar-size holes, while I ground the enamel from my teeth to keep from crying; and a great fire one night in the nearby slums which left a large portion of the community homeless; and falling in love with my cousins, Mabel and Margaret Bomar, who were more than twice my age at the time, I do not remember anything about Haines. Oh yes, the *geechee*, those descendants of runaway slaves and Indians who lived in the Georgia and Florida swamps; and Maud, the mule, who bit me seriously on the nose for stealing her corn, which I would roast and eat; and Pomp, the geechee mascot, startling the school one morning with, "O, Milaney, Milaney, de gote done dead." Yes, there was a goat, but he was "done dead." And fighting my cousin, Will Porter, at the instigation of the older boys.

My father bought a car, a secondhand Studebaker, in Memphis during the last year of the war and became the only car owner in our county in Mississippi. I learned to drive it but my legs weren't long enough to reach the pedals and I knocked down several picket fences in the school.

My mother used to take us for rides in the country with a student driving, but we got into so many controversies with the cracker farmers of the county by frightening their mule teams that my father was dismissed from the school and driven from the state. And I must confess I find white people just the same today, everywhere I have ever been, if a black man owns a big and expensive car they will hate him for it. Of course part of that was due to my mother's attitude; she always carried a pistol on our car rides through the country, and whenever a cracker mule driver reached for his rabbit gun she beat him to the draw and made him drop it.

My father got the same job in the Branch Normal College in Pine Bluff, Arkansas, which has later become known as the Arkansas A. & M. I don't know where it derived its first name—evidently it was the black "branch" of a white "nominal" college; anyway, it was the Arkansas state school for blacks.

Joe and I were enrolled in what was known as the first year of college. I was twelve and he was thirteen and our classmates were in their twenties. There was a roll call at the beginning of each class. A student named Jerry Ramsey told me that he wouldn't be to class the next day and when the professor called his name I was to say he'd gone to Memphis chasing whores. I didn't know what "whores" were, but I knew "hoers" were always needed to hoe the cotton and chop the corn. So when Jerry's name was called the following day I stood up and said loudly, "He's gone to Memphis chasing hoers." The ignorant professor, thinking I knew what I was saying, called me to the front of the class and attempted to punish me; and I began fighting him. He got me down on the floor and began beating me and my brother came to my help. It caused quite a scandal in the school.

A couple days later, when our botany class was taking a walk through the woods, the class belle, a girl of about twenty-five, fell in beside me and asked,

"Didn't you really know what they were?" Blushing, I said, "Sure." I remember her looking at me curiously.

I remember that we lived in a house near the railroad tracks some distance from the school and we used to hop the freight trains and ride as far as the crossing just outside the school grounds if any should pass.

Joe and I almost died of smallpox the first year we lived there. We broke out in pustules all over our bodies, inside our nostrils, on the palms of our hands, the soles of our feet; our eyes became spotted. Our father was at school when it was discovered that our high fever was due to smallpox. Along with our mother we were quarantined in our house, and our father was not permitted to come beyond the front fence for the duration. Our mother saved us from permanent scars by tying our hands inside feather pillows and keeping us covered with carbolic salve. We had had chicken pox in Mississippi and had been vaccinated against smallpox, but it didn't help. When we recovered, mother burned all of the bedding, the mattress, and all of our clothing and possessions that had been in the room during the period of our illness.

Like all schools in those days, Branch Normal College covered a large area in the wide angle made by the crossing of the Southern and Yellow Dog Railroads. It was an Arkansas adage—*where the Southern crosses the Yellow Dog.* The school grounds were enclosed by various types of fences and all of the school buildings were built of wood. Only the president, whose name I have forgotten, lived within the campus. I have vague memories of baseball and football games and the older boys fighting the professors and throwing stones through the windows of the buildings in resentment, and vaguer memories of school rooms and classes. My father was required to conduct academic classes in addition to his mechanical classes; his subject was Negro history. He used a number of textbooks and reference books on Negro history which I have never seen since.

Each year, toward the end of the term, the school presented a rehearsed performance for the parents of the students, to demonstrate the various avenues of education it offered. Students with the highest grades were chosen to demonstrate their skills and special techniques in the school auditorium, so the parents could get an idea of what we were learning. Some recited parts from plays, speeches of great Negro educators, lines from Homer, etc.; others demonstrated the mixing of bread dough, how to chop the weeds from the young cotton, the proper way to hold the leg of a mule while shoeing it. Some discoursed on the future of the combustion engine, others on the stability of the horse; and no program was ever concluded without a debate on which was the more destructive, fire or water.

That year, 1922 or 1923, Joe and I were chosen to give the chemistry demonstration. We were permitted to choose whatever demonstration we wished. It was not too long after the end of the First World War, and we had discovered how to make "torpedoes" from a mixture of ground saltpeter (potassium nitrate), ground charcoal (carbon), and ground glass (silica), which we would put on the railroad tracks for the engines to run over and explode with a loud bang. The ingredients were pulverized separately with mortar and pestle and at the last stage carefully mixed and made to explode by carefully packing the powder into an empty shotgun shell and throwing it against a concrete wall.

I do not remember why we chose that particular feat; it had little to do with our chemistry course. It was probably my choice; I was always the show-off, the adventurer. However, as was customary, I did something naughty—perhaps said a "swear word" in my mother's presence, or was disobedient, or "sassed" her—and my mother punished me by forbidding me to take part. I had looked forward to the performance and she knew that no punishment would be greater than forbidding it. Years later, when I was serving time in prison and used to see the signs—*Spitting on the floor is forbidden . . . Talking at night is forbidden . . . Taking food from the dining room is forbidden . . . Whistling is forbidden*—I was reminded of this. It had been a mistake. My brother had needed me. It was a delicate and dangerous performance.

When he began to mix the ground glass into the other ingredients, working alone, the contents of the whole mortar exploded in his face.

That one moment in my life hurt me as much as all the others put together. It still does, a half century later. I loved my brother. I had never been separated from him and that moment was shocking, shattering, and terrifying. I vaguely remember the confusion. I leaped to Joe's aid and fell down a flight of stairs. Next, I remember, we were squeezed into the back seat of a Stutz touring car—my mother and father and Joe and myself—and were hurtling through the night. Lights of other cars followed. We pulled into the emergency entrance of a white people's hospital. White clad doctors and attendants appeared. I remember sitting in the back seat with Joe watching the pantomime being enacted in the car's bright lights. A white man was refusing; my father was pleading. Dejectedly my father turned away; he was crying like a baby. My mother was fumbling in her handbag for a handkerchief; I hoped it was for a pistol. Joe was strangely silent. We took him to the black people's hospital. No one there seemed to know exactly what to do. Finally his face and eyes were bandaged and he was put to bed. His face was not disfigured but he was blinded.

Five days later my mother took him to St. Louis so he could be treated in Barnes Hospital. My father and I moved from our home and took rooms close to the school entrance; I don't remember whether we had owned the house or not. Suddenly it was summer; the school term was over and the summer school for teachers had begun. My father was made acting president that summer while the president was away. He let me take turns in driving the Fordson tractor for the farm. I felt big and important driving the tractor. I became thirteen years old that summer. The young black women teachers eyed me appraisingly. I played tennis with them. I developed a great passion for one young mulatto woman, who let me take her to the movies. I fought my father when he tried to curb me. I fell in love with a young brownskin girl in town, but her family did not approve of my taking her out at night.

My father had the use of the school Ford, and each Sunday he drove us early to the Baptist church, where he taught Sunday school and served as a deacon. After Sunday school I would skip church if I could and go out and sit in the Ford in the shade of a tree and entertain my sycophants. I was a big shot to all the other little black children who went to Sunday school because I was from the college and drove the school tractor during the week, and sometimes the school Ford on Sundays. The little black girls offered their bodies. In the South, black girl children reach puberty at nine or ten years old and at thirteen they are mating like rabbits. They are not a bit ashamed of lying on their backs and opening their legs and offering their nappy pussies. They don't care who knows as long as it's kept from their parents and the "old folks." Church picnics were the best occasions for them to go off in the woods with the boys. The boys would return and show how "greasy" their penises were to prove their manhood. The girls would name each boy she had lain with. Strangely enough, it was not that summer I lost my virginity. Their shamelessness repulsed me; I felt disgusted by their casual fornication. I must have been a puritan all my life. Then as now, I consider the sexual act private. I do not want my sexual experiences to be made public. I do not care for women who discuss the sexual behavior of men in public, or vice versa. I don't want to hear about it.

My father bought a house in St. Louis on Taylor Avenue within walking distance of the one black high school, Wendell Phillips, and the Overton beauty products company known as Poro College, which made hair straighteners and skin lighteners and creams and scents for Negro women. He resigned in the fall and moved us to St. Louis. I was back in Missouri again. We had left Jefferson City when I was four years old. During the nine years which followed I had lived in Cleveland briefly, Alcorn, Mississippi, in Augusta, Georgia, and Pine Bluff, Arkansas.

I was assigned to the second year of high school in St. Louis. Joe was going out to Barnes Hospital daily for treatment—the doctors were attempting to remove the scar tissue from the corneas of his eyes—and he had enrolled in the Missouri State School for the Blind and was learning Braille and how to play the clarinet. Although the public schools in St. Louis were strictly segregated, both white and nonwhite males and females attended the school for the blind. Revealing, isn't it?

I remember St. Louis as a strange big city where I played football, baseball, soccer, basketball, any game that you can name, with suicidal intensity. The other boys on the playground either ganged up on me or refused to play with me; the gym teacher stopped me from playing all games in school. I broke my right shoulder blade, which healed out of place and still looks deformed; my left ear was half torn from my head; all of my teeth were chipped. I cut classes and roamed alone through the strange big city, spending hours in the railroad station watching the trains come and go. I was unpopular with my teachers, disliked by the students; I was lonely, shy, and insufferably belligerent.

The first winter in St. Louis was very cold; it was said to be one of the coldest winters on record. The Mississippi River, which flowed through St. Louis, dividing East St. Louis from St. Louis proper, froze over that winter, and the big drays drawn by broad-beamed Percheron horses crossed on the ice. I have never met anyone who believes this. I know it sounds very like the school of whales that Hemingway sighted off the coast of Cuba. But I distinctly remember standing on the bridge and seeing the brewery carts passing on the ice beneath me.

We had hot-air central heating in our house, but the coal was delivered to a back shed fronting on the alley, and it was my job to bring it into the basement. I didn't mind the cold. I used to take Joe bobsledding down the hill from the museum in Forest Park; once we stayed out so long my toes were frostbitten and I barely escaped losing them; thick layers of dead tissue peeled off eventually.

I do not remember my father having any particular job at that time. We were all so concerned with the welfare of Joe that the significance of his unemployment entirely escaped me. Later I learned that he had been working as a waiter in one of the big beer halls.

After two years the doctors at Barnes Hospital said they could do no more for my brother's eyes. Scar tissue completely covered the cornea in one eye, but in the other he still retained a little vision; he could tell light from dark and he could distinguish large objects—such as people—in motion at short distances, and he could read the large numerals on a wristwatch if he held it about two inches from his eye. They said there was a danger of completely destroying his vision and even his eyes if they attempted to remove more scar tissue.

For a time my parents entertained a wild idea of fitting Joe's "good eye" with some sort of telescopic lens, but that proved impractical. My father was suffering from the frustrations of unemployment and Jim Crow, and as there was no longer any benefit to be had for Joe in St. Louis, he took us to Cleveland, Ohio, where he had two married sisters and a brother.

In 1913, when we left Jefferson City, Missouri, he had parked us for a half year with his sisters while he secured the post in Alcorn, and I had vaguely pleasant memories of Joe and me in kindergarten. And once, before I was born, he had worked for a firm in Cleveland that built Pullman cars, and on the whole his reminiscences inspired hope. But when we returned he soon discovered there was little difference from living in St. Louis.

Cleveland was the first city in which I lived that was in the "North." I do not remember any legal segregation in housing or education, but most blacks lived in ghettos and sent their children to the public schools in the ghettos. Most of the unskilled jobs in the factories and steel mills were taken by imported foreign labor from Poland, Hungary, and other European countries.

First we lived with Aunt Fanny and Uncle Wade Wiggins. Their son, Gerald, was about a year younger than me, but he was a "mamma's boy" and I couldn't tolerate him. Uncle Roddy was a federal meat inspector and lived out in a white neighborhood; his job had great status among blacks.

My mother didn't get along with my father's people. While my father was a professor in various black state colleges in the South, he had helped his sisters and brothers-in-law to go North and get established, and my mother felt they owed him a debt of gratitude. Instead they patronized him because he was unemployed. Then there was the question of color. Even during slavery, the light-complexioned house slaves, who were sired by either their masters or their overseers, considered themselves superior to the black slaves who worked the fields, partly because of their superior "white" blood and partly because they considered themselves more beautiful, more intelligent, and of a higher class. This color class within the black race prevailed long after the slaves were freed, and there are still remnants of it left among black people. The "light-bright-and-damn-near-white" blacks were offered the best jobs by whites; they maintained an exclusive social clique, their own churches, their own manners and morals. A marriage between a black man and a light-complexioned woman had the status of an interracial marriage with legal consent.

My father's people suspected my mother of looking down on them because they were black. Maybe she did. They hated her. She hated them. My father was in the middle. Poor Dad.

The Wigginses lived in a mixed neighborhood off Hough Avenue, near the Cleveland Indians' baseball park. I remember my cousin Gerald hustling tips parking cars in his front yard during the Indians' home games.

I entered East High School, which was located a great distance from the Wiggins house, but it must have been the high school for the district. Strangely, although other black families lived in the neighborhood, there were only three other black students at East High while I was there; perhaps the other black families didn't have any children eligible for high school. One of the black students, Billy Williams, was not only the star quarterback for East High but the star football player for all Cleveland.

My mother took Joe away from the Wiggins house and found living quarters with a stranger in a distant part of the city. I don't think my father ever forgave her for that; that was the beginning of the ill feeling which led to their divorce.

My father began doing carpentry and small construction jobs. Then he and mother bought a house jointly way out in the white neighborhood of Glenville, not far from Uncle Roddy's and right across the street from Glenville High School. It's a black ghetto now, but at that time it was a middle-class Jewish neighborhood.

We moved into our house in the fall. I was in my last term in high school and wasn't required to change schools. I was sixteen years old and still a virgin. I remember standing behind the curtains of the parlor windows and masturbating at the sight of the big-tittied Jewish girls when they came out of school.

Joe was attending a school for the blind, preparatory to entering a public high school the following term. Readers for him, paid by the hour, were employed by the state.

I made only a grade of 56 in my final examination in Latin, but through a clerical error 86 was given as my grade; I was passed and graduated in January 1926, and had received my high school diploma before the mistake was discovered. My parents received an urgent letter from my Latin teacher requesting that I return the following term and review the course, but I refused and nothing was done about it.

Any graduate of a public high school in Ohio was eligible to attend Ohio State University. I planned to matriculate in September and study medicine. To earn money for my matriculation fees and other expenses over and above what my parents could afford, I took a job in the Wade Park Manor—a chichi hotel overlooking Wade Park—as a busboy. The dining-room staff was black. Mr. Smith, the headwaiter, was a small, quick, elegant brownskinned man who attended the same church as my father and was perhaps of the same age. He was extremely well liked by all the white guests; perhaps he was an Uncle Tom. I didn't think about such things in those days. Perhaps my father was one too.

My job was to go up to the rooms and suites and collect the wheel trays when the clients had finished breakfast or lunch. I rolled them into the service elevator, two or three at a time, and brought them back to the kitchen, which seemed as large as the waiting room in the Cleveland railway station.

Two young women sat in a glass booth facing the elevators and checked the trays of the room service waiters before they went upstairs. The young women were good-looking and white. Most of the young black waiters flirted with them; they resumed the flirtation to a select few. One good-looking brownskin boy, a busboy like myself, was their favorite. I don't know whether any of the waiters had ever scored with either of them, but if not, it wasn't because they didn't try.

From the first day the girls began flirting with me. Other waiters noticed. Their previous favorite was furious.

It was during that week that I lost my virginity. They got me so excited that I was no longer satisfied with masturbation; I went to the black ghetto and paid money to an old fat ugly whore sitting on a stool outside her hovel on Scovil.

Scovil Avenue ran from Fifty-fifth Street to Fourteenth Street on the edge of the black ghetto and was the most degraded slum street I had ever seen. The police once estimated that there were fifteen hundred black prostitutes cruising the forty blocks of Scovil Avenue at one time. The black whores on Scovil for the most part were past their thirties, vulgar, scarred, dimwitted, in many instances without teeth, diseased, and poverty-stricken. Most of the black men in the neighborhood lived on the earnings of the whores and robbed the "hunkies." They gambled for small change, fought, drank poisonous "white mule," cut each other up, and died in the gutters. It was nothing unusual to see a black man lying in the gutter, drunk and bleeding and dying. "Don't touch him, man, don't touch him! They might think you did it," everyone warned. "They" generally meant the police, but it could mean his whore, his relatives, his friends, if he had any.

I must explain how Scovil happened; otherwise it's unbelievable. With the beginning of the steel mills in the Cuyahoga River Valley, which was to become one of the most despicable industrial ghettos in the world, foreign labor was imported from the underdeveloped countries of Eastern Europe—Poland, Rumania, Hungary, Czechoslovakia, and others. Years later when I wrote the history of Cleveland for the Cleveland Guide compiled by the Ohio Writers' Project (WPA), I came across a news item from a daily newspaper in the 1860s or 1870s describing how the owner of the "Newstead" Steel works drove to the freight station in his "elegant" buggy to pick up a freight-car load of immigrants to work in his mills, which he herded through the city like cattle. These foreign steel-mill workers, who could not speak a word of English, were quartered in shacks bordering on the black ghetto. They had left their women behind. A large section of Cleveland was inhabitated by these squat, thick, foreign men unattended by women.

But those immigrants, although ignorant and quite often debased, who did not speak a word of English, earned money and eventually sent for their families and some of their children and grandchildren became ranking politicians and millionaires, while the blacks—many of whom were descended from runaway slaves dropped off in Cleveland by the Underground Railroad and had been educated and accepted members of the community for several generations—were totally unemployed by industry. From all the research I did on Cleveland history, I never discovered any reason for this except that they were black, and foreign white labor objected to working with black men whose ancestors had been slaves.

These foreign laborers invaded the black ghetto in search of women and food in such great numbers that a majority of the black women either became whores or lived with the foreign men as mistresses-housekeepers-cooks. The laborers became known as "hunkies"—whether it was a diminutive of "Hungarian" I never discovered. Anyway, the majority of the foreign laborers in the steel mills were Polish.

The black men did not object to their women being whores; black slave women had always been whores of a kind, or at least always vessels for the white man's lust. When the hunkies bought the black women for sexual purposes they were called "Johns." The black men simply preyed on the hunkies for their livelihood, robbed the hunkies, beat them, sometimes killed them, and lived on the money their women made as whores.

This became the absolute and irrevocable sociological pattern for Scovil Avenue, called the Bucket of Blood.

And that was where I went to lose my virginity when I became so excited by the playful flirtations of the white girls at the Wade Park Manor.

I had been with the hotel a couple of weeks and had just gotten sufficiently adapted to the job so that I wasn't always tense and nervous and afraid I'd drop a tray or do something wrong, when one morning I stopped in front of the closed elevator doors to kid with the "checkers," as the girls were called, trying to screw up my courage to ask one for a date. Realizing what I wished to do, they laughingly steered the conversation to topical chitchat, and began recounting the happenings when the famous Hollywood dog star Rin Tin Tin had had a suite there. It was with a sense of let-down that I turned away and pulled open the elevator doors and, looking at them accusingly, stepped inside.

I fell past the floor below and the high-ceilinged basement, between thirty and forty feet. I landed upon the heavy steel plate of the springboard that is at the bottom of every elevator shaft. I didn't lose consciousness. I remember the sensation of falling through space and landing on a solid platform with the feeling of my body spattering open like a ripe watermelon.

I remember calling for help in a tiny voice. My mouth felt as though it were filled with gravel. Later I discovered that it was only my teeth.

My chin had hit something that cut the flesh to the bone, broke my lower jaw, and shattered all my teeth. My left arm hit something and both bones broke just above the wrist so that they came out through the skin, dead white with drops of blood in the bone fractures. My spine hit something and the last three vertebrae were fractured.

The waiters came to pull me out, peering over the lip of the shaft with the flattened planes and whitened eyes of black faces in shock, and I remember crying out when they seized my broken arm. Then several jumped down into the shaft and lifted me out as tenderly as though I were a newborn baby. I remember seeing Mr. Smith's shocked face and tears flowing down the faces of the two white girls; then the ambulance came and I was rushed to the nearest hospital—a big, new, modern hospital—on 105th Street, facing the park.

I remember the expressions of regret on the aquiline faces of the two staff doctors who walked slowly toward the ambulance, shaking their heads while the red-faced driver expostulated dramatically. It occurred to me that a scene was being re-enacted, that I had seen it all before in the white hospital in Pine Bluff, Arkansas, when my brother was rushed there and the white staff doctors had turned him away. So in Cleveland three years later, in 1926, I too was turned away, because there was no space, no empty bed, but I was given a massive injection of morphine.

Then I was taken to Huron Road Hospital on Euclid Avenue, near Eightieth Street, and given a bed in a large crowded ward, and the Ohio State Industrial Commission doctors were sent for.

I was bleeding internally but my broken bones took precedent and I was wrapped in a body cast; my left arm was put in a cast and my broken teeth were anesthetized and my jaw wired. I still remember the names of the three Industrial Commission doctors: Steele, Castle, and Eisenbray. Dr. Eisenbray was the bone specialist, Dr. Steele the diagnostician, and Dr. Castle the internist, if I remember correctly.

My mother arrived shortly after I was put into my cast. I was too filled with morphine at the time to notice the ravages of her hurt. And I was asleep when my father came.

That night I discovered that I could not urinate. My bladder swelled dangerously and Dr. Castle was summoned. He operated on me at 4:00 A.M., when the rest of the hospital was asleep; he opened my urethral canal where it had been ruptured and inserted a rubber tube to my bladder which emptied into a bottle beside my bed. The casts for my broken bones were not touched.

Joe came with my mother several days later. He knew all about accidents; he was cheerful. Mr. Smith and waiters from the hotel visited, and various executives whom I had never seen before.

The Ohio State Industrial Commission paid all of my hospital and medical expenses and put me on a pension of seventy-five dollars a month for total disability until such time as the doctors might designate my disability as partial. The hotel promised to continue my busboy's salary of fifty dollars a month.

It was determined by investigators for the Industrial Commission that the Wade Park Manor was entirely responsible for my accident because the elevator doors were defective; state law required that elevator doors should lock automatically and remain locked until the elevator became level with the floor; and on no account should it be possible to open the doors when the elevator was on another floor. Later I discovered that had I rejected the pension given me by the Industrial Commission I could have sued the hotel for a considerable sum of money. But when the Industrial Commission offered the pension and the hotel promised to continue paying my salary, my father persuaded me to sign the waivers to all rights for additional claims. My mother felt that I should have rejected the pension, and that became another topic of disagreement between my parents.

My father was born and raised in the tradition of the Southern Uncle Tom; that tradition derived from an inherited slave mentality which accepts the premise that white people know best, that blacks should accept what whites offer and be thankful, that blacks should count their blessings.

My mother, who looked white and felt that she should have been white, was the complete opposite. My mother was a fighter. She was a tiny woman who hated all manner of condescension from white people and hated all black people who accepted it. That much I inherited from her: I hate all manner of condescension from white people of whatever nationality—Americans, Frenchmen, Germans, Spaniards, Italians, Danes, Swedes, English, Dutch, whoever—all white people who are condescending toward me because I'm black.

But I respected my father and I did not consider him an Uncle Tom. I loved my mother with a strange fierce love which survived everything; but my father I respected. And while I loved my mother I obeyed my father. On his advice I signed away my rights.

I feel certain that my doctors did not expect me to ever walk again. But I fooled them all by getting out of the bed one morning without permission and walking as far as the window. Then I was measured for a back brace of leather with stainless steel supports, and the rubber tube was removed painfully from my urethral canal; it had become thickly encrusted with yellow crystals from leaking urine.

At the Huron Road Hospital, patients were not segregated by race, but the help was mostly white and resented attending black patients. The building was old and ugly, but the grounds, when I saw them, were lovely and green.

The patient beside me was a tall gaunt man who vaguely resembled my uncle Wade Wiggins. He was recovering from pneumonia and his wife, a pleasant woman, visited him daily. I had loaned him some of the blood-and-thunder books I had collected from visitors.

One morning his wife brought his clothes and informed him he could leave that afternoon. After lunch he finished reading a borrowed book before dressing to leave. Suddenly he died from a heart attack. One instant he was alive and the next he was dead. That shocked me.

The patient on the other side, also a black man, had blood poisoning, and his left arm was terribly bloated. It was threaded with strips of cloth to drain the poison, and was kept in a glass vat containing some sort of medication. The day following the death of the pneumonia patient a blood clot broke loose in a vein and began a slow journey to his heart. The doctors couldn't stop it. Perhaps nowadays they could have performed a transplant. But in those days he knew he was going to die. He began reciting the Lord's Prayer about nine o'clock that night in a husky anguished voice and the next morning before dawn he died. It wasn't his death that affected me so much that time; it was the sound of his voice reciting the Lord's Prayer through the night.

I was happy to leave that hospital. I was happy to return to our new house—new to us—in the white neighborhood. Joe had enrolled in East High School, which I had just left. We didn't live in the district but I suppose he was permitted to attend the public school of his choice because of his blindness. I didn't see much of him. I spent most of my time massaging my left wrist to restore its articulation and learning how to walk again with my harness. My brace consisted of two long bars of stainless steel, which flanked my spine and were held in place by straps that passed beneath my crotch and armpits and around my neck and shoulders and were buckled to a leather plate down my chest and stomach. I felt like a trussed fowl when I put on my brace. At the same time I began having my teeth filled, crowned, and repaired entirely by the Industrial Commission dentist.

The doctors employed by the Industrial Commission had private practices also; it was similar to socialized medicine. They accepted Industrial Commission patients for a prescribed fee paid by the state. The dentist to whom I had been assigned had formerly been a professor at the state dental college; he was conscientious and highly skilled. He began using gold in my fillings and crowns, but the cost was more than the state would pay, and he was ordered to use amalgam, which he refused to do, so I was transferred to another dentist. But the work he did lasted many years.

I was saving my money to enter Ohio State University that fall, father was working at odd jobs, and Joe was attending East High, when suddenly Mother became angered by my signing away my right to sue the hotel; she felt they had taken advantage of my youth and inexperience and race. She went to the hotel and created a considerable row; the hotel stopped paying me my fifty dollars a month salary. She and my father had a furious quarrel over this. She called him spineless and a bootlicker, which doubtless he was, but it created an intolerable atmosphere in our house. I was happy when September came and I could go off to college.

I entered Ohio State University in Columbus in September 1926. A high school diploma from any high school in the state was all that was required to matriculate. We were given quite extensive examinations to determine our intelligence quotients. I was later told that I had the fourth highest I.Q. of that year's entrants, and I must confess I felt proud.

Black students could not live in the school dormitories, and all the fraternity houses within the environs of the campus were strictly Jim-Crowed. The nearest a black student came to getting inside one of them was as a waiter or dishwasher. But many of the black householders in the environs took black students as roomers, and some also furnished board. I boarded in a rooming house several blocks away which also boarded a few coeds.

There were two fraternities and two sororities for the six hundred or so black students, but they met in the city's black neighborhood bordering on Long Avenue, which was several miles from the campus.

I bought a coonskin coat for three hundred dollars, a knickerbocker suit, a long-stemmed pipe, and a Model T Ford roadster, and I became a collegian. Because of my injury I was exempted from ROTC, which was compulsory for two years, and I did not have to buy the ROTC uniform, which other freshmen wore. Freshmen were also required to wear felt beanies with the school colors, but the white upperclassmen who enforced this rule could not tell that I was a freshman because I never wore a uniform, so I didn't have to wear a beanie either; many students thought I was an upperclassman.

I would have been a great success with the pretty black coeds if I had had more experience. Also, having to wear a backbrace humiliated me. It wasn't long before I discovered the whores in the ghetto.

In Columbus the whores were quite different from those I had known in Cleveland. Some of the whores in Columbus were young and beautiful, or so I thought. One in particular, a girl named Rose with whom I was trying to win a home, as the saying went, used to say, "You got an awful lot of steam for a li'l boy." And it was true.

One of the freshmen in my class was Stanton DePriest, son of Oscar DePriest, the black congressman from Chicago. He was a tall, light-complexioned, languid boy who tried for the basketball team, but didn't make it, although he could play well enough. I felt important to be considered Stanton's friend, and I used to lend him my car. Naturally he took advantage of me and sometimes used to keep my car for weekends, when I needed it myself, and drive down to the black A. M. E. college, Wilberforce, to see the girls.

Of the two black fraternities, Alpha Phi Alpha and Omega Phi Psi, the Alphas were more popular in the North, the Omegas in the South. I became pledged to the Alphas and was initiated by being blindfolded and thrown into the lake in the park at the end of Long Street in the upperclass black neighborhood; then, with the others, I became a Sphinx; the following year I would become a lifetime fraternity brother.

The sororities were the Kappas and the Deltas; they pledged all the stylish, light-complexioned girls, and their older members were noted for their enviable marriages and distinguished works.

However, the fraternity and sorority circle was the arbiter of all the social functions of the black students. There were lots of house parties, and most of the black girls were experienced and willing, and with my roadster and coonskin coat I could have scored on all occasions. But I had developed an inferiority complex and felt shy in their company. I preferred older, amoral women.

I went to see all the black musicals on Warren Street, which was the next street over from Long and ran through the worst of the black slums. So many soul brothers killed each other for one reason or another on Warren Street that it was known as The Burma Road. There were two movie theaters in the ghetto, the most pretentious on Long Street. I will always remember a tall brown-skinned man with slicked-down hair who used to sing *Moonlight on the Ganges* during the intervals, and the students who patronized that theater would try to imitate him. All the movie theaters in downtown Columbus and the white neighborhoods either segregated blacks in the upper balconies or did not receive them at all. And no white restaurants served blacks anywhere in the city, not even those near Ohio State University. I always tightened up inside whenever I passed one of them.

The white students didn't know exactly what to make of me. I dressed and behaved like the "Yes We Are Collegiate" students; I wore my coonskin coat and smoked my pipe and drove my Model T roadster, and yet I was black, a member of the inferior race. I rarely spoke to white people, and never unless I was addressed first by them, and yet I would find them always looking at me. I ignored them. I didn't hate white people then; I simply didn't need them, didn't want to know them, and always felt that they couldn't reject me any more than I could reject them.

I took pretty black coeds for drives in my car, driving so fast the manifold became white-hot; and went to see the slim black girls in the black musicals—Josephine Baker and Ethel Waters in *Running Wild* and others, now deceased who became rich and famous. I always sat in the front row. Sometimes I went backstage after the show to look into their muddy, sexy brown eyes up close and smell their musky femininity. I saw Greta Garbo and John Gilbert in *Flesh and the Devil*, and helped to pull down the stadium gates before the Ohio State–Michigan University football game in 1926. There had been famous black players on Ohio State's football team in the past, but there were none that year. Black students could star in any of the school athletic activities, but they could not live in the school dormitories on the campus, nor eat in any of the restaurants near the campus, nor attend the movie theaters, nor visit or become a member of the white fraternity houses. Yet this was Columbus, Ohio, where all forms of racial discrimination were prohibited by state laws.

I did not do very well in my studies. I was depressed by the white environment. Ohio State had quarter terms, and the first ended shortly before Christmas. I had already been in a fistfight with my laboratory instructor and no longer went to the lab; I turned in a blank form for my German examination; I had failing grades in all my other courses; my attendance was poor, my attitude was wrong, my interest was lacking. Freshmen who failed the first quarter were generally dropped from the university. As I prepared to return to Cleveland for the Christmas holidays, I fully expected to be dropped. But for reasons which I have never known, I passed. And now I had to go back. But by then I was tired of Ohio State University and its policy of discrimination and segregation, fed up with the condescension, which I could never bear, and disgusted with myself for my whoremongering and my inability to play games, my instinctive withdrawal from intimacy, and my schizophrenic impulses to be inconspicuous and conspicuous at the same time. It was much later in life that I came to understand I simply hadn't accepted my status as a "nigger."

Chester Himes

(1909–1984)

www

The son of a teacher, Chester Himes **Web** spent his youth in Missouri, Mississippi, and Arkansas. Himes attended Ohio State University, was expelled, and was later convicted of armed robbery. In prison, Himes began writing mystery stories in the style of Dashiell Hammett. His first novel, If He Hollers, Let Him Go (1945), began a series of works that critiqued racism and labor relations in America.

TOPICS FOR CRITICAL THINKING

1. In what various ways does the return to the past function in the excerpt?
2. To what ends does the narrative trace the seamier side of life in twentieth-century America?
3. What is the narrator's attitude toward his inability to succeed?

TOPICS FOR CRITICAL WRITING

1. In what ways does heritage translate into opportunity in the narrator's experience?
2. Write a portrait of the narrator based on the material he presents in the excerpt.

W. S. PENN

This Close, Coyote

(1995)

This Close, Coyote
I

Some people say "KI-yote," it's true, but to us his name has always been "Ki-YO-tee." As our song says, "Coyote, coyote, nothing but coyote."

This also is true, and it is said this way:

I was thirteen when the barber laid bare my high forehead, waxing a roll of hair to roll like a Dreamer's curl across my widow's peak. Only the curl felt good. The rest felt naked, bare, exposed to rain, and the elemental cruelty of chewed gum stuck in my hair by boys who instinctively picked on anyone who was different. And I was different. But at thirteen, I had no idea how. I didn't look that much different. I was not as different as the black kids who looked and dressed the part. My friends were Mexicans or thugs, neither of which ever achieved sufficient numbers at school to be securely a minority from which I might be excluded. Once I had battled the aphasic thugs to the ground, sat on their chests, and made them try in their wavering white voices to chant one of my songs, we were as good of friends as I ever had—which means we said "Hi" to each other, hung out behind the gym at lunch where we smoked and told old jokes, and left each other alone. And alone I liked to be: I came from a culture that was neither transported nor downtrodden; it had been truly removed and all but destroyed but now was mostly just plain ignored outside of Saturday afternoon movies, and what I saw in the movies made me ashamed.

Father was ashamed, too, and a measure of his solitude was that I didn't know he was. Whenever the subject came up—and it did come up, what with Grandfather living nearby and with Father's brother enshrining pictures of Young Joseph, the Nez Perce Chief, all over his bungalow—Father looked away, into the distance, across the playground or football field. I never felt as though I could ask, "Dad, why do I feel so alone?" or after a week of school with my friends, "Dad, why would I rather be alone?" It was a split: on the one hand, feeling an aloneness akin to loneliness I'd try to join, dancing the Mexican Hat Dance eagerly in cultural studies or playing games like basketball with an uncanny, almost innate ability to target the hoop with the ball. And yet after the dance was over and all of us stood around grinning, some sheepishly, having enjoyed ourselves together, or after the hoop game ended and the boys pounded me on the back with congratulation, I felt, well, uncomfortable. I smiled. They wanted me to be one of them. And though just minutes ago I had wanted to be one of them, I found little joy in being one with them, especially because I knew—somewhere way behind my eyes and underneath the words I gave them—that I could not be like them.

This wasn't the way blacks describe the feeling of being the only black in a room of whites. It came out of race, perhaps, but it was not racial. It was why, when finches flew across the street, I called out greetings to them, "Good morning, Juncos! How are you being?" It was why of all animals, my favorite was the frog, and why to this day I wear a scarab-frog necklace around my neck. It was why Father looked away from the mention of Indian things, perhaps. It was not a feeling that came from being different on the outside, the way blacks become different on the inside because of the way people treat the outside. There was that, I suppose, but it was later, secondary to my inside feeling that not only was I different but I was uncomfortable not being different. I could succeed, be a part of the Great Society around me, just like black kids were beginning to do; but where the black kids, the Chicano kids, the transformed, rehabilitated thugs and thuggettes seemed happy to be a successful part, it depressed the hell out of me. Somewhere inside of myself I knew that the measure of success was not false—not necessarily—but that it was not mine.

Thus it is that Indians fail. It is not that they cannot do it. It is because they reach a point beyond which they cannot summon the heart to travel. I've seen Indian college students read and understand Heidegger, Binswanger, Sartre, and Ortega y Gasset as easily as they understand the movements of junco or salmon and yet fail to attend the course's final examination—and for that failure, they do not get A's for recognizing the true relation of philosophy to examinations. Choosing to return to their homes before the school term was officially over, leaving college to take care of itself, they fail the course. I've seen the same students return to college the following year, only to bother not to turn in the final English essay because their brother called them home. I've heard professors say that if they can't cut it, then they should receive failing marks. I've heard other professors say they just need counseling, help integrating into the college environment, role models of Indian professors and then they will be successful. And I've heard a full range of sayings in between, even from my father's, my sister's, and yes, my own, mouth—and they are all wrong. If you are a Pit River, a Modoc, an Osage, Flathead, or a Nez Perce—especially a Nez Perce, who knows with his heart—and you are enrolled in a class—English, philosophy, wildlife management—and your heart calls you home, you are right to go.

I've seen my father, denying his Indianness with every fiber and vein, come This Close to success. In the world of money and work, he spent seventeen years getting up early and driving downtown on the Santa Ana Freeway, an Indian man riding a Spanish general to a Saxon building where he plugged his knees into a desk like all the other desks, smiling when one of his friends stuck gum in his hair, looking forward to the weekend when he could mow lawn or mend fence and on Sunday take us to see his father and mother. My mother, who liked the week, felt indifferent to Saturdays, and hated Sundays, was glad when Grandfather and Grandmother decided to pack up their objects and move four hundred miles to live next door to my uncle. I sometimes wonder whether she'd have so gladly bought new slip covers and curtains if she'd realized that, within a year, Father would have our objects packed and move us all northward to be close to his parents. We would have lived next door, probably, except Mother put her foot down, and we skidded to a halt some seventy miles short, close enough to resume Sunday visits without having to live, as Mother so eloquently put it, in a hellhole like Napa.

Mother was embittered by the notion that in less than three years, with just a little more gum in his hair, Father would have had full retirement from the company he had labored for all those years. She thought she could see that his heart had called Father home, and she was bitter towards Grandmother. Grandmother, not Grandfather, was the one who said day-to-day things, who gave things quick and immediate shape in unstoried words, so perhaps Mother had reason. But the blame was too great, swelling like the bitterness in Mother's heart, until she could accuse Grandmother of wanting Father to fail. "That was why she had them move north in the first place," Mother would say. "She was evil," she'd say later, after Grandmother was cut like a carnation from the earth. "Less than three years. Can you imagine?" she was still likely to ask, even after she and Father had been divorced by bitterness. "A witch."

Perhaps Mother was right. Perhaps Father's heart had called him home. But as Nu-mi-pu, as a nontreaty Nez Perce, it was in his blood to carry Home with him wherever he went—or, more precisely, wherever he was forced to go. There was something else at work, some power Mother did not see, could not see—indeed, which I never saw until it had worked in me, and even then I didn't see it, I only heard it, felt it in my heart while I made up excuses to satisfy Them. It was the power to be true. It meant that for seventeen years, Father had smiled when they put gum in his hair. He had come to believe in the value of gum, in what he contributed to society by helping an oil company extract and refine and add lead to fossil fuels or develop new chemicals which would rid the world of pests, and he could rattle off a list of things that would not have been but for this contribution. When he quit, he did not quit because he'd changed his mind. These things matter to him forty years later just as much as they mattered to him then, and I've seen him envelop his wife's head in a spraycloud of pesticides to free her from the nagging buzz of a housefly; proof that he does not believe in "all this nonsense about carcinogens." The only change in him is that he has great difficulty smiling, and he has, over the years, quit just about every group he ever joined. So what made him give up full retirement, give up all the smiling he had done?

It was not changing his mind. Nor was it the heart calling him home, as powerful as that might have been. I know this. I know that after three years of graduate school at the University of California at Davis, after smiling my way right up to doctoral examinations, after believing completely and wholly in the importance of the seventeenth and twentieth centuries, after reading white, black, Hispanic, and Indian writers who were alive all around me until I could chew gum with the angriest gay black man in the Confucius Bar at New York's MLA, after being able to quote, proudly, whatever the seriousness of the occasion, "I have my J&B. The J&B company keeps manufacturing it, case after case, year in and year out, and there is, I am told, no immediate danger of a dearth," making Donald Barthelme's *Sadness* into a kind of deflective shield, after filling out every possible triplicated form in the world, one summery day I packed up my old Volkswagen with my objects and drove eight hundred miles north to Port Townsend Washington. I never thought of it as quitting or dropping out. Indeed, years later, I discovered you needed to ask their approval to leave and that, the way General Howard had pursued the Nez Perce and destroyed their provisions, they made it impossible for me to return peacefully and take up where I had left off; they were too angry over the fact that I had just left in the first place, as though my sudden leaving were a judgment of their value and proof of my character. I certainly did not think of it as failing. I thought of it as a success. "There was no one fit to examine me," is what I said to people who asked why. But that was only an excuse they could understand, both in its meaning and its sheer Coyote arrogance. What I meant was, I came This Close to success by another measure and realized—as it appeared in a dream—my own measure was all that mattered to me. And it mattered in a way that meant something other than criticism of their measure. Let them have their measures. I knew deep down inside that, given the chance, they'd shoot Snowbird from the sky or blow up summery frogs in a celebration of Independence. At least a part of their measure meant death. How much of the dream were you willing to give up to death in order to succeed. I'd have liked to succeed—more, perhaps, than my father throughout those seventeen-plus years—enough to cut my hair crew cut, keeping only the waxed Dreamer's curl in front. But even at thirteen, I could not let the curl go completely, although I could keep the dream fairly hidden or disguised.

II

It was my girlfriend who said repeatedly, "You'll finish your degree" with the same authority someone else might say, "You'll no longer walk the earth one day." She was a white girl, a kind and generous and loving normal person to whom I'd whispered, giving shape in words to what was in my heart, "I don't know I can do it." It never entered her head that I wasn't capable of doing it, and it clearly never dawned on her that the inability was not intellectual but emotional, almost physical. My saying that I didn't know I could do it was an inadequate and unfair way to try to tell her that it was not my head but my heart that might keep me from doing it, that my heart which knew the world held secret a dream—unsaid, undefined, unending—in which I could measure myself by their stick only so far. After three years my heart was telling me that I had just about reached the end. If I got my degree before that end was reached, it would be fine; but the coup-stick end of these ways and days was no longer a mirage out there, it had shape and dimension in here. I could see it in the same way Chief Joseph saw it, fearing it, knowing it was coming, and yet, recognizing that the path which has been traveled until you can see its end cannot suddenly be altered and made into a different path, secretly rejoicing in its coming if that was what was to be. Joseph did everything he could while not signing away the land by yet another treaty to make peace for his band. Even camped at the top of White Bird Canyon, he had a white flag flown on a pole outside his lodge, a sign to the volunteers edging up the canyon that he desired peace. But in his heart, tired of the ways his people had been measured and the measures changed, he knew that when the volunteers fired on the scouts observing their movements, he would, if not rejoice, feel relief. He would be true to the path's end which would no longer be unclear and wavering like the shadow of Snowbird or the afterimage of Coyote who is gone but as sharp as war.

Graduate school was not life or death, and to use Joseph to explain me, thereby comparing myself to him, was—as I learned in school to say—"literally absurd." To explain this to my girlfriend in these terms would have drawn from her the same confusion it later drew from editors: "Wha . . . huh?" So when she told me that I would finish, and rolled over, cupping my genitals with her buttocks and resting her cheek on my biceps, I could only give her a whisper. "I hope you're right."

With all my heart, I hoped she was right, as much if not more than Father hoped Mother was right if she ever said to him, "Don't worry, you'll make retirement." It's an If but not so big an If. Probably, given the vituperation Mother expressed about Father's having given up full retirement because of that evil woman my grandmother, Mother said it as many times as my girlfriend said it. Nothing else would account for the vehemence of her vituperation but long expectation suddenly disappointed. After the first several times telling Father not to worry and receiving no reply, or none more expressive than "I hope you're right," Mother must have thought the matter settled. Or, when Father said "I hope you're right," perhaps Mother replied, "Is that a threat? What do you mean by that, you *hope* I'm right?"

I opt to re-remember the former, even though Mother was a white woman whose sense of family was perverted by suspicion and greed and whose sense of marriage was skewed by a family dedicated to divorce. I forget the latter because it is possible Father thinks he has said what he has to say. Riding that Mexican general's freeway downtown to the Saxon building, the Indian man dreams, doubling back over the same territory, making sense of it, describing it, saying what has to be said until he expects the person to whom he has said it all to understand what is true. Chief Joseph riding to a meeting with General Howard holds the meeting with the general before he even arrives, and the understanding is so good and perfect that the meeting seems almost unnecessary—and Joseph takes his time and arrives three days late. What do three days matter when the understanding has already been achieved? It is such a perfect understanding that Joseph believes that General Howard has had the same dream, has spoken and heard the same words, and their meeting is only a formality, a show for the people who do not understand—

the journalists and reporters, the squatters, prospectors, thieves, the army wives who write letters to St. Louis about savages hanging about laughing at Christmas carols during this wretched season at Fort Lapwai.

When the eighteenth annual Christmas Party rolled around, Father mentioned to Mother that he was thinking about not going. "You have to go," Mother replied.

"But. . . ," Father said.

"No buts about it," Mother said. "If you don't, they'll think you don't like and respect them."

That was sufficient to end the conversation: not wanting people to think he didn't like them when he did was a powerful argument for going. A Nez Perce can respect his worst enemy, as long as that enemy is true and not conniving or hypocritical, ever as much as Joseph respected Howard, whose heart he knew, but not Sheridan, whose heart was convenient. Father had spent the energy of seventeen years saying to himself that his enemies at work were not convenient but true. He respected them. He liked many.

This time Mother rides the Santa Ana Freeway with Father. It is a happy drive because all the words Father has needed to say to Mother to explain what was going on inside of him have already been said. There is no tension. To complete the vision, only Mother's presence where the words have been said and resaid was necessary, and there she is, beside him in the finned Plymouth, all dressed up in muted colors and simple jewelry with, finally, someplace to go. Father is so content that he takes no notice of the discordant notes in Mother's orchestrated anger when he refuses to pay a valet to park the car and they have to walk a long block from the covered garage beyond the building. Her lips are pursed. He sees that. But he smiles. "What warrior pays a boy to park his horse?" he thinks, assuming Mother's lips will unpurse at the thought and her mouth grin with his. He leads her in to the Christmas party.

The party is held in the central reception room, a large open area off which spin the corridors of offices. The hall from the elevator is like a Huron gauntlet, men and women raising their champagne glasses threateningly and calling out Father's name instead of inflicting blows with clubs or feet. The light is bright like the winter sun, reflecting off the cold crust of the walls. By the time Father and Mother pass the third group of glass raisers, Father flinches; at the fifth group, his head ducks involuntarily; Mother casts him a worried angry look. At the colon of the hall, where the corridor opens onto the bright and decorated main room, Mother squeezes in smiling as Father stops. To her, it is a room of gaiety and noise, of smells and sounds of people having fun together. To him, it is a web and tangle of different stories—of so many different stories that each one seems a lie. Each is true in its way, but said in a crowd like this, words gets lost, tangled into other stories, rise quiet to the heat of ceiling lights and fall like lies to the floor, unheard.

Afraid of trampling on their stories, Father physically cannot enter that room. His best friends are there. He sees one talking to the president, and he makes a start for the corner they're standing in. Stops. A woman he cares little for nods and smiles at him tentatively; she is willing to let bygones be gone, he can tell, and he takes a step or two in her direction and then falters and returns to the edge of the corridor. He bites his lip. Then he grins and stands there, grinning until he can no longer hold the grin, and he lets his face relax into an open inexpressive look, a look that says neither "Look at all this fun" nor "I need to go potty." Just a look that says, "Wha . . . huh."

When on the drive home Mother says, bitterly, "Well that was fun," and Father says, "I'm glad," he means it every bit as much as when he says, just before pulling into our driveway to bed down the Plymouth for the night, "I hope you're right." In between "That was fun" and "You'll make retirement" there was a whole conversation in which Father explained why he might not finish out the year in the Saxon building, how finishing twenty years no longer seemed to matter. Poor Mother never heard these explanations.

Their perfection would have been spoiled, anyway, the way it was when, Berkeley a dissonant chord of lights behind us as my girlfriend and I drove into the rich darkness of the hills, I tried explaining how I'd rather be shot through the teeth with a Henry rifle than sell Death Insurance for a living.

"It's life insurance," she replied, her head turned away, her voice bouncing off the passenger window of her car while I drove.

"It insures I'll live?"

"No."

"It insures I'll live longer?"

"No."

"It insures someone will get a lot of money if I die."

"Yes."

"Best not to tell them about it, hey?"

"I hate you sometimes."

"I pay someone money so when I die they give a lot of it to someone else. So what it insures is my death, not my life. If it was life insurance it'd pay me to stay alive. Imagine. Every birthday some guy in three pieces comes by and . . ."

"I'm gonna kill you."

"I should warn you. I'm uninsured."

"It was my Christmas party!" she exclaimed.

"I don't believe in Christmas."

"I work with them. I have to see them every day. They were nice to you. They all tried to make you feel welcome. No, but all you could do was stand in the corner and sneer."

"It was a grin."

"It was a sneer."

Grin. But once I'd passed a mirror at a party and happened to catch my face grinning, and ever since I understood how to some people the grin and gruff of Coyote looked like snarl and sneer. "All right," I said. "I'm sorry."

"Huh," she said, willing to forgive me right now but wanting to say some things she felt obliged to say. Nez Perce, I was finding out, were not the only ones given to having conversations in their dreams. Women do it too. "If you were really sorry, you'd change."

"You're right," I said, wondering how people changed more than their words without dying first. Coyote, the arrogant buffoon, dies, tricked by his own trickster nature; fox steps over him five times saying words only fox may know, and he is reborn. "I'm sorry."

"You'll try?"

"What?"

"To change?"

"If that's what you want," I said dully. There was warning in my voice, threat, change. Frog preparing to bury himself beneath the mud of a Sonoran Season, dead to the world as July and August peeled the desert to its vibrant core. But how?

"I don't think I can do it," I said as we left an Oakland A's game. It had felt good and queer to sit in the private box of her father's company beside third base. Good, for the privilege. Queer, because I did not belong among the Day Care and Mutual Funds of the other privileged in the box. One man kept talking Fidelity to me, a topic I coped with by nodding until it dawned on him that I had no idea what he was talking about. "I'm talking money," he said. "Ah," I said, glancing at his wife. "I see."

"You can do it. You are not a failure," my girlfriend said.

"No, indeedy," I said.

"Good," she said.

It was this goodness that made me say to her, that loving and generous and kind normal person, when she asked if I didn't want to come over to her house and at least talk about my decision to leave school and town and her that night, "No." The words had all been said too many times.

I felt bad as I drove north with sinking heart into the mud-dark night. All the time and energy she had put into me would be a waste for her. If I were lucky, though, she'd think me the failure.

III

This is better than true: By the time I was fifteen, my hair had grown back to a respectable length. In between, I found God, the Christian God, the one whose magic is to divide himself into three forms and pounce upon the world when it isn't looking. The Front Man they use to steal your land. The one they believe has a Reason for the horrid awful thing that has just happened to them and who keeps the happy things a mystery. He must have been a real trickster to watch the volunteers route Looking Glass under the white flag of truce, not long after so many of the Nez Perce had willingly taken up Christianity and its Book. Its magic seemed so powerful.

God explained why I was different. And he forgave me. Every Sunday, I rose early and walked across town where I sat outside the church and watched the old people park their cars by sonar, backing into one car, then reversing forward into another, turning the steering wheel this way and that until, within five feet of the curb, they were satisfied. God forgave me for enjoying the vaudevillian antics of the near-dead.

He also forgave me—sternly, I might add, with a black-and-white suit of words from the minister who caught me—for nipping a couple of cookies from the kitchens on my way to Sunday school. And he taught me, after the first time, to rearrange the cookies to look as though none were missing, a skill that has given me knowledge in return. I know if someone has gone through my medicine cabinet or my drawers; I know what someone's medicine cabinet contains even though not a single label is turned or changed on the bottles and vials. I can be in your house and not disturb your dust.

Most of all, he forgave me Cindy. She was two years older than I was with a round, open, freckled face. She believed just the right amount. She spoke in tongues, but she did not throw herself on the floor and writhe like a savage. Cindy sang in the choir, and when I heard her singing and surprised her in the bushes, across the stream from church, God was there. He looked away at the local Sparrow when her blouse fell open and a breast dropped into my hand; He blinked, slowly like a window shade drawing down, as her pleated skirt drew up. Afterwards, she knelt in prayer, and I believed from the fervor of her voice that God forgave her. Me, well, maybe there was a little doubt in His mind about me. Try as I may, these cookies were a bit more difficult to rearrange. I fell asleep to the song of crickets while Cindy prayed and dreamed of mallard duck girls giggling after copulation.

The real magic of Cindy's God was that he let me be so sure he existed in triplicate that I could walk into a room of strangers and smile, certain that I was superior to anyone who saw in me anything other than a Christian. I belonged to the Youth Group. We played basketball against other Youth Groups and won. We staged wholesome musicals for the church community. We went on retreats where I got to teach Cindy how to feel the animals watching us while she prayed excitedly. We planned a mission for the summer, taking our Triceratops God down to the Navaho (with Hopi Land) Reservation in Arizona and, while doing Good Works, preaching people into silence, if not acceptance and conversion.

At Second Mesa the bus parked below the village perched like Peregrines or Red Tails along the rim of the mesa. The broad road, hot and white with July, the gravel sharp and glittering, the dust thin and pervasive. We followed a path until we were among the village kids who were as happy to see us as a truckload of Mars Bars. Cindy handed me her camera, posed herself, hugging two of the kids, and said "Chee . . . eee . . . eee. . . ." Her smile, almost natural at first, turned hard with effort. "Sah," she said. "Gee whiz," she scolded me. "Take the picture."

The kids were happy to be hugged all over again. They giggled. An old woman stopped in a doorway and watched.

"Chee . . . eee . . . e . . . ee . . . eee. Sah."

I held the camera. It sweated in my hand as I drew a bead on Cindy and the two kids. But I could not pull the trigger.

"Gee whillikers. You're hopeless," Cindy said with as much anger as her Christian heart could muster. "Give the camera to Steven. Steven will you take my picture?"

I relinquished the camera to Steven, who snapped off a couple of rounds, and then handed the camera over to Cindy.

"You're a real failure as a photographer," Cindy joked as we walked through the village to the quonset hut the girls were to paint a donated green. "An utter and complete, useless failure."

I joined the boys, digging trenches and holes, laying sewer pipe and planting a septic tank.

That night, Cindy wanted to be shed of me. I left her in the vestibule of the mission church and hiked back out towards Second Mesa. I turned back silently when I ran into Indians guarding their fields below the mesa walls and met Steven coming in from a roll beneath the Pleiades with Cindy.

"Hi," Steven said nervously, sniffing snot made to run by the clear night air. "There's KI-yotes out there," he added, as if to explain his nervousness.

I grinned.

"Where you headed?"

"Bed."

He was relieved.

But before dawn he was shaking me awake in my sleeping bag. "Cindy's sick," he hissed.

"Wha'd you expect?"

"Wha . . . ? Huh?" Steven said.

The following day, Cindy felt pale and hot and rested on the air-conditioned bus as we took pick and shovel and continued scarring the earth for sewer trenches. Steven worked close to me, almost severing my toe with the point of his spade. Sweat dripped into the folds of my eyes, and periodically I had to pause with the pick and catch my breath, wiping the sting and looking out at the hot fluid haze of the desert. A hawk floated on currents of air drafting up the side of the mesa. Saguaro Cactus threw their arms up at the white sky. Somewhere in the canyon, frogs were buried three feet below the earth's surface, waiting patiently for the Rains to invite them to the surface to join the celebration.

The old woman appeared in her doorway, again, watching us. Watching me. As I turned back to my pick, raising it with the joy of one who belongs, on a mission, doing Good Works, a feeling much like fear, like the anxiety of night falling dreams, riffled through my veins. I looked at Steven, at the way his stubby penis swayed in the stretch cloth of his cutoff sweatpants, his knees you wouldn't wish on a camel. I looked at the other boys, secure in their sun-block and boots, secure in the goodness of their work. I remembered Steven, in the middle of a close basketball game at the Youth Group hall, twisting with epilepsy; as people rushed to his side, I stood apart and watched. I saw the pictures of opening night and my eyes, my musical eyes that shone like crystals among the other eyes of the chorus, and remembered how I—the lead—was supposed to walk out in front of the curtain and in all seriousness sing, "Phoebe! What are you doing?" Except for the afternoon wedding of Cary Costello, my sister's friend, and the gay man with the champagne tray, I might have succeeded. I could not be sure whether I got so drunk because I was scared or because I felt This Close to success at doing something Father or Grandfather never would have done, put themselves before a boast of audience, an audience joyful and willing to accept anything I did as the authentic actions of people like me. And I reheard Cindy, as she and I sought a private arbor, crashing through the undergrowth on the retreats, intent on our arrival and not the journey. That was why Steven's stubby penis was so pointed, today, in his sweatpants.

As I raised my pick to strike again, I saw the old woman through the sting of sweat, watching, watching, and I dropped my pick. I walked to her in her doorway.

"Wha-huh," she said. "The boy who walks alone."

She motioned me indoors.

Her name was Laura P. (She warned me never to reveal what the P. stood for.) I made her my grandmother in a book, and although she never was, in most ways she is. The inside of her home was dark, and the mantle was a shrine with candles, red-white-and-blue bunting draped in symmetrical half moons on either side of a triptych of photographs of John F. Kennedy. The kitchen at the back was brightened by an unshuttered window, and I sat on a bar stool as she fed me fried donuts and piki, a fragile bluecorn roll of flake the size of a tortilla. The sweet toasty lingering taste of piki comes to my mouth even now, and I have often wished I kept the things she told me more in my mind.

The truth is, I knew what this woman said, have known it, and will always know it, without tense or time, in my heart. I ate piki with her that day and the next, and then our grim Christian bus began its roundabout way back to where we came from. In my suitcase I had packed ten rolls of piki she gave me, and a small clay bowl, thrown and etched with sticks and glazed with signs. In my heart I carried a hidden joy, wanting to remain behind and yet longing to be at home.

Cindy rode the bus more ill than ever beside Steven Shovel-Toes, and that evening in Jerome when I offered to go off with her and she ceremoniously and weakly told me no, her words rose up the presbytery to meet the undusted words of her elders, tangled in them, and fell to the floor at my feet. My heart was full still with the words of Laura P. as Cindy explained it all to death. I bit my lip, grinned, and then unable to hold the grin any longer, let my face relax into inexpression. I felt neither bitterness nor jealousy but only an odd and historied contentment that the path had reached its measure. A touch of sorrow that Cindy never would be healed. But what could I do? I had offered.

"Wha-huh," I said, leaving the church, passing the Grouped Youth playing Frisbee in the twilight, and climbing the Cleopatra mine.

By the mine was a ghost town. By now, probably, the ghosts have been driven out, their stories ironed smooth, and the town restored. Then, the feeling of being alone was sufficient for my joy as I climbed weather-grayed steps and dusk dark stones, weaving around and through the brush that had overgrown the old mine, trying to avoid the air shafts which were covered by rotted wood. I felt as though I had the coal of fire in my pants pocket as I sat on the steep mountainside and watched the last tines of light rake the valleys below. A dark-skinned man carried a coil of rope on his shoulder. He walked across a plateau below me, past a rundown Catholic church and into a wooden cabin nearby. A light flashed on in one room. He moved a chair into the center of the room, and then the curtains closed on the window. A priest emerged from the side of the church cassocked and hatted—one of those wide French-brimmed hats—his old body shaped like the hiss of an *S*, his head hung meditatively in sorrow or understanding. He, too, crossed the plateau and after knocking, entered the same cabin. Time unwound itself. I was still sitting there hunched over my knees like Ollokot (Frog) when I realized it was blanket dark, with the lights of the Pleiades and the reflection of the moon giving everything a crisp shadowy feel like the first dusting of snow gives a white fringe to the trees and rivers. My skin felt cold, but with a jacket coldness, and the chill didn't penetrate my dreaming bones. The light in the cabin was out; the church nearby was empty and dark, its batted belfry like a finger jutting up against the starlit canvas of the valley behind it.

It was quiet, as though I sat buried beneath the earth, except for the crickets chirruping away and the occasional hoot of an owl. Abruptly everything went dead, quiet. The crickets held their breath, and the wide-eyed owls fell silent. I froze, breathing slowly, stilly, the air shallow in my lungs, just enough to keep from gasping. Brush crackled. A stone tumbled loose and bounced all the way to the plateau below. Still I sat, and stiller. I felt no fear, only the expectation which, in the heart, is knowledge. To my right, an animal snuffled. A low growl.

And then a leap, and I saw him. He stood on a boulder not ten feet from me, still snuffling and growling, silvered with the dust of night light, his eyes burnished with reflection. He stared at me. I stared at him. He was this close. I didn't speak, at first, and then it all came back to me with a rush like water over Beaver's dam, and I felt flooded with words.

"Wha-huh," I laughed. "Ki-YO-tee. Ki-YO-tee."

W. S. Penn

(b. 1949)

www

An urban mixed-blood Nez Perce, W. S. Penn **Web** is the author of *The Absence of Angels* (1994) and *All My Sins Are Relatives.* (1995), from which this excerpt is taken. A writer of both fiction and nonfictional essays, he has been named Writer of the Year and Editor of the Year by the Woodcraft Circle of Native Writers and Storytellers.

TOPICS FOR CRITICAL THINKING

1. In what various ways does the narrator signal the difference between the native and Anglo cultures?
2. What are the functions of the coyote?
3. What are the various definitions of success and failure in the narrator's worlds?

TOPICS FOR CRITICAL WRITING

Define the narrator's view toward his adolescence and analyze both how that view is conveyed and the differences it makes in the portrait.

NICOLE BROSSARD

from *Surfaces of Sense* (1980)

I had thought that once I had settled into those blanks or so-called «lapses of memory», I could make all sorts of anecdotes appear in reality which otherwise may not be part of it.

Fiction was getting me nowhere. There was that tension and much later on *those peals of laughter*, so real that / yet memory. My entire memory bit into my day like a devourer of animals.

Today I know that all of that made sense: this sudden inclination to spend all my time on a sheet of paper grappling with the past and the imperfect. I imagine hunger. My hunger. My desire to get down to work and passionately begin the narrative song so familiar to Adrienne, to Gertrude and to Yolande. The words flowing from what they had foretold. From what they are, from what they wanted to be. Like the prolonging of an episode which I will somehow have to imagine. Which does not cause me any pain.

I then imagine my temptation to write down all those happenings which led me to read about existing conditions.

I had thought that if I insisted, *the Sun Incident*, *the Mauve Impression* or THE ARDENT FORM could fill the void. It was intense—and foreseeable that I should try to think of a title which would do justice to a few lives on which my life may have depended.

I knew that being afraid did not help to sort things out in the writing process. Quite the contrary, it sometimes made it impossible, in the way that one says: that woman has had an impossible life. I knew that chit-chat was not the answer either. But anecdotes! I was very attracted to Adrienne and Gertrude. To their anecdotes, in the hot July weather, when they told me about the city and America and the Amazons. Yolande, on the other hand, wrote to me. Short letters. Random marks on a sheet of paper. Occasionally we made our texts overlap. A fictive overlapping of she-animals. Superimposition.

I now believe that these things could have taken place in New York or Montréal, in the course of the last ten years—certainly, I had not foreseen such a complete reversal just when I imagined myself free in time and space; and, or so I thought, I had all the time in the world, all the time necessary in the shape of a belly or else that of tongues:_______________, energetically licking inorder to experience ____________ the salt and the texture_____________ or else fleeing far away from faces with yet another sentence: I had thought of making several distinctions between reality and realism but each day presented an obstacle: rain, sun—autumn again each day so real, each day filled up. With descriptions, precise usage, gestures and comments. Each day: and this would form the only certitude in my life—how did Gertrude come into the world?

I had just imagined that perhaps for months, reality would confront fiction. Would enter my life so easily, would cut into the nerve, like all those breakfasts which sooth the grey mornings seen through my eyes.

Not for a moment had I imagined that this book, which I hoped would be published in the autumn, could have been written in this way, in the pure chance of my encounters with Gertrude from America and Yolande from Here, who—they have never met except at this moment, to make real-life gestures with as much finesse as in books—incited me to bring about metamorphoses.

Each day, then, I imagined that I was thinking of Gertrude and Yolande and that my prose would take a different turn. Simply by knowing that on that day, there was rain in New York, in *the lace-work of the skyscrapers.* I imagined the damp pavement, refracting the neon-lights; the grey mists and the haze; the florist's shop where we bought the plant for Gertrude's birthday. I imagined the three of us, sitting in a restaurant, silent women around us and others, *roaring with laughter* at the way they spend their time, laughing at the fabled, throaty sounds they would create from the depths of the ultraviolet light. I imagined them in the rain acting out a street scene in the roles of housewives, slender and beautiful as Yolande described them in her last letter. Yolande—who always took the trouble to mention if, on that day, it had rained or the contrary. I suppose it was fairly important to her, for she never forgot to write her letters in pencil on rainy days. On other days, her letters were written in ink. Her obsession with the washed-out manuscript.

Started off in beautiful ink, beautiful prose and *the glint of gnashing teeth,* what remained of them.

As the days went by, I became increasingly convinced that the blank which they called a lapse of memory was only imaginary, or else the only plausible connection with the imaginary. I had given considerable thought to writing about this obsession of mine; and having finished my book, I thought I should not attach too much importance to it, since I had forgotten the main point at any rate, by believing that it was unimportant. But now and then I feel like coming back to it, as if this mystery (or lapse of memory) was trying to produce a fifth dimension in me. A different sense.

The mystery reappears every time the names Adrienne, Gertrude and Yolande come back to me. Even more deep-rooted in my life, in my memory. This does not happen by chance. I know it makes sense, very much like my attitude when I listen to Adrienne talking about the lunarbelly; and the terrible windy nights which wear her out, in the middle of the city on those nights when there is a full moon—even when she is only waiting for the bus.

I do not imagine anyone could be excused from finding a solution to this mystery.

This is the symmetry: anger and sadness when I reflect on the mystery, the imaginary blank; and begin to think about the enormous patch covered with graffiti, which goes so far back in time that it almost seems to be part of my unconscious, but known to me. Shiver—that patch of memory filled with the names which Yolande continually writes down at the bottom of her manuscripts. I am capable of everything, she says, using several expressions which it is not my business to describe. I only say that the face of Yolande was important since she agreed to show it and because more often than not, she was mistaken for someone else. For no apparent reason.

Each day, the book burned up patches of memory; and I say that the expression *the glint of gnashing teeth* referred to so many things and words all at once that strange certainties were finding their way into my memory, as if in a narrative.

Of course it is necesssary to remain detached so as not to be, one day—in a frenzy, before we even so much as suspect it—committed to the beacons of America, to a literary climate which lays claim to all rights. There must be urgent matters for us if we are to survive, if we are to cross into the tribes of Sirens and Northern Lights.

ALL FICTIVE ESCAPES ARE SO REAL.

So intense when the scenes intended to condition us are no longer sufficient and the lens focuses on the interior, inviting memory to spring up in *all possible forms:* global aesthetics / an overwhelming passion which nothing can encompass. Which is already no longer fiction. But instead the fictional expectation of a certainty, hardly out of place in the ultraviolet light.

Because I narrowly escaped the clutches of feverishness yesterday, I already know that today the atmosphere will be calm and I will continue to imagine what it will be like in New York in Adrienne's life, in the lives of her companions and lovers. I know that she will pour tea, just after eleven o'clock, and stroke her cat, *Siamese*, before beginning to meditate. To muse on those powerful currents of vitality which run through her and which animate her Amazon companions in the city and in the country. I know that Adrienne will want poetry or else Gertrude. I know that in the spiral of their writings she will find that turn of mind which stimulates her radical way of loving. I know that the city, like an endless Bowery, will go along Grove Street and that Adrienne's eyes will light up with distress signals. From one outcry to the next. I also know that I will find myself unable to write about the agitation which will suddenly come over Adrienne when the tea is cold and she sets the cup down on the saucer (with a slight clink). So, I will have to use my imagination and tackle the impossible task of putting on this page the words which will not betray her thoughts when she will say, as if to herself: the end of motherhood, the end of utopias. As if she were made aware by the lunar belly of certain mythical patterns favoring lucidity.

On that day I imagined my thoughts: attentive to the movements which unwind in a spiral pattern in books written by women. It was as if I were seized by that inner logic which endlessly calls on women to melt away / eject themselves from the initial shell, taking with them the rhythm and the sound of the waves, recurring, modulating, tearing themselves from the waters; fertile and unremitting in the cycle of birth and rebirth. Seeking the right frequency far away from the waters.

The spiral pattern opens out onto the unwritten. And the unwritten circulates, round and round, producing emanations like those at the door to an initiatory pathway.

wind, entwined in soft arms by beautiful arms, arcs of circles and the feminine cycle; celebration in the grasses of the moist presence of the spiral of the word repeated, never as before, resumed but like a prolonging in the water, a fluid continues along its course my love as visible as cyprine to the sense of touch which triggers desire: meditation.

this moment when: writing will allow.

I was thinking: will once again allow for continuity. The line which forms a loop, its curves of life, its curve of words and a great deal of gravity *if by chance* a wave of anecdotes happened to cut into reality where it meets fate, as if to control it better. Draw it slowly towards you, like a piece of information, without the sense of it all crumbling away: Adrienne's fingers juggling a pen.

I was also thinking of the other dimension to the spiral when it turns back on itself, causing delirium, completely fluid. When this happens, the woman writing in the spiral hears the waves generated by her own energy—waves which are inaudible under normal circumstances of reality, waves which travel through houses, assuming forms which are different to those which you would imagine. This is known as beginning to live in another way. Then the senses open up to the spiral and the spiral revolves around the lovers' arms, arcs of circles and the feminine cycle in the celebration of the grasses.

I had decided to solve one problem at a time.

NICOLE BROSSARD

(b. 1943)

www Poet and novelist Nicole Brossard **Web** was born in Montreal, Quebec. She published her first novel, *Aube a la saison* (*Dawning Season*) in 1965 and ever since has been a vocal artist and theorist, interested in the relations among language, the body, impression, and the politics of art and feminism.

TOPICS FOR CRITICAL THINKING

1. In what ways does this excerpt map the process of writing?
2. How does the passage enact the encounters between reality and fiction?
3. What might the phrase "All fictive escapes are so real" mean?

TOPIC FOR CRITICAL WRITING

Can there be such a thing as postmodern autobiography?

19

Writing Communities:

The Beats Web www

After the Second World War, a group of young writers who first met at Columbia University began to explore the joy of unfettered creativity. Inspired by jazz, the crazy potentials of language, the excitement of the road, and the utter ecstasy of knowledge, this group grew to include Jack Kerouac Web, Allen Ginsberg Web, Neal Cassady, William S. Burroughs Web, Gregory Corso, and later Lawrence Ferlinghetti, Amiri Baraka (LeRoi Jones) Web, Diane di Prima, Gary Snyder Web, Michael McClure, Bruce Conner, and Ann Waldman, all of whom gave voice to the tradition of twentieth-century avant-gardism. These artists congregated in Greenwich Village and later San Francisco. They wrote poetry and prose, made films, staged readings and theatrical "happenings," and generally spread a new excitement about art and language throughout New York and later American culture. Paradoxically, what began as a distinctly countercultural, even radical, movement eventually became—and has continued to be in the twenty-first century—a dominant social force. Fifty years ago, their identity as cultural icons became so established that magazines like *Time* and *Newsweek* wrote about their unconventional lifestyle and rich socialites used to "rent" beatniks to attend parties. Both their work and their personas, although not without their critics, became the subjects of both fascination and emulation. California beat Michael McClure associated with Jim Morrison of The Doors, who liked to think of himself as a beat poet; today, the images of Jack Kerouac and actor-photographer Dennis Hopper, have been appropriated by Gap to help sell khakis. Their images still exude hipness and style.

The beats were not, however, simply "arts-for-art's sake" writers. Much of their work contains a social critique stimulated by what they saw as a 1950s culture of repressiveness in America. The decade gave rise to a host of political and social events promulgating notions of conformity and convention, including the House of Un-American Activities hearings, which were led by Senator Joseph McCarthy and blacklisted Hollywood writers and others for their political beliefs; a cold war mentality that thrived on paranoia; the threat of the atomic bomb; the racial oppressions and segregations intrinsic to American culture; the destructive greed of corporations; narrow and conformist

Beat literature book rack at the Paperback Book Gallery, New York, 1960.

notions of family, sexuality, and identity; and the exploration of what constitutes a useful endeavor. If Jack Kerouac travels the country with Neal Cassady looking for the soul of jazz and the charms of the everyday citizen, if Allen Ginsberg looks for ways to make words sing, if Gary Snyder and Bruce Conner seek visionary experiences through Eastern religion or Native American culture, all extol the spirit of life and art. Their work represents a mixture of media—language, photography, film, jazz, and a liberated theater no longer kept inside the confines of traditional form and stage.

Beat art reflects all of these: it is a fusion of jazz rhythms and soulfulness with the liberations of humor, philosophy, and substances. But beat art is not simply an accident or the result of some kind of spontaneous generation. Beat artists were conscious of their methods and the meanings of what they did. Although their public image may have been one of unrestrained action, their art was the result of the thoughtful analysis of the relations of individuals to the world. If beat artists extolled spontaneity, it was because they realized they could not control much of what happened. Beat art made a virtue out of understanding that a 9-to-5 workaday world may not be life.

In other words, beat art—beat literature, in particular—embodies a philosophy of critical action. More often than not, beat literature "does" something by intervening in contemporary events, ideologies, or oppressions. Both Allen Ginsberg and Gregory Corso spoke out in poems against nuclear proliferation during the cold war era; Kerouac and Ginsberg, to name just two, wrote strong criticisms of American capitalism that, in many respects, are still relevant and are entirely compatible with critiques of multinational capitalism today; black beats like LeRoi Jones (who changed his name to Amiri Baraka shortly after the assassination of Malcolm X), Bob Kaufman, and Ted Joans saw beat culture as embracing black cultural forms and making an intervention in what was, at the time, a deeply segregated America. For all of these reasons and more, beat culture metamorphosed readily into the "free love" generation of the later 1960s, into the anti-Vietnam War and civil rights movements, and into many other social and political causes. Aesthetic innovation and social critique joined in the beat movement; coffee houses and alternative bookstores, folk rock, and independent film remain today some of its significant legacies.

WILLIAM S. BURROUGHS

The Finger

(n.d.)

Lee walked slowly up 6th Avenue from 42nd Street, looking in pawnshop windows.

"I must do it," he repeated to himself.

Here it was. A cutlery store. He stood there shivering, with the collar of his shabby Chesterfield turned up. One button had fallen off the front of his overcoat, and the loose threads twisted in a cold wind. He moved slowly around the shop window and into the entrance, looking at knives and scissors and pocket microscopes and air pistols and take-down tool kits with the tools snapping or screwing into a metal handle, the whole kit folding into a small leather packet. Lee remembered getting one of these kits for Christmas when he was a child. Finally he saw what he was looking for: poultry shears like his father used to cut through the joints when he carved the turkey at grandmother's Thanksgiving dinners. There they were, glittering and stainless, one blade smooth and sharp, the other with teeth like a saw to hold the meat in place for cutting.

Lee went in and asked to see the shears. He opened and closed the blades, tested the edge with his thumb.

"That's stainless steel, sir. Never rusts or tarnishes." 5

"How much?"

"Two dollars and seventy-nine cents plus tax."

"O.K."

The clerk wrapped the shears in brown paper, taped the package neatly. It seemed to Lee that the crackling paper made a deafening noise in the empty store. He paid with his last five dollars, and walked out with the shears heavy in his overcoat pocket.

He walked up 6th Avenue repeating: "I must do it. I've got to do it now 10
that I've bought the shears."

He saw a sign: Hotel Aristo. There was no lobby. He walked up a flight of stairs. An old man, dingy and indistinct like a faded photograph, was standing behind a desk. Lee registered, paid one dollar in advance, and picked up a key with a heavy bronze tag.

His room opened onto a dark shaft. He turned on the light. Black stained furniture, a double bed with a thin mattress and sagging springs. Lee unwrapped the shears, and held them in his hand. He put the shears down on the dresser in front of an oval mirror that turned on a pivot.

Lee walked around the room. He picked up the shears again and placed the end joint of his left little finger against the saw teeth, lower blade exactly at the joint. Slowly he lowered the cutting blade until it rested against the flesh of his finger. He looked in the mirror, composing his face into the supercilious mask of an 18th-century dandy. He took a deep breath, pressed the handle quick and hard. He felt no pain. The finger joint fell on the dresser. Lee turned his hand over and looked at the stub. Blood spurted up and hit him in the face. He felt a sudden deep pity for the finger joint that lay there on the dresser, a few drops of blood gathering around the white bone. Tears came to his eyes.

"It didn't do anything," he said in a broken child's voice. He adjusted his face again, cleaned the blood off it with a towel, and bandaged his finger crudely, adding more gauze as the blood soaked through. In a few minutes the bleeding had stopped. Lee picked up the finger joint and put it in his vest pocket, and walked out of the hotel tossing his key on the desk.

"I've done it," he said to himself. Waves of euphoria swept through him as he walked down the street. He stopped in a bar and ordered a double brandy, meeting all eyes with a level, friendly stare. Good will flowed out of him for everyone he saw, for the whole world. A lifetime of defensive hostility had fallen from him.

Half an hour later he was sitting with his analyst on a park bench in Central Park. The analyst was trying to persuade him to go to Bellevue, and had suggested they "go outside to talk it over."

"Really, Bill, you're doing yourself a great disservice. When you realize what you've done you'll need psychiatric care. Your ego will be overwhelmed."

"All I need is to have this finger sewed up. I've got a date tonight."

"Really, Bill, I don't see how I can continue as your psychiatrist if you don't follow my advice in this matter." The analyst's voice had become whiney, shrill, almost hysterical. Lee wasn't listening; he felt a deep trust in the doctor. The doctor would take care of him. He turned to the doctor with a little boy smile: "Why don't you fix it yourself?"

"I haven't practiced since my internship, and I don't have the necessary materials in any case. This has to be sewed up right or it could get infected right on up the arm."

Lee finally agreed to go to Bellevue for medical treatment only.

At Bellevue Lee sat on a bench waiting while the doctor talked to somebody. The doctor came back, and led Lee to another room where an intern sewed up the finger and put on a dressing. The doctor kept urging him to allow himself to be committed; Lee was overcome by a sudden faintness. A nurse told him to put his head back. Lee felt that he must put himself entirely in the care of the doctor.

"All right," he said, "I'll do what you say."

The doctor patted his arm. "Ah, you're doing the right thing, Bill." The doctor lead him past several desks, where he signed papers.

"I'm cutting red tape by the yard," the doctor said.

Finally Lee found himself in a dressing gown in a bare ward.

"Where is my room?" he asked a nurse.

"Your room! I don't know what bed you've been assigned to. Anyway you can't go there before eight unless you have a special order from the doctor."

"Where is my doctor?"

"Doctor Bromfield? He isn't here now. He'll be in tomorrow morning around ten."'

"I mean Doctor Horowitz."

"Doctor Horowitz? I don't think he's on the staff here."

He looked around him at the bare corridors, the men walking around in bathrobes muttering under the cold, indifferent eyes of an attendant.

"Why this is the psychopathic ward," he thought. "He put me in here and went away!"

Years later Lee would tell the story: "Did I ever tell you about the time I got on a Van Gogh kick and cut off the end joint of my little finger?" At this point he would hold up his left hand. "This girl, see? She lives in the next room to me in a rooming house on Jane Street. That's in the Village. I love

William S. Burroughs

her and she's so stupid I can't make any impression. Night after night I lay there hearing her carry on with some man in the next room. It's tearing me all apart . . . So I hit on this finger joint gimmick. I'll present it to her: 'A trifling memento of my undying affection. I suggest you wear it around your neck in a pendant filled with formaldehyde.'

"But my analyst, the lousy bastard, shanghaied me into the nuthouse, and the finger joint was sent to potter's field with a death certificate, because someone might find the finger joint and the police go around looking for the rest of the body.

"If you ever have occasion to cut off a finger joint, my dear, don't consider any instrument but poultry shears. That way you're sure of cutting *through* at the joint."

"And what about the girl?"

"Oh, by the time I got out of the nuthouse she'd gone to Chicago, I never saw her again."

Diane di Prima

from *Memoirs of a Beatnik* *(1988)*

You never do get to go *back* to anything, but it really takes a long time to learn that. . . .

When I stepped off the bus at 40th Street and Eighth Avenue, it was like arriving at a foreign port. The city, steaming and tropical, resounded with music: guitars, harmonicas, an occasional horn, radios blaring, children playing in the dark, women talking together on the sidewalks or stoops, or calling to each other from the windows. The night was pregnant with lust and violence, and the small, dark men stalked softly. It was a universe away from my world of home-fries and roadwork that I had left only an hour and a half earlier, and yet it was the same, exactly the same—crowded together and seen in the dark.

Downtown the streets were filled with youngsters who had made their way to the Village over the summer months. You could hear their drumming blocks from Washington Square, and when you stepped into the crowd around the fountain, you saw the young men barefoot and naked to the waist, and the young women, their skirts held high, stomping and dancing together in the heavy night.

I had no luggage and I had no pad. The apartment had been lost for non-payment of rent while I was away, and O'Reilley had moved my "stuff"—mostly books—to a West Tenth Street apartment where a little street-hustler-ballet-dancer named René Strauss lived. I joined the kids at the fountain, chanting and clapping, greeting friends and acquaintances, hearing the news. Finally the crowd thinned, the musicians all went home, and I wandered over to René's and fell out.

I spent the next few days casing the scene. The city was really crowded; there were, simply, no pads to be had, and rather than hassle I took to sleeping in the park.

At that time no laws had been passed limiting a citizen's right to access to public parks, no curfews were in effect. By two o'clock in the morning Washington Square was usually clear of its usual crowd: folksingers, faggots, and little girls from New Jersey on the make, and I would stretch out on the steps by the fountain and sleep peacefully until just after dawn, when a Park Department man with a big broom would come by and wake me. He swept my bed and went away again, and I and the half-dozen other people, all complete strangers, who shared these quarters, would exchange dazed greetings and go back to sleep till ten or so, when people started to arrive.

There was a regular crew of about eight of us who slept there, four to six of the eight being there on any given night, and we all got to know each other pretty well, as far as moods and habits and aura went, but we never spoke. Something about the intimacy of our shared space and the code of coolness in effect at that time would made it unseemly for us to know each other by name, or have anything more to say to each other than the minimum morning greeting. It would have been intrusion filling each other's turf and head with rattling chatter and conversation, and the inevitable unfolding of our emotional lives would have destroyed the space that the indifference of the city gave each and every one as her most precious gift.

At ten I would get up, stretch, look around me, and read for an hour or so till I was thoroughly awake. Then, stuffing all my accoutrements into the attaché case that served as my portable home and contained a raincoat, a toothbrush, notebooks, pens, and a change of underwear, I would pick it up and set off for the Chinese laundry on Waverly Place. I kept all my clothes there on separate tickets: one pair of slacks and one shirt on each ticket. I would take out a ticket's worth, and, carrying now attaché case and laundry package, I'd amble to Rienzi's, which opened at eleven, and order a breakfast, usually some kind of sweet and espresso coffee, though occasionally I'd splurge and treat myself to eggs and English muffins, or even some sausages or bacon. While the order was making, I'd find my way to the bathroom which was hidden away downstairs; down a rank, damp staircase with oozing walls, and along a corridor straight out of the *Count of Monte Cristo* to a tiny, cramped room, fortunately vaguely cleaned, where I would wash my face and feet and hands, brush my teeth, and change clothes, stuffing the dirty ones into a paper bag I carried in the attaché case for that purpose. Would then pull a brush through my hair and tie it up, and, feeling vaguely human, would grope my way up the stairs and to my breakfast.

Great pleasure it is to sit in an unhurried, uncrowded shop, drinking good, strong coffee and reading while your friends come in and out and the morning draws to a close and you write stray words in a notebook. I would linger as long as I could, usually a couple of hours, leaving finally to go to my afternoon's "work." The man to whom Duncan Sinclair had been selling his pictures, a real porn tycoon named Nelson Swan, had been busted, and that

Diane di Prima

market was dead for the moment, but I had found it simpler and pleasanter, though much less lucrative, to work for some of the older painters on the scene—painters who were one or two generations older than the abstract expressionists, and still used models.

They were gentle, friendly folk who had come of age during the depression and were given to painting what in the thirties had been known as "Social Realism"— people with a sad, haunting sense that the world had changed since their "day," and a persistent kindly determination to discover of what the change consisted. Most of them were within walking distance of Washington Square, and I would walk up to the studio where I was expected, stopping along the way to drop off the bag with my yesterday's clothes at the Chinese laundry. I would perch on a high stool, or recline on a couch, in Moses Soyer's studio, while his wife rattled in and out chattering and Moses told me the gossip about his other models: who was going to have a baby, who was leaving for San Francisco, and almost one could believe oneself in that haunting and haunted world of nineteeth-century Paris, would catch the bold and flashy faces from *La Bohème* out of the corner of one's eyes. The money I got for two hours modeling was enough to buy me dinner and next morning's breakfast and to take another outfit out of the laundry, and, as I had no other needs, I thought myself quite rich.

After a while a certain number of luxuries attached themselves to this routine: I met Victor Romero, a young photographer with a job and an apartment, and he gave me a key to his place, which had a shower; and occasionally I would work two jobs in one day and take René or O'Reilley out to dinner; and I got a card at the New York Public Library, which varied my reading considerably. . . .

JACK KEROUAC

Essentials of Spontaneous Prose *(1953)*

SET-UP. The object is set before the mind, either in reality, as in sketching (before a landscape or teacup or old face) or is set in the memory wherein it becomes the sketching from memory of a definite image-object.

PROCEDURE. Time being of the essence in the purity of speech, sketching language is undisturbed flow from the mind of personal secret idea-words, *blowing* (as per jazz musician) on subject of image.

METHOD. No periods separating sentence-structures already arbitrarily riddled by false colons and timid usually needless commas—but the vigorous space dash separating rhetorical breathing (as jazz musician drawing breath between outblown phrases)—"measured pauses which are the essentials of our speech"—"divisions of the *sounds* we hear"—"time and how to note it down." (William Carlos Williams)

SCOPING. Not "selectivity" of expression but following free deviation (association) of mind into limitless blow-on-subject seas of thought, swimming in sea of English with no discipline other than rhythms rhetorical exhalation and expostulated statement, like a fist coming down on a table with each complete utterance, bang! (the space dash)—Blow as deep as you want—write as deeply, fish as far down as you want, satisfy yourself first, then reader cannot fail to receive telepathic shock and meaning-excitement by same laws operating in his own human mind.

LAG IN PROCEDURE. No pause to think of proper word but the infantile pileup of scatalogical buildup words till satisfaction is gained, which will turn out to be a great appending rhythm to a thought and be in accordance with Great Law of timing.

TIMING. Nothing is muddy that *runs in time* and to laws of *time*—Shakespearian stress of dramatic need to speak now in own unalterable way or forever hold tongue—*no revisions* (except obvious rational mistakes, such as names or *calculated* insertions in act of not writing but *inserting*).

CENTER OF INTEREST. Begin not from preconceived idea of what to say about image but from jewel center of interest in subject of image at *moment* of

Jack Kerouac

writing, and write outwards swimming in sea of language to peripheral release and exhaustion—Do not afterthink except for poetic or P.S. reasons. Never afterthink to "improve" or defray impressions, as, the best writing is always the most painful personal wrung-out tossed from cradle warm protective mind—tap from yourself the song of yourself, *blow!—now!—your* way is your only way—"good"—or "bad"—always honest, ("ludicrous"), spontaneous, "confessional" interesting, because not "crafted." Craft *is* craft.

STRUCTURE OF WORK. Modern bizarre structures (science fiction, etc.) arise from language being dead, "different" themes give illusion of "new" life. Follow roughly outlines in out-fanning movement over subject, as river rock, so mindflow over jewel-center need (run your mind over it, *once*) arriving at pivot, where what was dim formed "beginning" becomes sharp-necessitating "ending" and language shortens in race to wire of time-race of work, following laws of Deep Form, to conclusion, last words, last trickle—Night is The End.

MENTAL STATE. If possible write "without consciousness in semitrance (as Yeats' later "trance writing") allowing subconscious to admit own uninhibited interesting necessary and so "modern" language what conscious art would censor, and write excitedly, swiftly, with writing-or-tying-cramps, in accordance (as from center to periphery) with laws of orgasm, Reich's "beclouding of consciousness." *Come* from within, out—to relaxed and said.

JACK KEROUAC

The First Word: Jack Kerouac Takes a Fresh Look at Jack Kerouac

My position in the current American literary scene is simply that I got sick and tired of the conventional English sentence which seemed to me so iron-bound in its rules, so inadmissable with reference to the actual format of my mind as I had learned to probe it in the modern spirit of Freud and Jung, that I couldn't express myself through that form any more. How many sentences do you see in current novels that say, "The snow was on the ground, and it was difficult for the car to climb the hill"? By the childish device of taking what was originally two short sentences, and sticking in a comma with an "and," these great contemporary prose "craftsmen" think they have labored out a sentence. As far as I can see it is two short sets of picturization belonging to a much longer sentence the total picturization of which would finally say some thing we never heard before if the writer dared to utter it out.

Shame seems to be the key to repression in writing as well as in psychological malady. If you don't stick to what you first thought, and to the words the thought brought, what's the sense of bothering with it anyway, what's the sense of foisting your little lies on others, or, that is, hiding your little truths from others? What I find to be really "stupefying in its unreadability" is this laborious and dreary lying called craft and revision by writers, and certainly recognized by the sharpest psychologists as sheer blockage of the mental spontaneous process known 2,500 years ago as "The Seven Streams of Swiftness."

In the *Surangama Sutra,* Gotama Buddha says, "If you are now desirous of more perfectly understanding Supreme Enlightenment, you must learn to answer questions spontaneously with no recourse to discriminative thinking. For the Tathagatas (the Passers-Through) in the ten quarters of the universes, because of the straight-forwardness of their minds and the spontaneity of their mentations, have ever remained, from beginningless time to endless time, of one pure Suchness with the enlightening nature of pure Mind Essence."

Which is pretty strange old news. You can also find pretty much the same thing in Mark 13:11. "Take no thought beforehand what ye shall speak, neither do ye premeditate: but whatsoever shall be given you in that hour, that speak ye: for it is not ye that speak, but the Holy Ghost." Mozart and Blake often felt they weren't pushing their own pens, 'twas the "Muse" singing and pushing.

But I would also like to compare spontaneous composition of prose and verse to the incomparable, heartbreaking discipline of the fire ordeal. You had to get through the fire "to prove your innocence" or just die in it "guilty"—there was certainly no chance to stop and think it over, to chew on the end of your pencil and erase something. O maybe you could pause a second or two for another direction but the trick was to act now (or speak now, as in writing) or forever hold your tongue.

In another sense spontaneous, or ad lib, artistic writing imitates as best it can the flow of the mind as it moves in its space-time continuum, in this sense it may really be called Space Age Prose someday because when astronauts are flowing through space and time they too have no chance to stop and reconsider and go back. It may be they won't be reading anything else but spontaneous writing when they do get out there, the science of the language to fit their science of movement.

But I'd gone so far to the edges of language where the babble of the subconscious begins, because words "come from the Holy Ghost" first in the form of a babble which suddenly by its sound indicates the word truly intended (in describing the stormy sea in *Desolation Angels* I heard the sound "Peligroso" for "Peligroso Roar" without knowing what it meant, wrote it down involuntarily, later found out it means "dangerous" in Spanish)—I began to rely too much on babble in my nervous race away from cantish cliches, chased the proton too close with my microscope, ended up ravingly enslaved to sounds, became unclear and dull as in my ultimate lit'ry experiment "Old Angel Midnight" (*Evergreen Review* and *Lui* in Paris in French). There's a delicate balancing point between bombast and babble.

And now my hand doesn't move as fast as it used to, and so many critics have laughed at me for those 16 originally-styled volumes of mine published in 16 languages in 42 countries, never for one moment calling me "sensitive" or artistically dignified but an unlettered literary hoodlum with diarrhea of the mouth, I'm having to retreat closer back to the bombast (empty abstraction) of this world and make my meaning plainer, i.e., dimmer, but the Space Age of the future won't bother with my "later" works if any, or with any of these millions of other things written today that sound alike.

To break through the barrier of language with WORDS, you have to be in orbit around your mind, and I may go up again if I regain my strength. It may sound vain but I've been wrestling with this anger problem with at least as much discipline as Jacob.

The little kid in the Lowell House at Harvard, whose professor I was for an hour, looked me right in the eye and asked, "Why do you have no discipline?" I said, "Is that the way to talk to your professor? Try it if you can. If you can you'll pull the rug out from everybody."

20 Stories for Further Reading

Anton Chekhov

Translated by Constance Garnett

The Lady with the Dog *(1899)*

I

It was said that a new person had appeared on the sea-front: a lady with a little dog. Dmitri Dmitritch Gurov, who had by then been a fortnight at Yalta, and so was fairly at home there, had begun to take an interest in new arrivals. Sitting in Verney's pavilion, he saw, walking on the sea-front, a fair-haired young lady of medium height, wearing a *béret;* a white Pomeranian dog was running behind her.

And afterwards he met her in the public gardens and in the square several times a day. She was walking alone, always wearing the same *béret,* and always with the same white dog; no one knew who she was, and every one called her simply "the lady with the dog."

"If she is here alone without a husband or friends, it wouldn't be amiss to make her acquaintance," Gurov reflected.

He was under forty, but he had a daughter already twelve years old, and two sons at school. He had been married young, when he was a student in his second year, and by now his wife seemed half as old again as he. She was a tall, erect woman with dark eyebrows, staid and dignified, and, as she said of herself, intellectual. She read a great deal, used phonetic spelling, called her husband, not Dmitri, but Dimitri, and he secretly considered her unintelligent, narrow, inelegant, was afraid of her, and did not like to be at home. He had begun being unfaithful to her long ago—had been unfaithful to her often, and, probably on that account, almost always spoke ill of women, and when they were talked about in his presence, used to call them "the lower race."

It seemed to him that he had been so schooled by bitter experience that 5
he might call them what he liked, and yet he could not get on for two days together without "the lower race." In the society of men he was bored and not himself, with them he was cold and uncommunicative; but when he was in the company of women he felt free, and knew what to say to them and how to

behave; and he was at ease with them even when he was silent. In his appearance, in his character, in his whole nature, there was something attractive and elusive which allured women and disposed them in his favour; he knew that, and some force seemed to draw him, too, to them.

Experience often repeated, truly bitter experience, had taught him long ago that with decent people, especially Moscow people—always slow to move and irresolute—every intimacy, which at first so agreeably diversifies life and appears a light and charming adventure, inevitably grows into a regular problem of extreme intricacy, and in the long run the situation becomes unbearable. But at every fresh meeting with an interesting woman this experience seemed to slip out of his memory, and he was eager for life, and everything seemed simple and amusing.

One evening he was dining in the gardens, and the lady in the *béret* came up slowly to take the next table. Her expression, her gait, her dress, and the way she did her hair told him that she was a lady, that she was married, that she was in Yalta for the first time and alone, and that she was dull there. . . . The stories told of the immorality in such places as Yalta are to a great extent untrue; he despised them, and knew that such stories were for the most part made up by persons who would themselves have been glad to sin if they had been able; but when the lady sat down at the next table three paces from him, he remembered these tales of easy conquests, of trips to the mountains, and the tempting thought of a swift, fleeting love affair, a romance with an unknown woman, whose name he did not know, suddenly took possession of him.

He beckoned coaxingly to the Pomeranian, and when the dog came up to him he shook his finger at it. The Pomeranian growled: Gurov shook his finger at it again.

The lady looked at him and at once dropped her eyes.

"He doesn't bite," she said, and blushed.

"May I give him a bone?" he asked; and when she nodded he asked courteously, "Have you been long in Yalta?"

"Five days."

"And I have already dragged out a fortnight here."

There was a brief silence.

"Time goes fast, and yet it is so dull here!" she said, not looking at him.

"That's only the fashion to say it is dull here. A provincial will live in Belyov or Zhidra and not be dull, and when he comes here it's 'Oh, the dulness! Oh, the dust!' One would think he came from Grenada."

She laughed. Then both continued eating in silence, like strangers, but after dinner they walked side by side; and there sprang up between them the light jesting conversation of people who are free and satisfied, to whom it does not matter where they go or what they talk about. They walked and talked of the strange light on the sea: the water was of a soft warm lilac hue, and there was a golden streak from the moon upon it. They talked of how sultry it was after a hot day. Gurov told her that he came from Moscow, that he had taken his degree in Arts, but had a post in a bank; that he had trained as an opera-singer, but had given it up, that he owned two houses in Moscow. . . .

And from her he learnt that she had grown up in Petersburg, but had lived in S—— since her marriage two years before, that she was staying another month in Yalta, and that her husband, who needed a holiday too, might perhaps come and fetch her. She was not sure whether her husband had a post in a Crown Department or under the Provincial Council—and was amused by her own ignorance. And Gurov learnt, too, that she was called Anna Sergeyevna.

Afterwards he thought about her in his room at the hotel—thought she would certainly meet him next day; it would be sure to happen. As he got into bed he thought how lately she had been a girl at school, doing lessons like his own daughter; he recalled the diffidence, the angularity, that was still manifest in her laugh and her manner of talking with a stranger. This must have been the first time in her life she had been alone in surroundings in which she was followed, looked at, and spoken to merely from a secret motive which she could hardly fail to guess. He recalled her slender, delicate neck, her lovely grey eyes.

"There's something pathetic about her, anyway," he thought, and fell asleep.

II

A week had passed since they had made acquaintance. It was a holiday. It 20 was sultry indoors, while in the street the wind whirled the dust round and round, and blew people's hats off. It was a thirsty day, and Gurov often went into the pavilion, and pressed Anna Sergeyevna to have syrup and water or an ice. One did not know what to do with oneself.

In the evening when the wind had dropped a little, they went out on the groyne to see the steamer come in. There were a great many people walking about the harbour; they had gathered to welcome some one, bringing bouquets. And two peculiarities of a well-dressed Yalta crowd were very conspicuous: the elderly ladies were dressed like young ones, and there were great numbers of generals.

Owing to the roughness of the sea, the steamer arrived late, after the sun had set, and it was a long time turning about before it reached the groyne. Anna Sergeyevna looked through her lorgnette at the steamer and the passengers as though looking for acquaintances, and when she turned to Gurov her eyes were shining. She talked a great deal and asked disconnected questions, forgetting next moment what she had asked; then she dropped her lorgnette in the crush.

The festive crowd began to disperse; it was too dark to see people's faces. The wind had completely dropped, but Gurov and Anna Sergeyevna still stood as though waiting to see some one else come from the steamer. Anna Sergeyevna was silent now, and sniffed the flowers without looking at Gurov.

"The weather is better this evening," he said. "Where shall we go now? Shall we drive somewhere?"

She made no answer. 25

Then he looked at her intently, and all at once put his arm round her and kissed her on the lips, and breathed in the moisture and the fragrance of the flowers; and he immediately looked round him, anxiously wondering whether any one had seen them.

"Let us go to your hotel," he said softly. And both walked quickly.

The room was close and smelt of the scent she had bought at the Japanese shop. Gurov looked at her and thought: "What different people one meets in the world!" From the past he preserved memories of careless, good-natured women, who loved cheerfully and were grateful to him for the happiness he gave them, however brief it might be; and of women like his wife who loved without any genuine feeling, with superfluous phrases, affectedly, hysterically, with an expression that suggested that it was not love nor passion, but something more significant; and of two or three others, very beautiful, cold women, on whose faces he had caught a glimpse of a rapacious expression—an obstinate desire to snatch from life more than it could give, and these were capricious, unreflecting, domineering, unintelligent women not in their first youth, and when Gurov grew cold to them their beauty excited his hatred, and the lace on their linen seemed to him like scales.

But in this case there was still the diffidence, the angularity of inexperienced youth, an awkward feeling; and there was a sense of consternation as though some one had suddenly knocked at the door. The attitude of Anna Sergeyevna—"the lady with the dog"—to what had happened was somehow peculiar, very grave, as though it were her fall—so it seemed, and it was strange and inappropriate. Her face dropped and faded, and on both sides of it her long hair hung down mournfully; she mused in a dejected attitude like "the woman who was a sinner" in an old-fashioned picture.

"It's wrong," she said. "You will be the first to despise me now."

There was a water-melon on the table. Gurov cut himself a slice and began eating it without haste. There followed at least half an hour of silence.

Anna Sergeyevna was touching; there was about her the purity of a good, simple woman who had seen little of life. The solitary candle burning on the table threw a faint light on her face, yet it was clear that she was very unhappy.

"How could I despise you?" asked Gurov. "You don't know what you are saying."

"God forgive me," she said, and her eyes filled with tears. "It's awful."

"You seem to feel you need to be forgiven."

"Forgiven? No. I am a bad, low woman; I despise myself and don't attempt to justify myself. It's not my husband but myself I have deceived. And not only just now; I have been deceiving myself for a long time. My husband may be a good, honest man, but he is a flunkey! I don't know what he does there, what his work is, but I know he is a flunkey! I was twenty when I was married to him. I have been tormented by curiosity; I wanted something better. 'There must be a different sort of life,' I said to myself. I wanted to live! To live, to live! . . . I was fired by curiosity . . . you don't understand it, but, I swear to God, I could not control myself; something happened to me: I could not be restrained. I told my husband I was ill, and came here. . . . And here I have been walking about as though I were dazed, like a mad creature; . . . and now I have become a vulgar, contemptible woman whom any one may despise."

Gurov felt bored already, listening to her. He was irritated by the naïve tone, by this remorse, so unexpected and inopportune; but for the tears in her eyes, he might have thought she was jesting or playing a part.

"I don't understand," he said softly. "What is it you want?"

She hid her face on his breast and pressed close to him.

"Believe me, believe me, I beseech you . . ." she said. "I love a pure, hon- 40
est life, and sin is loathsome to me. I don't know what I am doing. Simple people say: 'The Evil One has beguiled me.' And I may say of myself now that the Evil One has beguiled me."

"Hush, hush! . . ." he muttered.

He looked at her fixed, scared eyes, kissed her, talked softly and affectionately, and by degrees she was comforted, and her gaiety returned; they both began laughing.

Afterwards when they went out there was not a soul on the sea-front. The town with its cypresses had quite a deathlike air, but the sea still broke noisily on the shore; a single barge was rocking on the waves, and a lantern was blinking sleepily on it.

They found a cab and drove to Oreanda.

"I found out your surname in the hall just now: it was written on the 45
board—Von Diderits," said Gurov. "Is your husband a German?"

"No; I believe his grandfather was a German, but he is an Orthodox Russian himself."

At Oreanda they sat on a seat not far from the church, looked down at the sea, and were silent. Yalta was hardly visible through the morning mist; white clouds stood motionless on the mountain-tops. The leaves did not stir on the trees, grasshoppers chirruped, and the monotonous hollow sound of the sea rising up from below, spoke of the peace, of the eternal sleep awaiting us. So it must have sounded when there was no Yalta, no Oreanda here; so it sounds now, and it will sound as indifferently and monotonously when we are all no more. And in this constancy, in this complete indifference to the life and death of each of us, there lies hid, perhaps, a pledge of our eternal salvation, of the unceasing movement of life upon earth, of unceasing progress towards perfection. Sitting beside a young woman who in the dawn seemed so lovely, soothed and spellbound in these magical surroundings—the sea, mountains, clouds, the open sky—Gurov thought how in reality everything is beautiful in this world when one reflects: everything except what we think or do ourselves when we forget our human dignity and the higher aims of our existence.

A man walked up to them—probably a keeper—looked at them and walked away. And this detail seemed mysterious and beautiful, too. They saw a steamer come from Theodosia, with its lights out in the glow of dawn.

"There is dew on the grass," said Anna Sergeyevna, after a silence.

"Yes. It's time to go home." 50

They went back to the town.

Then they met every day at twelve o'clock on the sea-front, lunched and dined together, went for walks, admired the sea. She complained that she slept badly, that her heart throbbed violently; asked the same questions, troubled now by jealousy and now by the fear that he did not respect her sufficiently.

And often in the square or gardens, when there was no one near them, he suddenly drew her to him and kissed her passionately. Complete idleness, these kisses in broad daylight while he looked round in dread of some one's seeing them, the heat, the smell of the sea, and the continual passing to and fro before him of idle, well-dressed, well-fed people, made a new man of him; he told Anna Sergeyevna how beautiful she was, how fascinating. He was impatiently passionate, he would not move a step away from her, while she was often pensive and continually urged him to confess that he did not respect her, did not love her in the least, and thought of her as nothing but a common woman. Rather late almost every evening they drove somewhere out of town, to Oreanda or to the waterfall; and the expedition was always a success, the scenery invariably impressed them as grand and beautiful.

They were expecting her husband to come, but a letter came from him, saying that there was something wrong with his eyes, and he entreated his wife to come home as quickly as possible. Anna Sergeyevna made haste to go.

"It's a good thing I am going away," she said to Gurov. "It's the finger of destiny!"

She went by coach and he went with her. They were driving the whole 55
day. When she had got into a compartment of the express, and when the second bell had rung, she said:

"Let me look at you once more . . . look at you once again. That's right."

She did not shed tears, but was so sad that she seemed ill, and her face was quivering.

"I shall remember you . . . think of you," she said. "God be with you; be happy. Don't remember evil against me. We are parting forever—it must be so, for we ought never to have met. Well, God be with you."

The train moved off rapidly, its lights soon vanished from sight, and a minute later there was no sound of it, as though everything had conspired together to end as quickly as possible that sweet delirium, that madness. Left alone on the platform, and gazing into the dark distance, Gurov listened to the chirrup of the grasshoppers and the hum of the telegraph wires, feeling as though he had only just waked up. And he thought, musing, that there had been another episode or adventure in his life, and it, too, was at an end, and nothing was left of it but a memory. . . . He was moved, sad, and conscious of a slight remorse. This young woman whom he would never meet again had not been happy with him; he was genuinely warm and affectionate with her, but yet in his manner, his tone, and his caresses there had been a shade of light irony, the coarse condescension of a happy man who was, besides, almost twice her age. All the time she had called him kind, exceptional, lofty; obviously he had seemed to her different from what he really was, so he had unintentionally deceived her. . . .

Here at the station was already a scent of autumn; it was a cold evening. 60

"It's time for me to go north," thought Gurov as he left the platform. "High time!"

III

At home in Moscow everything was in its winter routine; the stoves were heated, and in the morning it was still dark when the children were having breakfast and getting ready for school, and the nurse would light the lamp for a short time. The frosts had begun already. When the first snow has fallen, on the first day of sledge-driving it is pleasant to see the white earth, the white roofs, to draw soft, delicious breath, and the season brings back the days of one's youth. The old limes and birches, white with hoar-frost, have a good-natured expression; they are nearer to one's heart than cypresses and palms, and near them one doesn't want to be thinking of the sea and the mountains.

Gurov was Moscow born; he arrived in Moscow on a fine frosty day, and when he put on his fur coat and warm gloves, and walked along Petrovka, and when on Saturday evening he heard the ringing of the bells, his recent trip and the places he had seen lost all charm for him. Little by little he became absorbed in Moscow life, greedily read three newspapers a day, and declared he did not read the Moscow papers on principle! He already felt a longing to go to restaurants, clubs, dinner-parties, anniversary celebrations, and he felt flattered at entertaining distinguished lawyers and artists, and at playing cards with a professor at the doctors' club. He could already eat a whole plateful of salt fish and cabbage. . . .

In another month, he fancied, the image of Anna Sergeyevna would be shrouded in a mist in his memory, and only from time to time would visit him in his dreams with a touching smile as others did. But more than a month passed, real winter had come, and everything was still clear in his memory as though he had parted with Anna Sergeyevna only the day before. And his memories glowed more and more vividly. When in the evening stillness he heard from his study the voices of his children, preparing their lessons, or when he listened to a song or the organ at the restaurant, or the storm howled in the chimney, suddenly everything would rise up in his memory: what had happened on the groyne, and the early morning with the mist on the mountains, and the steamer coming from Theodosia, and the kisses. He would pace a long time about his room, remembering it all and smiling; then his memories passed into dreams, and in his fancy the past was mingled with what was to come. Anna Sergeyevna did not visit him in dreams, but followed him about everywhere like a shadow and haunted him. When he shut his eyes he saw her as though she were living before him, and she seemed to him lovelier, younger, tenderer than she was; and he imagined himself finer than he had been in Yalta. In the evenings she peeped out at him from the bookcase, from the fireplace, from the corner—he heard her breathing, the caressing rustle of her dress. In the street he watched the women, looking for some one like her.

He was tormented by an intense desire to confide his memories to some 65
one. But in his home it was impossible to talk of his love, and he had no one outside; he could not talk to his tenants nor to any one at the bank. And what had he to talk of? Had he been in love, then? Had there been anything beautiful, poetical, or edifying or simply interesting in his relations with Anna

Sergeyevna? And there was nothing for him but to talk vaguely of love, of woman, and no one guessed what it meant; only his wife twitched her black eyebrows, and said: "The part of a lady-killer does not suit you at all, Dimitri."

One evening, coming out of the doctors' club with an official with whom he had been playing cards, he could not resist saying:

"If only you knew what a fascinating woman I made the acquaintance of in Yalta!"

The official got into his sledge and was driving away, but turned suddenly and shouted:

"Dmitri Dmitritch!"

"What?" 70

"You were right this evening: the sturgeon was a bit too strong!"

These words, so ordinary, for some reason moved Gurov to indignation, and struck him as degrading and unclean. What savage manners, what people! What senseless nights, what uninteresting, uneventful days! The rage for card-playing, the gluttony, the drunkenness, the continual talk always about the same thing. Useless pursuits and conversations always about the same things absorb the better part of one's time, the better part of one's strength, and in the end there is left a life grovelling and curtailed, worthless and trivial, and there is no escaping or getting away from it—just as though one were in a madhouse or a prison.

Gurov did not sleep all night, and was filled with indignation. And he had a headache all next day. And the next night he slept badly; he sat up in bed, thinking, or paced up and down his room. He was sick of his children, sick of the bank; he had no desire to go anywhere or to talk of anything.

In the holidays in December he prepared for a journey, and told his wife he was going to Petersburg to do something in the interests of a young friend—and he set off for S——. What for? He did not very well know himself. He wanted to see Anna Sergeyevna and to talk with her—to arrange a meeting, if possible.

He reached S—— in the morning, and took the best room at the hotel, in 75
which the floor was covered with grey army cloth, and on the table was an inkstand, grey with dust and adorned with a figure on horseback, with its hat in its hand and its head broken off. The hotel porter gave him the necessary information; Von Diderits lived in a house of his own in Old Gontcharny Street—it was not far from the hotel: he was rich and lived in good style, and had his own horses; every one in the town knew him. The porter pronounced the name "Dridirits."

Gurov went without haste to Old Gontcharny Street and found the house. Just opposite the house stretched a long grey fence adorned with nails.

"One would run away from a fence like that," thought Gurov, looking from the fence to the windows of the house and back again.

He considered: to-day was a holiday, and the husband would probably be at home. And in any case it would be tactless to go into the house and upset her. If he were to send her a note it might fall into her husband's hands, and then it might ruin everything. The best thing was to trust to chance. And he kept walking up and down the street by the fence, waiting for the chance. He saw a beggar go in at the gate and dogs fly at him; then an hour later he heard a piano, and the sounds were faint and indistinct. Probably it was Anna Sergeyevna playing. The front door suddenly opened, and an old woman came out, followed by the familiar white Pomeranian. Gurov was on the point of calling to the dog, but his heart began beating violently, and in his excitement he could not remember the dog's name.

He walked up and down, and loathed the grey fence more and more, and by now he thought irritably that Anna Sergeyevna had forgotten him, and was perhaps already amusing herself with some one else, and that that was very natural in a young woman who had nothing to look at from morning till night but that confounded fence. He went back to his hotel room and sat for a long while on the sofa, not knowing what to do, then he had dinner and a long nap.

"How stupid and worrying it is!" he thought when he woke and looked at the dark windows: it was already evening. "Here I've had a good sleep for some reason. What shall I do in the night?"

He sat on the bed, which was covered by a cheap grey blanket, such as one sees in hospitals, and he taunted himself in his vexation:

"So much for the lady with the dog . . . so much for the adventure. . . . You're in a nice fix. . . ."

That morning at the station a poster in large letters had caught his eye. "The Geisha" was to be performed for the first time. He thought of this and went to the theatre.

"It's quite possible she may go to the first performance," he thought.

The theatre was full. As in all provincial theatres, there was a fog above the chandelier, the gallery was noisy and restless; in the front row the local dandies were standing up before the beginning of the performance, with their hands behind them; in the Governor's box the Governor's daughter, wearing a boa, was sitting in the front seat, while the Governor himself lurked modestly behind the curtain with only his hands visible; the orchestra was a long time tuning up; the stage curtain swayed. All the time the audience were coming in and taking their seats Gurov looked at them eagerly.

Anna Sergeyevna, too, came in. She sat down in the third row, and when Gurov looked at her his heart contracted, and he understood clearly that for him there was in the whole world no creature so near, so precious, and so important to him; she, this little woman, in no way remarkable, lost in a provincial crowd, with a vulgar lorgnette in her hand, filled his whole life now, was his sorrow and his joy, the one happiness that he now desired for himself, and to the sounds of the inferior orchestra, of the wretched provincial violins, he thought how lovely she was. He thought and dreamed.

A young man with small side-whiskers, tall and stooping, came in with Anna Sergeyevna and sat down beside her; he bent his head at every step and seemed to be continually bowing. Most likely this was the husband whom at Yalta, in a rush of bitter feeling, she had called a flunkey. And there really was in his long figure, his side-whiskers, and the small bald patch on his head, something of the flunkey's obsequiousness; his smile was sugary, and in his buttonhole there was some badge of distinction like the number on a waiter.

During the first interval the husband went away to smoke; she remained alone in her stall. Gurov, who was sitting in the stalls, too, went up to her and said in a trembling voice, with a forced smile:

"Good-evening."

She glanced at him and turned pale, then glanced again with horror, unable to believe her eyes, and tightly gripped the fan and the lorgnette in her hands, evidently struggling with herself not to faint. Both were silent. She was sitting, he was standing, frightened by her confusion and not venturing to sit down beside her. The violins and the flute began tuning up. He felt suddenly frightened; it seemed as though all the people in the boxes were looking at them. She got up and went quickly to the door; he followed her, and both walked senselessly along passages, and up and down stairs, and figures in legal, scholastic, and civil service uniforms, all wearing badges, flitted before their eyes. They caught glimpses of ladies, of fur coats hanging on pegs; the draughts blew on them, bringing a smell of stale tobacco. And Gurov, whose heart was beating violently, thought:

"Oh, heavens! Why are these people here and this orchestra! . . ."

And at that instant he recalled how when he had seen Anna Sergeyevna off at the station he had thought that everything was over and they would never meet again. But how far they were still from the end!

On the narrow, gloomy staircase over which was written "To the Amphitheatre," she stopped.

"How you have frightened me!" she said, breathing hard, still pale and overwhelmed. "Oh, how you have frightened me! I am half dead. Why have you come? Why?"

"But do understand, Anna, do understand . . ." he said hastily in a low voice. "I entreat you to understand. . . ."

She looked at him with dread, with entreaty, with love; she looked at him intently, to keep his features more distinctly in her memory.

"I am so unhappy," she went on, not heeding him. "I have thought of nothing but you all the time; I live only in the thought of you. And I wanted to forget, to forget you; but why, oh, why, have you come?"

On the landing above them two schoolboys were smoking and looking down, but that was nothing to Gurov; he drew Anna Sergeyevna to him, and began kissing her face, her cheeks, and her hands.

"What are you doing, what are you doing!" she cried in horror, pushing him away. "We are mad. Go away to-day; go away at once. . . . I beseech you by all that is sacred, I implore you. . . . There are people coming this way!"

Some one was coming up the stairs.

"You must go away," Anna Sergeyevna went on in a whisper. "Do you hear, Dmitri Dmitritch? I will come and see you in Moscow. I have never been happy; I am miserable now, and I never, never shall be happy, never! Don't make me suffer still more! I swear I'll come to Moscow. But now let us part. My precious, good, dear one, we must part!"

She pressed his hand and began rapidly going downstairs, looking round at him, and from her eyes he could see that she really was unhappy. Gurov stood for a little while, listened, then, when all sound had died away, he found his coat and left the theatre.

IV

And Anna Sergeyevna began coming to see him in Moscow. Once in two or three months she left S——, telling her husband that she was going to consult a doctor about an internal complaint—and her husband believed her, and did not believe her. In Moscow she stayed at the Slaviansky Bazaar hotel, and at once sent a man in a red cap to Gurov. Gurov went to see her, and no one in Moscow knew of it.

Once he was going to see her in this way on a winter morning (the messenger had come the evening before when he was out). With him walked his daughter, whom he wanted to take to school: it was on the way. Snow was falling in big wet flakes.

"It's three degrees above freezing-point, and yet it is snowing," said 105
Gurov to his daughter. "The thaw is only on the surface of the earth; there is quite a different temperature at a greater height in the atmosphere."

"And why are there no thunderstorms in the winter, father?"

He explained that, too. He talked, thinking all the while that he was going to see *her*, and no living soul knew of it, and probably never would know. He had two lives: one, open, seen and known by all who cared to know, full of relative truth and of relative falsehood, exactly like the lives of his friends and acquaintances; and another life running its course in secret. And through some strange, perhaps accidental, conjunction of circumstances, everything that was essential, of interest and of value to him, everything in which he was sincere and did not deceive himself, everything that made the kernel of his life, was hidden from other people; and all that was false in him, the sheath in which he hid himself to conceal the truth—such, for instance, as his work in the bank, his discussions at the club, his "lower race," his presence with his wife at anniversary festivities—all that was open. And he judged of others by himself, not believing in what he saw, and always believing that every man had his real, most interesting life under the cover of secrecy and under the cover of night. All personal life rested on secrecy, and possibly it was partly on that account that civilised man was so nervously anxious that personal privacy should be respected.

After leaving his daughter at school, Gurov went on to the Slaviansky Bazaar. He took off his fur coat below, went upstairs, and softly knocked at the door. Anna Sergeyevna, wearing his favourite grey dress, exhausted by the journey and the suspense, had been expecting him since the evening before. She was pale; she looked at him, and did not smile, and he had hardly come in when she fell on his breast. Their kiss was slow and prolonged, as though they had not met for two years.

"Well, how are you getting on there?" he asked. "What news?"

"Wait; I'll tell you directly. . . . I can't talk." 110

She could not speak; she was crying. She turned away from him, and pressed her handkerchief to her eyes.

"Let her have her cry out. I'll sit down and wait," he thought, and he sat down in an arm-chair.

Then he rang and asked for tea to be brought him, and while he drank his tea she remained standing at the window with her back to him. She was crying from emotion, from the miserable consciousness that their life was so hard for them; they could only meet in secret, hiding themselves from people, like thieves! Was not their life shattered?

"Come, do stop!" he said.

115 It was evident to him that this love of theirs would not soon be over, that he could not see the end of it. Anna Sergeyevna grew more and more attached to him. She adored him, and it was unthinkable to say to her that it was bound to have an end some day; besides, she would not have believed it!

He went up to her and took her by the shoulders to say something affectionate and cheering, and at that moment he saw himself in the looking-glass.

His hair was already beginning to turn grey. And it seemed strange to him that he had grown so much older, so much plainer during the last few years. The shoulders on which his hands rested were warm and quivering. He felt compassion for this life, still so warm and lovely, but probably already not far from beginning to fade and wither like his own. Why did she love him so much? He always seemed to women different from what he was, and they loved in him not himself, but the man created by their imagination, whom they had been eagerly seeking all their lives; and afterwards, when they noticed their mistake, they loved him all the same. And not one of them had been happy with him. Time passed, he had made their acquaintance, got on with them, parted, but he had never once loved; it was anything you like, but not love.

And only now when his head was grey he had fallen properly, really in love—for the first time in his life.

Anna Sergeyevna and he loved each other like people very close and akin, like husband and wife, like tender friends; it seemed to them that fate itself had meant them for one another, and they could not understand why he had a wife and she a husband; and it was as though they were a pair of birds of passage, caught and forced to live in different cages. They forgave each other for what they were ashamed of in their past, they forgave everything in the present, and felt that this love of theirs had changed them both.

120 In moments of depression in the past he had comforted himself with any arguments that came into his mind, but now he no longer cared for arguments; he felt profound compassion, he wanted to be sincere and tender. . . .

"Don't cry, my darling," he said. "You've had your cry; that's enough. . . . Let us talk now, let us think of some plan."

Then they spent a long while taking counsel together, talked of how to avoid the necessity for secrecy, for deception, for living in different towns and not seeing each other for long at a time. How could they be free from this intolerable bondage?

"How? How?" he asked, clutching his head. "How?"

And it seemed as though in a little while the solution would be found, and then a new and splendid life would begin; and it was clear to both of them that they had still a long, long road before them, and that the most complicated and difficult part of it was only just beginning.

KATHERINE MANSFIELD

This Flower

(1919)

"But I tell you, my lord fool, out of this nettle danger, we pluck this flower, safety."

As she lay there, looking up at the ceiling, she had her moment—yes, she had her moment! And it was not connected with anything she had thought or felt before, not even with those words the doctor had scarcely ceased speaking. It was single, glowing, perfect; it was like—a pearl, too flawless to match with another . . . Could she describe what happened? Impossible. It was as though, even if she had not been conscious (and she certainly had not been conscious all the time) that she was fighting against the stream of life—the stream of life indeed!—she had suddenly ceased to struggle. Oh, more than that! She had yielded, yielded absolutely, down to every minutest pulse and nerve, and she had fallen into the bright bosom of the stream and it had borne her . . . She was part of her room—part of the great bouquet of southern anemones, of the white net curtains that blew in stiff against the light breeze, of the mirrors, the white silky rugs; she was part of the high, shaking, quivering clamour, broken with little bells and crying voices that went streaming by outside,—part of the leaves and the light.

Over. She sat up. The doctor had reappeared. This strange little figure with his stethoscope still strung round his neck—for she had asked him to examine her heart—squeezing and kneading his freshly washed hands, had told her . . .

It was the first time she had ever seen him. Roy, unable, of course, to miss the smallest dramatic opportunity, had obtained his rather shady Bloomsbury address from the man in whom he always confided everything, who, although he'd never met her, knew, "all about them."

"My darling," Roy had said, "we'd better have an absolutely unknown man just in case it's—well, what we don't either of us want it to be. One can't be too careful in affairs of this sort. Doctors *do* talk. It's all damned rot to say they don't." Then, "Not that I care a straw who on earth knows. Not that I wouldn't—if you'd have me—blazon it on the skies, or take the front page of the *Daily Mirror* and have our two names on it, in a heart, you know—pierced by an arrow."

5 Nevertheless, of course, his love of mystery and intrigue, his passion for "keeping our secret beautifully" (his phrase!) had won the day, and off he'd gone in a taxi to fetch this rather sodden-looking little man.

She heard her untroubled voice saying, "Do you mind not mentioning anything of this to Mr. King? If you'd tell him that I'm a little run down and that my heart wants a rest. For I've been complaining about my heart."

Roy had been really *too* right about the kind of man the doctor was. He gave her a strange, quick, leering look, and taking off the stethoscope with shaking fingers he folded it into his bag that looked somehow like a broken old canvas shoe.

"Don't you worry, my dear," he said huskily. "I'll see you through."

Odious little toad to have asked a favour of! She sprang to her feet, and picking up her purple cloth jacket, went over to the mirror. There was a soft knock at the door, and Roy—he really did look pale, smiling his half-smile—came in and asked the doctor what he had to say.

"Well," said the doctor, taking up his hat, holding it against his chest and 10
beating a tattoo on it, "all I've got to say is that Mrs.—h'm—Madam wants a bit of a rest. She's a bit run down. Her heart's a bit strained. Nothing else wrong."

In the street a barrel-organ struck up something gay, laughing, mocking, gushing, with little trills, shakes, jumbles of notes.

> That's *all* I got to say, to say,
> That's *all* I got to say,

it mocked. It sounded so near she wouldn't have been surprised if the doctor were turning the handle.

She saw Roy's smile deepen; his eyes took fire. He gave a little "Ah!" of relief and happiness. And just for one moment he allowed himself to gaze at her without caring a jot whether the doctor saw or not, drinking her up with that gaze she knew so well, as she stood tying the pale ribbons of her camisole and drawing on the little purple cloth jacket. He jerked back to the doctor, "She shall go away. She shall go away to the sea at once," said he, and then, terribly anxious, "What about her food?" At that, buttoning her jacket in the long mirror, she couldn't help laughing at him.

"That's all very well," he protested, laughing back delightedly at her and at the doctor. "But if I didn't manage her food, doctor, she'd never eat anything but caviare sandwiches and—and white grapes. About wine—oughtn't she to have wine?"

Wine would do her no harm. 15

"Champagne," pleaded Roy. How he was enjoying himself!

"Oh, as much champagne as she likes," said the doctor, "and a brandy and soda with her lunch if she fancies it."

Roy loved that; it tickled him immensely.

"Do you hear that?" he asked solemnly, blinking and sucking in his cheeks to keep from laughing. "Do you fancy a brandy and soda?"

And, in the distance, faint and exhausted, the barrel-organ: 20

> A brandy and so-da,
> A brandy and soda, please!
> A brandy and soda, please!

The doctor seemed to hear that, too. He shook hands with her and Roy and went with him into the passage to settle his fee.

She heard the front door close and then—rapid, rapid steps along along the passage. This time he simply burst into her room, and she was in his arms, crushed up small while he kissed her with warm quick kisses, murmuring between them, "My darling, my beauty, my delight. You're mine, you're safe." And then three soft groans. "Oh! Oh! Oh! the relief!" Still keeping his arms round her he leant his head against her shoulder as though exhausted. "If you knew how frightened I've been," he murmured. "I thought we were in for it this time. I really did. And it would have been so—fatal—so fatal!"

WILLIAM FAULKNER

Barn Burning

(1939)

The store in which the Justice of the Peace's court was sitting smelled of cheese. The boy, crouched on his nail keg at the back of the crowded room, knew he smelled cheese, and more: from where he sat he could see the ranked shelves close-packed with the solid, squat, dynamic shapes of tin cans whose labels his stomach read, not from the lettering which meant nothing to his mind but from the scarlet devils and the silver curve of fish—this, the cheese which he knew he smelled and the hermetic meat which his intestines believed he smelled coming in intermittent gusts momentary and brief between the other constant one, the smell and sense just a little of fear because mostly of despair and grief, the old fierce pull of blood. He could not see the table where the Justice sat and before which his father and his father's enemy (*our enemy* he thought in that despair; *ourn! mine and hisn both! He's my father!*) stood, but he could hear them, the two of them that is, because his father had said no word yet:

"But what proof have you, Mr. Harris?"

"I told you. The hog got into my corn. I caught it up and sent it back to him. He had no fence that would hold it. I told him so, warned him. The next time I put the hog in my pen. When he came to get it I gave him enough wire to patch up his pen. The next time I put the hog up and kept it. I rode down to his house and saw the wire I gave him still rolled on to the spool in his yard. I told him he could have the hog when he paid me a dollar pound fee. That evening a nigger came with the dollar and got the hog. He was a strange nigger. He said, 'He say to tell you wood and hay kin burn.' I said, 'What?' 'That whut he say to tell you,' the nigger said. 'Wood and hay kin burn.' That night my barn burned. I got the stock out but I lost the barn."

"Where is the nigger? Have you got him?"

"He was a strange nigger, I tell you. I don't know what became of him." 5

"But that's not proof. Don't you see that's not proof?"

"Get that boy up here. He knows." For a moment the boy thought too that the man meant his older brother until Harris said, "Not him. The little one. The boy," and, crouching, small for his age, small and wiry like his father, in patched and faded jeans even too small for him, with straight, uncombed, brown hair and eyes gray and wild as storm scud, he saw the men between himself and the table part and become a lane of grim faces, at the end of which he saw the Justice, a shabby, collarless, graying man in spectacles, beckoning him. He felt no floor under his bare feet; he seemed to walk beneath the palpable weight of the grim turning faces. His father, stiff in his black Sunday coat donned not for the trial but for the moving, did not even look at him. *He aims for me to lie,* he thought, again with that frantic grief and despair. *And I will have to do hit.*

"What's your name, boy?" the Justice said.

"Colonel Sartoris Snopes," the boy whispered.

10 "Hey?" the Justice said. "Talk louder. Colonel Sartoris? I reckon anybody named for Colonel Sartoris in this country can't help but tell the truth, can they?" The boy said nothing. *Enemy! Enemy!* he thought; for a moment he could not even see, could not see that the Justice's face was kindly nor discern that his voice was troubled when he spoke to the man named Harris: "Do you want me to question this boy?" But he could hear, and during those subsequent long seconds while there was absolutely no sound in the crowded little room save that of quiet and intent breathing it was as if he had swung outward at the end of a grape vine, over a ravine, and at the top of the swing had been caught in a prolonged instant of mesmerized gravity, weightless in time.

"No!" Harris said violently, explosively. "Damnation! Send him out of here!" Now time, the fluid world, rushed beneath him again, the voices coming to him again through the smell of cheese and sealed meat, the fear and despair and the old grief of blood:

"This case is closed. I can't find against you, Snopes, but I can give you advice. Leave this country and don't come back to it."

His father spoke for the first time, his voice cold and harsh, level, without emphasis: "I aim to. I don't figure to stay in a country among people who . . ." he said something unprintable and vile, addressed to no one.

"That'll do," the Justice said. "Take your wagon and get out of this country before dark. Case dismissed."

15 His father turned, and he followed the stiff black coat, the wiry figure walking a little stiffly from where a Confederate provost's man's musket ball had taken him in the heel on a stolen horse thirty years ago, followed the two backs now, since his older brother had appeared from somewhere in the crowd, no taller than the father but thicker, chewing tobacco steadily, between the two lines of grim-faced men and out of the store and across the worn gallery and down the sagging steps and among the dogs and half-grown boys in the mild May dust, where as he passed a voice hissed:

"Barn burner!"

Again he could not see, whirling; there was a face in a red haze, moonlike, bigger than the full moon, the owner of it half again his size, he leaping in the red haze toward the face, feeling no blow, feeling no shock when his head struck the earth, scrabbling up and leaping again, feeling no blow this time either and tasting no blood, scrabbling up to see the other boy in full flight and himself already leaping into pursuit as his father's hand jerked him back, the harsh, cold voice speaking above him: "Go get in the wagon."

It stood in a grove of locusts and mulberries across the road. His two hulking sisters in their Sunday dresses and his mother and her sister in calico and sunbonnets were already in it, sitting on and among the sorry residue of the dozen and more movings which even the boy could remember—the battered stove, the broken beds and chairs, the clock inlaid with mother-of-pearl, which would not run, stopped at some fourteen minutes past two o'clock of a dead and forgotten day and time, which had been his mother's dowry. She was crying, though when she saw him she drew her sleeve across her face and began to descend from the wagon. "Get back," the father said.

"He's hurt. I got to get some water and wash his . . ."

"Get back in the wagon," his father said. He got in too, over the tail-gate. His father mounted to the seat where the older brother already sat and struck the gaunt mules two savage blows with the peeled willow, but without heat. It was not even sadistic; it was exactly that same quality which in later years would cause his descendants to over-run the engine before putting a motor car into motion, striking and reining back in the same movement. The wagon went on, the store with its quiet crowd of grimly watching men dropped behind; a curve in the road hid it. *Forever* he thought. *Maybe he's done satisfied now, now that he has* . . . stopping himself, not to say it aloud even to himself. His mother's hand touched his shoulder.

"Does hit hurt?" she said.

"Naw," he said. "Hit don't hurt. Lemme be."

"Can't you wipe some of the blood off before hit dries?"

"I'll wash to-night," he said. "Lemme be, I tell you."

The wagon went on. He did not know where they were going. None of them ever did or ever asked, because it was always somewhere, always a house of sorts waiting for them a day or two days or even three days away. Likely his father had already arranged to make a crop on another farm before he . . . Again he had to stop himself. He (the father) always did. There was something about his wolflike independence and even courage when the advantage was at least neutral which impressed strangers, as if they got from his latent ravening ferocity not so much a sense of dependability as a feeling that his ferocious conviction in the rightness of his own actions would be of advantage to all whose interest lay with his.

That night they camped, in a grove of oaks and beeches where a spring ran. The nights were still cool and they had a fire against it, of a rail lifted from a nearby fence and cut into lengths—a small fire, neat, niggard almost, a shrewd fire; such fires were his father's habit and custom always, even in freezing weather. Older, the boy might have remarked this and wondered why not a big one; why should not a man who had not only seen the waste and extravagance of war, but who had in his blood an inherent voracious prodigality with material not his own, have burned everything in sight? Then he might have gone a step farther and thought that that was the reason: that niggard blaze was the living fruit of nights passed during those four years in the woods hiding from all men, blue or gray, with his strings of horses (captured horses, he called them). And older still, he might have divined the true reason: that the element of fire spoke to some deep mainspring of his father's being, as the element of steel or of powder spoke to other men, as the one weapon for the preservation of integrity, else breath were not worth the breathing, and hence to be regarded with respect and used with discretion.

But he did not think this now and he had seen those same niggard blazes all his life. He merely ate his supper beside it and was already half asleep over his iron plate when his father called him, and once more he followed the stiff back, the stiff and ruthless limp, up the slope and on to the starlit road where, turning, he could see his father against the stars but without face or depth—a shape black, flat, and bloodless as though cut from tin in the iron folds of the frockcoat which had not been made for him, the voice harsh like tin and without heat like tin:

"You were fixing to tell them. You would have told him." He didn't answer. His father struck him with the flat of his hand on the side of the head, hard but without heat, exactly as he had struck the two mules at the store, exactly as he would strike either of them with any stick in order to kill a horse fly, his voice still without heat or anger: "You're getting to be a man. You got to learn. You got to learn to stick to your own blood or you ain't going to have any blood to stick to you. Do you think either of them, any man there this morning, would? Don't you know all they wanted was a chance to get at me because they knew I had them beat? Eh?" Later, twenty years later, he was to tell himself, "If I had said they wanted only truth, justice, he would have hit me again." But now he said nothing. He was not crying. He just stood there. "Answer me," his father said.

"Yes," he whispered. His father turned.

"Get on to bed. We'll be there tomorrow." 30

To-morrow they were there. In the early afternoon the wagon stopped before a paintless two-room house identical almost with the dozen others it had stopped before even in the boy's ten years, and again, as on the other dozen occasions, his mother and aunt got down and began to unload the wagon, although his two sisters and his father and brother had not moved.

"Likely hit ain't fitten for hawgs," one of the sisters said.

"Nevertheless, fit it will and you'll hog it and like it," his father said. "Get out of them chairs and help your Ma unload."

The two sisters got down, big, bovine, in a flutter of cheap ribbons; one of them drew from the jumbled wagon bed a battered lantern, the other a worn broom. His father handed the reins to the older son and began to climb stiffly over the wheel. "When they get unloaded, take the team to the barn and feed them." Then he said, and at first the boy thought he was still speaking to his brother: "Come with me."

"Me?" he said. 35

"Yes," his father said. "You."

"Abner," his mother said. His father paused and looked back—the harsh level stare beneath the shaggy, graying, irascible brows.

"I reckon I'll have a word with the man that aims to begin to-morrow owning me body and soul for the next eight months."

They went back up the road. A week ago—or before last night, that is—he would have asked where they were going, but not now. His father had struck him before last night but never before had he paused afterward to explain why; it was as if the blow and the following calm, outrageous voice still rang, repercussed, divulging nothing to him save the terrible handicap of being young, the light weight of his few years, just heavy enough to prevent his soaring free of the world as it seemed to be ordered but not heavy enough to keep him footed solid in it, to resist it and try to change the course of its events.

Presently he could see the grove of oaks and cedars and the other flower- 40
ing trees and shrubs where the house would be, though not the house yet. They walked beside a fence massed with honeysuckle and Cherokee roses and came to a gate swinging open between two brick pillars, and now, beyond a sweep of drive, he saw the house for the first time and at that instant he forgot his father and the terror and despair both, and even when he remembered his father again (who had not stopped) the terror and despair did not return. Because, for all the twelve movings, they had sojourned until now in a poor country, a land of small farms and fields and houses, and he had never seen a house like this before. *Hit's big as a courthouse* he thought quietly, with a surge of peace and joy whose reason he could not have thought into words, being too young for that: *They are safe from him. People whose lives are a part of this peace and dignity are beyond his touch, he no more to them than a buzzing wasp: capable of stinging for a little moment but that's all; the spell of this peace and dignity rendering even the barns and stable and cribs which belong to it impervious to the puny flames he might contrive . . .* this, the peace and joy, ebbing for an instant as he looked again at the stiff black back, the stiff and implacable limp of the figure which was not dwarfed by the house, for the reason that it had never looked big anywhere and which now, against the serene columned backdrop, had more than ever that impervious quality of something cut ruthlessly from tin, depthless, as though, sidewise to the sun, it would cast no shadow. Watching him, the boy remarked the absolutely undeviating course which his father held and saw the stiff foot come squarely down in a pile of fresh droppings where a horse had stood in the drive and which his father could have avoided by a simple change of stride. But it ebbed only for a moment, though he could not have thought this into words either, walking on in the spell of the house, which he could even want but without envy, without sorrow, certainly never with that ravening and jealous rage which unknown to him walked in the ironlike black coat before him: *Maybe he will feel it too. Maybe it will even change him now from what maybe he couldn't help but be.*

They crossed the portico. Now he could hear his father's stiff foot as it came down on the boards with clocklike finality, a sound out of all proportion to the displacement of the body it bore and which was not dwarfed either by the white door before it, as though it had attained to a sort of vicious and ravening minimum not to be dwarfed by anything—the flat, wide, black hat, the formal coat of broadcloth which had once been black but which had now that friction-glazed greenish cast of the bodies of old house flies, the lifted sleeve which was too large, the lifted hand like a curled claw. The door opened so promptly that the boy knew the Negro must have been watching them all the time, an old man with neat grizzled hair, in a linen jacket, who stood barring the door with his body, saying, "Wipe yo foots, white man, fo you come in here. Major ain't home nohow."

"Get out of my way, nigger," his father said, without heat too, flinging the door back and the Negro also and entering, his hat still on his head. And now the boy saw the prints of the stiff foot on the doorjamb and saw them appear on the pale rug behind the machinelike deliberation of the foot which seemed to bear (or transmit) twice the weight which the body compassed. The Negro was shouting "Miss Lula! Miss Lula!" somewhere behind them, then the boy, deluged as though by a warm wave by a suave turn of carpeted stair and a pendant glitter of chandeliers and a mute gleam of gold frames, heard the swift feet and saw her too, a lady—perhaps he had never seen her like before either—in a gray, smooth gown with lace at the throat and an apron tied at the waist and the sleeves turned back, wiping cake or biscuit dough from her hands with a towel as she came up the hall, looking not at his father at all but at the tracks on the blond rug with an expression of incredulous amazement.

"I tried," the Negro cried. "I tole him to . . ."

"Will you please go away?" she said in a shaking voice. "Major de Spain is not at home. Will you please go away?"

45 His father had not spoken again. He did not speak again. He did not even look at her. He just stood stiff in the center of the rug, in his hat, the shaggy iron-gray brows twitching slightly above the pebble-colored eyes as he appeared to examine the house with brief deliberation. Then with the same deliberation he turned; the boy watched him pivot on the good leg and saw the stiff foot drag round the arc of the turning, leaving a final long and fading smear. His father never looked at it, he never once looked down at the rug. The Negro held the door. It closed behind them, upon the hysteric and indistinguishable woman-wail. His father stopped at the top of the steps and scraped his boot clean on the edge of it. At the gate he stopped again. He stood for a moment, planted stiffly on the stiff foot, looking back at the house. "Pretty and white, ain't it?" he said. "That's sweat. Nigger sweat. Maybe it ain't white enough yet to suit him. Maybe he wants to mix some white sweat with it."

Two hours later the boy was chopping wood behind the house within which his mother and aunt and the two sisters (the mother and aunt, not the two girls, he knew that; even at this distance and muffled by walls the flat loud voices of the two girls emanated an incorrigible idle inertia) were setting up the stove to prepare a meal, when he heard the hooves and saw the linen-clad man on a fine sorrel mare, whom he recognized even before he saw the rolled rug in front of the Negro youth following on a fat bay carriage horse—a suffused, angry face vanishing, still at full gallop, beyond the corner of the house where his father and brother were sitting in the two tilted chairs; and a moment later, almost before he could have put the axe down, he heard the hooves again and watched the sorrel mare go back out of the yard, already galloping again. Then his father began to shout one of the sisters' names, who presently emerged backward from the kitchen door dragging the rolled rug along the ground by one end while the other sister walked behind it.

"If you ain't going to tote, go on and set up the wash pot," the first said.

"You, Sarty!" the second shouted. "Set up the wash pot!" His father appeared at the door, framed against that shabbiness, as he had been against that other bland perfection, impervious to either, the mother's anxious face at his shoulder.

"Go on," the father said. "Pick it up." The two sisters stooped, broad, lethargic; stooping, they presented an incredible expanse of pale cloth and a flutter of tawdry ribbons.

50 "If I thought enough of a rug to have to git hit all the way from France I wouldn't keep hit where folks coming in would have to tromp on hit," the first said. They raised the rug.

"Abner," the mother said. "Let me do it."

"You go back and git dinner," his father said. "I'll tend to this."

From the woodpile through the rest of the afternoon the boy watched them, the rug spread flat in the dust beside the bubbling wash-pot, the two sisters stooping over it with that profound and lethargic reluctance, while the father stood over them in turn, implacable and grim, driving them though never raising his voice again. He could smell the harsh homemade lye they were using; he saw his mother come to the door once and look toward them with an expression not anxious now but very like despair; he saw his father turn, and he fell to with the axe and saw from the corner of his eye his father raise from the ground a flattish fragment of field stone and examine it and return to the pot, and this time his mother actually spoke: "Abner. Abner. Please don't. Please, Abner."

Then he was done too. It was dusk; the whippoorwills had already begun. He could smell coffee from the room where they would presently eat the cold food remaining from the mid-afternoon meal, though when he entered the house he realized they were having coffee again probably because there was a fire on the hearth, before which the rug now lay spread over the backs of the two chairs. The tracks of his father's foot were gone. Where they had been were now long, water-cloudy scoriations resembling the sporadic course of a lilliputian mowing machine.

55 It still hung there while they ate the cold food and then went to bed, scattered without order or claim up and down the two rooms, his mother in one bed, where his father would later lie, the older brother in the other, himself, the aunt, and the two sisters on pallets on the floor. But his father was not in bed yet. The last thing the boy remembered was the depthless, harsh silhouette of the hat and coat bending over the rug and it seemed to him that he had not even closed his eyes when the silhouette was standing over him, the fire almost dead behind it, the stiff foot prodding him awake. "Catch up the mule," his father said.

When he returned with the mule his father was standing in the black door, the rolled rug over his shoulder. "Ain't you going to ride?" he said.

"No. Give me your foot."

He bent his knee into his father's hand, the wiry, surprising power flowed smoothly, rising, he rising with it, on to the mule's bare back (they had owned a saddle once; the boy could remember it though not when or where) and with the same effortlessness his father swung the rug up in front of him. Now in the starlight they retraced the afternoon's path, up the dusty road rife with honeysuckle, through the gate and up the black tunnel of the drive to the lightless house, where he sat on the mule and felt the rough warp of the rug drag across his thighs and vanish.

"Don't you want me to help?" he whispered. His father did not answer and now he heard again that stiff foot striking the hollow portico with that wooden and clocklike deliberation, that outrageous overstatement of the weight it carried. The rug, hunched, not flung (the boy could tell that even in the darkness) from his father's shoulder, struck the angle of wall and floor with a sound unbelievably loud, thunderous, then the foot again, unhurried and enormous; a light came on in the house and the boy sat, tense, breathing steadily and quietly and just a little fast, though the foot itself did not increase its beat at all, descending the steps now; now the boy could see him.

"Don't you want to ride now?" he whispered. "We kin both ride now," 60
the light within the house altering now, flaring up and sinking. *He's coming down the stairs now,* he thought. He had already ridden the mule up beside the horse block; presently his father was up behind him and he doubled the reins over and slashed the mule across the neck, but before the animal could begin to trot the hard, thin arm came round him, the hard, knotted hand jerking the mule back to a walk.

In the first red rays of the sun they were in the lot, putting plow gear on the mules. This time the sorrel mare was in the lot before he heard it at all, the rider collarless and even bareheaded, trembling, speaking in a shaking voice as the woman in the house had done, his father merely looking up once before stooping again to the hame he was buckling, so that the man on the mare spoke to his stooping back:

"You must realize you have ruined that rug. Wasn't there anybody here, any of your women . . ." he ceased, shaking, the boy watching him, the older brother leaning now in the stable door, chewing, blinking slowly and steadily at nothing apparently. "It cost a hundred dollars. But you never had a hundred dollars. You never will. So I'm going to charge you twenty bushels of corn against your crop. I'll add it in your contract and when you come to the commissary you can sign it. That won't keep Mrs. de Spain quiet but maybe it will teach you to wipe your feet off before you enter her house again."

Then he was gone. The boy looked at his father, who still had not spoken or even looked up again, who was now adjusting the logger-head in the hame.

"Pap," he said. His father looked at him—the inscrutable face, the shaggy brows beneath which the gray eyes glinted coldly. Suddenly the boy went toward him, fast, stopping as suddenly. "You done the best you could!" he cried. "If he wanted hit done different why didn't he wait and tell you how? He won't git no twenty bushels! He won't git none! We'll gether hit and hide hit! I kin watch . . ."

"Did you put the cutter back in that straight stock like I told you?" 65

"No, sir," he said.

"Then go do it."

That was Wednesday. During the rest of that week he worked steadily, at what was within his scope and some which was beyond it, with an industry that did not need to be driven nor even commanded twice; he had this from his mother, with the difference that some at least of what he did he liked to do, such as splitting wood with the half-size axe which his mother and aunt had earned, or saved money somehow, to present him with at Christmas. In company with the two older women (and on one afternoon, even one of the sisters), he built pens for the shoat and the cow which were a part of his father's contract with the landlord, and one afternoon, his father being absent, gone somewhere on one of the mules, he went to the field.

They were running a middle buster now, his brother holding the plow straight while he handled the reins, and walking beside the straining mule, the rich black soil shearing cool and damp against his bare ankles, he thought *Maybe this is the end of it. Maybe even that twenty bushels that seems hard to have to pay for just a rug will be a cheap price for him to stop forever and always from being what he used to be;* thinking, dreaming now, so that his brother had to speak sharply to him to mind the mule: *Maybe he even won't collect the twenty bushels. Maybe it will all add up and balance and vanish—corn, rug, fire; the terror and grief, the being pulled two ways like between two teams of horses—gone, done with for ever and ever.*

70 Then it was Saturday; he looked up from beneath the mule he was harnessing and saw his father in the black coat and hat. "Not that," his father said. "The wagon gear." And then, two hours later, sitting in the wagon bed behind his father and brother on the seat, the wagon accomplished a final curve, and he saw the weathered paintless store with its tattered tobacco- and patent-medicine posters and the tethered wagons and saddle animals below the gallery. He mounted the gnawed steps behind his father and brother, and there again was the lane of quiet, watching faces for the three of them to walk through. He saw the man in spectacles sitting at the plank table and he did not need to be told this was a Justice of the Peace; he sent one glare of fierce, exultant, partisan defiance at the man in collar and cravat now, whom he had seen but twice before in his life, and that on a galloping horse, who now wore on his face an expression not of rage but of amazed unbelief which the boy could not have known was at the incredible circumstance of being sued by one of his own tenants, and came and stood against his father and cried at the Justice: "He ain't done it! He ain't burnt . . ."

"Go back to the wagon," his father said.

"Burnt?" the Justice said. "Do I understand this rug was burned too?"

"Does anybody here claim it was?" his father said. "Go back to the wagon." But he did not, he merely retreated to the rear of the room, crowded as that other had been, but not to sit down this time, instead, to stand pressing among the motionless bodies, listening to the voices:

"And you claim twenty bushels of corn is too high for the damage you did to the rug?"

75 "He brought the rug to me and said he wanted the tracks washed out of it. I washed the tracks out and took the rug back to him."

"But you didn't carry the rug back to him in the same condition it was in before you made the tracks on it."

His father did not answer, and now for perhaps half a minute there was no sound at all save that of breathing, the faint, steady suspiration of complete and intent listening.

"You decline to answer that, Mr. Snopes?" Again his father did not answer. "I'm going to find against you, Mr. Snopes. I'm going to find that you were responsible for the injury to Major de Spain's rug and hold you liable for it. But twenty bushels of corn seems a little high for a man in your circumstances to have to pay. Major de Spain claims it cost a hundred dollars. October corn will be worth about fifty cents. I figure that if Major de Spain can stand a ninety-five-dollar loss on something he paid cash for, you can stand a five-dollar loss you haven't earned yet. I hold you in damages to Major de Spain to the amount of ten bushels of corn over and above your contract with him, to be paid to him out of your crop at gathering time. Court adjourned."

It had taken no time hardly, the morning was but half begun. He thought they would return home and perhaps back to the field, since they were late, far behind all other farmers. But instead his father passed on behind the wagon, merely indicating with his hand for the older brother to follow with it, and crossed the road toward the blacksmith shop opposite, pressing on after his father, overtaking him, speaking, whispering up at the harsh, calm face beneath the weathered hat: "He won't git no ten bushels neither. He won't git one. We'll . . ." until his father glanced for an instant down at him, the face absolutely calm, the grizzled eyebrows tangled above the cold eyes, the voice almost pleasant, almost gentle:

"You think so? Well, we'll wait till October anyway." 80

The matter of the wagon—the setting of a spoke or two and the tightening of the tires—did not take long either, the business of the tires accomplished by driving the wagon into the spring branch behind the shop and letting it stand there, the mules nuzzling into the water from time to time, and the boy on the seat with the idle reins, looking up the slope and through the sooty tunnel of the shed where the slow hammer rang and where his father sat on an upended cypress bolt, easily, either talking or listening, still sitting there when the boy brought the dripping wagon up out of the branch and halted it before the door.

"Take them on to the shade and hitch," his father said. He did so and returned. His father and the smith and a third man squatting on his heels inside the door were talking, about crops and animals; the boy, squatting too in the ammoniac dust and hoof-parings and scales of rust, heard his father tell a long and unhurried story out of the time before the birth of the older brother even when he had been a professional horsetrader. And then his father came up beside him where he stood before a tattered last year's circus poster on the other side of the store, gazing rapt and quiet at the scarlet horses, the incredible poisings and convolutions of tulle and tights and the painted leers of comedians, and said, "It's time to eat."

But not at home. Squatting beside his brother against the front wall, he watched his father emerge from the store and produce from a paper sack a segment of cheese and divide it carefully and deliberately into three with his pocket knife and produce crackers from the same sack. They all three squatted on the gallery and ate, slowly, without talking; then in the store again, they drank from a tin dipper tepid water smelling of the cedar bucket and of living beech trees. And still they did not go home. It was a horse lot this time, a tall rail fence upon and along which men stood and sat and out of which one by one horses were led, to be walked and trotted and then cantered back and forth along the road while the slow swapping and buying went on and the sun began to slant westward, they—the three of them—watching and listening, the older brother with his muddy eyes and his steady, inevitable tobacco, the father commenting now and then on certain of the animals, to no one in particular.

It was after sundown when they reached home. They ate supper by lamplight, then, sitting on the doorstep, the boy watched the night fully accomplish, listening to the whippoorwills and the frogs, when he heard his mother's voice: "Abner! No! No! Oh, God. Oh, God. Abner!" and he rose, whirled, and saw the altered light through the door where a candle stub now burned in a bottle neck on the table and his father, still in the hat and coat, at once formal and burlesque as though dressed carefully for some shabby and ceremonial violence, emptying the reservoir of the lamp back into the five-gallon kerosene can from which it had been filled, while the mother tugged at his arm until he shifted the lamp to the other hand and flung her back, not savagely or viciously, just hard, into the wall, her hands flung out against the wall for balance, her mouth open and in her face the same quality of hopeless despair as had been in her voice. Then his father saw him standing in the door.

"Go to the barn and get that can of oil we were oiling the wagon with," 85
he said. The boy did not move. Then he could speak.

"What . . ." he cried. "What are you . . ."

"Go get that oil," his father said. "Go."

Then he was moving, running, outside the house, toward the stable: this is the old habit, the old blood which he had not been permitted to choose for himself, which had been bequeathed him willy nilly and which had run for so long (and who knew where, battening on what of outrage and savagery and lust) before it came to him. *I could keep on,* he thought. *I could run on and on and never look back, never need to see his face again. Only I can't. I can't,* the rusted can in his hand now, the liquid sploshing in it as he ran back to the house and into it, into the sound of his mother's weeping in the next room, and handed the can to his father.

"Ain't you going to even send a nigger?" he cried. "At least you sent a nigger before!"

This time his father didn't strike him. The hand came even faster than the 90
blow had, the same hand which had set the can on the table with almost excruciating care flashing from the can toward him too quick for him to follow it, gripping him by the back of his shirt and on to tiptoe before he had seen it quit the can, the face stooping at him in breathless and frozen ferocity, the cold, dead voice speaking over him to the older brother who leaned against the table, chewing with that steady, curious, sidewise motion of cows:

"Empty the can into the big one and go on. I'll catch up with you."

"Better tie him up to the bedpost," the brother said.

"Do like I told you," the father said. Then the boy was moving, his bunched shirt and the hard, bony hand between his shoulder-blades, his toes just touching the floor, across the room and into the other one, past the sisters sitting with spread heavy thighs in the two chairs over the cold hearth, and to where his mother and aunt sat side by side on the bed, the aunt's arms about his mother's shoulders.

"Hold him," the father said. The aunt made a startled movement. "Not you," the father said. "Lennie. Take hold of him. I want to see you do it." His mother took him by the wrist. "You'll hold him better than that. If he gets loose don't you know what he is going to do? He will go up yonder." He jerked his head toward the road. "Maybe I'd better tie him."

"I'll hold him," his mother whispered. 95

"See you do then." Then his father was gone, the stiff foot heavy and measured upon the boards, ceasing at last.

Then he began to struggle. His mother caught him in both arms, he jerking and wrenching at them. He would be stronger in the end, he knew that. But he had no time to wait for it. "Lemme go!" he cried. "I don't want to have to hit you!"

"Let him go!" the aunt said. "If he don't go, before God, I am going there myself!"

"Don't you see I can't!" his mother cried. "Sarty! Sarty! No! No! Help me, Lizzie!"

Then he was free. His aunt grasped at him but it was too late. He whirled, 100
running, his mother stumbled forward on to her knees behind him, crying to the nearer sister: "Catch him, Net! Catch him!" But that was too late too, the sister (the sisters were twins, born at the same time, yet either of them now gave the impression of being, encompassing as much living meat and volume and weight as any other two of the family) not yet having begun to rise from the chair, her head, face, alone merely turned, presenting to him in the flying instant an astonishing expanse of young female features untroubled by any surprise even, wearing only an expression of bovine interest. Then he was out of the room, out of the house, in the mild dust of the starlit road and the heavy rifeness of honeysuckle, the pale ribbon unspooling with terrific slowness under his running feet, reaching the gate at last and turning in, running, his heart and lungs drumming, on up the drive toward the lighted house, the lighted door. He did not knock, he burst in, sobbing for breath, incapable for the moment of speech; he saw the astonished face of the Negro in the linen jacket without knowing when the Negro had appeared.

"De Spain!" he cried, panted. "Where's . . ." then he saw the white man too emerging from a white door down the hall. "Barn!" he cried. "Barn!"

"What?" the white man said. "Barn?"

"Yes!" the boy cried. "Barn!"

"Catch him!" the white man shouted.

But it was too late this time too. The Negro grasped his shirt, but the en- 105
tire sleeve, rotten with washing, carried away, and he was out that door too

and in the drive again, and had actually never ceased to run even while he was screaming into the white man's face.

Behind him the white man was shouting, "My horse! Fetch my horse!" and he thought for an instant of cutting across the park and climbing the fence into the road, but he did not know the park nor how high the vine-massed fence might be and he dared not risk it. So he ran on down the drive, blood and breath roaring; presently he was in the road again though he could not see it. He could not hear either: the galloping mare was almost upon him before he heard her, and even then he held his course, as if the very urgency of his wild grief and need must in a moment more find him wings, waiting until the ultimate instant to hurl himself aside and into the weed-choked roadside ditch as the horse thundered past and on, for an instant in furious silhouette against the stars, the tranquil early summer night sky which, even before the shape of the horse and rider vanished, stained abruptly and violently upward: a long, swirling roar incredible and soundless, blotting the stars, and he springing up and into the road again, running again, knowing it was too late yet still running even after he heard the shot and, an instant later, two shots, pausing now without knowing he had ceased to run, crying "Pap! Pap!", running again before he knew he had begun to run, stumbling, tripping over something and scrabbling up again without ceasing to run, looking backward over his shoulder at the glare as he got up, running on among the invisible trees, panting, sobbing, "Father! Father!"

At midnight he was sitting on the crest of a hill. He did not know it was midnight and he did not know how far he had come. But there was no glare behind him now and he sat now, his back toward what he had called home for four days anyhow, his face toward the dark woods which he would enter when breath was strong again, small, shaking steadily in the chill darkness, hugging himself into the remainder of his thin, rotten shirt, the grief and despair now no longer terror and fear but just grief and despair. *Father. My father,* he thought. "He was brave!" he cried suddenly, aloud but not loud, no more than a whisper: "He was! He was in the war! He was in Colonel Sartoris' cav'ry!" not knowing that his father had gone to that war a private in the fine old European sense, wearing no uniform, admitting the authority of and giving fidelity to no man or army or flag, going to war as Malbrouck himself did: for booty—it meant nothing and less than nothing to him if it were enemy booty or his own.

The slow constellations wheeled on. It would be dawn and then sun-up after a while and he would be hungry. But that would be to-morrow and now he was only cold, and walking would cure that. His breathing was easier now and he decided to get up and go on, and then he found that he had been asleep because he knew it was almost dawn, the night almost over. He could tell that from the whippoorwills. They were everywhere now among the dark trees below him, constant and inflectioned and ceaseless, so that, as the instant for giving over to the day birds drew nearer and nearer, there was no interval at all between them. He got up. He was a little stiff, but walking would cure that too as it would the cold, and soon there would be the sun. He went on down the hill, toward the dark woods within which the liquid silver voices of the birds called unceasing—the rapid and urgent beating of the urgent and quiring heart of the late spring night. He did not look back.

Chester Himes

Lunching at the Ritzmore (1942)

If you have ever been to the beautiful city of Los Angeles, you will know that Pershing Square, a palm-shaded spot in the center of downtown, is the mecca of the motley. Here, a short walk up from 'Skid Row,' on the green-painted benches flanking the crisscrossed sidewalks, is haven for men of all races, all creeds, all nationalities, and of all stages of deterioration—drifters and hop-heads and tbs' and beggars and bums and bindle-stiffs and big sisters, clipped and clippers, fraternizing with the tired business men from nearby offices, with students from various universities, with the strutting Filipinos, the sharp-cat Mexican youths in their ultra drapes, with the colored guys from out South Central way.

It is here the old men come to meditate in the warm midday sun, and watch the hustle and bustle of the passing younger world; here the job seekers with packed bags wait to be singled out for work; here the hunters relax and the hunted keep vigil. It is here you will find your man, for a game of pool, for a game of murder.

Along the Hill Street side buses going west line up one behind the other to take you out to Wilshire, to Beverly Hills, to Hollywood, to Santa Monica, to Westwood, to the Valley; and the red cards and the yellow cars fill the street with clatter and clang. On the Fifth Street side a pale pink skyscraper overlooks a lesser structure of aquamarine, southern California architecture on the pastel side; and along Sixth Street there are various shops and perhaps an office building which you would not notice unless you had business there.

But you would notice the Ritzmore, swankiest of West Coast hotels, standing in solid distinction along the Olive Street side, particularly if you were hungry in Pershing Square. You would watch footmen opening doors of limousines and doormen escorting patrons underneath the marquee across the width of sidewalk to the brass and mahogany doorway, and you would see hands of other doormen extended from within to hold wide the glass doors so that the patrons could make an unhampered entrance. And after that, if your views leaned a little to the Left, which they likely would if you were hungry in Pershing Square, you would spit on the sidewalk and resume your discussion, your boisterous and heated and surprisingly-often very well-versed discussion, on defense, or on the army, or the navy, or that 'rat' Hitler, or 'them Japs,' or the F.B.I., or the 'so and so' owners of Lockheed, or that (unprintable) Aimee Semple McPherson; on history and geography, on life and death; and you would just ignore the 'fat sonsaguns' who entered the Ritzmore.

On this particular day, a discussion which had begun on the Soviet Union 5 had developed into an argument on discrimination against Negroes, and a young University of Southern California student from Vermont stated flatly that he did not believe Negroes were discriminated against at all.

'If you would draw your conclusions from investigation instead of from agitation, you would find that most of the discrimination against Negroes exists only in communistic literature distributed by the Communist Party for organizational purposes,' he went on. 'As a matter of plain and simple fact, I have yet to visit a place where Negroes could not go. In fact, I think I've seen Negroes in every place I've ever been—hotels, theatres, concerts, operas . . .'

'Yass, and I bet they were working there, too,' another young fellow, a drifter from Chicago, argued. 'Listen, boy, I'm telling you, and I'm telling you straight, Negroes are out in this country. They can't get no work and they can't go nowhere, and that's a dirty shame for there're a lot of good Negroes, a lot of Negroes just as good as you and me.'

Surveying the drifter from head to foot, his unshaven face, his shabby unpressed suit, his run-over, unpolished shoes, the student replied, 'Frankly, that wouldn't make them any super race.'

'Huh?'

10 'However, that is beside the point,' the student continued, smiling. 'The point is that most of what you term discrimination is simply a matter of taste, of personal likes and dislikes. For instance, if I don't like you, should I have to put up with your presence? No, why should I? But this agitation about Negroes being discriminated against by the Army and Navy and defense industries and being refused service by hotels and restaurants is just so much bosh.'

'Are you kidding me, fellow?' the drifter asked suspiciously, giving the student a sharp look, 'Or are you just plain dumb? Say, listen—' and then he spied a Negro at the edge of the group. 'Say, here's a colored fellow now; I suppose he knows whether he's being discriminated against or not.'

'Not necessarily,' the student murmured.

Ignoring him, the drifter called, 'Hey, mister, you mind settling a little argument for us.'

The Negro, a young brown-skinned fellow of medium build with regular features and a small mustache, pushed to the center of the group. He wore a pair of corduroy trousers and a slip-over sweater with a sport shirt underneath.

15 'Say, mister, I been tryna tell this schoolboy—' the drifter began, but the Negro interrupted him, 'I know, I heard you.'

Turning to the student, he said, 'I don't know whether you're kidding or not, fellow, but it ain't no kidding matter with me. Here I am, a mechanic, a good mechanic, and they're supposed to be needing mechanics everywhere. But can I get a job—no! I gotta stand down here and listen to guys like you make a joke out of it while the government is crying for mechanics in defense.'

'I'm not making a joke out of it,' the student stated. 'If what you say is true, I'm truly sorry, mister; it's just hard for me to believe it.'

'Listen, schoolboy,' the drifter said, 'I'll tell you what I'll do with you; I'll just bet you a dollar this boy—this man—can't eat in any of these restaurants downtown. I'll just bet you a dollar.'

Now that a bet had been offered, the ten or twelve fellows crowded about who had remained silent out of respect for the Negro's feelings, egged it on, 'All right, schoolboy, put up or shut up!'

'Well, if it's all right with you, mister,' the student addressed the Negro, 'I'll 20
just take this young man up on that bet. But how are we going to determine?'

They went into a huddle and after a moment decided to let the Negro enter any restaurant of his choice, and if he should be refused service the student would pay off the bet and treat the three of them to dinners on Central Avenue; but should he be served, the check would be on the drifter.

So the three of them, the student, the Negro, and the drifter, started down Hill Street in search of a restaurant. The ten or twelve others of the original group fell in behind, and shortly fellows in other groups about the square looked up and saw the procession, and thinking someone was giving away something somewhere, hurried to get in line. Before they had progressed half the length of the block, more than a hundred of the raggedy bums of Pershing Square were following them.

The pedestrians stopped to see what the commotion was all about, adding to the congestion; and then the motorists noticed and slowed their cars. Soon almost a thousand people had congregated on the sidewalk and a jam of alarming proportions had halted traffic for several blocks. In time the policeman at the corner of Sixth and Hill awakened, and becoming aware of the mob, rushed forth to investigate. When he saw the long procession from the square, he charged the three in front who seemed to be the leaders, and shouted.

'Starting a riot, eh! Communist rally, eh! Where do you think you're going?'

'We're going to lunch,' the student replied congenially.

For an instant the policeman was startled out of his wits. 'Lunch?' His 25
face went slack and his mouth hung open. Then he got himself under control. 'Lunch! What is this? I suppose all of you are going to lunch,' he added sarcastically.

The student looked about at the crowd, then looked back. 'I don't know,' he confessed. 'I'm only speaking for the three of us.'

Shoving back among the others, the policeman snarled, 'Now don't tell me that you're going to lunch, too?'

A big, raw-boned fellow in overalls spat a stream of tobacco juice on the grass, and replied, 'That's right.'

Red-faced and inarticulate, the policeman took off his hat and scratched 30
his head. Never in the six years since he had been directing traffic at Sixth and Hill had he seen anyone leave Pershing Square for lunch. In fact, it had never occurred to him that they ate lunch. It sounded incredible. He wanted to do something. He felt that it was his duty to do something. But what? He was in a dilemma. He could not hinder them from going to lunch, if indeed they were going to lunch. Nor could he order them to move on, as they were already moving on. There was nothing for him to do but follow. So he fell in and followed.

The Negro, however, could not make up his mind. On Sixth Street, midway between Hill and Olive, he came to a halt. 'Listen,' he pointed out, 'these guys are used to seeing colored people down here. All the domestic workers who work out in Hollywood and Beverly and all out there get off the U car and come down here and catch their buses. It ain't like if it was somewhere on the West Side where they ain't used to seeing them.'

'What has that got to do with it?' the student asked.

'Naw, what I mean is this,' he explained. 'They're liable to serve me around here. And then you're going to think it's like that all over the city. And I know it ain't.' Pausing for an instant, he added another point, 'And besides, if I walk in there with you two guys, they're liable to serve me anyway. For all they know you guys might be some rich guys and I might be working for you; and if they refuse to serve me they might get in dutch with you. It ain't like some place in Hollywood where they wouldn't care.'

When they had stopped, the procession behind them which by then reached around the corner down Hill Street had also stopped. This was the chance for which the policeman had been waiting. 'Move on!' he shouted. 'Don't block the sidewalk! What d'ya think this is?'

They all returned to the square and took up the argument where they had dropped it. Only now, it was just one big mob in the center of the square, waiting for the Negro to make up his mind.

'You see, he doesn't want to do it,' the student was pointing out. 'That proves my point. They won't go into these places, but yet they say they're being discriminated against.'

Suddenly, the drifter was inspired. 'All right, I'll tell you, let's go to the Ritzmore.'

A hundred startled glances leveled on him, then lifted to the face of the brick and granite edifice across the street which seemed impregnated in rock-like respectability. The very audacity of the suggestion appealed to them. 'That's the place, let's go there,' they chimed.

'That's nonsense,' the student snapped angrily. 'He can't eat at the Ritzmore; he's not dressed correctly.'

'Can *you* eat there?' the Negro challenged. 'I mean just as you're dressed.'

The student was also clad in a sweater and trousers, although his were of a better quality and in better condition than the Negro's. For a moment he considered the question, then replied, 'To be fair, I don't know whether they would serve me or not. They might in the grill—'

'In the main dining room?' the drifter pressed.

Shaking his head, the student stated, 'I really don't know, but if they will serve any of us they will serve him.'

'Come on,' the drifter barked, taking the Negro by the arm, and they set forth for the Ritzmore, followed by every man in Pershing Square—the bindle-stiffs and the beggars and the bums and the big sisters, the clipped and the clippers, the old men who liked to sit in the midday sun and meditate.

Seeing them on the move again, the policeman hastened from his post to follow.

They crossed Olive Street, a ragged procession of gaunt, unshaven, unwashed humanity, led by two young white men and one young Negro, passed the two doormen, who, seeing the policeman among them, thought they were all being taken to the clink. They approached the brass and mahogany doorway unchallenged, pushed open the glass doors, and entered the classical splendor of the Ritzmore's main lounge.

Imagine the consternation among the well-bred, superbly clad, highly-heeled patrons; imagine the indignity of the room clerk as he pounded on his bell and yelled frantically, 'Front! Front! *Front!*' Had the furniture been animate, it would have fled in terror; and the fine Oriental rugs would have been humiliated unendurably.

Outraged, the house officer rushed to halt this smelly mob, but seeing among them the policeman, who by now had lost all capacity for speech, stood with his mouth gaped open, wondering if perhaps it wasn't just the effects of that last brandy he had enjoyed in '217,' after all. Stupidly, he reached out his hand to touch them to make certain they were real.

But before he could get his reflexes together, those in front had strolled past him and entered the main dining room, while, what seemed to him like thousands of others, pushed in from the street.

The student and the Negro and the drifter, along with ten or twelve oth- 50
ers, took seats at three vacant tables. In unison the diners turned one horrified stare in their direction, and arose in posthaste, only to be blocked at the doorway by a shoving mass of men, struggling for a ringside view.

From all over the dining room the waiters ran stumbling toward the rear, and went into a quick, alarmed huddle, turning every now and then to stare at the group and then going into another huddle. The head waiter rushed from the kitchen and joined the huddle; and then the *maître d'hotel* appeared and took his place. One by one the cooks, the first cook and the second cook and the third cook and the fourth cook on down to what seemed like the twenty-fourth cook (although some of them must have been dishwashers), stuck their heads through the pantry doorway and stared for a moment and then retired.

Finally, two waiters timidly advanced toward the tables and took their orders. Menus were passed about. 'You order first,' the student said to the Negro. However, as the menus were composed mostly of French words, the Negro could not identify anything but apple pie. So he ordered apple pie.

'I'll take apple pie, too,' the student said; and the drifter muttered, 'Make mine the same.'

Every one ordered apple pie.

One of the fellows standing in the doorway called back to those in the 55
lobby who could not see.

'They served him.'

'Did they serve him?'

'Yeah, they served him.'

'What did they serve him?'

'Apple pie.' 60

And it was thus proved by the gentlemen of Pershing Square that no discrimination exists in the beautiful city of Los Angeles. However, it so happened that the drifter was without funds, and the student found himself in the peculiar situation of having to pay off a bet which he had won.

HISAYE YAMAMOTO

Seventeen Syllables

(1949)

The first Rosie knew that her mother had taken to writing poems was one evening when she finished one and read it aloud for her daughter's approval. It was about cats, and Rosie pretended to understand it thoroughly and appreciate it no end, partly because she hesitated to disillusion her mother about the quantity and quality of Japanese she had learned in all the years now that she had been going to Japanese school every Saturday (and Wednesday, too, in the summer). Even so, her mother must have been skeptical about the depth of Rosie's understanding, because she explained afterwards about the kind of poem she was trying to write.

See, Rosie, she said, it was a *haiku*, a poem in which she must pack all her meaning into seventeen syllables only, which were divided into three lines of five, seven, and five syllables. In the one she had just read, she had tried to capture the charm of a kitten, as well as comment on the superstition that owning a cat of three colors meant good luck.

"Yes, yes, I understand. How utterly lovely," Rosie said, and her mother, either satisfied or seeing through the deception and resigned, went back to composing.

The truth was that Rosie was lazy; English lay ready on the tongue but Japanese had to be searched for and examined, and even then put forth tentatively (probably to meet with laughter). It was so much easier to say yes, yes, even when one meant no, no. Besides, this was what was in her mind to say: I was looking through one of your magazines from Japan last night, Mother, and towards the back I found some *haiku* in English that delighted me. There was one that made me giggle off and on until I fell asleep—

> It is morning, and lo!
> I lie awake, comme il faut,
> sighing for some dough.

Now, how to reach her mother, how to communicate the melancholy 5
song? Rosie knew formal Japanese by fits and starts, her mother had even less English, no French. It was much more possible to say yes, yes.

It developed that her mother was writing the *haiku* for a daily newspaper, the *Mainichi Shimbun*, that was published in San Francisco. Los Angeles, to be sure, was closer to the farming community in which the Hayashi family lived and several Japanese vernaculars were printed there, but Rosie's parents said they preferred the tone of the northern paper. Once a week, the *Mainichi* would have a section devoted to *haiku*, and her mother became an extravagant contributor, taking for herself the blossoming pen name, Ume Hanazono.

So Rosie and her father lived for a while with two women, her mother and Ume Hanazono. Her mother (Tome Hayashi by name) kept house, cooked, washed, and, along with her husband and the Carrascos, the Mexican family hired for the harvest, did her ample share of picking tomatoes out in the sweltering fields and boxing them in tidy strata in the cool packing shed. Ume Hanazono, who came to life after the dinner dishes were done, was an earnest, muttering stranger who often neglected speaking when spoken to and stayed busy at the parlor table as late as midnight scribbling with pencil on scratch paper or carefully copying characters on good paper with her fat, pale green Parker.

The new interest had some repercussions on the household routine. Before, Rosie had been accustomed to her parents and herself taking their hot baths early and going to bed almost immediately afterwards, unless her parents challenged each other to a game of flower cards or unless company dropped in. Now if her father wanted to play cards, he had to resort to solitaire (at which he always cheated fearlessly), and if a group of friends came over, it was bound to contain someone who was also writing *haiku*, and the small assemblage would be split in two, her father entertaining the non-literary members and her mother comparing ecstatic notes with the visiting poet.

If they went out, it was more of the same thing. But Ume Hanazono's life span, even for a poet's, was very brief—perhaps three months at most.

One night they went over to see the Hayano family in the neighboring 10
town to the west, an adventure both painful and attractive to Rosie. It was attractive because there were four Hayano girls, all lovely and each one named after a season of the year (Haru, Natsu, Aki, Fuyu), painful because something had been wrong with Mrs. Hayano ever since the birth of her first child. Rosie would sometimes watch Mrs. Hayano, reputed to have been the belle of her native village, making her way about a room, stooped, slowly shuffling, violently trembling (*always* trembling), and she would be reminded that this woman, in this same condition, had carried and given issue to three babies. She would look wonderingly at Mr. Hayano, handsome, tall, and strong, and she would look at her four pretty friends. But it was not a matter she could come to any decision about.

On this visit, however, Mrs. Hayano sat all evening in the rocker, as motionless and unobtrusive as it was possible for her to be, and Rosie found the greater part of the evening practically anaesthetic. Too, Rosie spent most of it in the girls' room, because Haru, the garrulous one, said almost as soon as the bows and other greetings were over, "Oh, you must see my new coat!"

It was a pale plaid of grey, sand, and blue, with an enormous collar, and Rosie, seeing nothing special in it, said, "Gee, how nice."

"Nice?" said Haru, indignantly. "Is that all you can say about it? It's gorgeous! And so cheap, too. Only seventeen-ninety-eight, because it was a sale. The saleslady said it was twenty-five dollars regular."

"Gee," said Rosie. Natsu, who never said much and when she said anything said it shyly, fingered the coat covetously and Haru pulled it away.

15 "Mine," she said, putting it on. She minced in the aisle between the two large beds and smiled happily. "Let's see how your mother likes it."

She broke into the front room and the adult conversation and went to stand in front of Rosie's mother, while the rest watched from the door. Rosie's mother was properly envious. "May I inherit it when you're through with it?"

Haru, pleased, giggled and said yes, she could, but Natsu reminded gravely from the door, "You promised me, Haru."

Everyone laughed but Natsu, who shamefacedly retreated into the bedroom. Haru came in laughing, taking off the coat. "We were only kidding, Natsu," she said. "Here, you try it on now."

After Natsu buttoned herself into the coat, inspected herself solemnly in the bureau mirror, and reluctantly shed it, Rosie, Aki, and Fuyu got their turns, and Fuyu, who was eight, drowned in it while her sisters and Rosie doubled up in amusement. They all went into the front room later, because Haru's mother quaveringly called to her to fix the tea and rice cakes and open a can of sliced peaches for everybody. Rosie noticed that her mother and Mr. Hayano were talking together at the little table—they were discussing a *haiku* that Mr. Hayano was planning to send to the *Mainichi*, while her father was sitting at one end of the sofa looking through a copy of *Life*, the new picture magazine. Occasionally, her father would comment on a photograph, holding it toward Mrs. Hayano and speaking to her as he always did—loudly, as though he thought someone such as she must surely be at least a trifle deaf also.

20 The five girls had their refreshments at the kitchen table, and it was while Rosie was showing the sisters her trick of swallowing peach slices without chewing (she chased each slippery crescent down with a swig of tea) that her father brought his empty teacup and untouched saucer to the sink and said, "Come on, Rosie, we're going home now."

"Already?" asked Rosie.

"Work tomorrow," he said.

He sounded irritated, and Rosie, puzzled, gulped one last yellow slice and stood up to go, while the sisters began protesting, as was their wont.

"We have to get up at five-thirty," he told them, going into the front room quickly, so that they did not have their usual chance to hang onto his hands and plead for an extension of time.

25 Rosie, following, saw that her mother and Mr. Hayano were sipping tea and still talking together, while Mrs. Hayano concentrated, quivering, on raising the handleless Japanese cup to her lips with both her hands and lowering it back to her lap. Her father, saying nothing, went out the door, onto the bright porch, and down the steps. Her mother looked up and asked, "Where is he going?"

"Where is he going?" Rosie said. "He said we were going home now."

"Going home?" Her mother looked with embarrassment at Mr. Hayano and his absorbed wife and then forced a smile. "He must be tired," she said.

Haru was not giving up yet. "May Rosie stay overnight?" she asked, and Natsu, Aki, and Fuyu came to reinforce their sister's plea by helping her make a circle around Rosie's mother. Rosie, for once having no desire to stay, was relieved when her mother, apologizing to the perturbed Mr. and Mrs. Hayano for her father's abruptness at the same time, managed to shake her head no at the quartet, kindly but adamant, so that they broke their circle and let her go.

Rosie's father looked ahead into the windshield as the two joined him. "I'm sorry," her mother said. "You must be tired." Her father, stepping on the starter, said nothing. "You know how I get when it's *haiku*," she continued, "I forget what time it is." He only grunted.

As they rode homeward silently, Rosie, sitting between, felt a rush of hate 30
for both—for her mother for begging, for her father for denying her mother. I wish this old Ford would crash, right now, she thought, then immediately, no, no, I wish my father would laugh, but it was too late: already the vision had passed through her mind of the green pick-up crumpled in the dark against one of the mighty eucalyptus trees they were just riding past, of the three contorted, bleeding bodies, one of them hers.

Rosie ran between two patches of tomatoes, her heart working more rambunctiously than she had ever known it to. How lucky it was that Aunt Taka and Uncle Gimpachi had come tonight, though, how very lucky. Otherwise she might not have really kept her half-promise to meet Jesus Carrasco. Jesus was going to be a senior in September at the same school she went to, and his parents were the ones helping with the tomatoes this year. She and Jesus, who hardly remembered seeing each other at Cleveland High where there were so many other people and two whole grades between them, had become great friends this summer—he always had a joke for her when he periodically drove the loaded pick-up up from the fields to the shed where she was usually sorting while her mother and father did the packing, and they laughed a great deal together over infinitesimal repartee during the afternoon break for chilled watermelon or ice cream in the shade of the shed.

What she enjoyed most was racing him to see which could finish picking a double row first. He, who could work faster, would tease her by slowing down until she thought she would surely pass him this time, then speeding up furiously to leave her several sprawling vines behind. Once he had made her screech hideously by crossing over, while her back was turned, to a place atop the tomatoes in her green-stained bucket a truly monstrous, pale green worm (it had looked more like an infant snake). And it was when they had finished a contest this morning, after she had pantingly pointed a green finger at the immature tomatoes evident in the lugs at the end of his row and he had returned the accusation (with justice), that he had startlingly brought up the matter of their possibly meeting outside the range of both their parents' dubious eyes.

"What for?" she had asked.

"I've got a secret I want to tell you," he said.

"Tell me now," she demanded. 35

"It won't be ready till tonight," he said.

She laughed. "Tell me tomorrow then."

"It'll be gone tomorrow," he threatened.

"Well, for seven hakes, what is it?" she had asked, more than twice, and when he had suggested that the packing shed would be an appropriate place to find out, she had cautiously answered maybe. She had not been certain she was going to keep the appointment until the arrival of mother's sister and her husband. Their coming seemed a sort of signal of permission, of grace, and she had definitely made up her mind to lie and leave as she was bowing them welcome.

So as soon as everyone appeared settled back for the evening, she an- 40
nounced loudly that she was going to the privy outside, "I'm going to the *benjo!*" and slipped out the door. And now that she was actually on her way, her heart pumped in such an undisciplined way that she could hear it with her ears. It's because I'm running, she told herself, slowing to a walk. The shed was up ahead, one more patch away, in the middle of the fields. Its bulk, looming in the dimness, took on a sinisterness that was funny when Rosie reminded herself that it was only a wooden frame with a canvas roof and three canvas walls that made a slapping noise on breezy days.

Jesus was sitting on the narrow plank that was the sorting platform and she went around to the other side and jumped backwards to seat herself on the rim of a packing stand. "Well, tell me," she said without greeting, thinking her voice sounded reassuringly familiar.

"I saw you coming out the door," Jesus said. "I heard you running part of the way, too."

"Uh-huh," Rosie said. "Now tell me the secret."

"I was afraid you wouldn't come," he said.

Rosie delved around on the chicken-wire bottom of the stall for number 45
two tomatoes, ripe, which she was sitting beside, and came up with a left-over that felt edible. She bit into it and began sucking out the pulp and seeds. "I'm here," she pointed out.

"Rosie, are you sorry you came?"

"Sorry? What for?" she said. "You said you were going to tell me something."

"I will, I will," Jesus said, but his voice contained disappointment, and Rosie fleetingly felt the older of the two, realizing a brand-new power which vanished without category under her recognition.

"I have to go back in a minute," she said. "My aunt and uncle are here from Wintersburg. I told them I was going to the privy."

Jesus laughed. "You funny thing," he said. "You slay me!" 50

"Just because you have a bathroom *inside*," Rosie said. "Come on, tell me."

Chuckling, Jesus came around to lean on the stand facing her. They still could not see each other very clearly, but Rosie noticed that Jesus became very sober again as he took the hollow tomato from her hand and dropped it back into the stall. When he took hold of her empty hand, she could find no words to protest; her vocabulary had become distressingly constricted and she thought desperately that all that remained intact now was yes and no and oh, and even these few sounds would not easily out. Thus, kissed by Jesus, Rosie fell for the first time entirely victim to a helplessness delectable beyond speech. But the terrible, beautiful sensation lasted no more than a second, and the reality of Jesus' lips and tongue and teeth and hands made her pull away with such strength that she nearly tumbled.

Rosie stopped running as she approached the lights from the windows of home. How long since she had left? She could not guess, but gasping yet, she went to the privy in the back and locked herself in. Her own breathing deafened her in the dark, close space, and she sat and waited until she could hear at last the nightly calling of the frogs and crickets. Even then, all she could think to say was oh, my, and the pressure of Jesus' face against her face would not leave.

No one had missed her in the parlor, however, and Rosie walked in and through quickly, announcing that she was next going to take a bath. "Your father's in the bathhouse," her mother said, and Rosie, in her room, recalled that she had not seen him when she entered. There had been only Aunt Taka and Uncle Gimpachi with her mother at the table, drinking tea. She got her robe and straw sandals and crossed the parlor again to go outside. Her mother was telling them about the *haiku* competition in the *Mainichi* and the poem she had entered.

55 Rosie met her father coming out of the bathhouse. "Are you through Father?" she asked. "I was going to ask you to scrub my back."

"Scrub your own back," he said shortly, going toward the main house.

"What have I done now?" she yelled after him. She suddenly felt like doing a lot of yelling. But he did not answer, and she went into the bathhouse. Turning on the dangling light, she removed her denims and T-shirt and threw them in the big carton for dirty clothes standing next to the washing machine. Her other things she took with her into the bath compartment to wash after her bath. After she had scooped a basin of hot water from the square wooden tub, she sat on the grey cement of the floor and soaped herself at exaggerated leisure, singing "Red Sails in the Sunset" at the top of her voice and using da-da-da where she suspected her words. Then, standing up, still singing, for she was possessed by the notion that any attempt now to analyze would result in spoilage and she believed that the larger her volume the less she would be able to hear herself think, she obtained more hot water and poured it on until she was free of lather. Only then did she allow herself to step into the steaming vat, one leg first, then the remainder of her body inch by inch until the water no longer stung and she could move around at will.

She took a long time soaking, afterwards remembering to go around outside to stoke the embers of the tin-lined fireplace beneath the tub and to throw on a few more sticks so that the water might keep its heat for her mother, and when she finally returned to the parlor, she found her mother still talking *haiku* with her aunt and uncle, the three of them on another round of tea. Her father was nowhere in sight.

At Japanese school the next day (Wednesday, it was), Rosie was grave and giddy by turns. Preoccupied at her desk in the row for students on Book Eight, she made up for it at recess by performing wild mimicry for the benefit of her friend Chizuko. She held her nose and whined a witticism or two in what she considered was the manner of Fred Allen; she assumed intoxication and a

British accent to go over the climax of the Rudy Vallee recording of the pub conversation about William Ewart Gladstone; she was the child Shirley Temple piping, "On the Good Ship Lollipop"; she was the gentleman soprano of the Four Inkspots trilling, "If I Didn't Care." And she felt reasonably satisfied when Chizuko wept and gasped, "Oh, Rosie, you ought to be in the movies!"

Her father came after her at noon, bringing her sandwiches of minced ham and two nectarines to eat while she rode, so that she could pitch right into the sorting when they got home. The lugs were piling up, he said, and the ripe tomatoes in them would probably have to be taken to the cannery tomorrow if they were not ready for the produce haulers tonight. "This heat's not doing them any good. And we've got no time for a break today."

It *was* hot, probably the hottest day of the year, and Rosie's blouse stuck damply to her back even under the protection of the canvas. But she worked as efficiently as a flawless machine and kept the stalls heaped, with one part of her mind listening in to the parental murmuring about the heat and the tomatoes and with another part planning the exact words she would say to Jesus when he drove up with the first load of the afternoon. But when at last she saw that the pick-up was coming, her hands went beserk and the tomatoes starting falling into the wrong stalls, and her father said, "Hey, hey! Rosie, watch what you're doing!"

"Well, I have to go to the *benjo*," she said, hiding panic.

"Go in the weeds over there," he said, only half-joking.

"Oh, Father!" she protested.

"Oh, go on home," her mother said. "We'll make out for a while."

In the privy Rosie peered through a knothole toward the fields, watching as much as she could of Jesus. Happily she thought she saw him look in the direction of the house from time to time before he finished unloading and went back toward the patch where his mother and father worked. As she was heading for the shed, a very presentable black car purred up the dirt driveway to the house and its driver motioned to her. Was this the Hayashi home, he wanted to know. She nodded. Was she a Hayashi? Yes, she said, thinking that he was a good-looking man. He got out of the car with a huge, flat package and she saw that he warmly wore a business suit. "I have something here for your mother then," he said, in a more elegant Japanese than she was used to.

She told him where her mother was and he came along with her, patting his face with an immaculate white handkerchief and saying something about the coolness of San Francisco. To her surprised mother and father, he bowed and introduced himself as, among other things, the *haiku* editor of the *Mainichi Shimbun*, saying that since he had been coming as far as Los Angeles anyway, he had decided to bring her the first prize she had won in the recent contest.

"First prize?" her mother echoed, believing and not believing, pleased and overwhelmed. Handed the package with a bow, she bobbed her head up and down numerous times to express her utter gratitude.

"It is nothing much," he added, "but I hope it will serve as a token of our great appreciation for your contributions and our great admiration of your considerable talent."

"I am not worthy," she said, falling easily into his style. "It is I who should 70
make some sign of my humble thanks for being permitted to contribute."

"No, no, to the contrary," he said, bowing again.

But Rosie's mother insisted, and then saying that she knew she was being unorthodox, she asked if she might open the package because her curiosity was so great. Certainly she might. In fact, he would like her reaction to it, for personally, it was one of his favorite *Hiroshiges.*

Rosie thought it was a pleasant picture, which looked to have been sketched with delicate quickness. There were pink clouds, containing some graceful calligraphy, and a sea that was a pale blue except at the edges, containing four sampans with indications of people in them. Pines edged the water and on the far-off beach there was a cluster of thatched huts towered over by pine-dotted mountains of grey and blue. The frame was scalloped and gilt.

After Rosie's mother pronounced it without peer and somewhat prodded her father into nodding agreement, she said Mr. Kuroda must at least have a cup of tea after coming all this way, and although Mr. Kuroda did not want to impose, he soon agreed that a cup of tea would be refreshing and went along with her to the house, carrying the picture for her.

"Ha, your mother's crazy!" Rosie's father said, and Rosie laughed uneasily 75
as she resumed judgment on the tomatoes. She had emptied six lugs when he broke into an imaginary conversation with Jesus to tell her to go and remind her mother of the tomatoes, and she went slowly.

Mr. Kuroda was in his shirtsleeves expounding some *haiku* theory as he munched a rice cake, and her mother was rapt. Abashed in the great man's presence, Rosie stood next to her mother's chair until her mother looked up inquiringly, and then she started to whisper the message, but her mother pushed her gently away and reproached, "You are not being very polite to our guest."

"Father says the tomatoes . . ." Rosie said aloud, smiling foolishly.

"Tell him I shall only be a minute," her mother said, speaking the language of Mr. Kuroda.

When Rosie carried the reply to her father, he did not seem to hear and she said again, "Mother says she'll be back in a minute."

"All right, all right," he nodded, and they worked again in silence. But 80
suddenly, her father uttered an incredible noise, exactly like the cork of a bottle popping, and the next Rosie knew, he was stalking angrily toward the house, almost running in fact, and she chased after him crying, "Father! Father! What are you going to do?"

He stopped long enough to order her back to the shed. "Never mind!" he shouted, "Get on with the sorting!"

And from the place in the fields where she stood, frightened and vacillating, Rosie saw her father enter the house. Soon Mr. Kuroda came out alone, putting on his coat. Mr. Kuroda got into his car and backed out down the driveway onto the highway. Next her father emerged, also alone, something in his arms (it was the picture, she realized), and, going over to the bathhouse woodpile, he threw the picture on the ground and picked up the axe. Smashing the picture, glass and all (she heard the explosion faintly), he reached over for the kerosene that was used to encourage the bath fire and poured it over the wreckage. I am dreaming, Rosie said to herself, I am dreaming, but her father, having made sure that his act of cremation was irrevocable, was even then returning to the fields.

Rosie ran past him and toward the house. What had become of her mother? She burst into the parlor and found her mother at the back window watching the dying fire. They watched together until there remained only a feeble smoke under the blazing sun. Her mother was very calm.

"Do you know why I married your father?" she said without turning.

85 "No," said Rosie. It was the most frightening question she had ever been called upon to answer. Don't tell me now, she wanted to say, tell me tomorrow, tell me next week, don't tell me today. But she knew she would be told now, that the telling would combine with the other violence of the hot afternoon to level her life, her world to the very ground.

It was like a story out of the magazines illustrated in sepia, which she had consumed so greedily for a period until the information had somehow reached her that those wretchedly unhappy autobiographies, offered to her as the testimonials of living men and women, were largely inventions: Her mother, at nineteen, had come to America and married her father as an alternative to suicide.

At eighteen she had been in love with the first son of one of the well-to-do families in her village. The two had met whenever and wherever they could, secretly, because it would not have done for his family to see him favor her—her father had no money; he was a drunkard and a gambler besides. She had learned she was with child; an excellent match had already been arranged for her lover. Despised by her family, she had given premature birth to a stillborn son, who would be seventeen now. Her family did not turn her out, but she could no longer project herself in any direction without refreshing in them the memory of her indiscretion. She wrote to Aunt Taka, her favorite sister in America, threatening to kill herself if Aunt Taka would not send for her. Aunt Taka hastily arranged a marriage with a young man of whom she knew, but lately arrived from Japan, a young man of simple mind, it was said, but of kindly heart. The young man was never told why his unseen betrothed was so eager to hasten the day of meeting.

The story was told perfectly, with neither groping for words nor untoward passion. It was as though her mother had memorized it by heart, reciting it to herself so many times over that its nagging vileness had long since gone.

"I had a brother then?" Rosie asked, for this was what seemed to matter now; she would think about the other later, she assured herself, pushing back the illumination which threatened all that darkness that had hitherto been merely mysterious or even glamorous. "A half-brother?"

90 "Yes."

"I would have liked a brother," she said.

Suddenly, her mother knelt on the floor and took her by the wrists. "Rosie," she said urgently, "Promise me you will never marry!" Shocked more by the request than the revelation, Rosie stared at her mother's face. Jesus, Jesus, she called silently, not certain whether she was invoking the help of the son of the Carrascos or of God, until there returned sweetly the memory of

Jesus' hand, how it had touched her and where. Still her mother waited for an answer, holding her wrists so tightly that her hands were going numb. She tried to pull free. Promise her mother whispered fiercely, promise. Yes, yes, I promise, Rosie said. But for an instant she turned away, and her mother, hearing the familiar glib agreement, released her. Oh, you, you, you, her eyes and twisted mouth said, you fool. Rosie, covering her face, began at last to cry, and the embrace and consoling hand came much later than she expected.

Richard Wright

The Man Who Was Almost a Man *(1961)*

Dave struck out across the fields, looking homeward through paling light. Whut's the use talkin wid em niggers in the field? Anyhow, his mother was putting supper on the table. Them niggers can't understan nothing. One of these days he was going to get a gun and practice shooting, then they couldn't talk to him as though he were a little boy. He slowed, looking at the ground. Shucks, Ah ain scareda them even ef they are biggern me! Aw, Ah know whut Ahma do. Ahm going by ol Joe's sto n git that Sears Roebuck catlog n look at them guns. Mebbe Ma will lemme buy one when she gits mah pay from ol man Hawkins. Ahma beg her t gimme some money. Ahm ol ernough to hava gun. Ahm seventeen. Almost a man. He strode, feeling his long loose-jointed limbs. Shucks, a man oughta hava little gun aftah he done worked hard all day.

He came in sight of Joe's store. A yellow lantern glowed on the front porch. He mounted steps and went through the screen door, hearing it bang behind him. There was a strong smell of coal oil and mackerel fish. He felt very confident until he saw fat Joe walk in through the rear door, then his courage began to ooze.

"Howdy, Dave! Whutcha want?"

"How yuh, Mistah Joe? Aw, Ah don wanna buy nothing. Ah just wanted t see ef yuhd lemme look at tha catlog erwhile."

"Sure! You wanna see it here?" 5

"Nawsuh. Ah wants t take it home wid me. Ah'll bring it back termorrow when Ah come in from the fiels."

"You plannin on buying something?"

"Yessuh."

"Your ma lettin you have your own money now?"

"Shucks. Mistah Joe, Ahm gittin t be a man like anybody else!" 10

Joe laughed and wiped his greasy white face with a red bandanna.

"Whut you plannin on buyin?"

Dave looked at the floor, scratched his head, scratched his thigh, and smiled. Then he looked up shyly.

"Ah'll tell yuh, Mistah Joe, ef yuh promise yuh won't tell."

"I promise." 15

"Waal, Ahma buy a gun."

"A gun? What you want with a gun?"

"Ah wanna keep it."

"You ain't nothing but a boy. You don't need a gun."

"Aw, lemme have the catlog, Mistah Joe. Ah'll bring it back." 20

Joe walked through the rear door. Dave was elated. He looked around at barrels of sugar and flour. He heard Joe coming back. He craned his neck to see if he were bringing the book. Yeah, he's got it. Gawddog, he's got it!

"Here, but be sure you bring it back. It's the only one I got."

"Sho, Mistah Joe."

"Say, if you wanna buy a gun, why don't you buy one from me? I gotta gun to sell."

"Will it shoot?" 25

"Sure it'll shoot."

"Whut kind is it?"

"Oh, it's kinda old . . . a left-hand Wheeler. A pistol. A big one."

"Is it got bullets in it?"

"It's loaded." 30

"Kin Ah see it?"

"Where's your money?"

"What yuh wan fer it?"

"I'll let you have it for two dollars."

"Just two dollahs? Shucks, Ah could buy tha when Ah git mah pay." 35

"I'll have it here when you want it."

"Awright, suh. Ah be in fer it."

He went through the door, hearing it slam again behind him. Ahma git some money from Ma n buy me a gun! Only two dollahs! He tucked the thick catalogue under his arm and hurried.

"Where yuh been, boy?" His mother held a steaming dish of black-eyed peas.

"Aw, Ma, Ah jus stopped down the road t talk wid the boys." 40

"Yuh know bettah t keep suppah waitin."

He sat down, resting the catalogue on the edge of the table.

"Yuh git up from there and git to the well n wash yosef! Ah ain feedin no hogs in mah house!"

She grabbed his shoulder and pushed him. He stumbled out of the room, then came back to get the catalogue.

"Whut this?" 45

"Aw, Ma, it's jusa catlog."

"Who yuh git it from?"

"From Joe, down at the sto."

"Waal, thas good. We kin use it in the outhouse."

"Naw, Ma." He grabbed for it. "Gimme ma catlog, Ma." 50

She held onto it and glared at him.

"Quit hollerin at me! Whut's wrong wid yuh? Yuh crazy?"

"But Ma, please. It ain mine! It's Joe's! He tol me t bring it back t im termorrow."

She gave up the book. He stumbled down the back steps, hugging the thick book under his arm. When he had splashed water on his face and hands, he groped back to the kitchen and fumbled in a corner for the towel. He bumped into a chair; it clattered to the floor. The catalogue sprawled at his feet. When he had dried his eyes he snatched up the book and held it again under his arm. His mother stood watching him.

"Now, ef yuh gonna act a fool over that ol book, Ah'll take it n burn it up."

"Naw, Ma, please."

"Waal, set down n be still!"

He sat down and drew the oil lamp close. He thumbed page after page, unaware of the food his mother set on the table. His father came in. Then his small brother.

"Whutcha got there, Dave?" his father asked.

"Jusa catlog," he answered, not looking up.

"Yeah, here they is!" His eyes glowed at blue-and-black revolvers. He glanced up, feeling sudden guilt. His father was watching him. He eased the book under the table and rested it on his knees. After the blessing was asked, he ate. He scooped up peas and swallowed fat meat without chewing. Buttermilk helped to wash it down. He did not want to mention money before his father. He would do much better by cornering his mother when she was alone. He looked at his father uneasily out of the edge of his eye.

"Boy, how come yuh don quit foolin wid tha book n eat yo suppah?"

"Yessuh."

"How you n ol man Hawkins gitten erlong?"

"Suh?"

"Can't yuh hear? Why don yuh lissen? Ah ast yu how wiz yuh n ol man Hawkins gittin erlong?"

"Oh, swell, Pa. Ah plows mo lan than anybody over there."

"Waal, yuh oughta keep you mind on whut yuh doin."

"Yessuh."

He poured his plate full of molasses and sopped it up slowly with a chunk of cornbread. When his father and brother had left the kitchen, he still sat and looked again at the guns in the catalogue, longing to muster courage enough to present his case to his mother. Lawd, ef Ah only had tha pretty one! He could almost feel the slickness of the weapon with his fingers. If he had a gun like that he would polish it and keep it shining so it would never rust. N Ah'd keep it loaded, by Gawd!

"Ma?" His voice was hesitant.

"Hunh?"

"Ol man Hawkins give yuh mah money yit?"

"Yeah, but ain no usa yuh thinking bout throwin nona it erway. Ahm keeping tha money sos yuh kin have cloes t go to school this winter."

He rose and went to her side with the open catalogue in his palms. She was washing dishes, her head bent low over a pan. Shyly he raised the book. When he spoke, his voice was husky, faint.

"Ma, Gawd knows Ah wans one of these."

"One of whut?" she asked, not raising her eyes.

"One of these," he said again, not daring even to point. She glanced up at the page, then at him with wide eyes.

"Nigger, is yuh gone plumb crazy?"

"Aw, Ma—"

"Git outta here! Don yuh talk t me bout no gun! Yuh a fool!"

"Ma, Ah kin buy one fer two dollahs."

"Not ef Ah knows it, yuh ain!"

"But yuh promised me one—"

"Ah don care what Ah promised! Yuh ain nothing but a boy yit!"

"Ma, ef yuh lemme buy one Ah'll *never* ast yuh fer nothing no mo."

"Ah tol yuh t git outta here! Yuh ain gonna toucha penny of tha money fer no gun! Thas how come Ah has Mistah Hawkins t pay yo wages t me, cause ah knows yuh ain got no sense."

"But, Ma, we needa gun. Pa ain got no gun. We needa gun in the house. Yuh kin never tell whut might happen."

"Now don yuh try to maka fool outta me, boy! Ef we did hava gun, yuh wouldn't have it!"

He laid the catalogue down and slipped his arm around her waist.

"Aw, Ma, Ah done worked hard alla summer n ain ast yuh fer nothing, is Ah, now?"

"Thas whut yuh spose t do!"

"But Ma, Ah wans a gun. Yuh kin lemme have two dollahs outta mah money. Please, Ma. I kin give it to Pa. . . . Please, Ma! Ah loves yuh, Ma."

When she spoke her voice came soft and low.

"What yu wan wida gun, Dave? Yuh don need no gun. Yuh'll git in trouble. N ef yo pa jus thought Ah let yuh have money t buy a gun he'd hava fit."

"Ah'll hide it, Ma. It ain but two dollahs."

"Lawd, chil, whut's wrong wid yuh?"

"Ain nothin wrong, Ma. Ahm almos a man now. Ah wans a gun."

"Who gonna sell yuh a gun?"

"Ol Joe at the sto."

"N it don cos but two dollahs?"

"Thas all, Ma. Jus two dollahs. Please, Ma."

She was stacking the plates away; her hands moved slowly, reflectively. Dave kept an anxious silence. Finally, she turned to him.

"Ah'll let yuh git tha gun ef yuh promise me one thing."

"What's tha, Ma?"

"Yuh bring it straight back t me, yuh hear? It be fer Pa."

"Yessum! Lemme go now, Ma."

She stooped, turned slightly to one side, raised the hem of her dress, rolled down the top of her stocking, and came up with a slender wad of bills.

"Here," she said. "Lawd knows yuh don need no gun. But yer pa does. Yuh bring it right back t me, yuh hear? Ahma put it up. Now ef yuh don, Ahma have yuh pa lick yuh so hard yuh won fergit it."

"Yessum."

He took the money, ran down the steps, and across the yard.

"Dave! Yuuuuuh Daaaaave!"

He heard, but he was not going to stop now. "Now, Lawd!"

The first movement he made the following morning was to reach under his pillow for the gun. In the gray light of dawn he held it loosely, feeling a sense of power. Could kill a man with a gun like this. Kill anybody, black or white. And if he were holding his gun in his hand, nobody could run over him; they would have to respect him. It was a big gun, with a long barrel and a heavy handle. He raised and lowered it in his hand, marveling at its weight.

He had not come straight home with it as his mother had asked; instead 115
he had stayed out in the fields, holding the weapon in his hand, aiming it now and then at some imaginary foe. But he had not fired it; he had been afraid that his father might hear. Also he was not sure he knew how to fire it.

To avoid surrendering the pistol he had not come into the house until he knew that they were all asleep. When his mother had tiptoed to his bedside late that night and demanded the gun, he had first played possum; then he had told her that the gun was hidden outdoors, that he would bring it to her in the morning. Now he lay turning it slowly in his hands. He broke it, took out the cartridges, felt them, and then put them back.

He slid out of bed, got a long strip of old flannel from a trunk, wrapped the gun in it, and tied it to his naked thigh while it was still loaded. He did not go in to breakfast. Even though it was not yet daylight, he started for Jim Hawkins' plantation. Just as the sun was rising he reached the barns where the mules and plows were kept.

"Hey! That you, Dave?"

He turned. Jim Hawkins stood eying him suspiciously.

"What're yuh doing here so early?" 120

"Ah didn't know Ah wuz gittin up so early, Mistah Hawkins. Ah was fixin t hitch up ol Jenny n take her t the fiels."

"Good. Since you're so early, how about plowing that stretch down by the woods?"

"Suits me, Mistah Hawkins."

"O.K. Go to it!"

He hitched Jenny to a plow and started across the fields. Hot dog! This 125
was just what he wanted. If he could get down by the woods, he could shoot his gun and nobody would hear. He walked behind the plow, hearing the traces creaking, feeling the gun tied tight to his thigh.

When he reached the woods, he plowed two whole rows before he decided to take out the gun. Finally, he stopped, looked in all directions, then untied the gun and held it in his hand. He turned to the mule and smiled.

"Know whut this is, Jenny? Naw, yuh wouldn know! Yuhs jusa ol mule! Anyhow, this is a gun, n it kin shoot, by Gawd!"

He held the gun at arm's length. Whut t hell, Ahma shoot this thing! He looked at Jenny again.

"Lissen here, Jenny! When Ah pull this ol trigger, Ah don wan yuh t run n acka fool now!"

Jenny stood with head down, her short ears pricked straight. Dave walked 130 off about twenty feet, held the gun far out from him at arm's length, and turned his head. Hell, he told himself, Ah ain afraid. The gun felt loose in his fingers; he waved it wildly for a moment. Then he shut his eyes and tightened his forefinger. Bloom! A report half deafened him and he thought his right hand was torn from his arm. He heard Jenny whinnying and galloping over the field, and he found himself on his knees, squeezing his fingers hard between his legs. His hand was numb; he jammed it into his mouth, trying to warm it, trying to stop the pain. The gun lay at his feet. He did not quite know what had happened. He stood up and stared at the gun as though it were a living thing. He gritted his teeth and kicked the gun. Yuh almos broke mah arm! He turned to look for Jenny; she was far over the fields, tossing her head and kicking wildly.

"Hol on there, ol mule!"

When he caught up with her she stood trembling, walling her big white eyes at him. The plow was far away; the traces had broken. Then Dave stopped short, looking, not believing. Jenny was bleeding. Her left side was red and wet with blood. He went closer. Lawd, have mercy! Wondah did Ah shoot this mule? He grabbed for Jenny's mane. She flinched, snorted, whirled, tossing her head.

"Hol on now! Hol on."

Then he saw the hole in Jenny's side, right between the ribs. It was round, wet, red. A crimson stream streaked down the front leg, flowing fast. Good Gawd! Ah wuzn't shootin at tha mule. He felt panic. He knew he had to stop that blood, or Jenny would bleed to death. He had never seen so much blood in all his life. He chased the mule for half a mile, trying to catch her. Finally she stopped, breathing hard, stumpy tail half arched. He caught her mane and led her back to where the plow and gun lay. Then he stopped and grabbed handfuls of damp black earth and tried to plug the bullet hole. Jenny shuddered, whinnied, and broke from him.

"Hol on! Hol on now!" 135

He tried to plug it again, but blood came anyhow. His fingers were hot and sticky. He rubbed dirt into his palms, trying to dry them. Then again he attempted to plug the bullet hole, but Jenny shied away, kicking her heels high. He stood helpless. He had to do something. He ran at Jenny; she dodged him. He watched a red stream of blood flow down Jenny's leg and form a bright pool at her feet.

"Jenny . . . Jenny," he called weakly.

His lips trembled. She's bleeding t death! He looked in the direction of home, wanting to go back, wanting to get help. But he saw the pistol lying in the damp black clay. He had a queer feeling that if he only did something, this would not be; Jenny would not be there bleeding to death.

When he went to her this time, she did not move. She stood with sleepy, dreamy eyes; and when he touched her she gave a low-pitched whinny and knelt to the ground, her front knees slopping in blood.

"Jenny . . . Jenny . . ." he whispered. 140

For a long time she held her neck erect; then her head sank, slowly. Her ribs swelled with a mighty heave and she went over.

Dave's stomach felt empty, very empty. He picked up the gun and held it gingerly between his thumb and forefinger. He buried it at the foot of a tree. He took a stick to cover the pool of blood with dirt—but what was the use? There was Jenny lying with her mouth open and her eyes walled and glassy. He could not tell Jim Hawkins he had shot his mule. But he had to tell something. Yeah, Ah'll tell em Jenny started gittin wil n fell on the joint of the plow. . . . But that would hardly happen to a mule. He walked across the field slowly, head down.

It was sunset. Two of Jim Hawkins' men were over near the edge of the woods digging a hole in which to bury Jenny. Dave was surrounded by a knot of people, all of whom were looking down at the dead mule.

"I don't see how in the world it happened," said Jim Hawkins for the tenth time.

The crowd parted and Dave's mother, father, and small brother pushed 145
into the center.

"Where Dave?" his mother called.

"There he is," said Jim Hawkins.

His mother grabbed him.

"Whut happened, Dave? Whut yuh done?"

"Nothin." 150

"C mon, boy, talk," his father said.

Dave took a deep breath and told the story he knew nobody believed.

"Waal," he drawled. "Ah brung ol Jenny down here sos Ah could do mah plowin. Ah plowed bout two rows, just like yuh see." He stopped and pointed at the long rows of upturned earth. "Then somethin musta been wrong wid ol Jenny. She wouldn ack right a-tall. She started snortin n kickin her heels. Ah tried t hol her, but she pulled erway, rearin n goin in. Then when the point of the plow was stickin up in the air, she swung erroun n twisted herself back on it. . . . She stuck herself n started t bleed. N fo Ah could do anything, she wuz dead."

"Did you ever hear of anything like that in all your life?" asked Jim Hawkins.

There were white and black standing in the crowd. They murmured. 155
Dave's mother came close to him and looked hard into his face. "Tell the truth, Dave," she said.

"Looks like a bullet hole to me," said one man.

"Dave, whut yuh do wid the gun?" his mother asked.

The crowd surged in, looking at him. He jammed his hands into his pockets, shook his head slowly from left to right, and backed away. His eyes were wide and painful.

"Did he hava gun?" asked Jim Hawkins.

"By Gawd, Ah tol yuh tha wuz a gun wound," said a man, slapping his thigh. 160

His father caught his shoulders and shook him till his teeth rattled.

"Tell whut happened, yuh rascal! Tell whut. . . ."

Dave looked at Jenny's stiff legs and began to cry.

"Whut yuh do wid tha gun?" his mother asked.

"What wuz he doin wida gun?" his father asked.

"Come on and tell the truth," said Hawkins. "Ain't nobody going to hurt you. . . ."

His mother crowded close to him.

"Did yuh shoot tha mule, Dave?"

Dave cried, seeing blurred white and black faces.

"Ahh ddinn gggo tt sshooot hher . . . Ah ssswear ffo Gawd Ahh ddin. . . . Ah wuz a-tryin t sssee ef the old gggun would sshoot—"

"Where yuh git the gun from?" his father asked.

"Ah got it from Joe, at the sto."

"Where yuh git the money?"

"Ma give it t me."

"He kept worryin me, Bob. Ah had t. Ah tol im t bring the gun right back t me. . . . It was fer yuh, the gun."

"But how yuh happen to shoot that mule?" asked Jim Hawkins.

"Ah wuzn shootin at the mule, Mistah Hawkins. The gun jumped when Ah pulled the trigger. . . . N fo Ah knowed anythin Jenny was there a-bleedin."

Somebody in the crowd laughed. Jim Hawkins walked close to Dave and looked into his face.

"Well, looks like you have bought you a mule, Dave."

"Ah swear fo Gawd, Ah didn go t kill the mule, Mistah Hawkins!"

"But you killed her!"

All the crowd was laughing now. They stood on tiptoe and poked heads over one another's shoulders.

"Well, boy, looks like yuh done bought a dead mule! Hahaha!"

"Ain tha ershame."

"Hohohohoho."

Dave stood, head down, twisting his feet in the dirt.

"Well, you needn't worry about it, Bob," said Jim Hawkins to Dave's father. "Just let the boy keep on working and pay me two dollars a month."

"Whut yuh wan fer yo mule, Mistah Hawkins?"

Jim Hawkins screwed up his eyes.

"Fifty dollars."

"Whut yuh do wid tha gun?" Dave's father demanded.

Dave said nothing.

"Yuh wan me t take a tree n beat yuh till yuh talk!"

"Nawsuh!"

"Whut yuh do wid it?"

"Ah throwed it erway."

"Where?"

"Ah . . . Ah throwed it in the creek."

"Waal, c mon home. N firs thing in the mawnin git to tha creek n fin tha gun."

"Yessuh."

"Whut yuh pay fer it?"

"Two dollahs."

"Take tha gun n git yo money back n carry it to Mistah Hawkins, yuh hear? N don fergit Ahma lam you black bottom good fer this! Now march yosef on home, suh!"

Dave turned and walked slowly. He heard people laughing. Dave glared, his eyes welling with tears. Hot anger bubbled in him. Then he swallowed and stumbled on.

That night Dave did not sleep. He was glad that he had gotten out of kill- 205
ing the mule so easily, but he was hurt. Something hot seemed to turn over inside him each time he remembered how they had laughed. He tossed on his bed, feeling his hard pillow. N Pa says he's gonna beat me. . . . He remembered other beatings, and his back quivered. Naw, naw, Ah sho don wan im t beat me tha way no mo. Dam em all! Nobody ever gave him anything. All he did was work. They treat me like a mule, n then they beat me. He gritted his teeth. N Ma had t tell on me.

Well, if he had to, he would take old man Hawkins that two dollars. But that meant selling the gun. And he wanted to keep that gun. Fifty dollars for a dead mule.

He turned over, thinking how he had fired the gun. He had an itch to fire it again. Ef other men kin shoota gun, by Gawd, Ah kin! He was still, listening. Mebbe they all sleepin now. The house was still. He heard the soft breathing of his brother. Yes, now! He would go down and get that gun and see if he could fire it! He eased out of bed and slipped into overalls.

The moon was bright. He ran almost all the way to the edge of the woods. He stumbled over the ground, looking for the spot where he had buried the gun. Yeah, here it is. Like a hungry dog scratching for a bone, he pawed it up. He puffed his black cheeks and blew dirt from the trigger and barrel. He broke it and found four cartridges unshot. He looked around; the fields were filled with silence and moonlight. He clutched the gun stiff and hard in his fingers. But, as soon as he wanted to pull the trigger, he shut his eyes and turned his head. Naw, Ah can't shoot wid mah eyes closed n mah head turned. With effort he held his eyes open; then he squeezed. *Blooooom!* He was stiff, not breathing. The gun was still in his hands. Dammit, he'd done it! He fired again. *Blooooom!* He smiled. *Blooooom! Blooooom! Click, click.* There! It was empty. If anybody could shoot a gun, he could. He put the gun into his hip pocket and started across the fields.

When he reached the top of a ridge he stood straight and proud in the moonlight, looking at Jim Hawkins' big white house, feeling the gun sagging in his pocket. Lawd, ef Ah had just one mo bullet Ah'd taka shot at tha house. Ah'd like t scare ol man Hawkins jusa little. . . . Jusa enough t let im know Dave Saunders is a man.

To his left the road curved, running to the tracks of the Illinois Central. 210
He jerked his head, listening. From far off came a faint *hoooof-hoooof; hoooof-hoooof*. . . . He stood rigid. Two dollahs a mont. Les see now. . . . Tha means it'll take bout two years. Shucks! Ah'll be dam!

He started down the road, toward the tracks. Yeah, here she comes! He stood beside the track and held himself stiffly. Here she comes, erroun the ben. . . . C mon, yuh slow poke! C mon! He had his hand on his gun; something quivered in his stomach. Then the train thundered past, the gray and brown box cars rumbling and clinking. He gripped the gun tightly; then he jerked his hand out of his pocket. Ah betcha Bill wouldn't do it! Ah betcha. . . . The cars slid past, steel grinding upon steel. Ahm ridin yuh ternight, so hep me Gawd! He was hot all over. He hesitated just a moment; then he grabbed, pulled atop of a car, and lay flat. He felt his pocket; the gun was still there. Ahead the long rails were glinting in the moonlight, stretching away, away to somewhere, somewhere where he could be a man. . . .

Doris Lessing

A Woman on the Roof *(1993)*

It was during the week of hot sun, that June.

Three men were at work on the roof, where the leads got so hot they had the idea of throwing water on to cool them. But the water steamed, then sizzled; and they made jokes about getting an egg from some woman in the flats under them, to poach it for their dinner. By two it was not possible to touch the guttering they were replacing, and they speculated about what workmen did in regularly hot countries. Perhaps they should borrow kitchen gloves with the egg? They were all a bit dizzy, not used to the heat; and they shed their coats and stood side by side squeezing themselves into a foot-wide patch of shade against a chimney, careful to keep their feet in the thick socks and boots out of the sun. There was a fine view across several acres of roofs. Not far off a man sat in a deck chair reading the newspapers. Then they saw her, between chimneys, about fifty yards away. She lay face down on a brown blanket. They could see the top part of her: black hair, a flushed solid back, arms spread out.

"She's stark naked," said Stanley, sounding annoyed.

Harry, the oldest, a man of about forty-five, said: "Looks like it."

Young Tom, seventeen, said nothing, but he was excited and grinning. 5

Stanley said: "Someone'll report her if she doesn't watch out."

"She thinks no one can see," said Tom, craning his head all ways to see more.

At this point the woman, still lying prone, brought her two hands up behind her shoulders with the ends of a scarf in them, tied it behind her back, and sat up. She wore a red scarf tied around her breasts and brief red bikini pants. This being the first day of the sun she was white, flushing red. She sat smoking, and did not look up when Stanley let out a wolf whistle. Harry said: "Small things amuse small minds," leading the way back to their part of the roof, but it was scorching. Harry said: "Wait, I'm going to rig up some shade," and disappeared down the skylight into the building. Now that he'd gone, Stanley and Tom went to the farthest point they could to peer at the woman.

She had moved, and all they could see were two pink legs stretched on the blanket. They whistled and shouted but the legs did not move. Harry came back with a blanket and shouted: “Come on, then.” He sounded irritated with them. They clambered back to him and he said to Stanley: “What about your missus?” Stanley was newly married, about three months. Stanley said, jeering: “What about my missus?”—preserving his independence. Tom said nothing, but his mind was full of the nearly naked woman. Harry slung the blanket, which he had borrowed from a friendly woman downstairs, from the stem of a television aerial to a row of chimney-pots. This shade fell across the piece of gutter they had to replace. But the shade kept moving, they had to adjust the blanket, and not much progress was made. At last some of the heat left the roof, and they worked fast, making up for lost time. First Stanley, then Tom, made a trip to the end of the roof to see the woman. “She’s on her back,” Stanley said, adding a jest which made Tom snicker, and the older man smile tolerantly. Tom’s report was that she hadn’t moved, but it was a lie. He wanted to keep what he had seen to himself: he had caught her in the act of rolling down the little red pants over her hips, till they were no more than a small triangle. She was on her back, fully visible, glistening with oil.

Next morning, as soon as they came up, they went to look. She was already there, face down, arms spread out, naked except for the little red pants. She had turned brown in the night. Yesterday she was a scarlet-and-white woman, today she was a brown woman. Stanley let out a whistle. She lifted her head, startled, as if she’d been asleep, and looked straight over at them. The sun was in her eyes, she blinked and stared, then she dropped her head again. At this gesture of indifference, they all three, Stanley, Tom, and old Harry, let out whistles and yells. Harry was doing it in parody of the younger men, making fun of them, but he was also angry. They were all angry because of her utter indifference to the three men watching her.

“Bitch,” said Stanley. 10

“She should ask us over,” said Tom, snickering.

Harry recovered himself and reminded Stanley: “If she’s married, her old man wouldn’t like that.”

“Christ,” said Stanley virtuously, “if my wife lay about like that, for everyone to see, I’d soon stop her.”

Harry said, smiling: “How do you know, perhaps she’s sunning herself at this very moment?”

“Not a chance, not on our roof.” The safety of his wife put Stanley into a 15
good humour, and they went to work. But today it was hotter than yesterday; and several times one or the other suggested they should tell Matthew, the foreman, and ask to leave the roof until the heat wave was over. But they didn’t. There was work to be done in the basement of the big block of flats, but up here they felt free, on a different level from ordinary humanity shut in the streets or the buildings. A lot more people came out on to the roofs that day, for an hour at midday. Some married couples sat side by side in deck chairs, the women’s legs stockingless and scarlet, the men in vests with reddening shoulders.

The woman stayed on her blanket, turning herself over and over. She ignored them, no matter what they did. When Harry went off to fetch more screws, Stanley said: "Come on." Her roof belonged to a different system of roofs, separated from theirs at one point by about twenty feet. It meant a scrambling climb from one level to another, edging along parapets, clinging to chimneys, while their big boots slipped and slithered, but at last they stood on a small square projecting roof looking straight down at her, close. She sat smoking, reading a book. Tom thought she looked like a poster, or a magazine cover, with the blue sky behind her and her legs stretched out. Behind her a great crane at work on a new building in Oxford Street swung its black arm across roofs in a great arc. Tom imagined himself at work on the crane, adjusting the arm to swing over and pick her up and swing her back across the sky to drop her near him.

They whistled. She looked up at them, cool and remote, then went on reading. Again, they were furious. Or, rather, Stanley was. His sun-heated face was screwed into a rage as he whistled again and again, trying to make her look up. Young Tom stopped whistling. He stood beside Stanley, excited, grinning; but he felt as if he were saying to the woman: Don't associate me with *him*, for his grin was apologetic. Last night he had thought of the unknown woman before he slept, and she had been tender with him. This tenderness he was remembering as he shifted his feet by the jeering, whistling Stanley, and watched the indifferent, healthy brown woman a few feet off, with the gap that plunged to the street between them. Tom thought it was romantic, it was like being high on two hilltops. But there was a shout from Harry, and they clambered back. Stanley's face was hard, really angry. The boy kept looking at him and wondered why he hated the woman so much, for by now he loved her.

They played their little games with the blanket, trying to trap shade to work under; but again it was not until nearly four that they could work seriously, and they were exhausted, all three of them. They were grumbling about the weather by now. Stanley was in a thoroughly bad humour. When they made their routine trip to see the woman before they packed up for the day, she was apparently asleep, face down, her back all naked save for the scarlet triangle on her buttocks. "I've got a good mind to report her to the police," said Stanley, and Harry said: "What's eating you? What harm's she doing?"

"I tell you, if she was my wife!"

"But she isn't, is she?" Tom knew that Harry, like himself, was uneasy at 20
Stanley's reaction. He was normally a sharp young man, quick at his work, making a lot of jokes, good company.

"Perhaps it will be cooler tomorrow," said Harry.

But it wasn't; it was hotter, if anything, and the weather forecast said the good weather would last. As soon as they were on the roof, Harry went over to see if the woman was there, and Tom knew it was to prevent Stanley going, to put off his bad humour. Harry had grownup children, a boy the same age as Tom, and the youth trusted and looked up to him.

Harry came back and said: "She's not there."

"I bet her old man has put his foot down," said Stanley, and Harry and Tom caught each other's eyes and smiled behind the young married man's back.

Harry suggested they should get permission to work in the basement, and 25
they did, that day. But before packing up Stanley said: "Let's have a breath of fresh air." Again Harry and Tom smiled at each other as they followed Stanley up to the roof, Tom in the devout conviction that he was there to protect the woman from Stanley. It was about five-thirty, and a calm, full sunlight lay over the roofs. The great crane still swung its black arm from Oxford Street to above their heads. She was not there. Then there was a flutter of white from behind a parapet, and she stood up, in a belted, white dressing-gown. She had been there all day, probably, but on a different patch of roof, to hide from them. Stanley did not whistle; he said nothing, but watched the woman bend to collect papers, books, cigarettes, then fold the blanket over her arm. Tom was thinking: If they weren't here, I'd go over and say . . . what? But he knew from his nightly dreams of her that she was kind and friendly. Perhaps she would ask him down to her flat? Perhaps . . . He stood watching her disappear down the skylight. As she went, Stanley let out a shrill derisive yell; she started, and it seemed as if she nearly fell. She clutched to save herself, they could hear things falling. She looked straight at them, angry. Harry said, facetiously: "Better be careful on those slippery ladders, love." Tom knew he said it to save her from Stanley, but she could not know it. She vanished, frowning. Tom was full of a secret delight, because he knew her anger was for the others, not for him.

"Roll on some rain," said Stanley, bitter, looking at the blue evening sky.

Next day was cloudless, and they decided to finish the work in the basement. They felt excluded, shut in the grey cement basement fitting pipes, from the holiday atmosphere of London in a heat wave. At lunchtime they came up for some air, but while the married couples, and the men in shirt-sleeves or vests, were there, she was not there, either on her usual patch of roof or where she had been yesterday. They all, even Harry, clambered about, between chimney-pots, over parapets, the hot leads stinging their fingers. There was not a sign of her. They took off their shirts and vests and exposed their chests, feeling their feet sweaty and hot. They did not mention the woman. But Tom felt alone again. Last night she had him into her flat: it was big and had fitted white carpets and a bed with a padded white leather head-board. She wore a black filmy negligée and her kindness to Tom thickened his throat as he remembered it. He felt she had betrayed him by not being there.

And again after work they climbed up, but still there was nothing to be seen of her. Stanley kept repeating that if it was as hot as this tomorrow he wasn't going to work and that's all there was to it. But they were all there next day. By ten the temperature was in the middle seventies, and it was eighty long before noon. Harry went to the foreman to say it was impossible to work on the leads in that heat; but the foreman said there was nothing else he could put them on, and they'd have to. At midday they stood, silent, watching the skylight on her roof open, and then she slowly emerged in her white gown, holding a bundle of blanket. She looked at them, gravely, then went to the part of the roof where she was hidden from them. Tom was pleased. He felt she was more his when the other men couldn't see her. They had taken off their shirts and vests, but now they put them back again, for they felt the sun bruising their flesh. "She must have the hide of a rhino," said Stanley, tugging at guttering and swearing. They stopped work, and sat in the shade, moving around behind chimney stacks. A woman came to water a yellow window box opposite them. She was middle-aged, wearing a flowered summer dress. Stanley said to her: "We need a drink more than them." She smiled and said: "Better drop down to the pub quick, it'll be closing in a minute." They exchanged pleasantries, and she left them with a smile and a wave.

"Not like Lady Godiva," said Stanley. "She can give us a bit of a chat and a smile."

"You didn't whistle at *her*," said Tom, reproving. 30

"Listen to him," said Stanley, "you didn't whistle, then?"

But the boy felt as if he hadn't whistled, as if only Harry and Stanley had. He was making plans, when it was time to knock off work, to get left behind and somehow make his way over to the woman. The weather report said the hot spell was due to break, so he had to move quickly. But there was no chance of being left. The other two decided to knock off work at four, because they were exhausted. As they went down, Tom quickly climbed a parapet and hoisted himself higher by pulling his weight up a chimney. He caught a glimpse of her lying on her back, her knees up, eyes closed, a brown woman lolling in the sun. He slipped and clattered down, as Stanley looked for information: "She's gone down," he said. He felt as if he had protected her from Stanley, and that she must be grateful to him. He could feel the bond between the woman and himself.

Next day, they stood around on the landing below the roof, reluctant to climb up into the heat. The woman who had lent Harry the blanket came out and offered them a cup of tea. They accepted gratefully, and sat around Mrs. Pritchett's kitchen an hour or so, chatting. She was married to an airline pilot. A smart blonde, of about thirty, she had an eye for the handsome sharp-faced Stanley; and the two teased each other while Harry sat in a corner, watching, indulgent, though his expression reminded Stanley that he was married. And young Tom felt envious of Stanley's ease in badinage; felt, too, that Stanley's getting off with Mrs. Pritchett left his romance with the woman on the roof safe and intact.

"I thought they said the heat wave'd break," said Stanley, sullen, as the time approached when they really would have to climb up into the sunlight.

"You don't like it, then?" asked Mrs. Pritchett. 35

"All right for some," said Stanley. "Nothing to do but lie about as if it was a beach up there. Do you ever go up?"

"Went up once," said Mrs. Pritchett. "But it's a dirty place up there, and it's too hot."

"Quite right too," said Stanley.

Then they went up, leaving the cool neat little flat and the friendly Mrs. Pritchett.

As soon as they were up they saw her. The three men looked at her, re- 40
sentful at her ease in this punishing sun. Then Harry said, because of the expression on Stanley's face: "Come on, we've got to pretend to work, at least."

They had to wrench another length of guttering that ran beside a parapet out of its bed, so that they could replace it. Stanley took it in his two hands, tugged, swore, stood up. "Fuck it," he said, and sat down under a chimney. He lit a cigarette. "Fuck them," he said. "What do they think we are, lizards? I've got blisters all over my hands." Then he jumped up and climbed over the roofs and stood with his back to them. He put his fingers either side of his mouth and let out a shrill whistle. Tom and Harry squatted, not looking at each other, watching him. They could just see the woman's head, the beginnings of her brown shoulders. Stanley whistled again. Then he began stamping with his feet, and whistled and yelled and screamed at the woman, his face getting scarlet. He seemed quite mad, as he stamped and whistled, while the woman did not move, she did not move a muscle.

"Barmy," said Tom.

"Yes," said Harry, disapproving.

Suddenly the older man came to a decision. It was, Tom knew, to save some sort of scandal or real trouble over the woman. Harry stood up and began packing tools into a length of oily cloth. "Stanley," he said, commanding. At first Stanley took no notice, but Harry said: "Stanley, we're packing it in, I'll tell Matthew."

Stanley came back, cheeks mottled, eyes glaring. 45

"Can't go on like this," said Harry. "It'll break in a day or so. I'm going to tell Matthew we've got sunstroke, and if he doesn't like it, it's too bad." Even Harry sounded aggrieved, Tom noted. The small, competent man, the family man with his grey hair, who was never at a loss, sounded really off balance. "Come on," he said, angry. He fitted himself into the open square in the roof, and went down, watching his feet on the ladder. Then Stanley went, with not a glance at the woman. Then Tom, who, his throat beating with excitement, silently promised her on a backward glance: Wait for me, wait, I'm coming.

On the pavement Stanley said: "I'm going home." He looked white now, so perhaps he really did have sunstroke. Harry went off to find the foreman, who was at work on the plumbing of some flats down the street. Tom slipped back, not into the building they had been working on, but the building on whose roof the woman lay. He went straight up, no one stopping him. The skylight stood open, with an iron ladder leading up. He emerged on to the roof a couple of yards from her. She sat up, pushing back her black hair with both hands. The scarf across her breasts bound them tight, and brown flesh bulged around it. Her legs were brown and smooth. She stared at him in silence. The boy stood grinning, foolish, claiming the tenderness he expected from her.

"What do you want?" she asked.

"I . . . I came to . . . make your acquaintance," he stammered, grinning, pleading with her.

They looked at each other, the slight, scarlet-faced excited boy, and the 50
serious, nearly naked woman. Then, without a word, she lay down on her brown blanket, ignoring him.

"You like the sun, do you?" he enquired of her glistening back.

Not a word. He felt panic, thinking of how she had held him in her arms, stroked his hair, brought him where he sat, lordly, in her bed, a glass of some exhilarating liquor he had never tasted in life. He felt that if he knelt down, stroked her shoulders, her hair, she would turn and clasp him in her arms.

He said: "The sun's all right for you, isn't it?"

She raised her head, set her chin on two small fists. "Go away," she said. He did not move. "Listen," she said, in a slow reasonable voice, where anger was kept in check, though with difficulty; looking at him, her face weary with anger, "if you get a kick out of seeing women in bikinis, why don't you take a sixpenny bus ride to the Lido? You'd see dozens of them, without all this mountaineering."

She hadn't understood him. He felt her unfairness pale him. He stam- 55
mered: "But I like you, I've been watching you and . . ."

"Thanks," she said, and dropped her face again, turned away from him.

She lay there. He stood there. She said nothing. She had simply shut him out. He stood, saying nothing at all, for some minutes. He thought: She'll have to say something if I stay. But the minutes went past, with no sign of them in her, except in the tension of her back, her thighs, her arms—the tension of waiting for him to go.

He looked up at the sky, where the sun seemed to spin in heat; and over the roofs where he and his mates had been earlier. He could see the heat quivering where they had worked. And they expect us to work in these conditions! he thought, filled with righteous indignation. The woman hadn't moved. A bit of hot wind blew her black hair softly; it shone, and was iridescent. He remembered how he had stroked it last night.

Resentment of her at last moved him off and away down the ladder, through the building, into the street. He got drunk then, in hatred of her.

Next day when he woke the sky was grey. He looked at the wet grey and thought, vicious: Well, that's fixed you, hasn't it now? That's fixed you good and proper.

The three men were at work early on the cool leads, surrounded by damp drizzling roofs where no one came to sun themselves, black roofs, slimy with rain. Because it was cool now, they would finish the job that day, if they hurried.

JOHN UPDIKE

A & P

(1962)

In walks these three girls in nothing but bathing suits. I'm in the third checkout slot, with my back to the door, so I don't see them until they're over by the bread. The one that caught my eye first was the one in the plaid green two-piece. She was a chunky kid, with a good tan and a sweet broad soft-looking can with those two crescents of white just under it, where the sun never seems to hit, at the top of the backs of her legs. I stood there with my hand on a box of HiHo crackers trying to remember if I rang it up or not. I ring it up again and the customer starts giving me hell. She's one of these cash-register-watchers, a witch about fifty with rouge on her cheekbones and no eyebrows, and I know it made her day to trip me up. She'd been watching cash registers for fifty years and probably never seen a mistake before.

By the time I got her feathers smoothed and her goodies into a bag—she gives me a little snort in passing, if she'd been born at the right time they would have burned her over in Salem—by the time I get her on her way the girls had circled around the bread and were coming back, without a pushcart, back my way along the counters, in the aisle between the checkouts and the Special bins. They didn't even have shoes on. There was this chunky one, with the two-piece—it was bright green and all the seams on the bra were still sharp and her belly was still pretty pale so I guessed she just got it (the suit)—there was this one, with one of those chubby berry-faces, the lips all bunched together under her nose, this one, and a tall one, with black hair that hadn't quite frizzed right, and one of these sunburns right across under the eyes, and a chin that was too long—you know, the kind of girl other girls think is very "striking" and "attractive" but never quite makes it, as they very well know, which is why they like her so much—and then the third one, that wasn't quite so tall. She was the queen. She kind of led them, the other two peeking around and making their shoulders round. She didn't look around, not this queen, she just walked straight on slowly, on these long white primadonna legs. She came down a little hard on her heels, as if she didn't walk in bare feet that much, putting down her heels and then letting the weight move along to her toes as if she was testing the floor with every step, putting a little deliberate extra action into it. You never know for sure how girls' minds work (do you really think it's a mind in there or just a little buzz like a bee in a glass jar?) but you got the idea she had talked the other two into coming here with her, and now she was showing them how to do it, walk slow and hold yourself straight.

She had on a kind of dirty-pink—beige maybe, I don't know—bathing suit with a little nubble all over it and, what got me, the straps were down. They were off her shoulders looped loose around the cool tops of her arms, and I guess as a result the suit had slipped a little on her, so all around the top of the cloth there was this shining rim. If it hadn't been there you wouldn't have known there could have been anything whiter than those shoulders. With the straps pushed off, there was nothing between the top of the suit and the top of her head except just *her*; this clean bare plane of the top of her chest down from the shoulder bones like a dented sheet of metal tilted in the light. I mean, it was more than pretty.

She had a sort of oaky hair that the sun and salt had bleached, done up in a bun that was unravelling, and a kind of prim face. Walking into the A & P with your straps down, I suppose it's the only kind of face you *can* have. She held her head so high her neck, coming up out of those white shoulders, looked kind of stretched, but I didn't mind. The longer her neck was, the more of her there was.

5 She must have felt in the corner of her eye me and over my shoulder Stokesie in the second slot watching, but she didn't tip. Not this queen. She kept her eyes moving across the racks, and stopped, and turned so slow it

made my stomach rub the inside of my apron, and buzzed to the other two, who kind of huddled against her for relief, and then they all three of them went up the cat-and-dog-food-breakfast-cereal-macaroni-rice-raisins-seasonings-spreads-spaghetti-soft-drinks-crackers-and-cookies aisle. From the third slot I look straight up this aisle to the meat counter, and I watched them all the way. The fat one with the tan sort of fumbled with the cookies, but on second thought she put the package back. The sheep pushing their carts down the aisle—the girls were walking against the usual traffic (not that we have one-way signs or anything)—were pretty hilarious. You could see them, when Queenie's white shoulders dawned on them, kind of jerk, or hop, or hiccup, but their eyes snapped back to their own baskets and on they pushed. I bet you could set off dynamite in an A & P and the people would by and large keep reaching and checking oatmeal off their lists and muttering "Let me see, there was a third thing, began with A, asparagus, no, ah, yes, applesauce!" or whatever it is they do mutter. But there was no doubt, this jiggled them. A few houseslaves in pin curlers even looked around after pushing their carts past to make sure what they had seen was correct.

You know, it's one thing to have a girl in a bathing suit down on the beach, where what with the glare nobody can look at each other much anyway, and another thing in the cool of the A & P, under the fluorescent lights, against all those stacked packages, with her feet paddling along naked over our checkerboard green-and-cream rubber-tile floor.

"Oh Daddy," Stokesie said beside me. "I feel so faint."

"Darling," I said. "Hold me tight." Stokesie's married, with two babies chalked up on his fuselage already, but as far as I can tell that's the only difference. He's twenty-two, and I was nineteen this April.

"Is it done?" he asks, the responsible married man finding his voice. I forgot to say he thinks he's going to be manager some sunny day, maybe in 1990 when it's called the Great Alexandrov and Petrooshki Tea Company or something.

What he meant was, our town is five miles from a beach, with a big sum- 10
mer colony out on the Point, but we're right in the middle of town, and the women generally put on a shirt or shorts or something before they get out of the car into the street. And anyway these are usually women with six children and varicose veins mapping their legs and nobody, including them, could care less. As I say, we're right in the middle of town, and if you stand at our front doors you can see two banks and the Congregational church and the newspaper store and three real-estate offices and about twenty-seven old freeloaders tearing up Central Street because the sewer broke again. It's not as if we're on the Cape; we're north of Boston and there's people in this town haven't seen the ocean for twenty years.

The girls had reached the meat counter and were asking McMahon something. He pointed, they pointed, and they shuffled out of sight behind a pyramid of Diet Delight peaches. All that was left for us to see was old McMahon patting his mouth and looking after them sizing up their joints. Poor kids, I began to feel sorry for them, they couldn't help it.

* * *

Now here comes the sad part of the story, at least my family says it's sad, but I don't think it's so sad myself. The store's pretty empty, it being Thursday afternoon, so there was nothing much to do except lean on the register and wait for the girls to show up again. The whole store was like a pinball machine and I didn't know which tunnel they'd come out of. After a while they come around out of the far aisle, around the light bulbs, records at discount of the Caribbean Six or Tony Martin Sings or some such gunk you wonder they waste the wax on, six-packs of candy bars, and plastic toys done up in cellophane that fall apart when a kid looks at them anyway. Around they come, Queenie still leading the way, and holding a little gray jar in her hand. Slots Three through Seven are unmanned and I could see her wondering between Stokes and me, but Stokesie with his usual luck draws an old party in baggy gray pants who stumbles up with four giant cans of pineapple juice (what do these bums *do* with all that pineapple juice? I've often asked myself) so the girls come to me. Queenie puts down the jar and I take it into my fingers icy cold. Kingfish Fancy Herring Snacks in Pure Sour Cream: 49¢. Now her hands are empty, not a ring or a bracelet, bare as God made them, and I wonder where the money's coming from. Still with that prim look she lifts a folded dollar bill out of the hollow at the center of her nubbled pink top. The jar went heavy in my hand. Really, I thought that was so cute.

Then everybody's luck begins to run out. Lengel comes in from haggling with a truck full of cabbages on the lot and is about to scuttle into that door marked MANAGER behind which he hides all day when the girls touch his eye. Lengel's pretty dreary, teaches Sunday school and the rest, but he doesn't miss that much. He comes over and says, "Girls, this isn't the beach."

Queenie blushes, though maybe it's just a brush of sunburn I was noticing for the first time, now that she was so close. "My mother asked me to pick up a jar of herring snacks." Her voice kind of startled me, the way voices do when you see the people first, coming out so flat and dumb yet kind of tony, too, the way it ticked over "pick up" and "snacks." All of a sudden I slid right down her voice into her living room. Her father and the other men were standing around in ice-cream coats and bow ties and the women were in sandals picking up herring snacks on toothpicks off a big glass plate and they were all holding drinks the color of water with olives and springs of mint in them. When my parents have somebody over they get lemonade and if it's a real racy affair Schlitz in tall glasses with "They'll Do It Every Time" cartoons stencilled on.

15 "That's all right," Lengel said. "But this isn't the beach." His repeating this struck me as funny, as if it had just occurred to him, and he had been thinking all these years the A & P was a great big dune and he was the head lifeguard. He didn't like my smiling—as I say he doesn't miss much—but he concentrates on giving the girls that sad Sunday-school-superintendent stare.

Queenie's blush is no sunburn now, and the plump one in plaid, that I liked better from the back—a really sweet can—pipes up, "We weren't doing any shopping. We just came in for the one thing."

"That makes no difference," Lengel tells her, and I could see from the way his eyes went that he hadn't noticed she was wearing a two-piece before. "We want you decently dressed when you come in here."

"We *are* decent," Queenie says suddenly, her lower lip pushing, getting sore now that she remembers her place, a place from which the crowd that runs the A & P must look pretty crummy. Fancy Herring Snacks flashed in her very blue eyes.

"Girls, I don't want to argue with you. After this come in here with your shoulders covered. It's our policy." He turns his back. That's policy for you. Policy is what the kingpins want. What the others want is juvenile delinquency.

All this while, the customers had been showing up with their carts but, 20
you know, sheep, seeing a scene, they had all bunched up on Stokesie, who shook open a paper bag as gently as peeling a peach, not wanting to miss a word. I could feel in the silence everybody getting nervous, most of all Lengel, who asks me, "Sammy, have you rung up their purchase?"

I thought and said "No" but it wasn't about that I was thinking. I go through the punches, 4, 9, GROC, TOT—it's more complicated than you think, and after you do it often enough, it begins to make a little song, that you hear words to, in my case "Hello (*bing*) there, you (*gung*) hap-py *pee*-pul (*splat*)*!*"—the *splat* being the drawer flying out. I uncrease the bill, tenderly as you may imagine, it just having come from between the two smoothest scoops of vanilla I had ever known there were, and pass a half and a penny into her narrow pink palm, and nestle the herrings in a bag and twist its neck and hand it over, all the time thinking.

The girls, and who'd blame them, are in a hurry to get out, so I say "I quit" to Lengel quick enough for them to hear, hoping they'll stop and watch me, their unsuspected hero. They keep right on going, into the electric eye; the door flies open and they flicker across the lot to their car, Queenie and Plaid and Big Tall Goony-Goony (not that as raw material she was so bad), leaving me with Lengel and a kink in his eyebrow.

"Did you say something, Sammy?"

"I said I quit."

"I thought you did." 25

"You didn't have to embarrass them."

"It was they who were embarrassing us."

I started to say something that came out "Fiddle-de-do." It's a saying of my grandmother's, and I know she would have been pleased.

"I don't think you know what you're saying," Lengel said.

"I know you don't," I said. "But I do." I pull the bow at the back of my 30
apron and start shrugging it off my shoulders. A couple of customers that had been heading for my slot begin to knock against each other, like scared pigs in a chute.

Lengel sighs and begins to look very patient and old and gray. He's been a friend of my parents for years. "Sammy, you don't want to do this to your Mom and Dad," he tells me. It's true, I don't. But it seems to me that once you begin a gesture it's fatal not to go through with it. I folded the apron, "Sammy" stitched in red on the pocket, and put it on the counter, and drop the bow tie on top of it. The bow tie is theirs, if you've ever wondered. "You'll feel this for the rest of your life," Lengel says, and I know that's true, too, but remembering how he made that pretty girl blush makes me so scrunchy inside I punch the No Sale tab and the machine whirs "pee-pul" and the drawer splats out. One advantage to this scene taking place in summer, I can follow this up with a clean exit, there's no fumbling around getting your coat and galoshes, I just saunter into the electric eye in my white shirt that my mother ironed the night before, and the door heaves itself open, and outside the sunshine is skating around on the asphalt.

I look around for my girls, but they're gone, of course. There wasn't anybody but some young married screaming with her children about some candy they didn't get by the door of a powder-blue Falcon station wagon. Looking back in the big windows, over the bags of peat moss and aluminum lawn furniture stacked on the pavement, I could see Lengel in my place in the slot, checking the sheep through. His face was dark gray and his back stiff, as if he's just had an injection of iron, and my stomach kind of fell as I felt how hard the world was going to be to me hereafter.

Part IV
Writing About Literature

21 Writing About Literature

A well-known writer was once asked his opinion about a topic. He responded by saying that he could not possibly answer the question until he saw what he had written about it. The point is a particularly cogent one and very relevant to the composition of papers on literary topics: Essay-writing affords a reader the opportunity to organize ideas or responses, and to meditate deeply on the text or texts under consideration. Writing clarifies not only what is important about a text, illuminating what really matters to its construction, language, or meaning, but also what is important to the reader herself.

An essay, true to its origin in the French verb *essayer*, meaning "to try or attempt," communicates its author's efforts to convey his or her reflections about a text or group of texts. At the same time, these reflections constitute an attempt to persuade an audience of their interpretive validity and explanatory power. Writing about literature, therefore, is also writing about reading. But how to begin? What plan of attack will be most effective in conveying your ideas?

Getting Ready, Making Decisions

As your instructor will explain and as we outline in greater detail in Chapter 23, "Writing a Research Paper," a writer needs to consider a number of questions before typing the first word: What audience am I addressing? What do they know about the text I want to discuss? What language will be most effective or appropriate in communicating to this audience? In other words, what assumptions should I make about the *rhetorical situation?* A writer always weighs these and other questions carefully before beginning, considering each point of the triangle below.

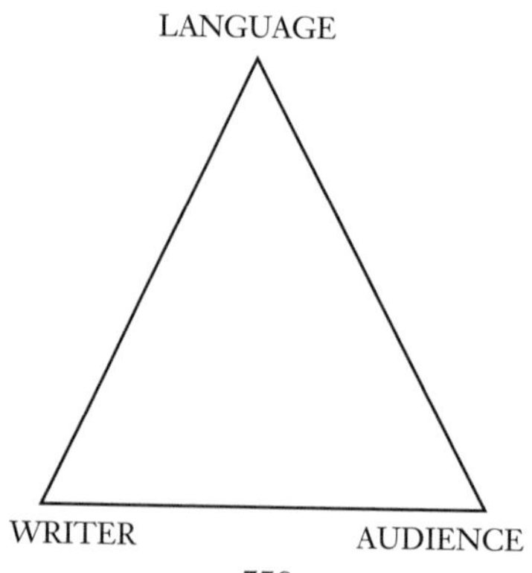

In preparing to write essays on literary topics, you should consider, among other things, who will read the paper and why. Assume that your audience is already familiar with the work you intend to discuss; thus, there is little reason to summarize the plot or rehearse the attractions or shortcomings of central characters if you are writing about a play or short story. Your audience knows, for example, that Hamlet meets a tragic fate and that Oedipus' last day as king of Thebes is not a happy one. What kind of language and evidence will be most effective in addressing this audience? What role do you as writer play? Generally, the answer is none at all. You are not a professor or academician, nor are you talking to a personal friend. You aren't in a locker room either, so select terms appropriate both to the occasion of the composition and the audience. This is especially true when crafting your thesis, the most significant aspect of your essay that your audience does *not* know.

The thesis embodies your purpose in writing the paper in the first place. Unlike, say, the occupation of a drama or film reviewer in a newspaper, your job in writing about literature is to persuade your audience of the significance of your topic to an understanding of the text you are discussing. The single statement most crucial to this enterprise is your *thesis statement.*

Thesis Statements

The thesis statement provides focus and purpose for the entire essay. Because it represents the most direct expression of your "big idea" about the literature you have read, the thesis statement may take longer to formulate than any other sentence you prepare. And it may take some time, some experimentation, and some trial-and-error before you arrive at the precise point you want to make. You may want to try such techniques as *freewriting* or *brainstorming,* where you put down on paper as quickly as you can whatever thoughts enter your mind about a topic. Don't stop to worry about punctuation or spelling—these can be corrected later. In a freewriting exercise, sometimes called "automatic writing," simply transcribe your thoughts into words on a page or screen, revising them later into more precise and compelling statements. The purpose of this exercise is invention: You are trying to purge your mind of thoughts on a topic, one of which may be refined later into a thesis statement.

You might also consider the thesis statement as the culmination of a process that narrows the topic: from a text to discuss, to a topic in or about the text, to a specific issue or reading. Suppose that the text is E. M. Forster's "The Road from Colonus." The subject or topic might be the story's imagery, and the thesis might argue for the importance of images of water. Or perhaps you have the opportunity to write about any aspect of Charlotte Perkins Gilman's "The Yellow Wall-Paper." The subject might be characterization, and the thesis might focus on questions about the narrator's sanity. Is the narrator crazy? Or are her responses to the wallpaper logical given the circumstances of her confinement? Or given the story's implied critique of gender relations, does the wallpaper represent the patriarchal system from which the narrator tries to escape? The same story and the same process of narrowing the scope of what will become your argument could lead you to focus on a different subject and thesis.

Argument in this context *is* the correct term. You should select a topic that you can develop into a persuasive argument, which begins with articulating a coherent, concise, and arguable thesis statement. Thesis statements have several distinctive features or criteria, as the following six points summarize. Test the thesis statement for your paper against these characteristics: Does your thesis meet all of the following? If not, what adjustments will make the statement more specific, more forceful, or more significant?

1. Thesis statements are statements of opinion, not statements of fact or intention.

Statement of Fact

> In Nathaniel Hawthorne's "The Birthmark," Aylmer meddles with nature.

As any reader of "The Birthmark" will readily concede, Aylmer does meddle with nature. Consequently, a research paper cannot be organized around a statement of this fact. Aylmer is a man who loves his wife, Boston is located in Massachusetts, and the Beatles are still popular—these facts do not require discussion or the presentation of evidence. They are self-evident.

Statement of Intention

> In my essay, I want to show you that Aylmer meddles with nature.

This sentence is not better than the first one. It not only fails to advance an opinion, but also is wordier than the statement of fact: "In my essay, I want to show you that" is particularly ineffective and verbose.

Statement of Opinion

> Since Aylmer is a perfectionist, his desire for perfection causes all of the story's unhappiness.

This sentence actually contains two opinions: that Aylmer is a perfectionist and that this perfectionism causes the events of the story to be unhappy. A number of the story's readers might disagree with both assertions, locating the story's motivations in problems of gender or scientific hubris. Often abstract terms like *unhappy* in the thesis spark disagreement or confusion, so be careful when inserting abstractions into theses. Nonetheless, this statement's assertion fits the first criterion of an effective thesis statement by stating an opinion, not a fact or intention.

2. A thesis statement advances an opinion about which informed and reasonable people might disagree. As is the case with the statement that Aylmer is a perfectionist, a thesis furthers an understanding about which informed readers might disagree. What would be the point of researching a topic about which everyone already possesses the same opinion? What would a reader of the paper learn that he or she does not know already? Thus, one way of testing a thesis is to present it to your classmates and determine if they all share your view. If they do, you need to keep working.

3. A thesis statement often contains an underlying rhetorical premise. By *rhetorical premise* we mean a concept or mode of understanding that implicitly structures or organizes the rest of the paper. In the 1960s, the rhetorician Randall Decker published a widely used textbook called *Patterns of Exposition*, which included chapters on comparison, process analysis, causality, definition, classification, and other rhetorical modes or premises. Such premises are frequently imbedded in the articulation of theses: Mr. Lucas's loss of insight in E. M. Forster's "The Road from Colonus" progresses through two distinct stages (this essay will follow the organizational strategy of process analysis); "The young boy's sudden insight at the end of James Joyce's 'Araby' is caused by the deflation of his fantasy" (this essay uses the organizational strategy of causality), and so on.

4. A thesis statement predicts, obligates, and controls what follows it. Rhetorician William Irmscher once made this point in a composition textbook, and its implications are still relevant today. Much like the title, a thesis suggests to a reader what course a research paper—or any essay, for that matter—will take. It *predicts*. It also *obligates* the writer to present evidence and discussion of the evidence consistent with the assertion; a writer cannot begin by claiming that Mr. Lucas experiences two distinct stages of loss, and then later argue that there are, in fact, four stages to his failure of insight. Finally, a thesis *controls* the kinds of evidence relevant to the essay's purpose. If the thesis addresses Mr. Lucas's loss of insight, then considering his daughter's motivations or the fate of the villagers would seem digressive unless they can be shown to contribute to his loss of perspective.

5. A thesis statement takes on a topic of significance, often the answer to an implicit question. Many graduate students we know, parodying a well-known Victorian writer's phrases the "Everlasting Yea" and the "Everlasting Nay," talk about the "The Everlasting So What?" This means, simply, that a thesis should argue a point of importance. "Mr. Lucas's loss of insight progresses through two stages"—so what? Why is this important? Notice, too, that all the examples we have used answer an unasked or implicit question, a "how" or "why" question: Why is the young boy in "Araby" so self-critical at the story's conclusion?

6. A thesis statement reflects theoretical or other assumptions that underlie your reading and, finally, the argument of the essay. All of the sample theses so far are based more or less on *formalist* premises: How is the plot constructed? How might a character's actions be explained? Why or how is an image, scene, or even a single word important to our understanding? Such questions quite properly involve close reading of the literary text, as they address one or more aspects of literary form. But, of course, as many of the chapters of *Understanding Literature* outline, other kinds of readings—and other premises for thesis statements—exist. They arise, in part, by asking different questions of the text: How is race or sexuality represented? How is social class or capitalism depicted? How does psychoanalytic theory, Marx's social theory, or feminist thought help explain a character's action or predicament? In other words, literature is more than a self-contained aesthetic object—or, to borrow a metaphor—it is more than an exceptionally "well-wrought urn." A literary text is also a social text, a historical artifact, a product made in a specific place, time, and culture. It can tell us much about these cultures and times as well.

These are, admittedly, difficult concepts that often lead to difficult questions and challenging thesis statements. But they must be asked and answered, because no writer—or reader—wants to waste his or her time on a topic of little consequence. If your paper addresses the actions of an important character, the implications of a major event or a significant *motif* (repetition in a poem, play, or story), then this close reading is likely to be important enough to make. If your essay concerns a matter of representation—how Africans are portrayed in Joseph Conrad's *Heart of Darkness*, how the city is represented in modernist fiction, how postmodern writers employ references to commodity culture—the chances are you can focus this interest into a significant thesis statement and thus respond effectively to the "Everlasting So What?"

And there's one other bit of good news, too—you're probably ready to write.

Writing

But how do you begin? If you're at all like the authors of this textbook, then you've probably asked yourself this very question scores of times. A thesis statement might be introduced in any number of ways, but it is actually easier to identify ways *not* to begin. The advice of rhetorician William Irmscher is again helpful in explaining three opening strategies to avoid at all costs.

1. The "panoramic" historical gesture. We've all read sentences like this one and tried to suppress our groans: "Since the dawn of time, man has pondered the nature of _______." This sentence is so trite and predictable that you can fill in the blank with any number of terms: *love*, *men*, *women*, *life*, and so on. But if it really is true that humans have puzzled over such weighty and complex matters for millennia, what chance do you have of resolving the matter in three to five pages? Obviously, this opening strategy—and that's what we are discussing, a strategy or tactic to present the thesis—has now lapsed into a parody of a profound utterance more likely to elicit laughter than respect.

The problem is, when you've stared into a blank computer screen for an hour, a sentence like this one starts to sound better and better—better than nothing. It isn't.

2. The appeal to Mr. Webster. Whenever a writer is really strapped for an opening gambit, this sentence starts to sound better as well: "According to *Webster's Dictionary*, realism is defined as . . . " Like the "panoramic" opener—and the "fact" that grandparents tend to die on the very day papers are due in a class like this one—this strategy has been overused. More important, the dictionary provides only a basic understanding of a term, its common meanings or denotations. Literary perceptions of a term like *realism* are far more complex and historically contingent than the definitions in most dictionaries.

3. Irrelevant biographical detail. Young writers sometimes feel that literary understanding always begins with the biography of the author; consequently, they begin essays with hackneyed sentences: "Samuel Beckett was born in Dublin, Ireland, in 1906." Fine. But save in the specific instance in which biography impinges directly upon reading, such a fact is not only superfluous, but irrelevant.

This was not always the case, which perhaps explains why the appeal to biography remains an attractive option for some students. In early twentieth-century British and American literary criticism, for example, biography often comprised the center around which interpretation revolved. In *The Human Approach to Literature* (1933), for example, William Freeman began a discussion of Chaucer's *Canterbury Tales* this way: "Geoffrey Chaucer, the sturdily-built man with the friendly brown eyes, was not merely a widely traveled Englishman who had passionately preserved his nationality, but a Londoner by birth and breeding."

Today, such opening strategies fail to introduce the real purpose of the essay and seem, well, almost silly. Chaucer's buff physique might be interesting, but surely it is not pertinent to a reading of his work. So why go there?

Fortunately, some devices *are* effective in introducing a thesis. You might begin with an epigraph, a brief quotation that encapsulates issues you feel are important to the text, and return to it in your opening paragraph (and later). You might start with a sensational detail, an anecdote, or a brief exchange of dialogue when discussing a play. Or, you might follow the instructions of countless composition texts by replicating the narrowing process discussed earlier, moving from a general subject, to a topic, to a specific statement.

The point is this: Thesis statements require introductions. The background of your "big idea" needs to be elaborated early in the essay and then, after your thesis is stated, you are ready to build a support structure for it. This is the body or argument of the essay.

Arguments and Admissible Evidence: Paraphrase and Quotation

Much like a lawyer in a criminal case who introduces materials into evidence and then "reads" the evidence in an attempt to persuade a judge or jury, writers of literary criticism marshal evidence carefully and discuss its implications. Persuasive arguments rely on well-chosen pieces of evidence and incisive analysis. The best kind of evidence is located in the literary text itself, parts of which will need to be summarized and paraphrased in the argument. For further discussion of paraphrase, see Chapter 23, "Writing a Research Paper."

But perhaps the most difficult task facing writers of all ages and experience is quoting from the text; that is, there will be occasions when a paraphrase or summary will not serve your needs. You will need to quote the original. But when? How much should you quote? What are the most graceful methods of integrating quoted excerpts into your own prose?

Let's take up this last question. In general, the same formula that makes for a good legal argument—evidence + analysis = guilt or innocence—applies in writing essays about literature. A prosecutor, for example, doesn't throw a weapon on a table and claim, "You see—that proves the defendant is guilty." Rather, a prosecutor examines the evidence, then builds an argument about it: Forensic analysis proves this is the murder weapon; the gun is registered to the defendant, who had a motive to kill the victim; the defendant was witnessed at the scene of the murder minutes before, and so on. If the lawyer is lucky, she might have eyewitnesses to depose, hair fibers or DNA evidence to present and discuss, and more: evidence + analysis = case. The same is true of building literary arguments: textual evidence (quotations or paraphrases) + your analysis = an argument.

To bring this to an even smaller, more precise case, consider the following:

your writing + quoted excerpts = complete sentence.

In other words, when quoting from a literary text don't simply drop a quotation between sentences; work to incorporate it into your sentence just as you attempt to integrate the piece of evidence into a larger argument. A citation should appear at the end of a quoted passage of any length (over a phrase or two), and usually this means that the citation appears at the end of a sentence. That is, try not to interrupt the sense of the sentence by placing page citations in the middle of clauses.

There are at least three proven ways of quoting effectively from a literary text.

1. Identification of the speaker + quotation. This method is employed in both popular and academic writing, usually for passages of four lines or less. Example: In Salman Rushdie's "At the Auction of the Ruby Slippers," the narrator explains, "We, the public, are easily, lethally offended. We have come to think of taking offense as a fundamental right. We value very little more highly than our rage, which gives us, in our opinion, the moral high ground." The positioning of the identification may be manipulated in any way that reads smoothly; for example, the narrator of "At the Auction of the Ruby Slippers" observes, "We the public, are easily, lethally offended." Again, variety of structure will enhance the readability of your essay. Don't begin every quotation with "The narrator says. . . ."

Because the introduction of the quotation specifies the origin of the passage, there is no need to identify it a second time by citing the author's name or the work's title in parenthesis. If, however, the identification fails to make this clear, then the author's name should appear in the citation. A full bibliographic entry should appear at the end of your paper in a section entitled "Works Cited."

2. The "block quotation" for longer excerpts. Any passage greater than four lines should be set off from the paragraph by indenting on the left side, a method that renders quotation marks themselves superfluous. Lines taken from stories should be quoted exactly as they appear in the original. Paragraph numbers, not page numbers, should be cited. For example, the narrator of Dorothy Parker's "The Waltz" reveals her attitude toward her oafish partner through a stream of running dialogue that contrasts with the dancers' actual conversation:

> *Oh, they're going to play another encore. Oh, goody. Oh that's lovely. Tired? I should say I'm not tired. I'd like to go on like this forever:*
>
> I should say I'm not tired. I'm dead, that's all I am. Dead, and in what a cause! And the music is never going to stop playing, and we're going on like this, Double-Time Charlie and I, throughout eternity. I suppose I won't care any more, after the first hundred thousand years. I suppose nothing will matter then, not heat nor pain nor broken heart nor cruel, aching weariness. Well. It can't come too soon for me. (17)

Note that, as in the above case, you must introduce the quotation, not simply "drop" it in the sentence.

In the example, a longer quotation is introduced by a complete sentence. But your responsibilities do not end here, because the quotation needs to be considered or "unpacked" thoroughly. After all, if the passage did not contain specific language that supports your argument, you would not have introduced it into evidence in the first place. Here, again, a balance between admissible evidence and your analysis is important. Remember: Quoting at length generally means discussing at length. This is entirely consistent with the logic that should inform your selection of the passage to quote: The very issues that led you to select the passage need to be conveyed to your reader.

3. Quoted phrases or "sound bites." Often you may want to quote only a word or phrase from the original. No problem. In these instances, take bits or "bites" of texts and work them smoothly into the syntax of your sentence. One suggestion might help: After quoting the bites, pretend that the quotation marks aren't there—that the bits are merely words in your sentence. Does it read smoothly and clearly as a sentence? If so, you have probably integrated the quoted excerpts well into your prose.

Examples

> Author of the most "enthusiastically applauded" writings by a black American, James Baldwin speaks "in an 'engaged' Black voice (Baker 63).

> Commenting that Mark Leyner was "perhaps the most notable embodiment of the 'avant-pop' sensibility of the nineties," Larry McCaffery suggests that Leyner's style is a "new form of 'realism'" (220).

> In *Heart of Darkness*, Marlow describes Mr. Kurtz as "at least seven feet long" with a "deep voice" (280, 281).

Note here that all three examples, in addition to crafting sentences that accommodate the quotations, employ different strategies of citation. The first example includes both a name and page number because the context does not identify the author of the quotation. The second example includes only a page number because the author's name—Larry McCaffery—is specified. The citation for the third example explains that the two phrases appear on different pages in the original.

In conclusion, select evidence carefully and present it in a meaningful pattern or logical order: Have you arranged it chronologically, in the order events occur in the literature you are discussing? Or have you elected to present the evidence in another way: from the least compelling example to the most compelling? From the easiest point to prove to the most difficult? In some other way? Paraphrase or summarize events as part of your argument—relevant events that provide a background or context for the specific argument you hope to build. When the language of the original is striking or so perfectly stated for your argument that you want to introduce it into evidence, follow the instructions we have just outlined. Last but not least, make certain that you have quoted *accurately:* word for word, punctuation mark for punctuation mark. Also, use the quotation fairly; in other words, make sure that it represents what you take to be the intent of the original.

If you do all of these things, there is an excellent chance the argument of your essay—your attempt at persuading your reader of the validity and importance of your thesis—will be successful.

Concluding

Like the creation of an effective introduction, the drafting of effective conclusions often poses a challenge. And, like trite introductions, ineffective conclusions are fairly easy to describe. Here's the worst:

> And, in conclusion, I have just shown you that Chester Himes's "Lunching at the Ritzmore" is about race relations.

Why is this such a weak statement? For several reasons. First, in a brief paper of three to five pages, it's fairly easy to determine that you are heading for a conclusion; you don't need to announce this. Second, the reader will decide whether you've made the case or not; the statement "I have just shown you" may in fact be inaccurate, because you might *not* have succeeded in making the case persuasively. Last, other than bringing the argument to a close, what is gained by this kind of sentence?

Fortunately, better concluding strategies exist. You might restate the thesis and offer a brief suggestion of its implications—or of matters related to the thesis that could not be admitted into your argument. Why is the thesis significant? What intellectual purchase or insight does it allow your reader? Such a tactic should not lead to a lengthy digression; rather, a strong thesis possesses a quality of interpretive richness that often exceeds the limits of the essay. Thus, in your conclusion you might outline briefly what other kinds of issues will be better understood because of your thesis statement. You might return to the epigraph or startling fact with which your essay began (assuming you employed one of these strategies). Or you might speculate briefly on how the field of evidence might have been expanded had you been afforded the opportunity of doing so.

Whatever strategy you use, remember that, like introductions, your conclusion for a short essay need not be overly elaborate. But you *do* need to bring the argument to closure.

Revision and Final Thoughts

Be sure to leave ample time to proofread your essay, which—we know—is advice easier to give than follow. Procrastination is the great enemy of revision. If you wait to begin your paper the night before it is due, the revision process will inevitably be compromised—or just totally nuked! So, get started early.

Then, after you have produced a rough draft, begin your revision process strategically. Does your essay satisfy the requirement of the assignment your instructor gave you? Is the title effective? Next, proceed to the largest elements of composition: arguments and paragraphs. Is the argument delineated in a logical and persuasive order? Are the paragraphs coherent, with immediately relevant topic sentences, evidence, and analysis? Is there an effective balance between evidence and discussion? Have you varied the lengths of quotations and your methods of introducing them? Have you created effective transitions between paragraphs and points of the argument?

Then, move to smaller matters, beginning with the problems your instructor has identified in previous essays. These differ from one writer to the next. Some have difficulty with sentence construction, others with phrasing and word choice, still others with spelling and punctuation. Recognize those areas of composition that have caused you difficulty in the past and revise them carefully. When writing on literary topics, again, accuracy is a crucial matter: Check every quotation against the original and make certain the citations are accurate. Also, be sure that you have followed your instructor's requirements in terms of pagination, presentation, and so on.

With any luck, this essay will prove a learning experience for you. How will you know what you think until you've seen what you have written?

22 Writing About Fiction

Just as any kind of writing helps writers clarify what they might think about a question, anyone who writes about fiction writes to explain, illuminate, enrich, deepen, connect, or even admire stories and novels. When scholars and literary critics write about fiction, they pose questions: What does this mean? How does this work? How is this fiction related to other works? How is this story related to its social and historical contexts? How does a work employ or describe sexual, gender, class, or racial relations? What does this fiction tell us about fiction in general or the act of reading or writing?

Experienced writers tend to answer such questions by providing a conclusion about how specific elements of a story or novel might express or convey an idea or produce an aesthetic effect. Like all good writers, they base their view on evidence from the specific fictional works under discussion, and perhaps from its historical context.

Another way writers offer ideas about understanding a story comes from using a particular set of assumptions that belong to one or another of the critical theories about literature. In this book, you have seen presented many different approaches (or theories) about literature including formalism, close reading, psychoanalytic criticism, feminist criticism, Marxist criticism, deconstruction, and reader response criticism. These critical approaches depend on slightly different sets of assumptions about how literary texts do what they do or arise partly from asking different questions about texts. For example, writers who want to study how a story's various parts—character, narrator, imagery, and style—work together to produce certain effects engage in analyses based on close reading. Writers exploring a psychoanalytic view ask how a story might reflect various tenets of psychoanalysis or illustrate or enact certain relationships in terms best understood through psychoanalytic categories.

Thoughtful writing about fiction enriches our understanding of how a story works. Such a thesis is seldom the only "truth" to be discovered about a story, since fiction is rich, embodies a broad range of values, and is open to multiple and even contradictory interpretations. Those who write about fiction, including students, join in an ongoing conversation about a text or the work of a writer.

An Ongoing Conversation

Criticism of fiction occurs in classrooms, among friends, and as part of a written exchange that takes place in newspapers, magazines, scholarly journals, and books. While some of this criticism takes the form of reviews in which a critic evaluates the quality of a story or novel, other criticism is more concerned with the questions listed above—with how stories work as stories. (See "Writing a Research Paper".) As more and more critics write about a particular text, other critics and students of literature read what they have written. Sometimes critics agree with one another; in that case, critics who have read and agree with what a previous critic has said will often cite the work of that critic as a part of their own arguments. Incorporating points another critic has already made enables scholars to build on what they have said to make other observations. Sometimes, however, critics will not agree with what another critic has said. In that case, scholars might merge a disagreement with another critic into the presentation of their own points.

Not all writing about fiction must become a part of this conversation. Essays for class sometimes ask you to engage with a literary work in various ways; the purpose of such assignments is to enable you to improve your reading, writing, and analytical skills. In this kind of writing, what is important is evidence that comes from the text as it is presented in a cogent argument with a clear, limited, specific thesis.

Drafting Your Essay

The conventional form for a discussion of a fictional text is an essay in which the writer presents a thesis and maps supporting arguments in the introductory paragraph or paragraphs, provides textual evidence throughout the essay's body, and concludes at the end. The introductory paragraphs are important because they indicate to readers what they can expect. If your thesis is clear and specific and if you map your supporting arguments, readers will know where you are going and will be gratified when you actually fulfill your promise. Introductory material is like a contract writers make with readers; it primes readers' expectations, makes them happy when the promises are fulfilled, and makes them angry or frustrated when the essay deviates from what it has promised.

The essay's body paragraphs present textual evidence incorporated into logical forms called arguments. These arguments may take several forms. They may be inductive (reasoning from a specific case to a more general conclusion) or deductive (reasoning from the general to the specific). In other words, writers may begin with a specific example—a character, an event in a story, an image—and in analyzing it, draw more general conclusions about the story. Or they may begin with a general principle or observation about a text and "prove" it by providing several more specific examples. Whether writers organize their arguments inductively or deductively, they always make certain assumptions about the nature of fiction and the ways stories work that affect not only the thesis they formulate, but the kinds of examples they use.

Essays on fiction end with a conclusion. In short essays, this conclusion should not simply reiterate what the writer has said, but also address the question "so what?" A conclusion might also help incorporate more specific material into a more general thesis (in an inductively organized essay) or might return to a restatement and clarification of a general principle (in a deductive essay).

Admissible Evidence

There are many kinds of evidence that writers can produce to support a thesis. Good evidence, however, is material that supports the thesis and provides some insight about the text under scrutiny. Good evidence is relevant to the thesis, is clear, or can be made clear through analysis. Kinds of evidence might include portions of the text itself, historical or biographical evidence, and conclusions of other critics. Evidence from primary texts (the story you are writing about) must often be analyzed to provide evidence. For example, if a particular image is the subject of the essay, then the writer must locate and sometimes analyze the appearances and uses of the image in the text. If the thesis involves a reading of gender or race or uses psychoanalytic principles, you may want to summarize examples taken from the story from the perspective of such a focus.

The presentation of evidence is crucial. Not only should its connection to the thesis be made absolutely clear in a topic sentence (which indicates the purpose and argument of a paragraph), its presentation must also be accurate. The passage should be exact and material that is elided or cut out should not be material that changes the meaning of a sentence or eliminates contrary evidence. Evidence should also be inserted at points where it best illustrates the point being made about it.

Textual evidence should be presented economically; that is, enough evidence should be there to make the point, but whole chunks of text inserted without commentary force readers to do the writer's work by making them locate what might be important in a quoted passage. Writers should always make the argument as easily accessible as possible. Don't make the reader do the work.

Summaries of narrative or character can be valuable rhetorical tools. Summaries are ways writers can organize aspects of a text that help make their argument. To be convincing, however, summaries should not distort the text too much; they should instead be a ground for agreement between the writer and the reader that at the same time provide a pretext for discussion and the development of further argument.

Outside sources may also provide evidence, as can historical context, biographical information, examples from other texts, or statements of authorial intent. In the case of any kind of evidence, the critic should ask the following questions:

1. What am I trying to show?
2. What does this evidence show?
3. Is this evidence relevant?
4. Does this evidence add something new to my argument?
5. Is this evidence consistent with the assumptions of my argument?

Though it may seem obvious that questions 1 and 2 should match, not asking these questions sometimes results in the presentation of evidence that does not relate to a thesis. Asking if evidence is relevant and if it adds something new are not only ways of double-checking 1 and 2, but also addresses the problem of too much evidence that provides too little support. Question 5 asks the writer to consider the kind of evidence being offered and prevents such problems as biographical evidence being used as support for an argument about textual language, for example, or material from another author being adduced as evidence of a text's use of a particular image. If a writer assumes, for example, that a text forms a consistent world in and of itself, how is evidence of historical context consistent with that kind of close reading? If a writer assumes that all of the relations within a story can be explained through the use of a class and economic analysis, how would the addition of an argument about psychoanalysis be consistent?

Final Thoughts

The purposes of writing about fiction, of course, are ultimately to learn something about how a particular story works as a story: how it makes its various meanings, how it composes its style, how its various formal parts (plot, character, narrator, point of view, imagery, structure) work together, how it reflects on its own sociohistorical context, how it might present views that either challenge or underwrite the status quo (or both).

Sample Student Essay

The sample essay below is an excellent example of a close reading of Colette's story, "The Hidden Woman," which appears in Chapter 13.

Ann Telford

English 50

Prof. Roof

May 12, 2002

When Reading Is about Writing:
Desire and Perception in Colette's
"The Hidden Woman"

He thinks the eel-like Pierrot is his wife. He follows her through the party, watching her dance with one, kiss another, drink champagne, put her hands on the neck of a woman. At the end he comforts himself with the idea that none of the Pierrot's gestures mean anything. Instead, she is merely being alone, "unknown, forever solitary and without shame, whom a little mask and a hermetic costume had restored to her irremediable solitude and her immodest innocence" (153). This husband, from whose point of view "The Hidden Woman" is narrated, is caught in his lie. Not only has he lied to his wife about attending the masked ball, he lies to himself about his wife's nature—and perhaps even about whether the Pierrot he follows is really his wife at all. For the husband, believing is seeing; what he sees is a reflection of his own guilt and desires. As he interprets the Pierrot as his wife and reads her actions as ultimately harmless (ultimately unthreatening to him), he shows the degree to which interpretation is more about the desires of the interpreter.

Why does the husband think he has the truth when the whole affair began with lies? After situating the husband at the masked ball, the story relates a flashback where the husband told his wife he would be out of town for the ball. The wife, with "shivers of disgust which made her hair, her delicate hands, and her chest in her white dress shudder at the sight of a slug or some filthy passer-by" performed her revulsion at the idea of attending (151). Since the story begins with the husband at the ball, we can only assume that he lied in order to be free to attend by himself. Like the husband, the story's readers must guess at why the wife lied, if the Pierrot is indeed the wife. But why would the husband suspect that she is his wife? What function does the Pierrot serve for him?

The husband thinks the Pierrot is his wife because he is guilty about his lie. In making his wife present as well, he makes her a partner in his own deceit. The evidence that the Pierrot is his wife is that she utters a little "ahem" "typical of his wife,"

Telford 3

and she pulls out a gold box like one he had given his wife, and she addresses him in a voice that sounds like hers "thinly disguised" (151–52). There is also, however, evidence to the contrary; the Pierrot is unidentifiable and it scratches "its thigh, with a free and uninhibited gesture" so unlike the wife that the husband is momentarily relieved. He encounters the Pierrot after he has been gazing at a scene of domination, a woman grasped by "the enormous square hands" of a Venetian lord (151). The husband's ability to penetrate the Pierrot's disguise is like the Lord grasping the woman with his hands. The husband is indeed the "Domino," the lord, the name used by the Pierrot to address him. But it is also possible—a possibility the husband ignores—that if the Pierrot is indeed his wife, she recognizes him.

The husband's interpretation of his wife's actions is one that initially worries him. He thinks "she's here for someone, with someone" (152). He follows her through the party, interpreting every meeting as a romantic tryst—her dance with the warrior, the Byzantine she kisses, the tussle with the wrestler, the dalliance with the Dutch girl. At the end of the story the husband comforts himself by interpreting all of these actions as meaningless. He has seen his wife as she would be if she thinks she's alone and she isn't unfaithful, but free and unfettered and perhaps more sensual than he thought (and certainly more than her first squeamish presentation). Finding a text in the suggestive Pierrot, the husband "reads" her actions and concludes that she is as he would want her. He also concludes that she is doing exactly what he is. If his initial identification of the Pierrot comes through guilt, his final analysis forgives them both.

Telford 4

As readers of this story, we are also asked to interpret the Pierrot's actions; through point of view we are aligned with the husband's perspective. We see his desire, but do we see our own? If we are sympathetic to the husband, we might not see the story's edge of irony that brings the astuteness of the husband's ideas into doubt. It is entirely possible, for example, that if the Pierrot/wife recognizes the husband, her actions are deliberate attempts to mislead and enrage him. She would also see him as a liar and might pay him back for his mendacity. After all, the Pierrot approaches the husband, not he her. If the Pierrot's actions are all accomplished with the idea that she has an audience, they gain an entirely different meaning, one the guilty hopeful husband cannot see. If we read from the side of the woman and if we assume she has knowledge, then her actions may mean nothing in themselves, but are deliberate attempts to show the husband what he deserves to see: her freedom, perversity, lack of discrimination, and unladylike character. He cannot fault her later without admitting he lied, but she will have taught him a lesson.

What lesson do the readers of the story learn? Do we know the ways we, too, are implicated in desire? If we see from the husband's perspective, we see that the Pierrot is as he thinks. If we stand apart from him, we might see that he is fooling himself. If we imagine events from the perspective of the Pierrot/wife, we play a little trick on him that will catch him with his own guilt. Perhaps readings of this story depend on the critics' desire to see the husband or wife vindicated, or perhaps, like the husband, our desire is for the text to be simple and fall into place.

23 Writing a Research Paper

Not to interpret is impossible, as refraining from thinking is impossible.

—ITALO CALVINO, *MR. PALOMAR* (1983)

This epigraph from Italo Calvino's novel, one chapter of which appears earlier in this book, seems uncannily accurate. For many of the phenomena we encounter in everyday life, however subtly, demand interpretation: menus, clothing styles, even the facial expressions of people we meet, to name just three. The interpretive process begins with reading, then moves to larger speculations, and, in the best of cases, leads to the formulation of answers to specific questions. What salad would go well with this entree? Why is this person frowning at me? What image does this suit or jacket and slacks ensemble project? In fact, many popular styles or recent "subcultures"—the Beat Movement, "Goth" culture, or the so-called punk rock movement of the 1970s—comprise a larger text to be read and interpreted. How is this music connected to that fashion, hairstyle, or lifestyle? What larger social or political statement is this subculture making, or not making? Consider, for example, all the things a term like *hip-hop* or *heavy metal* means. The list of things that might be interpreted is potentially endless.

Calvino's character Mr. Palomar, a compulsive reader and interpreter, knows this all too well. He contemplates waves, bodies on beaches, stellar constellations, the flight patterns of migrating birds—just about everything. Therein resides his problem: He has no rules to limit his interpretive activities; as a consequence, he drives himself to distraction by "reading" everything from the blades of grass and sea of weeds in his lawn to the kind of cheese he buys at a store. He is, in other words, both obsessed and adrift, a player immersed in a readerly game devoid of any organizing rules. And a game without rules quickly leads to chaos, which is one of the inferences *Mr. Palomar* seems to promote.

Fortunately, writing research papers on literature is a highly "ruleful" enterprise. Unlike Mr. Palomar's chaotic lawn, topics selected for research papers need to have clearly marked limits. Setting these boundaries, however, often poses one of the most difficult problems a writer faces, and this is merely one of the many decisions a research project demands. Some of these are relatively large, potentially complicated matters like "what is my topic?" and, even more central to most kinds of research papers, "what is my thesis statement?" Other decisions, like the one we just made about whether to quote directly or paraphrase a line from Calvino's novel, concern the smaller issues of a single sentence or paragraph. What would a paraphrase of this sentence sound like, and how should it be cited? Would it be more effective to render the passage as it appeared in the original?

This essay considers all of these questions and more. Throughout, however, as is the case in writing about literature without the benefit of research, we want to emphasize that at each step of the process—during the prewriting, writing, and revision stages—the composition of successful research papers depends on the writer's thoughtful decision making, the careful organization of reference materials, and a sincere effort to use these materials accurately. The best research writing is driven by the writer's intellectual curiosity about a subject, for writing based on research should result in increased knowledge for both the writer and reader of the paper.

As we described in Chapter 21, "Writing About Literature," the decisions that most influence the purpose and ultimate structure of a research paper are made during prewriting, before the first sentence is even drafted.

Prewriting

After being informed about the length of the assignment and its due date, the first question to be answered about a research project is this: What kind of essay am I being asked to write, a *review* or an interpretive *argument?* Most instructors will assign the latter, and the distinction between the two is crucial because it helps define your purpose in researching and writing about a topic, it determines who you are as a writer, and it suggests the kind of audience your paper is addressing. As in virtually every writing situation, from letters home to papers written for courses to portions of typical job applications, a writer at the prewriting stage needs to define as specifically as possible the purpose of the writing and the audience to whom it is directed.

The author of a *review,* a film review for example, regards his or her audience as *uninformed.* Because the audience has not seen the movie, the reviewer's job is largely descriptive and, finally, evaluative. For this reason, a reviewer of a feature film will almost always summarize the central plot or action, mention such features as the central characters, the actors' performances, and maybe even the film's musical score before rendering an opinion. And this opinion almost always pertains to the film's quality, its goodness or badness. That's the purpose of a review. The most influential reviewers, like Roger Ebert and the late Gene Siskel, can either breathe life into a movie's financial future or sound its death knell by giving it a "thumb's up" or a "thumb's down" verdict.

Reviewers, like all writers, make other decisions as well. What is the reading level of my audience? What language will most effectively communicate ideas to such readers? What other elements of my essay, such as the length and complexity of sentences or paragraphs, ought to be shaped for this particular group of readers? What kinds of evidence will be most persuasive in this particular rhetorical situation, and how should this evidence be presented?

By contrast, writers of critical essays define their audiences and purpose for writing quite differently. Such essays are addressed to *informed* readers, and the writer's task does not generally include commentary on a text's goodness or badness—indications of whether the writer liked it or not—but rather develops an idea, an opinion, about the text or texts under discussion. Because the reader of the essay, by definition, is familiar with the text, knows who the characters are and so on, the writers of research papers—and, indeed, most papers on literary topics—are not required to provide long summaries of the plot or action, descriptions of the central characters, and other features of the text. Instead, the paper attempts to advance a *reading*, an interpretation, of some aspect or aspects of the play, story, or poem by making a case for the validity of a particular understanding or intellectual "purchase" of the topic. This means that a research paper has to have a thesis statement.

Thesis Statements

The sentence that conveys the thrust of the writer's purpose—and, in fact, organizes the entire essay—is called the *thesis statement.* And while it is often the case that a precise thesis statement is formulated after a rough draft is produced, all research writing begins with at least some ideas about the topic to be undertaken and the direction the paper will take. But, as every writer also knows, finding that topic and refining the thesis are among the most difficult jobs a writer undertakes during prewriting.

By way of a brief review, here are the characteristics of a good thesis statement.

- A thesis statement is a statement of opinion, not a fact or statement of intention.
- A thesis statement offers an opinion about which reasonable people might disagree.
- A thesis statement usually possesses a rhetorical premise (comparison, process, classification, definition, and so on).
- A thesis statement predicts the progress of the paper and controls the evidence to be admitted.
- A thesis statement addresses a topic of interpretive significance, not a minor point.
- A thesis statement relies on theoretical or aesthetic assumptions.

All of these issues are described in greater detail in Chapter 21, "Writing About Literature." But when writing an essay based on research, one other component of thesis statements becomes relevant.

- A thesis statement enters its author into a critical conversation with other readers.

Unlike papers written solely from your own experience of a poem, short story, film, or play, a research paper inevitably leads to your consultation of other opinions. How have other readers before you understood Shakespeare's Hamlet, Joseph Conrad's Marlow and Kurtz, or Susan Glaspell's Iowa farmers? In some ways, this quality of a thesis statement becomes the most intimidating because, after all, if something is published in a book or academic journal, it must be correct. Right?

Wrong. A published essay or chapter of a book that analyzes the topic you want to explore need not be regarded as unimpeachable or exhaustive. In the case of materials printed on non-refereed Web sites, it may not even be any good. But such readings *do* exist and, as we will see, if you borrow anything from them—in any form—your indebtedness must be cited appropriately. The thesis of a research paper, in fact, responds in part to what "outside" sources you have found. But the best papers achieve more than a reiteration of source materials. They add to them, modify them, refocus them, even refute them. The sources you uncover during your research are much like the voices in a conversation into which your voice—your thesis statement—enters.

But how do you find this conversation in the first place? You start the research process by heading for the library.

Finding and Evaluating Sources

Your instructor will most likely stipulate the number of sources you need to consult for this assignment and may also restrict the kinds of materials you may use. One of the most controversial sources of information, whatever might be said of its convenience, is the World Wide Web, which can be "surfed" on topics ranging from Edgar Allan Poe to Michelle Cliff. Several realities make information taken from the Web potentially problematic: the possibility that it has not been "refereed," for instance, and the fact that information on Web sites may exist in cyberspace today and be gone tomorrow. By "refereed," we mean that an essay appearing in most academic books and journals has undergone "peer review": It has been evaluated and approved by experts in the field before being published. In the case of most academic presses, a book has not only been recommended for publication by experts, but also endorsed by a review board at the press. Unfortunately, most Web sites cannot guarantee such quality in the materials they post, with the exception of such refereed online publications as *Postmodern Culture* and *Workplace: The Journal of Academic Labor*.

In general, at least two factors can help you decide the quality of the material you have found: its date of publication and the reputation of the publisher. Journals and books published at reputable institutions (that is, colleges and universities you have heard of) have undergone peer review, as have books accepted by such major publishers as Houghton Mifflin, Norton, Macmillan, John Wiley, Harcourt Brace, and others. When in doubt about a potential source, ask your instructor.

Also, it is generally advisable—not to mention, efficient—to begin your search with recently published books and journal articles. Not because the last thing written is necessarily the best thing written, but because the bibliographies in these publications will lead you to potential sources published earlier. Obviously, starting your research with earlier materials will not be similarly enhancing of your bibliography. Here, again, exceptions exist. If, for example, you are interested in how New York audiences responded to the first production of Eugene O'Neill's *The Emperor Jones* in 1920 or how reviewers in the 1890s responded to several of Thomas Hardy's novels, then your investigation would most likely begin with the review of materials published then.

Finally, a number of indexes and bibliographies are helpful both in leading you to sources and in evaluating the sources you find. For example, the Modern Language Association (MLA) publishes the annual *MLA International Bibliography*, which lists works published about most American, British, and Western European authors during a given year. The *Reader's Guide to Periodical Literature* is similarly useful, because it indexes the contents of popular magazines, and the gateway site *Voice of the Shuttle: Web Page for Humanities Research* (if Internet sources are permissible for your assignment) can assist you in locating relevant materials on the Web. Most major city newspapers like the *New York Times* and the *Washington Post* are indexed and can prove indispensable sources for such materials as theater and film reviews. The *MLA Handbook for Writers of Research Papers*, 5th ed. (1999), whose documentation system we will summarize below, also recommends the *Book Review Index* and *Book Review Digest* as places you can go to find reviews of books you might want to consult. If you are preparing a research paper on a topic in American literature or culture, the annual volume *American Literary Scholarship* (*ALS*) could also prove valuable to you.

All of these reference books and much, much more are available in college and university libraries. And reference librarians are there to make your search for materials as painless and productive as possible; if you need assistance, don't hesitate to ask one for help.

Taking Notes from Sources

Remember that whatever sources you decide to use, it is your responsibility to paraphrase or quote from them accurately. Accuracy down to the last word or punctuation mark sounds like an easy enough goal to achieve, but it isn't. Imagine taking notes from a source when the phone rings, or when your roommate comes in and invites you to a party, or when someone next door puts on Eminem or Jimi Hendrix at high volume—any of these distractions could compromise your ability to record information accurately from a source. Further, after a week, a month, or more of reviewing and evaluating sources, it's easy to get confused about where certain material originated. If essential information from and about a source is not written down—and checked carefully—the possibilities of making mistakes increase dramatically. Of course, factors beyond your control may complicate your research: a book you are relying on may be called back to the library; a journal issue you found easily today may be missing tomorrow; and, as we have already mentioned, the Web site you discovered today may be quite different tomorrow.

For all of these reasons, it is essential that your note-taking system include at least the following information.

1. A *full* citation for every source. This means the author's complete name, title, publication information and, for articles or chapters of collected books, the full page run of the essay you intend to cite.
2. An indication for each entry that reminds you whether the information is a brief summary, an extended paraphrase of the original, or a direct quotation. The distinction between a paraphrase and a direct quotation is a crucial one and is discussed in the next section below.
3. A page number—or paragraph number for some Internet sites—for each note you take.
4. A note to yourself of exactly where you found the source, just in case you need to consult it later.

Quoting, Paraphrasing, and Avoiding Plagiarism

Once you have found sources relevant to your project and begin note-taking, you will need to decide whether to make a brief summary of the material, write a more extended paraphrase, or quote directly. Of course, you will probably do a combination of all three for many of the sources you find. The decision to quote or paraphrase involves several factors. Is the language of the original so striking that its precise phrasing is nearly as striking as its content? A sentence commonly found in histories of British drama like "The public theatre in England began in the later 1570s" might convey significant information, but its wording is hardly exceptional and need not be quoted. Whereas, Hamlet's famous soliloquy that begins "To be, or not to be, that is the question" (3.1.57) might prove awkward to restate and ineffective as well. "Should I, like, kill myself or maybe I shouldn't is what I'm trying to figure out" fails to capture the elegance of Shakespeare's line. Some passages, like the opening sentence of Samuel Beckett's novel *Murphy* (1957), are too cleverly phrased to be reduced to paraphrase: "The sun shone, having no alternative, on the nothing new." Others, like Salman Rushdie's description of the shame of colonized peoples from his novel *Shame* (1983), contain such vivid metaphors that you will probably want to quote it directly:

> Imagine shame as a liquid, let's say a sweet fizzy tooth-rotting drink stored in a vending machine. Push the right button and a cup plops down under a pissing stream of the liquid. How to push the button? Nothing to it. Tell a lie, sleep with a white boy, get born the wrong sex. (125)

You decide how best to use the material you find. Whether you quote or paraphrase, remember that you are obliged to explain the implications of this material when you write your paper.

When paraphrasing a passage, make certain that you not only convey its meaning accurately, but that you also restate it in your own words. This means, at the very least, revising the descriptive language of the original into your own prose. If you consciously recall taking a paraphrase from a source and using it in your essay, it must be cited, just as you would cite a direct quotation. Consider the following example, taken from Terry Eagleton's book *Crazy John and the Bishop and Other Essays on Irish Culture* (1998), which discusses the changing forms of modern art after World War II. Pay particular attention to the language Eagleton employs at the end of the excerpt to define aesthetic innovations and their origins.

Original Passage

> It is as though we can now recognize that, for example, simply because of the sharpening contradictions of naturalistic drama, there would have been a thrust beyond such theatrical realism, even if its names had not turned out to be Beckett or Pirandello or Ionesco. Someone, we feel, would have had to come up with free verse or musical dissonance or showing a face from five different angles simultaneously, just as once you have a variety of liquors it is hard not to think that cocktails were somehow preordained. Every cultural period provides us with a [host] of possibilities. . . . In post-war Europe, there were those authors gripped by a sense of spiritual exhaustion, writers who carved out a niche of anti-heroic debunkery, artistic exiles adrift between languages, and avant-garde experimenters in theatrical form. (Eagleton 297)

Paraphrase

> Naturalistic or realistic drama at the beginning of the twentieth century contained a number of ever-sharpening contradictions, so some innovative playwright inevitably would have gone beyond theatrical realism in terms of dramatic form. The same is true of all art in the period; someone would have had to come up with free verse in poetry, musical dissonance in composition, or showing a face from five different angles in filmmaking. Lots of aesthetic possibilities exist in every period. This is particularly true of Europe after World War II, where many authors, gripped by a sense of spiritual exhaustion, felt adrift between languages and led avant-garde experimentation, especially in a new theatre of anti-heroic debunkery.

Although this paraphrase accurately summarizes the original, it verges on *plagiarism* for at least two reasons: Highly descriptive phrases from the original appear without quotations marks, and no citation at the end identifies the source of these ideas. Notice that the quotation is followed by "(Eagleton 297)," signaling the origin of this material. If previous sentences clarified that Eagleton's book was the source, then only "(297)" would be necessary. But, again, *any material that you consciously recall taking from a source must be accompanied by a citation.* And, of course, fuller information about the source should appear in the "Works Cited" section at the end of the paper.

But this is only half of the problem with the above paraphrase. An equally significant failing is the writer's inability to rephrase important descriptions in Eagleton's paragraph: "sharpening contradictions," "gripped by a sense of spiritual exhaustion," "anti-heroic debunkery" and so on. Again, some language is, by its very nature, so basic and colorless that it really cannot be paraphrased. For example, "Abraham Lincoln was born in Kentucky and moved to Illinois when he was a small child" contains little descriptive language to rephrase. You cannot replace "born" with "came into this world" without risking verbosity; "moved" need not be changed to "migrated" or "transported." But phrases like "gripped by a sense of spiritual exhaustion" or "anti-heroic debunkery" in the original must be restated in your own words. The following paraphrase suggests one way to do this.

Paraphrase

> Contemporary scholars like Terry Eagleton emphasize the decline of dramatic realism in the early decades of the twentieth century, and the aesthetic experimentation that eventually took place not only in play writing, but in such other areas as poetry, musical composition, and filmmaking as well. So-called "free verse" in poetry and "musical dissonance" in musical composition were followed, in the years of soul-searching in Europe after World War II, by a variety of formal experiments in drama such as the writing of plays around anti-heroes and the creation of a dramatic mood on stage that matched the pessimism of the times. (297)

You may elect, as we have in the above paraphrase, to quote and paraphrase in the same paragraph. No problem—so long as the quoted portions are identified and are integrated smoothly into the syntax of your sentence. If you are at all confused about methods of quoting from the original, please review "Arguments and Admissible Evidence: Paraphrase and Quotation" in Chapter 21, "Writing About Literature."

Once you have formulated a thesis, however tentative and subject to refinement or tweaking; have found, evaluated, and taken notes from sources; and have made preliminary decisions about paraphrasing and quoting, you are probably ready to begin a rough draft. Of course, this stage of the research writing process means making more decisions, some of which are outlined in the following section.

Writing

Your trips to the library have helped you refine a thesis in which you feel confident; you have tested it against the criteria listed above and have asked informed readers (your classmates or instructor) to comment on its potential. After consulting the card catalogue at the library, indexes and bibliographies, and—perhaps—online sources, you have assembled a set of high-quality sources and taken accurate notes from them. You have read carefully the literary text or texts you intend to discuss, deciding what passages to incorporate into your argument; you have even made some preliminary decisions about which excerpts might be paraphrased and which should be quoted. Most important, you have allowed yourself sufficient time to write, rewrite, and revise some more. You are aware of the citation system you are supposed to follow and any other formal requirements outlined by your instructor: the recommended length of the essay, the placement of page numbers, and so on. You are well rested and comfortable.

You're ready to go! Well, almost.

Before you begin, reconsider the basic equation formulated in Chapter 21 and the ways in which your research will modify it. Here's the previous equation:

Your "reading" + textual evidence (paraphrase + quotation) = argument.

Writing that includes research material extends this equation as follows:

Your "reading" + textual evidence (paraphrase + quotation) + research (paraphrase + quotation) = argument.

Note that in both cases *your* analysis comes first, supported by concrete textual evidence. As we remarked earlier, a *balance* between your analysis and the evidence is crucial to the success of your paper. An argument with no evidence is no argument; an argument with only pieces of evidence left unexplained amounts to a mere patchwork of quotations and paraphrases. Effective arguments require both your organization and explanation of evidence—and, of course, the evidence itself must be presented clearly and concisely.

Most important, remember that the research you conduct only *supplements* your argument. That is to say, as is the case in writing any essay on a literary topic, your argument rests on your abilities to articulate a thesis statement and mount a convincing evidentiary case for it. Part of this evidence originates in the references you have consulted, but only a part and not necessarily the major part. And this prompts one more question:

What is your attitude toward this research and how does this affect your presentation of it in your argument?

As we mentioned earlier, not everything you read will be of equal quality, and you may not agree with everything you read. Fine. The question is, how do you present this information in your paper? The first answer is "with respect" and verbal grace.

After that, a number of possibilities exist. One common rhetorical tactic, for example, is called the "straw man" or "straw critic" approach in which a writer repeats a critical assertion only to modify or refute it. The purpose of the strategy is to create a "space" for the thesis or point of the argument by way of negation. Professional literary critics employ this strategy all the time, as the following passage from Richard H. Rodino's essay ("Authors, Characters, and Readers in *Gulliver's Travels*," *PMLA* 106 [October 1991]: 1054–70) on conflicting interpretations of Jonathan Swift's *Gulliver's Travels* suggests. Here, Rodino cites another scholar whose reading of the book, while incisive and useful, needs to be extended:

> Even a preliminary exploration of [conflicting views of *Gulliver's Travels*] requires an unusually complex understanding of the rhetorical relations involved. We must, for instance, go beyond Everett Zimmerman's pioneering description of the *Travels* as "a book not about a man who undergoes certain experiences but about a man who writes a book about experiences he has undergone"—a view that regards the reader simply as a receiver of meaning. . . . (1057)

In this passage Rodino expresses his admiration of Zimmerman's work ("pioneering description"), while at the same time insisting that his conception of the reader ought to be revised ("go beyond," "reader simply as a receiver").

The result is a respectful, yet strong statement of interpretive difference, which Rodino elaborates in his close reading of Swift's text.

On other occasions, broad critical agreement might exist, yet this consensus does not consider a text in which you are interested. Or, if it has been considered in such conversations, its significance hasn't been properly assessed. In such instances, you might indicate the principal parties in the conversation and then "clear a space" for your participation in the dialogue. This is the strategy Megan Sullivan uses to introduce her essay on recent women's films in Northern Ireland ("Orla Walsh's *The Visit* (1992): Incarceration and Feminist Cinema in Northern Ireland," *New Hibernia Review* 2 [Summer 1998]: 85–99):

> Following Pat Murphy, Anne Crilly, Margo Harkin, and Orla Walsh each have used film to critique nationalism and women's place in it. They also have taken great pains to suggest that nationalism itself is no longer women's primary concern; rather, they are concerned with day-to-day or material problems: censorship, the women's movement, class structure, and reproductive choice. Importantly, Crilly, Harkin, and Walsh invoke the site of the prison to suggest these concerns, and Murphy herself relies on the trope of incarceration to signal a young woman's emerging feminist consciousness. . . . Because her twenty-two minute film *The Visit* centers on the protagonist's physical and mental journey to visit her husband in prison, Walsh's film progresses furthest to argue for the significance of incarceration for nationalist women in Northern Ireland. (85)

This excerpt accomplishes several things at once. By alluding to several examples, it lends a sense of authority to the argument, suggesting that the writer really knows her subject. Like the "straw critic" approach, this more positive tactic also clears a discursive space for the writer's thesis. And, by returning to key terms in the essay's title, this passage reiterates elements crucial to the progress of the argument: "feminist cinema," Northern Ireland, and the importance of images of incarceration in these films.

However you choose to weave critical opinions into the fabric of your argument, do not let them overwhelm your presentation and analysis of textual detail. Introduce and enunciate the thesis statement, develop the evidence, and conclude—much as you would any other essay.

Revision

One unfortunate reality of research assignments is that while writers may spend weeks researching a topic and writing, many devote too little time to revising the argument, polishing the prose, and proofreading for mistakes. The revision stage, in fact, seems almost doomed to be given short shrift in most varieties of writing, yet its importance to the quality of the final product is indisputable. This is especially true of research papers.

Why? Because, as we have implied above, the process of conducting and writing a research paper is particularly vulnerable to human error. It isn't hard to understand why. Research writing includes more documents to read than most other kinds of writing, more material to process and organize, more quotations and decisions, more citations to foul up.

Our advice, consistent with that we have given earlier, is to read your draft carefully, checking in particular for some of the writing problems that have surfaced in earlier essays. This could mean checking all the transitions or topic sentences of paragraphs, sharpening the precision of your word selection, looking for spelling errors, and so on. By the time you write your research paper, you should have a fairly clear idea of the things you do well and those elements of your writing that need improvement. Remember that the root of word *revise* comes from the Latin meaning "look again," not "glance again" or "hurry through again." The very word, therefore, denotes a careful review of the entire project.

Research papers also add two significant elements to your list of "things to do" at the revision stage: Check the accuracy of every quotation in the essay—word by word, punctuation mark by punctuation mark—and verify that each entry in your "Notes" and "Works Cited" sections follow the *exact* format specified by your instructor. We are following the documentation system outlined in the *MLA Handbook for Writers of Research Papers*, 5th edition. If questions arise at any time in the process of researching or writing your paper, the *MLA Handbook* probably contains an answer. It is generally available in the reference section of college libraries or may be purchased from the Modern Language Association of America.

Because "Notes" and Works Cited" generally appear at the end of research papers, we will conclude with a brief discussion of their function and a listing of citation formats for the most common kinds of sources.

Notes and Works Cited

In the MLA citation system, "footnotes" and "endnotes" are greatly simplified. Why? Because instead of supplying a superscripted number for each citation and then listing each of these at the foot of the page or at the end of the essay, in the MLA system each reference in the text is followed by a parenthesis identifying the source and page number. So, to take the paraphrase from Terry Eagleton's book mentioned earlier, if the author of the excerpt is clear from the context—or if his name is specifically mentioned—you need only supply the page number at the end of the excerpt: thus, "(297)." If the source is *not* made clear by the context, then you must cite the author's last name and the page number: thus, "(Eagleton 297)." And, in cases in which you refer to two or more works by the same author, and the context does not specify the source of the excerpt, you must include the author's last name, an abbreviated title, and a page number: thus, "(Eagleton, *Crazy John* 297)."

That's about it. In this system of parenthetical or "internal" citation, the "Notes" section includes only extra information or brief asides—comments you might wish to make about a point raised in the essay that, in your judgment, is not important enough to include in the body of the argument. So, for example, suppose you had consulted several sources on literary experimentation after World War II, good sources but ones not so effective as Eagleton in explaining the topic. You might place a superscript after the passage from Eagleton and in your "Notes" section at the end of the paper direct your reader to these sources: thus,

Notes

[1]For further discussion of the origins of late modernist aesthetics and mid-twentieth-century "exhaustion," see Esslin and Miller.

You might even want to add a sentence or two to this entry distinguishing one source from another. Whatever the case, even if you only mention their names in one note, full information on Esslin and Miller must appear in the "Works Cited."

In the MLA documentation system of parenthetical citations, therefore, it is entirely possible to write a fine research paper without any notes at all. Not so with "Works Cited." Every work mentioned in notes, paraphrased or quoted in the body of the essay—and, of course, this includes the literary texts that form the nexus of your argument—must appear in the "Works Cited" at the end of the paper. Entries should be organized in alphabetical order by the author's last name (for a book written or edited by more than one person, you should use the last name of the first person listed on the title page). If an author is not listed for an article or essay, the first letter of the first major word in the title dictates its position in your "Works Cited."

Citation forms for the most commonly used kinds of sources follows.

A SINGLE-AUTHORED BOOK

Chávez, John R. *The Lost Land: The Chicano Image of the Southwest*. Albuquerque: U of New Mexico P, 1984.

TWO OR MORE BOOKS BY THE SAME AUTHOR

Jameson, Fredric. *The Political Unconscious: Narrative as a Socially Symbolic Act*. Ithaca: Cornell UP, 1981.

———. *Postmodernism, or, The Cultural Logic of Late Capitalism*. Durham, NC: Duke UP, 1991.

AN EDITED BOOK BY TWO OR MORE AUTHORS

Bérubé, Michael, and Cary Nelson, eds. *Higher Education Under Fire: Politics, Economics, and the Crisis of the Humanities*. New York: Routledge, 1995.

A TRANSLATED BOOK

Baudrillard, Jean. *Fatal Strategies.* Trans. Philip Beitchman and W. G. J. Niesluchowski. Ed. Jim Fleming. New York/London: Semiotext(e)/Pluto, 1990.

AN ARTICLE IN A SCHOLARLY JOURNAL

Newman, Karen. "Portia's Ring: Unruly Women and Structures of Exchange in *The Merchant of Venice.*" *Shakespeare Quarterly* 38 (1987): 19–33.

AN ARTICLE IN A MAGAZINE

Schlosser, Eric. "The Taking of the Presidency 2000." *Rolling Stone* 1 Feb. 2001: 36–38, 64.

AN ESSAY IN AN ANTHOLOGY

Onkey, Lauren. "The Passion Machine Theatre Company's Everyday Life." *A Century of Irish Drama: Widening the Stage.* Ed. Stephen Watt, Eileen Morgan, and Shakir Mustafa. Bloomington: Indiana UP, 2000. 223–35.

A MULTIVOLUME WORK

Lauter, Paul, et al., eds. *The Heath Anthology of American Literature.* 4th ed. 2 vols. Boston: Houghton Mifflin, 2002.

A FILM

North by Northwest. Dir. Alfred Hitchcock. Perf. Cary Grant, Eva Marie Saint, James Mason, Martin Landau, and Leo G. Carroll. MGM, 1959.

A LECTURE

Burke, Cynthia. "Tomorrow's English Majors." MLA Convention. Hynes Auditorium, Boston. 25 Apr. 2002.

AN INTERVIEW

Harold Bloom. Interview with Anthony Perro. *Weekend Edition.* Natl. Public Radio. WBUR, Boston. 10 June 1995.

AN E-MAIL

Tuttle, Robert. E-mail to the author. 2 May 2002.

CD-ROM

"Dickinson, Emily." *Discovering Authors.* Vers. 2.0. CD-ROM. Detroit: Gale, 1999.

A DOCUMENT WITHIN A DATABASE

"City Profile: San Francisco." *CNN Interactive.* 19 June 1998. Cable News Network. 19 June 1998.<http://www.cnn.com-TRAVEL/CITY.GUIDE/WTR/north.america.profiles/nap.sanfrancisco.html>

WEB SITE

Internet Public Library. 1 May 2002. 6 July 2002. <http://www.ipl.org/>.

Glossary

analepsis A literary term for shifts in chronology from the present to the past. In film, this practice is called a *flashback*.

antagonist A character who opposes the protagonist or whose actions conflict with the protagonist's aims or desires.

archetype The basic model for a particular character in a myth. Stemming from the Greek word *archetypos*, meaning "original pattern," an archetype in literature describes a symbolic image that is basic to the human experience of birth, death, fertility, disease, war, quest, and so on.

climax The moment of greatest emotional tension in a narrative. Usually, after events lead up to this point, they are resolved in the *denouement*.

close reading An engaged analysis and interpretation of a literary text that moves beyond a simple summary of the ideas or actions expressed in the work. A close reading often focuses on the specific words or figurative language used in a passage.

connotation The values, qualities, associations, and shades of meaning that a word acquires in contextual usage over time.

deconstruction The examination of how structures, language, and imagery work against or contradict themselves or other aspects of a story's expression.

denotation The literal meaning of a word or group of words rather than additional meanings those words might suggest (see *connotation*).

denouement The final resolution of a plot's conflict, generally occurring after the *climax* of the narrative.

diction The choice of words in prose, fiction, poetry, and drama.

diegesis The world of the story.

epiphany A sudden and overwhelming insight or recognition of a truth.

explication A critical interpretation of a text.

exposition The beginning of a story in which the characters and circumstances of the narrative are introduced.

feminist criticism The criticism that focuses on the politics and aesthetics of female experience and representation, as well as of gender generally.

first-person narrator See *narrator*.

formalism A kind of literary analysis that emphasizes using elements of form to interpret meaning.

frame narrator See *narrator*.

gay and lesbian criticism Analysis that focuses on issues of sexuality or the politics and aesthetics of gay experience and representation. It is part of a larger investigation of sexuality and gender called *queer theory.*

hyperbole A figure of speech using exaggeration for emphasis or effect.

hypertext Internet-based writing that contains links to other resources. Hypertext is performative because it requires readers to engage in a constant process of selection and arrangement that produces narrative.

image A suggestion of sensory phenomena.

imagery The use of language to evoke sensory experience.

in medias res In the middle of the thing (Latin). This term refers to starting a narrative in the middle of events rather than at the beginning.

intertextuality The various ways that texts refer to other texts.

irony A situation (dramatic irony) or phrasing (verbal irony) that performs something contrary to expectation. Dramatic irony occurs when the audience knows more about an incident than a character in a play does.

literary movement A set of ideas formulated by authors and critics about what literature should do and how it should be done.

Marxist criticism A form of analysis that studies representations of class, the ways literature enacts the effects of economic disparity, and the material conditions and contexts in which literature is produced. It is based on a labor theory of value advanced by the nineteenth-century German philosopher, historian, social scientist, and revolutionary Karl Marx.

metafiction A story about a story.

metanarrative A story that draws attention to the mechanisms of telling stories.

metaphor Figurative language that compares one word or thing in terms of another word or thing by way of direct transference.

mise en scène Put in the scene (French). Everything that a drama audience sees and hears, including set, costume, lighting, movement, and sound effects.

modernism A term used to describe various aesthetic movements in the late nineteenth and twentieth centuries, especially those prior to World War II. Modernism reacted against realistic representations of nineteenth-century literature as well as the conformity of commercial culture, in part by emphasizing stylistic experimentation.

monologue The spoken thoughts of a single character.

mood The atmosphere or feeling produced in a text, usually through descriptive language of places, people, and events.

motif Any significant repetition of images, symbols, language, actions, or other elements of a literary work.

myth criticism An approach to literary studies that analyzes characters and events as representative parts of archetypal, mythical patterns.

narrative A structure by which we make sense out of events by ordering them in a chain of cause-and-effect relations that play out in space and time.

narrator The voice of the person telling the story. Typically, the author selects a dominant narrative mode for each literary work, though some works may include multiple narrators and multiple narrative modes. A *first-person narrator* is a participating character in the story identified through the narrator's use of *I* or occasionally *we*. A *third-person narrator* is not explicitly present in the story but appears to recount events from a position outside the story, which is not explained or accounted for by the story. A *third-person omniscient narrator* is a narrator who has a complete, nearly godlike range of knowledge, including the thoughts and emotions of all characters. A *third-person limited narrator* is a narrator whose implied knowledge is limited to his or her subjective experiences. If a story involves more than one narrator, the first narrator is called the *frame narrator* (see Conrad's *Heart of Darkness* as an example).

naturalism A literary movement in which writers sought to render a realistic or scientific view of the human species.

New Criticism An approach to literary criticism that was followed by a group of American critics of the early and middle twentieth century who believed that analyzing the elements of a work was all that was necessary to understand it.

New Historicism An approach to literary analysis that focuses on the historical and cultural aspects of a text, asserting the importance of context and treating the text as a cultural document, not a literary icon.

Other The different. In both race and postcolonial criticism, the other is often constructed as a negation of white, European values. At times, the other is also made into an exotic or alluring figure of desire.

paradigms The models or patterns that make up the events in a story.

paraphrase A restatement in your own words of the main ideas, arguments, and thematic elements of a poem.

plot The purposeful arrangement of events in a story or play and the order in which they are presented. This arrangement of events may not necessarily follow the sequence in which they occurred but are usually presented for affective or causal reasons.

point of view The perspective from which people, events, and other details of a literary work are described.

popular culture The attitudes, customs, and folkways of ordinary, everyday people.

postcolonial criticism A set of theoretical issues emerging from the literature and culture of Europe's former colonies as they rebelled against colonial rule and asserted their own cultural and political independence, often by appropriating and recoding colonial discourse, national symbols, and other linguistic conventions of social distinction.

postmodernism A term used variously to characterize sets of aesthetic practices that break up any idea of unity, consistency, or singularity or that employs pastiche or other modes of borrowing. This term may also refer to postmodernist aesthetic practices or textual features.

prolepsis A flashforward.

protagonist A character that serves as the primary actor in a literary work and with whom readers are often invited to sympathize.

psychoanalytic criticism A critical approach that investigates the ways literary texts embody, enact, or illustrate dynamic relations within or among characters using concepts taken from psychoanalysis, particularly the work of Sigmund Freud and Jacques Lacan.

psychological criticism A critical approach that focuses on interpreting the psychological motivations of characters. Such an approach may adopt vocabularies from any of several psychological "schools" of thought such as the work of Sigmund Freud, Carl Jung, or D. W. Winnicott.

queer theory See *gay and lesbian theory.*

race criticism An approach to literary analysis that focuses on how racial difference is represented in the themes, characterizations, symbolism, settings, diction, and formal properties of literary texts.

reader response criticism An approach to literary analysis that focuses on the individual's response to literary texts and investigates the social conventions of reading that make up broader interpretive communities.

realism A literary movement and style that focuses on reproducing objective portraits of normal life through the use of a rigorous observation of human behavior in its social and material contexts.

reliability The degree to which readers can trust representations made by a narrator.

representation The act of using a word, image or pictorial sign to stand for something else. Representations have a shaping role in society insofar as they communicate perceptions, influence opinions, and build consensus, as well as determine attitudes and beliefs.

satire A literary work in which a person or group's vices, hypocrisies, or vanities are held up for ridicule or other comic criticism.

semiotics The study of how various signs (or signifiers) relate to one another in complex webs of meaning.

setting The physical, environmental, social, historical, and cultural contexts described in a story as the scene of its action.

stereotypes A character who represents a familiar type.

stock character A character that fills a predictable role that is conventional to certain kinds of drama. Westerns, for example, predictably offer readers and viewers a hero, a bad guy, a kind-hearted woman who either gambles or works in a saloon, and stereotypes of Native Americans.

story The collection of events that belong to the space and time of the world created by the text as well as events that are only suggested or implied in the text.

structuralist criticism Criticism that focuses on a story's structure as a way to understand how the story works.

style The distinctive manner of expression an author uses in a literary text.

subsystem A coherent group within a story.

symbol A concrete image, word, or thing, that refers to an abstract idea or condition. For instance, a wedding ring is a symbol of marriage.

theme The central idea or ideas suggested by a literary work.

third-person limited narrator See *narrator.*

third-person narrator See *narrator.*

third-person omniscient narrator See *narrator.*

tone A literary concept analogous to the tone of voice in spoken language.

unreliability The adjective applies to narrators whom readers may not trust to deliver unbiased information.

Credits

TEXT CREDITS

Achebe, Chinua, "The Sacrificial Egg": From *Girls at War and Other Stories* by Chinua Achebe, copyright © 1972, 1973 by Chinua Achebe. Used by permission of Doubleday, a division of Random House, Inc.

Anaya, Rudolfo, "A Story": From *The Silence of the Llano.* Copyright © 1982 by Rudolfo Anaya. Originally published by TQS Publications. Reprinted by permission of Susan Bergholz Literary Services, New York. All rights reserved.

Auster, Paul, *Ghosts*: From *Ghosts* by Paul Auster (Los Angeles: Green Integer Books, 1986). Copyright © 1986 by Paul Auster. Reprinted with the permission of the publisher.

Baldwin, James, "Previous Condition": Originally published in *Commentary.* Collected in *Going to Meet the Man* © 1965 by James Baldwin. Copyright renewed. Published by Vintage Books. Reprinted by arrangement with the James Baldwin estate; "Sonny's Blues": Originally published in *Partisan Review.* Collected in *Going to Meet the Man* © 1965 by James Baldwin. Copyright renewed. Published by Vintage Books. Reprinted by arrangement with the James Baldwin estate.

Balzac, Honoré de, "Sarrasine": From *S/Z* by Roland Barthes, translated by Richard Miller. Translation copyright © 1986 by Farrar, Straus & Giroux, Inc. Reprinted by permission of Hill and Wang, a division of Farrar, Straus & Giroux, LLC.

Barthes, Roland, "Sarrasine": From *S/Z* by Roland Barthes, translated by Richard Miller. Translation copyright © 1986 by Farrar, Straus & Giroux, Inc. Reprinted by permission of Hill and Wang, a division of Farrar, Straus and Giroux, LLC.

Beckett, Samuel, "The Calmative": From *Complete Short Prose: 1929–1989* by Samuel Beckett. Copyright © 1946 by Samuel Beckett. Used by permission of Grove/Atlantic, Inc.

Borges, Jorge Luis, "The Shape of the Sword": Translated by Donald A. Yates, from *Labyrinths* by Jorge Luis Borges, copyright © 1962, 1964 by New Directions Publishing Corporation. Reprinted by permission of New Directions Publishing Corporation.

Brossard, Nicole, *Surfaces of Sense.* Translated by Fiona Strachan. Coach House Translations, 1989. Pages 5–15. Reprinted by kind permission of Nicole Brossard.

Burroughs, William S., "The Finger": From *Interzone* by William S. Burroughs, introduction by James Grauerholz, copyright © 1989 William S. Burroughs. Used by permission of Viking Penguin, a division of Penguin Group (USA), Inc.

Calvino, Italo, "Mr. Palomar on the Beach: Reading a Wave": From *Mr. Palomar* by Italo Calvino, copyright © 1983 by Giulio Einaudi Editore, s.p.a., Torino, English translation by William Weaver, copyright © 1985 by Harcourt, Inc., reprinted by permission of Harcourt, Inc.

Cather, Willa, "Paul's Case": Reprinted from *Willa Cather's Collected Short Fiction, 1892–1912* edited by Virginia Faulkner by permission of the University of Nebraska Press. Copyright © renewed 1992, 1998 by the University of Nebraska Press.

Charters, Ann, "The First Word: Jack Kerouac Takes a Fresh Look at Jack Kerouac" and "Essentials of Spontaneous Prose": From *The Portable Jack Kerouac,* ed. Ann Charters, Viking, 1995. Reprinted by permission of Sterling Lord Literistic, Inc.

Chekhov, Anton, "The Lady with the Dog": From *My Life and Other Stories,* translated by Constance Garnett. Copyright © 1992. Reprinted by permission of Everyman's Library.

Cliff, Michelle, "The Store of a Million Items": From *The Store of a Million Items.* Copyright © 1998 by Michelle Cliff. Reprinted by permission of Houghton Mifflin Company. All rights reserved.

Colette, Sidonie-Gabrielle, "The Hidden Woman": From *The Other Woman* by Colette, translated by Margaret Crosland. Reprinted with the permission of Simon & Schuster Adult Publishing Group. Copyright © 1972 by The Bobbs-Merrill Company, Inc.

Cortázar, Julio, "Blow-Up": From *End of the Game and Other Stories* by Julio Cortázar, translated by Paul Blackburn, copyright © 1963, 1967 by Random House, Inc. Used by permission of Pantheon Books, a division of Random House, Inc.

Desai, Anita, "Studies in the Park": From *Games at Twilight.* Copyright © Anita Desai 1978. Reproduced by permission of the author c/o Rogers, Coleridge & White Ltd., 20 Powis Mews, London W11 1JN.

Di Prima, Diane, Excerpt from "Chapter 10, Summer": From *Memoirs of a Beatnik* by Diane Di Prima, copyright © 1969, 1988 by Diane Di Prima. Used by permission of Penguin, a division of Penguin Group (USA), Inc.

Faulkner, William, "A Rose for Emily": Copyright 1930 and renewed 1958 by William Faulkner, from *Collected Stories of William Faulkner* by William Faulkner. Used by permission of Random House, Inc.; "Barn Burning": Copyright 1950 by Random House, Inc. Copyright renewed 1977 by Jill Faulkner Summers, from *Collected Stories of William Faulkner* by William Faulkner. Used by permission of Random House, Inc.; "Golden Land": Copyright 1935 by Random House, Inc., from *Collected Stories of William Faulkner* by William Faulkner. Used by permission of Random House, Inc.

Fitzgerald, F. Scott, "Babylon Revisited": Reprinted with permission of Scribner, an imprint of Simon & Schuster Adult Publishing Group, from *The Short Stories of F. Scott Fitzgerald,* edited by Matthew J. Bruccoli. Copyright 1931 by The Curtis Publishing Company. Copyright renewed © 1959 by Frances Scott Fitzgerald Lanahan.

Forster, E. M., "The Road from Colonus": From *Collected Tales of E. M. Forster* by E. M. Forster, copyright 1974 by Alfred A. Knopf, a division of Random House, Inc. Used by permission of Alfred A. Knopf, a division of Random House, Inc.

Gilman, Charlotte Perkins, "The Yellow Wall-Paper": Reprinted by The Feminist Press in 1973.

Hemingway, Ernest: "Hills Like White Elephants": Reprinted with permission of Scribner, an imprint of Simon & Schuster Adult Publishing Group, from *The Short Stories of Ernest Hemingway.* Copyright 1927 by Charles Scribner's Sons. Copyright renewed 1955 by Ernest Hemingway.

Himes, Chester, "Lunching at the Ritzmore": From *The Collected Stories of Chester Himes.* Copyright © 1990 by Thunder's Mouth Press. Chester Himes, excerpt from *The Quality of Hurt: The Autobiography of Chester Himes,* Vol. 1., pp. 3–28. Copyright © 1971, 1972 by Chester Himes. Reprinted with permission of The Roslyn Targ Literary Agency, Inc.

Hurston, Zora Neale, "Sweat": As taken from *The Complete Short Stories* by Zora Neale Hurston. Introduction copyright © 1995 by Henry Louis Gates, Jr. and Sieglinde Lemke. Compilation copyright © 1995 by Vivian Bowden, Lois J. Hurston Gaston, Clifford Hurston, Lucy Ann Hurston, Winifred Hurston Clark, Zora Mack Goins, Edgar Hurston, Sr., and Barbara Hurston Lewis. Afterword and Bibliography copyright © 1995 by Henry Louis Gates, Jr. Reprinted by permission of HarperCollins Publishers, Inc. "Sweat" was originally published in *Fire,* November 1926.

Joyce, James, "Araby": From *Dubliners* by James Joyce, copyright 1916 by B. W. Heubsch. Definitive text copyright © 1967 by the Estate of James Joyce. Used by permission of Viking Penguin, a division of Penguin Group (USA) Inc.

Kafka, Franz, "A Hunger Artist": From *Franz Kafka: The Complete Stories* by Franz Kafka, translated by Willa and Edwin Muir, edited by Nahum N. Glatzer, copyright 1946, 1947, 1948, 1949, 1954, 1958, 1971 by Schocken Books. Used by permission of Schocken Books, a division of Random House, Inc.

Kureishi, Hanif, "Blue, Blue Pictures of You": From *Love in a Blue Time.* Copyright © Hanif Kureishi, 1997. Reproduced by permission of Rogers, Coleridge & White Ltd., 20 Powis Mews, London W11 1JN.

Lawrence, D. H., "The Horse-Dealer's Daughter": From D. H. Lawrence, *The Collected Short Stories.* Copyright © 1974. Reprinted by permission of Laurence Pollinger Limited and the Estate of Frieda Lawrence Ravagli.

Lessing, Doris, "A Woman on a Roof": From *To Room Nineteen: Collected Stories,* Vol. 1, 1978. Copyright © 1963 Doris Lessing. Reprinted by kind permission of Jonathan Clowes Ltd., London, on behalf of Doris Lessing.

Leyner, Mark, Selections from *My Cousin, My Gastroenterologist* by Mark Leyner, copyright © 1990 by Mark Leyner. Used by permission of Harmony Books, a division of Random House, Inc.

London, Jack, "The Law of Life"and "To Build a Fire": Reprinted with the permission of Scribner, a Division of Simon & Schuster, Inc., from *Jack London Short Stories, Authorized Edition with Definitive Texts,* edited by Earle Labor, Robert C. Leitz III, I. Milo Shepard. Copyright © 1991 by Macmillan Publishing Company.

Mansfield, Katherine, "The Garden-Party": From *The Short Stories of Katherine Mansfield* by Katherine Mansfield, copyright 1923 by Alfred A. Knopf, a division of Random House, Inc. and renewed 1951 by John Middleton Murray. Used by permission of Alfred A. Knopf, a division of Random House, Inc.

Márquez, Gabriel García, "The Handsomest Drowned Man in the World": Entire text from "The Handsomest Drowned Man in the World" from *Leaf Storm and Other Stories* by Gabriel García

Márquez. Copyright © 1971 by Gabriel García Márquez. Reprinted by permission of HarperCollins Publishers, Inc.

Melville, Herman, "Bartleby the Scrivener": From *Complete Stories,* ed. Jay Leyda, 1949, pp. 3–47, published by Random House, Inc.

Mena, María Cristina, "The Vine-Leaf": Reprinted with permission from the publisher of *The Collected Stories of María Cristina Mena* (Houston: Arte Publico Press—University of Houston, 1997).

Oates, Joyce Carol, "How I Contemplated the World from the Detroit House of Correction and Began My Life Over Again": From *Wild Saturday and Other Stories,* 1984. Copyright by the Ontario Review, Inc., 1993. Reprinted by permission of the author.

O'Connor, Flannery, "A Good Man Is Hard to Find": From *A Good Man Is Hard to Find and Other Stories,* copyright 1953 by Flannery O'Connor and renewed 1981 by Regina O'Connor, reprinted by permission of Harcourt, Inc.

Olsen, Tillie, "I Stand Here Ironing": Copyright © 1956, 1957, 1960, 1961 by Tillie Olsen, from *Tell Me a Riddle* by Tillie Olsen. Introduction by John Leonard. Used by permission of Dell Publishing, a division of Random House, Inc.

Parker, Dorothy, "The Waltz": Copyright 1933, renewed © 1961 by Dorothy Parker. First appeared in *The New Yorker,* from *Dorothy Parker: Complete Stories* by Dorothy Parker. Used by permission of Penguin, a division of Penguin Group (USA), Inc.

Penn, W.S., "This Close, Coyote": From *All My Sins Are Relative.* University of Nebraska Press, 1995. Copyright © 1995 by W.S. Penn. Reprinted by permission of The Barry-Swayne Agency.

Poe, Edgar Allan, "The Fall of the House of Usher": Reprinted by permission of the publisher from "The Fall of the House of Usher" in *Collected Works of Edgar Allan Poe: Tales and Sketches, Volume 2,* edited by Thomas Ollive Mabbott, pp. 392–422, Cambridge, Mass.: The Belknap Press of Harvard University Press, copyright © 1969 by the President and Fellows of Harvard College; "The Purloined Letter": Reprinted by permission of the publisher from "The Purloined Letter" in *Collected Works of Edgar Allan Poe: Tales and Sketches, Volume 3,* edited by Thomas Ollive Mabbott, pp. 392–422, Cambridge, Mass.: The Belknap Press of Harvard University Press, copyright © 1969, 1978 by the President and Fellows of Harvard College.

Rhys, Jean, *Smile Please: An Unfinished Autobiography,* Andre Deutsh, 1979. Chapter titled "Chorus Girls," pp. 106–113. Reprinted by permission of Sheil Land Associates, London.

Rushdie, Salman, "At the Auction of the Ruby Slippers" and "The Free Radio": From *East, West* © 1994 by Salman Rushdie, reprinted with the permission of The Wylie Agency.

Twain, Mark, "Story of the Bad Little Boy": From Walter Blair, ed., *Selected Shorter Writings of Mark Twain.* Copyright © 1962 by Houghton Mifflin Company. Used by permission; pages 43–50 from *The Autobiography of Mark Twain,* edited by Charles Neider. Copyright © 1917, 1940, 1958, 1959 by the Mark Twain Company, renewed in 1987. Copyright 1924, 1945, 1952, by Clara Clemens Samossoud. Copyright © 1959 by Charles Neider, renewed 1987. Reprinted by permission of HarperCollins Publishers, Inc.

Updike, John, "A & P": From *Pigeon Feathers and Other Stories* by John Updike, copyright © 1962 and renewed 1990 by John Updike. Used by permission of Alfred A. Knopf, a division of Random House, Inc.

Van Vechten, Carl, "A Note on Breakfasts": From Carl Van Vechten, *Sacred and Profane Memories,* pp. 211–221. New York: Alfred A. Knopf, 1932. Reprinted by permission of the Van Vechten Trust.

Walker, Alice, "Everyday Use": From *In Love & Trouble: Stories of Black Women,* copyright © 1973 by Alice Walker, reprinted by permission or Harcourt, Inc.

Woolf, Virginia, "Kew Gardens": From *A Haunted House and Other Short Stories* by Virginia Woolf, copyright 1944 and renewed 1972 by Harcourt Inc., reprinted by permission of the publisher; "Introduction" and "The Symbol": From *The Complete Shorter Fiction of Virginia Woolf,* by Susan Dick, copyright © 1985 by Quentin Bell and Angelica Garnett, reprinted by permission of Harcourt, Inc.

Wright, Richard, "The Man Who Was Almost a Man": From *Eight Men* by Richard Wright. Copyright 1940, 1961 by Richard Wright. Copyright renewed 1989 by Ellen Wright. Introduction by Paul Gilmore. Reprinted by permission of HarperCollins Publishers, Inc.

Yamamoto, Hisaye, "Seventeen Syllables": From *Seventeen Syllables and Other Stories.* © *Partisan Review,* November 1949, © Renewed Hisaye Yamamoto DeSoto, 1976. Kitchen Table: Women of Color Press, 1988. Rutgers University Press, 1998.

PHOTO CREDITS

Part opener: page 1, Metropolitan Museum of Art © ARS, NW #69.278.2; **Chapter 1:** page 4, © 2002 Cordon Art B.V.—Baarn-Holland. **Chapter 7:** page 164, Bettmann/Corbis. **Chapter 9:** page 333, Hulton-Deutsch Collection/Corbis #HU013742. **Chapter 10:** page 345, Metropolitan Museum of Art © ARS, NY #69.278.2; page 373, Cofield Collection, Southern Media Archive, Special Collections, University of Mississippi; page 375, Reprinted with permission of Joanna T. Steichen. Photo from George Eastman House. **Chapter 14:** page 492, Author's photo. **Chapter 15:** page 544, Matthew Mendelsohn/Corbis #ZIB70001159. **Chapter 18:** page 614, © 2003 Cordon Art B.V.—Baarn-Holland. All rights reserved. **Chapter 19:** page 664, © by Fred W. McDarrah; page 667, Allen Ginsberg/Corbis #AAGU001997; page 670, © by Fred W. McDarrah; page 672, © by Fred W. McDarrah. **Insert:** page 1, *top left,* Copyright Réunions des Musées Nationaux, Art Resource, NY #S01145238; *top right,* Scala/Art Resource, NY #S0156882; *bottom left,* Musée National d'art Modern, Paris © ARS, NY; *bottom right,* Barnes Foundation, Merion, PA; page 2, *top,* With permission of Henrietta Garnett. Digital photo courtesy Victoria University Library, Toronto; *bottom,* Scala/Art Resource, NY #S0027948; page 3, *top,* Copyright The Museum of Modern Art/Licensed by Scala/Art Resource, NY; *bottom left,* Copyright Tate Gallery, London/Art Resource, NY #S0040450; *bottom right,* Peter Willi/SuperStock #1330-1264-I-PIA; page 4, *top,* Giraudon/Art Resource, NY #S0137114; *bottom,* The Sidney and Harriet Janis Collection (580, 1967). Copyright The Museum of Modern Art/Licenses by Scala/Art Resource.

Index of Terms

Index of Authors and Titles